History CourseMate

Interested in a simple way to complement your text and course content with study and practice materials?

History CourseMate brings course concepts to life with interactive learning, study, and exam preparation tools that support *WCIV*.

Includes:
Integrated eBook, interactive teaching and learning tools, and Engagement Tracker, a first-of-its-kind tool that monitors student engagement in the course.

CourseReader

Create a custom ... using Cengage L...

With hundreds of ... CourseReader's easy ... preview, then select your customized stude... sourcebook. Each edited selection includes pedagogical support through a descriptive headnote, as well as critical-thinking and multiple-choice questions that assess students' understanding of the material.

For more information on **History CourseMate** and **CourseReader**, please contact your local Wadsworth Cengage Learning sales representative.

Value

WCIV offers full content coverage, review cards, and valuable material at **4ltrpress.cengage.com** – all at an unbeatable price whether you order one or both volumes, or the comprehensive text!

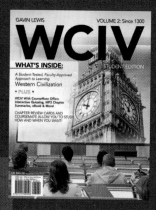

Comprehensive
978-1-111-34180-0

Volume 1
978-1-111-34234-0

Volume 2
978-1-111-34254-8

WCIV
Gavin Lewis

Senior Publisher: Suzanne Jeans

Senior Sponsoring Editor: Nancy Blaine

Associate Editor: Adrienne Zicht

Editorial Assistant: Emma Goehring

Media Editor: Robert St. Laurent

Executive Marketing Manager: Diane Wenckebach

Marketing Coordinator: Lorreen Pelletier

Marketing Manager: Caitlin Green

Senior Content Project Manager: Carol Newman

Senior Art Director: Cate Rickard Barr

Senior Print Buyer: Judy Inouye

Senior Text Rights Acquisition Specialist: Katie Huha

Senior Image Rights Acquisition Specialist: Jennifer Meyer Dare

Photo Researcher: Carole Frohlich and Elisa Gallagher/The Visual Connection Image Research, Inc.

Production Service: Lachina Publishing Services

Text Designer: Dutton &Sherman Design

Cover Designer: Studio Montage

Cover Image: The Colosseum, Rome, Italy © Jeremy Liebman/Workbook Stock/Getty Images

Compositor: Lachina Publishing Services

For product information and technology assistance, contact us at
Cengage Learning Customer & Sales Support, 1-800-354-9706

For permission to use material from this text or product, submit all requests online at www.cengage.com/permissions. Further permissions questions can be emailed to **permissionrequest@cengage.com**.

Library of Congress Control Number: 2010937496

ISBN-13: 978-1-111-34180-0
ISBN-10:1-111-34180-X

Wadsworth
20 Channel Center Street
Boston, MA 02210
USA

Cengage Learning is a leading provider of customized learning solutions with office locations around the globe, including Singapore, the United Kingdom, Australia, Mexico, Brazil, and Japan. Locate your local office at: **international.cengage.com/region**

Cengage Learning products are represented in Canada by Nelson Education, Ltd.

For your course and learning solutions, visit **www.cengage.com**

Purchase any of our products at your local college store or at our preferred online store **www.cengagebrain.com**

Printed in the United States of America
1 2 3 4 5 6 7 11 10

BRIEF CONTENTS

Kasuyoshi Nomachi/Pacific Press Photo; Scala/Art Resource, NY; Kevin Schafter/Corbis

Goran Tomasevic/AP Photo; Imperial War Museum, London/The Bridgeman Art Library; HIP/Art Resource, NY

CONTENTS

Scala/Art Resource, NY

Qwentes Italia srl/TIPS Images

The Granger Collection, New York

PART II MEDIEVAL CIVILIZATION, 500–1300 148

Bardo Museum Tunis/Gianni Dagli Orti/The Art Archive

Scala/Art Resource, NY

De Agostini/SuperStock

Image copyright © The Metropolitan Museum of Art/Art Resource, NY

Library of Congress. Rare Books Special Collections Division

Library of Congress LC-USZC4-5275

20 | Intercontinental Revolutions, 1700–1825 378

21 | Ideologies and Power Struggles, 1815–1871 396

Alinari/Art Resource, NY

The Royal Institution, London/The Bridgeman Art Library

© Gallery Oldham. Object number 10.67/1. Given by Mrs. S Leek, 1967. Photographer: Sean Baggaley

Interfoto/Alamy

Redferns/Getty Images

Brendan Howard/Shutterstock

Fabrice Coffrini, Pool/AP Photo

{ Explore It Your Way! }

"I liked how you could access the eBook online; you could do your reading anywhere."
– Ashlee Whitfield, Student, Grand View College

"I liked the questions that were asked (reflection questions, multiple choice) at the end of each of the supplementary documents that were attached to the eBook chapters. They helped me reflect on what I read."
– Ashley Mariscal, Student, University of Texas at Brownsville

"I liked the different options that you had: two different books, the eBook and the regular one. There were eBook links you could click on to find further information about that subject in the chapter plus good review questions at the end."
– Rachel Montieth, Student, Grand View College

We know that no two students read in quite the same way. Some of you do a lot of your reading online.

To help you take your reading **outside the covers** of **WCIV,** each new text comes with access to the exciting learning environment of a robust eBook containing **over 300 tested online links to:**

- **Primary source documents**
- **Interactive maps**
- **Web links for further investigation**
- **Interactive quizzes**
- **Audio resources**
- **Historical simulation activities**
- **Images**
- **Field trips**
- **Video**

THE ANCIENT WORLD,

3000 B.C.–A.D. 500

An essential first step toward understanding the past is to divide it up into periods—longer or shorter stretches of time that mark off important stages in the development of human activities and ideas. Of course, activities and ideas are complex things that change continually, so that the stages of their development are often difficult to recognize. In addition, what makes such stages "important" is to some extent subjective—it depends on what seems important about the past to ourselves, looking backward from the present day. All the same, we have to define historical periods as accurately and objectively as possible, for unless we do so, we cannot arrange facts about the past into any meaningful pattern.

The generally agreed-upon large-scale pattern of Western history is made up of three main periods, each more or less aligned with the lifetime of one or more civilizations that have played a leading part in Western history. The 3,500 years of the early civilizations of Mesopotamia, Egypt, Greece, and Rome make up the ancient period (3000 B.C.–A.D. 500). The thousand years of Christian Europe (500–1500) are the Middle Ages— the "in-between times" separating the ancient from the modern period (1500 to the present). This last period consists of the five hundred years (so far) of the rise of the modern West and the resulting changes in civilization across the world.

The dates that mark off these periods are simply convenient benchmarks, and nothing in particular happened at any of them. At each of them, however, large-scale and fast-moving

 What Is Western Civilization? (www.cengagebrain.com) Learn more about the meaning of "the West," "Western," "civilization," and "civilizations" in study material for this book

changes were taking place in many fields of activity and ideas, so that the transition from one era of civilization to the next was well under way. However, the fact that a particular historical period began and ended with spectacular changes does not mean that in between everything stayed the same. On the contrary, massive changes took place within these large-scale periods, so that historians often divide them into smaller-scale ones—"early," "middle," "late," and so on. Except in the case of the modern period, however, such changes within large-scale periods were never quite as far-reaching as those under way at the beginning and ending dates.

In the case of the ancient period, the initial sudden and world-changing development was the rise of the earliest civilizations in Mesopotamia and Egypt, which took place over several centuries around 3000 B.C. Over many centuries, most peoples in the region of southwestern Asia and northeastern Africa took to and adapted these earliest civilized ways. Political structures formed in this region that ranged from city-states (small self-governing communities) to great empires. Technical skills developed that were as varied as ironworking and alphabetic writing. Religious beliefs arose that were as different from each other as the worship of god-kings by the Egyptians and the monotheism of the Israelites (Jews). All these features were taken up by later Western and non-Western civilizations.

Eventually, peoples farther west adopted civilized ways of life and formed them into new patterns as they did so, until the brilliant Mediterranean civilization of Greece and Rome (often called "Greco-Roman") emerged and went through its own lengthy development.

Greco-Roman civilization was the first that today counts as geographically and culturally "Western." Citizen participation in government; the disciplines of science, philosophy, and history; magnificent new styles of architecture; works of art and literature that conveyed human experiences and perceptions with unprecedented vividness and power—all originated with the Greeks. The Romans then imitated and developed these and other achievements of Greek civilization to the point where they equaled and sometimes surpassed the Greeks. Rome, in turn, became an inspiration and model for civilization's further development—above all in Western Europe, the future heartland of Western civilization.

In two basic respects, however, Greco-Roman civilization had more in common with older civilizations than with later Western ones. First, like nearly all ancient peoples, the Greeks and Romans worshiped not one God but many gods and goddesses. Second, besides adapting the old established government model of city-states, the Greeks and Romans also continued the rival tendency of older civilizations to form vast empires ruled by limitlessly powerful monarchs. The final result was the mighty Roman Empire, which united the Mediterranean lands and Western Europe, as well as Egypt and some of Mesopotamia, under one rule. In these ways, Greco-Roman civilization was both "Western" and "ancient."

Eventually, over about three hundred years around A.D. 500, there came another series of world-changing events. The peoples of the Roman Empire converted to Christianity, with its belief in one almighty God. The empire itself was then broken apart by less advanced European peoples invading from the north, and by Arab conquerors from the south who brought with them another religion that worshiped one God—Islam. Countless traditions of ancient civilization persisted, but the changes were drastic enough for two new patterns of civilization to arise, whose future destinies would be closely linked. One was the non-Western civilization of Islam. The other, and the next in the Western succession, was that of Christian Europe.

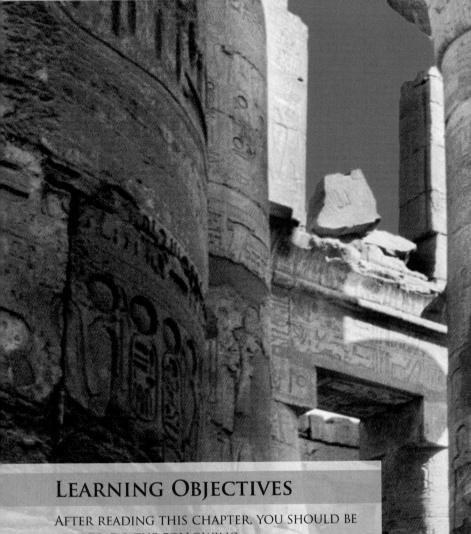

CHAPTER 1

FROM PREHISTORY TO CIVILIZATION,
3000–1200 B.C.

LEARNING OBJECTIVES

AFTER READING THIS CHAPTER, YOU SHOULD BE ABLE TO DO THE FOLLOWING:

LO¹ Trace the key developments of prehistory, from the emergence of our human ancestors to the beginnings of village life.

LO² Explain why the society that grew up in Sumer is considered one of the first civilizations, and describe later developments in Mesopotamia.

LO³ Contrast the ancient civilization of the Nile with that of the Tigris-Euphrates, and discuss the defining features of Egyptian life.

"LANGUAGE, RELIGION, ART, TECHNOLOGY, FARMING, FAMILY LIFE, AND VILLAGE COMMUNITIES—ALL THESE BASIC FEATURES OF HUMAN EXISTENCE ORIGINATED IN PREHISTORIC TIMES." Even the earliest civilizations were a very recent turn in the long road of human evolution and development. Accordingly, this chapter begins long before ancient times, with **prehistory**—the millions of years in which human beings appeared on the earth, spread across the planet, and advanced in organization and skills. Language, religion, art, technology, farming, family life, and village communities—all these basic features of human existence originated in prehistoric times.

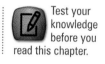
Test your knowledge before you read this chapter.

This earliest development led around 3000 B.C. to the rise of the first civilizations—those of Mesopotamia and Egypt. In these lands, located not far from each other in southwestern Asia and northeastern Africa, there appeared complex social and economic structures, effective and lasting governments, writing systems capable of expressing any thought, compelling religious beliefs, impressive scientific and technical achievements, and sophisticated literary and artistic styles, all of which influenced many later civilizations, both Western and non-Western.

What do you think?

With the development of agriculture and the move away from a hunting and gathering way of life, the quality of human life improved.

Strongly Disagree   Strongly Agree

1	2	3	4	5	6	7

The achievements of these first civilized peoples soon began to spread to their neighbors—a two-way process in which both sides were active. To come into contact with civilization at all, simpler societies had to be at least wealthy enough to be worth trading with or conquering. They took the initiative in learning the skills of civilization, themselves had skills that civilized peoples were glad to learn, and often invaded and conquered civilized neighbors—but that, too, brought them under the influence of civilization. Furthermore, they usually combined their own traditions with the types of civilization that they adopted. Thus, as civilization spread, it was liable also to change.

In these ways, by 1200 B.C., there came into existence an international region of civilization, with many local versions of Mesopotamian and Egyptian traditions.

« **The Temple of Amon** This temple, constructed about 1600 B.C. near the Egyptian city of Thebes, remains the world's largest religious building even today. In the Hypostyle Hall (Hall of Columns), a gigantic porchlike structure leading from the temple's outer courtyard to a series of inner shrines where the actual worship took place, priests prepared themselves to perform the holy rituals of the god.

This region stretched right across the lands where southwestern Asia met northeastern Africa, including the eastern shores of the Mediterranean Sea—and there was no reason for the spread of civilization to stop there.

LO¹ Before Civilization: The Prehistoric Era

Compared with the age of the human race, civilization is a very recent development. If we reduce the time since the first humanlike species appeared (about 2.5 million years ago) to the period of a twenty-four-hour day, the five-thousand-year era of civilization takes up less than the last three minutes! It took thousands of centuries of developing physically and completing a series of successful responses to the environment before human beings were at last able to take the first important steps toward civilization. But humans did not as yet produce written documents, the main material of actual history, so this lengthy time span is called the *prehistoric era*.

The Origins and "Ages" of Human Beings

The beginning of the prehistoric era can be only approximately dated, for prehistory began with the human race itself. The era ended with the rise of civilized societies producing permanent written records, but these societies arose at different times in different regions of the world, so that prehistory has no single worldwide ending date.

Excavations of fossils (remains of organisms) indicate that the earliest humanlike species probably appeared in East Africa. Over hundreds of thousands of years, new species evolved that gradually took on the various physical features and mental capacities that are unique to the human race. Humans began to walk on two legs, thereby releasing their hands to make and use tools and weapons. Their body hair thinned out and their digestions weakened, so that they needed clothing, cooking, and fire. Their brains grew larger, making possible language and abstract thought, as well as complex manual and physical skills.

About 200,000 years ago, probably in southwestern Africa, there appeared a human species that seemingly possessed more of these features than any other, and over tens of thousands of years it replaced all of them. Eventually, this type of human spread beyond Africa into

> "*If we reduce the time since the first humanlike species appeared (about 2.5 million years ago) to the period of a twenty-four-hour day, the five-thousand-year era of civilization takes up less than the last three minutes!*"

CHRONOLOGY

2.5 MILLION YEARS BEFORE THE PRESENT (B.P.)	Appearance of first humanlike species
200,000– 150,000 B.P.	Scientists have traced our genetic ancestry to a "Scientific Eve" living in Africa at this time
50,000 B.P.	Scientists theorize that humans began migrating out of Africa around this time
8000–4000 B.C.	Agricultural Revolution
3500–3000 B.C.	Rise of first civilizations in Mesopotamia and Egypt
2400 B.C.	Sumer falls to Sargon of Akkad; Sumerian civilization continues under a succession of foreign rulers
1600 B.C.	The Hittites dominate Anatolia
1100 B.C.	End of the New Kingdom in Egypt; Egyptian civilization continues under a succession of foreign rulers

Europe and Asia and then made its way across a "land bridge" that at that time linked the eastern tip of Asia with Alaska to colonize the Americas. By about 14,000 years ago, it had become the worldwide human race of the present day.

As the various human types developed and spread, their tools were mainly chipped from durable stone, so many of them have survived more or less undamaged down to the present. Tools improved over time, and these changes can often be dated by studying the earth layers where tools are found, or by laboratory tests. Accordingly, the stages of prehistory have come to be customarily divided according to the stages of tool development.

The earliest (and longest) prehistoric period is called the **Paleolithic (pay-lee-oh-LITH-ik—Old Stone) Age.** This era began with the earliest human types. With the appearance of present-day humans, the pace of progress in tool development speeded up. Stone tools became stronger, sharper, and more specialized for different tasks. By 8000 B.C., they had advanced

"The Human Family Tree" (http://channel.nationalgeographic.com/channel/human-family-tree) Learn more about human migration and your deep ancestry.

so far in southwestern Asia and northeastern Africa, as well as in neighboring regions including Europe, that archeologists call the subsequent period the **Neolithic (nee-oh-LITH-ik—New Stone) Age**.

When metals replaced stone as the principal tool material in these regions, the Neolithic Age was followed by the Bronze Age (about 3000–1000 B.C.) and then the Iron Age (after 1000 B.C.). Other regions of the world passed through similar stages at later periods, either by imitating and adapting these earliest advances or through independent invention.

The Hunting and Gathering Way of Life

Throughout the Paleolithic Age, all human beings lived as migratory (wandering) hunters, fishers, and gatherers of edible plants, sheltering in caves, in temporary huts, or in the open if the climate was favorable. Most likely their way of life was much like that of hunters and gatherers who have been studied by anthropologists in recent times.

To find food, protect themselves, and rear their children, they would usually have combined into small bands of perhaps twenty to thirty people. Individuals might leave one band to join another, and family groups of men, women, and their children might form within a band, with their own tools and weapons, their own stores of food and supplies, and their own spaces for shelter. Plants and animals, however, did not belong to anyone until they were gathered or killed, nor did the land on which the plants and animals were found—though the band as a whole would try to keep other bands out of the territory that it ranged.

Most likely there was a rough division of labor between men and women. Men would have been mainly responsible for hunting, for making the tools and weapons that were needed for killing and butchering animals, and for whatever violence was needed to protect or expand the band's territory. But most of the food that a band needed to survive would have come from plants, and it was women who were mainly responsible for gathering plants, as well as for the technologies required to store them and prepare them for eating.

Women would also have been mainly responsible for taking care of young children, but there would have been fewer of these than in later times. With no easily digestible cereal or milk foods available, children would have had to be breast-fed until they were old enough to eat normal adult food, and since women are less likely to conceive while breast-feeding, during that period they would produce fewer children. As the main providers of food, and with few children to take care of, women probably enjoyed much the same status and power within the hunting and gathering bands as men did.

As well as struggling to provide food and shelter for themselves and their offspring, early humans seem to have sought to understand and explain the natural world and their own destiny. They made regular rows of markings on pieces of stone or bone, probably to record the passage of time as measured by the movements of the sun, moon, and stars, which they probably saw as living beings with power to help or hurt. On the walls of caverns they painted lifelike images of large animals, as if these beasts, too, had power and could perhaps be influenced by magical rituals (see photo). Sometimes early humans buried their dead, presumably because their fellow humans were still in some way important to them even when no longer alive. The beginnings of what we today call science, art, and religion date back to these early times of the human race.

Paleolithic (Old Stone) Age
The earliest and longest period of prehistory, when humans used simple stone tools.

Neolithic (New Stone) Age
The period of human history characterized by advances in stone tool-making and the beginnings of agriculture.

Cave Paintings These images of wild beasts were painted about 25,000 years ago deep in a cave in southern France. Nearer the entrance, people had their dwellings. To judge from animal bones found in their garbage piles, they did not hunt these beasts; instead, perhaps they worshiped them. Layers of paint suggest that the paintings were continually restored, so they must have been very important objects.

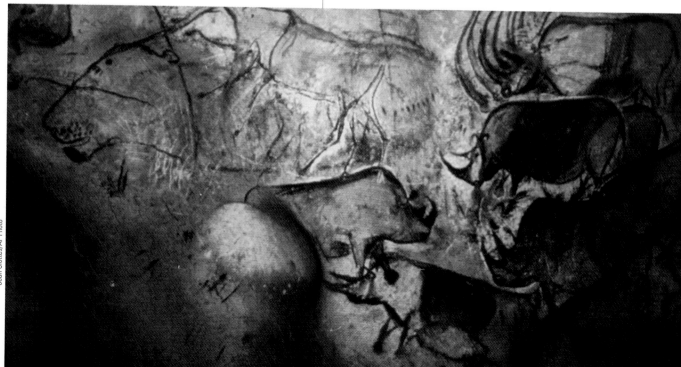

The Agricultural Revolution

The Neolithic advances in tool-making were only part of much wider alterations in human ways of life—the shift from the hunter-gatherer pattern to settled agrarian (farming) life. This giant step involved the cultivation of plants, the taming of animals, and the appearance of many new skills and technologies to adapt plants and animals to human needs—a whole series of discoveries that together are called the **Agricultural Revolution**.

Among the consequences of this change were a massive increase in the supply of food and a steep rise in population;

the replacement of hunting and gathering bands by families and village communities as the basic human groups; the growth of hereditary differences of wealth, status, and power within communities; and new and less equal relationships between men and women. This new way of life was extraordinarily resilient. It formed the basis of all civilizations and the majority of simpler societies right down to modern times, and it is still to be found in many parts of the world today.

Climate, Skills, and Technologies

The Agricultural Revolution took place not once but several times throughout the world; the first such revolution, however, began in southwestern Asia (see Map 1.1). Along with farming and the domestication of animals, there arose a whole range of new technologies to make the products of the fields and pastures fit for human use. Bread, beer, wine, cheese, edible oils, woven cloth, leather, pottery for cooking and storage (see photo), bricks for house building—all

Map 1.1 **Southwestern Asia**

Humankind's first Agricultural Revolution began in the lands of the Fertile Crescent, where farmers could depend on regular rainfall. To the south of the crescent's curving border, where rainfall was irregular, farmers eventually learned to use river water for irrigation. The resulting abundant crops provided the wealth for the world's first civilization. © Cengage Learning

Interactive Map

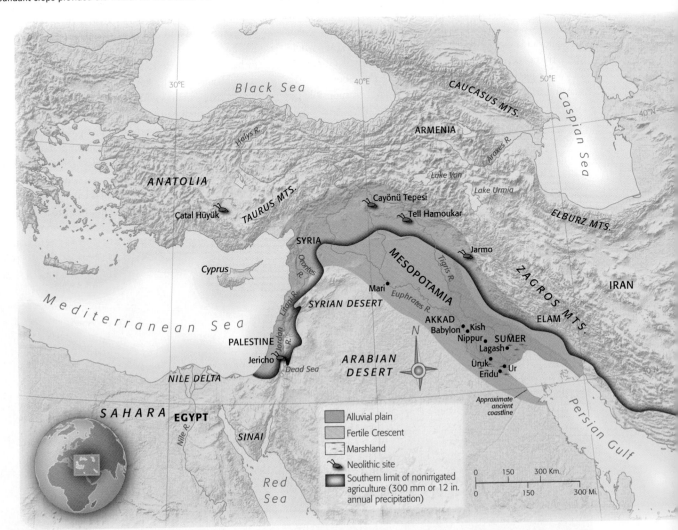

SEVERAL TRENDS CONTRIBUTED TO THE BEGINNING OF AGRICULTURE:

New Environmental Conditions

* Around 10,000 B.C., the planet was warming and the ice sheet that covered much of the Northern Hemisphere began to melt and withdraw northward.

* Southwestern Asia emerged as a region with a mild climate, fertile soil, and a good water supply—key elements for cultivating crops.

* Wild grasses that bore nourishing seeds flourished naturally in the grasslands above the river valleys of the region.

The Development of Techniques for Domesticating Plants

* Women of hunting and gathering bands, who were responsible for plant food, were probably the ones who noticed that the seeds of wild grasses could sprout into plants, and they began tending garden patches.

* By choosing to put back into the soil the seeds of those grasses that grew best and were easiest to harvest, cultivators helped breed (over many generations) wheat and barley.

* Tools were fashioned to make farming possible on a large scale. Stone-bladed hoes loosened the soil for seeding, and flint-edged sickles cut the edible seeds from the stalks.

The Development of Techniques for Domesticating Animals

* Wild dogs were the first animals to be tamed—probably by the men of hunting bands.

* Sheep, goats, pigs, and cattle were domesticated to provide meat, wool, skins, and milk.

* Toward the end of the Neolithic Age, humans began to use oxen for farming, along with a new tool—the plow. The oxen and plow made it possible to cultivate larger fields and feed more people.

* With the invention of the wheel, oxen were also used to pull carts and transport goods and people.

of these items of food, clothing, and equipment that we take for granted today were first used by the early farmers of this region. These technological advances, in turn, helped bring about a new way of life for the human race.

Villages and Families

Looking after crops required more or less permanent settlements, and around 6000 B.C. the first agricultural villages appeared in southwestern Asia—clusters of houses made of adobe (sun-dried bricks), where there lived anything up to two or three hundred people. Excavation of the ruins of these settlements, and study of traditional farming communities in recent times, give clues to the way of life that grew up in the villages—one that no longer revolved around migratory bands but around settled families and communities.

Each house, with its living and storage space, would have belonged to a family group of men, women, and children. The equipment and supplies, plants and animals, and also the sections of field that were needed for farming would also have belonged to the family, as well as to

following generations of its offspring. Over the generations, some families might add to their share of these goods, and others might lose them to their neighbors. Within the villages, family relationships, ownership and inheritance of property, hereditary differences of wealth and status, and climbing and slipping on the social ladder became much more important than in earlier times.

But families also needed each other. There were many tasks, such as house building and animal herding, that they could not do on their own. Families could not continue across the generations unless the sons and daughters of different families formed

Neolithic Storage Jar Pottery making, developed at the time of the Agricultural Revolution, made possible the storage of plant and animal products that were now available in much larger quantities than before. In addition, as with this jar, which was made in present-day Iran about 4000 B.C., pottery surfaces gave painters a new medium for artistic creation. Image copyright © The Metropolitan Museum of Art/Art Resource, NY

polytheism
The belief in many gods
and goddesses.

stable partnerships. They could not prevent or settle disputes with each other, or even among their own members, without agreed-upon rules that all families would obey and uphold, for example, those of inheritance or marriage and divorce. For all these reasons, families in villages could only exist as part of communities. Over many generations, the life of village communities and families came to be regulated by complex systems of tradition, custom, and authority, out of which the law and government of civilized societies would ultimately grow.

Among the most important traditions and customs that governed the life of villages and families would have been those connected with religion. Archeologists excavating larger villages sometimes find buildings bigger than ordinary houses, with a layout much like that of temples of later civilizations. Most likely an ancient belief in powerful beings who could influence the world and humans had already evolved into **polytheism**, the belief in countless humanlike gods and goddesses. Villagers would want to have at least one such being become part of their community. They would build this being a house where he or she could live among them, be served and honored with offerings and sacrifices, and in return watch over and protect them.

> *"Over many generations, the life of village communities and families came to be regulated by complex systems of tradition, custom, and authority, out of which the law and government of civilized societies would ultimately grow."*

Neolithic villages also needed each other. Villagers from smaller settlements would come to pay their respects to the powerful gods and goddesses in larger ones. Resources like clay that was good for making pottery were not to be found in every village, so neighboring villages would negotiate rules for their use and combine to defend them against outsiders. Other necessities and luxuries of village life were even more thinly scattered, and had to travel long distances from producers to consumers. Flint for sickle blades, obsidian (an unusually hard mineral) for knife blades and drill bits, and mother-of-pearl for bracelets and necklaces were traded over hundreds of miles. Out of cooperation among Neolithic villages there grew the organized governments of later times, and far-flung networks of Neolithic trade and travel provided the routes along which civilization would one day spread.

Men, Women, and Farming

Study of traditional farming societies also suggests that the Agricultural Revolution was accompanied by a lasting shift in the pattern of relations between men and women. Probably this was in part the result of a new division of labor between the genders, and partly also of the new importance of families and households.

The Agricultural Revolution made men, for the first time, the main suppliers of food. Domesticated animals—the larger ones mostly herded by men—were a far more important resource than wild ones. In addition, probably because plowing needed large animals, it was done by men, so that they took over the provision of plant products as well. Meanwhile, milk and cereals were providing food that very young children could digest, so that women were weaning babies earlier and becoming pregnant more often. Far more of women's time and effort was taken up with producing and rearing the larger numbers of people that farming could support.

This change, in turn, obliged women to concentrate on tasks that could be accomplished in and around the home and that could be combined with looking after young children. Among these were garden cultivation and the care of small farmyard animals, everything to do with food preparation, from grain grinding to cooking, and the management of the household. Tasks that required distance from the home for any length of time came to be done mainly by men, such as tending to field crops and herd animals, trade and travel, and fighting. As the main providers of basic necessities, and as the ones who were most active outside the household, men were likely to be main decision makers within households, and in the community's affairs.

In addition, now that families had their own wealth and status within communities, they wanted to hand these on to their offspring. That made it important to make sure that children were in fact the offspring of the men and women of the family. Since it was women who ultimately produced the children, it was their behavior that most needed to be surveyed and controlled—both by themselves and also by men.

Male dominance would usually have had its limits, however. Within village communities, women from prominent families could expect deference from men of humbler families. Women's work was just as essential to the wealth of households as men's work, and women and men had demanding expectations of each other. As in all face-to-face relationships, the real decision-making power within households might not in fact lie with those whom the community values said were the masters. And village women would be able to get out and about enough to form their own "public opinion," talk to their men accordingly, and thereby have a say in the decisions of the community.

Still, the distinction between "men's work" and "women's work" persisted, as did the acceptance by men and women of the rightfulness of some kind of male dominance. It was not until the rise of industrial societies and liberal values in modern times that these traditions began to change.

Villages and Civilization

Over many centuries, the Agricultural Revolution spread outward from its region of origin—including to the peoples of Europe, who adapted wheat and barley to the cooler and wetter conditions of their region. In Africa, tropical Asia, and eventually also the Americas, separate agricultural revolutions based on local crops such as yams, rice, corn, and potatoes brought settled village life to the humans of those regions as well. In this way, the small agricultural community, with its farms and families, its customs and traditions, its trusted religious rites, and its inequality between women and men, became the typical way of life of the human race throughout much of the world.

With the emergence of the village way of life, humans were ready for their next social and cultural leap: the rise of the first true civilizations. This was not a simultaneous worldwide development. On the contrary, throughout human history, it has only rarely happened that a prehistoric society of farmers and villagers has evolved on its own into an advanced civilization. The best-known "cradles of civilization" of this kind are the river valleys of the southwestern Asian land of Mesopotamia and the northeastern African land of Egypt about 3500 B.C., where the earliest known civilizations arose; those of northern India and northern China about a thousand years later; and the plains, forests, and mountain valleys of Central America and the Andes toward 500 B.C. All of these played major roles in world history, but the Western civilization of modern times is directly descended from the early civilizations of Mesopotamia and Egypt.

LO² The Earliest Cities: Mesopotamia

The civilizations of Mesopotamia (mes-oh-puh-TAY-mee-uh) and Egypt emerged at about the same time (from roughly 3500 B.C. onward), seemingly independent of each other. They lasted for more than 3,000 years—1,000 years longer than the time span between their disappearance and the present day. Their massive inheritance of cultural achievement, technical and scientific knowledge, and religious belief has been drawn on throughout the subsequent history of Western civilization. For many centuries, all direct knowledge of ancient Mesopotamia and Egypt was lost, but in recent times, archaeologists dug up their cities and scholars deciphered their writing systems and languages. As a result, recorded history now goes back almost to the beginnings of these earliest known civilizations. In the case of Mesopotamia, it is even possible to reconstruct how civilization arose out of the earlier village life of the region.

Sumer

The scene of this development was a vast plain stretching between two great rivers, the Tigris and the Euphrates (see Map 1.1 on page 8). The area bounded by them forms the heartland of the modern states of Syria and Iraq, but in ancient times, the Greeks called it Mesopotamia, "the land between the rivers."

> "*Nurtured by a favorable environment and then toughened by harsher conditions, there grew up in southern Mesopotamia a new kind of society, so much more complex than the older one that today it counts as one of the world's first true civilizations.*"

Landscape, Climate, and Cities

About 3500 B.C., several thousand years after the Agricultural Revolution began, Mesopotamia and the region surrounding it already had many prosperous villages. But the leap to civilization began in a much smaller area: the southernmost portion of Mesopotamia, where the twin rivers ran close to each other before entering the Gulf. In ancient times this district was called Sumer (SOO-mehr).

Sumer was a land of rivers and swamps with little rainfall, and to live there, the local farmers relied on irrigation. Seasonal river flooding deposited water and rich silt (earth materials containing plant nutrients) that had washed down from distant hillsides; the villagers diverted the water onto their fields and palm groves, which were the most productive in all of Mesopotamia. But the sheer size of the rivers made them hard to control, so that villages and patches of cultivation were actually fewer and farther between than elsewhere in the region.

What began the rise to civilization was a change in the local climate, which became slightly colder and drier about 3500 B.C. With less water flowing through them, the twin rivers, especially the Euphrates, became easier to harness for irrigation. The effects were dramatic. Archeological surveys of ancient settlements indicate that between 3100 and 2900 B.C., the population of this area expanded tenfold. Many new villages were founded, and some older ones grew into small towns. Dense clusters of villages and towns sprang up, which came to be grouped around still larger settlements—the first true cities in the history of the world, with populations estimated as high as 40,000 people.

It seems to have been about this time that the Sumerians arrived in southern Mesopotamia as immigrants or conquerors coming from an unknown earlier homeland. Very likely, they were attracted to their new homeland by its growing wealth and fertility, as the environment there began to change. They

dynasty
A line of rulers from the same family.

city-state
An independent state that consists of a city and its surrounding settlements and countryside.

settled in and ruled over the communities of the region, including its growing cities, each of which became the seat of government for a surrounding area of towns, villages, and countryside.

Eventually, as the landscape continued to dry out and water actually became scarce, the wealth and population ceased to grow. But the cities responded to new problems with new solutions. They built large-scale, centrally controlled water conservation and irrigation systems, and fought wars against each other and against foreign raiders and invaders for control of scarcer resources. Governments developed that were powerful enough to plan and organize these undertakings. Nurtured by a favorable environment and then toughened by harsher conditions, there grew up in southern Mesopotamia a new kind of society, so much more complex than the older one that today it counts as one of the world's first true civilizations.

Priests, Kings, and Others

Cities and their satellite towns and villages needed far more direction and control than before, and more productive agriculture provided a surplus that enabled some people to live without personally farming the land. As a result, there developed in Sumer two of the distinguishing features of civilization: many specialized crafts and many ranks of prestige, authority, and power.

Within the various crafts and social ranks, families intermarried and produced offspring so as to continue over generations just as families had always done. But hereditary differences of wealth and status, and distances up and down on the social ladder, were much greater—and the number of families at the top of the ladder, compared to those lower down, was far smaller.

At the top of the system of ranks stood the priesthood. As Sumerian communities became larger and wealthier than ever before, they devoted much of their new resources to the service of the gods and goddesses, and a class of hereditary servants of these mighty beings arose. The servants of the gods directed the building of unprecedentedly large temples to house the gods and goddesses, employed craftsmen to furnish the temples with costly and beautiful works of art, managed vast properties, introduced technological innovations, and were responsible for the invention of writing. In Sumer, the priesthood led the process of social, technical, and cultural innovation out of which civilization emerged.

In time, however, as the waters retreated and resources grew scarcer, there arose another group of leaders—military chieftains and warriors, who fought the cities' wars and thereby rose to wealth and power. By 2500 B.C., each city had a supreme ruler bearing the title of *lugal* or "great man." In effect, the "great men" were kings, with power not only in war but also in peacetime governance. Like everyone else, they did their best to keep their power and position in their families, and they became founders of **dynasties** (family lines of rulers). Their relationship with the priests seems to have been one of both partnership and competition. Like the priests, the kings claimed that they ruled as servants of the gods. To make sure of divine support, they built temples and took a leading part in temple rituals, and later myths and epics portrayed them as personally beloved of gods and goddesses.

In this way, each city of Sumer acquired its own government and army, independent of—and fiercely competitive with—others of its kind. The city, together with its surrounding towns, villages, and countryside, formed a new kind of community, far larger and more complex than had ever existed before: a **city-state**. From time to time, one of these city-states would gain dominance over the others, but none was able to hold this position for long, and their struggles lasted down to 2400 B.C. Such clusters of competitive city-states would arise in many future times and places—among the Phoenicians on the eastern Mediterranean coastline, in ancient Greece, and in Italy of the Middle Ages and Renaissance (pp. 32–33, 51–59, 195, 263–264).

Below the priests and kings were other people whom the newfound wealth of Sumer had partly or wholly freed from working the land. Excavations have uncovered the remains of specialized workshops that made pottery and metal goods. Early written documents mention skilled artisans employed in temples and palaces to make textiles, weapons, works of art, and many other items for use by priests and rulers. The priests and rulers, and later on professional merchants, also turned to trade on a larger scale than ever before. They set up trading stations hundreds of miles up the twin rivers, where they exchanged the luxuries of civilization for materials that could not be found in the river valleys, such as metals, timber, and stone.

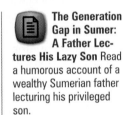 **The Generation Gap in Sumer: A Father Lectures His Lazy Son** Read a humorous account of a wealthy Sumerian father lecturing his privileged son.

Sumer, however, like every civilized society until recent times, was still overwhelmingly made up of farmers. Ninety percent of the population, including most of the people in the big cities, worked on the land. Most farmers were tenants working for the temple priests, the king, and other wealthy and powerful people who now had ultimate control of the land. Farming families still had enough control of land and other resources to provide for themselves and even to prosper. However, they had to yield large amounts of produce for the upkeep of priests, kings, and artisans, or they had to deliver it to vast temple storehouses from which the community could draw in time of famine or siege. If they failed to prosper or to hand over the expected produce, whole families might be sold (or parents would sell themselves or their children) into slavery as farmhands, artisans, or domestic servants.

In this way, the civilized society of Sumer allowed farmers to go on living their already traditional family and community way of life. However, they could do so only on condition of giving up much of the wealth they produced to those who ranked above them in a newly complex society—and under penalty of having their family and community life destroyed if they failed to do so. Over thousands of years until the rise of modern industrial society, the details of how wealth was extracted from farmers would vary in countless ways, but the basic pattern of a small minority of nonfarmers extracting wealth from a vast majority of farmers would always be the same. Without it, civilization could not have existed.

Men, Women, and Civilization

As the ladder of prestige, authority, and power grew longer, women as well as men were found on the topmost rungs. High-ranking women came to occupy many of the positions of command over lower-ranking men that they would fill in later civilized societies, but the upper ranks had their own forms of inequality that also had a long history ahead of them.

The Sumerian language had a word *nin*, meaning "lady," to distinguish women of high rank from those lower down, and such ladies were important in religion, politics, and government. The temple rituals of male gods were entrusted mainly to unmarried priestesses. Often they were the daughters of kings, who thereby hoped to gain power in the temples (p. 18). Likewise, kings' wives were often daughters of other kings, sent by their fathers who ruled "foreign" city-states to establish family ties between dynasties. Their husbands entrusted large estates to them, with many men and women at their beck and call. Tomb excavations at the city of Ur revealed that when the king's wife Pu-abi died about 2500 B.C., serving women, men from her bodyguard, and other manservants took poison so that they could go on serving their mistress in the world of the dead.

Priestesses, king's wives, and other married ladies, however, were not the equals of their husbands. Unlike the priests of goddesses, priestesses had no power outside their temples. Only one woman is known to have actually ruled a city-state and founded

(above, center) **A Sumerian Banquet** This scene of high life was made by a cylinder seal—an engraved roller used to mark clay jar stoppers while they were soft. Below, hunters bring in a trussed-up animal for a feast. Above left, an upper-class couple drinks beer through straws. By drinking from the same vessel they show togetherness, and the straws enable them to drink from beneath the scum-covered surface of the unfiltered beer. The University Museum, University of Pennsylvania, Image #152079, object #30-12-2

a dynasty, the lady Ur-Bau of Kish—and since the Sumerians had no word for "queen," she had to rule as a "great man."

Lower down the social ladder, written documents give history's first glimpse of what women and men expected of each other in family and household. As part of their training, scribes (writing experts) copied out lists of everyday proverbs, using different versions of the Sumerian language for those supposed to be spoken by women and by men. Sometimes the proverbs express romantic hopes: "A plant sweet as a husband does not grow in the desert." "May Inanna [the goddess of love and fertility] make a hot-limbed wife lie beside you! May she bestow upon you broad-armed sons!" There were also disappointments: "A thriftless woman in a house is worse than all demons," and an idle husband was no better: "A dog moves, a scorpion moves, but my man does not move." The household division of labor, and the contentment and dissatisfaction of both women and men to which it might lead, were already taken for granted.

Business documents and lists of trades and crafts suggest that the newly arisen specialist skills of civilization were practiced mostly by men—even though many of them were carried on around the home, where women could perfectly well have worked at them too. The one type of business that seems to have been carried on mainly by women was innkeeping, perhaps because it fitted into the pattern of women being responsible for everything to do with the preparation of food and drink. Most likely, the belief in the precedence of men over women was already so well established that it seemed natural for men to be the main practitioners of new skills and for women to be their helpers.

In any case, the Sumerians seem to have already followed the principle that the most active and creative roles in trades and crafts, reading and writing, and the fine arts and intellectual life were the province of men. Over the centuries, there would be many exceptions to this rule. Widows would take over family businesses, fathers would train daughters for lack of sons, and gifted and educated women would receive praise and encouragement from at least some of the people around them. But the principle as such survived unchallenged in all civilized societies until recent times.

Wheels, Plows, and Metals

Ancient civilizations had no monopoly on technical inventiveness, and the Sumerians

Bronze Age
The period from around 3000 B.C. to 1000 B.C. in which bronze, a mixture of copper and tin, was widely used for tools and weapons—the first metal to be so used.

cuneiform
A system of writing developed by the Sumerians that consisted of wedge-shaped impressions made by a stylus (a scratching tool made of reed) on clay tablets.

pantheon
The leading gods and goddesses of a people, believed to be a family group.

benefited greatly from a series of innovations, originating in socially and politically less complex societies, that changed the ways of life of many peoples across Asia, Africa, and Europe from about 3500 B.C. onward. Among these were the wheel and the plow (pp. 20, 46), which early written documents indicate were widely used in Sumer by 3000 B.C. Another such innovation, which revolutionized the making of tools and weapons, was the development of metalworking. Over thousands of years, people in the metal-bearing mountains of Anatolia had found out how to mine and work copper. Sometime before 3000 B.C., they had learned to alloy (blend) copper with tin to make bronze, a metal that was hard and strong enough to replace stone as the main material for tools and weapons. By 3000 B.C., the use of the new metal had spread to Sumer. Mesopotamia, as well as many other lands of western Asia, northern Africa, and eastern Europe, had entered the **Bronze Age**. Several other metals besides copper and tin—notably gold, silver, and lead—were also being worked for use or decoration. But bronze remained the king of metals until the development of iron tools and weapons after 1000 B.C. (p. 32).

Accounting and Poetry: The Birth of Writing

In addition, the Sumerians themselves developed one of the world's first systems of writing. The origins of this historic innovation were surprisingly humdrum. Nearly all of the earliest known written documents of Sumer (dating from about 3100 B.C. onward) are accounting records, providing information on supplies delivered to temple storehouses or consumed by temple officials. It seems that writing was developed in response to the increased prosperity of Sumer and the increased need for direction and control—both of which the wealthy and powerful Sumerian priesthood would have been particularly well aware of.

Sumerian writing grew out of a simpler record-keeping system used by Neolithic villagers, based on clay counters with *pictograms* (drawings of objects, such as sheep or bales of cloth) scratched into them. In the Sumerian temples, which had much more property to keep track of and consequently a greater need for detailed records, the pictograms were simplified so that they could be more easily and quickly drawn. Eventually, each symbol became no longer a picture but simply a group of wedge-shaped marks; hence

Cuneiform Learn about how cuneiform was deciphered in this video.

Sumerian writing is known as **cuneiform** (kyoo-NEE-uh-form), from *cuneus*, Latin for "wedge."

Meanwhile, some symbols came to be used as *logograms* (standing for whole words) and *phonograms* (standing for the individual sounds that make up words). Just as important, the new symbols were no longer written singly, each on its own small counter. Instead, any desired combination of symbols was scratched with a sharpened piece of reed, or stylus, into a larger piece of moistened clay, known as a tablet. The tablet was then dried to form a permanent record of complicated transactions involving any number of items.

As a result of all these improvements, the system had outgrown its original purpose. By 2600 B.C., a writer could produce a visual statement not just of business dealings but of anything that was spoken. Writing was a highly skilled task that was practiced only by professional scribes, who had to master hundreds of symbols and many complex rules for using them. "A scribe whose hand can keep up with the mouth, he is indeed a scribe!" said a proverb. But so valuable was the practice of writing that other peoples of Mesopotamia and neighboring lands later borrowed the cuneiform symbols, adapted them to their own languages, and used them for thousands of years, until cuneiform writing was gradually replaced by alphabetic writing after 1200 B.C. (p. 33).

Great Gods and Goddesses

As Sumerian communities grew larger and more complex, some of their deities (gods and goddesses) grew more mighty and splendid than ever before. Countless lesser deities were still worshiped, but at the center of each Sumerian city stood a magnificent temple where one of the great gods or goddesses was believed to make his or her home. There the divine being was honored and served by priests and priestesses as well as by the community in general, and was trusted to protect and preserve it in return. Enki, the god of the life-giving river waters, was worshiped in Eridu at the mouth of the Euphrates. Nanna, the moon god, had his temple up the river at Ur. At Uruk, a short distance beyond Ur, stood the shrine of the goddess Inanna, where solemn ceremonies yearly reenacted her marriage to the god Dumuzi, rising from the ground at harvest time as her fertility-bringing bridegroom. Together, these and other deities formed a **pantheon** (from the Greek words for "all the gods")—a close-knit family group of leading deities wielding power over the whole land.

A Mesopotamian Creation Myth: Earth, Gods, and Humans Read a Sumerian creation story.

The Sumerians had countless traditions, found in myths, temple hymns, and prayers, about their gods and goddesses. These traditions did not amount to a single consistent belief system, and of course, other peoples had different deities and told different stories about them. But the general Sumerian way of thinking about the gods and goddesses was widely shared by ancient civilizations until the rise of the belief in one God, or monotheism (p. 37).

The gods and goddesses were holy, inspiring love and fear in humans because there was nothing that did not depend on them: the fury of storms and war, the abundance of fields and flocks, the survival of great cities, dreams in the night, or sexual desire. They were not necessarily righteous: they might get drunk, have brawling quarrels, or be unfaithful to each other with other deities or with humans. Yet this made no difference to their holiness, for they were above mere human rules and regulations. For example, revered deities were said to practice incest involving all combinations of siblings, parents, and children.

Furthermore, as high and holy as the gods were, there was no fixed boundary between them and humans: gods and humans could interbreed and produce offspring, mighty heroes could achieve immortality and become divine. And traditions about the gods and goddesses changed according to the needs and hopes of their worshipers: rulers and priests in a newly dominant city-state might proclaim their community god or goddess mightier and holier within the pantheon than anyone had suspected before.

In dealing with these mighty beings, there were some basic rules that it was both righteous and prudent to follow. In order of importance, these rules were first, wholeheartedly to serve and honor the god or goddess of one's own community; second, to pay great respect to any other deity, great or small, native or foreign, who might influence one's fate; and third, to observe justice in dealings with other humans.

Immortality after death was a gift that the gods occasionally gave to humans of the highest rank, like the king's wife Pu-Abi. For most people, however, the only true life was life on earth—a life that was brief, hard, uncertain, and utterly dependent on the will of the gods. Creation myths told how the gods and goddesses had fashioned humans out of clay for their service, had sent a flood to destroy them when they grew annoyingly numerous, but had then felt pity and changed their minds. Among the specialists whom Sumerian wealth supported were those who sought clues to the changeable will of the gods: seers who knew the meaning of dreams, priests who studied the shape and size of inner organs of sacrificed animals, and astronomers who observed the movements of the sun, moon, and stars.

This same view of the relationships between mortals and gods is often found in the most famous of Sumer's literary legacies, its **epics**—

The *Epic of Gilgamesh* Describes a Great Flood Read about the Great Flood in the Epic of Gilgamesh.

long poems telling of gods and heroes and their ambitions and struggles. Most of the Sumerian epics concern the career of an early king, Gilgamesh (**GIL-guh-mesh**). Although Gilgamesh was probably a real person, in epic poetry he becomes a half-human, half-divine character who embodies the values and aspirations of the people of Sumer. He fights for his city-state; slays hostile humans and animals; and displays bravery, cunning, and a sense of fairness and mercy. The king's quest for immortality—a principal theme of the epic—ends in failure, as it does for most people. The epic of Gilgamesh, along with many other Sumerian literary works, was preserved, translated, and rewritten throughout the three thousand years of Mesopotamian civilization.

Still, in time, the Sumerians came to a more hopeful belief: that the great gods and goddesses took a personal interest not only in city-states and their rulers but also in ordinary human beings. These "personal gods" watched closely over their devotees, rewarding them with prosperity and punishing them with hardship depending on their deeds. According to a proverb, "A man's personal god is a shepherd who finds pasture for him. Let him lead him like a sheep to the grass where he can eat." This declaration of trust in divine power would echo down to the present day.

epic
A long poem or tale telling a story of gods and heroes from earlier times.

Numbers and Measurement

Besides writing, the practical needs of civilized Sumer in cultivation, irrigation, and commerce led to historic innovations in mathematics and science. The Sumerians devised the basic processes of arithmetic: multiplication, division, and the square and cube root. It was they who first divided the hour into sixty minutes, the minute into sixty seconds, and the circle into 360 degrees. They also found out how to calculate the length of the hypotenuse of a right triangle and worked out the method for calculating the area of a rectangle.

Sumerian Temple Statuettes These miniature statues, the largest of them 30 inches high, date from about 2700–2600 B.C. Each statue represents a worshiper who has donated it to the deity of the temple. By placing these images of themselves in the temple, worshipers proclaimed their loyalty to the deity and hoped to gain his or her protection and support. Courtesy of the Oriental Institute of the University of Chicago

ziggurat
A massive stepped tower topped with a temple dedicated to the city's chief god or goddess.

In addition, the well-organized Sumerians, even more than earlier peoples, needed to track the passage of time, as measured by the movements of the sun, moon, and stars. Besides, the sun, moon, and stars were deities whose movements should be carefully watched. Accordingly, Sumerian astronomers devised a calendar—a system for recording days, months, seasons, and years. The calendar's basic unit was a month of twenty-nine days—about the time between two full moons—with the months divided into seven-day weeks.

But the astronomers were also aware of a difficulty with this calendar. They knew that the sun and the stars seem to circle the earth at different speeds, so that it takes about 365 days for the sun to return to the same position relative to the stars. But twelve 29-day months do not add up to this solar (sun) year—and the seasons, so vital to farming, depend on the sun, not the moon. Keeping the months in step with the seasons was a major scientific and practical problem, which the Sumerian astronomers dealt with by adding in an extra month every few years.

Temples and Statues

The raising of huge temples to gain the favor of the gods or palaces to display the power of kings was a challenge that brought forth some spectacular monuments—all of them made of mud brick (adobe), since there was no other building material available in the river valleys of Mesopotamia.

Remains and records show that temples were the most distinguished structures. Typically, a temple consisted of an enclosure placed atop a man-made "mountain," a kind of step-pyramid called a **ziggurat** (see photo). The first level of the ziggurat at Ur was a solid mud-brick mass some 50 feet high and 200 by 300 feet at its base. It supported two ascending set-back levels, the higher one serving as a pedestal for the temple where the deity was thought to live. A structure of this type was probably the model for the Bible's Tower of Babel, with its "top in the heavens."

This general type of mountain-temple has reappeared throughout the world over long stretches of time, notably in Mexico and India, and perhaps, in all cases, it reflects similar beliefs about the relationship of the human and the divine. The hundred-step ramps of the ziggurat suggest a sacrificial climb as the worshiper approaches the deity, or perhaps the descent of the deity from heaven to be present among the people; the sheer mass of the monument symbolizes the power and rank of the god in comparison with ordinary mortals.

Inside Sumerian temples were many statues of both divine and human beings. Like all ancient peoples, the Sumerians thought that depicting persons or objects was a deed of magic

The Chogha Zanbil Ziggurat Ziggurats continued to be built for many centuries after Sumerian times. This one, east of Sumer in present-day Iran, was built about 1250 B.C. It is the best-preserved Mesopotamian ziggurat—about 100 yards on each side, and 170 feet high. Originally it had **two more levels on top.** © AISA Archivo Iconografico, Barcelona, Spain

that would bring these into actual being. Images of the main god or goddess, as well as of lesser deities that were connected with the main one in myth and ritual, ensured that these would all be present in the temple. Priests and priestesses, kings and their wives and children, as well as humbler worshipers who wished always to be in the presence of the deities, had larger or smaller statues there too (see photo).

Sumerian sculptors displayed extraordinary skill in creating highly stylized humanlike forms. In all the statues, the most prominent feature is the eyes; the pupils are magnified enormously, perhaps reflecting the dominance of eye function in human perception and communication (see photo). Because durable stone was hard to come by in Mesopotamia, sculptors often used sandstone or clay, adding shells, alabaster, and semiprecious stones for dramatic effect. Other artisans crafted exquisite jewelry and metalwork, chiefly for use in the temples and palaces.

Civilization in Mesopotamia

Almost as soon as it arose, the civilization of Sumer began to spread. Through trade and travel, through peaceful immigration and warlike invasion, peoples throughout southwestern Asia encountered, imitated, and adapted the new and more complex way of life that had originated in Sumer. For more than three thousand years, the traditions of Sumer provided a common basic pattern of civilization in a region that eventually stretched from the borders of India westward to the Mediterranean and Black Seas.

> "218. If a physician performed a major operation on a freeman with a bronze lancet and has caused the freeman's death, or he opened up the eye-socket of a freeman and has destroyed the freeman's eye, they shall cut off his hand. 219. If a physician performed a major operation on a commoner's slave with a bronze lancet and has caused his death, he shall make good slave for slave."
>
> —from The Law Code of Hammurabi, ca. 1800 B.C.

Farmers and Nomads

The first peoples to feel the pull of Sumerian civilization were of course those who lived close by, in or near Mesopotamia itself (see Map 1.1 on page 8). Many of these peoples farmed the upstream valleys of the Euphrates and Tigris Rivers. They mostly spoke Semitic languages, which were very different from the Sumerian tongue but closely related to the present-day Arabic and Hebrew languages.

But the up-river farmers were not the only neighbors of Sumer. In the dry plains in and around Mesopotamia where the floodwaters could not reach, there were Semitic-speaking peoples who followed a very different way of life. The Sumerians called them the ones "who know not grain"—wandering **nomads** who lived from their flocks and herds, traded for plant food with farmers, but did little or no farming themselves.

The nomadic way of life was no throwback to the era of hunters and gatherers. It arose in many parts of Asia and Africa in the wake of the Agricultural Revolution, as farmers moved out onto open grasslands that were not good for raising crops but could support large numbers of animals. Nomads lived in family groups that formed part of larger communities not unlike those of farmers, but to find fodder and water for their herds, they had to be continually on the move. In southwestern Asia, they roamed a region that stretched from the plains of Mesopotamia hundreds of miles southward into present-day Arabia.

From time to time, misfortunes such as overpopulation, famine, or war caused the nomads to spill out into the farmlands of Mesopotamia as immigrants or invaders. They constantly threatened the cities of Sumer, but nomads who broke in usually adopted the way of life that they found there. In Mesopotamia and beyond, nomads as well as farmers played a part in the spread of civilization and influenced civilization as it spread.

nomads
Groups whose social organization and livelihood are based on raising and herding livestock over large stretches of land.

Mesopotamian Empires: Akkad and Babylon

While the Sumerian city-states struggled with each other, nearby farming peoples northward up the main rivers and eastward on various tributaries were benefiting from the same climate changes that had brought wealth to Sumer, as well as from growing networks of trade and travel. A civilized way of life emerged throughout Mesopotamia and its eastern borderlands that was modeled on that of Sumer. More and more city-states joined in an ever-wider struggle for power across Mesopotamia. From time to time, short-lived Sumerian empires arose that claimed to rule "from the Lower Sea to the Upper Sea"—from the Persian Gulf to the Mediterranean.

 Art of the First Cities in the Third Millennium B.C. (http://www.metmuseum.org/toah/hd/trdm/hd_trdm.htm) Learn more about the art of the first cities.

The expanded world of Mesopotamian civilization was too large for any Sumerian city-state to control for long, however. About 2350 B.C., Sargon of Akkad, a Semitic-speaking territory immediately up-river from Sumer, overthrew the last Sumerian empire and replaced it with one of his own. Like later empire builders—the Romans in their relations with the Greeks, for instance (p. 118)—he could not help looking up to the conquered people whose traditions had most influenced his own. He called himself ruler of "Sumer and Akkad," and bound himself by close family ties with the Sumerian city-state of Ur. His daughter Enheduanna—a Sumerian, not a Semitic name—became high priestess in the temple of Nanna, the city's chief god, and was probably the author of several hymns in praise of the goddess Inanna, written in the Sumerian language.

Even so, Sargon's empire fell in its turn, and there followed a new period of struggles for control over Mesopotamia. A Semitic nomad people, the Amorites, moved into the farmlands along the rivers in large numbers, and their chieftains became kings of city-states. The Sumerian language ceased to be spoken in everyday life, though it continued to be used by priests and scholars for the next two thousand years of Mesopotamian civilization. From now on, however, the main language of Mesopotamia, in writing and probably also in speech, was the Semitic tongue of Akkad, whose prestige had outlasted Sargon's empire. Rulers issued orders and merchants transacted business in Akkadian, and the gods and goddesses were usually called by Akkadian names—Inanna was now Ishtar, for instance, and her bridegroom Dumuzi was Tammuz.

About 1900 B.C., the power struggles once again ended in the rise of an empire, which this time lasted for three hundred years. Its rulers were the Amorite kings of the formerly Sumerian city of Babylon—most famously Hammurabi (**ham-moo-RAH-bee**), who reigned about 1700 B.C. So impressive was his authority that under his rule the Creation myth was revised, and Marduk, patron god of the city of Babylon, was portrayed as the Maker of all things. Marduk eventually became the foremost deity of Mesopotamia. Some of his priests even proclaimed that all other deities were no more than different forms of this one and only supreme god.

King Hammurabi's Laws

Among Hammurabi's acts of royal power was the issue of the best-known collection of laws of ancient Mesopotamia. Hammurabi's law code was based on earlier codes issued by Sumerian kings, which themselves were probably written forms of earlier oral customs and traditions. No other law code has been recovered so completely, however, and it gives a vivid picture of a mighty ruler claiming to control the workings of a civilized society (see photo).

The code is engraved in cuneiform writing on a seven-foot-tall black stone pillar; a carving at the top shows the Babylonian god of justice, Shamash, speaking the laws to King Hammurabi. As the chosen servant of Shamash, the king could lay claim to exceptional stature among humans: "The great gods have called me, I am the salvation-bearing shepherd, whose staff is straight . . . to proclaim justice in the land, to settle all disputes, and heal all injuries." Countless future monarchs would claim to rule as doers of justice in the name of divine power.

To settle disputes and heal injuries in the complex society of Mesopotamia took many laws—above all, laws regarding crime and punishment. Death, most often by drowning, was a common penalty. An innkeeper who failed to report customers who used her saloon to plan a crime, for example, or a soldier who hired a substitute for war service and did not pay him, must lose their lives. And for the lesser crime of assault, "If a man puts out the eye of another man, his eye shall be put out. If he breaks another man's bone, his bone shall be broken." Evidently, civilized Mesopotamians were hard even for "salvation-bearing shepherds" to control except by spectacularly brutal punishments.

But fearsome penalties could only work if offenders were found out. To encourage accusers to come forward, they received the proceeds of any fines levied; to discourage false accusations, if a suspect was found innocent, the accuser was executed. Guilt and innocence were decided by "judges" and "elders," who could require witnesses and oaths. Should a matter come down to one man's word against another's, however, the suspect must jump into the Euphrates. If he sank and drowned, he was guilty, "but if the river proves that he is not guilty, and he escapes unhurt, then he who brought the accusation shall be put to death."

Almost fifty of Hammurabi's laws dealt with family life. The main intent here was seemingly the by now traditional one of making sure that families would continue over generations by controlling the behavior of women and keeping property mainly in the hands of men (p. 10). There were careful provisions, for instance, about inheritance by the sons of concubines (female bedfellows) of married men. This was an important matter in well-off families, where husbands often kept concubines—for pleasure, as status symbols, or because they had not fathered sons

The State Regulates Health Care: Hammurabi's Code and Surgeons Read a sample from Hammurabi's law code.

(above, center) **A King and His God** The top of the pillar on which King Hammurabi's laws are inscribed shows the Babylonian god Shamash (seated at right) giving the laws to Hammurabi. It expresses the Mesopotamian concept of kingship, which persisted in Western civilization down to modern times—that kings, though mortal, rule as servants of divine power and must therefore be honored and obeyed. Reunion des musees nationaux/Art Resource, NY

with their wives. But a wife taking a lover was quite a different matter. "If the finger is pointed at a man's wife about another man, but she is not caught with the other man, she shall jump into the river for her husband"—that is, she must let the river prove her guilt or innocence.

Still, in well-off families, women were bearers of family honor and were given in marriage with **dowries**—money and goods that they brought to their new households. It would be a family disgrace and a waste of family wealth if these women were left entirely without rights. If a husband deserted or neglected his wife, "so that she says, 'You are not congenial to me,' . . . she shall take her dowry and go back to her father's house."

In this way, Hammurabi's laws privileged men within family, marriage, and inheritance but gave women enough rights to uphold the status of the families from which they came. Specific provisions of family law would vary immensely in future centuries, but their general intent would be much the same as Hammurabi's for 3,500 years until recent times.

Likewise, the penalties and procedures of Hammurabi's laws, which were probably already ancient in his time, had a long history ahead of them. A thousand years after Hammurabi, the Israelites still punished some offenses on the principle of retaliation, or "eye for eye, tooth for tooth" (p. 42). Three thousand years after the Babylonian code, jumping into water and other

types of ordeal or "judgment of God" were routine procedures of English common law (p. 189). Retaliation and ordeal seemed natural and god-given to societies that could not afford prisons and had no knowledge of scientific detection.

dowry
Money and goods given by a woman's family to her new household when she marries.

The Expansion of Mesopotamian Civilization

The Babylonian empire eventually fell apart in its turn, but other empire builders followed. By 1600 B.C., the Kassites, a farming people from the mountains east of the Tigris, had conquered most of Babylonia. Like earlier invaders, they adopted the Mesopotamian pattern of civilization and dominated the region for four hundred years down to 1200 B.C.

Meanwhile, the civilization that had begun in Sumer flourished and spread not only in Mesopotamia but also far beyond—westward to the Mediterranean coast, northward through Anatolia toward Europe, and eastward toward India (Map 1.2). The spread of civilization through these regions happened partly through normal processes of trade and travel. But

Map 1.2 Southwestern Asia and Northeastern Africa about 1200 B.C.

By this date the lands where Africa and Asia meet had become a region of many powerful states, linked together by trade, travel, cultural influences, and warfare. Peoples on the fringes of this region, including the villagers of Europe, were already feeling the effects of its wealth and power. © Cengage Learning

 Interactive Map

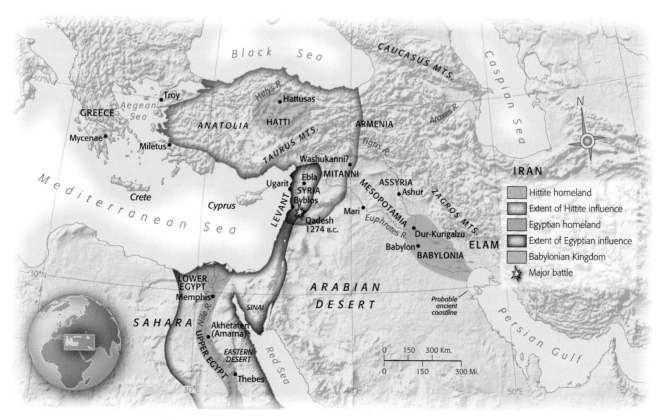

steppes
Vast semiarid grasslands or plains.

Moo-Cow on Wheels Wagons and chariots were not the only early devices that moved on wheels. When Neolithic farmers in eastern Europe learned of the world-changing device, they used it to make state-of-the-art toys—in this case, a cow that toddlers pulled round a village in present-day Ukraine in the fourth millennium B.C. The Museum of National Cultural Heritage 'PLATAR,' Kiev. Photo: ImagoRomae, Rome

it also resulted from the far-flung migrations of another group of nomadic peoples who lived farther north in the grasslands of what is today southern Russia: the *Indo-Europeans*.

Indo-European Peoples and Languages

Like the nomads of southwestern Asia, those of the **steppes**, as the northern grasslands are called, often settled in farming lands. Again and again, over many centuries between 4000 and 1000 B.C., they moved as immigrants, raiders, and invaders into territories that stretched from western Europe, by way of Mesopotamia, deep into India—hence the name Indo-European. Everywhere they moved, Indo-European peoples gave up their nomadic way of life for farming, while the peoples among whom they settled came to speak the closely related languages of the newcomers. This was a lasting change, though these languages developed away from each other over time. Present-day languages as different as English and Bengali, or Russian and Spanish, are all derived from those spoken by the prehistoric Indo-Europeans.

The Indo-European way of life differed from that of southwestern Asian nomads in one important respect: it revolved around an animal that was native to the steppes, the horse. Around 3800 B.C., the steppe peoples had begun keeping the horse for its meat and hide. By 3500 B.C., they had harnessed it to the earliest known wheeled vehicles, which in time evolved into a formidable new weapon of war, the horse-drawn chariot carrying warriors armed with bows and arrows, spears, and axes. By 1200 B.C.—having bred the horse to be larger and stronger than before—the steppe peoples would learn to ride it. The warriors of Mesopotamia and Egypt would need to learn these skills from the Indo-Europeans, often through painful experiences of defeat in war.

From about 2500 B.C. onward, the pace of Indo-European migration out of the steppes grew faster. Many of the migrants moved westward through Europe, including Greece, where their encounter with Mediterranean peoples influenced by Egypt led to the earliest beginnings of Greek civilization (p. 49). Others raided deep into Mesopotamia, until they settled down and founded kingdoms in the region's northern and western borderlands.

The Hittites

The most powerful and longest-lasting of the Indo-European-ruled kingdoms was that of the Hittites in the land of Hatti in Anatolia (see Map 2.1). In this land of mountains, forests, and high plains, the most valuable resources were metals: copper, gold, and silver were plentiful, though tin was scarce. For centuries, local peoples and then Indo-European newcomers had struggled for control of the mining districts, the routes by which

tin was imported to make bronze (p. 14), and the profitable export routes to Mesopotamia, as well as to Syria and Palestine on the eastern shore of the Mediterranean.

By about 1600 B.C., the Hittite kings had won this competition and dominated almost all of Anatolia with the help of powerful nobles living in mountaintop strongholds. They acquired authority as effective as that of any Mesopotamian king and regulated the affairs of their subjects with law codes almost as detailed as Hammurabi's.

With the wealth they acquired from the trade in metals, the Hittites built an army of charioteers and well-trained infantry numbering as many as thirty thousand men, and fought wars with Egypt to control Syria and Palestine. In the heavily fortified cities of the Hittite homeland, priests tended to gods and goddesses who were partly Hittite and partly Mesopotamian. Scribes adapted cuneiform writing to the Hittite language, and translated Babylonian versions of the tales of Gilgamesh and other Mesopotamian heroes. The scribes also composed letters in Akkadian for the kings to send to foreign rulers—for the Semitic tongue of Mesopotamia had become the international language of trade and diplomacy in a region of civilization that by 1200 B.C. stretched across southwestern Asia and northeastern Africa from the Indian Ocean to the Mediterranean Sea (see Map 1.2 on page 19). And among the rulers with whom the Hittite kings corresponded most often were their partners and rivals who ruled the other great civilization that had arisen at the same time as Mesopotamia—the pharaohs of Egypt.

LO³ Land of the Pharaohs: Egypt

During the Neolithic Age, the people of the Nile had moved toward civilization in response to the same influences that gave rise to the cities of Sumer, but Egyptian civilization was more stable than that of Mesopotamia. Political and sectional conflicts did not usually break the country's unity, and for many centuries foreign invasions were few and far between. Occasional times of trouble and change provided an invigorating challenge. Cultural influences from abroad were welcomed or

Map 1.3 **Ancient Egypt**

Egyptian civilization grew up in a thin strip of fertile land where the Nile crosses the North African desert, and in the broader region of the river's delta. Beyond these "Two Lands" of Upper and Lower Egypt lived wealthy and powerful African and Asian peoples. In the New Kingdom, Egypt dominated and influenced many of these peoples as well; later on, some of them in turn conquered Egypt.
© Cengage Learning

Interactive Map

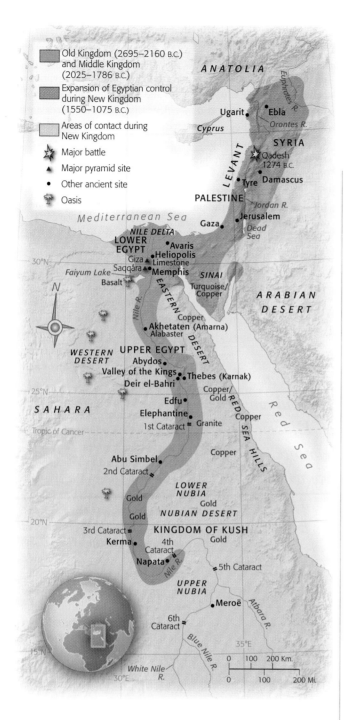

The Nile and the "Two Lands"

Egypt stretches along the lower reaches of the Nile's four-thousand-mile course from Central Africa to the Mediterranean Sea (see Map 1.3). The country is divided into two sections, called by the ancient Egyptians the "Two Lands." Upper Egypt is a narrow strip of fertile land, five hundred miles in length and averaging no more than twelve miles in width, that stretches alongside the river as it flows across the North African desert. Lower Egypt is a fan-shaped pattern of waterways, or delta, formed by the Nile in the last hundred miles before it reaches the sea.

The Nile played a role in Egypt similar to that of the Euphrates and Tigris in Mesopotamia. The cycle of labor and of life itself depended on its annual flooding and receding, and the "gift of the Nile" provided the wealth for the earliest Egyptian civilization. About the same time that the Sumerian city-states arose, Egypt witnessed the consolidation of increasingly wealthy communities, scattered along the river, into two kingdoms of Upper and Lower Egypt.

kept at arm's length, as seemed best to the literate elite. The traditions of Egyptian civilization became so strong that they flourished even in its last thousand years, when the country was repeatedly invaded and for long periods under foreign rule.

The Narmer Palette This palette was used for grinding makeup for divine images in an Upper Egyptian temple about 3100 B.C. The intertwined necks of two tethered beasts around the grinding area are believed to symbolize the union of the Two Lands. Above them, a king wears the crown of Upper Egypt; in front of him, some of the earliest known hieroglyphs give his name—Narmer—an army parades, and beheaded corpses are lined up. Evidently unification was not a peaceful process. Werner Forman/Art Resource, NY

pharaohs
The rulers of ancient Egypt.

Then, around 3100 B.C., the Two Lands were unified under a single king, seemingly in brutal warfare (see photo). The country's rulers from then on are usually known as **pharaohs (FAY-roh)**—a name derived from the Egyptian word for "palace," which they used to mean "the king" in the same way that "the White House" is today used to mean "the president." One of the early pharaohs built a new capital at Memphis, south of the delta and close to the boundary between the Two Lands, as the center of government. Thus, unlike Mesopotamia, Egyptian civilization, almost from the start, was linked with a single state under a single ruler.

Government by a God-King

The Egyptians, like other polytheistic peoples, recognized no hard-and-fast boundary between humans and gods, and in the case of the pharaoh, they took this belief much farther than the Mesopotamians. For the Egyptians, the pharaoh was to be obeyed as a man given power by the gods and venerated as a god who dwelt among men.

In his double capacity as god and man, the pharaoh had awesome responsibility and power. The stability and harmony of their state, the Egyptians believed, was part of the stability and harmony of the universe as a whole. The judges dealing out impartial justice in the courts, the tax collectors collecting no more from the peasants than was due, the Nile flooding in exactly the right amount to deliver its riches on schedule, even the sun rising on time in the morning and setting on time in the evening—all were simply different aspects of this same universal stability and harmony, which the Egyptians called *maat* (muh-AHT). It was up to the pharaoh to uphold all these aspects of *maat* against the forces of chaos and confusion.

> "*Hail to thee, O Nile, that issues from the earth and comes to keep Egypt alive! Hidden in his form of appearance, a darkness by day, to whom minstrels have sung. He that waters the meadows which Re created, in order to keep every kid alive. He that makes to drink the desert and the place distant from water: that is his dew coming down (from) heaven.*"
>
> —from The Hymn to the Nile, ca. 1350–1100 B.C.

god was always linked with or actually present in the person of the pharaoh.

Just as important as the pharaoh's divine nature was his nature as a human being. Alone among humans, the Egyptians believed, it was he whom the gods and goddesses had appointed to conduct the rituals and sacrifices that won their favor and made sure that they did their work of upholding the universe. Of course, thousands of priests daily served the gods and goddesses in hundreds of temples up and down the Two Lands. But they did so only as delegates of the pharaoh: not even the most trivial prayer or sacrifice was of any effect unless done in his name.

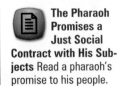

The Pharaoh Promises a Just Social Contract with His Subjects Read a pharaoh's promise to his people.

Likewise, all of Egypt was deemed to belong to the pharaoh as his personal property. Official monuments usually gave all credit for success in peace and war to his wisdom and prowess and to the favor in which the gods held him. Furthermore, the whole of Egyptian society was organized in such a way as to be under the pharaoh's control and responsive to his will.

At the highest level, the pharaoh maintained a vast household that was also his central administration. Throughout the Two Lands, the pharaoh had at his disposal an army of lesser officials, who qualified for their posts by a lengthy training as scribes (writing experts). Service to the ruler, rather than any kind of private activity, was the main path to wealth and power. Foreign trading expeditions, mining, and other large enterprises were carried on at the pharaoh's orders by groups recruited from his household. Peasants toiled as sharecroppers on the pharaoh's land and were drafted in thousands to build the temples with which he alone would win the favor of the gods, and the tomb where he alone would lie for all eternity.

But pharaohs took seriously the responsibility that came with their power. "Well tended are men, the cattle of god," King Khety III told his son and heir Merikare in a document of advice written about 2200 B.C.; ". . . he made for them rulers in the egg, leaders to raise the backs of the weak." In the opinion of this god-king of Egypt, rulers were made for their subjects, not the other way round. And the Egyptians certainly expected their ruler to deliver benefits for themselves and their families. Throughout the Two Lands, people bought and sold, bequeathed

Tending the "Cattle of God"

As a god, every pharaoh was identified in different ways with three of the country's ruling deities. By birth, he was the son of the sun-god Re, the king of all the other gods and goddesses. At his succession, he became the incarnation (living embodiment) of Horus, the falcon-headed ruler of the sky. When he died, he became one with Osiris, who reigned as pharaoh of the underworld. Thus, one or other mighty

and inherited land, houses, and goods, treating these as individual and family possessions regardless of the pharaoh's ultimate ownership—and the pharaoh's judges, who ruled on property disputes, evidently agreed. Officials and priests built tombs for themselves and their wives with inscriptions boasting of their virtuous deeds, and handed on their positions to their sons—all with the pharaoh's knowledge and approval.

Men and Women Under the Pharaohs

The women who were closest to the pharaoh, the King's Mother and the King's Principal Wife, also had a touch of divinity, for it was a god who made them pregnant and a god to whom they gave birth. Probably to show the godlike nature of the ruling family—since Egyptian deities, like Sumerian ones, were said to practice incest—the King's Principal Wife was often also his sister or half-sister. In addition, the mother and the principal wife had their own lands and households, and were among the few people besides himself whom the pharaoh sometimes commemorated in monuments for successes achieved under his rule.

The pharaoh had many other wives besides his principal one, most of them daughters of high officials and foreign rulers with whom he condescended to form family ties. Most of these wives lived apart from the pharaoh and were even put to work as weavers, but if one of them caught his eye or he had no sons with his principal wife, the junior wife might in time rise to holiness and power as a King's Mother.

Only very rarely, however, did a woman wield the full authority of a pharaoh. The most successful of these rulers, Hatshepsut (hat-SHEP-soot), reigned as "king" shortly after 1500 B.C., like the Sumerian ruler Ur-Bau five hundred years earlier (p. 13). Even so, Hatshepsut's name was eventually erased from monuments, probably because a female pharaoh was thought to undermine *maat*.

Lower down among the ordinary "cattle of god," women as well as men were entitled to benefit from the pharaoh's rule. Daughters inherited property equally with sons, and wives could divorce their husbands. Daughters could not usually inherit government and temple positions, but priests made sure that their wives were prestigiously employed in their temples as "Great Ones of Musical Troupes," directing the worship of the gods with music and song.

Unlike in Sumer, there are no records of women's expectations of men, but men were certainly expected to respect the women in their families. A book of "wisdom" (advice on the conduct of life) written about 1800 B.C. tells sons and husbands: "Support your mother as she supported you; she had a heavy load in you, but she did not abandon you. When you were born . . . she was yet yoked to you, her breast in your mouth for three years. As you grew and your excrement disgusted, she was not disgusted, saying 'What shall I do!' . . . Do not control your wife in her house, when you know she is efficient; don't say to her, 'Where is it? Get it.' . . . Do not go after a woman, let her not steal your heart."

But this advice still assumed that the wife was responsible to the husband rather than the other way round—and, of course, that there were plenty of bad women who were set on stealing him away from her. In tomb carvings of married couples, the wife is usually depicted smaller compared to her husband than she would naturally be, and is placed at his left—the humbler side.

Gods, Humans, and Everlasting Life

Many Egyptian deities, tracing back to the Stone Age, were originally conceived in the form of animals; during historic times, the divine images often had animal heads or bodies. The sky-god Horus, for example, is usually depicted with the head of a falcon, and the pharaoh himself is sometimes portrayed, as in the Great Sphinx (see photo), with a human head on a lion's body. Other important gods included the sun-god Re and the wind-god Amon, who came to be worshiped as a combined god, "Amon-Re, King of the Gods." Sometimes the two were even joined together with a third, the craftsman-god Ptah, to make a single, overwhelmingly mighty deity.

This custom of worshiping different deities in a single combined form probably arose from the way in which Egypt itself had come into being. The Egyptian deities had originally been local ones, and as the different communities of the Nile

The Great Sphinx This famous monument, carved out of solid rock in the royal burial area at Giza, expresses the Egyptian belief in the pharaoh as god-king. The sphinx's body is that of a lion, symbolic of the god Re, and its face is that of King Khafre (c. 2500 B.C.), who as pharaoh was thought of as the "living image" of the god. The pyramid to the left of the sphinx is Khafre's royal tomb. To the sphinx's right is the pyramid of Khafre's father Khufu.

THE SOUL DECLARES ITS INNOCENCE

By about 2000 B.C., the judgment of the soul after death and eternal life for those judged righteous became widely accepted beliefs. The newly dead were thought to travel by night through tests and ordeals in the underworld before rising to life in the morning with the sun-god Re. Papyrus documents with rites and spells that they would need to help them on their way were placed in their coffins for their guidance. Here, the soul declares its innocence of many forms of wrongdoing before Osiris, king of the dead.

The soul addresses Osiris by different names. The "Two Truths," "Two Daughters," and "Two Eyes" in these names are truth itself and righteousness; *Wennofer* means "eternally righteous." An *arura* is a measure of land area.

THE DECLARATION OF INNOCENCE

To be said on reaching the Hall of the Two Truths so as to purge [name] of any sins committed and to see the face of every god:

Hail to you, great God, Lord of the Two Truths!
I have come to you, my Lord,
I was brought to see your beauty.
I know you, I know the names of the forty-two gods
Who are with you in the Hall of the Two Truths,
Who live by warding off evildoers,
Who drink of their blood,
On that day of judging characters before Wennofer.
Lo, your name is "He-of-Two-Daughters,"
(And) "He-of-Maat's-Two-Eyes."
Lo, I come before you,
Bringing Maat to you,
Having repelled evil for you.
I have not done crimes against people,
I have not mistreated cattle,
I have not sinned in the Place of Truth,
I have not known what should not be known,
I have not done any harm.
I did not begin a day by exacting more than my due,
My name did not reach the bark of the mighty ruler.
I have not blasphemed a god,
I have not robbed the poor.
I have not done what the god abhors,
I have not maligned a servant to his master.
I have not caused pain,
I have not caused tears.
I have not killed,
I have not ordered to kill,
I have not made anyone suffer.

I have not damaged the offerings in the temples,
I have not depleted the loaves of the gods,
I have not stolen the cakes of the dead.
I have not copulated nor defiled myself.
I have not increased nor reduced the measure,
I have not diminished the arura.
I have not cheated in the fields.
I have not added to the weight of the balance,
I have not falsified the plummet of the scales.
I have not taken milk from the mouth of children,
I have not deprived cattle of their pasture.
I have not snared birds in the reeds of the gods,
I have not caught fish in their ponds.
I have not held back water in its season,
I have not dammed a flowing stream,
I have not quenched a needed fire.
I have not neglected the days of meat offerings,
I have not detained cattle belonging to the god,
I have not stopped a god in his procession.
I am pure, I am pure, I am pure, I am pure!

EXPLORING THE SOURCE

1. What sorts of things should a person avoid doing in order to please the divine judges? Which is more important to avoid, transgressions against the gods or against fellow humans?

2. What might be the reason that almost all of the soul's declarations are negative: "I have not . . ."?

Source: Miriam Lichtheim, trans. and ed., *Ancient Egyptian Literature*, pp. 131–133 Copyright © 2006 by the University of California Press. Reprinted with permission of the University of California Press.

combined to form a single state, it made sense to believe that the god or goddess of one community was the same as that of another with which it was now united.

In fact, Egyptian priests and rulers often speculated that, behind all the different deities they worshiped, there lay a single divine power: one god who had created all the others, perhaps, or who ruled, protected, and nourished all the nations of the world. A pharaoh of the New Kingdom, Akhenaten, who identified the supreme god with the Aten, the shining disk of the sun, took this idea so far that he actually tried to abolish the worship of other leading deities. He failed in this "religious revolution," but even so, Egyptian polytheism always had an underlying urge toward the opposite form of belief, monotheism.

Unlike Mesopotamian religion, that of Egypt came to offer a growing hope of immortality. At first, it was believed that only the pharaoh was immortal, though he could confer everlasting life on his close associates. But a time of troubles at the end of the Old Kingdom after 2200 B.C. (p. 27) inspired a creative new idea: local administrators who now held power independently of the pharaoh came to expect that they would also live independently of him after death. Even when the rulers regained their power, this belief in wider access to the afterlife continued to grow. Every person, it was now believed, possessed a supernatural life force or soul (*ka*) that persisted after the body died; and preserving the body (through mummification) and providing it with comforts in the tomb would help it in the life to come.

The hope of immortality strengthened ethical ideas in Egyptian religion—the belief that the gods expected righteous behavior from humans. By 1800 B.C., Egyptians had come to believe that the soul of every deceased person had to stand before Osiris, the ruler of the underworld, for judgment. The soul recited its good deeds and denied doing anything evil. The heart (character) of the person was then weighed in a balance to measure the soul's truthfulness. If the soul passed this test, it was admitted to everlasting life in a garden paradise; otherwise, it was cast into the crocodile jaws of a monster.

The Writing of the Words of God

Writing arose in Egypt, as it did in Sumer, along with civilization itself, but the initial impulse was different. Instead of the record-keeping needs of an expanding economy, what brought about writing was the religious needs of rulers as they rose to become god-kings. The earliest Egyptian writing, the **hieroglyphs** (from the Greek for "sacred carvings"), was devised about 3100 B.C. as part of carvings and paintings intended to honor the pharaohs. By having themselves depicted together with a god who was promising them immortality, for example, the pharaohs believed that they could cause the god to actually make that promise, in a magical world beyond the accidents of time and place. Obviously, the magic would be all the more effective if the god's actual words could be "depicted."

Probably for this reason, the hieroglyphs were actual pictures of real-life or mythical creatures and objects (for examples, see photo on page 27), but most of these pictures also stood for whole words or separate sounds of words. The words they were used to represent were always religious, and they were mostly found in temples and other monuments; in fact, the Egyptian name of the hieroglyphs was "the writing of the words of god."

> **hieroglyphs**
> The earliest Egyptian writing, in which pictures stood for whole words or separate sounds of words.

Soon after the invention of the hieroglyphs, "shorthand" versions of the characters were developed that could be much more easily and quickly written—the *hieratic* (priestly) script. In spite of its name, the hieratic script was used not only by priests but also for general literary and record-keeping purposes. Much later, around 700 B.C., an even faster shorthand, the *demotic* (popular) script, came into use. Like cuneiform writing, all the Egyptian scripts employed hundreds of characters according to complex rules, but they could communicate anything that could be thought or said. Thus, writing became as much part of the everyday life of civilization in Egypt as it was in Mesopotamia.

Most Egyptian writing, especially the hieratic and demotic scripts, was not chiseled into stone but done with ink on papyrus, a paperlike material made from the stems of the water-grown papyrus plant. The convenience of ink and papyrus for everyday writing was soon recognized everywhere, including in Mesopotamia, where it gradually replaced clay tablets and styluses (p. 14). Papyrus scrolls (rolls) became the books of the ancient world.

 **Advice to Ambitious Young Egyptians: Rise Above the Masses, Become a Scribe!** Read about the perks of being an Egyptian scribe.

Much of Egypt's literary writing served religious purposes, for example, tales about the gods and books of rituals and spells to aid the passage of the soul to the afterworld. But virtually all forms of literature arose: philosophical essays, books of "wisdom" (p. 23), tales of adventure, romances, texts on medicine and magic, poems, and songs. The Egyptians excelled in the scope and quantity of their literary creations.

Calendars and Sailboats

Egyptian civilization, like that of Sumer, both needed scientific and technical knowledge and had specialists who could provide it. Surviving texts explain how land surveyors and architects computed the areas of fields, the volumes of various shapes, and the properties of pyramids. Likewise, astronomers created a calendar with twelve equal months of thirty days and five "free" days at the end to make up the 365 days of the solar year (p. 16). This was the most successful solution yet devised to the problem of keeping the months in step with the seasons, and its basic principles are still used in the present-day calendar.

The Egyptians were also knowledgeable in practical medicine. They understood nothing of germs or infections and believed that sickness was caused by demons entering the body. But alongside magic formulas and priestly exorcists were some healing drugs and trained physicians and surgeons. The

Egyptians also developed systematic procedures for handling cases of illness, wrote books about diseases, and established medical libraries and schools. One reason for the superiority of their medical techniques, no doubt, was the anatomical knowledge (unique in the ancient world) derived from their practice of mummification. Prior to embalming with special preservatives, the body of the deceased was opened and the internal organs (except the heart) were removed.

Egyptology Online (www.egyptologyonline.com/mummification.htm) Learn more about the Egyptian practice of mummification.

The Egyptians were also eager to improve water transportation along their main artery, the Nile. They built larger boats than the traditional dugout canoes by fastening wooden planks together to make the hulls. To propel these heavy craft upstream, by 3100 B.C. they equipped them with masts and sails to catch the wind, which in the Nile Valley usually blows against the current of the river. The Sumerians also used river sailboats, but by 2500 B.C. the Egyptians had adapted these sailboats to travel the open sea to the Mediterranean's eastern shoreline, a source of timber and other valuable products. In this way, the Mediterranean became a highway that would one day stretch from its eastern shores to northern Africa, southern Europe, and the Atlantic Ocean (pp. 32–33).

Pyramids and Temples

The most spectacular Egyptian technical feats, however, were in the field of building. Their inspiration here was mainly religious—above all, the fact that their god-king (and as time went on, many other important personages) must have a stone tomb as a resting place for all time. The best-known tombs are the giant royal **pyramids**—the masterpieces of practical engineering (and social discipline) that come most readily to mind when we think of Egypt.

The great age of pyramid building was in the early centuries of Egyptian civilization, and the largest of them was built by order of King Khufu (often known by his Greek name, Cheops), who ruled about 2650 B.C. Located at Giza (near modern Cairo), the Great Pyramid measures 476 feet in height and 760 feet on each side of its base (see photo on page 23). This mountain of stone consists of some 2.3

million cut blocks, each weighing about 5,000 pounds. The sides of the pyramid were originally coated with polished marble, but that was stripped away by Muslim rulers in the Middle Ages to build the mosques and palaces of Cairo. (The royal tomb within was robbed by thieves in ancient Egyptian times.) Close by is the Great Sphinx, another type of monument, carved soon afterward for another king, Khafre (Chephren). The enormous head of this man-beast, cut from the cliff of the valley wall, rises 66 feet from its base.

Building the Great Pyramid Learn how the Great Pyramid was built in this video.

Later on, the pyramid-building urge faded, but pharaohs still poured resources into gigantic building projects—above all, temples. Temple buildings were usually constructed of horizontal beams held up by columns. The method was very suitable for stone structures, and Egyptian builders had easy access to immense supplies of stone.

The temple of Amon at Karnak (far up the Nile near the city of Thebes) was begun about 1530 B.C. and completed about 1300 B.C. The largest religious building ever constructed, it covered a ground area of about 400 by 110 yards or 10 acres, large enough to contain four of the huge Gothic cathedrals that were built more than 2,500 years later in Europe. The roof of the main hall rests on 134 columns, each made of stone drums carved with hieroglyphs; the central columns are 70 feet high and 12 feet in diameter (see photo on page 4). As the builders intended, the gigantic proportions of Karnak were worthy of one of Egypt's greatest gods, and of the rulers who worshiped him.

Sculptors and painters did much of their work for the interiors of royal and noble tombs. Stone statues of the individuals entombed and of members of their households made them present within the tombs; paintings on tomb walls with scenes of everyday life related to the career of the deceased made those scenes take place in the afterlife. Though

King Menkaure (Mycerinus) and His Queen, 2500 B.C. The queen has her arm protectively around her husband, a typical pose in Egyptian statues of married couples that testifies to the status and power of upper-class women. The king's pose, with arms at his sides, fists clenched, and left foot forward, remained typical of Egyptian male statues for thousands of years and influenced early Greek sculpture (see photo on page 65). King Menkaure (Myerinus) and queen, Egyptian, Old Kingdom, Dynasty 4, reign of Menkaura, 2490-2472 B.C., Greywacke, 142.2 x 57.1 x 55.2 cm, 676.8 kg, Museum of Fine Arts, Boston, Harvard University – Boston Museum of Fine Arts Expedition, 11.1738. Photograph © 2011, Museum of Fine Arts Boston

Isis, Guide of Souls In this tomb painting, Isis leads Nefertari, Principal Wife of the New Kingdom pharaoh Ramses II (about 1250 B.C.), into the land of the dead. The goddess's headdress combines the cow's horns of nurturing fertility and the sun disk of light and power. The picture and the accompanying hieroglyphs remained mostly in darkness, but the Egyptians believed they would bring about what they depicted and described—the continuation of Nefertari's life into eternity. Valley of the Queens, Thebes/Giraudon/The Bridgeman Art Library

lifelike, these representations were seldom naturalistic (the way persons and objects normally look to the eye). Sculptured portraits, for example, had to be made according to set rules. Rather rigid postures were required, and the figures were placed so as to be viewed from the front (this is known as "frontalism"). Usually the left foot was placed forward; wigs and beards were treated in a standard stylized manner. Yet the human quality of these statues comes through all the same (see photo).

This humanistic quality is evident also in tomb paintings, from which we have learned many details about Egyptian civilization. There was no attempt to provide perspective (the illusion of depth) in these pictures; artists were free to arrange their compositions as they thought best within the assigned space. What mattered most was that a painting must reflect established knowledge of the object and must be shown from the angle that best revealed that knowledge. For example, the face is always shown in profile, except for the eye, which is shown as it appears frontally. Shoulders and torso are viewed from the front, legs and feet in profile (see photo).

By depicting the various parts of a human body from the different angles at which each of them was most fully seen, the artist could make a person most fully present on a two-dimensional surface, even if the whole body was not seen, as it would be in real life, from a single viewpoint. In any case, the Egyptian painters, within their rules, developed techniques of line, design, and color that were extraordinarily effective.

The Rhythm of Egypt's History

To hold the Egyptian state together for many centuries on end was no easy matter. From time to time the balance of the Two Lands was upset by weakling pharaohs, boy-pharaohs, and disputes over the succession; by disloyal courtiers and self-seeking officials; and by rivalries among powerful families and unruly communities. Whole dynasties were cut down by failure to produce heirs, or sometimes by violent turnovers. In all, over three thousand years, no fewer than thirty dynasties ruled Egypt. There were even periods of total collapse when the Egyptian state dissolved into fragments, each with its own self-proclaimed pharaoh. But to the Egyptians, such a state of affairs seemed profoundly abnormal and wrong. Sooner or later it must give way to the harmony of *maat*, under a single all-powerful god-king.

As a result, the Egyptian state enjoyed lengthy periods of stability and unity, interrupted by briefer intervals of turmoil. After several hundred years of early state building, the power of the pharaohs first reached its height in the period

 Simulation to Learn About Ancient Cultures (http://college.cengage .com/history/049509286x/ student/assets/simulations/ simulations/wcrc_ simulations_ch01.html) Participate in a simulation of life in ancient Egypt as an Old Kingdom farmer or a New Kingdom warrior.

known to modern scholars as the Old Kingdom, beginning about 2700 B.C. In total command of the country's resources, having few foreign enemies to contend with, and seeking an everlasting resting place, the pharaohs of the Old Kingdom were the builders of the pyramids.

About 2200 B.C., however, a series of weak pharaohs allowed local officials to gain independent hereditary power in the regions that they controlled. Egypt remained in turmoil until about 2050 B.C., when a dynasty from the up-river city of Thebes brought the whole country under its rule, to form the Middle Kingdom.

By this time, the world outside Egypt was changing, with the spread of Semitic tribes and the growth of powerful states in Mesopotamia and Anatolia. Accordingly, the god-kings of Egypt faced a new challenge as part of their general task of upholding *maat*: that of what they called "treading on" foreign nations. The pharaohs of the Middle Kingdom rose to this challenge and poured the spoils of their conquests into building magnificent new temples. Finally, however, internal conflict was renewed about 1800 B.C. Semitic immigrant tribes known as the Hyksos (**HIK-sohs**) were able to move into Lower Egypt, and the Middle Kingdom came to an end. The Hyksos adapted to Egyptian civilization, and for a time their chieftains ruled Lower Egypt as pharaohs.

Native Egyptian pharaohs continued to rule Upper Egypt from Thebes, and in 1600 B.C. they were able to defeat the Hyksos rulers and bring the nation into its imperial era, the New Kingdom. More than ever before, the rulers of Egypt acted as conquerors. Their armies moved south into Nubia and vied with the Hittites of Anatolia (pp. 20) for control of Palestine and Syria. Along with this aggressive warfare and bid for military glory came more open contact with the world beyond the Nile: for example, the pharaohs took to breeding horses and riding—or at least, having themselves depicted riding—chariots, just like their Hittite rivals (see photo).

Yet again, the wealth of the world went to the benefit of the gods and goddesses of the Nile. No longer builders of pyramids, the pharaohs of the New Kingdom instead had their massive tombs hewn out of solid rock in the Valley of the Kings near Thebes, and they constructed vast new temples like that of the

"I Crushed a Million Countries by Myself, on 'Victory-in-Thebes,' 'Mut-Is-Pleased,' My Horses" A scene from the Battle of Qadesh in Syria (1274 B.C.), as described by the New Kingdom pharaoh Ramses II. The Egyptians have fled before a Hittite army—except for the pharaoh, who prays to Amon-Re for help, lashes his horses' reins round his waist, drives against the foe, and scatters them. Ramses' version was carved on temple walls throughout Egypt; meanwhile, however, the Hittites also claimed victory. DEA/G. Dagli Orti/Getty Images

Theban god Amon at Karnak. Partly because of this dedication of wealth to religion, however, the power of the priests eventually came to overshadow that of the pharaohs. This, together with the inability of the then ruling dynasty to produce heirs, led to the end of the New Kingdom about 1100 B.C.

After the New Kingdom, Egypt often became a victim of invaders from elsewhere in Africa, from Mesopotamia, and eventually from Europe. It was dominated at different times—though with intervals of independence—by its western and southern neighbors, the Libyans and the Nubians, and by the Assyrians of Mesopotamia (pp. 34–35). In 525 B.C. Egypt became a province of the empire of Persia (p. 35); from 333 B.C. it was ruled by the Greeks; and finally, in 30 B.C., it was conquered by the Romans (pp. 83, 101).

Even so, Egyptian civilization continued to flourish. Libyan and Nubian rulers were much influenced by Egyptian ways even in their homelands, and they governed as genuine pharaohs, upholding the country's power and independence against Mesopotamian enemies. The Persians and Greeks had their own traditions of civilization, but they still found it wise to rule Egypt in accordance with the country's traditional beliefs and customs. The last great temples of the Nile were built after 250 B.C. by Greek kings acting as Egyptian pharaohs, to uphold the stability and harmony of the universe by tending to the needs of the gods.

Still, Egypt no longer "trod on" foreign peoples but instead was often one of the trodden. The reason had to do with great changes that began in the lands between the Indian Ocean and the eastern Mediterranean around the time that the New Kingdom ended—changes that gave the advantage in skills, wealth, and power to peoples outside Egypt.

 Listen to a synopsis of Chapter 1.

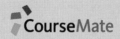 **Access to the eBook with additional review material and study tools may be found online at CourseMate for WCIV. Sign in at www.cengagebrain.com.**

CHAPTER 2

KINGS OF KINGS AND ONE GOD,
1200–300 B.C.

LEARNING OBJECTIVES

AFTER READING THIS CHAPTER, YOU SHOULD BE ABLE TO DO THE FOLLOWING:

LO¹ Describe how the period from 1200 to 900 B.C. was one of both crisis and innovation in the lands between the Indian Ocean and the Mediterranean Sea.

LO² Contrast the Assyrian and Persian methods of conquest and rule, and describe the achievements of these first universal empires.

LO³ Trace the evolution of the Jewish religion as a new kind of faith in one God.

"NEW SKILLS AND INTERNATIONAL CONTACTS HELPED MAKE IT POSSIBLE FOR CONQUERING PEOPLES TO BUILD 'UNIVERSAL' EMPIRES, WHICH RULED LARGER TERRITORIES THAN EVER BEFORE."

Around 1200 B.C., a new era began in the lands between the Indian Ocean and the Mediterranean Sea, when the region underwent a massive crisis. It was weakened by internal conflicts, nomadic peoples attacked it from north and south, and old-established kingdoms were swept away.

Gradually, the region recovered from the crisis, but it was different from before. It possessed new skills that would be basic features of many future civilizations, such as the use of iron and alphabetic writing. It was more closely knit together by trade and travel across networks of flourishing commercial city-states. And these new skills and international contacts helped make it possible for conquering peoples to build "universal" empires, which ruled larger territories than ever before. From time to time, there were spectacular reversals of fortune when one empire fell and another arose to take its place. But the idea took hold that it was normal for the region to have a single mighty ruler.

In this changing environment after 1200 B.C., there also appeared a new religious belief, that of monotheism, which proclaimed a single almighty God as the creator and ruler of the world. Monotheism was mainly the belief of one people, the Jews, and developed among them over many centuries of triumph and disaster in regional power struggles. By 300 B.C., the Jews were wholeheartedly committed to belief in the one God, and their beliefs and practices included many features of later monotheistic religions.

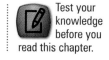 Test your knowledge before you read this chapter.

What do you think?

Monotheism represents an advance over the polytheism of Egypt and Mesopotamia.

Strongly Disagree						Strongly Agree
1	2	3	4	5	6	7

≪ "I Am Darius, the Great King, King of Kings" This scene illustrates a Persian king's account of his deeds, carved into a cliffside at Behistun in present-day western Iran about 500 B.C. The king tramples a defeated rebel while captives representing conquered peoples stand before him, and the winged disk of divine power hovers above. At the time, Darius's empire stretched from Egypt and Anatolia to the borders of India.

Iconotec/Photolibrary

31

LO¹ Crisis and Recovery

Civilized societies have often been beset by internal problems and outside invasions, but often these troubles have ended not in collapse but in renewal. This was what now happened to the lands between the Indian Ocean and the Mediterranean Sea, as three hundred years of chaos forced the development of world-changing technical skills as well as empires of unprecedented size.

A Time of Troubles

Around 1200 B.C., the Hittite kingdom in Anatolia (pp. 20) fell to mysterious invaders who arrived by land and sea from the coasts and islands of the eastern Mediterranean. These invaders had perhaps been displaced by overpopulation and war among the peoples of Europe. From Anatolia, they went on to attack Syria, Palestine, and finally Egypt, where they were known as the "Sea Peoples" and where they were eventually repelled or assimilated. At about the same time, the Kassite kings of Mesopotamia were overthrown by invaders from farther east, who, however, were not strong enough to replace them as rulers of that entire region. Of the three great powers of the region, two had been destroyed, and the third, Egypt, was badly weakened.

New groups of Semitic nomads took advantage of the power vacuum to move into Mesopotamia. The northern part fell to the Aramaeans (ar-uh-MEY-ans), from the barren lands between the river valleys, and the south to the Chaldeans (kal-DEE-uhns) from Arabia. In Anatolia, meanwhile, the disruption of the trade in metals that had supplied much of the wealth for civilization led to several centuries of decline and decay, made worse by new invasions of nomadic peoples from farther north.

New Skills and New City-States

Out of the turmoil, however, came more advanced technical skills and a more intensive pattern of trade and travel, than ever before.

The Advent of Iron

In the devastated lands of Anatolia, metalworkers who were short of the imported tin that they needed to alloy with copper to make bronze began to take an interest in another metal: iron. This metal was far more plentiful than copper or tin, but it was difficult to smelt (extract from rock) and work. Forced by necessity, the bronzesmiths started to experiment with improved processes for smelting iron, as well as hardening and toughening it, until they ended with a metal that was superior to bronze and available in far larger quantities. In this way,

> **"In the devastated lands of Anatolia, metalworkers who were short of the imported tin that they needed to alloy with copper to make bronze began to take an interest in another metal: iron."**

CHRONOLOGY

1200–900 B.C.	Invaders from the Mediterranean and others from lands east of Mesopotamia assault the lands between the Indian Ocean and the Mediterranean Sea; Egypt is badly weakened; Hittites and Kassites fall
	Phoenicians develop sea trade; Aramaeans develop overland trade; alphabet spreads
	Beginning of Iron Age
	King David makes Jerusalem his seat of government
900–600 B.C.	Assyrian Empire
587 B.C.	Jerusalem falls to the Chaldeans; Jewish Diaspora intensifies
550–330 B.C.	Persian Empire
	Hebrew Bible evolves

Anatolia and neighboring lands moved from the Bronze Age to the Iron Age.

Phoenicians, Aramaeans, and the Alphabet

On the Mediterranean coast, another Semitic-speaking people, the Phoenicians (fi-NEE-shuhns), benefited from the absence of great powers. The Phoenicians had traditionally lived by seaborne trade, above all with Egypt, and they seem to have been in some way subject to the pharaohs. Now, however, their seaports became wealthy and independent city-states.

The Phoenicians used the forests in their coastal mountains—the famous "cedars of Lebanon"—to build ships that were no longer the converted riverboats of the Egyptians (p. 26). Instead, they had stout internal timber frameworks to strengthen their hulls against wind and wave. Merchant vessels were escorted by purpose-built seagoing warships propelled not only by sails but also by crews of oarsmen, sitting in two rows one above the other, to provide speed and maneuverability. In battle, they sank enemy vessels with bronze-tipped rams projecting from their bows or hooked up alongside and put soldiers aboard.

In their seaworthy vessels, Phoenician merchants ranged throughout the Mediterranean and out into the Atlantic as far as the British Isles in search of timber, metal, and slaves. They set up trading stations on the coastlines of Africa and Spain that eventually turned into colonies (see Map 3.2 on page 50). Both as traders and as settlers, the Phoenicians linked the peoples of southern Europe with the region of civilization between the Indian Ocean and the Mediterranean Sea.

Meanwhile, in Mesopotamia, the Aramaean and Chaldean nomads adapted, like so many invaders before them, to the civilization that had grown up between the rivers. The Aramaeans in particular established a network of prosperous city-states that dominated the land trade of the region in the same way that the Phoenicians controlled its sea links to the west. And both the Aramaeans and the Phoenicians played a vital role in the transmission of a new and easily learned writing system: the **alphabet**.

Alphabetic writing seems to have developed out of a drastically simplified version of Egyptian hieroglyphs used as early as 1900 B.C. by Semitic immigrants and captives in and around Egypt. Instead of the hundreds of signs and complex rules in hieroglyphic and cuneiform writing, this system had only thirty letters, each representing a single basic sound of speech. Other Semitic peoples, including the Aramaeans and Phoenicians, then started using the alphabet. As the Aramaeans took over inland trade, their tongue, with its alphabetic writing, replaced Akkadian as the international language. Meanwhile, Mediterranean peoples who became advanced enough to feel the need for writing,

above all the Greeks, learned the Phoenician version of the alphabet and adapted it to their languages.

LO² Universal Empires: Assyria and Persia

New skills and more intensive trade and travel eventually made it possible for new great powers to arise that would build larger empires than ever before. In an era of limited intercontinental contacts, it was natural for the peoples between the Indian Ocean and the Mediterranean Sea to think of their large and diverse region as "the world," and for the new conquerors to think of themselves as world rulers. Consequently, the empires that they built are often called "universal" (worldwide) **empires**.

Assyria

The Assyrians had lived for centuries in a small homeland along the middle and upper reaches of the Tigris River (Map 2.1 on page 35), more or less successfully holding off powerful neighbors such as Babylonia and the Hittites. But after 1200 B.C., the Assyrians saw an opportunity to fill the regional power vacuum—to begin with, by controlling the profitable trade routes between western Asia and the Mediterranean. As they gradually accomplished this aim, they began to conceive of the larger goal of a universal empire. As one of their rulers would declare, "I am the legitimate king of the world . . . of all four rims of the earth . . . king of kings."

The rise of Assyria began shortly after 900 B.C. with the takeover of Aramaean city-states in northern Mesopotamia. Then the Assyrians struck north and west and took over the southern portion of Asia Minor, as well as Syria, Phoenicia, and part of the Israelite territories in Palestine. By 700 B.C., they had also added the Chaldean-ruled territories of southern Mesopotamia, including Babylon,

alphabet
A writing system in which each letter represents a basic sound of speech.

empire
A territory larger than a kingdom, including many different peoples, and governed by a single ruler (an emperor or empress) or by a single community such as a city-state.

Erich Lessing/Art Resource, NY

≪ **Long-Distance Haulage** Phoenician ships haul cedar logs while sea creatures look on. The logs are beginning a lengthy journey by sea, river, and road from the Mediterranean land of Lebanon to the palace of the Assyrian King Sargon II, far upstream on the River Tigris, where they will end up as roof beams. The king, who reigned about 700 B.C., was proud of importing these large items from a distant land; this depiction comes from his palace.

infantry
Soldiers who fight on foot.

cavalry
Soldiers who fight on horseback.

to their possessions. The empire reached its greatest extent in the seventh century B.C., when the rest of Palestine and most of Egypt fell under its control (Map 2.1 on page 35).

The Assyrians were not a numerous people, but they partly made up for this by innovations in military organization, tactics, and weaponry. All adult males were subject to military service, and war was glorified and pursued as the principal business of the kingdom. The army relied on the combined striking power of chariots, light **infantry** (archers and slingers), and massed heavy infantry clad in bronze helmets and armor and wielding iron swords and spears. Eventually, the Assyrians made use of another innovation, brought by nomadic invaders from the steppes: horse-riding **cavalry**. Their engineers also devised battering rams, undermining, and movable siege towers to break down the defenses of cities (see photo).

As an aid to conquest and to hold down the peoples they conquered, the Assyrians pursued a policy of deliberate terror—skinning and mutilating, impaling, burning alive, and displaying stacks of human skulls. The Assyrians were not the first conquerors lovingly to depict their own bloody deeds (see photo on page 21), and they were certainly not the last to use systematic atrocities to build and maintain their empires. But Assyrian palace art proclaims their acts of violence in exceptionally vivid and explicit images and inscriptions.

Even so, the task of holding such a widespread empire was, in the long run, too much for a small people. The imperial masters relied increasingly on drafted or hired troops drawn from subject peoples, but in the end their strength drained

> *"With battle and assault I stormed the city, I took it. Eight hundred of their fighting men I struck down with the sword, with their corpses I filled the streets of their city, with their blood I dyed their houses. Many men I captured alive with my hand, and I carried off great spoil from them; the city I destroyed, I devastated, I burned with fire."*
> —Ashurnasirpal II, ca. 875 B.C.

An Assyrian Emperor's Resume: Ferocious Conquests a Specialty Read an Assyrian ruler's account of how he dealt with a disloyal kingdom.

Ancient Near Eastern Art: New Light on an Assyrian Palace (http://www.metmuseum.org/explore/anesite/html/el_ane_newfirst.htm) Learn more about Assyrian palace art.

 Simulation to Learn About Ancient Cultures Participate in a simulation of life as a warrior in Nineveh in 664 B.C.

away. Finally, they were overcome by a rebellion of the Chaldeans of Babylon, aided by invaders from the north and east. In 612 B.C., their high-walled capital at Nineveh, on the Tigris, was broken into and burned. Most of their army and royal family were wiped out, and the Assyrians sank into obscurity, never to rise again.

All the same, the Assyrian kings succeeded in building the largest regional empire so far. This was the first truly imperial government. Conquered lands were usually organized as provinces, with Assyrian nobles appointed as governors by the king. Some local rulers were permitted to keep their lands, in return for regular payments and under the watchful eyes of Assyrian officials. Systematic intelligence and administrative reports flowed to the capital city of Nineveh from all corners of the empire—helped by a well-developed road system, for the Assyrians were forerunners of the Persians and Romans in grasping the importance of good roads for great empires (pp. 36, 115).

 Everyday Life in Assyria: Labor, Loans, Litigation, and Illegality Read how disputes were resolved in an Assyrian court of 678 B.C.

The Assyrians continued the traditions of Mesopotamian civilization in literature, culture, and the arts and played a vital role in transmitting them to future generations. The world's first known great library was established by the Assyrian ruler Ashurbanipal (ah-shoor-BAH-nee-pahl) at Nineveh (NIN-uh-vuh) about 650 B.C. It contained some twenty thousand tablets with cuneiform texts in the Sumerian as well as the Akkadian languages, and provided the key to present-day knowledge of ancient Mesopotamia when it was excavated in the nineteenth century A.D.

Persia

The power vacuum left by the fall of Assyria was briefly filled by the Chaldean rulers who had liberated Babylonia and who went on to conquer lands as far away as Palestine. But this Neo-Babylonian Empire, as modern scholars call it, soon fell victim to yet another empire-building people, the Persians.

The Persians, together with their neighbors the Medes, were peoples of Indo-European origin (p. 20) who had moved into the territories to the east of Mesopotamia from about 1000 B.C. onward. Media and Persia formed the western part of a vast plateau, much of it desert and fringed to the north and west by mountain ranges that stretched all the way to India. But

Siege Warfare Assyrian engineers adjust a chain holding a battering ram that they will swing against a city gate, and tunnelers undermine the walls. Defending archers take aim against the besiegers, attacking archers counter them, and defenders fall from their perches. Assyrian methods of attacking fortified positions continued to be used by armies for two thousand years down to the invention of cannon. British Museum Photo © Michael Holford

used either name, "Persians" or "Medes," to describe the new universal rulers. Thus, in his very first step, Cyrus showed that instead of terrorizing his opponents like the Assyrians, he would seek to win them over by reasonable and decent treatment. Within twenty years after his victory over the Medes, Cyrus was in control of every land from the Indus Valley to the Mediterranean. Four years later (525 B.C.), his son Cambyses added Egypt and Libya to the new empire, making it by far the largest that had ever arisen in the region (see Map 2.1). The Persians were able to hold together this vast empire for two centuries using different methods than the Assyrians.

dualism
The belief in two supremely powerful beings or forces, one good and the other evil, whose conflict shapes the destiny of the world and humans.

 Simulation to Learn About Ancient Cultures Participate in a simulation of life in ancient Persia as a government official in Cyrus's empire or a solder for Darius and Xerxes.

the region was rich in metals, and farmers there had adopted ingenious methods of exploiting underground water sources. As the wealth and population of the Medes and Persians grew, their rulers began to take an interest in the civilization of Mesopotamia and to intervene in its power politics.

The Persians' rise to empire began when their king Cyrus conquered the Medes in 550 B.C. and took them into partnership for further conquests—on such equal terms that the Greeks

Persian Religion: Good, Evil, and Salvation

In religion, the Persians began to break away from traditional polytheism, and their beliefs probably influenced the monotheism of the Jews. The Persian religious thinker Zoroaster (ZAWR-oh-as-ter), who is believed to have lived in the seventh century B.C., preached faith in one God, the author of both good and evil. His followers turned this faith into a **dualism** that

Map 2.1 **The Assyrian and Persian Empires**

The Assyrians and then the Persians built larger empires than ever before in the lands where Asia and Africa meet. About 660 B.C. the Assyrian Empire included all of Mesopotamia, the Mediterranean's eastern coast, and much of Egypt; in 500 B.C. the Persians ruled most of the region between southeastern Europe, northeastern Africa, and the borders of India, as well as vast lands of nomadic peoples in central Asia. © Cengage Learning

 Interactive Map

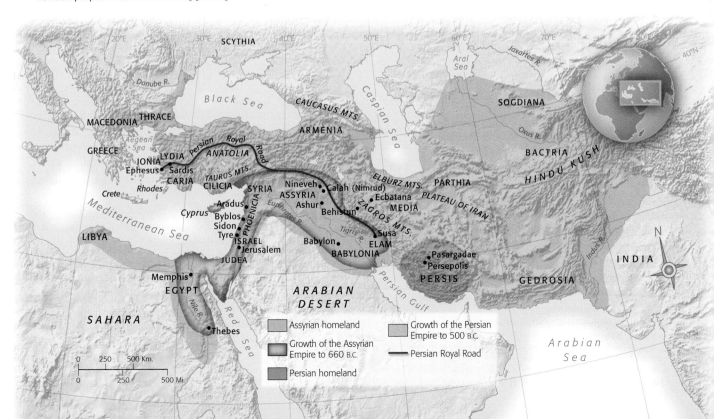

MULTIPLE FACTORS HELD THE PERSIAN EMPIRE TOGETHER FOR TWO CENTURIES:

The Kingship Tradition

· The Persian ruler won the loyalty of his subjects in Mesopotamia by operating within their kingship tradition. He was the "King of Kings," identified with divine will and justice though not himself thought of as a god.

· The "King of Kings" held his subjects in awe: he sat on a gold and blue throne, dressed in purple cloth and laden with jewels, in a huge palace where ordinary mortals were required to lie, face down, before him.

Partnerships with Local Powers

· Positions as King's Friends (leading officials and courtiers), satraps (governors of provinces), and army commanders were generally filled by wealthy landowners and leading warriors. The nobles could look to the king for honors and rewards if they served him well, and the king in turn could make use of their wealth and power in his service.

· The King's Sons and King's Daughters were regularly married off to noble children. The King's Wives played politics behind the scenes, vying to get their sons into positions of power. This pattern of partnership between the ruler and the nobles reinforced by family ties, with the women of the royal court wielding power that buttressed that of the king, was a precedent for many future monarchies, including those of Europe.

Military Might

· Similar in organization and weaponry to the Assyrians, Persian troops constituted the backbone of the heavily armed infantry, which operated together with bow-wielding cavalry and charioteers.

· Large supporting forces, including fleets of warships, were drawn from the conquered populations—Syrians, Phoenicians, Egyptians, and Greeks.

Tolerance of Local Customs

· Taxes and military supplies were rigorously collected, but local customs, languages, and religions were left alone.

As a result, rebellions were unusual, though the Greeks and Egyptians never fully accepted Persian rule.

A Strong Bureaucracy

· The realm was divided into some twenty provinces (satrapies). The satraps ruled with a light hand, under the guiding principles of restraint and tolerance.

· Royal inspectors, the "king's eyes," supervised the work of the satraps and reported directly to the royal palace. They followed existing practice by writing their reports in Aramaic.

· An excellent road system eased the flow of reports and goods between the provinces and the capital (see Map 2.1 on page 35).

· The Persians adopted the use of coins (invented by the Lydians of Asia Minor in the seventh century B.C.) to make payment of taxes easier.

---

taught that the world was the scene of two rival forces: Ahura Mazda, god of goodness and light, and Angra Mainyu, demon of evil and darkness. Righteous humans would go to the heavenly courts of Ahura Mazda upon their death; the wicked would go to hell with Angra Mainyu. At the end of time, however, a savior would appear, miraculously born, to prepare the way for Ahura Mazda's triumph. Angra Mainyu would be made harmless, and all of humanity, including even the captives in hell, would be raised to enjoy eternal bliss. These beliefs were proclaimed in a revered collection of holy writings, the Avesta.

 Virtual Tour of Persepolis (http://www .letsgoiran.com/ persepolis/persepolis- travel-guide) Take a tour of Persepolis.

Babylonian astronomers continued, with Persian encouragement, to advance their knowledge of the heavens; one result

was their learning how to calculate and predict eclipses of the moon. Persian art and architecture were chiefly adaptations of existing styles and techniques. The most magnificent example, the royal palace at Persepolis, was a successful combination of building and sculptural elements from Assyria, Babylonia, Egypt, and Greece.

The Persian Empire lasted for two hundred years until it was brought down by yet another world conqueror, Alexander the Great, and the Persians gave way to yet another ruling people, the Greeks (pp. 82–83). But in those two centuries, the Persians brought their subject peoples unity, peace, and the freedom of movement and ideas that unity permits, while allowing them to maintain their own identities. United yet diverse, enriched by many different cultural traditions that had grown up over the centuries, the Persian Empire was a high point of three thousand years of civilization in the lands between the Indian Ocean and the Mediterranean Sea.

LO³ The Jews and Monotheism

Of all the changes that took place in the lands between the Indian Ocean and the Aegean Sea after 1200 B.C., one of the most momentous was the appearance of a new kind of religious belief. Alongside traditional polytheism, there appeared the belief in one God, or **monotheism**.

 Religion Facts (for Judaism and Zoroastrianism) (http://www.religionfacts.com) Learn more about Judaism and Zoroastrianism.

The new belief involved far more than just the question of how many divine beings were to be worshiped. The one God was thought of as eternal, almighty, all-knowing, the creator of the whole universe, infinitely good, pure spirit yet somehow masculine. He would give humans prosperity and happiness so long as they worshiped and obeyed him alone, rejected all other gods and goddesses, and behaved righteously toward each other. If they did not, he would punish them with misfortune and misery, and for unsearchable reasons he also allowed evil to befall even those who were righteous in his sight. One day, however, he would send a mighty redeemer who would deliver the righteous from all evil, to live in blessedness forever. Meanwhile, his worshipers would form a community united in knowledge of him and obedience to his commands, and guided by holy writings and by specially qualified believers.

Several peoples had beliefs that were forerunners of monotheism and may have influenced its rise. About 1800 B.C., the Egyptian pharaoh Akhenaten had worshiped a single divine power that ruled the whole universe, though his innovations had been rejected after his death (p. 25). A thousand years later, the Persians saw the world as a place of struggle between mighty good and evil forces (p. 35). But above all, monotheism developed out of the beliefs and practices of the Jews and their experiences of triumph and disaster as their region of the world collapsed into chaos, recovered from the crisis, and came under the rule of universal empires.

One Land and Many Gods: The Israelites

For many centuries of their early history, the Jews lived in a single territory, the land of Palestine on the eastern shore of the Mediterranean Sea (Map 2.2). With its rocky landscape, its hot, dry summers, and its cold, wet winters, Palestine had only a limited amount of agricultural wealth to provide a foundation for civilized life. Over many centuries from about 3000 B.C. onward, however, farmers in Palestine and many other Mediterranean lands had learned to get the most from their soil by growing grain together with olive trees and grapevines.

The peoples of Palestine and nearby lands had learned from the ways of life of Anatolia, Egypt, and Mesopotamia, and in recent centuries the Hittites and the Egyptians had fought many wars for empire over them (p. 28). They spoke and wrote Semitic languages (p. 17), and they had links of trade and travel with nearby and distant lands. They had their own pantheon of gods and goddesses, whose chief and father, El, was called by such names as "the Most High" and "El of the Covenant." The ideas of a supreme god and of covenants (formal promises of protection and loyalty binding together the god and the communities that worshiped him) were seemingly important ones in this traditional religion.

> **monotheism**
> The belief in a single, all-powerful, and all-knowing God.

> "*United yet diverse, enriched by many different cultural traditions that had grown up over the centuries, the Persian Empire was a high point of three thousand years of civilization in the lands between the Indian Ocean and the Mediterranean Sea.*"

Israel and Its Gods

When the great regional upheaval began, Palestine was caught in the general turmoil. Archeological surveys indicate that the region's thinly populated hill country, lying inland from the Mediterranean coast, filled up with settlers. The remains of their tools and buildings suggest that the newcomers came from the coastlands of Palestine itself as well as from other nearby lands, probably to escape troubles in these less sheltered regions. By 1200 B.C., many of the settlers formed a distinct people. Their name is first mentioned in a monument that an Egyptian pharaoh set up about that date, listing them among defeated enemies: Israel.

The Israelites, as they were usually called at this time,[1] had traditions of much older origins, which were recorded many centuries later in the Hebrew Bible (the Old Testament of the Christian Bible). These traditions spoke of lengthy travels from Mesopotamia to Egypt, beginning with a first forefather,

---

[1]Israel ("He Who Strives with God") was a name taken, according to tradition, by Abraham's grandson. Until about 500 B.C., it was the name used by the people that claimed descent from him, though sometimes they were called Hebrews (from a Semitic word meaning "wanderer"). The name Jews (from the part of Palestine known as Judah) came into use after 500 B.C. The language of the Jews at all periods is known as Hebrew.

Abraham; and of escape from oppression in Egypt and wanderings in the desert that lay to the south of Palestine, led by a great prophet, Moses. Both as a wandering and as a settled people, the Bible says, the Israelites were guided and protected by a mighty god, Yahweh, who had covenanted with them to bring them prosperity and victory so long as they served and honored "no other gods before me."

The Bible also records, however, that the Israelites regularly "lusted after other gods." At first, these deities were probably the traditional gods and goddesses of the nearby lands from which the Israelite settlers came, whom they saw nothing wrong in worshiping alongside Yahweh. As the Israelites developed into a separate people from their neighbors, however, their traditions of distant origins and Yahweh's guidance became increasingly important to them. They called him sometimes Yahweh and sometimes El, as if they thought of the two supreme gods as one and the same. But in time his name became too holy even to speak, and usually he was called simply "the Lord."

Even so, many or most Israelites did not give up the worship of other deities. Instead, they continued to follow the polytheistic tradition that it was righteous and prudent for humans to worship not just the chief deity of their own community but all gods and goddesses who might influence their destinies (p. 15). Priests and prophets might speak of "The Lord, whose name is Jealous," and ask, "Who is God, except the Lord?" But it took many centuries for the Israelites to decide that the priests and prophets were right.

David, Solomon, and the Temple

Initially, the Israelite settlers led a simple village way of life without central government. As their region recovered from the crisis, however, their society became more complex. In the power vacuum left by the collapse of the Hittite kingdom and the weakening of Egypt, they fought, allied, and intermarried with neighboring peoples, led by war chieftains who grew into hereditary kings. Finally, about 1000 B.C., there came a time of triumph, when King David conquered the important settlement of Jerusalem and made it his seat of government.

 (http://www.pbs.org/wnet/heritage/episode1/presentations/1.6.1-1.html) Listen to a biblical account of the Israelites' conquest of Canaan in the late thirteenth century B.C. and discover how archeologists investigate that story.

As in every other kingdom, the royal city became the home of the god that the rulers served. David's son Solomon built the Temple in Jerusalem—a magnificent house for Yahweh, where priests served him with plentiful offerings and sacrifices like any other leading deity. Like other deities, too, Yahweh was present in his Temple—but not in the usual form of a "graven image," for he had forbidden his people to make any such objects of worship. Instead, in the midst of the Temple there stood the Ark of the Covenant, a wooden chest sheathed in gold that was at once a container for writings of Yahweh's covenant with Israel and the throne and footstool of the unseen god. But Solomon also made

sure not to neglect other mighty deities. He built several other sanctuaries near Jerusalem, among them one for Ashtoreth, the local version of the ancient fertility goddess Ishtar (p. 18).

Kings and Prophets

As Israelite society became more complex, it also became more liable to conflict. Resentment grew against its newly powerful kings, and when Solomon died about 950 B.C., most of Israel rebelled. Yahweh's people were divided between two kingdoms: a larger one, Israel, under new rulers; and the southern kingdom of Judah, including Jerusalem, still ruled by kings of David's line.

With kings now ruling as servants of divine power, questions of which divine power they were to serve became more urgent and divisive than before. Most rulers continued to worship other deities alongside Yahweh, but time and again, Yahweh's prophets openly resisted the traditional-minded kings and

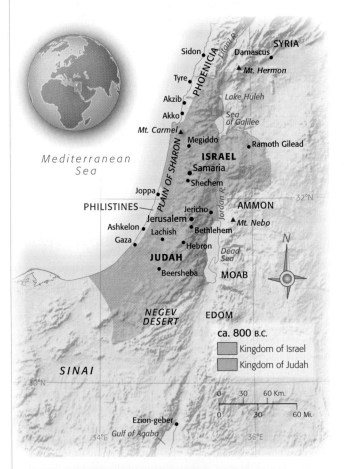

Map 2.2 The Israelites and Their Neighbors

About 1200 B.C. the Israelites lived mostly inland from the eastern Mediterranean coast. They were a farming people, unlike their seafaring neighbors, the Phoenicians, and their rivals the Philistines, who controlled most of the actual coastline. By 800 B.C. they had expanded but also divided into two kingdoms, Israel and Judah, which then became victims of the conquering Assyrians and Babylonians. © Cengage Learning

Interactive Map

threatened them and their subjects with Yahweh's wrath. The prophets also denounced such features of social life in Israel and Judah as kings who stole the property of their subjects, judges who sold verdicts, and rich landowners who took over the farms of debt-ridden peasants. Prophets were sometimes deeply involved in power struggles within the two kingdoms, and one of them, Elisha, even sponsored the bloody overthrow of a dynasty in Israel.

But what motivated the prophets was always the belief that Yahweh was not being properly worshiped and obeyed. Above all, they condemned idols—the images and other objects on which worshipers of the gods and goddesses focused their love and fear of divine power. Idols, said the prophets, were "abominations"—not just forbidden by Yahweh's "jealousy" but unworthy of worship because the beings they represented were evil or powerless. Yahweh's people, the prophets declared, must finally choose between him and the rival deities. The prophet Elijah, reproaching worshipers in the kingdom of Israel who turned to the weather-god Baal in time of drought about 850 B.C., asked them: "How long will you go limping with two different opinions? If the Lord is God, follow him; but if Baal, then follow him."

> " *How long will you go limping with two different opinions? If the Lord is God, follow him; but if Baal, then follow him.* "

Many Lands and One God: The Jews

Yahweh's people went on "limping with two opinions" all the same, until Mesopotamian world conquerors reached out to destroy the Israelite kingdoms. In 722 B.C., the Assyrians conquered the kingdom of Israel and made it a province of their empire. After Assyria's fall, the Chaldeans invaded Judah, and in 587 B.C. they captured Jerusalem and destroyed the Temple. Both disasters were followed by massive deportations to Mesopotamia, and when Judah fell, many of its people left for Egypt. Villagers in Palestine still worshiped Yahweh, but they were leaderless and mixed with settlers brought in by the conquerors. Priests, scribes, warriors, landowners, and many people of lower rank were now in exile.

God, His People, and the Nations

It was exactly these disasters that first made the monotheistic belief in Yahweh the dominant religion of his people. Most of the exiles from Israel and many from Judah lost their identity as Yahweh's people and merged with the nations among whom they were scattered. The only worshipers left to him were those who truly believed that he was the one almighty God that the prophets had proclaimed him to be. The true believers now listened to new prophets, who declared that, far from proving Yahweh's weakness, the disasters were proof of his worldwide power. The deportations and the Temple's destruction were God's punishment of his people for breaking their covenant with him. According to "the word of the Lord" as proclaimed by Isaiah about 700 B.C., even the mighty Assyrian king was merely "the rod of my anger."

Furthermore, he who punished could also forgive. If the Israelites turned their hearts back to God and fulfilled their covenanted duties to him, then sooner or later, in the words of Jeremiah (600 B.C.), "He who scattered Israel will gather him." Prophecies said to be by Isaiah declared that God would send a great king of David's line to deliver his people from oppression and evil, or perhaps a "suffering servant" who would take their sins upon himself. When that day came, the Temple would be rebuilt as "a house of prayer for all peoples," evil and suffering and war would cease, and "the earth shall be full of the knowledge of the Lord, as the waters cover the sea." The conquering universal empires that had destroyed the traditional Israelite nation would give way to a benign universal empire ruled by an Israelite king, in which all nations would unite in the worship of the one God.

Sure enough, when the Persians overthrew the Chaldeans and established the largest and most tolerant empire so far, they permitted the exiles to return to Palestine. By 515 B.C., the Temple was rebuilt, and again Yahweh was served with offerings and sacrifices in the city of David—though the "Holy of Holies" was now an empty chamber, since the Ark of the Covenant had not survived the troubles.

Many prophecies were still unfulfilled, however. God had not restored his people to their whole land, but only to Judah, from which they took their name as Jews. Instead of a God-sent king, the Jews were governed by the high priests of the Temple, appointed by the Persian rulers. Furthermore, most Jews did not return but continued to live in what came to be known as the **diaspora** (dahy-AS-per-uh). In Mesopotamia, and later in Judah as well, they gave up Hebrew as their everyday tongue in favor of the internationally spoken Aramaic language, and in Egypt, they eventually came to speak Greek.

If the scattered Jews were to survive as the chosen people of the one God until the day of full deliverance arrived, they must make drastic changes in their religious practices so as never again to break their renewed covenant. These changes began among the exiled remnant in Babylon, were enforced on the villagers of Judah by returning exiles, and eventually spread to Egypt to form a new pattern of worship and life for Jews in every land.

The Holy Writings

To make sure that they strictly observed their covenant with God, more than ever before the Jews needed to put in writing the terms of the covenant and the history of God's dealings with

diaspora
The dispersion of Jews to countries outside of Palestine.

JERUSALEM BESIEGED: THE ASSYRIAN KING SENNACHERIB'S ACCOUNT

Sennacherib had the story of his royal deeds written down in many copies, one of which was found in A.D. 1830 in the ruins of his palace in Nineveh. Here he describes how in 701 B.C. he crushed a widespread rebellion by his vassal kings in Palestine and Syria, supported by Assyria's rival "great power," Egypt. One of the rebels was King Hezekiah of the Israelite kingdom of Judah. Sennacherib could not take Jerusalem, but he inflicted great casualties on the Israelite army and forced Hezekiah and other rebels into submission. Sennacherib is rather vague about the events at Jerusalem; for a contrasting account by the Jewish prophet Isaiah, see the document link below.

"Tamartu-presents" are gifts given by a defeated enemy; "katru-presents" are gifts by way of regular tribute.

In my third campaign I marched against Hatti. Luli, king of Sidon, whom the terror-inspiring glamour of my lordship had overwhelmed, fled far overseas and perished. The awe-inspiring splendor of the "Weapon" of Ashur, my lord, overwhelmed his strong cities such as Great Sidon, Little Sidon, Bit-Zitti, Zaribtu, Mahalliba, Ushu, Akzib and Akko, all his fortress cities, walled and well provided with food and water for his garrisons, and they bowed in submission to my feet. I installed Ethbaal upon the throne to be their king and imposed upon him tribute due to me as his overlord to be paid annually without interruption.

As to all the kings of Amurru—Menahem from Sam-simuruna, Tubalu from Sidon, Abdiliti from Arvad, Urumilki from Byblos, Mitinti from Ashdod, Buduili from Beth-Ammon, Kammusun-adbi from Moab and Aiarammu from Edom, they brought sumptuous gifts and—fourfold—their heavy tamartu-presents to me and kissed my feet. Sidqia, however, king of

Ashkelon, who did not bow to my yoke, I deported and sent to Assyria, his family-gods, himself, his wife, his children, his brothers, all the male descendants of his family. I set Sharru-ludari, son of Rukibtu, their former king, over the inhabitants of Ashkelon and imposed upon him the payment of tribute and of katru-presents due to me as overlord—and he (now) pulls the straps of my yoke!

In the continuation of my campaign I besieged Beth-Dagon, Joppa, Banai-Barqa, Azuru, cities belonging to Sidqia who did not bow to my feet quickly enough; I conquered them and carried their spoils away. The officials, the patricians and the common people of Ekron—who had thrown Padi, their king, into fetters because he was loyal to his solemn oath sworn by the god Ashur, and had handed him over to Hezekiah, the Jew and he [Hezekiah] held him in prison, unlawfully, as if he [Padi] be an enemy—had become afraid and had called for

them. Documents already existed that told of God's promises and commands to his people and his dealings with them before the exile. Probably during and not long after the exile, these writings were combined and edited to produce books that in time came to be accepted as holy by Jews everywhere. Many new works, mostly telling of God's utterances through his prophets and his raising up and casting down of rulers and nations, were written from the time of the exile onward that also came to be considered as truthfully revealing God's deeds and will.

By sometime after 200 B.C., all the books of the present-day Hebrew Bible had been written, though it took until after A.D. 200 for Jewish leaders to settle on the **canon**—the exact list of works to be considered holy. In this way, the Hebrew Bible came into being—not as a single book, but as a collection of books that grew over many centuries.

Partly because the Hebrew Bible evolved in this way, it often makes contrasting statements about the one God. In one

book, for example, Yahweh insists to Moses on getting his share of every slaughtered animal, yet in another God declares to a prophet after the exile: "I desire steadfast love and not sacrifice, the knowledge of God rather than burnt-offerings." And many Bible stories depict Yahweh as a relentless war-god, while other stories tell of God's goodness to all nations, including even the terrible Assyrians.

"In the Beginning . . .": The Hebrews Explain Creation Read the Bible story of how God created the world.

Many of the features of God as portrayed in the Hebrew Bible were not new. Other peoples in the lands between the Indian Ocean and the Aegean Sea had already worshiped mighty creators of heaven and earth, inconceivably ancient and mysterious holy beings, dreadful judges of the righteous and the wicked, loving "shepherds" of individual humans, majestic wielders of supreme divine power, and deities to whom they were bound by covenants (pp. 15, 18, 25). But no earlier god had had all these features at once, and few had been without

help upon the kings of Egypt and the bowmen, the chariot-corps and the cavalry of the king of Ethiopia, an army beyond counting—and they actually had come to their assistance. In the plain of Eltekeh, their battle lines were drawn up against me and they sharpened their weapons. Upon a trust-inspiring oracle given by Ashur, my lord, I fought with them and inflicted a defeat upon them. In the melee of the battle, I personally captured alive the Egyptian charioteers with their princes and also the charioteers of the king of Ethiopia. I besieged Eltekeh and Timnah, conquered them and carried their spoils away. I assaulted Ekron and killed the officials and patricians who had committed the crime and hung their bodies on poles surrounding the city. The common citizens who were guilty of minor crimes, I considered prisoners of war. The rest of them, those who were not accused of crimes and misbehavior, I released. I made Padi, their king, come from Jerusalem and set him as their lord on the throne, imposing upon him the tribute due to me as overlord.

As to Hezekiah, the Jew, he did not submit to my yoke, I laid siege to 46 of his strong cities, walled forts and to the countless small villages in their vicinity, and conquered them by means of well-stamped earth-ramps, and battering-rams brought thus near to the walls combined with the attack by foot soldiers, using mines, breeches as well as sapper work. I drove out of them 200,150 people, young and old, male and female, horses, mules, donkeys, camels, big and small cattle beyond counting, and considered them booty. Himself I made a prisoner in Jerusalem, his royal residence, like a bird in a cage. I surrounded him with earthwork in order to molest those who were leaving his city's gate. His towns which I had plundered, I took away from his country and gave them over to Mitinti, king of Ashdod, Padi, king of Ekron, and Sillibel, king of Gaza. Thus

I reduced his country, but I still increased the tribute and the katru-presents due to me as his overlord which I imposed later upon him beyond the former tribute, to be delivered annually. Hezekiah himself, whom the terror-inspiring splendor of my lordship had overwhelmed and whose irregular and elite troops which he had brought into Jerusalem, his royal residence, in order to strengthen it, had deserted him, did send me, later, to Nineveh, my lordly city, together with 30 talents of gold, 800 talents of silver, precious stones, antimony, large cuts of red stone, couches inlaid with ivory, nimedu-chairs inlaid with ivory, elephant-hides, ebony-wood, boxwood and all kinds of valuable treasures, his own daughters, concubines, male and female musicians. In order to deliver the tribute and to do obeisance as a slave he sent his personal messenger.

EXPLORING THE SOURCE

1. What methods did the Assyrians use to bring the rulers of the region back into line?

2. Why does Sennacherib take full responsibility for and boast openly of the brutal deeds of his armies? How does this contrast with present-day behavior of commanders whose armies commit brutal deeds?

Source: James B. Pritchard, ed., *Ancient Near Eastern Texts Relating to the New Testament*, 3d ed. (Princeton, N.J.: Princeton University Press, 1969), pp. 287–288.

 Jerusalem Besieged: The Prophet Isaiah's Account of Sennacherib's Siege Read a contrasting account of the siege by the prophet Isaiah.

---

humanlike weaknesses and vices or been considered the only deity to be worshiped.

Men and Women in the Bible

One divine feature that the Hebrew Bible leaves no doubt about is that God is best described as masculine and that he is to be served by male priests. All the same, the Bible's creation story says that humans were made by God "male and female" in his own image. In the Bible, both women and men share a likeness to God.

A vast range of different relationships between men and women appears in the Bible. In early wars in Palestine, the Bible says, Deborah the prophetess and Barak the warrior jointly led Israel to victory—but the treacherous Delilah used womanly wiles to coax the mighty Samson into revealing the secret of his strength, and then betrayed him to Israel's enemies. A rapist and his victim, God-given law decreed, must both be stoned to death unless the woman had cried out for help. A good wife

is "far above rubies," said a proverb—that is, a wife who could run a large farm on her own while her husband spent his time as a prominent citizen "sitting among the elders of the land."

These and many other proverbs, laws, and stories provided examples of relations between men and women to be imitated or avoided in many future centuries of Western civilization. All of them took for granted a prevailing inequality that was much the same as in any other society at the time.

Where the Bible is exceptional, however, is in telling a story of how inequality began. God formed Eve, the first woman, says the Bible, from the flesh of Adam, the first man. It was Eve who gave in to temptation and persuaded Adam to eat the fruit of the tree of knowledge against God's command, and as part of her punishment, God decreed that her husband would rule over her. Scholars disagree about the exact meaning of the story, but it does seem to say that some kind of male dominance is God-given. The story does not say that Eve's disobedience was worse than Adam's, however, and nowhere does the Hebrew

Bible say that women as a group are weaker or more sinful than men as a group because they are "daughters of Eve." These ideas were developed from the Bible story in later times.

A People Apart: The Law

The single most important part of the Hebrew Bible was its first five books, called the Torah ("Instruction" or "Law"). Much of the Torah was a vast legal code, collecting all the laws that Yahweh was said to have given to Moses. The code covered every field of life, including crime and punishment, marriage and divorce, debt and credit, the conduct of worship, ritual purity (bodily cleanliness in the presence of God), and righteousness in general. Included in the Law were the Ten Commandments, the punishment of some offenses on the principle of "eye for eye, tooth for tooth" as in Hammurabi's code (p. 18), the requirements of male circumcision and the purification of women after childbirth, and the prohibition on eating the flesh of animals considered unclean.

Many of the laws were generally similar to those of other peoples, but the laws of ritual purity were exceptionally strict. It was normal for polytheistic worshipers to purify themselves before sacrificing, but the Jewish laws applied to the whole

> *"Monotheism was one of the two longest-lasting legacies to later civilizations from the changing world between the Indian Ocean and the Aegean Sea after 1200 B.C."*

people all the time. The reason was that God's covenant was with the whole people, and they must all obey his commands if he was to fulfill his promises. Accordingly, the Jews now began rigorously obeying the Law. And because obeying the Law was so important, for the first time the Jews took to keeping apart from Gentiles (non-Jews)—refusing, for instance, to intermarry or eat with them.

In addition, to avoid any influences from Gentile religious practices, the worship of God with offerings and sacrifices was now supposed to take place only in the Temple in Jerusalem. Outside the holy city, the religious practice of the Jews came to consist mainly of study of the holy writings and prayer and praise to God. It became customary for them to meet for these purposes on the Sabbath, the seventh day of the week, which God had commanded to be kept holy. The buildings where they met for prayer and study, and the congregations that met in these buildings, came to be known as **synagogues** (from the Greek word for "meetinghouses"). An elite of synagogue leaders grew up—men who could read and write and who were respected in their congregations for obeying, understanding, and interpreting the Law. These religious guides replaced the prophets, and gradually came to rival the Temple priests, as leaders of the Jews.

Heedful of the Bible and obedient to the Law, the Jews became what they had never been before, a people separate and apart from other peoples and forming their own widely scattered but closely knit community, the "House of Israel." But

≪ **"Be Pure and Take Heed"** This letter from Hananiah, a Jewish official of the Persian king, instructs Yedaniah, a commander of Jewish soldiers in Upper Egypt, how to celebrate Passover. Hananiah is particularly strict about leavened bread: "Let it not be seen among you; do not bring it into your houses, but seal it up during those days." The letter dates from 419 B.C., when Temple priests in Jerusalem were eager to standardize religious practice in the Diaspora. Bildarchiv Preussischer Kulturbesitz/Art Resource, NY

their apartness, the Jews believed, would not last forever. The prophecies of the advent of a redeemer-king and the conversion of the Gentiles found their way into the Bible as authoritative statements of what God had in store for the human race as a whole. Meanwhile, Gentiles could "join the House of Israel" by accepting all the obligations of the Law. Gentiles could even live as "God-fearers" on the margins of Jewish congregations, believing in the one God without full observance. The Jews saw themselves as preserving and deepening a closeness between humans and God that would one day be shared by all nations.

In these ways, many present-day features of Judaism came into existence in Persian times, and some of these features were inherited by Christianity and Islam. These monotheisms, too, would have authoritative holy writings, and ministers of religion who acted as leaders of congregations and interpreters of the writings. Both would despise the gods and goddesses as imaginary or evil. They would expect the conversion of the human race to one belief in one God. They would look forward to the advent of a God-sent man of power who would rule in

blessedness forever. And they would await the day of his coming as organized worldwide communities of believers.

For the moment, these were the beliefs of a scattered minority in a world where most people worshiped the traditional gods and goddesses. Still, monotheism was one of the two longest-lasting legacies to later civilizations from the changing world between the Indian Ocean and the Aegean Sea after 1200 B.C. The other was the adoption of a civilized way of life by a European barbarian people living on the region's northwestern edge: the Greeks.

 Listen to a synopsis of Chapter 2.

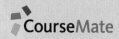 **CourseMate**

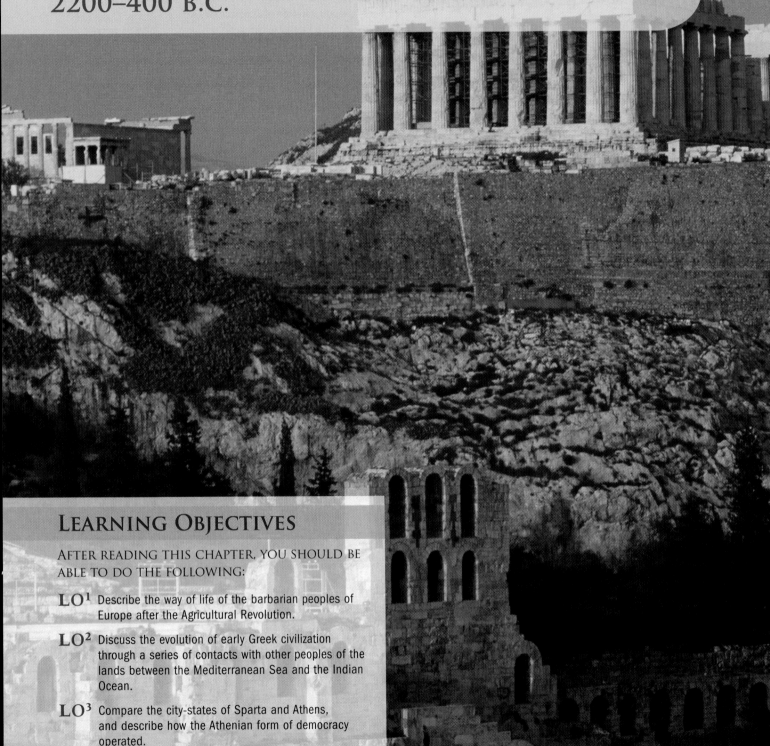

CHAPTER 3

THE FIRST EUROPEAN CIVILIZATION: THE GREEKS, 2200–400 B.C.

LEARNING OBJECTIVES

AFTER READING THIS CHAPTER, YOU SHOULD BE ABLE TO DO THE FOLLOWING:

LO¹ Describe the way of life of the barbarian peoples of Europe after the Agricultural Revolution.

LO² Discuss the evolution of early Greek civilization through a series of contacts with other peoples of the lands between the Mediterranean Sea and the Indian Ocean.

LO³ Compare the city-states of Sparta and Athens, and describe how the Athenian form of democracy operated.

Kevin Schafer/Corbis

> "WITHIN CLASSICAL GREEK CIVILIZATION THERE APPEARED IDEAS, ART FORMS, AND TYPES OF GOVERNMENT WHOSE INFLUENCE ON WESTERN CIVILIZATION HAS LASTED DOWN TO THE PRESENT DAY."

The Greeks began as one of many European **barbarian** peoples—that is, they had a distinctive way of life, based on farming and warfare, that was widespread in western Europe. About 2000 B.C., they began to migrate into Europe's southeastern region, within easy reach of the peoples of Asia Minor, Mesopotamia, and Egypt. As a result, the Greeks began to share in and adapt the more advanced ways of life of the peoples they encountered—something that would happen to European barbarian peoples over and over again in the next three thousand years.

The earliest Greek civilization was very much an offshoot of the ways of life of their eastern neighbors. It shared in the crisis and recovery of the lands between the Mediterranean Sea and the Indian Ocean (pp. 32–33) and finally emerged as "classical" Greek civilization about 800 B.C. Every feature of this renewed Greek civilization was still deeply influenced by their neighbors, but this time, the Greeks had created something new and distinctive. Within classical Greek civilization, there appeared ideas, art forms, and types of government whose influence on Western civilization has lasted down to the present day.

In particular, Greek city-states were the first to practice citizen participation in government—on a restricted basis in oligarchies like Sparta and on a much freer and wider basis in democracies like Athens. The city-states also traded and colonized along the northern coastlands of the Mediterranean Sea, and brought their distinctive civilization to many barbarian peoples of Mediterranean Europe—above all, Italy. They were also innovators in warfare, developing methods of fighting by land and sea that, shortly after 500 B.C., enabled them to preserve their independence against the mighty kings of Persia, the universal rulers of the time (pp. 35–36)—a role in which the Greeks would eventually replace them.

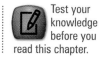

Test your knowledge before you read this chapter.

What do you think?

The practice of citizen participation in government is the most important legacy of ancient Greece.

Strongly Disagree						Strongly Agree
1	2	3	4	5	6	7

« **Citadel and Shrine** The Athenian Acropolis was already ancient when its temples were rebuilt after Persian invaders destroyed them in the fifth century B.C. The Parthenon (right) was the "Place of the Maiden"—the "home" of the city-state's virgin goddess, Athena. The Erechtheum (left) was named after Erechtheus, a mythical early god-king whom democratic Athens still venerated. The fortress wall dates from the Middle Ages, but follows the line of one built shortly before the temples.

LO¹ The European Barbarians

Over three thousand years up to the time of the Persian Empire, civilization had spread from its Sumerian and Egyptian homelands right across southwestern Asia and northeastern Africa, and other regions of civilization had also arisen in India, China, and the Western Hemisphere. Elsewhere, however, most people still lived the prehistoric village life that had emerged from the Agricultural Revolution (pp. 8–11), including in the lands stretching two thousand miles northwestward from the eastern Mediterranean Sea that we today call Europe.

The rulers, priests, and scribes of lands between the Indian Ocean and the Mediterranean Sea probably thought of these early Europeans merely as distant suppliers of raw materials and slaves and as occasionally troublesome raiders and invaders. Yet, it was out of the encounter between the peoples of prehistoric Europe and their southeastern neighbors that Western civilization would eventually be born.

The Earliest Europeans

Even before this historic encounter, the way of life of the peoples of Europe had undergone many changes and advances. By 4000 B.C., farming and village life had spread throughout the continent. With them came an increase in population and wealth, and by 3500 B.C. there were peoples in western Europe who were numerous and well organized enough to construct ceremonial monuments consisting of circles and rows of huge upright boulders, as well as massive earthen tombs and fortifications. Many of these **megalithic** structures (from the Greek words for "large boulder") have survived to the present day. Underneath some of the earthworks, archaeologists have discovered traces of furrows in the soil on which they were originally built—evidence that the peoples of this region were the first to use a revolutionary agricultural tool, the plow (p. 9).

Perhaps the most impressive single early European achievement was Stonehenge, a huge open-air monument built by a prosperous farming and trading people in the west of England, probably as a religious center. It was repeatedly rebuilt over a

 An interactive exploration of life in Europe during the Iron Age, created by the BBC (http://www.bbc.co.uk/history/ancient/british_prehistory/launch_gms_ironage_life.shtml) Explore life in prehistoric Europe in this interactive game.

3500 B.C.	Megalithic structures constructed in Europe
2500 B.C.	Indo-European nomads from the steppes migrate into Europe; European barbarian way of life evolves
2200 B.C.	Minoan civilization takes root in Crete; Greeks arrive in southeastern Europe
1600 B.C.	Greek fortified settlements along the Aegean develop Mycenaean civilization
1400 B.C.	Destruction of Minoan towns
1200 B.C.	Mycenaean civilization falls; beginning of "Dark Ages" of Greek history
800 B.C.	Recovery in the Aegean; Greek city-states form
494–445 B.C.	Persian Wars
460–430 B.C.	Golden Age of Athens

period of several hundred years, until it reached its final form about 2000 B.C. The monument consists of about 160 massive boulders, weighing up to 50 tons each, all of which had to be dragged many miles to the site. Forty of the largest boulders were trimmed with stone tools to form neatly rectangular structural components. These were set upright with others placed horizontally on top of them as crosspieces. Together with the other boulders, they were arranged in four circular or horseshoe-shaped groups one inside the other, all carefully aligned to the movements of the sun and the moon. The structure, much of which is still standing today (see photo on page 47), is testimony to the level of wealth, organization, and skills reached by the peoples of prehistoric Europe.

 Stonehenge Decoded, a National Geographic Special on New Findings (http://channel.nationalgeographic.com/episode/stonehenge-decoded-3372#tab-Overview)] Learn about the latest discoveries and theories regarding the mystery of Stonehenge.

The Barbarian Way of Life

The early Europeans cannot have had any sense of a common identity, but in time most of them came to share a distinctive way of life. This was probably the result of migrations of Indo-European nomads from the steppes (grasslands) that bordered Europe on the east (p. 20). From about 2500 B.C. onward, Indo-European peoples moved into Europe just as they did into Asia Minor and Persia, and under the influence of the newcomers, the settled peoples of the region began to form into new ethnic

Stonehenge The most famous of megalithic structures was built by a farming and trading people in the west of England about 2000 B.C., contemporary with the beginning of the Babylonian empire in Mesopotamia and the founding of the Middle Kingdom in Egypt. The wealth, skills, and organization to build great monuments were no monopoly of the peoples of the Euphrates, the Tigris, and the Nile.

groups whose way of life was a mixture of their traditional patterns and Indo-European influences.

Instead of their earlier tongues, the peoples of the region began to speak languages of Indo-European origin that were the distant ancestors of Greek and Latin, as well as of most European languages today. In other ways, too, their way of life underwent important changes. Throughout much of Europe, there appeared elites of warriors—often Indo-European–style charioteers and horsemen—whose lives centered around strength and courage, comradeship and loyalty, contests and battle. In addition to the deities of earth and fertility and the dominant mother-goddesses that many European peoples had traditionally worshiped, the warriors turned to gods of fatherhood and thunder, metalworking and war. When a leading warrior died, his horses and chariot, his bronze (or later, iron) swords and daggers, and his gold and silver drinking cups would all go to the grave with him—presumably so that he could go on riding, fighting, and drinking as a comrade of the gods in the afterlife.

Next to the warrior would lie his wife, with her jewelry and her fine textiles and utensils, so that she, too, could go on fulfilling her role in the afterlife—that of presiding over a household made wealthy by farming and war. She may even have been thought of as sharing in her husband's delights. To judge from the reports of Greek and Roman writers about the barbarian peoples of their time, women shared the warrior values of their menfolk. They went to war along with the men—not only to bring them food and bind their wounds but also to force them back into the fight if they panicked, and sometimes to join in the fighting themselves.

> *"When a leading warrior died, his horses and chariot, his bronze (or later, iron) swords and daggers, and his gold and silver drinking cups would all go to the grave with him—presumably so that he could go on riding, fighting, and drinking as a comrade of the gods in the afterlife."*

Even for the most warlike Europeans, however, the main business of life was farming, adapted in various ways to the different regions of the continent. They lived in villages or in big farmsteads that housed several related families; generally, the settlements were widely scattered, for the population was much thinner than in Egypt or Mesopotamia. Groups of villages or farmsteads formed **tribes**, held together by common interests, traditions, and real or mythical ties of kinship. A tribe would meet from time to time to conduct its business and celebrate the festivals of local deities, and would often build itself a massive earth and timber hilltop stronghold. Tribes would often have more or less powerful hereditary chieftains, whom Greek and Roman observers thought of as kings or (more rarely) queens.

Tribes, in turn, formed loose alliances under warrior kings or queens of exceptionally powerful tribes, together with their battle comrades. In good times, the tribal groupings fought each other for metals, slaves, and other items that brought prestige to their possessors or could be exported to Asia Minor, Mesopotamia, or Egypt in return for some of the luxuries of civilization. In bad times, overpopulation and famine sometimes drove them to massive armed migrations such as those of the Sea Peoples (p. 32). Either way, these groupings were mostly temporary. Tribes would join or leave them as suited their hopes and needs, and defeat—or disputes over the rewards of victory—often caused them to fall apart.

In this way, Europe came to be inhabited by peoples who spoke mostly Indo-European languages; who were skilled in farming, metalworking, trade, and warfare; and who were fairly well organized on the local level, but had no cities, written records,

Map 3.1 **The Greek Homeland**

The Greeks settled in mainland Greece from about 2000 B.C. onward, coming as migrants from somewhere farther north. Between 1200 and 800 B.C. they spread to the islands and eastern coastlands of the Aegean Sea. In later times, Greeks continued to migrate across Europe and Asia from the western Mediterranean to the borders of India, but the Aegean region remained the center of the Greek world. © Cengage Learning

Interactive Map

or fixed structures of government. The prehistoric peoples who followed this way of life are customarily called the European barbarians. The word comes from the Greek *barbaros*, which originally meant "non-Greek." Today, people often use the words "barbarian" and "barbaric" to describe those they believe to be less intelligent, refined, or humane than themselves. Scholars, however, use the word with no contemptuous overtones to mean the tribal groups and the way of life that emerged in Europe from about 2500 B.C.

One by one, over a period of three thousand years from 2000 B.C. right down to A.D. 1000, the European barbarian peoples came into contact with civilization. As with the earlier spread of civilization to the farming and nomad peoples of Mesopotamia and Anatolia (pp. 17, 19), the contacts were sometimes peaceful and sometimes warlike, and if the contacts were warlike, the barbarians were sometimes the conquerors and sometimes the victims. But the results were always the same: one by one, the barbarians adopted the ways of life of the civilizations they encountered. The chieftains and warriors of one era became the leaders of civilization in the next, often adapting and changing the form of civilization they had acquired. In this way, civilization eventually spread throughout Europe.

The first such European barbarian people to make contact with civilization were the Greeks. As a result of their encounter with peoples to their south and east from 2000 B.C. onward, the Greeks developed a distinctive civilization of their own—the first to emerge in Europe, and the first that counts as definitely "Western."

LO² The Aegean Encounter

The scene of this encounter was a region stretching from mainland Greece across the Aegean (eh-GEE-uhn) Sea, with its many islands, to the western coastlands of Asia Minor (Map 3.1). The farming wealth of the Aegean region, like that of Palestine (p. 37), came from a combination of grain fields, vineyards, and olive groves that was common throughout the Mediterranean lands. In addition, southeastern Europe was rich in metals and in timber for shipbuilding, so that the Aegean peoples also lived from metalworking, lumberjacking, trade, and piracy. Well before 2000 B.C., the Aegean had come to be a fringe region of civilization, inhabited by relatively advanced and prosperous peoples—none of whom, as yet, were Greeks.

Minoan Civilization

About 2200 B.C., a distinct civilization, known today as Minoan (from Minos, a legendary king), arose on the Aegean island of Crete. Minoan civilization drew its wealth from control of the surrounding seas and from thriving trade with many eastern Mediterranean lands, above all Egypt. As in Egypt, trade was controlled by the rulers, whose business records were written in a script developed locally under Egyptian influence. The ruins of luxurious palaces, as well as elegant jewelry and other surviving objects (see photo), suggest a wealthy and pleasure-loving society in which women played a prominent role—a society devoted to spectacular games resembling present-day bullfights.

 Francesco's Mediterranean Voyage, Crete Tour the archeological sites of Minoan civilization in this video.

 Artifacts from Minoan Crete in the Heraklion Museum's Collection (http://ancient-greece.org/images/museums/heraklion-mus/index.htm) Explore the art of the Minoans.

(above, center) **The "Master of the Animals"** This Cretan gold pendant, made about 1700 B.C., shows a powerful being with geese in each hand, and bull's horns looming behind him. The depiction of his body and the lotus flowers at his feet show Egyptian influence. The elegance of this piece of jewelry, and no doubt its luck-bringing power, were valued far from its homeland. It was found in the Greek island of Aegina, 200 miles across the sea from Crete. The Ancient Art and Architecture Collection

The Arrival of the Greeks: Mycenaean Civilization

At the time that Minoan civilization arose, great changes were taking place in the lands that stretched for thousands of miles to the north and east of Crete. Many Indo-European peoples were on the move, and about the same time that the Hittites conquered Anatolia (p. 20), another Indo-European–speaking people arrived in the Aegean—the Greeks.

There is no way of knowing exactly when, where, or how the Greeks developed into a separate ethnic group, but at the time that they made their way into their new homeland, they seem to have been a European barbarian people much like any other. They settled among the people that they found in their new homeland, developed a way of life that combined their own traditions and local ones, and eventually came under the influence of nearby Crete. By 1600 B.C., Greek chieftains had established fortified settlements along the mainland's southern shore and on some of the islands, and these settlements had become the centers of a new civilization—the Mycenaean civilization, so called from Mycenae, the first site to be excavated in modern times.

The Mycenaean Greeks were a warlike people whose leading warriors rode into battle in horse-drawn chariots and who protected their settlements with massive walls. They buried their rulers in huge, stone-lined underground chambers together with rich treasures of bronze weapons, as well as magnificent gold and silver jewelry and eating and drinking vessels. The Mycenaeans also adopted many features of Minoan civilization, including its writing, which they adapted to their own early version of the Greek language.

But the Mycenaeans also struggled with the Minoans for control of the commerce of the eastern Mediterranean. The rivalry ended about 1400 B.C. with the destruction of the Minoan towns, perhaps as a result of Mycenaean conquest. Crete became Mycenaean in civilization and eventually Greek in language, and the riches of every land between Egypt and the Black Sea now came by ship to the Mycenaean chieftains of the Greek mainland.

The "Dark Ages"

Mycenaean civilization lasted until shortly after 1200 B.C., when it fell victim to the same regional crisis that involved the downfall of the Hittites and the attacks of the Sea Peoples on Egypt. Exactly what happened in the Aegean is unknown. Perhaps, as later Greek tradition declared, new groups of warlike Greeks overran the region, or perhaps the Mycenaean chiefdoms were weakened by overpopulation and war, and themselves supplied uprooted warriors to the Sea Peoples. What is certain is that around 1150 B.C. Mycenae was sacked and all the other fortified settlements were deserted. The population dropped, the ships

colony
In ancient Greece, a new city-state settled in an oversea territory by a group sponsored by a city-state located elsewhere.

oracle
A priest or priestess who was believed to give answers that were inspired by a god or goddess to questions from worshipers at a temple.

> *"The minstrels' listeners absorbed the traditional values that the heroic songs celebrated—the values of a warrior aristocracy that was at home on both land and sea."*

no longer sailed, and writing fell out of use. The crisis led to the eclipse of civilization for nearly four centuries—a period known as the "Dark Ages" of Greek history.

But the Greeks themselves survived and even expanded their territory: many of them settled across the Aegean on the western coast of Anatolia, which became part of the Greek homeland. In addition, many earlier religious and cultural traditions lived on. Minstrels sang songs of heroic deeds done in the days of "golden Mycenae"—above all of a grand expedition of allied chieftains from Greece to besiege and capture the flourishing city of Troy on the northwestern coast of Anatolia. And the minstrels' listeners absorbed the traditional values that the

heroic songs celebrated—the values of a warrior aristocracy that was at home on both land and sea.

The Renewal of Greek Civilization

By about 800 B.C., the Aegean region, like the lands to its south and east was on the way to recovering from the crisis. Again the population expanded—so rapidly this time that it outran the food supply. Newly forming Greek city-states sent out expeditions to found **colonies**. For two centuries, emigration continued, until by 600 B.C., Greek city-states dotted the coastlines from the Black Sea westward to Spain, and the Greeks had joined the Phoenicians as the leading commercial and seafaring nation of the Mediterranean (Map 3.2).

All the same, the Greeks maintained a sense of oneness, which was expressed above all in their common religion. From all over the Mediterranean, Greek athletes came to compete in the Olympic Games, held every fourth year in honor of Zeus at Olympia in southern Greece. Warriors and statesmen visited the **oracle** of the sun-god, Apollo, at Delphi in central Greece to learn whether their undertakings would succeed. Ordinary

Map 3.2 **Greek and Phoenician Overseas Migration**

IIn the eighth and seventh centuries B.C., as their wealth and population grew, the Greeks joined the Phoenicians as traders, travelers, and settlers across the sea. By 600 B.C., Greek city-states flourished along the coasts of southern Italy and Sicily, Gaul and Spain, North Africa, and the Black Sea. As the philosopher Plato said shortly after 400 B.C., "We Greeks live around the sea like frogs round a pond." © Cengage Learning

Interactive Map

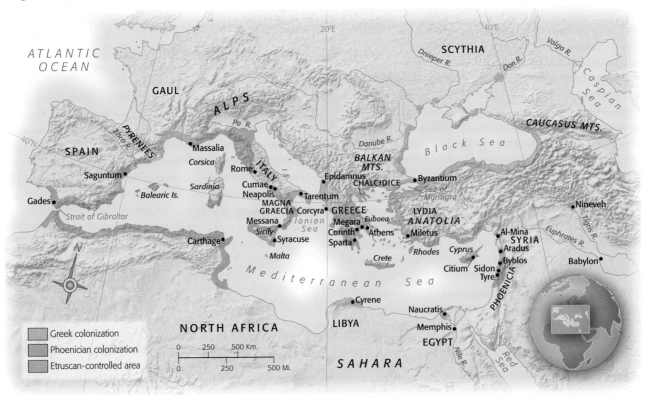

people went on pilgrimage to Eleusis, not far from Athens, to gain the hope of eternal life by sharing in the rites of the fertility goddess, Demeter. These practices, all dating from not long after 800 B.C., formed the main binding force in the renewed civilization of the Greeks.

As much as it inherited from the Aegean past, this renewed civilization was very different from the old one—mainly as a result of new influences from the changing lands to the south and east. From wealthy kingdoms that had arisen in Anatolia on the ruins of the Hittite state, Greek settlers on the coast learned the use of iron tools and weapons as well as coined money. From the Phoenicians, Greek sailors imitated the latest shipbuilding and naval warfare techniques. From the Phoenicians, too, the Greeks relearned the art of writing—this time in its new alphabetic form, with adaptations to fit the needs of the Greek language (for all these innovations, see Chapter 2). Greek mercenary soldiers, serving in the armies of Egyptian pharaohs defending their independence against Assyria (p. 34), came home with stories of huge stone temples and lifelike stone statues, which stirred the architectural and artistic ambitions of the increasingly wealthy rulers of the homeland. And Greeks who fought in the Babylonian armies that destroyed Jerusalem and scattered the Jews (p. 39) brought back knowledge of Babylonian astronomy, as well as of supposedly reliable ways of discovering the will of the gods from the shape and size of inner organs of sacrificed animals.

 Speak like an Ancient Greek: The Ancient Greek Alphabet with Audio Files (http://www.pbs.org/empires/thegreeks/igreeks/speak.html) Hear what the ancient Greek alphabet sounded like.

In the early development of their civilization, the Greeks began by doing what the Babylonians, the Hittites, and countless other peoples had done before them. After migrating into a region that brought them into contact with the civilizations that had begun in Mesopotamia and Egypt, they learned from these civilizations and then adapted what they learned to their own needs. But the Greeks went on to change what they learned so drastically that they created something new and different. Alongside Mesopotamia and Egypt there now appeared a third great civilization: that of classical Greece.

LO³ Citizens and Communities: The Greek City-States

With the recovery of Greek civilization, the tribal communities of the Dark Ages began to develop into city-states. Communities of this kind had often arisen before, for example, among the Sumerians and Phoenicians at times when there was no powerful kingdom or empire to limit their independence (pp. 12, 32). But the social and political development of the Greek city-state (often known by its Greek name, *polis*) took this type of community in unprecedented new directions.

Greek city-states were small places, generally consisting of no more than a town and a few square miles of surrounding countryside. Athens and Sparta, each about the same size as a couple of U.S. counties, were giants among city-states. The population of both town and country ordinarily numbered only a few thousand, though Athens may have reached as many as 250,000. Where possible, the town was built around a hill, at the top of which stood an **acropolis**—a combination of fortress and temple precinct.

> **acropolis**
> The high fortified citadel and religious center of an ancient Greek town.

Both fortresses and temples were vitally important to the Greek city-states. They were fiercely competitive communities that continually fought one another, and their single most important civic activity was the worship of the god or goddess on whom each community was thought to depend. Athens, for example, was the city of the goddess Athena, and from the Athenian acropolis her temple, the Parthenon, or "Place of the Maiden" (since mythology said that she was a virgin), overlooked the whole city (see photo on page 44).

In their small size, their competitiveness, and their reliance on community gods and goddesses, Greek city-states were much the same as those of the Sumerians or Phoenicians, but they differed in one important respect: for the Greeks, the city-state was a community in which all of its members had a share and in which all were entitled to participate to a greater or lesser extent. The Greek language is the first that is known to have had a specific word for a member of such a community: *politēs*, or "citizen."

City-States and Citizens

The notion of citizen participation seems to have originated partly in geography. The Greek city-states first developed at exactly the time that the Assyrians were reaching for power westward from Mesopotamia (pp. 33–34), but Greece was protected by many miles of land and sea. With no universal empire to keep them in order, the city-states were free to struggle among themselves. Furthermore, they occupied a land that was far less wealthy than Mesopotamia or Phoenicia. In their conflicts with one another, they could not afford professional soldiers or large cavalry forces.

An Athenian "Owl" That was the slang name of this tetradrachma (four-drachma coin), because of the owl, the sacred bird of Athena, on the reverse ("tails" side). On the obverse ("heads" side) the goddess herself wears a warrior's helmet. The coin, the size of a U.S. dollar, is pure silver—four days' pay for a skilled Athenian worker. Tetradrachmas were mass-produced in wealthy fifth-century B.C. Athens, and became the main international currency of the Mediterranean. Courtesy of the Trustees of the British Museum

hoplite
A heavily armed and armored citizen-soldier of ancient Greece.

phalanx
A unit of several hundred hoplites, who closed ranks by joining shields when approaching the enemy.

monarchy
A state in which supreme power is held by a single, usually hereditary ruler (a monarch).

oligarchy
A state in which supreme power is held by a small group.

triremes
Massive fighting vessels with three banks of oars, used to ram or board enemy ships.

tyranny
Rule by a self-proclaimed dictator (a tyrant).

democracy
In ancient Greece, a form of government in which all adult male citizens were entitled to take part in decision making.

Instead, they came to rely mainly on infantry armies made up of their own male citizens.

Citizens who could afford to serve as **hoplites** ("men-at-arms") equipped themselves with bronze helmets and armor, round shields, long spears with iron blades, and short iron swords.

> " *Alongside Mesopotamia and Egypt there now appeared a third great civilization: that of classical Greece.* "

They fought in formidable shock units of several hundred men each, known as **phalanxes**, or "rollers." Poorer citizens fought as light-armed infantry, harassing the enemy ahead of the phalanx's charge or covering its vulnerable flanks. This way of fighting was not new; in fact, much of the hoplites' equipment seems to have been modeled on that of Assyrian heavy infantry. But among the Greeks, it was ordinary male citizens fighting in this way on whom the city-states depended for survival. In the words of the poet Alcaeus about 600 B.C., "Not stone and timber, nor skill of carpenter, but brave men who will handle sword and spear—with these you have city and walls." And if sword- and spear-handling men wanted to participate in other community activities besides warfare, they could not very well be told to mind their own business.

The sense of the city-state as a community of all its citizens was reinforced by tradition and myth. Each city-state was believed to have been founded and developed by a family or clan descended from a divine or semidivine founder—in the case of Athens, King Theseus, the offspring of the sea-god Poseidon and the mortal princess Aethra—and most of its citizens claimed to trace their ancestry back to common forefathers. Citizenship was in fact a matter of birth: the status of a father usually determined that of his children. Thus, the citizens could think of themselves as distantly related members of one big family. They saw no more reason for conflict between the individual and the state than between the individual and the family. The "good life" for the individual was a life of active participation in civic affairs—including the government of the city-state.

Monarchy, Oligarchy, Tyranny, Democracy

In the earliest times of classical Greek civilization, the communities that would become city-states were ruled by kings (tribal chieftains) and their leading companion warriors, as described in the epics of Homer (p. 68). But with the development of citizen armies, **monarchy** (government by kings) gave way to new forms of government that distributed power more widely among male citizens. One of these forms was **oligarchy** (from the Greek for "rule by a few"). In this form, a minority of citizens dominated the government, and the power of the majority was limited in various ways. Many city-states in mainland Greece were oligarchies, above all Sparta.

But other city-states, particularly those that developed into large commercial centers, gave far more power to the majority. In such cities, the common people (in Greek, the *dēmos*) were too numerous and active to ignore, and the ruling groups were often divided among factions that competed for the commoners' support. Besides, big commercial cities needed navies as well as armies and depended in wartime on even the poorest citizens as oarsmen in the **triremes**. These were massive fighting vessels that fought in the Phoenician style, by ramming or boarding enemy ships, but had three banks of oars instead of two. Since each trireme needed 170 men to row it, there was no way that a city-state could maintain a powerful fleet without the willing cooperation of the commoners.

In these large city-states, social conflicts sometimes led to the emergence of **tyranny**—the rule of a "tyrant," or self-proclaimed dictator who held power partly by force, partly by exploiting internal divisions, and partly by providing efficient government. But tyranny was often only a passing phase on the way to **democracy** (literally, government by the common people), in which all government decisions were made by the majority of male citizens. The most powerful and successful of democratic city-states was Athens, but there were many others, particularly among the Greeks of Asia Minor and elsewhere on the Mediterranean coastline.

Like most tight-knit communities, Greek city-states were in many ways narrow and exclusive. Women generally participated in the community's affairs on a much more limited basis than men, immigrants were almost never awarded citizenship, and slavery was widespread. When a city-state sent some of its citizens overseas to found a colony, the new settlement became a separate, independent state. And when one city conquered another, it extended its control but not its citizenship. In the end, these tiny states exhausted one another through endless rivalry, jealousy, and war. But in the course of their warfare, they developed exceptional organizational and fighting skills that enabled them to hold their own even against the world-conquering Persians.

Although the Greek city-states had many features in common, each was individual in character and had its own personality. That was true, in particular, of the two communities that dominated much of the Greek world during the heyday of the city-states in the fifth century B.C., Sparta and Athens.

Sparta: The Military Ideal

The Spartans were the descendants of Greeks who had conquered part of the southern mainland, the territory of Laconia (see Map 3.1 on page 48). By the eighth century B.C., they were a minority of landholders (less than ten thousand adult males) ruling over a majority of **helots**, descendants of earlier Greek immigrants who were bound to the land by the Spartan state and compelled to work for the landholding citizens. Since much of the land in their territory of Laconia was infertile, the Spartans pushed westward into the broad and fertile plains of Messenia and turned the Greek inhabitants of that region into helots as well. As a result, the Spartan citizens were outnumbered by the noncitizens about ten to one.

The conquerors became prisoners of their own success. Though the Laconian helots were relatively well treated and even fought in the army, the Messenians were harshly exploited, never accepted their defeat, and often rebelled. To hold down the helots, the Spartan citizens had to accept a government system that put them under almost total domination by a few among themselves.

When and how the Spartans developed their government system is unknown, but by the fifth century B.C., policy decisions had been taken over by a council of elders—some thirty men from leading families who had to be at least sixty years of age and were chosen by the citizens for life. There were also two "kings"—actually high priests and army commanders—whose positions were hereditary in different families. The main executive authority, however, was held by five officials, elected annually and usually also elderly, who were called *ephors* (overseers). Although there was an assembly that was open to all adult males of the citizen minority, those who attended were not even permitted to debate. Instead, the council of elders drew up all proposals and then presented them to the assembly for approval or disapproval only—and this was given not by vote but by a shout. Thus, the Spartan government was a leading example of oligarchy.

The Spartan Way of Life

Along with this government system there went a way of life that dedicated male citizens entirely to the service of the state. The citizens' farms were worked by the helots, and a middle class of immigrant aliens took care of industry and trade. Meanwhile, the citizens devoted themselves to the one calling that was permitted to them by law: that of full-time hoplite warriors. Boys were taken from their families by the state at the age of seven; they were taught manly behavior and reading and writing and were started on a lifelong routine of physical toughening and military training. They were permitted to marry after age twenty—in fact, bachelors were punished—and the state encouraged the mating of the best human specimens. Even married men, however, were required to live in barracks until they reached the age of thirty. They might then have some home life, but they still had to take their chief meal each day at a soldiers' mess.

> **helots**
> Noncitizens forced to work for landholders in the ancient city-state of Sparta.

 Spartan Practices of Child Rearing Read how Spartans raised their children.

Girls were also required to participate in drills and exercises that were designed to develop them into healthy, child-bearing women. But the state did not control women as rigorously as men, and for long periods they lived apart from their husbands, so that they led relatively free and active lives. As in all other city-states, however, they could not take part in assembly meetings or hold government positions.

The freedom of Spartan women aroused both admiration and disapproval among other Greeks, depending on how they thought it affected the power of the city-state. Sometimes, Spartan women won praise for sharing the militaristic ideal of their menfolk. The story was told of the Spartan mother whose parting words to her son, as she sent him off to battle, were that she expected him to return to her either with his shield (that is, as a victor) or on it (as a corpse). But in the fourth century B.C., when Sparta began to lose battles, the philosopher Aristotle claimed that the women, neither disciplined by the state nor controlled by their husbands, thought only of private and family interests and were useless in time of war.

To protect their harsh and rigid way of life, the Spartans tried to seal off their city-state from outside influences. Sparta had little contact with foreigners; it discouraged trade and showed

A Winner in the Heraean Games? This bronze statuette of a female runner is looking backward, as if at other runners behind her. Perhaps she is ahead in one of the women's foot races in honor of Zeus's consort Hera that were held alongside the Olympic Games. Most likely she and most of her rivals were Spartans—the only city-state where women regularly underwent athletic training. Courtesy of the Trustees of the British Museum

aristocrats
Members of prominent and long-established Athenian families.

visitors little hospitality. But most Spartans were willing to pay a high price to preserve their system. With its well-trained and highly disciplined citizen army, Sparta not only held down the helots but was for several centuries the leading city-state of mainland Greece.

Many other city-states, including important centers like Corinth and Thebes, were also oligarchies, but their way of life was more easygoing. The power-holding "few" were generally the wealthiest citizens, who monopolized public office. But there were middling and poor citizens as well as wealthy ones, and the assemblies in which the "many" gathered had more power of debate and initiative than in Sparta. But even the most liberal oligarchy gave far less power to the majority of citizens than the main alternative form of government, democracy, as practiced most famously in Athens.

> "*Instead of softening their feet with shoes, his rule was to make them hardy through going barefoot.... Instead of pampering them with a variety of clothes, his rule was to habituate them to a single garment the whole year through, thinking that so they would be better prepared to withstand the variations of heat and cold.*"
>
> —Xenophon, describing the rules of the Spartan Lycurgus, ca. 400 B.C.

Athens: Freedom and Power

To the Athenians, the Spartan life was not worth living. One of their favorite jokes was that the life led by the Spartans explained their willingness to face death. The contrasts between the two cities are endless. Sparta was agricultural and landlocked; Athens carried on a prosperous commerce and had direct access to the sea. Sparta had the more powerful army; Athens's chief strength was its navy. Sparta sought cultural isolation; Athens welcomed foreign ideas and visitors. Sparta was a tightly controlled society; the Athenians were proud of their free way of life. The Spartans cultivated physical fitness and military courage; from Athens flowed daring inventiveness, glorious literature, and stunning creations of mind and hand.

But Athens was also a warlike community—and exactly because it had wider horizons than Sparta, it was more ambitious for conquest. Athenian democracy not only brought freedom for ordinary citizens and stimulation for artists, writers, and thinkers; for a time, it also brought exceptional power for the city-state in its struggles with its rivals.

Aristocrats and Commoners

The Athenian homeland was the peninsula of Attica in the central region of mainland Greece (see Map 3.1 on page 48). In the period of renewal of Greek civilization about 800 B.C., many old-established communities in Attica merged to form a single city-state that was known by the name of the most important community, Athens.

Over the next three centuries, Athens grew to become the wealthiest and one of the most powerful of Greek city-states—largely thanks to the growth of its overseas trade. Attica's large area (by Greek standards) of fertile countryside made it a producer and exporter of wine and oil, and this helped Athens to become a trading and manufacturing center. Workshops sprang up where Athenian citizens, immigrants, and slaves worked side by side to produce weapons, pottery, and articles of silver, lead, and marble. Ships from Athens and many other Greek and Phoenician cities carried these products to lands stretching from Spain to Palestine and from Egypt to the south of present-day Russia. The ships returned with metal, timber, and grain, for as the city grew, the countryside could no longer supply the food and raw materials that it needed.

With more people and greater wealth came social and political conflicts. The disputes were usually between the increasingly powerful and wealthy **aristocrats**—descendants of prominent and long-established Athenian families that had traditionally ruled the city-state—and the increasingly numerous *dēmos*. It was out of these conflicts that democracy was born.

Athenian aristocrats prided themselves on being exceptionally excellent human beings—"the fine and noble ones," as they called themselves—as a result of both breeding and education. They were not a closed caste, but their families married mostly among themselves. Their boys were trained for physical fitness with exercises and sports, and as young men of eighteen, they were assigned to special companies for two years of military and civic training. But they were supposed to be outstanding in mind as well as body, and private schools or tutors taught them public speaking, music, and the works of Homer and other poets.

Some aristocratic girls also got an education, particularly if they were sent off to live for a few years before marriage with one of the groups of young women who served in the temples of various goddesses. But most were kept at home without formal education until they were handed over in their middle teens to aristocratic husbands in their early thirties to continue the "fine and noble" bloodlines.

Besides their feeling of superiority, however, Athenian aristocrats had a strong sense of citizenship and responsibility to the community. The best way to show their distinction,

AN ATHENIAN SPENDTHRIFT

In ancient Athens there were no district attorneys, and it was the business of the individual male citizen to prosecute a crime that had come to his knowledge by publicly accusing the perpetrator in a speech before a court. In 345 B.C. a citizen by the name of Timarchus intended to charge the well-known orator Aeschines with accepting bribes from King Philip of Macedonia. However, Timarchus had a bad reputation for loose living, and under Athenian law, such men could not speak in public. In his own law court speech Aeschines charged Timarchus with loose living and painted a very unflattering portrait of a man who had squandered his inheritance. In the process Aeschines gave a picture of the way of life of a not so "fine and noble" upper-class Athenian man.

The demes that Aeschines mentions were wards in the city of Athens or townships in the nearby countryside. Liturgies were public duties, such as maintaining and commanding warships, that wealthy men were expected to carry out at their own expense. A drachma was a silver coin equivalent to a day's pay for a skilled worker; there were 6 obols to a drachma and 100 drachmas to a mina.

When this (property) [which had come to his use through his connections with a certain Hegesander] too had disappeared and had been squandered in gambling and gluttony . . . and his abominable and wicked nature always maintained the same appetites, and in an excess of incontinence imposed command upon command and dissipated wealth in his daily life, then he turned to consuming his paternal estate. Thus not only did he eat it up, but if one may use the expression, he even drank it up. Not for a proper price did he alienate his several possessions, nor did he wait for the opportunity of gain or advantage, but he used to sell for whatever price a thing would bring, so strenuously did he pursue his pleasures. His father had left him an estate from which another man might even have discharged the expensive and gratuitous public functions [liturgies], but he could not even maintain it for his own advantage. He had a house behind the Acropolis, another in the outlying district, in the deme Sphettus; in the deme Alopece another place, and in addition slaves who were skilled in the shoemaker's trade, nine or ten of them, each of whom brought this man an income of two obols a day, and the foreman of the shop three obols; also a woman slave who understood how to weave the fibre of Amorgos, and a man slave who was a broiderer. There were some, too, who owed him money, and besides he possessed personal property. . . . The house in town he sold to Nausicrates the comic poet, and afterward Cleaenetus the trainer of choruses bought it of Nausicrates for twenty minas. The estate in the country was sold to Mnesitheus of the deme Myrrhinus. It was a large farm, but fearfully run to weeds under the management of the accused. As to the farm at Alopece, which is eleven or twelve stadia distant from the walls (of Athens), when his mother entreated and begged him, as I learn, to let it alone and not sell it, but if nothing else, to leave it for her to be buried in,—for all that, even from this place he did not abstain, but his farm too he sold, for 2000 drachmas. Furthermore of the woman slaves and the domestic slaves he left not one, but has sold everything.

EXPLORING THE SOURCE

1. What can we learn from the speech about the kind of property and activities that provided the wealth of upper-class Athenians?

2. Is there any reason to suppose that Aeschines may be exaggerating this man's irresponsible behavior?

Source: G. W. Botsford and E. G. Sihler, eds., *Hellenic Civilization* (New York: Columbia University Press, 1915), pp. 508–509.

---

they thought, was by fighting as leading warriors in the citizen army and navy and by paying for many city-state expenses, notably religious festivals and warships, out of their own pockets. In addition, the aristocrats needed the commoners as willing rank-and-file warriors, and they also had their own bitter rivalries that led them to look to the commoners for help against each other. In conflicts with the aristocracy, the *dēmos* could generally find aristocrats to lead them whom they respected and who wanted their support.

From Monarchy to Democracy

As a result, Athens passed through several stages of political growth, beginning with monarchy and including both oligarchy and tyranny. But the upshot was the extension of political power to all adult male citizens, with the aristocrats becoming leaders instead of rulers.

In the century after the coming of democracy, there were two turning points in the life of Athens and the rest of Greece.

SEVERAL FACTORS CONTRIBUTED TO THE DEVELOPMENT OF DEMOCRACY IN THE ATHENIAN CITY-STATE:

Class conflicts led to Solon's reforms, a first step in extending power beyond wealthy landholders

- The aristocrat Solon was appointed about 600 B.C. at a time of crisis when poorer citizens were losing their farms through debt. They demanded a share of political power.

- Solon altered the constitution to give decision-making power to the Assembly, open to all male citizens.

- Aristocrats retained the sole right to public office.

Rivalries within the upper class led one of the rivals, Cleisthenes, to introduce full democracy

- Cleisthenes opened public office to all adult male citizens.

- The Assembly of all male citizens was given ultimate power to make government decisions.

- The newly empowered commoners increased their commitment to the state by agreeing to man a new fleet of warships.

- Wealthy and educated men continued to serve as military and political leaders.

- Democracy unleashed the enthusiasm and commitment of all social groups, and it was this that for a time would make Athens a "great power."

The first was the Persian Wars, in which Athens led the Greek city-states to victory. This success was followed by Athens's Golden Age (460–430 B.C.), a period of the highest confidence, power, and achievement. That period was cut short by the second turning point, the Peloponnesian (**pel-uh-puh-NEE-zhuhn**) War between Athens and Sparta, in which Athens was defeated and never recovered its earlier confidence and power. Still, Athens continued as a democracy right down to 338 B.C., when it came under the control of Macedonia (**mas-i-DOH-nee-uh**), and it remained a center of historic achievements in art and thought even after it lost its independence.

The Persian Wars

In the sixth century B.C., the Persians conquered a realm that stretched from the border of India to the Nile and the Aegean. For the first time, a universal empire had come within striking distance of the Greeks, and the Persians were able to bring the Greek city-states in the west of Asia Minor under their rule. When the Athenian upstarts aided a rebellion by these city-states, the Persian king, Darius I, determined (about 494 B.C.) to extend his control into mainland Greece.

Darius, and later his son Xerxes I (**zurk-seez**), sent two expeditions by land and sea against the mainland Greeks; the Persians lost the first decisive battle to the Athenians at Marathon in 490 B.C. Ten years later, in a sea battle off the island of Salamis near Athens, the Athenian navy smashed the Persian fleet (supplied mainly by the Phoenician city-states, the former rulers of the sea). On land, a small Spartan force held up Xerxes' army

in their renowned suicidal stand at Thermopylae (480 B.C.), and the main body of Spartan hoplites later routed the Persians in the pivotal land battle of Plataea. But it was Athens that went on to liberate the Greeks of Anatolia from Persian rule, and by 445 B.C., when final peace was made with Persia, Athens was the controlling power of the Aegean Sea.

The courageous and resourceful little state had demonstrated surprising capacity in fighting the Persian forces. At the height of the wars, the Athenians had fled their homes and watched the enemy burn their city to the ground, but they had come through victorious. With their victory came a new-felt power. How had they, so few in number, turned back the power of the King of Kings, with his millions of subjects? To the Athenians, there could be only one answer: they and their free institutions were superior. Democracy, it seemed, could not only nurture thinkers and artists; it could also win wars.

The leader of democratic Athens after the victory over Persia was another aristocrat, Pericles. By virtue of his personal influence and his long tenure in important elective offices, he held power during much of the thirty-year period of Athens's Golden Age, and it was in his time that democracy flourished

Greece Endangered: The Persians Cross the Hellespont Read how the Persians built a bridge to cross from Asia Minor into Greece.

Interactive Demonstration of Persian Bridge Construction (http://edsitement .neh.gov/PersianBridge_ flash_page.asp) See how the bridge to Greece was constructed.

most in Athens. Though the government system worked very differently from those of twenty-first-century democratic states, it nevertheless provided a precedent and example of democracy in action that have lasted—like the word itself—down to the present day.

The Workings of Democracy: The Assembly

In Athenian democracy, ultimate government power rested in the Assembly of adult male citizens. All major decisions were made there: for peace or war, for sending out expeditions, for spending public money, and for every other aspect of public affairs. Even the building of the Parthenon was decided not by any religious authority but by the Assembly. Meetings were held about once a week, and the number of citizens present was usually less than five thousand. Although many more were eligible to attend, men who lived in the country districts of Attica were often unable to come to town. At first, the Assembly met in the marketplace (*agora*) of Athens; later it met on the slopes of a nearby hill (the Pnyx). Voting was usually by a show of hands, and a simple majority determined the outcome. Anyone present could propose subjects for discussion, but most often, the Assembly debated proposals put before it by a smaller group, the Council of Five Hundred, which was also charged with executing the Assembly's decisions.

Debates in the Assembly were often spirited. Naturally, knowledgeable and convincing public speakers, distinguished battle commanders, patriotic contributors of triremes to the navy, and pious suppliers of animals for sacrifice to the gods were the most likely to be listened to. That was why most leading politicians were wealthy and well-educated aristocrats. But the ordinary members of the Assembly were highly critical and not always polite, and it took a shrewd and skillful leader like Pericles to win and hold the favor of the Assembly.

The Workings of Democracy: Officials and Courts

As an additional check on aristocratic power, the Council of Five Hundred and the roughly one thousand public officials that it supervised—tax collectors, building inspectors, and the like—were nearly all chosen annually by lot. Since these officials were paid for their services, poor men as well as rich could afford to serve, and the wealthy and well educated had no chance of monopolizing public office. The state covered the cost of official salaries by court fines, customs duties, an annual tax on aliens, and various sales taxes, since the rich preferred their contributions to go to more spectacular items that gained them credit with their fellow citizens.

The Athenians did not, however, trust to lot in selecting their chief military officers. These were the Ten Generals (*Stratēgoi*—literally "force commanders"), who were chosen each year by vote of the male citizens. They commanded the army and the navy, managed the war department, and exercised extensive control over the treasury. The Ten Generals chose their own chairman; the popular Pericles was elected general by the citizens and chairman by his fellow generals for sixteen years in succession. Since there were so many generals, there was little chance of a military takeover of power. And if any of them seemed to be becoming too ambitious, he risked **ostracism**: the Assembly could exile him or any other citizen for ten years by simple majority vote that required no proof of actual wrongdoing.

The Athenians also trusted to chance—or the will of the gods, as expressed by the drawing of lots—in the administration of justice. The court for each trial was made up of five hundred men chosen by lot from a long list of names. This made bribery or coercion difficult and guaranteed a broad cross section of citizen judgment. There was no judge to decide questions of law; the Athenian court was judge and jury combined. By majority vote, it ruled on all issues of procedure, legal interpretation, guilt or innocence, and type of punishment. There were no lawyers either, but every citizen argued his own case—though if he could afford it, he could hire some well-known orator to write his speech for him.

Civic and political participation was therefore part of the Athenian way of life for adult male citizens—but adult male citizens were a small minority of the population of Athens. Estimates suggest that during the Age of Pericles, out of Athens's quarter-million population, there were about 40,000 adult males who qualified. The rest of the population was made up of adult female citizens, adult noncitizens (resident aliens and slaves) who actually outnumbered the citizens, and of course children. Adult males probably made up no more than one-fifth of the total adult population, and the other four-fifths—female citizens, as well as aliens and slaves of both sexes—had no say in the city-state's democratic government.

Women in Athens

Most of what is known of the life of Athenian citizen women comes from surviving law court speeches composed by famous orators; in other words, it reflects conditions in families (from small farm and business owners up to the "fine and noble" elite)

> **ostracism**
> Banishment for ten years by majority vote of the Athenian Assembly.

> *"Where our rivals from their very cradles by a painful discipline seek after manliness, at Athens we live exactly as we please, and yet are just as ready to encounter every legitimate danger."*
>
> —Pericles, according to Thucydides, ca. 404 B.C.

that could afford to hire speechwriters. In some ways, the relationships of women and men in these families showed much the same patterns of inequality as anywhere else; in other ways, the relationships were actually more unequal than elsewhere.

Within marriage, the sexual liberty of the husband was taken for granted. In addition to his wife, he had access to his household slaves as concubines, as well as to public prostitutes. If he found his wife boring and could afford to do so, the husband might take up with more engaging female companions (*hetaerae*). These women, usually noncitizens from Asia Minor, were schooled in the arts of conversation and entertainment. The most famous of them was Aspasia, the consort and mistress of Pericles.

 **An Athenian Crime of Passion: A Cuckolded Husband Exacts the Ultimate Revenge** Read an Athenian husband's tale of finding his wife with her lover.

In addition, the husband could without dishonor fall in love and have sexual relationships with teenage boys—preferably only one of them. When the boy grew up, a relationship of this kind was supposed to turn into ordinary friendship, and male homosexuality between "consenting adults" was regarded as unmanly (though not wicked). Within these limits, homosexuality played an important part in the lives of well-to-do Greek men.

These Athenian customs, including love between men and boys, were found among other ancient peoples. In some other respects, however, women from well-off families in democratic Athens led a more restricted life and had fewer rights than in many other Greek city-states, as well as in Persia and Egypt. They were not supposed to socialize with men other than their fathers, brothers, and husbands; male visitors to a house had to keep to a special "men's room." If a woman left the house, she had to be escorted by a close male relative or be in a group with other women; and she had to have a specific reason, such as buying supplies or taking part in public religious celebrations. Women held property under the control of a male "guardian"—usually a father, brother, or husband—and they could plead in the law courts only through these guardians.

On the other hand, women were highly visible in an area of family and community life that was just as important as politics and law—the worship of the gods. It was aristocratic Athenian girls and women who every four years wove a new robe for Athena's sacred image on the Acropolis and brought it to her temple in solemn procession—the high point of the community's service to its beloved goddess. And in 480 B.C., when the Athenians were evacuating their city ahead of the approaching Persians, it took the priestess of Athena to persuade the citizens to hurry by convincing them that the goddess herself had already left.

 Women in Classical Greece (http://www.metmuseum.org/toah/hd/wmna/hd_wmna.htm) View images of women in ancient Greece.

Not much is known of women's life lower down the social scale or outside the city. *Hetaerae* were not despised, and they were entitled to generous gifts from their lovers. Sometimes they passed on their profession to their daughters, thereby forming independent though insecure female "dynasties."

Poor townswomen certainly worked in trades outside the home as weavers, innkeepers, and vendors in the marketplace. And rich or poor, no countrywoman could have done the "women's work" (p. 10) of the farms if she had lived under the same restrictions as well-off women in the city. In any case, no woman could take part in the proceedings of the Assembly or the law courts, let alone hold public office.

Aliens

The fifty thousand or so resident aliens were a very varied group. Some were wealthy businessmen, or independent women like Aspasia, who socialized on equal terms with the "fine and noble" citizens. Many were owners of stores and workshops, hardly different from citizens in the same lines of business. Many others were freed slaves who often went on working in the households of their former owners as artisans, laborers, domestic servants, concubines, and prostitutes.

Freeborn aliens were mostly Greeks and were still citizens of their city-states of origin even though their families might have lived in Athens for generations. If they were freedmen or freedwomen (ex-slaves), they were mostly non-Greeks or their descendants. Resident aliens in Athens bore all the obligations of citizenship but were entitled to only some of the benefits. They had to register with the government, pay taxes (including a special tax levied only on them), and (if male) do military service. They could sue Athenians in the law courts, and they shared on an equal footing in the community's worship of the gods, but they could not take part in Assembly meetings or hold government office. Their status was similar to that of resident aliens in the United States at the present day, except in one all-important respect: they had next to no chance of ever becoming citizens.

Still, freeborn aliens from elsewhere in Greece evidently preferred permanent second-class status in Athens to first-class status in their home city-states. And as resident aliens, ex-slaves gained a secure position in a community where they had lived for many years if not all their lives.

Slaves

The hundred thousand or so slaves in Athens were also a very diverse group, not all of them living lives of total subjection and powerlessness. "Fine and noble" citizens gave talented slaves an education and kept them as tutors to their sons; state-owned slaves worked as clerks in government offices, and even as policemen charged with such duties as corralling citizens from the marketplace to the meeting field on Assembly days.

Most slave owners were small businesspeople and farmers who kept only a few slaves and often worked side by side with them. Masters and (with the approval of their guardians) mistresses often freed their slaves: either they allowed them to work on their own account and save money to buy themselves free, or they freed them in their wills as a reward for faithful service. A slave concubine might even persuade her master to free her during his lifetime and make her his wife. Most Athenians did not expect deference from slaves. One of the few who did, an anonymous writer of Pericles' time or not long afterward, complained that slaves would not even get out of citizens' way on the streets.

But there were many for whom slavery was a truly inhuman condition. Slaves, both female and male and usually young, were kept as prostitutes in brothels or as domestic servants who had to double as concubines. Others—perhaps as many as ten thousand male slaves—worked in the silver and lead mines, where they were sure to die sooner rather than later from overwork, metal poisoning, or cave-ins. Most slaves were non-Greeks, or the descendants of non-Greeks, who had been uprooted from their homelands by war, and of course, all slaves were property that could be bought and sold. Their price ranged from ten minae (about ten pounds of silver, or a couple of years' wages for a skilled free worker) down to half a mina, depending on age, strength, skills, and looks. The slaves, therefore, represented an important part of the wealth of democratic Athens.

Democracy Within Traditional Civilization

The Athenian laws and customs concerning women, aliens, and slaves were not a special feature of democracy as such. They were the local version of traditional values and practices that the Athenians shared with most of the world at the time. But of course, democracy implies equality—yet so far as is known, no one in Athens ever complained that the treatment of women, aliens, and slaves was undemocratic.

The exclusion of female citizens from the community's decision making, for example, seems to have caused Athenian men no uneasiness whatever. Near the end of Athens's Golden Age, Pericles spoke at the funeral of citizen-soldiers fallen in the Peloponnesian War against Sparta (p. 80); and the historian Thucydides, following a Greek tradition of putting revealing words into the mouths of historical characters (p. 71), turned the speech into a famous proclamation of the values of Athenian democracy. Thucydides makes the Athenian statesman praise the democratic community for expecting all male citizens to be active in its service: "we regard him who takes no part in public duties not as unambitious but as useless." But the exact opposite applies to the widows of the fallen: they must remember that "the greatest glory will be hers who is least talked of among the men, whether for good or for bad." Thucydides was himself an Athenian, and the words he gives to Pericles certainly reflect the male citizens' way of thinking.

 The Funeral Oration of Pericles Read Thucydides' version of Pericles' funeral oration.

This was not because Athenian men failed to value women as members of the community. In narrating the destruction of

an Athenian force in Sicily later in the war with Sparta, Thucydides lists three precious things of which Athenian generals always reminded their soldiers to stiffen their courage when defeat was looming: "wives, children, and the gods of the forefathers"—in that order. But tradition said that the community was made up of families—of partnerships between men and women in which men were the senior partners and the ones responsible for running the community. The fact that running the Athenian community had become the business of all the men was simply not seen as a reason to make it the business of women as well.

True, the playwright Aristophanes staged two famous comedies in which he depicted women making decisions for the democratic city-state. In *Lysistrata*, the women of Athens and Sparta go on a sex strike to force an end to the war that their husbands are fighting; in *The Assemblywomen*, the wives actually take over the government. But comic dramatists often made their point by imagining the world turned ridiculously upside down. Aristophanes was a critic of democracy who disapproved of war with Sparta, and he probably wanted to shame the male citizens by showing them what seemed to them and to him a grotesque and impossible scene: women running the city-state, and doing no worse than the men.

What Athenian women themselves thought of democracy is unknown. However, well-born ancient Greek women sometimes broke the bounds of custom by studying and teaching philosophy, and a few of them expressed their views on the female role in the family and the community. In what is left of their writings, even these thinkers took for granted that the public life of city-states was male territory that women should not enter. According to Phyntis, probably writing after 300 B.C., "The activities proper to man are to command armies, to govern cities, to lead the people with rousing speeches. Those which are particular to woman are to look after her house, to stay at home, to wait for and to serve her husband." No ancient Greek woman is known to have criticized the exclusion of women from public life—or the institution of slavery, or permanent second-class status for immigrants—as women and men began to do when democracy returned in the West more than two thousand years later.

But the modern revival of democracy was part of a whole series of massive changes in basic features of civilization—religious beliefs, cultural values, economic systems, and family and social life, as well as government structures. Ancient Greek democracy, by contrast, had a brief "window of opportunity" to exist within a traditional civilization most of whose other basic features remained unchanged. That is the greatest difference between ancient democracy and that of the present day.

 Listen to a synopsis of Chapter 3.

(above, center) Just Married A sixth-century B.C. Athenian vase painting shows newlyweds riding a donkey-cart away from the bride's home, where the ceremony has taken place. They are going to the groom's home, where his mother is waiting to greet them. The best man, who has helped the bridegroom fetch the bride, rides with them; tonight he will stand guard outside the marriage chamber. Image copyright © The Metropolitan Museum of Art/Art Resource, NY

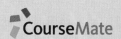

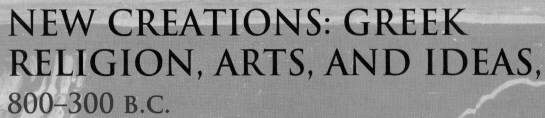

CHAPTER 4

NEW CREATIONS: GREEK RELIGION, ARTS, AND IDEAS, 800–300 B.C.

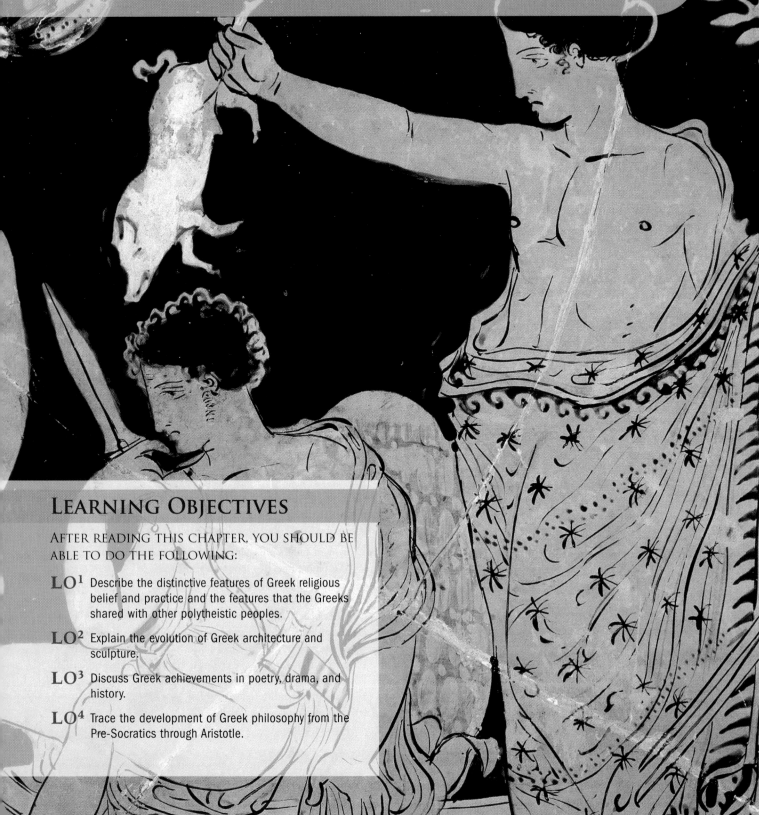

LEARNING OBJECTIVES

AFTER READING THIS CHAPTER, YOU SHOULD BE ABLE TO DO THE FOLLOWING:

LO¹ Describe the distinctive features of Greek religious belief and practice and the features that the Greeks shared with other polytheistic peoples.

LO² Explain the evolution of Greek architecture and sculpture.

LO³ Discuss Greek achievements in poetry, drama, and history.

LO⁴ Trace the development of Greek philosophy from the Pre-Socratics through Aristotle.

"THE RISE OF GREEK CIVILIZATION WAS ACCOMPANIED BY AN OUTBURST OF ARTISTIC AND INTELLECTUAL CREATIVITY."

The rise of Greek civilization was accompanied by an outburst of artistic and intellectual creativity. Greek architecture, sculpture, literature, and philosophy grew from three sources: their religious traditions, their encounter with the peoples of the lands between the Mediterranean Sea and the Indian Ocean, and the community life of their city-states.

Greek religion had a great deal in common with the beliefs of other polytheistic peoples and was directly influenced by the Greeks' southern and eastern neighbors, but the Greek gods and goddesses had a lifelike and human quality that helped inspire a lifelike and human art and literature. The need to honor these gods and goddesses, the wealth of city-states like Athens, and the example of the temples and statues of Egypt produced architecture and sculpture that stressed grace and movement yet was also solemnly impressive. The imported skill of alphabetic writing made it possible to record Greek poets' direct and vivid views of adventure and war, gods and fate, and personal feeling; dramatists actually showed their city-state audiences the characters and events they presented. And Greek thinkers, reflecting on their nation's religious traditions, the turbulent politics of the city-states, and the diverse international region in which they lived, began a quest for explanations of divine power, the natural universe, community life, and human behavior that has lasted in the West down to the present day.

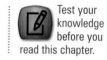

Test your knowledge before you read this chapter.

What do you think?

The arts of the Greeks are the standard by which all arts should be judged.

Strongly Disagree | | | | | | Strongly Agree
1 | 2 | 3 | 4 | 5 | 6 | 7

<< **"Guest of My Holy Hearth and Cleansed by Me of Blood-Guilt"** In a vase painting, the god Apollo holds high a slaughtered piglet; the blood drips onto the hand of Orestes, which holds the sword he used to kill his own mother Clytemnestra. The deed was retribution at Apollo's command for Clytemnestra's murder of Orestes' father Agamemnon, but the stain of matricide must still be washed away. Revenge and justice, divine retribution, pollution and cleansing, and sacrifice were among features of Greek religion that inspired tragedies such as Aeschylus's *Oresteia* trilogy.

LO¹ Greek Gods and Goddesses

The Greeks, like other polytheistic peoples, had no single set of beliefs about how the gods and goddesses were to be worshiped or about their plans for and demands on the human race. Traditional myths of the deities' personalities and deeds were preserved in the works of early poets, among them Homer, and lived on in poetry and art for thousands of years. Above all, however, Greek religion was a way for people and communities to understand and if possible influence the workings of the universe and human destiny—a way that many generations of Greeks found consoling and compelling.

Gods and Goddesses

The Greeks worshiped countless deities, who they believed could wield their power for good or ill on individuals, families, and city-states, so that it was vital to win their favor. "Impiety"—openly denying or insulting a deity—was a crime punishable by death, for it might bring divine revenge upon the community that tolerated it.

The gods and goddesses lived close by—lesser ones in homes, fields, streams, seas, and forests, and many of the great ones on top of Mount Olympus, the highest peak of Greece (see Map 3.1 on page 48). There, behind a veil of clouds, Zeus, the ruler of the sky, presided over a divine family. Zeus shared overlordship of the world with two of his brothers: Poseidon, ruler of the sea, and Hades, or Pluto, king of the underworld—a dark, forbidding place where spirits of the departed lingered for an uncertain period.

 Hesiod's Works and Days Assesses the Human Condition Read a Greek story of the gods' role in creating the human race.

The gods and goddesses displayed human frailties and emotions, including ambition, lust, pride, and vengefulness. Zeus, for instance, came from a line of divine fathers and sons who had struggled for power by such means as castrating and swallowing each other. All the same, the deities expected righteousness from humans. The king of the gods in particular was regarded as the upholder of such virtues as abiding by oaths and welcoming the stranger—as Homer said, "All wanderers and beggars come from Zeus."

As Zeus embodied the patriarchal (fatherly) principle, his wife Hera embodied the matriarchal (motherly) principle. She was regarded as the protector of womanhood and marriage, though in accordance with the belief that the gods were above mere human taboos (p. 15), she was also Zeus's sister. Zeus himself was far from a faithful husband. Greek poets told, for example,

> "The gods and goddesses displayed human frailties and emotions, including ambition, lust, pride, and vengefulness. Zeus, for instance, came from a line of divine fathers and sons who had struggled for power by such means as castrating and swallowing each other."

CHRONOLOGY

CA. LATE NINTH CENTURY B.C.	Homer's *Iliad* and *Odyssey*
SIXTH CENTURY B.C.	Poetry of Sappho; Pre-Socratic philosophers
FIFTH CENTURY B.C.	Parthenon constructed; works of Aeschylus, Sophocles, and Euripides
LATE FIFTH TO FOURTH CENTURY B.C.	Socrates, Plato, and Aristotle

how a lesser goddess, Leto, presented him with a splendid pair of twins—the handsome Apollo and his sister Artemis (Diana). Apollo, later associated with the sun, was widely worshiped as the god of poetry, music, art, and manly grace. Artemis, associated with the moon, was the goddess of wild nature, a hunter, and the model of athletic girlhood.

 Illustrated List of Greek Gods and Goddesses (http://www.greek-gods.info/greek-gods/) Learn more about all of the Greek gods and goddesses.

Athena, another of Zeus's offspring, was an armed and warlike virgin, though also linked with skill and wisdom. Aphrodite, on the other hand, the goddess of beauty and love, had many lovers among gods and humans, including the fierce war-god, Ares. But the god of war, "the curse of men," preferred the thrill of killing to the pleasures of lovemaking. Hermes, though, was the "friend of man"—the messenger of the gods, gliding on winged sandals over land and sea and guiding humans in every undertaking as well as on the way to the underworld.

The Worship of the Gods

The temple, the chief place of worship, was designed as a "home" where the god or goddess could live among the community that he or she protected. The deity was deemed to be present in the temple, usually in the form of a holy image that was tended by priests or priestesses who were appointed by the community or inherited their positions.

Ceremonies were usually performed in front of the temple, where the worshipers presented the priest or priestess with gifts—pottery, garments, whatever might be pleasing to the god or goddess. They also offered up prayers and animal sacrifices to win divine favor and assistance. After an animal had been ceremonially slaughtered and roasted and the aroma had reached the nostrils of the deity, the priest or priestess and the worshipers ate the meat in a common sacred meal. The worshipers also followed the Mesopotamian practice of judging the attitude of the gods to important undertakings from the shape and size of the victim's inner organs.

Oracles

Another way to discern the divine will was to consult an oracle—a person through whom a god or goddess was deemed to speak directly to humans. The most trusted oracles in all Greece were the priestesses of Apollo who lived at Delphi (see Map 3.1 on page 48). Politicians, generals, heads of families went or sent to Delphi for advice on such matters as whether or not to undertake a military campaign or what they must do to end a plague. A priestess would fall into a trance, relay the question to Apollo, and then utter the answer received from him. The utterance was usually unclear and had to be interpreted for the questioner by a priest. The Delphic oracles won a high reputation for accuracy, partly because the advice and predictions were in such vague, ambiguous terms that they could be made to fit almost any later event.

Mysteries

In these ways, the gods and goddesses offered mortals a glimpse of their will and ways of gaining their favor and help. What most of them did not provide was any promise of life other than the one on earth. There was no general expectation of immortality for humans and no system of rewards and punishments after death.

But some deities were more generous—above all, the wine god Dionysus (**dahy-uh-NAHY-suhs**) and the fertility goddess Demeter. These deities were associated with the "death" and "rebirth" of grapes into wine and seed into grain crops, and their followers believed that they could share in this death and rebirth by experiences such as becoming intoxicated with wine or drugs, eating a sacred meal, and witnessing a dramatic representation of death and resurrection. At the end of such rites, the worshiper sensed a mystic union with the deity and the assurance of everlasting life.

The rites were called **mysteries** because worshipers had to be initiated (solemnly admitted) to take part in them and must never reveal what they experienced. But tens of thousands of people took part, and in Athens, festivals of Dionysus and Demeter were as thronged as those of Athena and Zeus. These mystical experiences had compelling power—so much so that in spite of the vast numbers of people who shared them over many centuries, the details of what happened in them are today mostly unknown.

The Glory of the Gods

The Greeks shared the general features of their religion, including oracles and mystery cults, with many other ancient polytheistic peoples (pp. 14–15). Some of their actual gods and goddesses, like Zeus, had come with them as they moved into their new homeland, but others were deities that they had come across in the course of their migrations and international contacts. Athena, for example, was worshiped in the territory of Greece before the Greeks arrived. Adonis, one of Aphrodite's divine lovers, was a god originally worshiped in Sumer (p. 14), who "died" each year and was ceremonially mourned by women in every city from Athens to Babylon—his name came from the Semitic word *adon*, meaning "lord."

But as with other features of their civilization, the Greeks made something distinctive out of what they learned from other peoples. Wherever their deities originated, the Greeks generally gave them lifelike personalities and a lifelike appearance, modeled on those of human beings but far more "glorious"—a favorite Greek word of praise for gods and goddesses. An ancient hymn called Athena "the glorious goddess, bright-eyed, inventive, unbending of heart, pure virgin, savior of cities, courageous"; Apollo was "strong-shouldered," Demeter was "rich-haired," Aphrodite was "laughter-loving." The need to honor beings like these, so splendid and yet so human, helped inspire an art and literature that sought to depict the human quality in gods and the godlike features of humans.

LO² Architecture and Sculpture

As the early Greeks grew wealthier and their society grew more complex, Greek builders grew ambitious—and since community activities were more important than private affairs, they put their best efforts into public structures. They built open marketplaces enclosed by covered **colonnades** (rows of columns); outdoor amphitheaters (see photo on page 69) for dramatic festivals; and open-air gymnasiums, race courses, and stadiums. But their supreme architectural achievement was the temple.

Up to the sixth century B.C., even the most important buildings were usually made of wood. Gradually, however, limestone and marble took the place of timber in public structures. Impressed by the splendid temples of Egypt, the Greeks borrowed the Egyptian system of building stone structures from horizontal beams resting on vertical columns, but they developed the system in a new direction—toward a blend of solidity with graceful proportions.

Temple Building: The Parthenon

Early Greek temples had a rather heavy appearance, as in the sixth-century temple at Paestum in Italy (see photo on page 64). Gradually, however, the proportions of the temple, and of the columns especially, were refined. The most splendid result of this development was the Parthenon of Athens (see photo). In this shrine for Athena, a perfect balance of architectural features was achieved.

mysteries
Secret rites involving death, rebirth, and the promise of everlasting life.

colonnade
A series of regularly spaced columns, usually supporting the upper section of a structure.

≪ An Early Temple This temple of the goddess Hera is one of a group of shrines, overlooking the sea not far south of Naples, that formed the religious center of a Greek colony, Paestum. The temple was built in the sixth century B.C., when Greeks were settling in large numbers in the fertile and thinly populated coastal lands of southern Italy and Sicily. It has the massive appearance typical of early Greek stone temples.

≫ The Parthenon Rebuilding the temple of Athena after its destruction by the Persians was a cherished project of Pericles. It was he who about 448 B.C. persuaded the Athenian Assembly to authorize its construction and to employ two well-known architects, Ictinus and Callicrates. They achieved a combination of solidity and gracefulness that has made the Parthenon a model of classic dignity and beauty from ancient times to the present day.

The Parthenon was designed about 450 B.C. by the architects Ictinus and Callicrates (**cuh-LI-krateez**) as part of Pericles' plan for rebuilding the Acropolis after the Persians had destroyed the earlier sacred structures there. Though ravaged by time and war, it still embodies the Greek ideal of architectural perfection. It is not a huge structure, measuring only 100 by 230 feet, but it was perfectly suited to its purpose and position.

The exterior columns of the Parthenon form a continuous colonnade on all four sides of the temple. The interior consists of two rectangular chambers. The larger one was the actual chamber of the goddess, where she was present in the form of her holy image. The smaller chamber contained the treasury of Athens—as close as possible to the goddess herself, so that it would be under her protection day and night. The roof of the building was gabled (slanted) and supported by a wooden framework. It was closed at each end by a triangular slab of marble, called the pediment.

The wonder of the Parthenon comes, in part, from the painstaking details of its design. Subtle curves, rather than straight lines, avoid any impression of stiffness. The diameter of each column, for instance, diminishes gradually as it rises to its capital (carved top) in a slightly curving line. The Greek builders had discovered that a perfectly straight profile makes a column look too rigid. They had also found that by adjusting the spacing between columns, they could improve the

A virtual tour of the Parthenon, hosted by Columbia University (http://www.dkv.columbia.edu/vmc/learning/)] Take a virtual tour of the Parthenon.

visual effect of the entire structure. Hence, in the Parthenon, the space between each corner column and the column next to it is less than the space between other columns, and this gives a feeling of extra support at the points of extra stress. The fact that the designers went to such pains to satisfy the demands not only of engineering but of aesthetics as well is testimony to their desire for a building as glorious as the goddess who lived in it.

Images of Gods and Humans

The Greeks' passion for beauty and their interest in human forms are clearly reflected in their sculpture. Only a few originals—and these in mutilated condition—have come down to us. But hundreds of copies of Greek statues, produced in Roman times by Greek artisans, still survive, and have served through the centuries as models for Western sculptors.

 The Art of Classical Greece, ca. 48–323 B.C. (http://www.metmuseum.org/toah/hd/tacg/hd_tacg.htm) See more images of Greek gods and humans.

Early Greek statues, like their buildings, reveal an Egyptian influence. This is still seen in the many statues of young men, probably victorious athletes, that have been unearthed in Greece (see photo). Such statues were often placed in temples, thereby making the athlete into a personal "servant" of the god or goddess, in thanksgiving for victories in contests such as the Olympic Games. The pose of the statue, with arms hanging at the sides, fists clenched, and left foot forward, imitates Egyptian sculpture (compare photo on page 26). The nudity, however, and the smiling face—reproducing the nakedness of Greek athletes and expressing the joy of victory—are Greek innovations.

But Greek sculptors grew dissatisfied with this kind of representation and turned steadily toward greater naturalism, movement, and grace. The statues carved during the fifth century B.C. were chiefly of gods and goddesses; like the deities themselves, they resembled mortals—not actual individuals, but idealized men and women.

Phidias, the most highly respected sculptor of Athens in the Golden Age, was put in charge of the Parthenon sculptures. It was he who carved from wood the gigantic statue of Athena (some 35 feet tall) that was placed in the main inner chamber. Although the original was lost long ago, ancient descriptions tell us that it was richly decorated with ivory, gold,

> **"** *The statues carved during the fifth century B.C. were chiefly of gods and goddesses; like the deities themselves, they resembled mortals—not actual individuals, but idealized men and women.* **"**

and jewels. Phidias also planned and supervised carvings on the marble pediments and the marble frieze (band) that ran around the outside of the inner chambers. Fragments of this sculpture are still in existence (see photo on page 66). They show a solemn procession to the Parthenon in honor of Athena—the high point of Athens's religious year. The sense of ease and motion and the splendid proportion and form are evident even in these fragments.

Better known is *The Discus Thrower* by Myron, another sculptor of the time of Phidias (see photo on page 66). The original bronze casting has been lost, but the figure was so much admired that many marble copies were made. In this statue, Myron chose to portray the athlete at the moment before he made his supreme effort, so that he would appear dynamically poised and in full self-control. The statue is not an accurate picture of a real discus thrower; rather, it is an ideal representation of the male figure—a masterpiece of line and form.

After about 400 B.C., Greek sculptors tended toward a more natural style, as well as a wider choice of subjects. The leading developer of this new style was Praxiteles (**prak-SIT-l-eez**). His most famous work, *Hermes with the Infant Dionysus* (see photo), shows Hermes smiling down at Dionysus and Dionysus reaching up toward Hermes, yet both of them are so perfectly and gracefully balanced that they seem lifelike and godlike at the same time.

It was probably also Praxiteles who broke with the tradition of portraying women and goddesses fully clothed and introduced an entirely new subject of sculptural art—the naked or half-naked female body. The famous *Aphrodite of Melos (Venus de Milo)* of about 100 B.C. (see photo) shows the goddess with her body slightly twisted, her weight on her right leg, and her left knee thrust forward, keeping her low-slung garment from slipping off her hips. Yet this complex pose is so perfectly balanced that it produces an effect of goddess-like serenity and power.

Along with the trend toward a more natural style there developed an interest in portraiture, emotional expression, and

The Parthenon Frieze The horsemen are riding in solemn procession to the Parthenon as part of the yearly festival of Athena. Ancient peoples often decorated temples with scenes of religious ceremonies, probably as a magical way of making sure that the deity would always be receiving worship. The carvers of the frieze, supervised by the renowned sculptor Phidias, brought to this tradition the freedom and gracefulness of the newly developed Greek style of sculpture.
British Museum, London/The Bridgeman Art Library

The Discus Thrower This statue was much admired in the ancient world, and this is one of several marble copies made in Roman times. The bronze original, which does not survive, was made by Myron, a contemporary of Phidias, about 450 B.C. Unlike the early statue shown on page 65, with its conventional pose, this is an idealized study of the naked male body in action. Alinari/Art Resource, NY

>> Hermes with the Infant Dionysus This is the only surviving Greek statue known to be an original work by a famous master—the fourth-century B.C. sculptor Praxiteles. The statue was found in the nineteenth century A.D. in the ruins of the temple of Zeus at Olympia, exactly where the travel writer Pausanias had seen it 1,700 years earlier. Alinari/Art Resource, NY

representation of ordinary people—street vendors, dancers, and common soldiers. Exact likenesses became popular, and more and more statues showed intense emotion.

Probably the most famous example of this kind is the marble group known as *Laocoön and His Sons* (about 50 B.C.). According to legend, the Greeks had schemed to take Troy by hiding soldiers inside a giant wooden horse offered as a gift, and

Venus de Milo This famous statue, probably dating from about 100 B.C., was found by a fisherman on the Aegean island of Melos in A.D. 1820. Enough is left of her arms to suggest that she was holding something at eye level. A polished shield, in which to contemplate herself? A golden apple, awarded by the mortal Paris when judging her beauty against that of Athena and Hera? Nobody knows for sure. Reunion des Musees Nationaux/Art Resource, NY

the priest Laocoön (ley-OK-oh-on) had warned his fellow Trojans not to bring the horse into the city. But Athena, who favored the Greeks, sent two deadly serpents to crush the priest and his sons (see photo). The sculpture depicts the scene as one of desperate struggle and despair, yet also of perfect balance and proportion. In a distant future, this later style of sculpture would deeply influence the art of seventeenth-century Europe (compare photo on page 347).

LO³ Poetry, Drama, and History

As soon as the Greeks relearned writing (p. 51), they began using it to record traditional myths and tales. Later on, as their way of life developed, they wrote down poems praising winners in athletic contests and other matters of importance to an increasingly educated upper class. Then came dramatic performances and law court speeches that emerged from the life of city-states, above all Athens, as well as historical accounts of the conflicts among the city-states and between the Greeks and other peoples. The various kinds of poetry were exceptionally wide-ranging in their themes and expressive in their language; drama, speechmaking, and history were entirely new forms of the spoken or written word.

Epic and Lyric Poetry

The earliest type of Greek poetry was the epic—a long poem telling a story of gods and heroes in the national past. Such poems dated back two thousand years before the Greeks to the Sumerian *Epic of Gilgamesh* (p. 15), and many more were produced in the West for two thousand years afterward. Sometimes epics were based on ancient traditional tales that had been passed down orally (by word of mouth) before being written down, like the French *Song of Roland* (p. 238). Sometimes an epic was the written creation of a single author, like the *Aeneid* of the Roman poet Virgil (p. 108). Either way, the greatest epics became treasured possessions of the peoples among whom they originated—sources of national pride, of subjects for later poets, and of moral guidance.

Homer

The two surviving early Greek epics, the *Iliad* and the *Odyssey*, were believed by the Greeks themselves to be the work of a single author, Homer, who came from one of the Greek settlements in Asia Minor and lived perhaps about 800 B.C. Most likely, Homer worked with traditional tales sung with instrumental accompaniment by illiterate minstrels, who would have partly memorized and partly improvised them. Every minstrel and every generation had a different version, and what Homer probably did was to combine the tales into two great narrative poems, setting his stamp on them more than any minstrel before him. In addition, Homer or others soon after him had access to the new skill of alphabetic writing, so that his version became the standard, which has lasted for thousands of years.

Laocoön and His Sons According to a first-century A.D. Roman writer, Pliny the Elder, this statue was the work of three sculptors from the island of Rhodes—Athenodorus, Hagesander, and Polydorus—about a century before, and in Pliny's time it belonged to the emperor Titus. Fourteen centuries later, in 1508, it was dug up in a Roman vineyard and became the property of the popes. Timothy McCarthy/Art Resource, NY

The general setting of his poems is the Trojan War, a struggle between early Greeks and the defenders of Troy (Ilium) in Asia Minor that supposedly took place in the twelfth century B.C. The *Iliad* concentrates on the events of a few days in the tenth and last year of the war, telling the story of the wrath of the Greek hero Achilles and its consequences for the Greeks and Trojans. Homer's sequel, the *Odyssey*, skips the overthrow and destruction of Troy and tells the story of the ten-year journey home of one of the Greek heroes, the wily and brave Odysseus, king of the island of Ithaca off Greece's northeastern coast. The *Iliad* and *Odyssey* are not just tales of war and adventure. Like earlier epics, they also deal with deep questions about humanity and its place in the universe—with mortals and gods, morals and fate. In addition, more than any other epic poet before or since, Homer paints an unforgettable picture of human life as a whole.

Family life, for instance, is deeply important to Homer. The *Iliad*'s warrior heroes have aged fathers and mothers who love them and are afraid for them. They are happily married, and sometimes their wives wholeheartedly nurture any children they may happen to have had with slave women—a wifely deed that Homer evidently considered both praiseworthy and unusual. By contrast with this loving family life, the poem's scenes of strife and slaughter seem all the grimmer, and the heroes' bloody deaths are all the more tragic.

The Trojan Hero Hector Prepares to Meet His Destiny Read the moving story of the Trojan hero Hector's farewell to his family in the *Iliad*.

Likewise, Odysseus's adventures would not be so gripping without their longed-for goal of homecoming. His escape from a monster's cave, his defeat of a wicked enchantress, his survival through storm and shipwreck each take him a step closer to reunion with his wife and son—and to bloody revenge on strangers who have moved into his palace, tried to alienate his wife's affections, and plotted his son's death.

Furthermore, Homer's characters are no dim mythical figures, but human beings with many lifelike twists and turns of human nature. Priam, king of Troy, beside himself with grief and terror as he makes ready for a perilous nighttime journey to beg the body of his son Hector from the fierce Achilles, flies into a nervous rage at his remaining sons and cruelly tells them they are all worthless in comparison with the one he has lost. Penelope, Odysseus's faithful wife, dreams about his would-be rivals as her "pet geese," as if she cannot help being fond of the men who

> " *And her husband had pity to see her, and caressed her with his hand, and spoke and called upon her name: 'Dear one, I pray you be not of oversorrowful heart; no man against my fate shall hurl me to Hades; only destiny, I suppose, no man has escaped, be he coward or be he valiant, when once he has been born.* "
>
> —from the *Iliad*

have been keeping her company in his absence. And Homer shows his characters not only doing heroic deeds, but also taking care of the everyday business of life—building boats, washing laundry, roasting pork, making cheese. With their panoramas of adventure and war, their deep questions about human existence, their understanding of human nature, and their countless lifelike details, the *Iliad* and *Odyssey* have been an inspiration not only to the Greeks but to Western literature right down to recent times (p. 521).

Lyric Poetry

The Greeks created lyric poetry as well as epic poetry. It is called **lyric** because it was normally sung to the playing of a lyre (a plucked, harplike instrument). A lyric poem was a short work by a single author, who probably improvised it and improved it over time before writing it down. A good deal of lyric poetry was composed for public occasions— notably, praise of athletes and the wealthy backers who paid for their training and equipment. But much lyric poetry was also personal, expressing individual thoughts and feelings about life, love, patriotism—even the pleasures of wine.

An Illustrated Essay on Music in Ancient Greece, Metropolitan Museum (http://www.metmuseum.org/toah/hd/grmu/hd_grmu.htm)] Learn about lyres and the music of ancient Greece.

Solon, the Athenian lawgiver (p. 56), was as famous for his poetry as for his statesmanship. One of his verses is a proud defense of his record in politics. Referring to Athenians he had released from slavery, he wrote, "These I set free; and I did this by strength of hand, welding right law with force to make a single whole. So have I done, and carried through all that I pledged." But Solon's favorite subject was individual happiness and how it is won and lost. Foreshadowing later Greek dramatists, he advised his listeners "to call no man happy until the day of his death." Every life is uncertain, takes unexpected turns, and must be judged in its entirety.

One of the most admired of lyric poets was Sappho, an aristocrat from the Aegean island of Lesbos who lived about the same time as Solon. She spent much of her life away from home, in the neighboring land of Lydia in Asia Minor, where she had family connections, as well as in distant Sicily, where she spent years of exile after a local tyrant (p. 52) ousted her family from power.

A Lyric Poem Laments an Absent Lover Read Sappho's poem to Aphrodite, goddess of love.

Many of Sappho's poems celebrate erotic love, especially of the young women living in the temples of various goddesses where she presided (p. 54). Hence the use of the word *lesbian* in referring to women of her sexual temperament, which was not disapproved by the ancient Greeks, any more than the accepted form of male homosexuality (p. 58). No doubt because of the many partings in Sappho's life, one of the themes of her poetry is that of love sharpened by distance: "Some say cavalry, and others claim infantry or a fleet of long oars is the supreme sight on the black earth. I say it is the one you love . . . Anactoria is far, and I for one would rather see her warm supple step and the sparkle of her face than watch all the dazzling chariots and armored hoplites of Lydia."

A New Art Form: Drama

Other peoples had epic tales and poems of personal feeling, but it was in Greece that drama began. In addition to being read or sung, drama was acted out, and its tighter structure gave it unity and impact. It enabled the audience to see with a sense of detachment the common destiny of themselves and others.

The comedies and tragedies were presented during the festival of Dionysus in open-air amphitheaters. The theater of Athens was located on a slope of the Acropolis. Rows of seats, arranged in a semicircle, descended from the top of the hill to the orchestra—a pattern that was repeated in many city-states, and is best preserved at Epidaurus, in the south of Greece (see photo). Beyond the orchestra, across the open end of the theater, stood a *skéné*, or actors' building (the origin of the word *scene*); in front of it was a porch, or platform, from which the speakers usually recited their lines.

The Greek actors wore masks that identified their roles and were shaped to help them project their voices. All of them were men, though women seemingly were in the audience. The performances were colorful, with grand speeches, music, graceful dancing and singing, and rich costumes and headdresses. There was no curtain or lighting and very little scenery. The author himself wrote the music as well as the text and also trained the cast. During the standard three-day festival of Dionysus, dramatic performances began each morning and lasted until nightfall. Usually, three playwrights competed on successive days, and a prize of great honor was awarded to the one who was judged best.

 Ancient Greek Theater (http://www.richeast.org/htwm/Greeks/theatre/theatre.html) Learn more about Greek costumes, acting, and staging.

Tragedy: Gods and Humans, Morals and Fate

The three tragic playwrights most honored in ancient times, and still revered today, all lived in Athens in the fifth century B.C.

The Theater of Epidaurus Constructed by Polyclitus the Younger in the fourth century B.C. for dramatic contests in honor of the healer-god Asclepius, this theater is still in use today. The benches, seating about eight thousand people, surround the orchestra, and behind it are the foundations of the *skéné*. A person speaking in a normal voice from the *skéné* can be clearly heard seventy yards away in the rear of the theater. Robert Harding Picture Library/SuperStock 1890-20893

DRAMA EVOLVED IN ANCIENT GREECE IN TWO DIRECTIONS:

The Origins of Tragedy

- Greek **tragedy** grew out of ancient religious ceremonials. It began in the sixth century B.C. as part of the annual spring festival in honor of the god Dionysus.

- During the spring festivals, it was customary for a choral group to sing hymns about the gods and heroes of Greek legend. As the chorus sang, it danced in dignified fashion around a circular plot of ground called the *orkhēstra* (derived from the Greek word for "dance," and the origin of the word orchestra).

- Drama was born when the leader of the chorus was permitted to step out from the group and carry on a kind of conversation (in song) with the chorus.

- By the beginning of the fifth century B.C., the choral dramas might have several individual characters, although no more than three actors plus the chorus took part at any one time. Thus the ancient, repetitive ceremonial became a medium for expressing new ideas.

The Origins of Comedy

- The rites in honor of Dionysus included not only solemn dances and chants but also raucous processions and frenzied revels. It was out of these celebrations that Athenian **comedy** was born.

- The earliest comedies were crude slapstick performances, but gradually they became biting topical satires—though always heavily spiced with bedroom and toilet jokes.

- The most successful writer of Greek comedy was Aristophanes. He used his plays to make fun of local politicians, poets, and philosophers with whom he disagreed—as well as the politics and government of Athenian democracy, as in *Lysistrata* and *The Assemblywomen* (p. 59).

Aeschylus, Sophocles, and Euripides wrote nearly three hundred plays, although only about thirty have survived.

The earliest tragic dramatist was Aeschylus, whose plays transform suffering and death into inspiration and the will to live. In the Orestes trilogy—*Agamemnon*, the *Libation Bearers*, and the *Eumenides*—Aeschylus's central theme is the family crimes of the royal house of Atreus. The plot, well known in Greek legend, revolves around the murder of King Agamemnon by his wife Clytemnestra when he returns from the Trojan War. The murder is partly an act of revenge for Agamemnon's sacrifice of their daughter so that the gods will give a fair wind for the Greeks to sail to Troy at the beginning of the war; but in turn their son Orestes murders his mother. Father, mother, and son can all justify their acts, but all are nonetheless guilty. To Aeschylus, these crimes and the suffering they bring are divine punishment for violations of the moral order. In the final play of the trilogy, Athena herself intervenes to protect Orestes from pursuit by the Furies, the divine avengers of the murder of parents, and to stop the terrible cycle of crime and punishment (see photo on page 61). Revenge is transformed into the justice of the city-state, and Orestes is restored to respectability. Audiences left with the feeling that individuals pay for their crimes—that the gods and the moral law are hard but that one can face fate bravely and nobly.

Because Sophocles reflected the Greek ideal of "nothing in excess," he has been called the "most Greek" of the three playwrights. In the tragedy, *Oedipus the King*, Oedipus thinks he can avoid his fate, which has been foretold by the Delphic oracle of Apollo. A man of good intention, he tries to escape from the shocking prophecy that he will kill his father and marry his mother. But in the end, the truth of his moral crimes, which he has committed unknowingly, is brought to light by his own insistent searching. He realizes at last the folly of his conceit and savagely blinds himself as punishment for the foulness of his deeds.

 Sophocles on the Wondrous Abilities of Human Beings Read a speech from Sophocles' tragedy, *Antigone*.

Euripides, the youngest of the great Greek tragedians, probably had the deepest insight into human character. He was also considered something of a radical, for he challenged the traditional religious and moral values of his time. He opposed slavery and showed the "other side" of war. In *The Trojan Women*, the battle ends with a broken-hearted old woman sitting on the ground holding a dead child in her arms. Euripides was keenly sensitive to injustice, whether of the gods or of mortals, and he pleaded for greater tolerance, equality, and decency.

History

All ancient peoples celebrated events and deeds of the past. Minstrels sang of epic deeds, rulers built monuments boasting of their victories, priests chronicled the doings of the deities they served. But Greek writers were the first to try to separate fact from fiction and to analyze in depth the human causes of events.

The "father of history," Herodotus (huh-ROD-uh-tuhs), was born in 485 B.C. in Halicarnassus, a Greek city on the shore of Asia Minor. A great traveler, he visited various parts of the Persian Empire—Mesopotamia, Syria, and Egypt. He also toured Greek colonies from the Black Sea to southern Italy. Having grown up in the time of the Persian Wars (p. 56), he decided to set down a record of that struggle and of the events that led up to it.

Herodotus called his work the *Historia*, which means, in Greek, "investigation," and he set out to separate fact from legend, to write an account based on direct observation and evidence. The sources he used were not all reliable, to be sure, but he usually warned his readers when he was passing along doubtful information. Most of the *Historia* is a survey of the entire region of eastern Europe, Egypt, and Persia that formed the background to the wars: political and military affairs, social customs, religious beliefs, and leading personalities. In the final portion of his work, he tells the story of the Persian Wars in a manner sympathetic to both Persians and Greeks, though presenting it as an epic contest between slavery and freedom.

A generation later, the Athenian Thucydides (thoo-SID-i-deez) took the writing of history to a higher critical level in his history of the long and cruel war between Athens and Sparta that had broken out soon after their joint victory over Persia (Chapter 5). An exiled general of Athens, he had traveled widely to gather information during the war. His subject matter is far more limited than that of Herodotus, but his account has greater unity and depth. And he excluded all suggestion of supernatural interference; history, he was convinced, is made by human beings, and human nature could be understood through careful study of the past. He presented his facts from both sides, showing the reader the causes, motives, and consequences of the war. But his work is more than military history; it deals with the still-relevant questions of imperialism, democracy, and the whole range of social relations.

Both Herodotus and Thucydides were influenced by existing traditions of Greek literature, especially the epics of Homer. For example, both historians put speeches into the mouths of leading figures like Pericles (p. 59) that were never actually spoken but reveal their personalities and motives, just as Homer did with many of his characters. But history also sprang from another source: the search by Greek thinkers for explanations of the

> *"O god—all come true, all burst to light! O light—now let me look my last on you! I stand revealed at last—cursed in my birth, cursed in marriage, cursed in the lives I cut down with these hands!"*
>
> —from Oedipus the King

world and humans that would be more logical and convincing than religious tradition provided.

LO⁴ The Founders of Philosophy

The earliest Greek philosophers (in the sixth century B.C.) began by looking for alternatives to the traditions about the gods and goddesses. They found it hard to believe that lightning was a bolt from Zeus, or that a god who repeatedly deceived his wife would care about humans abiding by oaths. But if not, what was the real cause of lightning? Why should people be righteous? And what were the gods really like? Greek thinkers did not reach final answers to questions like these and even argued fiercely whether final answers were possible at all. But they began a quest for answers that has influenced Western thought and science ever since.

Thinking About the Universe: The Pre-Socratics

To answer questions about lightning and everything else that happens in nature, early Greek thinkers (now known as the **Pre-Socratics**) wanted to know what material things are made of. They were sure that everything they saw around them must be made of a few basic elements, but they could not agree on what these elements were. Around 600 B.C., Thales of Miletus (in Asia Minor) theorized that water was the basic element—it filled the sea, rivers, and springs; it fell from the sky; it was found in the flesh and organs of animal bodies. Though later philosophers rejected Thales' belief that everything can be reduced to water, they agreed that he was on the right track. Some believed the prime substance to be air or fire; others concluded that there are four basic elements: earth, air, fire, and water.

But during the fifth century B.C., Democritus of Abdera (in Thrace, a territory on the Aegean's northern coast) developed the theory that all things are formed by combinations of tiny particles, so small that they are both invisible and indivisible. He called them *atoms* (from the Greek for "can't be cut up"). Democritus's atoms are identical in substance but differ in shape, thus making possible the great variety of objects in the world. They are infinite in number, everlasting, and in constant motion. They account, said Democritus, for everything that has been or ever will be. Democritus offered no evidence to prove the

tragedy
A type of play in which the main character suffers a terrible downfall.

comedy
A type of play characterized by humor and a happy ending.

Pre-Socratic philosophers
The modern label given to ancient Greek philosophers before Socrates.

Sophists
A group of professional teachers who argued that truth is relative and that it was more important to have a persuasive argument than a sound one.

Socratic method
A form of inquiry involving questions and answers intended to lead from uncertainty to truth.

existence of atoms, but the fact that he could arrive at this idea demonstrates the far-reaching achievement of Greek reasoning.

Likewise, in the fifth century B.C., Hippocrates of Cos (an island in the Aegean) challenged traditional supernatural explanations of illness. He insisted that natural causes be looked for and that natural means be used to treat disease. He was one of the first physicians to stress the influence of the environment (climate, air, and water) on health. He also claimed that the human body contains four "humors" (fluids): blood, phlegm, yellow bile, and black bile. When these are in proper balance, the individual enjoys normal health. But when the balance becomes disturbed, the physician must use his skill to restore it. This theory was accepted in the West for more than two thousand years and was only proven incorrect in modern times.

Meanwhile, the philosopher Parmenides of Elea (in southern Italy) tackled the controversial issue of permanence versus change in the world. He convinced himself that everything in the universe must be eternal and unchangeable. Change requires motion, he reasoned, and motion requires empty space. But empty space equals nonexistence, which by definition does not exist. Therefore, he concluded, motion and change are impossible. Parmenides readily admitted that some things *appear* to move and change; but this must be an illusion of the senses, he said, because it is contradicted by logic. And logic, the Greek philosophers thought, is the most reliable test of truth.

Logic did not always lead to the same answers, however. In contrast to Parmenides, Heraclitus of Ephesus (in Asia Minor) insisted that the universe, instead of standing still, is in continuous motion. He declared that a person cannot step into the same river twice—a disturbing claim, for if everything is constantly changing (including ourselves), how can we gain true knowledge of anything? Heraclitus's answer was that the universe was ultimately understandable—that all its changes were governed by what he called Reason (in Greek, *logos*, from which the word *logic* derives), which was also present in the human mind. But so far as is known, he did not explain exactly how humans could use the Reason in their minds to understand the ever-changing universe.

> "Socrates did not believe it necessary to observe and collect data in order to find knowledge; on the contrary, he had a deep conviction that truth is implanted in the mind and cannot be seen in the changing world around us. The function of the philosopher is to recover the truth that lies buried in the mind."

No Final Answers: The Sophists

Suggestions like these led many Greeks to abandon the effort to find certain knowledge of anything. A group of professional teachers, called **Sophists** because they claimed to make their pupils wise (*sophos*), played a leading part in this shift. Most of them visited various cities of the Mediterranean area to earn their living. When they settled in Athens, as many did, they held more cosmopolitan views about the world than did ordinary Athenian citizens. Prominent among the Sophists was Protagoras. He is famous for having declared, "Man is the measure of all things, of what is and of what is not." Completely skeptical (doubting) of general truths, even about the gods, he insisted that truth is different for each individual. What was true (or right) for a Spartan might well be false (or wrong) for an Athenian.

The Sophists thus rejected the established view that there existed a common, "objective" reality that all persons can grasp in the same way. They concluded, therefore, that it is pointless to look for certain knowledge about either nature or morals. Because truth is relative to each individual, it is important only to know what one finds agreeable and useful, such as the arts of persuasion or how to achieve success.

As news of these teachings circulated in Athens and elsewhere in Greece, the citizens were shocked and alarmed. Such ideas smacked of impiety (disrespect for the gods) and threatened to subvert the laws and moral code of the state. Protagoras protested that his theories did not call for the denial of authority and cautioned his pupils, "When in Athens, do as the Athenians." Social order, he agreed, requires reasonable conformity to the laws of the community, whether or not they are absolutely true or right. But the citizens were not reassured. It upset them to think that one person's ideas are as "true" as another's. And the laws of gods and mortals, they argued, cannot be properly respected and upheld unless people believe them to be genuinely true and just.

Truth Beyond This World: Socrates and Plato

The greatest teacher of the fifth century was Socrates, who met the Sophist view of how to get on in life with the full force of his intellect and will. He was convinced of the existence of a higher truth, though he did not claim to know this truth but spoke of himself only as a seeker after knowledge. He believed that knowledge must proceed from doubting, and he was forever posing questions and testing the answers people gave him. Because of this, the Athenians often mistook Socrates for a Sophist, and he shared in their unpopularity.

The Socratic Method

This "Socratic method" of questioning is simply a procedure for reaching toward truth by means of a dialogue or directed discussion. Socrates cross-examined his friends on their definitions of justice, right, and beauty, moving them constantly toward answers that seemed more and more certain. Socrates did not believe it necessary to observe and collect data in order to find knowledge; on the contrary, he had a deep conviction that truth is implanted in the mind and cannot be seen in the changing world around us. The function of the philosopher is to recover the truth that lies buried in the mind.

Socrates' search for truth sustained him in the face of death itself. In the dialogue of the *Phaedo*, his pupil Plato describes the final hours of his teacher. Condemned to death by an Athenian jury on charges of corrupting the youth and not worshiping the gods of Athens, Socrates faces his fate cheerfully. He does so because he believes the soul is immortal, though during life it is hindered by the troubles and "foolishness" of the body. Death brings release for the soul and the opportunity to see the truth more clearly than before. And for Socrates, the real aim of life is to know the truth, rather than to seek the satisfactions of the body.

Socrates: Death Is a Good Thing Read Socrates' thoughts on death as he hears his death sentence.

Plato: The Doctrine of Ideas

Almost all we know about Socrates' views comes to us through Plato, who wrote masterly literary works in the form of dialogues in which Socrates usually appears as the chief speaker. It is difficult to say where the ideas of Socrates end and those of Plato begin, but it seems clear that Plato took up and developed the main thoughts of his teacher. Plato was born in or near Athens, traveled widely through the Mediterranean lands, and founded a school at Athens in 385 B.C. The Academy, as it was called, became the most influential intellectual center of the ancient world. It endured after its founder's death for over nine hundred years, and it served as a model for similar schools in other cities.

Plato continued Socrates' attack on the Sophist theory of truth as changeable and different for each person. Returning to the controversies of earlier Greek thinkers about what things were made of and about the question of permanence and change, Plato felt that the imperfect surface of things conceals a perfect and eternal order.

In his famous "Doctrine of Ideas," Plato conceded that everything that we actually see around us is just what the Sophists suggested: imperfect, changeable, and different in appearance to every individual. But above and beyond it, Plato asserted, is the real world of perfect Ideas or Forms, which exist unchanged through all the ages. There are, for example, the Ideas of Man, Horse, Tree, Beauty, the State, Justice, and the highest of all Ideas—Goodness. These exist independent of individuals and can be known to them only through the mind. Plato speculated that the universe as we see it is the work of a *demiurge* (from the Greek for "craftsman")—a divine but imperfect being whose creation could only be a distorted reflection of the Ideas. Philosophers should turn away from things as we see them and focus on the discovery and contemplation of the perfect, the eternal, the real.

The Ideal Community

True to his belief in a perfect world beyond the world as we perceive it, in the best known of his dialogues, the *Republic*, Plato presented an image of the perfect city-state—which he probably never expected to replace imperfect existing ones. Such a community, according to Plato, would need to be guided by truthful principles as interpreted by philosophers. An aristocrat who grew up during the Peloponnesian War, which brought Athens's Golden Age to an end (pp. 80–81), Plato admired Spartan institutions and had contempt for democratic ways. The institutions of a perfect community should aim not at complete individual freedom and equality but at social justice and order. In the community, just as in the human body, every part should do the job it was designed to do. The foot should not try to become the head—nor the head the stomach. Only then would friction, envy, and inefficiency—the chief sources of human and social sickness—be eliminated.

To reach this objective, Plato felt, the city-state must be structured according to natural capacities. The bulk of its citizens would make up the class of Workers (producers), who would be sorted into various occupations according to their aptitudes. Above them would be the Guardian class, which would be trained in the arts

<< **"Snub-Nosed and Pop-Eyed"** This portrait bust, believed to date from about twenty years after Socrates died, is true to Plato's description of his teacher and friend. Plato also compared Socrates with Athenian statues of the pot-bellied, balding god Silenus—which, however, opened up to reveal that they contained golden images of the noblest deities. Vatican Museums/Art Resource, NY

PLATO ON THE EQUALITY OF WOMEN AND MEN IN HIS IDEAL CITY-STATE

Like Plato's other works, his description of the ideal city-state, the *Republic*, is written in the form of a fictional dialogue (conversation) between Socrates and his friends. Here, the subject is the "virtue" (the excellence as human beings) of women and men—especially in the guiding elite of Guardians—and the activities that women should share with men as Guardians. Socrates and his friend Glaucon are discussing how Socrates would argue against someone who disapproves of women being active alongside men in such pursuits as government, warfare, and athletics.

Next, we shall ask our opponent how, in reference to any of the pursuits or arts of civic life, the nature of a woman differs from that of a man?

That will be quite fair.

And perhaps he, like yourself, will reply that to give a sufficient answer on the instant is not easy; but after a little reflection there is no difficulty.

Yes, perhaps.

Suppose then that we invite him to accompany us in the argument, and then we may hope to show him that there is nothing peculiar in the constitution of women which would affect them in the administration of the State.

By all means. . . .

And can you mention any pursuit of mankind in which the male sex has not all these gifts and qualities in a higher degree than the female? Need I waste time in speaking of the art of weaving, and the management of pancakes and preserves, in which womankind does really appear to be great, and in which for her to be beaten by a man is of all things the most absurd?

You are quite right, he replied, in maintaining the general inferiority of the female sex: although many women are in many things superior to many men, yet on the whole what you say is true.

And if so, my friend, I said, there is no special faculty of administration in a state which a woman has because she is a woman, or which a man has by virtue of his sex, but the gifts of nature are alike diffused in both; all the pursuits of men are the pursuits of women also, but in all of them a woman is inferior to a man.

Very true.

Then are we to impose all our enactments on men and none of them on women?

That will never do.

One woman has a gift of healing, another not; one is a musician, and another has no music in her nature?

Very true.

And one woman has a turn for gymnastic and military exercises, and another is unwarlike and hates gymnastics?

of government and war. From this disciplined class would be chosen, with the greatest care, the rulers of the state.

The Guardians would be no privileged upper class, but would lead austere and regulated lives of total devotion to the state. Matings among them would be arranged by the state, to ensure the production of superior offspring. Any infant showing a physical defect would be left to die of exposure, and healthy infants would be taken from their mothers and placed in a community nursery. Parents would not be permitted to know their own children, nor would they be allowed to possess personal property. The education of the Guardians was to be closely controlled. Only the "right" kind of music, art, and poetry would be taught, so that pupils would receive the desired moral indoctrination. Those selected to be the rulers would have additional training in philosophy and would serve a period of political apprenticeship before taking their places as directors of the state. All this was necessary, thought Plato, if they were to become truly selfless and dedicated to the welfare of the whole community.

The Abolition of the Family

The Guardians would be both male and female, and among the rulers there would be both "philosopher-kings" and "philosopher-queens." This was not because Plato found the existing treatment of women oppressive. On the contrary, he believed that the existing system was too

Certainly.

And one woman is a philosopher, and another is an enemy of philosophy; one has spirit, and another is without spirit?

That is also true.

Then one woman will have the temper of a guardian, and another not. Was not the selection of the male guardians determined by differences of this sort?

Yes.

Men and women alike possess the qualities which make a guardian; they differ only in their comparative strength or weakness.

Obviously.

And those women who have such qualities are to be selected as the companions and colleagues of men who have similar qualities and whom they resemble in capacity and in character?

Very true.

And ought not the same natures to have the same pursuits?

They ought.

Then, as we were saying before, there is nothing unnatural in assigning music and gymnastic to the wives of the guardians—to that point we come round again.

Certainly not. . . .

Well, and may we not further say that our guardians are the best of our citizens?

By far the best.

And will not their wives be the best women?

Yes, by far the best.

And can there be anything better for the interests of the State than that the men and women of a State should be as good as possible?

There can be nothing better.

And this is what the arts of music and gymnastic, when present in such manner as we have described, will accomplish?

Certainly.

Then we have made an enactment not only possible but in the highest degree beneficial to the State?

True.

Then let the wives of our guardians strip, for their virtue will be their robe, and let them share in the toils of war and the defence of their country; only in the distribution of labours the lighter are to be assigned to the women, who are the weaker natures, but in other respects their duties are to be the same. And as for the man who laughs at naked women exercising their bodies from the best of motives, in his laughter he is plucking a fruit of unripe wisdom, and he himself is ignorant of what he is laughing at, or what he is about;—for that is, and ever will be, the best of sayings, *That the useful is the noble and the hurtful is the base.*

EXPLORING THE SOURCE

1. How did Plato justify allowing women to participate as Guardians in the governance of his ideal city-state, and what kind of activities did he want them to take part in?

2. Why did Plato think that it was desirable for women to share fully in the activities of his ideal city-state?

Source: Plato, *Republic* 5, trans. Benjamin Jowett, *Dialogues of Plato*, 3d ed. (London: Macmillan, 1892), 3:147–150.

easy on women, because it exempted them from the main burdens of citizenship. Women were well able to bear these burdens, Plato believed, because their abilities—including as warriors—were basically the same as those of men. On the average, he thought, women's abilities were not so strong as men's, but this made no difference to the fact that a city-state that did not make use of women in the same way as it made use of men "is only half a state, and develops only half its potentialities."

Plato applied this idea only to the Guardians, among whom breeding and education would produce superior females and males as thinkers, fighters, and rulers. For the Workers, whose tasks and abilities were on a lower level than those of the Guardians, he though that traditional family life was still best.

And in another work, the *Laws*, where Plato was more interested in making recommendations for existing city-states than in imagining ideal alternatives, he advised that women should be deliberately educated in the belief that their abilities were different from men's, so that traditional family and community life could run smoothly.

Plato was the first thinker to imagine an alternative to the way of life based on communities made up of families that had grown up with the Agricultural Revolution (pp. 9–10). At least among a restricted elite, his alternative involved the abolition of the family, the equality of women and men, and the complete subordination of the individual to the community. The belief that these three things go together has inspired many radical social reformers—and horrified their opponents—over the centuries. Plato was also the first thinker to claim that the idea of a fundamental difference in abilities between men and women is a socially convenient myth—a claim that is basic to much of modern feminism.

Analyzing This World: Aristotle

Born in Stagira on the Aegean's northern coast, Aristotle made his way early to Plato's Academy in Athens; years later, he founded a school of his own there—the Lyceum (335 B.C.). Far more than his teacher, Aristotle was interested in the evidence of the senses. He was, in fact, the greatest collector and classifier in antiquity. His interests ranged from biology to poetry, from politics to ethics.

Aristotle accepted Plato's general notion of the existence of Ideas or Forms, but he held that the things around us are also a part of reality, a kind of raw material given their different shapes and purposes by the Forms. By logical thinking, people can gain knowledge of these purposes, and thereby approach closer to God—whom Aristotle conceived as pure spirit and the source of the Forms. For this reason, he worked out systematic rules for logical thinking that have been respected by philosophers for centuries.

Classifying Human Beings

In accordance with his theory that all things have a purpose, Aristotle taught that every organ and creature should function according to its design—including human beings. Like Plato, he thought that different human beings were designed for different functions. For each of them, "virtue" (human excellence) consisted in perfectly fulfilling these functions, so that virtue meant different things for different types of humans. But Aristotle worked out in much more detail than Plato what this meant for existing communities, and unlike his master, he accepted as true the idea that men and women have basically differing abilities.

The highest kind of human excellence, Aristotle believed, was to be found in the activities of ruling over other humans and pursuing knowledge of the Forms and of God. This, he thought, calls for a harmonious balance of faculties (abilities) of both body and mind. In general, excellence in a particular activity lies somewhere between extremes. True courage in battle, for example, lies somewhere in between cowardice and foolhardiness. Likewise, a truly beautiful work of art is one that is "just right"—it cannot be improved either by adding something or by taking something away. Aristotle warned that his advice did not apply to things that are good or bad in themselves. Truth and beauty, for example, should be sought in the highest degree, while murder, theft, and lying are evil in any degree. But in most activities, each man should find, through trial and self-criticism,

the desired mean (midpoint) between extremes. This has come to be called the **Golden Mean**—not a pale average or a mediocre standard, but the best performance of mind and body working together in harmony.

This kind of virtue, however, was only to be achieved by a small minority of the human race, namely, freeborn Greek men with at least some wealth and education. The virtue of other humans lay in performing various lower, though still essential, functions. Non-Greeks, for instance, were not designed for highest excellence, and that was what made them suitable as slaves. For them, virtue meant willingness to perform dull and heavy tasks, thereby freeing their masters to pursue higher forms of excellence. Likewise, Aristotle said that "the male is by nature superior, and the female inferior," and that though both possessed virtue, their virtue was of different kinds; for instance, "the courage of a man is shown in commanding, of a woman in obeying." In this way, Aristotle used the new methods of philosophical reasoning to claim that the existing Greek pattern of community and family life was no hardship and did not need to be replaced by an ideal alternative society, but was part of the proper order of the universe.

Real-World Communities

Aristotle believed that communities, too, had a purpose. Their function was to create the conditions in which virtue could flourish, but there was no single way of doing this. In his classic work, the *Politics*, Aristotle examined existing city-states, analyzed and evaluated the major types of political organization, and recognized that there are differences in local conditions and classes of inhabitants. He considered government by one man, by a few, and by many all legitimate, if devoted to the general welfare; each needs to serve the interests of all social groups if it is to survive; and any type of government becomes a "perversion" when the rulers pursue their own interest alone. (The worst government of all, he thought, is a perversion of rule by the many.) Under whatever constitution, Aristotle favored a strong role for the middle class of citizens. The more numerous poor, he stated, lack experience in directing others; the very rich are not used to obeying. The middle class knows what it is both to command and to obey and may be counted on to avoid political extremes.

 Aristotle on Politics Read a passage in which Aristotle analyzes different forms of government.

Aristotle's explanation of the order of the universe and human inequality had vast influence on Western philosophy, science, and everyday thinking for many centuries until recent times. His ideal of a highest human excellence that only a few can reach—though with the few no longer consisting of well-to-do men of a particular nation—is still influential today. And his method of analyzing and comparing the features and development of government systems is basic to modern political science.

 Listen to a synopsis of Chapter 4.

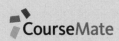

"I think this book is totally cutting-edge... it's making learning fun again."

- Scotty Williamson, Student at Middle Tennessee State University

WCIV was designed for students just like you – busy people who want choices, flexibility, and multiple learning options.

WCIV delivers concise, focused information in a fresh and contemporary format. And... **WCIV** gives you a variety of online learning materials designed with you in mind.

At **CengageBrain.com**, you'll find electronic resources such as audio downloads and online flash cards for each chapter. These resources will help supplement your understanding of core Western Civilization concepts in a format that fits your busy lifestyle.

Visit **CengageBrain.com** to learn more about the multiple **WCIV** resources available to help you succeed!

CHAPTER 5

GREATER GREECE: THE HELLENISTIC ERA, 400–30 B.C.

LEARNING OBJECTIVES

AFTER READING THIS CHAPTER, YOU SHOULD BE ABLE TO DO THE FOLLOWING:

LO¹ Trace the crisis of the Greek city-states and the rise of Macedonia.

LO² Explain how Hellenistic-era Greek culture gained international leadership but was also influenced by the peoples the Greeks ruled.

LO³ Contrast the Epicurean and Stoic philosophies of the Hellenistic era.

"THE GREEKS HAD EVOLVED FROM A BARBARIAN PEOPLE ON CIVILIZATION'S NORTHWESTERN EDGE TO BECOME THE DOMINANT NATION OF A REGION THAT STRETCHED FROM ITALY TO PRESENT-DAY AFGHANISTAN."

Throughout history, clusters of independent city-states have sooner or later come under the power of stronger neighboring rulers, and the Greek city-states were no exception. The longest and most brutal of their many conflicts, the Peloponnesian War between opposing alliances under Athens and Sparta, led to the end of the heyday of the city-states around 400 B.C. As a result, they eventually fell under the rule of the Greek-influenced northern kingdom of Macedonia.

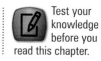 Test your knowledge before you read this chapter.

This did not mean the end of Greek civilization or of Greek power in the world, however. On the contrary, King Alexander of Macedonia led the Greeks to the conquest of Persia, and though his empire split up after his death, its separate territories came to be ruled by spectacularly wealthy and powerful Greek kings.

What do you think?

Greek civilization would have endured longer if the Greeks had not overreached.

Strongly Disagree						Strongly Agree
1	2	3	4	5	6	7

By 300 B.C., Greek civilization had entered a new phase, the Hellenistic (**hel-uh-NIS-tik**) era, in which theirs was the leading international culture but their way of life was also influenced by the peoples they ruled. And the Greeks themselves had evolved from a barbarian people on civilization's northwestern edge to become the dominant nation of a region that stretched from Italy to present-day Afghanistan.

≪ **A Hellenistic Buddha** This carving was made in Gandhara, in the borderland between present-day Pakistan and Afghanistan, about A.D. 100. Buddha is guarded by Vajrapani, the heroic symbol of his spiritual power. But Buddha's hairstyle, and his gown with its delicate folds, are Greek; and Vajrapani has the nude pose and the club of a Greek hero, Heracles. Following Alexander's conquests, Greeks had long ruled this region, and Buddhist art still felt their influence.

LO¹ The Crisis of the City-States

After several centuries of growing confidence and power, the Greek city-states were caught up in a massive conflict growing out of rivalry between Athens and Sparta. The Athenians called it the "Peloponnesian" war because their chief enemies were Sparta and its allies in the southernmost region of mainland Greece, the Peloponnesus, and neighboring areas (Map 5.1). There had been earlier conflicts between Sparta and Athens, but the long struggle that opened in 431 B.C., and lasted until 404 B.C., ended with the defeat of Athens and the weakening of Sparta.

The Peloponnesian War

Like all competitive city-states, those of Greece continually fought each other, with the more powerful ones struggling to dominate the others. Sparta, with its well-trained army, was traditionally the most powerful city-state in mainland Greece. The Persian Wars, however, made Athens first Sparta's equal partner and then its rival.

CHRONOLOGY

431–404 B.C.	Peloponnesian War between the alliances of Sparta and Athens
359 B.C.	King Philip II of Macedonia comes to power; moves to control Greece
338 B.C.	End of democracy in Athens
334 B.C.	Alexander III begins expansion of empire
323 B.C.	Alexander dies; empire is divided; Hellenistic era begins
200 B.C.	Internal rebellions and external invasions begin to weaken Greek rule
30 B.C.	Roman conquest of Egypt; the Hellenistic world lives on under Roman rule

Map 5.1 The Peloponnesian War

The war was a conflict between the land power of Sparta and its allies, mainly in southern Greece, and the sea power of the Athenian alliance of city-states in the coasts and islands of the Aegean. It was hard for either side to strike a decisive blow until Athenian naval losses in Sicily, as well as money and supplies from the still mighty Persian Empire, enabled Sparta to build a navy that could defeat Athens. © Cengage Learning

Interactive Map

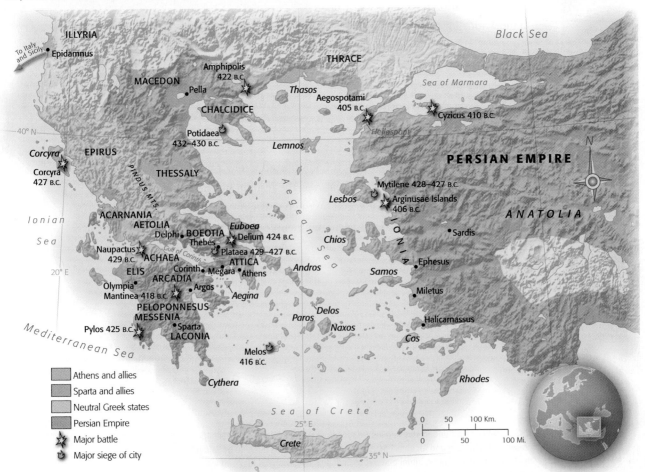

THE REASONS WHY...

SEVERAL FACTORS CONTRIBUTED TO ATHENS LOSING THE PELOPONNESIAN WAR:

Natural Disaster and Poor Leadership

- In 430 B.C., a terrible plague struck Athens, killing thousands of inhabitants, including Pericles himself.

- Athens recovered, but leadership of the city passed to reckless politicians who spurned Sparta's offers of compromise and "peace without victory."

Damaging Losses

- In 413 B.C., Athens lost two-thirds of its fleet in an expedition against Sparta's ally Syracuse.

- With help from Persia (which considered Athens their greatest threat), Sparta built a navy to challenge Athens's now smaller fleet.

- The Spartans crushed the Athenian fleet in 405 B.C. at the battle of Aegospotami in the straits between the Aegean and the Black Sea.

- Their navy destroyed and needing grain supplies from overseas, the Athenian citizens were starved into surrender (404 B.C.).

 The Plague Strikes Athens Read a vivid account of the plague's toll.

Once the defeat of Xerxes' invasion in 480 B.C. made mainland Greece safe from attack, Sparta dropped out of the fighting. Athens, however, formed an alliance of city-states to go over to the offensive, which most of the Greek city-states on the Aegean coasts and islands eventually joined (Map 5.1). Members agreed to contribute money annually for the construction of triremes (p. 52), which were placed under Athenian command. The city thus gained control of several hundred vessels with their crews—by far the largest fleet to sail the Mediterranean at the time.

In 445 B.C., after the Greek city-states of Anatolia had been freed from Persian rule and the Persians had accepted defeat, Athens nevertheless forced its allies to go on sending money, thereby turning them into tribute-paying subjects. Many of the city-states of mainland Greece were provoked by the Athenians' behavior—especially as these city-states were generally ruled by oligarchies, and the Athenians usually insisted that their subject cities practice democracy. The smaller mainland cities appealed to the Spartans to put a check on Athens. At last, the Spartans decided to support their ally, Corinth, which had become involved in a naval war with Athens, and the Athenians took up

 Athens Demands Tribute from Its Allies Read how the Athenians planned to collect tribute from their allies.

"To the north of Greece, a power was rising, the kingdom of Macedonia, that would soon put an end to the independence of the city-states. But under Macedonian leadership, the Greeks would enjoy a brief moment of unity that would enable them to replace the Persians as the dominant nation of the lands stretching from Asia Minor and Egypt to the borders of India."

the challenge. In the words of the historian Thucydides, what had brought on the conflict was the fact that "the Athenians had grown great and inspired fear in the Spartans, thereby compelling them to war."

In the course of the war (431–404 B.C.), the Athenians, under the guidance of Pericles, at first showed caution and sound strategy. The city of Athens and its nearby harbor, Piraeus, formed a single stronghold. The Spartans, unbeatable on the battlefield but not equipped for siege warfare, often raided Attica but could not capture the city itself or cut its links with the sea.

Meanwhile, the Athenians used their navy to guard the sea routes that supplied them with grain and to raid Sparta and its allies. Despite its strengths, however, Athens would eventually fall to Sparta.

Defeated, the Athenians gave up all their outlying possessions, pulled down their defensive walls, and became forced allies of Sparta under a harshly ruling oligarchy. But Sparta, too, had lost both men and resources, and could not prevent Athens from eventually returning to democracy and regaining its independence. With both rivals weakened, the city-states returned to their traditional pattern of continual struggle. Thebes tried unsuccessfully to replace Sparta and Athens as the dominant city-state, and even Persia, for a time, wielded effective influence in mainland Greece.

Meanwhile, Greek civilization continued to flourish. The works of Plato and Aristotle, for instance, date from the era that followed the end of the Peloponnesian War. Plato's search for an ideal city-state was perhaps partly inspired by the doubts and questionings in Athens following defeat—but in spite of the upheaval, Aristotle did not doubt or question the superiority of the Greeks in human excellence to all other peoples. In fact, the Greeks and their way of life were about to become more important in the world than ever before. To the north of Greece, a power was rising, the kingdom of Macedonia (mas-i-DOH-nee-uh), that would soon put an end to the independence of the city-states. But under Macedonian leadership, the Greeks would enjoy a brief moment of unity that would enable them to replace the Persians as the dominant nation of the lands stretching from Anatolia and Egypt to the borders of India.

The Rise of Macedonia

Macedonia was a border territory between Greece and still-barbarian peoples farther north in Europe, and though the Macedonians were probably native Greek-speakers, they and the Greeks regarded each other as different nations. The country was ruled in the traditional manner, by kings and warrior nobles. But it was also larger and richer in resources than any city-state, and its kings had always admired the Greeks and longed to associate themselves with them.

In 359 B.C., Macedonia came under the rule of King Philip II, a ruler of broad vision who was determined to gain control of the city-states and to lead the Greeks and Macedonians in a united force against the weakening empire of Persia. In the course of fighting against barbarian peoples to the north, he strengthened his army by adopting Greek phalanx tactics, improving the weapons of his hoplites, and building up a stronger cavalry force than any city-state possessed. Meanwhile, he made careful plans for infiltrating and conquering Greece. Philip's agents worked to prevent the city-states from joining forces against him. One eloquent Athenian, Demosthenes, recognized the peril and repeatedly warned his fellow citizens. But the traditional reluctance of the city-states to work together, combined with their failure to take the new menace seriously, played into Philip's hands.

At last, he was ready to move. Through diplomacy and military pressure, Philip thrust into northern and central Greece. The Athenians, aroused at last, formed an alliance with the Thebans in an attempt to stop him. It was too late. At the battle of Chaeronea (338 B.C.), the Macedonians won a decisive victory. What remained of Greek independence was left for Philip to decide.

The Macedonian king used his newly won power wisely, letting the Greek city-states govern themselves so long as they installed oligarchies and acted as loyal allies. Philip, now at the head of a powerful alliance, vowed to avenge the insults and injuries inflicted on Greek temples and sanctuaries by the invading Persians more than a century before (p. 64). But as he stood at the very brink of fulfillment, he was assassinated in 336 B.C. His son, Alexander III, only twenty years old, succeeded him and proceeded to carry out his father's grand design.

LO² The Greeks as a Ruling Nation

In 334 B.C., Alexander crossed into Asia Minor to launch the campaign that would make him one of the greatest conquerors in history. True, the Persian Empire had declined in military power, but the combination of heavily armed phalanxes, fast-moving cavalry, and Alexander's

HIP/Art Resource, NY

≪ **The Stag Hunt** This 6-foot-by-6-foot mosaic, dating from the late fourth century B.C., is part of a townhouse floor in the Macedonian capital, Pella. The lettering says "Gnosis made this." Only a very wealthy house owner could have ordered this luxurious walking surface, and only a very fashionable artist would have been allowed to sign it so conspicuously. Wealthy clients and fashionable artists were prominent features of the Hellenistic era.

daring and genius succeeded beyond anyone's expectations. His army of about 35,000 Macedonians and Greeks—small in comparison with what it accomplished, though far larger than that of any individual city-state—broke the power of the Persian king within four years. Asia Minor, Syria, Egypt, and Mesopotamia fell before him (see Map 5.2 on page 84). Pushing on through Persia to the frontiers of India, Alexander was checked only by the grumbling and protests of his own men. At the age of thirty-three, he died from the combined effects of fever (perhaps cholera) and a drinking bout—in the city of Babylon, which he had chosen for his imperial capital.

 Alexander the Great Remembered: Visions of Divinity Read an unflattering description of Alexander by one of his contemporaries.

 Biography of Alexander the Great http://www.biography.com/articles/Alexander-the-Great-9180468?part=0) Learn more about Alexander's life and conquests.

Alexander's Empire and Its Breakup

Alexander had hoped to found the latest in the succession of universal empires (pp. 33–37). This one would be held together by common values and a common way of life, in which Greek influences would predominate but would be blended with features of the local civilizations. He founded cities in the regions he conquered and sent Greeks or Macedonians to colonize them. Their military garrisons would serve to maintain order in the surrounding countryside, and the cities themselves would serve as cultural "melting pots." He made Greek the official language and distributed Greek books and works of art throughout his empire, hoping to spread Hellenic ideas and values. He also encouraged intermarriage and led the way himself by marrying a Persian princess, Roxana.

But after Alexander's death, his empire was soon divided. Though he left a son, the boy fell victim to power struggles among his father's leading generals. In twenty years of bitter warfare, three major states emerged, each ruled by a dynasty of kings descended from one or other of the Macedonian commanders Antigonus, Ptolemy, and Seleucus. The Antigonid kingdom was based on Macedonia itself; the Ptolemaic kingdom held Egypt and nearby lands; and the lands stretching eastward from Syria formed the Seleucid kingdom. Alongside these three dynasties, other rulers, Macedonian, Greek, and non-Greek, carved themselves smaller shares of territory (see Map 5.2).

> ❝*He accomplished greater deeds than any, not only of the kings who had lived before him but also of those who were to come later down to our time.*❞
>
> —Diodorus of Sicily on Alexander's legacy

 An Unfortunate Method of Royal Succession: Imperial Rule Shall Go "To the Strongest" Read an account of Alexander's death and his words on succession.

The three leading dynasties continued to be rivals and, from time to time, fought each other on a scale that dwarfed even the Peloponnesian War. As a result of these rivalries, the city-states of Greece itself managed to regain some freedom of action. But their citizen armies and navies were no match for the massive forces of Greek mercenary soldiers and slave-rowed warships that the "great powers" maintained, and the city-states generally bowed to whichever was strongest at any given time. Only in the western Mediterranean did truly independent city-states survive—many of them Greek, but others non-Greek, like the Phoenician outpost of Carthage and the native Italian community of Rome.

> **Hellenistic**
> Refers to the "international" period of Greek history, when much of the Mediterranean and southwestern Asia was under Greek rule.

The Hellenistic Kingdoms

In the centuries of the emergence of the city-states, Greeks had already emigrated westward across the Mediterranean. Now, summoned by Alexander's successors, who needed them as soldiers, officials, and traders, they migrated eastward as well. By 200 B.C., Greeks were scattered across the world from the coasts of Spain to the borders of India.

Greeks and Non-Greeks

In Mesopotamia and Egypt in particular, the Greeks now lived side by side with ancient civilizations from which their own had partly arisen. A new era in the history of Greek civilization had begun—one for which historians have invented the term **Hellenistic** (from a Greek word meaning "to behave like a Greek").

Actually, few non-Greeks behaved completely like Greeks. Greek became the international language of business and government, which ambitious non-Greeks would learn so as to get ahead in those fields. But ancient local traditions of civilization continued to flourish. In Egypt, for example, temples were built and decorated, and gods and goddesses were tended within them, all according to age-old tradition, as if the several hundred thousand Greeks who now lived in the country had never arrived; even the Greek kings were venerated and obeyed by the Egyptians as native pharaohs. As for the Greeks, they were mostly content to study Homer by the banks of the Nile, or to applaud Athenian tragedies performed by traveling actors in amphitheaters in Syria and Lebanon that looked exactly like those of Greece itself (see photo on page 69)—or of Sicily and Spain.

 Oppression in Alexander's Empire: Cleomenes, Satrap of Egypt Read a description of the misdeeds of a Greek official in Egypt.

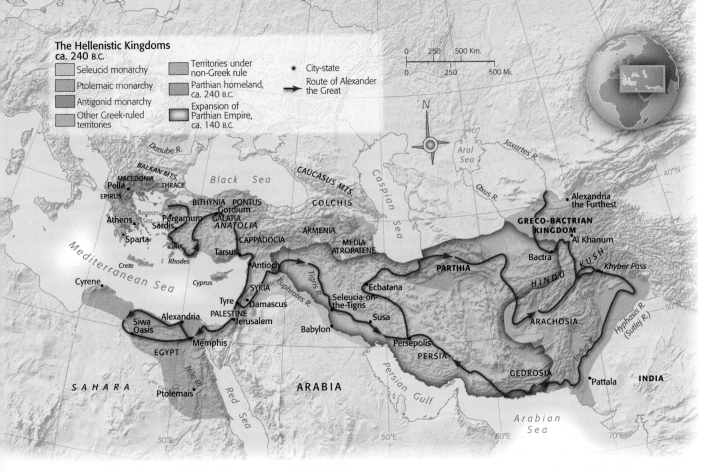

Map 5.2 **The Hellenistic Kingdoms**

With the conquests of Alexander, the Greek world expanded 2,000 miles eastward. Even though Alexander's empire fell apart after his death, much of it remained under the rule of Greek kings, and Greek cities sprang up from Egypt to the borders of India. The Greeks and their culture remained a dominant influence in much of the region for a thousand years until the rise of Islam in the seventh century A.D. © Cengage Learning

 Interactive Map

Still, in the long run, the fact that the Greeks were now an internationally dominant nation could not help but bring about changes in their way of life. With the immense resources at their disposal, the Greek rulers were able to support researchers in many fields and to build libraries that preserved the legacy of their nation for future generations. With their new and wider horizons, Greek scholars studied the past and present of many of the lands they now lived in, and non-Greek scholars sometimes wrote the histories of their nations in Greek. Hellenistic civilization achieved great things in science and technology, geography, history, and literary scholarship, as well as carrying on the earlier achievements of the Greeks in philosophy and the arts.

In the long run, too, the Greeks could not help absorbing influences from the nations they now dominated—above all, in the field of religion. The Hellenistic world abounded with international gods and goddesses—for example, the Egyptian deities of the underworld and fertility, Isis and Osiris. The Greeks believed such deities to be the same as their own, only in foreign guise: thus, Isis was identified with Demeter, who had much the same powers among the Greek gods and goddesses (p. 63). But the foreign versions of the gods and goddesses came to seem to the Greeks themselves more powerful, holy, and helpful to humans than the native ones. Later these international deities were even

more widely worshiped in the Roman Empire, and their worship was a precedent for the spread of Christianity (p. 119).

Kings, Queens, and Cities

The political forms of the Hellenistic world were also different from those of the Greek past. The city-states of Greece still had strong community traditions, and wherever Greeks emigrated eastward they founded new cities that kept up many of these traditions. The fate of communities now depended not on citizen armies, navies, and governments, however, but on good relations with the monarchs who ruled the world.

The monarchs, for their part, needed vigorous Greek local communities to underpin their power. However, they preferred these communities to be run by citizens who were few enough to be easily controlled and rich enough to keep the rest of the people satisfied by paying out of their own pockets for religious festivals, public entertainments, and other community business. Wealthy citizens hungry for local prestige and power were glad to take on the responsibilities and expense, so that narrow oligarchies

 The Art of the Hellenistic Age and the Hellenistic Tradition (http://www.metmuseum.org/toah/hd/haht/hd_haht.htm) View the artistic legacy of the Hellenistic Age.

A FEMALE PHILOSOPHER: HIPPARCHIA OF MARONEIA

This account of Hipparchia comes from a collection of biographies of notable thinkers written in the third century B.C. by Diogenes Laertius. Hipparchia, her brother, and her husband lived shortly before 300 B.C. in a town in the north of Greece that was under the rule of King Lysimachus of Macedonia. They belonged to the Cynic school of philosophy, which believed in striving for virtue by living a simple and natural life rather than chasing after the socially approved goals of wealth, fame, and power. The school's name came from the Greek word for "dogs," because conventionally minded people scorned the Cynics for their "doglike" existence.

"Leaving the shuttle near the warp" means suddenly breaking off from work. A shuttle is a device used to interweave a thread (called the warp) with other threads to make cloth.

Hipparchia, the sister of Metrocles, was charmed along with others by the doctrines of this school. She and Metrocles were natives of Maroneia. She fell in love with the doctrines and the manners of Crates, and could not be diverted from her regard for him either by the wealth or the high birth or the personal beauty of any of her suitors; but Crates was everything to her. She threatened her parents to make away with herself, if she were not given in marriage to him. When entreated by her parents to dissuade her from this resolution, Crates did all he could; and at last, as he could not persuade her, he arose and placing all his furniture before her, he said: "This is the bridegroom whom you are choosing, and this is the whole of his property. Consider these facts; for it will not be possible for you to become his partner, if you do not apply yourself to the same studies and conform to the same habits as he does." The girl chose him; and assuming the same dress as he wore, went with him as her husband, and appeared with him in public everywhere, and went to all entertainments in his company. Once when she went to sup at the house of Lysimachus, she attacked Theodorus, who was surnamed the Atheist. To him she proposed the following sophism: "What Theodorus could not be called wrong for doing, that same thing Hipparchia could not be called wrong for doing. But Theodorus does no wrong when he beats himself; therefore Hipparchia does no wrong when she beats Theodorus." He made no reply to what she said, but only pulled her gown. Hipparchia was neither offended nor ashamed, as many a woman would have been; but when he said to her:

> Who is the woman who has left the shuttle So near the warp? [Euripides]

She replied: "I, Theodorus, am the person; but do I seem to you to have come to a wrong decision, if I devote that time to philosophy which otherwise I should have spent at the loom?" These and many other sayings are reported of this female philosopher.

EXPLORING THE SOURCE

1. In what ways did Hipparchia's and her husband's way of life go against the expected behavior of women and married couples at the time? Why should Cynic spouses in particular have broken the rules in this way?

2. Why should an exceptionally famous, wealthy, and powerful man like King Lysimachus have invited a female Cynic? Given her principles and way of life, was it right for her to accept?

Source: G. W. Botsford and E. G. Sihler, eds., *Hellenic Civilization* (New York: Columbia University Press, 1915), p. 665.

became the commonest form of Greek community government. Democracy passed out of existence, not to be revived in the West for two thousand years.

Royal courts rather than citizen assemblies were now the real centers of government and politics, where officials, generals, and members of ruling families competed to reach the highest levels of power, wealth, and fame. As in earlier monarchies, women wielded power as wives, concubines, mothers, and sisters of kings, and occasionally as rulers on their own. In Greek cities, property-owning women contributed generously to community expenses alongside men, though in smaller numbers. Like men, they were honored with public monuments and public acclaim, thereby bringing prestige to their families. In this way, monarchy and oligarchy enabled some women to gain fame by doing what democracy had frowned on—getting themselves talked about by men (p. 59).

The Greeks venerated their mighty kings and queens as living gods and goddesses, with divine titles that proclaimed them

metropolis

In ancient times, an exceptionally large city that was both a ruler's seat of government and an international hub.:

doers of good, protectors from harm, members of harmonious families, and visible to humans: the Revealed God, the Father-Loving God and Goddess, the Savior God, the Benefactress Goddess (see photo). In Egypt, where the rulers were also pharaohs, they took up the local tradition of marriage between royal brother and royal sister, as myth declared was customary among gods and goddesses. But in Greek religion, too, the dividing line between humans and gods had always been porous, and incest was considered a mark of divinity (p. 62). The Greek version of divine rulership built on their own as well as non-Greek beliefs, and reflected both the self-confidence and the insecurity of a people that had so suddenly risen to international power.

The economy of the Hellenistic age was also different from that of earlier times. Large kingdoms encouraged large-scale production and trade. The Greeks had carried on a far-flung commerce, ranging from the Black Sea to Gibraltar, but now the gates were opened eastward as far as India. The vast new market stimulated enterprise: huge fortunes were made, banking and finance were expanded, and a kind of capitalism took shape. The rulers of the great states had a keen interest in business affairs. They promoted commerce by aiding navigation and transport and made up their expenses by taxing the enterprises. Although wages and general living standards remained low, the growth of industry and trade created many new jobs in the cities. As a result, thousands of peasants moved from the countryside into the urban centers of the eastern Mediterranean.

Large seaport cities such as fifth-century B.C. Athens were nothing new, but some cities—especially those that were centers of royal government as

well as of trade and industry—now grew to unprecedented size. The biggest and most famous such **metropolis** ("mother-city") was Alexandria, founded by the conqueror himself near the delta of the Nile River, in Egypt. Alexandria soon outgrew Athens in size and wealth and came to rival it as the cultural hub of the Greek world. For centuries, its marvelous library and "museum"—a kind of research institute endowed by the rulers—were centers of scholarship and scientific study.

 Tour the Sites of Ancient Alexandria (http://www.egyptologyonline.com/alexandria.htm) Take a virtual tour of Alexandria.

> " *The Greek version of divine rulership built on their own as well as non-Greek beliefs, and reflected both the self-confidence and the insecurity of a people that had so suddenly risen to international power.* "

The Benefactress Goddess On this ritual wine jug, Queen Berenice II of Egypt holds a horn of plenty, the symbol of royal beneficence, and pours out an offering to the gods. Berenice II married King Ptolemy III, the Benefactor God, in 249 B.C and seemingly shared his royal power. That was probably why her son King Ptolemy IV, the Father-Loving God, had her poisoned when he took over in 221 B.C. The J. Paul Getty Museum, Villa Collection, Malibu, California Unknown, Fragmentary Oinochoe, about 243-221 B.C., Faience, Object: H: 22.2 (8³⁄₄ in.)

The End of the Greek Kingdoms

From about 200 B.C. onward, the Greeks began to lose their position as international rulers. They lost their hold on the lands stretching eastward from Mesopotamia to the borders of India, which were taken over by invaders from the steppes (p. 20), most notably the Parthians, who formed a sizeable empire on the territory of present-day Iran (see Map 5.2 on page 84). Unsuccessful Egyptian rebellions and a successful Jewish one (p. 125) further weakened Greek rule. Meanwhile in the west, a non-Greek city-state was growing more powerful than Athens had ever been, and more powerful even than the Hellenistic kingdoms—Rome. The Romans gradually took over Greece itself, Anatolia, and other eastern Mediterranean territories, and in 30 B.C. they conquered Egypt, the last surviving Greek-ruled kingdom.

Even so, Hellenistic culture lived on under Roman rule. It was among the Greeks that the Romans found the philosophy, science, literature, and art that were to inspire their own achievements, as well as the political forms of universal monarchy and divine rulership that they adopted in their own empire (pp. 104–105). Within the Roman Empire, the eastern Mediterranean remained a distinct region dominated by Greek civilization. When that empire finally divided, its Greek-dominated eastern half continued for several centuries until the Muslim conquest. Even then, the Greek legacy was preserved by the empire of Byzantium, acquired by Arab conquerors, and ultimately taken over by Christian Europe.

LO³ Hellenistic Thinkers: The Individual and the Universe

Even in the Hellenistic world, Athens continued to be the headquarters of philosophy. Earlier arguments about the workings of the universe continued, but they were given a new twist. Perhaps because the small world of the city-state now seemed to thinkers less important than the larger world beyond it, they were more concerned than before with the place of individual humans within the vastness of the universe.

Epicureanism

One answer to this problem was **Epicureanism (ep-i-kyoo-REE-uh-niz-uhm)**, a philosophy based on the teachings of Epicurus **(ep-i-KYOOR-uhs)**, who taught in Athens around 300 B.C. Epicurus's view of the universe was based on that of Democritus of Abdera (p. 72), who had declared that all matter is made up of atoms. Epicurus claimed that the shape and character of every living and nonliving thing result from the chance motions of these tiny particles, and there is no governing purpose on earth or in the heavens.

In such a universe, Epicurus believed, the only logical aim for the individual is to strive for personal happiness. As a guide in the search for happiness, Epicurus proclaimed the principle that happiness equals pleasure minus pain, and that the best way to secure happiness is by decreasing pain rather than by increasing pleasure. And the deepest source of human pain, Epicurus taught, is fear, the "ache of mind and heart."

 Materialist Ethic: The Principal Doctrines of Epicureanism Read some principles for a happy life from Epicurus.

Fear, in turn, feeds on ignorance and superstition, which for Epicurus included all forms of worship of the gods. The gods, he thought, are themselves chance groupings of atoms who live far from humans and have no concern for them. They certainly do not grant humans eternal life, for when the atoms that we are made of go their separate ways, there is nothing left of us. But that is exactly why death is not to be feared: "Death, usually regarded as the greatest of calamities, is actually nothing to us; while we are here, death is not, and when death is here, we are not."

 Epicurus, His Philosophy and Legacy (http://www.epicurus.info/) Learn more about Epicurus and his philosophy.

The pursuit of pleasure is more difficult than the avoidance of pain. Epicurus warned that what he called "dynamic" (restless) pleasures such as eating and drinking are usually self-defeating, for these pleasures only stimulate the appetite for more of them, which acts as a fresh source of pain. Rather than feed such appetites, he thought it wiser to discipline them and instead cultivate the "passive" (quiet) pleasures, such as literature, recollection and meditation, personal friendship, and the enjoyment of nature. He shunned the pursuit of wealth or public office, for it often brings disappointment, trouble, and pain. Epicurus valued, above all, calmness, poise, and serenity of mind.

Stoicism

A rival Hellenistic philosophy was **Stoicism** (STOH-uh-siz-uhm), named after the porch (*stoa*) in Athens where Zeno, the founder of Stoicism, taught about 300 B.C. Zeno believed that far from being the result of chance motions of atoms, the universe is pervaded and upheld by a living force, which he called by various names: "Divine Fire," "Providence," "God," and "Reason" (in Greek, *logos*). This idea came from an earlier thinker, Heraclitus (p. 72), but Zeno made it much more of a guide for understanding the place of the individual in the universe than Heraclitus is known to have done.

The Reason of the universe, Zeno and his followers thought, was present in everything orderly and good—the movement of the stars in their courses, the growth of seeds into plants, the righteousness and wisdom of human beings. Harmony and happiness, declared the Stoics, are achieved by understanding this Reason, accepting it by self-discipline, and living in accordance with it, all of which means striving for virtue rather than pleasure. Virtue of this kind is not the possession of any particular nation, gender, or social class, because all human beings share the spark of Reason that upholds the universe. The only qualification is to study philosophy so as to understand the "natural law"—the mutual rights and duties that make it possible for individuals and communities to live in accordance with Reason. And all human beings are capable of this study. An Athenian Stoic, Chrysippus, is supposed to have said around 250 B.C. that "both slaves and women must be philosophers."

Stoicism and Epicureanism were very different ways of thinking, and their supporters argued fiercely for many centuries. Both views made sense in different ways in the vast and diverse world of the Hellenistic kingdoms, and they continued to make sense in the even vaster and more diverse world of the state that followed them, the Roman Empire.

 Listen to a synopsis of Chapter 5.

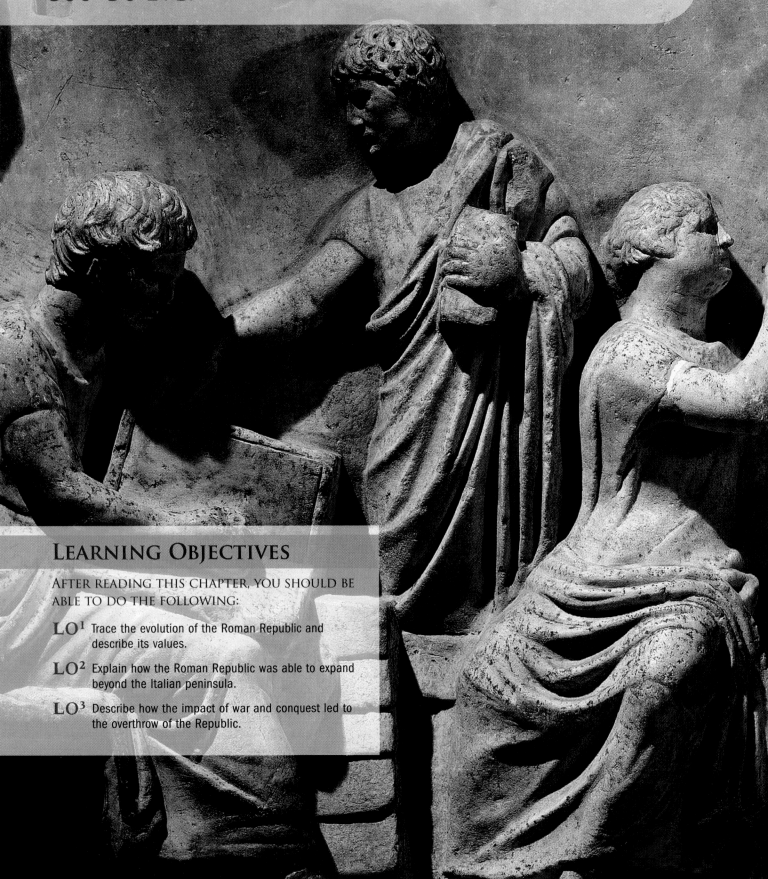

CHAPTER 6

THE RISE OF ROME,
800–30 B.C.

LEARNING OBJECTIVES

AFTER READING THIS CHAPTER, YOU SHOULD BE
ABLE TO DO THE FOLLOWING:

LO¹ Trace the evolution of the Roman Republic and
describe its values.

LO² Explain how the Roman Republic was able to expand
beyond the Italian peninsula.

LO³ Describe how the impact of war and conquest led to
the overthrow of the Republic.

"MANY GREAT EMPIRES HAD COME AND GONE BEFORE THAT OF ROME, BUT NO CONQUERING KING, AND CERTAINLY NO CITY-STATE, HAD ACQUIRED SUCH A VAST DOMAIN AND HELD IT FOR SO LONG."

The rise of Rome began as a continuation of Greece's early westward expansion through the Mediterranean Sea, which brought the Greek model of civilization to the peoples of Italy during the eighth century B.C.

The Romans not only imitated Greek civilization but also improved on it, at least so far as government and warfare were concerned. About 500 B.C., Rome became a Greek-style city-state that was no longer ruled by kings, but the Roman government system—the Republic, as they called it—was for several centuries more stable and more effective than any in Greece. The war-fighting methods of Roman armies were more consistently successful than those of the Greeks, and Rome's treatment of conquered enemies was usually more generous. As a result, in five centuries Rome became the center of an empire that stretched from the borders of Mesopotamia to the Atlantic Ocean. But by that time, endless expansion had also led to social conflict, political crisis, civil war, and unstable rule by powerful army commanders—until one of these commanders, Augustus Caesar (**SEE-zer**), managed to turn military rule into a workable system of government by one man.

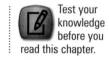

Test your knowledge before you read this chapter.

What do you think?

Rome built a great empire because of the exceptional virtue and public spirit of its citizens.

Strongly Disagree   Strongly Agree

1	2	3	4	5	6	7

Musee du Louvre, Paris/Gianni Dagli Orti/The Art Archive

≪ Taking the Census The Roman Republic held five-yearly censuses, in which the citizens had to come in to be counted. A carving from about 100 B.C. shows a citizen carrying a folded writing tablet in case he needs to look up the detailed information about his household and property that the census taker is asking him for and writing down. On the citizen's answers will depend his tax liability, his military service, and his actual membership in the Roman People, the united citizenry of the city-state.

LO¹ City-State and Empire: The Roman Republic

Many great empires had come and gone before that of Rome, but no conquering king, and certainly no city-state, had acquired such a vast domain and held it for so long. What features of the government and way of life of the Romans enabled them to outdo all that had gone before them?

Italy and Its Peoples

In the era of Indo-European migrations, when the Hittites moved into Asia Minor and the Greeks into the Aegean, other tribes moved into Italy. They arrived in a Mediterranean land with farming resources that were basically similar to those of Greece or Palestine (pp. 37, 49), but able to support a larger population—and in time, larger armies. In addition, Italy was situated astride the Mediterranean, commanding every direction: southward and eastward to the territories of Greek, Egyptian, and Mesopotamian civilization, northward and westward to the lands of barbarian Europe.

The Indo-European settlers formed various tribal groups, among them the Latin people of central Italy. Some of the Latins settled near the mouth of the Tiber River (see Map 6.1), building a cluster of dwellings on low-lying hills along the river—the famed "Seven Hills." Around 750 B.C., these settlements joined to form a single city-state, Rome. The Latins, of course, were only one of many peoples that lived in Italy, two of which were

CHRONOLOGY

NINTH CENTURY B.C.	Etruscans move into Italy
EIGHTH CENTURY B.C.	First Greek colonies in southern Italy; settlements near the mouth of the Tiber River join to form the city-state of Rome
SEVENTH CENTURY B.C.	Etruscans conquer Latium
500 B.C.	Rome overthrows Etruscan rule
450 B.C.	Twelve Tables, first written Roman legal code
264–146 B.C.	Punic Wars between Rome and Carthage
250 B.C.	All of Italy south of the River Po is in Roman hands; plebeians share political rights with patricians
202 B.C.	Rome wins control of western Mediterranean
FIRST CENTURY B.C.	Most non-Romans in Italy win citizen rights; Romans expand into the eastern Mediterranean and then into western Europe
44 B.C.	Julius Caesar becomes dictator for life; members of the Senate assassinate him
31 B.C.	Octavian's forces defeat Antony and Cleopatra; Octavian becomes supreme ruler of Rome

to have a decisive influence on the growth of Roman civilization: the Etruscans and the Greeks.

The Etruscans were non–Indo-European immigrants who arrived in Italy from somewhere to the east about the ninth century B.C. They gained control of territory to the north of the Latins that the Romans called Etruria, established city-states under the rule of kings, and built up a civilization that combined native features and influences from Greece and farther east (see photo). In the seventh century B.C., they conquered Latium, and

≪ Etruscan Gold This foot-long gold cloak clasp comes from the tomb of an Etruscan warrior-noble who died about 650 B.C. Lions, an animal not found in Italy but often seen on art objects from ancient Anatolia and Mesopotamia, walk across its upper plate. The perfect workmanship, the weight of precious metal, and the exotic beasts are testimony to the skills, wealth, and international contacts of a people who deeply influenced Rome and for a long time ruled it. Scala/Art Resource, NY

for a time, Etruscan kings ruled Rome itself. From the Etruscans, the Romans adopted such features as a gridiron street plan for cities, gladiatorial combats, and the masonry arch.

The Romans also borrowed directly from the Greeks. As part of their expansion across the Mediterranean (p. 50), the Greek city-states had begun to plant colonies in southern Italy as early as the eighth century B.C., and these spread northward up the coast almost to the borders of Latium (see Map 6.1). It was from these neighbors that the Latins first learned the alphabet and gained knowledge of the life of Greek city-states.

 Illustrated Essays on the Etruscans (http://history-world.org/etruscans.htm) Learn more about the ancient Etruscans.

The Roman Republic: The Senate and the People

Under the influence of the Etruscans and the Greeks, the Romans acquired the skills that enabled them to build their unique political institutions. At first, their city-state was ruled on the Etruscan model by powerful kings, including actual Etruscan conquerors. The king was advised by a council of elders called the Senate (from the Latin *senex*, meaning "old man"), whose members he appointed. Usually, he chose from among the **patricians** or "men with fathers"—that is, with fathers who already belonged to this hereditary group of leading families. When a king died, his suc-

Map 6.1 **Rome in Italy**

Rome began as one among many Italian city-states, located in Latium, the territory of one among many Italian ethnic groups. In 250 years, Rome united Italy under its leadership by a system of alliances, by migration and settlement, and by roads that speeded the movement of goods, news, and above all armies. Rome would later apply these methods of unification in many lands of Europe, Africa, and Asia. © Cengage Learning

 Interactive Map

cessor was chosen by the Senate from among its own members, subject to approval by an assembly of all male citizens. The assembly's approval, however, was automatic, for apart from the king, it was the Senate and the patricians who dominated the city-state.

Around 500 B.C., Rome overthrew its Etruscan rulers, and the monarchy was also abolished. The government of the Roman city-state became officially the "people's business"—in Latin, *res publica*, from which the word *republic* is derived. Like Greek city-states, the Roman **Republic** underwent a long and turbulent development under the influence of social struggles between aristocrats and commoners. The result, however, was a system of government that was neither a Greek-style democracy nor an oligarchy, but a mixture of both.

Patricians and Plebeians

The aristocratic side in the conflicts of the Republic was of course the patricians. On the other side were the **plebeians** (from the Latin *plebs*, meaning "the common people")—everyone who did not belong to patrician families, including workers, small farmers, and even quite wealthy citizens.

In the earliest times of the Republic, the "people's business" was in practice run by the **Senate**, an assembly of about three hundred heads of patrician families. Two among the senators functioned as **consuls** ("colleagues"), wielding for a year at a time the military and government power that had formerly belonged to the kings. The consuls now appointed senators, and they also chose their own successors, though they were careful to choose men who would be acceptable to the Senate. The one-year terms of the consuls, and the fact that there were two of them (each empowered to veto the other's lawmaking proposals), were a guarantee against a revival of monarchy. The Romans were so eager to avoid this possibility that the practice grew up of appointing two or more men for one-year terms to every magistracy (public office). This slowed down government decisions and actions, but in time

of emergency the consuls, on the advice of the Senate, could appoint a **dictator**, with full power to give orders and make laws for a maximum period of six months. With this exception, the Republic's original government system kept power in the hands of the patrician group as a whole.

The plebeians at first deferred to patrician rule, but as Rome grew and the plebeians became more numerous and often wealthier, they began to resent being treated as second-class citizens. They put pressure on the patricians in various ways, including through acts of passive resistance and threats to secede and start a rival settlement. The conflicts were often bitter, but the plebeians never lost the feeling that they depended on the leadership of the Senate. Furthermore, Rome, like the Greek city-states, relied on its own citizens as fighting men, so that the Senate could not forever deny the plebeians a share in government. As a result, over more than two hundred years, the Republic developed a government system that both maintained the leadership of the Senate yet also admitted the plebeians to power.

Among the chief complaints of the plebeians was that they lacked legal protection. Before the fifth century B.C., there had been no written code of law. Instead, the sacred traditional laws were passed down orally and interpreted by judges, who were, of course, patricians. About 450 B.C., in response to the plebeians' demand, the laws of Rome were set down in writing. The new code was said to have been engraved on twelve slabs of wood or bronze and mounted in the chief public square, the Forum, for all to see. These "Twelve Tables" (so called from the old-fashioned English word for such a slab) served as the foundation for the elaborate system of Roman law that grew up in later centuries.

 A Tour of the Roman Forum (http://www.italyguides.it/us/roma/rome/ancient_roman_empire/roman_forum.htm) Take a tour of the Roman Forum.

Not long afterward, new plebeian assemblies came into being alongside the existing one that soon gained far greater power. One of the new bodies, in which residents of the city of Rome predominated, won the right to elect consuls subject to confirmation by the Senate. The other, in which farmers from outside the city had a larger say, began electing their own magistrates, called **tribunes**. The tribunes eventually gained the power to initiate laws in their assembly and veto laws passed by the Senate.

Step by step, the patricians gave way to the plebeians, until by 250 B.C. the distinction between the two groups no longer much mattered in politics and government. By then, plebeians were eligible for all public offices including that of consul, they had won admission to the Senate itself, and they had even acquired the right to marry into patrician families.

"Mixed" Government

The struggles and compromises between patricians and plebeians produced a system of government that was bafflingly complex. Instead of abolishing an old institution, the Romans usually found it politically less divisive to install a counterweight—the two plebeian assemblies alongside the old one, or the tribunes alongside the consuls. But the resulting system showed extraordinary flexibility and resilience. The Roman "mixed" government, as it was called on account of its combination of oligarchic and democratic features (p. 52), was widely admired in ancient times and continues to influence government systems today. The separation of powers in the U.S. Constitution derives ultimately from the checks and balances between different branches of government in the Roman city-state.

But ultimate leadership of the Republic still rested in the hands of the Senate, and though plebeians could now join the Senate, only the wealthy could afford to do so. In yet another precaution against abuse of office, senators and would-be senators had to follow a complex career path from lower-ranking magistracies to higher ones, in which leapfrogging ranks was frowned upon or was actually illegal. Many of these magistracies were elective, and to get votes, a candidate had to spend large sums for displays and popular entertainments. In addition, he needed to follow the long-standing Roman practice of supporting **clients** ("hangers-on"). These were normally less wealthy citizens, who were protected and paid by a rich **patron** in return for personal services and campaigning. And once a candidate got himself elected, he had to pay the costs of his magistracy out of his own pocket, since it carried no salary. In this way, the Senate, originally an oligarchy of birth, became an oligarchy of wealth.

No matter how restricted a group the Senate might be, however, until the final centuries of the Republic, it governed firmly and effectively. The senators set long-range policies and made immediate decisions on pressing matters, appointed and instructed the military leaders of the Republic, received foreign ambassadors, and concluded treaties. They supervised finances and investigated high crimes. In all these ways, they exercised wide powers with general consent.

> *"The separation of powers in the U.S. Constitution derives ultimately from the checks and balances between different branches of government in the Roman city-state."*

Republican Values

The "mixed government" of Rome, like Athenian democracy and Spartan oligarchy, was not just a government system but part of a way of life. The values that inspired this way of life were expressed in traditional stories of the heroic deeds of early times that were mostly fictional, and in laws like the Twelve Tables that were no doubt often broken. All the same, for many centuries the Romans judged themselves according to these values, which thereby influenced their behavior and achievements.

The Roman Republic (http://www.metmuseum.org/toah/hd/romr/hd_romr.htm) See republican values reflected in the arts.

The City and the Gods

Some Roman values were common to all ancient city-states—notably the belief that even more than on government systems, the community's survival and prosperity depended on a god or goddess who was thought to take a particular interest in its destiny. As the Romans came into closer contact with neighboring peoples, they came to see some of these gods and goddesses as wielding worldwide power, though foreigners might worship them under different names and tell different stories about them.

By the time of the Republic, Rome had a special relationship with three deities, whose joint temple stood on the Capitol, the city's fortified citadel and equivalent of a Greek city-state's acropolis (p. 51). These deities were the sky-god Jupiter, whom the Romans believed was the same as the Zeus whom nearby Greek city-states worshiped; his consort, the fertility goddess Juno (the same as Hera); and Minerva (Athena), goddess of skill and wisdom. Responsibility for maintaining the "peace of the gods"—Rome's good relationship with these and many other deities—belonged to the **pontiffs**, a group of priests headed by the supreme pontiff (*pontifex maximus*), who were leading magistrates of the Republic.

client
A person who provides personal services in return for money and protection from a patron.

patron
A wealthy person who supports others with money and protection in exchange for personal services.

pontiff
In ancient Rome, one of the Republic's leading priests.

Citizens and the Community

The Romans shared other values specifically with Greek city-states. These values included the belief that it was the right and duty of the men of the community to fight its wars, and hence also to share in its government; and the community solidarity that came from the fact that high-born as well as low-born citizens bore the burden of war (pp. 52, 54-55). As in Greek city-states, too, the men took it for granted that the women of Rome had no right or duty to share in politics and government, and that women needed guardians for all legal transactions—"because of their light-mindedness," as the Twelve Tables declared.

Law in Early Roman Society: The Regulation of Women and Family Read some laws concerning women in ancient Rome.

But other values were distinctive to Rome—among them, the qualities that the Romans most admired in the leaders of their city-state. Many stories were told of the simple country life that such men led, and of their contempt for self-seeking. Around 450 B.C., it was said, when Rome was facing defeat in wars against neighboring tribes, the patrician Cincinnatus was plowing a field on his farmstead when a deputation arrived to summon him to serve as dictator. A couple of weeks later, having

paterfamilias
The "family father" in ancient Rome, who had unlimited power over his household.

matron
Title of honor given to a married woman in ancient Rome.

led the citizen-soldiers to victory, he resigned his office and went back to finish the plowing on which his family's survival depended.

The Community and the Family

Instead of devoting his life directly to the city-state as in Sparta, a Roman man belonged first of all to a family and a clan (a group of families descended from a real or mythical forefather). Clans and families, in turn, were held together by fathers—in particular by men who had the status of *paterfamilias* (**pey-ter-fuh-MIL-ee-uhs**) or "family father." The paterfamilias wielded unlimited power—including the power of life and death—over everyone in his household, as well as over sons and daughters who left his household upon marriage. Only his wife might not be completely subject to him—if she was still subject to the authority of her own father. The *genius* of the paterfamilias—the life-giving and life-upholding fatherly power that he embodied—was sacred and was worshiped by all in the household, including himself (see photo).

The Romans revered the power of fatherhood not only in family life but also in the community life of their city-state. The senators addressed each other in session as "conscript fathers"—men recruited to wield fatherly authority for the good of the Republic. In fact, Roman community life was seen as a kind of family life on a larger scale. One of the Republic's most important deities, besides those worshiped on the Capitol, was Vesta, the goddess of hearth and home. In every household, the fire in the hearth was sacred to Vesta and was only put out if the family moved. In addition, the Vestal Virgins, a group of six patrician women, devoted thirty years of their lives to tending the goddess's everlasting fire in her temple on the Forum, on behalf of the outsized "household" of Rome itself.

 Cato the Elder Educates His Son Read a glowing description of how a paterfamilias treated his family.

Motherhood, too, was revered in Rome. A married woman bore the title of **matron**—in Latin, *matrona* or "lady mother." Her "Juno"—the divine force of fertility and nourishment that she embodied—was worshiped in the household alongside her husband's genius. She was supposed to live in subordination to her husband, but through strength of personality and authority with her menfolk, she was also expected to contribute to the community as well as the family.

The founding myth of the Republic itself told how Rome's uprising against its Etruscan king began when a matron, Lucretia,

was raped by the king's son and killed herself—just as a Roman man might do if he faced unbearable shame. As the historian Livy told the story five centuries later, Lucretia first made clear to her husband and brother that she expected them to avenge her—"if you are men." The ideal matron demanded from the men of her family hard work, courage as warriors, devotion to duty—all the moral qualities that the Romans summed up in the word *virtus*, or "manliness." In this way, women were expected to help make sure that men had the qualities they needed to keep the Republic strong.

LO² Roman Expansion

The Romans were, above all, a military people—patriotic farmer-soldiers. Their first wars were against the neighboring Etruscans, competing Italian tribes, and barbarian invaders. Then, as the Romans secured their position at home, they began to reach out for territories and allies. One of Rome's main assets in this effort was its superior army.

Allies and Colonies

The Romans were shrewdly generous in their treatment of defeated enemies. More often than not, these were given the status of allies, keeping their local laws, government systems, and armies under ultimate Roman authority. The Romans also

>> **A Household Shrine** A temple painted on an inside wall of a house in Pompeii, south of Rome, is the dwelling place of powerful beings. Two *lares* (**LAH-rayz**–protective gods), dance and brandish drinking horns. A fatherly genius holds an incense box and a ritual wine-pouring dish, and covers his head in preparation for sacrifice on behalf of the household. A snake, symbol of the fertility of the soil, wriggles along the ground. Alinari/The Bridgeman Art Library

THERE WERE SEVERAL REASONS WHY THE ROMAN ARMY WAS SO EFFECTIVE:

Better-Prepared Soldiers

- At the beginning of the Republic, the citizens usually served for short periods and without pay. But in the course of numerous wars that were fought ever farther from home, the Romans began to pay their citizen draftees so as to permit longer campaigns and better training.

Better Military Tactics, Adapted from the Enemies They Encountered

- They wore light armor and carried large, oblong shields.

- Rather than using long thrusting spears like the hoplites (p. 52), they attacked their enemies from a distance with javelins before closing in for hand-to-hand fighting with swords.

- By 250 B.C., Roman soldiers fought in small units of about one hundred men (centuries), each under the command of a centurion.

- The centuries were combined into bigger units, of which the largest was the legion, of about four thousand; thus Roman armies were highly maneuverable yet also well coordinated, unlike the unwieldy Greek phalanxes.

A Strong Military Culture

- The Roman army combined iron discipline with treatment of the soldiers as citizens who deserved respect.

- The soldiers elected their own centurions, yet once chosen, a centurion had almost absolute power.

- Penalties for cowardice or neglect of duty were harsh; on the other hand, there were generous rewards and promotions for the brave and victorious.

---

tightened their control over the Italian peninsula by creating a network of colonies of settlers from Rome—generally discharged citizen-soldiers and their families. Both the colonists and the allies raised soldiers on the same scale as Rome itself, and the allies often provided light infantry and cavalry, which the Romans lacked. In this way, the Roman forces increased in strength and striking power in step with their conquests—an important advantage for an expanding empire. Rome had its share of incompetent commanders and panicky soldiers, but however disastrously its armies might be defeated, there were always other armies to take their place.

The Roman colonists enjoyed rights of citizenship that were almost equal to those of citizens who lived in Rome itself. In time, the allies began to demand full integration with Rome, and early in the first century B.C., some of them took up arms when the demand was at first denied. Following these Social Wars ("Wars against the Allies," from the Latin *socius*, "ally"), most non-Romans in Italy gained Roman citizenship, and the status of "ally," separate from the Romans, disappeared. Thus, Rome, unlike the exclusive Greek city-states, became an expanding, absorptive political entity.

The Punic Wars

Roman methods of conquest and administration paid handsome dividends, for by 250 B.C., all of Italy south of the River Po (see Map 6.1 on page 91) was in Roman hands. But this success brought Rome into collision with a rival city-state beyond the sea: Carthage, on the north coast of Africa.

Founded about 700 B.C. by Phoenician colonists (pp. 32-33, 50), Carthage had become an oligarchic and empire-building republic similar to Rome and had spread its influence across North Africa, southern Spain, Sardinia, Corsica, and Sicily (see Map 6.2). It was the Carthaginians' interest in Sicily, lying between Africa and Italy, that brought them into conflict with the Romans. The Greek city-states of Sicily had for centuries been struggling with Carthage for control of the island, and the Romans had inherited the struggle when they took over responsibility for protecting their Greek allies. But ultimately what was at stake was the command of the whole western Mediterranean.

The Punic Wars (from *Poeni*, the Latin name for the Phoenicians) were waged on land and sea in three vicious rounds between 264 and 146 B.C. In the first phase of the struggle, after many years of exhausting warfare, Rome was able to force Carthage out of Sicily, but the North African city kept the rest of its empire. In the second (and decisive) phase, the Carthaginian general Hannibal invaded Italy, defeated several Roman armies, and brought Rome to the brink of defeat. But the loyalty of the Romans' allies, the perseverance of their own forces, and their greater manpower—for they were able to draw citizen and allied soldiers from all of Italy, while Carthage relied on smaller mercenary armies—enabled them to triumph. At the end of the Second Punic War in 202 B.C., Carthage was disarmed and helpless.

Eventually, fearing a Carthaginian revival, Rome provoked a third war, and in 146 B.C., Carthage was captured after bitter fighting. In a final act of vengeance, the Senate ordered the city

Map 6.2 Roman Expansion

Notice the rhythm of Rome's expansion: 250 years to unify Italy (500–264 B.C.); 140 years of much faster growth from the outbreak of the Punic Wars to the death of Gaius Gracchus (264–121 B.C.); 140 years of triumphant conquest even as the Republic collapsed (121–44 B.C.) and Augustus took over (44 B.C.–A.D. 14); and in the following century of imperial monarchy, the gradual end of conquest (A.D. 14–117). © Cengage Learning

Interactive Map

to be leveled, its people sold into slavery, and even the ground on which it had stood to be solemnly cursed. But this was only an epilogue to the main struggle. Already in 202 B.C., Rome had won control of the western Mediterranean.

 Cato the Elder: "Carthage Must Be Destroyed" Read Greek historian Plutarch's account of who instigated the third war against Carthage.

Conquering an Empire

The former possessions of Carthage in Sicily, Spain, and Africa became the first Roman provinces. These administrative units did not enjoy the status of Rome's allies in Italy; instead, they were ruled as conquered lands by proconsuls (governors—from the Latin words for "stand-in for a consul") appointed by the Senate. They paid tribute to the Roman state, contributed "auxiliary" units of cavalry and light infantry to the Roman forces, and provided opportunities for influential Roman citizens to build up private fortunes. It was not until the time of Augustus, after 27 B.C., that the provinces began to share in the benefits of Roman order. In addition, some local rulers survived by becoming client kings, bound to Rome by ties of allegiance and support like those between Roman patrons and clients, though in the first century A.D. their kingdoms were mostly absorbed into the empire as normal provinces. One way or another, for the Romans the conquest of the western Mediterranean meant an enormous increase in both resources and military power.

The result was a spectacular increase in the pace of expansion. In the previous 250 years, from 500 B.C. to the outbreak of the Punic Wars, the Romans had unified most of Italy; in the next 250 years, they would spread their rule from the eastern Mediterranean to the British Isles (see Map 6.2).

In Spain and neighboring territories in the south of Gaul, Rome for the first time gained a substantial foothold among the peoples of barbarian Europe, which they soon began to expand. But even before the final defeat of Carthage, venturesome Romans were looking also to the eastern Mediterranean for new areas to exploit. The prospects in that direction were promising, for the Hellenistic kingdoms (pp. 86-87) were beginning to lose their grip.

Rome's first involvement was in Greece, and it grew out of a special invitation. Around 200 B.C., ambassadors from various Greek city-states appealed to Rome for aid in resisting the king of Macedonia, who had been allied with Carthage. Moved by admiration for Hellenic culture as well as by greed, the Romans

> *"In the course of endless maneuvering and fighting, the Romans carved one province after another out of the eastern Mediterranean and made many a local ruler into a client king, until by the early first century B.C., they were supreme in the region. From Gibraltar to Jerusalem fell the shadow of mighty Rome."*

replied by sending an army. Their professed aim was to secure the liberties of the proud and quarrelsome Greek cities and then to withdraw. But they soon began to actively intervene in the politics and conflicts of the Hellenistic kingdoms. In the course of endless maneuvering and fighting, the Romans carved one province after another out of the eastern Mediterranean and made many a local ruler into a client king, until by the late first century B.C., they were supreme in the region. From Gibraltar to Jerusalem fell the shadow of mighty Rome.

proletarian In ancient Rome, a propertyless but voting citizen.

LO³ The Overthrow of the Republic

Already by the end of the Punic Wars, Rome ruled an empire far larger than that of any earlier city-state, yet the Republic's decisions were still supposed to be taken in person by arms-bearing citizens. The Senate, the people's assemblies, and the magistrates they chose now wielded unchecked power over millions of people—both noncitizens who had no right to a share in government, and citizens who lived far from Rome and mostly had no voting rights. Furthermore, war and conquest had disrupted the traditional social order in Italy, the heartland of the newly arisen empire, while the political leaders and ordinary voters in Rome used their power mainly in their own interests. As a result, Rome's city-state government system gradually broke down, and a universal monarchy replaced it like those that ruled every other vast empire.

The Impact of War and Conquest

Rome's triumphs abroad had a profound effect on society at home. In former days, the farmer-soldier had been the backbone of the state. But the social and economic revolution that followed the Punic Wars changed all that.

Proletarians, Profiteers, and Slaves

The Punic Wars and then the endless further conquests enormously increased the burden of military service on the Roman farmer-soldiers. Once drafted, they now served for years at a time until the particular conflict for which they had been called up came to an end. Many never came back; those who did often found their farms spoiled by neglect. Some farmers remained stubbornly on their land, but most gave up, sank to the status of **proletarians** (mere "producers of offspring"—the lowest class of Roman citizens), and drifted into the cities. There they could expect to receive free food and public entertainments at the expense of well-to-do citizens who thereby won prestige and power. Rome itself, with its wealthy rival politicians eager to gain the support of these propertyless but voting citizens, was particularly generous with "bread and circuses," and grew to become one of the Mediterranean's great metropolis cities (p. 86).

Meanwhile, a new social group was rising to prominence in Italy. It consisted of war profiteers of various sorts—contractors to the armed forces and dealers in loot and slaves. They used their wealth to buy up ruined farms, restock them, and turn them to new purposes. Small plots on which independent farmers had raised grain were often merged into large estates for use as vineyards, olive groves, or pasturelands for livestock. The new owners, who operated their holdings as capitalistic enterprises, had little interest in the displaced farmers, either as tenants or as hired hands, when they could use gangs of slaves, who had become plentiful and cheap as a result of Rome's conquests overseas.

By 150 B.C., slaves made up nearly one-third of the population of Italy. They labored mainly on the large estates, where they were often treated little better than beasts of burden. In the cities, slaves were secretaries and tutors in the households of the rich and powerful, domestic servants, and workers in every kind of business, including prostitution. A slave owner had a right to a slave's earnings, but he or she sometimes permitted the slave to withhold a portion. By this means, some slaves saved enough money to purchase their freedom and with it Roman citizenship. In addition, during their lifetimes or in their wills, owners often freed their slaves as a reward for loyal service. These freedmen or freedwomen were expected to continue in the service of the former owners or their families, but ex-slaves sometimes succeeded in business and became founders of wealthy families themselves.

The Aristocracy

At the topmost levels of society, patrician families still enjoyed the highest social prestige, but they now mingled with successful plebeian families to form a single, fabulously wealthy and powerful aristocracy.

Some of these "noble Romans" combined traditional virtues with a newly refined and cultured way of life, providing models that aristocrats and would-be aristocrats would imitate for many centuries. Such was Scipio Aemilianus, the conqueror of Carthage in 146 B.C. Scipio was a descendant of an ancient patrician clan and a battle-winning general who, in the best Roman tradition, passed up the limitless money-making opportunities offered by his military commands and other high offices. In addition, he

was well read in Greek philosophy and literature and generously sponsored early Latin poets and dramatists.

Such, too, was Cornelia, patrician wife of a plebeian, Tiberius Gracchus. She lived up to the ideal of a Roman matron as a *univira*—a "one-husband woman"—spending her life as a widow after Tiberius's death and seeing to the education of her sons in the manly virtues. But the household that she headed without a husband (and seemingly without a guardian) was a center of social life and Greek culture, and her letters to her sons were much admired as early examples of elegant Latin writing.

Even the noblest Romans had to scramble to make sure they got their share of the spoils of empire, however, and the traditional stability of households sometimes gave way to the interests of aristocratic "dynasties." Regardless of the ideal of fatherhood, men with sons to spare gave them up for adoption by men without sons. In this way, the givers of sons saved themselves the vast expense of launching young men on a political career and forged alliances with the aristocrats whose families they saved from extinction. The ideal of matronhood, too, was sometimes sacrificed to politics. Husbands divorced wives for the sake of more profitable family alliances—and wives, sure of the backing of fathers and brothers for more politically useful marriages, did the same to their husbands.

In general, aristocratic women seem to have had more choice than before over whether to observe the traditional constraints. They shared in the social life of their husbands in a way that would have been unthinkable in Greece. "Who among the Romans is ashamed to take his wife to a supper party? And which mother of a family does not hold the first place in the house and does not go out among crowds of people?" asked Cornelius Nepos, a writer of the first century B.C., comparing Roman customs to the segregated social life of the Greeks (p. 58).

> "*The ideal of matronhood was sometimes sacrificed to politics. Husbands divorced wives for the sake of more profitable family alliances—and wives, sure of the backing of fathers and brothers for more politically useful marriages, did the same to their husbands.* "

The Gracchi

Caught up in the scramble for the spoils of empire, the wealthy aristocrats in the Senate had little interest in finding ways to solve the Republic's problems. On the contrary, toward the end of the second century B.C. the Senate put a violent end to the Republic's most determined reform effort, that of Tiberius and Gaius Gracchus (the Gracchi brothers).

Tiberius and Gaius, the sons of the famous Cornelia, thought that a partial solution to Rome's troubles would be to resettle many of the city's poor, as well as discharged army veterans, on small farms and to provide a public subsidy of grain for those who remained in Rome. Such a program, they hoped, would raise the number of independent farmers and reduce the gap between rich and poor. Though unable to win Senate support for these measures, the Gracchi proposed them directly to a plebe-

ADVICE ON MANAGING SLAVES

Columella, an agricultural writer of the first century B.C., wrote a handbook for landowners on agricultural techniques and estate management. One of the key components of estate management was the effective control and exploitation of the labor force, most of whom were slaves. With the decline of the traditional free farmer, Roman cities became increasingly dependent upon the agricultural output of large estates worked by such labor forces. Thus Columella's advice was of importance not only to individual landowners but also to Roman society at large.

After all these arrangements [for buildings, tools, etc.] have been acquired or contrived, especial care is demanded of the master not only in other matters, but most of all in the matter of the persons in his service; and these are either tenant-farmers or slaves, whether unfettered or in chains. He should be civil in dealing with his tenants, should show himself affable, and should be more exacting in the matter of work than of payments, as this gives less offence yet is, generally speaking, more profitable. . . .

The next point is with regard to slaves—over what duty it is proper to place each and . . . what sort of tasks to assign them. So my advice at the start is not to appoint an overseer from that sort of slaves who are physically attractive, and certainly not from that class which has busied itself with the voluptuous occupations of the city. . . .

But be the overseer what he may, he should be given a woman companion to keep him within bounds and yet in certain matters to be a help to him; and this same overseer should be warned not to become intimate with a member of the household, and much less with an outsider, yet at times he may consider it fitting, as a mark of distinction, to invite to his table on a holiday one whom he has found to be constantly busy and vigorous in the performance of his tasks. He shall offer no sacrifice except by direction of the master. Soothsayers and witches, two sets of people who incite ignorant minds through false superstition to spending and then to shameful practices, he must not admit to the place. He must have no acquaintance with the city or with the weekly market, except to make purchases and sales in connection with his duties. . . .

In the case of the other slaves, the following are, in general, the precepts to be observed, and I do not regret having held to them myself: to talk rather familiarly with the country slaves, provided only that they have not conducted themselves unbecomingly, more frequently than I would with the town slaves; and when I perceived that their unending toil was lightened by such friendliness on the part of the master, I would even jest with them at times and allow them also to jest more freely. Nowadays I make it a practice to call them into consultation on any new work, as if they were more experienced, and to discover by this means what sort of ability is possessed by each of them and how intelligent he is. Furthermore, I observe that they are more willing to set about a piece of work on which they think that their opinions have been asked and their advice followed.

EXPLORING THE SOURCE

1. How does Columella advise the landowner to treat slaves, and why?

2. What class of people does Columella expect the overseer to come from, and what possible problems with overseers should the landowner guard against?

ian assembly. Tiberius, who was elected tribune of the people in 133 B.C., initiated the reform effort. But his term as tribune, limited by custom to one year, did not allow sufficient time to carry through his long-range program. Moreover, the Senate attacked him as a dangerous troublemaker. Tiberius decided to stand for reelection as a tribune, which gave his opponents an excuse to instigate and condone his murder, along with the murder of hundreds of his supporters. His younger brother, Gaius, carried forward the reform crusade, but he, too, fell under attack by the Senate and met a violent death in 121 B.C.

The reform movement was defeated, but for the first time, it had brought into question the traditional government system of the Republic and the power of the Senate. Soon the Senate would face new challengers who were not so easy to eliminate: the armies that had conquered Rome's empire, and the commanders who led them.

Soldiers, Warlords, and Civil War

With the changes in Rome's society and politics, the character of its armies and their commanders also changed. Instead of the farmer-soldiers of old, it was now landless and propertyless proletarians who were drafted to fill the ranks of the legions. This new type of soldier proved just as courageous and tough as the old one, and throughout the first century B.C., Rome's empire expanded faster than ever (see Map 6.2 on page 96). But Rome's citizen-soldiers were now "semiprofessionals" who fought largely in the hope of bettering themselves through pay, loot, promotion, and above all grants of land or money to provide them with a living when they were discharged. And small farms for veterans were precisely what the Senate had shown itself too greedy and shortsighted to provide.

Instead, the soldiers began looking for these benefits to their own commanders. As in the past, the commanders were mostly senators themselves, but now they stood to gain an edge in the scramble for wealth and power. Many army commanders turned into what amounted to independent warlords, sure of the personal loyalty of their soldiers and hence more powerful than the Senate itself. Since there was usually more than one such warlord at any given time, their rivalries led to bouts of destructive civil war, in each of which the winner became the one and only supreme warlord and hence the one and only ruler of Rome—a tyrant like the strongman rulers of the Greek city-states (p. 52), but on a vastly larger scale. But government by supreme warlords was bound to be brief and unstable—unless one of them could turn military dictatorship into legitimate power.

The first of the civil wars took place between 88 and 82 B.C. The main contenders were two rivals for political influence and army command, Gaius Marius and Lucius Sulla. Marius, a plebeian, claimed to represent the interests of the people and the common soldiers, while the patrician Sulla had the support of the Senate. In fact, both warlords set aside the republican government while they settled their dispute by military force. After vicious fighting in Greece, Italy, and Spain, and after Marius had sickened and died, there was no one left to challenge Sulla, and he was appointed to the unprecedented position of dictator for an indefinite term (see photo).

Sulla abolished the traditional limits on the power of the Senate but also made sure to pay off his soldiers with generous land grants. In reality, the only unlimited power in Rome was his own. He ruled by terror, making systematic use of proscription—an outlawry procedure involving the public posting of the names of those selected for death and the confiscation of their property. The victims included many senators as well as men of lower standing—opponents, possible opponents, and anyone who was rich enough to make it worthwhile to eliminate him. After two years, Sulla felt safe enough to retire from office, and he died in 78 B.C.

Rome's first experiment with one-man rule had not been encouraging, and the Senate and the other institutions of the Republic returned to their traditional functioning. Soon, however, a new generation of army commanders and would-be army

>> **"To Lucius Cornelius Sulla the Fortunate, son of Lucius, Dictator, from the Fundanian Reservoir Ward."** The Romans believed that a man's good fortune was a sign of divine favor, which people could share in by honoring and obeying him. By installing a statue of Sulla and carving this dedication on its pedestal, prominent citizens in a district of Rome could at least hope to avoid the very bad fortune of becoming victims of his reign of terror. Departmento de Historia, Universidad de Navarra, Pamplona/Visual Connection Archive

commanders was struggling for power. Among them was the man who would become Rome's most spectacular warlord and its second and more statesmanlike, though ultimately unsuccessful supreme ruler, Julius Caesar.

Julius Caesar

Julius Caesar came from an old patrician family that had come down in the world, and he entered the city's politics as a young man determined to regain the fame and power of his ancestors. As he grew in maturity and experience, however, he also came to identify Rome's key problems at home and abroad. In the social struggles, he sided with the poorer citizens and used his influence with them to advance his own cause. But he was also a flexible politician, and in 60 B.C. he began to collaborate with Gnaeus Pompeius (Pompey), an officer promoted by Sulla who had conquered many eastern Mediterranean lands. The two allies formed a **triumvirate** ("Three-Man Board"), together with another former henchman of Sulla, Marcus Crassus, that was for a time the dominant political force in Rome.

Foreign Conquest, Civil War, and Supreme Power

With the help of his new friends, Caesar won an appointment as proconsul of a province that included the southern regions of Gaul, a territory stretching all the way from northern Italy and the Mediterranean coast to the Rhine River and the Atlantic Ocean (see Map 6.2 on page 96). The Gauls, as the inhabitants were called, were a branch of the Celtic peoples, the predominant barbarian ethnic group across most of western Europe and the British Isles. The Gaulish tribes outside the Roman-ruled areas were powerful enough that they might one day become dangerous to Rome and were wealthy enough to be a tempting target. In eight years of brilliant and brutal campaigns, Caesar conquered Gaul and even made forays into Britain and Germany. By 50 B.C., most of western Europe was under Roman rule, and Caesar had built a powerful army personally devoted to himself.

Meanwhile, on Rome's eastern frontier, Crassus had led an army to crushing defeat by the neighboring empire of Parthia (p. 86), while Pompey had stayed in Rome, growing increasingly jealous of Caesar's success. Finally, with Pompey's support, the Senate ordered Caesar to disband his army and return to Rome.

Instead, he decided to come back with part of his army, in defiance of Roman law. It was the beginning of another round of far-flung civil wars.

Pompey was hastily commissioned to defend the Senate, but his forces were no match for Caesar's veterans. Forced to flee from Italy, Pompey was later defeated by Caesar in Greece and murdered in Egypt, where he had taken refuge. After subduing supporters of Pompey and other opponents in Egypt, Anatolia, Africa, and Spain, Caesar returned to Rome in triumph in 46 B.C. The Senate now hailed him, however reluctantly, the Father of the Fatherland—a title recently invented for the Republic's most admired statesmen.

Simulation to Learn About Ancient Rome Participate in the power struggle between supporters of Caesar and Pompey in an online historical simulation.

Caesar moved swiftly to make himself supreme ruler of the Republic. He had himself appointed to most of the leading magistracies, either simultaneously or in quick succession: tribune, supreme pontiff, consul, and dictator for a ten-year term. The people's assemblies continued to exist, but they did little more than endorse Caesar's proposals. The Senate, now enlarged by his own appointees, paid him noble compliments, and its members vowed to risk death in defense of his person. For his part, Caesar showed respect to the Senate but treated it as a mere advisory body.

Caesar used his new powers to attack the grave problems facing Rome. He took care to keep the loyalty of the soldiers and prevent the rise of rival warlords, by resettling war veterans on farmlands in Italy and the provinces. He extended Roman citizenship to parts of Gaul and Spain and appointed citizens from the provinces to the Senate. He gave the Romans splendid public buildings and roads, and introduced reforms into every department of administration.

Assassination and Another Caesar

Romans at home and abroad applauded Caesar's deeds, but there remained a stubborn core of senators who were disturbed by his successes. Their concern deepened further when in 44 B.C. he secured a vote from the Senate making him dictator for life. Caesar never ruled by terror like Sulla, but he also showed no sign of giving up his high position as Sulla had done. On the contrary, he raised himself even higher, permitting a religious cult to be established in his honor and wearing the purple robe of the ancient Roman kings. In the view of the diehard senators, Caesar had become a Greek-style tyrant—and there was a traditional and honorable way of getting rid of tyrants. On the Ides of March (March 15), 44 B.C.,

Caesar appeared in the Senate house, unarmed and unguarded, according to his custom, and a crowd of senators struck him down with their daggers.

Caesar's murder did not restore the Republic; instead, his death produced yet another crop of warlords and yet more bouts of civil war. The main contenders were Mark Antony, once a commander under Caesar and now a consul; the leading assassins, Brutus and Cassius; and Caesar's grandnephew and adopted son, the youthful Octavian Caesar.

Mark Antony and Octavian were rival loyalists of Caesar, and each managed to attract some of Caesar's legions, which they used to fight a brutal war against each other in Italy. Then, however, they joined forces against Caesar's assassins; formed another triumvirate together with a lesser warlord, Marcus Lepidus; eliminated opponents in a new reign of terror in Rome; and defeated Cassius and Brutus in battle in Greece. The triumvirs declared that they intended to "restore the Republic," but they also had the Senate proclaim Julius Caesar a "Divine Being" (*divus*)—not quite a god like Jupiter, but far above any ordinary mortal. The murdered dictator had become a founding hero, whose memory would inspire all future supreme rulers of Rome.

A Man of Unlimited Ambition: Julius Caesar Read an account of the buildup to Caesar's assassination.

The partners then divided the Roman world, with Octavian based in Rome, Lepidus in North Africa, and Mark Antony in Alexandria. Their cooperation soon turned to rivalry, however, and the balance of power began swinging toward Octavian. Antony's passionate love affair with Queen Cleopatra, one of the last descendants of the Greek rulers of Egypt, made him unpopular in Rome, and his efforts to win prestige by making conquests on the eastern frontier ended in failure. Meanwhile, Octavian pushed Lepidus out of power and successfully began expanding Rome's frontiers northward toward the Danube (see Map 6.2 on page 96).

Finally, in 31 B.C., the rulers of the two halves of Rome's empire went to war. Octavian's forces defeated those of Antony and Cleopatra in a decisive naval battle near Actium off the western coast of Greece. Antony and Cleopatra returned to Egypt, and within a year, both had committed suicide. Octavian was now the supreme warlord—the third to rule Rome, and the one who finally managed to turn military dictatorship into legitimate and permanent monarchy.

Listen to a synopsis of Chapter 6.

> *"But that which brought upon him the most apparent and mortal hatred was his desire of being king; which gave the common people the first occasion to quarrel with him, and proved the most specious pretence to those who had been his secret enemies all along."*
>
> —Plutarch, from
> *The Life of Julius Caesar*

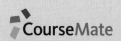

CHAPTER 7

THE ROMAN PEACE,
30 B.C.–A.D. 235

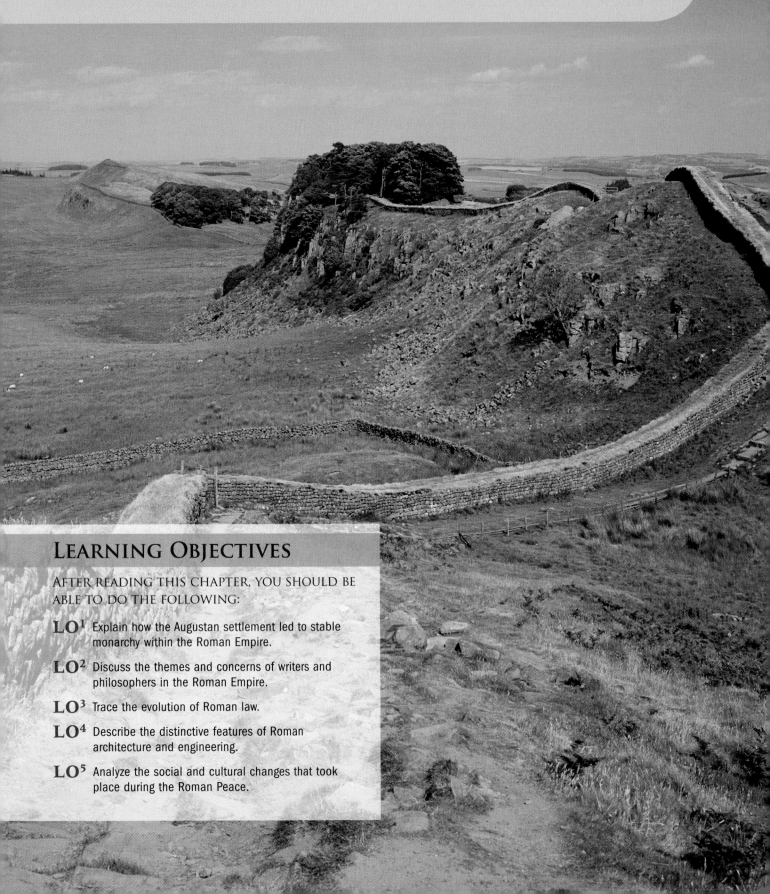

LEARNING OBJECTIVES

AFTER READING THIS CHAPTER, YOU SHOULD BE
ABLE TO DO THE FOLLOWING:

LO¹ Explain how the Augustan settlement led to stable
monarchy within the Roman Empire.

LO² Discuss the themes and concerns of writers and
philosophers in the Roman Empire.

LO³ Trace the evolution of Roman law.

LO⁴ Describe the distinctive features of Roman
architecture and engineering.

LO⁵ Analyze the social and cultural changes that took
place during the Roman Peace.

"THE ERA OF THE ROMAN PEACE WAS ONE OF MASSIVE SOCIAL, RELIGIOUS, AND CULTURAL CHANGES THAT WOULD FORM A NEW PATTERN OF WESTERN CIVILIZATION."

Augustus's new system of government kept many features of the Roman Republic, allowed subject peoples a good deal of self-rule, and brought Rome's destabilizing expansion to a halt. The result was two hundred years of stability that modern scholars call the Roman Peace.

Within the empire, the Roman version of Greco-Roman civilization prevailed in the Western territories, and the Greek version was dominant in the East. Roman literature and art, philosophy and law, architecture and engineering were often inspired by Greek models, but Roman achievements in these fields eventually equaled or surpassed those of the Greeks and became just as much an inspiration and model for future Western development.

In many ways, the dominant international civilization undermined the traditions of other peoples of the empire. In the West, the native languages of conquered European barbarian peoples began to be replaced by Latin; in the East, Egyptian hieroglyphic writing fell out of use. But the empire's most revered international gods and goddesses came from Egypt and other lands of the eastern Mediterranean or beyond the empire's eastern frontier, and the language of new Latin speakers began a lengthy evolution into the Latin languages of the present day. The era of the Roman Peace was one of massive social, religious, and cultural changes that would form a new pattern of Western civilization.

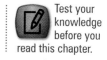 Test your knowledge before you read this chapter.

What do you think?

The era of the Roman Peace was a high point in the history of Western civilization.

Strongly Disagree						Strongly Agree
1	2	3	4	5	6	7

《 **Hadrian's Wall** Constructed at the order of the emperor Hadrian between A.D. 122 and 128, this frontier wall was originally ten feet or more high. It ran for seventy miles right across the island of Britain, between the Roman Empire (on the right) and what the Romans called the *barbaricum*—barbarian territory. The barrier helped keep barbarians out, but it also marked a self-imposed limit on Roman expansion.

103

LO¹ The Rule of the Emperors

Soon after Octavian's triumph at Actium, the Senate conferred on him a new title, Augustus ("Revered One"), the name under which he has gone down in history. Now that he was supreme ruler, Augustus intended to stay in power, reconstruct the failed government of the Roman city-state, and keep its empire together. The main lines of the "Augustan settlement" had emerged by 27 B.C., the year generally accepted as the end of the Republic and the beginning of the rule of the Roman emperors.

The Augustan Settlement

At the time, Augustus did his best to make it seem as if no such historic change was under way. He again proclaimed the goal of restoring the Republic (p. 100) and set about consolidating his supreme rule as much as possible within the traditional government and political framework.

The First Citizen

Unlike Sulla and Caesar, Augustus refused the offer of a long-term dictatorship and referred to himself simply as **princeps** ("first citizen"), a traditional name for prominent leaders who were considered indispensable to the Republic. From time to time, he served terms in leading magistracies such as consul, censor, and supreme pontiff, though the only one that he continuously held, and used as the legal basis of his power, was that of tribune of the people.

By arrangement with the Senate in 27 B.C., Augustus was confirmed as commander in chief (*imperator,* from which the English word *emperor* is derived) of the armed forces, which included civil and military control of all provinces with garrisons. In return, he permitted the Senate to supervise Italy and the city of Rome, as well as provinces where no soldiers were stationed. On his way to supreme power, he had proscribed and put to death many opponents in the Senate and replaced them with his friends and allies. Now he could afford to consult the Senate frequently and give it genuine government power.

The people's assemblies, on the other hand, lost what remained of their power to elect magistrates and make laws. The people of Rome did not oppose this, for they had lost confidence in the traditional system and trusted Augustus to rule in their interests as they had trusted Caesar before him. True to his policy of not breaking openly with tradition, Augustus still summoned the assemblies from time to time, but later emperors did not bother even with this formality. In "restoring" the Republic, Augustus

 The Roman Empire: In the First Century (http://www.pbs.org/empires/romans/index.html) Learn more about the Roman Empire in the first century in this interactive site.

was careful not to bring back the "mixed" government that had once been the source of its stability and vitality.

The Divine Being

In spite of avoiding Caesar's open exercise of supreme power, Augustus followed the dictator's even more arrogant-seeming example of accepting religious worship of himself.

After Augustus won supreme power, Greek cities in Anatolia began building shrines and sacrificing to "Rome and Augustus"—worshiping Rome itself as divine, and Augustus as a god-sent human being who embodied Rome's beneficent rule. Augustus was not the first powerful Roman to be worshiped in this way, but this time the practice spread well beyond Anatolia—with Augustus's permission and often with his encouragement. Shrines of Rome and Augustus sprang up throughout the empire, with prominent local citizens competing to serve as priests. Finally, when he died, the Senate declared him a Divine Being like Julius Caesar. It soon became customary for emperors to be worshiped in their lifetimes and to be deified (declared divine) when they died.

Augustus also acquired the title of Father of the Fatherland and took seriously the fatherly duty of supervising the behavior of his "household"—especially of the upper classes in Rome. He had laws passed against adultery by women and against both men and women who failed to marry; another law exempted mothers of more than three children from the requirement of guardianship. Poets and artists depicted him and his wife Livia as models of Roman family life, with Livia in the role of chaste and strong-minded "matron" of the Fatherland. Livia, who outlived Augustus, was also deified upon her death—the first of several emperors' wives to be honored in this way.

Of course, there was a good deal of make-believe in all this. The Roman upper classes went on living their free and easy way of life in spite of the moralizing from on high. As a matter of fact, Augustus and Livia themselves both got divorced in order to marry each other, and they never managed to have children together. And emperors themselves did not always take their divinity seriously. A later ruler, Vespasian (**ve-SPEY-zhuhn**), who was known for his cynical sense of humor, is supposed to have said on his deathbed: "Oh no, I think I'm turning into a god!"

Still, the Romans already believed that there was something divine about every paterfamilias and every matron; and they regarded community life as a kind of large-scale family life (p. 94); and most other peoples of the empire had similar beliefs. For Romans and non-Romans alike, the rule of one man was actually easier to accept if they could think of him as worthy of divine worship as well as human honor, and as a traditional paterfamilias married to a traditional matron. Augustus's claim to divinity and his fatherly moralizing strengthened his own rule, as well as the whole new system of monarchy that he founded.

 A Critical Assessment of the Reign of Augustus Caesar Read a vivid contemporary account of how Augustus handled power.

Reform, Reconstruction, and the End of Expansion

Ensuring peace and stability involved not only changing the way the Roman city-state worked but also reorganizing the whole of Rome's empire. There must be no more grasping governors and dishonest officials arousing fury among the subject peoples, and no more ambitious commanders making themselves into independent warlords with the help of discontented soldiers. Accordingly, Augustus began a whole series of large-scale reforms.

First, he brought the system of government appointments under his personal control. Here, too, he avoided breaking with tradition. Just as before, ambitious men from wealthy families made their way up a ladder of civil and military ranks in Rome and the provinces, and many of them were still appointed to their positions by the Senate. But none of them got far unless he performed competently, honestly, and loyally to the satisfaction of the princeps.

Second, Augustus showed respect for local institutions and encouraged provincial leaders to fulfill their responsibilities. He kept control over the affairs of the empire as a whole in Rome, but he left local affairs to the individual provinces, which in turn delegated a great deal of power. Greek city-states, Roman colonies, Celtic tribes, and countless other communities all ran their own day-to-day business, and it is estimated that the entire empire needed no more than a couple of thousand Roman officials to run it. Over several centuries and across a vast empire, corrupt and oppressive government was still common enough, but seemingly not so systematic and outrageous as under the Republic.

Third, Augustus reorganized the army to ensure the loyalty of the rank-and-file soldiers. After the battle of Actium, Mark Antony's troops came over to Augustus, who found himself at the head of a combined army of 600,000 men. Half were Roman citizens serving in about sixty legions, and the rest were noncitizens serving in auxiliary units (p. 97). Such a large army was impossible to pay for or keep under control, so Augustus quickly cut the troop strength in half and paid off the men he discharged with grants of land and money.

Then Augustus gradually brought about his single most drastic reform. Previously, soldiers had been mostly draftees who served for the duration of any particular war in units that were disbanded when a war ended. But by the end of his rule, all his soldiers were volunteers, serving for fixed terms of twenty-five years in permanent units. In this way, he hoped to make the army stable and reliable, since every man served by his own choice and knew exactly when to expect his release and his discharge grant. Soldiers in auxiliary units, which still made up about half the army, were not entitled to discharge grants, but later emperors began giving them something just as valuable: Roman citizenship (see photo on page 121). And every soldier swore obedience to the princeps personally and looked to him for pay and veterans' benefits.

 "An Army Marches on Its Feet": Basic Training in the Roman Army Read how volunteer soldiers were trained for marches and combat.

In this way, Augustus and his successors broke with the Roman tradition of citizen-soldiers to create the world's first professional standing army. The new model army was never completely proof against mutinous soldiers and treasonous commanders, but on the whole, it was loyal enough to the reigning princeps to give him a monopoly on military power.

> *"Augustus and his successors broke with the Roman tradition of citizen-soldiers to create the world's first professional standing army."*

The End of Roman Expansion

Even after Augustus's troop cuts, his army was still far larger than the forces that Rome had usually maintained in the past. He kept part of his army—the legion-sized Praetorian (**pree-TAWR-ee-uhn**) Guard—in Rome to back up his power at the empire's center, but he moved most of his forces to the frontiers of the empire, for he fully intended to continue Rome's tradition of seemingly endless conquest. Egypt, the lands stretching from Italy and Greece to the River Danube, a wide swath of Germany to the east of the Rhine (Map 6.2, p. 96)—all these territories were added to the empire by Augustus's legions. However, toward the end of his reign, Augustus turned against any further expansion—a change that had momentous long-term consequences for Rome's empire.

THE ADVENT OF MONARCHY BROUGHT FIVE CENTURIES OF ROMAN EXPANSION TO AN END:

A military disaster prompted new thinking on expansion

- In A.D. 9, recently conquered peoples in central Europe and Germany beyond the Rhine rebelled against the Romans, and an entire Roman army was destroyed by German barbarian insurgents.

- This loss forced Augustus to realize that his army had been overstretched by conquests and that a still larger army would be so expensive and so uncontrollable as to endanger his power.

Augustus advised his successors not to expand

- After his death in A.D. 14, Augustus's will was found to contain a recently added clause advising the Senate and his successors that the empire should be confined within its existing boundaries.

- Most of Augustus's successors followed his advice because they, too, found expansion too risky and destabilizing. In the next century, only a few large independent territories were permanently added to the empire (Map 6.2, p. 96).

The army's mission was changed from conquest to defense

- The army's 300,000 men were stationed in hundreds of permanent encampments along what came to be thought of as the permanent frontiers of the empire.

- Though Roman forces often campaigned beyond the frontiers, it was nearly always to deter or punish attackers from the other side.

 Historical Simulation of a Soldier's Life on the Roman Frontier Experience life as a soldier on the Roman frontier.

>> **Marcus Caelius, First Centurion** This senior officer served for thirty years in Augustus's reformed army before perishing in the German rebellion of A.D. 9. His body was not found, but the inscription on this monument built by his brother says hopefully: "His bones may be interred here." He holds his centurion's baton and wears his many battle honors. Also commemorated are his two freedmen (ex-slaves) who died with him. Evidently his bond with them was close. LVR-LandesMuseum Bonn

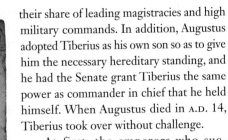

Permanent Monarchy

Augustus was convinced that if Rome's new peace and stability were to last, the changes he had made in its government system must continue after his death. For that to happen, he must settle in advance on someone to replace him—and this chosen successor must come from his own family. He himself would never have come to power if Julius Caesar had not made him his son, and the soldiers of the army, who were represented in Rome by the Praetorian Guard, felt a hereditary loyalty to the descendants of Caesar. Given the importance to the Romans of clan and family ties—which could be by adoption as well as by blood (p. 98)—if the position of princeps were to last, it must be hereditary.

Having no sons of his own, Augustus finally settled on Tiberius, Livia's son from her first marriage, as the next princeps. Tiberius was already experienced in government and trusted by the army, for Augustus had made sure that men of his family got

their share of leading magistracies and high military commands. In addition, Augustus adopted Tiberius as his own son so as to give him the necessary hereditary standing, and he had the Senate grant Tiberius the same power as commander in chief that he held himself. When Augustus died in A.D. 14, Tiberius took over without challenge.

At first, the emperors who succeeded Tiberius during the first century A.D. emerged—usually after vicious family infighting—from among the descendants of Julius Caesar and were then accepted by the Senate as Tiberius had been. Eventually, Caesar's last descendant, the notorious Nero, was overthrown after a tyrannical reign, but by that time, the Romans had become so used to one-man rule that no one seems to have thought of restoring the Republic. Instead, after a brief and brutal civil war among rival army commanders in A.D. 69, the winner— the humorous but also able and determined Vespasian—founded another dynasty, the Flavians (from Vespasian's full Latin name, Titus Flavius Vespasianus).

Near the end of the first century, the Flavian dynasty, too, came to an end following the assassination of another tyran-

 Nero's Death Precipitates "The Year of the Four Emperors" Read a Roman historian's account of corruption under Nero.

nical emperor, Vespasian's son Domitian (**duh-MISH-uhn**). Again, there was no thought of restoring the Republic, and the Senate appointed as princeps one of its own members, the aged and highly respected Nerva. Since Nerva had no sons and was unknown to the army, to avoid another civil war he adopted a leading general, Trajan, who took over peacefully upon Nerva's death in A.D. 98.

Subsequent rulers for much of the second century happened to have no sons by blood who survived them, so they, too, adopted sons whom they also designated (proclaimed) as their successors. Such an adopted son immediately became a junior emperor with what had by now become the imperial title **caesar**, and when his senior colleague died, he took full charge as **augustus**. This custom of "adoption and designation" produced a long series of outstanding emperors: Trajan, "the best of rulers," as he was called; the cultured and energetic Hadrian; the wise and dutiful Antoninus; and the philosopher-statesman Marcus Aurelius (**aw-REE-lee-uhs**).

Toward the end of the second century, however, the line of emperors by adoption and designation came to an end when Commodus, Marcus Aurelius's son by blood, outlived him, ruled irresponsibly, and was eventually murdered. Once again, civil war brought a new dynasty to power—this one founded by a capable and ruthless general of North African origin, Septimius Severus. His male descendants clung to power well into the third century in spite of rival generals and their own murderous quarrels, mainly thanks to their shrewd and determined mothers. All these women were close relatives of Septimius's wife Julia Domna, who came from a wealthy and cultured Syrian family. Some of them were publicly honored as "mother of the Senate," "mother of the camps," and even "co-ruler." Never before had Rome, with its reverence for public fatherhood (p. 94), paid the same honor to public motherhood—let alone to that of women from an eastern province.

In this way, Augustus's governing structure endured until the troubled times of the late third century (pp. 135–136). In spite of occasional upsets, the system always righted itself, for the soldiers, the ordinary Roman citizens, and the subject peoples all found a single all-powerful ruler far more helpful to their interests and needs than a greedy oligarchy. Even the upper classes found their pursuit of wealth and power on the whole safer and more predictable when it was supervised by the princeps. In this way, the Augustan settlement brought two hundred years of relative stability and prosperity that have gone down in history as the *Pax Romana*, the era of the **Roman Peace**.

LO² Literature and Thought in the Roman Empire

As Rome's conquests brought it into closer contact with the Greek world, the Romans began to share in the cultural traditions of Greece, and Latin joined Greek as a language of literature and thought. In the empire's eastern provinces, there was a great deal of writing in other languages such as Egyptian, Hebrew, and Aramaic, but most of it was for everyday and business purposes or dealt with religious belief and worship. Anyone who wanted to write in the literary forms and the fields of thought and study developed by the Greeks nearly always wrote in one or other of the international languages.

Literature in Latin and Greek

The rise of Latin began with a Greek ex-slave, Livius Andronicus, who in the third century B.C. translated Homer's *Odyssey* and several Greek dramas. Very soon, native Roman authors began to write in these and other traditional Greek literary forms, but they used these forms to express distinctively Roman values and experiences. Their works became in turn revered models for expressing the values and experiences of future European nations.

The Republic

Most of the earliest Latin literary works no longer exist, but many comedies staged in the third and second centuries B.C. by Plautus and Terence are still performed today. Their works were based on Greek comedies of the Hellenistic era, adapted to the rough-and-tumble tastes of Roman audiences.

Like their models, Plautus and Terence did not deal with topical subjects as Aristophanes had done (p. 70). Instead, they concentrated on the timeless themes of love and money. Their plays had complicated plots involving such characters as skinflint fathers, spendthrift and lovelorn sons, disillusioned but good-natured *hetaerae* (p. 58), beautiful young slave women who turn out to be the long-lost daughters of fabulously wealthy foreigners, and fast-talking slave men who juggle everyone else through to happy endings. What gave the Roman comedies their charm was their clever variations on the standard formulas, their humorously wise reflections on ordinary life and human nature, and the fact that audiences enjoyed being beguiled by what they knew perfectly well was wishful thinking. Terence himself had one of his characters say: "My life isn't like the comedies, where everything turns out well!"

The troubles of the first century B.C. were disastrous for the Republic but inspiring for writers. Men who were themselves involved in political feuding and military adventures produced notable works of history. Julius Caesar, for instance, wrote narratives of his own campaigns that were impressively sober and factual, and thereby convincingly advertised his battlefield genius. Outside politics, Catullus, a translator of Sappho (pp. 69–70), learned from her how to express deep passions in a brief space—but the passions he expressed were bitter as well as beautiful. "I hate and I love!" began one of his poems, inspired by a tempestuous affair with a free-living aristocratic woman.

The widest-ranging literary achievement of the late Republic was that of Cicero (**SIS-uh-roh**), an opponent of Caesar and a sympathizer with the dictator's assassins who was proscribed and killed on the orders of Antony and Octavian (p. 101). Trained as an orator in Athens, he put his skills to use in Rome, making magnificent Latin speeches in political and high-society trials and in Senate debates on matters of state. He was also a fascinating letter writer, a skill that was traditionally linked with oratory, since letters were often written to instruct and persuade. Besides serious reflections on life, however, his letters were full of news, gossip, and personal feeling. In addition, he wrote longer works on government, morals, and theology in which he explained and evaluated the ideas of Hellenistic philosophers, and thereby made Latin into a language of philosophy on a level with Greek.

The Empire

With Augustus's creation of a stable monarchy and the Republic's troubles still recent, writers found two themes both politically timely and genuinely inspiring: nostalgia for the supposedly simple and virtuous Roman past, and celebration of Rome's destiny as ruler and lawgiver of a peaceful world. These themes were most famously dealt with by a historian, Livy, and a poet, Virgil.

Livy's vast work, *From the Founding of the City*, narrated the entire eight hundred years of Rome's history up to the rise of Augustus. Its story was a patriotic but also a tragic one, of the community values and personal qualities that had made Rome great and the gradual decay of those values and qualities up to

The Power of Myth: Livy and the Rape of Lucretia Read Livy's retelling of the Roman legend of Lucretia.

Livy's own times, when "we can bear neither our diseases nor their remedies." Livy told a majestic story with memorable vividness, and his basic understanding of the Republic's history has survived to the present day.

Virgil's great epic poem, the *Aeneid* (**ih-NEE-id**), retells a Roman myth of the exile hero Aeneas (**ih-NEE-huhs**), who fled the destruction of Troy by the Greeks, wandered across the sea like Homer's Odysseus (p. 100), and redeemed Troy's defeat by making a new home in Italy that became the city of Rome. The myth expressed both Rome's need for a link with the traditions of the Greeks and its sense of rivalry with them, but Virgil's version is also a prophecy of Rome's imperial destiny. One of the stopping places on Aeneas's journey is the underworld, where he is shown a vision of his heroic descendants. These men are destined to take his city from humble beginnings to worldwide rule that "will bring good order joined to peace."

> "*But this is the kernel of my advice: Treat your inferiors as you would be treated by your betters. And as often as you reflect how much power you have over a slave, remember that your master has just as much power over you.*"
>
> —Seneca, ca. 50 A.D.

Besides triumph, however, the *Aeneid* is also full of what its hero calls "unspeakable woe": exile and separation; deaths of beloved kin and comrades and of worthy foes; the suicide of the queen of Carthage, whom Aeneas loves and leaves on his way to found the city that will one day destroy hers. Virgil's moving images of grief and pain, and his sense of the tragedy and cruelty of conquest, give depth and solemnity to his celebration of empire and make his tale truly heroic (see photo on page 109).

Two other poets of Augustus's reign, Horace and Ovid, were also eloquent spokesmen of Roman tradition and the blessings of empire, as well as of less momentous concerns. Many of Horace's lyric poems celebrate simple pleasures shared with friends, or comment ruefully on human foolishness. But for Horace, always aware of the shortness of human life, these seemingly trivial matters are deeply important. He conveys the joy and sadness that lie behind them in memorable images that make them, as he said of his own poems, "more lasting than bronze."

Ovid wrote long poems that told of such matters as Greek nymphs changing shape to escape lustful gods, lucky and unlucky days for Roman officials to issue laws, advice to men on how to seduce women, and advice to women on how to be seduced by men. Ovid was a master of shifting moods—irony and humor, sorrow and despair, cynical relish, and delight in human and natural beauty. His "how to" poems on seduction, celebrating the manipulative ways of men and women in Roman high society, displeased Augustus in his role as guardian and model of Roman family life, and Ovid spent his last ten years banished to a remote town on the west coast of the Black Sea.

In the century after Augustus, when one-man rule came to be taken for granted, writers became more detached and critical about Rome. The historian Tacitus (**TAS-i-tus**), for example, wrote disillusioned analyses of the workings of the

Noble Savages: Rome Encounters the Germans Read Tacitus's account of daily life among the barbarians.

imperial monarchy, as well as respectful treatments of barbarian peoples that Rome encountered. Following the ancient convention of inventing speeches for historical characters (p. 71), he made a British chieftain rally his warriors against a Roman army with a devastating condemnation of Rome's hypocrisy and oppression: "They call robbery, slaughter, and plunder by the lying name of empire; they make a desert, and they call it peace!" It was a very different view of Roman imperialism from Virgil's.

At about the same time, Juvenal brought to a new level of bitterness the tradition of lamenting Rome's moral decline, in a series of satirical poems on life in the capital. In Juvenal's Rome, aristocratic fathers of families go slumming in bars and brothels: meanwhile, their

"Some God Preserves Your Life for Greater Deeds" This wall painting from Pompeii shows a scene from the *Aeneid*. Aeneas has been struck by a javelin in a battle in Italy, and he comforts his young son Ascanius while his comrade Iapyx tries to remove the blade. Invisible to them, Aeneas's divine mother Venus swiftly heals her son's wound, and Iapyx tells him that this must be a god's work, so that Aeneas may fulfill his high destiny.

Erich Lessing/Art Resource, NY

wives enjoy the same pleasures at home, in between meddling in "matters of men's concern" like athletics, politics, and literature. Jumped-up freedmen elbow aside respectable Romans in the crowded mansions of the rich and famous, the lower classes are anesthetized with "bread and circuses," and foreigners—especially Greeks, Syrians, and Jews—are overrunning the natives. With scornful relish, Juvenal portrayed a city that in gaining an empire, had lost its traditions and identity to the peoples it ruled.

Greek Writers

Like the Romans, authors writing in Greek—which included both native Greeks and non-Greeks from the eastern provinces—both worked within their own traditions and had to come to terms with powerful foreign influences. In their case, however, the foreign influences were those of Rome itself.

The first Greek writer to encounter Rome in this way was the historian Polybius, who came to Rome as a hostage in the course of the conquest of Greece during the second century B.C. He befriended leading Romans, and his history sought to explain Rome's rise to supremacy over the Mediterranean world. Like Livy (who based a good deal of his history on Polybius), he admired Roman community values and personal qualities, but he also stressed the balance of power between Rome and its rivals, its style of warfare, and its city-state institutions. It was Polybius who first described the Republic as a "mixed government," combining the democratic commitment of all

citizens to the state with the experience and farsightedness of a stable oligarchy.

Two centuries later, another victim of Rome who became its friend, Josephus, wrote the history of the great Jewish revolt against Rome and its bloody suppression in A.D. 62–70 (p. 125). Josephus was himself a leader in the revolt who changed sides but remained a Jewish believer. Traditionally, the Jews had explained disasters as punishment by God for their sins (p. 39), but Josephus narrated this one much as Thucydides had narrated Athenian defeats in the Peloponnesian War (p. 71), as a human event resulting from human causes. Roman oppression, he thought, had fostered Jewish extremism and vice versa. Oppression and extremism had finally exploded into a disaster that had prevented or delayed the Jews from getting what Josephus believed God intended for them: an honored position under the Romans, whom God had raised up as world-ruling protectors of the Jews just as he had earlier raised up the Persians.

The broadest-ranging of Greek writers was Plutarch, who in the late first and early second centuries wrote well over a hundred short works on history, philosophy, and religion. Plutarch believed in the Stoic philosophy of achieving happiness by striving for virtue (p. 110), and in his most famous work, *Lives of the Noble Greeks and Romans*, he "compared and contrasted" the moral qualities of pairs of famous soldiers and statesmen of both nations. He explained the different strengths and weaknesses of his characters, but usually avoided finding a Greek generally more virtuous than a Roman or vice versa. In this way, Plutarch celebrated the partnership between Greece and Rome without taking sides in their rivalry.

Later in the second century, Lucian of Samosata, a Syrian from the Euphrates frontier who thoroughly mastered Greek culture, made fun of every kind of folly and pretentiousness in every class of society. Among his many targets were wealthy Romans who hired Greek philosophers as hangers-on to make themselves look well educated—as well as the philosophers they hired, for allowing themselves to be used in this demeaning way. His depiction of life in the mansions of the Roman rich and famous was much the same as Juvenal's, but it was seen from the opposite viewpoint—with Romans as the exploiters and Greeks as the foolish victims.

Epicureanism and Stoicism

In the era of the Roman Peace, Greeks and Romans came to share common traditions in philosophy as well as literature. These traditions originated with Plato, Aristotle, and other early Greek thinkers, but in Hellenistic times, Greek thinkers had become more concerned with the place of the individual within the universe (p. 86), and it was these later ideas that strongly influenced the Romans.

Epicureanism

One Hellenistic thinker widely revered in Rome was Epicurus, who claimed about 300 B.C. that everything in the universe was formed by the chance motion of atoms with no ultimate purpose, and that people should learn to live without fear, cultivate peace of mind, and accept the nothingness of death (p. 86).

The chief Roman promoter of Epicurus's teachings was Lucretius (**loo-KREE-shuhs**) (first century B.C.), who articulated them in a long poem *On the Nature of Things*. The poem is also a hymn to Epicurus himself, whom Lucretius praises for having liberated the human mind from superstitious fears. Later on, many poems of Horace celebrating private pleasures temperately enjoyed among friends, and many satires of Lucian targeting gullible religious believers, were also influenced by Epicureanism.

Epicureanism was not just a way of thinking but a way of life—one that involved giving up excitement, ambition, and sensual pleasure, and that needed training to live it properly. Groups sprang up across the Greek world and later the Roman world to study and follow Epicurus's example under the guidance of experienced practitioners, with the motto: "We will be obedient to Epicurus, according to whom we have made it our choice to live." It was a choice for a disciplined and directed life like that of Christian monks and nuns (p. 132), but one without immortality or gods.

Stoicism

The Hellenistic philosophy that most deeply influenced Rome, however, was Stoicism, with its belief in a purposeful universe functioning according to a plan of goodness that all humans can understand through reason, and that all humans must obey by living virtuously (p. 87).

The followers of Stoicism ranged from the orator and statesman Cicero, through Epictetus, a Greek freedman who had been a learned slave in Nero's court, to an actual emperor, Marcus Aurelius, who sought to embody Plato's dream of the philosopher-king (see photo on page 144). Day by day, while commanding his legions in fierce frontier wars, he set down his innermost thoughts in a little book, called *Meditations* (thoughts to himself). Stoicism, as formulated by Marcus Aurelius, was quite in accord with the ancient Roman virtues. "Let it be your hourly care," he advised, "to do stoutly what the hand finds to do, as becomes a man and a Roman, with carefulness, unaffected dignity, humanity, freedom, and justice." All people, whether emperors or slaves, must do their duty as it falls to them. Thus nature's plan is served, and the individual's life is blended with that of the universe.

In accordance with this principle, some writers of Roman times stressed the equal abilities and mutual duties of men and women. Plutarch wrote a lengthy essay, *On the Virtue of Women*, to prove the truth of Plato's doctrine that male and female virtue were the same (pp. 74-75). Seneca, tutor and adviser to Nero, even proclaimed in a letter to a friend the untraditional belief that "a man does wrong in

A Wealthy Stoic Urges Humane Treatment of Slaves Read Seneca on the just treatment of slaves.

> "*The earth occupies the central position in the cosmos, and all heavy objects move toward it.*"
>
> —Ptolemy, ca. 50 B.C.

philosophy involved the study of human groups including households, "a woman shaped by philosophy" would better understand "household management, the good provision of family needs, and the command of servants." The notion that sharing in traditionally male activities would make women more skillful at traditionally female tasks had a long history ahead of it, right down to the beginnings of modern feminism.

requiring chastity of his wife while he himself is having affairs with the wives of other men."

But Stoic philosophers expected that women, unlike Plato's philosopher-queens, would usually exercise their virtue within their traditional duties. Musonius Rufus, a Roman thinker of the first century A.D., believed that because

Roman Women: Following the Clues (http://www .bbc.co.uk/history/ ancient/romans/roman _women_01.shtml) Learn more about the roles of women in ancient Rome.

Science and Medicine

Unlike literature and philosophy, science under the Roman Empire remained mostly a Greek pursuit, and Alexandria continued as the hub of scientific and medical works. It was there, in the second century A.D., that the Greek astronomer and geographer Claudius Ptolemy (**TOL-uh-mee**) compiled his *Almagest*. The title is Arabic, meaning "the greatest," for the book was neglected in Europe after the fall of Rome but continued to be studied and admired by Muslim scholars. Bringing together the accumulated learning of the Greeks about the earth and the heavenly bodies, Ptolemy set forth a model of the universe that was generally accepted in the West until the Scientific Revolution of the seventeenth century (pp. 357–359).

A Geocentric Explanation: The Earth Must Be Stationary Read a selection from Ptolemy's description of the universe.

Of equal influence was a series of books written about the same time by a Greek physician, Galen of Pergamum (in Asia Minor). Galen stressed the importance of personal hygiene to health, and his views on anatomy and physiology were accepted until the emergence of scientific biology in the seventeenth century.

Women of Substance: Midwifery Training Read a passage from another Greek physician, Soranus, on the training of midwives.

LO³ Roman Law

The Romans were vigorous originators in the field of law, and their most enduring contribution to Western institutions lay in legal theory and practice. Beginning as a city-state guided by its own unwritten customs, the Romans gradually developed the idea that the law should not simply follow the traditions of a particular community but should reflect "universal reason"—what human reason discovers to be right at all times and in all places.

The Evolution of Roman Law

Rome's first written law code, the Twelve Tables (p. 92), remained the basis of Roman law for centuries, but it was continually adapted in accordance with Rome's increasingly complex needs. After 366 B.C., a special magistrate, called a praetor (Latin for "person in charge"), was elected annually to administer justice to the citizens of Rome. He was expected to follow the Twelve Tables, but at the start of his term, he was required to announce his own interpretation of the law. Through this decree and through his daily decisions, he adapted the original laws to the cases before him.

By 246 B.C., another praetor was established to deal with disputes between Roman citizens and noncitizens under Roman jurisdiction. This official could draw on the various foreign laws, as well as on Roman law, in arriving at fair decisions and settlements. Thus there grew up, in the days of the Republic, two distinct bodies of law: the "law of citizens," or *jus civile*, and the "law of peoples," or *jus gentium*.

But by the first century A.D., with Rome's empire much larger and dealings between citizens and noncitizens more intensive, the basic provisions of the two bodies of law had been brought close together. After 212, when all free inhabitants of the empire were declared Roman citizens (p. 121), the dual system disappeared. By then, the law recognized a class distinction between "worthier" and "humbler" citizens, but one system prevailed throughout the empire.

Under the empire, the laws of the Republic were further expanded by the decrees and interpretations of rulers and also by the writings of legal experts. The praetors of the Republic, who were not professional lawyers, had begun consulting men who were "skilled in the law" (*jurisprudentes*), and emperors regularly appointed outstanding legal scholars in this role. The opinions of these experts on individual cases, and their commentaries (explanations of existing laws), had much the same authority as actual laws.

The Idea of Natural Law

Most of the jurists were well-educated men who felt at home with Stoic philosophy. They observed that the laws of nations had many elements in common and that the laws themselves were gradually fusing into the single law of the empire. This similarity in legal ideas among the peoples of the empire coincided nicely with the Stoic belief that the just and orderly plan of the universe as a whole also applied to human communities.

From this, the jurists argued that the laws of actual communities should operate according to this "natural law." Cicero, in the *Laws*, observed, "Law and equity have been established not by opinion but by nature." The regulations of states that do not conform to

> " *Cicero, in the* Laws, *observed, 'Law and equity have been established not by opinion but by nature.* "

reason, he declared, are not truly laws and do not deserve obedience. This doctrine of natural law gives added authority to laws that citizens regard as right but opens the door to rebellion in the case of laws they believe to be wrong. It has repeatedly been used both ways in the history of the West—most notably, in the U.S. Declaration of Independence (pp. 381–382).

Codification of the Laws

Roman law grew naturally over many centuries, and it was only very late in the empire's history, after several earlier efforts, that the sixth-century emperor Justinian succeeded in combining the long-standing accumulation into a single orderly code. To do justice to the law's complexities, Justinian's *Corpus Juris Civilis* (*Body of Civil Law*) consists of several parts. The *Digest* summarizes judicial opinions and commentaries; the *Code* is a collection of statutes from Hadrian to Justinian himself; the *Novels* ("additions") include imperial statutes enacted after the publication of the *Code*; and the *Institutes* ("instruction") summarize the basic principles of Roman law. Justinian's great codification became the foundation for the legal systems that were later developed throughout Europe. Hundreds of millions of people today live under systems that are modeled, in whole or in part, on Roman law as found in Justinian's code.

LO⁴ Architecture and Engineering

There is no more impressive proof of the Romans' sense of power and permanence than their architecture. After centuries of erosion and vandalism, the ruins of Roman buildings still stand across the empire's former territories, all the way from the Euphrates to the Atlantic. Egyptian pharaohs and Hellenistic rulers had already built vast buildings, but the Romans outdid them in the sheer amount of construction and their combination of grandeur, elegance, and display.

Arches, Vaults, and Domes

For truly impressive buildings, the Romans found the Greek style of columns and beams (p. 63) inadequate. Instead, they preferred the arch, vault, and dome. All these forms dated back to ancient Sumer, but the Romans exploited and developed them on an unprecedented scale.

The Romans realized that an arch formed of bricks, stones, or poured concrete could carry a far heavier load than a stone beam supported at either end by a column. And they discovered that a row of arches built side by side, and more rows built on top of the first one, could carry a bridge or an **aqueduct** across a deep valley (see photo on page 115).

> **aqueduct**
> A channel or tunnel used to convey water across a distance, usually by gravity.

vault
An arch made deeper to produce a tunnel-shaped enclosure.

A **vault** is an arch made deeper to produce a tunnel-shaped enclosure, which can be of any desired length but admits light only at the two ends. To overcome this difficulty, Roman architects devised the cross-vault, which permits light to enter from the sides as well. It consists of one or more short vaults intersecting the main vault at right angles. This kind of structure can be carried to a great height and can be made to enclose a huge space with no need for supporting members between floor and ceiling (see photo).

The dome, resting on a cylindrical wall or on a circle of supporting arches, could also be used to create a vast and uncluttered interior. A large dome was built from a series of progressively smaller horizontal rings of brick, stone, or concrete. When completed, the parts formed a single unit firmly set in place (see photo).

Wealthy Romans lived in townhouses and country mansions that were extremely comfortable and luxurious, as we can tell from the remains of the splendid houses at Pompeii, not far south of Rome, which was buried by an eruption of Mount Vesuvius in A.D. 79. Excavations have revealed homes designed on an Etruscan plan, with a central court (*atrium*) partly open to the sky, as well as fountains, sculptures, wall paintings, mosaics, and metalware. The great mass of the urban populations, however, lived in *insulae* ("islands")—crowded and often shoddily constructed apartment buildings with half a dozen or so floors. Examples of these have been uncovered at Ostia, a port and suburb of Rome.

Cross-Vaulting: The Baths of Diocletian The *frigidarium* ("cold-water hall") of public baths built in Rome by the emperor Diocletian about A.D. 300 was remodeled by Michelangelo nearly thirteen hundred years later as a church. The Renaissance architect was able to make use of the vast space created by the Roman cross-vaults—the intersecting arches of the ceiling.

≪ **The Pantheon** "Thanks to its dome it resembles the vault of heaven itself," said a Roman writer of this building. That was what the emperor Hadrian and his architect Apollodorus of Damascus wanted, in order to build a temple that would be worthy of "all the gods." The result was this unprecedented dome, which remained the world's largest for more than a thousand years after it was built about A.D. 120.

Forums, Basilicas, and Temples

The grandest Roman buildings were public ones. Every major city of the empire had a public square—a **forum**—that served as a civic center. The Roman Forum, for example, was a marketplace in the early days of the Republic, but it was gradually transformed into an impressive meeting place with handsome statues, temples, and halls of government. Overlooking the Forum was the sacred Capitoline Hill, topped by the temple of Jupiter, Juno, and Minerva, while across the Forum, on the Palatine Hill, stood the palaces of the emperors.

Several emperors constructed their own forums in Rome as memorials to themselves. One of these, the Forum of Trajan, was built early in the second century A.D. on a spacious site near the Capitoline Hill. Symmetrically laid out, it included a large area for shops, an imposing public hall, a library, and a temple dedicated to the deified emperor. Dominating all the rest was the towering marble Column of Trajan, with a spiral sculptured band 3 feet across and 650 feet long depicting the emperor's conquest of Dacia (present-day Romania), the last substantial addition to the empire.

Most of the public meeting halls in Rome and the other cities of the empire were built in the style of the **basilica (buh-SIL-i-kuh)** or "imperial hall" (from *basileus*, the Greek word for "emperor"). This was a long rectangular building with a wide central aisle or "nave" and narrower side aisles. By lifting the roof of the center aisle higher than the roofs of the side aisles, the architects were able to admit light through a series of "clerestory" windows. At one or both ends was a semicircular structure called an apse, which was frequently walled off from the center aisle and used as a chamber for courts of law. In the fourth century, when Christians began building public houses of worship, they adapted the basilica to their own needs. The congregation stood in the open rectangular area, and the apse was used to house the altar and sacred objects. This plan of church architecture persisted for centuries (see photo).

The usual Roman temple was built on much the same plan as Greek ones, but the most impressive of all Roman temples, the Pantheon (Temple of All the Gods) in Rome, has a different design. The Pantheon consists of a round central hall capped by a vast concrete dome (see photo on page 112). To carry the great weight of the dome, the rotunda wall was built 20 feet thick. The height of the dome and its diameter are identical (140 feet), and the dome is pierced by a 30-foot hole or "eye" at the top that serves as the source of light. The single doorway is approached through a Greek-style porch. From the outside, the Pantheon has a squat, heavy appearance, but the interior gives a dramatic impression of space and buoyancy.

> **forum**
> A public square that served as a civic center in ancient Roman towns.
>
> **basilica**
> A type of building with a wide central aisle (nave), narrower side aisles, and a semicircular chamber (apse) at one or both ends of the nave; originally used for government halls and later for churches.

Sant'Apollinare in Classe This church in the Italian seaport of Classe was built by the local bishop about A.D. 540 to honor his predecessor Saint Apollinaris. It is modeled on a traditional Roman type of public building, a basilica, but it dates from sixty years after the last emperor reigned in Rome. The church's construction was a sign of the town's continuing prosperity in spite of the empire's troubles. Siepmann/Photolibrary

Baths and Arenas

Elaborate structures were erected in the empire's cities to satisfy the recreational needs of the people. Particularly popular were the public bathhouses, which were equipped with steam rooms and small pools filled with hot, lukewarm, or cold water. The emperors also courted popular favor by donating magnificent pleasure palaces that housed not only baths but also large indoor and outdoor swimming pools, gymnasiums, gardens, libraries, galleries, theaters, lounges, and bars. Because these recreational centers were especially attractive to the lower classes and to idlers, their reputation in polite society was not altogether respectable.

 Public Space in an Urban Setting: The Sounds of a Roman Bath Read a short humorous account of the sounds coming from a Roman bath.

The best-preserved pleasure palace in Rome is the complex of buildings known as the Baths of Diocletian, built in the late third century A.D. One of its surviving halls, constructed on the cross-vault principle, is 300 feet long, 90 feet wide, and 90 feet high (see photo on page 112). It is estimated that the baths could accommodate three thousand bathers in lavish surroundings of gilt and marble.

One of the most popular pastimes of the Romans was watching the chariot races of the circus and the gory combats of the arena. Although every city of the empire had places for these mass entertainments, the most famous arena was the Colosseum of Rome (see photo). This huge structure, which covers about six acres and seated more than fifty thousand spectators, was the largest of its kind. The crowds made their way to their seats through some eighty entry vaults, and the stairways were arranged so that the stadium could be emptied in minutes.

 Animation: The Colosseum: Building the Arena of Death (http://www.bbc.co.uk/history/ancient/romans/launch_ani_colosseum.shtml) Get a closer look at the Colosseum in this interactive animation.

A variety of materials was used in the construction of the Colosseum. Key areas of stress, such as archways and vaults, were generally of brick; other sections were of concrete and broken stone. The outer enclosure was built of three rows of arches topped by a high wall of stone blocks. Sockets set inside the high wall held great poles, on which protective awnings could be mounted. A coating of marble originally covered the exterior of the Colosseum, but the marble (and other building material) was carried off over the centuries for use in other structures.

Underneath the arena floor, which was made of wood covered with sand, lay a maze of corridors, chambers, and cells where animals and people (mainly slaves or criminals) awaited their turn at combat. The entertainments were lengthy affairs, lasting from early morning until dark. Wealthy donors seeking popularity—above all, emperors themselves—usually paid the bills, including the cost of food and refreshments.

 Art of the Roman Empire 27 B.C. to A.D. 393 (http://www.met museum.org/toah/hd/roem/hd_roem.htm) View the art of the Roman Empire.

Statues and Portraits

Like forums, baths, and arenas, works of sculpture were also used by the Roman rulers as a medium of propaganda. They might relate the events of a military campaign like Trajan's conquest of Dacia, or they might proclaim an ideal of imperial rule, like a famous bronze statue of Marcus Aurelius on horseback (see photo on page 115). The strength and eagerness of the horse express the power and authority of the rider who controls

The Colosseum A new imperial dynasty, the Flavians, built this arena about A.D. 80 to win popularity in the city of Rome by providing mass entertainment on a spectacular scale. The entertainment—mainly gladiatorial combats, wild beast hunts, and mock sea battles—continued until A.D. 523, when the city's decay ended them. The Colosseum then served as a "stone quarry" for newer buildings, but the structure was so huge that it took a thousand years to reduce it to the size seen here.

The Pont du Gard Completed in 19 B.C. as part of a 30-mile aqueduct supplying the city of Nemausus in southern Gaul (present-day Nîmes, France), this bridge carried a water channel for 300 yards across the 160-foot valley of the River Gard. The bridge is built of accurately cut stones that hold together by their own weight without cement, yet the structure is so strong that the bottom row of arches carries a roadway used by modern motor vehicles.

it, and the rider's high-browed, bearded face (modeled on depictions of Greek philosophers) and his outstretched arm speak of wisdom and mercy.

Most Roman portraits, however, are extremely lifelike, and sculptors carried farther than ever before the Hellenistic tradition of making a portrait bear the mark of an individual personality. A bust from about 80 B.C., for instance, depicting an unknown patrician, is a fine study of character—in this case, an aged but strong-minded, shrewd, and perhaps grimly humorous noble Roman (see photo on page 116).

Aqueducts and Roads

More than any other Western people until recent times, the Romans were builders of infrastructure—works other than actual buildings that served practical needs. To supply their cities with water, they built great aqueducts leading down from distant mountain springs. Much of the way, the water descended through pipes or channels in the mountains or hills, but across a valley or a plain it flowed in a channel carried by an aqueduct, engineered so that the water flowed steadily by force of gravity alone. The famous Pont du Gard (see photo) is part of a Roman aqueduct that once carried water in a 900-foot covered channel 160 feet above a river valley in southern Gaul.

Perhaps the most impressive infrastructure achievement of the Romans was their wide-ranging network of roads. Like the Assyrians and Persians before them (pp. 34, 36), they needed a swift and reliable means of overland movement to control, defend, and expand their empire. Over the centuries, they built or improved some 50,000 miles of roads, reaching out from Rome to the farthest corners of the empire. The typical roadbed was about 15 feet wide and 5 feet deep. Broken stone and gravel were packed down to form a foundation and then carefully graded to ensure solidity and good drainage. The surface was usually of dirt, except in the neighborhood of towns, where traffic was heaviest and thick blocks of hard stone were used.

The army, government officials, and the emperor's messengers had priority in the use of the strategically planned system of roads, but roads were also open to the public in general. The roads were regularly patrolled, and on the major arteries there was a stable every 10 miles and a hostel every 30 miles for the use of official travelers. Land travel under Rome's rule was easier than it had ever been before or than it would be again for nearly fifteen hundred years.

Emperor Marcus Aurelius This bronze equestrian (horse-riding) statue has inspired many other masterpieces since it was set up in Rome about A.D. 165 (see photo on page 299). Michelangelo, who designed the statue's present pedestal, was supposedly so taken with the horse's lifelike quality that when the pedestal was ready he commanded the animal to walk forward onto it.

LO⁵ Rome and Its Peoples

For two centuries, Rome's imperial monarchy brought unaccustomed government stability to the peoples living between the Euphrates and the Atlantic. But the era of the Roman Peace was also one of massive social and cultural change, which continued in the far less peaceful and stable two centuries that followed. Under the rule of the emperors, ancient traditions withered and died, new religious beliefs emerged that spread through the empire and beyond, new languages came into use that today are spoken across the world. The Roman Peace was an era of creative and destructive encounters among the peoples of the empire that permanently altered their patterns of civilization.

The Empire's Size and Structure

At the time of its greatest extent during the second century A.D., the Roman Empire measured nearly 3,000 miles from east to west and nearly 2,000 miles from north to south (Map 7.1), and its population was perhaps as high as 70 million. At the time, only the empire of China had a population as large as Rome's (though probably not larger), and no other human group under a single government was as large as these two.

The Empire and the World

As large as it was, the empire included less than half of Europe and far smaller amounts of Africa and Asia. Its survival therefore depended partly on the balance of power among nearby and distant peoples across the Eastern Hemisphere.

In spite of its name, the era of the Roman Peace saw plenty of frontier wars, but there were no enemies strong enough to make permanent breaches in Rome's defenses. To the south, the desert tribes of northwestern Africa were no more than small-scale raiders; in the Nile Valley, the Nubian rulers were mostly friendly. The Germanic barbarian tribes beyond the European

> "Since the city was not adorned as the dignity of the empire demanded, and was exposed to flood and fire, Augustus so beautified it that he could justly boast that he had found it built of brick and left it in marble. He made it safe too for the future, so far as human foresight could provide for this."
>
> —Suetonius, first century A.D.

frontier (p. 135) were still not powerful enough to invade the empire. The chief antagonist in the east was the empire of Parthia, carved by nomadic invaders out of territories beyond the Euphrates that had once been conquered by Alexander. On the eastern frontier, Parthia was a serious rival, but it was a mere "regional power" compared with the intercontinental empire of Rome.

Beyond Parthia, the Romans had sea links to India and Ceylon (si-LON), and on the lower Danube, they were in touch with the horse-riding nomads of the steppes (p. 20). But for the time being, the steppe peoples fought mainly with each other or with Rome's Asian counterpart, the empire of China. As for China itself, then enjoying power and prosperity under the Han dynasty as great as those of Rome itself, it was a distant land, known to the Romans only through the reports of middlemen in the overland silk trade. Thus, the intercontinental balance of power among the peoples and states of Asia, Africa, and Europe for the moment favored the peace and stability of the Roman Empire.

Cities of the Empire

Although the empire was administered through some forty provinces, the basic unit of government and of social and economic life was the city. Where cities existed in conquered territories, the Romans strengthened them as centers from which to control the surrounding districts; where there were no cities, the Romans created new ones in the image of Rome.

The cities of the empire were bound together by a network of sea lanes and highways, with Rome, the magnificent capital, at the center. During the prosperous second century, nearly a million people lived there. Augustus is said to have found Rome a city of brick and to have left it a city of marble. And the emperors who followed him lavished gifts on the capital, building temples, forums, arenas, monuments, public baths, and palaces to honor themselves and to please the populace. There were, in addition, the elegant private estates of the wealthy, both in the city and in its suburbs. True, most of the people lived in overcrowded tenements. But Rome gave a stunning impression of affluence and grandeur.

In the empire's eastern territories, the old-established Greek metropolis cities of Alexandria in Egypt (p. 86) and Antioch in Syria were not much smaller than Rome. Hundreds of smaller Greek or Greek-dominated cities of the eastern Mediterranean led their

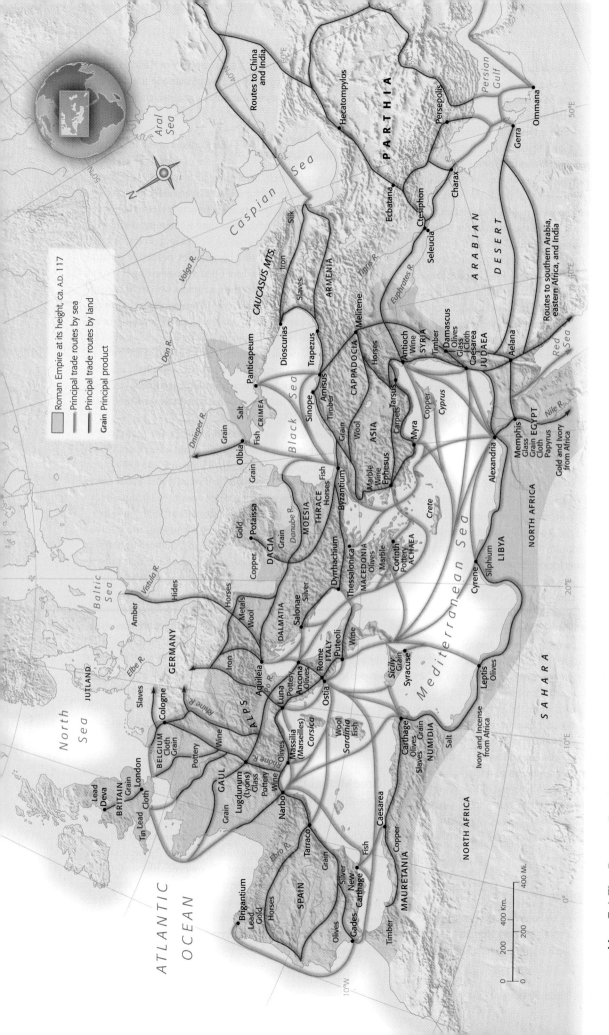

Map 7.1 The Roman Empire at Its Height

The map shows the empire at the beginning of Hadrian's reign. The road network stretches from Britain to the Middle East. But transport by water is even more efficient, and the Mediterranean, the Rhine, and the Danube are highways, not barriers. The network of trade and travel does not stop at the empire's frontiers but stretches deep into barbarian Europe, down the Red Sea to Arabia and India, and across the Middle East and central Asia all the way to China. © Cengage Learning

Interactive Map

traditional community life, ruled by oligarchies that now obeyed the Roman emperor instead of Hellenistic monarchs (pp. 84–85). The cities of the West—Italy, Gaul, Spain, Britain, and northwestern Africa—strove to become miniature Romes. Each had its forum, baths, arenas, and temples, as well as its governing council of wealthy townsmen modeled on the Roman Senate.

Unlike in Rome, however, in many of these cities, the governing elite still had to struggle for the votes of the people. In Pompeii (p. 112), professionally painted election signs on houses excavated by archeologists bear witness to hard-fought campaigns. "Terentius Neo asks your vote for Cuspius Pansa as Commissioner of Streets, Temples, and Public Buildings!" announced a well-off bakery owner. Women had enough public standing among the townsmen to join in campaigning, though they could neither vote nor be elected. "Fabia asks your vote for Caius Secundus for the Two-Man Judicial Board. He's worthy!" said a sign at the doorway of a respected matron. And sometimes campaigns went negative: "Marcus Cerrinius Vatia for Streets, Temples, and Buildings Commissioner—the small-time hoodlums ask your vote for him!" In this way, traces of the Republic's "mixed" government survived under Rome's imperial monarchy.

The Imperial Economy

As the Romans conquered their empire, they were able to expand along far-flung networks of trade and travel that already linked the lands surrounding the Mediterranean and nearby areas of western Europe. In the era of the Roman Peace, these networks grew into an empire-wide economy. Olive groves in Spain supplied oil to the citizens of Rome; legions stationed on the Danube received part of their grain rations from North Africa; workshops in Gaul turned out cheap earthenware bowls, jugs, and lamps for use in households throughout the empire.

Large markets also encouraged technical invention. Water-powered mills to grind grain, screw-operated presses to extract oil from olives and juice from grapes, light wooden barrels instead of heavy earthenware jars to carry oil and juice once they were pressed—these and many other devices first came to be commonly used in the Roman Empire. Such inventions made production and transportation easier and more convenient, but perhaps the single most notable Roman contribution to ease and convenience came in the field of reading and writing. Sometime in the first century A.D., the Romans began to make books with pages that could be turned as one read, instead of the traditional lengthy scrolls that had to be wound from one roller to another. By the end of the empire, the new reading device was on the way to replacing the old one, and has remained standard in the West ever since.

The Empire's Peoples

The Roman Empire was home to countless different peoples, but broadly they formed four main groups: Romans, Greeks, non-Greek peoples of the eastern Mediterranean, and the less complex societies of Europe and northwestern Africa. Out of the relationships, both friendly and hostile, among these groups there arose new forms of civilization, many of which have lasted down to the present day.

Romans and Greeks

The Romans owed many basic features of their civilized life to Greece. When the Greeks came under Roman rule, their influence on the conquerors only grew, for Greece alone could satisfy the intellectual tastes, the desire for sophisticated entertainment, and the need for models of elegance and refinement that developed in Rome along with increased wealth and power.

Like many peoples who come under pervasive outside influences, the Romans also developed a long-lasting tradition of fear and resentment against the foreigners who were supposedly diluting their identity and undermining their traditional way of life. Cato, an aristocrat of the same generation as the admirers of Greek culture Scipio and Cornelia (p. 98), called the Greeks "a quite worthless people. . . . When that race gives us its literature, it will corrupt all things." Two and a half centuries later (about A.D. 100), the poet Juvenal proclaimed, in effect, that Cato's prophecy had come true: "I can't stand a Rome that's turned into Greece!"

But in between Cato's time and Juvenal's, the Latin tongue had been enriched by borrowings and adaptations from Greek to become a sophisticated language of literature and philosophy; Roman writers had been inspired by Greek traditions to create works of prose and poetry that often outdid what the Greeks were producing at the time; and Roman officials governing eastern provinces had the advantage of knowing the international language of the region. The Romans had become partners and rivals of the Greeks in a common civilization that today is often called "**Greco-Roman**"—one that was also the empire's dominant international civilization.

For the Greeks, too, partnership between themselves and the Romans brought many benefits. True, they were now a subject people in a foreign empire, but in cultural matters, at least, they could feel themselves to be senior partners. All-powerful emperors often prided themselves on their fluent knowledge of Greek, but the Greeks never felt that knowledge of Latin was essential to being an educated person. Cato and Juvenal might resent this—but they, too, made sure to master the language and culture of the nation they resented.

Greeks and non-Greeks in the East

Partnership with the Romans meant that imperial rule actually safeguarded Greek dominance in the empire's eastern territories. Throughout those lands, the Greek language and culture wielded compelling influence on non-Greeks. The Jewish thinker Philo of Alexandria combined the sacred traditions of his own people with Greek philosophical thought to interpret the meaning of the Jewish holy writings. Roman army units stationed in Egypt used Greek for their lists of supplies ordered and soldiers available for duty—and so did Jewish believers in Jesus when they wrote the gospels.

For some eastern Mediterranean peoples, the combined impact of Greek culture and Roman power brought wrenching changes. Among the Jews, it gave rise to disputes and power struggles out of which both present-day orthodox Judaism and Christianity emerged (see Chapter 8). In addition, the empire's international civilization undermined the three-thousand-year-old traditions of Egypt. The Egyptian belief system, centered on the pharaoh as the upholder of the entire universe (p. 22), no longer made sense now that their country was a mere outlying province of a foreign empire. Perhaps for this reason, many other Egyptian traditions faded away—for example, their writing system. Shortly before A.D. 400, hieroglyphs were carved on a temple wall for the last time, and not long after, no Egyptian could read the ancient writing. But the Egyptians produced more documents and books than ever before, now that they read and wrote their language in the easily learned Greek alphabet.

The ways of Greece and Rome also changed under the impact of non-Greek ways, however—especially in the all-important field of religion. The international civilization needed international deities, and during the era of the Roman Peace, the most widely beloved and worshiped of these was the Egyptian goddess, Isis. Mighty and mysterious queen of the dead, yet also loving and merciful protectress of the living, she was approachable through secret rites in which rich and poor, men and women, slave and free could all gain her help in this world and her gift of eternal life.

The worship of Isis spread widely through the eastern Mediterranean lands in the centuries of Greek rule and Roman takeover (p. 84). Eventually, it reached Rome, where the Senate and the first emperors issued prohibitions against what seemed to them a subversive and un-Roman cult. By A.D. 100, however, Isis had a splendid temple in Rome, fitted out with genuine hieroglyphic carvings from Egypt—though Greek and Roman images of her generally played down her foreign origin (see photo). By A.D. 200, her worship had spread throughout the western half of the empire. Lucius Apuleius, a Roman lawyer from North Africa and author of works on philosophy as well as of a famous tale of magical adventure, *The Golden Ass*, praised Isis as the mightiest of deities: "The gods above adore you, the gods below do homage to you, you set the orb of heaven spinning around the poles, you give light to the sun, you govern the universe, you trample down the powers of Hell." It was the first but not the last time

>> **A Roman Image of Isis** In token of her origin, the goddess holds up a sistrum, a kind of rattle that was used in Egyptian temple processions, but her headdress and hairstyle, her clothing and her ritual wine jug, are all Greek (compare an Egyptian depiction, p. 27). Isis has been repackaged to meet Greek and Roman ideas of what a goddess should look like—thereby inspiring reverence from the emperor Hadrian, who kept this image in his mansion near Rome. Vanni/Art Resource, NY

that the empire's rulers resisted and then accepted a religion that originated among one of their subject peoples.

Romanization
The process of cultural change in which non-Romans adopted Roman ways.

Romans and Conquered Barbarians

From Spain, Gaul, and Britain all the way eastward to the Black Sea, Rome ruled a vast region of European barbarian peoples (Map 7.1 on page 117). Many of them were wealthy and highly skilled—especially the widespread Celtic tribes of western Europe (p. 100)—and the Romans had learned a great deal from them. Much of the armor and weaponry used by Roman armies, for instance, was adapted from the equipment used by Celtic warriors in Gaul and Spain. Town life and the use of writing had spread among some tribes, and if they had kept their independence, in time they would probably have developed their own local versions of Greco-Roman civilization.

Instead, the barbarians were conquered, and Roman soldiers, officials, and colonists moved in, bringing with them their language and culture. The Romans were perfectly willing to share all this on equal terms with wealthy native chieftains, landowning warriors, and traders, so long as they accepted imperial rule.

The result was a wide-ranging and mostly peaceful process of cultural change known as **Romanization**.

Already under Augustus, according to the Greek geographer Strabo, the native people in prosperous riverside towns of southwestern Spain were known as "toga wearers" (clothed in Roman-style robes), who had "completely changed over to the Roman way of life, not even remembering their own language anymore." Four centuries later, the language of country dwellers as well as townspeople, in most of the European barbarian lands that Rome had conquered, was Latin.

But the international Latin language had many native words in it—not because the new speakers were slow learners, but because the way the Romans themselves spoke their language changed to accommodate what they learned from the peoples they conquered. The Celtic peoples of Gaul, for instance, used a kind of four-wheeled horse-drawn wagon called a *carros*, which could transport far more and far heavier goods than the flimsy two-wheeled Roman carts. The Romans began to use these wagons, and having no word for them, used the Gaulish one, pronounced Latin-style: *carrus*. Many of the peoples ruled by Rome went on speaking Latin after the empire fell apart, though the pronunciation changed yet again: two thousand years later, speakers of Spanish, Portuguese, and Italian call a wagon a *carro*—and English speakers, whose language is heavily influenced by Latin (p. 238), call an automobile or a railroad vehicle a *car*.

Rome and Its Peoples **119**

TURNING CONQUERED PEOPLES INTO ROMANS: GNAEUS JULIUS AGRICOLA

Gnaeus Julius Agricola was governor of the Roman-held part of Britain late in the first century A.D., put down rebellions there, and conquered additional territory. He was the father-in-law of the historian Tacitus, who wrote his biography. In this selection, Tacitus describes Agricola's peacetime activities as governor of the province. Tacitus's depiction is probably too good to be true, but it shows how he thought high Roman officials ought to behave when dealing with recently conquered and still rebellious "provincials" (non-Roman peoples), and what he thought of the process of Romanization itself.

The mention of "dancing attendance at locked granaries" refers to abuses of the practice of collecting taxes in the form of grain for the needs of the army. Tribes were forced to buy the grain from distant granaries and deliver it to distant army camps, which evidently enabled corrupt officials and grain dealers to make a profit.

Agricola was heedful of the temper of the provincials, and took to heart the lesson which the experience of others suggested, that little was accomplished by force if injustice followed. He decided therefore to cut away at the root the causes of war. He began with himself and his own people: he put in order his own house, a task not less difficult for most governors than the government of a province. He transacted no public business through freedmen or slaves: he admitted no officer or private to his staff from private feeling, or private recommendation, or entreaty: he gave his confidence only to the best. He made it his business to know everything; if not, always, to follow up his knowledge: he turned an indulgent ear to small offences, yet was strict to offences that were serious: he was satisfied generally with penitence instead of punishment: to all offices and positions he preferred to advance the men not likely to offend rather than to condemn them after offences.

Demands for grain and tribute he made less burdensome by equalising his imposts: he cut off every charge invented only as a means of plunder, and therefore more grievous to be borne than the tribute itself. As a matter of fact, the natives used to be compelled to go through the farce of dancing attendance at locked granaries, buying grain to be returned, and so redeeming their obligations at a price: places off the road or distant districts were named in the governor's proclamations, so that the tribes with winter quarters close at hand delivered at a distance and across country, and ultimately a task easy for everyone became a means of profit to a few. . . .

In order that a population scattered and uncivilised, and proportionately ready for war, might be habituated by comfort to peace and quiet, he would exhort individuals, assist communities, to erect temples, market-places, houses: he praised the energetic, rebuked the indolent, and the rivalry for his compliments took the place of coercion. Moreover he began to train the sons of the chieftains in a liberal education, and to give a preference to the native talents of the Briton as against the plodding Gaul. As a result, the nation which used to reject the Latin language began to aspire to rhetoric: further, the wearing of our dress became a distinction, and the toga came into fashion, and little by little the Britons were seduced into alluring vices: to the lounge, the bath, the well-appointed dinner table. The simple natives gave the name of "culture" to this factor of their slavery.

EXPLORING THE SOURCE

1. Describe the policies of Agricola in Britain. How do they compare with those of recent and present-day conquerors in dealing with peoples under their control?

2. In Tacitus's view, how far did Agricola succeed in turning conquered peoples into the best kind of Romans, and how far was Romanization an improvement in their way of life?

Source: Tacitus, *Agricola* 19–21, trans. Maurice Hutton, Loeb Classical Library (London: Heinemann, 1914), pp. 203–207.

>> Proof of Citizenship This bronze plaque is one of a pair recording a grant of citizenship to Reburrus son of Severus (third line from bottom), upon his discharge from the Roman army on January 19, A.D. 103. Reburrus, a native of Spain, served in a cavalry unit in the west of Britain, and retired in the rank of decurion—commander of a thirty-man troop. The document lists many other locally stationed units whose new veterans became new citizens that day, gives the names of witnesses, and adds that it is an authentic copy of an original kept in Rome. For Reburrus, this was important proof that he had risen into the empire's ruling nation. Archaeological Museum Carnuntum, Austria

In ways like these, out of the encounter between the Romans and conquered barbarians there began to grow many worldwide languages of the present day.

Citizenship and Identity

Under the Republic, Rome had learned to be generous in awarding its citizenship to the peoples of Italy, but in the provinces, only a scattering of people were Roman citizens. Under the emperors, however, many provincials of middle-class social rank or higher were granted citizenship. These included important people who made themselves useful in local government, children of legally recognized marriages between male citizens and noncitizen women, and veterans of auxiliary army units (see photo).

Non-Romans who became citizens gained valuable advantages, such as the right of appeal against decisions of Roman officials, immunity from torture if they were suspected of crimes, and entry to government and army careers that might take them as far as the Senate. Above all, new citizens gained a new identity as Romans while remaining leading members of their non-Roman communities. About A.D. 150, Aelius Aristides, a Greek orator and Roman citizen, told an audience in Rome that included the emperor Antoninus: "You have divided all the people under your rule into two parts, . . . making citizens of all those who are more cultured, noble, and powerful, indeed making them your own kin, while the rest are in the position of subjects and the governed." And of course, the

> *"Once the great majority of people throughout the empire were granted citizenship, the legal distinction between 'worthier' and 'humbler' citizens became all the more important."*

rulers expected these "more cultured, noble, and powerful" people to be guided by their identity as Romans in governing "the rest."

In A.D. 212, the emperor Caracalla (kar-uh-KAL-uh) extended citizenship to all freeborn inhabitants of the empire. Probably he wanted to make it easier to levy taxes on poorer people and draft recruits into the army at a time when new outside threats and internal conflicts were bringing the Roman Peace to an end. But by Caracalla's time, a legal distinction was already growing up in regions like Italy, where most free inhabitants had long been citizens, between "worthier" citizens—aristocrats, government officials, and the military, including common soldiers—and "humbler" ones, which meant everyone else. Once the great majority of people throughout the empire were granted citizenship, the legal distinction between "worthier" and "humbler" citizens became all the more important.

In this way, the population of the empire continued to be "divided into two parts." The wealthy, educated, arms-bearing, and mostly town-dwelling few, with their common identity as leading Romans, held the empire together. The unprivileged, mostly country-dwelling majority, on the other hand, paid heavily for the splendor of the emperor, the upkeep of the army, and the beautification of the cities. At least among the elite, however, citizenship in a vast empire undoubtedly inspired a new sense of belonging to the human family. As Aristides told his hearers: "You have given the best proof of the ever-repeated saying: 'The earth is everyone's mother and everyone's common fatherland.'"

Which vision of Rome was closest to the truth—Aristides' worldwide fatherland or Juvenal's city swamped by its subject peoples, Virgil's bringer of order and peace or Tacitus's empire of plunder and slaughter? All these visions reflected different realities of an empire that forced itself on many peoples, made them live together more or less peacefully, and brought great changes to both rulers and ruled—changes that continued for centuries after Rome's peoples went their separate ways.

 Listen to a synopsis of Chapter 7.

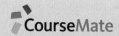

CHAPTER 8

THE CHANGING WORLD OF ROME: EMPERORS, CHRISTIANS, AND INVADERS,

200 B.C.–A.D. 600

EGO VERI SUM TAS ET VIA VITA

LEARNING OBJECTIVES

AFTER READING THIS CHAPTER, YOU SHOULD BE ABLE TO DO THE FOLLOWING:

LO¹ Describe the effects of Roman rule on the development of Judaism.

LO² Trace the development of Christianity during the Roman Peace.

LO³ Explain the problems facing the Roman Empire beginning in the third century, describe how the emperors responded, and discuss how their efforts failed in the Western half of the empire.

LO⁴ Discuss how Christianity became the dominant religion of the empire, and describe how the Church became a powerful organized community in partnership and rivalry with the state.

Erich Lessing/Art Resource, NY

"INSTEAD OF DYING, THE MEDITERRANEAN CIVILIZATION OF GREECE AND ROME BEGAN TO SPREAD AMONG MANY STILL-BARBARIAN NORTHERN PEOPLES, UNTIL IT BECAME THE CHRISTIAN EUROPE OF THE MIDDLE AGES."

The greatest single change that began among the peoples of the empire during the era of the Roman Peace was the spread of a new form of monotheistic religion, Christianity. The new religion began as a group within Judaism at a time of division and uncertainty among the Jews arising out of their encounter with the international civilization of Greece and Rome. In two centuries, Christianity developed away from Judaism to establish its own scattered, empire-wide community, the Catholic Church, which was already well on the way to forming the beliefs and practices that it would keep for centuries to come.

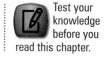

Test your knowledge before you read this chapter.

Meanwhile, the empire helped bring changes to peoples living outside as well as inside its borders. In particular, the Germanic barbarians of northern Europe became wealthier, more highly organized, and militarily stronger as a result of living as Rome's

neighbors during the era of the Roman Peace. From about A.D. 200, they became such a formidable threat that the emperors could hold them off only by building up the army, replacing self-rule by centralized government, and openly ruling as absolute monarchs—changes that, in the long run, failed to hold the empire together, but had lasting results for the future development of the West.

In addition, the empire was still strong enough to bring about the last and greatest of the changes in civilization that took place under its rule. As long as Rome had prospered, the emperors had taken little notice of Christianity's growth and spread; in the empire's time of troubles, they sometimes harshly persecuted it and sometimes deliberately tolerated it. Now, in the course of the empire's restructuring, they took Christianity into partnership as the official and majority religion.

Eventually, the burden of government and the army became too heavy to bear, the barbarian attacks grew too fierce to be resisted, and the empire began to collapse.

◄◄ **Christ Victorious** This mosaic in a chapel in the Italian city of Ravenna dates from about A.D. 500, when Rome was beset by invaders and Christians were bitterly divided over belief. Christ is shown as a youthful and steadfast Roman soldier, wearing the purple cloak of an emperor, and carrying his cross like a shouldered weapon. His open Bible proclaims: "I am the way, the truth, and the life."

123

Gentiles
A term for non-Jews; Christians used it to refer to worshipers of the gods and goddesses.

Over about a century down to A.D. 500, the entire western half was gradually taken over by Germanic invaders. But the Germanic rulers of the West accepted the Latin-speaking culture and Christian religion of Rome, and Rome's territories in the East survived as the long-enduring, Greek-ruled empire of Byzantium. Instead of dying, the Mediterranean civilization of Greece and Rome began to spread among many still-barbarian northern peoples, until it became the Christian Europe of the Middle Ages.

LO¹ The Jews in the World of Greece and Rome

Christianity began as one of many Jewish religious groups, each of which had its own answer to a disturbing question that faced the Jews as a whole: What was the will of God for his people in a world that was dominated by the international civilization of Greece and Rome?

True, the Jews believed that God had already revealed his will to them through prophets and holy writings (pp. 39–43). God, it seemed, wanted the Jews to live scattered through the world under the rule of more powerful peoples, but united in his worship as a single community under the ancient name of Israel. Around them, God would raise up and cast down world-ruling nations, but he would preserve and protect his people as long as they obeyed his Law. They must live righteously, structure their social institutions such as marriage according to his requirements, observe strict practices of ritual purity such as circumcision, and worship him in his Temple in Jerusalem.

But the worship of the one God was not for the Jews alone. One day, God would send his people a mighty redeemer—his Messiah (from the Hebrew for "Anointed One"), as the redeemer began to be called after about 200 B.C. There was no way of knowing when that day would come, but when it did, all the Jews would be gathered in their homeland and all peoples would come to the knowledge of the one true God.

Meanwhile, the Jews were a prominent people both inside and

CHRONOLOGY

63 B.C.	Jewish kingdom comes under Roman rule
CA. A.D. 30	Death of Jesus
A.D. 50–60	Paul's letters to Christian communities
A.D. 70	Temple in Jerusalem destroyed by Romans
A.D. 235–284	Series of short-reigning Roman emperors
A.D. 285	Diocletian takes control, begins reforms
A.D. 313	Edict of Milan formally ends persecution of Christians
A.D. 370	Huns enter eastern Europe; barbarians forced from frontier into empire
A.D. 378	Visigoths defeat Romans at the Battle of Adrianople
A.D. 410	Alaric and the Visigoths loot Rome
A.D. 476	Last Western Roman emperor deposed

> "One day, God would send his people a mighty redeemer—his Messiah (from the Hebrew for 'Anointed One'), as the redeemer began to be called after about 200 B.C. There was no way of knowing when that day would come, but when it did, all the Jews would be gathered in their homeland and all peoples would come to the knowledge of the one true God."

outside the Roman Empire. Many were townspeople and peasants in the homeland of Judaea in Palestine, but the majority lived in the Diaspora ("dispersion"): their congregations thrived in the cities of every Mediterranean land and beyond the empire's frontiers in Mesopotamia. They did not go out of their way to make converts, but **Gentiles** (JEN-tie-uhls) (non-Jews) sometimes either became full Jews or shared Jewish beliefs as "God-fearers" without complete obedience to the Law. Both in Judaea and the Diaspora, leaders of prayer to God and study of the holy writings held wide authority. The Temple in Jerusalem, with its long-lived dynasties of priests and its endless round of sacrifices, was one of the world's most magnificent shrines.

In all these ways, the place of the Jews in the world, and their future role in leading the human race to God, seemed assured. But in recent times, the world had begun to change, and the old answers had come to seem less certain.

Jewish Disputes in a Changing World

The change began in the second century B.C., when the Greeks started to lose their place as rulers of the lands between the Mediterranean Sea and the Indian Ocean, and for the first time since the days of David and Solomon almost a thousand years before, a powerful Jewish kingdom arose. The new state emerged from a heroic and brutal twenty-five-year struggle against a Greek king of Syria who had tried to prohibit Jewish worship. The struggle was led by the priestly family of the Maccabees, who became the new kingdom's rulers.

Eventually, the dynasty fell victim to family disputes, and the Romans stepped in, capturing Jerusalem in 63 B.C. Even so, the kingdom survived, and its most famous ruler, Herod the Great, reigned as a client king (p. 97) in allegiance to the new masters of the world for more than thirty years.

Yet the new kingdom produced discontent and division among the Jews. Most of the kings also held the office of chief priest of the Temple and used it to bolster their power. In addition, they made the Jewish peasants pay heavily for their building projects and their wars. Furthermore, they were deeply influenced by the international Greco-Roman civilization, even in religion. Herod, for instance, rebuilt the Temple to be more splendid than ever before, but in Caesarea, his kingdom's Mediterranean seaport, he built another temple—of the emperor-worshiping cult of Rome and Augustus (p. 104).

Many of the leaders of prayer and study who were now so influential with ordinary Jews distrusted the rulers and the Temple priests. They usually called on the people to obey the rulers and their Roman overlords and to make offerings in the Temple, but to some extent, they stood apart from other Jewish authorities. Perhaps for this reason, they came to be known as Pharisees, from a Hebrew word meaning "separators." Other groups separated themselves far more drastically from the rulers and the Temple, and set up communities in which they led lives of rigorous ritual purity and self-denial. Many of these groups believed that the Messiah would come sooner rather than later. He would be no peaceful uniter of the human race in the worship of the one God, but a warlike divider who would sweep away Greeks, Romans, Jewish kings, and all other Jews who did not accept him, leaving his loyal followers to live forever in blessedness under his rule.

Eventually, the Romans broke up the Jewish kingdom and made Judaea a province of the empire. Rome respected Jewish religion as the Greeks and Persians had mostly done, but its taxation was heavy and its governors were corrupt, inspiring hatred among the peasants and hope among those who expected that these troubles heralded the

 The Jewish Guerrillas' Last Stand: The Fall of Masada Read about the Jewish last stand and mass suicide at Masada.

advent of the Messiah. The result was two massive uprisings that were crushed by the legions and also resulted in religious disaster. The first ended in A.D. 70, with the destruction of the Temple, and the second in A.D. 135, with Jerusalem turned into a Roman city—complete with a shrine of Jupiter on the Temple site—that Jews were not allowed to enter. The traditional Temple worship had come to an end, never to be resumed.

 Jewish Revolt Against Romans, A.D. 66–70 (7:11) (http://www.pbs.org/wgbh/pages/frontline/video/flv/generic.html?s=frol02p584&continuous=1) Learn more about the Jewish revolt of A.D. 66–70 in this video.

Rabbinic Judaism

The end of the Temple worship was far from meaning the end of Judaism, however. Instead, the Jews continued the life of prayer, praise, and obedience to the Law that had grown up alongside the Temple worship and that now completely replaced it as the heart of Jewish religion.

The Pharisee leaders of prayer and study in Palestine had opposed both revolts, and events had proved them right. Favored by the Romans, who still tolerated Jewish religion even while they crushed the strivings for independence, the leaders of prayer and study became more revered than ever among the Jews. It became customary to address them as "My teacher!"—in Hebrew, *rabbi*.

The rabbis strove to end the disputes among the Jews by enforcing a consensus on belief and practice that all should follow. About the middle of the second century, they established the canon (authoritative list) of religious writings that Jews were to accept as written at God's command. Out of over fifty works that were more or less widely revered, the rabbis agreed on thirty-nine that were to be regarded as genuinely holy—the ones that make up the present-day Hebrew Bible. Meanwhile, their interpretations of and additions to the Law themselves acquired binding legal authority, and were collected about A.D. 200 in a book known as the "Repetition" (*Mishnah*). Later on, two enormous works explaining and expanding the Mishnah appeared, each of which was known as a "Commentary" (*Talmud*).

Judaism was now entirely based on the Bible and the rabbis' interpretations of the Law rather than on the Temple worship, and it was the rabbis who from now on led the Jews, rather than priests, prophets, or kings. This new, "rabbinic" form of belief and practice has remained the basic pattern of Judaism down to the present day. Rabbinic Judaism still foretold the future coming of the Messiah, the gathering of God's people in the homeland, and the turning of the entire human race to the true worship of the one God. But the spread of monotheism to become the dominant belief of the Roman Empire and many other lands began with a Jewish splinter group that believed that the Messiah had already arrived.

"The Priesthood Shall Be Theirs by a Perpetual Ordinance." This painting from a third-century A.D. synagogue in the eastern frontier town of Dura Europos shows the consecration of Moses's brother Aaron and Aaron's sons as hereditary priests during the Israelite wanderings in the desert. Aaron's name is in Greek letters, and the tabernacle, God's movable dwelling place, looks like a Greek temple. The Jews of Dura Europos could not escape contemporary influences, but the ancient covenant with God was still the center of their faith.

LO² Christianity in the Era of the Roman Peace

In its first two hundred years, Christianity acquired many lasting features of its belief and practice. The development of the new religion involved not only the Christians themselves, but also the Jews among whom it began, the Gentiles whom it sought to convert, and the environment of the Roman Empire through which it mainly spread.

Jesus

It was during the period of Jewish conflict and dispute leading up to the destruction of the Temple in A.D. 70 that Jesus lived and taught. What is known of him is found in the gospels (books of "good news") named after his followers Matthew, Mark, Luke, and John, which are thought to have been written between forty and seventy years after he died about A.D. 30. Most likely the gospel authors retold stories about Jesus that they found in earlier documents, or that had come down to them by word of mouth. Scholars debate how much these stories reflect Jesus's actual words and deeds, but some basic gospel traditions about him certainly dated back to his lifetime or not long afterward.

In any case, the authors of the gospels felt no need to set down all the details of Jesus's life, but focused on his birth, the brief years when he was a wandering preacher in Judaea, and his death and its aftermath. This was all that was necessary to show Jesus in two roles: as teacher explaining God's purposes, and as Messiah sent by God.

The Teacher

The gospels, written at a time when the Jewish majority and the believers in Jesus were turning against each other, portray him as an outright opponent of other Jewish groups. What is known of the teachings of these groups, however, suggests that Jesus had much in common with them, though with shifts of emphasis that made his message very much his own.

Like the Pharisees, Jesus obeyed the Law, visited the Temple, and called for acceptance of Roman rule, while standing apart from the Temple priests. Like the Pharisees, too, he appealed to a long-standing Jewish tradition of warning that true righteousness meant more than just obeying the strict ritual commands of the Law. However, Jesus took this tradition farther than ever before. He taught that even the most faithful righteousness according to the Law fell far short of what was necessary to please God. One must love not only one's friends but one's enemies; one must refrain not only from adultery but from lustful

The Gospel According to Matthew: The Sermon on the Mount Read Jesus's teaching from the Sermon on the Mount.

thoughts; one must not only avoid coveting one's neighbor's goods but give away all possessions and trust in God to "give us this day our daily bread." In short, one must "be perfect, as your heavenly Father is perfect."

Exactly because of this, Jesus made a point of associating with people whom sticklers for the Law thought of as highly displeasing to God—"prostitutes, tax collectors, and sinners." Furthermore, the entourage of eager hearers that accompanied him on his travels included women who broke the bounds of custom by leaving their homes and families to follow him. Sinners, Jesus taught, longed for God's forgiveness, which alone could admit them to his kingdom; and in God's kingdom, marriage and family would count for nothing. For Jesus's biggest difference with the Pharisees, as the gospels describe it, was that, like the radical Jewish groups, he proclaimed that "the kingdom of God has come near"—in fact, that, with himself, it had already arrived.

The Messiah

The gospels tell of Jesus's many signs and wonders. His birth to the Virgin Mary in fulfillment of prophecy; the descent upon him of the Spirit of God, which in Jewish belief had given life to Adam and guided the prophets; his miracles of healing that filled the crowds who saw and heard of them with joy and sometimes with terror—all are reported in the gospels as proof that he was Israel's redeemer.

But the Jesus of the gospels is a different kind of redeemer from the one that most other messianic (Messiah-expecting) Jewish groups hoped for—in some ways more benign, but in other ways even more terrible. He has not come to deliver just the Jews, but to fulfill the traditional prophecy that the whole human race will turn to the one God. He will redeem his people, Jew and Gentile, not as a warrior king but as a victim, by offering himself for one of the traditional purposes of sacrifice: to reconcile sinful humans with the divine power that they have displeased. But he also warns that "I have not come to bring peace, but a sword," and that when he comes again he will separate the righteous and the sinners "as a shepherd separates the sheep and the goats." Those who have believed and repented will live with him forever; for those who have rejected or ignored him, there will be eternal "weeping and gnashing of teeth."

Furthermore, in the gospels, Jesus calls himself both "Son of Man"—an ancient term for a human as against a divine being—but also "Son of God," and he proclaims that "The Father and I are one." He seems to be saying that he is both human and divine, and that he and God are somehow different and yet the same. And Jesus sometimes calls God's guiding Spirit "he," as if the Spirit were not just God's "breath"—the original meaning of the word—but a divine being in his own right. In these ways, the gospels announce a drastic change in the traditional Jewish understanding of the one truth about the one God.

To the Temple priests and the Roman rulers, popular preachers and miracle workers were a dangerous nuisance, particularly if they were suspected of claiming to be the Messiah. Accordingly, the priests arrested Jesus and the Romans crucified him, their standard method of executing the most despised criminals.

But then, say the Gospels, came Jesus's most spectacular signs and wonders of all: an empty tomb, appearances to witnesses, return to God who had sent him, and the descent of God's guiding Spirit upon his closest followers. For these followers, the age of the Messiah had already begun, when the Gentiles would finally turn to the God of Israel; and they saw themselves as the Messiah's **apostles** (from the Greek word for "messenger")—sent out by him to fulfill his command: "Go into all the world and proclaim the good news to the whole creation."

But what exactly was the "good news" that they were to proclaim? What did it mean in practice for the worship and daily life of believers? And who had the authority to proclaim the good news and tell believers how to live? Very soon, Jesus's followers started to wrestle with these questions. Out of their arguments and soul-searching there grew a movement that would change the religious outlook and the power structure of Western civilization.

 **From Jesus to Christ: The First Christians** (http://www.pbs.org/wgbh/pages/frontline/shows/religion/) Find out what archaeologists and others have discovered about the life of Jesus and the rise of Christianity.

Paul

In the thirty years after Jesus's death, his apostles worked hard to proclaim his "good news." Groups of believers sprang up in cities where Jews and Gentiles lived side by side—from nearby Antioch and Damascus, across Anatolia and Greece, all the way to Rome itself. This success brought Jesus's believers face to face with a first momentous question: To be accepted into the Messiah's coming kingdom, must Gentiles obey the Law's requirements of ritual purity?

Gentiles and the Law

In heated debates among leading apostles a few years after Jesus's death, the most forceful advocate of freedom from the Law was a Jew from a city in Anatolia, Paul of Tarsus. Paul had recently come to Judaea as a studious Pharisee and opponent of the new belief, but a vision made him a passionate believer in Jesus as Messiah and in his own work as an apostle—above all to the Gentiles. In a quarter-century of hard journeys by land and sea, he founded many groups of believers in Anatolia and Greece, driven on by the conviction that there was not much time for the Gentiles to turn to God before the Messiah would come again.

During his travels, Paul kept in touch by letter with distant groups of believers. Some of his letters, written between about A.D. 50 and A.D. 60 in Greek, the international language of Jews and Gentiles alike, are the earliest surviving documents of the new belief. In them, Paul gave guidance, tried to settle quarrels, and argued against the views of rival missionaries—including about the still disputed question of Gentiles and the Law.

For Paul, freedom from the Law was part of the changes that God had in store for the whole human race in the age of Christ—his Greek word for the Messiah. It was no longer "circumcision"—Paul's shorthand term for strict obedience to the Law—that made a person righteous in the sight of God. Instead, a person must have faith in Christ—in his self-sacrifice, his resurrection, and the day of his coming again. In the short time until that day came, let Jewish believers by all means live under the Law and Gentile believers not do so, so long as both understood that living or not living under the Law was beside the point. As Paul wrote to believers in Galatia, an inland territory of Anatolia: "in Christ Jesus neither circumcision nor uncircumcision counts for anything; the only thing that counts is faith working through love."

But how was it that not all who heard the gospel believed it? Paul himself had come to see the light; others seemingly no wickeder than he had rejected that light. This must be the doing of God himself: as Paul said in a letter to believers in Rome, "So then he has mercy upon whomsoever he chooses, and he hardens the heart of whomsoever he chooses." In that case, faith must be a gift granted or withheld by God for his own secret reasons, so that God determined in advance who would be saved and who would be damned. This doctrine of **predestination** was to become a feature of Christianity that many believers rejoiced in, others tried to soften, but few rejected outright (pp. 143, 318).

The Life of Early Believers

When writing to a group of believers in a particular city, Paul often called it by a Greek name used by Jewish congregations outside Judaea—*ekklēsia*, which literally means "assembly," but when used for believers in Jesus is usually translated as "church."

Within these earliest churches, there was no formal structure of authority and power. Apart from Paul himself, who claimed that his guidance was to be heeded because Christ had chosen him as an apostle, the main leaders were relatively wealthy heads of households in whose homes the worshipers met. Alongside these "house-church" leaders, however, there was room for many others who claimed special "gifts" from the Holy Spirit—such as prophets who gave guidance directly from God, and deacons (from the Greek for "servants") who organized festivities and helped the poor and sick. As befitted groups that saw themselves as forerunners of Christ's kingdom, women acted alongside men in every role from house-church leaders to deacons. Paul spoke of women who "have struggled beside me in the work of the gospel"—though he was also nervous about their becoming too prominent in worship.

Already the churches' worship included two formal services, both centering on Jesus as Messiah: baptism and a sacred common meal that came to be called the Eucharist ("Thanksgiving").

Baptism, the dipping of converts in water to purify them before God and admit them to the community of his worshipers, was a long-standing Jewish tradition. For believers in Jesus, however, it had a new meaning, the washing away of sin itself and becoming members of Christ's kingdom. For this reason, not only converts were baptized but also adult people who had been brought up as believers. In the Eucharist, the worshipers shared bread and wine in accordance with Jesus's command to his disciples at the Last Supper before he was crucified. In this way, believers were united with each other and with Christ, and celebrated his death as the central event of the age of the Messiah.

The Churches and the World

The believers in Jesus belonged not only to churches but also to other human groups—families, cities, the Roman Empire. They therefore faced a difficult problem of how they should live their lives from day to day. Should they live as part of "this world"—human society, with its imperfect human institutions, such as government and marriage? Or should they live as if Christ's kingdom had already arrived, recognizing no rule except his, and freed from Adam and Eve's burden of marriage and toil?

Paul gave guidance on this problem too, usually trying to find compromises between the way of life of this world and that of the coming kingdom. Both men and women, he said, should best live unmarried—that is, as virgins—but those who had no gift to do so must marry and not deny each other sexual satisfaction, for "it is better to marry than to be aflame with passion." Likewise, believers should not "take each other to court before the unrighteous," but they must accept government authority, for governments "have been instituted by God." Other differences of power and status in human society were also God-given: "Wives, be subject to your husbands as you are to the Lord. . . . Slaves, obey your earthly masters . . . as you obey Christ."

Yet Christ would soon return and do away with these differences—in fact, where believers gathered, his kingdom was already here. As believers were told at baptism services in Paul's churches, "There is no longer Jew nor Greek, there is no longer slave nor free man, there is no longer male nor female; for all of you are one in Christ Jesus."

> "*There is no longer Jew nor Greek, there is no longer slave nor free man, there is no longer male nor female; for all of you are one in Christ Jesus.*"

The Break with Judaism

Even during Paul's lifetime, he reproached his fellow Jews for distrusting his vision of Jews and Gentiles "all one in Christ Jesus," and after he died about A.D. 60—probably beheaded in Rome as a Jewish troublemaker—the vision faded.

To most Jews, the belief in a crucified Messiah who was himself divine seemed insulting to God, and the majority of new believers were Gentiles. Then came the Temple's destruction in A.D. 70, which most believers in Jesus took as God's abandonment of the Jews for rejecting the Messiah. Not long afterward, the believers in Jesus began calling themselves by a name originally given them by Gentile disbelievers, but which was now useful to mark them as a separate group—"Christians." For the Christians, the human race was now divided into three groups: the Jews, God's former chosen people; the Gentiles, a word that Christians still often used to describe worshipers of the gods and goddesses; and themselves, who were Gentiles no longer but God's new chosen people.

Still, by proclaiming faith rather than the Law as the bond between God and his people, Paul opened the way for a community of believers in one God to grow up that was drawn not from one but from many nations. Furthermore, Paul showed how this international community of believers could coexist with everyday human society, yet still think of itself as part of Christ's coming kingdom. This would become increasingly important as another part of Paul's vision faded, and it came to seem likely that Christ would not be returning, and everyday human society would not be ending, anytime soon.

The Church

As the years passed and Christ did not return, his believers did not lose their faith that he would one day come—and meanwhile, there was more time for them to proclaim his good news. But as Christianity grew and spread, this faced the churches with yet another problem: How could they be sure that they were truly obeying Christ's commandments and rightly proclaiming his good news when there were more churches scattered over wider regions, and when Christ's first coming was fading into a distant past?

Clergy and Laity

Early in the second century, out of the shifting leadership exercised in the earliest churches by whoever was deemed to have some special "gift," types of leaders began to appear who wielded firmer authority. Churches began to choose bishops (from the Greek word for "overseers") as permanent chiefs; priests (from the Greek for "elders") who assisted the bishops in teaching and worship; and deacons, who now also gained official standing.

Partly, this organization developed because churches were growing larger than before, but the new officials were far more than just managers. Early in the second century, Bishop Ignatius of Antioch, traveling under arrest to Rome to be put to death as a Christian, wrote to believers in the Anatolian port city of Smyrna: "Follow, all of you, the bishop, as Jesus Christ followed the Father; and follow the priests as the apostles. Moreover, revere the deacons as appointed by God. . . . Whatever the bishop approves is also pleasing to God, so that everything you do will be secure and valid." Surely, Ignatius thought, Christ would not leave his people without guides and rulers whom they should obediently follow until his second coming—and deacons, priests, and above all bishops were those Christ-appointed guides and rulers.

In the course of the second century, this "threefold ministry" spread through the churches. All male believers had a say in choosing ministers, though the ministers themselves, especially the bishop, and wealthy and prominent church members often had the largest say. Bishops as well as priests and deacons were usually married men who in poorer churches had to earn a living in some business or profession. All the same, the ministers came to form a group apart, the **clergy**—from a Greek word meaning "allotment," probably indicating that they specially belonged to God—as against the **laity**, from the Greek word for "people."

Now that the churches had formal rulers, women lost some of the share of leadership that they had held in the earliest churches. They still worked as deacons taking care of the poor and the sick, and wealthy women wielded weighty influence as owners of houses where Christian gatherings were held—for until the fourth century, there were no purpose-built Christian places of worship (see photo on page 130). Women as well as men were revered if they fell victim to persecution or lived lives of Christian self-denial. But women did not rule churches as priests or bishops—since formal rulership, according to the standards of everyday human society that the churches now observed, belonged in principle only to men.

The Canon of Scripture

For Christians to be sure of God's purposes and commands, they also needed writings that they could rely on as truthfully revealing his deeds and will. To begin with, all they had were the Jewish writings, which they continued to accept as holy. But of course, though these were deemed to foretell the coming of Christ, they did not record the actual deeds and sayings of Jesus or of the apostles who were next to him in holiness.

Collections of Jesus's sayings were probably compiled within twenty years of his death, and the four present-day gospels were written in the second half of the first century, as believers became more widely scattered and living memory of Jesus faded away. Meanwhile, churches that received letters from Paul preserved some of them, passed on copies to other churches, and revered them as the work of an inspired apostle. Many other gospels, letters, and prophecies appeared in the late first and early second centuries that claimed to be the work of this or that apostle.

By the end of the second century, some of these works, above all the present-day gospels and Paul's letters, were so revered that readings from them and sermons explaining the readings had become a regular feature of Christian worship services, and they were beginning to be thought of as a new group of holy writings alongside the Jewish ones—the "New Testament." The name came from the Latin *testamentum* or "covenant," since these writings were deemed to tell of God's "new covenant" with the Christians, as opposed to the Old Testament, which told of his "old covenant" (pp. 37, 38) with the Jews.

> **clergy**
> Church ministers—bishops, priests, and deacons—who guide the laity.
>
> **laity**
> Those members of the Church who are not clergy.

"The One Who Believes and Is Baptized Will Be Saved" A few blocks from the Dura Europos synagogue (photo on page 126), Christians met in a converted house. This reconstruction of their baptistry (christening room) includes original paintings and decorations. Catechumens ("persons under instruction," usually adults) kneel in the tub under the arch as water is poured on them from the pitcher. The wall images show women approaching Jesus's empty tomb: through baptism believers will share in his resurrection. Yale University Art Gallery, Dura-Europos Collection

Like the rabbis with the Hebrew Bible, the bishops had to decide which of many would-be holy writings truly deserved to be part of the New Testament. Since there was no way of knowing for certain which works had been written by apostles, the bishops usually accepted works that had been long revered by many churches. On the other hand, if a work went against their understanding of what Christian writings "ought" to say, they rejected it. In this way, they took until about A.D. 400 to settle on the present-day New Testament canon of twenty-seven books.

The Catholic Church

Apart from the churches that Paul and others founded in this or that city, his letters speak of "the Church" founded by Christ himself, meaning the entire body of believers awaiting Christ's second coming. As the Christian churches broke away from the wider community of Israel that bound together the Jewish congregations, they became increasingly aware of belonging to this wider body of their own. Early in the second century, they began to speak of it as the Catholic (from the Greek for "worldwide") Church.

During the second century, this "worldwide" Church came to operate as a fairly well coordinated network within the Roman Empire. Bishops wrote to each other a great deal and visited each other when they could, and sometimes came together in groups to discuss and decide on matters of common concern. But the Catholic Church was more than just a way for widely scattered bishops to keep in touch. Only by following the Catholic consensus, the bishops came to believe, could they be sure that they were acting rightly as guides and rulers—for the Church as a whole was guided and ruled by God himself. Late in the second century, Irenaeus, bishop of Lyon in southern Gaul, declared: "Where the Church is, there is the Spirit of God, and where the Spirit of God is, there is the Church."

Orthodoxy and Heresy

Sizable minorities of Christians, classified by modern scholars as Gnostics (from the Greek word for "knowledge"), did not agree that Christ must have appointed guides and rulers for his people. Instead, they said, believers must look for knowledge of God inside themselves, and to do so, they must give up unspiritual human activities like marriage and children, and lead a life of strict self-denial. Those who did not lead such a life must expect to spend eternity with God more or less hidden from them.

Furthermore, the Gnostics thought, Jewish traditions were no guide to knowledge of God. Jesus's perfect heavenly father

THE TRUTH ABOUT CHRISTIAN WORSHIP

As Christianity spread in the first two centuries after Jesus, it earned the suspicion of the Roman state and of worshipers of the gods and goddesses throughout the empire. Many misunderstood the act of communion as an act of ritual (or even real) cannibalism, and since the empire's welfare was thought to depend on the "peace of the gods," Christianity's rejection of the traditional deities seemed to endanger the whole of society as well as the state. In this document, dating from about A.D. 150, the well-educated convert Justin of Caesarea offers a description of early Christian practices in an effort to allay some of these suspicions.

All who are convinced and believe that what is taught and said by us is true, and promise that they are able to live accordingly, are taught to pray and with fasting to ask forgiveness of God for their former sins; and we pray and fast with them. Then they are brought by us to where there is water, and they are reborn in the same manner as we ourselves were reborn. For in the name of God, the Father and Lord of the universe, and of our Savior Jesus Christ, and of the Holy Ghost, they then are washed in the water. . . .

After thus washing the one who has been convinced and has given his assent, we conduct him to the place where those who are called the brethren are assembled, to offer earnest prayers in common for ourselves, for him who has been enlightened, and for all others everywhere, so that we, now that we have learned the truth, may by our works also be deemed worthy of being found to be good practitioners and keepers of the commandments, and thus be saved with eternal salvation. When we end our prayers we greet each other with a kiss. Then bread and a chalice of wine mixed with water are brought to the one who presides over the brethren; and he takes it, and offers up praise and glory to the Father of the universe, through the name of the Son and the Holy Ghost; and he gives thanks at length for our being deemed worthy of these things by Him. When he has finished the prayers and thanksgiving, all the people present express their assent, saying "Amen." . . . And when he who presides has celebrated the eucharist [thanksgiving], and all the people have expressed their assent, those called among us deacons allow each one of those present to partake of the bread and wine and water for which thanks have been given, and they bring it also to those not present. And this food is called among us the eucharist. . . .

And on the day called Sunday there is a gathering in one place of all who dwell in the cities or in the country places, and the memoirs of the Apostles or the writings of the prophets are read as long as time allows. Then when the reader is finished, he who presides gives oral admonition and exhortation to imitate these excellent examples. Then we all rise together, and offer prayers; and, as stated before, when we have ended our praying, bread and wine and water are brought. And he who presides similarly offers up prayers and thanksgiving, as far as lies in his power, and the people express their approval by saying "Amen." And each receives a share and partakes of the food for which thanks have been given, and through the deacons some is sent to those not present. The prosperous, if they so desire, each contribute what they wish, according to their own judgment, and the collection is entrusted to the one who presides. And he assists orphans and widows, and those who are in need because of illness or any other reason, and those who are in prison, and strangers sojourning with us; in short, all those in need are his care.

EXPLORING THE SOURCE

1. What were the main worship practices in early Christian communities?

2. How similar do the worship practices seem to those of the present day?

Source: From Roman Civilization: Selected Readings by Naphtali Lewis and Meyer Reinhold, eds. Copyright (c) 1955 Columbia University Press. Reprinted with permission of the publisher.

could not have created either the imperfect everyday world or the imperfect human race that lived in it. That had been the work of a lesser and perhaps even evil divine being—and it was this being, not the true supreme God, whose deeds and commandments were described in the Jewish holy writings. Jesus, in the Gnostic view, had been sent by the supreme God, but he, too, was not really part of this imperfect world. His life in the

body, troubled by hunger in the wilderness and suffering the agony of crucifixion, was mere appearance. He had not come to sacrifice himself for the whole human race, but to provide mystical knowledge of the supreme God to a minority of devotees.

The belief in a perfect spiritual world that people could only find inside themselves, and an imperfect outer world formed by an imperfect creator, came from a non-Christian philosopher, Plato (p. 73), but it fit in with the Christian belief in God working on the soul from within. Gnosticism was a strong movement throughout the second century and beyond, and Gnostic and Catholic Christianity may well have developed out of conflict with each other. But Christians who believed that Jesus was the longed-for Messiah of the Jews, that he had fully shared in the everyday human condition, and that everyday believers could become equal members of his kingdom naturally made the most converts. It was Catholic Christianity that became the predominant version of the new religion.

All the same, the Gnostics were active and articulate, and the disputes between them and the bishops were as fierce as between Christians and Jews, for in both cases, what was at stake was the one truth about the one God. The bishops, said the Gnostics, were "empty ditches," with no water of truth flowing in them; the Gnostics, said the bishops, were "wolves" preying on Christ's flock. In their struggle against Gnostic "ravings," the bishops insisted all the more on their authority as guides and rulers backed by the Catholic consensus, and they barred from the New Testament canon many would-be holy writings expressing Gnostic views. This, the bishops believed, was their duty as guardians of **orthodoxy** (from the Greek words for "right opinion") against **heresy** (from the Greek word for "school of thought"), which the bishops redefined to mean "false belief."

Philosophy and Faith

In this way, the bishops held on to much of the inheritance of Jewish tradition—disputing ownership of it with their rival heirs, the rabbis, and defending it against the Gnostics who wanted to renounce it. Still, with their belief in the divinity of Christ, orthodox Christians had themselves departed from the Jewish understanding of the one truth about the one God. For guidance in the search for a new understanding, these Christians, too, were tempted to turn from Jewish tradition to the wisdom of the Gentiles—to Greek philosophers whose own search for truth had led them away from the traditional gods and goddesses. But did the Gnostic use of Plato mean that the wisdom of the Gentiles could only lead Christians astray?

Tertullian, a successful lawyer from Africa who became a fierce advocate for Christianity late in the second century, certainly said so. "Heresies," he said, "are themselves instigated by philosophy. . . . What has Athens to do with Jerusalem? What has the Academy [the school where Plato taught] to do with the Church? What have heretics to do with Christians? We have no need of curiosity once we have Christ Jesus, nor of inquiring once we have the Gospel."

But the fact was that in their quest for a truthful understanding of divine power the Greek philosophers had developed ideas that orthodox Christians could not do without. Most notably, many

Greek thinkers believed that the entire universe was upheld by a living divine "Reason" or "Word" (in Greek, *logos*) that was present also in human beings (pp. 72, 87). This concept fit in well with orthodox belief. It helped explain how such a distant and mysterious being as God could be involved in every detail of the universe, and could even take human form: Christ must be none other than the *logos* through whom God created and upheld all things.

Already about A.D. 100, John's gospel hailed Christ as the *logos*, and Tertullian himself used the same idea to argue that Christ was both God and man. So did Justin of Caesarea, a Roman citizen from Palestine who became a Greek-style philosopher and then a Christian, but who always admired the Greek thinkers and their search for truth. They had lived, he said, "according to the *logos*"; in fact, philosophers like Socrates, whom the Athenians had put to death for not worshiping their gods, "are Christians, even though they were thought atheists." Eventually Justin followed Socrates' example: he was put to death in Rome about A.D. 165.

Asceticism

Whatever they thought about the Greek philosophers, orthodox Christians could not ignore the idea that self-denial was the best way to God. Paul himself had said that virginity was better than marriage, and the bishops gladly admitted that it was right for Christians to live in this world as they would in Christ's kingdom, by denying the demands and passions of the body—just so long as such exceptional strivers did not claim that Christ would bar from his kingdom believers who lived the everyday life of society.

By the end of the second century, there were many such orthodox self-deniers or **ascetics** (from the Greek word for the strenuous training of an athlete). The Greek physician Galen, an opponent of Christianity, reported that Christian ascetics stood comparison with followers of non-Christian philosophers like Epicurus who strove for mastery over the passions (p. 110). Christians, he said, "include not only men but also women who refrain from sexual intercourse all through their lives; and they also number individuals who, in self-discipline and self-control in matters of food and drink, and in their keen pursuit of righteousness, have reached a level not inferior to that of genuine philosophers."

Christianity and Rome

Judaea had strong links to Jews in two empires—eastward in Parthia and westward in Rome. However, Paul and many other early missionaries came from the world of the eastern Mediterranean, where both Jews and Gentiles were influenced by the international culture of Greece. Probably for this reason, in the era of the Roman Peace, Christianity spread mainly westward, and its destinies became entangled with those of Rome and its rulers.

The Spread of Christianity

By the end of the first century, there were about fifty Christian churches, mostly in the towns and cities of Syria, Palestine, and western Anatolia. Probably these churches included many people who still considered themselves Jews, as well as Gentile doubters of the power, goodness, or existence of the gods and goddesses.

As the rabbis created a new consensus within Judaism, the numbers of Jewish converts tapered off, and Christianity drew for its growth mainly on Gentiles. Mostly it seems to have spread through face-to-face contacts. Neighbors grew curious about the way of life of people next door; wives wore down husbands, and husbands exerted authority over wives; traders from distant cities chatted with business acquaintances after bargaining was done; slaves followed along willy-nilly with masters and mistresses; parents brought up their children as believers and began baptizing them as newborns. As a result, by the end of the second century, the network of churches in the original eastern territories had grown denser, and there were expanding footholds in Egypt and North Africa as well as toeholds in Italy and Gaul (Map 8.1).

For those who converted, the idea of Jesus as the Messiah was a life-changing truth that gave hope of eternal blessedness. Christianity was not the only international religion that offered this hope, and probably far fewer people became Christians than joined in the worship of Isis, for example (p. 109). But the crowds who took part in the Egyptian mysteries went their separate ways after the ceremonies were over, and did not stop worshiping other gods and goddesses. Christian converts, on the other hand,

became lifelong members of close-knit communities and were lost to the worship of the gods and goddesses—as were their offspring after them. As long as Christianity gained a more or less regular trickle of converts, it was bound to grow and spread.

As often happens with close-knit minorities that share and seek to spread religious hope, Christians were exceptionally generous and helpful toward each other and outsiders, notably honest in their business dealings, and impressively courageous in the face of persecution. That, at least, was what they boasted, and Lucian of Samosata (p. 109), a second-century Greek writer who was no lover of any kind of religion, agreed with much of what they claimed.

> The activity of these people, in dealing with any matter that affects their community, is something extraordinary; they spare no trouble, no expense. You see, these misguided creatures start with the general conviction that they are immortal for all time, which explains the contempt of death and voluntary self-devotion which are so common among them; it was impressed on them by their original lawgiver [Jesus] that they are all brothers

Map 8.1 **The Spread of Christianity**

The map shows areas in which Christian churches were thickly scattered at different dates. Christianity spread slowly during the Pax Romana down to A.D. 200, much faster in the troubled times between A.D. 200 and 300, and fastest of all in the era of imperial favor and barbarian invasions between A.D. 300 and 600. © Cengage Learning

Interactive Map

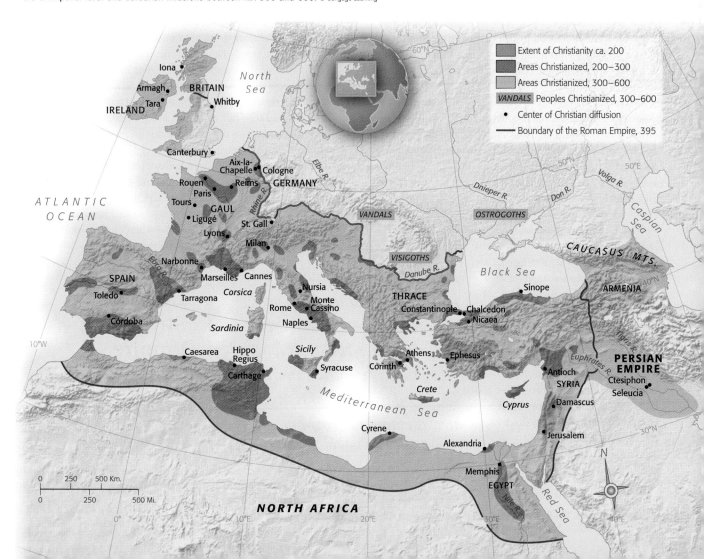

martyr
A person who is celebrated for accepting death rather than renounce his or her religious beliefs.

from the moment that they are converted, and deny the gods of Greece, and worship the crucified man of wisdom, and live after his laws.

It was this solidarity based on shared hope that gave Christians the self-confidence to call themselves the "Catholic Church" even though they were a small and scattered minority—fewer than the Jews, disliked by most Gentiles, and harassed by the rulers.

The Rulers and Christianity

As soon as the rulers of Rome became aware of Christianity, they viewed it with deep suspicion—as did the majority of worshipers of the gods and goddesses. Christians were disturbers of the "peace of the gods" (p. 93), who refused to take part in the traditional public worship on which the safety of communities and of the empire was thought to depend, and they refused to venerate the emperor as representative of divine power (pp. 104-105). Instead, they worshiped a man who had died a criminal's wretched death on the orders of lawful Roman authority; and they did so behind closed doors, with ceremonies that were said to include loathsome practices such as ritual cannibalism.

True, the Jews also denied the gods and goddesses, but theirs was an ancestral belief that they did not usually try to spread. Christians, on the other hand, actively sought to alienate people from the empire's traditional worship and to recruit them into what a high Roman official, Gaius Pliny, writing to Emperor Trajan early in the second century, called "a grotesque and deviant cult movement."

To begin with, however, Christians were a tiny minority, and busy officials had more urgent problems to deal with. On imperial orders, they followed a policy of "Don't ask, don't tell," acting only against Christians who were denounced to them by accusers who openly identified themselves. The action that officials took in such cases was extraordinarily mild, from their point of view: any suspect who sacrificed to the gods was released with no further investigation into his or her past conduct.

For a suspect who refused, however, the penalty was death—and the reward, Christians believed, was eternal blessedness with Christ whose suffering the suspect had shared. The church of which the steadfast victim had been a member would yearly commemorate the day of his or her death and revere the burial place—since the remains of executed criminals were usually released to family or friends—as a "victory monument." Word of the "victory" would go to other

churches, the "victorious one" would be honored by Christians across the empire as a **martyr** (from the Greek for "witness"), and the martyr's church would gain in standing within the Catholic Church as a whole. In this way, persecution gave Christianity a sense of struggle and triumph, without being systematic enough to crush it.

Late in the second century, as Christianity became more widespread, so did persecution. Across the empire, from Smyrna in Asia Minor to Lyon in Gaul, Christians were dragged to amphitheaters and sadistically tortured or devoured by wild beasts, for the entertainment of crowds whose fury against the "atheists" often forced the hands of Roman officials. These crackdowns were local and generally short-lived, but they were a sign that the rulers and the majority were taking Christianity more seriously.

 A Christian Martyr Awaits Her Impending Fate Read the moving story of Perpetua as she faces martyrdom.

Defending Christianity

In response, Christians began writing "apologies"—from the Greek word for a law court defense, in this case against the charge of disturbing the "peace of the gods."

Apologists countered this charge in two ways. First, they poured scorn on the gods and goddesses as nonexistent or (more often) as wicked demons. But secondly, in line with Paul's statement that governments were instituted by God, they insisted that Christians revered the empire and the emperor, and that they prayed to God for both—and since the God to whom Christians prayed was the only true one, it was they who were actually upholding Rome. As Tertullian told the worshipers of the gods and goddesses: "Caesar is more ours than yours, appointed as he is by our God." True, at Christ's return Rome and the world would come to an end amid hideous disasters, but as Tertullian admitted, "We [Christians] have no desire to go through such things, and so long as we pray for them to be delayed, we are helping Rome to endure." After two centuries in which Christ had not returned, Christians were beginning to have a stake in the survival of the empire that persecuted them—and this was happening at a time when the empire itself was coming under threat.

> "*Christian converts became lifelong members of close-knit communities and were lost to the worship of the gods and goddesses—as were their offspring after them. As long as Christianity gained a more or less regular trickle of converts, it was bound to grow and spread.*"

LO³ The Struggling Empire

Early in the third century A.D., a new and harsher era began for Rome. Already under Marcus Aurelius (p. 107), there had been signs of trouble to come, as epidemic disease spread through the empire and on the Danube frontier barbarian peoples mounted larger and better-organized attacks than ever before. Then, the emperors themselves began to lose their secure hold on power.

The Problems of the Empire

Following Marcus's death and the murder of his son Commodus, the new ruling dynasty founded by Septimius Severus (p. 107) gradually fell apart. The men and women of Severus's family struggled among themselves and were challenged by ambitious army commanders. In hopes of keeping their soldiers loyal, both they and their rivals faithfully followed the deathbed advice that Severus was said to have given his sons, to "pay off the soldiers and forget about everyone else."

The resulting gifts and pay raises had to be paid for by increasing taxes and debasing the coinage (cutting its gold and silver content). "Humbler" citizens paid more for the upkeep of the "worthier" elite than ever before, at the same time that prices were rising in step with the decreasing value of money. Insecure rulers, expensive armies, and poverty-stricken citizens, in turn, made it all the harder for the empire to deal with renewed attacks by the unconquered barbarian peoples who lived to the north of its European frontiers.

The Germanic Barbarians

These were the Germanic peoples, the latest ethnic group of European barbarians to live on the fringes of civilization and grow in skills, wealth, and power, just like the Celts, the Romans, and the Greeks before them.

The Germanic peoples seem to have originated in Scandinavia and northern Germany, but by the time of Caesar they had spread into the broad area between the Baltic and North Seas and the Rhine-Danube frontier. In the third century A.D., they moved into eastern Europe as well. The Romans called this whole region *Germania*—a much larger area than the Germany of the present day (see Map 6.2 on page 96).

Like all European barbarians, the Germanic peoples were not just fierce warriors but also hard-working farmers, shrewd traders, and skilled craftspeople (pp. 46–48). Roman writers, notably Tacitus, describe them as having a relatively free way of life, with villages run by assemblies open to all free males. Groups of villages formed tribes, which often fought for control of land and trade under the leadership of war chieftains and their war bands, groups of leading warriors who pledged themselves to follow a chieftain and defend him with their lives. The chieftain, in turn, supported the warriors and gave them a share in the spoils.

After Germanic resistance in Augustus's time brought the empire's expansion to a halt, the two sides became permanent neighbors (p. 106). There were many frontier wars, but Romans and barbar-

ians also lived peacefully side by side. Germanic stockbreeders sold meat and hides to Roman army supply officers, important chieftains received subsidies and were awarded citizenship, and warriors fought in the legions as well as the war bands. Ironically, the more the Germanic barbarians came under Roman influence, the more dangerous they were to the empire.

war bands Groups of leading barbarian warriors who pledged themselves to follow and defend a chieftain in exchange for support and a share of the spoils.

The Crisis of the Empire

When Severus's dynasty finally collapsed shortly before the middle of the third century, the combination of overstrained resources, power struggles, and growing barbarian strength brought about a crisis that almost destroyed the empire. Again and again, provincial armies fought to advance their favorite candidates, and many of the battle-hardened generals who came to power in this way proved to be effective leaders. But this did not save them from violent death, and their terms of office were generally short. In the half-century after the end of Severus's dynasty, the emperorship changed hands on average once every two and a half years.

Meanwhile, barbarian tribal confederacies devastated the empire's European territories from Gaul to the Black Sea. Even lands far from the frontiers, such as Spain, Greece, and Italy itself, were looted by barbarian war bands. Farther east, the Parthian kingdom (p. 116) had been overthrown by a revived Persian kingdom, whose rulers looked to rebuild the great empire of earlier centuries (pp. 34–37) at Rome's expense and now devastated the empire's eastern frontier territories.

Sometimes, barbarian and Persian invaders profited from each other's attacks and from the empire's civil wars. At other times, failure to cope with invaders caused the downfall of emperors and civil wars among rival would-be replacements. Either way, ordinary citizens were being ruined by taxes, rising prices, looting by invaders, and supply requisitions by Roman armies. The empire seemed caught in a vicious downward spiral.

 Villagers' Petition: Save Us from Our Protectors Read a village's plea to the emperor for relief from the demands of Roman armies and officials.

The Gundestrup Cauldron The metal workmanship of this two-foot-wide first-century B.C. silver cauldron is Thracian (from present-day Bulgaria). The images of a bearded god holding humans in his hands are probably Celtic (of the then-dominant ethnic group in Europe north of the Alps). It ended up buried in a field in Denmark, at the other end of Europe from its place of manufacture—evidence of the skills, wealth, and long-distance contacts of European barbarian peoples. Erich Lessing/ Art Resource, NY

INCREASED CONTACT WITH ROME MADE THE GERMANIC TRIBES STRONG ENOUGH TO CHALLENGE THE EMPIRE:

- Whether they fought for or against Rome, the Germanic warriors learned the empire's methods of fighting and adopted its weapons.

- In the second century A.D., the tribes began to form larger confederacies (tribal groupings) led by powerful chieftains and their war bands.

- Thriving on warfare, wealthy from loot or Roman subsidies, and eager to spend their wealth on the luxurious trappings of the upper-class Roman way of life, the members of the war bands became an elite that stood apart from the average Germanic warrior-tribesmen.

- With the ability to field armies as large as twenty thousand warriors, the tribal confederacies had formidable war-making capacity, both against each other and against Rome.

Restructuring the Empire: Diocletian

At last, in A.D. 284, a ruler came to power who had the shrewdness and good fortune to avoid sudden death and the vision and determination to rescue the failing empire. Diocletian was born in Illyria—a territory to the south of the middle stretch of the Danube that had become a main recruiting ground for the empire's overstretched armies (see Map 7.1 on page 117). He was the son of a freed slave who enlisted in the ranks, worked his way up, was at last proclaimed emperor by his troops, and subdued all rivals who contested his claim to the throne. After a reign of some twenty years, he retired voluntarily to a palatial estate at Split, in his native Illyria.

Already before Diocletian, hard-pressed emperors had found Augustus's power-sharing arrangements with the Senate, the aristocracy, and the cities to be a nuisance (pp. 104, 105). But they had mostly improvised new arrangements during their brief reigns, and

>> **All for One, and One for All** These contemporary sculptures show Diocletian, Maximian, Constantius, and Galerius, the four emperors who jointly ruled Rome from A.D. 293 to 305. The statues, set into an outside corner of Saint Mark's Cathedral in Venice, previously stood in separate pairs on a building in Byzantium. But their identical appearance and soldierly clothing, their embraces and their hands on their sword hilts, all convey a message of forces united to uphold Rome's empire come what may. Scala/Art Resource, NY

Diocletian was the one who systematically reorganized the Augustan settlement to build a new government structure—one based on the imperial bureaucracy, the army, and his sacred imperial authority.

The Government and the Army

Partly because the empire was threatened from so many directions, and probably also to win the support of commanders who might become his rivals, Diocletian made unprecedented use of the old system of senior and junior emperors (p. 107). He ruled the empire's eastern territories from Nicomedia, close to the Bosporus (see Map 7.1 on page 117). In 286, he appointed a fellow general, Maximian, as joint ruler to govern the empire's western territories from Milan, which was closer than Rome to the threatened frontiers. From then on, emperors only rarely ruled from Rome, though they still honored it as the empire's founding city. In 293, these two senior emperors or *augusti* each acquired a junior colleague (a *caesar*), who was entrusted with his own region carved out of his augustus's territories and who would one day become an augustus in his turn (see photo).

The most urgent problem that Diocletian and his colleagues faced was that of coping with more numerous and better-armed Germanic barbarian raiders, as well as with Persian attacks spearheaded by forces of heavily armed and armored cavalry. Diocletian began a series of reforms to meet these threats that, by early in the fourth century, produced what amounted to a new Roman army. The old legions were broken up into smaller units; infantry arms and armor were lighter and fortifications much stronger than before. Cavalry—in particular, Persian-style heavy cavalry, the forerunners of the knights of the Middle Ages—was far more important than in the days of the legions.

All this required an increase in troop strength to perhaps 400,000 men—one-third higher than in Augustus's time. To reach these numbers, more and more of the soldiers had to be recruited from the barbarians, and in time many of them became loyal Romans and rose to positions of high command.

The emperors also strengthened their grip on their territories by dividing them into more and smaller provinces—about a hundred in all—with much greater power over local affairs than before. Cities were made strictly responsible to the provincial authorities, and leading citizens were compelled to take over government duties, above all tax collection—and made personally responsible for shortfalls. The provinces were grouped into twelve units called **dioceses** (from the Greek word for "administration") that were in turn grouped into the four regions that the augusti and caesars ruled. It is estimated that the new government structure employed perhaps as many as 20,000 officials—ten times the number under Augustus. One of its main tasks was to carry out regular surveys of the empire's population and wealth and thereby ensure a higher tax yield to provide for Rome's larger army.

Diocletian knew that if the empire was to bear the increased burden of his army and bureaucracy, he must restore its prosperity. A tough old soldier, Diocletian tried to deal with economic problems by giving orders, many of which were ineffective or pointless. To check inflation, he issued an edict freezing the price level of all basic commodities, and to reduce tax evasion and banditry, he ordered that important occupations such as those of soldier, baker, and farmer be made hereditary. Both these sweeping decrees were widely disregarded and probably hindered Rome's recovery from war and invasion, if they had any effect at all.

All the same, Diocletian, his colleagues, and his successors managed to restore order in the empire and on the frontiers. They did so by breaking the limits on the size of the bureaucracy and the army that every emperor since Augustus had more or less kept to, and by imposing on the citizens a heavy burden of tax payments and supply deliveries. A thousand years later, their innovations would be studied and imitated by many European rulers when they, too, wanted to collect more taxes to pay for larger armies.

Sacred Monarchy

As a pious Roman, Diocletian believed that army and government reforms were not enough: the empire also needed to keep the support of divine power, which for him meant the traditional gods and goddesses of Rome. He built or restored many temples, and unlike earlier emperors, who had merely accepted veneration of themselves as sharing in the larger divinity of Rome (p. 104),

Diocletian called himself "Jupiter-like," while Maximian was "Hercules-like." The rulers believed themselves to be specially linked to these two gods, and expected the empire's citizens to revere them accordingly.

Diocletian's court ceremonial matched his new divine status. In Nicomedia, Diocletian built a two-thousand-room palace, set in a vast park. On state occasions, he sat on an immense throne beneath a canopy of Persian blue and the glittering emblem of the sun, wearing a crown of pearls. Visitors lay flat on the floor before his sacred person, and reported proudly, in documents describing their life histories, that they had "adored the purple"—that the emperor had actually let them kiss the hem of his purple robe. In this way, Diocletian's efforts to add majesty and mystery to the emperorship were successful. Whatever all-too-human struggles might have brought him to his high position, he deserved reverence as a representative of divine power.

Among the emperor's subjects, only two groups refused to accept that the emperor was himself divine. One was the Jews, whose devotion to the one God was respected as part of their ancient national traditions. The other was the Christians, who had newly turned against the gods and goddesses of Rome and whose numbers had increased spectacularly in the empire's time of troubles.

The Palace of Diocletian at Split (http://www.croatiatraveller.com/Heritage_Sites/Diocletian'sPalace.htm) Take a tour of Diocletian's palace at Split, a UNESCO World Cultural Heritage site.

Christianity in Rome's Time of Troubles

By A.D. 300, there were several million Christians among the 60 million people of the empire, so that they were perhaps as large a minority as the Jews. Probably the empire's misfortunes made Christianity seem more convincing than before, and this gave continued momentum to a natural process of growth. More Christians meant more face-to-face contacts, more conversions, and more offspring, so that the increase in numbers grew continually larger and faster.

The increase was not the only change in Christianity. The new religion spread to the Western half of the empire, with many churches in prosperous towns of Africa and Spain, Italy and Gaul, and the Danube and Rhine frontiers (see Map 8.1 on page 133). Most Christians still lived in the East, but Latin joined Greek and various tongues of the empire's eastern borderlands as a language of Christian literature and church services. Bishops of larger cities with larger churches gained authority over bishops of smaller cities with smaller churches, and bishops of the largest cities became leaders of "blocs" of bishops throughout whole regions of the empire. The bishops of Antioch and Alexandria wielded this influence in the eastern parts of the empire, and the bishops of Rome in the western territories.

Furthermore, Christianity was reaching into Rome's ruling elite, and the new religion's leaders were themselves becoming an elite. According to the renowned Egyptian thinker and teacher Origen, Christianity now attracted "even rich men and persons in positions of honor, and ladies of refinement and high birth"—probably ladies in particular, since they did not have public careers that might be endangered by unwise conversion. Big-city churches became large-scale organizations: about the middle of the century, Bishop Cornelius of Rome claimed that his church had more than 150 full-time clergy and supported 1,500 widows and other poor people. And complaints surfaced that Christian leadership was becoming an object of worldly ambition and pride. "In many so-called churches, especially in large cities," said Origen, "one can see rulers of the people of God who do not allow anyone, sometimes not even the noblest of Jesus' disciples, to speak with them on equal terms."

In these ways, Christianity was not just spreading within the empire, but growing together with it. That, in turn, faced the rulers with a choice. Should they try to uphold the "peace of the gods" by more systematic repression of Christianity, or should they take the Christians at their word and let them alone to pray to their God for the safety of the empire?

Given the overwhelming problems that the emperors had to cope with, the second course was much the easiest, and most of them followed it. In the half-century before Diocletian, two of the many short-reigning emperors launched empire-wide campaigns of persecution, but each was more or less formally called off by the next emperor. The numerous Christians who had not been steadfast could repent, though there were fierce disputes over how far this applied to priests and bishops. Christians who had lain low could come into the open, churches had their confiscated property returned by the government, and those who survived were inspired by the memory of the martyrs who had borne witness to the faith. Both persecutions ended with the Christian churches becoming larger and more numerous than ever.

Diocletian, too, left the Christians alone until near the end of his reign, when he undertook the most systematic persecution of all. The persecution continued for several years after he left office in 303, but to be successful, it would have taken a united long-term effort by all his fellow emperors. Instead, not all of them agreed that repression was the best way to deal with Christianity, and in any case, power struggles broke out among them as soon as he retired from office. After years of warfare, by 324 one among the various claimants to power, Constantine I, had defeated all rivals and became the founder of a new dynasty.

Restructuring the Empire: Constantine

Constantine carried forward most of Diocletian's government and army reforms. He built up the army to perhaps as many as half a million troops, some in mobile armies inland and others in central reserve forces in the imperial capitals. To help pay for the extra soldiers, he introduced a new gold coinage that kept its value for many centuries. Like Diocletian, he shared power with fellow emperors, though in his case, they were his sons; and he began building an Eastern capital, the city of New Rome, later called Constantinople, strategically located on the straits between Europe and Asia.

Constantine and Christianity

Constantine's one historic innovation was in the empire's relationship with Christianity. In 313, when he already ruled the empire's Western territories, he and the incumbent Eastern emperor issued the Edict of Milan, once again formally ending persecution and proclaiming complete freedom of worship throughout the empire. As between repressing and tolerating Christianity, the emperors had again made the second choice. But Constantine went on to make a third, and entirely new choice. He began to actually favor Christianity, thereby opening the way for it to become the religion of Rome.

Exactly how and when Constantine came to believe in the Christian God is unknown. His own story was that during the wars that brought him to power, he began using the cross of Jesus as a battle standard—because, he said, he had one day seen the cross hovering above the sun with the words written on it, "Conquer by this sign!" In any case, just like Diocletian, Constantine wanted to win for the empire the support of the divine power that ruled the universe, and to strengthen his authority as emperor by identifying himself with that power—only the power he had in mind was the one God whom the Christians worshiped. Of course, as a Christian, he could not expect to be venerated as a god himself. Still, he retained the majesty and mystery of Diocletian's court, and bishops themselves expressed reverence for him. In a speech before the emperor, his friend and biographer Bishop Eusebius of Caesarea once made a point-by-point parallel between Constantine as ruler of Rome and Christ himself as ruler of the universe.

The Burden of Empire

The Christian version of sacred monarchy had a long history ahead of it. Right down to the nineteenth century, European monarchs would claim to wield power as the chosen ones of God. But Christianity could not solve the urgent problems of the Roman Empire. Rivalries and warfare among emperors and would-be emperors, and frontier wars against barbarians and Persians, continued regardless of religion.

Above all, Christianity did not alter the fact that the empire of Diocletian and Constantine was drawing too heavily from its most precious asset: the willingness of the citizens to bear the burden of keeping it going. Particularly in the West, high taxation and rising prices were as destructive and demoralizing in the long run as the most savage barbarian attacks.

In the third century, many cities of the Western empire had become heavily fortified outposts whose citizens had lost all real self-government. In the fourth century, the cities became centers of social life for wealthy landowners and of Christian religious life, and they found a new source of civic leadership in the clergy. But urban life no longer flourished as it had in the days of the Roman Peace.

Meanwhile, the country dwellers, bankrupted by the endless demands of the tax collectors, came under the domination of a tiny elite of landowners—those who were wealthy enough to carry the burden of taxes or influential enough to gain tax exemptions. The debt-ridden peasants sold out to these wealthy men and became sharecroppers or laborers—giving up part of their harvest or doing farmwork in return for continuing to occupy their holdings. Though they were not human property like the slaves who worked alongside them (p. 98), the peasants became bound to their landlords by ties of personal obedience and subjection. The landowners usually dealt with the government on behalf of their peasants, often shielding them from the tax collectors as best they could, if only in order to exploit the peasants more effectively themselves (see photo).

In spite of their power and wealth, there were limits to the sacrifices that the landowners were willing to make for the emperor. Ever since the troubled times of the third century, emperors had kept them out of the most important government positions. Lower-ranking officers, common soldiers, and barbarian chieftains were promoted to high army commands and leading official positions, while landowners had to be content with wielding local power as counts—officials in charge of a city and its surrounding territory—and as bishops.

Both as counts and as bishops, the landowners were strongly attached to the ideal of Rome and far from disloyal to the emperors, but in practical politics, what counted most for them was not the empire as a whole but their local power and local responsibilities. In reaction against the overmighty state of Diocletian and Constantine, some of the features of the western Europe of the Middle Ages were already beginning to appear—notably the institution of serfdom (p. 193) and the involvement of the Church in matters of worldly government.

The Germanic Invasions of the West

Thanks to the reforms of Diocletian and Constantine, the empire held off barbarian attacks for most of the fourth century. During this time, there was plenty of brutal and exhausting warfare between the Romans and their barbarian neighbors, but in many ways, they were becoming increasingly alike. Leading Romans began to take up barbarian ways: even the

A Year on Lord Julius's Country Estate A fourth-century A.D. mosaic shows a North African mansion surrounded by scenes of country life. At bottom, left to right, a garden boy offers spring flowers to his mistress while she chooses jewelry; a secretary hands his master a scroll addressed "To Lord Julius"; and a fruit picker carries the fall plum harvest. At top, children in winter hoods beat olives out of trees; the mistress fans herself as she arranges a summertime table, and grain grows tall.

Bardo Museum Tunis/Gianni Dagli Orti/The Art Archive

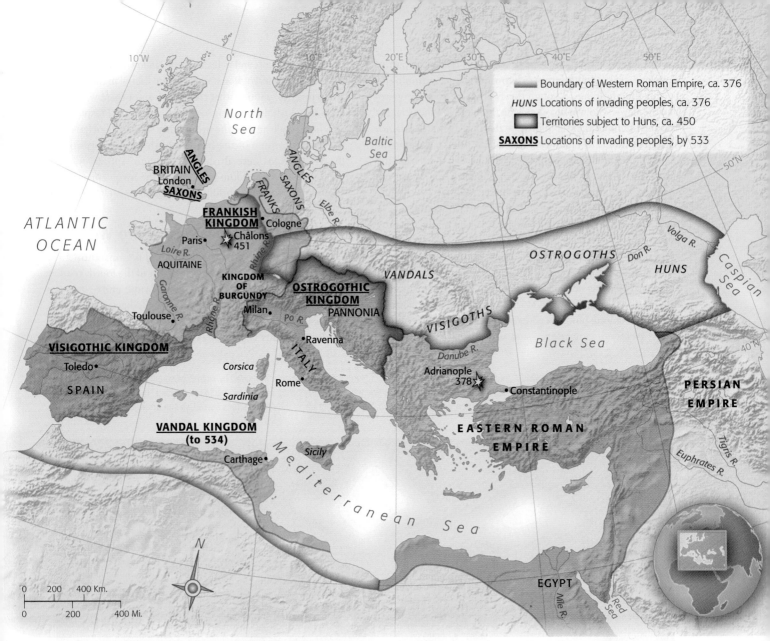

Map 8.2 **Invasions of the Western Empire**

The map shows the locations of the main invading groups when the invasions started in A.D. 376, and the regions that they came to occupy in A.D. 533—after 150 years of struggles with the Romans, with each other, and with less successful invading groups, and just before Eastern Roman efforts at reconquest began. © Cengage Learning

Interactive Map

emperors, when not dressed for court ceremonies, now wore the cloak, tunic, and pants of Germanic chieftains. Some tribal confederacies became Christian, though in the bitter fourth-century conflicts over Christian belief, they mostly adopted the Arian version of the new religion that Rome itself eventually rejected (pp. 145–146).

In this way, the stage was being set for a "merger" between Rome and the barbarians. When it came, the merger involved the entire Western half of the empire and took more than a century to accomplish. Sometimes it took the form of bloody conquest; sometimes, too, it resembled a peaceful takeover.

The Opening Moves

The Germanic barbarians began to move in on the empire not because of any deliberate plan of invasion but as a result of a

shift in the intercontinental balance of forces that had helped Rome endure for so long (p. 116). Shortly before the beginning of the Christian era, a nomadic people living to the north of China, the Huns, had been defeated in conflicts with other nomads who were backed by the Chinese emperors. As a result, they began to move away westward across the steppes, and as often happened with nomad peoples, once they had left their homeland, they gradually migrated and fought their way farther westward, picking up other tribes on the way.

Finally, in 370, they burst into Europe. Though earlier nomad conquerors had ruled parts of Eastern Europe, none had been so well organized, ruthless, and ambitious as the Huns. For three-quarters of a century, they dominated a region stretching from Europe's eastern borders all the way to the Rhine (Map 8.2), causing turmoil among the barbarian peoples of the region. Some tribal confederacies joined the Huns, others were destroyed, and others migrated away from them.

Among those who migrated were the Visigoths, a Christian tribal confederacy living on the lower Danube who in 376 begged to be admitted to Roman territory. Their plea was granted, but the starving tribespeople were ruthlessly oppressed by corrupt Roman officials and provision merchants. Finally, the Visigoths went to war, and at the battle of Adrianople, their horsemen won a crushing victory over the imperial foot soldiers, killing the emperor Valens. His successor, Theodosius I, decided to make the best of the situation. First, he gave the Visigoths a substantial grant of land, and then he used them as allies against a rebellious army commander in the West.

When Theodosius died in 395, he left the empire to his two sons, one ruling the West from Milan and the other ruling the East from Constantinople. It was by now traditional for emperors to arrange for more than one successor to rule within what they still thought of as a single empire, but from now on, there were two continuous lines of rulers in East and West. Meanwhile, the Visigothic chieftain Alaric began to exploit the weakness of Theodosius's successors to gain even more land and power in the empire. Sometimes he played off the Eastern against the Western emperor, sometimes he helped them both against Roman foes, and sometimes he made or threatened to make war on them. Sensing the greater weakness of the West, Alaric finally concentrated his efforts there, and in 408 he led the Visigoths into Italy.

Meanwhile, the West was being penetrated from another direction. In 406 and 407, taking advantage of the Western emperor's problems with the Visigoths, several other Germanic tribal confederacies crossed the frontier on the Rhine River. By 410, they had spread far and wide into Gaul and Spain. In that year, too, the Visigoths, angered by what Alaric saw as the Western emperor's unreasonable refusal to grant them land and Roman civil and military titles, captured and looted Rome itself. Such a thing had not happened in eight hundred years, but it would happen twice again in not much more than a century.

The Crumbling of the Western Empire

During the fifth century, the story of these opening moves in the barbarian takeover was repeated over and over again. The leaders of the tribal confederacies were not deliberately trying to destroy the empire but rather to extract concessions from its rulers. Depending on circumstances, they would fight the Romans or each other or make deals with emperors or local Roman commanders—and the Romans were ready to deal. Rival emperors or would-be emperors sought the help of the invading tribal confederacies in wars against each other, and Eastern emperors troubled by barbarian armies persuaded them to move to the West. Even when the Romans defeated some barbarian group, they simply settled the invaders within the frontiers. And in 451, at the battle of Châlons, Romans and Germans fought side by side to hold off an invasion of Gaul by the Huns under their famous ruler Attila. Within two years, Attila was dead and his people began to retreat back into Asia and disperse.

In any case, by the time the Huns disappeared, not much of the Western empire was left to save. The last Western emperor, Romulus Augustulus, was a teenage boy installed in 475 by his father, a rebellious Roman general, and deposed the next year by a barbarian mercenary commander who did not even bother to kill him.

By the early sixth century, the Western empire had been carved up into a number of territories, each dominated by one or another Germanic tribal confederacy. The Visigoths had moved right across the empire to occupy Spain; the Ostrogoths now held Italy; Africa belonged to the Vandals; the Franks were supreme in most of Gaul as well as across the Rhine, in the western lands of barbarian Germany; and the Angles and Saxons had sailed across the North Sea to conquer Britain (see Map 8.2). Most of the Germanic ruling chieftains had won some kind of recognition and official titles from the Eastern emperors in Constantinople and were in theory the emperor's subordinates. In practice, however, they ruled as independent kings. The kings gave their leading warriors vast landholdings, and the mass of tribal fighters received freehold homesteads.

All the same, Roman normality continued, and the empire's international civilization lived on. Except for the Angles and Saxons in Britain, the invaders were a small minority of the population, and their chieftains and leading warriors revered Rome's way of life. Roman institutions continued to function in the service of the Germanic kings. Roman landowners had to give up a great deal of land to Germanic settlers, but they still had enough left to live cultured lives in their country mansions. Bishops, emperors, and Germanic kings built splendid new churches (see photo on page 113), and in Rome itself, crowds still enjoyed bloodthirsty entertainments in the Colosseum. The main change was that, to the relief of ordinary citizens, tax collectors and army requisition officers came around less often than before.

Meanwhile, in the East the Roman Empire lived on: the emperors in Constantinople still saw themselves as successors of Augustus, and were deferred to as such by the barbarian kings of the West. And in both East and West, Christianity kept the position it had won since Constantine, as the imperial religion of Rome.

LO⁴ Imperial Christianity

In the two hundred years after Constantine, regardless of the empire's problems and the barbarian takeover, Christianity won and kept its position as the religion of the rulers and the masses. But the issues that it had faced in earlier centuries did not go away, and some of them became more urgent and divisive than before. Christian arguments and soul-searching continued, and Christianity developed features as a majority religion many of which have lasted to the present day.

The Twilight of the Gods

Roman rulers had persecuted the Christians as disturbers of the "peace of the gods," but Christians had all along claimed that the truth was exactly the other way around: it was the one true

God with whom Rome must be at peace, and it was the traditional worshipers who were disturbing the peace. Nearly all emperors after Constantine were Christians, who therefore felt responsible to God and the empire for discouraging what they now began to call pagan worship. (In Latin, *paganus* meant a country dweller or a civilian, and most Christians were town dwellers who often thought of the Church as a kind of army.) But actually eliminating traditional religion took time.

The Shift to Christianity

To start with, Constantine began honoring the one God in the same way that emperors had used to honor the gods and goddesses—with splendid buildings. Magnificent Christian places of worship built on the model of imperial basilicas (public halls—p. 113) rose at the burial places of martyrs to rival the temples—for example, the Basilica of St. Peter in Rome (see photo). Temple funds were confiscated to help pay government expenses—which now included subsidies to churches for their charitable work. Meanwhile, bishops devised splendid public festivities to compete with celebrations of gods and goddesses. For instance, Western bishops began celebrating Christmas on December 25—a date not mentioned in the gospel accounts of Jesus's birth that was the same as that of a joyous sun-worshiping festival that greeted the lengthening of daylight. Now that Christianity was prominent and respectable, it seemed much more convincing to many more people than before.

But Christian emperors, like pagan ones before them, had too many other problems to try to systematically crush by force the worship they viewed as disturbing the peace. "Let them have, if they please, their temples of falsehood," said Constantine of the traditional worshipers, and the old and new religions continued alongside each other for several decades after he died in 337. In the 380s and 390s, however, there came a tipping point. The emperor Theodosius issued a series of decrees on such matters as canceling pagan holidays and closing temples—and by that time, Christians were numerous and powerful enough in the cities to save him the trouble of systematic enforcement. Mobs, often egged on by bishops, began smashing images, attacking worshipers, and demolishing temples or commandeering them for use as churches. The Parthenon in Athens, for instance, the 800-year-old temple of the virgin goddess Athena, became a church of the Virgin Mary.

By early in the fifth century, open worship of the gods and goddesses was unusual in the cities, and in the fifth and sixth centuries, it retreated in the villages as well. Regardless of the barbarian takeover of the West, landowners built village churches, appointed parish (local) priests, gave land to support the priests and maintain the churches, and used their power to deter their dependent peasants from the traditional rites. "Beat them . . . cut off their hair . . . bind them in iron shackles," advised Caesarius, a sixth-century bishop of Arles in southern Gaul. One way or another, by A.D. 600 the Church organization was well established in the countryside, and Christianity was probably the religion of the majority in most of the territories that belonged or had once belonged to the Roman Empire (see Map 8.1 on page 133).

The Jews in a Christian World

For the Jews, the shift to Christianity made no difference to their belief in themselves as a minority living among Gentiles who did not know the one truth about the one God. Christians by now mostly believed that God himself was punishing the Jews for rejecting the one truth about him, by scattering them across the earth and depriving them of his presence in the Temple, while they misguidedly submitted to the burden of the Law. Thus, by actually suppressing Judaism, Christians would be going against the judgment of God.

Saint Peter's Basilica, Rome This painting of the church constructed at Constantine's command in the mid-fourth century A.D. was made by assistants of the Renaissance artist Raphael just after the building was demolished to make way for the present one. The scene, showing Constantine "donating" to the pope the power to rule the West, is fictional (pp. 292–293), but the view of the thronged and splendid interior is authentic. Compare the modest house-church of only a century earlier (see photo on page 130).

Scala/Art Resource, NY

Christian mobs did sometimes attack Jews as well as pagans (p. 147), but Theodosius ordered that Jewish religious practices be tolerated, and the bishops did not oppose him. All the same, Jews were forbidden to seek converts or to build new synagogues, intermarriage between them and Christians was severely punished, and they were excluded from government service. In this way, there began an ambivalent Christian policy toward the Jews that was to continue for centuries to come—one of harassing, restricting, and humiliating them while not usually seeking to convert or destroy them as a people.

Christian Thinkers and the Shift to Christianity

Coercion of pagans probably worked because, from the pagan point of view, Constantine and his successors seemed to have broken the "peace of the gods" and gotten away with it. The gods and goddesses, it seemed, were weak, or evil, or did not exist—in which case, what was the point of resisting Christianity?

But then the Western frontiers started to give way, and though no one at the time knew how far that process would go, it was accompanied by a deeply troubling event, the sacking of Rome by the Visigoths in 410. If the God whom the Christians worshiped held worldwide power, both pagans and Christians asked, how was it that he allowed the Roman Empire, which was now so devoted to him, to suffer such a blow?

The Two Cities: Augustine

The thinker who answered this question was a pagan convert and bishop from North Africa, Augustine of Hippo (see Map 8.1 on page 133).

Augustine's conversion was not an easy one. In his *Confessions*, he describes it as a long struggle to turn away from rival philosophies to which he was strongly attracted, as well as from a life of pleasure to which he was compulsively addicted. Like Paul, Augustine believed that his change of life and belief was the work of Christ himself: "For so completely didst thou convert me to Thyself that I desired neither wife nor any hope of this world, but set my feet on the rule of faith."

Like Paul, too, Augustine believed that God predestines those who are to belong in his kingdom and those who will be excluded. Late in his life, he spelled this out. Humans, he argued, cannot influence God's choice of whom to save and whom to damn, for hopeless sinfulness is part of their biological inheritance, passed down from Adam by sexual intercourse. It is God alone who enables his chosen ones, though undeserving, to do good, avoid evil, and receive a place in his kingdom. Augustine's explanation became the classic statement of the doctrine of predestination for future generations of believers.

In his monumental book, *The City of God*, Augustine assured the faithful that the sack of Rome was a spectacular confirmation of basic Christian teachings. All of humanity, he said, is divided into two communities. The first is the "Earthly City" of those who are moved by love of self; the second is

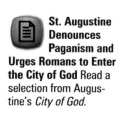 **St. Augustine Denounces Paganism and Urges Romans to Enter the City of God** Read a selection from Augustine's *City of God*.

the "Heavenly City" of the saved, who are moved by love of God. The members of these two communities live mixed together in the present world, but the first will suffer everlasting punishment with the devil, while the second will live eternally with God.

The Heavenly and Earthly cities were not the same as the Church and the empire. Augustine thought that many Christians would not be saved and that God had raised up Rome as a protector of both earthly life and orthodox Christianity. But in an era when Christian worldly evildoers lived alongside Christian zealous believers, and when the empire was struggling to survive, Augustine's arguments made sense. He had adapted to Christianity the ancient Jewish understanding of their place among the Gentiles. Scattered through the world, the citizens of the Heavenly City should live within whatever empires God might raise up and cast down, but they could never fully belong to these. As the Roman Empire continued to fall apart in the West, Augustine's belief only became more compelling.

"Plundering the Egyptians": Christianity and Greco-Roman Culture

Even while emperors and bishops were suppressing the traditional worship, educated Christians faced the problem of what to do with the art and literature with which it was so closely connected. Already Christians had differed over whether they should rely on Greek philosophers for guidance in understanding their own beliefs. But what about the poetry of Homer and Virgil, the oratory of Demosthenes and Cicero, and the art of Phidias and Praxiteles?

In the fourth century, this question became more urgent than before, as pious Christians struggled for the allegiance of the educated elite. How could they command the respect of the elite without being knowledgeable in Greek and Roman culture, and how could they argue persuasively without the skills of eloquence in speech and writing that were a basic part of that culture? But, as the Egyptian Christian ascetic Antony (p. 144) said, "in a person whose thought is pure there is no need for writing"—and it was hard to study Greek and Roman culture without taking a worldly delight in it that might taint the purity of one's thoughts.

To solve this dilemma, learned Christians turned to Old Testament stories of how the Israelites had taken and used the possessions of their enemies—for instance, when they escaped from oppression in Egypt they had "plundered the Egyptians" of gold and silver and fine clothing. In the same way, Christians must plunder all that was good and useful in the international culture of Greece and Rome, and reject all that was useless and wicked.

Among those who followed the Israelite example was one of the greatest of Christian scholars, Jerome, who lived about the same time as Augustine. Born in Illyria (see Map 7.1 on page 117), he went to Rome, studied Latin and Greek, and developed a guilty love of pagan literature; but at the orders of the pope, he also used his knowledge to revise the existing Latin translation of the New Testament by comparing it with the original Greek version. That left the Old Testament, however, which had originally been written in Hebrew and had been translated into Latin from a Greek version originally made by Jewish scholars.

hermit
An ascetic who lives alone, removed from ordinary society.

monastery
The residence of an ascetic community.

Finally, Jerome decided he must be either a "Ciceronian" (an admirer and imitator of Cicero, the renowned orator, thinker, and letter writer of the Roman Republic—p. 108) or a Christian. He left Rome for the Holy Land, where he learned Hebrew—a rare accomplishment for a Gentile. Then he harnessed his new knowledge to the mighty Christian task of translating the Old Testament directly into Latin. His new version eventually became part of the Vulgate (the "commonly used version"), the standard Bible of the Church in the West. Meanwhile, Jerome wrote Latin letters to his friends that combined the intimacy and eloquence that he had learned from Cicero's letters with Christian guidance—as well as not-so-Christian malice against people he disliked. In ways like these, Jerome and other learned Christians were able to distance themselves from the pagan culture of Greece and Rome yet also preserve and benefit from its legacy.

"White Martyrdom": Hermits, Monks, and Nuns

There had always been Christian men and women who lived an ascetic life, breaking the ties that bound them to this world—pleasure, comfort, marriage, and children—and living a life of prayer and self-denial that bound them to the world to come. Usually, they had lived their lives in families and households and had helped out with tasks such as teaching and charity in the churches to which they had belonged.

As Christianity grew in the third century, many more people followed the path of "white martyrdom" (without the shedding of blood, as opposed to "red martyrdom"). Furthermore, they did so more radically, withdrawing from family, household, and everyday church life. And when Christianity became the imperial religion, this kind of asceticism became a mass movement.

Partly, this was because many more wealthy people than before were pious believers. A rich gentleman like Anthony, who late in the third century gave all his possessions to the poor, lived alone in the Egyptian wilderness, and dug himself a garden plot like a field hand, was obeying the commandment of Jesus and imitating his humility. Likewise, Macrina, a well-off lady in Anatolia in the mid-fourth century, used her property to set up a community of like-minded virgins who shared the work, food, and bedding of the maidservants. And poorer believers welcomed a life where toil, hardship, strict obedience, and floggings—all normal features of ascetic communities—were not just a result of injustice or bad luck but steps on the narrow path to God's kingdom.

Men and Women Alone with God; Ascetic Brothers and Sisters

Many ascetics were solitary seekers after God or **hermits** like Anthony—or like Mary the Egyptian, a free-living young woman from Alexandria in the fourth century who took a pleasure trip to Jerusalem, repented of her way of life in the holy city, and heard an inner voice: "If you cross over Jordan you will find real peace!" She crossed the river eastward out into the desert and lived there for forty-eight years, often struggling with sexual thoughts "as though with wild beasts." In the fourth and fifth centuries, many believers moved out into the eastern deserts, as well as into the forests and mountains of Italy and Gaul, hoping through hardship and inner struggle to come to the joyful awareness that "I and God—we're alone in the world."

Hermits tended to attract followers, however, and not everyone who wanted to live an ascetic life was eager to do so completely on their own. Women's ascetic communities or **monasteries** dated back to the third century, and one of the earliest monasteries for men was founded early in the fourth century on an island in the Nile by Pachomius, a former soldier. He laid the place out like an army camp and imposed a strict schedule, hard manual work, and fierce discipline on his "recruits."

In the centuries of the shift to Christianity and the barbarian takeover, many revered ascetics founded monasteries across the Mediterranean lands and western Europe, and two in particular devised ways of life for ascetic communities that were disciplined but more varied and harmonious than that of Pachomius and came to be followed by women as well as men. About 360, Basil of Caesarea, a younger brother of Macrina, founded a monastery on one of his family's estates in Anatolia. In 529, after the Western empire's collapse, an Italian nobleman, Benedict of Nursia, founded the monastery of Monte Cassino on a towering hilltop south of Rome.

 The Rule of St. Benedict: Work and Pray Read a short passage from Benedict's *Rule*.

Both Basil's and Benedict's monks combined regular services of prayer and praise to God by day and night with labor in the fields, at handicrafts, or in study—for as Benedict said, "Work is prayer." New members had to spend a period as "novices," to make sure that they were up to the ascetic life, before taking perpetual vows of poverty, chastity, and obedience. They were to live in harmony as "brothers" under an abbot (from the Hebrew word for "father"), whom they were bound to obey but whom they would themselves elect. Within a few centuries, Benedict's rule (regulations for ascetic community life) became the model for both monks and nuns in the West, and Basil's rule became the model in the East.

Ascetics and the World

In the age of imperial Christianity, however, even those who sought distance from the world could

> " *Idleness is the enemy of the soul. And therefore, at fixed times, the brothers ought to be occupied in manual labour; and again, at fixed times, in sacred reading.* "
> —Benedict of Nursia, A.D. 529

not help remaining a part of it. The religion whose founder had said that "Many are called, but few are chosen" was now the faith of millions, and believers could no longer look to the gods and goddesses in the daily business of life. For help in finding a place in the world to come as well as for guidance in this world, ordinary Christians often looked to ascetics.

The ascetic feats of hermits, for example, gave them compelling authority over ordinary Christians. The deserts of Egypt and Syria were not far from the river valleys with their towns and villages, so hermits were actually easy to visit and consult. One of the most famous hermits of the fifth century was Simeon Stylites (the "Pillar-Dweller") of Syria. In an effort to limit his contacts with visitors who wished to witness his holiness, he lived for many years on a small, unenclosed platform at the top of a pillar (see photo). This did not prevent crowds of pilgrims—including the Eastern emperor himself—from seeking Simeon's advice on personal and business matters as well as spiritual ones.

When Simeon died, the nearby city of Antioch fought off an effort by distant Constantinople to get hold of his body, and preserved it in a splendid building, according to what was by then a well-established custom of venerating "white martyrs," like "red martyrs," after their deaths. The dead Simeon was a **saint** (literally, a "holy person") who was both close to God in his kingdom and yet watched over the city where his body was preserved, and who could intervene with God at the request of humans, as a favored official might intervene with the emperor at the request of ordinary citizens.

Monks and nuns, too, had their saints, and their communities came to be considered essential to the well-being of Christianity as a whole. Ordinary Christians could be helped into heaven by their prayers—or by giving a son or daughter to God, so that in time, the majority of monks and nuns came to be "draftees" rather than volunteers. At the command of bishops, rank-and-file monks swarmed out of their monasteries to destroy temples or intimidate believers in rival versions of Christianity. And leading monks often became bishops, for their closeness to God made it seem likely that they would best withstand the money-making and power-abusing opportunities that were now open to rulers of the Church.

Rival Orthodoxies

Ever since the first disputes over Gentile converts and the Jewish Law, Christians had argued over the beliefs and practices of their religion. After the second-century rise of the Catholic Church, the arguments became for a while less bitter and widespread, but exactly in the era of Constantine they became fiercer than ever before.

Partly, this was because the arguments concerned basic and long-held ideas about the God and the Christ in whom Christians believed. God, they thought, was not just the almighty

Creator and Father. God was also the world-upholding and world-redeeming Son, and the Holy Spirit, the guide of individual believers and the whole Church. Furthermore, the eternal divine Son was also Jesus the mortal human being. Yet Christians also believed that there was only one true God, and that there was an infinite divide between God and humans. Was there some logical way in which God could be both one and three, and Christ could be both God and human?

The Arian and Nicene Faiths

On the whole, Christians had managed to live with this problem until about the time that Constantine came to supreme power, when a learned priest in Alexandria, Arius, proposed a solution. The Son, said Arius, was indeed divine, but since he was also human, he was not the equal of the Father, but had been brought into being by the Father as part of his plan for the universe. This view was acceptable to many bishops and ordinary believers in the Eastern empire. To many others in the East, however, and to the vast majority in the West, it seemed a wicked heresy that made Christ more human than divine. And if the bishops could not agree among themselves, who was to say which view was orthodoxy and which was heresy?

This was a tormenting situation for believers who needed to be sure of the one truth about the one God, including for the newly Christian emperor Constantine. Accordingly, in A.D. 325 he took the unprecedented step of summoning the bishops to a general council at Nicaea in Asia Minor. He hoped that the Holy Spirit would guide them to the truth, which they would then proclaim with their united authority.

Pushed by the emperor's longing for consensus, the bishops drew up a formal **creed** (statement of belief) restating the traditional beliefs in a way that rejected the Arian view—in particular, the Son was "of the same being as the Father" and yet "was made flesh, becoming human." But not long after the council broke up, this "Nicene" consensus (as proclaimed at Nicaea) began to unravel. Eastern bishops sympathetic to Arius felt that this wording suggested there was no difference between the Father and the Son, and once back in their cities they in turn opposed the creed as a heresy. The disputes soon restarted, and continued for nearly three centuries.

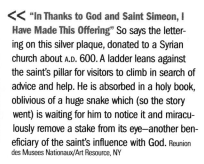

<< **"In Thanks to God and Saint Simeon, I Have Made This Offering"** So says the lettering on this silver plaque, donated to a Syrian church about A.D. 600. A ladder leans against the saint's pillar for visitors to climb in search of advice and help. He is absorbed in a holy book, oblivious of a huge snake which (so the story went) is waiting for him to notice it and miraculously remove a stake from its eye—another beneficiary of the saint's influence with God. Reunion des Musees Nationaux/Art Resource, NY

hierarchy
In Christianity, the clergy with their system of ranks from highest to lowest.

patriarch
In early Christianity, the five leading bishops—those of Rome, Alexandria, Antioch, Constantinople, and Jerusalem.

Three Centuries of Conflict

What kept the arguments going was not just the importance of the actual issues but also the new position of Christianity itself. Divisions among Christians now involved whole populations and their powerful bishops, as well as rivalries among the bishops themselves. The emperors were also involved, both as Christian believers with their own views and as rulers who needed the Church's support—and rival emperors were liable to have differing views. And most Christians by now agreed that there ought to be a Catholic consensus on belief, so that the rival faiths battled all the more fiercely to capture the consensus for themselves. A fourth-century observer, Ammianus Marcellinus, himself a pagan but mostly respectful of Christianity, said of the disputes: "No wild beasts are such dangerous enemies to man as Christians are to one another."

History of Arian Doctrine (http://www.earlychristian history.info/arius.html) Learn more about the Arian doctrine and its followers.

By the end of the fourth century, the arguments and power struggles had played out in such a way that most bishops in the empire were prepared to reject the Arian faith. But the fifth-century Germanic invaders had mostly been converted to Christianity by Arian missionaries, and as rulers of the West, they kept their faith for a century or more until they finally adopted the Nicene faith of their Roman subjects. Meanwhile, many eastern bishops who opposed the Arian faith swung to the opposite extreme, and declared that since Jesus was the divine Son of God, he was not really or only secondarily a human being—and they, too, proclaimed their faith to be orthodoxy and other faiths to be heresy.

Christian arguments and power struggles continued in Egypt, Syria, and other eastern lands until the seventh century, when the Arabs conquered the region and brought a new mono-theism, Islam. The overwhelming majority in the remaining Christian lands was committed to the Nicene faith, and in this way it became more or less unchallenged orthodoxy. In spite of all objections, Nicene Christians insisted that the only way to describe God and Christ was by fully accepting the seemingly opposed ideas of one and three, divine and human. God was a Trinity of three separate "persons" who were nevertheless a single "being." Jesus was the almighty and eternal Son, but he was just as much a human being subject to change and death. This understanding of God, as above and beyond what seems logical to the human mind, has remained basic to Christianity ever since.

> "*Corrupt and unworthy bishops, and zealous and saintly ones, would be among the most hated and the most beloved figures in the public life of Christian peoples for many centuries to come.*"

Bishops and Emperors

Already before Constantine, Christianity had been growing together with Rome, but now, with the shift to Christianity, Rome had two closely interlocking power structures. One was that of the empire, headed by emperors, officials, and army commanders, and the other was that of the Church, headed by the bishops.

The Bishops

The Church's power structure or **hierarchy** (from the Greek words for "sacred government") from deacons to bishops was already well developed before Constantine, but now it grew several new layers. Big-city bishops were formally recognized as "metropolitans" or "archbishops" with authority over bishops of neighboring smaller cities. The authority of the bishops of Rome, Antioch, and Alexandria over wide regions of the empire was also formally accepted, and in the fifth century, the bishop of the empire's new Eastern capital of Constantinople gained the same status. Together with the bishop of the holy city of Jerusalem, these leading bishops acquired the title of **patriarch**, which had earlier only been used for Abraham and other revered early Israelites (from the Greek for "forefather"). These arrangements were mostly legislated by councils of the whole Church, six of which met in various Eastern cities from the fourth to the sixth centuries. All of them were called in connection with the struggles over belief, but they also dealt with questions of Church organization.

Within their cities, bishops were now just as important as the local imperial officials, the counts. They presided over awe-inspiring services in imposing public buildings. They controlled massive resources of land and money, built up by contributions from wealthy donors and supplemented by government subsidies. This wealth enabled them and their clergy to live comfortably and to provide society's main safety net for sick and poor people. They socialized with local landowning families, to which they themselves often belonged; a bishop's position was a valuable family asset, and in any case, many landowners now felt the same devotion to the Church that they had traditionally felt for the empire. Bishops also wielded strong influence over ordinary believers, who still had a say in choosing them alongside the local clergy and wealthy and prominent local men and women. They could unleash riots against pagans, heretics, Jews, and sometimes each other: in A.D. 366, fighting between supporters of two rival candidates to become bishop of Rome left 137 dead in a single day.

Naturally, there were bishops who valued their positions, as Ammianus Marcellinus put it, because "they are sure of rich gifts from upper-class ladies, they can ride in coaches, dress splendidly, and serve such lavish dishes that their cuisine outshines royal banquets." But he also allowed that there were bishops "whose extreme frugality in eating and drinking, their simple clothing, and their downcast eyes, prove to the eternal deity and his genuine worshipers the purity and modesty of their lives." Corrupt and unworthy bishops, and zealous and saintly ones, would be among the most hated and the most beloved figures in the public life of Christian peoples for many centuries to come.

The Emperors

Apart from the actual clergy, there was now one more level in the hierarchy—the emperors. The Christian rulers of Rome considered themselves instruments of God and responsible to him for the welfare of their subjects, including in the world to come. That gave them the right to a large say in the Church's doings, and besides, the Church had become so powerful that they could not rule effectively without this influence.

It was emperors, not bishops, who called general councils, which often fell into line with the version of the faith that the incumbent ruler preferred. Arian-leaning emperors banished and replaced Nicene-leaning bishops and vice versa. Bishops hung around imperial courts, hoping to persuade emperors to favor their version of the faith or to appoint their friends and family members to well-paid government jobs. A succession of Eastern emperors was able to build up the bishops of their capital city, Constantinople, to patriarch status against the resistance of the bishops of Rome, Alexandria, and Antioch. And in cities like Constantinople that were close under the eye of an emperor, it was he, rather than the local clergy and people, who chose the bishop.

Bishops did sometimes defy emperors. Bishop Athanasius of Alexandria, for example, was an unbending supporter of the Nicene faith about the middle of the third century. He spent years in hiding from Constantine's Arian-leaning son Constantius, writing attacks on the emperor as a heretic and persecutor who interfered in Church matters that were none of his business. Near the end of the century, Bishop Ambrose of Milan on two famous occasions made the emperor Theodosius actually do his bidding. First of all, he refused to continue with a service that Theodosius was attending until the emperor agreed to drop punishments he had ordered for a Christian mob that had destroyed a synagogue in a town on the Euphrates frontier. Later, he persuaded the emperor to repent humbly and publicly for having ordered an army massacre of rioters in a town in Greece.

 An Emperor Brought to Heel: St. Ambrose and Emperor Theodosius Read Bishop Ambrose scolding the emperor Theodosius.

When emperors stepped out of line by favoring heretics, giving Jews equal protection with Christians, or committing atrocities against Christian citizens, the balance of power between them and bishops could shift. Furthermore, the barbarian takeover and the end of the rule of the emperors in the West led to a larger shift in the balance, not only between emperors and bishops, but also among the bishops themselves—the growing authority of the bishops of Rome.

The Popes

In the East, where Christianity began, many cities could claim a connection with Jesus himself and his most revered early followers. In the West, there was only one such city, Rome. Rome was the place of martyrdom not only of Paul, the apostle to the Gentiles, but also of Peter, whom Jesus had called "the rock on which I will build my Church." As a result, the bishops of Rome were uniquely respected by Christians in the West, and other bishops often accepted their advice and instructions. But most Christians were still to be found in the empire's Eastern lands, where the bishops took most seriously the advice and instructions of the bishops of Antioch and Alexandria. In case of dispute, the Easterners usually "agreed to differ" with the distant Roman bishops.

The fourth-century changes in Christianity brought the Roman bishops greater authority in the West than ever before. There were more believers to look up to them, the hierarchy that took their advice and instructions was more powerful and better organized, and since emperors no longer governed from Rome, there was no one in the city itself who outranked them. Above all, in the disputes over belief the Roman bishops and the Western hierarchy were usually Nicene believers, while Eastern bishops argued and general councils wavered. Surely, thought many in the West, the best judge of orthodoxy and heresy was no council, and no emperor to whose wishes a council might bow. About the middle of the fourth century, the Roman bishops began quoting Jesus's words to Peter as proof that they were the supreme Christ-appointed guides of the whole Church, East and West.

In the fifth century, as the Western empire collapsed and the Eastern empire continued to be troubled by disputes over belief, the Roman bishops insisted more and more on their guiding role in the Church. At the end of the century, Bishop Gelasius told an Eastern emperor: "Twofold are the ways in which this world is mainly ruled: by the sacred authority of bishops and by the imperial power. The burden on the priests is heavier, because they will be accountable to the Lord at his judgment even for the souls of rulers . . . in matters of religion you should not take the lead but rather submit." And when Gelasius spoke of bishops, he had in mind "specially the Vicar [deputy] of the blessed Peter." Not long after Gelasius's time, the Vicars of Peter acquired a title that marked how special they were. Traditionally, Christians had often respectfully called priests and bishops "daddy" (in Latin, *papa*), to show their childlike love for their spiritual fathers. Now, Westerners stopped using that name except for the bishop of Rome, who became the one and only *papa*—the pope.

Meanwhile, the Eastern emperors went on taking the lead in religious matters in the lands they ruled, and rather than submitting to the popes, they built up the patriarchs of Constantinople to become leading bishops in the Eastern empire. The popes and the patriarchs shared the Nicene faith and considered themselves to belong to one undivided Church. In both West and East, the power structures of the rulers and the Church continued to be tightly interlocked. Patriarchs sometimes resisted Eastern emperors, and popes sometimes deferred to Western kings. But in the East, the rulers reigned over an empire where they were just as responsible for their subjects' salvation and the orthodoxy of the Church's beliefs as the clergy—and in the West, the popes were beginning to carve out for themselves and the clergy a separate and higher realm.

 Listen to a synopsis of Chapter 8.

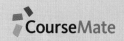

MEDIEVAL CIVILIZATION,

500–1300

The conversion to Christianity of the peoples of the Roman Empire and the Germanic invasions of the empire's western territories were completed by about the year 500. Together with the conquest of lands stretching from Spain to the borders of India by Islam in the seventh century, they bring us to a new phase of Western history. These shifts in civilization opened the thousand years of the Middle Ages—the "in-between times" separating the ancient from the modern period (p. 2).

Geographically, the Middle Ages were the European phase of Western development, when a new and distinctive civilization emerged on the soil of Europe, spread throughout that region, and reached the highest levels of cultural achievement. In religion, this was the era when the Christian faith and Church spread through all of Europe and set the tone of Western civilization in every activity. In government and social life, it was the heyday of an elite whose power came mainly from the fact that its members were owners of land and leaders of warriors— the social group that came to be known, on account of its overwhelming prestige, as the nobility. It was also a time when Western civilization came into closer touch with the other civilizations of the Eastern Hemisphere than before, but was inferior to them in wealth, practical knowledge, and social organization.

In these ways, the Christian Europe of the Middle Ages was very different from the secular-minded, democratic, and world-dominating West of the present day.

The modern West is separated from the Middle Ages by a new series of spectacular shifts in civilization that began about two hundred years before 1500 (the "official" end date of the Middle Ages), went on for more than a century afterward (see Part Three), and were followed by yet more shifts that have continued down to the present (Parts Four and Five). Because of these shifts, Christian Europe is often regarded today as the most alien of the Wests of the past. The word *medieval* (from the Latin for "Middle Ages," *medium aevum*) is often used to mean the same as "brutal," "superstitious," "closed-minded," "unhygienic," and other unpleasant adjectives that people today like to think no longer apply to Western civilization.

In fact, many of the things that are thought of today as typically "medieval" in the bad sense were widespread features of traditional civilization in general. Disease, poverty, and torture were just as common in ancient Greece and Rome, for instance, as in the Middle Ages, and in reality they are also normal features of present-day civilization. Christian Europe also shared many of its more praiseworthy features with other civilizations. It inherited many of its cultural and intellectual traditions from ancient Greece and Rome and developed these traditions in many creative ways. In spite of religious hatreds, Christian Europe also learned a great deal from the neighbor and rival civilization of Islam. But the civilization with which Christian Europe has the most in common, in spite of all shifts and changes, is the present-day West.

The list of basic features of the West of today that originated in medieval times is a long one. It was in the Middle Ages that Western civilization first came to be made up of many ethnic groups, each with its own version of a common culture, and of many independent states, all competing fiercely with each other. English, Spanish, and most of the other languages of the West were first spoken and written in the Middle Ages. England, France, Russia, and many other present-day European countries first came into existence and practiced the earliest forms of representative government. Christianity itself remains the overwhelmingly predominant religion of the West. Everyday practices of today, such as arranging lists in alphabetical order so as to make the items easy to find, or putting hops into beer to make it taste interestingly bitter, also began in medieval times. In all these and many other ways, the modern West is still the child of the Christian Europe of the Middle Ages.

CHAPTER 9

AFTER ROME,
500–700

LEARNING OBJECTIVES

AFTER READING THIS CHAPTER, YOU SHOULD BE
ABLE TO DO THE FOLLOWING:

LO¹ Describe the way of life of the Germanic barbarians,
and discuss their role in preserving and spreading
Roman and Christian civilization.

LO² Trace the expansion and contraction of the Eastern
empire, and explain how Byzantium served as the
main custodian of ancient Greek culture while also
sponsoring new art and architecture.

LO³ Discuss the emergence of Islam as a new religion
and culture, and explain why the rise of Islam was an
important event for European peoples.

The Granger Collection, New York

> **"THE UPHEAVAL OF THE EARLY MIDDLE AGES ENDED NOT IN A COLLAPSE OF CIVILIZATION BUT IN ITS RENEWAL, AND THE FIRST TWO EARLY MEDIEVAL CENTURIES SET THE PATTERNS FOR HOW THIS RENEWAL WOULD LATER TAKE PLACE IN WESTERN AND EASTERN EUROPE."**

The two centuries after the fall of Rome were a time of turmoil in Europe that would continue for five hundred years—a half-millennium that counts as the "early" part of the Middle Ages. As with the upheaval in ancient civilization two thousand years before (pp. 32–33), the upheaval of the early Middle Ages ended not in a collapse of civilization but in its renewal, and the first two early **medieval** centuries set the patterns for how this renewal would later take place in western and eastern Europe.

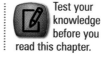

Test your knowledge before you read this chapter.

In the Germanic kingdoms that had taken over the western half of the Roman Empire, Roman institutions gradually stopped working, cities ceased to be centers of trade and social life, and warfare became more important than education and culture in the lives of the upper classes. But missionary-monks brought Christianity and Roman traditions to peoples beyond the empire's old frontiers, and in the largest Germanic kingdom, carved out of Roman and barbarian lands by the Franks, the kings ruled in partnership with warrior-landowners and Church leaders. Both the missionaries and the Frankish rulers created precedents for spectacular later renewal in western Europe.

Meanwhile, the Roman Empire's surviving eastern half contributed to western Europe's chaos by efforts at reconquest, and then itself came under attack by newly powerful neighbors. By 700, the emperors in the eastern capital, Constantinople, ruled only Anatolia and a few patches of land in Europe, and their state had become more Greek than Roman. To mark the difference, the remaining empire is today usually called by its capital's original Greek name, Byzantium (**bi-ZAN-tee-uhm**).

What do you think?

The early medieval period was a "dark age" in Western history.

Strongly Disagree						Strongly Agree
1	2	3	4	5	6	7

« The Baptism of Clovis An ivory plaque made about A.D. 900 depicts the founding event of the Kingdom of the Franks four centuries earlier. The conquering chieftain Clovis is humbly naked and up to his waist in water. The Roman aristocrat Remigius, bishop of Reims, touches Clovis's head as he speaks the words of baptism. Clotilde, Clovis's already Christian queen, looks on; the Holy Spirit, in the form of a dove, brings holy oil in token of God's blessing upon the fusion of Frank, Roman, and Christian.

medieval
Refers to the distinctive civilization of the Middle Ages, which developed in Europe after the disintegration of the Roman Empire and before the emergence of the modern West.

noble
A member of the warrior-landowner group that formed the elite of medieval Europe.

However, Byzantium was still a powerful state and a center of Christianity and Greek culture. From Byzantium, renewal would spread to the ethnic group of barbarians that took over most of eastern Europe, the Slavs, and Byzantine cultural impulses would reach both halves of Europe. And the empire kept up links of trade and travel across the Middle East and northern Africa, in spite of losing those regions to the Arabs with their new monotheism, Islam.

The Muslim conquest of Christian Syria, Palestine, and North Africa redefined Christianity as geographically European for the rest of the Middle Ages, and it led to many centuries of warfare between Christians and Muslims. But as Europe renewed itself, it would also find in Islam a source of trading wealth and cultural inspiration, and a gateway to more distant civilizations of the Eastern Hemisphere. Apart from Christianity, the religion that would have the greatest impact on medieval Europe in war and peace would be Islam.

LO¹ The Germanic Kingdoms of the West

The Germanic invaders of the West were a small minority who in time were mostly assimilated by the Roman peoples they conquered. All the same, some of their traditions lasted, and these same traditions persisted more strongly among Germanic peoples farther north in Europe who did not enter the empire. Either way, the way of life of the Germanic barbarians influenced various features of civilization in western Europe, alongside Roman culture and institutions and Christianity.

The Germanic Barbarians

Over several centuries of close contact with Rome, the Germanic peoples had developed an elite of powerful chieftains and their war bands of leading warriors (p. 135). When they took over the empire's western territories in the fifth century, the chieftains shared newly acquired land with

> "The Germanic takeover actually led to the spread of Roman and Christian civilization beyond Rome's frontiers."

CHRONOLOGY

FIFTH CENTURY	Angles and Saxons invade Britain
486	Clovis leads Frankish confederacy against Romans and rival Germanic invaders in Gaul
527–565	Reign of Emperor Justinian in the Eastern empire
542	Plague hits Egypt, then spreads throughout the Mediterranean area and much of western Europe
568	Lombards conquer most of northern Italy
570–632	Life of Muhammad
595	Missionaries sent by the pope begin to convert the pagans of England
711	Muslim invasion of Spain
800	Slavs occupy almost all of eastern Europe

the members of their war bands, who became owners of vast properties. They took up Roman ways and often intermarried with Roman aristocrats, but they also changed the way of life of the relatively unmilitary Roman landowners to form a new elite of warrior-landowners. Landownership and war leadership came to be marks of what came to be called the **nobles** for the next thousand years.

More "democratic" tribal institutions, notably regular assemblies of rank-and-file warriors and farmers (p. 135), did not long survive the move into the Roman Empire. Even among the tribes that did not move into the empire, the spread of Christian and Roman civilization increased the power of chieftains and their favored warriors at the expense of tribal assemblies. All the same, a tradition of popular participation in government continued, especially in the field of law and justice. In many western European countries in the early Middle Ages, groups of ordinary freemen would be summoned and sworn to reveal their collective knowledge of the truth, in such matters as identifying the originator of a blood feud, establishing ownership of property, or accusing wrongdoers.

Many Germanic pagan traditions persisted in folklore and symbolism even after the adoption of Christianity. Thus, in the English language, the names of Tiu, the Germanic war god;

Woden, who was thought to take a special interest in the affairs of the human race; Thor, the thunder god; and Frigg, the fertility goddess, are still honored in the names of four days of the week: Tuesday, Wednesday, Thursday, and Friday. Even the climactic day of the Christian calendar received its name, in many northern lands, from Eostre, the ancient Germanic goddess of spring.

Perhaps the most important result of the Germanic takeover was that, in the long run, it led to the disappearance of the already crumbling frontier between Roman and barbarian Europe. In Germany, the Low Countries, and the Scandinavian lands farther north, there remained many Germanic peoples who had not moved into the Roman Empire. These barbarians now began to look southward in their turn for trade, conquest, Roman culture, and Christianity. Meanwhile, the Germanic rulers of former Roman lands were less cautious than the Romans had been about expanding their power north and east of the Rhine and Danube Rivers. In this way, the Germanic takeover actually led to the spread of Roman and Christian civilization beyond Rome's frontiers.

The Kingdom of the Franks

In not much more than two centuries, many of the Germanic kingdoms fell victim to Byzantine efforts at reconquest, to the power of Islam, or to each other. However, two Germanic groups that established themselves for the long term, the Anglo-Saxons and the Franks, together with the non-Germanic Irish, played a leading role in preserving and spreading Roman and Christian civilization.

England and Ireland

From the area that is now Denmark and northwestern Germany, two tribal groups, the Angles and the Saxons, sailed over the North Sea and invaded Britain during the fifth century (see Map 8.2 on page 140). They overran the native Britons and established several kingdoms of their own. Unlike in other conquered regions of the Roman Empire, it was the natives who were assimilated by the invaders, except in outlying territories that came to be known as Wales and Scotland. In the rest of Britain, Germanic dialects and customs took firm root, and the country came to be known as "the land of the Angles," or England. Though pagan when they first settled, most of the Angles and Saxons became Christian during the seventh century, partly as a result of missionary efforts sponsored by the papacy from 595 onward and partly under the influence of two neighboring, already Christian nations: the Irish and the Franks.

Ireland was the first territory outside the frontiers of Rome to which Christianity spread when the empire collapsed. A remnant of the Celtic peoples who had dominated much of western Europe centuries earlier (p. 100), the Irish had never been conquered by Rome. In the turmoil of the fifth century, Patrick, a native Briton who had been captured by Irish raiders, brought Christianity to the island, and Christian monasteries soon came to dominate the tribal life of the country. Under their influence, a unique Irish civilization grew up, based on the Christian faith, Roman literature, and the heritage of Irish barbarian culture. This civilization, in turn, came to influence much of western Europe during the early Middle Ages.

Clovis and the Franks

The most powerful Germanic kingdom was that of the Franks, who were to give their name to modern France. The Franks were originally a loose tribal confederacy along the lower Rhine River, just outside the Roman frontier. In 486, as the Western empire was falling apart, a Frankish chieftain, Clovis, led the confederacy in campaigns against the Romans and rival Germanic invaders in Gaul. From then on, Clovis's family, the **Merovingians** (from the Frankish word for "children of Merovech," their mythical forefather), were the ruling dynasty of all the Franks. Clovis and his successors pushed southward and also eastward from their original homeland, until they ruled all of present-day France and much of western and southern Germany (see Map 8.2 on page 140). As the Franks became Christian and adopted Roman ways, so also did some of their subject tribes to the east of the Rhine. In this way, the spread of Christian and Roman civilization beyond the empire's former frontiers began on the mainland of western Europe.

> **Merovingians**
> The first ruling dynasty of all the Franks, founded by Clovis and named after his family's mythical forefather, Merovech.

 In Search of Ancient Ireland (http://www.pbs.org/wnet/ancientireland/index.html) Explore the truth behind Irish legends and learn more about Irish influences on western Europe.

Anglo-Saxon Treasure Shortly after A.D. 600 a local ruler was buried aboard a ship in a mound at Sutton Hoo, near the eastern English seashore. Among the treasures buried with him was a locally made purse covered by this eight-inch-long lid, decorated with images of men, wolves, and eagles and delicate abstract patterns, all made of gold, garnets, and colored glass. Anglo-Saxon England was a land of skilled craftspeople and of wealthy rulers who were at home on both land and sea.
Courtesy of the Trustees of the British Museum

THE CONVERSION OF ENGLAND: INSTRUCTIONS TO MISSIONARIES

In 595, Pope Gregory I the Great sent a Roman monk, Augustine, to convert the Anglo-Saxon kingdom of Kent, a territory in southern England. About 150 years afterward, the Anglo-Saxon monk Bede of Jarrow included in his *Ecclesiastical History of the English People* a letter from Gregory to the leader of a later group of missionaries, giving instructions to be conveyed to Augustine on how to make Christianity easier for pagans to adopt. Gregory's strategy involved building the new faith by using the foundations of the old one.

When Almighty God shall bring you to the most reverend Bishop Augustine, our brother, tell him what I have, after mature deliberation on the affairs of the English, determined upon, namely, that the temples of the idols in that nation ought not to be destroyed, but let the idols that are in them be destroyed; let holy water be made and sprinkled in the said temples; let altars be erected, and relics placed. For if those temples are well built, it is requisite that they be converted from the worship of devils to the service of the true God; that the nation, seeing that their temples are not destroyed, may remove error from their hearts and, knowing and adoring the true God, may the more familiarly resort to the places to which they have been accustomed.

And because they have been used to slaughter many oxen in the sacrifices to devils, some solemnity must be substituted for them on this account, as, for instance, that on the day of the dedication, or of the nativities of the holy martyrs whose relics are there deposited, they may build themselves huts of the boughs of trees about those churches which have been turned to that use from temples, and celebrate the solemnity with religious feasting, no more offering beasts to the devil, but killing cattle to the praise of God in their eating, and returning thanks to the Giver of all things for their sustenance; to the end that, whilst some outward gratifications are permitted them, they may the more easily consent to the inward consolations of the grace of God.

For there is no doubt that it is impossible to efface everything at once from their obdurate minds, because he who endeavors to ascend to the highest place rises by degrees or steps and not by leaps. Thus the Lord made himself known to the people of Israel in Egypt; and yet he allowed them to use the sacrifices which they were wont to offer to the devil in his own worship, commanding them in his sacrifice to kill beasts to the end that, changing their hearts, they might lay aside one part of the sacrifice, whilst they retained another; that whilst they offered the same beasts which they were wont to offer, they should offer them to God, and not to idols, and thus they would no longer be the same sacrifices.

EXPLORING THE SOURCE

1. What would have been the benefits of this method of conversion as opposed to using more aggressive tactics? What would have been the disadvantages?

2. Are you familiar with any present-day Christian practices that originated from pagan roots?

Source: James Harvey Robinson, ed., Readings in European History (Boston: Ginn, 1904), 1:100–101.

Clovis now began to build a stable system for governing his territories. He shared the conquered land with his leading warriors but made sure that the lion's share went to himself and his descendants. He let the existing Roman elite of landowners, counts, and bishops keep much of their property and their positions in church and state. He further strengthened his rule by converting to the Nicene Christianity (p. 145) of his Roman subjects (see photo on page 150). At a time when many Germanic invaders were Arian Christians, this won him the enthusiastic support of the bishops, who revered him as a God-sent ruler—a Frankish Constantine. The imperial partnership of bishops and rulers continued, with two important changes from Roman times:

the kings always obeyed the bishops and never commanded them in matters of faith, but from now on it was the kings, not the local clergy and people, who chose the bishops.

Kings, Warrior-Landowners, and Bishops

and the example of the Roman emperor Constantine—he divided his territories among his sons, each of whom became the king

History of the Franks: An Early Frankish King and His Wives Read the story of Frankish King Lothar's romantic entanglements.

When Clovis died, however, much of what he had done to restore stability was destroyed. Following Germanic custom—

of his share of the royal inheritance. But what worked well enough in a loosely organized tribal society, and in an empire with a strong government structure, spelled trouble in a Germanic kingdom, where leading warriors and Roman landowners were merging into a powerful new elite. The local kings often quarreled over their shares of the royal inheritance, and this gave leading warrior-landowners a chance to play off one king against another. To win their support, the kings had to appoint them to positions as counts and bishops, grant them royal lands, and give them the right to control their lands without royal interference.

As a result, a vicious circle set in. As the rulers' lands, revenues, and control over the government and the Church gradually dwindled, they were forced to depend still more on the leading warrior-landowners and to concede them still more land and power. By the end of the seventh century, the Merovingian kings were mere puppets of their chief officials, the **mayors of the palace**. The mayors were themselves usually the heads of powerful factions among the warrior-landowners. But these factions feuded ferociously with each other, and there was usually more than one rival mayor, each associated with one or another rival king, so that even the power of the mayors was insecure. In consequence, the authority of the central government became increasingly weakened, with each warrior-landowner family acting as a power unto itself.

> "*The imperial partnership of bishops and rulers continued, with two important changes from Roman times: the kings always obeyed the bishops and never commanded them in matters of faith, but from now on it was the kings, not the local clergy and people, who chose the bishops.*"

Compared with the Roman Empire in its most glorious days, the Frankish kingdom was a feeble political structure, yet its role in the building of European civilization was important. The Merovingian kings and warrior-landowners were Christian believers and respecters of Roman culture. True, in the sixth and seventh centuries, they gradually ceased to be the well-educated rulers and aristocrats of imperial times; in fact by 700, they were usually illiterate. But they invested a great deal of their resources in monasteries that harbored learning, culture, and religion, and they sent many of their own sons and daughters to become monks and nuns. The Franks passed these beliefs and practices on to neighboring Germanic peoples to the east and north, often with the help of Anglo-Saxon and Irish missionaries.

Furthermore, in spite of the Frankish kingdom's history of conflict and disintegration, it set important precedents for later European government and politics. Within the kingdom, the main elements of the feudal state, with its decentralized authority and its constant interplay

> "*In one form or another, monarch, nobles, and churchmen would dominate political and social life in most European countries down to the nineteenth century.*"

of monarch, powerful nobles, and leading churchmen, were already coming into existence. In one form or another, monarch, nobles, and churchmen would dominate political and social life in most European countries down to the nineteenth century.

LO² The Eastern Empire and Its Neighbors

While Germanic kings ruled the West, the emperors in Constantinople still ruled a mighty empire in the East, stretching from the Danube to the Euphrates and the Nile (Map 9.1 on page 156). The Eastern empire still worked on the pattern laid down by Diocletian and Constantine. It had an all-powerful emperor surrounded by a splendid court, a centralized bureaucracy, and massive armies and navies recruited from within the empire and from neighboring barbarian peoples. Unlike the Western lands, the Eastern empire's territories were wealthy enough to support this burden. The Eastern emperors still saw themselves as Roman, and claimed authority over East and West alike. But when they seriously tried to enforce this claim, instead of growing, their empire began to shrink.

From "Eastern Empire" to "Byzantium"

Reconquest and New Invasions

In the fifth century, the Eastern emperors were too busy holding their existing frontiers and dealing with Christian religious disputes to try to reconquer territory in the West. But in 527 Justinian came to power—a ruler of extraordinary talent and determination, with a program of what he called "renewing the empire." Part of his program was peaceful and long-lasting—notably the codification of Roman law, the *Corpus Juris Civilis* (p. 111), which still forms the foundation of the legal systems of most Western countries today. But Justinian was also intent on restoring the empire to its traditional

URBS CONSTANTINOPOLITANA NOVA ROMA.

>> "The City of Constantinople, New Rome" Landward and seaward walls protect the city on its triangular spit of land. An equestrian statue of Constantine commemorates the city's founder. The dome of a church (predating Justinian's as yet unbuilt Hagia Sophia) dominates the urban landscape. This illustration, from a list compiled about A.D. 400 showing the locations of Roman government agencies and army units, presents an image of Constantinople as an impregnable fortress of Christianity and empire that would remain truthful for many centuries. Bodleian Library Oxford/The Art Archive

best organized of European states—a model of civilization for eastern European peoples, and in spite of religious differences, a source of cultural inspiration for western Europe.

Byzantine Culture and Architecture

Byzantium inherited from the Hellenistic past the internationally dominant Greek culture of the eastern Mediterranean, and even when the Greeks lost their cultural leadership to the new, Arab-dominated civilization of Islam, Byzantium continued to serve as the main custodian of Greek culture, pagan as well as Christian. Much of the literature of ancient Greece was conserved in archives and libraries, and Byzantine scholars added their own commentaries and summations. Greek learning continued to serve as the foundation of education. Though Justinian closed the schools of Athens, one of the last outposts of pagan philosophy, a great Christian university grew up in Constantinople.

Byzantium also contributed to the education of western Europe. All through the Middle Ages, there was constant interchange between East and West—by way of clergy, warriors, pilgrims, traders, and scholars. There was not much love lost between "the Greeks" and "the Franks," as they called each other. But right down to the Renaissance (Chapter 16),

 The Glory of Byzantium (http://www.metmuseum.org/explore/Byzantium/byzhome.html) Learn more about the art of Byzantium.

western European scholars looked to Byzantium for knowledge of Greek language and literature, and in the Middle Ages, many western European artists and architects looked up to those of Byzantium as their masters.

Visitors from the West were dazzled by the artistic treasures and the magnificent churches and palaces of Constantinople, the "city of cities." Above all, they were impressed by Justinian's mighty cathedral of Hagia Sophia (Holy Wisdom) with its huge main dome resting on four giant arches (see photo). Never had so large a dome been supported in this way until the Greek architect-mathematicians Anthemius of Tralles and Isidorus of Miletus designed this structure. The dome was described by the historian of Justinian's reign, Procopius of Caesarea, as "marvelous in its grace, but . . . utterly terrifying. For it somehow seems to float in the air with no firm support, but to be poised aloft to the peril of those inside it."

 Hagia Sophia: The Heart of Constantinople Read another description of how Hagia Sophia appeared to sixth-century viewers.

Built in only six years' time under the urging of the impatient emperor, Hagia Sophia is one of the world's architectural wonders—proof of the Eastern empire's exceptional cultural vitality, engineering skill, and religious commitment. The building inspires, in its own way, the sense of marvel and holy mystery that the cathedrals of Europe were to achieve centuries later, and it has served as a model for countless religious buildings—both churches and mosques.

The Cathedral of Hagia Sophia Justinian's cathedral, later a mosque and now a museum, was the work of two architect-mathematicians, Anthemius of Tralles and Isidorus of Miletus. Using their knowledge of the geometry of curves, they designed a dome supported by arches high in the air that remained a model for both church-builders and mosque-builders for more than a thousand years.

LO³ A New Monotheism and a New International Civilization: Islam

At the same time that Rome and Byzantium were beginning to evolve different versions of European civilization, the largest single section of the old Roman Empire, its lands in northern Africa and on the eastern shore of the Mediterranean, developed in an entirely different direction. This region became the seat of a new and different form of civilization as a result of another great invasion—this time, from Arabia. The Arabs brought a militant faith and succeeded in building a brilliant and distinctive culture—both known by the name of Islam.

The Arabs and Muhammad

> **"Built in only six years' time under the urging of the impatient emperor, Hagia Sophia is one of the world's architectural wonders—proof of the Eastern empire's exceptional cultural vitality, engineering skill, and religious commitment."**

At the opening of the seventh century, most of the Arabs were nomadic tribespeople. Because they conquered and adapted to an advanced civilization, there is a parallel between their role in the Mediterranean world and that of the Germanic invaders in western Europe. But the Arabs, instead of being converted by the Christians they conquered, were fired with a monotheistic zeal of their own, and most of the peoples they overcame eventually accepted their version of the one truth about the one God.

Muhammad, the founder of the faith, was born about 570 in Mecca, a trading center near the western coast of Arabia. He apparently grew up with no formal education, but he did learn something of the teachings of Judaism and Christianity, which had sifted down from Palestine and Syria. When he was about forty years old, he turned from his life as a merchant to become a hermit. Spending days in solitary meditation, he began to experience visions that he believed to be direct revelations from God—in Arabic, *Allah*. In one of these visions, the archangel Gabriel directed him to carry these messages to his people, and from that time on, he abandoned all other activities.

Most Arabs, however, were polytheists, and Muhammad's insistence that "there is no God but Allah, and Muhammad is his Prophet" proved offensive to them. He became especially unpopular in the city of Mecca, where a building known as the Kaaba housed images and a black stone considered holy by the Arabs. When he denounced this shrine, he was branded a blasphemer and a disturber of the peace. Faced with this opposition, Muhammad left Mecca in 622 and fled northward to Yathrib (later renamed Medina, "City of the Prophet"). This event marks the beginning of the Islamic calendar and is known as the **Hegira**.

Hegira
Muhammad's flight from Mecca to Medina, an event that marks the beginning of the Islamic calendar.

 The Constitution of Medina: Muslims and Jews at the Dawn of Islam Read a selection of Muhammad's rules for the community of believers in Medina.

In Medina, Muhammad was able to preach freely, and his band of disciples began to grow and to follow his example of preaching complete submission to the will of Allah as revealed to him. The Arabic word for submission is *islam*, and the word for one who has submitted is *muslim*. These are the terms used to identify, respectively, the faith and the believer.

Like Abraham and Moses, the Israelite servants of the one God whom Muhammad revered, he was a warrior and ruler as well as a prophet. He was persuaded through revelation that the use of force, if necessary, against unbelievers was one of many forms of religious "striving" (in Arabic, *jihad*) that were approved by Allah. (Other forms of *jihad* included everything from unwarlike efforts to convert unbelievers, through the struggle for justice in society, to the individual's striving for personal righteousness.) Soon Muhammad was

The successor to Muhammad as leader of the Islamic religion and people.

caliphate
The empire of the caliph.

mosque
A Muslim house of worship.

Koran
The sacred book of Islam (the scholarly letter-for-letter version of the spelling in the Arabic alphabet, *Qur'an*, is also used in English today).

Five Pillars of Faith
The fundamental religious duties of Muslims, as stated in the Koran.

minaret
A slender, free-standing tower next to a mosque from which a muezzin (crier) calls the faithful to prayer.

leading his followers in successful warfare against the Meccans, and the Prophet returned to Mecca in triumph. He ordered that all the images in the city be destroyed, but he preserved the Black Stone as a symbol of the new faith. Attracted by his militant methods and by his vision of bringing the whole world under Islam, the desert tribes began to flock to his leadership. By the time of his death in 632, he had extended his personal control over a large portion of Arabia.

The Arab Empire

Once the pattern of expansion had been established, the movement spread with lightning speed. Muhammad had left no son to inherit his mantle, so his disciples chose a successor (**caliph**) from among his close relatives. Family connection with Muhammad was accepted from the beginning as a mark of political legitimacy, in the same way that Jewish Temple priests had claimed descent from Moses's brother Aaron.

Under the first two caliphs, Abu Bakr and Omar, the Arabs carried their holy war to neighboring lands. Commanders and warriors alike were driven on by a religious sense of mission and contempt of death, expansion helped hold together the recently united Arabs, and each victory brought hope of yet more conquests. Besides, the Arabs' main opponents, Byzantium and Persia, were weakened by their endless wars against each other, and Christian religious disputes were causing many bishops and ordinary believers in Egypt and Syria to turn against their rulers in Constantinople. Within a decade after Muhammad's death, the hard-riding Arab horsemen conquered Persia and took Egypt and Syria from the Byzantine Empire, and within a century, their empire (**caliphate**) (from the Arabic word for "successor" of the Prophet) stretched from Persia to Spain (Map 9.2).

Finally, Islam's warlike expansion came to a halt. In 718, Arab besiegers gave up a year-long blockade of Constantinople after suffering huge casualties from starvation and disease; in 732 a Muslim raiding army that had moved far into the Frankish kingdom was intercepted and forced to retreat (p. 167). But where the warriors stopped, the traders took over. By 1000, Arab merchants, looking in distant lands for exotic goods to bring to the centers of the Islamic world, had spread the religion of

 Islam: Empire of Faith/Jewels of Architecture (http://www.pbs.org/empires/islam/featuresjewels.html) Take a video tour of Islamic architecture.

the Prophet to gold- and ivory-producing kingdoms in western Africa, to the spice islands of East Asia, and to empire-building Turkish nomads in Central Asia.

Though determined to drive out paganism and eager to convert all peoples to their faith, the Arabs offered toleration to Jews and Christians (upon payment of a special tax). Within a few generations, however, most Christians in the conquered territories embraced Islam. There were legal and social advantages in becoming Muslims, and the religion appealed to many Christians. The conversion was to prove lasting; except for Spain, the lands that fell to the Arabs are still lands of the **mosque**.

Islam and Christianity

What were the teachings of this new faith? A radical monotheist, Muhammad never claimed divinity for himself but insisted only that he was the last and greatest of Allah's prophets, for Allah was the same God that Jews and Christians worshiped and who had already spoken through prophets from Abraham to Jesus. Instead of claiming that he was introducing a new religion, he insisted that his work was the fulfillment of the old, just as Jesus had claimed that his work was the fulfillment of Judaism. His message, as recorded in the **Koran**, might be viewed in this light as a sequel to the Old and New Testaments. But in the same way that Christians believed that the Jews had gone astray from the one truth about the one God, Muslims believed that Christians had also gone astray. From the Muslim viewpoint, Christians were worshipers of three or more divine beings, who endlessly wrangled over doctrine and had tainted Jesus's message with pagan superstition.

The central spiritual appeal of Islam is its stress on the oneness of God. Most of the Koran is given over to describing and praising Allah, who alone is the supreme reality, all-knowing and all-powerful. The true believer must submit unreservedly to Allah's will as expressed through the Prophet. This can be done simply and without doubting; unlike Christianity, Islam raised no questions concerning the nature of God (pp. 145–146).

Similarly, there were no arguments over what made up the sacred canon (authorized holy books). Muhammad's revelations were memorized by his disciples and written down in final form shortly after his death; this original Koran, in Arabic, remains the only version studied by Muslims, whatever their native language. Shorter than the New Testament, it is a poetic book, which millions have memorized (hence its name, which in Arabic means "Recitation").

Religion Facts (for Islam) (http://www.religionfacts.com/islam/index.htm) Learn more about the Muslim faith.

Islamic Social and Ethical Ideas

Muhammad's ethical teachings are in the tradition of Judaism and Christianity, and the Koran repeats many of the proverbs and stories of the Bible. Because the Prophet had a practical mind, the model life that he described is within the reach of the faithful. While stressing love, kindness, and compassion, he did not insist on self-denial beyond the powers of most people. He

A long siege; Muslims forced to withdraw

Map 9.2 The Expansion of Islam

The swiftest Muslim conquests came in the century after Muhammad, when Islam united under its rule nearly all the lands once held by Alexander and nearly half the lands once held by Rome. Thereafter, resistance on the western and eastern fringes of Islam, as well as its own disputes and power struggles, slowed further expansion. All the same, a new world of religion and culture had come into being, stretching from Spain to the borders of India. © Cengage Learning

Interactive Map

saw no particular virtue, for instance, in sexual abstinence. He did, however, try to moderate the ancient practice of polygamy by declaring that a man should have no more than four wives at a time. No limit was set on the number of concubines a man might have. Though women possessed some property rights, Muslim society was (and is) a "man's world."

Still, in Islam, both men and women stand as equals before Allah—though in practice, religious scholars and holy men enjoy special respect and authority. There are no saints mediating between humans and God , and because there are no priests, there are no mysterious rites that only priests can perform. To increase the worshiper's concentration on Allah, statues and images are banned from Muslim art. In the mosque (from an Arabic word meaning "to worship"), there is nothing that resembles an idol.

Obligations of the Faithful

The religious duties of Muslims, known as the **Five Pillars of Faith**, are clearly stated in the Koran. The first is the familiar profession of belief, "There is no god but Allah, and Muhammad is his Prophet." By accepting and repeating these words, the convert is initiated into the faith.

Daily prayer—at dawn, midday, midafternoon, sunset, and nightfall—is the second duty. At the appointed hours, from atop slender **minarets** (towers), the muezzins (criers) call upon the

faithful to bow down, turn toward Mecca, and say the prayer in Arabic. The prayer itself usually includes the short opening verse of the Koran, praising Allah and asking for guidance along the "straight path." This formula is repeated many times each day. The only public religious service is the midday prayer on Fridays, which must be attended by all adult males (and is closed to females). Inside the mosque, standing in self-ordered rows, the congregation prays aloud in unison; then the leader, a layman, delivers a brief sermon. After the service, normal everyday activities may be resumed.

The third duty is giving to the poor. At first, almsgiving was practiced as an individual act of charity, but it gradually developed into a standard payment. In the Islamic states, the money was collected through regular taxation and was used to help the needy and to build and maintain the mosques. The usual amount was one-fortieth of the individual's income.

Fasting, the fourth pillar of faith, ordinarily is confined to *Ramadan*, the ninth month of the Muslim lunar (moon-based) calendar (p. 16). It was during Ramadan that Allah gave the Koran to the archangel Gabriel for revelation to Muhammad. For thirty days, no food or drink may be taken between sunrise and sunset. Fasting, which was not practiced by the Arabs before Muhammad, was adopted from Jewish and Christian custom.

Finally, every Muslim who can afford it must make a pilgrimage to the Holy City of Mecca at some time during his or her

EUROPEANS BENEFITED IN A NUMBER OF WAYS FROM CONTACT WITH ISLAM:

- Islam spread in every direction from its Arabian origin, forming an intercontinental region of trade and travel that linked the peoples beyond its borders more closely than before. Europe thereby became part of a group of civilizations that stretched all the way to China and Japan.

- Arab traders traveled between Spain and western Africa and between Egypt, Syria, China, and the East Indies; as a result, exotic goods came within reach of merchants from Europe.

- Scholarly and scientific discoveries from other civilizations reached Europe through Islam as well. For example, what we now call Arabic numerals came to Europe from India by way of Islam, and this innovation freed mathematicians from the awkward Roman system.

- Muslim scholars also made advances in knowledge that came to be known in Europe. In the field of medicine, a noteworthy contribution was the *Canon* of Avicenna (ibn-Sina), a summary of the medical knowledge of his time (eleventh century).

- Great centers of learning sprang up in the Islamic world, notably at Cairo (Egypt), Toledo (Spain), and Palermo (Sicily), and western European scholars made their way to Spain and Sicily. From Arabic translations—retranslated into Latin, the scholarly language of western Europe, by Spanish and Sicilian experts—the scholars recovered many of the treasures of Greek philosophy and science that had been forgotten in western Europe for centuries.

- Western artisans and builders were also impressed by what they discovered in Muslim countries. Muslim architects devised a graceful variation on the traditional rounded Roman arch that was also a technical improvement by making it pointed (see photo on page 163)—a form that was taken up by their western European colleagues to produce some of the noblest Christian houses of worship ever built, the Gothic cathedrals.

---

life. Over the centuries, this practice has had a unifying effect on the different peoples that embrace Islam. Rich and poor, black and white, Easterner and Westerner—all come together in the Holy City.

In the early stages of Muslim history, a sixth duty was required of all able-bodied men: participation in *jihad*, in the sense of war against unbelievers. It was this requirement that sparked the first explosive conquests of the Arabs. Each caliph believed it his obligation to expand the frontiers of Islam and thus reduce the infidel "territory of war."

The Five Pillars of Faith are only the minimum requirements of Islam. In all things, true believers must seek to do the will of Allah as revealed in the Koran. They must also believe that God has *predestined* the ultimate fate of all humankind, to be revealed in the Last Judgment. Muhammad left vivid descriptions of hell and heaven. Unbelievers will burn eternally in a great pool of fire; believers who die in sin will also suffer there for a time but will finally be released. In the end, all Muslims (male and female)—who have accepted Allah—will enjoy the pleasures of paradise. Muhammad, drawing from Persian sources, pictured paradise in sensual terms as an oasis of delight, with sparkling beverages, luscious fruits, and dark-eyed beauties.

Religious and Political Divisions

In spite of the comparative simplicity of Muhammad's teachings, they were open to conflicting interpretations as the years passed. The major disagreements arose over the principle of succession to the caliphate, religious doctrines, and the proper way of life for Muslims.

The main division was between the **Sunni** and the **Shia**, a division that still disturbs the Muslim world. The Sunni (from the Arabic word for "example"—followers of the example of the Prophet) were associated with the Umayyad dynasty, which seized the caliphate in 661 and moved the capital of Islam from Medina to Damascus, in Syria. They accepted as valid certain traditions that had grown up outside the Koran. On the other hand, the Shia (from the Arabic

The Qur'an: Muslim Devotion to God Read the description of the Last Judgment from the Koran.

> "*Lo! the Day of Decision is appointed—the day when there shall be a blowing of the trumpet, and ye shall come in troops, and the heavens shall be opened, and be full of gates, and the mountains shall be removed, and turn into [mist].*"
>
> —from the Koran

The Ibn Tulun Mosque, Cairo Pointed arches, more stable than round ones of the same height, were a feature of Muslim architecture that developed from about A.D. 800 in what is now Iraq. They were used in the courtyard of this mosque, built on the orders of an Egyptian ruler, Ahmed ibn Tulun, shortly before A.D. 900. Italian traders visiting Cairo would have brought word home of this new style of arch construction, so that Ibn Tulun's mosque is an ancestor of medieval Gothic cathedrals.

for "followers"—followers of their founder, Muhammad's cousin Ali), held strictly to the Koran and insisted that only descendants of the Prophet could become caliphs. The Abbasid family, who were Shia Muslims, gained power in 750 and moved the capital again, this time to the new city of Baghdad (see Map 9.2) on the River Tigris in Mesopotamia.

After the eighth century, the Arab empire began to break up. The ousted Umayyad family established itself in Spain and broke off political connections with Baghdad. Similarly, a descendant of Muhammad's daughter Fatima later declared himself an independent caliph in control of Egypt, Syria, and

> *"The rise of Islam was almost as important an event for European peoples who remained Christian as for those of Africa and Asia who actually became Muslims."*

Morocco. Provinces in Arabia and India also fell away, until by 1000 the Abbasid ruler controlled only the area surrounding Baghdad.

In spite of these religious and political divisions, Muslim civilization reached its height in the ninth and tenth centuries. The Islamic achievements of this period built on earlier Greek, Syrian, and Persian traditions. But out of this blend there emerged a distinctive new international culture that replaced those of Greece and Persia in the lands stretching from northern Africa to the borders of India, and eventually spread, with Islam itself, to a vastly larger area.

Sunni
Members of the branch of Islam associated with the Umayyad dynasty, who accepted as valid certain traditions that had grown up outside the Koran.

Shia
Members of the branch of Islam that held strictly to the Koran and insisted that only descendants of the Prophet could become caliphs.

The Muslim Legacy to the West

The rise of Islam was almost as important an event for European peoples who remained Christian as for those of Africa and Asia who actually became Muslims. The Islamization of North Africa and much of the eastern Mediterranean lands had the effect, for many centuries, of confining Christianity, and many traditions of Greco-Roman civilization, to the territory of Europe. The Christian European peoples now lived on the fringes of a mighty intercontinental civilization that was inspired by an opposing version of the one truth about the one God, and that included many more lands with ancient traditions of civilization, and many more centers of wealth and power, than half-barbarian Europe.

It was no wonder, then, that for Europe, Islam was a formidable enemy. For a thousand years, Christians and Muslims fought bitter wars against each other. The warlike prowess of medieval European society was steeled by the continual conflict; European states such as the Frankish kingdom and Byzantium devoted much of their energies to it; and the struggle with Islam eventually led to European overseas exploration and empire building (Chapter 15). Yet Islam was also a neighbor from which Europe benefited in many peaceful ways, and the rise of Islam furthered the renewal of civilization in Europe.

Córdoba (History and Culture) (http://www.muslimheritage.com/topics/default.cfm?ArticleID=454) Learn about Córdoba, the largest city in medieval Europe after Constantinople.

Listen to a synopsis of Chapter 9.

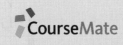

CHAPTER 10

EUROPE TAKES SHAPE,
700–1000

LEARNING OBJECTIVES

AFTER READING THIS CHAPTER, YOU SHOULD BE ABLE TO DO THE FOLLOWING:

LO¹ Trace the rise of the Carolingian dynasty and explain the significance of the Carolingian Renaissance and the coronation of Charlemagne.

LO² Describe the collapse of Charlemagne's empire and the rise of western Europe and Byzantine eastern Europe in the ninth and tenth centuries.

"BY 1000, CIVILIZATION HAD SPREAD THROUGHOUT EUROPE, AND THE THREE-THOUSAND-YEAR-OLD EUROPEAN BARBARIAN WAY OF LIFE HAD COME TO AN END—THE VICTIM OF ITS OWN SUCCESS."

Shortly after A.D. 700, the renewal of European civilization in the West began with the rise to power of a new dynasty in the Frankish kingdom, the Carolingians. In the Frankish ruling partnership of kings, nobles, and the Church, the Carolingians made themselves very much the senior partners. Around A.D. 800, the Carolingian warrior-king Charlemagne was able to conquer barbarian peoples in central Europe, encourage a revival of education and scholarship among the clergy, and take the title of Roman emperor. In the end, Charlemagne's empire fell apart, but the rulers of its easternmost section soon became powerful in their own right, as the Holy Roman emperors.

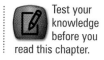

Test your knowledge before you read this chapter.

Meanwhile, the renewal also got under way in the East, where Byzantium regained some of the ground it had lost to Arab, Slav, and nomad invaders. Where it could not reconquer, it began to project its influence well beyond its frontiers by converting many eastern European peoples to Christianity—sometimes on its own initiative, and sometimes at the plea of their increasingly powerful rulers.

During the era of renewal, barbarian and nomadic peoples, notably the Norsemen and Hungarians, continued to raid, conquer, and settle in lands that had once belonged to Rome or where Roman influence had already spread. As with earlier invasions, however, what enabled these peoples to make such inroads was the fact that they were already growing in organization and skills, and they ended by adopting the way of life of the peoples they attacked. By 1000, civilization had

What do you think?

The popes acted in the best interest of the Church when they allied with the Frankish kings.

Strongly Disagree						Strongly Agree
1	2	3	4	5	6	7

◄◄ **Charlemagne** The mighty Frankish ruler appears on his coffin enthroned, and only a little lower than Christ. Churchmen stand respectfully beside him: Pope Leo III (left), who crowned him Emperor of the Romans in A.D. 800, and Archbishop Turpin of Reims, his warrior-companion in medieval epic. The Holy Roman Emperor Frederick II had the coffin made in 1215, but Charlemagne himself would probably have been pleased with this image. Certainly this is how medieval emperors, competing with the popes for supremacy in Western Christendom, wanted to see him.

Scala/Art Resource, NY

165

Carolingian
The Frankish dynasty founded by Charles Martel in the eighth century, as successors to the Merovingians.

spread throughout Europe, and the three-thousand-year-old European barbarian way of life had come to an end—the victim of its own success (pp. 46–49).

Because they were conquerors rather than conquered, however, most of the once-barbarian peoples formed separate kingdoms that were independent of the older civilized lands. As a result, the renewed European civilization was one of many vigorous ethnic cultures and many powerful competing states. And it renewed itself in two variant forms, named after the different branches of ancient traditions and Christianity that inspired them—the "Latin" West and the "Greek" East.

LO¹ The Carolingians

By A.D. 700, the kingdom of the Franks, once the most powerful state in western Europe, was seemingly falling apart. It was divided among rival kings of the Merovingian dynasty, each controlled by a "mayor of the palace" (head of the royal household) who wielded whatever government authority was left, while competing factions among the nobles scrambled for wealth and power (pp. 154-155).

 The Decline of the Merovingians Read a critical description of the powerless Merovingian kings.

Finally, however, one particular family that had become exceptionally wealthy and powerful in the continual factional struggles gained the hereditary position of one and only mayor of the palace throughout the Frankish kingdom. Like the kingship, the mayoralty was liable to be divided between heirs, but in 714, an out-of-wedlock son of the family by the name of Charles laid claim to the position and won it in several years of civil war. He thereby became the ancestor of a new dynasty, the **Carolingians** (from the Frankish word for "children of Charles").

The Carolingians rebuilt the Frankish kingdom, and although their power melted away in its turn, their achievements outlasted them. It was they who began the rise of western Europe to become the heartland of Western civilization.

The Rise of the Carolingian Dynasty

Charles was a ruthless and warlike ruler who went down in history as Charles Martel ("Charles the Hammer"). But in the power struggles of Frankish warrior-landowners it was important to reward followers as well as to crush opponents. Rewarding followers meant giving them gifts of land—but not from one's own family possessions, the main source of a ruler's wealth and power. Some of the land could come from defeated opponents,

CHRONOLOGY

732	Charles Martel forces an Arab army to retreat from Frankish kingdom
751	Pope Zachary approves the transfer of royal power from the Merovingian king to Pepin, a Carolingian
756	Donation of Pepin seals the alliance between the Frankish kingdom and the papacy
768–814	Reign of Charlemagne
780	Charlemagne sets up a palace school in Aachen
800	Pope Leo III crowns Charlemagne "Emperor of the Romans"
CA. 800	Charlemagne conquers the barbarian peoples in central Europe; Norsemen begin raids along coastline of western Europe; Byzantium regains control of Greece, begins to push against Slavs and Arabs
843	Treaty of Verdun divides the Frankish kingdom among Charlemagne's three grandsons
871	King Alfred leads the Anglo-Saxons of England against the Danish Viking invaders
911	Last direct descendant of Charlemagne dies in eastern Frankish kingdom
962	Otto I of eastern Frankish kingdom is crowned emperor in Rome; beginning of Holy Roman Empire
987	Hugh Capet replaces last Carolingian in western Frankish kingdom (France)
988	Prince Vladimir of Kiev converts to Christianity
1000	Viking journeys across Atlantic to Iceland, Greenland, and "Vinland" (North America)
1066	Norman conquest of England

but to be truly generous, it was necessary to find some additional source of property to distribute, and Charles found it in lands belonging to the Church.

Charles was a generous donator of land to favored monasteries, but bishops and abbots often belonged to noble families that he distrusted. Surely, he felt, it was right for him to take Church property that might be misused for a bad political purpose, namely to oppose him, and use it for a good political purpose, namely to strengthen him as a Christian ruler. Charles was not the first powerful believer to think this way, and he would not be the last. But he commandeered Church resources on an unprecedented scale—not only to reward supporters, but also to give land to foot soldiers who served him in peace and war (see photo on page 168).

Not long after Charles took power, he faced a historic challenge—and a historic opportunity—when Arab invaders from Spain took over some of the kingdom's southern borderlands. In 732, an Arab army moved out of the occupied territory on a large-scale raid far north into the Frankish kingdom. Charles intercepted them near the town of Tours and forced them to retreat. The Christian nobles of the south, who had been practically independent rulers of their lands, accepted the authority of their rescuer, and in hard campaigning over the next twenty years, the invaders were forced back into Spain. The expansion of Islam had come to a halt, and the whole of the Frankish kingdom was under a single effective rule—though the rule was that of a mayor of the palace who called himself "chief and army commander of the Franks," and not that of a king.

> "*Except for his empty title, and an uncertain allowance for his subsistence, . . . there was nothing that the king could call his own, unless it were the income from a single farm, and that a very small one, where he made his home, and where such servants as were needful to wait on him constituted his scanty household. When he went anywhere he traveled in a wagon drawn by a yoke of oxen, with a rustic oxherd for charioteer.*"
>
> —Einhard, on the last Merovingian kings, ca. 825

The Alliance of the Franks and the Papacy

Charles Martel's son, Pepin, decided that the time had come for the actual power in the kingdom to be recognized as the legal power. But it was not a simple matter to take the crown from the Merovingian descendants of Clovis. Though they were only figureheads, they were respected as the rightful possessors of the kingship, and all the powerful men of the kingdom—bishops, nobles, and mayors of the palace—had sworn loyalty to them.

In search of a way to take over the kingship that would be seen as legitimate (rightful and lawful), in 751 Pepin turned to the generally accepted highest religious authority, Pope Zachary. For a pope to be consulted on a transfer of royal power actually widened the papacy's authority, and a grateful new Frankish king might be a valuable ally. With papal approval, the last Merovingian king was sent to live out his life as a monk, the assembled Frankish nobles chose Pepin to replace him, and Pepin was anointed (holy oil placed on him) by Archbishop Boniface of Fulda, a monk and missionary in the kingdom's eastern lands who was close to both Pepin and the pope.

This was the first time in the history of any western European kingdom that a king began his reign with a solemn religious ceremony. The ceremony was patterned after the inauguration of Byzantine emperors, which in turn imitated the consecration of the Israelite kings at God's command as described in the Old Testament. It is not certain that Pepin also underwent coronation (placing a crown on his head) like the Israelite and Byzantine rulers. But against the hereditary legitimacy of the Merovingians, Pepin certainly now claimed a special holiness and authority from God. Both coronation and anointing soon became the normal inauguration ceremony for kings throughout Europe. In this way, kings proclaimed that their power came from God, though in the Middle Ages, the popes always stressed that this divine authority was conferred by the Church.

A few years later, Pope Stephen II came in person to the Frankish court and anointed Pepin as well as his two sons—an additional precaution to make sure that the Carolingians could legitimately continue as a royal dynasty. In return, Stephen won promises of military help against the papacy's Italian neighbors, the Lombards, whose king was trying to take over the lands around Rome that the popes ruled (p. 157). Accordingly, in 756 Pepin crossed the Alps, defeated the Lombards, and transferred a strip of territory right across central Italy to the governing authority of the pope (Map 10.1 on page 169).

By the so-called Donation of Pepin, the popes acquired a legal basis for authority over a much wider region than before, and they ruled their new territory for over a thousand years—until the unification of Italy in 1870. But at about the same time as Pepin's gift, the papacy began to claim far wider power. The papal court produced a document that had supposedly been issued by the Roman emperor Constantine when he left Rome for a new capital in the East (p. 138). In the document, Constantine made over to the popes the rule of the entire West, acknowledged their supremacy over the entire Church, and recognized their superior dignity to emperors. In the fifteenth century, the Donation of Constantine, as it came to be called, was shown to be a forgery (pp. 292-293), but as late as the sixteenth century, popes used it as a basis for claiming power over emperors and kings.

Meanwhile, however, the Donation of Pepin sealed the alliance between the Frankish kingdom and the papacy, the two

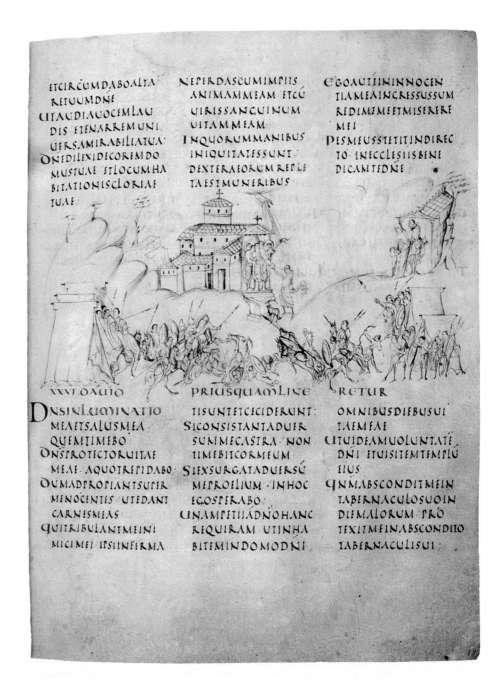

Carolingian Foot Soldiers
A picture in the Utrecht Psalter, a book of psalms made in a northern French monastery about A.D. 830, illustrates Psalm 27: "Though an army encamp against me, my heart shall not fear." Soldiers with spears and round shields, some helmeted, some bareheaded, but otherwise unarmored, spill out of tents and brandish their weapons at a church, where a priest welcomes a believer to take sanctuary. Charles Martel's soldiers would have looked much the same a century before. Bibliotheek der Rijksuniversiteit, Utrecht

strongest forces in the West. The outcome of this alliance was the "Roman" empire of Charles the Great.

Charlemagne

Charles, Pepin's son and Charles Martel's grandson, was a towering figure, celebrated in history and legend under the name of Charlemagne—the French version of "Charles the Great." Through the force of his personality and the challenges of a forty-six-year reign, he contributed mightily to the evolution of western Europe.

 Charlemagne (http://www .youtube.com/ watch?v=qJBKGVR dhy8) Watch a short film on Charlemagne's legacy.

Descendant of Frankish barbarian invaders, warrior against heathens and Muslims, and holder of the revived office of emperor, Charlemagne personified the merging of Germanic, Christian, and Roman elements in western European civilization.

Conquests: Italy, Germany, Spain

Charlemagne was almost constantly at war. Ruthless and cruel in battle, he fought not only for territory and spoils but also for what he considered the higher goals of Christianity and universal order. As a result, he expanded the boundaries of both Christianity and Frankish power outward in all directions by military force.

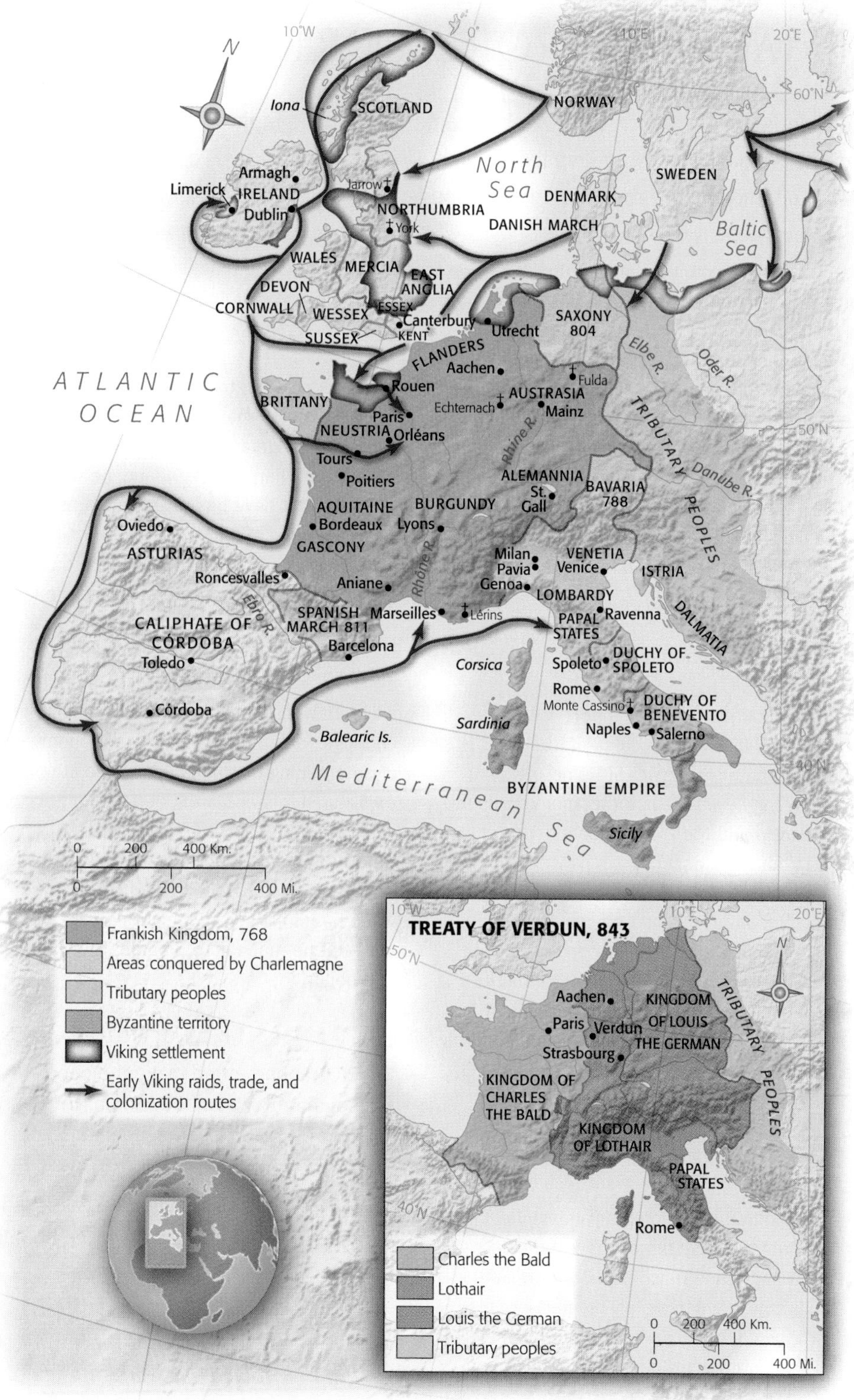
N
10°W
0°
10°E
20°E
60°N
50°N
40°N
Iona
SCOTLAND
NORWAY
SWEDEN
North Sea
DENMARK
DANISH MARCH
Baltic Sea
Armagh
Limerick
IRELAND
Dublin
Jarrow
NORTHUMBRIA
York
WALES
MERCIA
EAST ANGLIA
DEVON
CORNWALL
WESSEX
ESSEX
SUSSEX
Canterbury
KENT
Utrecht
SAXONY 804
ATLANTIC OCEAN
FLANDERS
Aachen
Fulda
Elbe R.
Oder R.
BRITTANY
Rouen
Echternach
AUSTRASIA
Mainz
Paris
NEUSTRIA
Orléans
Rhine R.
TRIBUTARY PEOPLES
Tours
Poitiers
ALEMANNIA
St. Gall
BAVARIA 788
Danube R.
AQUITAINE
Bordeaux
BURGUNDY
Lyons
Oviedo
ASTURIAS
GASCONY
Milan
Pavia
VENETIA
Venice
ISTRIA
Roncesvalles
Aniane
Rhône R.
Genoa
LOMBARDY
CALIPHATE OF CÓRDOBA
Ebro R.
SPANISH MARCH 811
Marseilles
Lérins
PAPAL STATES
Ravenna
DALMATIA
Barcelona
Toledo
Corsica
Spoleto
DUCHY OF SPOLETO
Rome
Monte Cassino
DUCHY OF BENEVENTO
Córdoba
Sardinia
Naples
Salerno
Balearic Is.
Mediterranean Sea
BYZANTINE EMPIRE
Sicily
0 200 400 Km.
0 200 400 Mi.
Frankish Kingdom, 768
Areas conquered by Charlemagne
Tributary peoples
Byzantine territory
Viking settlement
Early Viking raids, trade, and colonization routes
TREATY OF VERDUN, 843
Aachen
Paris
Verdun
Strasbourg
KINGDOM OF LOUIS THE GERMAN
KINGDOM OF CHARLES THE BALD
KINGDOM OF LOTHAIR
TRIBUTARY PEOPLES
PAPAL STATES
Rome
Charles the Bald
Lothair
Louis the German
Tributary peoples
0 200 400 Km.
0 200 400 Mi.

Map 10.1 **Charlemagne's Empire**

Charlemagne ruled far less territory than the original Roman emperors, but he widened the strip of Christian lands that stretched between the Islamic world and the pagan barbarians and nomads of northern and eastern Europe. Furthermore, his empire was twice the size of contemporary Byzantium. Even after his death and his empire's gradual collapse, the new boundaries of Christendom did not shrink, and the balance of power within Christendom did not swing back to the East. © Cengage Learning

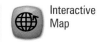

Interactive Map

CHARLEMAGNE: A WORD PORTRAIT

This description of Charlemagne's behavior and habits comes from a biography of the emperor written by a well-educated courtier, Einhard, who knew Charlemagne well. It gives an intimate view of someone who seemed larger than life in his own time and was celebrated in history and legend for centuries afterward.

Charles was large and robust, of commanding stature and excellent proportions, for it appears that he measured in height seven times the length of his own foot. The top of his head was round, his eyes large and animated, his nose somewhat long. He had a fine head of gray hair, and his face was bright and pleasant; so that, whether standing or sitting, he showed great presence and dignity. Although his neck was thick and rather short, and his belly too prominent, still the good proportions of his limbs concealed these defects. His walk was firm, and the whole carriage of his body was manly. His voice was clear, but not so strong as his frame would have led one to expect. . . .

He took constant exercise in riding and hunting, which was natural for a Frank, since scarcely any nation can be found to equal them in these pursuits. . . .

He wore the dress of his native country, that is, the Frankish; [and] he thoroughly disliked the dress of foreigners, however fine; and he never put it on except at Rome. . . .

In his eating and drinking he was temperate; more particularly so in his drinking, for he had the greatest abhorrence of drunkenness in anybody, but more especially in himself and his companions. He was unable to abstain from food for any length of time, and often complained that fasting was injurious to him. On the other hand, he very rarely feasted, only on great festive occasions, when there were very large gatherings. The daily service of his table consisted of only four dishes in addition to the roast meat, which the hunters used to bring in on spits, and of which he partook more freely than of any other food.

While he was dining he listened to music or reading. History and the deeds of men of old were most often read. He derived much pleasure from the works of St. Augustine, especially from his book called *The City of God*. . . .

While he was dressing and binding on his sandals, he would receive his friends; and also, if the count of the palace announced that there was any case which could only be settled by his decision, the suitors were immediately ordered into his presence, and he heard the case and gave judgment as if sitting in court. And this was not the only business that he used to arrange at that time, for he also gave orders for whatever had to be done on that day by any officer or servant.

He was ready and fluent in speaking, and able to express himself with great clearness. He did not confine himself to his native tongue, but took pains to learn foreign languages, acquiring such knowledge of Latin that he could make an address in that language as well as in his own. Greek he could better understand than speak. Indeed, he was so polished in speech that he might have passed for a learned man.

He was an ardent admirer of the liberal arts, and greatly revered their professors, whom he promoted to high honors. In order to learn grammar, he attended the lectures of the aged Peter of Pisa, a deacon; and for other branches he chose as his preceptor Albinus, otherwise called Alcuin, also a deacon,—a Saxon by race, from Britain, the most learned man of the day, with whom the king spent much time in learning rhetoric and logic, and more especially astronomy. He learned the art of determining the dates upon which the movable festivals of the Church fall, and with deep thought and skill most carefully calculated the courses of the planets.

Charles also tried to learn to write, and used to keep his tablets and writing book under the pillow of his couch, that when he had leisure he might practice his hand in forming letters; but he made little progress in this task, too long deferred and begun too late in life.

EXPLORING THE SOURCE

1. Biographers often make the people they write about seem better than they actually were. Does Einhard's portrayal of Charlemagne seem "touched up" or lifelike, and why?

2. Which of Charlemagne's activities described here had the greatest importance for the European future, and why?

Source: James Harvey Robinson, ed., *Readings in European History* (Boston: Ginn, 1904), 1:126–128.

Not all of Charlemagne's victims were pagans or Muslims. When advised by the pope that the Lombards were again threatening papal territory, he led his armies into Italy in 774 and broke the Lombard power. Now, he called himself king of the Lombards as well as king of the Franks, and gained control of northern Italy (see Map 10.1 on page 169).

His hardest campaigns, which lasted some thirty years, were against the Saxons. Some of these Germanic barbarians had crossed the North Sea to Britain in the fifth century, but the rest still lived on the northeastern boundary of the Frankish kingdom (see Map 10.1 on page 169). Unlike the Saxons in England, they clung stubbornly to their heathen religion. Charlemagne, encouraged by the Church, was determined to transform the Saxons into Christian subjects. He succeeded, but only after laying waste to Saxony, massacring countless captives, and deporting thousands of families in other parts of his empire. At last, the Saxons accepted Christianity, and the Frankish clergy moved in to establish bishoprics and monasteries.

 Christianity at the Point of a Sword: The Saxon Settlement Read Charlemagne's harsh orders for dealing with the pagans of Saxony.

Farther south, Charlemagne attacked the nomadic nation of the Avars, who had invaded central and eastern Europe in the sixth century (p. 171). As with the Huns before them, the defeat of the Avars caused most of them to retreat and disperse, but they left behind Slavic tribes who had accompanied them on their campaigns of conquest. The eastern borderlands of Charlemagne's empire now marked an ethnic divide between Germanic and Slavic peoples that has lasted, more or less, to the present day.

Government: The Church and the State

Charlemagne concerned himself with domestic matters as well as with military campaigns. As a Christian ruler, he worked to strengthen the leadership of the Church and extend its activities. He did not intervene in matters of belief like the Byzantine rulers, but he appointed bishops and issued reform orders to the clergy. In addition, like every ruler since Constantine, he needed the help of the Church to reinforce his own power. He treated bishops and abbots as agents of his government and saw to it that they received copies of all his decrees.

Like earlier rulers back to late Roman times, Charlemagne governed through local officials called **counts** (p. 139). Each count represented the crown in a given region, his *county*. He presided over a court that met once a month, collected fines, and in time of war called out the warriors of his county. Sometimes,

> **"***If any one of the race of the Saxons hereafter concealed among them shall have wished to hide himself unbaptized, and shall have scorned to come to baptism and shall have wished to remain a pagan, let him be punished by death.***"**
>
> —Charlemagne

for purposes of defense, several counties were grouped into a larger unit headed by a **duke**.

Counts and dukes traditionally came from the local landed nobility, and their positions were a valuable asset that they might use in the interest of their own families rather than in the service of the ruler. As a check on these officials, Charlemagne appointed royal inspectors, who visited all his territories once a year. Traveling in pairs (a nobleman and a clergyman), they investigated the performance of the counts and dukes and reported their findings to Charlemagne. By acting vigorously in response to this intelligence, he succeeded in holding together his far-flung empire.

Because there was no general system of taxation, Charlemagne had to draw most of his revenue from the crown lands, which he kept as his own. He held thousands of estates, most of them concentrated between Paris and the Rhine River (see Map 10.1) where his noble ancestors had first built up their power. Understandably, he was keenly interested in the efficiency with which his properties were managed, and he prepared detailed instructions for the guidance of his royal stewards (estate managers).

 Inspecting the Imperial Domains: The Capitulary de Villis and an Estate Inventory Read Charlemagne's detailed instructions for managing his estates.

Art and Literature: The Carolingian Renaissance

Charlemagne made his capital at Aachen, which was surrounded by productive crown lands in the heart of the ancient Frankish territories. His palace chapel, which still stands, was the first important stone building to be erected north of the Alps after the fall of Rome (see photo). This fact in itself indicates the slow recovery of the West. The chapel was modeled on the church of San Vitale in Ravenna, a Byzantine outpost on Italy's east coast. The king was so impressed when he first saw San Vitale, with its dome supported on arches and its glistening mosaics, that he directed his builders to duplicate the plan in his own capital. Thus,

Charlemagne's Palace Chapel Built about A.D. 800 in Charlemagne's capital at Aachen in the west of present-day Germany, the chapel imitates an earlier Byzantine building in Italy. However, the designer was a Frankish architect, Odo of Metz, who evidently possessed sophisticated knowledge and skills. The chapel remained for many centuries an imperial shrine and a monument to the dream of a revived Roman Empire.

the art of Constantinople found its way to Aachen and the Frankish heartland.

Charlemagne was also concerned over the low level of education and scholarship in his realm and issued a decree instructing bishops and abbots to improve the training of the clergy. In Aachen itself, around 780, he set up a palace school that would become a center of intellectual activity.

 An Illustrated Guide to the Aachen Cathedral (http://www.sacred-destinations.com/germany/aachen-cathedral) Tour Charlemagne's chapel in Aachen.

The school came under the guidance of a monk named Alcuin, the leading scholar of his day, whom Charlemagne had called from the cathedral school of York, the finest in England. The students, like most of those who received any kind of schooling at the time, all belonged to the clergy. It was still unusual even for high nobles and rulers to be literate: Charlemagne himself only learned to read as an adult and never mastered the art of writing.

Alcuin trained a staff of expert scribes (copyists), who brought back the monastic tradition of reproducing ancient

BOTH THE POPE AND CHARLEMAGNE DESIRED CHARLEMAGNE'S CORONATION:

The Pope's Reasons

- The pope needed a strong protector in Italy, and there was also the possibility that the Franks themselves might prove dangerous.

- By crowning the emperor, the pope defined the relationship between the restored (Western) empire and the Church.

- Charlemagne received the crown from the hand of the pope, thereby putting the emperor under obligation to the papacy—and what the papacy had given, it also had a right to withdraw.

Charlemagne's Reasons

- Though Charlemagne may have been surprised by the circumstances of his crowning, there is no evidence that he was displeased.

- Under his rule, the Frankish state had become large and strong enough to lay claim to being a restored version of the Roman Empire. The coronation ceremony seemingly confirmed the truth of this idea.

- The coronation gave Charlemagne even greater power as a ruling figure. He could claim a special holiness and authority from God.

---

manuscripts. Most of the ancient Roman works that survive today have come down from Carolingian copies preserved in monastery libraries, and the easily readable handwritten letters designed by the Carolingian scribes still form the basis of today's lowercase letters. In copying, the monks naturally concentrated on Christian authors, but they also preserved pagan literature. Christian tradition encouraged the reading of pagan works that were morally and intellectually improving (pp. 143-144), but monks sometimes stretched the limits of what was allowed. Alongside works on philosophy and morals by the high-minded Cicero, they also carefully copied the how-to poems on seduction of the disreputable Ovid (p. 108).

Alcuin also established a course of studies, based on that of the monastic and cathedral schools, for selected young men of the Frankish nobility. The faculty of the school at Aachen was made up of distinguished scholars drawn from all over Europe. Many of their pupils became outstanding teachers themselves in other intellectual centers of present-day Germany and France. Though Charlemagne's empire barely survived him, the "Carolingian Renaissance" of the arts and scholarship provided a lasting impetus to the cultural development of Europe.

The Restoration of the "Roman Empire"

The most dramatic event of Charlemagne's rule was his coronation as "Charles Augustus, Emperor of the Romans." The event took place on Christmas Day, 800, while the Frankish king was attending Mass in Saint Peter's Basilica in Rome. Supposedly, he had not planned the coronation beforehand; his biographer, Einhard, reports that Pope Leo III, without warning, placed the crown on his head and declared him emperor.

The restored empire in fact had a very different structure from the old one. It was much smaller than the Western half of ancient Rome; missing were North Africa, Sicily, Spain, and Britain, though lands east of Rome's Rhine frontier were part of Charlemagne's realm. In Charlemagne's territories, there was no single citizenship, no unified law, no professional civil service, no standing army, and few cities, and the roads had fallen into disrepair.

Even so, Charlemagne's coronation was a truly historic event. There was, after all, another "Roman emperor" in Constantinople. At the time, an empress, Irene, was reigning over Byzantium, contrary to strict Roman tradition under which females were considered ineligible to rule. The pope may therefore have seized the moment to elevate Charlemagne to a "vacant" throne. But in any case, by accepting the title of emperor, Charlemagne was not just restoring the old empire. For the first time, a barbarian-descended western European king was claiming equality with, or even supremacy over, the Eastern emperors. Between the Byzantine East and the barbarian West, the balance was beginning to shift.

LO² The New Pattern of Europe

After Charlemagne died in 814, the promise of order and stability that his rule had held out faded in the dusk of renewed civil

serf
A peasant bound to work for a landowner—a lifelong hereditary status—as a condition for hereditary possession of a small farm.

vassal
A warrior who agreed to serve a greater warrior in exchange for secure possession of land.

wars and invasions. Yet, out of the collapse of his empire emerged the main features of medieval European civilization that would govern Western life and thought until the fifteenth century.

The Collapse of Charlemagne's Empire

One of the main reasons for the Carolingian rulers' success so far was that they had escaped having to follow the custom of sharing the mayoralty and then the kingship with other heirs. Both Pepin and Charlemagne had brothers, but Pepin's brother voluntarily became a monk and Charlemagne's brother conveniently died. Likewise, it was good for the dynasty's future that Charlemagne had only one surviving son, Louis. The new emperor reigned well enough to go down in history as Louis the Pious, but unfortunately for the dynasty, he had three sons who survived him. During his lifetime, he tried to break with custom and hand on most of his inheritance to his eldest son, Lothar, but this effort led to warfare with his younger sons.

Renewed Division and Renewed Invasions

Finally, after Louis's death, his sons arrived at a settlement that marked an important early stage in the development of the countries of western Europe. By the Treaty of Verdun (843), Lothar was confirmed as emperor and given a middle section of the empire stretching from present-day Holland to northern Italy. The second son, Louis, received the section east of the Rhine, which would one day become Germany. Charles, the youngest son, inherited the western section, the nucleus of France. But the treaty did not prevent continued fighting among Louis's sons and their descendants. The middle section soon disappeared, with most of its territory ultimately taken over by the rulers of the eastern section.

 Collapse of the Carolingian World: Partition and Invasion Read a medieval account of the events surrounding the Treaty of Verdun.

The disintegration of Charlemagne's empire was accelerated by ferocious attacks from outside. In the Mediterranean, Muslim raiders from North Africa had taken over Sicily and Sardinia. They preyed on shipping, struck at the coastal towns of Italy and southern France, and made off with everything they could carry. In 846, they captured Rome and looted Saint Peter's Basilica, the central church of the Christian West.

On the eastern frontier, there appeared yet another nation of Asiatic nomads, the Magyars or Hungarians (Map 10.2). They took over the same territory that the Huns and Avars had occupied before them—a large plain about halfway along the course of the River Danube, which still makes up present-day Hungary. From here, they sent raiding expeditions throughout Germany, sometimes striking as far as the Netherlands and southern France. For much of the tenth century, they kept central Europe in turmoil.

The Norsemen

The strongest blows came from Scandinavia, home of the Norsemen or Vikings ("men of the North" or "pirates" in their own language). The Norsemen were the northernmost branch of the Germanic peoples, and with the northward spread of Christianity and Roman culture, it was their turn to live on the fringe of civilization. By the ninth century, like the Greeks in their encounter with the people of the eastern Mediterranean many centuries before (pp. 49-53), they had become a formidable nation of seafarers, traders, and warriors, and their population had grown beyond what the harvests of their northern homeland could support. Consequently, they struck out on what proved to be the last great barbarian invasion of civilized Europe.

From 800 on, the high-prowed longboats of the Norsemen began to appear all along the coastline of western Europe (see photo on page 176). The warriors who leaped ashore demanded tribute from the inhabitants and carried off what they could. From the coasts, they moved up the rivers and carried their raids deep into the interior. Finally, the Viking raids turned into regular campaigns of conquest in which they seized and settled whole territories.

The western Viking tribes, the Norwegians, mainly sailed westward and took over much of Scotland and Ireland; by 1000, their westward urge had taken them across the Atlantic to Iceland, Greenland, and "Vinland" (North America). The southernmost tribes, the Danes, generally moved southward to the coastlands of the North Sea and the Channel: England, France, and the Netherlands. The Anglo-Saxons were forced to surrender the eastern half of England (the Danelaw) to the invaders, and the Frankish rulers were compelled to yield a large territory along the Channel that was called, after the Norsemen, the duchy of Normandy (see Map 10.2).

Meanwhile, the eastern Vikings, the Swedes, traveled across the Baltic Sea and then upriver to a watershed region far inland, where other rivers led them hundreds of miles south to the Black Sea. They won power over the Slavic tribes who had settled this vast region of eastern Europe, and in 860 their longboats attacked Constantinople.

The Great Lords

Throughout the territory of Charlemagne's empire, the struggles among his descendants, as well as barbarian and Muslim attacks, made violence and danger more than ever a normal condition of life. Everywhere, people turned from the distant and helpless rulers to whoever was near enough and strong enough to offer them some protection. Free peasants bound themselves and their descendants to labor on the lands of local warriors as **serfs** (p. 193). Lesser warriors agreed to serve greater ones in war and peace as their **vassals** (pp. 184–185) and in turn received from the greater warriors secure possession of land. Everywhere, effective power came to be exercised by the strongest warrior nobles who could gain the allegiance of the largest number of lesser warriors to swell their armies. They could then use their armies to win control of the most important resources: land, the labor of peasants, and the goods and treasure obtainable by trade or looting.

The leading warrior-nobles also increased their power at the expense of the rulers. Partly by grants from Carolingian rivals who sought their support, and partly by simple seizure from feeble kings, the leading nobles took over royal lands, collected royal revenues, and exercised royal powers of justice. And they treated all these new resources and powers, as well as the rights they acquired over lesser warriors and peasants, as family property. The hereditary possessor of such a property was known as a **lord**. The leading lords also took over such former royal offices as duke and count and converted these into hereditary titles.

Finally, in both the eastern and the western Frankish kingdoms, the succession to the kingship itself came to be settled through election by the great lords. When the direct descendants of Charlemagne died out—in the eastern kingdom in 911 and in the western kingdom in 987—the great lords chose

> **lord**
> The hereditary possessor of lands, revenues, and powers over lesser warriors and peasants.

Map 10.2 **Invasions of the Ninth and Tenth Centuries**

Muslim sailors attacked the Christian coastlines of the western Mediterranean. Magyar horsemen raided westward from the middle Danube, the traditional staging area for nomad invaders of Europe. Norsemen traveled the coasts and rivers of western Europe, made lengthy river voyages across eastern Europe to the Black Sea, and "island-hopped" across the Atlantic to North America. But converted Norse and Magyar settlers in parts of eastern and western Europe eventually helped to strengthen Christendom. © Cengage Learning

Interactive Map

primogeniture
The custom of passing along the bulk of family property to the eldest son.

new (and powerless) kings from among themselves.

The Rise of Western Europe

The collapse of Charlemagne's empire did not mean the end of civilization in Europe. On the contrary, as with the fall of Rome in the fifth century, the end of empire and barbarian invasions actually led to civilization's wider spread.

Government itself did not simply disintegrate but developed into new and, in the long run, more effective forms. The great lords, eager to pass on their newly acquired powers and possessions to their descendants, began to give up the custom—previously followed by nobles as well as kings—of dividing their properties among their children. Instead, during the eleventh century, the custom grew up of handing the bulk of the property to the eldest son. This was known as the right of **primogeniture** (from the Latin for "firstborn"). As a result, dynasties of great lords emerged that were able to control fairly stable blocks of territory over several generations.

Sooner or later, any individual dynasty would usually fall victim to defeat in war or failure to produce male heirs. As a group, however, the great lords came to constitute a class of regional potentates, presiding effectively over a chaotic but dynamic warrior society. They defended their possessions against Norsemen, Hungarians, and Arabs; they undertook counteroffensives, such as the reconquest of Spain or the Crusades; and they fought continually against each other.

But these lords did more than wage wars. They generously endowed monasteries and supported movements of reform and reorganization in the Church. They pushed the peasants on their lands to carve new farms and villages out of the wilderness

The Gokstad Ship This Viking longboat was buried with its owner in Norway about A.D. 900 and was dug up and restored in 1870. It has a mast to hoist a sail and 32 oar holes along the top edge of the hull. The 75-foot-long boat probably carried 64 warrior-oarsmen rowing in shifts, with wooden chests for their clothes and bedding that doubled as rowing benches, on lengthy open-air trips on stormy seas and treacherous rivers. In 1893, a replica of this vessel crossed the Atlantic. University Museum of Cultural Heritage, Oslo

that at that time covered much of Europe, and they took a hand in founding towns as centers of trade and industry. The role of these leading nobles in the building of medieval European civilization was an important one.

Barbarian Conquerors and the Spread of Civilization

Even where barbarian invaders conquered and settled, as so often before, they ended by adopting the civilization of their new homelands. Furthermore, the very same Norse and Hungarian attacks that helped demolish the power of the Carolingians also led to the appearance of new forms of royal government to defend whole countries against the invaders (p. 178).

In the main western European territories seized by the Vikings—the Danelaw and Normandy—the Norse settlers agreed to become Christian in return for recognition of their conquests by the English and French kings. In England, Danes and Anglo-Saxons—both ethnically Germanic—became so mixed in language and customs that within a few generations they were hard to tell apart; in Normandy, the sons and daughters of the invaders already spoke the language into which the Latin of that region had evolved in the centuries since the fall of Rome—French. From England and France, and under the influence of the Holy Roman Empire, Christianity and Roman civilization spread back to the Norse homelands, so that by 1000 Norway, Denmark, and Sweden were on the way to becoming Christian kingdoms.

Among the Norse conquerors, the Normans in particular had a great impact on the development of civilization in the West. In 1066, Duke William of Normandy conquered the Anglo-Saxon kingdom of England, coming not as a barbarian invader but with his banners blessed by the pope, as a claimant to the country's Christian kingship. Building on the institutions of the Anglo-Saxon kingdom, the Norman conqueror and his successors made innovations in the fields of administration and justice that have influenced the laws and government of England, and of countries inheriting English traditions, down to the present day (pp. 189–190).

 The Bayeux Tapestry (http://www .bayeuxtapestry .org.uk) Explore the Bayeux Tapestry, depicting the Norman invasion of England.

 Losing to William the Conqueror: One Abbey's Experience Read an account of one abbey's hardships after William conquered England.

Meanwhile, other Normans acting independently of their dukes wrested Sicily from Muslim control, and together with warriors from other parts of France, they reinforced Christian efforts at the reconquest of Spain. In this way, the descendants of pagan barbarian conquerors became the leaders of the western European counteroffensive against Islam.

In central Europe, barbarian conquerors were absorbed in much the same way as farther west. After their defeat by Otto I in 955, the Hungarians still held a large region between the Holy Roman Empire and Byzantium (see Map 10.3). Instead of retreating and dispersing as earlier defeated nomads had done, the Hungarians held on to the territory they had conquered, and won acceptance from the Holy Roman Empire by adopting its Western Christianity and culture. During the ninth and tenth centuries, so did the rulers of various groups of Slav tribes that in earlier centuries had settled in the lands on the empire's eastern borders (pp. 156-157): the Poles, Czechs, and Slovaks, and farther south, the Slovenes and Croats.

For many barbarian peoples, contact with civilization was divisive. Leading warriors often clung to traditional pagan beliefs, and they rightly suspected that their rulers would swell from mere chieftains into kings who would demand obedience in peace as well as war. In Scandinavia, Poland, and Hungary, the coming of Christianity led to rebellion and civil war, and the triumph of the new religion was military as well as spiritual. But the upshot was that the ninth- and tenth-century invasions ended with the boundary of Western Christianity expanding northward into Scandinavia and a long way into eastern Europe and the Balkans (see Map 10.3).

The Rise of Byzantine Eastern Europe

Beyond the boundary of Western Christianity, the same general pattern prevailed, of successful barbarian peoples attacking civilized states yet also reaching toward the religion and way of life of their victims. The difference was that the Christianity and civilization they were reaching for were those of Byzantium.

In Byzantium, as in western Europe, central power grew stronger under the stress of external attack from the seventh century onward as the emperors reorganized their administrative and military system. By about 800, Byzantium had regained control of Greece from the Slavs, and its rulers were experts in playing the Slav tribes and nomadic invaders of eastern Europe against each other. During the ninth and tenth centuries, with many setbacks, Byzantium gradually pushed northward against the Slavs and eastward against the Arabs.

The Conversion of the Slavs

In dealing with the Slavs, the Byzantines did not rely on warfare and diplomacy alone. Among the Slavs, like the Germanic tribes before them, migration and war had fostered a wealthy and powerful elite of chieftains and warriors. This elite might fight against Byzantium, but also wanted to participate in its way of life. Byzantine armies and navies could never banish the Slav threat, but the Christian religion and the Greek heritage might at least bring the Slavs under the empire's spiritual and cultural sway.

In the ninth and tenth centuries, the Byzantine emperors and leading clergy of the Eastern Church deliberately set about the task of bringing Christianity and Greek culture to the Slavs. So eager were the Byzantines to make their message acceptable that they even allowed the Slavs to worship in their own language, rather than in Greek—unlike the Western Church, which usually insisted that no other language than Latin be used in public worship. Byzantine monks also adapted the Greek alphabet to the sounds of the Slav language. The result was the Cyrillic alphabet

NEW FORMS OF ROYAL GOVERNMENT AROSE IN ENGLAND, THE HOLY ROMAN EMPIRE, AND FRANCE IN RESPONSE TO THE NORSE AND HUNGARIAN ATTACKS:

England

- In the ninth century, King Alfred of the southern kingdom of Wessex led all the Anglo-Saxons in resistance to the Danes. Even though he had to concede the Danelaw to the invaders (see Map 10.2 on page 173), it remained under his overlordship.

- Alfred's tenth-century successors were able to recover the lost territory and, for the first time, build a united English kingdom.

Holy Roman Empire

- In the eastern Frankish kingdom, the great lords badly needed strong leadership against the Hungarians, and finally, they permitted the most powerful family among them, the dukes of Saxony, to fill the office of king.

- The ablest of that family, Otto I, defeated the Hungarians decisively in 955, ending their raids into Germany.

- Otto next reclaimed the "Roman" imperial title, which had fallen into disuse, and was crowned emperor by Pope John XII at Rome in 962. Actually, Otto's holdings included only Germany and the northern and central regions of Italy, and the empire he founded came to be known as the Holy Roman Empire of the German Nation, or the Holy Roman Empire (Map 10.3).

- The Holy Roman emperors were never consistently able to enforce the principle of hereditary succession against that of election by the great lords, but they remained powerful down to the later Middle Ages, and the empire itself lasted until 1806.

France

- In the western Frankish kingdom, Hugh Capet, count of Paris, replaced the last Carolingian king in 987.

- Though Hugh wielded little power outside the area of northern France that he controlled as count, he did at least succeed in persuading the great lords to elect his son king during his own lifetime.

- Later Capetian rulers managed to get rid of election altogether and hand on the kingship—whole and undivided, like the rest of their possessions—by hereditary right.

- Having thereby won "independence" from the other great lords, the Capetians would lead the way, by the thirteenth century, to the establishment of a strong hereditary monarchy in France (pp. 187–188).

---

tsar
The Slav term for emperor, from the Latin *caesar.*

(named for the missionary Cyril, one of the leaders in the project of converting the Slavs); it has remained the standard script in Russia and several other Slav countries ever since.

These Byzantine gifts of religion, culture, and literacy were usually combined with others that were just as appealing: military alliances, commercial treaties, and prestigious imperial titles for the Slav chieftains. In the long run, the combination proved irresistible. One by one, the chieftains invited Byzantine missionaries to their lands or came in person to Constantinople to be baptized. As in

 Russian (Cyrillic) Alphabet and Audio Pronunciations (http://listen2russian.com/lesson01/a/index.html) See the Cyrillic alphabet and hear the Russian pronunciations.

western Europe, pagan warriors often clung to their traditional customs, but their opposition faded away or was crushed. More serious competition came from the Western Church, which was able to attract the westernmost Slav tribes into its orbit. Elsewhere, it was Byzantium that triumphed.

The Balkans

In the Balkans, for a time, Byzantium had a formidable rival. North of Byzantium's recovered territory of Greece, many Slav tribes had been united into a powerful state by yet another nation of nomadic invaders, the Bulgars. The Slav majority eventually assimilated their overlords and accepted Christianity from Byzantium. Even so, the Bulgarian **tsars** (the Slav version of the Latin title *caesar*, inherited by Byzantium from ancient Rome) struggled with the Byzantine emperors for control of the Balkan region. Around 1000, in the last of many brutal wars,

Map 10.3 **Europe About 1000**

The division between Christian Europe and pagan barbarian Europe has almost vanished. Slavs, Norsemen, and Magyars have formed Christian kingdoms on the model of their neighbors and former victims. More convert peoples have followed the model of the Latin than of the Greek Church, so that the boundary between the two runs a long way east. To the south, the rival monotheism of Islam has yielded little ground. Europe is taking shape between the Atlantic, the Mediterranean, and the River Volga. © Cengage Learning

 Interactive Map

Byzantium finally conquered Bulgaria, though in language and culture the Bulgarians remained Slavic.

To the west of the Bulgarians there lived another Slavic tribal group that had become Christian under Byzantine influence, the Serbs. Long overshadowed by the powerful Bulgarians, the Serbs were now able, for the first time, to build a unified state, whose rulers soon came into conflict with the rulers of the neighboring Slav people to the west, the Croats. In addition, between Serbia and Croatia there now ran the dividing line between Western and Eastern Christianity; and while the Serb rulers counted as subject to Byzantium, from about 1100, Croatia was ruled

> "*Then we went on to Greece, and the Greeks led us to the edifices where they worship their God, and we knew not whether we were in heaven or on earth. For on earth there is no such splendor or such beauty, and we are at a loss how to describe it. We know only that God dwells there among men, and their service is fairer than the ceremonies of other nations.*"
>
> —A Russian visitor to Constantinople, A.D. 987

by the kings of Hungary. Thus, although the Serbs and Croats were closely related tribal groups whose descendants still understand each others' languages today, they eventually developed into separate and sometimes rival nations.

Russia

Byzantium's greatest success was with the Slavs of northeastern Europe, between the Baltic and Black Seas. These Slavs came to be known by the name of a group of Swedish Vikings who conquered them in the ninth century: the Rus or Russians. The Swedish conquerors formed their territories into a powerful state that they ruled from the important commercial center of Kiev (see Map 10.3). Like the Norse conquerors of Normandy, those of Russia quickly adopted the language and customs of their subjects (in this case, Slavic), but they did not lose their Viking appetite for trade and warfare.

The main trading partner of the Russians, and the target of many of their raids, was Byzantium. Either way, the Russian rulers admired the empire's way of life and respected its ancient glory. Finally, in 988, Prince Vladimir of Kiev made a bargain with Byzantium: in return for the exceptional honor of marriage to the emperor's own sister, he threw down the pagan idols of Kiev and was baptized into the Eastern Church. Thus Russia became the easternmost of the states that shared in the religious and cultural heritage of Byzantium.

By 1000, most of the eastern European peoples formed a religious and cultural community like that of western Europe—but one that looked to Constantinople instead of to Rome. What held this community of Byzantine-influenced states together was not, as in western Europe, the inheritance of Roman civilization, the Western Church, and obedience to the pope. Instead, it was the inheritance of Greek civilization, the Eastern Church, and reverence for the Byzantine emperor (or in some cases his actual overlordship). In this way, as Europe took shape, it developed different variants of a common civilization in its western and eastern regions.

> *"Christianity and the inheritance of Greece and Rome, in spite of all divergences between Rome and Byzantium, gave European civilization its basic unity. Numerous different ethnic groups and independent states supplied the vigor of diversity and competition, as well as the destructive urge to conflict and domination."*

 Holy Russia/ The First Flowering of Christianity (http://mini-site.louvre.fr/sainte-russie/EN/html/1.2.html Holy Russia) View the earliest Christian art of Russia.

 Religious Competition in Kievan Russia Read the medieval story of Vladimir of Russia's conversion to Christianity.

The End of the Barbarian Way of Life

By 1000, the turmoil of the ninth and tenth centuries had produced a surprising result. For three thousand years, Europe had been both the meeting place and the arena of conflict between civilized and barbarian peoples; and now this lengthy era had more or less come to an end. It took another four centuries for the last remaining pagan tribes along the southern and eastern coastlands of the Baltic Sea to be converted. But otherwise, all of Europe had come within the orbit of civilization, and this civilization had already developed distinctive features that have characterized it ever since. Christianity and the inheritance of Greece and Rome, in spite of all divergences between Rome and Byzantium, gave European civilization its basic unity. Numerous different ethnic groups and independent states supplied the vigor of diversity and competition, as well as the destructive urge to conflict and domination. All these features would be inherited to a greater or lesser extent by the modern West.

 Listen to a synopsis of Chapter 10.

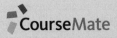
Access to the eBook with additional review material and study tools may be found online at CourseMate for WCIV. Sign in at www.cengagebrain.com.

« **"He Fell in Battle, in the East in Garthar"** This carved stone commemorates Torstein, the leader of a Swedish warrior band that fought in "Garthar"—Russia—probably for Yaroslav the Wise, a warlike ruler of Kiev about 1050. The inscription is written in runes, the ancient alphabet of pagan Scandinavia, but the monument is marked with a cross. At a time when Christian kingdoms were forming across northern Europe, converted Vikings were fighting and dying in the service of their rulers. Swedish National Heritage Board/Visual Connection Archive

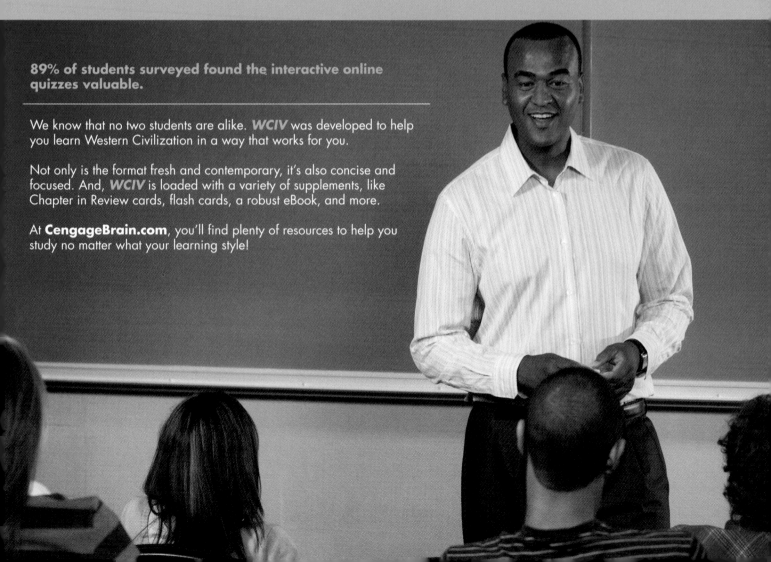

{ Learning Your Way }

89% of students surveyed found the interactive online quizzes valuable.

We know that no two students are alike. *WCIV* was developed to help you learn Western Civilization in a way that works for you.

Not only is the format fresh and contemporary, it's also concise and focused. And, *WCIV* is loaded with a variety of supplements, like Chapter in Review cards, flash cards, a robust eBook, and more.

At **CengageBrain.com**, you'll find plenty of resources to help you study no matter what your learning style!

MANORS, TOWNS, AND KINGDOMS,
1000–1300

LEARNING OBJECTIVES

AFTER READING THIS CHAPTER, YOU SHOULD BE
ABLE TO DO THE FOLLOWING:

LO[1] Describe how feudalism worked to govern social and
political relationships in the Middle Ages.

LO[2] Discuss the operation of a manor.

LO[3] Explain how the rural-based civilization of the early
Middle Ages became a city-based civilization.

> "BESIDES NEW PEOPLES AND NEW KINGDOMS, THE FIVE HUNDRED YEARS OF UPHEAVAL THAT FOLLOWED THE FALL OF ROME ALSO PRODUCED NEW SKILLS AND NEW SOCIAL STRUCTURES."

Besides new peoples and new kingdoms, the five hundred years of upheaval that followed the fall of Rome also produced new skills and new social structures. The new kingdoms continued to be ruled in partnership by rulers, warrior-landowners, and Church leaders, but in many of them, the interplay of these power wielders came to be regulated by rules and customs so formal and binding that they had the force of law. In this way, a new pattern of social life and government arose—that of feudalism. Between 1000 and 1300, feudalism enabled some of the new kingdoms to become well-organized states.

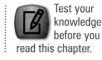

Test your knowledge before you read this chapter.

Meanwhile, turmoil in the countryside gave rise to the institutions of serfdom (an unfree but farm-holding peasantry) and the manor (a type of agricultural estate). These institutions gave both peasants and landowners an incentive to grow more crops, at the same time as inventive ironworkers were developing new and more effective farming tools. The result was three centuries of growth in population and wealth, which kings, nobles, and Church leaders were able to use for purposes of government, warfare, religion, and culture.

The increase of farming wealth, together with closer contacts with the world outside Europe, in turn led to an increase in trade and a revival of urban life. Roman towns revived, new ones grew up in once-barbarian lands, the network of trade routes and commercial centers grew extensive and close-meshed, and in regions where rulers were weak, independent city-states appeared for the first time since the rise of Rome.

What do you think?

Feudalism fostered greater inequality than we experience in contemporary society.

Strongly Disagree						Strongly Agree
1	2	3	4	5	6	7

« **Sir Geoffrey Luttrell** A fourteenth-century English knight prepares for the battle or the joust. His wife, Agnes de Sutton, hands him his helmet; his daughter-in-law, Beatrice le Scrope, holds his shield. The shield, and the clothing of the rider and the horse, display the Luttrell coat of arms; on Agnes it is combined with the Sutton coat of arms, and on Beatrice with that of the Scropes. The three families form a warrior-landowner network linked by marriage, and the married ladies approve and support their knightly warrior.

These changes affected all of Europe, but the "Greek" East still contended with nomad invasions and Muslim expansion. For this reason, change was most spectacular in the "Latin" West, which now rose to become the heartland of a renewed civilization, as brilliant as any in the past.

LO¹ Feudalism

The word **feudalism** was coined by historians long after the end of the Middle Ages, to describe the type of government institutions, as well as the general social and political relationships, that existed at that period among warrior-landholders in much of Europe. Feudalism originated in northern France during the tenth century, following the breakup of the Carolingian empire. Warrior-landholders elsewhere who found that it met their needs, as well as conquering Norman warriors (p. 177), brought it to many other countries. By the twelfth century, not only France but also England, the Holy Roman Empire, Spain, Sicily, and even Byzantium were governed according to feudal principles.

Feudalism was not a tidy unified system, but it always worked according to two basic principles, each affecting one of the two things that were of most concern to warrior-landholders—warfare and land.

As warriors, feudalism bound them by personal ties of mutual trust and loyalty. Lesser warrior-landholders were supposed to show loyalty to a greater one, enabling him to rely on them as his personal army; but the greater warrior-landholder was expected to show them loyalty in turn, protecting and helping them individually so that they would not have to stand against enemies on their own.

As landholders, feudalism bound members of the upper class together by giving them mutual rights over and interests in the most important of all resources, the land and the peasants who worked it. Lesser warrior-landholders did not actually "own" their land but "held" it on condition of doing military and other service to a greater one, who in turn was obligated to guarantee and protect the lesser ones in the secure hereditary possession of their estates.

For leading warriors to provide for their soldiers by giving them land was nothing new, but the soldiers who now had to be provided for were not just the infantry of Charles Martel's time (p. 167), but heavily armed and armored horse warriors (see photo on page 182). Heavy cavalry warfare was first practiced by the Persians and spread to the Romans and then the Arabs, who in turn "taught" it to their European opponents. Along the way, it was made easier by the invention of stirrups—iron foot

CHRONOLOGY

1152–1190	Reign of Holy Roman Emperor Frederick I Barbarossa
1180–1223	Reign of King Philip Augustus of France
1199–1216	Reign of King John of England
1204	France's Philip Augustus seizes Normandy and other French possessions of the English kings
1215	King John of England signs the Magna Carta, granting new rights to barons and subjects in general
1300	Population of Europe hits 100 million

rests hanging from a saddle—which were brought to the Middle East and Europe by nomad invaders. Stirrups gave horsemen a more stable platform from which to wield their weapons. As a result, during the eleventh century, heavy cavalry became the main striking force of armies.

In English, these warriors came to be called *knights*, from a Germanic word meaning "servant." But to provide for just one such "servant," with all his training and equipment, took a good deal of land and and a good many peasants. Through feudal ties, kings and great lords could assure themselves of the services of knights by guaranteeing them the hereditary control of land and peasants that made them, too, part of the ruling warrior-landholder class.

Relationships of the same kind also existed between rulers of countries and the great lords within the countries they ruled. Since the great lords had taken over so much of the powers of government (p. 175), it was only through these ties that monarchs were able to hold their countries together. In any country, in fact, there existed a host of miniature governments, each ruled by one or another great lord and loosely associated under the monarch by the ties of feudalism. In spite of its decentralized operation, feudal government afforded some measure of security and justice for millions of Europeans, and held many countries of Europe together as political units, for five hundred years. It even succeeded in producing powerful states, in which effective central authority was grafted onto the decentralized feudal structure with its stress on mutual rights and responsibilities between holders of power and those subjected to them.

The Feudal Compact

At first, the practice of exchanging property for personal service was extremely vague, consisting of unwritten agreements among greater and lesser landholders that were subject to a wide range of interpretations. By the eleventh century, however, the **feudal compact**, or contract, as this aspect of feudalism is called, had evolved into a fairly standard arrangement. Whoever granted land to someone stood in the position of lord; the grantee was his vassal (from another word for "servant"); and the land granted was called a **fief** (from a word for "property"—in Latin, *feudum*, from which *feudalism* is derived).

Besides possession of land, the fief carried with it government responsibility and power. The vassal was expected to protect the inhabitants of his fief, collect revenues, and dispense justice. In this way, political authority was linked to landholding. In addition, each vassal, in return for the benefits of his fief, owed important obligations to his lord.

 The Feudal Contract: Mutual Duties of Vassals and Lords Read a medieval account of the mutual duties of vassals and lords.

Chief among these was military service. A vassal was expected to serve his lord in person, and the holder of a large fief was required, in addition, to furnish knights—his own vassals—as well as foot soldiers. In this way, the kings and the great lords, who found it impracticable to pay for standing armies, were able to raise fighting forces when needed. At first, the vassal's obligation to fight when called on by his lord was unlimited, but gradually, it was set by custom at about forty days' service each year.

The holder of a fief was also obliged to serve on the lord's court, which was usually held once a month. This court heard disputes among the lord's vassals, often over land and interpretations of feudal rights, as well as criminal charges. The lord presided in all cases, and his vassals acted as judges. It then became the lord's duty to enforce their decision, but should the losing party refuse to accept it, armed conflict could result. In this way, a lord and his vassals formed a community, with shared responsibility and power.

Under the feudal compact, a lord had no general right to collect taxes from a vassal or the peasants who lived on the vassal's fief, but in some strictly defined circumstances, a vassal was required to make payments to his lord. After receiving his fief, he normally paid its first year's income to the lord. When the lord's eldest son was knighted (see next section) or his eldest daughter was married, or if the lord was captured in battle and had to be ransomed, the vassal had to make payment. In addition, for a given number of days each year, the lord and his family and attendants could demand food, lodging, and entertainment from the vassal.

Homage and Knighthood

The granting of a fief, with all its requirements, was accompanied by the vassal's doing **homage** to his lord (see photo on page 196). Usually, the vassal knelt down, put his hands between those of his lord, and offered himself as the lord's "man" (in Latin, *homo*). The lord accepted the vassal's homage, told him to rise, and embraced him. Next, it was customary for the vassal to make a Christian vow of fealty (faithfulness). The lord, in exchange for the declaration of vassalage, customarily presented his vassal with a clod of earth or some other object symbolizing the right to govern and use the fief.

With its use of symbol and ritual, its hand-clasping and embracing and taking of vows, the act of homage was not unlike a wedding. In fact, the intention was much the same: to reinforce a legally binding contract between two individuals by a strong personal bond—one that would survive disputes, conflicts, and even the occasional breach of the terms of the contract.

The feudal contract remained in effect so long as lord and vassal honored their mutual obligations or until one of them died. By the custom of primogeniture (p. 176), their eldest sons then inherited the positions of lord and vassal. But whenever one of them died, new ceremonies of homage were necessary.

Since kings and great lords led their forces in person as heavy cavalry soldiers, they, too, came to regard themselves as "knights," and by the eleventh century, knighthood came to be an honorable status shared by the entire feudal elite. Before a young man could qualify for this status, he had to serve an apprenticeship as squire to a respected knight—preferably someone other than his own father, so that he could forge loyalties and friendships beyond his own family. The young man would then be knighted—initiated into the professional caste of warriors, usually by being presented with a sword by an already qualified knight.

This ceremony soon developed spiritual and religious overtones. By the middle of the twelfth century, the knight's sword was usually placed on an altar before the presentation, implying that the knight was obliged to protect the Church. By the thirteenth century, the ritual was normally performed in a church or a cathedral, rather than in a manor house or a castle. The initiate spent a night of vigil and prayer before the day of the ceremony, emerging from the ritual as a "soldier of Christ."

When a vassal died and left an heir who was not a qualified knight, special arrangements had to be made. If the heir was a son who had not yet attained his majority, the lord would normally serve as guardian until the youth could qualify as a knight and become his vassal. If the sole heir was a daughter, the lord would serve as guardian until he found her a knightly husband. Then her husband, through the act of homage, would receive the fief as the lord's new vassal. Such marriages were one of the chief means of expanding individual and family power during the feudal age, and women continued to fulfill one of their ancient traditional functions in family politics, of binding

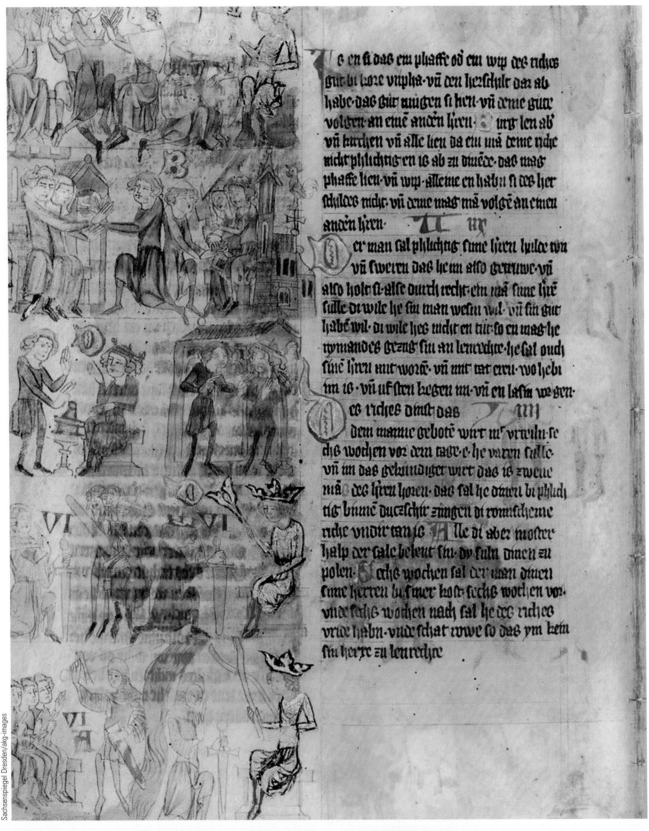

Doing Homage These pictures from the *Saxon Mirror*, a thirteenth-century German law book, illustrate sections on rights of giving and holding fiefs. In the second picture down, kneeling vassals and seated lords clasp each others' hands. One vassal has the shaven head of a clergy member, and the givers of fiefs are clergy and ladies—groups for whom the law made special provision. In the third picture down, a vassal swears allegiance to a lord (both laymen) on a casket containing relics, and dutifully welcomes the lord into his house.

together higher-ranking and lower-ranking power wielders. When a vassal died leaving no heir, the fief reverted to the lord, who could keep it for himself or grant it to a new vassal on the same terms.

The Feudalization of the Church

Because of the close interlocking of the Church hierarchy and the ruling power structure, land held by the Church was naturally also bound up in the feudal pattern. Church lands were held as fiefs by archbishops, bishops, and abbots who had sworn fealty to counts, dukes, princes, or kings. But how could clergymen be warriors on the field of battle? They were not trained knights, and Church law forbade the shedding of blood by the clergy.

The higher clergy were usually the sons of noblemen and familiar with the ways of war. During the ninth and tenth centuries, in fact, they often ignored the Church prohibition and fought in person. Archbishop Turpin, in the epic *Song of Roland* (p. 238), wields his sword against the infidel and dies a hero's death along with Charlemagne's lay vassals. However, with the reform movement of the eleventh century (pp. 208-211), clerical vassals were directed to satisfy their military obligations by assigning portions of their properties as fiefs to vassals who pledged to perform the required military services.

Feudal States

Feudal relationships also existed between rulers of countries and the great lords within the countries they ruled. Since the great lords had taken over so much of the powers of government, however, any feudal monarch who wanted to be truly the ruler of his country faced daunting problems. It was only in his hereditary family territories within his kingdom that he was entitled to do justice, levy taxes, recruit knights, and in general, exercise government authority. Outside these territories (the "royal domain"), it was the great lords, or **barons**, as they were called, who held these powers. Of course, all the barons were vassals of the monarch as overlord, holding their properties as fiefs on condition of doing him military service and bound to him by the personal tie of homage. But it was hard for the monarch to compel them to meet their obligations, given that their combined knightly armies—and often those of individual barons—were larger than his own.

All the same, a feudal monarch did have certain assets on which to build. One was the fact that the barons actually needed an effective overlord to settle their quarrels and lead them in war. A king could use the authority he gained in this way to favor cooperative vassals and undermine obstructive ones. He would use every chance to increase the size of the royal domain so that his personal wealth and power would grow to outweigh those of his vassals. And if things went wrong, the barons rebelled, and he was defeated, he was almost certain not to be killed or overthrown. For of all the warrior-landholders in his country, he alone was holy: chosen by God, crowned, anointed like King David of old, and even credited with the miraculous power to heal disease by his mere touch.

A feudal monarch who built up his assets in this way could not only be a powerful ruler but also create government institutions to ensure that his power would outlive him. In this way, there developed within feudalism effectively governed states, of which the most important were the Holy Roman Empire, France, and England. All of these states were vulnerable to disruptions of various kinds—above all, resistance and rebellion on the part of barons and disputes with the Church, which was both a partner and a rival institution. As a result, throughout medieval times and beyond, the balance of power in the ruling partnership of kings, nobles, and Church leaders constantly shifted. In one and the same country, kings might be feared and respected rulers in one generation, and helpless figureheads in the next.

But only the Holy Roman Empire was permanently weakened by these problems. France and England, in spite of many ups and downs of royal power, survived as strong states into modern times and provided models of statehood for other European countries.

> **baron**
> A great lord who exercised government authority over vast family territory.

> *"Of all the warrior-landholders in his country, the king alone was holy: chosen by God, crowned, anointed like King David of old, and even credited with the miraculous power to heal disease by his mere touch."*

France: The Strengthening of Monarchy

In France, the homeland of feudalism, for more than a century the descendants of Hugh Capet (p. 178) had enough to do ensuring that the kingship would remain in their family and strengthening their control of the royal domain, a 50-mile stretch of countryside around the city of Paris. Outside that area, the barons governed their territories—often ably and effectively—and struggled for power among themselves, paying little heed to the wearer of the crown.

In the twelfth century, however, the power of the rulers began to grow—mainly because outside threats caused the barons to cluster more closely as vassals around their overlord, the king. The Holy Roman emperors coveted territory in eastern France and even dreamed of restoring the united empire of Charlemagne. In the south, militant heretics, the Albigensians (al-bi-JEN-see-uhns) (p. 212), challenged Catholicism and feudalism alike. Above all, France was threatened with gradual takeover by rival foreign rulers who were also overmighty French vassals: the kings of England.

THE HOLY ROMAN EMPERORS LOST POWER AS FEUDAL MONARCHS GRADUALLY OVER TIME:

- Their control of Church positions was disrupted when the Church reasserted its independence.

- The great lords lost the habit of looking to the emperors for leadership.

- The emperors diverted energy and resources in a vain attempt to establish power bases in Italy, from which they hoped to overawe both their German vassals and the popes.

- The great lords gained the power to elect emperors, and from the middle of the thirteenth century onward, they chose emperors who would leave them alone.

- Each fief, bishopric, and city in the empire became in practice a small independent state. While individual states might be fairly powerful, none would be as formidable as the large feudal states of France and England.

It was in the duel with the English kings that a powerful French monarchy was forged. Ever since Duke William of Normandy (a territory that was part of France) had conquered England in 1066, his descendants had been fully independent kings of England yet also, so far as their French possessions were concerned, vassals of the king of France. In the twelfth century, by marriage and inheritance, the English kings added to Normandy a whole series of other fiefs that gave them control of the entire western half of France. Although they were vassals, they were easily powerful enough to destroy their overlords. Therefore, as a matter of survival, their overlords set out to destroy them.

It was King Philip Augustus who finally succeeded in this undertaking. Patiently, late in the twelfth century, he exploited his powers as overlord against his dangerous vassals, rallying other French barons against them, and hearing appeals from the English king's own French vassals against high-handed acts by their overlord. He even encouraged the disobedient and warlike sons of his English rival, Henry II, in rebellions against their own father. The climax of Philip's campaign came in 1204. Using feudal procedures, he declared one of Henry's successors, King John, a rebellious vassal in his capacity as duke of Normandy. Philip then confiscated that territory and summoned his other vassals to come with their knights to enforce the judgment. Normandy and other French possessions of the English kings were conquered—and many of them were added to the French king's royal domain. Though the English kings still held extensive fiefs in southwestern France, it would be more than a century before they again challenged the French monarchy.

> *"Each prince shall possess and exercise in peace according to the customs of the land the liberties, jurisdiction, and authority over counties and hundreds which are in his own possession or are held as fiefs from him."*
>
> —Emperor Frederick II, 1231

The French kings had become the most powerful warrior-landholders in their country, to whom even the greatest barons looked for leadership, and this, in turn, gave them the chance to build a strong state. The thirteenth-century King Louis IX, courageous crusader, generous giver to the poor, fighter against injustice and corruption in his own government, who was eventually recognized by the Church as a saint, was also the mightiest ruler in Europe. His royal courts were open to all free subjects, regardless of the courts maintained by barons in their fiefs. Paid officials throughout the country enforced the king's decisions, carried out his orders, and saw to it that the central power of the king overrode the local power of the barons. Even so, Louis kept the barons' support—because he personally was a model of the Christian warrior virtues that they admired and because on the whole he stayed within the limits of feudal custom and tradition. Louis and later thirteenth-century French kings still operated in many ways as feudal overlords, but they also laid the foundations of the absolute monarchy of later times.

 Young Philip Augustus Masters a Vassal Read how Philip Augustus dealt with an insubordinate vassal early in his reign.

The Holy Roman Empire: The Weakening of Monarchy

In the same centuries that the kings of France changed from figurehead rulers to truly powerful monarchs, the Holy

Roman emperors moved in exactly the opposite direction. The empire's founder, Otto I (p. 178), and his tenth-century successors had been able to exploit from the start the kind of assets that it took the French kings generations to acquire. The emperors already owned massive domain territories, and the great lords needed their leadership against outside enemies, above all the Slavs and Hungarians. In addition, the emperors controlled the Church, thus ensuring that bishops and abbots, with their extensive properties and large knightly armies, would be agents of the ruler's power throughout the empire.

True, for a long time, the lords were outright owners of their territories, rather than holding these on condition of service to the ruler. But the twelfth-century emperor Frederick I Barbarossa ("Red-Beard"), a contemporary of Philip Augustus and Henry II, remedied this. He obliged the great lords to accept the status of vassals to him as overlord, holding their territories as fiefs. Like Philip Augustus, he deprived an overmighty vassal, Duke Henry the Lion of Saxony, of his fief, and then drove him into exile. The empire, too, it seemed, was on its way to becoming a powerful feudal state.

However, the emperors faced a persistent and formidable adversary: the popes. In Charlemagne's time and for long afterward, the popes had been willing to accept the protection of the emperors and often their supervision. But with the eleventh-century Church reform movement, the popes began to seek independence from and even supremacy over the emperors. In the long run, the monarchy became weak and the Holy Roman Empire was fragmented.

Concessions to the German Princes Read the list of concessions that a thirteenth-century Holy Roman emperor had to make to the German princes (local rulers).

> " *Walter Trenchebof was asserted to have handed to Inger of Faldingthrope the knife with which he killed Guy Foliot, and is suspected of it. Let him purge himself by water that he did not consent to it. He has failed and is hanged.* "
>
> —from a document of the English Royal Courts (ca. 1201–1214)

writ
In medieval England, a written royal order to a sheriff.

ordeal
In medieval Europe, a method of judging guilt or innocence by subjecting suspects to tests that were deemed to reveal the "judgment of God."

England: The King's Government and the Common Law

In England, feudalism from the start actually favored the growth of royal power. It was Duke William of Normandy who introduced feudalism when he conquered England. As the leader of a victorious army, he could structure his relations with his vassals to his own advantage as king. He kept no less than one-sixth of the country in his own hands as royal domain. He also set up his leading Norman vassals as barons in England, with generous fiefs; however, these mostly consisted not of solid blocks of territory but of smaller areas scattered across the country. As a result, they were practically impossible to govern without central government services that only the king could provide. Furthermore, earlier native English rulers had already devised a fairly efficient government system. The whole country was divided into counties, or *shires*, with a royal official, the *shire reeve* (sheriff), transacting business in accordance with written royal orders or **writs**.

William's successors, particularly the contemporary and rival of Philip Augustus, King Henry II, built on this basis the most complex and efficient of medieval states. On the whole, they got the cooperation of the barons because the state provided both the barons and lesser folk with services that they could not provide for themselves. Most notably, by the beginning of the thirteenth century, the king was providing his subjects with standardized justice operating according to standardized rules and precedents (the "common law").

A Sampling of Criminal Cases Read a sampling of criminal cases and jury decisions.

The king's legal experts, or *justices*, regularly traveled the country to hear cases. When a justice would arrive in a county to hold a court session, the sheriff would summon sworn groups of freemen known as *juries* (from the Latin *jurare*, "swear an oath"), to give truthful evidence before the justice that would establish the rights and wrongs of disputes over property, or to present before him those suspected of serious crimes.

Criminal suspects were normally sent for trial by **ordeal** (from a Germanic word meaning "judgment"). Ordeals involved such procedures as "purging oneself by water"—being tied up and lowered into a pit full of water after a priest had blessed it and asked God to reveal his judgment. Suspects who sank were thought to have been miraculously "accepted" by the water and therefore to be innocent; those who floated had been "rejected" and were therefore guilty. Ordeals were common throughout Europe and dated back at least to the ancient Babylonian King Hammurabi (p. 18). Early in the thirteenth century, however, the Church paralyzed the criminal justice systems of many countries by declaring ordeals superstitious and ungodly. Most governments responded by reviving investigative methods of Roman law,

Magna Carta
The "Great Charter" or agreement between the king of England and the country's barons.

estates
In the Middle Ages, the groups that made up society: often defined as those who pray, those who fight, and those who work.

> ❝No free man shall be arrested or imprisoned or disseised [dispossessed] or outlawed or exiled or in any way victimized, neither will we attack him or send anyone to attack him, except by the lawful judgment of his peers or by the law of the land.❞
>
> —from Magna Carta, 1215

including torture, but in England the king's legal experts thought up a new procedure. From now on, the guilt or innocence of suspects would be determined by summoning juries of a new kind, who would render a verdict, under the guidance of the justice, on the truth of testimony given by others. In this way, the feudal English state inaugurated the modern jury system.

With these and other changes in law and administration, the English kings extended their power over everyone throughout their country. But they were still feudal rulers whose power came from their overlordship of vassals, and their innovations also led to problems and tensions that exploded early in the thirteenth century into a major political crisis.

The Crisis of English Feudal Monarchy: Magna Carta

The English rulers used their new government machinery not just to benefit their subjects but also to exploit the resources of the country to the fullest—above all, to maintain armies that would protect their possessions across the sea in France. Henry II and his elder son Richard I (the "Lion-Hearted") made their English subjects pay heavily for these wars. They even stretched their powers as overlords to demand money as well as military service from their vassals. But at least they were mostly victorious—an important quality in a feudal overlord. In 1204, however, Richard's younger brother, King John, lost Normandy and other French lands to Philip Augustus and subsequently failed to win them back. As a result, he lost the respect of his vassals— "Lackland," they scornfully called him—and he had to rule by increasing oppression and terror.

Between overlords and vassals, outright oppression and terror were always counterproductive: the end result, in 1215, was a rebellion on the part of many leading barons in which the king found himself deserted and alone. But the barons, true to feudal tradition, could not bring themselves to kill or depose their crowned and anointed king. Instead, following complex negotiations, the armed barons came to an agreement with their king that was enshrined in a famous document: **Magna Carta**, the "Great Charter."

 Magna Carta: The Great Charter of Liberties Read a selection from Magna Carta.

What the barons wanted from the king was not for him to dismantle his efficient government machine. Rather, they wanted him to ensure that it worked to their benefit, by operating within the traditional feudal framework of mutual rights and responsibilities between overlord and vassals. Some of the king's concessions were of historic importance. He promised that in the future, should he need to collect money from his vassals other than for the traditional feudal purposes of knighting his eldest son, marrying his eldest daughter, or ransoming himself, he would do so only with the consent of a council composed of the vassals themselves. And he also promised that he would not deprive any free man of life, liberty, property, or protection of the law, "unless by lawful judgment of his peers or by the law of the land."

Of course, King John granted all this because he could only get the armed barons to demobilize by promising whatever they demanded. He and the barons were soon at war again, and conflicts of this kind continued to break out regularly during the thirteenth century. But at the end of every conflict, as a trust-building gesture, the Great Charter would be solemnly renewed, and in time, it became part of the political instincts of kings and barons alike.

Only a powerful king heading an effective government, they came to believe, could ensure peace, justice, and prosperity in the kingdom. But as overlord, the king must respect the rights of his vassals—including their right to share with him the responsibility for governing the country—and he must strictly observe his own legal procedures. The king, then, was under the law, and he needed the consent of at least his leading vassals before taking measures that were not expressly part of his legal rights. In this way, out of the collision between the newly powerful state and the traditions of feudalism, England took its first steps toward constitutional and parliamentary government.

 Time Traveler's Guide to Medieval England (http://www.channel4.com/history/microsites/H/history/guide12/part02.html) Learn more about the politics, culture, and society of medieval England.

LO² Peasants and Lords

In the Middle Ages, society was often thought of as being divided into three **estates** (social groups), each making its particular contribution to the welfare of the whole. Highest were "those who pray"—the clergy, whose lives were the most honorable because they were the guardians of people's souls. Next came "those who fight"—the feudal nobility, from mighty kings to simple knights, who protected life and property. Lowest in status were "those who work"—the common people in town and countryside, including everyone from wealthy merchants and lawyers to landless farm workers, whose labors supported the clergy and nobles as well as themselves.

The people of this low estate had little political voice and even less social prestige, but it was they who made possible the achievements of medieval civilization. Like every great civilization before it—those of Sumer and classical Greece, for example (pp. 11-12, 50)—the civilization of medieval Europe owed its rise to an increase of population and agriculture and a growth of cities and trade. These developments provided the wealth for a complex society, a well-organized government, and a brilliant culture. Accordingly, it is to the life, labor, and forms of community of "those who worked" that we now turn—beginning with the most numerous group, probably forming 90 percent of the population in most countries: the ones who worked in the countryside.

The Manorial Estate

In medieval Europe, most of the agricultural population worked as members of families that occupied small farms—that is, they belonged to the type of rural social group that is known as peasants. But the peasant families did not work their farms individually, nor did they own them as private property. Instead, the principal farming property and social unit was the **manor**, usually belonging to a member of the feudal nobility or to a Church institution. A relatively humble member of the nobility—a simple knight, for instance—might possess no more than a single manor or even a fraction of one. A great fief, on the other hand, consisted of hundreds of manors. And so far as the peasants were concerned, anyone who owned a manor, no matter how high or low his status in the feudal hierarchy, was their lord.

Manors ranged in size from about 300 acres to perhaps 3,000. The average manor was probably about 1,000 acres, supporting some two or three hundred people. It had to be large enough to

manor
The principal farming property and social unit of a medieval community, usually belonging to a member of the feudal nobility or to a Church institution.

>> **A Wheeled Plow** This one belonged to a peasant in Moravia (present-day Czech Republic) in the eighteenth century, when such plows were still standard equipment. As the plow moves, the colter (the vertical blade behind the wheels) slices through the earth; the plowshare then rips the earth up from underneath; and the moldboard (beneath the handles) shoves against the earth, turning it over so tht it settles as loose and fertile soil. The wheels make it easier for animals to pull this complex earth-breaking device.

Courtesy, Moravian Provincial Museum, Brno

three-field system
A method of crop rotation designed to maintain the fertility of the soil and to provide for a regular supply of fall and spring crops.

> "*The rise of trade and the growth of cities, the emergence of national states, the struggles between religious factions—all seem to have had slight effect on the basic patterns and rhythms of rural life.*"

support the people who lived in it and to enable its lord to fulfill his feudal obligations, but it could not be so large as to be unmanageable as a farming unit.

Farming Methods: Wheeled Plows and the Three-Field System

The productive heart of the manor consisted of crop-growing fields (arable fields or plowland). Crop yields were tiny by today's standards, but they had been boosted by technical innovations that had spread widely through much of western Europe since the fall of Rome, regardless of the turmoil of the times.

Ironworking had become so common that blacksmiths were to be found on most estates, turning out sturdy tools that made it easier to clear forests and work the soil. In particular, iron was used to make soil-cutting parts for big wheeled plows that turned over the wet, heavy soils of northern Europe far more thoroughly than earlier types of plow (see photo on page 191). Iron horseshoes and new types of harness made it possible to use horses as work animals, though the less powerful but hardier oxen were more often used. Water-powered grain-grinding mills, first used on a large scale in the Roman Empire and widespread throughout much of Europe by 1000, relieved peasant women from endless hours of grinding grain by hand—time that they could devote to more productive women's work (p. 10) such as taking care of farmyard animals, spinning, and weaving (see photo on page 194).

The most important innovation that increased the agricultural wealth of western Europe was the **three-field system** of cultivation. The manor's plowland was divided into three large, unfenced fields. In a given farming year, one of these fields would be planted in the fall with crops, mainly wheat and rye, that took about nine months to grow and ripen; another in the spring, with crops such as barley and oats that needed six months or less; and the third would be left fallow (unplanted), to regain its fertility. Late in the summer, the fall and spring crops would all be harvested, and in the fall, the fallow field would be planted. In the following spring, the previous fall field would be planted, and the previous spring field would be left fallow for the whole year; and in the third year, the three fields would be rotated yet again. Thus, each year, two-thirds of the arable lands were in use while one-third was lying fallow. This simple conservation measure helped to maintain the fertility of the soil.

Individual peasants did not have compact farms assigned to them. Instead, they held long, narrow strips in each of the three fields. In this way, peasant families had a regular supply of fall crops and spring crops each year, more fertile and less fertile land was evenly distributed among families, and plowmen could work more efficiently because they did not have to turn their teams so often. This layout, together with the regular crop rotation, meant that the peasants must farm cooperatively, planting and harvesting the same crops in the same field at the same time.

Land and Buildings

Besides plowland, a manor needed woodland for fuel, meadowland (grass-grown areas to provide hay for work animals), and pasture where sheep and cattle grazed. Only a small section of the estate was occupied by the homes of the village, with thatched or tiled roofs and timber, brick, or plaster walls according to local conditions and the wealth of the peasants; windows were shuttered but not glazed, since glass was an expensive luxury. Around these cottages were sheds and gardens where the village women raised vegetables, hens, rabbits, and pigs.

Many villages had a manor house for the lord, as well as a church or priest's house. If there was no church or the lord did not actually live in the manor—or if the "lord" was not an individual person but an institution such as a monastery or bishopric—there would at any rate be barns to collect the produce that was the lord's due. Then there were the mill and the smithy, as well as a bake oven and a wine press. All were provided by the lord for a fee, usually paid in the form of produce—for example, a share of the grain that a peasant brought to be ground, or of the resulting flour. In addition, the priest, the miller, the blacksmith, and the baker had their own holdings.

 The Medieval Village of Wharram Percy (http://loki.stockton.edu/~ken/wharram/wharram.htm) Take a guided tour of the archeological site for Wharram Percy, a medieval village.

 Alwalton Manor: An Inventory Read an inventory of a manor belonging to an abbey, including the people who lived on it and the days of labor and payments in goods and money that they owed the abbot.

The People of the Manor

The records of village life prior to the thirteenth century are meager. But we do know that in those mute centuries, the basic habits of work, law, worship, and play evolved into established custom. And we have abundant evidence that village life as it existed in the thirteenth century persisted with little change for the following five hundred years. The rise of trade and the growth of cities, the emergence of national states, the struggles between religious factions—all seem to have had slight effect on the basic patterns and rhythms of rural life.

The Lord and His Family

The lord of the manor was presumably guided by the rules of God and by custom; in any case, his word was law. Whether a simple knight or a noble of high degree, he was often away from home for long periods of time. He was a warrior as well as a landlord and had his feudal obligations to fulfill. When he was not performing those duties, his favorite pastime was hunting. He typically took little direct interest in farming and left the management of his lands and local justice to his overseers (*stewards* or *bailiffs*). The lord's wife spent most of her days in the manor house supervising the servants, household operations, and entertainment of guests. If she was a lady of high rank, she might also act as a partner in the conduct of her husband's political and administrative affairs.

The lord normally took about half the total production of the estate—mainly crops from strips in the open fields that the peasants cultivated for him, and also payments from them of household and garden produce. He also maintained a reserve of grain in his barns so that in years of crop failure he would be able to provide the peasants with food and seed. He could not allow them to starve, for aside from humane considerations, they represented his labor force.

Peasants and Serfdom

Most of the peasants were serfs (from Latin *servus*), whose special status and ties to the soil were inherited. The origins of serfdom can be traced back to the western provinces of the Roman Empire in the third and fourth centuries (pp. 138-139); by 1000, serfdom had spread beyond the empire's former frontiers and was normal throughout most of Europe. During the turbulent times of the early Middle Ages, whole communities of farmers had placed themselves under powerful warriors for protection (p. 174). In addition, in territories that had once belonged to the Roman Empire, many serfs were descended from earlier generations of slaves who had worked on the estates of great landowners (p. 98)—*servus*, in fact, originally meant "slave." In their case, serfdom represented an improvement in status. Nevertheless, a serf was legally unfree.

The main duty of the serfs was to cultivate the strips in the open fields that belonged to the lord. In addition, they could be called on to build roads, clear forests, and do other work.

 Life in Medieval Europe (http://www.youtube.com/watch?v=pypbyC548dw) Watch a re-creation of peasant life in medieval Europe.

Their work obligation or **labor service** was usually reckoned in time rather than specific duties, and mostly varied between two and three days in the week. In addition, they had to give the lord fixed amounts of any valuable items that they produced, such as spun yarn or poultry (see photo on page 194). The serfs' children were likewise bound to the manor; no members of their families could leave the estate or marry without the consent of the lord. A serf's eldest son normally inherited the rights and duties of his father.

Peasants whose ancestors had managed to avoid serfdom had the status of *freemen*. This did not necessarily mean that they were better off; some, in fact, lived on the edge of starvation. If the freeman farmed land, he did so as a farm tenant, paying rent to the lord in the form of a share of his crop. The lord could evict a freeman whenever he saw fit, whereas a serf could not legally be separated from his land.

Manors and serfdom were the medieval European way of fulfilling the traditional purposes of farming communities ever since the earliest civilizations—to provide for the needs of both the families who farmed the land and the elite who lived off their labors. Serfdom persisted in many countries until the nineteenth century; much is known about the life of serfs in these later times, and there is no reason to suppose that in the Middle Ages it was basically different. Kings and nobles might look down on peasants as a mass of humble toilers, but each village had its own hierarchy of families with larger and smaller holdings, as well as families with no land at all. Better-off families married into each other, dressed up for family and religious occasions, and lent each other tools and work animals. They gave handouts of food and clothing to landless families, became godparents to their children, and hired them as farmhands—whom they then sent to labor on the lord's land, rather than perform this humbling duty themselves. For serfs, too—at least, the better-off ones—had their pride.

Manorialism and Increasing Wealth

In its time, manorialism was a highly successful form of economic and social organization. More secure than freemen, with far greater property rights than slaves, and benefiting from a relatively productive farming system, the serfs had an incentive to found families and increase the amount of land they farmed. Partly for these reasons, the emergence of manorialism by 1000 was followed by three centuries of agricultural boom. Throughout Europe, the serfs cut down forests, drained swamps, and brought grasslands under the plow. Thousands of new villages sprang up, and by 1300 the population of Europe had risen from roughly 40 million to about 100 million.

labor service
The work that a serf was required to do as a condition of holding a farm. It included cultivating the lord's crops and performing other tasks such as building roads or clearing forests.

acozdo pfalterio: cum cantico

Women's Work A fourteenth-century peasant woman feeds chicks and a hen, part of the labor around the house and farmyard that was done by women in medieval Europe as in every traditional agricultural society. Under her arm she carries a distaff for spinning raw linen or wool into yarn, so that the moment she is finished with the chickens she can get back to spinning—slow but money-earning work, as she will sell the yarn, or cloth that she will weave from it, to a traveling merchant. © British Library Board, Add. 42130, f. 166v

This **internal colonization**, as it is called, was very much in the interests of the lords, as it increased the amount of productive land that they controlled. Usually, it was they who founded new manors on uncultivated land and moved serfs into them. But to get the cooperation of the serfs, the lords had to offer them concessions, such as larger holdings, smaller crop deliveries, and fewer days of labor service. In time, the lords even found it preferable to turn their serfs into free tenants, paying rent in produce or cash. (The lords, however, usually retained manorial powers of government and justice, as well as ultimate ownership of the land.) In western Europe, this eventually led, by the end of the Middle Ages, to the almost complete disappearance of serfdom (p. 255).

In addition, European society became much wealthier and also more complex and diverse. As the population swelled and peasants and lords both prospered, commerce and industry also began to grow, and the number of people who made a living by these activities increased. Alongside the manor, the typical community of peasants and lords, there appeared another type of community, formed by merchants and craftspeople: the town.

LO³ Trade and Towns

As the towns grew, an expanded cast of medieval characters appeared there, consisting of merchants, bankers, lawyers, artisans, and unskilled laborers. As was normal in even the wealthiest societies before modern times, these groups made up only a fraction of the population (on average probably less than 10 percent by 1300), but their importance in medieval Europe was out of all proportion to their numbers.

In some areas, notably northern Italy, where trading opportunities were particularly rich and the authority of the feudal ruler, the Holy Roman emperor, was usually feeble, the towns grew into cities. They extended their power over the neighboring countryside, acquired their own armies and navies, and thus became true city-states. More commonly, the towns had to find themselves a place within the existing structure of feudal monarchy. But their place was an important one: it was in the towns that kings set up their government offices, bishops built their cathedrals, and scholars gathered to form universities (pp. 233-235). Thus, the rural-based civilization of the early Middle Ages became a city-based civilization, like those of earlier Greece and Rome—or neighboring Byzantium and Islam.

> "*Throughout Europe, the serfs cut down forests, drained swamps, and brought grasslands under the plow. Thousands of new villages sprang up, and by 1300 the population of Europe had risen from roughly 40 million to about 100 million.*"

internal colonization
The process of cultivating and settling in formerly wild land in medieval Europe.

overland through Spain or, more commonly, through Venice and other port cities of northern Italy (Map 11.1 on page 198). Constantinople was the main source of luxury goods, which found a growing market among European aristocrats. Those who could afford them sought spices (pepper, ginger, and cinnamon); silks and satins; precious jewels; statues; and rugs and tapestries.

In return for these imports, the Europeans began to export woolens and linens, horses, weapons and armor, timber, furs, and slaves. (The word *slave* is derived from *Slav* because Slavs, captured in wars among themselves or with their German and Hungarian neighbors, often ended up being sold by Italian merchants in the slave markets of Byzantium and the Muslim world.) From all parts of Europe, caravans carried goods across the Alps, chiefly to Milan, Pisa, and Venice, for transshipment further east. Northern Italy thus became the commercial gateway between western Europe and the rest of the Eastern Hemisphere.

The Growth of Trade

As the medieval agricultural boom got under way, the lords of manors and even better-off peasants had more to spend on the luxuries that the towns had to offer. Likewise, with some assurance that crops could be marketed in the towns, peasants and lords had an additional incentive for increasing farm output. Church lords and nobles, instead of consuming all the food and supplies that the peasants produced for them, sold some of the produce in the towns in return for cash; or instead of receiving their income in goods and services, they freed their serfs and charged them rents to be paid in money—for money was now seen as the key to new comforts and delights.

Long-Distance Trade

Many luxuries came from the Mediterranean world and the wider intercontinental world to which the Mediterranean gave access. Byzantium and Islam, which dominated the sea's eastern and southern shores, were vigorous commercial societies and manufactured elegant articles for export; in addition, they controlled trade routes that led overland across Central Asia to China and by sea across the Indian Ocean to India and the spice islands of East Asia (pp. 271-272). Their merchandise was brought to western Europe

Famous Makers and European Centers of Arms and Armor Production (http://www.metmuseum.org/toah/hd/make/hd_make.htm) Learn more about arms and armor production in medieval Europe.

Industry and Technology

The wool and textile industries provided the bulk of European exports. These industries centered in the Low Countries, where conditions were favorable for sheep raising. In time, this region gained fame also for its manufacture of woolen cloth, and Flemish producers finally had to turn to outside sources of raw wool to satisfy their needs. After the thirteenth century, both in England and on the mainland of Europe, there was a growing cash market for wool. English farmers and landlords met this demand by converting more of their holdings into pastureland, and in this way, became participants in the new trading economy.

The increase in wealth brought about by the growth of agriculture and trade also fostered a spirit of technical progress, which was shared not only by "those who worked" but also by "those who fought" and "those who prayed."

Enterprising craftsmen, wanting to save labor and increase production in their workshops, devised ingenious mechanisms to adapt the waterwheel, long used for grinding grain, to all sorts of other tasks. Hammering raw iron to remove impurities, beating rags into pulp to make paper, stamping on woolen cloth to thicken it—all these and many other manufacturing processes came to be done by water-powered machinery. Feudal lords wishing to besiege the castles of their rivals equipped their forces with trebuchets—huge wooden contraptions that

FROM MERCHANT TO HERMIT: THE CAREER OF *ST. GODRIC OF FINCHALE*

Godric of Finchale, who lived in the eleventh and twelfth centuries, began as a trader and ended his life as a hermit (a solitary seeker after God) in the north of England. His biographer Reginald of Durham describes the steps by which Godric rose from being a small-time peddler to a successful and wealthy merchant, and then turned away from the world, in an era when the medieval economy was growing and commerce was turning into big business.

When the boy had passed his childhood years quietly at home, then, as he began to grow to manhood, he began to follow more prudent ways of life, and to learn carefully and persistently the teachings of worldly forethought. Wherefore he chose not to follow the life of a husbandman [farmer] but rather to study, learn, and exercise the rudiments of more subtle conceptions. For this reason, aspiring to the merchant's trade, he began to follow the chapman's [peddler's] way of life, first learning how to gain in small bargains and things of insignificant price; and thence, while yet a youth, his mind advanced little by little to buy and sell and gain from things of greater expense. For, in his beginnings, he was wont to wander with small wares around the villages and farmsteads of his own neighbourhood; but, in process of time, he gradually associated himself by compact with city merchants. Hence, within a brief space of time, the youth who had trudged for many weary hours from village to village, from farm to farm, did so profit by his increase of age and wisdom as to travel with associates of his own age through towns and boroughs, fortresses and cities, to fairs and to all the various booths of the market-place, in pursuit of his public chaffer [bargaining]. He went along the highway, neither puffed up by the good testimony of his conscience nor downcast in the nobler part of his soul by the reproach of poverty. . . .

Yet in all things he walked with simplicity; and, in so far as he yet knew how, it was ever his pleasure to follow in the footsteps of the truth. For, having learned the Lord's Prayer and the Creed from his very cradle, he oftentimes turned them over in his mind, even as he went alone on his longer journeys; and, in so far as the truth was revealed to his mind, he clung thereunto most devoutly in all his thoughts concerning God. At first, he lived as a chapman [peddler] for four years in Lincolnshire, going on foot and carrying the smallest wares; then he travelled abroad, first to St. Andrews in Scotland and then for the first time to Rome. On his return, having formed a familiar friendship with certain other young men who were eager for merchandise, he began to launch upon bolder courses and to coast frequently by sea to the foreign lands that lay around him. Thus, sailing often to and fro between Scotland and Britain, he traded in many divers wares and, amid these occupations, learned much worldly wisdom. . . .

Then he purchased the half of a merchant-ship with certain of his partners in the trade; and again by his prudence he bought the fourth part of another ship. At length, by his skill

used the counterweight principle to hurl boulders weighing as much as a ton. And bishops and abbots, desiring their cathedral and monastery towers to be heard as well as seen across miles of countryside, urged on metalworkers to develop methods of large-scale bronze casting that would produce monster bells. The spurt of technical progress that began in the Middle Ages continued and accelerated without a break until it ended in the Industrial Revolution of the eighteenth and nineteenth centuries (pp. 256-258, 422-425).

The Location and Appearance of Towns

Towns usually appeared at places where land and water routes converged: sheltered harbors, junctions of highways, or confluences of rivers. Often, there were already settlements at these places that welcomed merchants and craftspeople—government centers of kings and great lords, cathedrals of bishops, Viking trading posts, and ancient cities that had survived the fall of Rome. In some parts of Europe, particularly "frontier" areas such as eastern Germany, new towns were deliberately founded. Kings and nobles cooperated in founding them on account of their strategic value, but rarely took part in their actual government. In other regions, the townspeople had to struggle for many generations to win from the rulers, great lords, and bishops a degree of self-government for their communities.

However a town came into being, it needed walls—in fact, the word *town* derives from the Anglo-Saxon *tun*, meaning "fortified enclosure." If an existing settlement grew into a town,

in navigation, wherein he excelled all his fellows, he earned promotion to the post of steersman. . . .

For he was vigorous and strenuous in mind, whole of limb and strong in body. He was of middle stature, broad-shouldered and deep-chested, with a long face, grey eyes most clear and piercing, bushy brows, a broad forehead, long and open nostrils, a nose of comely curve, and a pointed chin. His beard was thick, and longer than the ordinary, his mouth well-shaped, with lips of moderate thickness; in youth his hair was black, in age as white as snow; his neck was short and thick, knotted with veins and sinews; his legs were somewhat slender, his instep high, his knees hardened and horny with frequent kneeling; his whole skin rough beyond the ordinary, until all this roughness was softened by old age. . . .

And now he had lived sixteen years as a merchant, and began to think of spending on charity, to God's honour and service, the goods which he had so laboriously acquired. He therefore took the cross as a pilgrim to Jerusalem, and, having visited the Holy Sepulchre, came back to England by way of St. James [of Compostella]. Not long afterwards he became steward to a certain rich man of his own country, with the care of his whole house and household. But certain of the younger household were men of iniquity, who stole their neighbours' cattle and thus held luxurious feasts, whereas Godric, in his ignorance, was sometimes present. Afterwards, discovering the truth, he rebuked and admonished them to cease; but they made no account of his warnings; wherefore he concealed not their iniquity, but disclosed it to the lord of the household, who, however, slighted his advice. Wherefore he begged to be dismissed and went on a pilgrimage, first to St. Gilles and thence to Rome the abode of the Apostles, that thus he might knowingly pay the penalty for those misdeeds wherein he had ignorantly partaken. I have often seen him, even in his old age, weeping for this unknowing transgression. . . .

Godric, when he had restored his mother safe to his father's arms, abode but a brief while at home; for he was now already firmly purposed to give himself entirely to God's service. Wherefore, that he might follow Christ the more freely, he sold all his possessions and distributed them among the poor. Then, telling his parents of this purpose and receiving their blessing, he went forth to no certain abode, but whithersoever the Lord should deign to lead him; for above all things he coveted the life of a hermit.

EXPLORING THE SOURCE

1. How did Godric start out as a trader, and what were the main stages of his commercial career? What does this tell about the ways of achieving business success around 1100?

2. Does Godric's decision to give up the life of a merchant seem to you reasonable or foolish, and why?

Source: Reginald of Durham, "Life of St. Godric of Finchale," in *Social Life in Britain from the Conquest to the Reformation*, ed. G. G. Coulton (Cambridge: Cambridge University Press, 1918), pp. 415–420.

its fortifications were lengthened to make room; if a town was newly founded, it soon acquired walls. The remains of these town walls may still be seen in many of the old cities of Europe, notably Carcassonne in France, Avila in Spain, and Rothenburg in Germany.

Rothenburg, Germany's Model Medieval Village (http://www.roadstoruins.com/rothenburg.html) Tour the medieval town of Rothenburg, Germany.

Understandably, space was at a premium in these towns. Streets and passageways were kept as narrow as possible so that a maximum number of buildings could be erected within the walls, and the buildings themselves had as many stories as safety would permit. Even so, as the numbers of townspeople increased, many of them took the risk of living outside the walls, and towns grew *suburbs* (from the Latin for "beneath the walled town"). Both inside and outside the walls, housing was painfully cramped—tighter, sometimes, than the space in peasants' cottages. There was very little town planning, and sanitation was notoriously poor. From the very earliest times, European cities faced problems of congestion, traffic jams, infectious diseases, slums, and devastating citywide fires.

Nevertheless, there was a certain order in most medieval towns. By the thirteenth century, a typical pattern had appeared. The town was usually dominated by the towers or spires of its main church. Next in importance were the town hall and the buildings of the various trading and industrial organizations, the guilds. The heart of the town was the central marketplace with its stalls selling produce from the nearby countryside,

Map 11.1 Trading Routes and Towns, ca. 1100

With Europe's medieval economic boom well under way, the network of land and sea routes and important towns is still densest in areas that once belonged to the Roman Empire—through southern and western Europe and across the Mediterranean to the Islamic world. But the network has also extended to places that were far from civilization in Roman times—Scandinavia and the Baltic, and eastern Europe as far as Russia. © Cengage Learning

Interactive Map

Major route of trade and commerce
Grain-growing region
Wine-producing region
Coal Primary product

locally manufactured goods, and luxury items from distant lands (see photo). The marketplace and nearby streets were likely to be lined with houses where families lived, worked, and sold what they made—all in the same building, since most industry and commerce, like farming, was carried on by small family businesses.

The Life of Townspeople

Unlike the peasants, all townspeople were legally free, but the towns had a social structure of their own. At the top were the leading merchants and moneylenders and the heads of the guilds.

Beneath them were skilled artisans and clerks, and at the bottom were apprentices and unskilled laborers.

The members of the highest group dominated civic affairs and constituted a new element in European society, which gained in wealth and power as the centuries passed. But except in regions like northern Italy where the cities were truly the dominant force in society, even the wealthiest and most powerful townspeople were regarded as legally and socially inferior to the clergy and the nobility.

Because the whole pattern of life in the towns was different from that of the feudal estate, a new plan for government had to be devised for the new communities. The townspeople

Scala/Art Resource, NY

≪ **The Ravenna Gate Market, Bologna** An early fifteenth-century picture shows a market specializing in textiles just inside the walls of a north Italian city. Cloths are displayed on counters, hang from ceilings, and lie around in unopened bales. A porter bends under his load and a storekeeper waits for customers; one woman inspects merchandise and another has made up her mind to buy. A crucifix presides in its shrine over the busy commercial scene.

charter
A document granting rights and privileges to a person or institution—in particular, a document permitting the establishment of a town and allowing the townspeople to establish their own rules and government in exchange for regular payments of money to the grantor.

guild
An organization of merchants or craftspeople who regulated the activities of their members and set standards and prices.

master
A craftsman who had the right to operate workshops, train others, and vote on guild business.

journeyman
A licensed artisan who had served an apprenticeship and who was employed by a master and paid at a fixed rate per day.

apprentice
A "learner" in the shop of a master.

> *"In the first place, that no one of the trade of spurriers shall work longer than from the beginning of the day until curfew rings out at the church of St. Sepulcher, without Newgate; by reason that no man can work so neatly by night as by day. . . . And further, many of the said trade are wandering about all day, without working at all at their trade; and then, when they have become drunk and frantic, they take to their work, to the annoyance of the sick, and all their neighborhood as well."*

—from regulations of the Spurriers' Guild (makers of spurs for horses) of London, 1345

sought special **charters**—documents that would free them from the customary obligations of the feudal relationship and would permit them to establish appropriate rules of their own. These charters, granted by the king, nobleman, or bishop holding authority over the area, recognized the citizens of the town as a collective group or *corporation*, with legal privileges and powers. In return for these privileges, and in place of feudal services, the corporation made regular payments of money to the grantor. The form of government differed from one town to another, but in most places, control rested in the hands of a governing council and a mayor. Though voting rights (for adult males only) were often quite liberal, it was uncommon for any but the leading families to hold important offices.

 New Regulations: No Work After Sundown Read a sampling of regulations from the spurriers' (spur makers) guild.

The Guilds

The governing council imposed strict political control on the community. Legally, the citizens of a town were free individuals, but the idea of collective responsibility and regulation was accepted in town and countryside alike. Merchants and craftspeople formed special organizations called **guilds**. The guilds limited production and sale of goods to their members, upheld standards of business practice and quality of merchandise, and set prices for every commodity.

The principal organization in most towns was the merchant guild, which established rules for the times and places at which goods could be sold, weights and measures, and grades and prices of goods. At first, the merchant guild included most of the tradespeople in a given town. With growing specialization, however, one group after another split off from the parent unit to form independent craft guilds: weavers, dyers, tailors, carpenters, masons, silversmiths, bakers, barbers, and the like. By the thirteenth century, there might be as many as thirty or forty guilds in a single town.

The primary function of a craft guild was to supervise the production of goods and the training of artisans. Craftsmen were classified as **masters**, **journeymen**, and **apprentices**. Only masters had the right to operate workshops and train others; they alone were voting members of the guild and directed its policies, and their coveted status was won by other craftsmen only after long experience and proof of excellence. Before the masters admitted a journeyman to their rank, they customarily required him to submit an example of his workmanship—his *masterpiece*. Journeymen were licensed artisans who had served an apprenticeship. They were employed by the masters and were usually paid at a fixed rate per day (in French, *journée*). Before becoming a journeyman, an individual was obliged to work for a specified period of time, ranging from two to seven years, as an apprentice (learner) in the shop of a master. In return for their labor, apprentices received only food and lodging. Though women of the towns were permitted to perform some skilled and unskilled services, they were generally excluded from guild membership.

The guilds also performed charitable and social functions. If a member fell sick, was put in jail, or got into some other kind of trouble, he could count on help from the guild brotherhood. The guilds provided proper ceremonies on the occasions of births, marriages, and funerals; they conducted social affairs; and they celebrated Church festivals as a body. Each one, moreover, honored a particular saint who was associated by tradition with a given craft—Saint Joseph, for example, was honored by carpenters. The guilds often dedicated altars or chapels in the town church to their special saints. In all their varied activities, they embodied the corporate and community spirit so characteristic of medieval society.

 Listen to a synopsis of Chapter 11.

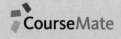

CHAPTER 12

WESTERN CHRISTENDOM AND ITS NEIGHBORS, 1000–1300

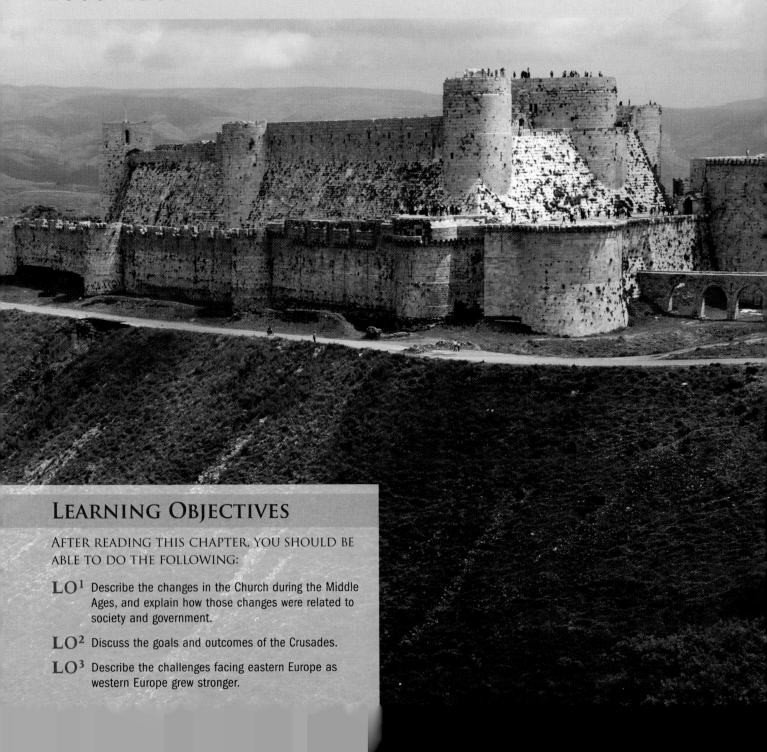

LEARNING OBJECTIVES

AFTER READING THIS CHAPTER, YOU SHOULD BE ABLE TO DO THE FOLLOWING:

LO¹ Describe the changes in the Church during the Middle Ages, and explain how those changes were related to society and government.

LO² Discuss the goals and outcomes of the Crusades.

LO³ Describe the challenges facing eastern Europe as western Europe grew stronger.

> **"THE SINGLE MOST IMPORTANT INFLUENCE ON MEDIEVAL EUROPE WAS RELIGION—SO MUCH SO THAT EUROPEANS AT THE TIME USUALLY CALLED THEIR PART OF THE WORLD NOT BY A GEOGRAPHICAL NAME BUT BY A RELIGIOUS ONE—'CHRISTENDOM.'"**

As with earlier civilizations, the single most important influence on medieval Europe was religion—so much so that Europeans at the time usually called their part of the world not by a geographical name but by a religious one—"Christendom." In the early Middle Ages, two regions had developed within Christendom: a western region looking to Rome, and an eastern one looking to Constantinople (p. 180). Christians in both regions still saw themselves as belonging to a single Church, and in both regions, the conversion of barbarian peoples, the rise in population, the agricultural boom, and the revival of trade brought the Church more territory, believers, and wealth. But as with other features of the renewal of European civilization, the renewal of Christianity brought the greatest changes in the West.

One feature of this Western renewal was an upsurge of new developments in the Church's beliefs, practices, and organization. More humanly appealing forms of devotion appeared that made heaven seem more accessible to believers and strengthened the authority of the clergy who controlled this access. New groups of monks and nuns were founded—some to make up for the failings of existing groups that had been spoiled by increasing wealth, and others to adapt to the needs of the growing towns.

All these changes gained approval and backing from the popes, who were striving to bring the whole Church under their central control. Their efforts ran into determined resistance from their partners and rivals, the rulers of the western European feudal states. All the same, the popes acquired such authority that they became for a time the most powerful rulers in western Europe.

Test your knowledge before you read this chapter.

What do you think?

The Crusades are an example of the misuse of religion.

Strongly Disagree   Strongly Agree

| 1 | 2 | 3 | 4 | 5 | 6 | 7 |

« Krak des Chevaliers The "Fortress of the Knights" was built in the twelfth-century Holy Land by crusading warrior-monks, the Knights Hospitalers. To the east beyond the castle lay Muslim-held land; this side belonged to the County of Tripoli, a crusader foothold on the Mediterranean coast that the castle helped protect. With its double walls, its state-of-the-art round towers that had no vulnerable corners, and its 2,000-strong garrison, the castle withstood besiegers such as the renowned Muslim commander Saladin for more than a century.

Nick Ledger/Alamy

sacrament
In Christian worship, a ceremony meant to grant divine aid to sinners.

grace
In Christian belief, divine aid to sinful men and women without which they cannot be saved.

Religious renewal and that of civilization in general also combined to produce two other features of Western Christendom: bitter internal conflicts and an urge toward outward expansion. New heresies arose that denied the authority and holiness of the clergy. Christian resentment of Jews in the growing towns led to frequent explosions of anti-Jewish violence. And beyond the frontiers of Western Christendom stood yet more religious enemies—above all, Islam.

Accordingly, Western Christendom also invested its newfound skills in formidable attacks on its religious foes. The Church tribunals of the Inquisition devised complex procedures of investigation and punishment to enforce religious conformity. Rulers of powerful feudal states used their government machinery to expel the Jews from entire countries. And the main forces in medieval society—the Church, the feudal warriors, and the towns—combined to undertake a series of unprecedented long-distance expeditions against religious enemies—the Crusades.

These holy wars failed in the most famous of the purposes for which they were fought: to regain the Holy Land permanently from Islam. They led to a split with Eastern Christendom, which came to be seen in the West as a religious opponent because it would not accept the rule of the pope. But the Crusades also brought colonists and missionaries to conquered territories in Muslim Spain and remaining pagan regions in eastern Europe, as well as traders to seaports in the eastern Mediterranean. In this way, the Crusades set a precedent of colonizing and converting non-Christian lands, and of long-distance overseas trade, which was to be followed by empire-building western European nations at the end of the Middle Ages.

LO¹ The Western Church

Both halves of the Church inherited their basic features from the early Christianity of the Roman Empire (Chapter 8), but within the Western Church, many of these features developed

CHRONOLOGY

910	Monastery of Cluny is founded; beginning of the Cluniac reform
1054	Disputes between the Eastern (Orthodox) and the Western (Catholic) Churches result in mutual excommunications
1095	Pope Urban II launches the First Crusade
1098	Abbey at Cîteaux founded; beginning of the Cistercian order
1099	Crusaders take Jerusalem; Latin Kingdom of Jerusalem established
1122	Investitures Dispute between the pope and emperor is settled in a power-sharing compromise
1170–1221	Life of Dominic, founder of Dominican order
1181–1226	Life of Francis, founder of Franciscan order
1187	Saladin crushes army of Latin Kingdom; regains Jerusalem for Muslims
1204	Constantinople looted by western crusaders; Latin Empire of Constantinople founded
1231	Pope Gregory IX establishes the Inquisition to find and try heretics
1261	Byzantine emperor regains Constantinople

in new ways—both shaping and responding to other changes in the government and society of western Europe.

The Church's Worship

Church worship took on even greater significance in the Middle Ages as a path to divine aid in this world and the afterlife.

The Sacraments

Ever since the earliest days of Christianity, believers had undergone ceremonies that they believed were necessary to admit them to Christ's kingdom (p. 128). Over many centuries, the number of these ceremonies had increased in East and West alike, but Western religious thinkers developed a specific theory of how many such ceremonies there were and how they worked.

The Western Church recognized seven **sacraments** (from the Latin word for "holy"). All of them were traced back to gospel commands and sayings of Jesus, who had established them as a means of **grace**—divine aid to sinful men and women without which they could not be saved.

Four of the sacraments must be undergone by all believers. Through *baptism* a person gained entry to Christ's kingdom (usually as an infant) and was cleansed of the stain of sin. *Confirmation* was administered to baptized people later on, to confirm them in their acceptance of baptism and strengthen them in faith. *Penance* involved confession to a priest and acceptance of a penalty, thereby cleansing believers of recently committed sins and making them worthy to receive the *Eucharist* ("Thanksgiving") or *Mass* (probably from the Latin for "dismissal," because the congregation was told to leave at the end of the service). The Church taught that at a certain moment in the rite, the bread and wine were transformed in their inmost nature ("substance") into the body and blood of the Savior, while keeping the outward appearance of bread and wine—a process known as **transubstantiation** ("transfer of substance"). The recipients, united with each other and with Christ himself, would be aided in doing good and resisting evil.

The other three sacraments were not compulsory for all believers. Through *extreme unction* ("final anointing") Christians in danger of death were granted final forgiveness of sins, but death was too unpredictable for everyone to receive this sacrament. *Ordination* was the sacrament whereby a bishop made a person a priest with the miraculous power to administer sacraments. The seventh sacrament was *matrimony*, the joining together of husband and wife so long as they both lived; the Church did not permit divorce, though widows and widowers could remarry.

Ever since Christianity began, believers had had to contend with the problem of how to keep their standing as members of Christ's kingdom if they sinned after baptism. The seven sacraments, guaranteeing believers divine aid and forgiveness throughout their lives, broadened the narrow path to salvation. And the actual sacraments were accompanied by many other practices and observances that made God and his kingdom more accessible to sinful humans.

Jesus the Human

It was a basic doctrine of Christianity that Christ the Son of God and Jesus the human being were one and the same person, but Christian worship had traditionally stressed the Savior's role as God. Early medieval art usually portrayed him as the risen Christ sitting in royal dignity upon the heavenly throne (see photo on page 206). Sometime after the year 1000, a new view began to prevail. It emphasized Jesus's human experiences—his struggles, humiliations, and sufferings. Both theologians (religious thinkers) and the common people drew fresh meaning from the suffering of their Lord, recognizing in his agony their own anguish and miseries. Artists increasingly showed the dying Savior hanging heavily from the Cross. Gradually, the crucifix, which aroused in pious hearts the deepest feelings of compassion and love, became the most popular devotional object (see photo on page 207).

Medieval Images of Christ from the Getty Museum (http://www.getty.edu/art/gettyguide/displayObjectList?sub= 2032280) View a gallery of medieval images of Jesus.

In the same way, the infant Jesus in early portraits appears as a kingly figure, but during the Middle Ages he was made to look like any infant held in the arms of a loving mother. And his mother, Mary, was presented in an ever more tender and human light.

transubstantiation
In Catholic belief, the process of "transfer of substance" in the Mass, whereby bread and wine are transformed in their inmost nature ("substance") into the body and blood of Christ while keeping their original outward appearance.

The Virgin Mary and the Saints

The cult of the Virgin was exceedingly popular in the Middle Ages. The monasteries played a leading role in developing it, but ordinary people responded warmly to the appeal of Mary. Aside from her role as the Mother of God, she personified the Christian ideals of womanhood, love, and sympathy. During an upsurge of religious fervor in the twelfth and thirteenth centuries, many of the great new cathedrals were dedicated to Mary. A rich literature and a host of legends came into being that told of the countless miracles of the Virgin. She was pictured as loyal and forgiving toward all who honored her and ready to give earthly benefits and heavenly rewards to those who prayed to her. And the opinion gained ground among believers, though it was not yet officially accepted by the Church, that Mary, unlike all other humans, was completely free of sin.

Medieval Images of Mary from the Getty Museum (http://www.getty.edu/art/gettyguide/displayObjectList?sub= 2032407) View a gallery of medieval images of Mary.

No other human was considered sinless, but ever since early Christian times, it had been customary to revere apostles and martyrs as especially close to God. Later on, exceptionally devoted hermits, monks, and nuns, as well as exceptionally pious laypeople (ordinary believers), also came to be regarded as saints (holy people). In this way, the numbers of saints increased over the centuries, so that by medieval times, the Church revered several thousand of them. Most of them had first gained the reputation of sainthood in the places where they had spent their lives; local bishops and heads of monasteries had supported or led public opinion; and reverence for them had then spread more or less widely. In the thirteenth century, another step became necessary: the pope himself must canonize a person (formally identify him or her as a saint).

A Comprehensive List of Catholic Saints and Angels (http://www.catholic.org/saints/) Learn more about the lives and legends of Catholic saints.

Christians traditionally showed the saints the special honor of veneration (deep reverence). Veneration was not the same as worship (which was reserved for God), but it did include praying to saints for their favor and help. Saints, in turn, could intercede (plead with) God to miraculously grant a human need, whether

Christ on His Throne This late-twelfth-century statue is carved in a tympanum (a space above a doorway) in the west façade of the cathedral of Saint-Trophîme in the southern French town of Arles. Christ is crowned as a king and seated upon a throne as he blesses the world and holds a Bible on his knee. He is surrounded by winged creatures symbolic of the Evangelists (authors of the Gospels)—an angel (Matthew), a lion (Mark), an ox (Luke), and an eagle (John). Scala/Art Resource, NY

recovery from sickness, rain in time of drought, or victory in battle. God was believed to grant such requests to show both his power and the holiness of the saint who made it.

Hardly any act was undertaken in the Middle Ages without first calling upon these Christian heroes who could influence God himself. Moreover, some of their power was thought to stay on earth in their real or alleged clothing, possessions, and bodily remains (*relics*) (see photo on page 208). Oaths and treaties were sworn on relics; townspeople carried them in religious processions, and knights often inserted them in the hilts of their swords. People traveled hundreds of miles on pilgrimage to the shrines of famous saints where their relics were preserved to ask for favors or give thanks for help received.

The Saints and Purgatory

Above all, the saints could also give benefits in the other world. Since early times, Christians had prayed for the dead, as if the path to salvation continued after death and souls still needed help to travel it. Out of this practice, there developed the belief in **purgatory**—a place where souls that were not hopelessly sinful would be cleansed of sin before entering God's kingdom. The cleansing process was long and painful, including fire that, in the words of the fourth-century thinker Augustine (p. 143), "will be harder to bear than anything a human being can suffer in this life."

life-size wood carving made for Archbishop
Gero of Cologne toward the year 1000, is
one of the earliest appearances in art
of the figure of Christ suffering on the
Cross. Traditionally, artists had treated
the Crucifixion as a scene of the
divine Savior triumphing over death.
Here, by contrast, Jesus is shown with
his arms stretched back, his knees
giving way, and his head hanging
down—a human being in the last
agony of a cruel death. Erich Lessing/Art
Resource, NY

purgatory
In Catholic belief, a
place where souls that
are not hopelessly sinful
will be cleansed of sin
before entering God's
kingdom.

indulgence
A reduction in the time
a person must spend in
purgatory, issued by the
pope.

But God would shorten the
suffering of the "Poor Souls" in
response to the earnest prayers
of believers, of monks and nuns
whose way of life brought them
closer to him, and above all, of
the saints who surrounded him in
heaven. In the eleventh century, the
popes began issuing **indulgences**—
reducing the time a person must spend
in purgatory so long as that person demonstrated true repentance for sin. God, it
was believed, would honor the pope's action in
consideration of the accumulated holiness of the
saints and of Christ himself, which made up for the failings of
sinners. In ways like these, medieval practices made the path of
salvation easier to travel.

The Clergy

Ever since Christianity became the religion of Rome, the clergy
had been one of the most powerful groups in society, and
events in Western Christendom
since the fall of Rome had caused
their power to grow greater still.
As barbarian peoples became
Christian, bishoprics, parishes,
and monasteries sprang up among
them. As bishoprics and monasteries accumulated land, bishops
and abbots became full partners
in government and politics with
kings and great lords, and as feudal relationships developed, they
became leading vassals like the
barons (p. 187). As feudalism grew into a system of government,
illiterate kings and great lords depended on the clergy to staff
their government offices. And as the path to salvation became
easier to travel, more than ever the clergy became guides and
gatekeepers on the path. Practices grew up that symbolized
their special status apart from and above the laity. At the Mass,

*"Gradually, the crucifix, which
aroused in pious hearts the
deepest feelings of compassion
and love, became the most
popular devotional object."*

laypeople received only bread, while
the clergy received both bread and
wine; popes and bishops insisted
that ordained priests be celibate
(unmarried).

Corruption in the Church

But exactly because the clergy were so
wealthy and powerful, they were deeply
entangled with the society that they were supposed to be guiding. The choice of bishops,
abbots, and even parish priests was too important
to be left to the Church. Instead, kings and great lords
maneuvered relatives and political allies into bishoprics, and
landowners who founded monasteries and parishes gained the
hereditary right to appoint abbots and parish priests. Often, the
appointers also took the Church's welfare into consideration,
and the appointees turned out to be zealous religious guides—but
often, too, the appointees turned out to be zealous political
operatives or zealous devotees of the luxury and pleasure to
which wealth and power gave access. The increased power of
clergy as gatekeepers on an easier
path to heaven likewise opened
the way to moneymaking abuses—
the sale of fake relics, and indulgences exchanged for cash without
real repentance.

Medieval believers were well
aware of these problems; in fact,
throughout the Middle Ages, no
one was more generally despised
and detested than corrupt and
unworthy members of the clergy.
From time to time, public opinion
would revolt against corruption in the Church, and there would
be a cleanup campaign. As with every cleanup campaign in every
era, sooner or later the hue and cry would die down and the
problem would return. Still, medieval struggles against Church
corruption were genuine movements of religious striving, and
because the Church was so important in society, they also had

>> **Saint Andrew's Sandal** Gold, ivory, pearls, and precious stones cover this reliquary (relic casket), and a life-size hammered-gold sandaled foot tells of a revered object inside—the sole of a sandal said to have belonged to Jesus's disciple Andrew. Archbishop Egbert of Trier in western Germany, who commissioned the casket about A.D. 1000, used it as an altar for saying Mass when away from a church. Portable altars for important people, and reliquaries in the shape of the relics they contained, were common in medieval times. Scala/Art Resource, NY

massive social and political consequences—especially the first great struggle, in the tenth and eleventh centuries.

The struggle began at a time when the Carolingian empire was collapsing, and no ruler was able to wield wide-ranging power over the Western Church mainly for the Church's benefit, as Charlemagne had done (p. 171). Corruption in the Church was on the rise, and so were distrust and anger against the clergy—against bishops who bought their positions from great lords and let their parish priests live as illiterate drunkards; and against high-living abbots of wealthy monasteries who let their monks neglect their prayers and books and take the vow of chastity lightly. But it was also religiously devoted abbots, allied with earnest-minded great lords and conscientious bishops, who were the first leaders of the campaign for reform.

Cycles of Reform: Cluny and Cîteaux

The most far-reaching reform effort was undertaken by the monastery of Cluny (**KLOO-nee**), founded in Burgundy (in eastern France) in 910 by the duke of Aquitaine (**AK-i-teyn**). The first abbot, Berno, set out to revive the strictness of the Benedictine rule (regulations for monks and nuns—p. 144), which was followed by many monasteries in Western Christendom, and his efforts were carried on by a series of extraordinary abbots. Many new monasteries were founded and old ones were reformed on Cluniac principles throughout western and central Europe, with generous support from lords and bishops who were attracted by Cluny's reputation for holiness.

To protect individual monasteries from falling under local political influences, the Cluniac monks placed themselves under the direct authority of the pope. For the same reason, the abbots of Cluny did not allow newly founded monasteries to become independent, as Benedictine monasteries had traditionally been. Instead, they were "daughter houses" subject to the "mother house," and the priors (deputy abbots) who governed them were appointed by the Great Abbot of Cluny.

From Cluny, the movement for reform spread to all parts of the clergy. Cluniac monks became bishops, **simony** (the selling of Church services or offices) was exposed and reduced, and the behavior of parish clergy was more strictly controlled. But in the end, Cluny's very success brought about its decline as a model of reform. By the twelfth century, surrounded by mounting wealth and influence, the monks of Cluny slipped into the ways of material ease.

Repeating the Cluniac pattern, a new **religious order** (group of monasteries following the same way of life) now appeared. This order also arose in Burgundy, with the founding of an abbey at Cîteaux (**SEE-toe**) in 1098. Its daughter houses expanded spectacularly under the leadership of Bernard of Clairvaux (**KLER-voe**), who was to promote the Second Crusade of 1147–1149. The Cistercians (from *Cistercium*, the Latin name of Cîteaux) wore white robes to distinguish themselves from the black of the Benedictines. There was acute rivalry between the two orders, with the Cistercians at first deploring the riches of Cluny. But the white robes, too, became soiled by economic success, gifts, and worldly power. Within a century of the abbey's founding, the Cistercians had fallen to the comforts of wealth.

A New Kind of Holiness: The Friars

Early in the thirteenth century, a young Italian, Francis of Assisi, felt himself called to live his life in imitation of Christ. The son of a wealthy merchant, Francis followed Jesus's gospel command and gave up his home, his fine clothing, and the security of his family. For a thousand years, many strivers after holiness had done the same, but usually they had gone into the wilderness to live alone as hermits. Francis, however, walked the highways and city streets, begging for food and lodging and preaching as well as praying.

Soon he was joined by like-minded companions, forming a company of twelve who took over an abandoned building near Assisi as a base from which they continued to wander, preaching the ideal of Christian love and brotherhood. A wealthy lady, Clare, became Francis's disciple, and women as well as men followed his way of life of "holy poverty." Married people who could not join the actual Franciscan friars (from the French word for "brothers") and "Poor Clare" sisters joined Francis's "Third Order" to follow his example as best they could.

In this way, Francis founded a movement of religious striving of a new kind—one that did not withdraw from the world, but was very much part of it. Within a century, there were groups of Franciscans and Poor Clares in towns and cities throughout western Europe. To do their work, these groups needed permanent living quarters and places of worship, and they disputed fiercely whether their ideal of poverty allowed them to own land and buildings. But this did not prevent them from becoming the most important single influence on the religious life of the burgeoning towns of Western Christendom (see photo on page 210).

Francis himself was a mystic—one who seeks God's truth through inner inspiration and revelation. He and his fellow mystics were doubtful of book learning and human reason. Of a contrary view was the Spaniard Dominic, a contemporary of Francis. Dominic was an intellectual, who saw the Christian faith as a reasoned approach to truth, and the order of friars he founded was devoted chiefly to scholarship, teaching, and preaching—their official name was the "Order of Preachers." Alarmed by the spread of heretical doctrines in his time, Dominic believed he could best serve the Lord by guiding the thoughts and education of Christians. Francis appealed mainly to people's hearts; Dominic appealed more to their minds. But Dominican communities and churches spread as widely as Franciscan ones, Dominican scholars were prominent in newly founded universities, and Dominican inquisitors were in charge of preventing the spread of heresies.

 The Franciscan Archive (http://www.franciscan-archive.org/index2.html) Learn more about the life of Francis and his followers.

"My Last Will and Testament," Francis of Assisi Read Francis's guidance to his followers about how to carry on after his death.

> "Medieval struggles against Church corruption were genuine movements of religious striving, and because the Church was so important in society, they also had massive social and political consequences."

> "Francis founded a movement of religious striving of a new kind— one that did not withdraw from the world, but was very much part of it."

The Papal Monarchy

The greatest changes in the Western Church involved the papacy itself. Traditionally, the popes were obeyed throughout Western Christendom in matters of belief and worship but had little or no governing power, such as over the appointment of clergy. Furthermore, as bishops of Rome, they were themselves chosen by the traditional method of election by the clergy and male believers of their bishopric (p. 129). In practice, this meant that local nobles controlled the elections, and their rivalries and intrigues had produced many disreputable popes.

However, as the Holy Roman emperors became powerful rulers and began to take an interest in the affairs of Italy (p. 178), they sometimes intervened to appoint their own candidates—most of them worthy and conscientious churchmen. It was one such imperial appointee, Pope Leo IX, a German bishop much influenced by Cluniac ideals, who, toward the middle of the eleventh century, first put the papacy at the head of the movement for Church reform.

The Independent Papacy: Gregory VII

To the more radical reformers, however, it seemed a wicked defiance of the will of God that the successors of Peter (p. 147) should be under the control of any worldly ruler, even reform-minded emperors. The chief promoter of this idea was the Italian Hildebrand. As archdeacon of Rome, a key position in the Church's administration, he proved himself a shrewd planner and tactician.

In 1059, thanks largely to Hildebrand's efforts, a new system was brought into being for the election of popes. From now on, the right to vote was to be restricted to the **cardinal** clergy—a small number of the ranking priests of Rome. The cardinals were appointed by the pope, and when a pope died, they met in seclusion to name his successor. Because they usually chose from their own membership, the body automatically furnished select candidates for the papal office. In this way, the voting process was to be insulated from any kind of lay influence, and the choice of the successor of Peter would hopefully be where it belonged—with the Holy Spirit, speaking through a group of clergy who were uniquely qualified to hear his voice.

The Popes and the Church

In 1073, the cardinals chose Hildebrand as Pope Gregory VII. Conditioned by his earlier training at Cluny, he applied himself to a sweeping reform of the Church. To bring this about, it was not enough for him to issue declarations; he must effectively govern the church to put reforming ideals into effect. He kept in touch with the bishops through continual correspondence—the papal letters run to thousands of volumes. He required bishops to make regular visits to Rome, which often involved weeks of arduous travel. He sent out papal legates (ambassadors) to conduct inquiries and see that the pope was being obeyed in the territories they visited. He also began hearing appeals against decisions of bishops on matters such as marriage and ownership of Church property.

All this activity needed an expanded headquarters in Rome. Under Gregory's guidance, the central administration of the papacy came to be handled through a number of bureaus, departments, and assemblies—called, collectively, the papal *curia* (court or council). The officers in charge of these agencies were usually chosen from among the cardinals and formed, in effect, a kind of "cabinet" for the pope. To finance the administration, countless payments started flowing to Rome: fees for appeals from bishops' courts, for dispensations (exemptions) from Church law, for acquiring Church positions, and for indulgences. In this way, Gregory and the popes who followed him built up what amounted to a complex international government system, financed by Church institutions and believers.

In building their power across Western Christendom, the popes were in some ways in the same position as rulers who were building their power across countries (p. 187). The popes, too, had certain assets to begin with—in their case, the Western consensus that they were the Christ-appointed guides of the whole Church. They also had means of compulsion against resisters. They could **excommunicate** opponents, thereby depriving them of the sacraments without which there was no salvation.

A Franciscan Preacher Bernardino of Siena, a fifteenth-century friar, is shown in a painting by a local artist, Sano di Pietro, preaching to a segregated crowd of men and women before his hometown's city hall. The gaunt-faced friar aims harsh words against their sins while holding up a symbol of hope—a plaque with the Greek letters *I H Σ*, the Holy Name of Jesus. Two centuries after Francis, his follower made crowds in Siena and throughout Italy kneel in shame and hope. Cathedral Treasury Trier, Photo: Rita Heyen

They could place whole regions under interdict, forbidding the conduct of Church services and thereby depriving whole populations of the sacraments. But these measures would not have worked if local clergy had not been willing to enforce them, and if local laity had not taken them seriously in the first place.

As with rulers, therefore, the main reason that the popes were able to grow powerful was that this seemed in the interest of the people over whom they wielded power—above all, because the popes were seen as leaders in the struggle for Church reform. Obedience to the papacy, it seemed, provided a guarantee that bishops and priests would be conscientious, monks and nuns would be saintly, and laypeople, whether kings and great lords or peasants and craftspeople, would honor the clergy. That suited both laypeople and clergy who wanted to see in the Church to which they belonged a true reflection within earthly society of God's heavenly kingdom.

But earthly society contained other powerful forces, notably the rulers who were also striving for increased power. And no ruler could be truly powerful without the influence in the Church that Gregory wanted to deny them.

Popes and Rulers

Ever since the time of Constantine, Christian teaching had given monarchs a sacred character as well as secular authority. The emperor Charlemagne, who was held up as a model, had appointed bishops and abbots to their offices and had employed churchmen as administrators and teachers in his palace school. The nobility and the clergy supported each other at all levels of feudal government. It was this relationship that Gregory and his successors sought to change.

The Investitures Dispute

By various historical arguments and documents, including the falsified Donation of Constantine (pp. 292–293), Gregory claimed to be the overlord of the rulers of western Europe. He declared, for example, that the Holy Roman emperor, Henry IV, was his vassal, on the grounds that Charlemagne, Henry's predecessor, owed his crown to Pope Leo III (p. 173). He objected particularly to Henry's control over the selection of German bishops, who were important fief-holders and vassals of the emperor. Henry was exercising a traditional right when he influenced their selection and invested (clothed) them with their symbols of office. Gregory insisted, however, that bishops were spiritual officers and could be invested with ring and staff, the symbols of their religious authority, only by the pope. What he sought, of course, was papal control over the elections themselves.

Gregory employed every means at his command to bring Henry down. He plotted with the emperor's enemies in Germany, excommunicated and deposed him (1076), and turned to the Normans in southern Italy for military assistance against Henry's forces. After his excommunication, Henry outmaneuvered his adversary by crossing the Alps in winter and appearing as a penitent before Gregory at the palace of Canossa in northern Italy. Standing barefoot in the snow, he begged the pope to forgive him for his offenses and restore him to communion with

 **The Concordat of Worms: Compromise Ends the Investiture Controversy** Read a selection from the Concordat of Worms, the compromise that ended the Investitures Dispute.

the Church. Gregory granted the request, but the contest shortly resumed, and the pope once again excommunicated Henry. In the long run, Gregory lacked sufficient armed power to transform occasional triumphs into lasting victory. The **Investitures Dispute**, as modern scholars call it, was settled later by compromise: Henry's successor agreed in 1122 to give to the pope the investiture of religious symbols, but he retained the emperor's traditional influence over the selection of German bishops.

> **Investitures Dispute**
> A conflict, originally between Pope Gregory and Emperor Henry IV, over who had the power to select the bishops of the Holy Roman Empire.

The Papacy at Its Height

Even so, the papacy's growing control over the Church gave it greater power against emperors and kings than ever before. During the reign of Innocent III, the papacy reached its height of prestige and power. Its strength was shown by the humbling of King John of England, who, after a bitter dispute with Innocent over the election of the archbishop of Canterbury, the kingdom's leading churchman, was forced to submit. In the course of the dispute, John was deposed; afterward, in 1213, he was granted the realm of England as a fief from Rome, but only after doing homage to the pope. Such was the international authority of Innocent III that John's subjection to the pope actually strengthened the king's hand in his disputes with his discontented barons (p. 190).

A century later, papal claims were carried even further by Pope Boniface VIII. He met his match, however, in King Philip (the Fair) of France. Philip, who was waging war against England, levied a tax on church properties in 1296. Boniface answered this bold move, which was contrary to existing law, with angry denunciations. The violent dispute reached its climax a few years later when Boniface issued a declaration titled *Unam sanctam*, which insisted that *all* secular rulers were subject to the pope and that the pope could be judged by God alone. (Papal declarations are named after their first two words in Latin, in this case "One Holy" [Catholic and Apostolic Church].) Boniface concluded, daringly, "We declare, state, define, and pronounce that it is altogether necessary to salvation for every human creature to be subject to the Roman pontiff." Yet Boniface's words did not prevail over Philip's deeds. Philip sent a military force across the Alps to seize the aged pontiff. Roughly treated and humiliated by the French soldiers, Boniface died soon afterward in 1303.

The popes had failed to win supremacy over secular rulers or even to put an end to the power of those rulers within the Church. In the partnership and rivalry of Church and state that had begun with Constantine, the balance would soon swing against them. Even so, the position of the papacy within the Church had permanently changed. The popes had won for themselves a position as true rulers of the Church, governing and supervising its operations, which they have kept to the present day.

Rebellion Against the Church

Rulers who opposed the increase in power of the papacy did not question the belief that Christ had founded the Church and appointed a clergy to guide it that was headed by the pope. As the Church grew stronger and better organized, however, there also appeared movements of rebellion against it—new or revived heresies that denied the Church's beliefs and despised the priests, bishops, and pope.

One of the most widespread of these, perhaps descended from the Gnostics of early Christian times (pp. 130–131), proclaimed that only spirit was good, whereas matter was by nature evil. It was the creation not of God himself but of a lesser or opposing being, the "King of the World," and it was this being that the Church served. Sexual intercourse, procreation, and the eating of meat, among other things, were forbidden to God's true devotees, the "Most Perfect Ones," though ordinary "Believers" were permitted an easier way of life. Beliefs of this kind spread widely in both Western and Eastern Christendom, and were always viciously persecuted. They were found in the Balkans throughout the Middle Ages; in the twelfth century, they were widespread in southern France, where they were called the "Albigensian heresy," named for the cathedral town of Albi.

Pope Innocent III proclaimed a crusade against the Albigensians (al-bi-JEN-seez), and French nobles from the north cruelly suppressed the rebellion by 1226. But heresy smoldered even after the crusade was over. To snuff out the remaining embers, Innocent's successor, Pope Gregory IX, established a permanent court for finding and trying heretics: the **Inquisition**.

> **"***We declare, state, define, and pronounce that it is altogether necessary to salvation for every human creature to be subject to the Roman pontiff.***"**
> —Pope Boniface, 1302 (?)

The Inquisition

The pope's grand inquisitor was placed at Carcassonne (kar-kuh-SON), in the south of France. He sent deputies, drawn chiefly from the new Dominican order, to the towns and cities of the area. In the public square of each place, the deputies would announce their mission and then call for people to testify regarding suspected heretics. In pursuing their inquiries, the deputies followed common judicial practice of the period in using torture to wring confessions from uncooperative suspects and in denying accused persons legal counsel and the right to call or confront witnesses. Proceedings were usually conducted in secret. Lucky prisoners would confess early, repent, and forfeit only their property.

Those who proved stubborn or who lapsed again into heresy after repenting were excommunicated and turned over to the civil authorities for more severe punishment, since Church law forbade the clergy to take life. Because heresy was often associated with popular discontent or rebellion, the civil authorities regarded it as equivalent to treason and therefore set the penalty of death for convicted heretics. The most common means of execution was burning at the stake—a means that symbolized the flames of hell that awaited unrepentant heretics, but also gave heretics a chance to make a final repentance as the flames reached higher and higher. They might then have time to beg for God's forgiveness and the salvation of their souls. But in no case would the fire be quenched; the body of a "confirmed" heretic was already forfeit.

 Links to Inquisition Sites (http://www.rarebooks.nd.edu/exhibits/inquisition/text/links.html) Delve into the trials and punishments of the Inquisition.

In the view of medieval churchmen, the end of rooting out heresy justified these cruel means. Even the "angelic doctor" of the Church, Thomas Aquinas (p. 236), held that extreme punishments were necessary to protect souls from the contamination of false beliefs, and the papacy established inquisitions in many regions suspected of heresy besides southern France. But the Inquisition was also open to the foulest abuses. To level the accusation of heresy became a convenient way of injuring or getting rid of personal enemies, and the accusers were never identified by the court. Besides, Church courts subject to the pope came to be unwelcome even to Catholic rulers after the end of the Middle Ages. Except in Spain and Portugal, where the Inquisition became in effect an arm of the government, rulers preferred to use methods of religious repression that were more safely under their control (p. 323).

LO² Western Christendom on the Offensive: The Crusades

To the south and east of Christendom, stretching from Spain to the Middle East and beyond, lay the lands of the rival monotheism of Islam. Before the Arabs had conquered them, most of these lands had been Christian, and as European civilization renewed itself, rulers and warriors in both halves of Christendom struggled to win some of them back. For several centuries, there was continual fighting on the borders of Christendom and Islam—in Spain, the Mediterranean islands, and Asia Minor. But late in the eleventh century, as Western Christendom became more powerful, skilled, and ambitious, it took aim at a more distant target—the Holy Land.

In the Christian understanding, "holy war" was a form of "just war"—and no war could be "just" unless it was declared by an authority with legitimate power over the entire community. Western Christendom in the late eleventh century had such an authority—the papacy. Once the popes took on the role of declarers of war against the enemies of Christendom, the stage was set for the most dynamic forces in western European civilization—the feudal warriors, the townspeople, and the Church—to cooperate in a vast but ill-fated enterprise: the **Crusades**.

Triumph and Tragedy in the Holy Land

Although crusades were proclaimed and fought in the Middle Ages against various religious enemies in different regions, the most important of them were directed against the Muslims in the Holy Land for the purpose of recapturing the birthplace of Christianity. These "great" Crusades were international mass movements that fired the imagination of all classes of society, mainly in the twelfth and thirteenth centuries. Though the Crusades in the Holy Land failed to achieve their aim, they provided a dramatic expression of the confidence and zeal of the renewed Western Christendom.

Western Christendom, Byzantium, and the Turks

The series of events that led to the Crusades had its beginning in Central Asia. In this period, when the civilizations and peoples of the Eastern Hemisphere were drawing closer together, Islam, like Christian Europe, was subject to invasion by increasingly powerful nomads of the steppes. During the ninth century, a nomadic people that had recently come to prominence in the steppes, the Turks, entered Persia from the north. They were quickly converted to Islam and, for more than a century, held control over a portion of the Islamic empire.

In the eleventh century, the Turkish Seljuk dynasty conquered Baghdad and won the title of sultan (ruler) from its caliph (p. 160). Members of this warlike family pushed westward from Baghdad into Syria, Palestine, and Anatolia. They established themselves as rulers of several small states in those areas and were less tolerant of Christian minorities than earlier Arab rulers had been. In particular, they began harassing the growing numbers of Christian pilgrims to the Holy Land.

While resentment mounted in western Europe against the infidels who ruled the holiest shrines of Christianity, to Byzantium the expansion of the Turks was a formidable new threat. It arose, moreover, at a time when its relations with Western Christendom were endangered by religious disputes. Various differences of belief and practice had grown up over the centuries between the two halves of the Church, but now a new and especially divisive issue appeared: as the popes built up their power in the West, they also insisted more than ever before on their supremacy over the whole Church. This brought them into collision with both the emperors and the patriarchs in Constantinople.

In 1054, in the course of these disputes, papal representatives in Constantinople formally excommunicated the patriarch, whereupon the document of excommunication was solemnly burned by the Greeks, and the patriarch in turn excommunicated

 Mutual Excommunication: Christianity Split Between East and West Read what each side of the Church had to say about the other in 1054.

the pope's representatives. At the time, neither side intended this as a complete break between the two halves of the Church. But they began to see each other, much more than before, as religious adversaries, and this eventually led to a lasting **schism** between the Catholic and Orthodox Churches.

Around this time, it became customary for the two halves of the Church to call themselves by different names, each of which had originally applied to the Church as a whole. The Eastern Church, which had overcome many internal disputes over belief, began to call itself specifically "Orthodox" ("rightly believing"). The Western Church, with its papacy that claimed to rule the whole Church, began to call itself specifically "Catholic" ("worldwide"). And the difference between the two halves was not just one of names. The Norman rulers of Sicily, having conquered the island from the Muslim Arabs, now went on to wrest southern Italy from Christian but "schismatic" (Church-splitting) Byzantium.

Now, on top of all these problems from its fellow Christians in the west, Byzantium suddenly found itself in deadly danger from its new Muslim neighbors to the east. In 1071, the Turks defeated a Byzantine army at Manzikert in eastern Anatolia (Map 12.1 on page 217) and then gradually moved westward toward the imperial capital itself. Finally, the eastern emperor, Alexius, decided to mend his relations with the Christian West and sent an appeal for help to Pope Urban II.

Preaching the Crusade

The pope heard the plea of Alexius's ambassador early in 1095 and found the idea of sending a rescue force to the East well suited to his own far-reaching aims. Heir to the Cluniac reform movement and to the policies of Gregory VII, Urban realized that a successful holy war against the Turks would do more than free the Holy Land and reopen the roads of pilgrimage. It would in all likelihood compel the Byzantine emperor, in repayment, to recognize the supremacy of the pope over the whole Christian Church. Moreover, the triumph would lift the prestige of the papacy to such a height that the ideal of Church supremacy over the state would surely be realized.

Inquisition
A Church tribunal that used complex procedures of investigation and punishment to enforce religious conformity.

Crusades
Holy wars declared by the popes against the enemies of Christendom.

sultan
A Muslim Turkish supreme ruler (from an Arabic word for "ruler").

schism
A division within the Christian Church mainly involving disputes over the powers of Church leaders rather than questions of actual belief.

THERE WERE SEVERAL MOTIVATIONS FOR THE WESTERN OFFENSIVE AGAINST ISLAM:

Religion

- War between Christians and Muslims and between Christians and pagans was already traditional, and the aim of offensive wars against Muslims was to reconquer lands that had been originally Christian.

- In the eleventh century, theologians redefined the Church's teaching about war against non-Christians.

- War against pagans and Muslims was no longer merely a necessary evil but a deed that was pleasing to God, and to die in the course of such a war was a form of martyrdom (similar to the Muslim doctrine of jihad, p. 162).

Feudal Land Hunger

- Kings and great lords were eager to enlarge their holdings and acquire land with which to reward their vassals.

- Among lesser warriors, many younger sons and landless knights dreamed of finding fiefs that would enable them to acquire the wealth and status of landholders.

- Therefore, feudal warriors went on the offensive, not just to eliminate enemies but also to conquer and colonize land. Any non-Christian nation, whether pagan or Muslim, was regarded as fair game for this purpose.

- During the tenth century, Norman warriors hastened to Sicily to reconquer it from the Arabs, and great lords and knights from all over Europe participated in the gradual reconquest of Spain.

Commercial Enterprise

- Conquest and colonization usually opened the way for trade and were therefore in the interests of towns-people as well as landholders.

- The pushing back of the frontiers of Islam cleared the western Mediterranean for the rising commerce of Christian Europe.

- In the eleventh century, while feudal knights were fighting to reconquer Spain and Sicily, the islands of Sardinia and Corsica were seized from the Arabs by an Italian city-state, Pisa.

Later in the year 1095, Urban used the Council of Clermont, in central France, as his forum for launching the First Crusade. Exactly what he said to the clergy who had gathered from all over France is uncertain. Different accounts, mostly written many years later, put different words into his mouth: about the blow to fellow Christians in the East whom the Muslims had "overcome in seven battles"; about the "base and bastard Turks" who had polluted Jerusalem, "the very city in which . . . Christ Himself suffered for us" (see photo); and about the opportunity for quarrelsome feudal warriors to save their souls by fighting for once in a just and holy war—"Let those who have been serving as mercenaries for small pay now obtain the eternal reward." Whatever the pope actually said, words like these must have been what the clergy in France and elsewhere in Western Christendom were saying—and what French feudal warriors and Italian seafaring traders were eagerly hearing.

Taking the Cross: The Path to the First Crusade Read how news of the crusade spread throughout Europe.

The crusading spirit possessed other classes of society as well. Early in 1096, a motley crowd of commoners set out from southern Germany for Constantinople. Their enthusiasm, sparked by the pope's call to arms, was whipped to a fury by a maverick preacher known as Peter the Hermit. The Peasants' Crusade, as it came to be called, distinguished itself chiefly by the massacre of Jewish communities along the way. Lacking provisions of their own, these commoners lived off the country as they marched. When they at last reached Constantinople, the Byzantine emperor grew alarmed and hastily ferried them across the Bosporus waterway to Anatolia. There, the Turks made quick work of the misguided peasants.

The First Crusade

Meanwhile, however, a more formidable force was assembling. French warriors, responding to the call of Urban (who was himself a French aristocrat), made up the main body of crusaders. Godfrey, duke of Lorraine, joined by other dukes, counts, and barons, set out in 1096 with an army of some fifteen thousand knights. It was this army of feudal warriors that fought and won the First Crusade, the only crusade that temporarily, at least, attained its goal.

The crusaders traveled down the Danube and then across the Balkans to Constantinople, where they met other groups of

◀◀ **Jerusalem the Golden** A map from about 1200 shows the city as a perfect circle surrounded by walls. Revered sites are labeled and imaginatively depicted, such as "Temple of Solomon" (top right in the circle); and "Golgotha," "Place of Calvary," and "Sepulcher of the Lord" with an empty coffin (lower left). Below the map, a crusader knight puts a Muslim knight to flight—the necessary bloodshed that will enable the Christian warrior to enter and possess the Holy City.

The amount of blood that they shed on that day is incredible.... Some of our men (and this was more merciful) cut off the heads of their enemies; others shot them with arrows, so that they fell from the towers; others tortured them longer by casting them into the flames. Piles of heads, hands, and feet were to be seen in the streets of the city.... It was a just and splendid judgment of God that this place should be filled with the blood of unbelievers, since it had suffered so long from their blasphemies.

With the help of fleets from Venice, Genoa, and other Italian cities, the crusaders moved on to take the coastal towns of Palestine and Syria. (For this aid, the Italians received, as they had hoped, rich privileges in the trade of the Middle East.) The various conquered territories were then drawn together into a loose feudal state, the Kingdom of Jerusalem. Baldwin of Flanders was chosen as its first king and accepted the usual homage and services of the landholding nobility. The feudalism of western Europe was thus transplanted to Outremer (**OO-truh-mair**)—"Overseas," as the French called the Christian beachhead in the Holy Land.

 Life as a Seljuk Turk During the First Crusade Experience life as a Seljuk Turk during the First Crusade.

 Muslim Life Under Christian Rule Read a Muslim's account of life under Christian rule.

knights that had taken different overland routes, and then crossed into Anatolia to confront the Turks (see Map 12.1 on page 217). On the way across Anatolia, they suffered terrible hardships, disease, and some defeats, but they were at last victorious. Their leaders, having turned back the Turkish threat to Constantinople, moved on to establish dukedoms in eastern Anatolia and abandoned their original plan to march on to Jerusalem. The survivors of lesser rank, however, insisted that the crusade be resumed. Responding at last to their demands, Raymond, count of Toulouse, advanced on Jerusalem and took the city, after a six-week siege, in 1099.

The crusaders' entry into the Holy City was an orgy of looting and killing of Muslims and Jews. One crusader reported in his journal:

 Frankish Arrogance in the Byzantine Court Read about the misbehavior of a Frankish knight in the Byzantine court of Constantinople.

The Struggle for the Holy Land

The First Crusade was followed by countless other expeditions, only some of which have been assigned a number by historians. Most of these later crusades to the Holy Land were intended not to expand the Christian territories but to defend them against fierce Muslim campaigns of reconquest. The Second Crusade (1147–1149)—called in response to Turkish success in recapturing part of the gains of the First Crusade—was inspired by a reforming monk, Bernard of Clairvaux. An extraordinarily persuasive man, he induced two leading feudal rulers, the king of France and the Holy Roman emperor, and thousands of fighting men to "take the Cross."

BERNARD OF CLAIRVAUX CALLS FOR A CRUSADE

In 1146, following Muslim gains at the expense of the Christian territories in the Holy Land, the widely revered Abbot Bernard of Clairvaux wrote an "open letter" to the clergy and people of Germany calling upon them to join a new crusade—what is now known as the Second Crusade. The letter would have been distributed widely enough to provide guidelines for local preachers. In this excerpt, Bernard explains how taking the Cross will be an aid to salvation, and discourages outbreaks against the Jews, which had been a feature of the First Crusade.

Behold, brethren, now is the accepted time, now is the day of salvation. The earth also is moved and has trembled, because the God of heaven has begun to destroy the land which is his. . . . And now, for our sins, the enemies of the Cross have raised blaspheming heads, ravaging with the edge of the sword the land of promise. . . . Alas! they rage against the very shrine of the Christian faith with blasphemous mouths, and would enter and trample down the very couch on which, for us, our Life lay down to sleep in death.

What are you going to do then, O brave men? What are you doing, O servants of the Cross? Will you give what is holy to the dogs, and cast your pearls before swine? How many sinners there, confessing their sins and tears, have obtained pardon, after the defilement of the heathen had been purged by the swords of your fathers?

What are we then to think, brethren? Is the Lord's arm shortened so that it cannot save, because he calls his weak creatures to guard and restore his heritage? Can he not send more than twelve legions of angels, or merely speak the word, and the land shall be set free? It is altogether in his power to effect what he wishes; but I tell you, the Lord, your God, is trying you. He looks upon the sons of men to see if there be any to understand, and seek, and bewail his error. For the Lord hath pity upon his people, and provides a sure remedy for those that are afflicted. . . .

But now, O brave knight, now, O warlike hero, here is a battle you may fight without danger, where it is glory to conquer and gain to die. If you are a prudent merchant, if you are a desirer of this world, behold I show you some great bargains; see that you lose them not. Take the sign of the cross, and you shall gain pardon for every sin that you confess with a contrite heart. The material itself, being bought, is worth little; but if it be placed on a devout shoulder, it is, without doubt, worth no less than the kingdom of God. Therefore they have done well who have already taken the heavenly sign: well and wisely also will the rest do, if they hasten to lay upon their shoulders, like the first, the sign of salvation.

Besides, brethren, I warn you, and not only I, but God's apostle, "Believe not every spirit." We have heard and rejoice that the zeal of God abounds in you, but it behooves no mind to be wanting in wisdom. The Jews must not be persecuted, slaughtered, nor even driven out. Inquire of the pages of Holy Writ. I know what is written in the Psalms as prophecy about the Jews. "God hath commanded me," says the Church, 'Slay them not, lest my people forget.'"

They are living signs to us, representing the Lord's passion. For this reason they are dispersed into all regions, that now they may pay the just penalty of so great a crime, and that they may be witnesses of our redemption. Wherefore the Church, speaking in the same Psalm, says, "Scatter them by thy power; and bring them down, O Lord, our shield." So has it been. They have been dispersed, cast down. They undergo a hard captivity under Christian princes. Yet they shall be converted at even-time, and remembrance of them shall be made in due season. Finally, when the multitude of the Gentiles shall have entered in, then "all Israel shall be saved," saith the apostle. Meanwhile he who dies remains in death.

I do not enlarge on the lamentable fact that where there are no Jews there Christian men *judaize* even worse than they in extorting usury,—if, indeed, we may call them Christians and not rather baptized Jews. Moreover, if the Jews be utterly trampled down, how shall the promised salvation or conversion profit them in the end? . . .

EXPLORING THE SOURCE

1. How does Bernard think that taking the Cross will help people to salvation?

2. What is Bernard's attitude to the Jews, and why does he think that it is wrong to use persecution and violence against them?

Source: James Harvey Robinson, ed., *Readings in European History* (Boston: Ginn, 1904), 1:33.

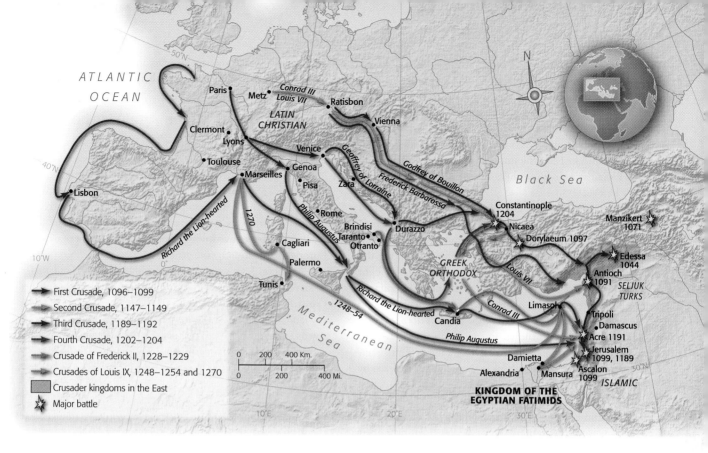

Map 12.1 **The Crusades, 1095–1270**

Western Christendom's efforts to conquer and hold the Holy Land, 2,000 miles away by land or sea, were on a vast scale. Large forces had not marched, sailed, and fought across such distances since the time of the Roman Empire—a sign of Western Christendom's growing wealth and skills. Crusades on this scale continued during the thirteenth century, but by 1300, the Muslims prevailed. © Cengage Learning

Interactive Map

The main force of this expedition was cut to pieces as it moved across Anatolia. Bernard, convinced that his cause was just, concluded that the failure must have been due to the sinfulness of the crusaders.

Bernard's view was accepted by his more ardent followers. Some of them went still further: they reasoned that if purity of the soul was a requirement for victory, young children would be the most favored of all crusaders. In accordance with this notion, thousands of innocent German and French boys marched off on the Children's Crusade in 1212. They never reached the Holy Land, however, for they fell victim to accident and disease or were captured by Christian slave dealers along the way—who mostly sold them to buyers in Muslim lands.

The climax of the struggles in the Holy Land came earlier, however, with the Third Crusade (1189–1192). Until not long before this crusade, most of the Muslim resistance to the invaders had come from Anatolia and Syria. Now, however, Muslim Egypt joined the struggle under its ruler Salah-ed-Din—Saladin, as the crusaders called him. Saladin was a pious Muslim, an ambitious statesman, and a formidable warrior who was a hero to Muslims and admired even by Christians. If he could expel the unbelievers from Jerusalem, to Muslims the "Glorious Place" from which the Prophet had ascended to heaven, he would both fulfill his duty of *jihad* and strengthen his position as the dominant Muslim ruler in the Middle East. Accordingly, in 1187, he crushed the army of the Latin Kingdom and went on to capture Jerusalem.

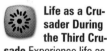

Life as a Crusader During the Third Crusade Experience life as a Christian warrior during the Third Crusade.

Once again, armies set out from the feudal kingdoms of western Europe—overland from the Holy Roman Empire and from France and England by sea routes that the Italian cities had opened across the Mediterranean (see Map 12.1). Saladin fought them all to a standstill, and finally, the most famous Christian warrior of the time, King Richard I of England ("the Lion-Hearted"; p. 190), had to make an agreement with the Egyptian ruler that left most of the Holy Land, including Jerusalem, in Muslim hands.

The Fourth Crusade and After

The Fourth Crusade, organized a few years later by leading French barons, involved a change of strategy: instead of going to the Holy Land, the barons made an agreement with the leading Italian seagoing city-state, Venice, to transport their army by sea to the center of Muslim power in Egypt (see Map 12.1 on page 217). But Venice was ambitious to dominate the eastern Mediterranean, a deposed emperor in Constantinople appealed for help from the crusaders, the Orthodox Church was seen as a religious rival, and besides, Constantinople would be an easier prize than the Egyptian capital, Cairo. Accordingly, the crusaders changed their plans, and in 1204 the imperial capital was stormed by the very men whose forefathers had promised its rescue a century before.

Untold treasures of gold, silver, and holy relics were seized during the subsequent looting. Vandalism and fire consumed irreplaceable works of Greek art and literature. The city and the empire's European lands were then divided among the chieftains of the crusade, and these remnants were brought together as the Latin Empire of Constantinople. The count of Flanders was proclaimed its first emperor, and a new patriarch was installed—one who was loyal to the pope in Rome. Venice secured special trading privileges, and the farmlands were shared out in feudal fashion among the plundering knights. Thus, long-desired and ill-concealed goals were momentarily realized by the papacy, the Venetians, and the French aristocracy—all at the expense of Byzantium.

The Latin Empire of Constantinople had an even briefer life than that of the Kingdom of Jerusalem. Byzantine emperors carried on in exile, clinging to a small piece of territory in Anatolia, and in 1261 they managed to regain Constantinople and the area around it. But Christendom's southeastern gateway was no longer defended by a powerful empire, so that the Turks eventually made their way through it; and the rivalry between the Western and Eastern Churches hardened into outright hostility.

Additional crusades intended to maintain or expand the Christian presence in the Holy Land continued throughout the thirteenth century. They all came to nothing, however, and the last Christian foothold, the fortress of Acre, fell in 1291. After that, the popes continued to proclaim crusades—against eastern European pagan peoples, against Christian heretics, and even against local rivals in Italian power struggles. From the fifteenth century, however, as European rulers built up centralized governments and became the main focus of loyalty within their countries, they no longer needed or wanted to act under the authority of the pope. Christians and Muslims, and later on Catholics and Protestants, still fought wars of religion against each other, but formal crusades became a thing of the past.

Western Christendom Against the Jews

The Christian expeditions against the East were accompanied by rising hostility toward the Jews. During the early Middle Ages, the Jews had continued to live in communities scattered across Christendom under the terms of a grudging decree of toleration by the Roman emperor Theodosius I, as well as in Muslim North Africa and the Middle East. They remained small in numbers, constituting perhaps 1 to 2 percent of western Europe's population by the year 1000.

Medieval Jews were usually forbidden to hold land, serfs, or slaves and were in fact a group entirely separate from the Christian social order. Cut off from the land, they mainly lived in the towns, where they were usually confined to their own quarters or *ghettos* (from the Italian word for a Jewish quarter) but were allowed to manage their own affairs. The professions, guilds, and most other occupations were closed to them, however, so they supported themselves in enterprises that were for the most part shunned by Christians—above all, moneylending.

 **A Charter for the Jews of Speyer** Read about the rights of one medieval Jewish community.

Despite the limitations on their freedom of action, some Jews rose to positions of power and distinction in commerce and royal administration. These individuals, however, could not match the achievements of the Spanish Jews, who were able to take refuge with tolerant Muslim local rulers when Christian ones turned against them, and vice versa. Notable Sephardic (from the Hebrew word for "Spanish") scholars, poets, philosophers, and statesmen made a golden age of Jewish history. They contributed, at the same time, to the intellectual development of Christian Europe by helping bring the wisdom of the ancient Greeks into circulation in the West.

The Crusades, however, brought a disastrous end to the relative security of Jews in much of Western Christendom. The First Crusade, launched in 1096, set off a spasm of religious fanaticism and violence. During the next two centuries, as prejudices against Jews were stirred

> **"I have therefore collected some Jews and located them in a place apart from the dwellings and association of the other inhabitants of the city; and that they may be protected from the attacks and violence of the mob, I have surrounded their quarter with a wall."**
>
> —The bishop of Speyer (Germany) on establishing a Jewish ghetto, 1084

up by Christian leaders, mob attacks on Jewish communities became commonplace.

Sporadic outbursts of anti-Semitic feeling had occurred in earlier times, but now the massacres became endemic. Ghetto laws became much stricter, and in 1215 the Fourth Lateran Council of the Church encouraged public humiliation of the Jews by ordering that they must wear a yellow patch or cap for identification. Punishment and intimidation often took the form of seizing and burning copies of the Talmud (ancient rabbinical commentaries on the Hebrew Bible; p. 125), on the ground that the contents were offensive to Christ.

At last, because they were thought to be an intolerable "contamination" to Christians, all Jews who refused conversion to Christianity were expelled from country after country: England in 1290, parts of Germany in 1298, France in 1306, Spain in 1492, and Portugal in 1498. Compelled to leave their property behind, thousands of Jews migrated to eastern Europe and Muslim lands.

 Philip Augustus Expels French Jews Read a medieval justification for expelling the Jews of Paris.

LO³ Western and Eastern Europe

In spite of their failure, the Crusades were mighty undertakings. In the Fourth Crusade, for example, 12,000 warriors and perhaps 1,000 horses sailed from Venice to Constantinople—as large a long-distance seaborne operation as the Romans themselves had ever undertaken. The crusade was a sign that in government effectiveness and industrial capacity, medieval western Europe was climbing back to the level of ancient Rome. On the other hand, eastern Europe was squeezed between nomad and Muslim invaders and the resurgent West. Europe was forming into two regions—a western heartland and an eastern periphery (outlying area) (see Map 12.2).

Byzantium and Orthodoxy

The differences between the two regions were partly religious and cultural, originating in the divergences between Roman and Byzantine civilization and the rivalry between the Catholic and Orthodox Churches, as they now usually called themselves. The Fourth Crusade and the capture of Constantinople in 1204 led to more than two hundred years of chaos in the Balkans, a region that Byzantium had earlier dominated, but which the Latin Empire of Constantinople and the restored Byzantine Empire were both too feeble to control.

Serbia and Bulgaria, both already important earlier in the Middle Ages (pp. 178–179), reappeared for a time as powerful independent kingdoms, but eventually they disintegrated as a result of disputes over the succession to their thrones and rivalries among their nobles. Other rulers held power over less prominent Balkan ethnic groups such as the non-Slavic Albanians and Romanians, which thereby took their first steps toward independent nationhood. Meanwhile, on the outskirts of the Balkans, powerful neighbors—Venice, Hungary, and the Turks—took advantage of the situation to gain power and influence in the region.

Yet the spiritual and cultural hold of Byzantium over the Orthodox peoples of eastern Europe was as strong as ever. The most successful Bulgarian and Serbian rulers took the title of tsar (emperor—p. 178), surrounded themselves with Byzantine pomp and ceremony, and dreamed of ruling in Constantinople. They established national "Bulgarian" or "Serbian" Orthodox (as opposed to "Greek Orthodox") churches and appointed "autocephalous" (independent) patriarchs to run these churches. They built splendid cathedrals and monasteries, where glowingly colored frescoes and icons (holy pictures) seemed to give believers a glimpse of the other world (see photo on page 221), and where monks wrote chronicles and lives of saints in the ancient Slavic religious language and the Cyrillic alphabet (pp. 177–178) used by all the national Orthodox churches. In many ways, the thirteenth and fourteenth centuries were the golden age of Slavic Orthodox culture.

As a result of the Fourth Crusade, this flourishing Orthodox world now viewed the Catholic Church as an enemy and a traitor to Christianity. The Bulgarian, Serbian, and restored Byzantine rulers sometimes struck bargains with the popes, submitting to papal religious authority in return for western military and political support. But these bargains never lasted, for suspicion and hatred of Rome were firmly anchored in the hearts of the Orthodox faithful. Thus the estrangement between the Catholic and the Orthodox Churches hardened into bitter religious hostility.

Eastern European States and Societies

The divergence between western and eastern Europe was also social, economic, and political. With the rise of a dynamic urban trading and industrial economy from 1000 on, western Europe forged ahead of the east. While the ruling families of western Europe came to accept the principle of primogeniture (p. 176) in the eleventh and twelfth centuries, those of eastern Europe continued to divide their lands among numerous heirs until the end of the Middle Ages, thereby weakening their dynastic power. Europe came to be divided into a group of politically and economically stronger western countries and a group of politically and economically weaker eastern countries. The second group included not only the Orthodox countries but also Catholic Poland and Hungary and the eastern territories of the Holy Roman Empire (see Map 12.2).

In the Middle Ages, the western countries gained many advantages from the countries on their eastern borders. For western Europe, the east provided territories for colonization and emigration and sources of foodstuffs and raw materials. In the twelfth and thirteenth centuries, crusaders from the Holy Roman Empire conquered many still-pagan tribes on the southern and eastern shores of the Baltic Sea (see Map 12.2). Throughout these eastern borderlands of the Holy Roman Empire and on into Poland and Hungary, masses of German colonists moved in, clearing the land for agriculture and founding new towns and cities—a migration that nationalist-minded German historians centuries later christened the "Drive to the East." Along with the migration of Germans, there was also a mass movement of Jews, fleeing eastward from western European persecution.

In the newly colonized territories, and throughout much of the rest of northeastern Europe, farmers grew grain and flax, and lumberjacks logged timber, for export westward. The towns functioned as trading outposts of German coastal cities that controlled the region's seaborne trade and eventually joined together in a cooperative trading organization, the *Hansa* (p. 253). Farther south, the commerce of Hungary, Serbia, Bulgaria, Byzantium, and the Black Sea regions (see Map 12.2) was controlled in the same way by the Italian city-states (p. 195).

Sometimes this western expansion into eastern Europe led to conflict. For more than two hundred years, the rulers of Poland vied for control of the Baltic coastlands with the Teutonic Knights, a group of crusading warriors that had led the German conquest of the pagan tribes of that region. The kings of Hungary likewise contested the hold of Venice on the eastern shores of the Adriatic Sea, Hungary's main outlet for seaborne commerce. In Bohemia, which was inhabited mainly by the Slavic Czechs, resentment at German immigration, along

Map 12.2 Europe about 1230

This small region of the world is crowded with kingdoms, princedoms, and self-styled empires. Many of these states will survive to the present through border changes, periods of foreign rule, and government and social revolutions; others, notably the Holy Roman Empire, will eventually disappear. One landmark of the early Middle Ages, Byzantium, has already almost vanished, and Islam is expanding into its former territories; at the other end of Europe, in the Iberian peninsula, Islam is retreating. © Cengage Learning

Interactive Map

Major battle

Boundary of the Holy Roman Empire

Erich Lessing/Art Resource, NY

The Lamentation of Christ Two Greek artists, Michael and Eutychius of Thessalonica, made this wall painting in 1295 for a church in a Balkan religious center, Ohrid. Disciples touch Christ's lifeless limbs, the Virgin Mary (at right) tears her hair, an angel clutches at his face. The painting shows human emotions and reactions in a manner quite new in Eastern Christendom—and new in Western Christendom when the Italian artist Giotto painted the same scene in the same manner ten years later (see photo on page 295).

with religious disputes, led eventually to a bitter internal and international struggle, the Hussite Wars (pp. 250-251).

But these conflicts were exceptional. So long as the rulers of eastern Europe did not feel directly threatened with the loss of their local power and independence, they usually accepted western immigration and commercial domination. The kings of Bohemia, Poland, and Hungary welcomed and even invited Germans and Jews to settle in their countries, for the sake of the increased prosperity—and increased tax revenues—that the newcomers brought. Noble landowners were glad to supply foodstuffs and raw materials to the west; and with the kings weakened by the division of their territories and family disputes, it was often the nobles who wielded the greatest share of power.

As a result of these migrations, social differences in eastern Europe came to be also ethnic. In any particular region, the peasants belonged to one ethnic group and the townspeople

to other groups—usually German, Jewish, and in the Balkans, also Greek—and it was not unusual for the nobles and rulers to belong to yet another ethnic group. In the Middle Ages, eastern Europe was, on the whole, more tolerant of ethnic and religious diversity than western Europe. But in modern times, under the impact of religious, nationalist, and class ideologies of western European origin—combined, in the Balkans, with the lasting effects of Turkish conquest (p. 251)—eastern Europe would be torn by savage strife.

Mongols, Tartars, and Russia

There was another important difference between eastern and western Europe: the eastern countries, unlike the western ones, were constantly exposed to attack by the nomadic peoples of the steppes. This threat reached its height in the thirteenth

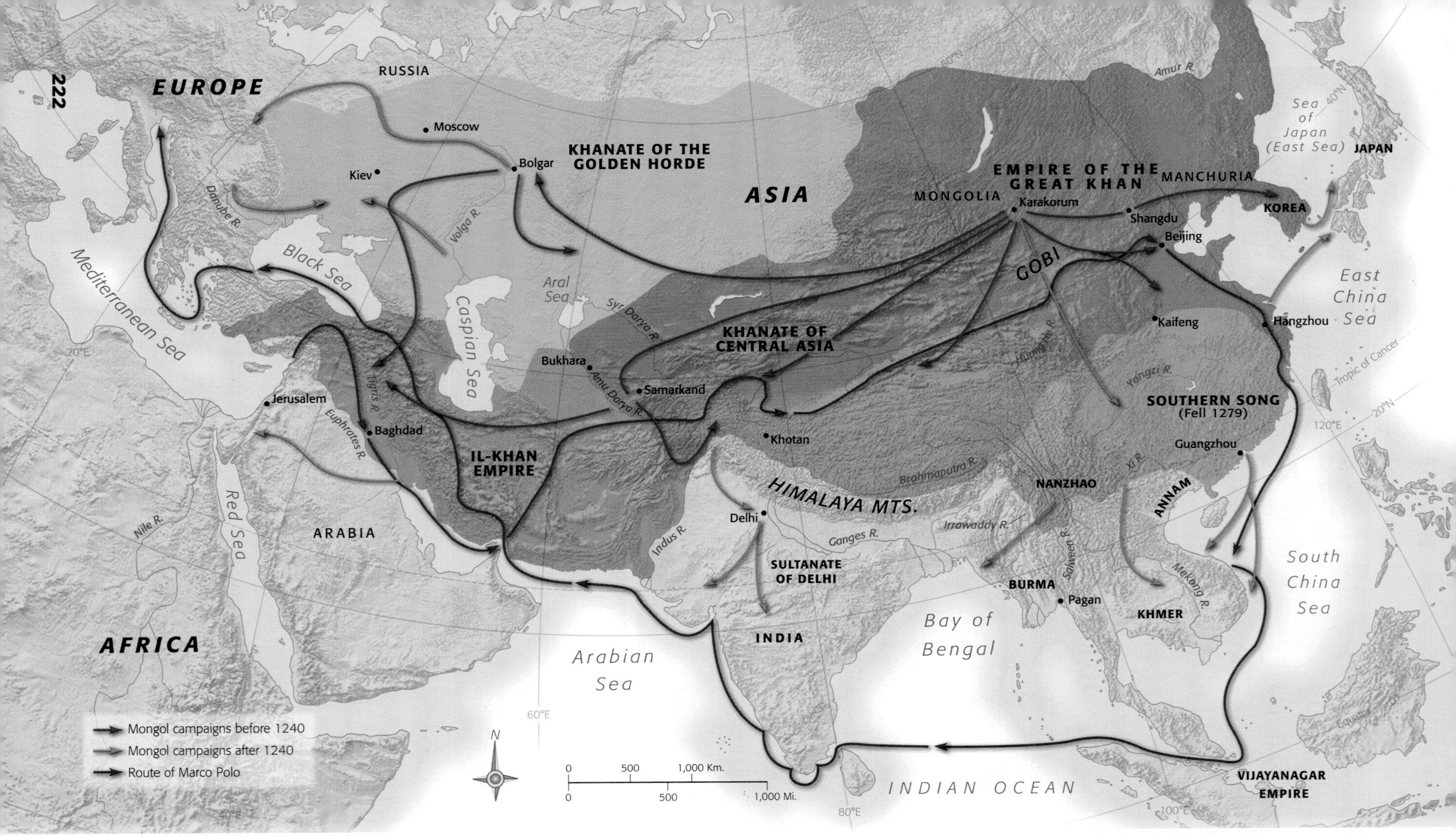

Interactive
Map

Map 12.3 The Mongol Empire

The Mongols built a larger empire than any conquering people before them, and held it securely for most of the thirteenth century. From his capital at Beijing, the Great Khan ruled China, Korea, and the Mongol homeland. Lesser khans, loosely subject to the Great Khan, ruled territories stretching across the steppes as far as Russia. For the first time in history, so far as is known, Europeans (including Marco Polo) could visit the eastern shores of Asia. © Cengage Learning

Mongol campaigns before 1240
Mongol campaigns after 1240
Route of Marco Polo

century when a pagan nomadic people from the Far East, the Mongols under Genghis Khan, built an empire that stretched from China to Europe (Map 12.3). Between 1237 and 1240, Genghis's grandson Batu Khan devastated much of eastern Europe and conquered Russia.

The Mongol Empire soon broke up, but Russia's ancient capital city of Kiev and most of the country's southern territories (present-day Ukraine) remained under the rule of a Muslim people ethnically related to the Turks and allied with the Mongols, the Tartars (known to the Russians, supposedly because of their luxurious encampments, as the "Golden Horde"). The northern regions, however, were held by native Russian vassals of the Tartars, most prominent among whom were the rulers of the city of Moscow and its surrounding territory.

Over the generations, even while acknowledging Tartar overlordship, Moscow extended its power over most of northern Russia. The new state was in close contact with the Byzantine-influenced Slavs of the Balkans and shared in their flourishing religious and cultural life, but its rulers already controlled far more people and territory than the Bulgarian and Serbian monarchs who so proudly called themselves tsars. Eventually, the Russian rulers would take—and keep—that title (pp. 251-252). In time, they would make their country as powerful as any of its western European rivals, but even they could not change the overall balance of power between the two halves of Europe, which has favored the West down to the present day.

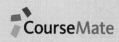 Listen to a synopsis of Chapter 12.

CHAPTER 13

THE CULTURE OF WESTERN CHRISTENDOM,
1000–1300

LEARNING OBJECTIVES

AFTER READING THIS CHAPTER, YOU SHOULD BE ABLE TO DO THE FOLLOWING:

LO[1] Describe the Romanesque and Gothic styles.

LO[2] Trace the renewal of intellectual life in medieval Europe.

LO[3] Discuss the evolution of medieval literature.

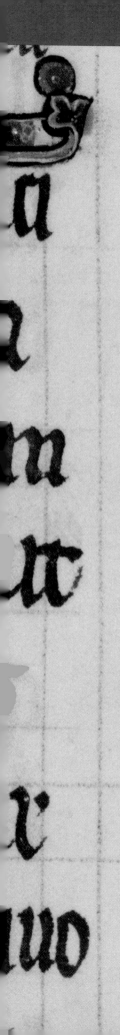

> "AS THE RENEWAL OF MEDIEVAL
> CIVILIZATION REACHED ITS PEAK, THE
> INSPIRATION OF RELIGION, COMBINED
> WITH INCREASING WEALTH, TECHNICAL
> PROGRESS, AND THE REVIVAL OF URBAN
> LIFE, CREATED THE CONDITIONS FOR
> BRILLIANT CULTURAL ACHIEVEMENTS."

As the renewal of medieval civilization reached its peak, the inspiration of religion, combined with increasing wealth, technical progress, and the revival of urban life, created the conditions for brilliant cultural achievements. Western Christendom invested much of its newfound wealth and skills in magnificent religious buildings—the churches and cathedrals of the Romanesque and Gothic styles. New urban institutions of learning, the universities, supplied skilled professionals to meet the needs of a complex society and also nurtured advances in knowledge and thought. Literacy became normal for nobles and better-off townspeople, who provided authors and a public for masterpieces of literature in both Latin and the developing vernacular (native) languages of Europe.

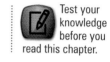

Test your knowledge before you read this chapter.

What do you think?

Medieval artists, scholars, and writers were more concerned with the afterlife than this life.

Strongly Disagree						Strongly Agree
1	2	3	4	5	6	7

By permission of the Warden and Fellows of Merton College Oxford. 157_MER_MS_269_f_140_v

≪ Understanding Aristotle In a thirteenth-century copy of a work by an ancient Greek, Aristotle, with explanations by a medieval Arab, Averroës, a medieval-style "E" begins the Latin word *Ens* ("Being"—a philosophical concept). Inside the "E," a Christian scholar contemplates a model of the universe, representing "Being," with a smile of confident understanding—thanks to colleagues who have translated the original Greek and Arabic into Latin. Medieval Western Christendom is reaching for knowledge across barriers of language and religion to both the pagan past and the Muslim present.

Romanesque
The "Roman-like" style of church architecture and sculpture in the eleventh and twelfth centuries.

LO¹ Architecture and Art

The creative force of medieval Christianity inspired spectacular achievements in the visual arts—above all, in architecture.

For several centuries after the Germanic invasions of the West, most new buildings north of the Alps were built of timber; the first stone structure of importance was Charlemagne's chapel at Aachen, completed around 800 (see photo on page 172). But the real beginning of medieval architecture came two centuries later. The end of invasions made it worthwhile to invest resources in large buildings with some assurance that they would not be looted and burned. There were more resources to invest as population, trade, and wealth increased. Greater security meant more travel, including by pilgrims visiting the shrines of saints, while reforming monks and pious rulers and nobles built hundreds of new monasteries. All of a sudden, great abbey and pilgrimage churches began to spring up.

The Romanesque Style

The style in which the new churches of the eleventh and twelfth centuries were built is known as **Romanesque** (Roman-like), because the church builders revived some basic features of ancient Roman architecture. But as usually happens when old traditions are revived, the builders of the Middle Ages used these Roman features in new ways to serve new purposes.

"Returning to the Cross"

Romanesque churches were ultimately based on the pattern of the Roman basilica (public hall), a long building with a nave (central hall) and side aisles, and an apse (a semicircular space) at one end. In late Roman times, Christians had used a

≪ Romanesque Structural Design As trade and travel revived after A.D. 1000, pilgrims on their way to the Spanish shrine of Jesus's disciple James at Compostela stopped off at the monastery of Vézelay in eastern France to honor relics said to be of another disciple, Mary Magdalene. The pilgrims' contributions helped the monks to build a splendid Romanesque church, completed in 1145. The light- and dark-colored round arches divide the ceiling into bays, and additional round arches running diagonally across the bays strengthen the structure. Dagli Orti/The Art Archive

more or less unchanged basilica plan for churches, (see photo on page 113) but in eleventh- and twelfth-century churches, chapels projected outward from the apse, and a transept ("cross-hall") intersected the nave at right angles. This "cruciform" (cross-shaped) plan provided more space for solemn Masses with many clergy; and in each chapel, worshipers could "talk one-on-one" with the saint to whom it was dedicated.

In addition, the cruciform plan had obvious symbolic meaning. When the faithful entered the church, they were "returning to the Cross." The façade (front) of the building usually had three main portals (entryways), symbolizing the Trinity. Whenever possible, the cross plan was located so that the nave ran from west to east, with the altar at the eastern end. Thus, the worshipers faced more or less in the direction of Jerusalem. Because of this symbolism and its suitability for changing religious practices, the cruciform plan remained the standard for large churches in Western traditions of Christianity until the rise of Modernist architecture in the twentieth century.

The actual structure of Romanesque churches also reused features of Roman models, notably high walls made of rows of rounded arches one on top of the other, and cross-vaults (diagonal arches intersecting each other) to lighten the weight of stone ceilings. Even so, ceilings were heavy. In the abbey church of Vézelay in eastern France, each cross-vault is made of 45 tons of stone. To carry this weight, the side walls have to be thick, with narrow slits for windows that widen on the inside so that shafts of light swing across the interior as the sun moves across the sky (see photo on page 228).

 Build an Arch Animation, BBC History (http://www.bbc .co.uk/history/interactive/ animations/arch/index_ embed.shtml) Learn how medieval masons built cathedral arches.

Romanesque buildings often included a new architectural feature, the tower, from which bells called the worshipers to prayer. In Italy, the graceful *campanile* (**kam-puh-NEE-lay**) (bell tower) stood by itself a few feet away from the church; elsewhere in Europe, the tower was an integral part of the main building. It was sometimes built over the crossing of the nave and the transept, but more commonly, a tower or a pair of towers formed part of the front of the building. In some areas, bell towers were capped by a soaring spire. Church towers remain to this day a symbol of Western Christianity.

Bibles in Stone

The new churches needed painting and sculpture, not just for decoration, but above all for the glorification of God and the instruction of the faithful. Overcoming the barrier of illiteracy, each medieval church was virtually a "Bible in stone." Nowhere is the contrast between the early medieval world and the ancient world more sharply displayed than in Romanesque sculpture. The "idealistic" style of the Greeks and the "naturalistic" style of the Romans (pp. 65, 115) are both absent. Few ancient statues were available to the sculptors of the eleventh and twelfth centuries; they took as their models the illustrated figures of medieval manuscripts.

The tradition of furnishing written documents with illustrations dates back to ancient Egypt, where scribes most likely used it for magical purposes—to give additional force to the rituals and spells that their manuscripts contained. The idea of illustrating books for the sake of increasing the effect of the text on the reader—to give visual form to the ideas it contained or simply to break the monotony of the endless procession of words on a page—seems to have originated not long after the invention of books with pages (p. 118). In the early Middle Ages, this kind of illustration flourished. Bibles and prayer books, volumes of poetry, even philosophical works and law books—all were "enlumined" ("lit up") with pictures (see photos on pages 182, 186, 224, 240).

The strange animal figures that often appear in Romanesque sculpture came directly from the northern barbarian tradition. Numerous books were available describing hundreds of imaginary beasts, and sculptors copied them in stone. The upper walls of Romanesque churches were studded with *gargoyles* (from a French word for "throat")—frightening monsters and demons whose open mouths spouted water draining from the roof.

 **Medieval Gargoyles from Across Europe** (http://quazen .com/arts/visual-arts/ gargoyles-glorious- gruesome-grotesques/) View a gallery of medieval gargoyles.

Romanesque sculptors mingled the natural and the supernatural, the earthly and the unearthly. Hence, the real may look unreal and the unreal real. To ensure that the idea or story they were illustrating would be correctly interpreted, sculptors relied heavily on symbols. Although they might show Saint Peter in a number of poses, they always identified him by giving him a set of keys, because of Jesus's gospel saying that he would give Peter the keys of the kingdom of heaven. Matthew was consistently shown as an angel, Mark as a lion (see photo on page 206). Having identified a figure with its traditional symbol, the artist could then treat it in an individual manner.

This freedom presented an opportunity for creativity quite unknown in ancient art. Romanesque sculptors were not bound to exacting artistic rules or naturalistic representations. This also permitted them greater liberties in overall composition—a freedom shared by painters and other artists of the period.

The Gothic Style

In less than two centuries, out of the Romanesque came the later style of the Middle Ages—the **Gothic**. This style showed itself first in architecture around 1150 and reached its prime by 1300, though splendid Gothic structures were built as late as the sixteenth century.

The term *Gothic* (from the Goths, fourth-century barbarian invaders of the Roman Empire) was invented in the sixteenth

Gothic
A style of architecture and art that evolved in the twelfth century, characterized by spaciousness, height, glowing illumination, and naturalistic images.

cathedral
The head church of a bishopric—from the Greek word for "seat" (of a bishop).

flying buttress
A supporting structure on the outside of a Gothic cathedral that arches over the roof of a side aisle.

century, when Greek and Roman models of culture were the most admired. It was originally applied to the culture of the Middle Ages in general and meant much the same as "barbaric." The name continues to be used, without the contemptuous overtones, to describe the style of architecture and art that is now recognized as the grandest expression of medieval civilization.

In the twelfth century, the era of the Crusades, the ruling papacy, and eager veneration of the Virgin Mary and the saints, the self-confidence and religious zeal of Western Christendom were on the rise. This mood found its outlet in Gothic churches, first of all, in new or rebuilt **cathedrals** (head churches of bishoprics) in the bur-

Chartres Cathedral Nave Window (http://www.gigapan.org/gigapans/22895/) View a stained glass window from Chartres Cathedral and zoom in for a closer look.

geoning towns of northern France—structures as ambitious and daring as the finest buildings of Greece and Rome.

The cathedrals were also the most eloquent expression yet devised of Christian belief. Their architects sought to meet the desire of twelfth-century clergy for buildings that would be a true image of the universe as they believed it to be: a vast structure, designed by its creator to be perfectly harmonious in every detail and glowing with light that flowed from God himself. Only buildings of this kind, the clergy thought, would truly lead the worshipers to the knowledge and love of God.

Cathedrals Learn more about medieval cathedrals.

Webs of Stone

Judged by this standard, Romanesque churches seemed inadequate. Their thick walls often gave a feeling of confinement, their massive arches seemed ill-proportioned, and their small windows did not provide a rich illumination. But any attempt to alter this pattern raised a difficult engineering problem. How could architects increase the spaciousness and height

≪ **Web of Stone** In Gothic cathedrals, structural stresses are transmitted mostly downward from intersecting stone ribs, shaped as pointed arches, to vertical pillars resting on bedrock. The spaces between the ribs and pillars are filled with brick or glass surfaces that carry no structural loads. At the thirteenth-century cathedral of Amiens in northern France, the system makes possible a nave that is 50 feet wide and 140 feet high. Angelo Hornak/Corbis

of a building, reduce the thickness of the supporting walls and arches, and enlarge the windows, given that walls had to be thick and windows had to be small to support a massive stone ceiling?

Part of the solution was to lighten the weight of the ceiling, and twelfth-century Romanesque builders had already found a way to do this. They marked off each rectangular bay (building section topped by a vaulted ceiling) with four vertical stone pillars. From the top of each pillar, they connected ribs of arching stone to the tops of the other three; then they filled in the ceiling areas between these ribs with a thin layer of brick. The weight of the roof was carried to the ground through the ribs and pillars, and little or no force was exerted on the areas between the pillars (see photo on page 226).

Gothic architects developed the full potential of the new method with the aid of two further innovations. One of these was the graceful pointed arch. This hallmark of the Gothic style had originally been devised by Muslim mosque builders and had been learned from them by Christian church builders (see photo on page 163). It turned out to be perfectly suited to

> "*Gothic architects thought of a large church not as a stone mass enclosing static space but as a web of stone with space and light flowing freely through it.*"

cathedrals, since it accentuated the vertical lines of a structure and lifted its vaults to greater heights than could be achieved with the round arch. With the pointed arch, the direction of thrust was more downward than outward, decreasing the danger that the supporting pillars would collapse.

Even so, a further innovation was needed to keep the soaring vaults from falling down—massive external stone buttresses (props). These buttresses could not be placed directly against the pillars of the nave because the side aisles, with their separate, lower roofs, stood in the way, so they stood outside the side aisles. They rose almost to the level of the nave ceiling and were connected to the pillars of the nave by stone ribs (see photo). Since the ribs seem to "fly" over the side aisles, these structures are called **flying buttresses**.

This revolutionary plan of construction enabled Gothic

Amiens Animated Glossary, from Columbia University (http://www.learn.columbia.edu/amiens_flash/) Explore the plan of a Gothic cathedral in this interactive site.

Flying Buttresses At the east end of the thirteenth-century cathedral of Le Mans in northern France, flying buttresses help prop up the upper part of structure while straddling lower parts that project outward—essentially, they are outward extensions of the internal web of stone. The buttresses also draw the eye upward, making the building look higher but also less massive than it actually is. R.Lamb/Robertstock.com

architects to lift roofs to soaring heights and to make windows into broad, softly glowing sheets of stained glass. They thought of a large church not as a stone mass enclosing static space but as a web of stone with space and light flowing freely through it.

From outside, such a building was also overwhelmingly impressive. It stood high above the houses huddled in the town, symbolizing the commanding position of the Church in the life of the community. As travelers approached the town, the first sight they saw on the horizon was the spire (or spires) reaching hundreds of feet into the sky. Then the whole of the cathedral would gradually come into view, and its flying buttresses, with their tangle of tall stone pillars and slanting ribs, would make the building look even loftier than it actually was. If the travelers were pilgrims, they would approach the west façade and reverently prepare to enter.

Gothic Sculpture The thirteenth-century Cathedral of Our Lady of Reims was the third to be built there since the Frankish chieftain Clovis had been baptized in the first one 800 years before (see photo on page 150). The west façade shows scenes from the Virgin's life in the new and lifelike Gothic style of sculpture. Left, the Annunciation: the Archangel Gabriel tells the Virgin Mary of the coming birth of Christ. Right, the Visitation: the Virgin (inner statue) is greeted by Saint Elizabeth, John the Baptist's mother.

Lifelike Images

Set into the façade were stone sculptures representing figures and scenes from the Bible, which the artists depicted in a much more lifelike manner than their Romanesque forerunners. Worshipers entering the northern French cathedral of Reims **(reemz)** , where the kings of France were crowned, would pass through a doorway above which a smiling Archangel Gabriel brought a solemn Virgin Mary the joyful yet awe-inspiring news that she would become the Mother of God, and the Virgin respectfully greeted the recognizably elderly Saint Elizabeth, the mother of John the Baptist (see photo). In keeping with the contemporary trend of emphasizing the human side of the beings whom Christians revered, Gothic sculptors were turning back to the aim of Hellenistic and Roman sculpture—to depict human emotion and interaction in stone.

Inside the cathedral, worshipers would be absorbed by the vastness, rhythm, and splendor of the interior, as well as by the many glowing colors in the stained-glass windows. These were huge "jigsaw puzzles" of pieces of glass that were colored while molten, cut to fit the design, and fastened together with strips of lead; important features like faces were then painted onto the surface of the glass. In the most renowned of French cathedrals at Chartres, worshipers would see "Our Lady of the Lovely Window," a seven-foot-high image of the Virgin Mary crowned and enthroned with the infant Jesus (see photo). The image proclaimed to them the contemporary cult of the Virgin as Queen of Heaven in a way that glowed with the light of divine

>> **"Our Lady of the Lovely Window."** Colored glass is an art form that dates back to ancient Egypt, and in the early Middle Ages both church builders and mosque builders began using it in windows. Muslim glassmakers devised complex abstract patterns, while their Christian counterparts created vivid representations of revered beings. This stained glass window in Chartres Cathedral depicts the Virgin Mary crowned and enthroned with the infant Jesus.

Giraudon/Art Resource, NY

UNIVERSITIES GRADUALLY TOOK OVER AS THE MAIN CENTERS OF EDUCATION AND STUDY:

Professional schools developed near Muslim and Byzantine centers of learning

- Medical instruction started at Salerno, in the south of Italy close to Muslim-ruled Sicily (and Muslim learning), in the ninth century.

- Late in the eleventh century, training in Roman law began in the northern Italian town of Bologna, not far from Ravenna, which had a long Byzantine tradition.

- The universities founded at these centers were professional schools that satisfied the demand for physicians and lawyers to serve Italian rulers and merchants, as well as the rising papal monarchy.

A new model university was established in Paris

- The university movement spread northward from Italy to Montpellier in southern France and to Paris.

- Europe's foremost institution of learning was established in Paris during the thirteenth century.

- Paris was the first to offer the four major curricula that were, for centuries, the main fields of university study: theology, law, medicine, and liberal arts.

New universities sprang up across Europe

- From Paris, the movement spread to England, Germany, and the rest of western Europe.

- By 1300, eighteen universities had been founded.

- By 1500, the total number of universities, many of which are still in existence, exceeded eighty.

revelation. And in its immensity, its harmonious beauty, and its glowing illumination, the cathedral as a whole conveyed to the worshipers something of the image of the universe and its creator that inspired the builders.

LO² Thought and Education

Medieval education, like the visual arts, was dominated by the Church. From the eighth to the twelfth century, members of the clergy made up the only literate and educated class of society, and even after that, they staffed virtually all the schools, libraries, and centers

> "*I have learned . . . that you do not study in your room or act in the schools as a good student should, but play and wander about, disobedient to your master and indulging in sport and in certain other dishonorable practices which I do not now care to explain by letter.*"
>
> —Father to son, thirteenth century

of higher learning. But the feudalistic and local character of the times counterbalanced what was, in theory, the monolithic force of the Church. The methods of long-distance communication were primitive, and the Church itself was made up of many authorities, orders, and factions. Although basically only a Catholic point of view could be professed in western Europe, a wide range of intellectual inquiry and debate was still possible.

During the troubled centuries immediately after the fall of Rome, the monasteries had conserved precious manuscripts and provided at least the basics of education to the clergy, the only class of society

"THEY MAY GO IN SAFETY": IMPERIAL PROTECTION FOR SCHOLARS

Already in the twelfth century, increasing numbers of scholars and students in Western Christendom needed to travel long distances to study. Travel was often dangerous, and safety for academics did not always improve once they reached their destinations. As foreigners without local status, scholars and students could find themselves at the mercy of local officials, merchants, and landlords. At a meeting of nobles and high clergy of the Holy Roman Empire in the Italian city of Roncaglia in 1158, Emperor Frederick I Barbarossa issued an order of protection for scholars. The order was a sign of the high value that leaders of the church and the state put on education and scholarship, which would soon lead to the development of formal institutions of higher learning—universities.

After a careful consideration of this subject by the bishops, abbots, dukes, counts, judges, and other nobles of our sacred palace, we, out of our piety, have granted this privilege to all scholars who travel for the sake of study, and especially to the professors of divine and sacred laws, namely: that they may go in safety to the places in which the studies are carried on, both they themselves and their messengers, and may dwell there in security. For we think it fitting that, so long as they conduct themselves with propriety, those should enjoy our approval and protection who, by their learning, enlighten the world and mold the life of our subjects to obey God and us, his minister. By reason of our special regard we desire to defend them from all injuries.

For who does not pity those who exile themselves through love for learning, who wear themselves out in poverty in place of riches, who expose their lives to all perils and often suffer bodily injury from the vilest men,—yet all these vexatious things must be endured by the scholar. Therefore, we declare, by this general and ever-to-be-valid law, that in the future no one shall be so rash as to venture to inflict any injury on scholars, or to occasion any loss to them on account of a debt owed by an inhabitant of their province,—a thing which we have learned is sometimes done, by an evil custom. And let it

be known to the violators of this decree, and also to those who shall at the time be the rulers of the places where the offense is committed, that a fourfold restitution of property shall be exacted from all those who are guilty and that, the mark of infamy being affixed to them by the law itself, they shall lose their office forever.

Moreover, if any one shall presume to bring a suit against them on account of any business, the choice in this matter shall be given to the scholars, who may summon the accusers to appear before their professors, or before the bishop of the city, to whom we have given jurisdiction in this matter. But if, in sooth, the accuser shall attempt to drag the scholar before another judge, even though his cause is a very just one, he shall lose his suit for such an attempt.

EXPLORING THE SOURCE

1. What specific abuses does Frederick seek to protect scholars against?

2. Why does Frederick think that scholars and students are worthy of respect and valuable to society?

Source: James Harvey Robinson, ed., *Readings in European History* (Boston: Ginn, 1904), 1:452

---

that was thought to have need for it. Around 800, Charlemagne gave strong support to the revival of interest in intellectual matters (pp. 172–173), and by 1200, it was again normal for nobles and businesspeople to be mostly literate. The monasteries still provided elementary education, and cathedral schools were beginning to respond to a growing desire for education in the towns. But the most significant development was the rise of the universities.

Medieval Universities

Unlike the old monastic schools, nearly all of the universities were located in important towns and cities, reflecting the connection between the rise of universities and that of trade and towns. Each university operated under the protection of a charter granted by a ranking official of the Church or the state (usually the pope or a king). Thus, the universities were freed, for the most part, from the jurisdiction of local courts and local clergy. One justification for this exempted status was that teachers and students came from all over Europe, making the universities truly international. The Latin word *universitas* simply meant any kind of organized group including guilds, and universities were organized much like guilds (pp. 200–201), with "masters" (the faculty) practicing in their fields of knowledge and teaching "apprentices" (the students).

The basic curriculum that was followed in all universities was taken over from the monastic schools, which, in turn, followed late Roman educational practices. The course of studies consisted of the seven *liberal arts* ("fields of knowledge befitting a free man"): grammar, rhetoric, and logic (the *trivium*); and arithmetic, geometry, astronomy, and music (the *quadrivium*—the names came from the Latin for "three roads" and "four roads" to knowledge).

Grammar, of course, meant Latin grammar. This was the language used by members of the clergy, lawyers, physicians, and scholars all through the Middle Ages. But the trivium went beyond the mechanics of language; it included the study of works of philosophy, literature, and history. The quadrivium was based

A Fourteenth-Century Classroom Henry of Germany, an internationally respected expert on Aristotle, explains a work by the Greek thinker to a class at the University of Bologna about 1350. Students in the front rows follow his lecture attentively; students farther back have other things on their minds.

on the reading of ancient scientific and mathematical texts and was almost entirely theoretical.

Whatever subject they were studying, the students had few books and no laboratories. They scribbled their lecture notes on wax tablets and then transferred them to sheets of parchment. More stress was placed on memorizing and analyzing a small number of highly respected books than on extensive reading (see photo).

The faculty lectured in their homes or in hired halls, and students lived independently, according to their means and tastes, though wealthy clergy and laypeople donated lecture halls, libraries, and dormitories. The first notable "college" of this kind was established in Paris about 1250 by Louis IX's chaplain, Robert de Sorbon, and the "Sorbonne" is still part of the University of Paris today. Still, college students—all men, of course, since most women were thought to have no need for formal education and professional qualifications—had a reputation for wildness throughout the Middle Ages.

College Students Write Home: Parents Respond Read the correspondence between medieval students and their parents.

The students in medieval universities earned their degrees on the basis of comprehensive oral examinations. After attending lectures and reading for several years in the subjects of the trivium, a student would ask to be examined by the members of the faculty. If he performed satisfactorily, he was granted the preliminary degree of Bachelor of Arts, a prerequisite for going on to the quadrivium. After several additional years of study, the student would present himself for examination once again. If he passed, he was awarded the degree of Master of Arts, which certified that he was qualified to teach the liberal arts curriculum.

The Latin word *doctor* (teacher) was customarily used for higher degrees in theology, law, and medicine. Each of these degrees normally required four or more years of study beyond the master's and was also awarded on the basis of the candidate's performance in an oral examination. The candidate usually presented a *thesis* or *theses* (one or more statements about a subject), which he defended before a faculty board.

Scholastic Thought

University faculty, as well as earlier teachers in monastery and cathedral schools, not only taught but also contributed to their areas of study, especially in what they considered the most important areas—theology and its allied field of philosophy. Because these thinkers worked in universities and schools, they were known at the time as **schoolmen**, and medieval thought in general is today called **scholastic**.

Like other features of the renewed culture of Western Christendom, scholastic thought was nourished by impulses from Christianity's rival monotheisms, Islam and Judaism. In the twelfth and thirteenth centuries, Arabic versions of many works of Aristotle, as well as books of Hellenistic science, mathematics, and medicine, were translated into Latin. So also were original writings and commentaries (books explaining works of earlier thinkers and developing their ideas) by leading Muslim and Jewish scholars (see photo on page 224).

Chief among the Muslim commentators on Aristotle was the twelfth-century philosopher Averroës ((uh-VER-oh-eez)—ibn-Rushd), a Spanish-born Arab. But many Christians (and many Muslims) were disturbed by his doctrine, drawn from Aristotle, that the universe had always existed and was therefore not created. He also denied the immortality of the human soul. More acceptable were the writings of Averroës's Jewish contemporary, also born in Muslim Spain, Maimonides (mahy-MON-i-deez) (Moses ben Maimon). His *Guide for the Perplexed* addresses the "big" religious and philosophical questions that confront believing Jews, Muslims, and Christians alike: What is the purpose of God's universe? Will it last forever? How is God's will related to natural causes? Maimonides' answers to such questions consist of a closely reasoned mixture of Aristotle, the Hebrew Bible, and traditional Jewish authorities.

> "*Should human faith be based upon reason, or no?*
> *Is God the author of evil, or no?*
> *Did all the apostles have wives except John, or no?*"
>
> —Peter Abelard, ca. 1135

Reason and Faith

Like Maimonides, the scholastics wanted above all to use the recovered Greek thought to deepen their understanding of their religious beliefs. Thus, Anselm, a learned Italian monk who became archbishop of Canterbury in England, put together arguments to prove logically the existence of God. In another book, written about 1100, he explained why God had chosen to take on human form as Jesus. Understanding and believing, Anselm thought, belonged together, and one could not properly have one without the other—though believing came first: "I believe," he said, "so that I may understand."

In the twelfth century, the French scholar Peter Abelard argued that the authorities of the Church should not be read without questioning, for they often contradicted one another. He demonstrated this in an influential writing that put many such conflicting answers to theological questions alongside one another; he called this work *Sic et Non* (Latin for "Yes and No"). Abelard insisted, therefore, that all

Sic et Non: Is It or Isn't It? Read a selection of Abelard's questions.

writings be subjected to the light of logic. "By doubting," he observed, "we come to examine, and by examining we reach the truth." Thus Abelard had returned to the position of Socrates, who had sought knowledge through persistent questioning (p. 72).

Words and Things

Though theological matters remained the focus of scholastic concern, medieval philosophers debated every subject under the sun—some grand and divine, some trivial and worldly. One of the most absorbing issues was that of "universals." Do "Man," "Horse," "Beauty," and "Justice" exist independently of particular things? Or are these words merely convenient symbols for referring to various classes of objects and characteristics? The argument paralleled the ancient one between Plato and the Sophists (pp. 72–73). Plato believed that Ideas (Forms) have a perfect and independent existence, while the Sophists thought that only particular things exist. In the Middle Ages, those who held that universals are real were called *realists*; those who declared that they are just names (*nomina*) were called *nominalists*.

The extreme realists attached little importance to individual things, and sought, through sheer logic or divine revelation, to know the universals. The extreme nominalists, by contrast, saw only specific objects and refused to admit the existence of unifying relationships among particular things. The realists tended to ignore the observed world; the nominalists could scarcely make sense of it.

Most scholars took a middle position on this question. Among the moderates, Abelard expressed a view that is still widely held today. It is called *conceptualism*. Abelard held that only particular things have an existence in and of themselves. The universals, however, are more than mere names. They exist as *concepts in individual minds*—keys to an understanding of the interrelatedness of things. Thus, the concept "Horse" exists in our minds and adds something to our understanding of all four-footed animals of a certain general type. Once we have identified such a creature, we can assign to it the specific features drawn from our concept. By means of many such concepts, based on individual observations, we can make the world (to a degree) comprehensible, manageable, and predictable.

Harmony of Faith and Reason: Aquinas

Thomas Aquinas (uh-KWAHY-nuhs), the greatest of the scholastic philosophers, was a moderate realist. Born near Monte Cassino (Italy) of an aristocratic family, he joined the order of Dominican friars in 1244. A brilliant pupil, he studied at Cologne and Paris and spent his adult life teaching at Paris and Naples. He wrote an enormous number of scholarly works, in which he sought to harmonize various approaches to truth and to bring all knowledge together. In his most comprehensive work, the *Summa Theologica* ("Theological Summary"), he clarified Church teachings about the nature of God and humanity.

 Summa Theologica: **On Free Will** Read a selection from *Summa Theologica*.

Following the lead of Anselm, Abelard, and other scholastics, Aquinas set a high value on human reason. By this time, the full impact of Aristotle (p. 76) had struck the schools and universities of Europe, and Christian teachings were being challenged, above all by Averroës. Instead of answering these arguments by denying the power of reason, Aquinas adopted Aristotelian logic and turned it to the defense of his faith. He sought to demonstrate that divine law—as revealed in the Bible—is never in conflict with logic, properly exercised. Both faith and reason, he argued, were created by God, and it is illogical to hold that God could contradict himself.

Aquinas's way of arguing involved dividing each major subject into a series of questions. For each, he explained the arguments for and against, in accordance with the usual scholastic method of presentation. The arguments are generally **deductive** in form—that is, they rely on reasoning from basic propositions assumed in advance to be true, because they are found either in the Bible or in the works of thinkers (both pagan and Christian) who are considered authoritative. He presented his own conclusion for each of the questions he posed—a conclusion that generally agreed with accepted Christian teachings.

The *Summa Theologica* is a masterful combination of quotations from Scripture, formal logic, and common sense. Aquinas's grand synthesis ("harmonization" of knowledge) stands as an impressive monument to the discipline and resourcefulness of the human mind.

Medieval Science

Besides the thought of Aristotle, the schoolmen also relearned from Muslim and Jewish experts the astronomy of Ptolemy and the medicine of Hippocrates and Galen (pp. 72, 110). Some became experts themselves and expanded on the ancient knowledge.

The German scholar Albert the Great (a teacher of Thomas Aquinas) wrote on the broad range of philosophical and theological questions that challenged thirteenth-century thinkers. But he also found time to observe systematically many of the animal species of western Europe, including bees, spiders, hawks, beavers, whales, and eels. Albert rejected medieval accounts of mythical animals like "griffins" and "harpies," simply because he had never observed any.

Robert Grosseteste, an outstanding English scholar of the same period, wrote commentaries on the Bible, Aristotle, and a wide variety of philosophical topics. But he wrote, too, about the sun, weather, tides, colors, comets, and other aspects of nature. Grosseteste was a pioneer teacher at the new Oxford University, where he helped establish the study of science and mathematics. A generation afterward, his pupil, Roger Bacon, continued to emphasize experimental methods. Bacon, who died in 1294, is remembered also for his predictions of such technological innovations as flying machines and powered ships.

The Legacy of Scholasticism

By the end of the thirteenth century, the intellectual life of Western Christendom had achieved a new vigor. The communities of university scholars had succeeded in their efforts to preserve and advance learning. The scholastic philosophers had refined the methods of logical thought and had laboriously collected, compiled, and classified sources of information. Above all, they had established the essentials of scholarship: comprehensive research and precise expression.

Modern thought owes much to these medieval seekers after truth. They built upon ancient Greek thought, reconciled it with Christian teachings, and absorbed new ideas from the Muslim and Jewish worlds. The twelfth-century thinker Bernard of Chartres once compared himself and his fellow scholars with the philosophers and scientists of ancient times. "We are dwarfs," he said, "standing on the shoulders of giants." There is modesty in this statement but also pride—pride in the fact that he and his colleagues could see a bit farther than their intellectual ancestors.

> **"We are dwarfs standing on the shoulders of giants. "**
>
> —Bernard of Chartres

LO³ Language and Literature

The international language of religion and thought, education and scholarship, and government and commerce in western Europe during the Middle Ages was Latin. Passed down from ancient Rome, it had been carried beyond the old Roman frontiers by the Church, and literary works were still written by and for people who knew Latin. But by now, no one knew Latin as their mother tongue, and in everyday life, people spoke local languages (**vernaculars**). These had developed in the early Middle Ages out of Latin itself and out of the languages of barbarian peoples in northern Europe. By the thirteenth century, the vernaculars were coming to be used in government and commerce, and they were already the main languages of literature.

Latin Writings

Medieval Latin did not usually follow the principles of ancient Roman "eloquence" (good style in speech and writing). Written and spoken Latin developed into a highly technical language of philosophy, administration, and law in which precision was more important than eloquence, and preachers and writers mostly used a modified Latin that itself became the medium for notable literary achievements.

The finest creations in medieval Latin were the prayers and hymns of the Christian worship services. Some of these were incorporated into the Mass and were notable for their poetic beauty, such as the *Stabat Mater*, the great hymn on the sorrows of the Virgin Mary: "At the Cross her station keeping, / Stood the mournful Mother weeping, / While her Son was hanging there."

Meanwhile, some ancient Roman authors were widely read. Christian writers who had lived at the time of the Roman Empire, such as Augustine and Jerome (pp. 143–144), were deeply studied for the religious guidance they offered. Some pagan authors, such as Cicero and Virgil (p. 108), were admired because it was felt that in spite of not possessing the faith, they taught valuable moral lessons. Furthermore, ancient eloquence was still admired. Hroswitha of Gandersheim (**hros-VIT-tuh, GAN-ders-hime**), a learned nun in tenth-century northern Germany, even confessed to preferring "the polished elegance of the style of pagan writers" to the Scriptures.

Furthermore, within the medieval "Age of Faith" there also flowed a powerful current of delight in earthly pleasures. According to Hroswitha, the most widely read of ancient writers was no Christian thinker or high-minded pagan but the playwright Terence (p. 107), in spite of the fact that his plays celebrated "the licentious acts of shameless women." In the tenth century, the vast majority of people who knew enough Latin to read Terence would have been monks and nuns—and it was monks and nuns who painstakingly copied his works and those of other "licentious" ancient authors like Ovid (p. 108), ensuring their survival alongside the works of Cicero and Virgil.

In this tradition, a great deal of medieval poetry in Latin celebrated eating, drinking, and lovemaking—often in a way that made fun of high-minded religious ideals. Many of these works were dedicated, tongue in cheek, to an invented holy patron, Saint Golias, and therefore are known as Goliardic poetry. The Goliardic poets were shy about revealing their names, but it is clear that they were men of learning, schooled in Latin and familiar with ancient literature. One of them looked forward to a boozily beautiful death: "Angels when they come shall cry, / At my frailties winking: 'Spare this drunkard, God, he's high, / Absolutely stinking!'"[1]

 Gaudeamus Igitur: Live While We Are Young Read a poem in celebration of youth and pleasure.

---

[1] From George F. Whicher, *The Goliard Poets.* Copyright 1949 by George F. Whicher. Reprinted by permission of New Directions Publishing Corporation.

> *"Let us live then and be glad*
> *While young life's before us!*
> *After youthful pastime had,*
> *After old age hard and sad,*
> *Earth will slumber o'er us. "*
>
> —from *Gaudeamus Igitur,*
> Anonymous, ca. 1175

Vernacular Writings

Literature in the vernacular tongues, however, spoke more directly even to those who knew Latin. In areas that had long been occupied by Rome, spoken Latin had evolved over many centuries into different local languages that already resembled such present-day Latin languages as Spanish, French, and Italian (pp. 119–120). In western Europe, north of the Roman imperial frontiers, former Germanic barbarian peoples (p. 135) spoke languages that were evolving toward languages of today like German, Dutch, and Swedish. Eastern Europe was occupied mostly by Slav peoples (pp. 156–157), whose speech was developing into present-day languages such as Russian, Polish, and Serbian.

European languages borrowed words from each other, as well as from Latin and Greek, and English borrowed more than any other language. English was originally the Germanic dialect of the Anglo-Saxon invaders of the island of Britain (p. 153). The later Danish and Norman conquests brought influences from Germanic languages spoken by the Vikings, as well as from French, which was spoken by the Normans. By the middle of the fourteenth century, Anglo-Saxon (Old English) had changed into what is now called Middle English. Out of this evolved modern English, a mixture of Germanic and Latin elements.

Epic and Romance

As with Homer's *Iliad* and *Odyssey* eighteen hundred years before, among the earliest medieval European vernacular written works were epic poems that grew out of traditional songs memorized and continually altered by generations of illiterate minstrels (p. 68). One of the most notable was the *Song of Roland,* written down around 1100 by an unknown author in northern France and based on *chansons de geste* (shahn-sawn duh ZHEST) ("songs of great deeds") about the hero-king Charlemagne and his companions. Like the epics of Homer, this poem about heroes of the past in fact expresses the values of the time at which it was written—in this case, the ideals of medieval Christian knights.

Its chief hero is Count Roland, nephew of Charlemagne. Roland personifies the warrior ideals of bravery, loyalty, and military prowess—and Christian faith in God and salvation. The field of battle runs red with the blood of the courageous, and Roland's fellow vassals observe strictly the code of honor and revenge. Many other national epics were written down in the eleventh and twelfth countries, such as the *Song of the Nibelungs* (NEE-buh-looongz) in Germany, the *Poem of the Cid* in Spain, and the *Lay of Igor's Host* ("The Ballad of Igor's Army") in Russia.

But the **troubadours** (nobles who created poems and accompanying music) did not confine themselves to epic tales. They also sang of "courtly" manners and romantic love (from *romance,* which originally meant a tale, as opposed to a learned work in Latin). For the first time since the days of the pagan authors, a poetry of passion appeared in Europe. Often, the passion was on an "elevated" plane. The romantic knight placed his ideal woman on a pedestal and adored her from afar—with thoughts of physical fulfillment repressed or postponed. Often, too, the knight was seduced by a female figure of power—King Arthur's unfaithful Queen Guenevere, or a well-wishing fairy lady in an enchanted castle—who found him irresistible for his beauty and "courtesy" (courtly manners). Either way, this "cult of love" also brought forth elaborate manuals of behavior for lovers. Courtly love, however, was a pastime for the nobility only; commoners were considered unsuited to the delicate art of romance. Even so, the code of conduct that held love as a noble ideal made a distinguishing mark upon the whole of Western culture.

 The Lay of Igor's Host: Warfare on the Russian Steppes Read a selection from the Russian national epic.

Clearly, the hearty masculine culture of the early Middle Ages was giving way to a more tranquil, confident, and leisurely society. The noble's castle was becoming less of a barracks for fighting men and more of a theater for refined pleasures. Aristocratic ladies were accorded more and more attention and were able to exercise greater control over the men. Most notable among such ladies was Eleanor, duchess of Aquitaine in southwestern France. Eleanor married King Louis VII of France, went on crusade with him, but agreed with him to have the pope annul the marriage, which had produced no sons. She then married King Henry II of England, had plenty of sons, but was imprisoned by him for supporting a rebellion against him by one of them. All the same, she ruled England for several years after Henry died while another son, King Richard the Lion-Hearted, went on crusade. Besides her deeds in politics, government, and war, Eleanor also reigned as the queen of courtly love and its laws of conduct.

 The Rules of Love? Read some observations about courtly love.

The feudal society of the Middle Ages is splendidly portrayed in the so-called Arthurian romances, a cycle of verse tales composed in the twelfth and thirteenth centuries by French and Norman writers. The central figure of the romances is King Arthur, a Celtic chieftain of sixth-century Britain who fought against the Anglo-Saxon invaders, and the tales are based partly on ancient Celtic lore. But the legends of Arthur's Round Table are told in the manner of the Middle Ages; they are tales of forbidden love, knightly combats, and colorful pageantry.

Among the most popular of the romance writers were Chrétien de Troyes (**kreh-t-YEN duh trwah**) and Marie de France. Both of them lived in the late twelfth century, and both enjoyed the patronage of Eleanor of Aquitaine. Chrétien's romances of Lancelot, Percival, the Holy Grail, and other Arthurian characters and themes set a pattern for the lore of King Arthur and his knights and ladies that has lasted down to the present day. Marie composed "lays," shorter tales than Chrétien's romances, that also dealt with combat, seduction, and love among knights and ladies at Arthur's court. According to an English monk who admired her work, her poems were "dear to many a count, baron, and knight . . . and her lays please ladies too, who listen to them with joy and good will."

Realism and Satire

Toward the close of the Middle Ages, the narratives of chivalric love became less fanciful and more realistic than the Arthurian tales. Most successful was the work of Christine de Pisan, the first woman to support herself entirely from her earnings as an author. Born in Italy, she spent most of her years at or near the French court in Paris. Her best-known story, *The Book of the Duke of True Lovers* (ca. 1400), reads much like the earlier aristocratic romances. But it is based on actual events rather than legend, and its lovers act in response to common sense rather than to the dictates of passion and the cult of love.

As with works in Latin, there was also a far less high-minded form of literature, which also originated in France—the *fabliaux* (FAB-lee-ohz) (**fables**). Frank, sensual, and witty, they ridiculed both courtly and priestly life. One of the most popular fables was *Aucassin and Nicolette*, by an unknown author. Its hero, Aucassin, spurns knighthood in order to pursue his passion for a beautiful young Muslim captive. Indifferent to his soul's salvation, he subordinates everything to his desire for union with Nicolette. He even prefers hell to heaven, on the ground that the company there will be more attractive and entertaining.

Drama

Medieval drama, like that of ancient Greece (p. 70), grew out of religion—in this case, reenactments of scenes such as Christ's birth and death that were part of Christmas and Easter worship. In the twelfth and thirteenth centuries, as the clergy sought to stress the humanness of holy people and holy events (pp. 205–206), the reenactments developed into independent performances in vernacular languages. **Passion plays** showed Christ's suffering and death, with the Jews usually cast as collective villains; **miracle plays** had plots involving happy endings brought about by the Virgin Mary; in **morality plays**, the characters were torn between noble virtues and tempting vices; and **mystery plays** were edifying dramas staged by guilds ("mystery" being a medieval word for a guild or craft). These plays often used slapstick and satire to help make their point, and they were often staged outside churches by troops of semiprofessional actors.

Chaucer and Dante

Two works of the late Middle Ages rise above ordinary classification. One is the *Canterbury Tales* of Geoffrey Chaucer, written in the fourteenth century. This collection of stories is in the general spirit of the fabliaux but includes all classes of society and a wide range of topics.

Born of a merchant family, Chaucer spent most of his life in the service of the English aristocracy. He read broadly, in Latin, French, and Italian as well as in English, and traveled extensively on the continent of Europe. His outlook was cosmopolitan and urbane, and he displayed a rare combination of scholarship, insight, and humor. In the *Tales*, a group of people exchange stories as they ride on a pilgrimage to the shrine of a revered saint, Thomas Becket, at Canterbury. The stories, of "good morality and general pleasure," appealed to all literate persons in fourteenth-century England. In them—and in the tellers of the tales, all of them typical people of the time (see photo on page 240)—they could see themselves and their society as in a mirror.

The other monumental work of the period is the *Divine Comedy* of Dante. A scholar and poet from the Italian city-state of Florence, Dante was deeply involved in the political and intellectual trends of his time, and his *Comedy* is a grand synthesis of medieval theology, science, philosophy, and romance.

Escorted by the Roman poet Virgil, Dante travels in his poem through the regions beyond the grave. He descends

> **passion plays**
> Dramatizations of Christ's suffering and death.
>
> **miracle plays**
> Dramas with plots involving miraculous happy endings brought about by the Virgin Mary.
>
> **morality plays**
> Dramas in which the characters were torn between noble virtues and tempting vices.
>
> **mystery plays**
> Dramas designed to edify and staged by guilds.

> **"** *They died for the Russian land. The grass withered from sorrow, and the saddened trees drooped earthward.* **"**
> —from *The Lay of Igor's Host*, Anonymous, tenth century

>> **"Upon an Ambler Easily She Sat"** Geoffrey Chaucer's *Canterbury Tales* was already a best seller as a handwritten book—eighty-four copies, an unusually large number, still exist today. This illustration from a luxury manuscript of about 1400 shows one of the pilgrim storytellers, the Wife of Bath. Forceful, independent, and five times married and widowed, she is depicted as Chaucer describes her, with wide-brimmed hat, hair in a net, and riding astride, not side-saddle as was expected of medieval ladies.

> *"XV. Every lover regularly turns pale in the presence of his beloved. XVI. When a lover suddenly catches sight of his beloved his heart palpitates. XVII. A new love puts to flight an old one. "*
>
> —from Andreas Capellanus, *The Art of Courtly Love*, ca. 1175

into the terrible Inferno (hell), where the damned suffer eternal punishments that fit their crimes. Then he moves on to Purgatory, where pardoned sinners suffer for a limited time until they are cleansed of guilt. At last, he is permitted to enter Paradise (heaven), where the blessed enjoy, in fitting ways, the gifts of God. For this final portion of the journey, Dante must leave the pagan Virgil behind. Now he is guided by the pure Beatrice, his ideal of Christian womanhood, who represents the blending of romantic and spiritual love that leads Dante at last to a climactic vision of God.

Dante called his work a "comedy" because he believed the story suggests a happy ending for all who choose to follow Christ. (Later admirers added the compliment "divine.") But apart from his spiritual quest, Dante had strong opinions on subjects ranging from poetry and astronomy to city-state politics and the conflict of the

 The Canterbury Tales: The Knight Read the description of the Knight from the *Canterbury Tales*.

popes and the Holy Roman emperors (he sided with the emperors). At every turn of his narrative, Dante makes sharp comments on the real and mythical characters from ancient Israel, Greece, and Rome to his own time whom he meets in the other world, and who serve as dramatic symbols for his ideas. Readers may agree or disagree with Dante's judgments, but they will long remember the vivid images created by his words. The *Comedy* is an intensely personal story, yet it is also the finest expression of the ideals and conflicts, the hopes and resentments, the strivings and failures of the Western Christendom of the Middle Ages.

 Listen to a synopsis of Chapter 13.

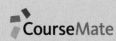

PART III

THE REMAKING OF EUROPE, 1300–1700

Unlike the Roman world, the Christian Europe of the Middle Ages did not "fall." There were no waves of invading barbarians, no collapse of empires, no decline of trade and cities. Instead, many old-established and gradually developing traditions of medieval civilization reached "critical mass"—and gradual development turned into spectacular change.

Two of the most famous events connected with this change, Christopher Columbus's voyage of 1492 and the beginning of the Protestant Reformation in 1517, took place around the year 1500. As a result, that year has become the benchmark date of the "end" of the Middle Ages and the "beginning" of the modern period (p. 2). In fact, however, medieval civilization began to change as early as 1300, and it took 350 years for a recognizably more modern pattern of civilization to appear. A whole series of further changes then followed, which have gone on right down to the present. Unlike the ancient and medieval periods, the modern period has so far been one of continual shifts in civilization, each just as massive as the ones before it.

In the three and a half centuries of the first series of modern shifts in civilization, Europe's social and political structures, as well as its place in the world, were all transformed. Out of the booming agriculture and bustling cities of the Middle Ages came the freeing of the serfs in western Europe and the rise of international banking and capitalism. The competition of powerful feudal states led successful rulers to rely on royal bureaucrats, mercenary armies, and national taxation rather than on the services of warrior-landowners. Late in the Middle Ages, this led many rulers to seek backing from their subjects through representative institutions, but by 1700, the most successful states were those where rulers governed on their own authority as absolute (unlimited) monarchs. The one exception was Britain, whose limited monarchy combined representative institutions, guarantees of subjects' rights, and effective state power.

Meanwhile, stronger links with the other civilizations of the Eastern Hemisphere brought technical ideas from distant lands that fourteenth- and fifteenth-century Europe turned into revolutionary advances—firearms, printing, clocks. And out of the urge to make intercontinental links even stronger, as well as the need to counter the growing power of Islam, came exploration and overseas empires, so that Christendom replaced Islam as the world's farthest-flung intercontinental civilization.

The changes in culture and religion were just as drastic, and their roots in the past were just as deep. Medieval scholars and thinkers had always felt themselves to be the heirs of Greece and Rome, and this finally led them into a determined effort to revive all that was left of the ancient traditions—the Renaissance. Out of this encounter with the Greco-Roman past came new ideals of human personality and behavior, new philosophical ideas, new questions about Christian belief and practice, and new forms of art and literature.

Likewise, the Catholic Church of western Europe, for all its stress on unity of faith, had a long-standing history of inner conflict that finally exploded in the religious revolution of the Protestant Reformation. Protestantism failed to take over the entire Church or even to remain a united movement, but out of its disunity came many new forms of Christian belief and practice. The Reformation also strengthened the state in its partnership with both the Catholic and the Protestant Churches, and in the long run, it helped make religious diversity and freedom of conscience accepted Western values.

All these changes also strengthened the position that western Europe had won in the Middle Ages as the heartland of Western civilization. The Renaissance and Reformation began in western Europe and hardly affected the Orthodox countries of the East. The centers of finance, trade, and technical innovation, as well as the rulers with the best-organized governments and armies, were all to be found in the West. It was the western European countries that reached overseas for trade and empire, while eastern Europe served as their buffer zone against the expanding Islamic land empire of the Turks.

These shifts in civilization were far from being a triumphant progress toward modernity. The international capitalist economy brought bitter class struggles and vicious repression in town and countryside, and in eastern Europe, it helped serfdom grow ever more oppressive. The short-term result of the Reformation was two hundred years of religious hatred, persecution, and war. Europe's closer links with the rest of the world led to devastating intercontinental epidemics, the destruction of the civilizations of the Western Hemisphere, and the beginning of the Atlantic slave trade. In all these ways, the era was as tormented as any in history.

All the same, by 1650, a new kind of civilization, possessing unprecedented technical skills, worldwide power, and a willingness to deliberately alter its own ways of life, was coming into being. Christian Europe was on the way to remaking itself into the modern West.

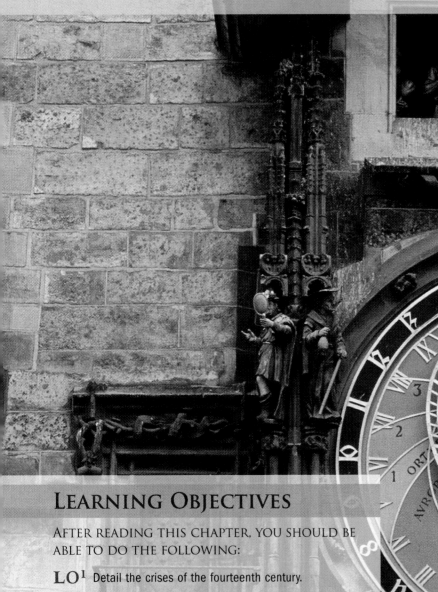

CHAPTER 14

BEGINNINGS OF A NEW EUROPE: THE LATE MIDDLE AGES, 1300–1500

LEARNING OBJECTIVES

AFTER READING THIS CHAPTER, YOU SHOULD BE ABLE TO DO THE FOLLOWING:

LO¹ Detail the crises of the fourteenth century.

LO² Trace the evolution of capitalism in the late Middle Ages.

LO³ Describe the technical advances that, for the first time, gave Europe worldwide technological leadership.

LO⁴ Identify the changes in government and politics that began in the late Middle Ages.

Francois Pugnet/Kipa/Corbis

"THE CRISES OF THE LATE MIDDLE AGES DID NOT STOP THE CONTINUING EVOLUTION OF CIVILIZATION IN WESTERN EUROPE, AND IN SOME WAYS THEY EVEN SPURRED IT ON."

In the late Middle Ages—the fourteenth and fifteenth centuries—Europe was shaken by a series of crises and disasters. The increase in population that had begun in the early Middle Ages broke through the limits of what existing farming methods could support, and the result was famine, social conflict, and peasant revolts. The Black Death, the famous mid-fourteenth-century outbreak of the plague, ravaged the entire Eastern Hemisphere and killed as much as a quarter of the people of Europe. The papacy became entangled in Church corruption and the rivalries of rulers, and the result was a long-enduring crisis of confidence in the holiness of the popes. Islam, now led not by Arabs but by convert peoples from the Asiatic steppes, once again went over to the offensive in its continual struggle with Christendom, and much of eastern Europe came under the rule of the Turks.

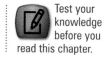 Test your knowledge before you read this chapter.

But these crises did not stop the continuing evolution of civilization in western Europe, and in some ways, they even spurred it on. Merchants reinvested their profits in industry and banking as well as trade, so that a capitalist sector of the economy began to appear alongside the agrarian and guild-based economy of the Middle Ages. Partly in order to serve the needs of this new economy, and helped by its ability to mobilize resources and create markets, late medieval inventors came up with a series of world-changing devices: three-masted sailing ships, firearms, printing presses, and mechanical clocks. All these inventions built on inspirations from Islam and East Asia, but for the first time, they gave Europe technological leadership among the civilizations of the world.

Capitalism and new technology also helped change the way in which rulers governed their countries. Rulers began to rely on taxes from their subjects and on

≪ **Telling the Time** On a clock installed in 1410 on the city hall of the central European city of Prague, a hand points to numbers on the outer ring that show twenty-four-hour time beginning at sunset—but since sunset changes from earlier to later and back again through the year, the outer ring turns very slowly back and forth to compensate. The clock shows much more timekeeping and astronomical information, all automatically. Revolutionary devices like mechanical clocks were among the many new beginnings of the later Middle Ages.

Jacquerie
A large-scale uprising of French peasants in 1358.

loans from bankers as well as on the services of vassals. New infantry weapons overthrew the battlefield supremacy of mounted knights. The invention of cannon made the castles of nobles vulnerable to attack, as well as being too expensive for anyone but leading rulers to afford. The Italian city-states came under the rule of efficient despotic governments that practiced the naked pursuit and use of power. The rulers of western European countries began to build up centralized governments, hire mercenary soldiers, and collect taxes directly from their subjects.

However, the feudal notion persisted that subjects had rights against rulers and that rulers could not do things that affected these rights without their subjects' consent. Accordingly, to get the backing of their subjects for their new measures, rulers in many countries began to summon representative assemblies—most famously, the English Parliament.

LO¹ The Fourteenth-Century Disasters

Famine, rebellion, war, and disease have been regular features of human society from prehistory to the present. In the Middle Ages, conflict and corruption within Christendom, and reverses in the continual struggle with Islam, were nothing unusual. But in fourteenth-century Europe, all these things happened one after another and on a massive scale, with aftershocks that continued into the fifteenth century and long afterward.

Famine, Rebellion, War, Disease

About the year 1300, the lengthy agricultural boom that had caused Europe's population to more than double over three centuries (p. 193) came to an end. Early in the new century, arctic cold and heavy rains swept across Europe, flooding farmlands and shortening the growing season. Because of the earlier growth in population and farming, there was no more wild territory that could be turned into productive fields, and the available farmland had reached the limit of what it could produce with the methods in use at the time. The resulting famines led to hostility between peasants and lords, lowered human resistance to disease, and disrupted agriculture and commerce.

Rebellion and War

In 1320, a peasant uprising started in northern France. Its leaders expressed the grievances of the poor and a religious hope that the lowly would overthrow the highborn and establish a

CHRONOLOGY

1300s	Famines and peasant revolts; changes in feudalism and manorialism; new weaponry begins to change warfare
1309–1377	The "Babylonian Captivity" of the popes in France
1338–1453	Hundred Years' War
1347–1350	The Black Death spreads across Europe
1378–1417	The Great Schism in Western Christendom; John Wiclif and Jan Hus lead movements that challenge the power of the clergy and papacy
1400s	Age of despots in Italy; capitalism and international commerce flourish; banking and merchant partnerships allow for large-scale enterprise; domestic system of production begins; "second serfdom" begins in eastern Europe
1450	Gutenberg develops printing with movable type
1453	Fall of Constantinople to Ottoman Turks
1462	Ivan the Great throws off the "Tartar yoke" in Russia
1492	Ferdinand and Isabella complete the reconquest of Spain
1500s	End of serfdom in England and most of western Europe; rise of national monarchies in Spain, France, and England
1513	Machiavelli writes *The Prince*
1526	Habsburg dynasty reaches greatest extent under Emperor Charles V

"Christian commonwealth" of equality for all. Farmers and poor people from the cities joined excited mobs as they made their way across the countryside. The rebels seized arms, attacked castles and monasteries, and destroyed tax records. Finally, after Pope John XXII had condemned the outlaws, mounted bands of knights ruthlessly slaughtered the weary peasants (see photo). But the resentment and anger of the poor persisted.

Another uprising occurred about a generation later, in 1358. It was called the **Jacquerie** (zhahk-REE), (from Jacques, the French for Jack—a slang name for a peasant). Kindled in a village near Paris, the revolt spread like wildfire across the country. At its peak, perhaps 100,000 men, women, and children were on

<< **Crushing an Uprising** This manuscript illustration shows the capture of a rebellious town in fourteenth-century France. Foot soldiers hack at rebels and throw them into a river; mounted knights patrol the streets, and noble ladies, dressed in the height of fashion, look on unconcerned. Snark/Art Resource, NY

the rampage. Though better equipped and better organized, the Jacquerie suffered the same fate as the earlier rebellions, with systematic burning, looting, and killing by both the peasants and the avenging nobles.

France was not alone in its ordeal. Similar uprisings occurred all over Europe throughout the century. In England, the Peasants' Revolt of 1381 followed the pattern of the Jacquerie. Marked by murders and burnings, it was finally crushed by the ferocity and treachery of the nobles and the king.

Adding to these miseries were lengthy struggles between the English and French kings, which began in 1338, continued with intervals for more than a century, and are known as the Hundred Years' War. The combats, which often consisted of large-scale English raids deliberately intended to inflict the maximum destruction, brought ruin to the farms and towns of France, the principal battlefield.

The Black Death

But the cruelest blow of all was the **Black Death**. This was the name given in Europe to a pandemic (universal) outbreak of a deadly disease, the bubonic (**byoo-BON-ik**) plague—from *buboes*, painful swellings that mark the disease's onset. The infection had already devastated much of Europe in the sixth century (p. 156). For several centuries, there were no more massive outbreaks, until one began in southwestern China about 1340 and spread in a few years throughout the Eastern Hemisphere (Map 14.1).

By about 1347, the plague reached the Black Sea region; from there, merchants from the city of Genoa brought it to Italy; and in about four years, it spread across Europe. Having had little or no prior contact with the infection, people were highly susceptible, and their capacity for resistance was weakened by widespread malnutrition. The plague killed perhaps a quarter of all the inhabitants of Europe during the fourteenth century (25 million out of a population of 100 million).

By the close of the fourteenth century, the effects of the plague had diminished, and life returned more or less to normal. But it was not until the sixteenth century that the population reached its earlier level, and the plague continued to flare up locally until the late seventeenth century. In addition to its toll in death and suffering, the plague had drastic economic, social, and psychological effects. Death became a universal obsession. Many people interpreted the plague as a punishment from God that called for severe personal penitence; some thought the end of the world was at hand. And the plague and the other catastrophes that had struck the people of Europe severely strained the medieval patterns of society.

 The Plague Hits Florence Read an eyewitness account of life in Florence during the plague.

 Black Death: The Lasting Impact (http://www.bbc.co.uk/history/british/middle_ages/black_impact_01.shtml) Learn how the Black Death changed life in England.

 Simon Schama Hosts a BBC Motion Gallery on the Black Death (http://www.bbc.co.uk/history/interactive/audio_video/) View a short video on "King Death" in England.

The Crisis of the Papacy

Besides these human disasters, the fourteenth century was also an era of crisis in the leading religious institution of Western Christendom, the papacy. Since about the year 1000, the popes

"Babylonian Captivity"
The period in which the popes resided in Avignon rather than Rome and were thought to be controlled by the French monarchy.

Great Schism
The division of Western Christendom into two competing groups, each with its own pope and college of cardinals.

had gained a new position as rulers with international governing power over the Catholic Church. They had done so partly by building on their traditional position as generally accepted guides in matters of belief and worship, and partly by putting themselves at the head of the eleventh-century movement for Church reform (pp. 210–211). As a result, they had become both partners and rivals of feudal rulers in the power structure of Western Christendom.

Exactly because the Church was so powerful, rivalries between popes and feudal rulers were often intense. Should clergy who committed crimes be tried by Church or royal courts? Could rulers levy taxes on the clergy to help pay the expenses of governing their countries, and could popes collect fees from believers to help pay the expenses of governing the Church? Popes and rulers naturally tended to have very different views on matters like these.

> *"And turn or tarry where I may, I encountered the ghosts of the departed."*
>
> —from Boccaccio, *The Decameron*

Furthermore, in spite of their supreme position in Western Christendom, the popes were liable to all sorts of pressures from below. There was pressure, for example, to do favors for cooperative rulers—especially the kings of France, who were usually on good terms with the papacy. Thirteenth-century popes appointed many French churchmen as cardinals (pp. 209–210), so that the papal court became divided between a French bloc and an Italian bloc.

Furthermore, now that the popes headed an international government, their officials were eager to enrich themselves from fees and bribes. Like all rulers at the time, popes found it hard to stamp out this practice, since the chance of fees and bribes was exactly what made officials willing to work in government—in fact, able but corrupt Church officials sometimes rose to become popes. As a result, in the never-ending struggle against Church corruption, the papacy was no longer seen as part of the solution, but as part of the problem. Around 1300, the pious Catholic Dante, in his story of his journey through the afterlife, told of meeting the recently deceased Pope Nicholas III in hell—stuck forever upside down into a hole, just as during his lifetime he had stuck into his purse the money he had made from selling Church positions.

The Babylonian Captivity and the Great Schism

Late in the thirteenth century, the papacy's relations with France

In the fourteenth century, disputes and pressures like these led to a historic shift in the relationship of popes and rulers.

temporarily soured, and in 1303, Pope Boniface VIII died after being humiliated by King Philip IV of France in a struggle arising out of a dispute over taxation of the clergy (p. 211). Shortly afterward, with powerful help from Philip, a French archbishop was elected as Pope Clement V. The new pope began by appointing nine new cardinals, all Frenchmen, giving the French bloc a majority at the papal court—and it was the cardinals who elected the pope. A few years later, Clement moved his court to Avignon, a papal holding on the Rhône River just east of the border of the French kingdom. For some seventy years, a succession of French popes reigned at Avignon.

Outside France, these popes were looked upon with suspicion and hostility. Because the pope holds office by virtue of his being the bishop of Rome, it seemed improper that he should reside anywhere but in the Eternal City, and the move confirmed a widespread feeling that the papacy had become a captive of the French monarchy. The Italian humanist Petrarch labeled the popes' stay at Avignon the "Babylonian Captivity," a reference to the forced removal of ancient Jewish leaders to Babylon.

More serious embarrassments to the Church were yet to come. In 1377, Gregory XI decided to return the papal court to Rome; upon his death there, a Roman mob pressured the cardinals into choosing an Italian as pope. But the French cardinals then fled the city, pronounced the election invalid, and chose a pope of their own. This one, with his supporting cardinals, moved to Avignon, while the Italian pope, with his cardinals, stayed in Rome. Each declared the other to be a false pope and excommunicated him and his followers.

For the next forty years (1378–1417), Western Christendom had two popes and two colleges of cardinals, each supported by competing groups of rulers: France and its allies recognized Avignon, while England and the German princes recognized Rome. The **Great Schism** (split), as this division is called, was at last settled by a general council of the Church at Constance in Switzerland, which deposed both rival popes and elected a new one. That, however, raised a new danger to the papacy—that its supremacy over the Church might be challenged by bishops acting collectively in council and swayed by the rulers who backed them.

 The Triumph of Conciliarism: End of the Great Schism Read a selection from the documents that announced the end of the Great Schism.

Powerful but Disrespected: The Fifteenth-Century Papacy

Fifteenth-century popes were able to fend off this danger. They astutely played rival rulers against each other and made compromises with them, whereby the rulers controlled leading Church appointments while letting the popes collect large sums from the Church in their countries. Meanwhile, the popes strengthened their control over the States of the Church, the territories that they ruled in central Italy. They made sure of a permanent Italian majority among the cardinals and became leading contenders in Italian power struggles.

But popes who made deals with rulers to skim off the Church's resources, and who acted as ruthless Italian power wielders, were in no position to restore confidence in the papacy's holiness. Halfway through the fifteenth century, the papacy repeatedly called for a crusade to liberate Constantinople, recently captured by the Turks, and no one responded. None other than Pope Pius II explained why not, in a speech to the cardinals: "People think all we want to do is to heap up gold. No

> "*People think all we want to do is to heap up gold. No one believes what we say. Like bankrupt tradesmen, we have no credit.*"
>
> —Pope Pius II

The Downfall of the Church: Condemnation of the Papacy During the Great Schism Read a fifteenth-century description of the greed of the pope and cardinals.

one believes what we say. Like bankrupt tradesmen, we have no credit."

In an era when the pope himself called the papacy "bankrupt," the question was bound to arise: Was this situation simply the result of mistakes and failings that could be corrected, or was there something basically corrupt and unholy about a powerful clergy headed by a ruling papacy? Late in the fourteenth century, some dissident religious thinkers gave the second, more radical answer. In England, the followers of John Wiclif became, for a time, a widespread movement, and the Bohemian supporters of Jan Hus were able to take and hold an entire country.

John Wiclif

A leading Oxford scholar and teacher, Wiclif was among the first to question openly the need for a priesthood. After a lifetime of study, Wiclif concluded that the Church was suffering from

Map 14.1 **The Spread of the Black Death**

The map shows the spread through Europe and neighboring lands of a disease that affected most of the Eastern Hemisphere. It arrived in the Black Sea region by overland routes across Asia. From there it spread in two years (1346–1347) from seaport to seaport along both shores of the Mediterranean and Europe's Atlantic coast. In a few following years it spread farther by way of seaports and inland trading cities from Ireland across Scandinavia all the way to Russia. © Cengage Learning

Interactive Map

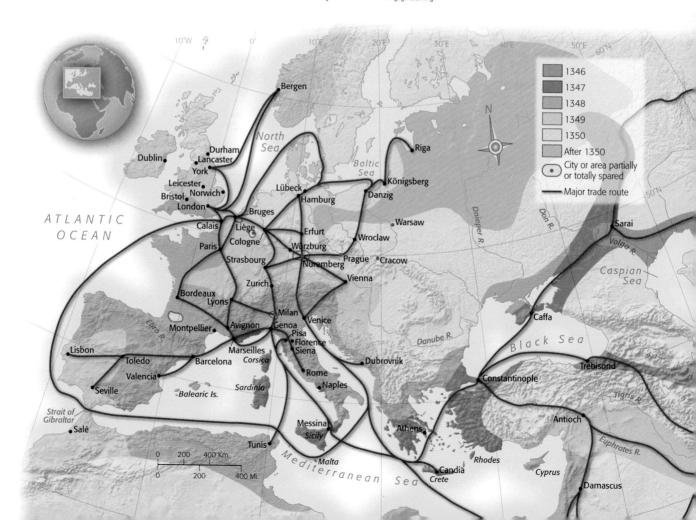

more than just the misbehavior of some of its clergy. He challenged the established role and powers of the clergy itself—arguing that God and Scripture (the Bible) are the sole sources of spiritual authority. To enable ordinary English people to read Scripture for themselves, he made an English translation of the Vulgate Bible (p. 144). Every individual, he said, can communicate directly with the Lord and can be saved without the aid of priests or saints.

For challenging the accepted doctrines of authority and salvation, Wiclif was condemned and forced to retire from teaching. Civil disturbances in England and the Great Schism in the Church saved him from more drastic punishment, and he had many followers in England, whom their opponents called Lollards (a slang word for "mumblers"—of prayers and foolish beliefs). The alarmed English Parliament introduced the penalty of burning for heresy, not previously known in the country, and systematic repression caused the Lollard movement to die out during the fifteenth century.

Jan Hus

The fate of the movement that began with Jan Hus was different. Hus was a priest and a professor at Charles University in Prague, in the central European kingdom of Bohemia (Map 12.2 on page 220). Already active in efforts to reform the clergy, he was inspired by the writings of Wiclif to launch stronger, more radical attacks. Hus had the support of most of his compatriots, partly because many of the clerics he criticized were Germans, whereas he himself and the majority of the population in Bohemia were Czechs (pp. 220–221).

Bohemia was part of the Holy Roman Empire, and Emperor Sigismund grew disturbed by the mounting agitation there. Hus was summoned by the Council of Constance in 1414 to stand trial on charges of heresy, and the emperor promised him safe conduct to and from the trial. After a long and cruel imprisonment in Constance, Hus was tried and found guilty. The emperor did not keep his promise of protection, and Hus, refusing to recant (withdraw) his beliefs, went to his death at the stake. The reaction in Bohemia was instantaneous. Anti-German and antipapal sentiments were inflamed. A bloody uprising erupted, which eventually took over the country and fought off Catholic campaigns against it. The Hussite armies carried on their banners the emblem of the chalice, the cup in which wine was offered at Mass, in token

 Czechs in History: Jan Hus, by Nick Carey for Radio Prague (http://www.radio .cz/en/article/37466) Read about present-day arguments over the still-controversial Jan Hus.

Map 14.2 The Ottoman Empire about 1500

The Ottoman dynasty began in 1300 as mere beys ("lords") of a hundred-mile stretch of land in northwestern Anatolia. By 1500, they had conquered their Muslim and Christian neighbors in Anatolia and the Balkans; the incumbent ruler now called himself *padishah* ("Lord of Kings"), and Christians, impressed by his power, called him the "Grand Turk." Yet this was only the beginning of Ottoman conquest; compare Map 14.5 on page 266. © Cengage Learning

 Interactive Map

of what became their defining belief, that laity and clergy alike—not just clergy as in the Church's practice (p. 207)—should receive both bread and wine. In spite of internal divisions, the Hussite movement persisted for more than a century and finally merged into the Protestant Reformation.

In the rest of Western Christendom, the consensus still prevailed that Christ had appointed the clergy to guide believers to salvation under the supreme authority of the pope, but the question of how to bring the reality of the Church closer to the ideal was widely debated. Given the Church's importance in society, any answer to this question must have wide-ranging social and political as well as religious consequences.

The Turks in Europe

At about the same time that the Mongol Empire began to break up (p. 223), a Middle Eastern empire began to form that would reach far into Europe—that of the Turks. By origin yet another nomadic people of the steppes, the Turks had entered the Middle East and become Muslims in the ninth century. Under the Seljuk dynasty in the eleventh and twelfth centuries, they had already conquered most of Anatolia. Then, in 1299, they came under the rule of a new dynasty, the Ottomans.

The Ottoman Conquests

Combining warlike prowess with exceptional diplomatic and governing skills, the **Ottoman Turks** expanded their empire by stages rather than all at once like the Mongols—and their first target was the chaotic and divided Balkans (southeastern Europe).

The Turks first landed in Europe in 1352 and quickly took over most of the limited territories that the restored empire of Byzantium still possessed. Within fifty years, the Bulgarians and Serbs were conquered, and the Albanians not long after that. There followed Byzantium's final destruction. In 1453, the last outpost of the thousand-year-old empire, Constantinople itself, was taken. The city founded by Rome's first Christian emperor became the capital of the Ottoman sultan, and Justinian's cathedral of Hagia Sophia was turned into a mosque. Outlying areas of the Balkans, such as Greece and the Romanian territories, still had to be "mopped up" (see Map 14.2). But by 1500, the Turks were ready to turn their attention to new targets: Hungary, the lands surrounding the Black Sea, and a huge swath of Arab countries stretching right across the Middle East and North Africa. Once again, as in the early Middle Ages, Christendom confronted a huge and expanding Islamic empire.

 The Fall of Constantinople to the Ottomans: A Lamentation Read the anguished words of a Byzantine commander upon losing Constantinople.

Christian Peoples in a Muslim Empire

For the Christian peoples of the Balkans, life as subjects of this empire had its advantages. The Turks brought unity and peace such as the region had hardly ever known since Roman times, and with unity and peace came prosperity, trade, and low taxes. Trade flourished and towns burgeoned. Constantinople, where a shrunken population had lived amid abandoned buildings at the time it was conquered, grew to a size of three-quarters of a million, thereby regaining its long-lost position as Europe's largest city.

Turkish rule even brought religious benefits, for the sultans, in accordance with Muslim principles (p. 160), tolerated other monotheistic religions. The Orthodox majority not only could practice their religion freely but were also sheltered by Turkish power from Catholic efforts to make them accept the supremacy of the pope. Furthermore, under Muslim law, the Orthodox faithful constituted a separate community, governed in secular as well as spiritual matters by their own religious leaders. As a result, the Orthodox bishops, headed by the patriarch of Constantinople, actually wielded greater worldly power under the Turks than they had ever enjoyed under the Christian emperors. Jews, too, fleeing Christian persecution around 1500 in Spain and Portugal, found the Turkish-ruled Balkans a haven of tolerance, and were far more prosperous and respected there than those who fled western Europe for Poland and Hungary.

All the same, most Christians in the Balkans now had a status of second-class citizens from which there was only one way of escape: conversion to Islam. Many people chose this escape, among them, noble landowners who wanted to maintain their privileged status; Christian heretics in Bosnia who were squeezed between the Muslim rulers and the traditional Orthodox persecutors; and Albanians moving out of their mountainous homeland along the Adriatic Sea into the nearby Serb-inhabited plain of Kosovo (pp. 601, 604).

There was one Christian group that was highly favored: the wealthy Greek upper class, which became a second ruling elite of the Balkans under the Turks. Now that they were freed from Venice's domination by Turkish power, Greek merchants and bankers controlled the region's trade and finance and provided men and ships for the Turkish merchant and war fleets. Likewise, Greek patriarchs and bishops held power throughout the Balkans, regardless of whether the local faithful were Greek or not. The other Orthodox nations of the Balkans now consisted almost entirely of peasants, with no leadership apart from their parish priests and monks.

In these ways, new religious and national divisions grew up in the Balkans. When Turkish rule grew weak and oppressive in the eighteenth and nineteenth centuries, and finally disappeared early in the twentieth century, this mixture would flare into frequent murderous conflicts.

Pushing Back Islam: Russia and Spain

The frontier between Christendom and Islam was a long one, and in spite of the Ottoman conquests, in other regions Christendom made gains. In the far northeast of Europe, Russian rulers in the city of Moscow had formed an extensive princedom as vassals of the Muslim Tartars

Europe's Largest Mosque The Selimiye (she-LEEM-ee-yeh) Mosque was built in the late sixteenth century at Edirne (eh-DAIR-neh), on the European side of the Bosporus, at the command of the Ottoman sultan Selim II. With its 200-foot minarets and its symmetrical structure topped by a dome that the architect, Mimar Sinan, intended to rival that of Hagia Sophia, the mosque symbolizes the splendor of the Ottoman Empire at its height. De Agostini/SuperStock

(p. 223), and in the fifteenth century, Ivan the Great threw off what has gone down in Russian history as the "Tartar yoke" and became an independent ruler—but not as a mere prince. He married Sophia, the niece of the last emperor of Byzantium, and took the title of tsar ("caesar"), the traditional Slav name for Eastern emperors. Those emperors had in turn been regarded as the legitimate successors of the emperors of ancient Rome, and accordingly, a Russian writer of Ivan's time referred to Moscow as the "third Rome." From Rome and Constantinople, the Christian imperial mission had passed to Moscow.

Meanwhile, at the other end of Europe, the Spanish rulers Isabella and Ferdinand completed another long-standing Christian mission. In 1492, they conquered Granada, the last Muslim territory in Spain, and soon inflicted on their Muslim subjects far more systematic repression than Balkan Christians endured under the Turks.

The Ottoman conquests outweighed these Christian gains, however—partly because the western European countries mostly left the Balkans to their fate. Western help was generally too little and too late, and was usually coupled with highly unwelcome demands that Orthodox rulers and their subjects submit to the pope. Up to 1500, what prevented the Turks from advancing still farther into Europe was mainly the huge size of their empire, which obliged them to fight wars on many other fronts besides Europe. With little effort of their own, the western countries were insulated from attacks from the east as they pursued the innovations that would create the modern West.

LO² The Birth of Capitalism

From about 1200 onward, European commerce began to develop a new feature: alongside guilds, craftspeople, and local traders, there began to appear international merchants who branched out into industry and banking. The troubles of the fourteenth century did not stop this development; in fact, they may even have speeded it up. Independent craftspeople, in trouble because of trade stoppages, might become employees of wealthy merchants who were better able to survive until times improved; kings fighting expensive wars, and popes moving money to Rome, both needed the services of bankers. An economic system began to come into being that was new to Europe: that of **capitalism**.

Trade and Capitalism

Italian merchants had taken the lead in the revival of trade in the eleventh century (p. 195), and in the thirteenth, they pioneered the development of capitalism. They dominated the profitable trade of the Mediterranean, and many of them made quick fortunes in their dealings. Finding that they could not spend all their profits immediately, they hit upon the idea of reinvesting the surplus.

This novel idea made it possible for successful traders to launch new, more ambitious enterprises. Soon, they were no longer traveling about as ordinary merchants but minding their account books at home. They extracted profits from their varied enterprises and reinvested them to gain yet more profits. Thus emerged the features that have characterized capitalism ever since: its boundless profit seeking and its dynamic spirit.

What the Italians achieved as the middlemen between Europe and Islam, the merchants of the port cities of Germany achieved in the Baltic Sea area. They found that by pooling their resources, they could build fleets and win joint trading privileges abroad, and by the fourteenth century, the leading towns of northern Germany had formed a commercial league, the *Hansa* (a German word for a group of merchants), which dominated the trade of northern Europe from England to Russia. The cities of the **Hanseatic League** monopolized the foreign trade of northern Germany and set up outlets in the trading centers of Russia, Poland, Norway, England, and the Low Countries. From these far-flung outposts, rich profits flowed to the capitalists of northern Germany.

The merchants of the Low Countries prospered too. The wharves of Antwerp and Bruges saw a steady stream of Italian ships carrying oriental spices and silks, as well as vessels from the Baltic loaded with furs, timber, and herring. The industries of England and western Germany also sent their products into the Low Countries. By the fifteenth century, a truly international commerce had developed—extensive enough to provide for the accumulation of profit surpluses and for the growth of a capitalist class.

Breaking Away from the Guilds

Traditionally, industry and commerce were locally regulated. Business owners ran their shops where they made and sold their products within a strict framework of rules set by the collective organizations to which they all belonged, the guilds (pp. 200–201). This system still worked well for businesses such as goldsmiths' and pharmacists' stores, which sold small amounts of items that took a great deal of skill and knowledge to produce. But with the growth of international trade, industries grew up that produced goods in large amounts and needed many semiskilled or unskilled workers. After about 1200, these industries began to cast off the shackles of the guilds.

In the woolens industry, for example, the traditional association of master weavers, journeymen, and apprentices had disappeared in many areas by 1400. The industry was taken over by enterprising merchants who bought the raw wool and put it out to semiskilled laborers for processing—first to spinners and then to weavers, dyers, and cutters in succession. The workers were paid by the piece or by measure, but ownership of the materials stayed with the merchants. They sold the finished cloth or garments in the international market at whatever price they could get. To avoid guild regulations, the merchants and their workers operated outside the cities—in suburbs beyond their walls, or actually in the countryside.

The wool merchants thus reaped the profits of both industry and commerce. They paid the laborers at a low rate and permitted them no say in running of the business. Moreover, the laborers were forbidden by law to organize or strike. This **"putting-out" or "domestic" system** destroyed the close relationship between master and journeyman that existed in the guilds. It made profit the sole concern of the entrepreneur and diminished the worker's sense of creativity. The antagonisms that grew up between these entrepreneurs and the workers, especially in Europe's biggest textile-producing region, the Low Countries, foreshadowed the fierce conflicts that were to mark the later industrial world.

International Banking

Large-scale international trade, wars, and movements of Church funds all required large-scale international methods of borrowing and transferring money. Merchants with extra capital on hand were glad to oblige, so long as they were well paid with interest and fees.

Moving Money

Often, the new methods of transferring money involved replacing actual gold and silver with paper (see photo on page 254). A Venetian who bought linen from Antwerp, for example, could avoid shipping cash to the Low Countries every time he placed an order by giving the cash to a Venetian merchant who had an office in Antwerp—with a bit extra for his trouble. In return, the merchant would give the linen buyer a **bill of exchange**—an order to the Antwerp office to pay the money to the linen seller. The buyer would then send the bill of exchange to the seller, who could get his cash from the Antwerp office—or he could endorse the bill (sign it on the back) and hand it over to someone else to whom he, in turn, owed money. Thus, the bill would become a kind of international paper money.

capitalism
An economic system that developed as entrepreneurs reinvested their surplus wealth (capital) in order to gain more profits.

Hanseatic League
A commercial league of the port cities of Germany that by the fourteenth century dominated the trade of northern Europe from England to Russia.

"putting-out" or "domestic" system
A system of production in which merchants supply workers with raw materials and pay them by the piece or by measure.

bill of exchange
A paper substitute for gold and silver used for long-distance business transactions.

Lending Money

Even more profitable than organizing money transfers for a fee was lending it at interest, and in the thirteenth century, large-scale moneylending became normal. In earlier times, moneylending had been on a small scale—partly because the economy was not so prosperous and partly because the Church condemned all interest-taking as usury (lending at an excessive rate). In consequence, lending at interest had been done chiefly by Jews, whose faith did not forbid it. This particular role of the Jews no doubt contributed to the periodic outbursts against them in Europe (pp. 218–219).

With the expansion of commerce, however, many people came to realize that lending was a useful and acceptable activity. The traditional argument against interest payments was based on a revulsion against taking high rates from individuals "in distress." But loans to businessmen engaged in profitable enterprises, or to kings and popes, were obviously of a different sort. These loans could be productive, and they exposed the lender to risks that justified some reward. Many theologians agreed that this kind of lending was not sinful, and the popes themselves were among the biggest borrowers. Consequently, small-scale Jewish moneylending was overtaken by large-scale Christian banking.

Keeping Track of Money

Moving and lending money was a complicated business, and to keep track of it Italian merchants about 1300 developed a new system of bookkeeping that involved keeping separate records or "accounts" for the resources and activities of a business, for example, cash in hand and items sold. Every transaction would affect two or more accounts and had to be subtracted (debited) in one account and added (credited) in another. Accounts had to be compared from time to time, and if debits and credits did not "balance" (equal each other), that indicated an error. The new system made it possible for owners to stay in control of their businesses from day to day and know how well they were doing over the long term. Without this method of **double-entry bookkeeping**, banks or any kind of large-scale business would have been very difficult to operate, and it is still the standard method of accounting today.

On Commerce and the Perfect Merchant: The Power of Bookkeeping Read the advice of an entrepreneur on the importance of bookkeeping.

A Genoese Loan with Interest Read a medieval loan document.

Banking Families

Large-scale financial business required a pooling of capital and of managerial talent. Merchants often formed **partnerships**—especially with their own relatives, or with business associates whom they made into relatives by strategic marriages. A group of relatives, well placed in cities across several countries, could best handle long-distance matters demanding secrecy and mutual trust, and could ensure the continuance of an enterprise.

In the thirteenth and fourteenth centuries, the largest of these international family businesses were based in Florence, which became the leading center of international finance. The Bardi and Peruzzi families, for example, lent huge sums to King Edward III of England, which financed the first campaigns of the Hundred Years' War. Later, Edward refused to repay the loans and thereby forced those families into bankruptcy—an occupational hazard for bankers who lent to rulers. But in the fifteenth century, a new house of bankers, the Medici (**MED-ih-chee**), emerged in Florence that restored the financial power of the city and came to dominate its political and cultural life as well.

Banking spread north from Italy to the rest of Europe. Jacques Coeur (**K-uh-r**), a French merchant who had made a fortune by trading in oriental

≪ **Financial Innovation** Fifteenth-century customers do business at a branch of Europe's leading firm of international bankers, the Medici of Florence. At right, a clerk hands out coins to a customer. At left, a clerk examines a piece of paper that a customer has handed him. Probably it is a recent financial innovation, a bill of exchange. This customer is having this Medici branch pay him money he is owed by another Medici customer in a foreign city, without the trouble and risk of shipping cash. The Granger Collection, New York

silks and spices, was appointed royal treasurer by King Charles VII of France in 1439, and he lent the king the money finally to expel the English from France. Taking advantage of his position at the court, Coeur acquired extensive holdings in mines, lands, and workshops and thus became one of Europe's most powerful international industrialist-bankers. In the end, rivalries at court caused his downfall, but the palace he built himself on a kingly scale still stands in his native town of Bourges.

The wealthiest banker of the era was Jacob Fugger of Augsburg in southern Germany, a region that in the fifteenth and sixteenth centuries was sharing in the prosperity of growing commerce. He invested in copper and silver mines in the Holy Roman Empire and Hungary—an industry where improved tools were enabling miners to dig more deeply and more efficiently. The leading entrepreneurs of the industry soon took control of smelting and metalworking as well as mining, concentrating the direction of all operations in a few hands, and the workers, who had formerly been independent producers, now became employees of capitalists like Fugger.

Jacob drew immense wealth from these and other enterprises and channeled the surplus into international banking. He ventured into buying, selling, and speculating in all kinds of goods, and he provided financial services to merchants, high clergy, and rulers. One of his most spectacular operations was to lend half a million florins (a sum of gold coins worth perhaps $60 million at today's value of gold) to King Charles I of Spain. The Spanish monarch used the money to become the Holy Roman emperor Charles V by bribing the imperial electors (p. 267). A good capitalist, Jacob was also a good philanthropist. He and his brothers built, as evidence of their piety and generosity, an attractive group of dwellings for the "righteous" poor of Augsburg. They still stand, near the center of the city, as a memorial to the Fuggers' wealth and charity.

Photos and Description of the Housing Complex Sponsored by the Fugger Brothers (http://www.historicgermany.com/4244.html) Tour the Fuggerei of Augsburg, Europe's oldest social housing complex.

Capitalism and Society

Successful international bankers like the Medici and the Fuggers gained social and political influence, and sometimes actual government power, equal to that of counts or princes. All the same, the European social order was still dominated by kings, nobles, and Church leaders. Europe was still basically an agrarian region where land and its products remained the main forms of wealth. Merchants and bankers sooner or later took their profits out of trade and finance, put them into land, and sought to acquire noble titles.

 A Lesson for Success in Business Read a successful merchant's advice to his children on working within the social order.

Masters and workers in industries like woolen textiles that outgrew the guild system were powerfully affected by growing capitalism, though there were many other industries where the traditional system continued unchanged. The new economy's influence was felt most strongly of all, however, in the countryside, affecting western and eastern Europe in strikingly different ways.

partnership
A type of business organization in which a group of entrepreneurs pool their capital and talent.

Western Europe: The End of Serfdom

Traditionally, serfs were required to cultivate the lord's demesne, the land reserved for his benefit. From about 1000 to 1300, as the population grew, landowners had generally lightened the burdens on serfs to get their cooperation in bringing new land under the plow (pp. 193–194).

Toward the end of the medieval period, the nobles often found it advantageous to rent out their demesnes to free tenants, who were now able to sell their produce at nearby markets and pay their rents in cash. The serfs preferred this arrangement because it released them from extra work; the lords preferred it because they could usually find cheap day labor and still have cash left over from the serfs' payments.

The next step was the emancipation (freeing) of the serfs. Now that the nobles no longer depended on forced labor, they were willing to grant the serfs freedom. In most instances, freed serfs remained on the land as tenants and in exchange for freedom paid the lords a lump sum or extra rent. But in so doing, they normally lost their former hereditary right to stay on the land, which meant that they could be evicted when their leases expired.

By 1500, serfdom had become a rarity in western Europe. The medieval lord, with his rights to the produce and services of the peasantry, had become a landowner living off his rents. Though many of the great estates remained intact, the pattern of relationships had been changed. The spirit of commercial enterprise had spread to the countryside.

Eastern Europe: The Second Serfdom

In eastern Europe, too, so long as the population was growing and more land was coming under the plow, nobles had lightened the burdens of serfdom as in the western countries. But even so, eastern Europe was more thinly populated than western Europe, with fewer nearby towns to provide a market for farm products. Nobles therefore depended heavily for their income on grain exports to the big cities of Germany and Italy, which were too far away for most peasants to reach them. Unable to rely on peasants to sell produce and pay them cash rents, the nobles (or their farm managers) had to sell the grain themselves, so they needed serfs to grow it for them—and when the Black Death drastically reduced the numbers of serfs, the nobles began to make the burdens of serfdom heavier than before.

> " *By 1500, serfdom had become a rarity in western Europe.* "

second serfdom
The term modern scholars use to characterize the revival of serfdom in eastern Europe after the Black Death.

magnetic compass
An instrument with a rotating magnetized needle that indicates magnetic north.

astrolabe
An instrument used to calculate latitude (a ship's position north or south of the equator) by determining the height of the sun and stars above the horizon.

carrack
The first three-masted sailing ship.

> *"Sea transport, warfare, book production, the measurement of time—all were revolutionized by the Europe of the late Middle Ages."*

This **second serfdom**, as modern scholars call it, prevailed in the eastern territories of the Holy Roman Empire, through Poland and Hungary, and on into Russia. In these countries, serfdom persisted down to the nineteenth century, further pushing apart the two halves of Europe.

LO³ Technology Breakthroughs

The rise of capitalism, like the rise of trade and towns earlier in the Middle Ages (pp. 195–196), went hand in hand with technical progress. Now, however, increased contact, both peaceful and warlike, with the intercontinental civilization of Islam exposed Europe to the often superior technology not only of the Arabs but of East Asia as well. Like many earlier peoples, the Europeans adapted and improved on advances that they learned from outside, and in this case, the result was a whole series of world-changing technical innovations. Sea transport, warfare, book production, the measurement of time—all were revolutionized by the Europe of the late Middle Ages.

Navigation and Ship Design

One of the basic needs of growing medieval trade, in an age when transport was far more efficient by water than by land, was for reliable methods of navigation—for sailors at sea to be able to know where they were and what direction they must sail in to reach the ports for which they were bound.

Building on geographical techniques developed by the Greeks and improved on by Arab scientists, European mapmakers began to produce accurate charts of the Atlantic and Mediterranean coastlines. New instruments of navigation came into use. One was the north-pointing **magnetic compass**, a Chinese invention that helped the navigator set and hold a ship's course. Another was the **astrolabe**, an astronomical instrument devised in ancient times and improved by Arab astronomers, which enabled the navigator to calculate latitude (a ship's position north or south of the equator) by determining the height of the sun and stars above the horizon. Both these aids to navigation were in common use on the seaways of Europe by the early fifteenth century. Soon they would help guide sailors across oceans to distant continents (see photos on pages 271 and 275).

Growing trade also needed ships that were large, strong, and easy to handle. Shipwrights in Venice and Genoa, whose craft had to be able to carry goods to and from western Europe, combined features of ship design from both the Mediterranean and the stormier Atlantic waters. They borrowed the triangular sails of their Mediterranean neighbors the Arabs, which made for easy maneuvering, as well as the stout hulls and square, wind-catching sails of Atlantic ships. The result was a new kind of vessel, the **carrack** (from the Arabic word for "merchant ship")—the first three-masted sailing ship, which appeared about 1400 and would soon become the workhorse of overseas exploration (see photo on page 268).

Carracks had a combination of speed, maneuverability, and seaworthiness that was unmatched by the vessels of the most advanced non-European civilizations. And eventually, three-masted ships would also become unbeatable fighting vessels, once they were equipped with another late medieval invention—the cannon.

Firearms

The Chinese invention of gunpowder first became known to Europeans in the twelfth century, when Christian warriors in North Africa and Spain found their Muslim foes using the quick-burning substance against them as an incendiary (fire-starting) weapon. The idea of confining the powder so that it would actually explode, and using the force of the explosion to hurl a projectile, seems to have been a European one. At any rate, "firepots" or "tubes" (Latin, *canones*) are first mentioned in Italian documents of the 1320s.

 Ancient Chinese Technology (http://library.thinkquest.org/23062/frameset.html) Learn more about Chinese inventions that were adapted by the West.

Up to around 1400, cannon were too small, inaccurate, slow to operate, and dangerous to their users to make much real difference to warfare, but in the fifteenth century, improvements came quickly. Makers of church bells began using their knowledge of large-scale bronze-casting methods to manufacture guns that were solid and safe to use. Ironworks started turning out cannonballs that were heavier in proportion to their size, more accurately spherical, and far quicker to make than stone ones. Carpenters devised wheeled gun carriages that made the weapons mobile and absorbed the recoil when they were fired. Water-powered hammermills were adapted to crush charcoal, sulfur, and dried animal droppings so as to produce gunpowder by the ton. Mathematicians tackled the problems of weight and motion involved in accurate aiming.

By 1500, cannon could be relied on to smash any stone castle or town wall—let alone the wooden hulls of sailing ships—and scaled-down versions of the big weapons were beginning to appear that were small and handy enough for a single soldier to load, aim, and fire.

Printing

European traders and warriors earlier in the Middle Ages had learned from the Muslims of peaceful as well as warlike Chinese inventions—most notably, of paper and woodcut printing. Paper, made mainly from rags that were beaten to a pulp with water and various chemicals and then dried into sheets in special frames, was much faster and cheaper to make than parchment (the skin of lambs or calves), the traditional European writing material.

Likewise, printing with woodcut blocks was faster than writing out books by hand. The process involved carving a whole page of text and illustrations in mirror image out of the surface of a single block of wood, then smearing the block with ink, and pressing a sheet of paper onto the block with a roller. By 1400, small books and items such as playing cards (an Arab pastime that had spread to Europe) were commonly produced in this way. But woodcut printing was an expensive way to produce large books with many pages, since hundreds of blocks had to be painstakingly chiseled and then thrown away when the job was finished.

Supposing, however, that each individual letter were made in mirror image on its own tiny block, many such blocks could then be put together to form the text of a page, and taken apart and reassembled any number of times to make new pages. The printing process would become fast and cheap, even for the longest books.

This had already occurred to printers in China and Korea, but the idea had never caught on there—partly because of the large number of characters in the Chinese writing system (used in both countries at the time), which made it hard to manage all the different blocks. When the same idea struck Johann Gutenberg, a businessman in the German city of Mainz, he had the basic advantage of living in a region that used an alphabetic writing system with relatively few characters (p. 33).

Even so, it took twenty years of tinkering and much technical wizardry to put the idea into practice. Gutenberg's greatest inspirations were to make the tiny single-letter blocks ("types") out of metal so that they could be quickly cast in molds rather than laboriously carved, and to adapt the centuries-old olive or grape press to apply quick and accurate pressure to the paper lying on the ink-smeared type. By about 1450, he had developed a reliable system of printing with "movable" (reusable) type.

The new method of printing, with its drastically reduced costs, for the first time made it possible to mass-produce books, and the international trading and credit networks of early capitalism enabled books to find a mass market. By 1500, there were more than a thousand printers at work in Europe, and nearly 10 million books had been printed (Map 14.3). The influence of the printed word was far wider than that of the written word had been before. The spread of religious and cultural movements like Renaissance humanism and the Protestant Reformation, the growth of powerful centralized governments with their need for law books and bureaucratic form documents, the expansion of business firms which also benefited from standardized paperwork—all were helped along by the Gutenberg printing process (see photo).

Clocks

Along with printed books and firearms, the late Middle Ages also saw the introduction of history's first widely used automatically operating machine, the mechanical clock. Automatic machines that modeled the motion of the sun, moon, and stars across the sky and thereby measured time had a long history in ancient Greece, China, and Islam, but they were unwieldy devices powered by the flow of water. Medieval European clocks seem to have been inspired partly by astrolabes, which used dials with revolving pointers as sighting devices to measure the motion of the sun, moon, and stars across the sky. Sometime late in the thirteenth century, inventors in various countries began tinkering with ways to make the pointer actually "imitate" these sky objects—in particular the sun—by moving around the dial. Since the hours and days were reckoned by the motion of the sun, the effect would be that the motion of the pointer would measure the passage of time.

Of course, for this to happen, the pointer would have to be made to turn by itself. Rather than flowing water, a falling weight, attached to a cord wound around a spindle, could provide the necessary turning power. But there would also have to be mechanisms to slow the weight's fall and "wind it up" again when there was no more cord left to unwind, and gearwheels to slow the turning motion still more, so that the pointer would move round the dial no more than once in a day.

It seems to have been mechanically minded English monks, looking for improved ways of regulating their communities' complex daily routines of work and prayer, who first came up with practicable solutions to these problems around 1300—and made their pointer-turning gearwheels also actuate a bell-striking mechanism to summon brethren who were out of sight. Falling weights were a far more convenient source of power than flowing water, and it was not long before the lives of townspeople, with their hours

≪ "We, the Undersigned Account-Masters in the Treasury of the United East India Company in Middelburg, Hereby Acknowledge . . ." On a bond issued by a Dutch company to Jacob van Neck, mayor of Amsterdam, who lent it 2,400 guilders at 8 percent for six months on November 22, 1622, all standard wording is printed and only the details are written in. The company was a huge enterprise that borrowed large sums from many lenders; printing greatly speeded its business operations.
Visual Connection Archive

Map 14.3 **The Spread of Printing**

The map shows the dates were printing presses were first set up in some of the most important of the 265 places where they are known to have been operating in 1500. Notice how fast printing spread, starting a dozen years after Gutenberg's press first went into operation in 1448. In the 1460s, 1470s, and 1460s, presses were established in 38 of the 53 places shown on the map. © Cengage Learning

Interactive Map

of work fixed by guilds or settled privately between capitalists and their employees, also came to be regulated by the new time-measuring machine. High in a tower of town hall or cathedral, it was visible to many as its hand (to start with, usually only one of them) moved, with no human intervention, in step with the movement of the sun itself; and everyone could hear the clock as it struck the changing hours of the day (see photo on page 244).

Clocks were machines that worked by themselves, printing presses turned out a complicated product in large quantities, and cannon released massive energy from small amounts of chemicals. In these ways, late medieval Europe set precedents for today's world of automation, mass production, and large-scale power generation. And already, by the end of the Middle Ages, firearms and new-style sailing ships were helping rulers to build stronger governments and sailors to explore and conquer across the world.

LO⁴ The New Politics

Economic and technical change enabled rulers to gain more control of their governments and armed forces than before (see Reasons Why).

Governments did not necessarily become more efficient as a result. Most officials were not paid from the central government treasury but were expected to charge the public fees, which they put directly into their own pockets. Tax collection was usually assigned to "farmers"—bankers who agreed to pay governments a fixed sum and were permitted to collect a larger amount and pocket the difference. Both practices were a license for every kind of fraud and corruption. Likewise, military contractors might take the money but not provide the soldiers—or they might provide the soldiers but not get their money, in which case the soldiers would mutiny for lack of pay.

THE GROWTH OF ROYAL POWER IN THE LATE MIDDLE AGES WAS FUELED BY SEVERAL DEVELOPMENTS:

The Rise of a Money-Based Economy

- Because all classes of society were able to make payments in money, it was easier for rulers to collect rents, levy tariffs on trade, and impose national taxes.

- Rulers had to decide what property to tax, hold kingdom-wide property surveys, and take measures against tax avoidance. Late Roman emperors had faced the same problems and recorded the solutions in their law codes (p. 137), which were eagerly studied by medieval lawyers.

- Rulers could also borrow large sums from bankers.

- With all this money available, rulers could buy the services of officials and mercenary soldiers rather than relying on help from their independent-minded vassals.

New Developments in Warfare

- New developments in warfare weakened the power of the feudal elite as it strengthened the rulers.

- With the invention of the longbow, the pike, and various types of axes, knives, and hooks on long poles, foot soldiers became more deadly (see photo on page 260).

- Cavalry soldiers were still needed in battle but were no longer the dominant force as in the era of knights on horseback.

- Cannon, which were so expensive that only governments could afford them, were able to smash through the walls of nobles' fortifications.

Furthermore, none of these developments deprived the nobles as a group of their leading place in society and government. In most countries, rulers found it too risky to tax the nobles and clergy, and the burden of national taxation was borne mainly by commoners. Officials and bankers usually invested their profits in land, and expected to be rewarded for their services to rulers with titles of nobility; and even men from ancient noble families could gain additional wealth and honor as royal officials or commanders of mercenary soldiers.

Sometimes, nobles were able to prevent the growth of royal government, as happened in the Holy Roman Empire, or to roll it back for a time, as in sixteenth-century France (p. 324). But countries that remained without strong central government for any length of time were bound to become dominated by more powerful neighbors, or even to be swallowed up by them. From the late Middle Ages on, the successful European countries would be ones where the traditional governing partnership of rulers, nobles, and Church leaders continued, but with rulers enjoying more direct control of their countries than under feudalism.

Building National Monarchies: France, England, and Spain

Among European rulers, those of France, England, and Spain took the lead in building nationwide power. Benefiting from the inheritance left by strong rulers of feudal times, helped by the increasing wealth and technical advancement of western Europe, and backed by growing national feeling, French, English, and Spanish rulers came into more direct control of their countries than ever before.

France: The Hundred Years' War

In France, the richest and most populous kingdom of Europe, with some 12 million inhabitants, the most powerful stimulant to national feeling was the **Hundred Years' War** (1338–1453). This lengthy off-and-on struggle with the English began when the king of England, Edward III, himself the grandson of a French king, laid claim to the throne of France. By 1420, the English had triumphed. Most of northern France was given to Henry V, now the English king, and the French also agreed to accept Henry as heir to their throne.

This humiliation at the hands of foreigners brought forth a surprising reaction among the French people, who had traditionally been indifferent toward feudal struggles. After the throne fell vacant, they found an inspiring leader in a peasant girl called Joan of Arc, who in 1429 persuaded Charles, the disinherited son of the former French king, to march to Reims, the ancient crowning place of French monarchs. Claiming divine guidance, Joan herself took command of a small military force

Hundred Years' War
A conflict between France and England over French territory that flared intermittently in the fourteenth and fifteenth centuries.

Estates-General
A French government assembly that represented the three estates (groups that made up society) of France—the clergy, the nobles, and the commoners—and that had the sole power to authorize new taxes.

and vowed to drive the English from the soil of France. The young prince, responding to Joan's appeal, was crowned in Reims Cathedral as Charles VII and went on to lead his armies to final victory over the English. Joan did not live to see that day, however. Soon after Charles's coronation, she was captured by the English, tried as a witch, and burned at the stake. The martyred Joan has been revered for centuries as the glorious symbol of French patriotism.

The Hundred Years' War was frightfully destructive to France and interrupted the growth of royal authority. But when it was over, Charles VII and his son, Louis XI, were able to build a stronger monarchy than ever before.

France: The King and the Nobles

In their efforts, the kings of France were able to take advantage of the new developments in warfare to build armies that were more than a match for any aristocratic opponent. Such armies required more revenue than the monarch had ever received through ordinary feudal dues, but Charles succeeded in raising this revenue. In preparing for his final thrust against the English, he summoned the **Estates-General** of France in 1439. This body, which represented the three estates, or groups making up society (p. 190)—the clergy, the nobles, and the commoners—had the sole power to authorize new taxes. In a burst of patriotic fervor, the Estates-General approved Charles's national army and voted a permanent tax for its support. This tax, called the *taille* ("cut"), was a kind of land tax levied mainly on commoners. With this substantial new revenue, supplemented by income from his own lands, Charles could now afford to act against nobles who opposed him. By deception, threats of force, and marriage alliances he brought the fiefs of powerful vassals back into the royal domain (his personal holdings).

Louis XI pursued his father's methods and more than doubled the size of the royal domain. His final victory was to win back the duchy of Burgundy, which had long been independent even though it was legally subject to the French crown. Its last duke, Charles the Bold, had tried to expand his holdings into a major state between France and Germany. But his plans had miscarried; and when he died without a male heir in 1477, Louis took over the duchy.

France: The King and the Church

While taming the nobility, Charles did not overlook the clergy. The archbishops, bishops,

The Granger Collection, New York

Infantry, Cavalry, and Artillery An early sixteenth-century woodcut shows state-of-the-art warfare. In front, opposing masses of foot soldiers wielding pikes and halberds (axes on poles) have come to grips; where they meet, there is a grim killing zone. Behind them, cannon are emplaced to bombard a walled town; to left of the town, more pikemen are shown, leveling their weapons for the charge. At rear, armored horsemen charge against each other in the traditional way.

and abbots themselves mostly came from noble families, and they wielded the vast wealth and power of the Church, which all Catholic rulers needed to have reliably on their side. But of course, Charles had a formidable competitor for control of the Church—the pope.

The French bishops and abbots had traditionally tended to act independently of Rome. They had no thought of overturning Catholic doctrines and institutions, but they resented the large proportion of Church revenues that was siphoned off by Rome, and the papal practice of filling important Church offices without consulting them. At the Council of Bourges in 1438, the clergy, with Charles's approval, formally declared the administrative independence of the "Gallican" (French) Church from the pope. The decree limited papal interference and forbade payments and appeals of local decisions to Rome. This move gave clear control of the Gallican Church to the French bishops under royal protection.

But the popes were too valuable as allies and too dangerous as opponents in international politics to be defied in this way. Louis XI revoked the decree, and his successor, Francis I, struck a new bargain with the pope. By the Concordat (treaty) of 1516, Francis secured the right to appoint French bishops

THE TRIAL OF JOAN OF ARC

As a teenage farm girl in the 1420s, Joan of Arc heard voices that she believed to be from Heaven telling her to drive out the English invaders who at that stage of the Hundred Years' War controlled most of France. She gained the confidence of the French king Charles VII, and in eighteen months of campaigning won a string of victories until she was finally captured. A French bishop allied with the English had a Church court convict her of a variety of religious offenses including witchcraft, and in 1431 she was burned at the stake. The trial was intended to discredit King Charles by showing that his armies' successes were the result of witchcraft. But the French eventually won the war, in 1455 the pope quashed the verdict on Joan, and in 1920 she was declared a saint.

This excerpt from testimony at Joan's trial mainly involves her victory over an English army that was besieging the city of Orleans, in which she took over from Count Jean de Dunois as leader of an assault on an English-held fortress commanded by Sir William Glasdale ("Classidas").

Joan [to her inquisitors]: When I was thirteen years old, I had a voice from God to help me govern my conduct. And the first time I was very fearful. And came this voice, about the hour of noon, in the summertime, in my father's garden. . . . I heard the voice on the right-hand side . . . and rarely do I hear it without a brightness. . . . It has taught me to conduct myself well, to go habitually to church. . . . The voice told me that I should raise the siege laid to the city of Orleans . . . and me, I answered it that I was a poor girl who knew not how to ride nor lead in war.

Jean Pasquerel [priest, Joan's confessor]: On the morrow, Saturday, I rose early and celebrated mass. And Joan went out against the fortress of the bridge where was the Englishman Classidas. And the assault lasted there from morning until sunset. In this assault . . . Joan . . . was struck by an arrow above the breast, and when she felt herself wounded she was afraid and wept. . . . And some soldiers, seeing her so wounded, wanted to apply a charm to her wound, but she would not have it, saying: "I would rather die than do a thing which I know to be a sin or against the will of God." . . . But if to her could be applied a remedy without sin, she was very willing to be cured. And they put on to her wound olive oil and lard. And after that had been applied, Joan made her confession to me, weeping and lamenting.

Count Dunois: The assault lasted from the morning until eight . . . so that there was hardly hope of victory that day. So that I was going to break off and . . . withdraw. . . . Then

the Maid came to me and required me to wait yet a while. She . . . mounted her horse and retired alone into a vineyard. . . . And in this vineyard she remained at prayer. . . . Then she came back . . . at once seized her standard in hand and placed herself on the parapet of the trench, and the moment she was there the English trembled and were terrified. The king's soldiers regained courage and began to go up, charging against the boulevard [line of defense] without meeting the least resistance.

Jean Pasquerel: Joan returned to the charge, crying and saying: "Classidas, Classidas, yield thee, yield thee to the King of Heaven; thou hast called me 'whore'; I take great pity on thy soul and thy people's!" Then Classidas, armed from head to foot, fell into the river of Loire and was drowned. And Joan, moved by pity, began to weep much for the soul of Classidas and the others who were drowned in great numbers.

EXPLORING THE SOURCE

1. Whose side are the witnesses testifying on, and how does their testimony support their case?

2. What image does the testimony give of Joan as a warrior?

Source: Used with permission of Madison Books from *Joan of Arc, By Herself and Her Witnesses* by Régine Pernoud, 1966; permission conveyed through Copyright Clearance Center, Inc.

and abbots. In return, the papacy was granted the first year's income of Church officeholders in France. The pope thereby gained additional revenue and the alliance of a powerful monarch; the king, outflanking his own clergy, brought the Church within his grip.

In these ways, French kings after the Hundred Years' War built up their power in their governing partnership with the nobles and the Church, but the partnership itself was as strong as

ever. Nobles who cooperated with the rulers kept their ancestral estates and inherited titles, were awarded favored positions as military commanders or civil officials, and were appointed to leading positions in the Church. Furthermore, the lands of nobles, together with those of the Church, were exempt from the *taille*. Wealthy bankers like Jacques Coeur gave financial aid to the kings and financed their military campaigns while townspeople generally favored the growth of royal power, but the ambition of most successful commoners was to join the nobility themselves.

From time to time, the kings summoned the Estates-General, but now that it had granted the kings permanent tax authority, it was no longer a necessary partner in royal government, and in the end, the rulers stopped calling it together. Meanwhile, the English kings were relying heavily on their own national representative body, the Parliament.

England: The King and Parliament

In England, as in France, the Hundred Years' War had strengthened national feeling, but the eventual defeat weakened the position of the monarch. In addition, in order to raise the substantial sums of money needed for the expeditions to France, the kings of England had had to make concessions to **Parliament.**

The origins of Parliament go back to the thirteenth century. Already in 1215, the Magna Carta had expressed the idea that the king needed the advice and consent of his barons before taking measures such as the levying of unaccustomed taxes (p. 190). Later in the century, as both king and barons sought to enlarge their bases of support in the country, the custom grew up of inviting representatives of the shires (counties) and boroughs (towns) to such meetings.

In 1295, Edward I held the precedent-setting "Model Parliament," and during the next century, Edward's successors called Parliament frequently in their need for additional funds to carry on the war in France (see photo). Parliament evolved into two chambers: the House of Lords and the House of Commons. In the Lords sat the great barons and clerics of the country—the king's leading vassals together with bishops and important abbots. In the Commons sat representatives of the shires and of certain towns, elected on open ballots by a small minority of the male population. The Lords were the more important house for several centuries, but the Commons would ultimately have the upper hand in lawmaking. Parliament only met when the king decided to call it, but he needed its consent for approval of new revenues, and its members took advantage of that to gain privileges and redress of their grievances. Unlike the French Estates-General, England's Parliament granted the king no permanent tax and often gave the king less than he asked. The king benefited too, however: measures that he and the Parliament agreed on became laws that must be nationally obeyed, for they were enacted not just by himself, but also "by and with the advice and consent of the Lords Spiritual and Temporal and of the Commons."

At the close of the Hundred Years' War, England suffered a series of calamities. Confidence in the crown was shattered by the defeat in France, and civil war began between noble factions led the houses (family lines) of York and Lancaster, which had rival claims to the throne. The Wars of the Roses (from the

heraldic emblems of the two sides) took place in several bouts of fighting for more than thirty years. A relative of the House of Lancaster, Henry Tudor, won the final bout in 1485, put a real end to the wars by marrying the Lady Elizabeth, heiress of the House of York, and as Henry VII began rebuilding royal power.

Henry and the rulers who followed him wielded unprecedented nationwide authority. But unlike the rulers of France, those of England continued to rely on Parliament, using it both as a safety valve for grievances and to give legitimacy to their actions. Parliament actually became more important and more deeply involved in government than before—a true partner of the rulers, though still the junior one.

The Unification of Spain

In the Middle Ages, the name "Spain" meant not a country but a region that included several separate countries, among them the Christian kingdoms (from east to west) of Aragon, Castile, and Portugal, and the Muslim

The Royal Collection © 2010, Her Majesty Queen Elizabeth II

The English Parliament At a ceremonial opening session, King Edward I (about 1300) is surrounded by visiting rulers of Scotland and Wales and by archbishops and high officials. In the middle, the Law Lords (high judges) sit on sacks of raw wool, a symbol of England's wealth. To the king's right and in front sit the Lords Spiritual (high clergy). To his left sit the Lords Temporal (leading nobles). The Commons, not shown, would be farther in front, standing in the presence of their betters.

state of Granada in the south. In 1469, however, Queen Isabella of Castile married King Ferdinand of Aragon, and "Spain" soon came to mean those two linked kingdoms, as against the separate kingdom of Portugal.

Between them, Isabella and Ferdinand brought independent-minded nobles into line and reformed the Church in their kingdoms, gaining the right to name its bishops. They conquered Granada and soon broke promises of tolerance they made to Muslims, as well as viciously repressing the Jews, who were forced to convert or leave the country. The Inquisition was established under strict royal control, and for two centuries it enforced Catholic religious conformity that came to be linked with an idea of nationhood as confined to those who were "pure of blood"—not tainted by Jewish or Muslim ancestors.

Under the descendants of Isabella and Ferdinand, Castile and Aragon remained legally separate kingdoms sharing one ruler, but the rulers governed from the Castilian capital, Madrid, and gradually turned Aragon into a province of their Castilian-dominated kingdom. In this way, a whole new country was brought into existence from the top down, by the marriage of two powerful late medieval rulers and the policies of themselves and their descendants.

State Power in Miniature: Italy

Ever since the end of the Roman Empire, Italy had been the scene of continual struggles for power among barbarian, Muslim, and Norman invaders, Byzantine and Holy Roman emperors, and the popes. As a result, Italy had become a permanently divided country (Map 14.4). Instead of developing across the whole country, state power was wielded on a smaller scale by city-states, popes, and kings. But these rulers often governed more efficiently than those of the larger countries, and the theory of unchecked state power was pioneered by an Italian, Niccolò Machiavelli (**NICK-oh-loh mak-ee-uh-VEL-ee**).

City-States and Despots

Northern Italy was officially part of the Holy Roman Empire, but the emperors were weak and distant, and the leading commercial cities were exceptionally wealthy and powerful. In the Middle Ages, the region developed into a cluster of self-governing city-states struggling against each other for survival and mastery, like the Greek city-states two thousand years before. The Italians certainly had a sense of nationhood like the French and English, but their strongest loyalty went to their city-states.

The internal politics of the Italian city-states were generally turbulent. The usual source of trouble was rivalry among factions: bankers and capitalists, rising rapidly in wealth, tried to take political control from the more numerous small merchants, shopkeepers, and artisans. At the same time, wealthy families competed with one another for special advantage. Out of the struggle, political strongmen had emerged during the fourteenth century. Sometimes they were invited to assume power by one or another of the factions; sometimes they invited themselves.

Conflicts between the elite and the common people, vendettas among upper-class families, and takeovers of power by strongmen had also been normal features of city-state life in ancient Greece (p. 52). In Greece, such takers of power were called tyrants; in reference to medieval Italy, they are today usually known as **despots**. Like Greek tyrants, Italian despots were often enlightened rulers and eager patrons of the arts; they were liable to assassination and overthrow; and they hoped to gain legitimacy by becoming hereditary rulers and founders of dynasties. The main difference was that Greek tyranny sometimes led toward democracy, whereas in Italy, rule by despots became widespread and permanent.

Partly, this difference was because the merchants and bankers of medieval Italian city-states were far wealthier and more powerful than the well-to-do upper-class citizens of ancient Greece. Furthermore, in Greece, the commoners had had strong political leverage because their city-states needed them as part-time warriors in the armed forces. In medieval Italy, however, the city-states came to rely on professional mercenary soldiers, recruited and trained by enterprising warrior-businessmen known as **condottieri** ("contractors"). With no sentimental attachments, condottieri generally sold their services to the highest bidder. On occasion, they turned down all bids and seized power for themselves. Either way, they provided the armed force that was needed to gain and hold power regardless of the commoners.

One of the most famous condottiere-despots was Francesco Sforza (**SFORT-suh**), who made himself ruler of Milan in 1450. Assuming the title of duke, which an earlier despot had purchased from the Holy Roman emperor, he governed from his moated fortress-palace. Under the shrewd policies of Sforza and his heirs, Milan enjoyed a half-century of peace and prosperity, and his descendants continued to govern Milan as hereditary dukes well into the sixteenth century.

The city of Florence remained officially a republic during the fifteenth century, but in the course of many upheavals, it developed into a despotism in practice. In 1434, authority settled in the hands of Cosimo de' Medici, heir to Europe's wealthiest banking family. He and his successors generally held no major political office, but they controlled the machinery of government through persuasion, manipulation, bribery, and force. The Medici advanced their own financial interests and the interests of their supporters, and treated rival groups harshly. The most illustrious member of the family, Lorenzo the Magnificent, was a man of extraordinary ability and artistic taste. Under his rule, late in the fifteenth century, Florence reached its peak as the cultural center of Italy. Later Medici rulers turned Florence into a hereditary dukedom like Milan.

Venice, too, remained a republic, and never came under the rule of a single despot. Instead, it was ruled by a kind of collective despotism that had been securely in power since the beginning of the fourteenth century. A small group of rich merchants

despot
The term applied today to a self-proclaimed dictator of medieval Italy.

condottieri
Warrior-businessmen of medieval Italy who recruited and trained professional mercenary soldiers.

managed to keep political control over the city and saw to it that the rest of the citizens were excluded from participation. The constitution of Venice, the envy of its less fortunate rivals, provided that the city be governed by councils and committees elected from and by the merchants. The official head of state was the *doge* (duke), who was chosen for life by the leading families. Though the doge was treated with respect, he had no independent authority.

Despotism in Central and Southern Italy

In the middle of Italy, the States of the Church, originating in the eighth-century Donation of Pepin (p. 167), were under the rule of the pope. In the south of the peninsula was the feudal Kingdom of the Two Sicilies, ultimately descended from territories conquered by the Normans in the eleventh century.

In the States of the Church, the pattern of despotism was the same as that in the rest of the country. The popes hired condot-tieri to strengthen their control of their territories, engaged in wars and alliances, enthusiastically sponsored scholarship and art, and used their office to further the wealth and rank of their families. Usually, the popes came from prominent families in Rome or elsewhere in Italy, and were the winners in intensive bouts of deal-making among the cardinals at each conclave (papal election). The process produced popes who were able politicians but not usually noted for holiness. Alexander VI, who reigned around 1500, wanted to found a dynasty like other despots. He and his out-of-wedlock son, Cesare Borgia, tried to carve out a territory for Cesare to rule, but Alexander's death and the election of a pope from a rival family put an end to the plan.

South of Rome, the Kingdom of the Two Sicilies was equal in area to all the rest of Italy (see Map 14.4 below). It was created in 1435 when King Alfonso of Sicily won a major victory in the Italian power struggle by acquiring the kingdom of Naples on the mainland and strengthened his control of his territories by the same methods as the popes. But Alfonso was also king

Map 14.4 **Fifteenth-Century Italy**

A thousand years after the fall of Rome, Italy is still in some ways the center of Europe. Two city-states, Milan and Florence, are Europe's main banking centers. Two others, Genoa and Venice, control Mediterranean empires and sea routes. The popes, rulers of the States of the Church, also govern the international Catholic Church. But the world of these "great powers" is threatened by still greater ones—the Ottoman Turks, France, and Aragon (in Spain), which already ruled the south of Italy. © Cengage Learning

Interactive Map

of Aragon, in the east of present-day Spain, and this link with a powerful outside kingdom in the end helped undermine the independence of the Italian states.

By the middle of the fifteenth century, the stronger Italian states had expanded their boundaries, absorbing weaker neighbors. A kind of balance of power developed among the three leading city-states, Milan, Florence, and Venice, together with the States of the Church and the feudal Kingdom of the Two Sicilies. It was the interplay of these states with each other and neighboring states, as well as the despotic methods of their rulers, that formed the background to the thought of Machiavelli.

The Theory of Absolutism: Machiavelli

In the late fifteenth and early sixteenth centuries, Italy was invaded by the kings of France and Spain, whose own governments were less efficient than those of the local despots but operated on a larger scale. For more than a century, the French and Spanish rulers fought each other for control of Italy and kept the country in turmoil. The Italian states were able to keep some of their independence by playing the rival invaders against each other, but Italy as a whole was more than ever before at the mercy of outsiders. Nearly two thousand years before, the crisis of the Greek city-states had helped inspire Plato and Aristotle to think deeply about politics and government; now, the crisis of the Italian states helped lead Machiavelli to the idea of **absolutism**, the theory that state power should be unlimited.

As a onetime diplomat and a close observer of Italian affairs, Machiavelli knew that despotic rule had put down internal dissension in Milan and his own city of Florence, but in relations among the Italian states, anarchy still reigned. If a despot could bring all of Italy under his rule, he believed, the country would benefit from effective government in the same way that individual states had done. But how to bring this about? In 1513, Machiavelli set down his basic views in a kind of how-to book, *The Prince*. At that time, the word *prince* was used to mean the ruler of a state, and Machiavelli intended his book as a guide for the despot who he hoped would one day liberate Italy.

 The Prince: Power Politics During the Italian Renaissance Read a selection from *The Prince*.

The Secularization of the State

Machiavelli's book marks a sharp turn in Western political thought. Medieval philosophers had seen government as one aspect of God's administration of human affairs: the Church and its officers direct Christians toward spiritual salvation, which is eternal; the state looks after their physical well-being, which is temporal (limited in time). Yet both branches of authority are subject to divine law.

Thomas Aquinas had discussed this matter in his *Summa Theologica* (p. 236). He reasoned that temporal power is invested by God in the people as a whole, who delegate it to suitable persons. The state, then, whether monarchical, aristocratic, or democratic, is not a power in itself. It receives its authority from God (through the people), and it must exercise its power for Christian purposes and in a Christian manner. To be sure, there

were just as many ruthless and unscrupulous rulers in the Middle Ages as in any other era, but their practices were condemned as a perversion of the state's true purpose.

Machiavelli met this doctrine head on and rejected it. He believed that Christian teachings, in general, did not contribute to good citizenship. In his *Discourses*, a commentary on the ancient Roman Republic, he claimed that the pagans had encouraged civic pride and service, whereas the early Christians had urged people to turn away from public affairs. The state, he thought, does not rest on any supernatural authority. It provides its own justification, and it operates according to rules that have grown out of the "facts" of human nature. He thereby removed politics from Christian belief and placed it on a purely secular (worldly) level.

The Pursuit of Power

Means, as well as ends, were a matter of concern to Machiavelli. As he saw it in *The Prince*, the central problem of politics is how to achieve and maintain a strong state. Much depends on the character of the citizens. He admired the Romans of the ancient Republic, but he concluded that a republican form of government could prosper only where the citizens possessed genuine commitment to the state. According to Machiavelli, the Italians of his day were "ungrateful and fickle, fakers, anxious to avoid danger, and greedy for gain; they offer you their blood, their goods, their life, and their children, when the necessity is remote; but when it approaches, they revolt." With citizens of such character, a strong state could only be founded and preserved by a despot.

Machiavelli advised that a ruler first turn his attention to military strength. He must devote himself to the training and discipline of his troops and must keep himself fit to lead them. Machiavelli had only contempt for the condottieri, for they had proved ruinous to Italy and incapable of defending the country from invasion. He advised the prince to build an army of citizens drawn from a reserve of qualified men under a system of compulsory military training, for their interests would be bound up with his own. Machiavelli thus introduced to modern Europe the ideas of universal male conscription (draft) and the "nation in arms."

Military strength is not enough in itself, however. For the prince must be both "a lion and a fox." The lion, Machiavelli explained, cannot protect himself from traps, and the fox cannot defend himself from wolves. A ruler, in other words, must have both strength and cunning. Machiavelli noted that the most successful rulers of his time were masters of deception. They made agreements to their advantage, only to break them when the advantage passed. He declared that the ruler should hold himself above normal rules of conduct—that the only proper measure for judging the behavior of a prince is his power. Whatever strengthens the state is right, and whatever weakens it is wrong; for power is the end, and the end justifies the means.

Machiavelli cautioned the prince never to reveal his true motives and methods, for it is useful to appear to be what one is

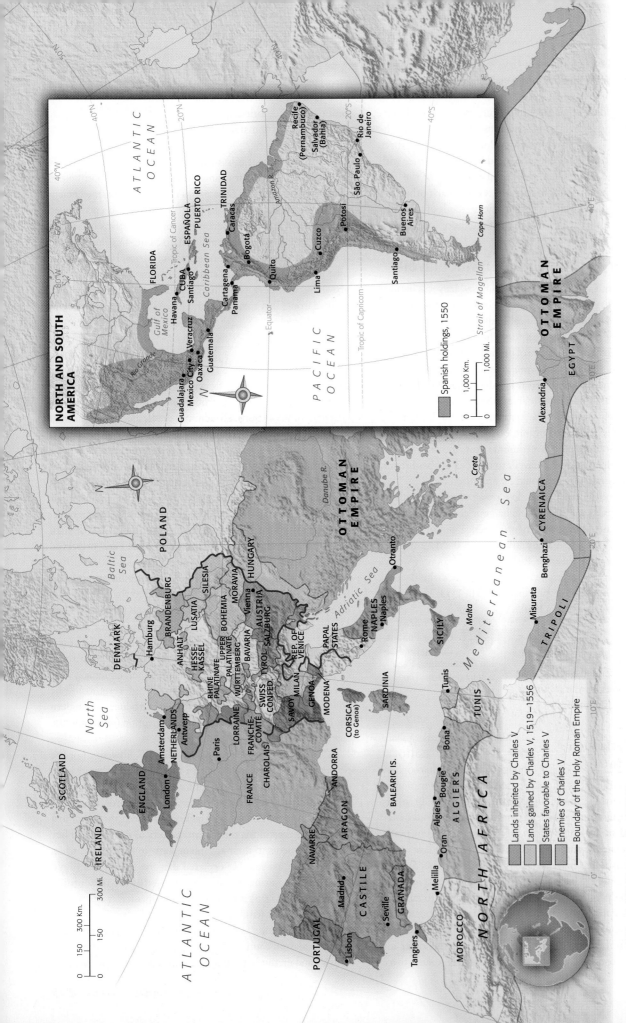

Map 14.5 Europe in 1556

In half a century, two dynasties have come to dominate Europe. The regional empire of the Ottoman Suleiman the Magnificent has expanded across southeastern Europe, North Africa, and Western Asia (compare Map 14.3 on page 259). Meanwhile, the Habsburg Charles V has acquired the first worldwide empire, with lands stretching from the Netherlands to Sicily, from Austria to Spain, and from California to Chile. The Habsburg-Ottoman rivalry also gives room for four competing middle-sized powers: England, France, Poland, and Russia. © Cengage Learning

Interactive Map

NORTH AND SOUTH AMERICA

- Guadalajara
- Mexico City
- Oaxaca
- Veracruz
- Guatemala
- Havana
- Santiago
- CUBA
- FLORIDA
- ESPAÑOLA
- PUERTO RICO
- TRINIDAD
- Caracas
- Cartagena
- Panamá
- Bogotá
- Quito
- Lima
- Cuzco
- Potosí
- Santiago
- Buenos Aires
- São Paulo
- Rio de Janeiro
- Salvador (Bahia)
- Recife (Pernambuco)

Gulf of Mexico
Rio Grande
Caribbean Sea
Amazon R.
ATLANTIC OCEAN
PACIFIC OCEAN
Tropic of Cancer
Equator
Tropic of Capricorn
Strait of Magellan
Cape Horn

Spanish holdings, 1550

0 — 1,000 Mi.
0 — 1,000 Km.

Europe legend

- Lands inherited by Charles V
- Lands gained by Charles V, 1519–1556
- States favorable to Charles V
- Enemies of Charles V
- Boundary of the Holy Roman Empire

European place names: SCOTLAND, IRELAND, ENGLAND, London, Amsterdam, Antwerp, NETHERLANDS, Paris, FRANCE, LORRAINE, FRANCHE-COMTÉ, CHAROLAIS, ANDORRA, NAVARRE, ARAGON, CASTILE, PORTUGAL, Lisbon, Madrid, Seville, GRANADA, Tangiers, MOROCCO, DENMARK, Hamburg, POLAND, BRANDENBURG, ANHALT, LUSATIA, SILESIA, HESSE-KASSEL, RHINE PALATINATE, UPPER PALATINATE, WÜRTTEMBERG, BOHEMIA, MORAVIA, BAVARIA, Vienna, AUSTRIA, SALZBURG, TYROL, SWISS CONFED., SAVOY, MILAN, GENOA, MODENA, REP. OF VENICE, PAPAL STATES, Rome, NAPLES, Naples, SARDINIA, CORSICA (to Genoa), BALEARIC IS., Melilla, Oran, Algiers, Bougie, Bona, ALGIERS, TUNIS, Tunis, SICILY, Malta, TRIPOLI, Misurata, Benghazi, CYRENAICA, EGYPT, Alexandria, OTTOMAN EMPIRE, HUNGARY, Crete, Otranto

North Sea, Baltic Sea, Adriatic Sea, Mediterranean Sea, ATLANTIC OCEAN, NORTH AFRICA, Danube R.

0 — 150 — 300 Mi.
0 — 150 — 300 Km.

not. Though the prince must stand ready, when necessary, to act "against faith, against charity, against humanity, and against religion," he must always *seem* to possess those qualities. Machiavelli summarized his advice to the ruler as follows:

> Let a prince therefore aim at conquering and maintaining the state, and the means will always be judged honorable and praised by everyone. For the vulgar [common people] is always taken in by appearances and the result of the event; and the world consists only of the vulgar, and the few who are not vulgar are isolated when the many have a rallying point in the prince.

 Famous and Provocative Quotations from Machiavelli (http://www.brainyquote.com/quotes/authors/n/niccolo_machiavelli.html) Discover fifty-eight provocative sayings from Machiavelli.

Building Dynastic Monarchy: The Habsburgs

One of the factors that enabled the city-states of northern Italy to build their independent power was the failure of the region's highest feudal overlords, the Holy Roman emperors, to turn their territories into an effectively governed state (pp. 188–189). In the empire's much larger territories north of the Alps, including Germany and neighboring lands, many local power wielders likewise gained more or less independent authority, and one particular dynasty, the Habsburgs, rose from local to Europe-wide—and ultimately worldwide—power.

The emperor's vassals north of the Alps included nobles with a bewildering array of ranks and titles, wealthy trading and industrial cities, and leading archbishops, all of whom governed their territories more or less independently of the emperor himself. The ranking vassals—three nobles, three archbishops, and the emperor's highest vassal, the king of Bohemia—had the status of permanent **electors**. When an emperor died, these seven men met to choose his successor. In spite of his limited power, the Holy Roman emperor was still the first in honor of European monarchs, so an imperial election often involved lengthy bargaining.

However, in the fifteenth century, the electors developed a habit of choosing emperors from one ruling family, the Habsburgs. The family originated in southern Germany; in the thirteenth century, they had become leading nobles as dukes of Austria, in the southeast of the empire; and from 1438 until the end of the Holy Roman Empire in 1806, every emperor came from the House of Habsburg. Even so, each Habsburg would-be emperor had to win over the independent-minded electors, and the fam-

> "No single dynasty had ever ruled so much of western and central Europe as the Habsburgs, and none in the history of the human race had ever ruled lands in both the Eastern and the Western Hemispheres."

ily's efforts to revive the imperial power were generally unsuccessful. The Habsburgs therefore also looked to build their power by marrying into ruling dynasties outside the empire.

Every ruling family made dynastic marriages, both as a way of cementing alliances and in hopes of one day gaining territory by inheritance. Of course, inheritance depended on accidents of birth and death in the families involved, and in the inheritance lottery, the Habsburgs were luckier than any other dynasty—above all in the early sixteenth century.

From fifteenth-century dynastic marriages, the youthful Charles of Habsburg inherited the Netherlands, Spain, Sardinia, Naples, and Sicily, besides the family's original territory in Austria. In 1519, he bought the votes of the electors with the help of a huge loan from the Fugger banking firm and became Emperor Charles V, and in the 1520s, Spanish conquests in the New World made him the ruler of a vast transoceanic empire (Map 14.5). Meanwhile, Charles's younger brother Ferdinand married the sister of the king of Hungary and Bohemia, and when the king died in battle against the Turks in 1526, Ferdinand was elected king by the nobles of those two countries. No single dynasty had ever ruled so much of western and central Europe as the Habsburgs, and none in the history of the human race had ever ruled lands in both the Eastern and Western Hemispheres.

But these far-flung lands were exceedingly hard to control. The emperor encountered an endless series of political, military, and personal frustrations, and he at last retired to a monastery in 1556. Before abdicating, Charles divided the Habsburg lands between two heirs. His son Philip was given Spain, the dynasty's other territories in western Europe and the Mediterranean, and the Spanish overseas empire. His brother Ferdinand inherited Austria, Bohemia, and Hungary, and was elected Holy Roman emperor.

Far from weakening the Habsburgs, the division of their territory into more manageable portions actually strengthened them. Working closely together, the Spanish and Austrian branches of the dynasty dominated Europe for a hundred years. It was they who sustained the Catholic Church against the Protestant revolt, fought the Turks to a standstill, and organized the Spanish empire in the New World (pp. 278–279, 328, 335–337). In these ways, the Europe and the world of today still feel the effect of their power.

elector
One of seven high-ranking vassals of the Holy Roman emperor with the authority to elect the emperor's successor.

 Listen to a synopsis of Chapter 14.

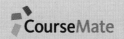

CHAPTER 15

WORLDWIDE EUROPE: EXPLORATION AND EMPIRE BUILDING,

1300–1800

LEARNING OBJECTIVES

AFTER READING THIS CHAPTER, YOU SHOULD BE ABLE TO DO THE FOLLOWING:

LO¹ Explain the developments outside and inside Europe that led to European efforts to find new routes to Asia.

LO² Discuss the stages of European exploration, from early voyages to overseas empires.

LO³ Describe the mutual impact between Europe and the rest of the world from the sixteenth to the eighteenth century.

> "THE RESULT OF THE EUROPEAN CONQUEST OF THE AMERICAS WAS A HISTORIC CHANGE IN THE POSITION OF EUROPE AMONG THE CIVILIZATIONS OF THE WORLD."

The beginnings of European worldwide exploration and empire building were linked with other changes of the late Middle Ages— the renewed Muslim offensive against Christendom, the capitalist pursuit of profit, new seafaring and war-fighting technology, and the competitive ambitions of powerful rulers. The explorers originally hoped to find routes to East Asia that would bypass the Venetian and Arab traders who controlled the existing routes, and to find distant allies against Islam. The first of these hopes came true, while the second turned out to be false. But the explorers also came into contact with the civilizations of the Western Hemisphere, which lacked many technologies and resources—as well as diseases—shared by the peoples of the Eastern Hemisphere, and were therefore easy to conquer.

Test your knowledge before you read this chapter.

The result of the European conquest of the Americas was a historic change in the position of Europe among the civilizations of the world. The capitalists of western Europe gained worldwide profits. The region's governments fought worldwide wars against each other for control of worldwide trade and empire. The Christianity of western Europe, both Protestant and Catholic, became a worldwide religion, for the first time outreaching Islam. At the same time, the eastern European countries became strong enough to hold off the Turks, stabilizing the land frontier with Islam and reaching across northern Asia to the Pacific, while the western countries broke out from Europe across the oceans to spread their influence around the globe.

What do you think?

Columbus's voyage across the Atlantic was the most momentous undertaking of late medieval Europe.

Strongly Disagree						Strongly Agree
1	2	3	4	5	6	7

≪ **A *Nanban* Carrack** To the Japanese, Europeans were *nanban*—"southern barbarians," since they came by way of southern Asia and their manners were crude by local standards. Still, the *nanban* were in some ways fascinating, among other things on account of their large, fast-sailing, and easily maneuverable ships. This painting by Kanō Naizen, a fashionable artist about 1600, shows a Portuguese carrack, the workhorse vessel of European worldwide trade and exploration, leaving port with wind-filled sails and its crew in their exotic Western costumes.

LO¹ Europe's Intercontinental Ambitions

Neither earlier Europeans nor fifteenth-century non-Europeans were ripe for long-term exploration and empire building in distant lands. A landing in North America by the Norwegian Leif Ericson in the course of the Viking migrations around 1000 made only a slight impression in Europe. Likewise, a fifteenth-century non-European venture, in which the Ming emperors of China sent several powerful fleets ranging across the Indian Ocean from the East Indies to the African coast, came in the end to nothing. But in the fifteenth and sixteenth centuries, Europe—or at least a group of leading western European countries—became hungry for contact with the outside world.

Wider Horizons

This hunger was partly the outcome of changes in the wider group of civilizations of which Europe had come to be a part. Ever since the rise of Islam and of the nomadic peoples of the steppes had linked the civilizations of the Eastern Hemisphere, Europeans had benefited in many ways from membership in this intercontinental grouping. They had tasted sweets, spices, and other luxuries from afar, and they had enjoyed exotic pastimes such as card games and chess. By the fifteenth century they were making use of non-European knowledge and inventions such as Arabic numerals, gunpowder, and printing—as well as mapmaking methods, navigational instruments, and models of ship design that would in time help them across oceans (pp. 256–258; see photos on pages 268, 271, and 275).

But until late in the thirteenth century, Europeans had known little of the distant lands from which these things came to them. The region they actually knew and lived in stretched from Greenland to North Africa and the Middle East. Revived knowledge of ancient Greek geography—another Arab import—had taught them more about the rest of the world than they knew before. They had a vague idea of the coastlines and islands of the Indian Ocean. They believed that Europe, Asia, and Africa formed a single huge landmass, surrounded by ocean that covered all the rest of the earth's surface. And they were well aware that the world as a whole was round. But the actual size of Asia and Africa, the geography of their interiors, and the peoples who lived in them were matters of fantasy and guesswork.

The Mongol Empire

In the thirteenth and fourteenth centuries, this European ignorance of the outside world began to change. The main reason was the rise of the intercontinental empire of the Mongols. As devastating as the Mongol conquests were to their victims in eastern Europe and to Muslim lands in Asia, once established, their empire maintained secure communications across the steppes for a hundred years (see Map 12.3 on page 222). For the first time, Europeans were able to visit the lands beyond Islam and return to tell what they had seen.

Marco Polo, a thirteenth-century merchant of Venice, contributed more than anyone else to Europe's awareness of the lands beyond Islam. Members of the Polo family, after establishing trading contacts with the Mongol Empire in western Asia, made the long trek from the Black Sea to Beijing, newly established as the Chinese capital by the Mongols. The Mongol ruler Kublai Khan welcomed the Polos with courtesy, and they later returned with Marco, who remained in China for many years before returning by way of Southeast Asia and the lands of the Indian Ocean. Once back in Italy, he wrote of his travels and revealed to astonished Europeans the fabulous wealth of **the Indies**—their name for the entire region of eastern and southern Asia.

Not long afterward, Europe received the same revelation about another hitherto unknown part of the world with which it did indirect business—West Africa (the lands in the bulge of Africa south of the Sahara). Early in the fourteenth century, Mansa Musa, the ruler of the powerful Islamic empire of Mali, fulfilling his obligation to visit Mecca, passed through Cairo, where there was a large Italian trading community. Soon the news reached Europe that the wealthy pilgrim had handed out so much gold by way of gifts that the gold-based Egyptian coinage had temporarily lost a quarter of its value. Much else was reported about Mansa Musa, his empire, and its resources (see photo).

 In the Footsteps of Marco Polo: A Journey Through the Met to the Land of the Great Khan (https://www.metmuseum.org/explore/Marco/index.html) View Marco Polo's journey through art and artifacts.

From this new knowledge of Asia and Africa, Europeans began to get a distinct idea of the distant lands and peoples of the Eastern Hemisphere—together with the uncomfortable but enticing feeling that among these lands and peoples, they were, so to speak, poor relations.

The Indies
The medieval European name for the region encompassing eastern and southern Asia.

Barriers to Trade and Travel

In the middle of the fourteenth century, the Black Death swept through Asia, Africa, and Europe, leading to an intercontinental decline in prosperity and trade. Disputes among the successors of Genghis Khan led to the gradual collapse of the Mongol

A European View of an African King The *Catalan Atlas* (about 1375) shows the African coastline with descriptions of harbors and landmarks; the radiating lines indicate compass directions, and the pebble-like band is the Atlas Mountains. Mansa Musa, "Lord of the Black People of Guinea" has a European-style crown and scepter; his right hand holds a gold nugget. A camel-riding Sahara nomad has his face wrapped against wind-blown sand. Just before exploration began, Europeans already had fair knowledge of some of the outside world. Art Gallery Collection/Alamy

Empire, and the rising power of the Turks (p. 251) blocked off the western end of the overland routes to the Indies. Trade and other contacts between Europe and Asia came to be channeled mainly through Egypt, where Italian and Arab merchants exchanged European textiles against the spices of the Indies. Thus, as Europe gradually recovered from the Black Death, it found the door to the outside world partly closed. But in the countries of western Europe, the effect was actually to increase their hunger for contact with distant lands.

Venice's Monopoly

Among the Italian city-states that had traditionally dominated the routes to the eastern Mediterranean (p. 195), competition to control the chief remaining link with the Indies grew intense. In the fourteenth century, the two largest cities, Venice and Genoa, fought a series of wars that ended in the victory of Venice. That city now became Europe's main gateway to the rest of the world. Venetian strongpoints and harbors were scattered along the coasts and islands of the eastern Mediterranean, guarding the sea routes, attracting the commerce of neighboring areas, and creating a Venetian trading monopoly in the region. But the Venetians not only traded; they also developed new resources. In the Venetian-owned island of Cyprus, a fabulously profitable crop of Middle Eastern origin, sugarcane, was grown on plantations worked by gangs of slaves imported from countries to the north of the Black Sea.

 Life in Fifteenth-Century Venice Make choices and experience the consequences in the role of a young man in fifteenth-century Venice.

In these ways, Venice set an example of empire building and colonial exploitation that was carefully studied by the increasingly powerful and prosperous countries of western Europe—even while they envied the city's newfound monopoly of links with the Indies. Meanwhile, Genoa was confined to the western Mediterranean and the sea routes leading from there to the lands of Europe's Atlantic coast. It was no coincidence that Christopher Columbus came from Venice's Atlantic-oriented rival city.

The Muslim Offensive

The fifteenth century also saw a hardening in western European attitudes toward Islam. The Muslim world, for so long the connecting link between Europe and other civilizations of the Eastern Hemisphere, came to seem an irksome obstacle now that western Europeans had some idea of what lay beyond it. At the same time, the Turkish drive into eastern Europe left no doubt that Islam was a more formidable adversary of Christendom than ever before—one against which it would be most desirable to find non-European allies. Somewhere in the world beyond Islam, there might be powerful Christian rulers, or non-Muslim

> "*Marco Polo, a thirteenth-century merchant of Venice, contributed more than anyone else to Europe's awareness of the lands beyond Islam.*"

ones ripe for conversion to Christianity, who would join Christendom's struggle against the followers of the Prophet.

Merchants, Rulers, and Clergy

To break Venice's trading monopoly and to find allies against Islam, a way must be found linking western Europe directly with the Indies. The prizes for whoever found the way would be glittering indeed. Western European merchants would become as rich as or richer than those of Venice. The region's ambitious rulers would make money by collecting taxes on the new trade or sponsoring trading ventures of their own—and more money meant more mercenary soldiers, less dependence on the nobles of their kingdoms, and last but not least, more power against each other. And of course, the rulers and merchants of each country intended that they and they alone would find the way, excluding the rulers and merchants of every other country just as Venice monopolized the existing Mediterranean route.

In addition, the rulers and merchants had the blessing and encouragement of the Church for any efforts to find allies against Islam and spread the gospel. Even in the European religious turmoil of the sixteenth century (see Chapter 17), both Catholic and Protestant missionaries, as well as rival Protestant churches and Catholic religious orders, would strive against each other to baptize the maximum number of converts.

LO² Breaking Out

In this way, the clergy's Christian zeal, the rulers' hunger for power, the merchants' instinct for profit, and the competitive spirit of all three groups combined to sharpen their desire to find a new way to the Indies. But did this new way exist at all, and if so, where was it to be found?

Portugal and Africa

The little kingdom of Portugal was the first to begin looking for a new way to the Indies. Carved by Christian warriors out of formerly Muslim lands during the reconquest of Spain, Portugal was a relatively poor country of farmers and fishermen, sandwiched between the larger and wealthier kingdom of Castile to the east and the Atlantic to the west—and one thing that seemed certain about any new route to the Indies was that it must go by way of the western ocean.

If Portuguese sailors were to be the ones to find the route, their country's standing among Christendom's competing kingdoms would be changed out of all recognition. The merchants of Portugal's capital city and main seaport, Lisbon, would become as rich as those of Venice, and richer than their rivals in Castile's main Atlantic seaport, Seville. Portugal's rulers would be able to shift the balance between their kingdom and

Castile, while also winning glory as Christendom's leaders in its struggle with Islam.

Besides, Portugal was close to the most likely region of the ocean to look for a new way to the Indies, southward along the coastline of Africa. Sooner or later, the coastline must surely turn northward, allowing a ship to sail on eastward to the Indies. Of course, no one knew exactly where the turn in the coastline would come, but at least there would be a coastline to follow. Sailors could stay close to land, fill their holds with food and water whenever they ran short and keep on going, or turn back and find their way home to report. And well before they reached the Indies, they would arrive in West Africa and do profitable direct business with the wealthy peoples who were known to live there.

Early in the fifteenth century, these hopes filled the mind of a younger son of the Portuguese royal family, who sponsored many expeditions along the African coast and has gone down in history as Prince Henry the Navigator. By 1460, Henry's sailors had occupied the nearby Madeira Islands and the Azores (**AY-zorz**) and had opened trade for gold, ivory, and slaves along the coast of West Africa. But then the prince died and the African coastline turned from going eastward toward the Indies to going southward, away from them. As a result, exploration came to a halt.

Twenty years later, an ambitious new king of Portugal, John II, took up where Henry had left off. New expeditions sailed, and in 1488, Bartolomeu Dias sailed farther south than any earlier Portuguese sailor until the coastline finally turned northward—and was still trending northward at the point where his crew grew nervous and made him turn for home. Still, the turn in the coastline was encouraging news, which seemed to justify King John's decision a few years earlier to reject an unorthodox proposal for a different way to the Indies made by an Italian residing in his kingdom—Christopher Columbus.

Spain Looks Westward

Columbus grew up in Genoa as the son of a weaver, but he found work with a family firm of international merchants that took him to Lisbon. There, he went into the business of making sea charts and accompanied ship captains on voyages down the African coast. Meanwhile, he studied the works of Marco Polo and of Muslim and ancient Greek geographers, and came to the conclusion that the shortest sea trip to the Indies would be not southward round Africa, but westward across the Atlantic Ocean.

In 1485, Columbus asked King John II for ships and men to make the trip, but the royal advisers on geography and navigation pronounced his plans unsound. The reasons they gave are unknown, but they certainly did not say that Columbus would fall off the edge of the earth. Most likely they disagreed with Columbus's unorthodox view that, going westward on the surface of the round earth, the Indies were only about 2,600 miles away—near enough for a ship to arrive without resupplying with food and water. The orthodox view, based on the work of the ancient Greek geographer Ptolemy (p. 110), was that the world was indeed round, but that the westward distance to the Indies

must be at least 10,000 miles. In that case, the crew of a ship that sailed that way would perish of thirst and hunger in the middle of the ocean, and probably this assessment was what led King John to refuse Columbus's proposal.

Not being a man to give up, Columbus turned to Queen Isabella, the ruler of Portugal's neighbor and rival kingdom of Castile, whose marriage to King Ferdinand of Aragon had made the two of them joint rulers of Spain (p. 263).

The Spanish monarchs had recently made an agreement with the Portuguese king whereby, in return for various concessions, they agreed not to permit their merchants to compete with Portuguese ones on the West African coast. Columbus's offer to find a way to the Indies that would bypass Africa as well as Venice and Islam was therefore a tempting one. But their advisers, too, said that Columbus was wrong, and they hesitated for several years until 1492, when he was about to leave to put his idea to the king of France. Isabella and Ferdinand could not face the thought of giving up to a rival monarch even a slim chance of gaining a monopoly of a quick and easy route to the Indies.

Sure enough, after a five-week voyage, Columbus sighted land at precisely the point where he expected to find the shores of the Indies (Map 15.1). Most geographers remained convinced that the western ocean was wider than Columbus believed, and that he had stumbled across uncharted islands well short of the Indies. But even that was very encouraging: it gave hope that a ship could take on food and water in the western islands and sail on to the Indies. Columbus finding land in the middle of the ocean was like Dias rounding the southern tip of Africa. Both Spain and Portugal, it seemed, were within reach of the longed-for destination but not quite there.

1492: An Ongoing Voyage (http://www.ibiblio.org/expo/1492.exhibit/Intro.html) Explore the impact of Columbus's voyage of 1492 on the worlds of Europe, the Americas, and Africa in this online exhibit.

Fulfillment and Frustration

Now that it seemed possible that there were two routes to the Indies, the Spanish and Portuguese monarchs agreed to respect each other's regions of exploration, trade, and conquest. In 1494, by the **Treaty of Tordesillas (tor-duh-SEE-yuhs)**, these rulers of countries that together occupied about one-third of one percent of the earth's surface agreed to divide the other ninety-nine and two-thirds percent between them. They established a demarcation line—a circle that passed through a point approximately 1,500 miles west of Cape Verde, the westernmost tip of Africa (see Map 15.1) and continued north and south right around the globe. The Portuguese would stay within the hemisphere to the east of that line, while the Spaniards would limit themselves to the hemisphere west of the line. Secured from each other's

Treaty of Tordesillas
The 1494 agreement between Portugal and Spain that established the boundary for each country's new territorial claim.

a

Breaking Out **273**

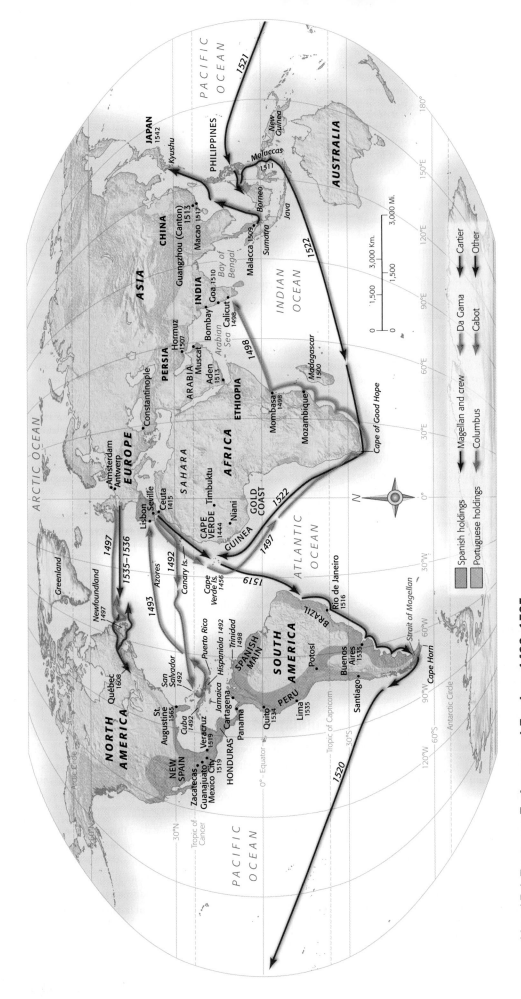

Map 15.1 European Explorers and Empires, 1492–1535

In the early sixteenth century Portuguese eastward explorers sailed round Africa, spread out across southern and eastern Asia, and began building an intercontinental network of trading footholds among powerful peoples and states. Westward explorers inspired by Columbus's dream of a shortcut to the Indies ranged the coastlines of the Americas, across the Pacific, and eventually around the world. Vast New World territories fell to conquerors from the least wealthy and powerful of the civilizations of the Old World. © Cengage Learning

 Interactive Map

interference by this agreement, the rulers and sailors of both nations set about finally winning the prize.

Portugal Finds the Way

to follow the same route as Bartolomeu Dias, but this time with four ships, two of them cannon-armed carracks (p. 256). Vasco continued beyond where Dias had turned back until he reached Arab trading cities in East Africa, and then sailed across the Indian Ocean to the west coast of India (Map 15.1). After almost a century, Portugal had found the way to the Indies.

Spain, the New World, and the Pacific

For the Portuguese, success came soon. In 1497, King John of Portugal sent Vasco da Gama

> *"Thirty years after Columbus, the Spaniards now knew that even the orthodox view of the westward distance to the Indies was an underestimate."*

Meanwhile, Spain was not so lucky. With hopes so high, an international boom in exploration across the western ocean got under way. Columbus himself made three more expeditions and found many more islands before he died in 1506, still believing he had found the Indies but not having reached any of the wealthy lands described by Marco Polo. Meanwhile, regardless of the Treaty of Tordesillas, in 1497 King Henry VII of England sent out a Genoese mariner, known to the English as John Cabot, who made landfall in or near Newfoundland. Shortly after Cabot's voyage, Portuguese sailors sailing southwestward in the Atlantic toward the line of demarcation found land on their side of the line (present-day Brazil). Spaniards searching westward across the Caribbean reached a coastline that did not seem to be that of an island, and in 1513, Vasco Nuñez de Balboa made his way across the Isthmus of Panama, thereby becoming the first European to see the Pacific Ocean.

No one as yet gave up hope of finding a quick and easy westward route to the Indies, but it was clear that vast lands stretched for thousands of miles across the western ocean. In 1508, a colorful description of some of these lands was printed under the title *The New World*. The book was based on letters by Amerigo Vespucci (ve-SPOO-chee), a mapmaker from Florence who had sailed with various explorers. It became a bestseller, and shortly afterward, a German mapmaker gave this New World what became its standard name, the "land of Amerigo," or America.

The climax of the exploration boom came in 1519, when the Holy Roman emperor Charles V, in his capacity as king of Spain (p. 267), accepted a proposal by a sea captain of Portuguese origin, Ferdinand Magellan, to find a southern route past the New World to the Indies. Magellan guided his fleet of five ships down the coast of South America. He managed the hazardous passage around the southern tip of the continent and then sailed northwestward into the Pacific. Following a frightful three-month crossing, during part of which his men lived on leather and rats, Magellan reached the island of Guam. With fresh provisions, he sailed on to the Philippine Islands, where he got involved in a conflict between local rulers and was killed. But the expedition pushed on across the Indian Ocean and westward around Africa, and the one remaining vessel finally returned to Spain in 1522 (Map 15.1). So far as is known, the ship's eighteen surviving crewmen were the first human beings ever to travel right around the world.

>> **Finding the Way** On a sixteenth-century astrolabe (p. 256), a navigator sights along the pointer to determine the height above the horizon of the sun or a star, and thereby to find out a ship's latitude (its position north or south of the equator). The ring and the disk beneath it revolve to compensate for the seasonal movement of the sun and stars. Instruments like this one helped make long exploring voyages possible. Courtesy of the Trustees of the British Museum

conquistador
Spanish conqueror of the New World.

Thirty years after Columbus, the Spaniards now knew that even the orthodox view of the westward distance to the Indies was an underestimate. The Indies were nearly 12,000 miles away, so that they lay mostly on the Portuguese side of the line of demarcation as it continued round the world from the Atlantic to the Pacific. But the New World, which had so far seemed a frustrating barrier to their westward search, was about to yield them wealth and power that more than made up for their disappointment in the Indies.

Conquering Overseas Empires

The Portuguese and Spanish discoveries were followed by empire building. A network of Portuguese harbors and citadels arose along the coastlines of the powerful peoples and states of the Old World, while Spain overthrew entire vulnerable civilizations in the New World.

The Portuguese in the Indies

As soon as Vasco da Gama returned to Lisbon with news of his success, the Portuguese began preparing to exploit their victory on the largest scale they could manage. In 1497, Vasco had set out with four ships; when he left Lisbon again in 1502, he commanded twenty, and from then on, Portuguese fleets regularly sailed the waters of the Indies. Within forty years, they made their way right across the Indies to the Spice Islands (Indonesia) and Japan.

On the way to the Indies, the Portuguese had encountered powerful West African kings and well-armed Arab city-states in eastern Africa. Now they met with fabulously wealthy local rulers in India and the Spice Islands, the well-run feudal state of Japan, and the huge empire of China. The few hundred soldiers aboard the Portuguese ships were no match for the local armies; their one advantage was at sea, with their cannon-armed carracks. The Portuguese negotiated for trading rights, seized outposts that were easy to defend against attack by land, and used their sea-fighting advantage against the Arab merchants who controlled the trade of the Indian Ocean.

By about 1540, the coastlines of the Eastern Hemisphere from western Africa to East Asia were dotted with Portuguese-controlled harbors, naval bases, and trading stations. The trade in spices, silks, and other luxury goods from India, the Spice Islands, and East Asia to Europe, as well as much of the regional trade of eastern and southern Asia, was in their hands. It was a repetition of what Venice had done in the eastern Mediterranean, only on an enormously larger scale—and, of course, to the great disadvantage of the Italian city. For it was the Portuguese who now monopolized the trade between Europe and the East, and it was Lisbon that was now Europe's gateway to the Indies (see Map 15.1).

Spain in the New World

While the Portuguese were building a far-flung imperial network in Africa and Asia, the Spaniards were founding modest farming settlements in the Caribbean islands and brutally enslaving the Native Americans of the region. Some of the newcomers moved westward, still hoping to find the way to the Indies but also attracted by rumors of nearby peoples rich in gold and silver. In 1519, the same year that Magellan set sail for the Indies, a former law student turned farmer and imperial official in Cuba, Hernán Cortés, finally came upon the reality behind the rumors, the Aztec Empire in Mexico.

An Aztec View of a Spanish Conquistador A traditional Aztec manuscript, one of the last to be made, shows a Spanish commander setting out to conquer a territory in western Mexico. A caption by an unknown Spanish writer explains: "In the year . . . 1529, Nuño de Guzmán left for Jalisco to subjugate that land; they claim that a snake came out of the sky saying that hard times were coming for the natives with the Christians going over there."

© Foundation for the advancement of Mesoamerican Studies Inc., www.famsi.org

CORTÉS ON THE PEOPLES OF THE NEW WORLD: REPORTS TO CHARLES V

Hernán Cortés often had bad relations and even armed conflicts with local Spanish officials in the Caribbean and fellow conquistadors. It was therefore important for him to gain and keep the good will of the Holy Roman emperor Charles V, who was also king of Spain and its empire in the New World. In these excerpts, from the second and fifth of a series of lengthy reports that Cortés sent to Charles, he describes the former Aztec capital city of Tenochtitlán (present-day Mexico City) and his activities during an expedition to Honduras.

This great city of Tenochtitlán is built on the salt lake. . . . It has four approaches by means of artificial causeways. . . . The city is as large as Seville or Córdoba. Its streets . . . are very broad and straight, some of these, and all the others, are one half land, and the other half water on which they go about in canoes. . . . There are bridges, very large, strong, and well constructed, so that, over many, ten horsemen can ride abreast. . . . The city has many squares where markets are held. . . . There is one square, twice as large as that of Salamanca, all surrounded by arcades, where there are daily more than sixty thousand souls, buying and selling . . . in the service and manners of its people, their fashion of living was almost the same as in Spain, with just as much harmony and order; and considering that these people were barbarous, so cut off from the knowledge of God and other civilized peoples, it is admirable to see to what they attained in every respect.

It happened . . . that a Spaniard saw an Indian . . . eating a piece of flesh taken from the body of an Indian who had been killed. . . . I had the culprit burned, explaining that the cause was his having killed that Indian and eaten him which was prohibited by Your Majesty, and by me in Your Royal name. I further made the chief understand that all the people . . . must abstain from this custom. . . . I came . . . to protect their lives as well as their property, and to teach them that they were to adore but one God . . . that they must turn from their idols, and the rites they had practised until then, for these were lies and deceptions which the devil . . . had invented. . . . I, likewise, had come to teach them that Your Majesty, by the will of Divine Providence, rules the universe, and that they also must submit themselves to the imperial yoke, and do all that we who are Your Majesty's ministers here might order them. . . .

EXPLORING THE SOURCE

1. What is Cortés's attitude to the indigenous peoples of Mexico and Honduras, and how does he expect to make them obey him?

2. How would the information that Cortés gives in these letters help him gain the king's approval?

Source: *Fernando Cortes: His Five Letters of Relation to the Emperor Charles V*, trans. Francis A. MacNutt (Cleveland, Ohio: A. H. Clark, 1908), 1:256–257, 2:244.

Cortés's conquest of the Aztecs was both daring and cruel. The Aztecs were a civilized people who boasted rich cities, splendid temples and palaces, superb artistic creations, and a well-organized government. They suffered serious disadvantages, however. They had no iron weapons, no horses, and no firearms. The government was oppressive and constantly threatened by rebellious subject peoples. Finally, like all the peoples of the New World, the Aztecs had not been exposed to European diseases; they therefore lacked resistance to the deadly smallpox germs that the invaders brought with them.

As a result, Cortés was able to do in the New World what was impossible for the Portuguese in the Indies—with only a few hundred soldiers of his own, to overthrow an empire. By 1521, the last Aztec emperor, Moctezuma, was dead; his capital city of Tenochtitlán (**teh-noch-tit-LAN**), which was probably larger than all except a handful of European cities, had been destroyed and was being rebuilt as Mexico City; and Cortés was governing in the name of the distant Spanish king, with the title of captain-general and governor of New Spain.

Within a decade, Cortés and other **conquistadors (kon-KEY-stuh-dors)** (conquerors) expanded New Spain to include most of Central America, from the Rio Grande to Panama (see photo on page 209 and Map 15.1), and another, Francisco Pizarro, then moved into South America. Learning of gold and silver in the Inca territories, he organized an

 The Battle Between the Spanish and the Aztecs Experience the battle between the Spanish and Aztecs in your choice of role in this simulation

 "Ice Treasures of the Incas" (http://www .national geographic.com/ features/96/mummy/) Learn more about the civilization of the Incas before their encounter with Pizarro.

EUROPEANS HAD CERTAIN ADVANTAGES OVER THE NATIVE AMERICANS:

Technologies Built Up by Many Old World Civilizations

- About 4,500 years had passed since the civilizations of Sumer and Egypt had first arisen, whereas it was only about 2,500 years since the earliest civilizations had appeared in the Western Hemisphere.

- European benefited from armor made of iron, a metal first worked in the Middle East, and the gunpowder for their weapons had been invented in China.

- Europeans brought horses, which had first been domesticated in Central Asia.

Greater Resistance to Smallpox and Other Diseases

- The diseases that Europeans brought with them were common throughout the Eastern Hemisphere but were unknown in the Americas.

- It is believed that, having no resistance to these diseases, the indigenous population was reduced by as much as 90 percent in the first hundred years of European rule—a staggering blow to their ability to resist.

---

expedition with royal approval. The Inca Empire, like that of the Aztecs, rested upon an advanced society; it stretched southward along the Andes Mountains from Ecuador through the modern states of Peru and Bolivia. Pizarro discovered, however, that the empire was torn by internal unrest and infected with smallpox—to which his own soldiers had greater resistance. Like Cortés, he made the most of the situation. Armed with superior weapons, Pizarro's men captured the ruler, Atahualpa (ah-tah-WAHL-pa) and held him for an extravagant ransom. After Pizarro had received tons of gold and silver, carried in from all parts of Peru, he had his prisoner baptized a Christian and then had him strangled. He next marched to the magnificent Inca capital of Cuzco (KOOS-koh), looted it, and took over the empire in 1534.

LO³ Europe Encounters the World

In 1580, thanks to an earlier dynastic marriage, the Spanish ruler King Philip II inherited the kingdom of Portugal. From the Spanish farming settlement of Valparaiso in the south of Chile to the Portuguese trading outpost of Nagasaki in Japan, people in every continent now acknowledged him as their ruler. Persia, Rome, and China had built mighty regional empires; never before had an empire stretched across the world. The empire lasted only sixty years until Portugal regained its independence, but still, it was a symbol of Europe's sudden worldwide impact—an impact that took different forms in different regions of the world.

The Americas: The Triumph of Europe

In the sixteenth century, the impact of the Europeans was felt above all in the Western Hemisphere. The confrontation between the Europeans and the Native Americans was a clash between the Old World and the New World in which the advantage was overwhelmingly on the side of the former.

Building Spain's Empire

After the era of conquest and plunder was over, the Spaniards undertook two tasks—of exploiting the wealth of the conquered lands, and of making them Christian. Like the Portuguese in the Indies, they, too, had a model to follow, but in their case, it was not Venice but the empire in which they had themselves been a subject nation more than a thousand years before—Rome.

Like the Romans in Spain, the Spanish settled in the Americas by tens of thousands, bringing with them their language and their way of life and founding cities on the model of the cities of their homeland. Like the Romans, they were willing to intermarry and share their way of life with the indigenous elite, and a colonial upper class of Spanish or Hispanicized townspeople and landowners grew up, while most of the indigenous population lived as unfree peasants subject to compulsory labor and tribute payments. Like the Roman emperors, the Spanish kings governed their empire through a relatively small number of aristocratic officials, chief among them the **viceroys** of New Spain and Peru—"viceroy" meaning "stand-in for the king," just as in Rome "proconsul" had meant "stand-in for a 'consul" (p. 97). And the Spanish New World, like Roman Spain, was a source of immense wealth to its owners. Central American farmers produced valuable crops like tobacco, cocoa, and dyestuffs, and the silver mines of Peru helped make the Spanish kings the strongest in Europe.

Meanwhile, Spanish bishops and clergy attended to the conversion of the people to Christianity, using, in the New World, the same methods that bishops and clergy had used in the Roman Empire after the conversion of Constantine (p. 142). The shrines of gods and goddesses were destroyed or turned into churches, and other traditions deemed idolatrous, such as the ancient writing system of the Maya people of Central America, were abolished. Devoted missionaries preached to New World peoples demoralized by conquest and disease, and encouraged cults of local saints, both Spanish and indigenous. Towns were centers of Christianity from the start, and more gradually, missionaries, soldiers, and landowners enforced it in the villages as well.

As in Europe, many traditional beliefs and practices survived in more or less Christian guise, especially in the countryside. But from now on, the accepted, respectable, and official religion of Spain's New World empire was Catholic Christianity, just as its accepted, respectable, and official language and culture were Spanish. On the ruins of the indigenous civilizations, a variant of Western civilization grew up that has flourished down to the present day.

The exploitation of empire took a different course in the Caribbean islands and in the Portuguese territory of Brazil. These regions were thinly populated, and the Native Americans quickly succumbed to the maltreatment and disease of the invaders. They were replaced, over time, by millions of Africans brought to the Western Hemisphere as slaves, and for that reason, their history is closely linked with that of Africa.

 **An Ambassador's Report: The Costs of Wealth from the Indies** Read an account of how the Spanish profited in New Spain

Spanish Colonial Art from the Denver Art Museum (http://www.denverartmuseum.org/explore_art/collections/collectionTypeId—90) See how the Christian art of Spain was transformed in the Americas.

> *"The Europeans held no massive advantage that would have enabled them, as a handful of newcomers, to undermine the Asian civilizations."*

 A Dominican Voice in the Wilderness: Preaching Against Tyranny in Hispaniola Read how a missionary urged the Spanish to halt the mistreatment of Caribbean peoples.

viceroy
In the Spanish colonies of the Americas, a high-ranking official who governed as a "stand-in for the king."

Asia: The Limits of European Power

While the impact of the Europeans in the Western Hemisphere was catastrophic, in Asia it was at first hardly noticeable. The reason, once again, was that the peoples of Asia and Europe belonged to the same group of civilizations. The Europeans had most of their knowledge and skills, and even their diseases, in common with the peoples they encountered; in fact, the wealth of India and the statecraft of China, for example, were superior to their own. Thus, the Europeans held no massive advantage that would have enabled them, as a handful of newcomers, to undermine the Asian civilizations. Apart from the Spaniards in the Philippines, Europeans were unable to conquer and Christianize any Asian territories other than their tiny commercial footholds.

Missionaries like the Jesuit father (pp. 321-322) Francis Xavier traveled incredible distances and learned many languages to preach the gospel throughout the Indies. But without the help of conquering armies, cultural shock, and deadly diseases as in the New World, the success of Christianity depended on whether the local rulers tolerated, accepted, or rejected it.

China and Japan

At first, many rulers tolerated Christianity, partly because the missionaries also brought new technology and science in an era when Europe was, for the first time, gaining an edge in these fields over the other Old World civilizations. But as in pagan Rome (p. 134), Christianity rejected practices on which the rulers and the people believed that the good order of the state, society, and the universe depended—such as the honor due to Hindu gods and goddesses, the veneration of the Chinese and Japanese emperors as divine, and the Chinese practice of ancestor worship.

Around 1600, the Japanese rulers began systematic persecution in regions where Christianity had taken hold, and soon drove the new religion deep underground. Meanwhile, Jesuits in China convinced themselves that reverence for ancestors and the emperor were not the same as worshiping them as divine, so that converts need not give up these basic traditions of Chinese civilization. But early in the eighteenth century, the papacy rejected the Jesuit compromise, and the Chinese government responded by banning Christianity. In both China and Japan, every other kind of European activity was also strictly controlled—a sure sign that the rulers took the Europeans seriously as a potential source of disruption. It was not until the nineteenth century that

Western countries became strong enough to force the rulers to change their policies (pp. 462–463).

Africa and the Slave Trade

In the last major area of the world where the Europeans were newcomers, Africa south of the Sahara, they also encountered civilizations and cultures that they could not destroy. In West Africa, powerful Islamic states had existed for centuries, and at the time of the arrival of the Europeans, central and southern Africa were also advancing in prosperity and sophistication.

Stable governments and powerful tribal chiefdoms, centered on permanent capital cities like Timbuktu in western Africa or Zimbabwe in the southeast, were an increasingly common feature of the region. Iron, horses, and of course Old World diseases were more or less familiar throughout most of Africa. Even with their firearms, when Europeans tried to conquer black African nations, they were generally defeated. Thus, they had to treat the rulers of the region as partners to be dealt with on the basis of mutual interest, rather than as victims to be destroyed.

Above all, this mutual interest lay in trade. Black African rulers had traditionally built their power partly on the control of those resources of their region that were most highly valued in the outside world, namely, gold, ivory, and slaves. European traders had originally been attracted to Africa, above all, by the lure of gold, but following Venice's example, they soon began buying slaves to work on sugar plantations—in this case, located in various newfound islands of the Atlantic.

 The African Slave Trade Make choices and experience consequences in this simulation about life in Africa during the fifteenth century.

Then, in the sixteenth century, the rulers of the new European empires in the Americas turned from plunder to developing new sources of wealth. In Brazil, the Caribbean, and North America, there was land suitable for growing not only sugar but also other profitable crops like tobacco, coffee, and later cotton; but there were few indigenous inhabitants who could be compelled to grow them. However, all along the Atlantic coast of Africa were densely populated regions with rulers who continually fought for control of the region's resources.

The result was the appearance of the most massive and systematic traffic in human beings that the world had ever seen: the African slave trade (Map 15.2). Between 1523, when the first Africans were shipped across the Atlantic, and the 1880s, when the trade finally came to an end, at least 12 million people were transported from Africa to the Americas.

This was also the most systematically brutal of all forms of slavery. Captured by enemy warriors in the course of plundering their villages, the victims—mostly young men, though young women were also taken—were marched down to the nearest coastal trading station and sold to European (mainly Portuguese, English, and Dutch) dealers. They were packed lying on their backs into the holds of the slave ships for a voyage of many weeks: at least one in six could expect to die on the way. Once arrived and sold to a plantation owner, another one in three could expect to be dead of overwork and underfeeding within three years. But that did not matter to the owners. Until competition among traders drove up the price in the late eighteenth century, new slaves could always be bought cheaply from the African suppliers.

 An Eyewitness Describes the Slave Trade in Guinea Read a Dutch captain's account of the slave trade on African soil.

 An African Slave Relates His First Impressions upon Boarding a Slave Ship Read an African's account of conditions on a slave ship.

The Impact of the Slave Trade

For Africa, the result of the slave trade was a debilitating loss of human resources. Many other warlike and rapidly advancing societies, including that of medieval Europe (p. 195), had profited by selling captives to foreigners as slaves. But to do so on such a vast scale helped bring to an end several centuries of social and political development in black Africa. For the Americas, the result was a corresponding gain, especially from the late eighteenth century, when the African survival rate began to rise. In the end, a distinctively African element emerged in the culture of many nations from Brazil to the United States.

For the western European countries that ran the slave trade, the result was enormous profits that helped make them the economic center of the world. In addition, the unchecked exploitation of Africans led to the growth of the belief in white racial superiority and the related feeling that the rest of the world was at Europe's disposal to do with as it wished. It was these notions that helped fuel the intensive imperialism of the nineteenth and twentieth centuries (p. 459).

> "Between 1523, when the first Africans were shipped across the Atlantic, and the 1880s, when the trade finally came to an end, at least 12 million people were transported from Africa to the Americas."

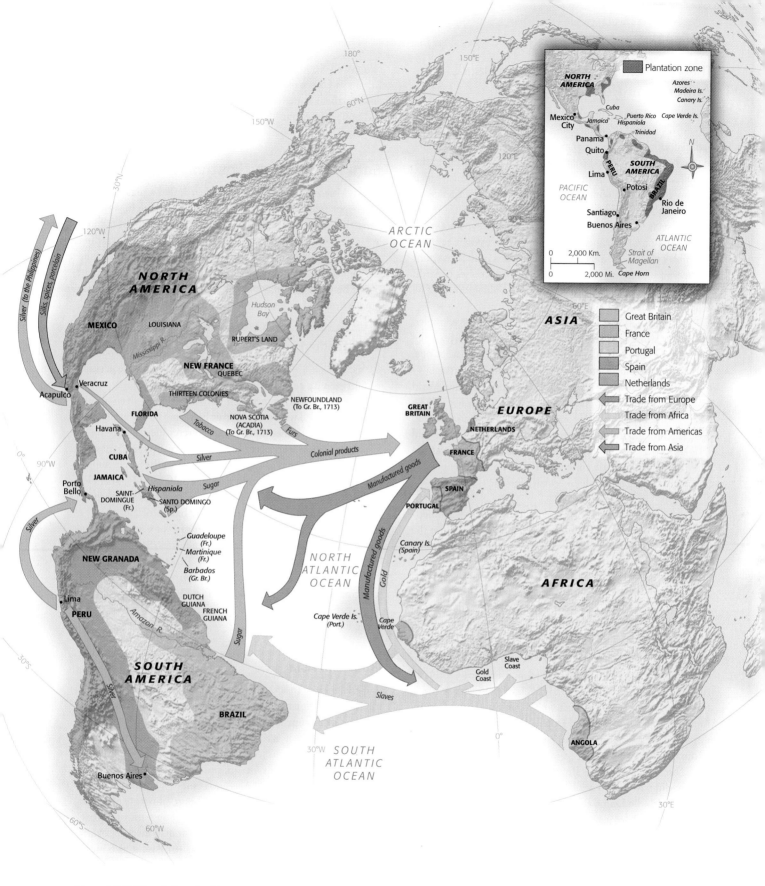

Map 15.2 **The Atlantic Economy about 1750**

A far-flung trading system has grown up across the western ocean. The system has three main components: the trade in sugar and tobacco from plantations in the eastern coastlands and islands of the Americas to Europe; the trade in slaves from western Africa to the Americas to work the plantations; and the trade in manufactured luxuries and necessities from Europe to the Americas and Africa in exchange for sugar, tobacco, and slaves. © Cengage Learning

Interactive Map

The New Empire Builders: England, France, and Holland

As soon as news of Columbus's and Vasco's successes arrived in Europe, the rulers, nobles, and merchants of the ambitious national monarchies of England and France began scheming to join in the search for a route to the Indies. Later on, in the second half of the sixteenth century, most of the Spanish-ruled territory of the Low Countries rebelled and won its independence (p. 324). The new state, commonly known as Holland (from the name of its largest province), became the most dynamic commercial nation of Europe. For most of the sixteenth century, the efforts of these powerful seagoing nations of northwestern Europe were overshadowed by the fabulous successes of Spain and Portugal. But three such competitors could not forever be kept on the sidelines.

Around 1600, the English, French, and Dutch redoubled their efforts to gain a share of world trade and empire. They explored the coastlines of North America and northern Europe, vainly searching for a "northwest" and "northeast passage"—routes to the Indies that would bypass the regions of the world controlled by Portugal and Spain, in the same way as those countries had bypassed Venice and Islam. (Though such routes do exist, they are too icebound to have been used by sixteenth- and seventeenth-century ships.) More successfully, the northwestern countries began to settle colonists in areas not yet occupied by Spain and Portugal, mainly in North America.

Europe's Worldwide Wars

In addition, the new competitors began to encroach on the trade and territories held by the Spanish and Portuguese themselves. An era of "world wars" began, in which European armies and navies fought for control of distant overseas lands (Map 15.3).

By the end of the seventeenth century, England, France, and the Netherlands had successfully stepped into the inheritance of Portugal and Spain. They dominated the trade of East Asia, and most of Portugal's possessions there were now in the hands of the Dutch or the English. They had taken over many Caribbean islands, and Dutch ships carried much of the overseas trade of the Portuguese and Spanish empires in South and Central America. English, French, and Dutch colonies in North America were thriving, with those of the English already harboring tens of thousands of settlers.

The three newcomers struggled as fiercely with each other as they did with Spain and Portugal. During the eighteenth century, with the Dutch exhausted by wars within Europe, the overseas struggle narrowed to one between France and Britain (the union formed by England and Scotland in 1707; p. 344). Every major eighteenth-century war, including those of the American and French Revolutions, was part of a worldwide conflict between these two most powerful western European nations. By 1800, in spite of the loss of its American colonies, Britain had come off best. It had won the position it was to keep down to the twentieth century, as the world's leading commercial and imperial nation.

Europe's Eastern Frontier

When Vasco da Gama first arrived in India, a messenger he sent ashore told local Arab merchants: "We came in search of Christians and spices"—in search of allies in Christendom's struggle with Islam as well as of intercontinental trading wealth. The explorers never found those religious allies, but all the same, by 1700 their efforts had helped shift the balance of power between Christendom and Islam, and Europe had broken out eastward on its land frontier as well as westward overseas.

Christendom and Islam

As a result of Spain's conquest and conversion of the peoples of the New World, the position of Christianity among the world's religions was transformed. After many centuries in which Christianity had been almost entirely confined within the narrow limits of Europe, it replaced Islam as the world's farthest-flung intercontinental religion.

In addition, the silver mines of Peru financed massive Spanish armies, navies, and subsidies to allies that helped Christendom against Islam in Europe itself. In 1571, Spain led an alliance of Christian seagoing states of the Mediterranean that defeated a Turkish fleet at the battle of Lepanto on Greece's western coast, ending a century of Ottoman naval domination of the Mediterranean. Likewise, Spanish money and troops stiffened resistance to the Turks in central Europe by the Austrian branch of the Habsburg dynasty to which the Spanish kings also belonged (p. 267). After 1600, the Ottomans pushed no farther into Europe, and by 1700, they were losing ground.

Russia in Asia

Farther north, the Russian tsars pursued their own Christian imperial mission (p. 252). In the sixteenth century, they conquered their Muslim former overlords, the Tartars, who lived on the borders of Europe and Asia. The vast eastward wilderness of Siberia, with a tiny indigenous population, was now open to Russian fur traders and settlers. By 1700, the tsar's rule stretched all the way to the Pacific Ocean, and Russians would soon enter the New World by way of Alaska. Together with contemporary conquests by the powerful Qing (Ching) emperors of China, the Russian advance brought to an end thousands of years of nomad domination of the steppes and nomad invasions of the settled peoples of Europe and Asia (p. 20). And it also meant that yet another huge region of the world formed part of a European empire.

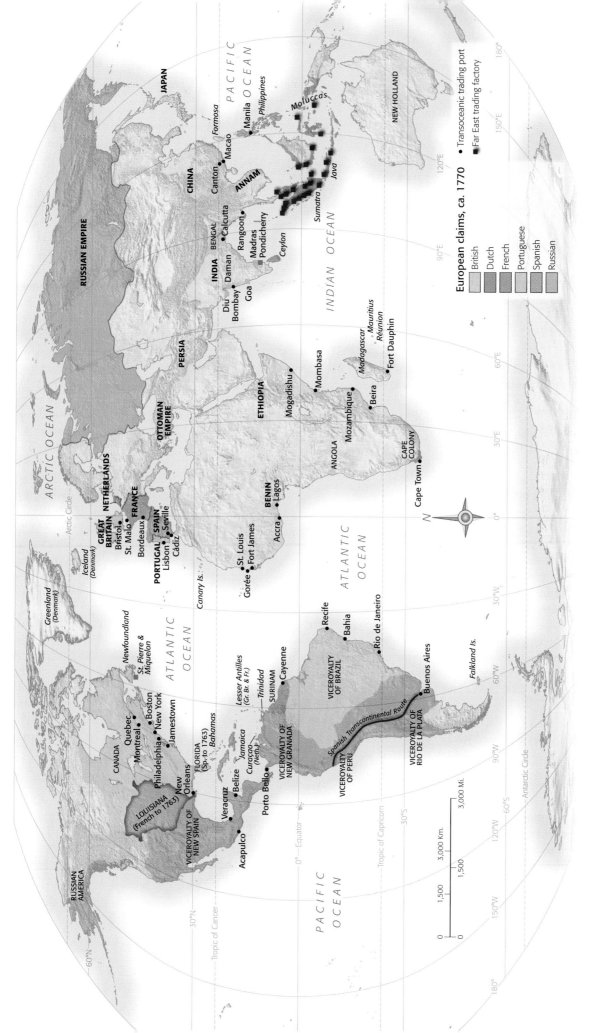

Map 15.3 Worldwide Trade and Empire About 1770

Three centuries after Columbus, European rule has spread through the Americas, Russia stretches eastward to Alaska, European trading footholds dot the coasts of Africa and Asia, and Britain has replaced Spain as the leading worldwide power. Soon there will be drastic changes in this global pattern centered on Europe: independence in the Americas, imperialistic conquest in the interior of Africa and Asia, and new centers of trade and empire in North America and East Asia. © Cengage Learning

Interactive Map

European claims, ca. 1770

- British
- Dutch
- French
- Portuguese
- Spanish
- Russian

• Transoceanic trading port
■ Far East trading factory

The World's Impact on Europe

The growth of worldwide trade and empire was one of the main forces that remade Europe into the modern West—not only because it spread European power and influence around the world, but also because of its effect on the economy, the power structure, and the outlook of Europe itself.

The Columbian Exchange

Partly this was a result of the worldwide movement of plants, animals, diseases, and people between the New and Old Worlds, which brought many changes to Europe. Sugar, a rare luxury in the Middle Ages, was an everyday item by 1700, after this Old World crop, and the slave-worked plantation system of cultivating it, had been established in the New World. By 1800, European peasants had taken to growing corn and potatoes—New World crops that were hardier and produced larger harvests than wheat and rye—and the population was growing faster than before. And this was only part of a worldwide process—the **Columbian Exchange**, as it is called today, because it began with Columbus's voyages. By 1800, for instance, "golden apples" had become a daily food in Italy and "fruit of Paradise" were common in central and eastern Europe, while in Iran people were eating "foreign plums" and in China, "barbarian eggplants"—all of them local names for another New World crop, tomatoes.

Europe and Worldwide Capitalism

In addition, as worldwide trade increased, profits accumulated; and the huge investments required for long voyages and colonial ventures brought handsome gains to bankers and capitalists. The flow of gold and silver from the New World stimulated general business activity. By 1600, the volume of money in existence in Europe had risen to nearly $1 billion (in today's terms). This larger supply of coins promoted trade and strengthened the incentive of all classes to produce for the market, and it also made for price inflation.

This, in turn, gave an added push to business, for merchants and investors are eager to buy goods and properties when they see that prices are moving upward.

Furthermore, as Britain, France, and Holland became the main trading gateways between Europe and the rest of the world, the center of prosperity and power shifted from Italy to northwestern Europe. Venice, Florence, and Milan were still wealthy trading cities, but Antwerp, Amsterdam, and London became the leading financial centers of expanding world commerce, and they took over as the leaders in the development of banking and capitalism. These cities had the first organized "money markets" in which large private and government loans were arranged. Exchange houses arose there for trade and speculation in commodities, currencies, bonds, and stocks. Stocks began to appear in the seventeenth century with the creation of **joint-stock companies**, the forerunners of the modern corporation; these companies made it possible to raise large sums of capital for long-term investment (see photo on page 257). Though limited at first to trading ventures, joint-stock companies were later formed in the mining and manufacturing industries.

The triumph of capitalism was assured by the acceleration of trade and production. The wealth of Europe mounted steadily, and the variety and quantity of goods increased with every day. New products and habits, formerly unknown in Europe, were introduced from both America and Asia. Oriental furnishings and exotic art objects began to appear in the homes of the privileged classes. Chinaware, tea, coffee, chocolate, and citrus fruits became necessities for middle-class people. And tobacco, rum, and eventually potatoes, tomatoes, and corn were consumed by peasants and workers as well.

In these ways, Europe, whose people made up a tiny fraction of humanity, became the headquarters of a worldwide system of trade, travel, and finance and was in a position to seize and exploit vast areas of the globe. In no other period of history has a major cultural group enjoyed so favorable a ratio between its population and its available resources. Although the Europeans were to squander this advantage on endless wars, it served to lift their standard of living and their sense of power.

> *"In no other period of history has a major cultural group enjoyed so favorable a ratio between its population and its available resources."*

Europe's New Self-Confidence

In addition, the growth of Europe's worldwide power increased its self-confidence against the other peoples of the world. Medieval Christendom had been sure of possessing the one truth about the one God, but it had been surrounded by peoples whose worldly skill, knowledge, and power were greater than its own. Now, Europe had not only spread its religion far and wide but had outdone the rest of the world in these nonreligious respects as well. For that matter, it had also outdone in worldly skill, knowledge, and power the non-Christian peoples of the past to whom even Christians had been accustomed to look upon with awe—the Greeks and Romans. This was not the first time that a people had felt itself superior to other peoples of the past and present, but it was the first time that this had happened on a worldwide scale.

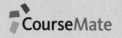 Listen to a synopsis of Chapter 15.

CHAPTER 16

REVIVING THE PAST AND CHANGING THE PRESENT: THE RENAISSANCE, 1300–1600

LEARNING OBJECTIVES

AFTER READING THIS CHAPTER, YOU SHOULD BE ABLE TO DO THE FOLLOWING:

LO¹ Describe how Renaissance humanism offered a new set of values based on ancient models.

LO² Discuss how humanist ideals and the ancient past shaped the visual arts of the Renaissance.

LO³ Explain how humanist ideas were spread to a larger audience through vernacular literature.

"THE BEST OF RENAISSANCE LITERATURE AND ART PROVIDES AN IDEAL OF BEAUTY AND AN UNDERSTANDING OF THE HUMAN CONDITION THAT WILL NEVER CEASE TO CONSOLE AND INSPIRE."

From about 1300 onward, scholars, thinkers, writers, and artists began taking to a new level the existing medieval habit of borrowing ideas and knowledge from ancient Greece and Rome. This endeavor began in Italy, but by 1600 most of the educated elite of western Europe had come to share in it. To those who took part in the endeavor, it seemed so exciting that they came to speak of literature, thought, and the arts as having been "reborn," and today we still call the movement by the French word for "rebirth"—the **Renaissance.**

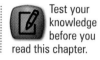

Test your knowledge before you read this chapter.

The Renaissance involved far more than simply resurrecting the past, however, for there was no way that the admirers of Greece and Rome could separate themselves from the living civilization of their own day and age—the Western Christendom that had grown up in the Middle Ages. The Renaissance, in fact, was an encounter between Western Christendom and the Greek and Roman past—an encounter that brought about an extraordinarily diverse cultural achievement.

Renaissance scholars rediscovered the ancient ideal of the fully developed human being whose character was formed by literary study and education, and traders and bankers, lords and ladies, and even popes and bishops tried to live up to this ideal. Thinkers looked for an ultimate truth that would reconcile the pagan wisdom of Greece and Rome with Christian faith, and sought to renew Christianity by bringing it back to its roots in the ancient world. Painters and sculptors used and improved on the methods of ancient artists to make saints and angels come alive before believers' eyes. Writers longed to "equal or surpass the ancients" in the beauty of their Latin style, but they wrote just as eloquently in French, English, and many other native languages of Europe. And most often, what they wrote about was the life and characters of their own or recent times—the hypocrisy and

What do you think?

The artists and thinkers of the Renaissance have had greater influence than any earlier age on the culture of today.

Strongly Disagree						Strongly Agree
1	2	3	4	5	6	7

« Scholars and Thinkers A painting by Domenico Ghirlandaio portrays four renowned leaders of the Renaissance in Florence about 1490. From left: Marsilio Ficino, reviver and adapter of the thought of Plato; Cristoforo Landino, writer on the much-discussed theme of the life of action versus the life of contemplation; Angelo Poliziano, scholar and poet in Greek, Latin, and Italian; Demetrius Chalcondylas, responsible for the first printed edition of Homer's *Iliad* and *Odyssey.*

Renaissance
From the French word for "rebirth," the term for the period beginning around 1300 when scholars, artists, and writers revived and adapted the traditions of the Greco-Roman past.

humanists
From the Latin *humanitas*, the word Renaissance scholars used to define themselves as seekers of human excellence through the study of Latin and Greek works.

virtù
Human excellence, as conceived by Italian humanists.

corruption of monks, for example, or the tragic flaws of an all too thoughtful prince of Denmark.

By reviving and adapting the traditions of the Greco-Roman past, however, the scholars, thinkers, writers, and artists of the Renaissance also changed the traditions of the European present—and thereby contributed in many ways to the remaking of Christian Europe into the modern West. Their efforts to renew Christianity helped bring about both the Protestant Reformation and the reform and reaffirmation of Catholicism. Their rediscovery of ancient mathematical knowledge and military tactics helped make possible the Western revolutions in science and warfare. Their ideals set precedents for basic cultural values of today—belief in the ennobling effect of education, literature, and art on the human personality; respect for unfamiliar ways of life and thought; and distrust of received wisdom and preconceived ideas. And though the writers and artists of the modern West have traveled far from the aims and methods of their Renaissance forerunners, the best of Renaissance literature and art provides an ideal of beauty and an understanding of the human condition that will never cease to console and inspire.

LO¹ The Humanist Enterprise

Throughout the Middle Ages, thinkers, writers, and scholars had looked up to "the ancients," as they called the Greeks and Romans, and had drawn on their achievements. Latin had never ceased to be the international language of Western Christendom, which most literate people knew well. Monks had carefully copied the works of Roman writers, and had sometimes imitated them in works of their own. Scholastic philosophers had leaned heavily on the thought of Aristotle. Dante told of being guided round the other world by Virgil; less high-minded readers had taken pleasure in the how-to poems on seduction of Ovid. But Renaissance scholars undertook to study and imitate the works of the ancients on an unprecedented scale, and actually to revive the way of thinking and living that they found in these works—above all, the values of what today is called *humanism*.

CHRONOLOGY

(time spans are life dates)

1266?–1337	Giotto, pioneering artist of the early Renaissance
1304–1374	Petrarch, poet and pioneer of humanist revival
1313–1375	Boccaccio, author of *Decameron* and humanist scholar
1377?–1446	Brunelleschi, architect and sculptor who revived the building traditions of ancient Rome and developed geometrical rules of perspective
1386?–1466	Donatello, pioneering sculptor of *The Feast of Herod* and statue of Gattamelata
1401–1428?	Masaccio, one of the first painters to apply Brunelleschi's rules of perspective
1440	Lorenzo Valla demonstrates that the Donation of Constantine is a forgery
1450	Cosimo de' Medici founds the Platonic Academy in Florence; scholars include Marsilio Ficino and Pico della Mirandola
1445–1510	Botticelli, Platonist and painter of *The Birth of Venus*
1447–1576	Titian, Venetian painter of *Venus of Urbino*
1452–1519	Leonardo, artist, inventor, and symbol of Renaissance ideal
1466?–1536	Erasmus, author of *In Praise of Folly* and corrected version of New Testament
1475–1564	Michelangelo, painter, sculptor, architect of Renaissance masterpieces
1490–1553	Rabelais, popular satirist whose works were condemned by authorities
1533–1592	Montaigne, influential French essayist and skeptic
1564–1616	Shakespeare, English playwright

The Appeal of Humanism

Cicero, the Roman orator, letter writer, thinker, and statesman (p. 108), had used the word *humanitas* as a shorthand term for the powers of reasoning, creation, and action that distinguish human beings from animals. Such human excellence, he thought, is best nurtured and expressed through literature (including his-

HUMANIST IDEALS APPEALED TO VARIOUS MEMBERS OF SOCIETY:

The Secular Elite

- Kings, nobles, bankers, and city-state despots hoped to imitate the elegance, refinement, and heroic achievements of the elite of Greece and Rome (see photo).

High-Ranking Clergy

- In an era when popes and bishops were also devoted to elegance, refinement, and worldly achievements, they, too, looked up the ancients with a new level of sympathy.

Middle Classes

- Middle-class people who could afford time and leisure for study had the satisfaction of feeling that their human excellence put them on a level with kings, nobles, bankers, despots, and bishops.

tory, philosophy, and oratory). Renaissance scholars, following Cicero's lead, took ancient Latin and Greek literature as a guide to human excellence, and accordingly, they described themselves as **humanists**.

This ideal of human excellence—*virtù*, as the Italian humanists called it—was generally earnest, high-minded, and optimistic about human nature. It overlapped with some traditional values of the Middle Ages, for example the ideal of the chivalrous warrior, but it ran counter to the ideal of the saintly ascetic and to the Christian view of the human race as utterly sinful and dependent on divine mercy. The new ideal certainly did not drive out the traditional ones. Many people rejected humanist values, and many people "compartmentalized," living as both humble and repentant Christians and self-confident imitators of the ancients.

In many ways, too, the urge to revive the ancients actually worked together with the urge to reinvigorate Christianity. Italian humanists often sought to combine Christian belief with ancient

(above, center) **The Triumph of Fame** The Florentine painter Giovanni Lo Scheggia depicts Fame as a living ancient Roman statue, greeted by horsemen in fifteenth-century war gear as trumpets sound fanfares in all directions. The scene appears on a birth tray—a souvenir tray presented by the father to the mother of the newborn Lorenzo de' Medici (p. 263) in 1449. It symbolizes his parents' Renaissance hope that he will gain fame, the reward of human excellence, as timeless and worldwide as that of the ancients. Image copyright © The Metropolitan Museum of Art/Art Resource, NY

ideals; humanists in other countries looked back to early Christianity, which had developed in the world of ancient Greece and Rome, as a model to which the Christianity of their own time should return. And artists throughout Europe used the lifelike methods of ancient art to give a new reality to the holy events and holy people they depicted. In these ways, humanist ideals helped bring change to Christianity—though they also sometimes acted as a substitute for it.

The Pioneers: Petrarch and Boccaccio

Humanism began in Italy in the fourteenth century—a land where trade, industry, finance, and city life were more highly developed than anywhere else in Europe, but also a land that felt keenly the problems and disasters of the late Middle Ages. The country was torn apart by the conflict between the Holy Roman emperors and the papacy; the popes themselves abandoned Rome, and when they returned, they were challenged by rival popes in France; factional rivalries and class conflicts made city-states almost ungovernable; and a quarter of the population was carried off by the Black Death.

What a difference from the days when the Roman ancestors of the Italians had ruled a vast empire as mighty warriors and self-sacrificing citizens, inspired to virtue and wisdom by splendidly eloquent thinkers, poets, and orators! Of course, Rome had also had plenty of corrupt rulers, class conflicts, epidemic diseases, and civil wars—and it had fallen in the end, as its ruined buildings in countless Italian cities testified. But in this dark time for medieval Italy, the thought of Rome's fall only made Italians more nostalgic for the bright side of the ancient past and more eager to revive its glories.

Petrarch

Francesco Petrarca (Petrarch) (PEE-trahrk), the pioneer of the humanist revival of the past, was born in 1304 in an exiled Florentine family. Urged by his father to study law, he turned instead to a life of reading and writing, and eventually came upon some of Cicero's works. Surely, Petrarch thought, the pagan Cicero, with his eloquence, wisdom, and commitment to public life, was a better guide to human excellence than the Christian thinkers of his time, the schoolmen (p. 235), arguing in the universities over trivial details in pedantic technical Latin. Inspired by his encounter with Cicero, he began a quest to discover the world of ancient Roman authors who had been neglected, ignored, and forgotten, to imitate their Latin eloquence, and to adopt their values.

Letter to Posterity: Petrarch Writes His Autobiography Read Petrarch's account of how he became a humanist.

Petrarch undertook a search for manuscripts in monastic and cathedral libraries all over Italy and in France and Germany as well. He arranged for the works he found to be copied, and built up his own collection of ancient works. His private library, the first of its kind, became a model for humanist scholars and well-to-do people who sympathized with their aims. Later humanists continued his search, so that by 1500 almost all the surviving ancient Roman works had been recovered—and were more widely available than ever before, thanks to printing.

In his own life, too, Petrarch identified with the ancients. Though he was a busy man and spent much of his time in cities and at the courts of aristocrats, he

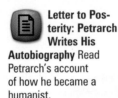

"*The greatest kings of this age have loved and courted me. They may know why; I certainly do not.*"

—Petrarch, from his *Letter to Posterity*

expressed a love of solitude and the peace of nature. But this was a different solitude from that of the hermit; it was closer to the model of the statesman and scholar Cicero. Petrarch spent his private hours not meditating and praying but studying literature; for isolation without books, he declared, was "exile, prison, and torture." And he took the ancient works he studied as models for his own works, writing poems, dialogues, and letters in Latin patterned after the style of Cicero and Virgil.

Yet Petrarch also carried on many traditions of the medieval world in which he lived. When he was growing up, Dante was still writing the *Divine Comedy*, and in some ways, Petrarch continued where Dante left off. He, too, wrote in Italian, most notably his love poems to Laura, a beautiful young married woman whom he idealized in the tradition of medieval courtly love, just as Dante had idealized Beatrice (p. 240). And Petrarch

was a devout Catholic, who firmly believed that love of the ancients and Christian faith belonged together. Among his beloved ancient writers was the early Christian thinker Augustine (p. 143)—who Petrarch claimed had been inspired to one of his great statements of Christian faith by reading Cicero. Nearly a thousand years before, another early Christian, Jerome, had believed himself to face a choice between being a Christian and a "Ciceronian." For Petrarch, a Ciceronian was actually the best kind of Christian.

Boccaccio

One of Petrarch's fourteenth-century followers, Giovanni Boccaccio (boh-KAH-chee-oh), the son of a Florentine banker, also wrote Italian works that carried on medieval traditions. In his case, the traditions were the less high-minded kind that originated in fabliaux and Goliard poetry (pp. 237, 239). The characters in *The Decameron*, Boccaccio's best-known work, tell tales borrowed from various countries of Europe and the Islamic world, involving sensual escapades, deceits, and clever revenges.

But Boccaccio was also an earnest humanist scholar, who searched far and wide for ancient manuscripts like Petrarch. Among his prized discoveries was a work of the Roman historian Tacitus (p. 108), which he uncovered in the monastery library at Monte Cassino. When he first saw the neglected condition of the archives there, he burst into tears. And going beyond Petrarch, he also learned ancient Greek—a language only a few western European scholars had studied since Roman times. To be "learned in both languages" (Latin and Greek) remained an unusual accomplishment, but enough humanist scholars followed Boccaccio's example for most surviving ancient Greek works to be available in print by 1500.

Boccaccio also wrote in Latin—most notably, two collections of short biographies intended to provide edifying examples of virtue and vice, *On Famous Men* and *On Famous Women*. Collections of this kind dated back to ancient times, but Boccaccio was the first to write one dealing with women. His collection ran from Eve, through figures of ancient history and myth, to Queen Joan of Naples, a powerful fourteenth-century ruler. In this way, he put important women of his own time on the same level of extraordinary virtue and vice as those of the ancient past—and putting important people of the late Middle Ages on the same level as the ancients was one of humanism's main attractions.

Renaissance Ladies and Gentlemen

Petrarch's and Boccaccio's high valuation of ancient eloquence and virtue won them fame in their own time and soon spread through Italy, evidently because it answered a widely felt need.

By the early fifteenth century, leading Italian humanist scholars were celebrities, greeted by eager devotees of the revived ancient lore as they journeyed from town to town, and rewarded with influential positions as tutors to noble children and professors of rhetoric at universities.

Guarino da Verona and Vittorino da Feltre

One of the most notable humanist academics was Guarino da Verona, who studied Greek in Constantinople and was eventually appointed to the University of Ferrara, not far from Venice. His lectures drew enthusiastic students from all over Italy and the rest of Western Christendom—among them a pioneer of humanist education below the university level, Vittorino da Feltre.

In Mantua, another town near Venice, with the support of the local feudal lord, Vittorino opened a boarding school for boys that was so renowned for its kind treatment of students and its individual attention to their development that it was known as the "Pleasant House." Study of ancient authors and instruction in Latin eloquence were balanced by training in music and athletics. The students came from poor as well as wealthy families, and Vittorino aimed to turn them into young men who were mentally and physically able to live a life of fruitful citizenship inspired by wisdom and virtue, like the revered Roman and Greek ancients. But this ideal was combined with traditional Christian piety: Vittorino's students attended daily prayer services and regularly went to Mass.

> "*Battista and Federico were examples of a powerful new Renaissance ideal—the active, responsible, learned, elegant, and Christian lady and gentleman.*"

member of a brotherhood of noble warriors founded by a fourteenth-century king of England and inspired by medieval tales of King Arthur and his knights—as well as a builder of elegant palaces in the latest, Roman-influenced architectural style. And he often stopped by a convent in the town of Urbino to hold uplifting religious discussions with the nuns.

His duchess, Battista Sforza (from the ruling family of Milan, p. 263), also combined eloquence and action. At the age of sixteen, she delivered a public speech in Latin before Pope Pius II, and the pope, who was himself a leading humanist scholar, found her performance "most elegant." And a neighboring lord who was Federico's enemy complained of how good she was at running the dukedom in her husband's absence: "This woman definitely has too much wisdom and foresight—enough to rule the kingdom of France!" Battista and Federico were examples of a powerful new Renaissance ideal—the active, responsible, learned, elegant, and Christian lady and gentleman.

Like all ideals, this one was hard to put into practice. Duke Federico could sometimes be very ungentlemanly—for instance, when he gave underhand support to an abortive plot to murder the ruler of Florence, Lorenzo de' Medici. Not that he had anything personal against Lorenzo, but in the political situation in Italy at the time, the Florentine despot's elimination seemed a sound business move. On a less sinister level, Baldassare Castiglione, a nobleman whose book *The Courtier*, published

Duke Federico and Duchess Battista

Among Vittorino's students was a noble boy, Federico da Montefeltro, who went on to become duke of Urbino, near Florence, from the 1440s to the 1480s (see photo). Duke Federico was a battle-winning condottiere (p. 263) and a splendid Latin orator, a careful administrator of his dukedom and a collector of a huge library of ancient and medieval learning. He was a Knight of the Garter—a

>> **Battista Sforza and Federico da Montefeltro** Renaissance portraits of married couples generally put the husband "first"—on the viewer's left—and the wife "second"—on the right. But in this portrait from about 1470 by the Florentine painter Piero della Francesca, the order is reversed. Otherwise, the right side of Federico's face would be visible, and Piero would have had to falsify the portrait by painting in Federico's missing right eye, poked out by an opponent's lance in a tournament in his youth.
Scala/Ministero per i Beni e le Attività culturali/Art Resource, NY

in 1528, became the standard work on how to live the gentlemanly and ladylike ideal, found it necessary to warn courtiers who attended banquets not to start food fights. But the ideal's widespread appeal, to middle-class women and men as well as to nobles, guaranteed it a long future.

Humanist Thought: Back to Plato

Now that humanist scholars had direct access to ancient Greek thought, they began to pay attention to other philosophers besides Aristotle—most notably, to Plato (pp. 73–76). Aristotle still ruled in the universities because his methods of logic were so useful to scholastic thinkers. But ever since Petrarch, humanists had despised the schoolmen as quibblers without real wisdom, and besides, Plato had a quality that humanists deeply admired and Aristotle definitely lacked—eloquence. Here was philosophy that was at the same time literature and literature that was philosophy. For the humanists, Plato became the new master.

The New "Academy"

Florence was the leading center for Platonic studies. Cosimo de' Medici, yet another learned Renaissance ruler, founded the Platonic Academy there about 1450. The Academy served as a center for the translation of Plato's writings and discussions of his philosophy. Named after Plato's own circle of disciples, it consisted of only a few select scholars, subsidized by the Medici, and their circle of friends. Yet, the influence of the Academy was widely felt—in art, in literature, in science, and in the Renaissance undertaking of reconciling Christianity with pagan wisdom.

 Nicolo Nicoli: A Humanist's Passion for the Classics Read about the humanist Nicolo Nicoli, friend of Cosimo de' Medici.

Marsilio Ficino was the shining light of the Academy (see photo on page 286). Chosen by Cosimo at an early age, he was carefully educated and then installed in a villa in the hills near Florence. From that time until his death, he devoted himself to translating Plato's writings and explaining his doctrines. He presided over polite seminars at the villa and corresponded with notables all over Europe, seeking to demonstrate that Platonic teachings were in agreement with Christianity.

Pico della Mirandola, a disciple of Ficino, went beyond his master and attempted a synthesis (a bringing together) of all learning. This genius of the age knew Arabic and Hebrew as well as Greek and Latin, and he studied Jewish, Babylonian, and Persian writings. He refused to ignore any source of truth merely because it was not labeled "Christian," and he emphasized human freedom and capacity for learning.

> "For the humanists, Plato became the new master."

All the same, he believed, like Plato, that humans had become separated from their divine home of pure spirit by some accident of prehistory. Though each soul (spirit) had fallen prisoner to matter (the body), it struggled for liberation and a return to God. This view corresponded to the Christian doctrine of the Fall and the human longing for salvation.

 **A Renaissance Oration on Human Dignity (Mirandola)** Read Mirandola on human nature.

Platonism, Art, and Science

Platonic beliefs also deeply influenced Renaissance art. The feeling for natural beauty, said the Platonists, came from the soul's remembrance of the divine beauty of heaven, and the emotion of physical love was part of a higher urge that moves humans toward the divine source of their being. According to the Florentine intellectuals, art stimulates appreciation of beauty, and love brings the individual closer to the ultimate goal of spiritual reunion with God. Some of the finest Renaissance artists, notably Botticelli and Michelangelo, were absorbed by this idea. And in science, the Platonic notion that the soul may ascend to God by contemplating the visible universe helped inspire the Polish astronomer Nicholas Copernicus to place the sun, which lights the universe, at the center, rather than the earth (p. 358).

Observation and Facts

The manuscripts of ancient writers that Petrarch, Boccaccio, and others collected were the latest of many generations of copies and were liable to contain many generations of copying errors—the results of slips of the pen or of misunderstandings of their meaning. With their deep knowledge of the ancient languages and cultures, humanists were often able to correct these errors and arrive at texts that were closer to what the ancient authors had originally written. This, as well as their rejection of scholasticism, with its system of knowledge based on authority and reason, led them to a more critical attitude toward the written word and greater attention to observed facts. Eventually, many later thinkers came to look for truth by observation, as well as by the related method of experiment (p. 360).

> "Whatever seeds each man cultivates will grow to maturity and bear in him their own fruit."
>
> —Pico della Mirandola from "Oration on the Dignity of Man"

Lorenzo Valla

One of the most notable triumphs of humanist knowledge of ancient languages and cultures was Lorenzo Valla's demonstration in 1440 that the Donation of Constantine was a forgery. This document, according to which the fourth-century Roman emperor Constantine handed over vast powers to Pope Sylvester before leaving Rome to build a new capital at Byzantium, had served for centuries as a basis for papal claims to secular supremacy over the West. Valla showed, however, that the Latin language of the Donation could not have been that of the fourth century but was more likely that of the eighth or ninth century. Furthermore, the document did not square with Valla's humanist knowledge of the period when it was supposed to have been issued. For instance, Constantine declares that the pope shall have supremacy over all "patriarchs," including the one at "Constantinople." How could this be, asked Valla, when at that time, Constantinople was not yet a city and had no patriarch?

Valla had no intention of attacking the religious claims of the popes as rulers of the Church, and Pope Nicholas V—himself a humanist, who founded the Vatican Library as a depository for ancient manuscripts—thought so highly of Valla that he brought him to Rome to translate the ancient Greek historian Thucydides into Latin (p. 71). Still, his exposé stirred a good deal of indignant disagreement. As late as the 1520s, Pope Leo X took the donation as genuine and had his private apartment decorated with a scene of the emperor humbly kneeling before the pope as he made his donation (see photo on page 142). But then Protestants started using Valla's work as ammunition against the papacy, and soon Catholics, too, accepted that it was false.

> *"And for what, after all, do men petition the saints except for foolish things?"*
> —from Erasmus, *In Praise of Folly*

Machiavelli and Leonardo da Vinci

The method of judging the genuineness of a document by the test of known facts had many other applications. Niccolò Machiavelli, basing his view of government and the state on recorded history and personal experience (pp. 265–267), used essentially the same method. So did the painter Leonardo da Vinci, who improved his skill in drawing human and animal bodies by dissecting cadavers and making on-the-spot sketches and comments in notebooks. He found dissection difficult and distasteful, but he insisted that observation was the only means to true knowledge. He also experimented with mechanics and drew up plans for ingenious practical inventions. A man of his times, Leonardo both typified Italian humanism and foreshadowed the age of observation and experiment.

 "Universal Leonardo" (http://www.universalleonardo.org/index.php) Discover the wide-ranging interests and investigations of Leonardo.

Humanism and Christian Practice: Erasmus

From 1400 onward, wealthy and educated people in every country of Western Christendom began to take notice of the Italian revival of the ways of thought and life of the ancients.

Scholars journeyed to the Italian centers of learning to learn eloquence and study Greek; leading Italian humanists became internationally famous and were invited to royal courts; Italian diplomats and representatives of banking firms brought word of the "rebirth" to the countries where they were stationed. By 1500, many countries beyond the Alps were home to humanist scholars who rivaled the Italians.

However, scholasticism was still vigorous in many of these countries, and university faculties often looked with disdain upon the humanist reverence for pagan literature and art. Some Oxford masters condemned humanist studies as "dangerous and damnable"—dangerous, that is, to the proper understanding and practice of Christianity. Devout Italian humanists like Petrarch had argued that ancient wisdom and Christian faith were two sides of the same coin. Less devout Italians had delighted too much in the rediscovered ancient lore to bother with its implications for Christianity at all. But humanists outside Italy, who were more likely to be denounced as un-Christian, threw the charge back at their opponents and claimed that it was they who had distorted Christianity.

The most influential of these humanist religious critics was a Dutchman, Erasmus **(uh-RAZ-muhs)** of Rotterdam. Born in 1466, as the out-of-wedlock son of a priest, he went to a school that was supervised by an order of devout laymen, the Brethren of the Common Life. The Brethren offered what seemed to them a purer alternative to traditional practices like devotion to the saints, veneration of their relics, and indulgences (pp. 205–207). These practices had always been open to abuse—by clergy who used them for moneymaking, and by believers who expected from them salvation without real repentance. Instead, the Brethren offered a pious, mystical Christianity, and taught that individual lives should be modeled on the example of Jesus. While subjecting themselves to rigid spiritual discipline, they also emphasized service and love. Erasmus was deeply touched by this early influence, and he adopted the "philosophy of Christ" as his lifetime ideal.

Retrieving Christian Truth

After school, Erasmus entered a monastery, but he soon left and took to the hand-to-mouth life of a wandering scholar. For years, he lived off tutoring jobs and handouts from friends, while he taught himself Greek, studied pagan and Christian ancient authors, and developed a forceful and humorous writing style in Latin—the language of all his books. Finally, he began to make a name for himself as an exceptionally learned humanist, and this gave him the standing to comment on religious and social issues of the time. Thanks to the new technology of printing, his books were bestsellers, and he became famous throughout Europe—deeply admired by some and deeply distrusted by others.

Like Petrarch, Erasmus was sure that true Christianity and pagan wisdom belonged together; in fact, he expressed this idea even more strongly. A character in one of his books invoked the Greek thinker Socrates with the words "Saint Socrates, pray for us!" Earlier Christians had revered Socrates and had even claimed him as a fellow believer because he had been put to death for doubting the pagan gods and goddesses, but no one before Erasmus had ever put an ancient philosopher among the saints. By doing so, Erasmus meant to say that what made a person holy was not by-the-book observance of the traditions and beliefs that had grown up in the Church over the centuries. Instead, it was love of truth and devotion to God—on which baptized Christians did not have a monopoly.

Erasmus did not doubt that the highest truth had been brought by Christ, but he also believed that Christians had forgotten or neglected Christ's message, or hidden it beneath layers of new beliefs and practices—just as the way of living and thinking of the pagan ancients had been forgotten, neglected, or distorted over time. And as with the works of pagan ancients, one way to get back to the original truth of Christianity was to purify its earliest writings of errors that had crept in over the centuries—above all, into the New Testament, which had originally been written in Greek.

Erasmus spent many years preparing a corrected version of the New Testament, which he published in 1516, along with his own Latin translation and commentary. This, he hoped, would lead to a clearer understanding of Christ's message—not only by the learned, but also by the unlearned, who would read or hear the message in translation. "Christ wanted his counsel and his mysteries to be spread around as much as possible," he wrote. "I would like all women to read the gospel . . . and I wish to God it was translated into the languages of all peoples. I wish to God that the plowman would sing a text of scripture at his plow beam, and that with this the weaver at his loom would drive boredom away."

Foolishness in Religion and Society

In addition, Erasmus learned from an ancient writer the use of mockery to drive his message home. He read with delight and translated into Latin the Greek works of Lucian of Samosata (p. 109), who had made a specialty of mocking every kind of pretentiousness and superstition in imperial Rome. Erasmus's most widely read work, *In Praise of Folly* (1509), did the same for the Europe of his own time. He portrayed Folly ironically as an all-powerful goddess, whose worshipers include warriors who think their bloody deeds are glorious, noblemen with nothing to be proud of but their family trees, and believers who pray to the saints to cure their toothaches or find their lost property but never dream of imitating the saints' holy way of life. It is Folly, in fact, who makes the wicked world go round.

 **Pope Julius II Excluded from Heaven (Erasmus)** Read Erasmus's attack on a worldly pope.

Sometimes, Erasmus could be much more explicit, as in an essay inspired by an ancient Roman saying about money-grubbers, "They demand tribute even from the dead":

> You can't be baptized . . . without paying for it. . . .
> They won't bless your marriage unless you pay;

they only hear your confession because they hope to make money from it. . . . They won't communicate the Body of Christ, except for money. . . . Among the pagans . . . there was at least a place where you could bury your dead without having to pay. Among Christians . . . if you have paid a great deal, you may lie and rot in the church in front of the high altar; if you have given stingily, you can be rained on with the common herd outside.

"They" were greedy clergy whom Erasmus accused of turning the salvation-bringing sacraments of the Church into a cradle-to-grave system for extracting money from the Christian faithful. In a thousand years of denunciation of Church corruption, no one had said anything more powerful.

Erasmus was not the only humanist to criticize both Christian practice and the social order. A few years after *In Praise of Folly*, his English friend Sir Thomas More published *Utopia*, a description of an invented island in the western ocean that revived Plato's tradition of imagining an ideal society where the problems of actual ones were all solved (pp. 73–75). The people of Utopia avoid oppression and class conflict by holding no private property; the men and women are educated alike so that all can develop their human excellence to the fullest; and they avoid religious persecution and war by tolerating all beliefs except atheism.

More's book was not a serious blueprint for social and religious change. Its title was a play on the similar-sounding Greek words for "Good place" and "No place," hinting that his description of a good society was pure fiction. Later on, as a high government official when the Protestant Reformation was getting under way, he supported the burning of heretics, and in the end, he laid down his own life rather than swear loyalty to the king as head of the English Church. Likewise, neither the Church nor society was much changed by Erasmus's sharp words. He wanted a purified Church, not a divided one, and when the Reformation started, he was just as critical of Protestant rage and violence as of Catholic greed and superstition.

All the same, Erasmus and More proclaimed a whole series of inspiring ideals—faith combined with toleration, religion cleansed of superstition, truth shared among all classes of society, peaceful achievement more admired than warlike deeds, society itself structured to avoid conflict and oppression. These were ideals by which future generations would come to judge themselves.

LO² The Renaissance in Art: Ancient Models for Modern Needs

In the visual arts, as in literature and thought, the Renaissance began in fourteenth-century Italy—in this case, in response to religious trends of the time. It was an era when clergy were stressing the human side of Christ and the saints, and Gothic sculptors in France had already made statues of saints that showed their emotions and interactions as they took part in holy events of Christian tradition (p. 231). Now it was the turn of Italian artists to make depictions so lifelike that they gave worshipers the feeling of being actual eyewitnesses of holy events, or even participants themselves. And in a land where so many Roman works of art survived, painters and sculptors soon began to turn to the ancient artists for models of lifelike depiction.

"Painting Restored to Life": Giotto

The pioneer of this new trend was the Florentine painter Giotto di Bondone, whose innovations brought him instant success and lasting fame. Prominent citizens, feudal lords, and above all the Franciscan friars, with their urge to involve people deeply in Christian belief and practice (pp. 208–209), ordered his works. Petrarch called Giotto (**JOT-toh**) a "genius," and more than a century later, another humanist scholar, Angelo Poliziano (see photo on page 286), wrote an inscription for his monument in Florence's cathedral: "Lo, I am he by whom dead painting was restored to life, to whose unerring hand all was possible, by whom art became one with nature."

A notable example of Giotto's methods of touching the hearts of worshipers is his *Lamentation* (see photo), one of thirty-seven scenes, mainly from the lives of Christ and the Virgin Mary, that he painted about 1305 on the inside walls of the newly built Arena Chapel in Padua, a town near Venice. The painting shows the Virgin Mary and some of Christ's followers in dramatic attitudes of grief as they mourn over the body of the crucified Savior. They stare into his face as if for a sign of life, touch his hands

> "*Giotto began a practice that generations of Renaissance artists continued—using methods of ancient art to create works that were uniquely their own and belonged to their time.*"

and feet as if they cannot let go of him, and show their grief in other lifelike ways, while the sky above is turbulent with mourning angels. Two of Christ's followers are seen from the back, a favorite device of Giotto's to give the feeling that a scene is really taking place before the viewer's eyes. What also gives this feeling is the clothing of the mourners, which hangs from their bodies in realistic folds, so that they seem solid and weighty although they are painted on a flat surface.

The details of the gestures and the clothing in the *Lamentation* come from Giotto's own imagination. However, he is known to have studied surviving Roman stone coffins with scenes from pagan mythology carved on them, as well as Bible scenes on the walls of churches dating from the time that Rome became Christian. Pagan or Christian, the ancient artists had used dramatic gestures and folds in clothing to depict solid figures expressing real emotions. In this way, Giotto began a practice that generations of Renaissance artists continued—using methods of ancient art to create works that were uniquely their own and belonged to their time.

Surpassing the Ancients: Brunelleschi, Masaccio, Donatello

Early in the fifteenth century, visual artists came under the direct influence of the burgeoning humanist movement—not only in painting, but in architecture and sculpture as well. The highest praise that humanist scholars awarded to a work of literature or art that pleased them was to say that it not only "equaled" but actually "surpassed the ancients." That was what fifteenth-century artists in some ways actually achieved.

Humanist Architecture: Brunelleschi

Among those who did so was a Florentine architect and sculptor, Filippo Brunelleschi (**broon-el-ES-kee**), who revived the building traditions of imperial Rome. In the Santo Spirito (Holy Spirit) Church in Florence (see photo on page 296), the columns and arches do not reach

Alinari/Art Resource, NY

≪ "*Dead Painting Restored to Life*" In his *Lamentation of Christ,* Giotto uses ancient techniques of arranging figures in groups and creating a three-dimensional appearance so as to create an image of overwhelming sorrow. His work also has roots in the medieval past, however—he has found a way to reproduce in two dimensions the naturalism and human interaction of Gothic sculpture (see photo on page 230).

SIR THOMAS MORE ON POWER POLITICS VERSUS GOOD POLICY

In this excerpt, the explorer of the New World island of Utopia (Greek for "No-place" or "Good-place"), Raphael Hythlodaeus ("Good-at-gabbing"), is speaking to More himself, who makes a brief comment at the end. Raphael contrasts the power politics of France with the good policy of Achoria ("Non-country"), a kingdom near Utopia that has given up foreign conquest.

The lands and cities that Raphael mentions to begin with are places in Italy, the Low Countries, and Spain that the French king wants to dominate. The royal advisers' suggestions include giving pensions (regular payments) to captains of German and "Switzer" (Swiss) mercenary soldiers, as well as to courtiers of foreign rulers. Sir Thomas More was an experienced diplomat himself, and his portrayal of French aims and methods is lifelike.

"Do not you think that if I were about any king, proposing good laws to him, and endeavoring to root out all the cursed seeds of evil that I found in him, I should either be turned out of his court or at least be laughed at for my pains? For instance, what could it signify if I were about the King of France, and were called into his Cabinet Council, where several wise men, in his hearing, were proposing many expedients, as by what arts and practices Milan may be kept, and Naples, that had so oft slipped out of their hands, recovered; how the Venetians, and after them the rest of Italy, may be subdued; and then how Flanders, Brabant, and all Burgundy, and some other kingdoms which he has swallowed already in his designs, may be added to his empire. One proposes a league with the Venetians, to be kept as long as he finds his account in it, and that he ought to communicate councils with them, and give them some share of the spoil, till his success makes him need or fear them less, and then it will be easily taken out of their hands. Another proposes the hiring the Germans, and the securing the Switzers by pensions. Another proposes the gaining the Emperor by money, which is omnipotent with him. Another proposes a peace with the King of Aragon, and, in order to cement it, the yielding up the King of Navarre's pretensions. Another thinks the Prince of Castile is to be wrought on, by the hope of an alliance; and that some of his courtiers are to be gained to the French faction by pensions. The hardest point of all is what to do with England: a treaty of peace is to be set on foot, and if their alliance is not to be depended on, yet it is to be made as firm as possible; and they are to be called friends, but suspected as enemies: therefore the Scots are to be kept in readiness, to be let loose upon England on every occasion:

Nicholas Sapieha/Art Resource, NY

upward to a vault as in medieval churches; instead, they march forward under a flat ceiling, on the model of churches that were built after Rome became Christian (see photo on page 113). And Brunelleschi followed the advice of Roman works on architecture written in pagan times, which stressed that all the dimensions of a building—its overall length, breadth, and height, as well as details such as the height and spacing of columns—must be related to each other in a harmonious system of proportion.

But Brunelleschi did all this for the same purpose as Gothic architects—to make his church reflect the harmony of the universe, and thereby give a glimpse of the mind of the universe's Creator. And in his most famous design, he used the Gothic methods of stone ribs and a pointed shape to raise the great dome of Florence's cathedral far higher than any Roman dome-builder could have imagined possible (see photo).

≪ **A Renaissance Church.** Of several churches that Brunelleschi designed, Santo Spirito is closest to his idea of what a religious building should look like. The church revives both Christian and pagan architectural traditions of ancient Rome and adapts them to the needs of fifteenth-century Florence.

and some banished nobleman is to be supported underhand (for by the league it cannot be done avowedly) who had a pretension to the crown, by which means that suspected prince may be kept in awe.

"Now when things are in so great a fermentation, and so many gallant men are joining councils, how to carry on the war, if so mean a man as I should stand up, and wish them to change all their councils, to let Italy alone, and stay at home, since the Kingdom of France was indeed greater than could be well governed by one man; that therefore he ought not to think of adding others to it: and if after this, I should propose to them the resolutions of the Achorians, a people that lie on the southeast of Utopia, who long ago engaged in war, in order to add to the dominions of their prince another kingdom, to which he had some pretensions by an ancient alliance. This they conquered, but found that the trouble of keeping it was equal to that by which it was gained; that the conquered people were always either in rebellion or exposed to foreign invasions, while they were obliged to be incessantly at war, either for or against them, and consequently could never disband their army; that in the meantime they were oppressed with taxes, their money went out of the kingdom, their blood was spilt for the glory of their King, without procuring the least advantage to the people, who received not the smallest benefit from it even in time of peace; and that their manners being corrupted by a long war, robbery and murders everywhere abounded, and their laws fell into contempt; while their King, distracted with the care of two kingdoms, was the less able to apply his mind to the interests of either.

"When they saw this, and that there would be no end to these evils, they by joint councils made an humble address to their King, desiring him to choose which of the two kingdoms he had the greatest mind to keep, since he could not hold both; for they were too great a people to be governed by a divided king, since no man would willingly have a groom that should be in common between him and another. Upon which the good prince was forced to quit his new kingdom to one of his friends (who was not long after dethroned), and to be contented with his old one. To this I would add that after all those warlike attempts, the vast confusions, and the consumption both of treasure and of people that must follow them; perhaps upon some misfortune, they might be forced to throw up all at last; therefore it seemed much more eligible that the King should improve his ancient kingdom all he could, and make it flourish as much as possible; that he should love his people, and be beloved of them; that he should live among them, govern them gently, and let other kingdoms alone, since that which had fallen to his share was big enough, if not too big for him. Pray how do you think would such a speech as this be heard?"

"I confess," said I, "I think not very well."

EXPLORING THE SOURCE

1. Does More want you to get the impression that cynical power politics is a special feature of France?

2. Why do Raphael and Moore both think that the French king and his advisers wouldn't welcome advice to change to Achoria's policy?

Source: Thomas More, "Dialogue of Counsel," in *Ideal Commonwealths: Comprising More's Utopia, Bacon's New Atlantis, Campanella's City of the Sun, and Harrington's Oceania*, introd. Henry Morley (New York: Colonial Press, 1901), pp. 22–24.

Florence Cathedral Medieval and Renaissance styles combine in a majestic and harmonious group of buildings. A late-thirteenth-century architect, Arnolfo di Cambio, designed the nave exterior in Romanesque style. The interior, and Giotto's fourteenth-century bell tower, are Gothic. The fifteenth-century dome, designed by Filippo Brunelleschi, is 375 feet high including the lantern (the structure on top)—nearly 200 feet higher than its tallest ancient predecessor, Justinian's Hagia Sophia (see photo on page 159).

Vanni Archives/Corbis

perspective
Methods for creating the illusion of three-dimensionality on a flat surface, which Renaissance artists improved by the use of exact geometrical rules.

Fooling the Eye: Masaccio

That was not the only way in which Brunelleschi improved on ancient models. He also devised an accurate system of **perspective**—of depicting three-dimensional scenes on a flat surface. The new system used exact geometrical rules to determine how the size and shape of objects should change, depending on how far away they are supposed to be from the viewer and on the angle at which the viewer is supposed to be looking at them. Like so many other late medieval inventions, this one was based on knowledge that came from outside Europe—in this case, discoveries by Muslim scientists in the basic geometry of light and vision. The result was that Renaissance artists could give a three-dimensional look to their paintings that was more convincing than ancient artists had ever been able to manage.

One of the first painters to use the new system was Brunelleschi's friend Masaccio (**muh-SAH-chee-oh**). In 1427, in the Church of Santa Maria Novella (New Saint Mary's) in Florence, he painted the Holy Trinity with the Virgin Mary, Saint John, and the donors of the painting—the wealthy citizens who paid for it (see photo). The subject matter was common enough, but Masaccio followed Brunelleschi's rules to give a "real-life" view of the donors kneeling outside the Roman-style arch and columns, the figures grouped round the crucified Christ and God the Father just inside them, and the high vault fading into the background. As viewers stood back from the wall, they must have gasped at what seemed to be a group of sculptured

Surpassing the Ancients Countless late medieval pictures showed scenes like this one, but Masaccio's version (about 1425) is framed by correctly designed ancient columns and an arch like those of Brunelleschi (see photo on page 296). Masaccio has also followed Brunelleschi's rules of perspective to give a "real-life" view of the scene. No ancient artist could create such a convincing illusion of height and distance.

figures placed outside and inside a hollow space in the church's wall.

Humanist Sculpture: Donatello

About the same time as Masaccio painted his three-dimensional scene, another friend of Brunelleschi, the sculptor Donatello, made *The Feast of Herod* as part of the baptismal font (holy-water basin for christenings) of the cathedral in the nearby city of Siena (see photo above). Donatello shows the climax of a Bible story: the Jewish King Herod, at the urging of his stepdaughter Salome, has ordered the beheading of John the Baptist, the forerunner and baptizer of Christ, because John

◀◀ The Feast of Herod Donatello's bronze relief was made about the same time as Masaccio's wall painting (see photo above). Like the painting, it uses perspective to make the scene more lifelike and has a background of Roman arches and columns. In Giotto's tradition, it is a dramatic scene with individual figures expressing similar emotions—in this case, disgust and horror—in different ways. Scala/Art Resource, NY

Gattamelata The Venetian condottiere Erasmo da Narni acquired the nickname "Gattamelata," meaning "Honey-sweet Cat," on account of his combination of a mild manner, sweet talk, and deep cunning, which enabled him to take unwary fellow condottieri by surprise in negotiation and war—activities that often went together. In this statue, Donatello turned the "Honey-sweet Cat" into an updated version of an ancient Roman emperor.
Scala/Art Resource, NY

has condemned the king's unlawful marriage to Salome's mother. Now Herod and his guests, seated at the banquet table, recoil in horror as Salome shows them the severed head.

The sculpture, carved in clay and then cast in bronze, is a relief—a flat panel with the human figures raised above the surface. The human figures stand out vividly, but Donatello has also created a marvelous illusion of depth. One can look through the rounded arches to Herod's musicians and beyond, through other archways, into the far background. Donatello knew well Giotto's methods of conveying dramatic emotion, he had made a careful study of surviving Roman carvings, and he had mastered Brunelleschi's rules of perspective. All this helped Donatello to create a memorably vivid and terrible scene.

In Donatello's time, a Roman custom was coming back into fashion under humanist influence—commemorating the human

excellence of an important man by placing a statue of him in a public space. Twenty years after *The Feast of Herod*, Donatello won a commission to make a statue of Gattamelata, a leading condottiere who had recently died in Padua. Donatello's model for Gattamelata's monument was a famous ancient statue of the emperor Marcus Aurelius in Rome, which shows him as a weaponless philosopher-ruler restraining an eager mount (see photo on page 115). But since Marcus's time, the world had changed, and Donatello's statue shows a heavily armed and armored soldier astride a ponderous charger. Donatello revived the Roman sculptors' practice of emphasizing a man's power and dignity by putting him on the back of a horse, but he changed the ancient image of peaceful rule over a vast empire into one of warlike power in a land of competing city-states.

Portraits, Nudes, and Ancient Myths: Botticelli, Leonardo

Later in the fifteenth and in the early sixteenth centuries, humanism opened up to artists a whole range of revived ancient art forms, including portraits of individual people, the naked human body, and scenes of Greek and Roman mythology.

The Female Nude: Modest and Erotic Venuses

Sandro Botticelli (bot-i-CHEL-ee), a fifteenth-century Florentine, did much of his work for the Medici rulers and was very much influenced by the Platonism of their Academy. Earthly beauty, said the Platonists, was a reflection of divine beauty, and the human love of beauty came from the longing for the ideal world beyond everyday appearances. In ancient times, poets had sometimes praised the love goddess, Venus, not as an erotic being but as an image of divine beauty, and sculptors had developed a tradition of carving the nude Venus so that her nakedness was divine and noble rather than alluring—a "modest Venus." Renaissance poets had revived this tradition, and Botticelli expressed it in visual form in his most famous work, *The Birth of Venus* (see photo on page 300).

In ancient mythology, Venus was born from the sea foam off the island of Cyprus, and in Botticelli's painting, Zephyrus, god of the West Wind, wafts her toward the land, while a nymph starts to fling a garment about her. The goddess covers her nakedness as best she can, her face suggests deep thought, and she seems to glide above the sea shell that floats her toward the shore. Her beauty is no image of bodily desire, but one of spiritual love that springs from the mind of God.

Once Botticelli had made female nudes respectable, however, artists soon began painting them in ways that were frankly sensual. The Venetian painter Titian is a notable example. In his *Venus of Urbino* (see photo on page 300), which he painted in 1538, he used his supreme mastery of Renaissance artistic techniques to give this painting its sensual power. Perspective makes the

 The Nude in the Middle Ages and the Renaissance (http://www.metmuseum.org/toah/hd/numr/hd_numr.htm) View examples of the nude by other Renaissance masters.

viewer feel the closeness of the naked woman by showing the depth of the room behind her. Her left hand emphasizes rather than covers her nakedness. The arrangement of the figures makes a contrast between the woman boldly gazing at the viewer and her servants who turn away, thereby adding to the intimacy of her glance. This is not the spiritual Venus of Botticelli; in fact, she is probably not meant to be Venus at all. The picture acquired its title long after it was painted, and seems originally to have been a gift to the bride of a sixteenth-century duke of Urbino—a gift that celebrated the erotic side of the marriage bond.

Modest Venus In Botticelli's *Birth of Venus*, the figure of Venus is inspired by Hellenistic statues depicting her as modest rather than erotic—compare her thoughtful eyes with the bold glance of Titian's *Venus of Urbino* (see photo below).

Representing the Individual: Portrait Painting

Ever since Petrarch had called Giotto a genius, humanists had admired artists for possessing *virtù* that put them on a level with statesmen, warriors, orators, thinkers, and scholars. Leonardo da Vinci became a symbol of this ideal of the artist on the highest level of human excellence. The out-of-wedlock son of a Florentine lawyer and a peasant woman, he apprenticed with a painter (since painting was a business that worked on the guild system, pp. 200–201), made a name for himself as an engineer as well as an artist, and worked for the rulers of Milan and Venice and then for the pope. He ended his life in France, in a splendid mansion put at his disposal by his close friend, King Francis I.

Leonardo was an exceptionally close observer of anatomy, physiology, and nature. He put all this to use in his painting, and where he reached the limits of what could be observed, he combined lifelike depiction with an element of mystery—most notably in his portrait of the wife of a wealthy Florentine silk merchant, the *Mona Lisa* (see photo opposite).

Portraits of individuals were another revived ancient art form, and Leonardo believed, in accordance with the humanist ideal, that "the good painter has essentially two things to represent: the individual and the state of that individual's mind." It is not certain how much the sitter actually looked like her portrait, since Leonardo worked on it for years after he left Florence. All the same, in the *Mona Lisa*, Leonardo put his advice into practice. His skill of eye and hand gives the illusion of life to the sitter's physical appearance yet also creates a veiled, misty effect. His artistic perception probes her inner nature—including the element of mystery at the core of every human personality. This revealing yet mysterious quality is what has given the portrait its enduring fascination and fame.

Leonardo also painted traditional religious scenes, including *The Last Supper*, completed in 1497 (see photo opposite). He used his skills of accurate observation and lifelike depiction to

Erotic Venus Titian's *Venus of Urbino*, with its memorable depiction of the female nude as an image of desire, was most likely a suggestive wedding gift from a newly married Italian noble to his bride. Scala/Art Resource, NY

Mona Lisa Lisa del Giocondo, known for short as Mona Lisa ("Madam Lisa"), was twenty-four years old in 1503 when Leonardo da Vinci began painting this portrait, which her merchant husband intended as a gift to celebrate the birth of their second son. The couple never took delivery, for Leonardo worked on the picture on and off until he died in 1519. Evidently the commission set him off on a creative quest that took him the rest of his life to complete. Scala/Art Resource, NY

convey the reaction of the disciples when Jesus said, "One of you will betray me." To convey the drama of this moment, he also used the "stagecraft" skills of Giotto and Donatello. He made countless preliminary drawings, "rehearsing" individual disciples in expressions and gestures of protest, astonishment, disbelief—and in the case of Judas, the betrayer (third from left), obstinate defiance. But even with the agitation and tension of the recorded instant, the painting forms a harmonious whole centered on Jesus, whose foreknowledge of betrayal and death leaves him wholly tranquil.

>> **"Is It I?"** Leonardo's *Last Supper* depicts the disciples reacting to Jesus' announcement that one of them will betray him, and extracts the maximum drama from that moment. For the Milan monks who commissioned this work for their dining hall, it was an unforgettable reminder of the most sacred of all meals. Scala/Art Resource, NY

The Artistic Climax: Michelangelo

Renaissance artists were often painters, sculptors, and architects all at once, and the mightiest achievements in all three fields were those of Michelangelo Buonarroti. Artists at the time saw his work as the climax of art's "restoration to life" that had begun with Giotto. "Truly," said his pupil Giorgio Vasari, "his coming was . . . an example sent by God to the men of our arts, so that they might learn from his life the nature of noble character, and from his works what true and excellent craftsmen ought to be."

Michelangelo was the son of an official and property owner in Florence. When he showed a talent for painting, he was apprenticed to a leading artist who recommended him to Florence's ruler Lorenzo de' Medici. Lorenzo helped him get a good humanist education, including in Platonic thought. He had a thorny personality, liable to fits of suspicion of colleagues as well as to a sense of sin and rage at life; but he was also a person of enormous energy and persistence as well as exceptional artistic skill. All of this, he poured into his masterpieces of sculpture, painting, and architecture.

 A Model for Judas: Leonardo Paints *The Last Supper* Read how Leonardo defended his working method on The Last Supper.

 Portraiture in Renaissance and Baroque Europe (http://www.metmuseum.org/toah/hd/port/hd_port.htm) View examples of portraiture by other Renaissance masters.

 Keeping Michelangelo Happy: "We Love You from the Heart" Read a patron's soothing letter to Michelangelo.

The Male Nude: David

Michelangelo's single best-known work of sculpture is in another ancient tradition that had recently been revived by Donatello, the depiction of the naked male body. In 1499, following a political overturn in the Florentine city-state, by way

of celebration the new rulers commissioned the twenty-six-year-old Michelangelo to carve a larger-than-life-size statue of the ancient Israelite King David, to be placed in Florence's main square. Because of his youthful feat of killing the giant Goliath, David was a traditional symbol of Florence, which prided itself on fighting off such neighboring "Goliaths" as the popes.

The rulers gave Michelangelo an 18-foot-high block of marble, and he set to work first of all with pencil and paper, to figure out, in numerous sketches, exactly how he would depict the Israelite hero. Then he took up his chisel, and with furious energy, he "liberated" an entirely original form from the stone. Statues usually showed David with the head of the defeated Goliath at his feet, but Michelangelo carved him dauntlessly facing the approaching giant. Michelangelo was inspired by serenely balanced poses that he had seen in Roman copies of Hellenistic statues, but this David is not at rest. His balanced pose and his measuring glance are those of a fighter poised to swing into ferocious combat (see photo).

David With one statue, Michelangelo tells a whole Bible story. The youthful Israelite hero is naked and unarmored, for the armor of the Israelite King Saul was too heavy for him; and he is armed only with a sling, for "the Lord does not save by sword and spear." He confidently measures with his eye the Philistine warrior-giant Goliath, for he knows that "This very day the Lord will deliver you into my hand."

The Soul and Its Maker: The Creation of Adam

Michelangelo's greatest work of painting came about by accident, after he was called to Rome in 1508 by Pope Julius II—himself a Renaissance man of *virtù* who was no saint, but a statesman, general, and patron of the arts. The pope wanted Michelangelo to make him a monumental tomb, but complications arose, and instead, Julius asked Michelangelo to paint the Sistine Chapel, so called after its fifteenth-century builder, Pope Sixtus IV. Its walls had been painted by earlier masters, including Botticelli, but the ceiling remained blank.

Michelangelo much preferred sculpting to painting, but he plunged into the new task with extraordinary vigor. The work took him four years to complete, covered about 10,000 square

"Let Us Make Humankind in Our Image" Michelangelo's *Creation of Adam* shows the beginning of the human race, and also its destiny according to Christian belief. Adam, the first man, is stirred to life by the finger of God; Eve, the first woman, and Christ, the redeemer of Adam and Eve's sin, are waiting to fulfill their part in God's plan.

feet, and included more than three hundred figures. It was the largest work ever painted by a single artist.

The main feature of the ceiling is a series of nine panels showing the stories of the Creation and the Flood, among them *The Creation of Adam* (see photo). God, borne by angels on a rushing mighty wind, reaches toward the first man; the mortal body stirs and reaches toward God; and the immortal soul passes from its divine originator to its human recipient. In the crook of God's arm, the still uncreated Eve looks intently toward Adam, the mother of humankind gazing upon its father. Beyond her, God's finger rests on the infant Christ, humankind's future redeemer. Adam's nakedness both follows the Bible story and is in the ancient tradition of celebrating the male body; God and Adam reaching toward each other reflect the Platonic

 **Vatican Museum's Video and Slide Tour of the Sistine Chapel** (http://mv.vatican .va/3_EN/pages/x-Pano/ CSN/Visit_CSN_01.html) Tour the Sistine Chapel and see all of Michelangelo's frescoes.

understanding of the divine origin of the soul and the soul's longing for God. In these ways, Michelangelo's depiction gives visual form to a humanist version of Christian beliefs about the human race and its creator.

Outdoing the Ancients: The Dome of Saint Peter's

Later in life, having won fame as a painter and a sculptor, Michelangelo turned to architecture, and here, too, he produced a supreme masterpiece—the dome of Saint Peter's Basilica. In 1503, Pope Julius II decided to tear down the thousand-year-old basilica of the Roman emperor Constantine (p. 142) and replace it with a more splendid building. His chosen architect, Donato Bramante (**bruh-MAHN-tey**), planned a dome that would dwarf that of another ancient Roman structure, the Pantheon (see photo on page 112), but died before he could carry out the work. In 1547, Michelangelo was put in charge.

The floor plan was for a colossal structure laid out in the form of a Greek (square) cross, with a central dome as the crowning feature. Inspired by Brunelleschi's dome in Florence (see photo on page 297), Michelangelo planned one even steeper and higher—one that would tower over every other building in the Eternal City. Although he died before Saint Peter's was completed and the floor plan was later changed, the dome was finished according to his designs (see photo). Equal in diameter to

"You Are Peter, and on This Rock I Will Build My Church" The saying of Christ to Peter is carved in Latin on the inside of the dome of the rebuilt St. Peter's Basilica, as well as Christ's following words: "I will give you the keys of the kingdom of heaven." Michelangelo's dome, with its solemn splendor and its dizzying height, symbolized the claim of the papacy to supremacy over Christendom at a time when Christendom was for the first time becoming truly worldwide. James Morris/Art Resource, NY

the dome of the Pantheon and 300 feet higher, Michelangelo's dome sets the crown on the most daring of Renaissance undertakings—not just to bring the ancients back to life, but to destroy one of their most revered buildings in order to outdo them.

LO³ Ancient Traditions and Modern Languages: Renaissance Literature and Drama

Humanist scholars believed that their activities benefited the whole human race, and they had always been eager to spread their ideas. Until about 1500, however, their audience was mostly made up of people who could read Latin. In the sixteenth century, as printing made books cheaper and more widely available, humanists took the opportunity to reach a much wider audience—and that meant using the vernacular (native) languages of Europe. They translated ancient works and those of Erasmus and More, and they began writing original works in every language of Western Christendom—works that were then, in turn, translated into every other language. Vernacular literature, one of the great cultural creations of the Middle Ages, now felt the influence of the humanists, and of the ancients whom the humanists had reawakened.

The Liberty-Loving Humorist: Rabelais

In France, the first vernacular author to become widely popular was François Rabelais (**RAB-uh-ley**), an enthusiastic humanist with a talent for satire and parody. Though his books were condemned by religious and civil authorities, they became and remained bestsellers.

Like Erasmus a generation earlier, Rabelais knew the Church and the universities from the inside. From a middle-class family, he had entered a Franciscan monastery in order to become a scholar. But he was a rebel from the beginning; his absorption in ancient literature disturbed his superiors and led to trouble. He switched from one religious order to another, for a time wore the garb of a priest, studied at various universities, and later took up law and medicine. His career, like his writing, followed no visible plan. With a vast appetite for life and learning, he was the personification of a vigorous and spontaneous humanism.

Though Rabelais loved the ancient works and knew them intimately (especially those of Rome), he had no taste for high-minded ideals, and he detested all rules and regulations. One should follow, he insisted, one's own inclinations. Rabelais thus represented a humanism that did not copy ancient models (or any other) but stood as a purely individualistic philosophy. Rejecting the doctrine of original sin (and most other doctrines), he stressed natural goodness; he held that most people, given freedom and proper education (in the lore of the ancients), will live happy and productive lives.

This idea is central to Rabelais's great work, *Gargantua and Pantagruel*. The story, about two imaginary giant-kings, was printed in several volumes beginning in 1538. He wrote the work primarily for amusement, because he believed that laughter (like thought) is a distinctively human function. However, in telling of the heroes' education and adventures, he voiced his opinions on the human traits and institutions of his time. In a tumble of words, learned and playful, he mingled serious ideas with earthy jokes and jibes.

Monasticism was a prime target for Rabelais, as it was for Erasmus. Its stress on self-denial, repression, and regimentation was to him inhumane and hateful. He had Gargantua give funds to a "model" institution that violates monastic practices in every possible way. At this "abbey of Thélème," with its fine libraries and recreational facilities, elegantly dressed men and women are free to do as they please. Monks, hypocrites, lawyers, and peddlers of gloom are barred from the abbey; only handsome, high-spirited people are admitted.

Rabelais disliked pretense and deception and praised the natural instincts and abilities of free persons. Rejecting the ascetic ideal, he expressed humanism in its most robust and optimistic form. In doing so, he also anticipated the modern appetite for unlimited experience and pleasure.

The Skeptical Essayist: Montaigne

Michel de Montaigne (**mon-TEYN**), born a generation after Rabelais, lived through the troubled times of religious struggle between Protestants and Catholics and shared Rabelais's keen interest in the ancients. But his temperament was nearer that of Erasmus. Both men remained loyal to the Catholic Church, and both were dedicated scholars, though Montaigne was more secular-minded and detached than Erasmus.

A Life of Contemplation

The son of a landowning family near Bordeaux in southern France, Montaigne received a superb education. His father held public office, traveled abroad, and believed in a humanistic upbringing for his children. When his father died, Montaigne inherited the family estate and was able to retire at the age of thirty-eight to his library of a thousand books. The ideal humanist way of life was one that combined "action" and "contemplation" (quiet study and thought) like that of Cicero the statesman and thinker. Montaigne, however, chose contemplation, reading and rereading the Latin authors (and some Greeks in translation). As he read, he "attempted," as he put it, to write down briefly and clearly the ideas that came into his mind. The French word for "attempt" is *essai*, and at that time the English word **essay** had the same meaning. It was Montaigne who gave the word its usual modern meaning—a brief and thoughtful discussion of a subject.

Ancient writers like Seneca and Plutarch had written what amounted to essays, and so had Erasmus. But they had written in Latin and Greek, and always on solemn themes, whereas Montaigne wrote in clear and eloquent French on topics ranging from "Freedom of Conscience" and "The Greatness of Rome" to "Drunkenness," "War-horses," and "Not Pretending to Be

Sick." Montaigne's essays usually began with the opinions of traditional authorities, with quotations from their works, and went on to explain his own views. Sometimes he would present opposing answers to a given question and then suggest a compromise solution—or perhaps no solution at all.

Michel de Montaigne on the Fallibility of Human Understanding Read an excerpt from a Montaigne essay.

Montaigne did not try to change the minds of his readers but wrote in large measure for his own satisfaction. And because the essays were based on his own experiences and thoughts, they were also a form of autobiography. As he put it himself, in a note "To the Reader": "I want to be seen in my simple, natural, and ordinary style, without effort or artifice; for it is myself that I paint"—like a Renaissance artist making a self-portrait. That only added to his essays' appeal. Readers enjoyed the feeling of getting to know the ideas and character of an interesting person, and the fact that there was no pressure to share his ideas actually made them more appealing. His more than a hundred "attempts" to express the results of his life of private study and thought were printed beginning in 1580 and had an immense public impact.

The Uncertainty of Judgment

Montaigne wrote often of the limits of reason in efforts to comprehend the universe: neither theology, the wisdom of the ancients, nor science can provide final answers to the "big questions." "Of the Uncertainty of Our Judgment" is the title of one of his essays.

The human mind, observed Montaigne, is erratic; and the senses, which are unreliable, often control the mind. Beliefs, no matter how firmly held, cannot be regarded as constant, for they, too, have their seasons, their birth and death. His **skepticism** (doubting and inquiring attitude, from the Greek word for "inquiry") had a history dating back to ancient Greek thinkers. By reviving this attitude, Montaigne challenged the self-assurance of both Christians and earlier humanists. The uncertain character of knowledge, he thought, ought to teach us that claims to absolute truth are unjustified, and that persecuting people for differing beliefs is wrong. In the midst of frightful struggles between Catholics and Protestants that raged through sixteenth-century France, Montaigne could see that war and homicide are often the outcomes of unwarranted certainty in thought and belief, and pleaded eloquently for skepticism and tolerance.

Like many skeptics, exactly because of his distrust of claims to certainty Montaigne was a conservative, who believed that firm authority was indispensable to peace and order. Though he cherished independence of thought, he did not rebel against established institutions—one of his essays is "On Never Easily Changing a Traditional Law." Instead, he hoped that those

> *"It is impossible to find two opinions exactly alike, not only in different men, but in the same man at different times."*
>
> —Michel de Montaigne, from his *Essays*

who held power would see the light, ultimately, of moderation and decency. In any event, he stuck to his personal philosophy and remained aloof from other people. In the quiet and security of his library, Montaigne could meditate on one of his favorite sayings: "Rejoice in your present life; all else is beyond you."

The Master Dramatist: Shakespeare

Along with many other ancient traditions, the humanists revived that of drama—especially Roman drama. Comedies of Plautus and Terence (p. 107), with their complicated plots and happy endings, and tragedies by the Roman thinker Seneca that were full of strong emotions and spectacular bloodshed, were widely read and were sometimes performed at the courts of rulers. In addition, medieval popular drama was still a living art form, and as in so many other fields, the Renaissance combined both ancient and medieval traditions—notably in England, and above all, in the work of William Shakespeare.

The Business of Drama

As Shakespeare's friend (and rival playwright) Ben Jonson said, he knew "small Latin and less Greek." But by Shakespeare's time (around 1600), humanists had translated most of the writings of ancient Greece and Rome, and morality and mystery plays were still being performed. For a generation already, English playwrights had used and expanded on both highbrow ancient themes and lowbrow popular ones, in a vernacular language enriched by borrowings from the eloquence of Greece and Rome. The English drama had universal appeal—from the well-educated rulers Queen Elizabeth I and King James I, who sponsored troops of actors to perform the new plays, to the rowdy audiences in London's newly built theaters.

The new theaters were unlike those of ancient Greece or Rome, which had been religious or public structures with room for tens of thousands of spectators, and with all expenses paid by wealthy citizens (see photos on pages 69 and 104). London's **Globe Theater**, by contrast, held a maximum of three thousand people with considerable overcrowding. Furthermore, it was an admission-charging private business, in which Shakespeare himself owned a one-eighth share, located in a theater and red-light district safely across the River Thames from London itself.

 A Virtual Tour from the Official Site of the Globe Theater (http://www.shakespeares-globe.org/virtualtour/) Tour London's Globe Theater.

Circular in outward plan, the theater faced inward on a large courtyard (see photo). The "groundlings," who had paid the cheapest admission, stood or sat in the yard itself, and the quality folk sat in covered galleries. The technical equipment was minimal. Behind the stage were curtains from behind which Polonius could spy on Hamlet, and a balcony where Juliet could be overheard by Romeo; costumes were usually those of the time; and lighting was unnecessary, since this was an open-air theater and performances were given in the afternoon. However, there were occasional special effects that could go badly wrong. In 1613, a cannon that was fired to liven up a battle scene set the roof of the Globe alight, and the theater burned to the ground.

Acting, however, was already a skilled craft. Its aim, according to Shakespeare himself, was "to suit the action to the word, the word to the action," and thereby "to hold the mirror up to nature"—just like Renaissance painting. What distorted the mirror, however, was that women were not supposed to appear on stage, so that female parts were played by boys. But so strong was the desire for lifelike performance that this would soon change. Half a century after Shakespeare's time, women were as prominent on stage as men, even though the feeling persisted that they did not really belong there. Well-known actresses were both idolized for their star quality and condemned for following a disrespectable profession.

"All the World's a Stage"

Like all commercial playwrights, Shakespeare looked for subjects that would excite his audiences, and he generally did not have to invent these for himself. Translated ancient works told of the larger-than-life heroes and villains of Greece and Rome. Patriotic historians narrated the triumphs that England had enjoyed and the disasters it had overcome in the Middle Ages. Sensational storytellers told of the doings of Italians, with their reputation as great lovers and great villains. Geographers described fantastic islands in the western ocean. In addition, Roman comedies and tragedies and

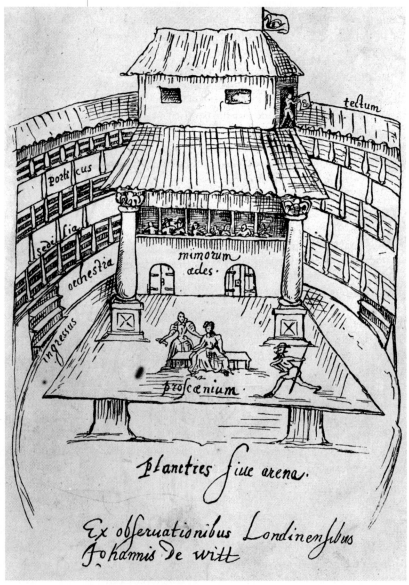

>> **An Elizabethan Playhouse** This sketch of the Swan Theater, of similar construction to the Globe and located in the same London theater district, was made by a visiting Dutchman in 1596. It shows a play under way on the "proscenium" in front of the "actors' building." The lower classes fill the "level space or arena" in front; upper-class spectators climb an "entry" stairway to the "orchestra"; and the middle classes climb higher to the "seating" or the "gallery" directly under the "roof" (top right label).

medieval morality plays provided Shakespeare with models of drama that he could combine at will. "All the world's a stage" says one of Shakespeare's characters—and with his vast range of themes and styles, Shakespeare made those words come true.

The basic plot of his tragedy *Hamlet*, for instance, comes from a medieval Danish tale: Hamlet finds out that his uncle the king, who is also his stepfather, has gained the crown and the queen by secretly murdering his father. Like a character in a medieval morality play (p. 239), Hamlet is faced with a choice, but the choice is one between the Renaissance alternatives of contemplation and action, as he hesitates to take revenge upon his uncle. The result is a series of spectacular deaths, as in Roman tragedies—in this case, eliminating all the main characters, including Hamlet himself. Without these sources and models,

Hamlet would not be *Hamlet*. But it was Shakespeare's deep insight into human nature and the uniquely expressive eloquence of his language that made *Hamlet* and so many of his other plays, as Ben Jonson said, "not of an age but for all time."

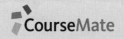

Listen to a synopsis of Chapter 16.

CourseMate

Access to the eBook with additional review material and study tools may be found online at CourseMate for WCIV. Sign in at www.cengagebrain.com.

CHAPTER 17

NEW CHRISTIANITIES: THE REFORMATION, 1500–1700

LEARNING OBJECTIVES

AFTER READING THIS CHAPTER, YOU SHOULD BE ABLE TO DO THE FOLLOWING:

LO¹ Describe the background of the Protestant Reformation.

LO² Trace the evolution of Lutheranism from the Ninety-five Theses to the Religious Peace of Augsburg.

LO³ Discuss the core tenets of Calvinism and its impact on the Reformation.

LO⁴ Outline how the Catholic Church responded to the Protestant challenge.

LO⁵ Explain how the religious wars of the Reformation period led to a new, secular European state system.

"THE EMERGENCE OF PROTESTANTISM WAS THE GREATEST SINGLE CHANGE IN WESTERN RELIGION SINCE THE END OF ANCIENT PAGANISM."

The **Protestant Reformation** was yet another spectacular change that grew out of the gradual shifts in Western Christendom during the late Middle Ages. In particular, resentment at corruption and abuse among the Catholic clergy that involved the papacy itself began to discredit the religious beliefs and practices on which the power of the clergy and the popes was based. When Martin Luther proclaimed that the Church was leading souls to hell rather than heaven, and must be reformed along lines of Christian freedom and equality, his individual protest soon turned into a mass movement.

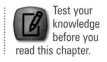

Test your knowledge before you read this chapter.

As Luther's protest spread, however, his followers interpreted his message of reformation in different ways. John Calvin proclaimed a more thoroughgoing break with Catholic tradition, in the name of return to the pure truth of the gospel. Radical groups of reformers claimed that Christian freedom and equality were not just spritual, but applied to society and government as well. These issues seemed to affect the salvation of souls just as much as the disputes between reformers and traditionalists, and the arguments among reformers were just as bitter. Instead of changing the whole Church, the reformers—the Protestants, as they came to be called—split into many different churches, each with its own beliefs and organization.

What do you think?

The Protestant Revolution weakened Christianity in western Europe.

Strongly Disagree						Strongly Agree
1	2	3	4	5	6	7

Meanwhile, by far the largest of the churches was still the Catholic Church. In response to the Protestant challenge, it rallied around its traditional beliefs and practices as the only way to heaven, and around the traditional authority of the papacy as the only guide of Christians. It acted against some of the worst abuses that had brought the clergy into contempt, and regained the trust of many rulers and many believers. And although it lost most of northern Europe to Protestantism, it gained millions of new believers in Latin America.

《 **The Lord's Supper** A Protestant painter, Lucas Cranach the Elder, shows Jesus and his disciples sharing the Last Supper as friends around a table. The odd man out is Judas, to whom Jesus gives the bread that marks him as the betrayer. The disciple taking a cup of wine—the cup that was so important to Protestants in the Communion service—is Martin Luther, wearing the beard he grew in hiding as an outlawed heretic. For Cranach, Luther is worthy to sit among the original twelve.

Church of St. Marien, Wittenberg, Germany/The Bridgeman Art Library

Protestant Reformation
A religious mass movement against the Catholic Church that gave rise to Protestant Christianity.

Most reformers, as well as Catholics, still believed that all Christians should belong to one Church that was allied with the state, so religious disputes also led to persecution and war. These conflicts were further embittered by nonreligious rivalries among rulers and within their countries. About 1650, however, more than a century of religious-political struggles ended in stalemate. Alongside the existing rival Christianities of Catholicism and Orthodoxy, there now existed the third Christianity of Protestantism, itself divided into many different sub-Christianities. The emergence of Protestantism was the greatest single change in Western religion since the end of ancient paganism. It was also one that affected nonreligious areas of civilization, as the Reformation interacted with other changes involved in the remaking of Europe.

The Reformation strengthened both Protestant and Catholic rulers in their partnership with the churches, since it was the rulers above all who had the power to choose and uphold one or other religion. But Calvinists trying to take over kingdoms often championed the rights of subjects against rulers, and radical sects kept alive the belief that Christian freedom and equality applied to this world as well as the next. Likewise, the Reformation at first blighted many ideals of the Renaissance, such as tolerance and understanding among religions and optimism about the possibilities of human nature. But as religious stalemate set in, the idea of toleration revived and was even strengthened by the Protestant belief in freedom of conscience. As the struggles of the churches died down, all these ideas began to get a wider hearing.

LO¹ The Christian Background

For more than a thousand years before the Reformation, the majority of Christians had agreed upon certain basic beliefs about how they would make their way to heaven. They would do so as members of a community founded by Christ himself, the Church, and by taking part in various holy ceremonies that the Church practiced. They accepted that Christ had appointed the clergy as guides and rulers of the Church, and had established its hierarchy of bishops, priests, and lower ranks. They trusted

CHRONOLOGY

1517	Luther's Ninety-five Theses attack the sale of indulgences
1521	Excommunicated by the pope, Luther refuses to recant his beliefs before the Diet of Worms; he translates the Bible into German while under the protection of Frederick of Saxony
1522	Luther returns to Wittenberg; his new version of Christianity gains adherents
1529	Holy Roman Emperor Charles V reaffirms decree prohibiting new religious doctrines in Germany; Lutheran rulers protest and acquire label of "Protestants"
1530s	Armed alliances of Lutherans and Catholics form within the Holy Roman Empire; Augsburg Confession sets out beliefs of new Evangelical Church
1534	Pope Paul III launches Catholic Reformation; England's Parliament passes the Act of Supremacy, breaking ties with the pope
1536	John Calvin's *Institutes of the Christian Religion* is published and widely read; Calvin settles in Geneva, where he establishes a model community
1539	The Society of Jesus (Jesuits) becomes an official Catholic order
1545–1563	Council of Trent meets periodically to initiate Catholic Church reform
1553	Queen Mary launches persecution of English Protestants
1555	Religious Peace of Augsburg allows each ruler within the Holy Roman Empire to choose either Catholicism or Lutheranism for his territory
1562	Beginning of wars between Catholics and Huguenots in France
1588	English defeat Spanish Armada
1598	Edict of Nantes guarantees toleration and military forces for Huguenots
1618–1648	Thirty Years' War devastates Germany, ends with Peace of Westphalia

that monks and nuns, and the saints in heaven, were closer to God than ordinary believers, and could help ordinary believers into heaven by interceding with God for them.

This consensus had not prevented many furious disputes over belief and struggles for power from arising within Christendom, and in the Middle Ages, the Church had already come to be divided between the Catholic West and the Orthodox East (p. 219). Furthermore, in both halves of Christendom there had always been heretics who disagreed with the consensus. Even so, the consensus had survived these challenges, until in the sixteenth-century Catholic West, it broke down.

Many long-standing developments within Western Christendom contributed to this breakdown. In the Middle Ages, changes in religious practices that were intended to ease believers' path to heaven had increased the power of the clergy as gatekeepers on this path—and also increased the temptation for them to exploit this power for political and money-making purposes. The international power of the popes had grown as they rose to become effective rulers of the Catholic Church—and increased power saddled them with increased responsibility for everything that was wrong with the Church. Banking and capitalism made it easier for popes and clergy to exploit the growing wealth of Western Christendom—but also made it easier for landowners, merchants, and rulers of countries to do the same, and to look upon the Church as an unwelcome competitor.

Corruption in the Church, resentment at unworthy clergy, and quarrels between the clergy and other power wielders were nothing new in Western Christendom, and these problems had sometimes provoked zealous mass movements of renewal and reform within the Church. In the fifteenth century, grassroots movements like the Brethren of the Common Life (p. 293) were committed to Catholic piety, and in Spain, Isabella and Fredinand sponsored reform of the clergy. To become truly a mass movement, however, reform had to have the wholehearted backing of the popes. In the fifteenth century, the popes were too busy with power struggles in Italy, and with holding off challenges to their control of the Church by increasingly powerful rulers of countries, to bother much with Church reform.

Instead of provoking renewal and reform, therefore, the problems of the Church began to inspire doubts that it was guiding Christians rightly, and searches began for the true path to salvation. Renaissance humanists contrasted the Church's wealth and corruption with the simple holiness of early Christianity, and insisted that many beliefs that had grown up over the centuries hid the truth that Christ had originally proclaimed (pp. 293–294). Heretic movements grew up that sought to weaken or abolish the clergy's rule, and to change or eliminate many practices and ceremonies (pp. 249–251). By the end of the fifteenth century, furthermore, humanists and heretics had

a new means of spreading their doubts and disagreements to a mass audience, with the advent of printing.

As with many massive and sudden changes in human affairs, no one expected the Reformation until it actually happened. But in many ways, the time was ripe for a religious mass movement that would not be one of reform and renewal within the thousand-year-old consensus, but a revolt against the consensus as such.

LO² The Revolt of Luther

One person who certainly did not expect the Reformation before it happened was the one who began it, Martin Luther. All the same, his own early life was shaped by his search for the true path to salvation, and eventually, he became the leader of a religious revolt motivated by resentment at the clergy and the papacy and by rejection of the traditional beliefs and practices as the way to heaven.

Luther's Search for Salvation

Luther was the son of a well-to-do mine operator in the north German town of Eisleben (see Map 17.1) who wanted him to study law. But he was deeply afraid for his own salvation, and like many pious Catholics who felt that way, he defied his father's wishes and entered a monastery, in the traditional belief that as a monk he would be more pleasing to God than as an ordinary Christian.

For centuries, the Church had taught that praying, fasting, strict obedience to superiors, and abstinence from sex and marriage that made up the ascetic way of life of a monk (p. 144) were "good works"—righteous deeds that were pleasing to God. Together with God's grace, received through the sacraments, they would "justify" Luther (free him from the penalty of sin and admit him to salvation). But no matter how strictly he fasted, prayed, and punished himself, his sense of being unpleasing to God persisted. To give him something else to think about, the head of his monastery sent him to study theology at the nearby University of Wittenberg. After receiving his doctor's degree there in 1512, he stayed on as a professor of theology.

At Wittenberg, Luther began to discover his path to spiritual peace—not in the pronouncements of popes, revered monks, or earlier Christian thinkers, but in humanist fashion, by going back to the words of Christ and the apostles themselves. Above all, he was struck by the words of Paul, in a letter to early believers in Rome: "The one who is righteous will live by faith." Luther took these words to mean, as he later wrote, that "by grace and sheer mercy God justifies us through faith"—an idea that "became to me a gate to heaven." He had been right all along to feel that his "good works" as a monk had not made him pleasing to God. Because of the sinfulness that all humans inherited from Adam and Eve, no one could deserve salvation through his or her

> **"** *As with many massive and sudden changes in human affairs, no one expected the Reformation until it actually happened.* **"**

Interactive Map

Map 17.1 Catholics and Protestants in 1555

The map shows the religious division of Europe when the Reformation was approaching its height. The Lutheran and Anglican Reformations are dominant in much of northern Europe, and the Calvinist Reformation is gaining in the Netherlands, Scotland, France, and Hungary. But the rest of Western Christendom is still mainly Catholic, and a Catholic religious revival and the support of local rulers will soon bring the spread of Protestantism to an end. © Cengage Learning

Predominant religion in 1555

- Lutheran
- Calvinist (Reformed)
- Church of England
- Roman Catholic
- Orthodox
- Muslim
- ▲ Spread of Calvinism
- ▲ Huguenot center
- Ottoman Empire, 1566

Map labels

ATLANTIC OCEAN

North Sea

Baltic Sea

Mediterranean Sea

Black Sea

Adriatic Sea

Danube R.

NORWAY 1536/1607

SWEDEN

DENMARK

IRELAND

SCOTLAND 1560
- Edinburgh John Knox, 1505–1572
- Penetration of Calvinism to England after 1558

ENGLAND 1536
- Oxford John Wyclif, 1320–1384
- London
- Plymouth

NETHERLANDS
- Amsterdam
- Antwerp
- Brussels
- Münster

FRANCE
- Rennes
- Nantes Edict of Nantes, 1598
- Orléans
- La Rochelle
- Bordeaux
- Toulouse
- Marseilles
- Avignon

- Noyon Birthplace of John Calvin, 1509–1564
- Paris
- Strasbourg
- Edict of Worms, 1521

SAXONY
- Hamburg
- Wittenberg Martin Luther
- Eisleben Birthplace of Martin Luther, 1483–1546
- Erfurt
- Leipzig
- Marburg
- Birthplace of John Calvin

BRANDENBURG

PRUSSIA

LITHUANIA
- Riga
- Helsinki
- Stockholm
- Copenhagen
- Bergen

POLAND
- Warsaw

HOLY ROMAN EMPIRE
- Nuremberg
- Speyer
- Stuttgart
- Augsburg
- Munich
- Zurich Ulrich Zwingli, 1484–1531
- Basel
- Geneva John Calvin
- Trent Council of Trent, 1545–1563

BOHEMIA
- Prague Jan Hus, 1369–1415

MORAVIA

AUSTRIA
- Vienna

HUNGARY
- Buda
- Pest

ITALY
- Milan
- Pavia
- Genoa
- Pisa
- Florence
- Venice
- Rome Roman Inquisition established, 1542
- Naples
- Bari

Corsica
Sardinia
Sicily

SPAIN
- Madrid
- Toledo
- Granada
- Seville
- Valencia
- Barcelona
- Loyola Birthplace of Ignatius Loyola, 1491–1556

PORTUGAL
- Lisbon

Balearic Is.

MOROCCO

ALGIERS

TUNIS

OTTOMAN EMPIRE

WALLACHIA

MOLDAVIA

BESSARABIA

TRANSYLVANIA

BULGARIA

SERBIA
- Belgrade

GREECE

OTTOMAN EMPIRE

Dublin

Scale

400 Mi.
400 Km.
200
0

N

60°N
50°N
10°W
0°
10°E
20°E
30°E

deeds. Only faith in salvation through Christ and humble trust in God's mercy could "justify" a person—and because of human sinfulness, no one could acquire faith by his or her own efforts, but must receive it as a free gift of God's mercy. We are saved not by works, concluded Luther, but by *faith alone*. If God has given us that faith, we will live as righteously as human sinfulness allows—not because we need to but because we want to.

Luther's Rebellion

The idea of **justification** by faith alone brought Luther immense personal relief, but when he began to apply it to the institution of the Church, he grew troubled. If people received faith as a free gift from God, were not the claims of the clergy to guide people to salvation untrue? If the way of life of monks and nuns was not pleasing to God, what good was it either to themselves or to ordinary believers for whom they were supposed to pray? If the saints themselves had done nothing to deserve God's favor but had simply benefited from his mercy, what was the use of praying to them and making pilgrimages to their shrines? And if these beliefs were deceptive, must not the traditional path to heaven in fact be leading believers to hell?

> **"***Thus those preachers of indulgences are in error who say that by the indulgences of the Pope a man is freed and saved from all punishment.***"**
>
> —No. 21, from the Ninety-five Theses

The Provocation: The Sale of Indulgences

For several years, Luther kept his views to himself, until in 1517 a Dominican friar (p. 209), Johann Tetzel, arrived in Wittenberg on important papal business. Tetzel was a seller of indulgences—grants of time off purgatory issued on the authority of the pope, which believers could obtain both for themselves and also for other people who were already dead (pp. 206–207). People who obtained indulgences were supposed to show sorrow for their sins, but they also had to pay a fee, and popes in need of money would initiate international indulgence-selling campaigns. In this case, the proceeds were to go to the rebuilding of Saint Peter's Basilica in Rome, and Tetzel's catchy sales slogan was allegedly "As soon as the gold in the casket rings, the rescued soul to heaven springs!"

In his indignation, Luther prepared a public statement about indulgences in the form of **"Ninety-five Theses"** (propositions for academic debate). Cautiously but unmistakably, he attacked not just the sale of indulgences but also the whole idea that he believed lay behind them—that the pope could commit God to show mercy in consideration of the merits of deserving persons, when in fact God's mercy was the free gift of his almighty power, which no person could possibly deserve.

Originally, Luther seems to have publicized his theses in the traditional way for professors who wanted to hold debates, by nailing a single handwritten copy to the door of the Wittenberg Castle church. Soon, however, the theses were printed in thousands of copies, and were setting off a chain reaction of dissent and rebellion throughout Germany.

The Split with Rome

Pope Leo X, an able and cultured Italian despot like many popes at the time, hoped to settle this "squabble among monks," as he called it, by having a reply to Luther published, whereupon Luther published a reply to the reply. That led to yet more publications on both sides, in the course of which Luther stood by the radical consequences of his belief in justification by faith alone and proclaimed them as Christian truth. In addition, he appealed outside

justification
In Christian theology, the process whereby a person is freed from the penalty of sin and admitted to salvation.

Ninety-five Theses
Luther's 1517 argument against the sale of indulgences and the ideas that lay behind the practice.

On Aplas von Rom kan man wol selig werden durch anzaigung der götlichen hailigen geschryfft.

≫ **"One Can Be Saved Without an Indulgence from Rome, as Proven by God's Holy Scripture"** In a woodcut from a Lutheran pamphlet of about 1520, a friar holds an indulgence festooned with seals, believers pay up and a cashier rakes in the money, and Christ has departed the Cross, leaving only a crown of thorns. The pope's coat of arms behind the preacher leaves no doubt about who is to blame for this evil, and the slogan at the top drives home the message. © British Library Board, 3906.b.55

Diet of Worms
The assembly of the Holy Roman Empire before which Luther refused to recant his beliefs.

Anabaptists
Radical Protestants who opposed infant baptism and also held various other beliefs that were opposed to beliefs that other Protestants still had in common with Catholics.

sect
In religion, a small group that sees itself as part of a minority of true believers apart from the rest of society.

the ranks of the clergy to secular wielders of power and to Christians in general. In his *Address to the Christian Nobility of the German Nation*, he spoke of the equal "priesthood" of all baptized Christians. In this and other documents, he claimed that not just indulgences, but also an unmarried clergy set apart from and above other believers, as well as monks and nuns, saints and relics and pilgrimages, were all devices of the devil to lead believers away from the true path of salvation. So, too, was the idea of the papacy as the single Christ-appointed guide and ruler of the Church. Instead, Christians should listen to the voice of God himself, speaking to them through the Bible and within them through their own consciences.

Likewise, Luther declared, most of the Church's seven sacraments—the holy ceremonies that helped believers to salvation (pp. 204–205)—were a deception. Using the humanist test of early Christian practice as found in the New Testament, he claimed that Christ had established only two sacraments: baptism and the Eucharist. And he denied the Catholic doctrine of transubstantiation—that in the Eucharist, the priest brings about a miraculous change of bread and wine into the body and blood of Christ. Luther taught, instead, that Christ was present *along with* the bread and wine, and that it is not the priest who makes Christ present, for God is present everywhere and always. Furthermore, it was a wicked violation of Christ's command that only clergy should receive both bread and wine in the Eucharist.

"My Conscience Has Been Taken Captive by the Word of God"

In 1520, Leo finally ordered Luther excommunicated, and Luther responded by burning the document of excommunication before the city gates of Wittenberg. The clergy now called on the Holy Roman emperor Charles V to seize Luther, since it was considered the duty of the civil ruler to punish confirmed heretics, but Luther by now had such widespread support that the emperor hesitated. In particular, the local ruler of Saxony, the elector Frederick (one of the rulers who elected the emperor, p. 267) favored Luther, and insisted that Luther receive a hearing before the Imperial Diet. (The Diet was the assembly of the local rulers and self-governing cities of the empire—in German, *Reichstag* or "imperial day," because it was called for a particular day; the English word *diet* comes from the Latin word for "day.")

 "Martin Luther: The Reluctant Revolutionary" (http://www.pbs.org/empires/martinluther/) Learn more about Luther's life and the other major players in his story.

At the **Diet of Worms** (a city in western Germany where the Diet met) in 1521, Luther was given a last chance to recant his heresies. He refused, in words that became the motto for the Reformation appeal against Church tradition to the Bible and individual conscience: "Unless I am convinced by the testimonies of the Holy Scriptures or evident reason (for I believe neither in the Pope nor councils alone, since it has been established that they have often erred and contradicted themselves), I am bound by the Scriptures cited by me, and my conscience has been taken captive by the Word of God, and I am neither able nor willing to recant, since it is neither safe nor right to act against conscience. God help me. Amen."

The Diet then condemned Luther and issued a decree prohibiting all new religious doctrines within the Holy Roman Empire, and the emperor ordered him branded an outlaw. Frederick, however, sent soldiers to "kidnap" Luther as he left Worms and took him secretly to a castle at Wartburg in Saxony, where Luther remained for about a year working on a German translation of the Bible. His "people's" version of Scripture was printed in hundreds of thousands of copies, and helped shape the modern German language as well as Protestant doctrines.

Reforming the Church

When Luther returned to Wittenberg, he found himself the leader of a mass movement that included local rulers, clergy, townspeople, and peasants, and he set about turning this movement into a reformed Christian church. This involved him in a struggle on two fronts—against Catholics who sought to suppress his protest, and against people who wanted to take his protest in directions of which he disapproved.

 Pastor Luther Confronts His Flock Read an excerpt from one of Luther's sermons in Wittenberg.

The Anabaptist Sects

Many of the second group went under the general name of **Anabaptists** (from the Greek words for "baptize again"). They insisted that baptism was meaningful only after someone old enough to comprehend Christian doctrines had made a voluntary confession of faith. They therefore opposed infant baptism and held that adult Christians who had been baptized as infants must accept the rite again. Baptism of adults had been normal among the earliest Christians; but the earliest Christians had been a tiny minority in a pagan world, mostly made up of people who had in any case converted as adults. The custom of infant baptism had grown up as Christians became numerous and then a majority, and one tradition that Luther still took for granted was the belief that everyone should belong to a single organized Church.

The Anabaptists, by contrast, were not a single organized group but a collection of **sects**—small groups that saw themselves as part of a minority of true believers apart from the rest of society. They varied considerably in their ideas, which often proved troublesome to established society. Some applied New Testament teachings literally to their own times, refused military service, and sought to establish a more egalitarian community. As among the earliest Christians, women were often prominent in their worship, though they were usually the wives of male leaders. Some sects advocated acts of violence against "ungodly" persons and against officials who declined to punish them.

Luther, however, was determined not to let changes in the Church spill over into the rest of society. In 1524, he responded angrily to a peasant revolt that swept through Germany. The serfs were seeking relief from new burdens laid upon them by their feudal lords, especially in eastern Germany, and often used slogans of Christian freedom and equality derived from Luther's protest. But Luther urged the aristocracy to put down the violent uprising without mercy, to slay the rebels as they would "mad dogs." He later admitted that it was he who had commanded the slaughter of the peasants: "All their blood is on my head. But I throw the responsibility on our Lord God, who instructed me to give this order." (Luther also urged harsh measures against Jews, reinforcing the popular anti-Semitism of his times.)

 Luther Rages Against the "Murdering and Robbing Bands of Peasants" Read Luther's condemnation of the peasant revolt.

Luther was equally severe with the Anabaptists. He considered them "blasphemers" and believed that they, like persons guilty of rebellion against the state, should be executed. In fact, Lutherans and Catholics alike brutally persecuted the Anabaptists, for they both believed in a Church that included everyone, was integrated with the existing society, and was allied with the state. But would this Church be Catholic or Lutheran? That depended on the wielders of power in the existing society—the local rulers in the Holy Roman Empire, and the emperor Charles V himself.

 An Anabaptist Martyr Takes the Stand Read the testimony of an Anabaptist who refused to recant his beliefs.

War and Stalemate

In 1529, Charles and the Catholic members of the Imperial Diet reaffirmed the earlier Worms decree prohibiting all new religious doctrines in Germany. The Lutheran rulers protested this action and acquired the name "Protestant," which in time came to be used for all the rebellious creeds. Meanwhile, in the 1530s, armed alliances of Lutheran and Catholic rulers formed within the empire and eventually went to war.

Which side a particular territory found itself on depended on several factors—Lutheran and Catholic religious leadership, the convictions and interests of its ruler, and its distance from the southern power base of the emperor. Generally, rulers in southern Germany upheld Catholicism in their own territories and were willing to defend it by force. They were less eager to help Charles crush the Lutheran rulers in the north, however, for fear that he would become too powerful and turn his loose imperial authority into real control over them. As a result, several bouts of warfare ended in a truce known as the **Religious Peace of Augsburg** (1555), in which the Diet agreed to leave each ruler free to choose either Catholicism or Lutheranism for his

territory—which in practice meant that the northern territories were mostly Lutheran, while the southern ones remained Catholic. The Catholics had failed to crush the Lutheran revolt, but the Lutherans had failed to reform the Church throughout the empire. It was a foretaste of what would eventually happen between Protestants and Catholics on the scale of Western Christendom as a whole.

The Evangelical Church

Meanwhile, in the Lutheran territories the **Evangelical** (gospel-following) **Church**, as it was usually called, came into being. It was an organized institution like the Catholic Church, though of course with a different set of beliefs that were set out in the **Augsburg Confession** of 1530. Luther did not believe that God had established any particular structure for the Church, except that, like any organized institution, its workings must be orderly. The only people who could guarantee orderliness were rulers, so in each Lutheran territory, the ruler appointed superintendents to oversee the religious establishment—thus subordinating church to state. The formerly Catholic religious buildings and grounds were assigned to the new churches, but the extensive landholdings of bishoprics and monasteries were taken over by the rulers.

The Evangelical Church had neither monks and nuns, nor veneration of saints and relics, and its ministers were expected to marry. Luther himself married a former nun, Katharina von Bora, the daughter of a poverty-stricken nobleman who had handed her over to a convent at the age of five. Soon after the indulgences dispute began, she led a group of nuns in an escape from the convent with Luther's help, and eventually became his wife. As a married woman, in between bearing six children she managed a large property that the Saxon elector had handed over to Luther for religious and charitable purposes. She was among the first of many generations of busy and forceful wives of Protestant clergy—the kinds of wives who were "above rubies," according to the Old Testament proverb (p. 41). She and Luther seem to have made each other happy—though at least once when he annoyed her, she told him: "Before I put up with this, I'd rather go back to the convent and leave you and all our children!" By his acts and teachings, Luther raised the value placed on marriage and upheld the rights of wives to sexual satisfaction; he did not, however, urge any basic changes in the social role of women.

The Evangelical worship service was not much different from the Catholic service, except in two all-important respects. Both ministers and people received bread and wine in the

Religious Peace of Augsburg
An agreement to end religious wars within the Holy Roman Empire by allowing rulers the freedom to determine the faith (Lutheran or Catholic) of their territories.

Evangelical Church
The name given to the church formed by Luther; from *evangelical*, meaning "gospel-following."

Augsburg Confession
A document detailing the beliefs of Luther's Evangelical Church.

THE RELIGIOUS PEACE OF AUGSBURG

In 1555, both Catholics and Lutherans came to the Diet of the Holy Roman Empire (the empire's parliament-like assembly) in the German city of Augsburg, to bring an end to twenty-five years of religious warfare in the empire. Electors (local rulers who chose the emperor), other rulers ranking as princes, high-ranking noblemen, bishops and other leading clergy, and representatives of important cities attended. The Catholic Ferdinand of Habsburg, ruler of the Habsburg territories in central Europe, presided on behalf of his brother the Holy Roman Emperor Charles V. The result of the Diet was an agreement for mutual toleration between opposing versions of Christianity that lasted for more than fifty years.

The various groups at the Diet are referred to here as "estates"; an individual belonging to any one of them is called an "estate." "His Roman Imperial Majesty" is Charles V; "we" and "us" are Ferdinand himself, referring to himself in the plural as was customary for monarchs.

In order that . . . peace, which is especially necessary in view of the divided religions, as is seen from the causes before mentioned, and is demanded by the sad necessity of the Holy Roman Empire of the German nation, may be the better established and made secure and enduring between his Roman Imperial Majesty and us, on the one hand, and the electors, princes, and estates of the Holy Empire of the German nation on the other, therefore his Imperial Majesty, and we, and the electors, princes, and estates of the Holy Empire will not make war upon any estate of the empire on account of the Augsburg Confession and the doctrine, religion, and faith of the same, nor injure nor do violence to those estates that hold it, nor force them, against their conscience, knowledge, and will, to abandon the religion, faith, church usages, ordinances, and ceremonies of the Augsburg Confession, where these have been established, or may hereafter be established, in their principalities, lands, and dominions. Nor shall we, through mandate or in any other way, trouble or disparage them, but shall let them quietly and peacefully enjoy their religion, faith, church usages, ordinances, and ceremonies, as well as their possessions, real and personal property, lands, people, dominions, governments, honors, and rights. . . .

On the other hand, the estates that have accepted the Augsburg Confession shall suffer his Imperial Majesty, us, and the electors, princes, and other estates of the Holy Empire, adhering to the old religion, to abide in like manner by their religion, faith, church usages, ordinances, and ceremonies. They shall also leave undisturbed their possessions, real and personal property, lands, people, dominions, government, honors, and rights, rents, interest, and tithes. . . .

But all others who are not adherents of either of the above-mentioned religions are not included in this peace, but shall be altogether excluded. . . .

No estate shall urge another estate, or the subjects of the same, to embrace its religion.

But when our subjects and those of the electors, princes, and estates, adhering to the old religion or to the Augsburg Confession, wish, for the sake of their religion, to go with wife and children to another place in the lands, principalities, and cities of the electors, princes, and estates of the Holy Empire, and settle there, such going and coming, and the sale of property and goods, in return for reasonable compensation for serfdom and arrears of taxes, . . . shall be everywhere unhindered, permitted, and granted. . . .

EXPLORING THE SOURCE

1. What are the limits on the religious toleration that this agreement guarantees?

2. What reason is given here for establishing religious toleration?

Source: James Harvey Robinson, ed., *Readings in European History* (Boston: Ginn, 1904), 2:114–116.

Eucharist, in token of the Christian equality between them; and the language was German, so that God could be understood when he spoke to the people. Art and music, and above all the singing of hymns, many composed by Luther himself, added to the impact of the reading and explanation of the Word of God in the Bible.

LO³ The Calvinist Movement

Luther's rebellion soon found sympathizers outside the Holy Roman Empire, but only in Scandinavia—the northern kingdoms of Denmark, Norway, and Sweden—did actual rulers support him and reform the Church on his model. In other regions, there was no way that he could control the rebellion that he had started. Anabaptist sects multiplied across Europe from the Low Countries to Poland and Hungary in spite of persecution. And among reformers who held to the idea of a single Christian Church to which all must belong, leadership passed to a Frenchman with more radical ideas than Luther about the Church's beliefs, practices, and organization—John Calvin.

Calvin: The International Reformer

Younger than Luther by some twenty-five years, Calvin was the son of a well-off lawyer. His father saw to it that he got a good education in Paris, where he gained knowledge of theology, law, and humanist scholarship. To begin with, he was a pious Catholic, but in 1533, as he later put it, "God by a sudden conversion subdued and brought my mind to a teachable frame."

In fear of persecution, he left France and lived in various cities of the Holy Roman Empire that were sympathetic to reform, while he put his early learning and his newfound conviction into writing the *Institutes of* ("Introduction to") *the Christian Religion*. In spite of its title, the book was a detailed and systematic statement of reformed Christian belief as Calvin understood it.

In 1536, the same year that Calvin published the *Institutes*, he settled down in the Swiss city of Geneva (see Map 17.1

The Reformed Temple, Lyon A christening begins at a Calvinist church in the southern French city during the 1560s. In a barn-like structure, well-dressed men and women sit mostly apart, and there are no holy images though the coats of arms of local worthies are displayed. A pulpit takes the place of an altar. A dog gazes faithfully and attentively up at the preacher.
The Granger Collection, New York

on page 312). Like the rest of Switzerland, Geneva was part of the Holy Roman Empire, and it had just revolted against the local ruler, a bishop. The city was in political and religious turmoil, but Calvin soon achieved dominance in the community and held it until his death in 1564. Reformers all over Europe read the *Institutes* in the original Latin and in translation, and came to Geneva to see how Calvin's version of a reformed Church worked in practice. Calvinism soon became the leading Protestant force across Europe from Scotland to Hungary.

Predestination: The Saved and the Damned

Calvin was very close to Luther in his basic beliefs, but there was a real difference in what they chose to emphasize. For Luther, it was the question of the soul's salvation, which led him to the doctrine of justification through faith alone. For Calvin, it was God's almighty power and human wickedness, which led him to stress the doctrine of **predestination**.

God, declared Calvin, foreknows and determines everything that happens in the universe. It follows that he determines who shall be saved and who shall be forever lost. All people, inheriting hopeless sinfulness from Adam and Eve, would disobey God if left to their own puny powers. But God gives to those he "elects" (chooses) the ability to persevere in his service. The rest, for his own mysterious reasons, he allows to fall. Calvin unflinchingly defined this doctrine in his *Institutes*:

> Predestination we call the eternal decree of God, by which he has determined in himself, what he would have become of every individual of mankind. For they are not all created with a similar destiny; but eternal life is foreordained for some, and eternal damnation for others. Every man, therefore, being created for one or the other of these ends, we say, he is predestinated either to life or to death.

Against the charge that God could not be so unfair as to condemn most of humankind to damnation, Calvin admitted that this was "an awe-inspiring decree." But he insisted that no one actually deserves salvation, and that it is only through God's gracious mercy that some are saved.

Predestination was a traditional Christian belief, which the revered early thinker Augustine had insisted on and which had first been stated by Paul himself (pp. 128, 143). Catholic thinkers mostly accepted that God chose whom to save, but they also believed that he left people free to do good works that would help them into heaven. How God could do both these opposite-seeming things was a divine mystery that human reason could not solve, and which it was best to be cautious about discussing. Luther also accepted predestination, but avoided stressing it for fear of discouraging believers. Calvin, on the other hand, proclaimed predestination as starkly as possible and made it the driving force behind a new and powerful international Protestant movement.

The Reformed Church

Calvin's opponents sometimes argued that predestination destroyed all incentive for following a righteous Christian life, and that it made membership in a Church unnecessary for salvation. Calvin insisted, however, that it was God's will that the elect should be saved through the Church, and that no one knows for certain who is elect and who is "reprobate" (condemned). All people must therefore live righteously as if they enjoyed God's favor, and they must all belong to the Church.

> "*Calvinism soon became the leading Protestant force across Europe from Scotland to Hungary.*"

The Presbyterian Hierarchy

Calvin accepted, with Luther, the principle of the "priesthood of all believers." The **Reformed Church**, as it was usually called, gave to its ministers no special powers that set them apart from baptized lay-people. But Calvin also believed, in the humanist tradition, that a God-given model for the workings of the Church was to be found in early Christian churches, with their officials chosen by the congregations (p. 128). Accordingly, the governance and worship of congregations were in the hands of elected elders, with a system of local, regional, and countrywide boards of elders above them. In this way, the Reformed Church held to the Catholic belief in a God-given hierarchy (Church structure), though the actual structure was very different. Whereas the Catholic hierarchy was **episcopal** (controlled by bishops, who at the time were mostly appointed by rulers and confirmed by the pope), the Reformed one was **presbyterian** (controlled by elected elders—from the Greek word for "elder").

Likewise in the humanist tradition, Calvin went behind the worship practices that had grown up over the centuries and insisted that worship be based on what he believed to be the rule of the earliest churches—"that no meeting of the church should take place without the Word, prayers, partaking of the Lord's Supper, and alms-giving." "The Word" meant Bible readings, sermons explaining them, and psalm-singing; the Lord's Supper was the sacrament of the Eucharist. Calvin agreed with Luther that the only sacraments are baptism and the Eucharist, and that all should receive both bread and wine. More radically than Luther, he declared that the presence of Christ in the Eucharist is spiritual, not physical.

The minister wore no splendid robes but a simple black gown—the equivalent of today's business suit. Calvin believed that art and ornamentation had no place in the Church; the awesome Catholic cathedrals, with their stained glass, statues, and splendid altars, he branded as pagan. Instead, Reformed "temples" (named after the Temple in Jerusalem) were modest structures, in which the pulpit often stood in place of the altar (see photo on page 317).

> *"Eternal life is foreordained for some, and eternal damnation for others."*
> —John Calvin

Church and State

However, Calvin did share Catholic ideas on the partnership of Church and state. He believed that the purpose of government was to regulate society according to the will of God, and that the Church was the appointed interpreter of God's will: "Great kings ought not to think it any dishonor to humble themselves before Christ, the King of Kings, nor ought they to be displeased at being judged by the Church. . . . They ought even to wish not to be spared by the pastors, that they may be spared by the Lord." That was similar to what Pope Gelasius had told a Roman emperor about the relationship between "the authority of bishops and the imperial power" more than a thousand years before (p. 147). But the Church authority that Calvin had in mind was that of the pastors (elders charged with teaching and worship), and the partner of the Church that he himself mainly dealt with was the town council of Geneva.

Among the council's duties as upholder of the Church, Calvin believed in traditional fashion, was the suppression of heresy. In 1553, Calvin was the driving force behind the council's trial and execution of a Spaniard, Michael Servetus, who challenged the doctrine of the Trinity (p. 146)—though the council applied the traditional penalty of burning at the stake against Calvin's wishes. In the Reformation, what was heresy and what was orthodoxy often depended on whose side one was on, but Servetus denied a belief that nearly all Christians still upheld. When he was arrested in Geneva, the Reformed town council received a request for his extradition from the Catholic Inquisition (p. 219) in France, which the council denied so that they could burn him themselves.

> *"The theater, because of its historical associations with paganism, was closed down in Geneva; art was seen as a distraction from God's word."*

 **"Calvin 500"** (http://www.calvin500.com/) Learn more about Calvin's life and beliefs.

"A Godly, Righteous, and Sober Life"

Another function of the Reformed Church, springing from Calvin's belief that all Christians must live according to God's commands, was to ensure that all Christians actually did so. With no sacrament of penance to wash away sin, and no monks, nuns, or saints in heaven to intercede for God's mercy, it was actually more important for the Reformed Church than for the Catholic Church to supervise every detail of its members' behavior.

Calvin criticized any form of decoration lest it lead to vanity and pride—and any form of card playing lest it lead to gambling. The theater, because of its historical associations with paganism, was closed down in Geneva; art was seen as a distraction from God's word. Drinking was condemned as a prelude to intoxication, and dancing was prohibited as a stimulant to desire. The clothing of women had to be plain and ample; the display of personal ornament or the exposure of flesh was a signal to lustfulness. In living such a strictly disciplined life, concluded Calvin, one follows the teachings of the Lord, who "condemned all those pleasures which seduce the heart from chastity and purity."

This strictness was not at all the same as the traditional idea of an ascetic life. Like Luther, Calvin thought that the way of life of the monk or nun, based on the belief that virginity, fasting, and poverty were good works, was a wicked delusion that must lead a person to hell. Instead, God's elect must live what England's Calvinist-influenced *Book of Common Prayer* (p. 325) called "a godly, righteous, and sober life," not an ascetic one. They must eat and drink in moderation, marry and be true to their spouses, accumulate wealth through hard work and thrift, and donate it generously to the relief of the poor. Calvin took for granted (as Luther and Catholic theologians did not) the functions of capital, banking, and large-scale commerce—though, in his day, the biggest merchants and bankers were mostly Catholic, like the Fuggers (p. 255).

To Calvin, a person's conscience was the main guide to living in accordance with God's commands. But if a person could not avoid wrongdoing, Calvin believed, it was up to other Christians to be their "brother's keeper." As chief pastor in Geneva, he used his pulpit to warn and frighten potential sinners. When his sermons failed, he resorted to compulsion. Offenders were hailed before the Consistory, an assembly of elders from the various congregations in Geneva, which might reprimand the accused or impose bread-and-water sentences upon them. Common offenses included profanity, drunken-

 Religious Law and Order in Calvin's Geneva Read Calvin's ideas about enforcing religious law and order.

ness, dozing in church, criticizing ministers, and dancing.

In this way, a style of life evolved in Geneva that was imitated by Calvin's followers across Europe. Urged on by the hope of being among the elect and the fear of being among the reprobate, the disciplined, active, and persistent Calvinists became the leaders in the international movement of Protestant reform in the second half of the sixteenth century—at the same time as the Catholics were finally putting their house in order.

LO⁴ Catholic Renewal and Reform

From the 1530s onward, the threatened heretic takeover of the Church galvanized the papacy into wholeheartedly backing reform, while devoted priests founded new religious orders that rallied believers to the Church. The long-delayed Catholic movement of renewal and reform got under way—a movement that today is usually called the **Catholic Reformation**.

The Reforming Popes

By the 1530s, Luther's protest could no longer be seen in Rome as a "squabble among monks," and in 1534, a new pope, Paul III, committed himself seriously to reform. He launched an overhaul of papal administration and ordered a report by a committee of cardinals on abuses among the clergy that was so shocking that he kept it secret. His most decisive measure, however, was to summon a general council of bishops to settle the deep troubles facing the Church.

For the papacy, this was a risky move. The Church had a thousand-year-old tradition of holding general councils to deal with disputes, but councils had often made compromises between opposing beliefs, or they had bowed to the wishes of secular rulers, or they had set themselves up as rival authorities to the popes (pp. 145–146, 248). On the other hand, such a meeting might be able to set the course for a program of Catholic reform and renewal with the papacy at its head. That was what happened on this occasion (see photo).

The Council of Trent

The **Council of Trent** met in the northern Italian city of that name, with lengthy interruptions, over a period of some twenty years (1545–1563). Papal ambassadors presided over the sessions, and the pope had to approve the council's decisions. The growing bitterness of the religious divide meant that Protestants were unwilling to attend and were eventually not permitted to do so. All this enabled the papacy to ensure that the council would do what it wanted.

The council acted vigorously against corruption and wrongdoing within the Church. Bishops were ordered to regain strict discipline over their clergy and to provide better education for the priesthood by establishing seminaries (theological schools). The council passed decrees against simony (the sale of Church positions) and pluralism (the holding of more than one Church office at a time). Simony was already a Church offense, but making pluralism illegal was something new, and from now on, both prohibitions were taken more or less seriously. The council also outlawed the

≪ Heresy Crushed A wall painting in a Roman church by a local painter, Pasquale Cati, shows the Council of Trent at work. A panel of cardinals discusses with a bishop, a secretary takes notes, and the Holy Spirit descends to inspire the proceedings. In front, female figures representing Christian virtues—Charity, for instance, nurtures two children—surround a majestic lady representing the Catholic Church, who tramples the demon of Heresy beneath her feet. Santa Maria in Trastevere, Rome/The Bridgeman Art Library

selling of indulgences while affirming that the spiritual grace granted by indulgences was genuine.

On the other hand, the council uncompromisingly upheld traditional beliefs and practices. The special powers of the priesthood, the role of the papacy, the seven sacraments, the doctrine of transubstantiation, the veneration of saints and relics, the belief in purgatory, and above all, the necessity for salvation of good works as well as God's grace—all were specifically confirmed. At the same time, the council condemned the opposing Protestant doctrines. The result was to make orthodoxy clearer than before but also narrower, and to leave Catholic theologians with less freedom of interpretation than in earlier times. In an era of religious struggle, however, that was another sign of the council's success.

 The Council of Trent and Catholic Reformation Read a selection from the Council of Trent.

The Jesuits

Like earlier reform movements, this one also needed people who were willing to devote their lives to it, and who would rally ordinary believers to the Church by methods suited to the political, social, and cultural conditions of their time. That was what the Cluniac and Cistercian monks, and later the Franciscan and Dominican friars, had done in the Middle Ages. Now it was the turn of the Jesuits.

Ignatius Loyola

Ignatius Loyola, the founder of the Jesuits, grew up in Spain, the one country in Western Christendom where reform had already got under way in the late fifteenth century. Cardinal Ximenes (**hi-MEH-nes**), archbishop of Toledo, had mounted a rigorous campaign to improve the morals and education of the clergy, the Inquisition had ruthlessly enforced orthodoxy against heretics, Jews, and Muslims, and pious rulers from Isabella and Ferdinand onward had overseen these efforts. Like Luther and Calvin, Loyola underwent a profound religious experience as a young man, but it sent him in exactly the opposite direction—to a life of total dedication to the Catholic Church.

Loyola was of noble birth and had an early career as a soldier. But in 1521—the same year that Luther stood before the Diet of Worms—he was fighting in defense of a castle when a cannonball badly wounded him in both legs. In the months of agonizing surgery and tedious convalescence that followed, he turned his warrior instincts of loyalty and courage from the king's service to that of Jesus. He wanted to do some great feat for his new "commander," but he was not sure what it should be. He learned Latin, preached on street corners in cities in Spain, lived for a time as a hermit in a cave, studied theology at the

"To attain the truth in all things, we ought always to hold that we believe what seems to us white to be black, if the Hierarchical Church so defines it."

—from Loyola's *Spiritual Exercises*

University of Paris, and thought seriously of moving to the Holy Land and converting the Muslims. Finally, he and a few companions went to Rome, were welcomed by the reforming Pope Paul III, and put themselves at his service for whatever he might order them to do. In 1539, they became an official religious order, the Society of Jesus, with the mission "to employ itself entirely in the defense of the holy Catholic faith."

Jesuits The Society of Jesus, a Catholic order founded by Ignatius Loyola with the mission to defend the Catholic faith.

"Thinking with the Church"

When Loyola died in 1556, the Society of Jesus had grown to about 1,000 members; two centuries later, there were about 20,000 Jesuits. They were carefully selected and rigorously schooled in the same absolute devotion to Jesus that Ignatius himself felt, using methods of prayer and meditation that he explained in his book of *Spiritual Exercises*. ("Exercise," in those days, usually meant "military training.") The *Exercises* included "Rules for Thinking with the Church," among them "Laying aside all private judgment, we ought to keep our minds prepared and ready to obey in all things the true Spouse of Christ our Lord, which is our Holy Mother, the Hierarchical Church." These were very different words from Luther's at the Diet of Worms.

But as purposeful as the Jesuits were in their training and goals, in their methods they were extraordinarily flexible. As revivalist preachers, they stirred crowds of believers with passionate sermons on the torments of hell and the bliss of heaven, the sufferings of Jesus and the miracles of the saints.

As father confessors, they steered the lives of sinners one at a time, using kindly and understanding methods and thereby ensuring that their guidance would be welcomed—including by rulers who could use their power to uphold the Church. As educators, they turned the sons of the middle and upper classes into Renaissance gentlemen with a humanist knowledge of the ancients (pp. 290–292), who also reliably "thought with the Church." As missionaries in China, they dressed and behaved like Chinese gentlemen, and became learned in the literature and thought of that country (pp. 279–280). In ways like these,

 Spiritual Exercises: A Manual for Christian Training Read a selection from Loyola's Spiritual Exercises.

 "History of the Jesuits" (http://www .historyworld.net/ wrldhis/PlainText Histories.asp?historyid =ab30#1577) Learn more about the experiences of the early Jesuit missionaries.

the Jesuits imitated the apostle Paul, who once said that to spread the gospel he had "become all things to all people." That was what enabled them to rally believers to the traditional faith in a changing and expanding Europe.

With popes committed to reform and renewal, a definite course set by the Council of Trent, and the purposeful flexibility of the Jesuits, in the second half of the sixteenth century, the Church moved from stagnation and defensiveness to a bold offensive. Its vigorous response to the Protestant challenge prevented further losses, and the religious divisions of about 1560 (see Map 17.1 on page 312) generally remain today. But it took another century before all sides accepted the divisions as more or less final—a century not just of religious debate, but also of religious repression and religious war.

LO⁵ Religion, Politics, and War

In spite of all the Reformation changes, most of the contending religious groups held to two traditional beliefs. The first was that there must be only one Church, proclaiming one religious truth, to which all people must belong. The second was that rulers and other power wielders must be partners of the Church, helping it to uphold religious truth and guide people to salvation. Now that there was no longer a single religion but several "religions," as they were called, each with its own version of truth, these beliefs in unanimity and partnership actually made for conflict.

In every country, there were also humanists who were in principle against settling religious disputes by force, as well as statesmen who feared that religious repression and war would weaken their countries in nonreligious struggles. But they got a hearing only at times when the rival religious groups had fought each other to a standstill and compromise of some kind seemed inevitable. And even when compromises came about, new religious disputes and nonreligious conflicts supplied new reasons for war.

As a result, wars of religion were fought in three main stages, each inspired by the main religious movements of the time and intertwined with fierce nonreligious conflicts. First came the wars in the Holy Roman Empire arising from the spread of Lutheranism, which ended in the first effort at religious compromise, the Peace of Augsburg of 1555. Then, in the second half of the sixteenth century, the spread of Calvinism resulted in civil and international wars involving the Netherlands and France. Finally, as the Catholic Reformation gathered strength, Catholic efforts to recover lost territory led, in the first half of the seventeenth century, to new struggles in the Holy Roman Empire that reached their height in the Thirty Years' War.

When the Thirty Years' War ended in stalemate, efforts to change the religious balance internationally came to seem so costly and destructive that they were finally seen as clearly harmful to the nonreligious interests of whoever pursued them. As a result, in the second half of the seventeenth century, religion gradually ceased to play a role in international conflicts. In this way, out of the religious wars of the Reformation there grew a new, secular European state system.

Religious Repression

Repression of one kind or another was continually practiced by all sides throughout the era of the Reformation. It took two forms—outright persecution of rival religions using updated methods, and efforts to prevent ideas from spreading by restricting freedom of the press.

≪ **"Force Outbids Reason"** The motto at right gives the message of a cartoon of 1686, when King Louis XIV of France was persecuting Huguenots (French Calvinists). A "Missionary dragoon" (a mounted infantryman—label at bottom left) levels a musket to make a Huguenot sign a drumhead conversion. The dragoon's musket, loaded with a cross, is labeled "Invincible argument"; his sword is labeled "Penetrating argument." The caption at top makes clear that this is happening by order of the king. Bibliotheque Nationale, Paris/Giraudon/The Bridgeman Art Library

THE REFORMATION WAS AN ERA OF WIDESPREAD PERSECUTION, AND OF CIVIL AND INTERNATIONAL WARS OF RELIGION, FOR SEVERAL REASONS:

Attempts to Uphold Different Versions of Religious Truth

- Rulers and churches of dominant religions tried to repress rival religions as part of their duty of upholding religious truth, and to prevent rival believers from taking power and doing the same to them.

- Rulers of countries with different dominant religions made war on each other as part of their duty of upholding religious truth, and to avoid being conquered and persecuted themselves.

- Within countries, believers in out-of-power religions, facing a hostile partnership of Church and state, rebelled and sought help from sympathetic foreign rulers, hoping to become dominant themselves.

Nonreligious Reasons for Conflict

- Rulers continued their endless nonreligious struggles for power, land, and trading opportunities, as well as for personal, dynastic, and national glory.

- Rulers' partnerships with powerful subjects—especially nobles—also continued to be full of frictions.

- Religious disputes did not replace all these conflicts but became entangled with them.

- Religious and nonreligious rivalries reinforced each other, and wars of religion were all the longer and more embittered as a result.

New-Style Persecution

In the Reformation era, medieval methods of persecution mostly went out of style. Only in Spain, Portugal, and Italy did the traditional Inquisition and burnings at the stake continue, but elsewhere, persecution was "modernized" (see photo). Everywhere local clergy were on the watch for religious dissidents, but actual intimidation and punishment became the work of the state. In Catholic countries, troops would be billeted in Protestant districts to live at the people's expense and harass them into conforming; Protestant ministers would be given life sentences as galley slaves; and if all else failed, the Protestants of whole regions would be given the choice between conversion and expulsion.

Catholics in Protestant countries were also systematically persecuted. In England, for example, Catholic families could be ruined by huge fines for not attending Protestant services, and priests were sadistically put to death as traitors. In Catholic France and in Habsburg-ruled territories in the Holy Roman Empire, as well as in Protestant England and Scandinavia, these new kinds of persecution drove the rival religions deep underground.

> "Out of the religious wars of the Reformation there grew a new, secular European state system."

Religious Censorship

In every country, as the rulers became aware of the power of printed books to spread ideas, they tried to bring the new technology under their control. Printers were licensed by governments or guilds (pp. 200–201), and could lose their licenses and be sent to prison for publishing objectionable books; literature of the wrong religion belonged in this category, along with such material as attacks on rulers, revelations of scandals involving powerful people, and pornography. The most systematic censorship was established in Catholic countries by the Council of Trent. The council authorized an Index (list) of prohibited books, and established the Congregation of the Index to publish the list and keep it current. The Index remained in force until 1965, when it was dropped by order of the Second Vatican Council (p. 556).

But the printing industry was too large and diverse to be easily controlled. Printers could set up underground workshops; books that were prohibited in a country of one religion could be smuggled in from a country of another religion; printers in countries with easygoing censorship, notably Holland, did good business publishing books that were objectionable in countries

Huguenots
French Calvinists.

politique
A French term for the school of thought that put politics before religion and sought religious compromise for the sake of national unity.

of every religion. In religion, as in other fields, censorship was no more than a minor drag on the spread of ideas.

The Calvinist Wars: The Netherlands and France

In the late sixteenth century, reformers in many countries rallied to Calvin, and his version of Protestantism often found support from nobles who appreciated the limits he set to the authority of rulers. In Scotland, Calvinist nobles actually overthrew a ruler, Queen Mary; in Hungary, they resisted Habsburg power with the support of the Turks, who occupied much of that country. But the longest conflicts over Calvinism were in the Netherlands and France.

The Revolt of the Netherlands

The Low Countries, or Netherlands, were a center of trade and industry that formed a wealthy part of the Habsburg domains, and the region's powerful cities had a long-standing tradition of self-government. Protestantism first spread there from Germany and then grew rapidly under Calvinist leadership (see Map 17.1 on page 312). At about the same time, the Netherlands came under the rule of the Spanish Habsburgs, following the division of the territories of Charles V (p. 267), and in 1567, King Philip II of Spain responded to the spread of Calvinism with cruel repression. In addition to admitting the Inquisition to the area, he introduced harsh political and economic restrictions. In reaction to this challenge to their self-government, both Catholics and Calvinists rebelled in 1566 under the leadership of a local aristocrat and Habsburg official, William "the Silent," prince of Orange-Nassau.

There followed nearly half a century of wars, in which the Netherlands gradually divided. Spanish armies and growing Catholic mistrust of the Calvinists recovered the southern Netherlands for the old rulers and the old religion. But in the north, the defiant Calvinists, with English help, fought the Habsburg forces on land and sea. In 1581, they declared independence, but it took nearly thirty years before a truce gave them de facto Spanish recognition in 1609. A new country had appeared, the United Provinces of the Netherlands—often known as Holland, the name of its largest province.

Holland's commercial wealth made it a leading contender in European power struggles throughout the seventeenth century, and it became one of the main challengers of Spain and Portugal for control of worldwide trade and empire. It was governed as a loose confederation of provinces, with descendants of William the Silent presiding alongside many other competing power wielders as *stadtholders* (viceroys), the title of the former Spanish governors. There were still many Catholics in Holland, many disagreements among the dominant Calvinists, and many dissident Protestant groups. Persecution would risk renewed civil war in a small country that was still vulnerable to Spanish attack,

and would also be very bad for business. Instead, therefore, Holland became Europe's first country to hold consistently to a policy of religious toleration, though the government stayed under Calvinist control.

Civil War in France

Religion and politics were also mixed in France. Early in the Reformation, persecution by the Catholic rulers had kept Protestantism from spreading, but after the death in 1547 of King Francis I, the country had a series of weak rulers, and noble factions began to spring up that sought either to limit the monarch's power or to bring the government under their control. At about the same time, missionaries from Geneva began to spread their beliefs in France (see Map 17.1 on page 312). Soon, there was a growing **Huguenot (HYOO-guh-noh)** movement (a French slang word for "Swiss"), in which Calvinist ministers supplied religious fervor and powerful nobles provided military force.

The Huguenots never made enough converts or gained enough victories to take over the government, but the rulers were too weak, and had too many independent-minded Catholic nobles to deal with as well, to be able to crush them. The result was a series of civil wars and foreign interventions that continued on and off for most of the second half of the sixteenth century.

The very existence of France as a powerful independent country seemed to be threatened by religious struggles, and a school of thinking grew up, known by the French name *politique* ("political," because it put politics before religion), that sought religious compromise for the sake of national unity. Finally, King Henry IV, legitimate ruler by inheritance but also a Huguenot, brought the wars to an end by following a *politique* strategy. He defeated Catholic forces in battle but himself became a Catholic so as to win the loyalty of the strongest religion. To keep the support of the Huguenots, by the Edict of Nantes (1598) he guaranteed them civil rights, religious tolerance, and even the possession of military forces and strongholds.

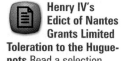 **Henry IV's Edict of Nantes Grants Limited Toleration to the Huguenots** Read a selection from the Edict of Nantes.

In this way, Henry was able to restore both national unity and royal power, but after his death, this second effort to keep religious disputes separate from political struggles broke down. The French rulers became fervent Catholics as the Catholic Reformation took hold, and Cardinal Richelieu (**ree-shuh-LYOO**), the powerful minister of Henry's successor, King Louis XIII, viewed the Huguenots as an obstacle to royal power—a "state within the state." In renewed civil war, he broke the military power of the aristocratic Huguenot faction. For the time being, Huguenots were still tolerated, but they now faced a strong Catholic government that favored those of its own religion. From a powerful faction under noble leadership, the Huguenots became a minority of middle-class townspeople and peasants.

England: A Middle Way?

In sixteenth-century England, shrewd and strong-willed rulers of the Tudor dynasty maintained the powerful monarchy that had emerged from the fifteenth-century Wars of the Roses (p. 262). But England was also caught up in the Reformation, and out of its rulers' efforts to reform the Church while not having their power undermined by religious struggles, there emerged yet another Christianity. **Anglicanism** (from the Latin for "English") borrowed from both Lutheranism and Calvinism but also kept many Catholic features. It was a compelling faith in its own right, which also for a time—but only for a time—saved England from civil war over religion.

"The King's Great Matter"

More than anyone else, it was an actual ruler, King Henry VIII, who opened the door to reform. For most of his long reign, he ruled as a Catholic king in partnership with the Church, and even earned the title "Defender of the Faith" from Pope Leo X for a book that he personally wrote attacking the beliefs of Martin Luther. Then, however, a royal family problem arose that involved the papacy and was also an issue in European power politics—the fact that his only surviving child with his queen, Catherine of Aragon, was a daughter. Powerful noble factions still lurked beneath the surface of the Tudor monarchy, and Henry feared that under a woman's rule, new civil wars would start. He must have a son; the queen was beyond childbearing age and had a young attendant, Anne Boleyn, who had caught his eye; so he needed the pope to annul his marriage so that he could marry Anne.

Popes had done favors of this kind for kings before, but the pope at the time, Clement VII, was under pressure from Catherine's powerful nephew, the Holy Roman emperor Charles V—and in the course of Italian power struggles, Charles had occupied Rome itself. Caught between Charles's wish to have England come under the rule of a relative and Henry's desire for a male heir, the pope decided to do nothing.

For six years, Henry pursued what the English called "the king's great matter" in Rome, until his patience finally ran out. He married Anne Boleyn in 1533, after his newly appointed archbishop, Thomas Cranmer, had declared his marriage to Catherine annulled. Clement promptly excommunicated the king and released Henry's subjects from their obligation of obedience to the crown. In the past, such papal actions had led to vicious power struggles with rulers, but no ruler had challenged the belief that the pope was the Christ-appointed head of the Church. Now, however, in the era of Luther's revolt, Henry "declared independence" from the papacy.

The Royal Supremacy

For this purpose, Henry did what English kings had got into the habit of doing, to rally the support of their subjects behind important measures—he acted with the "advice and consent" of the Parliament (p. 262). In 1534, Parliament passed the Act of Supremacy, which declared that the king was the "only supreme head on earth" of the Church of England. Additional acts forbade communication with and payments to the "bishop of Rome"; gave the crown the right to appoint bishops and abbots; and made refusing to swear to the king's supremacy an act of treason.

The king's break with the papacy encouraged English reformers inspired by Luther and Calvin to expect changes in traditional beliefs and practices as well. In some ways, Henry satisfied them—most radically, by abolishing monasteries and nunneries, confiscating their property, and selling it off to the profit of the crown. But in other ways, he remained a "defender of the faith." In 1539, he had Parliament pass the Act of Six Articles, which ordered penalties up to and including death for denying various traditional beliefs and practices such as transubstantiation and an unmarried clergy.

Meanwhile, Henry's search for a son, his changing love interests, and vicious rivalries at court led him to marry six wives in all, separate from two of them, and behead two others, including Anne Boleyn. When he died in 1547, he left three children, each with a different mother and a different religious upbringing. There were a young boy, Edward, and two adult daughters: Mary, the offspring of Catherine of Aragon; and Anne Boleyn's child, Elizabeth. In eleven years, all these children came to the throne in turn, and with each ruler, England officially changed its religion.

Anglicanism
The faith of the Church of England, with both Protestant and Catholic features.

Catholicism in Britain Before the Turn to Protestantism (http://www.bbc.co.uk/history/programmes/av/hob/hob_06.ram) Learn about the Catholic faith in England on the eve of Henry VIII's break with the Church.

"Henry VIII and the Reformation" (http://www.bbc.co.uk/history/british/tudors/) Learn more about Henry VIII, one of history's most colorful monarchs.

England Between Protestant and Catholic

Edward, as a male heir the first in the line of succession, was related through his mother to powerful noble factions that sympathized with reform. With Edward's uncle as regent (the king's guardian) and Archbishop Cranmer the main influence on questions of belief and practice, in 1549 Parliament passed the reforming Act of Uniformity. This law required that all Church services follow a uniform text, composed in English by Cranmer himself; this was then put into the *Book of Common Prayer*, which is still the basis of Anglican ritual. All subjects of the kingdom were required by the act to attend services regularly, and other forms of public worship were outlawed.

But in 1553 Edward died, and the traditionalist Mary became queen. Parliament repealed (undid) Edward's reforming laws and restored the traditional Latin services, and the pope formally pardoned Mary's subjects for their heresy. Protestant-minded bishops were replaced by Catholics, and several hundred reformers who refused to recant, including Cranmer, were burned at the stake. Furthermore, in hopes of producing a reliably Catholic heir, Mary wed Philip, the Habsburg heir to the Spanish throne.

As England's rulers shifted from one religion to the next, the Parliament, the clergy, and other power wielders mostly followed along. Unsuccessfully opposing the ruler would lead to terrible punishment, and whatever people's religious beliefs, they mostly also believed that God wanted them to obey the ruler, and that such obedience was the only guarantee of social order and national power. Besides, if they only lay low while the present ruler made unwelcome religious changes, there was always the chance that the next ruler would reverse them.

But Mary was the first ruler to put hundreds of people to death for religion, and by her marriage, she risked her kingdom becoming part of Spain's intercontinental Catholic empire. When she in turn died in 1558 and her reform-minded half-sister Elizabeth took over, the memory of "Bloody Mary" and the Protestant martyrs, as well as fear and envy of Spain, were pushing the kingdom in the Protestant direction.

The Elizabethan Settlement

Once again, Parliament undid its previous actions, reinstating Henry's Act of Supremacy and Edward's Act of Uniformity. Catholic-minded bishops were replaced by Protestants, and under their guidance, the clergy agreed on a new statement of belief, the Thirty-nine Articles. According to the articles, the English Church accepted the authority of the Bible, salvation by faith, only two sacraments, bread and wine for all in the Eucharist, and a married clergy like other Protestant churches. Like the Evangelical Church, it put itself under the authority of the ruler and urged that the belief in predestination not be stressed. Like the Reformed Church, it denied that Christ was bodily present in the Eucharist and particularly warned against sins such as idleness. Like the Catholic Church, it had a hierarchy headed by bishops who claimed authority from Christ himself. And like all three, it proclaimed itself the one and only Church to which all should belong.

This combination—the **Elizabethan Settlement**, as it is usually called today—was one that many believers could live with, but it also dissatisfied wholehearted traditionalists and thoroughgoing reformers alike. Now it was up to the queen, Parliament, and clergy to uphold the settlement against both groups.

The chief upholder of the settlement was the queen herself. Elizabeth was a learned and active Renaissance lady (pp. 290–292), whose reign laid to rest her father's fears about what would happen if a woman should rule. "I know I have the body but of a weak and feeble woman; but I have the heart and stomach of a king,

and of a king of England too," one of her soldiers remembered her as telling them when Spanish invasion threatened in 1588. Scholars debate how reliable his memory was, but the words certainly reflect what she wanted her male subjects to feel about her—protectiveness toward her as a woman, trust in her as a forceful commander, and pride in themselves as belonging to a nation that was at least as great as Spain. She never married, because depending on her bridegroom, that would have committed her to a fully Protestant or a pro-Catholic course, and she preferred to keep foreign rulers and dissidents at home guessing about her ultimate goals. Thereby she gained the aura of a "virgin queen"—married, so to speak, to her subjects. She was also lucky to have a forty-five-year reign, for a long-reigning strong ruler was a guarantee of stability.

For most of Elizabeth's reign, the main threat to the settlement came from the Catholic side. In 1570, after Elizabeth's forces had crushed a Catholic rebellion in the north of England, Pope Pius V declared her deposed, a step that in turn led her to begin systematically persecuting Catholics. About the same time, English merchants and sailors were breaking into Spain's New World empire, English volunteers (and eventually an official English army) fought on the Protestant side in the Netherlands, and Philip II of Spain began to think of conquering England as the key to Catholic victory across Europe.

 The Scaffold Speech of a Condemned English Jesuit Read the testimony of a Jesuit accused of treason in Elizabeth's England.

The crisis of Elizabeth's reign came in 1588, when Philip sent an invasion force against England that has gone down in history as the Spanish Armada. His big ships were held off by more maneuverable and better-armed English ones, and many were lost to storms on the way home. Protestants across Europe gave thanks to God, and medals were struck with mottos like "God Blew and They Were Scattered" and "Man Proposes, God Disposes" (see photo). The feeling grew among the English that God had singled them out as a Protestant people, the best hope of reformed Christendom, who would also be a great nation in the new worldwide Europe.

Even so, Elizabeth's religious settlement was not safe. The more England identified with Protestantism, the more influence the thoroughgoing Protestants gained—the **Puritans**, as their opponents called them, from their habit of complaining

"Man Proposes, God Disposes" A medal struck in Holland in 1588 celebrates England's defeat of the Spanish Armada. "Man" in the motto is Philip II of Spain, whose plan to conquer England God has disposed of by sinking his fleet. A Protestant Dutch family gives thanks to God for this deliverance, which means as much to them as to the English themselves. The destruction of the Spanish Armada was a victory for international Protestantism over international Catholicism. Library of Congress, Rare Book Special Collection

that the settlement did not meet the standards of the "pure gospel" as Calvin understood it. In the last years of Elizabeth's reign, she and her officials and bishops spent a great deal of time confiscating pamphlets against government by bishops and dismissing clergy who preached too forthrightly about predestination. In the next century, England would after all face a religious civil war—not between Protestants and Catholics, but among Protestants themselves (pp. 340–341).

The Catholic Counteroffensive: The Thirty Years' War

As Calvinism spread and the Catholic Reformation got under way in the Holy Roman Empire, the Peace of Augsburg began to break down. The Catholic rulers, guided by the Jesuits, stamped out the remnants of Protestant dissent in their territories, but the Lutheran rulers were weakened by bitter squabbles with Calvinist minorities. Sensing danger, some of the Protestant rulers joined together in an armed league in 1608, an action promptly countered by the formation of a Catholic league.

Local Rebellion: The Bohemian Revolt

As each camp eyed the other, revolt exploded in Bohemia, a self-governing kingdom within the Holy Roman Empire. Most of the people of Bohemia were Czechs who were both anti-German and antipapal, and the trouble there had its roots in the Hussite rebellion of the fifteenth century (pp. 250–251). During the sixteenth century, the Protestants of Bohemia had enjoyed toleration under moderate Catholic rulers of the Austrian branch of the Habsburg dynasty. But under a new Habsburg ruler, Ferdinand II, who zealously supported the Catholic Reformation, they feared that their religious and political rights were in jeopardy. Accordingly, in 1618, the Bohemian nobles announced their open defiance of Ferdinand and chose the Calvinist ruler of the Rhineland, a territory in the northwest of the empire, to be their king.

The Catholic league moved swiftly to help Ferdinand crush the poorly organized rebellion, and the support of the Spanish Habsburgs, as well as his election as Holy Roman emperor in 1619, gave him added strength. The imperial armies moved into the Rhineland to attack the possessions of the defeated rival Bohemian king. Ferdinand hoped to overthrow Protestantism throughout the empire and, in the process, to reverse the empire's gradual breakup and turn it into a powerful Catholic state under his own rule. And Catholic victory in the empire, so he and his Spanish relatives as well as the papacy hoped, would be the key to Catholic victory throughout Europe.

European War: The Struggle for the Empire

But what the Habsburgs hoped for, many other rulers—both Protestant and Catholic—feared. Among Protestant rulers, the king of Denmark decided to intervene in Germany to protect Lutheranism and to acquire territory for himself. He was promised help by the English and the Dutch, who also wanted to check the advance of Habsburg (and Spanish) power. Later, Sweden joined the struggle against Ferdinand. Meanwhile, the Catholic local rulers within the empire regularly lost enthusiasm for the struggle whenever it seemed that Ferdinand was too successful and might threaten their independence. Catholic France actually joined the war on the Protestant side. Richelieu wanted to build a powerful Catholic monarchy at home, but he was determined not to let Ferdinand do the same in the Holy Roman Empire.

All of the empire's neighbors became involved at one time or another, but the balance of forces was too even. None of the contenders was able to win a lasting victory, but it took thirty years, from 1618 to 1648, for them finally to give up hope of doing so. Germany was turned into a ghastly battlefield, endlessly fought over by mercenary armies. By the end of the **Thirty Years' War**, fighting, looting, famine, and disease had reduced the population by perhaps as much as one-tenth, and cities, towns, and villages were in ruins (see Map 17.2).

The End of Wars of Religion

The **Peace of Westphalia** (west-FEY-lee-uh), which concluded the war, is a landmark in European history. In Germany, the terms of the Peace of Augsburg were restored and extended to include Calvinism as well as Lutheranism and Catholicism. The local rulers within the empire won recognition as independent sovereigns, and Switzerland and Holland, which had once been part of the empire, were recognized as independent states. The empire itself continued with the Habsburgs as emperors, but they made no more efforts to turn it into a single state under their rule.

The European State System and International Law

The settlement, whose main provisions lasted until the nineteenth century, marked the emergence of the modern European state system.

Now that there was no longer a common faith and no hope of reimposing one, European countries and rulers more or less deliberately excluded religion from their conflicts. Rulers no longer thought of themselves as belonging to a single Christendom whose harmony was liable to be disturbed by quarrels arising from sinful human nature. Instead, they thought of themselves as sharing a single territory, Europe, whose "balance of power" depended on successful adjustment of mutually competitive interests.

The seventeenth century also saw the emergence of the idea and practice of international law, aimed at regulating relations

> **Thirty Years' War**
> A conflict between Catholics and Protestants in the Holy Roman Empire that engaged the major powers of Europe between 1618 and 1648.
>
> **Peace of Westphalia**
> Settlement ending the Thirty Years' War by extending religious freedom in Germany and recognizing the independence of Switzerland and Holland.

Map 17.2 Europe During the Thirty Years' War, 1618–1648

The war began as a religious and political struggle within the Holy Roman Empire, but the empire was a key area in the international conflict of Protestant and Catholic as well as in the dynastic and power struggles of its neighbors. Countries near and far joined in the war at one time or another, from Spain across western and northern Europe to Poland. © Cengage Learning

Interactive
Map

Legend:
- Austrian Habsburg lands
- Spanish Habsburg lands
- Other German states
- Swedish lands by 1648
- Ottoman Empire and tributary states
- Boundary of the Holy Roman Empire

among these independent states by mutual agreement. Some rulers, of course, were more careful than others in following the law, but the law at least provided standards that were widely respected. The classic statement of those standards is the *Law of War and Peace* (1625), written by the Dutch lawyer Hugo Grotius partly in response to the atrocities committed early in the Thirty Years' War. Though Grotius recognized war as a "legitimate" state of affairs, he distinguished between just and unjust conflicts and laid down some guidelines for "humane" methods of waging war. Grotius condemned such acts as poisoning wells, mutilating prisoners, and massacring hostages. Drawing on the ancient Roman principles of natural law (p. 111), he also spelled out the rights of neutral states and of civilians in war zones.

Religious wars were still occasionally fought. Late-seventeenth-century struggles between English-backed Protestants and French-backed Catholics in Ireland ended in more than a century of second-class citizenship for the Catholic majority. Repression of out-of-power religions also continued. In France in 1685, King Louis XIV formally revoked the Edict of Nantes, which guaranteed toleration for Huguenots, and tens of thousands of refugees "defected" to Protestant countries (see photo on page 322). But for the most part, religious disputes among Christians ceased to play the leading role in international and civil conflicts that they had played since the sixteenth century.

Continued Church-State Partnership

This did not mean that the traditional parnership between Church and state came to an end. Leading clergy of the dominant religion in each country were still appointed by the ruler, and still set the crown upon the ruler's head. Most Protestant rulers more or less officially controlled the Church, with wide powers of oversight and appointment. Many Catholic rulers held similar powers, and even set new limits on the pope's power, for example, to publish proclamations and decrees without their permission. Popes might protest, but in the now divided Western Christendom, they no longer openly struggled with Catholic rulers.

Meanwhile, with dominant religions by now secure, minority religions gradually came to be tolerated, but their believers were still second-class citizens, excluded from public service and university education. In eighteenth-century England, public officials had to swear that they did not believe in the doctrine of transubstantiation, which no Catholic could do without blasphemy; in Hungary, officials had to take their oath of office in the name of the immaculate (sinless) Virgin Mary (p. 205), which no Protestant could do without idolatry.

Eventually, the newly formed United States actually dissolved the partnership of Church and state, with the First Amendment to its Constitution declaring that "Congress shall make no law respecting an establishment of religion." Few European countries followed this example, but in the nineteenth century, they mostly granted religious minorities, Christian and non-Christian, full toleration and civil equality. Religious freedom and equality became generally accepted Western values, which were violated more often by supporters of new secular ideologies than by religious believers. Such, ironically, was the long-term result of the wars and persecutions of the Reformation era.

 Listen to a synopsis of Chapter 17.

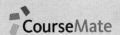

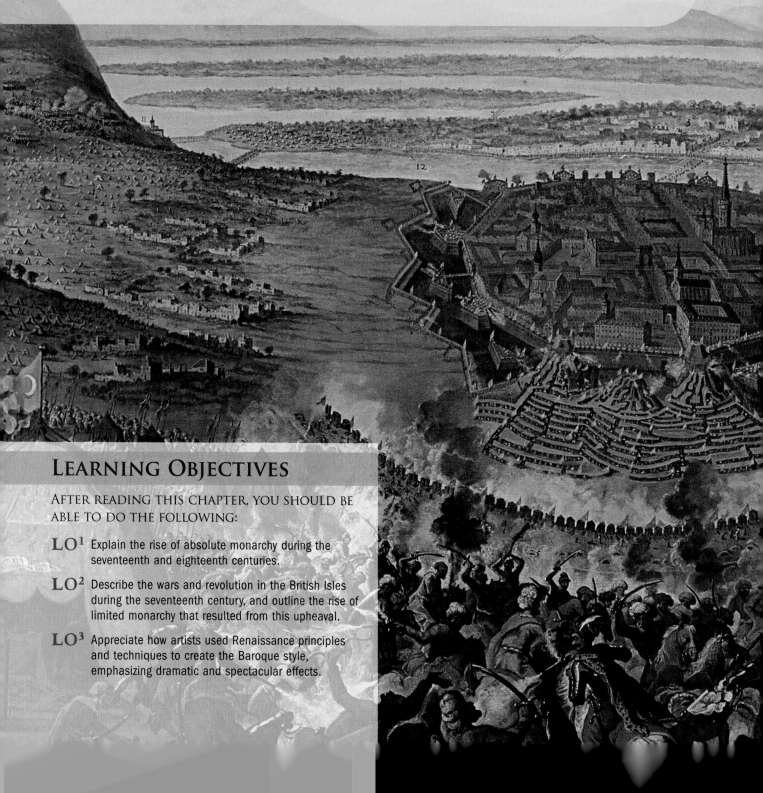

CHAPTER 18

RESTRUCTURING KINGDOMS: ABSOLUTE AND LIMITED MONARCHY,

1600–1700

LEARNING OBJECTIVES

AFTER READING THIS CHAPTER, YOU SHOULD BE ABLE TO DO THE FOLLOWING:

LO¹ Explain the rise of absolute monarchy during the seventeenth and eighteenth centuries.

LO² Describe the wars and revolution in the British Isles during the seventeenth century, and outline the rise of limited monarchy that resulted from this upheaval.

LO³ Appreciate how artists used Renaissance principles and techniques to create the Baroque style, emphasizing dramatic and spectacular effects.

"ABSOLUTE MONARCHY WAS AN IMPORTANT SHIFT IN THE POWER STRUCTURE OF WESTERN CIVILIZATION, BUT NOT A REVOLUTIONARY ONE."

In the fierce seventeenth-century European struggles, rulers came to believe that the only way to uphold government, religion, and social order was for them to gain complete supremacy within their kingdoms by casting off traditional restrictions on their power. They declared that they were not bound by established laws and customs, stopped calling representative assemblies, treated nobles and clergy at best as junior partners, and levied heavier taxes than ever before. They used the money mainly to build up well-equipped standing armies and navies, as well as to foster trade and industry and support science, scholarship, and art, thereby helping forward other Western changes. They often met with opposition as they restructured their kingdoms on this pattern of **absolute monarchy** (unlimited monarchy), but on the whole their subjects accepted them as providers of national security, upholders of religion, and distributors of favors and privileges.

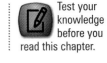

Test your knowledge before you read this chapter.

What do you think?

Governments that violate the rights of individuals should be overthrown.

Strongly Disagree						Strongly Agree
1	2	3	4	5	6	7

Absolute monarchy was an important shift in the power structure of Western civilization, but not a revolutionary one. It continued the growth of royal power that began in some countries in the late Middle Ages (pp. 259–263), and it kept many earlier features of kingship. Absolute monarchs still upheld the long-standing privileges of the nobility and clergy, and they still thought of their power as God-given—in fact, they claimed to be God's actual representatives, entitled to the same total obedience as himself. They were still intent on power and glory for themselves and their dynasties, and they proclaimed their power and glory more splendidly than ever with palaces built and decorated in the dramatic and spectacular style that had developed out of Renaissance art, the Baroque.

≪ **Attack and Counterattack** A city, ringed by a belt of cannon-resistant walls, has endured a three-month siege. Attackers have demolished a section of walls by digging trenches gradually close enough to tunnel under and explode mines. The city is ready to fall—but a relief army has broken into the besiegers' camp. The picture shows the Turkish siege of Vienna in 1683, but such scenes were normal in every war. The vast scale and expense of new and improved warfare helped drive the seventeenth-century restructuring of government.

absolute monarchy
Rule by a monarch (king or queen) that is not limited by traditional restrictions on power such as established laws, customs, and representative assemblies.

limited monarchy
A monarchy that shares power with a representative assembly and is bound by established laws.

Meanwhile, the British Isles were troubled throughout the seventeenth century by intertwined religious, national, and political struggles that reached their height in twenty years of war and revolution during the 1640s and 1650s. The religious conflicts were among Protestants as well as between Protestants and Catholics; the national rivalries involved three peoples of the region, the English, the Scots, and the Irish; and the political disputes pitted kings with absolutist leanings against the English Parliament, which sought a larger share in government.

The outcome of the struggles was yet another restructured kingdom—but on a different pattern from absolute monarchy. England and Scotland joined to form the kingdom of Great Britain, in which they enjoyed a fairly satisfactory partnership and their different forms of Protestantism were secure, while the neighboring, mainly Catholic kingdom of Ireland was ruled as a conquered country. The power of the British rulers diminished and the power of Parliament and the rights of subjects increased, yet under this system of **limited monarchy**, the government was more stable and stronger in both war and peace than before. Reflecting on the British upheavals, John Locke claimed that governments were appointed by societies to enforce the rights of individuals, and that governments that violated these rights could be legitimately resisted or overthrown. Locke's theory helped make the British experience a precedent for later changes in the power structure of many Western lands.

LO¹ Monarchs Supreme in the State: Absolutism

Throughout the Middle Ages, powerful and prosperous kingdoms had been ones where monarchs had the largest share of power in their partnership with nobles and the Church; when rulers lost control, the result was "failed kingdoms," beset by civil war and foreign invasion. Since then, the struggles of the Reformation and conflicts over worldwide trade and empire had greatly increased the stakes for kingdoms in having powerful rulers with armies and navies at the ready. Because of this

1600s	The Austrian Habsburg dynasty consolidates power in central and eastern Europe; Frederick William and his successor Frederick I develop the economic and military might of Prussia
1649	Charles I of England is executed; England becomes a Commonwealth without monarch or House of Lords
1643–1715	Reign of Louis XIV, the "Sun King," in France
1651	Thomas Hobbes describes absolute rule as the alternative to a warring "state of nature" in *Leviathan*
1660	The monarchy is restored in England under Charles II
1670	Jacques Bossuet argues for the divine right of kings in *Politics Drawn from Holy Scripture*
1682–1725	Reign of Tsar Peter "the Great" in Russia
1689	English Bill of Rights makes Parliament an equal partner of the ruler and guarantees many civil liberties
1690	John Locke's *Two Treatises on Government* rejects divine right and defends the right of rebellion
1691	The "Glorious Revolution" is completed in the British Isles, transferring power to the Protestant monarchs William and Mary
1707	England and Scotland become the United Kingdom of Great Britain

drive for military and economic dominance, absolute monarchy became the predominant form of government in seventeenth-century Europe.

Model of Absolutism: Louis XIV

Of all the seventeenth-century absolute monarchies, the most powerful, and for a long time the most successful, was France. The largest and wealthiest of the western European kingdoms, France had moved toward political centralization during the fifteenth century and collapsed into civil war following the Reformation (p. 324). But finally, a winner emerged from the wars—King Henry IV, who founded a new dynasty, the Bourbons (the name of one of their family properties).

MONARCHS GAINED UNLIMITED POWER DURING THE SEVENTEENTH CENTURY FOR SEVERAL REASONS:

The costs of equipping armed forces rose, as innovations in warfare continued from the late Middle Ages

- On land, small firearms (muskets) for foot soldiers became available; engineers devised both cannon-resistant fortifications and new ways of attacking such defenses (see photo on page 330).

- At sea, ships became large enough to carry whole batteries of cannon.

Military spending was necessary even in peacetime

- The long time it took to build ships and train their crews led governments to maintain standing navies.

- Mercenaries had been unreliable during the Thirty Years' War, so governments began to keep standing armies.

- Because of these expenses, rulers needed to tax their countries more heavily. They began to do so at their own discretion, without seeking the approval of representative assemblies.

Nobles and clergy accepted greater royal authority in exchange for favors

- Nobles received lucrative government, military, and Church positions.

- Both nobles and clergy were exempted from taxation.

- Landowners kept wide authority over peasants.

- Religious minorities were discouraged and granted second-class status at best.

Other classes of society also accepted increased royal power including

- Bankers who lent rulers money.

- Lawyers whom rulers employed as bureaucrats.

- Merchants and manufacturers who supplied rulers with food, clothing, and equipment for their armies.

- Even peasants whom rulers secured against unwelcome changes of religion.

As victors, the Bourbons were in a good position to rebuild royal power. Cardinal Richelieu, the astute minister of Henry's son Louis XIII, crushed the Protestant "state within the state" of the Huguenots, and appointed new regional officials known as *intendants* to see to it that royal orders and policies were carried out across the country. His aim, he declared, was "to make the king supreme in France and France supreme in Europe." Richelieu died in 1642, but his work was continued during the reign of Louis XIV.

 Richelieu Evaluates the State of the French Monarchy Read Richelieu's argument for crushing the Huguenots.

The King Supreme in France

Louis came to the throne as a boy in 1643. Boy kings were always a danger to royal power, but his mother, Anne of Austria, and another able minister, Cardinal Mazarin (**MAZ-uh-rin**), held the government together against revolts by noble factions. The rebels were a minority even among the nobles, and they were defeated and so discredited that their revolts were contemptuously called the Fronde—the

French word for "sling," since mobs used slings to throw stones at palace windows during the disturbances. By the time Louis personally took over the government in 1661, he was determined that never again would his power be hostage to his subjects. In a reign that lasted more than half a century, he built up a standing army that gave him a monopoly of military force, increased the numbers and powers of intendants, and eliminated the main legal restriction on royal power, the requirement for *parlements* (superior courts in Paris and the provinces) to officially register royal decrees before they went into effect.

 The Sun King Describes the State of France at the Dawn of His Reign Read Louis XIV's account of the early days of his reign

In these ways, Louis made himself "supreme in France," but his aim was not just to gain personal power. "I am the state," he is supposed to have said, but he put this differently on his deathbed: "I am going, but the state will remain." He might embody the state, but it was greater and longer-lasting than himself.

Furthermore, Louis never dissolved the traditional royal partnership with the nobles. They remained a privileged elite,

king himself. Rulers had always tried to attract leading nobles and win the admiration of their subjects by the splendor of their courts; Louis alone was the "Sun King," the dazzling center round which his court and kingdom revolved (see photo).

Louis also vigorously upheld the traditional royal partnership with the Catholic Church, on terms that put him very much in control. From earlier rulers, he inherited the power to appoint leading clergy, and he encouraged the clergy to think of themselves as a national "Gallican" Church, accepting the pope's authority in matters of belief and worship but otherwise self-governing. He put pressure on the Huguenots, France's large Calvinist minority, to convert, and in the 1680s, he turned to outright persecution. Finally, in 1685, he revoked Henry IV's Edict of Nantes that had guaranteed toleration, and thereby made the Huguenot faith illegal. Most Huguenots became nominal Catholics, but several hundred thousand took their skills as businesspeople and soldiers to Protestant countries.

Royal Power, National Culture, and National Prosperity

In spite of the attack on the Huguenots, Louis's reign was an era of splendid cultural creativity in France, for which some of the credit belonged to the king. His court nourished the architects and artists who built and decorated Versailles (pp. 348–349), and the composers, playwrights, and performers who created entertainments for royal occasions. Louis also favored the French Academy, founded by his father Louis XIII in 1635. Its members had acquired fame in many fields of literature and learning, and it was charged with "giving exact rules to our language, to render it capable of treating the arts and sciences"—so that French would be on a level with the traditional language of the arts and sciences, Latin. The Renaissance belief that creativity and knowledge are among the highest forms of human excellence still held sway (pp. 288–289), and increasingly, the arts and sciences were seen as the key to human power and prosperity as well. It was, therefore, Louis's business as an absolute monarch to foster them for his own splendor and the benefit of his subjects.

The king's splendor, his government bureaucracy, and above all his armed forces were expensive, but he also took measures to increase France's ability to bear the burden. His minister of finance, Jean Baptiste Colbert (kohl-BARE), strengthened the tax system and promoted economic development. Internal trade was aided by

Power and Fashion In Hyacinthe Rigaud's portrait, Louis XIV is a kingly figure with one hand on his hip, the other on his scepter, and his ermine-lined coronation robe cascading around him. The 63-year-old monarch also wears youthful-looking leg-hugging breeches; he personally designed his high-heeled red shoes, which became the correct style for men's footwear at court; and he places his feet as recommended by dancing masters. In an aristocratic society, being a leader of fashion was an important part of being an absolute monarch.

and he surrounded himself with men and women of the oldest and wealthiest noble families at his court, which he eventually settled in his newly built palace of Versailles (vehr-SIGH) . At the court, the nobles scrambled for the favor of the king and for the government, army, and Church positions that only he could award—and the wealth and luxury of the courtiers added to the splendor of the

 The Official French Government Site for the Palace of Versailles (http://en.chateauversailles.fr/homepage) Tour the Palace of Versailles.

 Colbert Promotes "The Advantages of Overseas Trade" Read Colbert's argument for founding colonies in the East Indies.

improved roads and waterways, colonies and trading companies were founded overseas, and French industries were sheltered by protective tariffs and export subsidies.

The purpose of Colbert's program was to increase employment, profits, and state revenues—and above all, to secure for France a favorable **balance of trade** with other countries. According to the prevailing theory of **mercantilism**, a country should sell to other countries goods of greater total value than it bought from them, so that foreigners must pay the balance in gold or silver. The more precious metals flowed into the country, the wealthier it must be, and the better able to bear the burden of royal taxation. Regulation of business was not new in Europe; the towns and guilds had practiced it for centuries (pp. 199–201). But regulation of trade by rulers, based on the belief that a country's wealth consisted in its stock of precious metals, was the first nationwide form of deliberate government intervention in the economy. This policy was well established in seventeenth-century France and other western European trading countries like Spain, Holland, and England.

> "*Louis alone was the 'Sun King,' the dazzling center round which his court and kingdom revolved.*"

France Supreme in Europe?

Louis had a passion for territorial expansion and a love of war and glory. His driving desire was to gain and hold France's "natural" frontiers—the Rhine River, the Alps, and the Pyrenees. During his long reign, Louis was able to push France's frontiers farther east and north than ever before, and when the Habsburg rulers of Spain died out, he was able, after many years of war, to win the succession for a branch of his own Bourbon dynasty. Throughout the eighteenth century, the size and strength of France and its alignment with Spain were basic facts of the balance of power (see Map 19.1).

Louis's opponents—above all Britain, Holland, and the Austrian Habsburgs—were able to limit his gains, however. Strong barriers to French expansion remained in the Netherlands and northern Italy. Louis had failed to make France "supreme in Europe," and at his death in 1715, France lay exhausted, its military power spent. Though it recovered and remained the most powerful single country on the mainland of Europe for another hundred years, the power and prestige of its absolute monarchy began a long decline that ended in revolution (pp. 383–387).

The Eastern Monarchies

Absolute monarchy could not prevent kingdoms from losing as well as gaining weight in the European balance of power. In 1600, the Spanish Habsburgs were the mightiest of absolute rulers, but by 1700, Portugal had overthrown their rule, the Protestants were entrenched in the Holy Roman Empire, and western European rivals had taken over much of the trade of the New World. Later, under its eighteenth-century Bourbon rulers, Spain became the junior partner of its former rival, France. Still, absolutism

did seem to guarantee religion, social order, and the survival of kingdoms—so much so that in the Holy Roman Empire, where the emperors failed to impose their absolute power, most local rulers governed their territories as minor absolute monarchs.

In addition, absolute monarchy enabled the rulers of countries farther east in Europe to become far more powerful than before. Since the Middle Ages, these lands had been less wealthy than those of western Europe, many of them were exposed to Turkish invasion, and most of the peasants (the vast majority of the population) were serfs (pp. 251–252, 255–256). In the seventeenth century, the eastern countries were troubled by the same kinds of conflicts as in the western countries— rivalries among rulers, civil wars among noble factions, religious struggles between Catholics and Protestants as well as between Catholics and Orthodox, and campaigns of persecution and massacre against Jews, who now lived in large numbers in the lands between Poland and Russia.

The rulers of Poland, earlier the region's strongest Christian kingdom, could not master the chaos. By the end of the century, they were paralysed by a representative assembly dominated by powerful nobles in which any single member could end a session and nullify any measures passed by calling out "I do not allow it!" But three other dynasties emerged from the turmoil that ruled their lands as absolute monarchies—the Habsburgs of Austria, the Hohenzollerns (**HOH-uhn-zol-ernz**) of Prussia, and the Romanovs of Russia. By exploiting their countries' resources more fully than before, they greatly increased their weight in the balance of power—both against rivals further west, and against the Turks.

Austria

The Austrian Habsburgs had traditionally been junior partners of their Spanish relatives, the Thirty Years' War had left them mere figurehead emperors of the Holy Roman Empire, and in spite of many years of war after the Spanish Habsburgs died out, they finally had to yield Spain to the Bourbons. But they were able to take over some of the Spanish Habsburg possessions in the Netherlands and Italy, they held their own hereditary lands in central and eastern Europe in spite of rebellions by Protestant nobles and peasants, and they gained territory from the Turks in Hungary and the Balkans (see Map 18.1).

By confiscating the lands of defeated Protestant nobles and selling them cheaply to Catholic followers, the Habsburgs were able to build up a loyal noble class in many of their lands. They did not interfere with the nobles' power over the serfs,

---

balance of trade
The relationship between a country's imports and exports; in a favorable balance, the value of exports exceeds imports.

mercantilism
An economic theory that measures a country's wealth by its stock of precious metals, accrued through a favorable balance of trade.

Map 18.1 The Balance of Power, 1725

Since 1648 (see Map 17.2 on page 327), a branch of France's Bourbon dynasty has replaced the Habsburgs as rulers of Spain and its empire. The Austrian Habsburgs, however, have reconquered Hungary from the Turks and kept former Spanish Habsburg territories in the Netherlands and Italy. Prussia now stretches from the Rhine to the eastern Baltic, where Russia is pushing westward. England and Scotland have formed the union of Great Britain, which is now the leading worldwide power. © Cengage Learning

Interactive
Map

which the nobles used both in their own interests and as agents of the central government. On these conditions, the nobles were willing to leave government decision making to the rulers and their advisers—who were in any case often leading nobles. Austrian absolute monarchy was less thoroughgoing than in France, but it was strong enough to keep the Habsburgs in the ranks of leading dynasties.

Prussia

The Hohenzollern dynasty rose to power from small beginnings in the Middle Ages, as vassals of the Holy Roman emperors. By the early seventeenth century, they were Protestant rulers of Brandenburg in the northeast of the empire, Prussia beyond the empire's border to the east, and several smaller territories in western Germany; eventually, the name "Prussia" came to be used for all these lands. At the Peace of Westphalia, the elector Frederick William (one of the rulers who elected the emperor, p. 267) gained additional lands.

In the next half-century, Frederick William and then his son Frederick I ruled their holdings as strict and dutiful absolute monarchs. They developed the economy—helped by thousands of Huguenot refugees from France—and raised a large and well-trained standing army. Prussia's noble landowners, like those of Austria, accepted the monarch's authority in return for complete control over their serfs, and supplied the ruler with loyal officials and a hereditary officer class. In 1701, Frederick joined the coalition against Louis XIV, for which the Habsburg emperor awarded him the title of king. By that time, Prussia had become the most efficient of all absolute monarchies, with a weight in the balance of power that was out of all proportion to its size and resources.

Russia

The most spectacular change in eastern Europe was the rise of Russia, which began early in the seventeenth century. In 1613, a new dynasty, the Romanovs, was summoned to power by the nobles in 1613 to end the "Time of Troubles," a period of civil war and foreign invasion like the struggles in France. The earliest Romanov tsars were pious supporters of their country's Orthodox religious traditions and generally ruled in cooperation with the nobles. This brought them stability at home and success in power struggles with their powerful neighbors, Poland, Sweden, and Turkey. These three rivals had other wars to fight in central Europe, the Balkans, and the Middle East, and none of them was Orthodox—the prevailing religion in many of the lands between the Black and Baltic Seas that the Romanovs coveted. The dynasty gradually increased its holdings in this region, while Russian traders and settlers spread across northern Asia to the Pacific Ocean, turning their country into an intercontinental empire (see photo, and Map 15.3 on page 282).

As Russia's power and its western contacts grew, its rulers began to pay attention to the changes under way in western Europe—the cultural innovations, the burgeoning of science and technology, the rulers who wielded absolute power as embodiments of the state. About 1700, Tsar Peter the Great determined to rebuild Russia on the western European model.

Peter's project involved a vast upheaval—one that he pushed forward, even while he fought savage wars against Turkey and Sweden that brought Russia to the actual shorelines of the Black and Baltic Seas (see Map 18.1). He continued to rule through nobles, but treated them as servants of the state rather than as partners with whom he shared power; the ranks and titles of nobles, instead of being hereditary, were determined by their positions in the tsar's service. He replaced Moscow as his capital with the new city of Saint Petersburg on the Baltic Sea, mainly designed by a French architect who had once worked for Louis XIV—but Peter's building project dwarfed even Versailles.

And he pressured the upper classes, who still wore medieval-style tunics and robes, to look like western Europeans—men should shave their beards and wear stylish jackets and pants, and women should have elegant coiffures and low necklines. Dress and hairstyles were no trivial matter. They were a symbol of Peter's determination to make Russia a part of the new civilization that was growing up in western Europe.

Peter was history's first "Westernizer," and like later Westernizers, he only partly changed the society over which he ruled.

Peter the Great Imposes Western Styles on the Russians Read Peter's decrees on men's clothing and shaving.

A Virtual Tour of St. Petersburg's Monuments (http://www.saint-petersburg.com/virtual-tour/index.asp) Take a virtual tour of St. Petersburg.

He overcame opposition by old-fashioned brutality, he had no thought of ending serfdom, and his changes gave rise to persisting debates: Did Russia's strength lie in imitating western Europe, or in its traditional Orthodox mission as the "Third Rome" (pp. 251–252) and in the unchanging life of its peasants? Still, with

(above, center) **Tsar Michael Fyodorovich's** *Shapka* This ceremonial headgear, made for the first tsar of the Romanov dynasty in 1627, imitates a Tartar-style *shapka* or cap of state given by a fourteenth-century khan to a vassal prince of Moscow (p. 223). The *shapka* was an inheritance from Russia's past as a subject land of an Asian empire; significantly, Peter the Great replaced it with a European-style crown modeled on that of the Holy Roman emperors. *Jevgeni German/Russian Picture Service/akg-images*

divine right
The idea that the monarch is God's representative on earth and is therefore entitled to total obedience and unlimited power.

its vast size, its modern absolute monarchy, and its enduring traditions, Russia now played a larger part in the power struggles and the cultural life of Europe than ever before.

Absolutist Ideas: Bossuet, Hobbes

In every traditional civilization, the power of monarchs was thought to be linked with divine power. Now that European monarchs were seeking to throw off all restrictions on their power, thinkers added a new twist to the old tradition—the idea of **divine right**.

> *"With its vast size, its modern absolute monarchy, and its enduring traditions, Russia now played a larger part in the power struggles and the cultural life of Europe than ever before."*

God's Lieutenants

Medieval monarchs had set themselves above their subjects by the religious ceremony of coronation (pp. 167, 173), but they usually accepted that God had set bounds to their authority. Divine right thinkers, however, dropped any notion of limits. The new view was pithily expressed by an actual ruler, King James I of England, early in the seventeenth century. "The state of monarchy," he lectured Parliament, "is the supremest thing on earth, for kings are not only God's lieutenants here below and sit upon God's throne, but even by God himself are called gods." King James did not mean to say that monarchs were actually divine, but he did claim that as God's "lieutenants" (representatives), they wielded the power of God himself and were therefore entitled to the same total obedience.

Later on, a favored bishop at the court of Louis XIV, Jacques Bossuet (**baw-SWE**), echoed King James's views in *Politics Drawn from Holy Scripture*, a booklet prepared about 1670 for the instruction of Louis's heir. Buttressing his arguments with many quotations from the Bible, he too declared that kings are "ministers of God" and that their power, being that of God himself, has no limits. "Kings should tremble then as they use the power God has granted them," lest they misuse what belongs to him—but "the ruler need render account of his acts to no one" except God. For "the ruler . . . is a public personage, all the state is in him; the will of all the people is included in his. As all perfection and all strength are united in God, so all the power of individuals is united in the person of the prince. What grandeur that a single man should embody so much!"

> *"For Hobbes, without the restrictions provided by government, human life would be 'solitary, poor, nasty, brutish, and short.'"*

Leviathan

Divine right had wide appeal in an era when monarchs—and most of their subjects—instinctively thought of royal power as God-given. But in the changing Europe of the seventeenth century, thinkers developed new ideas about what it was that upheld the power of rulers. Already in the Renaissance, Machiavelli had described how power was upheld only by the courage and cunning of those who wielded it (pp. 265–267). Now, Thomas Hobbes, a supporter of the Stuart kings in the British wars, developed a whole new theory of absolute power in his book *Leviathan* (**le-VYE-uh-thuhn**). He derived it not from God's command but from the competing desires and needs of individual human beings.

Drawing on the scientific advances of his time, Hobbes claimed that every human being is a kind of machine, driven by an instinctive need for self-preservation—and this need naturally brings these living machines into conflict with each other. In a "state of nature," with no coercive governing authority, the general human condition is a "war of every man against every man" and human life is "solitary, poor, nasty, brutish, and short." Hobbes did not base this view on any actual society of his own or earlier times; his dismal picture of the "state of nature" arose from his understanding of what drives the human machine.

Hobbes Describes the Natural State of War Read an excerpt from Leviathan.

Fortunately, said Hobbes, humans have a power of reason that enables them to provide an alternative to the anarchy of nature. Because they are selfish egoists, unable to trust one another, they cannot create a cooperative society of equals. What they can do is agree to surrender their individual strength to a higher authority, which alone will have the power to curb individual aggression. Hobbes believed that human society, the state, and civilization itself arose from an imaginary "contract" of each individual with all others: "I authorize and give up my right of governing myself, to this man, or to this assembly of men, on this condition, that thou give up thy right to him, and authorize all his action in like manner. This done, the multitude so united in one person, is called a COMMONWEALTH." The makers of this contract have come together out of pure self-interest. Their need for self-preservation alone is what moves them to form a state and accept total obedience to it.

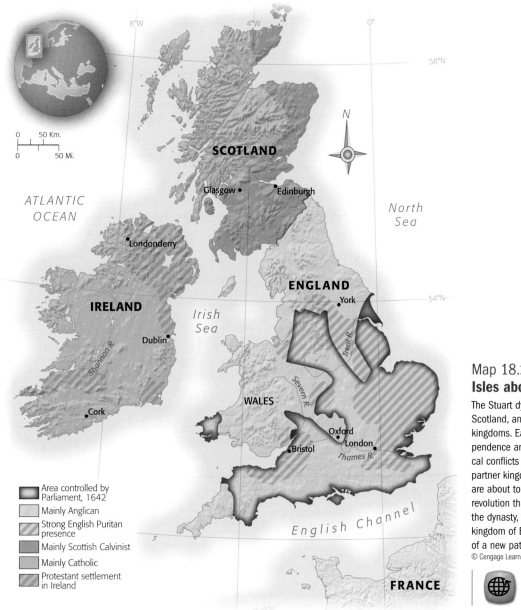

Map 18.2 **The British Isles about 1640**

The Stuart dynasty rules England, Scotland, and Ireland as separate kingdoms. Each is jealous of its independence and has religious and political conflicts both internally and with its partner kingdoms. The three kingdoms are about to enter an era of war and revolution that will end with the fall of the dynasty, the creation of the new kingdom of Britain, and the emergence of a new pattern of government.
© Cengage Learning

 Interactive Map

Map legend:
- Area controlled by Parliament, 1642
- Mainly Anglican
- Strong English Puritan presence
- Mainly Scottish Calvinist
- Mainly Catholic
- Protestant settlement in Ireland

Hobbes's argument did not find favor with supporters of absolute monarchy at the time, for he broke the traditional link between royal and divine power. But by doing so, he turned people's minds to the search for a kind of government authority that would not be based on the direct command of God.

LO² Monarchs and Parliaments: The British Constitution

In the Middle Ages, the British Isles had come to be divided among four countries (see Map 18.2). The island of Britain (or Great Britain, as its inhabitants often proudly called it) was shared between England and its neighbors, Wales on the west and Scotland on the north; and to the west of Britain lay the island of Ireland. The rulers of England, the largest country, often tried to gain power over the other countries, and by 1600 they had united Wales with England and ruled Ireland as a separate kingdom.

Meanwhile, in the sixteenth century the Tudor dynasty of England and the Stuart dynasty of Scotland had intermarried, and in the lottery of marriage and inheritance, it was the Stuarts who won. When the unmarried Queen Elizabeth I died in 1603, her cousin King James VI of Scotland became King James I of England. The British Isles were still divided among three kingdoms, but now they all had the same king—one, furthermore, who believed that "the state of monarchy is the supremest thing on earth."

gentry
In England, the class of landowners below the nobility.

The Breakdown of Traditional Monarchy

For James actually to rule supreme over his three kingdoms was no easy matter—particularly since the Reformation had added religious conflicts to their continuing national rivalries. Scotland had become fiercely Calvinist and shared Calvin's disapproval of bishops and his belief in the Church's right to pass judgment on kings (p. 319). In Ireland, a fiercely Catholic majority confronted a militant minority of English and Scottish Protestant settlers. In England, the Anglican compromise between Catholicism and Protestantism prevailed but was under attack from Calvinist-influenced Puritans (pp. 326–327), and this religious dispute made it hard for James to win the cooperation of the country's representative assembly, the Parliament.

Traditionally, the Parliament had been a valued but junior partner of the rulers in the government of England. It met for short periods when the rulers decided to summon it—usually when they needed its backing for important measures or money to carry them out, since Parliament had to approve the levying of taxes. Parliament assembled in two houses: nobles and Anglican bishops met in the House of Lords; and elected representatives of country districts and towns who were mostly **gentry** (nonnoble landowners) and wealthy businessmen sat in the House of Commons.

In other countries, the gentry would have counted with the nobles rather than the commoners, but because of the way feudalism had developed in medieval England, actual nobles were a small group of great lords. Neither nobles nor gentry were exempt from royal taxation, so neither of them needed absolute monarchy to help uphold tax privileges. Both groups wielded vast social and economic power, with the gentry usually deferring to the nobles, so that the House of Commons had traditionally followed the lead of the Lords. This system had worked well in the sixteenth century, but under James, it began to break down.

The Road to War

By James's time, the Commons were dominated by Puritans, whereas in the Lords, Puritan nobles were balanced off by Anglican bishops. James, however, who had already defended his royal power against Calvinists in Scotland, was determined to uphold the Anglican Church with its existing worship and bishops, and himself as its "Supreme Governor." Besides this religious disagreement, the Commons were against James's ideas of divine right, they disapproved of the corruption and extravagance of his court, and they distrusted his ability or willingness to uphold Protestantism internationally as the Thirty Years' War broke out on the mainland of Europe. When James asked them for grants to cover government deficits or support military interventions abroad, this led to arguments with Parliament in which the Commons rather than the Lords took the lead.

Under James's son, Charles I, these religious and political tensions built up still further. Charles used harassment and coercion to uphold the Anglican Church against the Puritans, and made the religious conflict worse by marrying a French Catholic princess. From now on, distrust between the Stuart kings and their English and Scottish subjects was heightened by the suspicion that what the rulers really wanted was to revive "popery." Unable to make the English Parliament do his bidding on new taxes, Charles stretched the law in various ways to raise money on his own authority. He brought critics and resisters before courts that ignored the legal safeguards, including jury trial, that had grown up in England since the Magna Carta of 1215 (p. 190).

> *"The state of monarchy is the supremest thing on earth."*
> —King James I

The Wars of the Three Kingdoms

Charles finally undermined his own position by overreaching in his other two kingdoms. In 1639, the Calvinist Scots rebelled against many years of Stuart efforts to impose Anglican-style worship and bishops on their country. For troops who could be relied on to crush the Scots, Charles began raising an army of Irish Catholics, but in 1640, to pay the expenses of war, he had no choice but to summon the English Parliament. The resentful Parliament, however, proclaimed its sympathy with the Scots and threatened Ireland with invasion—which in turn led to an Irish rebellion against English rule.

Meanwhile, the Parliament tried to make the weakened king bow to its will. It enacted unprecedented restrictions on his power: among other things, rather than calling parliaments when it suited him, the king must call them at least once every three years. In addition, it issued a "Grand Remonstrance" calling for a whole series of changes in government and religion. In the future, the king must respect the traditional liberties of subjects; his ministers and advisers must have the confidence of Parliament; the power of bishops must be curtailed; and "formality and superstition" must be eliminated from worship. Against the king's efforts to enforce Anglicanism and build absolute monarchy, the Parliament—with the Lords now following the Commons—was aiming at supremacy over the king in a Calvinist England. The traditional partnership of ruler and Parliament had broken down.

Parliament Chastises Charles I: The Grand Remonstrance Read an excerpt from Parliament's "Grand Remonstrance."

Finally, in 1642, Charles tried to personally arrest the parliamentary leaders, and finding them gone and the people of London aroused against him, he left the city for the nearby town of Oxford. The king and the Parliament raised opposing armies, and soon England, too, was at war.

The **Wars of the Three Kingdoms**, as they are called today, lasted on and off into the 1650s. In England, the wars pitted Puritans and opponents of arbitrary royal power against Anglicans and believers in obedience to God-given royal authority. In general, outlying northern and western regions were Royalists (supporters of the king), while the country's commercial and agricultural heartland in the south and east was for the Parliament. Of the most influential groups in the country, nobles mostly followed the king, the gentry were divided between the two sides, and businessmen mostly supported the Parliament. The Scots fought to uphold their Calvinist Church, and intervened in England and Ireland to prevent Royalist and Catholic victories there; and for Irish Catholics, the wars were ones of liberation against Protestant oppression.

To start with, the king's opponents did not fight to overthrow him, but to force him to do what they wanted. Gradually, however, the wars changed into a revolution—one that was centered in England. The fighting went badly for the Parliament at first, so it reorganized its forces into the "New Model Army," a force recruited mainly from volunteer **yeomen (YOH-muhn)** (independent small farmers) who were inspired by a Puritan zeal more radical than that of the Parliament itself. Whereas the parliamentary leaders looked to establish an English Calvinist Church in alliance with the monarchy, the soldiers were mostly Independents—believers in self-governing congregations of committed "saints," with no overall Church structure and no alliance with the state. These convictions were shared by the army's commanders—chief among them a middling landowner and novice soldier who in a few years taught himself a great deal about both war and politics, Oliver Cromwell.

The English Revolution

The new English army decisively defeated Charles's forces in 1646, and in 1648 it went on to take power from the Parliament, where the majority of members still hoped for a bargain with the imprisoned king. By that time, Cromwell and his fellow commanders had come to the conclusion that the king would never meet their religious and political demands, and finally they sent a detachment of soldiers to "purge" from the House of Commons all members but those who agreed with the army's views. The military takeover was followed by a truly revolutionary deed, when the surviving "Rump" Commons of some sixty members put the king on trial for treason (see photo).

In 1649, King Charles I, wearing his hat to show his disrespect for a court he did not recognize, faced his judges. No king had been put on trial before, let alone for treason—by seeking "to uphold an unlimited and tyrannical power to rule according to his will, and to overthrow the rights and liberties of the people of England." The sentence was also unprecedented—that Charles "be put to death, by the severing his head from his body." Ten days later, the sentence was carried out.

The "Rump" then declared the monarchy and the House of Lords abolished, and proclaimed England a "Commonwealth" (republic). But the beheaded monarch's family was safe in exile, and his supporters now recognized his eldest son as King Charles II. Accordingly, brutal warfare continued, mainly with the Scottish Calvinists who hoped for a compromise with their native dynasty, and with the Irish Catholics who looked to the Stuart monarchy to protect them against the Protestants.

By 1654, Cromwell's army had imposed its will on the entire British Isles, and he and his supporters now tried to remodel the region's nations according to their religious and political

A King on Trial Charles confronts a panel of judges selected by a committee headed by Cromwell. Security is tight: armed soldiers watch the public, and the president of the court, John Bradshaw, wears a steel-lined hat. The king will soon be beheaded, but at the Restoration, many of his judges will suffer the far worse penalty of hanging, drawing, and quartering. Bradshaw, having meanwhile died, will be dug up and his skull will dangle on a pole atop this very building.

Bodleian Libraries, University of Oxford, Ashmole 1689, Plate LXX

Restoration

Term applied to the reign of Charles II, in which the monarchy was restored (reinstated) in England.

Glorious Revolution

The regime change in which James II was replaced as monarch by his daughter Mary and her husband William, assuring Protestant rule in Britain.

views. There was no longer a state Church, and Protestants could believe and practice according to their consciences, with the major exception that Anglican worship and Anglican bishops were prohibited. So also was Catholicism, so that in Ireland, the majority lived outside the protection of the law. Taxes were efficiently collected and honestly spent—mainly on the standing army and on a large navy that restored England's standing in European and worldwide power struggles following the end of the Thirty Years' War.

But only a minority actively supported Cromwell's regime, and he found that he could maintain orderly government only through strong personal rule backed by the army. He tried to set up a permanent and legitimate system of rule that would outlast him and, in 1653, took the position of "Lord Protector"—a kind of substitute king. But this was not the kind of government that most of the Puritan and parliamentary opponents of Charles I had wanted, let alone his Anglican and Catholic supporters. In all three kingdoms, power wielders and humble people alike either resentfully obeyed the regime or served it without loyalty, while waiting for it to go away.

 The Oliver Cromwell Website (http://www.olivercromwell.org/index.htm) Learn more about the controversial figure of Oliver Cromwell.

The Growth of a New Order

Following Cromwell's death in 1658, his regime soon collapsed. His son took over as Lord Protector, but the young man was no soldier-politician like his father, and power drifted to Cromwell's military governor of Scotland, General George Monck. The canny general realized that the decision on a new regime must lie mainly with England—specifically with the nobles, gentry, and business interests that traditionally dominated the Parliament. Accordingly, the only way to establish a permanent and legitimate government would be through a Parliament including both Lords and Commons that was free to make its own decisions, and Monck marched his army into England to overawe opponents and make sure that this happened.

The Parliament met in 1660; it received from the would-be King Charles II promises of renewed partnership, pardon for opponents, and religious toleration; and it recognized him as the rightful ruler. He was warmly welcomed home in England, and was accepted also in Scotland and Ireland. The grateful monarch did not forget to make General Monck a duke.

The Restoration

The quarter-century of Charles's reign is known as the era of the Restoration. There was no going back to traditional monarchy, however, for the political, religious, and national rivalries that had led to revolution were not stilled. Under Charles's rule, there was bitter political strife in England between believers in God-given royal power and supporters of the rights of Parliament and subjects. In spite of the king's promises, the restored Anglican Church harassed English "Dissenters" (as Puritans were now called), bishops were imposed on Calvinist Scotland, and Protestants still had the upper hand over Catholics in Ireland. But Charles astutely maneuvered among the opposing groups in his three kingdoms, took advantage of the widespread fear of civil war and Puritan dictatorship, and avoided risky overreaching. By the end of his reign, he ruled free of parliamentary control and open opposition.

There remained, however, a persistent source of mistrust between the Stuart dynasty and most of its subjects—the specter of "popery." Charles had a Catholic mother and a Catholic queen, and most alarming of all, a Catholic convert brother, James—and since Charles's marriage was childless, James was the heir to the throne. In spite of fierce efforts by opponents of royal power to disinherit him, Charles's brother became king as James II in 1685.

The "Glorious Revolution"

Less cautious than Charles, James appointed Catholics to government, army, and court positions, and declared toleration for both Catholics and Protestant Dissenters. These measures went against acts of Parliament, so he claimed the right to "dispense with" (exempt people from) laws, and pressured power wielders throughout his kingdoms to support his measures. Partly in response to local uprisings but also to overawe peaceful opposition, he also maintained a standing army—the first since Cromwell's time. With these measures, James lost the trust of the Anglican clergy and believers, traditionally the strongest supporters of royal power, without gaining much loyalty from Protestant Dissenters, who were generally "popery's" bitterest foes.

Even so, it seemed best to the king's leading subjects to follow the traditional policy of waiting out an unwelcome reign. The fear of civil war and Puritan dictatorship was still powerful, and besides, James's likely heir was his Protestant daughter, Mary, who was married to William III, the stadtholder (p. 324) of Protestant Holland. In 1688, however, James's queen gave birth to a son who was baptized a Catholic. Faced with the prospect of generations of future Catholic rulers, a small group of influential nobles secretly invited William to land with an army in England. After William arrived, much of James's army deserted, and James quickly sailed for France. Parliament, alleging that James had abdicated (resigned as king), offered the throne to the welcome invader William and the Stuart heiress Mary as joint monarchs.

Soon after, Scotland accepted the English-made regime change—one that rid the Scots, too, of a Catholic king while maintaining a link through Mary with their native dynasty. Only Catholic Ireland stood by James, but he lost a final bout of religious and national warfare there to William, sailed away again, and spent the rest of his days in France. By 1691, the "**Glorious Revolution**," as it had already come to be called, was safe in all three kingdoms.

THE ENGLISH BILL OF RIGHTS

Even at the present day, Britain does not have a constitution consisting of a single document, but is governed under a collection of written laws and unwritten customs that has grown up over the centuries. One of the most important constitutional laws is the English Bill of Rights of 1689, passed by a parliament summoned by William III (mentioned here under one of his titles, the prince of Orange) after the "abdication" of James II. By consenting to this law, William and Mary as joint monarchs legally obliged themselves and their successors to rule in partnership with Parliament and to respect various rights of their subjects.

And whereas the said late King James II having abdicated the government, and the throne being thereby vacant, his Highness the prince of Orange (whom it hath pleased Almighty God to make the glorious instrument of delivering this kingdom from popery and arbitrary power) did (by the advice of the lords spiritual and temporal, and diverse principal persons of the Commons) cause letters to be written to the lords spiritual and temporal, being Protestants, and other letters to the several counties, cities, universities, boroughs, and Cinque Ports [five port towns on the English Channel, having special privileges], for the choosing of such persons to represent them, as were of right to be sent to parliament, to meet and sit at Westminster upon the two and twentieth day of January, in this year 1689, in order to provide such an establishment as that their religion, laws, and liberties might not again be in danger of being subverted; upon which letters elections have been accordingly made.

And thereupon the said lords spiritual and temporal and Commons, pursuant to their respective letters and elections, being now assembled in a full and free representation of this nation, taking into their most serious consideration the best means for attaining the ends aforesaid, do in the first place (as their ancestors in like case have usually done), for the vindication and assertion of their ancient rights and liberties, declare:

1. That the pretended power of suspending laws, or the execution of laws, by regal authority, without consent of parliament is illegal.

2. That the pretended power of dispensing with the laws, or the execution of law by regal authority, as it hath been assumed and exercised of late, is illegal. . . .

4. That levying money for or to the use of the crown by pretense of prerogative, without grant of parliament, for longer time or in other manner than the same is or shall be granted, is illegal.

5. That it is the right of the subjects to petition the king, and all commitments and prosecutions for such petitioning are illegal.

6. That the raising or keeping a standing army within the kingdom in time of peace, unless it be with consent of parliament, is against law.

7. That the subjects which are Protestants may have arms for their defense suitable to their conditions, and as allowed by law.

8. That election of members of parliament ought to be free.

9. That the freedom of speech, and debates or proceedings in parliament, ought not to be impeached or questioned in any court or place out of parliament.

10. That excessive bail ought not to be required, nor excessive fines imposed, nor cruel and unusual punishments inflicted. . . .

13. And that for redress of all grievances, and for the amending, strengthening, and preserving of the laws, parliament ought to be held frequently.

EXPLORING THE SOURCE

1. The bill lists some practices as "illegal," and others as the way government "ought" to be conducted. Why this difference?

2. Which of the bill's clauses would have been most effective in restraining the growth of absolute royal power, and why?

Source: *The Statutes: Revised Edition*, vol. 2 (London: Eyre and Spottiswoode, 1871), pp. 10–12.

The British Constitution

Meanwhile, in 1689, the English Parliament passed the Bill of Rights, which turned the Parliament from a junior partner to an equal partner of the ruler and guaranteed many civil liberties. This historic measure stated that the ruler could suspend laws, raise armies, and levy taxes only with the consent of Parliament; it also provided for frequent meetings of the lawmakers and unlimited debate within their houses. The Bill of Rights also guaranteed every citizen the right to petition the monarch, to keep arms, and to enjoy "due process of law" (trial by jury and freedom from arbitrary arrest and cruel or unusual punishment).

Under the Bill of Rights, the monarch was still the ultimate decider on government, military, and Anglican Church appointments, and was mainly responsible for foreign policy and the conduct of wars. But the monarch's power was explicitly limited by the requirements to cooperate with Parliament and to observe the rights of subjects. From now on, England was legally a limited monarchy, as against the absolute monarchies that prevailed on the mainland of Europe.

In religion, the Anglican Church remained the church of the majority and the monarchs, who in future could neither be Catholics nor marry Catholics. A Toleration Act gave freedom of worship to Protestant Dissenters, but government and army positions as well as university education were closed to them. From challengers of the government and religious order, they became accepted but second-class citizens.

In Scotland, similar measures limited the ruler's power and established toleration among Protestants, though in this case, it was the Calvinist Church that was the official church. The Scots also wanted to continue as a separate kingdom with the right to choose different rulers from England—a notion that horrified leading English politicians. By combining threats to cut off trade with offers of aid to bail the Scots out of a financial crisis, in 1707 they persuaded Scottish representatives to agree to a union of the two kingdoms. The union was deeply unpopular in Scotland, and English public opinion did not welcome it either. But in the new United Kingdom of Great Britain, both nations kept their religious and national identities and their different legal systems while sharing in worldwide trade and empire.

Of the original three kingdoms, the one that had suffered most from the seventeenth-century upheavals was Ireland. The wars there had been at least as devastating as the Thirty Years' War in Germany, and afterward, the country remained a separate kingdom with a long-lasting system of religious oppression. A small Anglican minority owned most of the land and ran the government and the official church; a larger minority of Protestant Dissenters were second-class citizens as in England; and the Catholic majority was mostly landless and rightless. The resulting conflicts and resentments have lasted down to the present day.

Even in Britain, the new order was far from equitable. The House of Lords, consisting of two hundred nobles and bishops, had as much power in the government as the House of Commons. The Commons themselves were elected by a small minority of the male population, who were easily bribed and intimidated by local nobles and gentry. And the monarchs, with the effective government power that they still wielded, could influence parliamentary votes by job offers and other favors.

All the same, the "British Constitution"—the collection of parliamentary acts and unwritten customs under which the government now operated—was felt to guarantee rights to the humble as well as the powerful, and became a focus of widespread patriotic pride. Furthermore, now that Parliament was an equal partner in government, it was far more generous with taxation and far less distrustful of the rulers than before, so that Britain kept its standing army and built a massive navy that gained the country worldwide supremacy. "Rule, Britannia! Britannia rule the waves!" ran a British patriotic song; "Britons never, never, never will be slaves!" In Britain, as in ancient Athens (p. 54), freedom went together with power.

Locke's Justification of Revolution

A byproduct of the British upheaval was John Locke's political theory, which would have a profound influence on future revolutions. Locke, who came from a Puritan family, grew up in the era of war and revolution. In the Restoration era, he joined the king's opponents and spent several years in exile, where he made notable contributions to philosophy (pp. 365–366). After the overthrow of James II he came home, and in 1690 he published *Two Treatises on* ("Studies of") *Government* in defense of the new order. The first treatise rejected the theory of divine right, and the second defended the right of rebellion and became an ideological handbook for revolutionists everywhere.

Like the absolutist thinker Thomas Hobbes, Locke believed that the miserable condition of people in the "state of nature" had given rise to an agreement to establish civil government, but Locke disagreed with Hobbes about the terms of the "social contract." Hobbes had argued that individuals must have turned over their entire "right of governing themselves" to the state as a means of securing order. Locke, on the other hand, believed in specific "natural rights"—a concept that grew out of the ancient belief in natural law (pp. 87, 111), and which he defined as being rights to life, liberty, and property. These rights are "natural" because they are natural features of being human, just as size, shape, and weight are natural features of physical objects, so that there is no way that people can give up any of them. Instead, what they transfer to society is the power to take measures to preserve their rights.

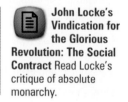 **John Locke's Vindication for the Glorious Revolution: The Social Contract** Read Locke's critique of absolute monarchy.

A society, said Locke, holds this power as long as the society lasts, but it delegates its power to a government, such as that of a monarch. Should a monarchy or any other type of government use its power to violate natural rights, the society is legally and morally entitled to resist. Who decides whether a government's action is in fact in violation of rights? "The people shall judge,"

Locke replied, and if a government refuses to yield to this judgment, the people have the ultimate right to resort to force—to "appeal to Heaven."

Thus, by building on ancient Greek and Roman ideas of natural rights and natural law, Locke constructed a "universal" political theory. Though it rested neither on scientific facts nor on actual historical events, it served to justify the "Glorious Revolution." In the next two centuries, Locke's ideas were heartily embraced by Thomas Jefferson and by many other revolutionary leaders as "self-evident" truths.

LO³ Art of Faith and Power: The Baroque

In the era of the Reformation and wars of religion, and of the growth of absolute and limited monarchy, Renaissance art evolved into a new style that today is called **Baroque**—a word that originally meant "elaborate" or "excessive." The name is used because painters and sculptors exploited to the limit new Renaissance skills such as accurate perspective (p. 298) for the utmost dramatic effect, while architects stretched the revived ancient rules of design and added an abundance of decorative features to their buildings. But the result was paintings and statues full of movement and excitement and sometimes of awe-inspiring mystery, as well as spectacularly magnificent churches and palaces.

> "*For he that thinks* absolute Power purifies Mens Bloods, *and corrects the baseness of Humane Nature, need read but the History of this, or any other Age to be convinced of the contrary.* "
>
> —John Locke

Baroque Painting and Sculpture: Rubens, Gentileschi, Rembrandt, Bernini

Baroque art first reached its full flourishing around 1600 in Catholic countries. The clergy of the Catholic Reformation valued dramatic and emotional presentations of religious scenes; absolute monarchs wanted their triumphant deeds to be spectacularly glorified; and depictions full of movement and drama added excitement to subjects from Greek and Roman mythology. The result was an outpouring of magnificent art, ranging from the mystical to the sensual.

Rubens

The leader of Baroque art was the Flemish painter Peter Paul Rubens (from Flanders, the southern part of the Low Countries, p. 324). As a young man, he studied in Italy, and then worked chiefly in his native Antwerp for international clients including the rulers of Spain, France, and England, for Flemish aristocrats and businesspeople, and for the Church. A man of enormous energy and versatility, he created fine portraits of royalty, nobles, merchants, and his own family; huge wall and ceiling paintings celebrating the owners of royal palaces; altar paintings dramatically depicting the central mysteries of the Catholic faith; and mythological scenes of vigorously cavorting gods and goddesses. So great was the demand for Rubens's work that he set up a well-organized workshop in which he trained specialists to paint certain elements—clothing, animals, or backgrounds. He supervised the production of each picture and himself finished the key features, such as faces and hands. He was blessed by good fortune and a happy disposition, and his paintings are charged with movement and vigor.

In his treatment of a subject from Greek mythology, *The Rape of the Daughters of Leucippus* (see photo on page 346), Rubens depicts Castor and Pollux, horse-riding sons of Zeus, kidnapping Phoebe and Hilaera, the daughters of a mortal king, as brides. The muscular riders reaching down to their struggling naked victims create an image of irresistible male passion overwhelming helpless womanhood. Even the horses, white in the original myth, are a more masculine-looking chestnut and gray. But on the left, and in the middle next to the head of the chestnut horse's rider, are mischievous boy-gods—Cupids. The kidnappers, too, are helpless—mere puppets of Cupid, whose name means "Desire."

Gentileschi

A very different depiction of women in relation to men was the work of an early seventeenth-century Italian painter, Artemisia Gentileschi (**jen-tee-LES-kee**). Her works were commissioned by rulers and admired by colleagues in Italy and abroad: among her clients were King Charles I of England and the Medici ruling family of Florence, where she was the first woman to be admitted to a renowned artistic institution, the Academy of the Arts of Drawing.

Gentileschi's painting *Judith Beheading Holofernes* (**ho-lo-FER-neez**) depicts a Bible story, of the beautiful Israelite widow Judith who made her way to the camp of an invading army, contrived for herself and her serving woman to be alone with the army commander when he was in a drunken stupor, and cut off his head with his own sword. Traditional depictions showed a demure Judith holding the general's head as a trophy; already a renowned Baroque artist, Caravaggio (**Cah-rah-VADZH-yo**) had broken with this tradition and shown the

Baroque
A style of art and architecture that emphasized the spectacular, magnificent, and dramatic, often with the purpose of proclaiming the glory of a state or church power.

and avoiding bright colors in favor of browns, dark reds, and golds. The effect is sober but revealing, as in a self-portrait that Rembrandt painted near the end of his life (see photo), in which he goes outside himself and looks inward. He shows himself, like any other sitter, in the dress and with the equipment of his calling. He flatters himself a little with a freehand-painted circle to proclaim his technical skill. But he mainly uses his skill to carry out Leonardo da Vinci's advice (p. 300), to paint "the individual's appearance and the state of his mind"—in this case an aging, weary, but still creative and powerful artist.

Rembrandt used the same methods in religious painting, for example, in his *Supper at Emmaus* (see photo), which shows the Bible story of the risen Christ revealing himself to two loyal followers after walking with them unrecognized to a village tavern near Jerusalem. Catholic artists usually depicted this scene in close-up, with the followers in poses of astonishment. But Rembrandt shows an intimate group in a corner of a shadowy room, with Christ's followers too absorbed by the sight of him to be amazed—perhaps, even, they have quietly and joyfully realized that they knew who he was all along. Rembrandt's deliberate understatement actually makes the unforgettable moment all the more dramatic.

The Rape of the Daughters of Leucippus Rubens depicts with relish the Greek gods Castor and Pollux voluptuously kidnapping their brides . . .

actual deed. But Gentileschi's painting is the most grimly vivid of all Baroque depictions, with the women's faces coldly ruthless, and Judith's pose giving a disturbing sense of the hard work involved in sawing through a man's neck while standing far enough away not to be spattered with blood (see photo). The grimness of the painting probably reflects a traumatic experience of Gentileschi's youth, a rape followed by a lengthy and sordid trial—an experience that creative imagination and artistic skill have turned into a memorably horrific Baroque scene.

Rembrandt

As Rubens was the artistic master of Catholic Flanders, Rembrandt van Rijn (**REM-brant, Rine**) was the master of the northern, Protestant part of the Low Countries—Holland. Like Rubens, though a generation younger, Rembrandt won recognition early in his career. After his beloved and well-to-do wife died in 1642, however, he fell into debt, his popularity vanished, and he turned more and more inward in his thoughts. Yet it was the dark days of tragedy and self-examination that made Rembrandt the most profound of Baroque artists. He made many portraits of Dutch townspeople, shunning dramatic poses

>> *Judith Beheading Holofernes* . . . and Gentileschi coldly observes the Israelite widow Judith and her serving woman hard at work sawing off the head of an Assyrian invader.

Portrait of the Artist Rembrandt made over 80 portraits of himself from youth to old age. His youthful self-portraits were often studies of different facial expressions that sold well and helped to make him well known, but as he grew older they turned into explorations of his own personality, of which this is one of the deepest.

Supper at Emmaus Catholic Baroque artists usually made this scene of Christ being recognized by two travelers into a moment of high drama, but Rembrandt, the sober Protestant, makes it into one of tranquil contemplation.

Bernini

Meanwhile, in Catholic Italy the dominant master was Giovanni Lorenzo Bernini, a sculptor of extraordinary technical skill. In the cold, hard medium of stone, Bernini succeeded in catching the fleeting instant, the throbbing passion, the rhythm of movement.

One such moment of passion that Bernini depicted was the experience of mystical union with God, as described by a sixteenth-century Spanish nun, Saint Teresa of Avila: "The pain was so great that I screamed aloud; but at the same time I wished the pain to last forever. . . . It was the sweetest caressing of the soul by God." In *The Ecstasy of Saint Teresa*, carved for a chapel in a church in Rome, Bernini boldly used theatrical devices to reenact the saint's words. The figures are poised on a cloud with no apparent support, divine rays (and actual light) flood down from above, a smiling angel pierces the saint with the arrow of divine love, and the saint's face echoes the commonest human experience of unbearable pleasure (see photo). The sculpture proves the truth of Bernini's proud claim: "I render marble as supple as wax, and I have united in my works the resources of painting and sculpture."

The Ecstasy of Saint Teresa Bernini's sculpture is set into the end wall of a chapel in a church in Rome belonging to the Carmelite nuns, a religious order of which Teresa had been a member. In theater box-like enclosures on the side walls, statues of members of a Venetian noble family that commissioned the chapel sit observing and discussing the scene of religious drama.

Baroque Architecture: Bernini, Le Brun, Wren

Baroque architects, as well as painters and sculptors, emphasized the spectacular, the magnificent, and the dramatic in their works. The buildings they created spoke of the glory and power of religions, rulers, and nations.

Bernini and Saint Peter's

Bernini was an architect as well as a sculptor, and late in his life, he fashioned Saint Peter's Square, the space in front of Saint Peter's Basilica in Rome. The approach to the church begins with Bernini's vast oval plaza (see photo). The plaza is linked with the basilica by a straight-sided space that widens toward the church's western entrance. The entire area is surrounded by rows of 60-foot-high columns, supporting a roof topped by giant-sized statues of saints. The plaza has an ancient Egyptian obelisk at its center that was brought to the city in the first century A.D. at the command of an emperor; it was moved in front of Saint Peter's and topped with a cross sixteen centuries later on the orders of a pope.

In this way, visitors entering the plaza are embraced, in Bernini's words, by "the maternal arms of Mother Church," and welcomed by many of its most revered men and women through the ages. At the Catholic Church's center, the architecture proclaims that the Church has outlasted Egypt, triumphed over Rome, and spread around the world to embrace the human race.

Le Brun and Versailles

While Bernini was proclaiming the glory of the Catholic Church in Rome, French architects were working in Versailles to do the same for Louis XIV and the French state that he embodied.

The king's new palace was built in the countryside near enough to Paris to allow easy access to the capital and far enough away for the king, his attending officials, clergy, and nobles, and their families and servants to form a self-contained community whose life revolved around the monarch. The palace therefore had to be exceptionally large: the buildings cover 17 acres, and the formal gardens, courts, parade grounds, and surrounding woods stretch over many square miles. The whole complex took the entire half-century of Louis XIV's reign to build, at staggering cost. Even so, the accommodation was basic even for courtiers, let alone for the palace staff, since 10,000 people had to be squeezed into the space.

The royal and public rooms, however, were lavish in the extreme. One of the most dazzling chambers is the Hall of Mirrors (see photo), designed by Charles Le Brun, whose genius for large-scale creations and his shrewdness in gaining and keeping the king's favor made him for many years one of the court's leading artists. The 80-yard-long marbled and mir-

The Church's Embrace Two hundred yards across, 300 yards long, and surrounded by 60-foot-high columns, the space in front of Saint Peter's Basilica designed by Bernini can accommodate a crowd of 300,000 people—a worthy setting for the most festive celebrations of the worldwide Catholic Church. Scala/Art Resource, NY

Erich Lessing/Art Resource, NY

≪ The Hall of Mirrors The symbolic meaning for France's friends and enemies of King Louis XIV's ceremonial chamber has been long-enduring. In this hall in 1871, the invading king of Prussia was proclaimed emperor of Europe's new dominant power, united Germany; and in 1919, France and its allies summoned the Germans back to sign the treaty ending the First World War.

Wren had visited France and Italy and studied the work of architects there, including Bernini, but he had to deal with Anglican clergy, who were conservative in their tastes and eager to avoid any suggestion of "popery." The new Saint Paul's had an awe-inspiring dome like Michelangelo's at Saint Peter's in Rome, as well as many Baroque features of design and decoration like the statues on the roof overlooking the entrance (see photo). But it also had old-fashioned features like the twin towers flanking the entrance as in Gothic cathedrals; and

 "Christopher Wren and St. Paul's Cathedral" (http://www .bbc.co.uk/history/british/ civil_war_revolution/ gallery_st_pauls.shtml) Examine Wren's plans for the new St. Paul's Cathedral.

rored chamber was intended for court ceremonies and festivities. The mirrors were themselves a luxury item that spoke of the king's magnificence, while they also multiplied the splendor of all the other decorations that they reflected. For the ceiling, Le Brun made huge paintings of Louis XIV's government achievements and victories over rival rulers, thereby proclaiming "the king supreme in France and France supreme in Europe."

Wren and Saint Paul's

Catholic clergy and absolute monarchs were not the only ones who appreciated the possibilities of Baroque architecture for proclaiming glory and power. In 1666, the Great Fire of London destroyed most of the city's medieval core, including the huge Gothic cathedral that dominated the urban skyline, Saint Paul's. The task of rebuilding the cathedral was given to an Oxford scholar who was mainly noted as an astronomer deeply involved in the burgeoning scientific discoveries of the time, Christopher Wren.

≫ Saint Paul's Cathedral With its stately mixture of Baroque and traditional design, the first cathedral built in England since the Reformation became a national shrine for the new United Kingdom of Britain and an enduring symbol of the nation in good times and bad (see photo on page 505).

A. F. Kersting/akg-images

instead of a huge plaza with an obelisk like Saint Peter's, it had a modest forecourt with a statue of Queen Anne, the British ruler at the time the cathedral was completed in 1710.

Saint Paul's is soberly majestic rather than lavishly spectacular—a restrained version of Baroque that was very suitable for an era when Britain was consolidating Protestant domination, strengthening parliamentary government, and rising to worldwide power. The stately new cathedral became a British shrine where national victories were celebrated and national heroes had their funerals, and Wren became a national hero himself. He is commemorated by a Latin inscription carved into the cathedral's floor: "If you seek a monument, look around you."

Painting Everyday Life: Brueghel

The Renaissance skills of lifelike depiction also opened up to painters new themes that called for realistic treatment, among them the everyday life of ordinary people. This kind of painting has come to be called **genre painting**, from the French *petit genre*, the "small kind" of art depicting scenes of ordinary life, as against the *grand genre*, the "grand kind" of art depicting scenes from religion, mythology, and history. In an era when accurate observation of the world was highly valued (pp. 292–293), "small" subjects came to be admired as well as the traditional "grand" themes.

One of the pioneers of genre painting was Pieter Brueghel (**BROI-guhl**), a sixteenth-century Flemish artist. Among Brueghel's everyday scenes were ones that showed, bluntly and honestly, the ordinary men and women who made up the bulk of European society—the peasants.

Medieval artists had sometimes shown peasants at work, not for their own sake, but to celebrate such themes as orderly government or the seasons of the year. But in his *The Wedding Dance* (see photo), Brueghel shows peasants at play—dancers uproariously flinging themselves about, quietly sociable groups of neighbors, everyone in their Sunday best. He is celebrating peasants themselves, with their spontaneous high spirits, their sense of community, their modest prosperity—and also their social pretensions. Some of the men wear tight-fitting pants complete with suggestively upstanding codpieces, as was the fashion among nobles of the day.

Painters in seventeenth-century Holland, with its well-off townspeople who were willing to spend money on works that

The Wedding Dance As in all traditional civilizations, peasants were the majority of Europe's population until the twentieth century, and not all of them were downtrodden. Brueghel's sixteenth-century depiction shows the well-fed and well-dressed elite of a village enjoying themselves.

Detroit Institute of Arts, USA/ City of Detroit Purchase/ The Bridgeman Art Library

realistically depicted the world they lived in, and its Calvinist Church that frowned on religious art, made a speciality of genre scenes. Dutch painters also specialized in two other newly prominent kinds of painting. One was landscapes—depictions of rural scenery for its own sake, not as background for the doings of saints and heroes. The other was still lifes—depictions of everyday objects in ordinary surroundings such as fruit in a bowl or musical instruments lying on a table. In this way, alongside the splendor of the Baroque, another kind of painting was growing up that foreshadowed Realism and Impressionism (pp. 449–451)—the nineteenth-century styles that would inaugurate a new age in Western art.

Listen to a synopsis of Chapter 18.

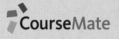

Access to the eBook with additional review material and study tools may be found online at CourseMate for WCIV. Sign in at www.cengagebrain.com.

THE RISE OF THE MODERN WEST,

1600–1900

The seventeenth, eighteenth, and nineteenth centuries were an era of further spectacular shifts in civilization, following upon those that had already altered the medieval pattern. These new shifts eventually brought into being all the basic features of the modern West.

In those three centuries, violent revolutions and peaceful reforms undermined Europe's traditional government structure of kings and nobles claiming authority from God. European settlers in North and South America revolted against their distant rulers and founded independent countries. The ancient institutions of slavery and serfdom were abolished. Secular ideologies—nonreligious systems of thought and belief—arose to challenge Christianity as

the central belief of Western civilization. The slow-moving pace of technical advance and scientific discovery turned into a headlong rush, and the traditional agrarian way of life gave way to an industrial society.

All these shifts in civilization sprang from the earlier ones that had already altered the medieval pattern. The rise of industrial society was made possible by the technical advances of the late Middle Ages, the worldwide markets opened up by overseas exploration and empire building, and the financial resources of burgeoning capitalism. The astronomers who overturned the traditional earth-centered model of the universe, and in the process developed new ways of gaining scientific knowledge in every field, were inspired by the Renaissance revival of ancient Greek

science and philosophy. The revolts and revolutions that shook the traditional order were reactions against the burdens and inequalities of absolute monarchy. The first of the secular ideologies, the Enlightenment belief in reason, progress, and human fulfillment in this world, was developed by eighteenth-century thinkers impressed by Europe's growth in knowledge, wealth, and power up to their own time.

In addition, the new shifts in civilization interacted with one another—usually in such a way as to drive all of them onward. The increase of scientific knowledge contributed to the rise of secular ideologies, and the resulting breakdown of consensus over Christian belief made it pointless for governments to claim to rule in the name of God. Industrialization speeded travel and brought mass media into existence, making it easier for political leaders to rally citizens of large countries to influence governments. Enlightenment principles helped inspire the abolition of slavery and serfdom, and millions of workers became free to move from plantations and villages into factories.

As a result of all these changes, a new kind of civilization grew up within the West that was different from all others of its own time and of the past, including the earlier "Wests" themselves. In this new civilization, the majority of the population lived in cities and worked in factories and offices rather than on farms, and the traditional division of status and power between men and women was beginning to break down. It was wealthy enough to have realistic expectations of health, education, leisure, and abundance for the masses as well as the elite. Its governments ruled in the name of the people and the nation, and had more control of their citizens' lives than ever before—compelling them to go to school, support-ing them in sickness and poverty, drafting them into the army. Citizens, in turn, were equipped with rights and freedoms that enabled them to wield greater power over governments than ever before, above all, through more or less democratically elected representative assemblies.

More than any earlier civilization, this one had a double and often conflicting view of the order of the universe and the destinies of the human race. It still regarded these things as the fulfillment of divine purposes to be interpreted through religion, but it also saw them more clearly than ever before as the outcome of natural processes to be understood through science. And it was the first civilization to pin its hopes and fears for its own future on the production of a limitless flood of technical advances and scientific discoveries.

In this civilization, the traditional understanding of the meaning and purpose of literature and art was also beginning to change. In its most admired works of art, the affirmation of generally accepted beliefs and values was beginning to give way to questioning. Recognizable depiction of the appearance of things was being replaced by the expression of the perceptions and inner world of the artist. Alongside the continuing influence of traditional styles and themes, a self-conscious break with the past was under way. The progress of science and technology was giving rise to new artistic media, as well as to a whole new area of artistic creation: mass entertainment.

The geography of the Western heartland had also changed. It was now to be found in those regions where the shifts in civilization had gone farthest, and whose wealth, power, and cultural influence had consequently grown the most—no longer western Europe alone, but also the formerly outlying territory of North America.

CHAPTER 19

NEW WORLDVIEWS: SCIENCE AND ENLIGHTENMENT, 1500–1800

LEARNING OBJECTIVES

AFTER READING THIS CHAPTER, YOU SHOULD BE ABLE TO DO THE FOLLOWING:

LO¹ Trace the beginnings of the Scientific Revolution.

LO² Describe the Enlightenment worldview.

LO³ Appreciate the Enlightenment spirit in literature and art.

LO⁴ Follow the development of Western music up to the Baroque and classical periods.

LO⁵ Discuss how the reform efforts of central and eastern European rulers reflected both Enlightenment ideals and power politics.

"A NEW UNDERSTANDING OF THE NATURAL UNIVERSE HELPED LEAD TO A NEW UNDERSTANDING OF HUMANITY AND GOD—THAT OF THE EIGHTEENTH-CENTURY ENLIGHTENMENT."

Among the most spectacular new shifts in civilization in the seventeenth and eighteenth centuries were the beginning of modern science and the emergence of the secular worldview of the Enlightenment—a nonreligious view of the universe's general purpose and meaning, and of the human condition within it. Under the influence of ideas that originally grew out of the Renaissance, investigators from Nicholas Copernicus to Isaac Newton brought about a revolution in one particular field of natural knowledge: astronomy.

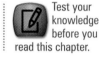

Test your knowledge before you read this chapter.

They did not just prove that the earth moved around the sun, but developed a whole new understanding of the universe as a vast self-regulating entity, whose rules of operation could be discovered by observation and experiment and described in

What do you think?

Ultimate certainty about the workings of the universe can one day be achieved.

Strongly Disagree						Strongly Agree
1	2	3	4	5	6	7

the language of mathematics. Thus, in addition to revolutionizing astronomy, the investigators launched the whole modern enterprise of scientific discovery.

This new understanding of the natural universe in turn helped lead to a new understanding of humanity and God—that of the eighteenth-century Enlightenment. In place of an almighty God who directed the workings of nature and the destinies of the human race, the writers and intellectuals of the Enlightenment put a remote deity who had created the universe, established its laws, and left it to itself. In place of faith in the unseen, they put human reason, which could limitlessly discover the unknown. In place of original sin and redemption, they put the ideas of progress and human perfectibility. The Enlightenment was the first serious challenge to Christian belief since ancient times, but it was also an attractive way of thinking that influenced all classes of society. Few people shed their religious beliefs, but even

≪ **Rearranging the Universe** A diagram in an atlas published in 1660 shows "The Universe According to the Copernican Hypothesis." The sun is at the center and the stars (marked by zodiac signs) on the outside, with the planets orbiting in between; only the moon orbits the earth, the third planet out. Jupiter, the fifth planet, has four moons, discovered by Galileo Galilei. But more than a century after Copernicus, his universe is still only a "hypothesis," not to be taken as certain fact.

nobles, bishops, and absolute monarchs began to work for such reforms as widespread education, religious toleration, and the abolition of serfdom.

In the cultural field, Europe continued its Renaissance revival of Greco-Roman art and thought, and continued to reinterpret the traditions of the ancients in accordance with its own changing needs. The order, clarity, and precision of classicism were suitable to an age of reason and exact science. The elegance and refinement of the eighteenth-century Rococo style reflected the luxurious court and noble life of the eighteenth century. In addition, after many centuries of improvements in musical instruments, composers from the Renaissance onward had more scope for creativity than ever before.

In some of its basic features, the seventeenth- and eighteenth-century West was still a traditional civilization. Farming remained the main source of wealth, the vast majority of the population still consisted of peasants, and absolute monarchy rested on the long-standing partnership of rulers, nobles, and churches. Even so, the changes in knowledge, thought, art, and government were impressive, and more than ever before, they radiated outward from the countries of western Europe.

LO¹ The Scientific Revolution

Ever since prehistoric hunter-gatherers began recording the movement across the sky of the sun, moon, and stars (p. 7), humans have sought knowledge of the workings of the universe in which they live—what is today called scientific knowledge. Over many centuries, their knowledge increased, but this happened in fits and starts, and often as a byproduct of religious belief and philosophical thinking. In just a few recent centuries, however, scientific knowledge has increased continuously and with unprecedented speed. And gaining such knowledge has become a basic undertaking of modern civilization—one that has helped drive other recent changes, notably the revolutions in industry and technology and the rise of secular ideologies alongside and often opposed to religion.

This speedup in the growth of scientific knowledge, and the accompanying change in the status of science within civilization, began in Europe in the sixteenth and seventeenth centuries,

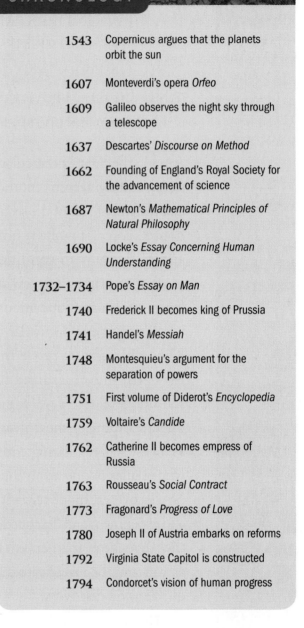

CHRONOLOGY

1543	Copernicus argues that the planets orbit the sun
1607	Monteverdi's opera *Orfeo*
1609	Galileo observes the night sky through a telescope
1637	Descartes' *Discourse on Method*
1662	Founding of England's Royal Society for the advancement of science
1687	Newton's *Mathematical Principles of Natural Philosophy*
1690	Locke's *Essay Concerning Human Understanding*
1732–1734	Pope's *Essay on Man*
1740	Frederick II becomes king of Prussia
1741	Handel's *Messiah*
1748	Montesquieu's argument for the separation of powers
1751	First volume of Diderot's *Encyclopedia*
1759	Voltaire's *Candide*
1762	Catherine II becomes empress of Russia
1763	Rousseau's *Social Contract*
1773	Fragonard's *Progress of Love*
1780	Joseph II of Austria embarks on reforms
1792	Virginia State Capitol is constructed
1794	Condorcet's vision of human progress

the era of what is today called the **Scientific Revolution**. The revolution itself started in a field of science where knowledge was already fairly precise and systematic, and problems in interpreting that knowledge were therefore fairly easy to see—astronomy.

The Universe of Aristotle and Ptolemy

For thousands of years, humans had taken great trouble to observe the heavenly bodies (sky objects) to the limit of what was possible with the naked eye. Partly this was because the reckoning of time, as well as navigation at sea, depended on this knowledge; just as important, it was because the heavenly bodies were thought to influence the destinies of individuals and communities. Pagan peoples believed that the heavenly bodies were gods and goddesses in their own right; and many monotheists believed that God had created the universe in such a way that every part of it—including the stars in their courses—influenced every other part—including human health and happiness upon the earth. Astronomers routinely and respectably doubled as astrologers, until the Scientific Revolution eventually forced the two activities apart.

Probably already in prehistoric times, sky-watchers were familiar with three basic features of the movements of the heavenly bodies. The first was that the heavenly bodies all seem to move across the sky in huge circles from east to west once a day. Secondly, the stars all move together at the same speed. Third, the sun, the moon, Mercury, Venus, Mars, Jupiter, and Saturn move slightly slower, so that they constantly shift backward against the stars. That was why they came to be known as *planets*, from the Greek for "wanderers."

Eventually, ancient Mesopotamian priests began to observe and measure these movements systematically. The priests discovered some of the complex but regular patterns in which the movements take place, and this enabled them to predict events such as eclipses. Ancient Greek and medieval Muslim thinkers improved the sighting instruments used for observing and measuring, as well as the skills of arithmetic and geometry needed for interpreting the measurements, and these achievements came to the knowledge of Christendom. In this way, by 1500 astronomy had developed one important feature of modern science—it was based on systematic observation and measurement, and on mathematics.

The Ptolemaic Theory

Ancient Greek thinkers also discussed how best to explain the observed movements of the heavenly bodies. Eventually, they arrived at a consensus view, first argued in the fourth century B.C. by Aristotle and explained in detail in the second century A.D. by Ptolemy (p. 110), in his handbook of astronomy, the *Almagest*. The **Ptolemaic (tol-uh-MEH-ic)** or **geocentric** (earth-centered) theory was accepted as authoritative by Muslim and Christian astronomers for more than a thousand years.

According to this explanation, the earth was a motionless sphere located at the center of the universe. Rotating around it were huge, rigid, but weightless and transparent spheres, nested one inside the other like the layers of an onion, that carried the heavenly bodies along in circular orbits. Closest to earth was the sphere that carried the moon; beyond were spheres carrying Mercury, Venus, the sun, Mars, Jupiter, and Saturn. Then came the sphere of the stars, carrying all of them at the same distance from the earth. Aristotle had taught that each sphere was moved by its own divine being, but Muslim and Christian thinkers believed that the "unmoved mover" of the system was the one God, who dwelt in the highest Heaven beyond the stars.

But what kept the earth, itself a very large object, motionless in the center of the universe? The answer, also derived from Aristotle, was that everything beneath the moon's orbit was made of a mixture of four basic materials or *elements*: earth, water, air, and fire. Each element had various "qualities" or features: earth, for example, was solid and cold, and it also had the feature

≪ Tycho Brahe's Observatory An illustration in a book by Tycho shows him pointing skyward beside a huge star-sighting device. When a star or planet passes overhead, the device's attendant calls out its angle above the horizon; the clock-watcher calls out the time; and the clerk writes both down. Such star-sighting devices were nothing new, but the clocks, Tycho boasted, "give not only the single minutes, but the seconds with the greatest accuracy." The exact measurement of both angles and time made Tycho's observations unprecedentedly reliable.
Maritime Museum Kronborg Castle, Denmark/Gianni Dagli Orti/The Art Archive

THE PTOLEMAIC (GEOCENTRIC) THEORY OF THE UNIVERSE ENDURED FOR CENTURIES IN THE ANCIENT, MUSLIM, AND CHRISTIAN WORLDS FOR SEVERAL REASONS:

The theory matched everyday observations and religious beliefs

- The earth felt as if it was motionless, whereas the heavenly bodies clearly looked as if they were moving in circles round it.

- The theory suited people's awe of the heavens by placing the heavenly bodies in a more perfect zone where everything moved in circles and nothing ever changed.

- It assigned the highest region of the universe to God, his angels, and the souls of the saved, and made God the ultimate mover of the whole universe.

- It placed imperfect humans in a lower region, where change and decay ruled.

The theory was adjusted to account for observations that did not fit the pattern of circular orbits around the earth

- Centuries of observation and measurement showed that the planets seemed sometimes to speed up on their paths around the earth, moving ahead of the stars for a while before slowing down and dropping behind them again.

- To explain this took complex adjustments, including having the planets move on epicyclical (looping) paths around the earth.

- Such adjustments upset the concept of the unchanging perfection of the heavens.

- However, astronomers thought of the adjustments as mere geometrical devices that were necessary to "save the appearances"—to make sense of the observations even though they might not be actually happening.

---

of belonging at the universe's center. That was why objects made mainly of earth, such as stones, felt heavy when picked up and fell when dropped: the earth in them was tending back to its natural place. Water's natural place was just above the earth, that of air above that of water, and that of fire above that of air.

Rearranging the Universe

Astronomers from Ptolemy onward knew that the theory did not exactly fit the observed movement of the heavenly bodies, but they accepted it all the same (see Reasons Why above). But then came the Renaissance, with its respect for observation as the way to truth and its understanding of the universe as truthfully revealing the mind of God (p. 292). Surely a universe whose appearance to observers did not convey the reality of its workings was absurd—or so it seemed to a Polish Church official and humanist scholar whose spare-time obsession was astronomy, Nicholas Copernicus (**koh-PUR-ni-kuhs**).

The Copernican Theory and Its Problems

Copernicus worked on his theory on and off for most of his life, and finally published his great work, *Concerning the Revolutions of the Celestial Bodies*, in the year of his death, 1543. Against the Ptolemaic theory, Copernicus claimed that the sun was at the center of the universe, and that the earth was a planet that orbited the sun and turned on its own axis as it did so. The seeming movement of the heavenly bodies westward across the sky was because the earth was itself turning eastward. The seeming speeding up and slowing down of the other planets was because they were seen from the moving viewpoint of the earth. Copernicus accepted that the planets were carried round the sun on spheres, and there were still details of the planets' movements that he could only explain by having them move on looping paths. All the same, he thought of his theory as no mere geometrical device, but as a true image of the universe's actual workings.

The **Copernican** or **heliocentric** (sun-centered) theory was not new. It was a refined version of a theory first put forward by the Greek astronomer Aristarchus in the third century B.C., which Copernicus knew because it was described by Ptolemy—who had also explained why, in his view, Aristarchus was wrong.

To turn on its own axis once a day, Ptolemy pointed out, such a large object as the earth must be revolving at vast speed. But how could it do that, with nothing to make it spin? Thinkers ever since Aristotle had agreed that for an object to move, something must be continuously causing it to move—even a thrown javelin, they thought, was pushed forward by the air after it left the thrower's hand. A heliocentric universe would be an absurd place where objects could move with nothing to push or pull them.

Furthermore, as Aristarchus and Copernicus both admitted, the only explanation of the observed movement of the moon was that it circled the earth while the earth circled the sun. Again, thinkers since Aristotle had believed that the entire universe revolved in one direction around a single central point. A heliocentric universe would be a monstrous place where one planet moved on a disordered path—constantly revolving around another planet, and changing direction as it did so.

In addition, if the earth was swinging around the sun in a huge circle, observers on the earth must be looking at any particular constellation (group of stars) at constantly changing angles—from sideways, then from directly opposite, and then again sideways. Objects seen at an angle look closer together than objects seen head-on, so how come the stars making up constellations did not seem to open out and then squeeze togther again as the earth moved past them? The only possible explanation would have to be that the stars were so far away that even the earth's movement around the sun hardly changed the angle at which they were seen. No one doubted that the universe was big, but a heliocentric universe would have to be absurdly and monstrously vast.

Making the Theory Fit the Appearances: Kepler

Copernicus did not answer Ptolemy's objections in a way that his fellow astronomers found convincing, and most of them saw no reason to go over to the heliocentric theory. All the same, the ideal of a simple and harmonious universe whose workings could be truthfully seen and understood was a compelling one. Perhaps, if observed even more systematically than before, the heavenly bodies would after all yield their secrets. That was the hope of a Danish nobleman, Tycho Brahe (**TEE-koh BRAH-eh**). Late in the sixteenth century, Brahe persuaded the king of Denmark and then the Holy Roman emperor to finance him in many years of sky-watching with the most accurate instruments ever constructed, on the understanding that he would furnish them with the most reliable horoscopes ever cast (see photo on page 357). His observations were then assembled and analyzed by his coworker, the German mathematician Johannes Kepler.

Kepler was convinced that God had created the sun as the source of all light, life, and movement in the universe, and had therefore placed it at the center. Sure enough, when he compared Ptolemy's description of the orbits of the planets with Brahe's newly precise observations, they did not fit—but it turned out that neither did Copernicus's. Did the planets perhaps move round the sun as Copernicus said, but in orbits of a different shape?

In many years of work early in the seventeenth century, Kepler developed a description that fit Tycho's observations exactly—one that needed no complex looping movements to make it work. The planets were moving around the sun in ellipses—oval curves that took them sometimes nearer the sun and sometimes farther away. As they neared the sun, they sped up; as they moved farther away, they slowed down; and planets with orbits farther out moved slower than those with orbits closer

in. All this Kepler described not in the vague language of words but in the precise language of geometry and numbers. Kepler's universe did indeed have a simple and harmonious structure that could be seen and understood by humans.

Piling Up Evidence: Galileo

Meanwhile, eyeglass makers in Holland had combined lenses of different shapes to create the first telescopes, and the invention soon came to the knowledge of an Italian professor of astronomy and devotee of Copernicus, Galileo Galilei. In 1609, Galileo built his own telescope, pointed it at the night sky, and became the first astronomer ever to study the heavenly bodies other than with the naked eye. What he saw provided powerful new evidence against the geocentric theory and the idea of the universe's workings with which it was linked.

The surface of the moon, it turned out, was scarred with mountains and craters, and from time to time, spots appeared and disappeared on the surface of the sun. So much for the idea that the heavens were a place of unchanging perfection quite unlike the earth. Jupiter was accompanied on its path across the sky by objects that sometimes sped past it and sometimes lagged behind it, but never strayed far from it—objects that Galileo realized, after a week of watching them, were moons. These "Medicean stars," as he christened them in honor of the Medici rulers of Florence (see photo on page 360), were also an argument in favor of the heliocentric theory: If Jupiter could move on an orbit with moons orbiting round it, why not the earth with its moon? And as Galileo peered into the night sky, thousands of previously unseen stars came into view. Surely these stars must be much farther away than the previously visible ones, and countless more must lie beyond the range of his telescope. The universe must indeed be unimaginably vast.

 Galileo Discovers the Moons of Jupiter Read Galileo on his discovery of the moons of Jupiter.

Galileo the "Heretic"

As Galileo piled up evidence against Aristotle and Ptolemy, this put him at the center of the first serious conflict between two traditional allies, science and religion. Some religious thinkers, including Luther and Calvin, had already objected to the heliocentric theory because it contradicted various Bible statements, for example: "The Lord . . . has established the world: it shall never be moved." True, there was a long-standing Christian tradition of not taking literally what the Bible said about matters like the earth's location in the universe—as the pious and learned Cardinal Cesare Baronio once said to Galileo, "The Scriptures teach us how to go to heaven, not how the heavens go." But many theologians in the strict Church of the Catholic Reformation were not so easygoing, and Galileo, though loyal to the Church, could not resist provocatively popularizing his views.

> **Copernican, heliocentric**
> Refers to the sun-centered theory of the universe's movements, argued by the sixteenth-century astronomer Nicholas Copernicus.

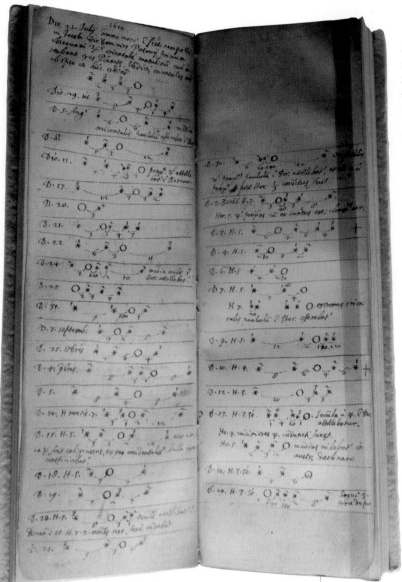

relevant to understanding the workings of a universe in which the earth orbited the sun. For example, there was the question how come, if the earth was moving in an orbit, objects fell toward it. Evidently this could not be because they tended toward the center of the universe, and Copernicus had already declared that the earth had a feature of "gravity" (heaviness) that caused objects to tend toward its own moving center. But how did gravity operate?

Galileo's Experiments: Interactive Lessons from NOVA
(http://www.pbs.org/wgbh/nova/galileo/expe_flash_1.html) Explore some of Galileo's experiments in this interactive site.

To find out, Galileo rolled highly polished metal balls down carefully smoothed grooves in sloping wooden ramps. The slope enabled him to measure the balls' rate of fall more easily than if he dropped them vertically, and the polishing and smoothing minimized the effect of friction. He thereby proved that no matter the balls' size, they all rolled down at the same speed but accelerated as they did so—in other words, the earth's gravity acted on them more strongly the nearer they came to its center. And like Kepler with the planets' orbits, he was able to describe this increasing strength of the earth's gravity in the exact language of mathematics.

Galileo did not invent this process of **experiment**—of answering a question about a natural process by making the process take place under conditions that make it measurable, while eliminating effects that might disturb the measurement. But his experiments were so imaginative and ingenious, and the questions they dealt with were so important to understanding how the universe worked, that he, more than anyone else, established experiments as a basic feature of science.

Galileo not only conducted actual experiments but also devised "thought experiments"—visualizing how objects

In 1633, the Inquisition in Rome found Galileo "vehemently suspect" of heresy by "holding as true the false doctrine taught by some that the sun is the center of the universe"; ordered him to "abjure, curse, and detest" that doctrine; and sentenced him to lifelong house arrest. His published works—and all others advocating the Copernican theory—were placed on the Index of Prohibited Books (p. 323). It was two centuries before Copernican works were dropped from the Index, and longer still before Pope John Paul II formally cleared Galileo of heresy in 1993, after criticizing "the error of the theologians of the time, when they maintained the centrality of the earth."

> **"The Scriptures teach us how to go to heaven, not how the heavens go."**
> —Cardinal Cesare Baronio

Galileo the Experimenter

Meanwhile, for the rest of his life, Galileo worked quietly on problems that were too earthbound to alarm the Inquisition, but eventually turned out to be highly

might behave under ideal conditions that he could not create. Supposing, for example, a totally smooth object were set moving on an equally smooth and absolutely level surface, in otherwise completely empty space, so that there would be no friction or air resistance to slow it down. Would it ever stop? Aristotle had taught that once whatever set an object in motion stopped acting on it, the object must instantly stop, but Galileo concluded that "a body moving on a level surface will continue in the same direction at constant speed unless disturbed." For Galileo, the possibility of objects moving with nothing to push or pull them, and doing so forever unless something stopped them, was entirely conceivable.

Visions of Scientific Progress

The era of Kepler and Galileo was one of bitter dispute and unwelcome perplexity, when evidence against the old consensus about the workings of the universe was piling up but a new consensus was not yet in place. Supporters and opponents of Aristotle, "Ptolemeans" and "Copernicans," argued fiercely, and Copernicans did not always agree among themselves—Galileo, for instance, insisted against Kepler that planets move in circles. As the English poet John Donne complained at the time,

> The sun is lost, and the earth, and no man's wit
> Can well direct him where to look for it.

However, two hundred years of exploration of the oceans and continents suggested that disputes about the earth's surface, at least, could be settled by investigation; gunpowder and the magnetic compass were proof of human ability to make use of natural processes; and printing had greatly accelerated the spread of knowledge. Was there some way that these precedents of increasing knowledge could be made to apply to the universe and its workings in general? Francis Bacon, an English scholar and lawyer who lived at the same time as Kepler and Galileo, was convinced that this could be done.

Inductive Science: Bacon

What held up the progress of knowledge, Bacon believed, was the traditional reliance on **deduction**—on reasoning from beliefs assumed in advance to be true, sometimes because they simply seemed self-evident, and sometimes because they had been stated by some revered ancient author such as Aristotle. Instead, Bacon favored **induction**—reasoning from observed facts to the principles and processes that lay behind them. There was a precedent for this in the practices of observation that had sprung up during the Renaissance, but Bacon wanted to turn these practices into a systematic undertaking for the increase of knowledge. By induction from careful observation and repeated experiments, investigators would reach general conclusions. New observations and experiments would then be undertaken that would permit further inductions to be made. In this way, he thought, the area of certain knowledge would steadily grow and the region of argument and dispute would steadily shrink.

Bacon was mistaken in many of his own scientific beliefs, and he was no brilliant experimenter like Galileo. All the same, his vision of scientific progress as cumulative, with one discovery leading to another, was a true prophecy—though today it is still an open question whether ultimate certainty about the workings of the universe can ever be reached (pp. 516–517).

Deductive Science: Descartes

Not long after Bacon, a Frenchman, René Descartes, proposed another way of arriving at certain knowledge—one that relied on deduction, but not from the kind of consensus beliefs that earlier thinkers had often started with. Descartes was the son of a lawyer who left him enough money to spend his life in study and thought, mostly outside France in the freer atmosphere of Holland. He was a brilliant mathematician, and in his *Discourse on Method*, published in 1637, he tried to apply to knowledge in general the methods of mathematics, which start with axioms (self-evident assumptions) such as the geometrical axiom that a straight line is the shortest distance between two points.

To find such a self-evident basic fact on which to build, Descartes began by doubting all existing ideas, a method of thinking known as "Cartesian doubt" (from the Latin version of its originator's name): if an idea could be questioned for any reason at all, it must be rejected as an axiom. Descartes was left with a single idea that he could accept absolutely—his own consciousness: "I *think*"—from which he deduced, "therefore I *exist*." From this starting point he set out to construct, by a series of logical steps, a complete picture of the universe up to and including God. And the vision of the universe he arrived at was a mathematical one, in which the movements and makeup of all material objects, human bodies as well as heavenly ones, could be measured and described in terms of geometry and number.

In this effort for a total picture of the universe, Descartes fell short of success. But his rejection of existing knowledge, intellectual authority, and traditional ways of reasoning undermined those old ways of looking at the world. And his vision of the universe as a vast machine in which everything was subject to measurement and governed by mathematical rules would deeply influence philosophy and religion as well as science.

"I think, therefore I exist."
—Descartes

experiment
Making a natural process take place under conditions that make it measurable, while eliminating effects that might disturb the measurement, in order to answer a question about the process.

deduction
Reasoning from beliefs assumed in advance to be true.

induction
Reasoning from observed facts to the principles and processes that lay behind them.

Science Beyond Astronomy: Harvey

Meanwhile, amid all the arguments, the growth of scientific knowledge was truly beginning to speed up, as distrust of traditional consensus spread from astronomy to other fields. Early in the seventeenth century, for example, an English medical doctor, William Harvey, disproved the theory of yet another authoritative ancient Greek thinker, Galen of Pergamum (p. 110), that blood was continuously produced and consumed by the body. Harvey did so partly by estimating how much blood the heart pumps each time it beats and how often it beats on average. His conclusion was that if all of this blood was newly made, the body would have to be making an impossible amount of blood—about a quarter of a ton every day. Most of the blood that the heart pumped must therefore be "old" blood that circulated again and again. In this way, Harvey applied astronomy's methods of measurement and number to the study of living beings and made a discovery that is basic to modern physiology.

Organized Science

At the same time, the pursuit of new knowledge was developing its own forms of organization separate from the traditional knowledge-pursuing institutions, the universities. Much of university study and teaching was necessarily taken up with subjects like theology, rhetoric, and law. In scientific fields like astronomy and medicine, the faculty—with notable exceptions like Galileo and Newton—tended to be traditionalists. It was not until the nineteenth century that universities would become leading centers of scientific research. Meanwhile, seekers after new knowledge formed their own groups, backed by wealthy patrons fulfilling their Renaissance duty of furthering the cause of learning.

Short-lived groups of this kind first appeared in Italy, but eventually the rulers of large countries beyond the Alps joined the trend, and set up what became permanent organizations for the advancement of science. The first of these was the Royal Society of London for Improving Natural Knowledge, established by King Charles II in 1662. Its members came from every wealthy and educated walk of life from nobles and churchmen to merchants and physicians, among them England's most notable scientific thinkers, including Newton. Strongly influenced by Bacon's idea for building up a total system of knowledge, the society aided experiments, listened to learned discussions, corresponded with foreign societies, and published a journal. These developments reflected the growing interdependence of scientific investigators. The isolated experimenter of the Renaissance like Leonardo da Vinci was giving way to a new type, and science was becoming a social enterprise.

The Royal Society also pinned on the progress of science a newly arisen hope—not just of approaching God by understanding the universe he had created, but also of using the universe's workings for human benefit. Bacon himself had declared that the increase of knowledge would increase human prosperity and power, and the society's charter (founding document) declared that it would devote itself to "further promoting by the authority of experiments the sciences of natural things and of useful arts, to the glory of God the Creator and the advantage of the human race."

Of course, anything that increased human prosperity and power in general would also do the same for kingdoms and their rulers. In 1666, King Louis XIV set up the Royal Academy of Sciences, the French counterpart of the Royal Society, at the suggestion of his finance minister, Colbert, whose responsibilities included fostering France's industrial and military resources. Rulers of other kingdoms soon followed the English and French examples. Science (the search for understanding of nature) and technology (the search for ways to control nature) began to experience a mutual attraction with the blessing of the state, though the actual marriage of the two had to wait until the nineteenth century (pp. 424–425).

The Universe of Newton

The thinker who finally put an end to arguments about the structure and workings of the universe was Isaac Newton. The son of a well-off English farmer whose exceptional abilities brought him a professorship at Cambridge University in his twenties, Newton finally broke with the traditional belief in a difference between the earth and the heavens that earlier investigators had undermined but not destroyed.

Sometime in the 1660s—inspired, so he later said, by the sight of an apple falling from a tree, though it did not actually hit him on the head—Newton began to ask himself whether the force in the moving earth that caused the apple to fall might act beyond the earth itself, perhaps even as far as the moon. That, however, raised another question. At such a distance, Galileo's rolling-ball experiment indicated, the earth's pull must be quite weak, but still, how come the moon did not fall to the earth like the apple? The reason could have something to do with Galileo's thought experiment concerning the tendency of objects to continue moving in a particular direction—an example of what Newton called inertia.

 An Essay on Newton's Life and Work (http://galileoandeinstein. physics.virginia.edu/ lectures/newton.html) Learn more about the genius of Newton.

In that case, the moon's orbit must be the result of a complex interaction between its inertial movement and the gravitational attraction between itself and the earth, the details of which were determined by the factors of mass, distance, and time—and the same interactions must surely apply between orbiting planets and the sun, and for that matter between the earth and falling apples. After many years of thought and observation, Newton was able to define these interactions in mathematical terms that fit in with both Kepler's mathematics of planets orbiting the sun and Galileo's mathematics of balls rolling down slopes.

Newton published his results in *Mathematical Principles of Natural Philosophy* in 1687. In this work, he showed the reality of the kind of universe that Ptolemy had deemed

 Sir Isaac Newton Lays Down the Ground Rules for the Scientific Method Read Newton's rules for developing valid scientific theories.

absurd—where objects could move without being pulled or pushed, where planets could orbit each other, and which was vast beyond imagining, so that even the sun had no special position within it. When Newton died in 1727, the poet Alexander Pope composed an inscription for his monument that sounded a very different note from John Donne's words of a century earlier:

> Nature and nature's laws lay hid in night;
> God said, "Let Newton be!" and all was light.

In fact, astronomers and physicists in the centuries since Newton have shown that the light he shed on the workings of the universe was only a partial one (p. 515). Still, from an outpost in a tiny corner of the universe, a human being had achieved truthful knowledge of some of its structure and discovered some of the rules according to which it worked. The methods of observation, experiment, and mathematics that had enabled him to do so had already brought truthful knowledge of some of the universe's other features, such as the living beings that inhabited it. New scientific knowledge had already improved the "useful arts," notably by enabling inventors to create steam engines for pumping ground water out of deep mines (p. 423). Bacon's vision of a continuous process of expanding knowledge with endless practical applications was becoming a reality.

> **worldview**
> A vision of the universe's general purpose and meaning, and of the human condition within it.

LO² Science, Religion, and Humanity: The Enlightenment

The revolution within science also led to revolutionary changes outside it, in the general ideas, values, and attitudes of society. For science gave to educated Westerners a radically new understanding of the workings of the universe, and on this basis, they constructed a new **worldview**.

The main propagators of this worldview were mostly not scientific investigators, but "people of letters," as they called themselves—writers of poetry and fiction, history and philosophy, and commentary on culture and public affairs. They came from both the nobility and the educated middle class, and most of the best-known of them lived in eighteenth-century France (see photo). Their opponents sarcastically called them *philosophes*—"philosophers," as in "self-proclaimed philosophers"—a name

People of Letters Distinguished guests attend a reading of a play by Voltaire in the mansion of Madame Geoffrin, one of the Parisian ladies who presided over enlightened social and intellectual life. The listeners include Diderot, Montesquieu, and Rousseau, and Voltaire is present in the form of a bust; a quarter of the guests are nobles, and one-eighth are women. Anicet-Charles-Gabriel Lemonnier painted this scene in 1812, nearly sixty years after it supposedly took place, but it gives a good view of the enlightened elite. Lauros/Giraudon/The Bridgeman Art Library

philosophes
The name given to eighteenth-century "people of letters" who embraced the Enlightenment worldview.

Enlightenment
The name for the century from 1687 to 1789, when a new "enlightened" view of humanity and God grew out of the new findings of science.

Deism
A religious belief that recognizes a Supreme Being but rejects the idea that such a deity influences nature and human destiny.

agnosticism
A position of uncertainty about the existence of God.

atheism
A position that denies the existence of God.

that with time lost its derogatory overtones, so that today they are known as **philosophes** in English as well as French.

The philosophes were so dazzled by Newton's brilliance that they considered themselves to be living in an unprecedented "age of light." It was this notion that gave rise to the term **Enlightenment** as a name for the century from 1687, the date of Newton's *Principles of Mathematics*, to 1789, the start of the French Revolution. Those who glimpsed the new vision of the universe thought of themselves as the "enlightened" ones, and they were eager to spread the light to others.

God and the Universe

The universe that the philosophes held up to view contrasted sharply with the traditional one. The most evident and disturbing difference was that the new universe extended through boundless space. Late in the seventeenth century, the devoutly religious French mathematician Blaise Pascal confessed, "I am terrified by the eternal silence of those infinite spaces." In those spaces, God had no obvious dwelling place from which he could move the heavenly bodies by his almighty will. Instead, the universe ran itself according to Newton's precise mathematical laws, with no need for divine intervention. As the French astronomer Pierre Laplace said, "Give me the present location and motion of all bodies in the universe, and I will predict their location and motion through all eternity."

God the Watchmaker

If the heavenly bodies were lumps of matter like the earth that influenced each other only through the force of gravity, it was hard to believe that they could influence human destiny, and educated people gradually stopped taking astrology seriously. But to some it also seemed that if God did not interfere with any aspect of the universe, it followed that Christianity, based as it was on the belief that he had appeared on earth as a human being, was also a myth. If so, then the different Christianities that had developed over the centuries, whether Catholic, Orthodox, or Protestant, were purely human creations based on incorrect thinking—or on fraud and superstition.

This did not mean that God did not exist. Common sense made it difficult for people to think of something as existing that had not been made, so the universe itself must have had a maker, namely God. As Newton himself said: "Gravity explains

the motions of the planets, but it cannot explain who set the planets in motion. God governs all things and knows all that is or can be done"—and he even suspected that as minor disturbances built up in the motion of the planets, God might intervene to correct them. But the philosophes generally believed—to use a comparison often made at the time—that God's relation to the universe was like that of a human watchmaker to a watch. Having designed the universe, built it, and wound it up, God had then left it to run on its own.

Deism, Agnosticism, and Atheism

This was a religion of sorts, but it broke with the traditional belief of monotheist and polytheist religion alike, that mighty divine beings influence nature and human destiny, and can in turn be influenced by humans. Vaguely labeled **Deism**, the new religion originated with a seventeenth-century English nobleman, Lord Herbert of Cherbury, who tried to revive what he thought were the natural and reasonable beliefs of the human race before it had been led astray by "the covetous and crafty sacerdotal order" (clergy) of different religions. There were five of these basic beliefs: the existence of a Supreme Power, the necessity of worship, the requirement of good conduct, the benefit of repentance of vices, and the existence of rewards and punishments after death.

Deism became popular with the philosophes, but for most churchgoers, it was an inadequate substitute for traditional religion. It lacked mystery, ritual, emotional appeal, and discipline. And it was offensive to the clergy of all denominations, for it challenged the authority of their sacred books, doctrines, and offices and accused them of fostering superstition for the sake of their own wealth and power.

By the close of the eighteenth century, Deism began to lose its appeal even for devotees of the Enlightenment. Many of them decided that there really is no need even for a creator. Watches might need watchmakers, but the universe was not a watch. It was the infinite totality of all existing things, which did not have to obey the rules that applied to watches and their makers in the tiny outpost of the earth. Very likely, the universe and its motion had always been and always would be, with no creator to set it going. This line of reasoning led some to say that they could not or did not know whether God existed (**agnosticism** or skepticism); others took it as certain fact that God did not exist (**atheism**). For the first time since Rome's conversion to Christianity, religious doubt became a force in Western civilization.

Traditional Religion and the Enlightenment

All the same, traditional religion continued to be the main influence on the way of life of most people in Europe. In fact, the age of the Enlightenment was also a time of religious revival. In different faiths, religious mass movements arose, inspired by beloved leaders whose preaching stirred up the fervor of many thousands of people. In Protestant England, for example, there was the Methodist minister John Wesley; in Catholic Italy, the Redemptorist father Alfonso Liguori; among the Jews of Poland, the Hasidic rabbi Israel ben Eliezer. All three had in common the ability to interpret the traditional beliefs of their respective religions in deeply personal and moving ways that made sense to ordinary believers. All of them, moreover, had a permanent effect on their respective faiths, through organizations of their followers who have continued their work down to the present.

But believers, including clergy, could not help being influenced by scientific discovery and the new worldview that claimed to be based on it. At the level of basic belief, they rejected the notions of the philosophes that science had made traditional religion harder to believe in, and that the clergy were "crafty and covetous" misleaders of the human race. But at the level of social and political thought, many of them could more or less accept such Enlightenment ideas as religious toleration, widespread education, or the use of scientific knowledge to improve the condition of the human race. It was through adaptations of this kind that the ideas of the Enlightenment spread beyond the relatively small circles of the philosophes, to become part of the general climate of opinion among educated people, and to some extent among working people in town and countryside, in eighteenth-century Europe.

Human Society

If God played an inactive role (or none at all) in the view of the philosophes, the place and powers of humans were dramatically enlarged. The universe's infinite spaces might be terrifying, but humans had explored those spaces by the use of their unaided reason, and through science and technology, they could improve their well-being on earth and press nature itself into their service. Worldwide travel and trade, printing and firearms had already changed the conditions of human life; Europeans, accustomed to look up to the "ancients" of Greece and Rome, could now claim to have outdone the ancients—and non-European peoples of their own time—in knowledge, wealth, and power. The English author Edward Gibbon, whose *History of the Decline and Fall of the Roman Empire* is still revered by scholars today, listed in his great work some of the improvements and advances that in his opinion secured Europe against the fate that had befallen Rome. He ended by declaring: "We may therefore acquiesce in the pleasing conclusion that every age of the world has increased and still increases the real wealth, the happiness, the knowledge, and perhaps the virtue, of the human race."

Even with a "perhaps," the claim that the human race was becoming more virtuous was a bold one, but many philosophes were willing to believe it. Nature, as revealed by Newton, was orderly and harmonious. Within the boundaries of human freedom, it seemed likely that people would choose good rather than bad—so long as they followed nature and reason. If they had not done so, this was the result of ignorance—because they

had failed to follow nature's ways and had made customs, laws, sanctions, and beliefs that twisted and shackled the individual. Humans would regain their birthright and advance in knowledge and virtue when the chains of unreason were broken.

The philosophes also had strong opinions about how to achieve this liberation of human capacities. They called for schools that would spread reason and knowledge among the masses; for reforming instead of sadistically punishing criminals; for an end to persecution in the name of what they thought of as rival religious myths; for rulers and nobles to recognize their common humanity with those over whom they wielded power. They mocked and protested against social institutions that they believed held back the improvement of the human race—most of all organized religion, but also serfdom and slavery, and occasionally (though much less often) the subordination of women to men. The philosophes inherited many of their criticisms and ideals from Renaissance humanists, above all Erasmus and Thomas More (p. 294). But unlike these earlier thinkers, the philosophes were no longer inspired by Christianity, and they believed that their ideals could become at least to some extent reality.

Human Nature

Along with their new views of the universe and society, the philosophes also had a new view of the human beings by whom the universe was inhabited and societies were formed. This view originated with the apostle of the Glorious Revolution in Britain, John Locke (pp. 344–345).

Locke had studied medicine, economics, political theory, and philosophy, and besides his political writings, he also wrote on the nature of human knowledge and perception. His ideas were especially persuasive, for he rested his case on the ordinary sense experience of his readers. Locke may not have been profound, and he was certainly not scientific. Nevertheless, his writings swept away many ancient beliefs and showed what the "new" reason could do when it was applied to questions about human beings and society.

In his *Essay Concerning Human Understanding* (1690), Locke stated that experience is the source of all knowledge—a view known as **empiricism**, from the Greek word for "experience." This was in line with Bacon's belief in induction, and it challenged convictions that knowledge is inborn, as Socrates and Plato had taught, or revealed by God, as Christianity claimed, or derived from self-evident principles, as Descartes thought. Locke supported a rival concept that is often called the *tabula rasa* ("blank writing tablet") theory, though he himself used a

> **empiricism**
> The view that all knowledge comes from experience acquired through the senses, as opposed to being inborn, revealed by God, or derived from self-evident principles.

> "The philosophes believed that God designed the universe, built it, and wound it up—and then left it to run on its own."

slightly different comparison. The mind at birth, he said, is like "white paper, void of all characters, without any ideas." The ideas that come to be written on this paper come from but one source: experience—that is, knowledge that comes to us through our senses and is then sorted and arranged by our minds. In this way, we learn to understand and control the world about us.

Locke's notion of the "thinking machine" suited the eighteenth-century view that people are shaped by their environment. Given that ideas come entirely from outside, it follows that if the correct environment is provided, people will receive only the "right" ideas. This suggests, in turn, that through the reform of institutions, especially education, rapid improvements can be made in human nature and society. These beliefs help explain the devotion of the philosophes to both science and education. To them, ignorance had replaced sin and the devil as the principal enemy. Sinners were to be redeemed not by the grace of God, but by human reason. Research had to be encouraged so that investigators could learn more; education had to be overhauled and extended so that the new knowledge could be carried everywhere.

The philosophes threw themselves into these endeavors with the enthusiasm and dedication of missionaries. The French man of letters Denis Diderot devoted twenty years of his life to the most ambitious of Enlightenment knowledge-spreading projects, the twenty-eight-volume *Encyclopedia, Or Systematic Dictionary of the Sciences, Arts, and Crafts*. He explained the project's aim in the entry for "Encyclopedia," speaking for himself and his hundreds of contributors: "to bring together the knowledge scattered across the face of the earth, to present it systematically to the people among whom we live, and to hand it on to those who will come after us; so that our descendants, in becoming better educated, will at the same time become happier and more virtuous, and so that we ourselves will not die without having deserved well of the human race."

Human Destiny: The Vision of Progress

Ideas of this kind led to a new view of human destiny. If it was true that "every age of the world has increased and still increases" the happiness and virtue of the human race, it followed that future ages would do the same—that progress was humanity's ultimate destiny.

This faith in progress was a new idea. The ancients, if they wished to think of something better than their own lives, had looked backward rather than forward, to a Golden Age when the gods first created the human race. Christianity and other monotheistic religions prophesied ultimate blessedness upon the earth, but only for some, and only after an age of hideous disasters. Even the humanists of the Renaissance, for all their high estimate of human capacity, had looked backward to Greece

and Rome as the time when that capacity had been most fully realized. Now, however, science, exploration, invention, and education all seemed to point the way toward an ever grander future.

The marquis de Condorcet **(kawn-dawr-SEH)**, a well-educated nobleman trained in mathematics and science, made the most eloquent statement of this new faith in progress. His *Sketch for a Historical Picture of the Progress of the Human Mind* was written, ironically, in 1794, a chaotic year of the French Revolution when Condorcet had broken with the more radical leaders of the revolution and was in hiding as a fugitive. But he wrote that his sorrow over temporary injustices and barbarities was overbalanced by his vision of the future.

 **Condorcet Affirms the Inevitability of Progress** Read Condorcet's proof that humanity will attain perfection.

Condorcet declared that nothing could stop the advance of human knowledge and power "as long as the earth occupies its present place in the system of the universe, and as long as the general laws of this system produce neither a general cataclysm nor such changes as will deprive the human race of its present faculties and its present resources." He forecast that rapid technological advances would lead to a world in which "everyone will have less work to do, will produce more, and satisfy their wants more fully." He saw the eventual achievement of equal rights for women, the abolition of poverty, and the ordering of economic affairs so that every individual, guided by reason, could enjoy true independence. And he predicted an end to warfare, declaring that wars would "rank with assassinations as freakish atrocities, humiliating and vile in the eyes of nature."

> **"***Our descendants, in becoming better educated, will at the same time become happier and more virtuous.* **"**
>
> —Denis Diderot

Forms of Government

The Enlightenment is an outstanding example of how ideas conceived by writers and intellectuals can have an overwhelming impact on practical affairs. In the long run, the philosophes helped to bring about massive changes in Western politics, government, and society. The philosophes' emphasis on reason, education, and progress naturally led them to judge the social and political institutions of their own time. Did these institutions, they asked, contribute to advancing the happiness and virtue of the human race? Needless to say, they mostly condemned what they found.

Separation of Powers: Montesquieu

Only one major European country met with some degree of approval from the philosophes. This was Britain, whose seventeenth-century troubles (pp. 339–345) had produced a government and social system that met their standards, at least in some respects. And they were deeply impressed by the theories of natural rights, the social contract, and limited monarchy that John Locke had used to argue for the rightness of Britain's "Glorious Revolution."

The most influential Enlightenment admirer of the British system of government was a Frenchman, the Baron de Montesquieu. A distinguished aristocrat, actively involved in political affairs of the nobility, he was deeply concerned about the dangers of any form of despotism. In *The Spirit of the Laws* (1748), he argued that there is no single form of government suitable to all times and places. But he insisted that some arrangement of checks and balances is essential in every type of government as a guard against tyranny. This idea dated back to the Roman Republic (pp. 92–93), but Montesquieu thought of Britain as the contemporary model of this principle, with its "separation of powers" as he called it—the division between the legislative, executive, and judicial branches of government—and the partnership among the monarch, the Lords, and the Commons. In fact, the formal and informal links among the British branches of government were closer than Montesquieu allowed, but his ideas had a direct impact on the writing of the United States Constitution pp. 382–383).

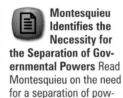 **Montesquieu Identifies the Necessity for the Separation of Governmental Powers** Read Montesquieu on the need for a separation of powers in government.

The General Will: Rousseau

The French-Swiss man of letters Jean-Jacques Rousseau lived at the same time as the philosophes and his ideas overlapped with theirs, but he also disagreed with them in ways that foreshadowed the nineteenth-century Romantic movement (pp. 404–405). He shared the Enlightenment belief in the basic goodness of human beings, but he rejected the idea that the history of the human race was one of increasing wealth and knowledge leading to increasing happiness and virtue. Instead, he believed that humans had been truly happy and virtuous in their original "state of nature" before societies existed, when people had lived for themselves according to their own natural goodness without exploiting or controlling each other (see photo). The formation of societies had certainly increased human capabilities, but had also deprived people of their natural freedom and thereby corrupted their natural virtue, and the result was the "rich and wretched nations" of eighteenth-century Europe. So how could humans form societies that would let them be wealthy, free, and virtuous?

Rousseau answered this question in his *Social Contract*, published in 1763. Like Hobbes and Locke, he believed that a society is founded on a mutual contract among the individuals who form it (pp. 338–339, 344–345). But his version of the contract ran: "Each of us puts his person and his whole power in common under the supreme direction of the general will, and in return we receive every member as an indivisible part of the whole." As an "indivisible part" of the whole community, every citizen would have an individual share in its **general will**, so that "each, coalescing with all, may nevertheless obey only himself, and remain as

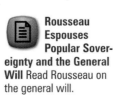 **Rousseau Espouses Popular Sovereignty and the General Will** Read Rousseau on the general will.

free as before"—and being free, the citizens would also be virtuous. Citizens should actively share in forming the general will, preferably by taking government decisions themselves in mass assemblies. But once the general will was formed, even citizens who disagreed with it must selflessly obey it, and those who disobeyed must be "forced to be free."

In this way, Rousseau tried to bridge the gap between obedience and freedom that exists in every society. Many thinkers since his time have argued that his ideas are in fact a recipe for dictatorship, since citizens are supposed to gain

general will
According to Rousseau, the collective wishes or desires of a society, which must be obeyed as part of the social contract.

 An Overview of Enlightenment Themes and Artifacts by the British Museum (http://www.britishmuseum.org/explore/galleries/themes/room_1_enlightenment.aspx) Investigate other Enlightenment themes and artifacts in the British Museum.

Jean-Jacques Rousseau Society, Geneva

"He Goes Home to His Equals" In an illustration in a work by Rousseau, elegantly dressed representatives of European civilization look in puzzlement at a loincloth-wearing African, who has bundled up and thrown away his own European clothing. The African has learned European ways, but that has only taught him that his own people's way of life is superior. The "equals" to whom he is returning are happier and more virtuous in their "state of nature" than the Europeans.

freedom through total obedience. But his ideal of a society that fostered wealth, freedom, and virtue all at once had a powerful influence—notably on the hopes and strivings of the French Revolution (p. 388).

LO³ The Enlightenment Spirit in Literature and Art

The new ideas in science and philosophy had a marked effect on the literature of the seventeenth and eighteenth centuries. The leading cultural fashion was **classicism**, an extension of Renaissance ideals given fresh force by the new stress on logic and universal laws. The leaders of classicism also sought to perfect exact forms of expression. Rejecting the force of current usage in determining what is "correct," they looked instead to recognized judges of style and taste, who based their verdicts on ancient models. In this way, it was hoped, modern languages would gain the precision and elegance of Greek and Latin as used by the most admired ancient writers. It was about this time, in fact, that ancient culture in general came to be described as "classical"—a word that derived from "class," and was used to mean not just ancient but supremely refined, orderly, elegant, and generally admirable, in the same way that today people who show those qualities are described as "classy."

Already in 1635, King Louis XIII of France had founded the French Academy as guardian of the French language (p. 334); in the late seventeenth and early eighteenth centuries, Nicolas Boileau (**bwah-LOH**) in France and Alexander Pope in England were respected critics, each of whom was regarded as the Newton of his art. Likewise, Bernard Fontenelle (**fawnt-NEL**), an eighteenth-century secretary of the French Royal Academy of Sciences, declared:

> The geometric spirit is not so tied to geometry that it cannot be detached from it and transported to other branches of knowledge. A work of morals or politics or criticism, perhaps even of eloquence, would be better (other things being equal) if it were done in the style of a geometer. The order, clarity, precision, and exactitude which have been apparent in good books for some time might well have their source in this geometric spirit.

And at the end of the century, Condorcet insisted that all forms of expression must accept "the yoke of those universal rules of reason and nature which ought to be their guide."

Classicism: Racine, La Fayette, Pope

Classicism had its strongest roots in France, inspiring one of the richest periods in French literature with outstanding authors in every branch of letters. Among the most notable was Jean

Racine (**ruh-SEEN**), France's greatest dramatic poet and a leading promoter of classicism.

Educated by a Catholic religious order, Racine received thorough training in Greek and Latin. His middle-class family wanted him to become a priest, but an urge to write poetry took him to Paris in 1663. When a poem written to Louis XIV brought him to the attention of the king, Racine's career was launched as both a playwright and a courtier.

The plots of Racine's tragedies were drawn mostly from ancient Greek themes and invariably centered on a single moral issue. Like other plays of the period, his were intellectual in nature, with long verse speeches and little action on stage. All the same, his plays gripped audiences at the time and ever since, as he put it himself, "by means of a simple plot, sustained by the violence of the passions, the beauty of the sentiments, and the elegance of the expression."

Another writer who combined violent passions and elegant expression was a lady of Louis XIV's court, the Countess de La Fayette. Her novel *The Princess of Cleves* is set in the royal court a century earlier—a place where "there were countless different ambitions and countless different factions, in which ladies played such a leading part that love was always mingled with business and business with love." In this setting, where the mixture of ambition and love makes straightforward feeling impossible, a tragedy plays out involving a young noblewoman, the older husband with whom she has made a prudent marriage, and a dashing young courtier with whom she is in love. Jealousy both justified and groundless, fear for one's reputation and standing at court, passion both welcomed and feared, lead to the husband's death and his widow's rejection of the young courtier; and the rest of her life, "which was quite short, furnished inimitable examples of virtue."

Early in the eighteenth century, an Englishman, Alexander Pope, wrote verse "essays" on various subjects, including *An Essay on Man*, which dealt with the place of humanity in the universe. Pope, a Catholic but strongly influenced by Deism, tried to reconcile the discoveries of science with the idea of a benevolent God—while admitting that there were limits on how far humans could understand the universe:

> All Nature is but art, unknown to thee;
> All chance, direction which thou canst not see;
> All discord, harmony not understood;
> All partial evil, universal good.

In lines like these, all having the same rhythm and all ending in pairs of rhymes, Pope expressed highly complex ideas. Racine used the same strict verse form in French to express his characters' ungovernable passions, and La Fayette made her characters give vent to their complex feelings in precise and balanced prose. The ability to express ideas and emotions in highly structured language was what gave classicism its compelling power and beauty.

Satire: Voltaire

In the era of the Enlightenment, one of the chief aims of people of letters was to digest important new ideas and put them in readable form for an ever-widening public—not only in books and in encyclopedias like Diderot's, but also in rapidly spreading newspapers and magazines.

The most successful and famous of such writers was Voltaire **(vohl-TAIR)**. The son of a Parisian lawyer, he was schooled by Jesuits, who evidently sharpened his talent for argumentation. But his real education began in England. In trouble in France because he had insulted a nobleman, Voltaire accepted exile across the Channel in 1726. Through private study and conversation, he quickly absorbed the ideas of English philosophy and politics.

When Voltaire returned to France, he began to write all sorts of works—plays, histories, poems, scientific surveys, and philosophical essays. The best known and most widely read of his more than a hundred books is the novel *Candide* (1759), a **satire** that reflects his reasoned outlook, his irony, and his strong convictions. The story is a swift-moving, rollicking caricature of an idea popularized by Pope—that "this is the best of all possible worlds." The "hero," Candide, is an innocent young man who has been brought up to believe that "everything is for the best." In the course of incredible misadventures, he learns differently. At the story's end, Candide and his companions are living on a small farm trying to shut out the stupidities and indecencies of the world. One of them concludes that the only way to do this is to "lose oneself" in some form of satisfying work. "It's the only way to make life endurable."

In the novel, Voltaire struck out with rapier and bludgeon at many targets: the bigotry and hypocrisy of organized religion, the atrocities of war, man's inhumanity to man. He expressed contempt for arbitrary authority and disgust with ignorance and prejudice. Though a man of the Enlightenment, he criticized many of the new ideas as well: he ridiculed "pseudo"-reason, which seeks to find "cause" and "effect" in every event, and turned the dream of progress into a nightmare.

Yet Voltaire had faith in the method of science and the power of reason. He stood courageously for freedom of expression; he admired simple honesty, moderation, humaneness, and tolerance. "Tolerance," he wrote in his *Philosophical Dictionary* (1764), "is the natural attribute of humanity. We are all formed of weakness and error; let us pardon reciprocally each other's folly. That is the first law of nature. It is clear that the individual who persecutes a man, his brother, because he is not of the same opinion, is a monster." If Voltaire sometimes grew bitter, it was because the world seemed so full of what he hated and so empty of what he loved. Like Erasmus, he was no revolutionist, but he and his fellow philosophes nevertheless helped prepare the ground for revolution.

> **"***It is clear that the individual who persecutes a man, his brother, because he is not of the same opinion, is a monster.***"**
>
> —Voltaire

Art of the Enlightenment: Rococo and Neoclassicism

During the eighteenth century, royal and aristocratic patrons grew tired of proclaiming their power and glory in the Baroque manner (p. 345). Instead, they preferred the intimacy and charm of the **Rococo** style (from *rocaille*, a French word for the pebble- or shell-lined walls of grottoes that were a fanciful feature of aristocratic garden design). In addition, the taste for classical orderliness, proportion, and restraint spread from literature to the visual arts. Ever since the Renaissance, artists and architects had combined and adapted features of ancient art and buildings rather than actually imitating them. Now, however, ancient principles were followed more strictly than before—so strictly that the classical style in the visual arts is today called **neoclassicism** (from the Greek for "new"—renewed or revived classical art). Rococo and neoclassical styles both corresponded to different aspects of the Enlightenment. On the one hand, the high pretensions of rulers and nobles were taken less seriously, even by themselves; on the other, neoclassical art stressed the "order, clarity, precision, and exactitude" that Enlightened people of letters so highly valued.

Rococo: Watteau and Fragonard

The French painter Antoine Watteau was the finest representative of the Rococo style. He came to Paris in 1715 and soon became famous for works that caught the spirit of refined ease and gallantry so dear to the hearts of French aristocrats. His *Music Party* (see photo on page 371) depicts a type of scene that he originated, and which the French Academy of Painting—yet another royal institution intended to set cultural standards—officially named "elegant entertainment." Fine clothes, beautiful young women, handsome young men, pretty children, friendly animals, a pleasant countryside, wine served by a "negro page" (an aristocratic status symbol in his own right), and music—all combine to form a stage-like tableau whose original title was *The Delights of Life*. But this is not a lifelike portrayal. It arises out of a dream world where ugliness is absent and beauty touches all—beauty, but also a hint of sadness. Destined to die in his thirties of tuberculosis, Watteau seems to have sensed the fleeting character of life and beauty.

More sensual and lighthearted—but no more realistic—were the paintings of Watteau's

National Gallery of Art Tour of the Rococo and Watteau (http://www.nga.gov/collection/gallery/gg54/gg54-main1.html) Take the National Gallery's tour of the Rococo and Watteau.

satire
A type of literature that uses irony, exaggeration, and wit to expose and ridicule human folly.

Rococo
A delicate, ornate, and fanciful style of architecture and painting of the eighteenth century.

neoclassicism
In the visual arts, a style that strictly follows the most admired models of ancient (classical) art, seeking to reproduce their orderliness, proportion, and restraint.

VOLTAIRE ON RELIGIOUS TOLERATION

On March 10, 1762, Jean Calas (**zhan cah-LAS**), a Protestant living in the city of Toulouse in the south of Catholic France, was executed for the murder of one of his sons who had intended to convert to the majority religion. The evidence against Calas was thin, and his judges were likely influenced by strong anti-Protestant feelings in Toulouse. To the last he insisted on his innocence and pardoned the judges for sending him to his death. All the same he was broken on the wheel—tied to a cartwheel, his limbs repeatedly broken between the spokes, and left to die—the standard French penalty for murderers.

Both Protestants and Catholics in many countries publicly condemned the verdict and contributed to a fund for Calas's family, and in 1765 a superior court exonerated him with the approval of King Louis XV. The main organizer of this early international campaign to arouse public opinion was Voltaire, who took the opportunity to resoundingly proclaim Enlightenment views on religious intolerance in general. This excerpt comes from a work that Voltaire published in 1763, his *Treatise on Tolerance*.

One does not need great art and skilful eloquence to prove that Christians ought to tolerate each other—nay, even to regard all men as brothers. Why, you say, is the Turk, the Chinese, or the Jew my brother? Assuredly; are we not all children of the same father, creatures of the same God?

But these people despise us and treat us as idolaters. Very well; I will tell them that they are quite wrong. It seems to me that I might astonish, at least, the stubborn pride of a Muslim imam or a Buddhist monk if I spoke to them somewhat as follows:

This little globe, which is but a point, travels in space like many other globes; we are lost in the immensity. Man, about five and a half feet high, is certainly a small thing in the universe. One of these imperceptible beings says to some of his neighbours, in Arabia or South Africa: "Listen to me, for the God of all these worlds has enlightened me. There are nine hundred million little ants like us on the earth, but my ant-hole alone is dear to God. All the others are eternally reprobated by him. Mine alone will be happy."

They would then interrupt me, and ask who was the fool that talked all this nonsense. I should be obliged to tell them that it was themselves. I would then try to appease them, which would be difficult. . . .

EXPLORING THE SOURCE

1. What argument does Voltaire make here against religious intolerance, and what does this suggest about the influence of science on religious disputes?

2. Why does Voltaire mainly imagine himself arguing about tolerance with non-Christian clergy?

Source: Excerpt from Voltaire, *Treatise on Tolerance*, 1763.

---

contemporary, Jean-Honoré Fragonard, who celebrated, among other themes, the frivolities of the nobility. In *The Meeting* (see photo), an eager young gentleman climbs a ladder to a terrace where he surprises an enticingly bashful young lady. She sits beneath a statue of Venus withholding a quiver full of love-arrows from an angry Cupid—who will, however, get his way in the end. Love, in this fantasy landscape of feathery trees, riotous flowers, and an antique statue, seems both playful and dreamlike.

Neoclassicism: Reynolds, David, Jefferson

In Britain, neoclassicism began with the work of Joshua Reynolds. He was a strong believer in universal standards of taste and excellence, though he looked to the Italian Renaissance for models just as much as to the ancients. In 1768, he became the first president of the Royal Academy of Art, the British equivalent of France's Academy of Painting, and he told his Academy: "I would chiefly recommend that an implicit obedience to the Rules of Art, as established by the practice of the great Masters, should be exacted from the young students."

Reynolds felt that historical or mythological subjects offered the greatest artistic challenge, but he made his fortune by painting the nobility, for example, the duchess of Hamilton (see photo on page 372). A pose like a classical statue, and a carving with a mythological scene, lend this great lady the ideal nobility of Greece and Rome, while her ermine cloak proclaims her an actual noblewoman. The duchess's high standing was recently acquired, however. She was one of two propertyless daughters of an Irish commoner family who went off to London, created a sensation by their beauty, and quickly made splendid marriages.

>> *The Music Party* In Watteau's scene of "elegant entertainment," the servant is cooling wine in a basin before serving it. The bottle is large and heavy, to contain the pressure from a new type of wine that was wildly fashionable among French nobles of the early eighteenth century, champagne.

To be painted by Joshua Reynolds in his neoclassical style was confirmation of her social triumph.

In France, too, neoclassicism took hold in the second half of the eighteenth century. Here the attraction of ancient art was not only aesthetic but also political. At a time when the hold of the absolute monarchy on its subjects' loyalty was weakening, classical art was often linked with other admired features of the ancient world. Among these were equal citizenship, manly virtue, and selfless commitment to the state as proclaimed by Rousseau, which had supposedly been embodied in the ancient Roman city-state before it grew wealthy and corrupt. In 1785, Jacques-Louis David (dah-VEED) exhibited in Paris a painting

> "*I would chiefly recommend that an implicit obedience to the Rules of Art, as established by the practice of the great Masters, should be exacted from the young students.*"
>
> —Joshua Reynolds

of Roman warriors, *The Oath of the Horatii* (see photo on page 372). The Horatius (huh-REY-shuhs) brothers swear on their swords, held aloft by their father, to fight to the death as Roman champions against three brothers from a rival city who are their relatives by marriage. David emphasizes the hard determination of the men by contrasting them with the soft and languishing women of the household, who mourn the coming bloodshed. The figures are "frozen" as if carved in marble, giving the picture's message of manly patriotism above womanly family feeling the timelessness of a classical statue. The painting foreshadowed the ideals of the French Revolution, in which David himself took part.

Neoclassicism also appealed to the increasingly wealthy and sophisticated British colonies in North

<< *The Meeting* This painting was one of a series, *The Progress of Love*, that Fragonard completed in 1773 for the mansion of Madame du Barry, King Louis XV's intimate female friend. The paintings did not please, and were returned—perhaps because, as a contemporary writer suggested, they hinted too broadly at "the adventures of the mistress of the house." Copyright The Frick Collection

<< *The Duchess of Hamilton* According to the English man of letters Horace Walpole, when the duchess appeared at court shortly after her marriage in 1752 "the crowd was so great, that even the noble mob in the drawing-room clambered upon chairs and tables to look at her." Joshua Reynolds painted her six years later, in between her husband's death her remarriage to another duke.

America, especially when they, like the ancient Romans, threw off the rule of a king. On a visit to the French town of Nîmes in the 1780s, Thomas Jefferson saw an ancient Roman temple, the Maison Carrée ("Square Building"), constructed seventeen centuries earlier to commemorate two grandsons of the Roman emperor Augustus who had been deified (declared divine) after their deaths (p. 104). Thinking that the temple had been built earlier, when Rome was still a republic, he gazed at it for hours at a time, he reported, "like a lover at his mistress." Jefferson was a man of letters and a talented architect as well as a statesman, and he took the Maison Carrée as his model for the Virginia State Capitol in Richmond (see photo). In this way, he reused a design that had served the cult of an all-powerful ruler's divine offspring to proclaim the "Roman" wisdom and virtue of the new American republic.

LO⁴ Music in Western Civilization

Music, with its mysterious ability to express and influence emotion, has always been a powerful force in human life, including the life of Western civilization. The ancient Israelites told of King David, whose youthful playing on the lyre (a harp-like instrument) would drive away an evil spirit that often tormented the mind of his predecessor King Saul; the ancient Greeks told of Orpheus (**OR-fyoos**), whose lyre so softened the hearts of the

>> *The Oath of the Horatii* According to the Enlightenment thinker Denis Diderot, "there is one thing that painting and poetry have in common: they should both be moral." Rococo painting disregarded this rule, but David's neoclassical painting of ancient Roman men putting the republic before family teaches a lesson of civic virtue. It was commissioned in 1784 by King Louis XVI, whose idea of civic virtue included loyalty to the monarchy, but the painting soon came to symbolize the values of revolutionary France. Reunion des Musees Nationaux/ Art Resource, NY

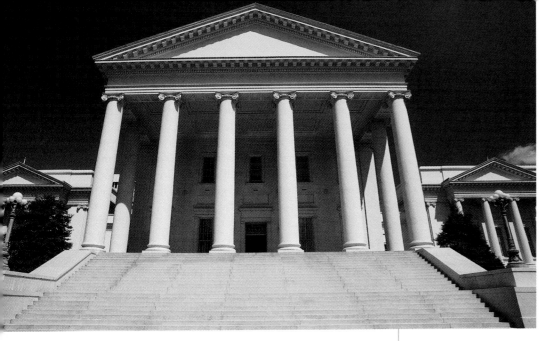

The Virginia State Capitol Thomas Jefferson designed this building in the 1780s while he was the U.S. envoy to France and was able to visit its original at Nîmes, as well as to get the help of a leading French designer, Charles-Louis Clérisseau. He was proud of his work: "Our new Capitol," he wrote ". . . will be worthy of being exhibited alongside the most celebrated remains of antiquity." Mark Karrass/Corbis

monophonic music
Music made up of a single tune.

homophonic music
Music made of a tune accompanied by harmonizing chords.

polyphonic music
Music made up of two or more independent and overlapping tunes.

relentless rulers of the underworld that they released his wife Eurydice (**yoo-REE-dee-see**) from their grip. Israelite psalms, Greek poetry and dramatic choruses, and later on the epics and love poems of medieval European minstrels were all sung with instruments playing along. And Aristotle, the great organizer of Greek knowledge, classified many ways in which different types of music could calm, sadden, or enliven the hearer's mood.

Greek thinkers also perceived the connection between music and number, studying the exact proportions in which the pitch of a sound (how high or low it is) varied according to the length of the plucked string or blown pipe that produced it. Music, these thinkers believed, was not just a way to influence emotions but a way for the mind to perceive the ordered structure of number and proportion on which the universe was built. For this reason, music was an important part of Greek and Roman education—a tradition that was kept up by medieval European universities, which listed music along with arithmetic, geometry, and astronomy in the quadrivium, the standard curriculum of higher studies.

In addition, the development of devices for producing musical sounds was an important field of technology. Inventors in Hellenistic Egypt figured out ways to use the force of water instead of human lungs to blow air through sets of pipes of different pitches, with the pipes opened and closed by keyboards—the first organs. As the peoples of Eurasia grew closer together during the Middle Ages, musicians from Europe all the way to Japan learned of a new method of making a string produce sound, invented among horse-riding archers in Central Asia—by sliding a horsehair bow across it. And in the Renaissance, keyboards were adapted to pluck sets of strings of different pitches, thereby producing instruments that were the ancestors of the harpsichord and the piano.

Ancient peoples also devised systems for writing tunes down, but almost nothing survives of this earliest musical notation. The oldest Western music that can still be heard today consists of religious chants for unaccompanied voices that were composed by monks in the lands ruled by Charlemagne in the eighth century A.D.. Their style of singing soon spread through Western Christendom, and came to be attributed to Gregory the Great, a revered pope about A.D. 600. Not long after the so-called Gregorian chant first appeared, the monks devised a system for writing it down that included horizontal lines to mark the intervals between higher and lower notes. The new system was improved upon to represent music more completely and exactly throughout the Middle Ages.

In the eleventh century, as medieval civilization emerged from its early time of troubles, a new and more complex form of music made its appearance in Europe. Ever since the ancient Greeks, music had been **monophonic**, consisting of single tunes, but now composers began to create **homophonic** and **polyphonic** music—where a tune was accompanied by harmonizing chords, or where several independent but harmonizing tunes were played or sung at the same time. Like other medieval traditions, these ones continued into the Renaissance. Hymns and masses, madrigals (love songs), and dance music were all performed in parts, with singers accompanied by a wide range of instruments.

By 1600, music had developed the unprecedentedly eloquent language of polyphony, a broader range of more expressive instruments than ever before, and a method of notation that was as accurate for sound as the alphabet for speech. Many centuries earlier, the Roman author Horace had boasted that his poetry was "a monument more lasting than bronze." Soon, European composers would be able to say the same of their music.

Baroque Music

Baroque composers used these musical resources for the same purpose as Baroque visual artists—to create the maximum dramatic

opera
A dramatic work combining text (libretto) and musical score, with grand characters, spectacular stage action, and striking musical effects.

oratorio
A religious story set to music with narrators and characters but no stage action.

cantata
A choral composition with musical accompaniment.

chamber music
Music originally intended for performance by small groups at aristocratic courts.

string quartet
A composition for four stringed instruments.

concerto
A composition for an orchestra and one or more solo instruments.

symphony
A lengthy and complex composition for an orchestra.

enlightened despotism
A form of absolute monarchy characterized by reforms intended to better the lives of citizens and strengthen the state.

effect. Their innovations were so sweeping that they referred to earlier music as the "old style" (in Italian, *stile antico*) and to their own as the "modern style" (*stile moderno*). Traditional polyphony had an even sound built of many complex parts; Baroque composers stressed a dominant melody with dramatic chords, played by ever-larger numbers and types of instruments—many of which reached their present-day form in the seventeenth century.

Perhaps the most important Baroque musical development was a new art form that used the expressive power of music to heighten the effect of dramatic speech and action: the **opera**. Its chief creator was an Italian, Claudio Monteverdi, who spent the earlier years of his life writing madrigals and masses in the "old style" but in middle age turned enthusiastically to the "modern style" and wrote at least eighteen operas beginning with *Orfeo* (*Orpheus*) in 1607. Operas were usually based on stories from history or myth with grand characters and spectacular action that lent themselves to striking musical effects. For Lent, when the Church forbade stage performances, Monteverdi and other composers also created **oratorios**—religious stories set to music with narrators and characters but no stage action.

Nearly a century passed before opera spread north of the Alps, but it finally did so thanks partly to the work of George Frideric Handel. Of German origin, Handel spent much of his youth in Italy before settling in England early in the eighteenth century. Admired by the king and aristocrats who acted as his patrons—and beloved also by the growing English middle classes who attended his performances—Handel was enormously successful in his adopted country, and died a wealthy man. Endlessly prolific and versatile, Handel could express in music almost any situation and emotion. These ranged from the sensual passion of many of his operas, through the magnificence of his works for royal occasions such as the *Music for the Royal Fireworks* (composed for celebrations at the end of a war), to the religious grandeur of his sacred music, notably the oratorio *Messiah*.

Meanwhile, another prolific German composer was writing in every form except opera. Handel's contemporary Johann Sebastian Bach was a giant of the Baroque period and one of the great musicians of all time. A devout Lutheran, he composed profound and inspiring **cantatas** (sung at services and based on each day's Bible readings) and oratorios. Bach was equally talented in secular music, creating superb **chamber music** (pieces for performance by small groups at aristocratic courts). He is notable for the power and grandeur of his expression and for his mastery of polyphonic themes.

The Classical Spirit in Music

In the mid-eighteenth century, the prevailing style of music changed—once again on the same pattern as in the visual arts. A reaction set in against the spectacular effects of seventeenth-century music, and in favor of the classical values of rationality and clarity.

Among the most gifted of the classical composers were Franz Joseph Haydn and Wolfgang Amadeus Mozart, both Austrians. Their music expressed a vast range of ideas and emotions, with all the more impact because, in the classical manner, it was carefully structured and proportioned, in forms that the two composers themselves originated or perfected. Chief among these were the **string quartet**; the **concerto** (kuhn-CHER-toh), in which a solo instrument plays against a larger group; and the **symphony**, in which a large group plays on its own. A piece of music by Haydn or Mozart in any of these forms leads its hearers along a musical pathway with many twists and turns of mood and expression, each of which, however, leads logically from one to the next to give the feeling of a complete and satisfying whole.

 Minnesota Public Radio's Site Devoted to Mozart's 250th Anniversary (2006) (http://minnesota.publicradio.org/about/features/2005/12/mozart/) Listen to Mozart's operas and symphonies.

LO⁵ Progress and Power: Enlightened Despotism

Enlightenment ideals also influenced the absolute monarchs, bureaucrats, and nobles who dominated most countries of eighteenth-century Europe. Many of them became dissatisfied with the very social and political order they ruled, producing a reform within the system that later historians called "**enlightened despotism**."

Enlightened Despotism in Prussia, Austria, and Russia

Among the most notable enlightened despots were several rulers of the leading absolute monarchies of central and eastern Europe, Prussia, Austria, and Russia. They sought to put into practice such enlightened reforms as religious toleration, wider access to education, and improvements in the condition of agriculture and the peasants—who in their territories were mostly serfs (pp. 255–256). Partly they did so because they shared the ideal of the human race progressing in knowledge, happiness, and virtue. But the enlightened despots were thinking also of their own power. They were well aware that a reformed state with well-fed, well-educated, and productive citizens, with believers in different faiths living peaceably side by side, and with the nobles acting as real social leaders rather than as pampered courtiers, would probably outmatch an unreformed state in both peace and war. And the absolute ruler of such a reformed state, they believed, would be more truly in control of his or her dominions than the divine-right rulers from whom they inherited their thrones.

> "*The only thing we inherit from our parents is animal life—king, count, townsman, peasant, there's not the least difference.*"
> —Joseph II of Austria

Prussia

Frederick II, who became king of Prussia in 1740, personified this combination of Enlightenment ideals and the pursuit of power. He was personally friendly with Voltaire and tolerated all religions in his officially Lutheran kingdom—partly because, as a Deist, he took none of their beliefs seriously. He abolished torture as a part of judicial procedure, and he made the Prussian peasants cultivate a New World crop that he was convinced would improve their well-being, the potato. And whereas Louis XIV of France had famously said "I am the state," Frederick described himself as "the state's first servant"—a citizen like everyone else whose role in serving the state happened to be that of commanding it.

But Frederick was also a warrior-king who was eager to add to the lands he inherited from his Hohenzollern ancestors (p. 337). *Der alte Fritz* ("Old Man Fred"), as his soldiers called him, was the battle-winning commander of Europe's best-trained army, whose discipline he upheld by the traditional methods of flogging and branding. He acquired the territory of Silesia (see Map 19.1) from Empress Maria Theresa of Austria at the beginning of his reign by an unprovoked attack, and he held it through a series of devastating wars. And like Louis XIV, he built himself a splendid palace not far from his capital city, Berlin—though he chose the daintily elegant Rococo style, and gave the palace an informal-sounding French name, *Sanssouci* ("Carefree"). With this combination of Enlightenment and power politics, Frederick made Prussia a power of the first rank in Europe.

Austria

Empress Maria Theresa blamed her loss of Silesia on the fact that early in her reign she found herself, in her own words, "with no money, no credit, and no army." Enlightened reforms seemed the best way to remedy this, and she made considerable progress in centralizing control of her territories, improving the administrative and tax systems, and limiting noble exploitation of the serfs so that the serfs would be able to pay higher taxes to the government. In this way, she built up an army that sometimes won battles against Frederick—with enough money left over to build her own Rococo palace outside her capital city, Vienna.

Maria Theresa also allowed her son Joseph to be educated in Enlightenment principles, and he became something of a philosophe. He once complained to his mother of the "prejudice that wants to make us believe that I am more honorable because my grandfather was a count. . . . The only thing we inherit from our parents is animal life—king, count, townsman, peasant, there's not the least difference." These were radical words, coming from a future emperor, and Joseph's actual reign was a high point of enlightened despotism. In ten years of whirlwind reform between 1780 and 1790, he introduced changes so drastic as to amount almost to a peaceful revolution (see photo on page 376). Among other things, the emperor, himself a Catholic believer, granted religious freedom to his Protestant, Orthodox, and Jewish subjects; abolished hundreds of Catholic monasteries and nunneries, with much of their funds going to schools and universities; and gave the serfs freedom to marry and leave their manors without the consent of the lords (though serfs were still bound to cultivate their lords' lands until 1848; p. 413).

Russia

Two empresses of the Romanov dynasty (p. 337), Elizabeth and then Catherine II, kept Russia under enlightened rule for most of the second half of the eighteenth century. In Russia, "Enlightenment" overlapped with "Westernization"—the acceptance in the Orthodox "Third Rome" (p. 252) of values and ways of life that originated in Western Christendom. Elizabeth, who came to the throne in 1741—just after Frederick and Maria Theresa—managed to bridge both worlds. She was piously Orthodox, but with her encouragement the nobles, whom her father Peter the Great had begun to Westernize by command, truly began taking to Western ways. Among other efforts for education and culture, she sponsored the founding of Russia's first university in Moscow, and approved a "General Plan for the Education of Young People of Both Sexes" that resulted in the establishment of a prestigious school for young noblewomen in St. Petersburg.

Catherine II was herself a Westerner—the daughter of a German nobleman, who gained the throne in 1762 after marrying a grandson of Peter. She corresponded with Diderot and Voltaire, shared their Deism, and was herself a woman of letters who wrote fiction, drama, and memoirs of her own life—though being an empress, she did not publish her works. She sponsored education and the arts on a magnificent scale, thereby helping propel Russia toward the leading role in European culture that it would gain and hold in the next century.

multinational state
A state in which no single ethnic group forms a majority of the population.

Still, enlightened reforms under the two empresses did not spread far beyond the Russian noble class. Catherine made changes in government and finance, but these had the effect of bringing the serfs under stricter control than ever without lightening the burdens placed on them by either the government or the nobles. And she dealt with a widespread peasant uprising by the traditional method of brutal reprisals and the public beheading of the main leader.

Both empresses also fought many wars. Those of Elizabeth were not particularly successful, but Catherine was a conqueror to rival Peter the Great. In wars against the Turks, many of whose subjects shared the Orthodox Christianity and Slavic ethnic origins of the Russians, she extended her territories to the south. On Russia's western frontier, she intervened in the neighboring country of Poland. Once one of the strongest powers in eastern Europe, Poland had failed to develop into either an absolute monarchy or an effective limited monarchy (p. 335), and between 1772 and 1795, it was partitioned (divided up) among its neighbors (Map 19.1). Russia gained the largest share, and the rest was taken over by Prussia and Austria—partly to prevent Russia from advancing still farther westward.

The Limits of Enlightened Despotism

For all their successes, Prussia, Austria, and Russia remained in some ways vulnerable. This was partly because their rulers built their power on societies that were not nearly so wealthy as the western European countries that controlled worldwide trade and empire. The Hohenzollern, Habsburg, and Romanov rulers put great efforts into reorganizing their governments, increasing the yield of taxes, and recruiting and training soldiers. Yet they could not fight wars for any length of time without massive financial help from Britain or France—help that these countries were usually eager to give, to enlist the central and eastern European powers as allies against each other.

Furthermore, like all efforts at reforming a system from within, enlightened despotism worked only so long as it did not go too far and too fast. Joseph II, the most radical of the despots, ended with his government paralyzed by the opposition of the nobles; the Prussian and Russian rulers, who did not meet such opposition, left many of their countries' traditional institu-

"Depiction of His Imperial Majesty Joseph II Personally Operating a Plow" Journeying through the province of Moravia one day in 1769, the enlightened emperor borrowed a plow from a serf beside the road and ceremonially plowed two furrows. The local lord immediately built a monument (at left), and the deed has gone down in the region's history as marking the beginning of the end of serfdom. A monument still marks the spot, and "Emperor Joseph's Plow" is preserved in a nearby museum (see photo on page 191). Bildarchiv Preussischer Kulturbesitz/Art Resource, NY

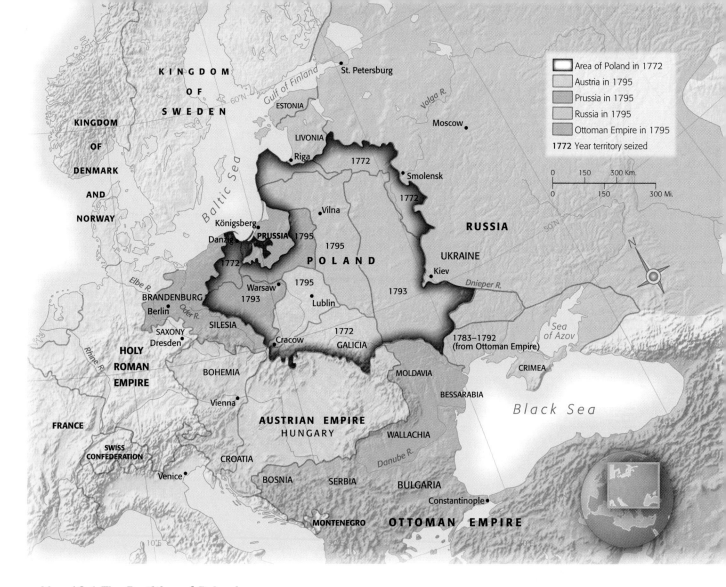

Map 19.1 **The Partition of Poland**

Under Catherine the Great, Russia gained lands from Poland and Turkey (mostly not inhabited by either Poles or Turks) that it held with brief intervals until the breakup of the Soviet Union in 1991; today these lands belong to Lithuania, Belarus, and Ukraine (see Map 32.1 on page 597). Prussia and Austria divided the Polish-inhabited lands, thereby setting a limit to Russia's westward expansion. © Cengage Learning

Interactive Map

tions unchanged. That was why serfdom survived in all three countries into the nineteenth century, even though freeing the peasants, as enlightened despots well understood, offered the greatest hope of modernizing their economies and making their countries truly wealthy and powerful.

In addition, the Habsburgs and Romanovs in particular had expanded into regions of eastern Europe that were ethnically very mixed. Once-powerful central and eastern European nations—Poles, Czechs, Hungarians, Ukrainians, and many others—were now under the rule of foreigners. Russia and Austria were not national but **multinational states** in which no single ethnic group formed a majority of the population. In the eighteenth century, serfdom and the subjection of nations to foreign rulers were generally accepted as legitimate, but in time, this would change. Serfdom would be abolished but leave an aftermath of

"Enlightened despotism worked only so long as it did not go too far and too fast."

social conflict, national rivalries would become ferocious, and in the end, the central and eastern European rulers would fall.

In the short term, however, these rulers gained more power then ever in their realms. Rulers of lands in western Europe and across the Atlantic were not so fortunate. Here, the Enlightenment became entangled with social and political conflicts that governments could not contain, and the reforming hopes of the philosophes turned into ideologies of revolution.

Listen to a synopsis of Chapter 19.

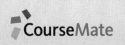

Access to the eBook with additional review material and study tools may be found online at CourseMate for WCIV. Sign in at www.cengagebrain.com.

CHAPTER 20

INTERCONTINENTAL REVOLUTIONS,
1700–1825

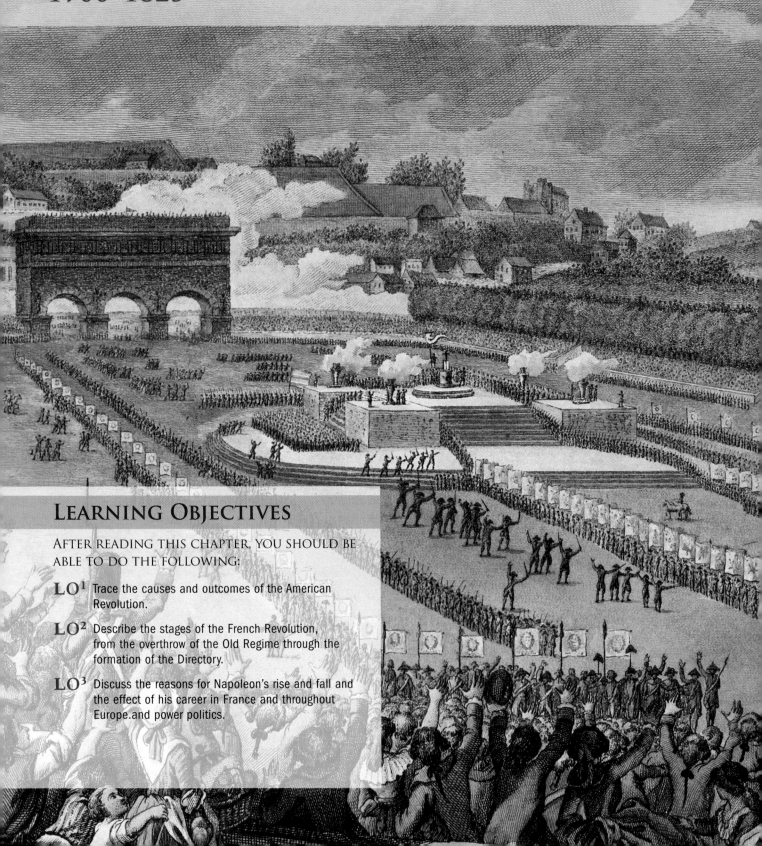

LEARNING OBJECTIVES

AFTER READING THIS CHAPTER, YOU SHOULD BE
ABLE TO DO THE FOLLOWING:

LO¹ Trace the causes and outcomes of the American
Revolution.

LO² Describe the stages of the French Revolution,
from the overthrow of the Old Regime through the
formation of the Directory.

LO³ Discuss the reasons for Napoleon's rise and fall and
the effect of his career in France and throughout
Europe.and power politics.

"THE RESULT OF THE AMERICAN AND FRENCH REVOLUTIONS WAS THE BEGINNING OF THE END OF THE TRADITIONAL WESTERN POWER STRUCTURE."

Revolutionary overthrows or attempted overthrows of entire religious, social, and political orders date as far back as the Hussite Wars in the Middle Ages and the Jewish revolts against ancient Rome (pp. 250–251, 125). But revolutions have become much more common in recent centuries as massive shifts in civilization have been accompanied by deep conflicts within the West and across the world.

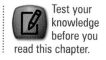

Test your knowledge before you read this chapter.

This speedup of revolutionary change began in sixteenth- and seventeenth-century Western Christendom, when the Reformation made churches and governments illegitimate in the eyes of those who did not share their religious beliefs, and inspired opposing religions with idealistic fury. At the same time, the rise of absolute monarchy provoked conflicts among lesser power wielders who either resisted or

What do you think?

Revolutionary ideals can never be fully achieved in practice.

Strongly Disagree						Strongly Agree
1	2	3	4	5	6	7

supported the kings, and the growing scale and cost of warfare led to struggles over who had the right to levy taxes and who had to bear the burden of paying them. Already in seventeenth-century Britain, conflicts of this kind led to the collapse of a traditional order followed by years of strife that set the pattern for later revolutions (pp. 339–345).

In the eighteenth century, monarchs still sought greater control of the lands they ruled, and the cost of warfare and the burden of taxes went on growing. Disputes among religious believers were no longer so explosive as before, but instead, disputes over the Enlightenment, or between different versions of the Enlightenment, provided the fuel for new and vicious ideological conflicts. A whole series of revolutions got under way both in Europe itself and in the new regions of Western civilization that had grown up across the Atlantic. The result was the beginning of the end of the traditional Western power structure that

《《 Revolutionary Celebration In Paris on July 14, 1790, 100,000 people celebrated the French Revolution's first anniversary. The revolutionary National Guard paraded, headed by the noble Marquis de La Fayette. At the Altar of the Fatherland (center) a high cleric, Bishop Talleyrand, celebrated Mass. King Louis XVI, present with Queen Marie Antoinette, swore to uphold France's new constitution. It was a glorious moment of unity before La Fayette and Talleyrand fled into exile and the king and queen went to the guillotine.

379

had developed fifteen hundred years before out of the merging of Greco-Roman civilization and the warrior societies of barbarian Europe.

The first of these revolutions was in British North America. It produced the United States, the first democratic republic to govern a large territory and the first community that did not practice a specific form of religious worship. But the North American republic was also a compromise designed to uphold the country's existing society and values—its many ex-colonial governments, its religious diversity, its commercial interests, and the institution of slavery. The result was a successful and adaptable new order, but the abolition of slavery was a revolutionary struggle that was still left to be fought.

At the end of the eighteenth century, Europe's most powerful absolute monarchy collapsed in France, and in the next quarter-century, the turmoil of revolution eventually spread through much of the region. Unlike the revolution in North America, the French Revolution ended not in compromise but in defeat—its foreign enemies victorious, France itself occupied, and its old rulers restored. But the shifts in civilization that had undermined the partnership of king, nobles, and Church in France could not be turned back, and defeat only continued the conflicts of the revolution—not just in France, but to a greater or lesser extent in the rest of Europe as well. The struggles over a new Western power structure were just beginning.

LO¹ Revolution in the New World: The United States

The overseas expansion of Europe had brought English settlers to the North American continent in the seventeenth century, many of them Puritans escaping harassment and coercion by the established Anglican Church (pp. 340, 342). Most of the settlers, after driving out the Native Americans and carving homesteads from the wilderness, inhabited the thirteen colonies of the Atlantic seaboard from Maine to Georgia. By 1770, the population of these colonies amounted to about 3 million. Viewed from London, they made up only a part of a far-flung empire that also included territories in the West Indies and India, and had a total population of 15 million.

The Colonies and the Empire

Like every empire-owning European country, Britain viewed its colonies mainly as a source of trading wealth that it would monopolize. But the costs to Britain for defense and administra-

CHRONOLOGY	
1776	Declaration of Independence
1783	United States of America is recognized as a sovereign nation by the Treaty of Paris
1787	U.S. Constitution drafted in Philadelphia
1789	The French National Assembly abolishes feudalism and the Old Regime; Declaration of the Rights of Man and the Citizen
1792	Austria and Prussia declare war on France; Jacobins take control and declare France a republic
1793	Louis XVI executed; the Terror begins
1794	Robespierre executed
1795	The Directory takes charge in France
1799	Napoleon becomes First Consul
1802	Napoleon becomes First Consul for Life
1804	Napoleon becomes Emperor of the French
1814–1815	Napoleon is banished to Elba, escapes, and is defeated at Waterloo

tion were heavy, the colonists broke through trading restrictions by means of wholesale smuggling, and they showed little desire to provide for their own military defense. After 1750, therefore, the British Parliament tightened the regulation of trade and the collection of taxes.

Not surprisingly, the colonists resented British efforts to collect existing taxes or to impose new ones. This was especially true after 1763, when the close of the French and Indian War—the American theater of one of many eighteenth-century worldwide struggles for trade and empire between Britain and France (p. 282)—brought victory to Britain and ended the threat of French conquest of the thirteen colonies. Instead, Britain itself came to seem an oppressive ruler that subordinated the colonists' well-being to imperial aims.

Parliament passed various new taxes and then repealed them in the face of American protests, with the exception of a tax on imports of tea, which it retained for symbolic reasons—to emphasize its right to tax British subjects everywhere. But the Americans, who sent no members to the distant Parliament, refused to admit that right. "No taxation without representation!" became the rallying cry of colonial protest. Some British politicians believed that the Americans were in the right, but most of them took the view that Parliament "virtually represented" the colonists—that it could act in their name even though they had no actual vote, just as it did with the huge majority of the British population who at the time had no right to vote. For the Parliament, the issue was its sovereign right to run the empire as it saw fit. For the colonists, it was government by consent—what they for the moment called "the rights of Englishmen."

 William Pitt Gives a Whiggish Defense of American Resistance to Taxation Read the British politician William Pitt's defense of American resistance to taxation.

American Independence and Its Worldwide Meaning

By 1774, the conflict had gone so far that the colonists had begun to commit acts of violence and sabotage (notably the Boston "Tea Party"), and the British responded with tough measures. Parliament passed what Americans called the **Intolerable Acts**, which closed the port of Boston and virtually canceled the charter of Massachusetts. Protests and opposition grew in Massachusetts, and shortly thereafter, representatives from all the colonies assembled at a **Continental Congress** in Philadelphia. There they drew up a statement of grievances and formed an association to cut off all trade with Britain. The conflict of words had given way to direct action.

Revolution and War

When the British governor of Massachusetts ordered its legislature dissolved, the legislators defiantly met again and raised a defense force of "Minutemen." The first clash of arms occurred in April 1775, when British troops looking for a stockpile of rebel weapons in Concord near Boston ran into fierce resistance and suffered heavy losses on their return march. Shortly afterward the Continental Congress reassembled. The Minutemen around Boston were enlisted as the core of a Continental Army, and George Washington, a distinguished officer of the Virginia colonial militia, was appointed its commanding general.

To begin with, the American leaders liked to think that they were fighting to force the British to compromise, and they even hoped that King George III would act as peacemaker. But as it became clear that the king and most British politicians were determined to settle the matter by force, the American war

> **"Using the language of the Enlightenment, Thomas Paine declared that America's subjection to England was 'contrary to reason.'"**

 "The American Revolution" (http://www.history.com/topics/american-revolution/videos#american-revolution) Hear different ideas about the significance of the American Revolution. (3:20)

aims changed. The new view was famously expressed early in 1776 by a shrewd revolutionary propagandist, Thomas Paine. Using the language of the Enlightenment, he declared that America's subjection to England was "contrary to reason." He went on:

> There is something absurd in supposing a continent to be perpetually governed by an island. In no instance has nature made the satellite larger than its primary planet; and as England and America, with respect to each other, reverse the common order of nature, it is evident that they belong to different systems. England to Europe; America to itself.

On July 4, the Continental Congress formally proclaimed the colonies' independence from Britain, and in 1777, it passed Articles of Confederation for the purpose of "securing the freedom, sovereignty, and independence of the United States."

The war dragged on for six years. Britain, though a leading European power, was hampered by long lines of communication and uneven generalship. The Americans suffered from the internal differences that normally divide revolutionists, and the Continental Congress was unable to provide enough troops, supplies, or money. Although the colonists fought bravely and endured severe hardships, they could hardly have won without the aid of foreign powers.

The French monarchy, eager to even the score with Britain after the humiliation of 1763, decided to aid the uprising, and the first significant American victory, at Saratoga, was won chiefly with French weapons. Impressed by the American success in that battle, the French became formal allies and declared war on Britain. Spain and Holland followed, swinging the European balance in the Americans' favor. The surrender of the encircled troops of Lord Cornwallis at Yorktown (Virginia) in 1781, which ended the British military effort, was forced by a French fleet controlling the waters offshore. Two years later, by the Treaty of Paris, the United States of America won recognition as a sovereign nation stretching from the Atlantic Ocean to the Mississippi River (see photo on page 382).

The Declaration of Independence

The most significant document of the Revolution was the Declaration of Independence of 1776. This masterpiece of revolutionary propaganda was drafted by Thomas Jefferson not just to appeal to Americans

Intolerable Acts
The American colonists' name for British legislation that curbed their economic and political activities.

Continental Congress
An assembly of representatives from the American colonies that provided leadership during the revolutionary crisis.

AMERICA TRIUMPHANT and BRITANNIA in DISTRESS

EXPLANATION.

>> **America Triumphant** An illustration in an almanac published in 1782 shows a majestic lady, America, "inviting the ships of all nations to partake of her commerce." Across from her, Britannia is "weeping at the loss of the trade of America." In between is "French, Spanish, Dutch &c. shipping in the harbours of America." The overthrow of British rule means that the United States is free to grow in wealth and power through trade—a welcome prospect, especially in seaports like Boston where the almanac was published. Library of Congress, LC-USZC4-5275

but to show "a decent respect to the opinions of mankind." In the spirit of the Enlightenment, Jefferson called upon the world to witness what the Americans were doing, and to understand what he saw as its worldwide meaning and purpose.

The declaration proclaimed the same principles that John Locke had already stated in defense of Britain's "Glorious Revolution" (pp. 344–345), but Jefferson condensed them into a single ringing paragraph:

> We hold these truths to be self-evident, that all men are created equal, that they are endowed by their Creator with certain unalienable Rights, that among these are Life, Liberty, and the pursuit of Happiness.—That to secure these rights, Governments are instituted among Men, deriving their just powers from the consent of the governed.—That whenever any Form of Government becomes destructive of these ends, it is the Right of the People to alter or to abolish it. . . .

The Americans, in fact, were no longer fighting just for "the rights of Englishmen." Instead, they were fighting for rights that belonged to the human race as a whole.

The Legacy of Revolution

After independence, the most pressing need of the former colonies was to agree on a plan for self-government. Each new state drew up a written constitution for itself, but there was disagreement over what form the union of the states should take. Having previously lived in separate colonies, many citizens preferred complete independence for their states but grudgingly accepted the idea of a loose union, as provided by the wartime Articles of Confederation. When the Confederation proved unable to meet the common needs of commerce and defense, the states sent delegates to Philadelphia in 1787 to revise the Articles. Instead, they drafted a new constitution aimed at forming a closer union, which the thirteen states approved after bitter debate.

The Constitution

The very act of Americans' framing their own basic law fired the imagination of European intellectuals. Here was Locke's social contract made real! Here also was a reasoned statement of the new doctrine of popular sovereignty (rule by the people). The preamble (introductory statement) identifies the sole source of civil authority in its opening words: "We, the people . . . do ordain and establish this Constitution for the United States of America." The new document also launched a successful experiment in **federalism**, in which power is shared between a central government and local governments, and neither may encroach on the authority of the other. The authors of the Constitution struck a balance between powers delegated to the central government and those reserved to the states, thereby intending to harmonize the requirements of centralized planning and power with the desire for self-government within each state.

To ensure that legitimate power did not degenerate into tyranny, and influenced by the workings of the ancient Roman Republic as well as by the ideas of Montesquieu on separation of powers (92–93, 366–367), the founders put their trust in a system of "checks and balances." The best protection against the human urge to power, they thought, is to establish separate political authorities and to leave them in jealous competition. Thus, the states were to keep a watchful eye on the national power; and within all gov-

 Official U.S. Government Site on the Constitution (http://www.archives.gov/exhibits/charters/constitution.html) Learn more about the making of the U.S. Constitution.

ernment units, a division of executive, legislative, and judicial powers was established.

Although the Constitution provides defenses against the invasion of individual rights, fears of an overly strong central government continued to be voiced by many citizens, and the Bill of Rights was added to the Constitution in 1791. Comprising the first ten amendments, it clarifies and extends the principles of the English Bill of Rights (pp. 342–343). Strongly supported by church leaders, freedom of worship and freedom from an established church head the list. Every person is also guaranteed freedom of expression, petition, and assembly; the right to keep and bear arms; security of person and home; and due process of law.

The U.S. Constitution was the earliest written constitution of a major country—and is the oldest still in use. It worked in the first place because, like the British system of government (p. 344), it provided for both the freedom of the people and the power of the state. Unlike in Britain, however, the people's freedom included democratic control of the government, and the state wielded power over a continental-sized territory that continued to grow. Amendments, judicial interpretation, and legislation adapted the government system to the massive social and political changes of two centuries—the closing of the frontier, the swelling of the population, the growth of giant industry, the rise of the United States to worldwide power, the admission of women to full citizenship. The Constitution is one of history's most notable examples of traditions that are long-lived because later generations both respect them and alter them.

> "*The U.S. Constitution was the earliest written constitution of a major country—and is the oldest still in use.*"

Slavery

In one respect, the system was not so easily adaptable, however. One-sixth of the population was African American slaves, mostly in southern states that threatened to stay out of the union if slavery was abolished. As a result, the Constitution as originally written in effect upheld slavery. The United States, whose revolutionary leaders were the first in the world to declare liberty a God-given right of the entire human race, became one of the last Western countries to abolish slavery, and then only as a result of a brutal civil war.

Other conflicts left over from the American Revolution were resolved more or less peacefully, largely because the main issues in the revolution had been between the country and its rulers an ocean away, rather than within the country itself. The situation was very different in France.

LO² Revolution in Europe: France

At the time of the American Revolution, the United States was part of an outlying region of Western civilization; France, by contrast, was a leading country of the Western heartland, and the real break in Western history came with the French Revolution. Taking place within crowded Europe, the French Revolution soon became international. As the nineteenth-century French political thinker Alexis de Tocqueville later wrote, "The French Revolution had no territory of its own; indeed, its effect was to efface, in a way, all older frontiers. It brought men together, divided them, in spite of law, traditions, character, and language— turning enemies sometimes into compatriots and kinsmen into strangers. . . ." And on balance, the French Revolution divided people more than it united them. Unlike in the United States, the revolutionary conflicts in France and beyond its frontiers pitted deeply rooted internal groups and institutions against each other, and the struggles among them did not end in a generally accepted new order until late in the twentieth century—if then.

The Changing Old Regime

Before the Revolution, France lived under a version of the same political, social, and religious order that had prevailed in western Europe since the early Middle Ages. In this traditional order, the rulers, the nobles, and the Church shared power over a predominantly agrarian society, where the land was the main source of wealth and most people were peasants.

The Three Estates

The superiority of the nobles and the Catholic clergy to the rest of the king's subjects was a legally recognized fact. The status of all French people in the eyes of the law depended on which of three "orders" or "estates" they belonged to: the First Estate, made up of about 100,000 clergy; the Second Estate, consisting of 400,000 nobles; and the Third Estate, which included the rest of the 26 million people of France. The members of the First and Second Estates enjoyed various privileges over those of the Third Estate, the most important of which was exemption from the *taille*, a tax on land and other property that was one of the government's main sources of revenue. Yet as lords of manors holding rights of government and justice, the nobles and clergy were able to extract much of the wealth they needed for their upkeep from the very same peasants who paid the largest share of taxes. In addition, the legal division of society expressed the feeling of nobles, in particular, that they stood far above the rest of the king's subjects: without noble status, even a wealthy banker, a learned judge, or a writer renowned throughout Europe was still a mere commoner.

Two things had traditionally kept this system from being so starkly unfair in practice as it was in principle. First, most members of the privileged orders had not really lived in splendid isolation above the rest of society. Besides bishops and abbots from noble families, there were tens of thousands of parish priests and nuns who lived and worked among the peasants and townspeople to whom they themselves belonged by birth. In addition to nobles who surrounded the king in his splendid

SEVERAL FACTORS CONTRIBUTED TO THE UNRAVELING OF FRANCE'S OLD REGIME:

Shifting Power at the Top

- Absolute monarchy depended very much on the character of the monarch.

- Louis XIV's successors did not have his dominating personality.

- Louis XVI, France's king when events boiled into revolution, was well meaning but indecisive.

- Nobles regained power at the court of Versailles, as courtier-nobles and courtier-clergy advised and influenced the king.

- The *parlements* (superior law courts in Paris and the provinces) reasserted their traditional right to limit the king's power by registering his decrees before they went into effect.

Pressures from Below

- By the late eighteenth century, the **bourgeoisie (boor-zhwah-ZEE)** were larger and wealthier than ever before.

- They began to feel restricted by their traditional humble position in the government and social order.

- Manufacturers were hampered by guild rules and price controls, which the monarchy maintained to keep the urban poor from rioting.

- Traders' profits were cut by government tariffs on goods passing from one province to another inside France.

- Nobles tried to prevent the sons of the bourgeoisie from entering military academies.

- Nobles objected to the royal practice of elevating the bourgeoisie by creating nobles of the hat.

The Enlightenment

- The literate public was inspired by the books of the philosophes but also felt cynicism and resentment at existing realities.

- Many royal advisers were tempted by the idea of turning France into an efficient and reforming enlightened despotism.

- Enlightened nobles, on the other hand, began to believe that their privileges had become a bar to progress.

- The lower social classes, especially the bourgeoisie, embraced the idea that all people were endowed with natural rights to freedom and equality.

---

court at Versailles (pp. 333–334), there were farm- and factory-managing nobles, ship-owning nobles, and even small-farmer nobles who plowed their own fields. And alongside "nobles of the sword" who prided themselves on their own or their forebears' prowess, there were "nobles of the gown" who earned law degrees and worked as judges and administrators.

Secondly, inequality was an accepted feature of society at all levels. In families high and low, brides promised to obey bridegrooms, and younger children were not supposed to marry before older ones. In the villages, peasants with larger holdings intermarried to form "dynasties" that looked down on families with smaller holdings or none at all. Rather than expecting equality for everyone, most people hoped for privileges for themselves, and over the centuries, the traditional order had to some extent satisfied this hope. Wealthy townspeople, for example, could buy official positions from the king that turned them into tax-exempt "nobles of the hat," looking down upon humble taxpaying commoners though still despised by nobles of the sword and the gown.

Oppressed peasants, religious dissidents, and discontented nobles had often rebelled when these safety valves had not worked, but the rebels had mostly wanted to make the existing order better serve their interests or ideals, not to destroy it. In the eighteenth century, however, France was undergoing changes that were causing pressures to build up and safety valves to become clogged. The result would be an explosion of unprecedented suddenness and violence. The existing order, still generally assumed to be permanent as late as the 1780s, would in the 1790s come to be seen as a thing of the past—the "**Old Regime.**"

War and Taxes

The hopes and resentments of the changing Old Regime came to a head in the second half of the eighteenth century, when the ruling partnership of king, nobles, and Church was strained to breaking point by disputes over the problem of paying for the country's wars.

The disputes began in 1763, after a worldwide war that had ended badly for France, thanks to defeats by Prussia's enlightened despotism and by Britain's limited monarchy. Like every absolute monarchy, that of France had traditionally met the growing cost of war both by increasing taxes and by heavy borrowing, but by the middle of the eighteenth century, these sources were reaching their limit. For more than a century, the burden on the main taxpayers, the peasants, had been increasing. Many landowners, worried that the peasants might react by skimping on payments to them, had recently been using their power as lords of manors to extract every penny that the peasants owed them. Meanwhile, as the monarchy's debts mounted, so did the cost of repaying them—which also had to be met by the taxpayers.

King Louis XV and his advisers did not believe that the problem could be solved at the expense of the peasants, who would revolt at yet another tax increase, or of the bankers, who might never again lend money if the government defaulted. That meant that the solution would have to come at the expense of the privileged orders, and as a first step, the government announced a tax on land belonging to nobles—an attack on their ancient privilege of tax exemption that even Louis XIV had never attempted. The nobles' response came from the Parlement of Paris, which told the king that "to levy a tax without consent" was "to do violence to the constitution of the French government" and to "injure . . . the rights of the Nation." This was language that had been heard a hundred years before from English Puritans and gentry, and would soon be heard again from North American colonists. But the ones who were using it now were members of the privileged orders of France.

This particular conflict ended in a compromise that enabled the government to raise enough new revenue to avoid bankruptcy. The basic problems remained, however, and for the next quarter of a century, the nobility and the monarchy struggled indecisively over reform of the public finances, which inevitably raised questions about reform of the government system in general. The problems remained unsolved, while both sides fell into the dangerous habit of publicly criticizing each other. Both absolute monarchy and the privileges of nobles and clergy became subject to discussion in the court of public opinion—which included the opinion of the wealthier and better-educated members of the Third Estate.

The Old Regime's Collapse

The final crisis came after the absolute monarchy fought another expensive war against Britain, this time in support of American independence. The war was successful but the debts were overwhelming, and in 1786, the government announced yet another reform plan, the centerpiece of which was a permanent tax on land, to be levied on all subjects alike.

 Imaging the French Revolution (http://chnm.gmu.edu/revolution/imaging/images1—14.html) View images of the French Revolution.

The Nobles Against the King

As usual, the privileged orders protested and resisted, and this time, they had a trump card to play in the battle for public support. In 1787, the Parlement of Paris declared that the new tax could not become law unless it was discussed and accepted by the ancient national representative assembly of France, the Estates-General. This body had been an important part of the government in the Middle Ages (pp. 260, 262), but as the rulers' power had grown, they had found it a nuisance and had not convened it since 1614. To revive it now, therefore, would in effect mean the dismantling of absolute monarchy.

With this proposal, the privileged orders briefly became the leaders of the nation against the king. Bourgeois who wanted a larger place in the power structure and freedom for industry and trade, the urban poor who were suffering from high food prices caused by bad harvests, peasants hoping for relief from taxes and payments to landowners—all could hope for redress of grievances from the Estates-General, and the demand that the king summon it became widespread and clamorous. Facing open disobedience from nobles, with tax revenues shrinking and bankruptcy threatening, and afraid to use force, in 1788 King Louis XVI agreed to summon a meeting of the Estates-General, to be held at Versailles the following year.

The Third Estate Against the Privileged Orders

As planning for the meeting went ahead, a split opened between the nobles and the bourgeoisie. Traditionally, the Estates-General had been an assembly of representatives of the First, Second, and Third Estates, with each estate meeting and voting separately. The consent of two out of three estates (as well as the king) was required for decisions to become law, so that the representatives of the clergy and nobility could outvote the representatives of the vast majority of the nation. In 1614, this had seemed fair enough, but in the age of the Enlightenment and bourgeois self-confidence, the lawyers and other professional men who emerged as spokesmen for the Third Estate wanted it revised. They argued that there should be twice as many representatives of the Third Estate as of the other two, and that all three estates should meet in a single assembly. The privileged orders would still have far more representatives than their numbers warranted, but reform-minded noblemen and lower-ranking clergy would vote with the Third Estate, so that the Third Estate would dominate the decision making.

The king granted the demand for double representation of the Third Estate, but the Parlement of Paris, to which the issue was referred, ruled in favor of the traditional voting method. The arguments continued, however, as elections got under way throughout France to choose the members who would represent the Third Estate. The members were chosen by provincial assemblies that were themselves elected on a fairly wide suffrage, including small businessmen and heads of peasant households—and by ancient custom, the assemblies also drew up "Registers of Grievances," based on consultations with local communities, to be presented to the king. Now, if not

 The Third Estate Speaks: The Cahier de Doléances of the Carcassonne Read the Cahier de doléances (Register of Grievances) prepared for the king by a provincial assembly.

National Assembly
The representative body created by members of the Third Estate after they quit the Estates-General.

Paris Commune
The new city government of Paris, with its own militia force, formed after the local uprising of 1789.

> "*The stage was set for a conflict that would involve not just the king, the privileged orders, and the bourgeoisie but also the entire nation.*"

before, the common people in general became aware that their votes might not carry as much weight as those of the nobles and the clergy. The stage was set for a conflict that would involve not just the king, the privileged orders, and the bourgeoisie but the entire nation (see photo).

After the session opened at Versailles in May 1789—to the accompaniment of riots caused by bad harvests and high bread prices in many parts of France—matters soon came to a head. Unable to persuade the two higher estates to sit and vote with them

as one body, the representatives of the Third Estate walked out of the Estates-General and declared themselves to be the "**National Assembly**" of France—the only true representatives of the people. This proclamation was the first act of actual revolution, for by law, the power to determine the procedure of the Estates-General rested with the king. Louis XVI was thereby faced with a crisis of decision.

Forced to choose between the nobility and the bourgeoisie, Louis sided with the nobility and locked the meeting hall of the building where the Third Estate had been sitting. But the Third Estate found another meeting place at an indoor tennis court nearby, and there they swore the "Tennis Court Oath," pledging not to return home until they had drafted a new constitution for France. Within a few days, the National Assembly was joined by many lower-ranking priests from the First Estate and by some of the nobles.

Having failed to persuade the opponents of the privileged orders to back down, Louis next tried to intimidate them by a show of force. Toward the end of June, he called some 20,000 soldiers to Versailles.

Parisians and Peasants Join the Struggle

The National Assembly was rescued by the people of nearby Paris—not just the wealthy bourgeois, but also the small business owners and their workers who made up the bulk of the city's population. Aroused by the threat to the Third Estate, crowds began to roam the streets in search of weapons, and on July 14, they attacked the Bastille (**bah-STEEL**), Paris's medieval fortress, state prison, and symbol of absolute power. The outnumbered garrison killed many attackers but finally surrendered, whereupon the crowd rushed in, stabbed the commander to death, sawed off his head, and paraded it on a spear point through the city streets.

Thoroughly alarmed, and doubting that his troops would fire on the people, Louis yielded. He sent his forces away from Versailles, directed the representatives of the privileged estates to sit in the National Assembly, and recognized a new city government in the capital, the **Paris Commune**, with its own militia force, the National Guard. Thus, the revolutionary movement was strengthened by a new and powerful influence—the Parisian populace.

The final blow to the Old Regime came from the largest social group in France, the peasants. At least since the elections, they had known of the issues at stake, and by late July, many of them knew that the Third Estate was in some way threatened. Earlier they had rioted to stop merchants exporting scarce grain from country districts, but now it was rumored that landown-

A Guide to the Significance of the Bastille in French History (http://www.discoverfrance.net/France/Paris/Monuments-Paris/Bastille.shtml) Learn more about the Bastille and the attack of July 14.

"Let's Hope This Game Ends Soon" A cartoon published during the conflict of the estates in 1789 shows a priest, a noble, and a peasant playing piggyback. The priest and the noble (the First and Second Estates) are comfortable; the peasant (the Third Estate) is the one who has had enough. Musee de la Ville de Paris, Musee Carnavalet, Paris/The Bridgeman Art Library

Á faut espérer q'eu jeu la finira ben tôt.

THE DECLARATION OF THE RIGHTS OF WOMAN AND THE FEMALE CITIZEN

This declaration is the work of Olympe de Gouges (**oh-LAHMP de goozh**), a woman of letters (p. 363) who in the 1780s wrote essays and dramas inspired by Enlightenment ideas. After the end of the Old Regime, she generally supported the measures of the National Assembly to turn France into a limited monarchy in which "the source of sovereignty is essentially in the nation," with one major exception: for her and for a small group of like-minded women and men, the wielders of the nation's sovereignty ought to include women.

In 1791, de Gouges published this document, worded like the ringing clauses of the Declaration of the Rights of Man and the Citizen, but including women. It was a striking way of showing up the inconsistency of most revolutionaries as well as most Enlightenment thinkers when they proclaimed universal human rights. Politicians of all factions disregarded or condemned her views—including the Jacobins, whose ruthless methods she also opposed. In 1793, they guillotined her on charges of counterrevolutionary conspiracy, and a report of her execution declared: "It seems the law has punished this conspirator for having forgotten the virtues that belong to her sex."

The mothers, daughters, and sisters, representatives of the nation, demand to be constituted a national assembly. Considering that ignorance, disregard of or contempt for the rights of women are the only causes of public misfortune and of governmental corruption, they have resolved to set forth in a solemn declaration, the natural, inalienable and sacred rights of woman. . . .

1. Woman is born free and remains equal in rights to man. . . .

3. The principle of all sovereignty resides essentially in the Nation, which is none other than the union of Woman and Man. . . .

4. Liberty and Justice consist of rendering to persons those things that belong to them; thus, the exercise of woman's natural rights is limited only by the perpetual tyranny with which man opposes her; these limits must be changed according to the laws of nature and reason. . . .

10. No one should be punished for their opinions. Woman has the right to mount the scaffold; she should likewise have the right to speak in public, provided that her demonstrations do not disrupt public order as established by law.

EXPLORING THE SOURCE

1. How does de Gouges's attitude to men compare with the Third Estate's attitude to the other two estates at the beginning of the Revolution?

2. What reasons does de Gouges give why women should have the same political rights as men? How do her arguments reflect Enlightenment thinking?

Source: Susan Grooge Bell and Karen M. Offen, eds., *Women, the Family, and Freedom: The Debate in Documents* (Stanford, Cal.: Stanford University Press, 1983), 1:105–106.

---

ers were gathering hired ruffians to attack the peasants. While many of the nobles were away at the capital, the peasants seized the initiative. During the "Great Fear" of late summer, they vandalized manor houses and destroyed the hated records of their required payments and services.

"Feudalism Is Abolished"

As the king had appeased the Paris populace, the National Assembly now tried to quiet the peasants. Many bourgeois, as well as nobles, held landed estates, and they realized that they would have to take drastic action to save their families and properties. On August 4, at a single night session, the National Assembly abolished the thousand-year-old arrangements whereby "those who fight" and "those who pray" lived off the labors of "those who work" (p. 190). Reform-minded noblemen led the way by surrendering their entitlement as lords of manors to peasant fees and labor, and their tax exemptions and advantages. A final decree, approved overwhelmingly, declared that "feudalism is abolished." The chief losers were, of course, the nobles; the beneficiaries were the peasants, who now had a substantial interest in defending the revolution.

Trying to Build a New France

Having abolished the Old Regime, the National Assembly swiftly issued a founding document for the new one, the Declaration of the Rights of Man and the Citizen. Like the English Bill of Rights and the American bill that the new U.S. Congress was discussing at this time, the French declaration listed various rights of citizens that the government must in future respect. But like the U.S. Declaration of Independence, it also proclaimed general principles, valid for the entire human race, of which France was in future to be an example.

The Rights of Man

Whereas Jefferson had drawn from Locke, however, the National Assembly drew mainly upon Rousseau. "Men are born and remain free and equal in rights. . . . The source of sovereignty is essentially in the nation. No body, no individual can exercise authority that does not proceed from it in plain terms. . . . The law is the expression of the general will. All citizens have the right to participate in the making of law, and its administration must be the same for all." The new France was to be a community of free, equal, and virtuous citizens, obedient to the law because it reflected the will of the whole community (p. 367). In the words of what later became a popular revolutionary slogan, France would be a land of "Liberty, Equality, Fraternity."

But what framework of government would enable France to become such a land? A whole spectrum of factions developed in the National Assembly with different views on this question. Some wanted the new government modeled after that of England, with an upper and a lower house, and a king with executive and veto powers. Others, fearing that this arrangement would give undue power to the nobility, wanted a single legislative chamber and a figurehead king. Still others wanted to abolish the monarchy altogether. To start with, this last group was a small minority, but as the National Assembly debated, events were unfolding that would soon bring the radicals to power.

> "*France would be a land of 'Liberty, Equality, Fraternity.*'"

Internal Conflict and Foreign War

For the transformation of France to be a peaceful process, the king would have had to consistently cooperate with the National Assembly and the nobles and the clergy would have had to be at least neutral, but exactly the opposite happened.

The king hesitated to accept either the Declaration of Rights or the Assembly's decrees abolishing feudalism until, in October 1789, 7,000 Parisian market women joined an armed march to Versailles to force King Louis XVI to act against high bread prices, approve the National Assembly's revolutionary measures, and come with his queen, Marie Antoinette, and the heir to the throne to live in Paris. After tense negotiations, the king agreed to all the demands. "Let's go get the baker, the baker's wife, and the little baker boy!" was the market women's slogan, expressing the contempt of the Parisians for

 Popular Revolution: The Women of Paris March on Versailles Read an account of the armed march on Versailles.

their once-absolute monarch. A few days later, the National Assembly followed the king to Paris, and the capital became more than ever the driving force in the continuing revolution.

The coercion of the king and his family, following the rioting of the Great Fear, in turn led to a mass exodus of nobles. Eventually, over 100,000 aristocrats left France, including more than half of the officers of the army, and began urging foreign powers to intervene. Meanwhile, the king resisted and then agreed to one revolutionary measure after another, and took part to spectacular public demonstrations of revolutionary fervor (see photo on page 378) while keeping in regular touch with the émigrés. Finally, in May 1791 the king tried to join the emigration together with his queen and his son, but they were captured near the northeast frontier and brought back to Paris in humiliation. For the time being the king continued in office, but he had lost all real authority.

This in turn led the Austrian emperor and the Prussian king to issue the Declaration of Pillnitz, stating that if Louis XVI was threatened and if the other European powers would join them, they would use force to protect Louis. The foreign rulers were busy at the time negotiating to divide Poland with Russia (p. 376) and meant their declaration simply as a warning, but from now on, the revolution faced the threat of foreign intervention.

Meanwhile, the National Assembly itself was busy alienating the one privileged group of the Old Regime that had mostly supported it, the lower-ranking clergy. The majority in the Assembly were influenced against actual Christian belief by Deism, but held to the French monarchy's ancient tradition of intervening in Church affairs (pp. 260–261, 334), and the combination produced the biggest religious split in France since the Reformation. The National Assembly confiscated the properties of the Church as a way to help deal with the government's continuing financial problems, and suppressed all monasteries, since monks and nuns were by Enlightenment standards "useless" members of society. To ensure the social usefulness of the rest of the clergy, in 1791 the Assembly passed the Civil Constitution of the Clergy, which turned priests and bishops into elected officials paid by the state and required them to take an oath of loyalty to the new arrangement. About half the clergy took the oath, but in the devoutly Catholic western and southeastern parts of France, most of them refused. Along with these clergy, peasants, who not long before might have been rioting against the nobles, now went into opposition to the revolution.

The Assembly further undermined itself with the new constitution, which went into effect in September 1791. Reflecting the growing distrust for the nobles and the king, the constitution provided for a single-chamber legislature, to be called the Legislative Assembly, and a suspensive veto for the king—he could only delay, not prevent, legislation. But well-to-do bourgeois politicians managed to exclude the poorest third of the male population from voting at all, while the other two-thirds were to vote for "electors" who would actually choose the members of the new legislature—and the electors had to be so wealthy that only 50,000 qualified as candidates in the first elections.

An untrustworthy king, noble emigrants pushing foreign rulers to intervene, Catholic opposition building up inside France with widespread popular backing, a constitution that broke the promises of the Declaration of the Rights of Man and the Citizen—all this led the Legislative Assembly to try to restore national unity by carrying the revolution abroad. More radical members pictured French armies carrying the banner of "liberation" into neighboring lands and uniting with native revolutionaries to overthrow established governments. Moderates, and even the king himself, hoped that victory would gain them popularity that they could use against the radicals. Accordingly, France declared war on Austria in April 1792, and soon was at war with Prussia as well. So began a period of international war and revolution that lasted for twenty-three years.

The Jacobin Takeover

France's army had been disorganized by the Revolution, however, and at first the war went against the French. There was panic, suspicion, and disorder in the capital and the provinces, causing power to drift toward the radical factions, of whom the most influential were members of the **Jacobin (JAK-uh-bin) Club**. (The name came from that of a building in Paris where the club met, which had belonged to the Jacobin religious order.) The club had been founded in 1789, and the mutual hostility between supporters and opponents of the revolution nourished its growth: by the end of 1792, it had half a million members in hundreds of local chapters throughout France, as well as close links with the Parisians. The Jacobins were not a united group, but in the crisis of 1792 their most radical members took the lead—those who stood for ruthless crushing of opposition to the revolution, as well as for full implementation of the principles of liberty and equality under the rule of the general will, including universal male suffrage and abolition of the monarchy.

The Jacobins also gained influence in the Paris Commune and among lower-class Parisians, among whom suspicion and anger were spreading. Late in the summer of 1792, rioters rushed the royal palace of the Tuileries, massacred the king's guards, and went on to threaten the Legislative Assembly. Later a band of enthusiastic army recruits invaded the Paris jails and seized a thousand or more prisoners who had been rounded up as suspected sympathizers with the aristocracy. After mock trials, these unfortunates were put to death. With Paris in uproar, most of the non-Jacobin members stopped attending the Legislative Assembly. Dominated now by Jacobins, the Assembly suspended the king from office and summoned a new constitution-making body, the **National Convention**, to be elected by all Frenchmen with no restrictions.

> **"**You are, from this moment, brothers and friends; all are citizens, equal in rights, and all are alike called to govern, to serve, and to defend your country.**"**
> —National Convention, 1792

The French Republic

In September 1792, the Convention met and proclaimed France a republic, after elections in which only a minority voted, for "counterrevolutionaries," as they were now beginning to be called, were unwilling to take part, and Jacobins kept voters they distrusted away from the polls. The winds of violence were beginning to sweep across France, and the Jacobins had taken power in the name of the general will in a bitterly divided nation. Furthermore, the Jacobins themselves remained divided, and the divisions soon came to the fore as the Convention debated the fate of the former king.

 The French Revolution Becomes a Universal Political Crusade Read a selection from the Convention's proclamation of 1792.

The Jacobin Dictatorship

One of the Convention's first acts was to put Louis on trial for treason, mainly on account of his dealings with emigrants and foreign powers. Unlike King Charles II of England a century and a half before (p. 341), Louis submitted to questioning and made a brief speech in his own defense before the Convention unanimously found him guilty. But was the penalty to be death? Many members, fearing that the king's death would further embitter opponents of the revolution, wanted to let the people decide through a referendum. In the end, the death penalty passed by a narrow margin, and early in 1793, Louis was beheaded by a newly adopted device, intended, in the humane spirit of the Enlightenment, to execute criminals without pain—the guillotine (see photo on page 390).

Meanwhile, the Convention had to uphold the revolution against foreign invasion and civil war. By this time, Spain and Britain as well as various smaller kingdoms had joined Austria and Prussia against revolutionary France. To oppose these enemies, the National Convention reorganized the army and approved the drafting of all able-bodied men and large-scale requisitioning of supplies. Against the well-drilled but slow-moving armies of their opponents, the French armies relied on larger forces of draftees, on bold leadership by swiftly promoted officers, and on the commitment of all ranks to defending France itself as well as its revolution. By the end of 1793, the new army

Jacobin Club
A French political organization that supported the revolution; its most radical members gained national power during the crisis of 1792.

National Convention
The legislative assembly in revolutionary France during its republican period.

Going to the Guillotine A contemporary print of the execution of Robespierre and his associates shows the whole process from the arrival of wagonloads of victims to the dumping of a headless body at the foot of the scaffold. After a couple of thousand guillotinings in Paris in two years, not many people pay attention to this routine event. Perhaps they would take more interest if they foresaw that with the death of the Terror's leading instigator, the guillotine will in future much be less busy.

had turned the tide of battle and had driven the invaders out of France.

The new armies also fought counterrevolutionary uprisings in the strongly Catholic parts of the country. Along with the armies came revolutionary trial courts to dispose of real and suspected enemies of the revolution in an "orderly" manner. In the period of what the Jacobins themselves called the **Terror**, as many as 40,000 heads fell under the guillotines. When guillotining was too slow for the number of people to be executed, the process was accelerated by firing squads, cannon loaded with musket balls, or barges with the hatches closed and then scuttled. The less well-organized counterrevolutionaries, on the other hand, preferred the more spontaneous method of mass lynchings.

To raise armies, gather supplies, and kill opponents took nationwide organization under strong central control. Local

> **"***Help us to strike great blows or you will be the first to feel them.*** Liberty or death: *reflect and choose.***"**
> —The Committee of Republican Surveillance in Lyons

 The Reign of Terror in the Provinces: Lyons Read a document warning the people of Lyons to support the Republic.

Jacobins provided the lower ranks, under the supervision of officials sent out from Paris who were mainly appointed by and responsible to the Convention's Committee of Public Safety. The committee, consisting of no more than a dozen members, became the heart and soul of the revolution, and itself came to be dominated by a high-minded and ruthless lawyer, Maximilien Robespierre (ROHBZ-peer).

Robespierre had plenty of rivals and opponents in the revolutionary camp. Many in the Convention had voted against the death penalty for the king and disapproved of mass executions. An atheist faction wanted to replace Christianity with a state-sponsored "Cult of Reason," as against the Deist "Cult of the Supreme Being" that Robespierre preferred. Would-be redistributors of wealth wanted economic as well as political equality, whereas Robespierre viewed private property as sacred. Feminists called for female and male citizens to participate equally in forming the general will, whereas Robespierre believed (like Rousseau) that feminine virtue was to be exercised within the home, and also suspected women of being more strongly attached than men to traditional Christianity. Convinced of his own revolutionary righteousness, Robespierre treated all these opponents as enemies of the revolution and sent many of them to the guillotine.

Robespierre on Republican Virtue Read Robespierre on the lofty ideals of the revolution.

In 1793, the republic needed a leader who was convinced that he was in harmony with the general will of the citizens and would stop at nothing to "force them to be free" (p. 367). But by 1794, the invaders had retreated and the uprisings had dwindled, yet Robespierre more than ever upheld his power through the guillotine. Finally, in June 1794 the Convention turned against Robespierre and sent him to the guillotine in his turn.

The Directory

France was still a republic with the Convention in charge, but Robespierre's opponents wanted a republic without one-man domination or riotous takeovers of power. In 1795, the Convention approved a constitution that again provided for citizens to vote for wealthy electors who would choose the legislature, along with a powerful executive headed by a board of five men called the **Directory**.

France under the Directory was a very different country from what it had been only six years earlier. The monarchy had been abolished, and feudal property rights, titles of nobility, and special privileges had been swept away. The traditional administration, with its chaotic mixture of royal authority and noble privilege, had been replaced by "departments"—units about the size of American counties. Craft guilds, labor organizations, and the mercantilist regulations of the late monarchy had all been scrapped.

But what kind of country France would become was still very uncertain. The leaders of the Directory were mostly ex-Jacobins who had themselves been involved in vicious repressions against nobles, clergy, and peasants; but they had also killed Robespierre and repressed his followers among impoverished urban workers. Furthermore, many sincere reformers had either dropped out of public affairs or been destroyed in the rivalry of factions, and the politicians who remained were mostly interested in gaining wealth through corruption and holding power regardless of the constitution. The new regime was therefore widely hated and despised by both counterrevolutionaries and thoroughgoing Jacobins, and distrusted even by people in the middle who might have been expected to support it.

LO³ Napoleon and the Revolutionary Empire

There was, however, one institution of the republic that inspired widespread trust and admiration—its army, which by 1799 had pushed far outside the borders. France's power had grown beyond what even Louis XIV had dreamed of, and its revolution had become international. It had gained territory on its frontiers with the Low Countries and Italy; beyond that, a belt of satel-

lite republics stretched north into Holland, east into Switzerland, and far southward to the toe of Italy (see Map 20.1). France had become a conquering republic like ancient Rome, and as with Rome, its republican institutions were beginning to be overshadowed by its battle-winning commanders—including General Napoleon Bonaparte.

the Terror
A period of politically motivated mass executions in republican France.

Directory
A five-man executive board that governed the French republic along with the National Convention.

Napoleon's Rise to Power

Napoleon Bonaparte was born on the Mediterranean island of Corsica in 1769, the year after the French monarchy had purchased the island from the Italian city-state of Genoa. As a result, he grew up as a Frenchman, and began an officer's career in the royal army not long before the army was torn apart by revolution.

Bonaparte sided with the revolution, distinguished himself as an artillery officer in the new Jacobin army, and in 1795 earned the favor of the Directory by using his gunnery expertise against counterrevolutionary rioters in Paris. The Directory promoted him to high command, and in startlingly successful campaigns, by 1797 he had made France dominant in most of Italy. In the same year, he sent one of his generals to help the Directory purge the legislature of members whom the leaders of the regime considered too eager for reconciliation with Catholic rebels. France had other generals who were dramatically victorious and politically astute, but none was so spectacular, cunning, and lucky as Bonaparte.

In 1799, Bonaparte plotted with some of the Directory's leaders to again purge the legislature—this time of Jacobin sympathizers—and also to change the system of government. The conspirators believed that only a strong government headed by a general with army backing could hold off both counterrevolution and Jacobinism, establish internal order, and defeat France's foreign enemies. Napoleon became First Consul, a title adapted from the ancient Roman Republic, and in practice ruled as a relatively popular military dictator. In 1802, he became First Consul for Life, and in 1804, he proclaimed himself Napoleon, Emperor of the French (see photo). As founder of a new hereditary monarchy, he hoped to both consolidate the revolution and satisfy his own ambition.

Consolidating the Revolution

Napoleon owed his rise to the overthrow of the Old Regime, and he declared himself a "son of the revolution." He despised inherited and artificial privilege and was impatient with the inefficiency of the former government. He favored equality of opportunity, with careers (like his own) open to talent. He readily embraced the revolutionary slogan of "Liberty, Equality, Fraternity," while interpreting its meaning in his own way. He

Napoleonic Code
The civil code of France, initiated by Napoleon, that reorganized French law and administration.

Emperor of the French A ten-inch porcelain plaque forms the centerpiece of a drawing-room table that Napoleon ordered at the height of his power in 1806. With his classical-style throne, his eagle-headed scepter, and his laurel wreath, the emperor is just as much a figure of power as King Louis XIV (see photo on page 334), but he seems less at ease in that role—as befits a ruler who has taken power by force instead of inheriting it by right. Lauren Lecat/akg-images

held referendums for his changes of status from general to First Consul to emperor, and his various constitutions gave voting rights to all adult males. But the referendums were rigged, and in elections the voters elected only lists of candidates, from which his government named the legislators and officials. From 1799 on, the one and only spokesman of the general will was Napoleon himself.

Napoleon's first task was to secure domestic peace and order. He silenced his opponents by means of deportations, "exposure" of alleged plots, and the efficient work of his secret police. But with a loyal army at his back, he did not have to be nearly so ruthless as the Jacobins. On the contrary, he declared a general political amnesty, and invited back to France all the emigrants who were willing to work faithfully for their homeland. He called to his service men of widely varying backgrounds, from royalist to regicide, who would cooperate in consolidating the new order.

In addition, Napoleon neutralized the most powerful force behind counterrevolution—Catholic resentment at measures against the Church. In 1801, he negotiated a concordat (treaty) with Pope Pius VII, formally accepting the Roman Catholic faith as the principal religion of the French. Church seminaries were reopened, monasteries and convents were reestablished, and public religious processions were again permitted. Priests who had remained loyal to Rome were recognized as legitimate, and those who had taken the oath to the revolutionary Civil Constitution mostly made their peace with the pope.

In return, the pope dropped claims to confiscated Church property, accepted that the clergy would be paid by the state, and recognized the French republic's right to nominate bishops as the kings had traditionally done. And when Napoleon became emperor, Pius attended his coronation and said a blessing—although by prior agreement, he did not crown Napoleon but let the emperor do it himself, to avoid the implication that the papacy was conferring the imperial power, as medieval popes had claimed against Holy Roman emperors (p. 211).

Napoleon was himself a nonbeliever, however, and he would not allow the Church to be the primary force in the shaping of citizens. The state, through its own schools, had to provide for the education and patriotic instruction of the young. He approved the earlier closing of Church schools by the National Convention, and put into effect its comprehensive plans for a national educational system. By 1808, his officials had completed the structure of state-supported primary and secondary schools as well as public institutions of higher learning. The entire system, supervised from Paris, remains the basis of French education to this day.

Napoleon also carried through the plans of revolutionary leaders for reorganizing French law and administration. French law, like that of most of Europe, was based on ancient Roman law codes (systematic collections of laws, p. 111), but a bewildering mass of new laws had grown up over the centuries. Napoleon's appointed commissions cut through this accumulation to produce a new code, named, like the Roman ones, after the emperor who ordered it to be drawn up—the **Napoleonic Code**. The code would become the new basis of law in much of Europe and the New World, and in later years, Napoleon regarded it as his most durable accomplishment. While in exile he wrote, "My true glory is not in having won forty battles; Waterloo has effaced the memory of so many victories. What nothing can efface, what will live eternally, is my civil code."

The Napoleonic Code Regulates Gender Read a selection of codes governing marriage and divorce.

Under Napoleon, the modern techniques of administering a centralized state took shape. The historic provinces of France, the local courts and offices, the administration of justice—all had been swept away by the revolution. Salaried officials ("prefects") responsible to the central government now presided over the cities and departments. The reform of public administration extended to taxation, expenditure, and money

> "*What nothing can efface, what will live eternally, is my civil code.*"
>
> —Napoleon

Map 20.1

Conquests of the French Republic

By 1799, revolutionary France and the leading European monarchies had been at war for seven years. The result was an expanded France and a belt of satellite republics, stretching from Holland (the "Batavian Republic") to Italy, mostly called by the names of their territories in Roman times.
© Cengage Learning

Interactive Map

Map legend:
- Boundary of France, 1789
- Boundary of French Republic, 1799
- France, 1789
- Territory annexed by 1799
- French satellite states, 1799

and banking; the day of the bureaucrat was at hand, and with it the equality of citizens before the law. All these changes were in keeping with the rationalism (logical thinking) of the Enlightenment and with bourgeois ideas of efficiency.

The Struggle for Europe

In spite of Napoleon's success in bringing peace and order to France, he was also the heir to a revolution that had destroyed the traditional order in France and neighboring countries and had upset Europe's balance of power in France's favor. Even without his fierce will and boundless ambition, it would have been hard for the other European powers to live with the new France. As it was, his rule brought more widespread turmoil and devastation to Europe than ever before.

France Supreme in Europe?

Napoleon's first challenge in foreign affairs after he came to power was to defeat a new alliance, including Britain, Russia, and Austria, that had come together to retake France's earlier gains. Again and again, Napoleon's swift-marching armies outmaneuvered their opponents, forced them to do battle at a disadvantage, and crushed them with heavy gunfire and massed infantry and cavalry attacks. By 1802, the allies had accepted defeat, but after a brief interval of peace the wars began again.

Once again the French armies won battle after battle, and by 1808, France had absorbed much of Germany and Italy and destroyed the ancient Holy Roman Empire. France's satellite states—several of them now ruled as kingdoms by Napoleon's brothers and other relatives—stretched from Spain to Poland.

Interactive
Map

Map 20.2 Napoleon's Europe

By 1810, France had absorbed much of Germany and Italy; its satellite states stretched from Spain to Poland; Austria, Prussia, and Russia were its obedient allies; and only Britain stood against it. When the ancient Roman Republic had given way to a single ruler, Rome's conquests soon slowed and then stopped, and its emperors had ruled for centuries. Napoleon's conquests reached right across Europe, but his empire lasted only a dozen years. © Cengage Learning

Map legend

- French empire
- Dependent states
- Allied with Napoleon
- At war with Napoleon
- ★ Major battle

Map labels

ATLANTIC OCEAN

North Sea

Baltic Sea

Black Sea

Mediterranean Sea

IRELAND

SCOTLAND

GREAT BRITAIN

ENGLAND

London

KINGDOM OF NORWAY AND DENMARK

KINGDOM OF SWEDEN

Stockholm

Copenhagen

St. Petersburg

RUSSIAN EMPIRE

Moscow

Smolensk

Borodino 1812

Kiev

SWEDISH POMERANIA

PRUSSIA

Lübeck

Hamburg

Bremen

Berlin

Königsberg

Danzig

Tilsit

Friedland 1807

GRAND DUCHY OF WARSAW

Elbe R.

Rhine R.

Neman R.

Danube R.

WESTPHALIA

Auerstädt 1806

SAXONY

Jena 1806

CONFEDERATION OF THE RHINE

WÜRTTEMBERG

BADEN

BAVARIA

Zurich

SWITZERLAND

Austerlitz 1805

Wagram 1804

Vienna

Pressburg

Buda

Pest

AUSTRIAN EMPIRE

OTTOMAN EMPIRE

Constantinople

Athens

ILLYRIAN PROVINCES

FRANCE

Brussels

Waterloo 1815

Paris

Lunéville

Amiens

Marseilles

KINGDOM OF ITALY

Milan

Marengo 1800

Genoa

Rome

Naples

KINGDOM OF NAPLES

Palermo

KINGDOM OF SICILY

Malta (Gr. Br.)

Corsica

Elba

Sardinia

Ionian Is. (Gr. Br.)

SPAIN

Madrid

PORTUGAL

Lisbon

Trafalgar 1805

GIBRALTAR (Gr. Br.)

Scale

0 200 400 Mi.
0 200 400 Km.

50°N

60°N

10°W

0°

10°E

20°E

30°E

Austria, Prussia, and Russia were France's forced allies (see Map 20.2). Napoleon, it seemed, was replacing the traditional Europe of many competing states and dynasties with a Europe in which a single state dominated the rest and a single international dynasty outshone all the others. The upstart emperor had almost brought about what the Bourbon kings had hoped for but never achieved (p. 335): a Europe in which France was supreme.

 Napoleon I "Enlightens" Spain Read Napoleon's call for revolutionary changes in Spain.

Resistance, Overreaching, and Downfall

There was, however, another country whose power had grown through the years of war—Britain. While French armies were conquering Europe, the Royal Navy consolidated Britain's worldwide supremacy. British seaborne forces took over colonies from France and its allies, while British blockading fleets strangled their overseas trade. In 1805, Napoleon prepared to invade Britain itself, but the renowned Admiral Horatio Nelson crushed the French and Spanish navies off Cape Trafalgar, near where the Atlantic joins the Mediterranean, and without warships to cover troop-carrying vessels, the emperor had to call off the invasion. Instead, Napoleon tried a counter-blockade against British trade by means of a Europe-wide embargo, the so-called **Continental System**. But the system hurt Europe more than Britain, and France's allies and satellites were not eager to enforce it. Britain remained a formidable enemy, to which every resister of French domination looked for help.

Napoleon's efforts to force the Continental System on reluctant Europe led in turn to disastrous defeats by enemies against whom his swift-moving methods of warfare did not work: Spain, Portugal, and then Russia. He invaded Spain and Portugal in 1807–1808 in part because he was unsure of their loyalty to the system. The French defeated the two kingdoms' regular armies, but the people continued to resist by means of what the Spaniards called the *guerrilla*, or "little war." Their tactics were those of ambush, surprise, and retreat before superior forces, and they were backed by Britain with money, supplies, and an expeditionary force of regulars. In years of devastating warfare, the guerrillas held down tens of thousands of troops that Napoleon badly needed elsewhere.

Likewise, Tsar Alexander I of Russia eventually stopped enforcing the Continental System, and in 1812, this led Napoleon to his fatal blunder, an invasion of Russia. In the face of his Grand Army of half a million French and allied troops, the outnumbered Russians mostly avoided battle and refused to negotiate even when he captured Moscow. Short of supplies, the Grand Army turned back, and was annihilated by starvation, disease, the terrible winter, and Russian guerrillas.

Following this defeat, Napoleon's forced allies turned against him, his own French subjects lost confidence in him, and soon it was France's turn to be invaded and conquered by all four of its main rivals—Russia, Prussia, Austria, and Britain. After abdicating as emperor in 1814, Napoleon was banished to the Mediterranean island of Elba. Escaping a short while later, he raised a new army in a foolish gamble against the odds of power. On the battlefield of Waterloo (in modern Belgium) in 1815, his last minutes as a maker of history ran out, and he was again shipped away—this time to the far-off British-owned South Atlantic isle of Saint Helena. There he died in 1821, a man of not much more than fifty.

Meanwhile, however, the revolution that had started in France, spread across Europe, and then seemed to be over was getting under way again.

Continental System
Napoleon's wartime strategy for weakening Britain by barring trade with Europe.

 PBS Companion Site to Its Program on Napoleon War (http://www.pbs.org/empires/napoleon/n_war/ibs/index.html) Play the Waterloo Interactive Battle Simulator.

 Listen to a synopsis of Chapter 20.

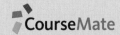

CHAPTER 21

IDEOLOGIES AND POWER STRUGGLES, 1815–1871

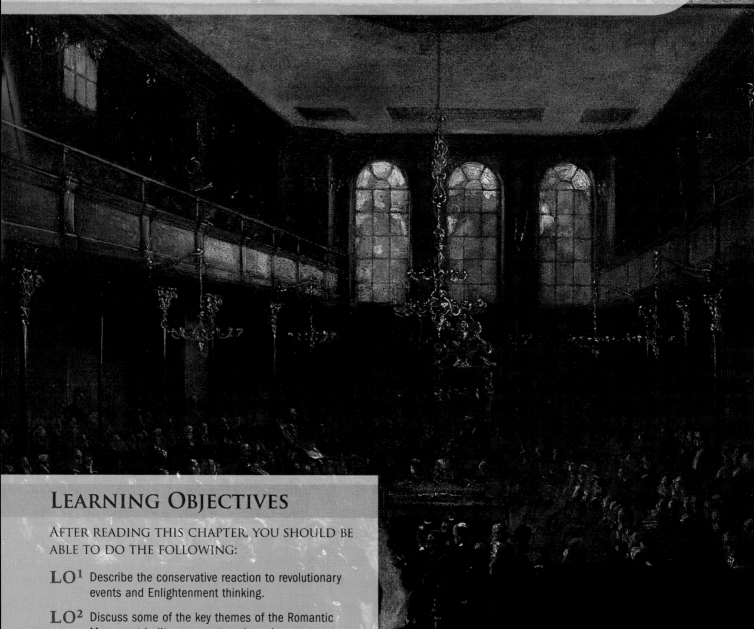

LEARNING OBJECTIVES

AFTER READING THIS CHAPTER, YOU SHOULD BE ABLE TO DO THE FOLLOWING:

LO¹ Describe the conservative reaction to revolutionary events and Enlightenment thinking.

LO² Discuss some of the key themes of the Romantic Movement in literature, art, and music.

LO³ Trace the spread of liberal democracy and nationalism in Europe in the mid-nineteenth century.

"IN THE MIDDLE OF THE NINETEENTH CENTURY, THE DISMANTLING OF THE OLD POWER STRUCTURE GATHERED SPEED."

In the first half of the nineteenth century, the struggles that accompanied and followed the French Revolution led to the rise of three new **ideologies** (systems of thought and belief) that were also international political movements: conservatism, liberalism, and nationalism. Out of the interaction of all three, a new Western power structure gradually began to develop.

Conservatism was the instinctive belief of rulers, nobles, clergy, and many of lower rank whom the turmoil of the French Revolution had turned against Enlightenment ideals. Conservatives proclaimed the virtues of tradition and community, and the limits on people's ability to change the world or govern themselves. At first, conservatives tried to uphold the traditional order by repression and force, but in time, they turned from resisting change to trying to guide it. They formed political parties that competed with liberals and nationalists for seats in representative assemblies. Rulers, for their part, hoping to avoid revolution and outdo one another in their continuing rivalries, reinvented themselves as leaders of social reform and national power.

Test your knowledge before you read this chapter.

What do you think?

Once people have experienced liberty and equality, it is impossible to maintain an authoritarian regime.

Strongly Disagree						Strongly Agree
1	2	3	4	5	6	7

Liberalism was the ideology of those who still supported Enlightenment ideals of reason and progress in spite of revolutionary turmoil. Middle-class business and professional people, as well as others of both higher and lower standing, were often liberals. They trusted that if individuals were given equal chances, control over the actions of governments, and the maximum freedom to pursue their own interests, the result would be a prosperous, harmonious, and efficient society. As a means of bringing this about, liberals put their faith in the British and American model of representative institutions, legally guaranteed rights and freedoms, and legally binding constitutions.

The rise of **nationalism** was a result of changes that revolution and liberalism brought to the long-standing Western tradition of different nations shar-

‹‹ **The First Reformed Parliament** A contemporary painting by Sir George Hayter shows the British House of Commons assembling after the 400-year-old voting system was reformed in 1832. Many of these men come from newly important industrial cities; thanks to earlier legislation, many are Catholics or non-Anglican Protestants (p. 344). But there are no women members or voters, and nearly nine-tenths of men cannot sit or vote either. Britain is still far from a democracy.

ideology
A system of thought and belief.

conservatism
In Europe after the French Revolution, an ideology that proclaimed the virtues of tradition and community, and the limits on people's ability to change the world or govern themselves.

liberalism
In Europe after the French Revolution, an ideology aligned with Enlightenment ideals of reason and progress, and the belief that liberty and equality will lead to prosperity and harmony.

nationalism
An ideology that advocates self-government and unity for the people making up a specific nation.

ing a common civilization. Revolutionaries and liberals acted in the name of the united and self-governing "people," but always "the people" meant the British, the American, or the French people—in other words, the people making up a specific nation. Self-government and unity, it seemed, were rights of nations just as much as of peoples. This ideal of the united and independent nation-state soon spread to the Germans and Italians, large but divided nations to whom it offered equality with other large nations like the French. It also appealed to nations living under imperial rule like the Poles, the Greeks, and European settlers in Latin America, to whom it held out the hope of developing their national cultures and interests as they saw fit.

All three political movements were influenced by a wider cultural trend, that of Romanticism. The Romantic movement began as a rebellion against some aspects of the thought and art of the Enlightenment. It valued emotion and imagination above reason, community above individualism, and spontaneity above established rules. Romantic thinkers stressed the limits of reason and observation as ways of knowing the world, or they looked for some higher reason to be found in history or nature rather than individual humans. Writers, painters, and musicians celebrated such themes as the drama of nature, the passions and torments of sensitive souls, the horrors of war, or the fleeting joys of youth. Romantics might be liberals or conservatives, depending on whether they saw untamed human fancy and feeling as a hope for the future or an endangered tradition of the past. They might be deeply religious or enthusiastically nationalist, according to whether they believed in Christianity or the nation as the guardian of community traditions.

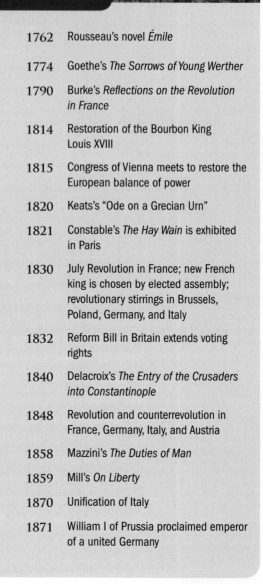

CHRONOLOGY

1762	Rousseau's novel *Émile*
1774	Goethe's *The Sorrows of Young Werther*
1790	Burke's *Reflections on the Revolution in France*
1814	Restoration of the Bourbon King Louis XVIII
1815	Congress of Vienna meets to restore the European balance of power
1820	Keats's "Ode on a Grecian Urn"
1821	Constable's *The Hay Wain* is exhibited in Paris
1830	July Revolution in France; new French king is chosen by elected assembly; revolutionary stirrings in Brussels, Poland, Germany, and Italy
1832	Reform Bill in Britain extends voting rights
1840	Delacroix's *The Entry of the Crusaders into Constantinople*
1848	Revolution and counterrevolution in France, Germany, Italy, and Austria
1858	Mazzini's *The Duties of Man*
1859	Mill's *On Liberty*
1870	Unification of Italy
1871	William I of Prussia proclaimed emperor of a united Germany

In the middle of the nineteenth century, the dismantling of the old power structure gathered speed. Eastern European serfdom, New World slavery, and the legal privileges of nobles and clergy were all abolished. Latin American empires disintegrated into independent nations, Germany and Italy were unified into powerful nation-states, and many subject nations of eastern European multinational empires laid claim to independence. In nearly every European country, rulers yielded a larger or smaller share of power to more or less widely elected representative assemblies. The original revolutionary countries—Britain, the United States, and France—evolved toward full democracy.

These changes came about through continued turmoil of revolution and war, as well as through peaceful reforms, and often the result was bitter social resentments and fierce international power struggles. In only two major countries, Britain and the United States, did a generally accepted new power structure arise. Elsewhere, the shape of the future Western social, political, and international order was still uncertain and contested. Would it live up to the ideals of liberalism and nationalism, or would it bring social, national, and international conflict on a scale never seen before?

LO¹ The Conservative Reaction

While Napoleon was making his dash from Elba to final defeat in the spring of 1815, rulers and diplomats were assembled at the glittering Congress (international conference) of Vienna, trying to restore Europe to what it had been before 1789 (see photo). But revolution and war had planted the seeds of a new order, and Europe would never again be the same.

Metternich and the "Concert of Europe"

Though many countries were represented at the Congress, its decisions lay in the hands of five major powers: victorious Britain, Russia, Prussia, and Austria, as well as defeated France, which was once again respectable under a new ruler.

Restoration and Legitimacy

Prince Clemens von Metternich, the chief minister of Austria, was the leading spirit of the conference. In 1810, when there seemed no alternative to accepting Napoleon's restructuring of Europe, Metternich had arranged a marriage between the conqueror and Maria Louisa, daughter of the Austrian emperor, but after Napoleon's defeat in Russia, Metternich threw Austria's weight against him. Austria thus came out of the wars in a victor's role; and Metternich, to clinch

"Europe's Rebirth through the Grand Union of Rulers in Vienna" At the Congress of Vienna, rulers and ministers of the great powers sit with papers, a map, and a globe of the world whose fate they are deciding. Emperor Francis I of Austria, the host, wears a white uniform; at far right, Talleyrand, representing defeated France, sits with the victors. Behind them, a crowd of lesser rulers waits to hear what the decision makers have in store for them.

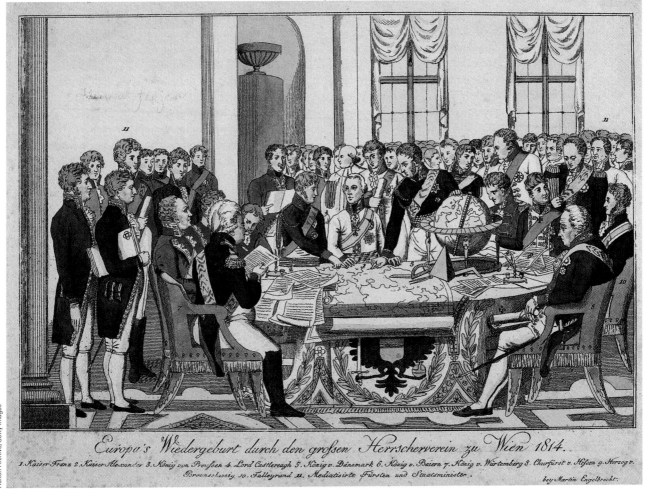

Europa's Wiedergeburt durch den grossen Herrscherverein zu Wien 1814.

1. Kaiser Franz 2. Kaiser Alexander 3. König von Preußen 4. Lord Castlereagh 5. König v. Dänemark 6. König v. Baiern 7. König v. Würtemberg 8. Churfürst v. Hessen 9. Herzog v. Braunschweig 10. Talleyrand 11. Mediatisirte Fürsten und Staatsminister.

bey Martin Engelbrecht.

the advantage, persuaded the allies to hold the congress in Vienna, the Austrian capital.

Metternich's cunning was matched by that of the leading French diplomat, Prince Talleyrand. Talleyrand had served as a bishop under Louis XVI, as a statesman of the revolution, and as Napoleon's foreign minister. When it appeared that the French emperor was overreaching himself, Talleyrand offered secret aid to Napoleon's enemies abroad, thereby preparing a place for himself in the postwar government. When the emperor fell, Talleyrand urged the victors to restore the Bourbons, the traditional royal dynasty of France. The allies were agreed on the necessity of restoring **legitimacy**—rightful rule according to established tradition, as opposed to that of revolutionary dictators and conquerors—which in France certainly meant the Bourbons. Louis XVI had been beheaded, and his young son, whom royalists recognized as Louis XVII, had died in 1795. In 1814, therefore, the eldest surviving brother of the executed king, who had been living as an émigré in England, took over as King Louis XVIII, and at once made the indispensable Talleyrand his foreign minister.

"The Indispensable Talleyrand" (http://www.hoover.org/publications/policyreview/14778531.html) Learn about the colorful life of Prince Talleyrand.

At Vienna, Talleyrand played skillfully on the differences among the four main victors. The chief concerns of the conference were to restore, so far as practicable, the legitimate holdings of all rulers and the European balance of power. That balance, which had been established by the Peace of Westphalia (see Map 17.2 on page 327), had aimed to secure the independence of European states by preventing one or more of them from gaining too much power. In the course of the Vienna congress, for example, Talleyrand joined Metternich and Lord Castlereagh of Britain in a secret pledge to go to war should Prussia and Russia carry through their joint plans for expansion in central Europe. When word of the agreement leaked out, a compromise plan was proposed and accepted.

The Congress of Vienna by no means restored the borders of Europe exactly as they had been before 1789. Most notably, there was no attempt to revive the Holy Roman Empire. Napoleon had given the final blow to the empire in 1806 and had merged many of the smaller German states into a league known as the Confederation of the Rhine. The Congress kept this general arrangement, which was joined by Austria and Prussia and renamed the German Confederation. Subject mainly to Austrian control, this grouping forestalled for the moment Prussian desires for dominance in Germany. The redrawn map of Germany and the

> *"All across Europe, patriotic societies arose to champion the cause of national unity and independence."*

rest of Europe (see Map 21.1) was to remain in effect, save for minor alterations, for half a century.

Europe After the Congress

In France itself, the effects of the French Revolution were not completely undone. Instead, Louis XVIII granted a constitution that made the country a limited monarchy. The legal, administrative, religious, and educational reforms of the revolution were retained. And beyond the borders of France, the ideas of liberalism could not be erased. Still less could Metternich prevent the rising sentiment of nationalism, which had been strengthened by the revolution's stress on "fraternity" and by Napoleon. The peoples of Germany and Italy, especially, were impressed by the power and accomplishments of the French "nation-in-arms" and exhilarated by the sense of national solidarity that came from resistance to the French conquerors. All across Europe, patriotic societies arose to champion the cause of national unity and independence.

For the time being, the rulers of most countries viewed liberalism and nationalism as threats to the restored "legitimate" order, and agreed at Vienna to keep a close eye on them. Metternich arranged a "Concert of Europe" (in actuality, a Quadruple Alliance of Austria, Prussia, Russia, and Britain) that would use diplomacy and force against moves to change boundaries or social systems. Accordingly, several congresses were called on Metternich's initiative to meet threats to the established order.

Constitutional Monarchy in France, Again Read Louis XVIII's remarks on the new French constitution.

But it was hard for the rulers to cooperate against liberalism and nationalism for long. Traditionally, the rulers were rivals, and it soon occurred to them that they could actually strengthen themselves by compromising with the new movements, and could even use them against each other. Already, following shattering defeats by Napoleon, the Prussian monarchy had abolished serfdom and begun drafting all male citizens for military training, thereby increasing the loyalty of the peasants and making its army into a version of the "nation-in-arms." Then, in the 1820s and 1830s, Prussia played a leading role in a customs union (usually known by its German name, the Zollverein [TSAWL-fer-ahyn]) that grew to include most German states, but not Austria. The union not only made possible free trade across Germany but also put Prussia, not Austria, at the head of a united German national undertaking. In the long run, the "Metternich System" was eaten away by rivalries at the top as well as by new revolutions from below.

A Poetic Tribute to the Zollverein Read a poet's tribute to the Zollverein.

Map 21.1 Europe in 1815

The peacemakers at Vienna tried to restore the old balance of power among European monarchies. Many small states in Germany and Italy were restored, and France itself lost none of its eighteenth-century territory (Map 18.1 on page 336). But in central Europe, instead of an empire that called itself Roman, there was now a confederation that called itself German, and within it, Prussia was far larger than before. A new Germany, a new Europe, and new wars and revolutions lay ahead. © Cengage Learning

 Interactive Map

The Rejection of Revolution and Rationalism: Burke

Opposition to liberal ideas was not confined to rulers, nobles, and clergy. The ideals of the Enlightenment had been dimmed by the realities of revolution and war, and many who had sympathized with the ideals now recoiled from the bloody cost of attempting to put them into practice. The liberals, who stressed science and reason, equality and democracy, now stood in opposition to those who stressed tradition and sentiment, aristocracy and authority—the conservatives.

One of the ablest spokesmen of the conservative point of view was the British thinker and statesman Edmund Burke. His *Reflections on the Revolution in France*, which appeared in 1790—soon after the revolution's outbreak but long before it reached its most radical phase—attacked its underlying ideas and has remained to this day an important statement of conservative principles (see Reasons Why).

Burke did not think, however, that institutions should remain frozen. He viewed society as an organism, and this led him to think in biological terms. Useless growths should be cut off, and new shoots and branches should be allowed to develop.

BURKE ATTACKED KEY IDEAS BEHIND THE FRENCH REVOLUTION:

Equality

- Rather than "natural rights," Burke believed that rights were an "inheritance" handed down through generations.

- The king, the lords, and every other group within the English social body had the right to enjoy the particular privileges and liberties passed on to them from "a long line of ancestors."

- Burke thus expressed his belief in aristocracy and attacked efforts made in the name of equality to interfere with "legitimate" privilege.

Reason

- Burke felt that each person's private stock of reason is pitifully small and therefore a poor guide to action.

- Traditional wisdom—deposited in the "general bank and capital of nations and ages"—was more reliable than knowledge gained through reason.

- Therefore, Burke believed, tried and tested institutions are better than those created by reformers out of their own minds.

Right of Revolution

- Burke rejected the Enlightenment idea that the state is an executor of the social contract, to be changed at the will of people.

- Burke saw the state as a divine creation, binding past, present, and future generations. The state, being sacred, must be regarded with awe and reverence.

- It should not be "hacked to pieces" by would-be innovators; such reckless-ness can lead only to anarchy.

- To Burke, anarchy is "ten thousand times worse" than the blindest and most stubborn government.

Faith in Human Goodness and Progress

- A devout Anglican, Burke believed that people are born with original sin.

- Only by strict social discipline, he believed, is the individual made decent and civilized.

- Once restraints are broken, people fall back to beastlike behavior.

- Thus, Burke argued, revolution leads to an intolerable chaos, which can be ended only by some form of despotism.

He was, therefore, a flexible conservative. He even stated that conditions in a given society might become such that a resort to revolution would be permissible. But it should never be a calculated action. The justification for revolution, he declared, must be "the first and supreme necessity only, a necessity that is not chosen, but chooses, a necessity paramount to deliberation, that admits no discussion, and demands no evidence." This, he believed, had been the case with Britain's Glorious Revolution of 1688, and even with the American Revolution—but not with the course that the French Revolution had taken.

A New Philosophical Synthesis: Kant, Hegel

The conservative reaction was also strong on the European continent, where the intellectuals of the Enlightenment were held responsible for the unhappy events of revolution and war. Defenders of the restored order concluded also that the weakening of religious faith had eased the way to social subversion. They therefore encouraged the revival of religious fervor that had arisen as a reaction to the secularism of the Enlightenment and the revolution. The Roman Catholic Church, tradition-ally conservative, played a leading role in this renewal of piety, morality, and respect for authority.

Kant: The Limits of Knowledge

European philosophy was affected even more deeply than religion by the reaction against eighteenth-century thought. A German professor, Immanuel Kant, was a key figure in the shift away from the outlook of the Enlightenment. Born in Prussia, he spanned in his long lifetime (1724–1804) the confident period of science and rationalism as well as the aftermath of disenchantment. His keen, analytical mind, coupled with a profound moral and religious sense, gave his philosophy its special shape.

Deeply impressed by the achievements of Newtonian science (pp. 362–363), Kant retained much of its belief in observation and reason, but he marked off areas of knowledge where religion and moral conviction applied. It was the skepticism of the eighteenth-century Scottish philosopher David Hume that first awakened Kant to the limitations of reason and observation as means of knowing. Hume had argued that science has no way of proving that one event *causes* another; it can only note that one event *is regularly followed* by another. This sequence may be

The Polish Prometheus An eagle wearing the insignia of the Russian Empire claws at the body of a Polish patriot after a failed nationalist uprising in 1831, just as in the Greek myth an eagle sent by Zeus tore daily at Prometheus, bringer of enlightenment to the human race. This painting by the French artist Horace Vernet condemns Russia for crushing the Polish forces of progress. But it also implies that just as Prometheus was finally unbound, so one day Poland—and other oppressed nations—will be free.
Akg-images

witnessed over and over again; yet the idea of causation remains a suggestion of the mind, not a proven fact.

Kant went further, asserting that even the objects that we perceive are a reflection of the mind. Kant criticized Locke's belief that knowledge comes from experience, received through the senses (pp. 365–366). He insisted that our minds, independent of experience, establish certain internal structures, which impose their patterns on our perceptions. For example, we have the concept of "time"—which cannot be perceived and is therefore a mental "construction," not something we actually experience. Yet this concept, along with many others, controls and puts in order all our observations.

From this, Kant concluded that scientific knowledge, though highly useful, is not knowledge of the "real" world but a creation of the human mind. While science thus provides a restricted means of knowing about material things, it cannot even ask questions about such issues as the existence of God, immortality of the soul, and moral responsibility. In these

> **"I had therefore to remove knowledge, in order to make room for belief."**
>
> —Immanuel Kant

vital matters, Kant declared in his *Critique of Pure Reason* (1781), the individual must rely chiefly on conscience and intuition.

Hegel: The Dialectic of History

In the early nineteenth century, another Prussian professor, Georg Wilhelm Friedrich Hegel (**HEY-guhl**), responded to the doubts and contradictions current among thinkers by trying to reconcile opposing philosophical tendencies within a unified system. To do so, he steeped himself in the study of history, convinced that true understanding of any subject—whether

historicism
The idea that the true understanding of any subject can be found only through examining its historical development.

Zeitgeist
Spirit of the Age, which according to Hegel inspires the entire politics, art, and religion of an era and is itself the fulfillment of a divine and logical Idea.

dialectic
Hegel's notion of the conflict of opposing ideas—the *thesis* and *antithesis*—that leads to a higher idea—the *synthesis*.

Romanticism
A cultural movement that stressed the limits of reason and observation as ways of knowing the world, and that valued emotion, imagination, community, and spontaneity.

politics, art, or religion—can be found only through examining its historical development. (This idea came to be known as **historicism**.) He saw the general history of an era as more than a collection of events; politics, art, and religion are related parts of a whole—guided by a unifying Reason, or Spirit of the Age (in German, *Zeitgeist*—TSAHYT-gahyst), which is itself the fulfillment in time of a divine and logical Idea.

The Idea may be invisible to most individuals before it takes shape as historical happening. Hegel illustrates this point by declaring, "Great revolutions which strike the eye at a glance [like the French Revolution] must have been preceded by a quiet and secret revolution in the Spirit of the Age, a revolution not visible to every eye. . . . It is a lack of acquaintance with this spiritual revolution which makes the resulting changes astonishing." The human individual, so precious to the philosophes, was reduced by Hegel to a relatively minor role in history. Great leaders, acting on their own purposes and passions, can nevertheless accomplish notable deeds by identifying themselves with a developing idea. In this way, Hegel would explain the greatness of a Caesar, a Jefferson, or a Napoleon.

Hegel's thought is related to that of Plato, with its Doctrine of Ideas (p. 73). Hegel's special contribution was his development of the notion of **dialectic**—the conflict of opposing forces—in history. He defined those forces as opposing ideas, which become ever more inclusive at successive stages of the struggle. The dominant idea at any given stage he defined as the *thesis*, which (because it is imperfect and incomplete) calls forth a negative or opposing idea—its *antithesis*. In the conflict between the two, neither is entirely destroyed; the opposing elements are reconciled and absorbed into a higher idea, the *synthesis*.

As an example of his theory, Hegel suggested that the idea of "oriental despotism" (embodied in such ancient states as Persia) had been opposed by the Greco-Roman idea of limited freedom; both were being superseded by the "German-Christian" idea of universal freedom. This freedom, however, was an ordered freedom governed by law, and therefore, it could only exist within the state, which Hegel believed was approaching perfection in the Prussian monarchy of his day.

Hegel discarded the eighteenth-century concept of progress as naïve. Instead, he insisted that history provides its own solu-

tions to problems that even the wisest of thinkers can understand only dimly. All the same, he regarded the dialectic of history as leading surely to a freer and happier condition for humanity. (This condition would not include equality for women, whom he regarded as, by nature, inferior to men.)

Hegel's thought was a blend of many elements that had previously been regarded as contradictory. It assigned value, on the one hand, to science, reason, and individual freedom—and on the other hand, to faith, intuition, and authority. As might be expected, this comprehensive philosophy had a broad appeal: Hegel's books provided stimulus and support for a wide range of ideas. After his death in 1831, his disciples branched off in many directions.

LO² The Romantic Spirit in Literature, Art, and Music

The reaction against the Enlightenment showed itself not only in philosophy but also in **Romanticism** in the arts. The Romantic movement included an extraordinary variety of creative expressions in the life and work of individual artists, some of whom were political and social conservatives, while others were supporters of liberalism.

Romanticism in Literature

The pioneer of Romanticism, as well as the inspirer of the ideals of the French Revolution (p. 388), was Jean-Jacques Rousseau. Though he lived during the Enlightenment, Rousseau was in many ways a rebel against it. A man of little formal education or personal discipline, Rousseau reacted spontaneously against the eighteenth-century emphasis on reason and science. Through a stormy career, which we know largely through his own *Confessions*, he found time to write hundreds of letters, as well as essays and books.

Rousseau's Appeal to the Heart

Rousseau's attacks on rationalism struck home because of the power of his language and his appeal to inner experience. Science, he declared, gives people knowledge that they are better off without. The only knowledge worth having is knowledge of virtue (moral goodness)—and for this, science is not needed. The principles of virtue are "engraved on every heart."

Readers who were unmoved by the theories of science and philosophy responded warmly to Rousseau's emotional outpourings. In his novel *The New Héloïse* (1761), the hero is madly in love with one of his pupils, but she must marry another. The two frustrated souls experience many temptations and torments that end only after the death of the heroine. The theme of passion and suffering became a mark of Romantic prose and poetry in the nineteenth century. Another theme of *The New Héloïse* is Rousseau's criticism of sophisticated society and his glorification of nature. The hero of the novel seeks relief from his anguish by wandering through a wilderness. This provides the author with an opportunity to fashion eloquent word pictures of lakes, mountains, and flowers, which inspired such Romantic nature poets as William Wordsworth.

Rousseau's individualism and his rejection of imposed patterns of behavior are best expressed in his novel *Émile* (1762). From infancy to manhood, the fictional Émile is cared for and taught in a manner contrary to the educational practices of the eighteenth century. Rather than forcing the boy into a succession of studies, his teacher encourages Émile to learn for himself. When the need or desire strikes him, the youngster asks for instruction in reading, writing, and nature studies. Meanwhile, he lives a spare, simple, athletic life in the country. The teacher refrains from punishing his pupil for destructive acts, confident that such errors will be corrected through the boy's own experience of consequent loss. There are no naturally bad boys; real vices are learned from "civilized" elders.

Rousseau held that girls as well as boys deserved a sound education. But it must be suited to the female role in life, which he sharply distinguished from the male role. In *Émile*, he states that girls should be taught only what they will need as women, namely:

> To please men, be useful to them, and make themselves loved and respected by them; to educate them when they are young, care for them when grown, counsel and console them, and make life agreeable and sweet to them. . . . The search for abstract and speculative truths, principles, and scientific laws is beyond the capacity of women; all their studies therefore ought to be of a practical sort.

Rousseau's permissiveness appealed to Romantic individualists and impressed a number of educational reformers. His religious sentiments, too, influenced succeeding generations. His was a Romantic brand of Deism (p. 364), rejecting theology and sacred books. As taught to Émile, this religion consisted of a simple faith in God and immortality. All that needs to be known about the deity and his commandments, wrote Rousseau, can be found in one's heart and in the study of nature.

Rousseau's insistence on the divinity and beauty of nature and on unrestricted human emotion was echoed by the writers of the early nineteenth century, and their typical means of expression was lyric poetry. As a literary form, lyric poetry traces back to ancient Greece—to Solon and Sappho (pp. 68–69). It was perfectly suited to the needs of Romantic writers, who desired to tell others of their innermost feelings and visions. Prose forms, especially the novel, also flourished, but many leading novelists were also poets.

English Romantic Writers

William Wordsworth was one of the first Romantic poets; his most moving verses deal with the excitement and meaning of wild nature. But Wordsworth sensed something beyond the colors and movements of a landscape. His perceptions of nature opened the way to moral and spiritual insights, and partly for this reason, he shared Rousseau's contempt for formal learning as well as his passion for nature. In "The Tables Turned," he wrote:

> Books! 'tis a dull and endless strife:
> Come, hear the woodland linnet,
> How sweet his music! on my life,
> There's more of wisdom in it. . . .
> One impulse from a vernal wood
> May teach you more of man,
> Of moral evil and of good,
> Than all the sages can.

Beauty, youth, and rebellion were common themes of three other poets—Keats, Byron, and Shelley—each of whom died young. John Keats saluted the ancient Greek ideal of beauty in a poem honoring a painted vase ("Ode on a Grecian Urn," 1820). Addressing this ancient work of art, Keats concludes with these words:

> When old age shall this generation waste,
> Thou shalt remain, in midst of other woe
> Than ours, a friend to man, to whom thou say'st,
> "Beauty is truth, truth beauty,"—that is all
> Ye know on earth, and all ye need to know.

Lord Byron (George Noel Gordon) lived a turbulent life of passion and adventure, corresponding to the Romantic quality of his writings. He died in 1824 at the age of thirty-six while taking part in the Greek war for independence from the Turks. In his poem *Don Juan* he proclaims his admiration for youth and his contempt for life "after thirty":

> "Whom the gods love die young" was said of yore,
> And many deaths do they escape by this:
> The death of friends, and that which slays even more—
> death of friendship, love, youth, all that is,
> Except mere breath; and since the silent shore
> Awaits at last even those who longest miss
> The old archer's shafts, perhaps the early grave
> Which men weep over may be meant to save.

Byron's young friend, Percy Bysshe Shelley, also lived an unconventional life—devoted to the cause of unrestricted personal freedom. Expelled from Oxford University because of his open profession of atheism, Shelley continued to rebel against all forms of authority. He spent his last years in Italy, where he composed his most eloquent poems. In one of these ("Hellas," 1822), he ends by expressing anguish over the human sufferings of the past and hope that a better world may be dawning (signaled by the Greek war for independence):

> Oh, cease! must hate and death return?
> Cease! must men kill and die?
> Cease! drain not to its dregs the urn
> Of bitter prophecy.
> The world is weary of the past,
> Oh, might it die or rest at last!

Shortly after writing this poem, at age thirty, Shelley drowned while sailing in the Mediterranean Sea.

Yet another English Romantic writer who died young was Emily Brontë. She and her sister Charlotte are best known as the authors of two of the most popular and widely read novels in the English language, Charlotte's *Jane Eyre* and Emily's *Wuthering Heights*. But Emily was also a poet of such Romantic themes as love and loss, the longing for death, and nature echoing human passions. In a poem of praise to God, she proclaims the Romantic belief that God and nature and human souls are all one and exist in and for each other:

> Though earth and man were gone
> And suns and universes ceased to be
> And Thou wert left alone
> Every existence would exist in Thee.

Emily's Romantic gift for making nature echo feeling appears also in *Wuthering Heights*. At the end of her tale of love and vengeance persisting through the generations, the fictional narrator tells how he heard of rumors that the ghosts of Catherine Earnshaw and Heathcliff walk the moorlands where their passion for each other played out. He visits the graveyard where both of them lie buried. "I lingered round them, under that benign sky: watched the moths fluttering among the heath and harebells, listened to the soft wind breathing through the grass, and wondered how any one could ever imagine unquiet slumbers for the sleepers in that quiet earth."

> *"The world is weary of the past, / Oh, might it die or rest at last!"*
>
> —Percy Bysshe Shelley

Goethe

In Germany, the leading literary figure was Johann Wolfgang von Goethe (**GUH-tuh**). Born in the middle of the eighteenth century, he grew up during the Enlightenment and lived on into the age of Romanticism. Goethe came from a well-to-do family of lawyers and administrators; his conversion to Romanticism took place while he was studying law at Strasbourg. He later became a member of the court of Saxe-Weimar, a small German duchy. He remained for most of his life in Weimar (**VAHY-mahr**), the capital of the duchy, where the duke's generosity allowed him freedom to study, travel, and write.

A man of high intelligence and feeling, Goethe wrote beyond the limitations of most Romantic authors. But his personal life was notably romantic—a series of passionate love affairs, many of which he described in his writings. Goethe's lyric poetry reflects his fascination with love, nature, and death. In prose, the most striking expression of his youthful Romanticism is *The Sorrows of Young Werther* (1774), which describes the extravagant sufferings of a forlorn hero tortured by frustrated passion.

Faust, a dramatic poem on which Goethe worked during most of his long life, parallels the conflicts and growth that took place in his personal development. Part One, published in 1808, retells the Renaissance legend of a learned professor, Doctor Faust, who bargained his soul with the devil in return for youth and power. Part Two, which was not published until after the author's death in 1832, carries Faust on a kind of philosophical excursion in search of man's ultimate purpose and way to hap-piness. The soul of the hero, in Goethe's poem, is saved at last because he loves God and humanity and tries, in spite of errors, to serve both. Goethe's Faust is a literary model of the "modern" individual who seeks to understand and experience the lowest and the highest and to harmonize sensual and spiritual urges.

Rebellion and Romance in Painting

In the era of the French Revolution, neoclassicism proclaimed the glory of the ruling power in the same way that Baroque art had earlier done. Jacques-Louis David, the painter of *The Oath of the Horatii* (p. 371), in the last years of the Old Regime, was elected to the National Convention and reached the height of his influence under Napoleon. The emperor thought neoclassicism suitable to his role as a "modern Caesar" and wanted the art and architecture of his reign to be different from the Baroque and Rococo styles of earlier French rulers. As "First Painter of the Empire," David made portraits of the emperor, supervised the national galleries, arranged imperial ceremonies, and saw to the licensing of artists who wished to exhibit their works.

After Napoleon's fall, neoclassicism remained influential in both art and architecture; Louis XVIII admired David in spite of his past and offered him a post as court painter, though David preferred to spend the rest of his life in Brussels, painting less political subjects. Already during the revolutionary era, however—and partly inspired by its turmoil and savagery—a reaction began against the values of the eighteenth century in the visual arts, as earlier in philosophy and literature.

Rebels Against Neoclassicism: Goya, Delacroix

One of the earliest rebels was Francisco Goya, a Spanish contemporary of David. His painting *The Third of May, 1808, at Madrid* (see photo) shows a scene from Napoleon's invasion of Spain. French soldiers are carrying out a reprisal for an attack by civilians the previous day, and Goya focuses on a single moment of horror. A group of prisoners, defiant, terrified, and prayerful, faces a firing squad. A minute before, they were among the background figures; in the foreground, we see what will become of them in another second. The executioners and their victims do not seem to be consciously posed, as in a Baroque or neoclassical painting, but in fact the picture is carefully arranged: the night sky, the buildings and hillside, and the line of soldiers bar the viewer's eye from escaping the central scene. In an era of revolutionary violence, Goya has depicted with extraordinary honesty man's inhumanity to man.

The Romantic style achieved its fullest expression in France during the generation after Napoleon's downfall. Its most brilliant exponent was Eugène Delacroix (**duh-la-KRWAH**). He was trained in the neoclassical style, but soon became an enthusiastic convert to the new style. "If by Romanticism is meant the free

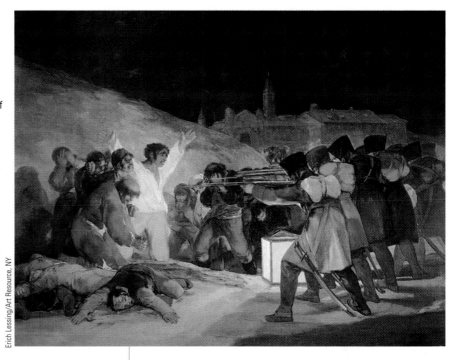

The Third of May, 1808, at Madrid
Goya never saw the scene depicted here, and he painted it six years later, as he told the Spanish government after the French armies had retreated, to "perpetuate by the means of his brush the most notable and heroic actions of our glorious insurrection against the Tyrant of Europe." But he created a scene that was not just pro-Spanish or anti-French, but a pitiless indictment of human cruelty in general.

expression of my personal feelings, my aloofness from the standardized types of paintings prescribed by the Schools, and my dislike of academic formulas," he wrote later, "I must confess that not only am I a Romantic but that I already was one at the age of fifteen!"

Delacroix excelled in the Romantic art of creating "atmosphere." In his historical painting *The Entry of the Crusaders into Constantinople* (see photo), like Goya, he depicts a grim event—in this case, the conquest of the city in the Fourth Crusade (pp. 217–218). But actual brutality is only the background to a menacing group of horsemen advancing on cowering Greeks. The sky is smoke-filled, the horsemen drag captives along, and the foremost horse—no noble beast in the tradition of equestrian images (see photo on page 299)—viciously threatens two

 Met Museum's Illustrated Thematic Essay on Romanticism in Painting (http://www.metmuseum.org/toah/hd/roma/hd_roma.htm) Learn more about Romanticism in the visual arts.

captives. Delacroix leaves the viewer to imagine what exactly may happen next, but everything suggests that it will not be good.

The Sublimity of Nature: Turner, Constable

The love of nature, which was a central feature of Romanticism, was best expressed in painting by the British artists J. M. W. Turner and John Constable. Turner's paintings are visionary rather than realistic. *The Fighting Téméraire* (see photo on page 408), painted in 1839, shows a scene that moved British patriots: the *Téméraire*, a sailing ship of Admiral Nelson's battle fleet, is being towed away to the breaker's yard. It is led to its inglorious fate by a squat black tug, symbol of the triumph of steam over sail, iron over timber, efficiency over beauty. But the painting also expresses the Romantic theme of the "sublime"—the awesome vastness of nature, of which humans and their doings are only a tiny part. The sailing ship fades into the sky above it, and the steam tug merges with its reflection in the sea. The scene is dominated, symbolically, by the setting sun and the glow

<< *The Entry of the Crusaders into Constantinople* Delacroix's painting is full of menace, conveyed in the Romantic manner not only by the actions and gestures of the conquerors and their victims but by scenery itself: against the background of a troubled sky and a sunlit city, the crusaders form a dark mass advancing upon the Greeks.

>> *The Fighting Téméraire* Though British-built, this ship had been given the name of a captured French warship ("Bold"), and it had acquired the nickname "Fighting" because it had been in the thick of the Battle of Trafalgar (p. 395). Now the gallant ship is fading into a glorious sunset that pervades both sea and sky. As with Delacroix's crusaders, in Turner's painting the scenery is part of the event.

that it casts over sky and sea. Turner's imaginative treatment of the sublimity of nature proved extremely popular; he sold hundreds of paintings and etchings and built up a fortune during his lifetime.

Turner's contemporary John Constable approached nature in a different manner. His love of the English countryside was akin to that of his good friend, the poet Wordsworth, but he studied nature with the eye of a scientist. His paintings were so

The Hay Wain "Constable is one of the glories of England. He is a genuine reformer, who has broken free of the well-trodden paths of earlier landscape painters." That was the verdict of Delacroix, who repainted the sky in one of his own paintings after he saw the sky in this painting at an exhibition in Paris.

strikingly different from the commonplace studio landscapes of the period that they created a sensation at first showing. When *The Hay Wain* (see photo) was exhibited in Paris in 1821, French painters were astonished by its truth to nature, and many set out to imitate Constable's technique.

Constable referred to Turner's works as "airy visions, painted with tinted steam," whereas he wanted nature to speak for itself, without artificial effects: "The sound of water escaping from mill dams, willows, old rotten planks, slimy posts and brickwork, I love such things. These scenes made me a painter." Limiting his subject matter almost entirely to rural scenes, he painted rich canvases with people and animals fitting into a larger landscape. *The Hay Wain*, with its carefully depicted wain (wagon), its farmhands, horses, and dog, its cottage and field with ripening crops, is a more human scene than Turner's misty seascape. But above there stretches a wide sky with billowing clouds whose light is reflected and transformed in countless ways by the details of the scene below—in accordance with Constable's belief that the sky is "the key note, the standard scale, and the chief organ of sentiment." For Constable, humans are very much a part of nature's larger harmony.

The Gothic Revival in Architecture

In the nineteenth century, architectural style became more and more a matter of individual taste or fancy. This was a time of vast activity in construction,

especially in the industrial cities; most of the older buildings still standing in Europe today were erected during the nineteenth century. They represent a variety of styles springing from several architectural revivals. The architect sometimes aimed at a "pure" style, sometimes at a mixed one, and sometimes at an original design. But by midcentury, certain associations had developed: banks and government buildings, for instance, were usually built in the neoclassical manner; churches and colleges, in the Gothic.

Of the various styles, the Gothic is most often associated with Romanticism. The **Gothic revival** first appeared in Britain before the French Revolution, as a reaction to the neoclassical architectural style. After the turn of the nineteenth century, the Romantic Movement gave new force to the Gothic revival. The outstanding example of this period is the Houses of Parliament in London (see photo). When the old building burned down in 1834, the lawmakers, remembering that British liberties and Parliament itself traced back to the thirteenth century, decided to rebuild it in the medieval style. No medieval government building had looked so impressively regular and symmetrical as this one, however. Three hundred years of Baroque and neoclassical architecture had inspired the instinctive belief that to express the pride of nations, buildings had to be orderly in appearance. Like the Renaissance revivers of Roman architecture before them, the Romantic revivers of Gothic architecture adapted an earlier style to ideas and needs of their own time.

> "*The sky is 'the key note, the standard scale, and the chief organ of sentiment.'*"
>
> —John Constable

the Romantic spirit, and his later works are marked by heightened drama, suspense, and brilliant climaxes. Beethoven never lost control of his musical themes, however, and he followed established musical forms throughout most of his life; his works throb with energy but are contained within an orderly pattern.

Orchestral compositions in the Romantic style called for more volume and range of sound than earlier works; Beethoven's orchestra was nearly twice the size of Haydn's. Although few new instruments were introduced—with the notable exception of the modern piano—the number of strings, winds, and percussion instruments was enlarged. Melodies were highly expressive and original, harmonies were rich and often **dissonant**, and rhythms were subject to sudden or subtle changes.

Leading Romantic composers were an Austrian, Franz Schubert; a Pole, Frederic Chopin (**SHOH-pan**); a Frenchman, Hector Berlioz; and a Russian, Peter Ilich Tchaikovsky (**chahy-KAWF-skee**). The high point of Romanticism, however, appeared not in the symphony hall but in the opera house. Richard Wagner (**VAHG-ner**), born

Gothic revival
An architectural style of the nineteenth century that borrowed from the medieval Gothic but with more symmetry and regularity.

dissonant
Creating a sense of tension, instability, and unrest.

Romanticism in Music: Beethoven, Wagner

The eighteenth-century classical style in music stressed order, grace, and clarity; the nineteenth century cast off restraint and released the emotional power of music. The classical style did not disappear altogether, but it was submerged in the tide of Romanticism. Ludwig van Beethoven, born in the western German city of Bonn in 1770, bridged both styles. His early works are similar to those of Haydn and Mozart, but he responded to

>> **The Houses of Parliament** At the far end, stretching away from the clock tower (Big Ben, with its "hoarse"-sounding chime produced by a crack in the bell) is the House of Commons; at the near end, in line with the House of Commons, is the House of Lords. On the side farthest from the River Thames is the medieval Westminster Hall; the rest of the Houses of Parliament is a single nineteenth-century building, intended to proclaim the power and antiquity of the British constitutional monarchy.
London Aerial Photo Library/Corbis

in the German city of Leipzig in 1813, created a new concept of opera—or music-drama, as he preferred to call it. He stressed above all the Romantic idea of the unity of thought and feeling and believed that this unity should be reflected in all art forms. He had contempt for art as mere entertainment or spectacle—"effects without cause." His new kind of opera, which was modeled on the performances of Greek tragedy (pp. 70–71), joined poetry, music, scenery, and action into one unified whole.

Wagner's "Ring cycle," a sequence of operas drawn from Germanic legend, best illustrates his idea of form. Here the drama—which is concerned with the curse of gold and the lust for power—is central. Voices and orchestra combine to carry forward the powerful themes; instead of writing separate speeches, arias, choruses, and accompaniments, Wagner created an "endless melody" out of all the musical elements. His music is rich and complex, full of passion and suspense, wholly Romantic.

 **Excerpts from LA Opera Production of** *Das Rheingold* (http://www.losangelesopera.com/production/0809/rheingold/index.aspx) View excerpts from the first opera in Wagner's ring cycle (3:10)

Italian opera, too, reflected the new stress on emotion and the enlarged capabilities of the orchestra. Giuseppe Verdi (VAIR-dee), Wagner's artistic rival, is probably the most successful of operatic composers; his spectacular *Aïda* (ah-EE-duh) has been performed more often than any other opera. Verdi chose plots that focused on the most elemental human feelings and set them to thrilling vocal music. A political activist, he also used stories in his operas that inspired the rising desire for liberty and nationhood in Italy.

 NPR Music's Introduction to Verdi's *Aïda* (http://www.npr.mobi/templates/story/story.php?storyId=112115431) Listen to the story of Verdi's Aïda.

LO³ The Spread of Liberal Democracy and Nationalism

The defeat of revolutionary France and the conservative reaction that followed slowed the momentum of liberal and national revolution, but in the long run, could not reverse it. The forces of change were too strong to contain. These included the resentment of the middle classes against absolutism and privilege, continued deprivation among the urban poor, the growing discontent of eastern European serfs, and the appeal of liberal Romantic ideas to educated young people of all classes. On the other side, the conservative rulers, divided by traditional power rivalries and inclined to waver between repression and reform as the best way of preventing renewed violent revolution, were not so united and determined as they seemed. Down to 1871, the nineteenth century saw the gradual crumbling of conservative resistance and the emergence of a new Europe, dominated by the hopes and ideals—and the ambitions and rivalries—of liberalism and nationalism.

Revolution and Reform

In the first decade after the Congress of Vienna, most liberal and nationalist uprisings in Europe were quickly suppressed (as in Naples, Spain, and Russia). Revolutionary successes were achieved only in Greece (against the Ottoman Turks; pp. 251–252) and overseas, where the Spanish and Portuguese colonies in Latin America gained their independence by 1825. But the European struggle began to turn with the victory of liberal forces in France in 1830.

Even with the restoration of the Bourbon king, Louis XVIII, in 1814, France had preserved the principal reforms introduced by the revolution and Napoleon. Louis reigned as a constitutional monarch, with a legislature that represented the restored nobility and well-to-do members of the business class—an arrangement close to what the moderate bourgeois had sought in 1789. It was threatened in 1824, however, when Louis was succeeded by his brother, Charles X.

As Count of Artois, Charles had been a leader of the émigrés who had urged other European nobles and princes to attack revolutionary France after 1789. After becoming king, he and his reactionary friends moved to turn back the clock. They sought to require the government to make annual payments to nobles whose lands had been confiscated during the revolution, and they favored a return of clerical influence in education and politics. Charles himself, proud and stubborn, was contemptuous of the popular criticism his measures caused. When the elective Chamber of Deputies refused, in 1830, to bend to his will, Charles dissolved the Chamber, censored the press, and changed voting rights to strengthen the power of the nobles.

The French Revolution of 1830

Paris responded to this revival of absolutism by throwing up barricades in the streets. The "July Revolution" of 1830 lasted only a few days, for the troops and police refused to fire on the populace. Charles, who had no desire to share the fate of Louis XVI, promptly abdicated and left for England. The rebels now found themselves divided on what to do next. The workmen, students, and intellectuals who had hoisted the revolutionary tricolor (red, white, and blue flag) at the city hall demanded that the monarchy give way to a republic. The bourgeois politicians, however, opposed such a change, feeling that their interests would be safer under a constitutional monarchy. All they wanted was a different kind of king, one who would serve their purposes. The politicians found such a man in Prince Louis-Philippe, who, though a member of the Bourbon family, had fought on the side of the revolution in the 1790s before the Jacobins took power. They persuaded an aged and respected national hero, the Marquis de Lafayette, to support Louis-Philippe. This helped to make the "left-wing" Bourbon prince acceptable to those who wanted a republic.

The reign of Louis-Philippe brought a modest extension of liberal and democratic practices. Though the number of voters was still only a small fraction of the total citizenry, it was double what it had been before. The chief significance of the July Revolution was that it decisively ended the threat of counterrevolution in France and shattered the principle of legitimacy, hallowed at Vienna in 1815—Louis-Philippe became king upon the invitation of an elected Chamber of Deputies. The French thus struck a blow against the Metternich System, and their success encouraged liberals and patriots elsewhere.

The European Revolutions of 1830

The first uprising outside France occurred in the Low Countries. Ever since the Reformation, this territory had been divided between Holland in the north, and a southern part that had belonged first to the Spanish and then to the Austrian Habsburgs (pp. 324, 325). The two halves had been reunited by decision of the Congress of Vienna, in hopes that they would jointly serve as a barrier to the French. But the north was mainly Protestant, while the south was mainly Catholic, and had a large French-speaking population that resented the required use of the Dutch language.

Discontent with the Dutch king, William I, led to street riots in Brussels shortly after the July uprising in France. At first, the southern leaders demanded only local self-rule, but when William took up arms against them, they declared for complete independence, and with French and British backing, they managed to hold off the Dutch. Finally, in 1831 an international conference in London provided for an independent country, with a German prince as constitutional monarch. The new country was named Belgium (after the Belgae, a people who had lived there in Roman times), and its independence and neutrality were guaranteed by the major powers.

Polish patriots, meanwhile, had tried and failed to regain the independence they had lost to Russia, Austria, and Prussia in the eighteenth century (p. 376). At the Congress of Vienna, most of Poland had been given over to Russian control as a separate kingdom—under the personal rule of Tsar Alexander I. Early in 1831, the Polish assembly of nobles (the Diet) rejected Alexander's successor Nicholas I as their king; Nicholas sent a large army and crushed the brave but divided Polish forces (see photo on page 403). Revolutionary stirrings were also put down by force in 1830 in various parts of Germany and Italy. But the widespread agitations demonstrated that liberal and nationalist forces were rising throughout Europe, kept in check only by political repression and military measures.

Liberal Reform in Britain

Liberal ideas and practices made a striking advance in Britain, where substantial change could be brought about through legislation. Already during the 1820s, Parliament moved away from a mercantilist economy toward free international trade. It also gave to Catholics and dissenting Protestants political rights equal to those of

Political Reform Comes to Great Britain, with a Nobleman's Support Read a fiery argument for the Reform Bill.

Anglicans. But the most significant single act was the Reform Bill of 1832, which altered the voting franchise and the system of representation in the House of Commons.

The act assigned seats to growing industrial cities at the expense of "rotten boroughs" and "pocket boroughs"—tiny places with a few easily bribed or intimidated voters. The individual right to vote remained tied to property ownership, but more lenient requirements almost doubled the number of eligible voters to about 800,000 adult males. The new voters were chiefly of the middle class; the Reform Bill raised its share of power in the Commons to roughly that of the landed gentry (p. 340). It also opened the door to further liberal and democratic reforms during the ensuing decades, though it was almost a century before the vote was extended to women. Although the British achieved this transformation without revolution or civil war, at critical moments the threat of violence was no doubt decisive. In 1832, for example, the Reform Bill was driven through Parliament under the pressure of street demonstrations and signs of possible insurrection.

Some of these pressures came from the British "Radicals" of the time, who wanted to go far beyond the liberals in overhauling British society and politics. The Radicals—chiefly from the working class, along with some of the new industrialists like Robert Owen (p. 442)—were both philosophical and action-minded. Inspired by such older writers as the American Tom Paine and their own countryman Jeremy Bentham (p. 414), they demanded radical changes in voting laws, Parliament, courts, prisons, the Anglican Church, and the privileges of the House of Lords. Many of these changes were brought about later in Britain. But for the time being, in 1832, the controlling powers in Parliament showed enough skill to permit mild reforms rather than face the risk of rebellion.

The French Revolution of 1848

On the European continent, the strongholds of privilege proved more unbending. Rather than submit to change or attempt to guide its course, the conservatives generally sought to repress it. Liberal and nationalist discontent continued to build up, however, and another and more widespread series of explosions came in 1848 (see Map 21.2).

In France, Louis-Philippe, the "citizen-king," had become exceedingly unpopular. The critics of the government fell into two groups: the radicals, heirs to the Jacobins of the 1790s, who wanted to discard the monarchy and establish a republic with universal voting rights, and the liberals, who wanted only a limited extension of voting rights. Had Louis-Philippe yielded to the liberals, he could have gained broader support and kept his crown. But he stubbornly rejected any constitutional change, and in February 1848, the streets of Paris bristled once again with barricades.

Once again the royal troops refused to march against the people, and the king sensibly sailed for England. The victors were again split between monarchists and republicans, but this time the disagreement developed into deeper civil conflict. The republican leaders of Paris were concerned about social as well as political reforms. They spoke for the growing number of workers who had been drawn into the capital. The victims of low income, insecurity, and poor working conditions, the workers were generally anticapitalist and antibourgeois.

In 1848, the republicans in Paris overcame monarchist opposition and forced the proclamation of a republic. They then arranged for the election, by a universal male vote, of a Constituent Assembly to frame a new constitution for France. The Assembly, which met in May, no doubt represented the sentiment of the nation as a whole, which was much less radical than Paris. It favored democratic political changes but no substantial social or economic reforms. This view was assailed by the aroused workers of the city, most of whom wanted the government to establish industrial workshops as a means of providing employment.

Fearing that the majority of the Assembly would reject their demands, groups of workers attacked it, and yet again the barricades went up (see photo). This time, however, the result was very different. An ugly class war started in Paris, and some 10,000 people were killed or wounded in several days of bloody street fighting. The regular army, called upon to defend the Assembly, crushed the revolt and thereby earned the bitterness of most of the urban workers. The bourgeois, for their part, were shaken by the threat of social revolution.

After those bloody "June Days," the Constituent Assembly drafted a new constitution that provided for a legislature and a president with strong powers. Presidential elections were soon held, and the victory went to the candidate who promised the most to both sides in the civil struggle.

Prince Louis Napoleon Bonaparte, a nephew of the famous Corsican, represented himself as standing for both social order and social change. Capitalizing on his family name, he swamped his rivals and became president. Three years later, he brought about the dissolution of the legislature and had himself elected for a new term of ten years. In 1852, this shrewd politician proclaimed himself emperor; since the original Napoleon had had a son, also Napoleon, who had died in 1832, the new emperor took the title of Napoleon III.

The Austrian and German Revolutions of 1848

The cycle of revolution and counterrevolution was repeated beyond the borders of France. In central Europe, liberal demands were mixed with nationalist hopes. Revolutionists rushed into the streets in a dozen capitals, proclaiming political rights and calling for the unity and independence of their own national groups. Monarchs and ruling classes were at first frightened by these demonstrations and generally responded by offering concessions or new constitutions. But the protesting movements lacked the internal cohesion and the organized force

Urban Warfare On June 25, 1848, a dweller on the Rue Saint-Maur in central Paris made this daguerreotype (early photograph) of barricades of cobblestones neatly piled up by insurgents in readiness for street battle. To overcome such well-built defenses, a contemporary account said, the army "marched up with cannon to each barricade, and once its strength loosened, charged at the bayonet, killing all whom they found either in arms, or with their faces blackened with powder." That was what happened here on June 26.
Giraudon/The Bridgeman Art Library

Map 21.2 Revolutions of 1848–1849

Earlier revolutions had usually broken out in one country at a time, but in the charged atmosphere of Europe after 1815, revolutions spread fast. In 1848, the collapse of the French monarchy led to outbreaks in cities across Germany, Italy, and the Austrian Empire, where both middle-class people and urban workers called for government and social reform and for national liberation and unification. They mostly failed to achieve their aims, but they set the pattern for future change in Europe. © Cengage Learning

Interactive Map

needed to hold their gains. When it became clear that they could be stopped by military action, the authorities recovered their poise, withdrew their concessions, and put down the rebels with troops and police.

Nevertheless, the movements of 1848 had significant consequences. The Austrian Empire felt the greatest shock, a warning of things to come. Until 1848, Prince Metternich had remained the outstanding leader of "legitimacy" and conservatism. Yet a liberal uprising in Vienna so unnerved him that he hurriedly resigned as imperial chancellor and departed for London. Within two years, imperial troops had suppressed the disturbances in the Habsburg domains, and Metternich could return to Vienna to write his memoirs. But he was no longer in power, and the Metternich System was broken. Furthermore, to ensure the loyalty of the vast peasant majority in its realm, the Austrian monarchy actually upheld one liberal reform, the abolition of serfdom. Russia was now the only major country where the peasants were still not free.

Nationalist aspirations, though frustrated, were intensified throughout central Europe. Hungarians, Czechs, Italians, Serbs, Croats, and Romanians became more dissatisfied within the Austrian Empire. Many Germans, meanwhile, were looking toward the creation of a large united German state. The various German territories sent delegates to Frankfurt in 1848 with the aim of setting up a German federal union. Political disagreements, power rivalries, and the suspicion of the existing authorities frustrated its work, and it broke up in 1849 having achieved nothing. Nationalist sentiment had nonetheless been stirred, and within a generation, a united Germany would be created by the more "realistic" methods of diplomacy and war.

The Liberal Ideal: Mill

The hopes and ideals of the liberal movement had a long ancestry going back through the Enlightenment beliefs in natural rights, reason, and progress to the Renaissance hopes of Erasmus and

BETWEEN GERMANY AND RUSSIA: A CZECH NATIONAL LEADER REFUSES TO JOIN THE GERMAN NATION

František Palacký (**FRAHN-ti-shek PAH-lat-skee**) was a leading historian and scholar of Slav languages who was thrust into politics by the revolutions of 1848. He was a Czech, a member of the majority nation in the small central European kingdom of Bohemia. That kingdom was one of many lands that the Habsburg dynasty had acquired over the generations and formed into the empire of Austria—a multinational empire in which German and Hungarian officials and nobles traditionally wielded power over many other nations, including the Czechs.

Some Austrian lands, including Bohemia, had once also belonged to the Holy Roman Empire, and therefore became part of the German Confederation of sovereign states under local rulers ("princes" in this document), which replaced that empire in 1815. The rest of Austria lay to the south and east of the confederation's borders, on either side of the River Danube, all the way to the frontiers of the Russian and Ottoman Empires (see Map 21.1 on page 401). In 1848, German revolutionaries assembled in the city of Frankfurt, hoping to unify the confederation's member states into a single nation-state, Germany—a plan that would have involved breaking up the Austrian Empire and making the Czechs part of the self-ruling German nation. Accordingly, the Frankfurt Assembly invited Palacký to attend. In this letter, he refuses the invitation and gives his reasons.

I am unable, gentlemen, to accept your invitation for my own person, nor can I send any other "trustworthy patriot" in my stead. Permit me to give you, as briefly as possible, my reasons.

The object of your assembly is to establish a federation of the German nation in place of the existing federation of princes, to guide the nation to real unity, to strengthen the sentiment of German national consciousness and in this manner expand the power and strength of the German Reich. . . . I am not a German. . . . I am a Czech of Slavonic blood. . . . That nation is a small one, it is true, but from time immemorial it has been a nation by itself and depends upon its own strength. . . . If . . . anyone asks that, over and above this heretofore existing bond between princes, the Czech nation should now unite with the German nation, that is at the very least a novel demand, devoid of any historical or juridical basis, a

More for a just and rational society (pp. 284, 364–365). But nineteenth-century liberals were also bitterly aware that "Liberty, Equality, Fraternity" had led to bloodshed and dictatorship. They became more respectful of history than Enlightenment thinkers had been, observing that human rationality is not sufficient to overcome, in a short time, the lasting power of old institutions and habits of thought. They were also more wary of popular tyranny, concluding that the will of the majority can be as wrong and oppressive as that of a despot. Many liberals emphasized, finally, that freedom must be guided by morality if it is not to go astray.

In Britain, the leading country of peaceful liberal reform, John Stuart Mill was the foremost spokesman of this more tempered doctrine of liberalism. His conceptions of personal freedom, precisely and eloquently expressed, have had a persistent appeal to people everywhere who admire the ideal of liberty.

Mill was a follower of Jeremy Bentham, the founder of a philosophy called **utilitarianism**. According to Bentham, the most acceptable way of evaluating social institutions is to measure their total utility (usefulness) to all the affected individuals—looking to "the greatest good of the greatest number." Mill defended this view, explaining that the measurement of the "greatest good" must take into account that some goods are higher and more desirable than others. He believed that the highest goods can be reached only under conditions of personal freedom, and he set out to specify those conditions and work for their achievement. Mill's carefully reasoned essay *On Liberty* (1859) remains the classic statement of the historic liberal view of individual rights in relation to society.

The book accepts Aristotle's conviction that the purpose of human life is the harmonious development of one's abilities (p. 76). This purpose, declared Mill, requires two conditions: "freedom" and "a variety of situations." He would give to each individual, therefore, the utmost freedom in relation to society and the state. Each person's freedom he regarded as sacred: "The only purpose for which power can be rightfully

demand to which I, so far as I personally am concerned, would not feel justified in acceding until I receive an express and authentic mandate to do so. . . .

The second reason which prevents me from taking part in your deliberations is the fact that, according to all I have so far learnt of your aims and intentions as publicly proclaimed, it is your irrevocable desire and purpose to undermine Austria as an independent empire and indeed to make her impossible for all time to come—an empire whose preservation, integrity and consolidation is, and must be, a great and important matter not only for my nation but also for the whole of Europe, indeed for humanity and civilization itself. . . .

You know that in the Southeast of Europe, along the frontiers of the Russian Empire there live many nations widely differing in origin, in language, in history and in customs—Slavs, Wallachians [Romanians], Magyars [Hungarians], and Germans, not to speak of Turks and Albanians—none of whom is sufficiently powerful of itself to offer successful defiance to the superior neighbor on the East forever. They could only do so if a close and firm tie bound them all together as one. The vital artery of this necessary union of nations is the Danube. The fulcrum of power of such a union must never be moved from this river if the union is to be effective and to remain so. Assuredly if the Austrian state had not existed for ages it would have been incumbent upon us in the interests of Europe and indeed of humanity to endeavor to create it as soon as possible. . . .

. . . in the unhappy blindness that has long afflicted her, Austria has long failed to recognize the real juridical and moral basis of her existence, and has denied it; the fundamental rule, that is, that all the nationalities and all the religions under her sceptre should enjoy complete equality of rights and respect in common. The rights of nations are in truth the rights of nature. No nation on earth has the right to demand

that its neighbors should sacrifice themselves for its benefit, no nation is under an obligation to deny or sacrifice itself for the good of its neighbor. Nature knows neither dominant nor subject nations. If the bond which unites a number of diverse nations in a single political entity is to be firm and enduring, no nation must have cause to fear that the union will cost it any of the things it holds most dear. On the contrary, each must have the certain hope that in the central authority it will find defence and protection against possible violations by neighbors of the principles of equality. Then will every nation do its best to delegate to that central authority such powers as will enable it successfully to provide the aforesaid protection. I am convinced that even now it is not too late for this fundamental rule of justice, this *sacra ancora* [sacred anchor] for a vessel in danger of foundering, to be publicly and sincerely proclaimed in the Austrian Empire and energetically carried out in all sectors with the consent and support of all. . . .

. . . I must briefly express my conviction that those who ask that Austria, and with her Bohemia should unite on national lines with Germany, are demanding that she should commit suicide—a step lacking either moral or political sense. . . .

EXPLORING THE SOURCE

1. Does Palacký approve of German unification? Why does he not want the Czechs to take part in it?

2. What does Palacký think is wrong with Austria? Why does he want to reform Austria rather than seek independence for the Czech nation?

Source: S. Harrison Thomson, *Czechoslovakia in European History*, 2d ed. (Princeton, N.J.: Princeton University Press, 1953), pp. 44–46, 207–208.

exercised over any member of a civilized community, against his will, is to prevent harm to others." Mill justified this position not by resorting to Locke's doctrines of natural rights and the social contract (pp. 344–345) but on the utilitarian ground that freedom is essential to the greater happiness of the individual and the species.

He included females as well as males in his philosophical judgments. His partner in writing *On Liberty* and other major works was a woman, Harriet Taylor. A close intellectual associate for many years, she at last became his wife. Mill, unlike other writers of the nineteenth century, viewed women as equal to men in intelligence. He helped found the first woman's suffrage society in Britain in 1867 and published, soon after, *The Subjection of Women*, a persuasive statement of the case for female political rights.

Mill abhorred the drift toward large bureaucracies and cultural

 **Political Reform Taken to Its Logical Conclusion: Rights for Women** Read Mill on women's rights.

conformity. The state itself, he insisted, is worth no more than the individuals who make it up: "A State which dwarfs its men, in order that they may be more docile instruments in its hands even for beneficial purposes, will find that with small men no great thing can really be accomplished." He opposed increases in public services by government, even when done for the benefit of individuals. He preferred that citizens and groups act on their own initiative to forestall the "deadening hand" of centralized power and uniformity.

But Mill's first concern was the preservation, at any cost, of liberty of thought and discussion. This, he thought, is crucial to the health of the individual and society. He denied the right of any government, popular or despotic, to interfere with free expression: "If all mankind minus one were of one opinion, and only one person were of the contrary opinion, mankind would be no more justified in silencing that one person, than he, if he had the power, would be justified in silencing mankind." The evil of forbidding the expression of an opinion is more than the injury

utilitarianism
A philosophy that evaluates institutions and actions by considering whether they serve the "greatest good of the greatest number."

state
A territory and population under a sovereign government.

nation
A self-aware ethnic and cultural group associated with a particular territory.

statism
The view that the individual's first duty is obedience to the state.

to an individual, Mill asserted: it hurts the human race, and it hurts those who dissent from the opinion more than those who hold it. "If the opinion is right, they are deprived of the opportunity of exchanging error for truth; if wrong, they lose, what is almost as great a benefit, the clearer and livelier impression of truth, produced by its collision with error."

The Nationalist Ideal: Mazzini

Liberalism and nationalism were allied movements, but nationalists gave priority to national unity and independence over individual freedom. Except in some countries of western Europe, the boundaries of states—that is, territories and populations under sovereign governments—were not the same as those of nations—that is, self-aware ethnic and cultural groups (see Map 21.3). The Germans and the Italians lived under many more or less powerful independent rulers, and in the empires of eastern Europe—Austria, Russia, and Turkey—many subject nations lived under the rule of a single imperial power. In these nations, the desire for national unity and independence overshadowed all other aims.

Nationalists did not despise individual freedom, but the history of the freest countries—Britain, France, and the United States—seemed to show that freedom itself was rooted in the unity and independence of the nation. Unlike Mill, who took Britain's power for granted, nationalists on the European mainland did not glorify the individual, free of interference by the state; they regarded the building of a powerful state as the necessary means to full nationhood and individual realization.

The special form and tone of this idea, in the first half of the century, were expressed by the Italian patriot Giuseppe Mazzini. Though inspired by the humanitarian and egalitarian ideals of the Enlightenment, Mazzini was caught up in the Romantic and nationalist passion of his own generation. In him, the "religion of liberty" became the "region of the fatherland."

The nationalist ideal, as described by Mazzini, was linked to a concern for all humanity that originated in the Enlightenment.

> **Young Italy: A Dream of Republican and National Unity** Read Mazzini's passionate call for an Italian republic.

He set forth his feeling in a series of essays, *The Duties of Man*, written at midcentury and directed to the Italian working class. "You are men," Mazzini told his readers, "before you are citizens or fathers." The "law of life" requires that individuals embrace the whole human family in their love, confessing their faith in the unity and brotherhood of all peoples. But the lone individual, declared Mazzini, is powerless to work for the benefit of all: "The individual is too weak, and Humanity too vast." Effective action requires fraternal cooperation among individuals who can work together—those of a common language and culture—in other words, a nation. Starting with this line of reasoning, Mazzini went on to glorify the nation as divinely created for serving humanity.

Mazzini saw the independent nation as a promoter of individual liberty and equality: "A Country is a fellowship of free and equal men. . . . The law must express the general aspiration, promote the good of all, respond to a beat of the nation's heart." But in fact, the push for national strength through unity often reduced freedom, especially when freedom involved dissent from national objectives. Nationalism could readily become **statism**, as it did north of the Alps. The historian Heinrich von Treitschke (**TRAHYCH-kuh**), writing later in the century, declared that the individual's first duty is obedience to the state. This influential professor at the University of Berlin gave academic and philosophical respectability to the German drive for discipline, unification, and dominance.

> "*The law must express the general aspiration, promote the good of all, respond to a beat of the nation's heart.*"
>
> —Giuseppe Mazzini

The Achievement of National Unification

The unsuccessful liberal-nationalist uprisings of 1830 and 1848 had failed because of inadequate organization and power. It is significant that the eloquent Mazzini, who labored tirelessly to rid Italy of foreign occupation, spent most of his years as a revolutionary exile. Mazzini lived to see the achievement of a united Italy in 1870, but his liberal ideals were far from realized. Italian unification came about as part of a wider struggle that also brought about German unification and was mostly conducted not by peaceful change or popular uprisings but by wars among states.

Germany

The practical means to national unification were most forcefully demonstrated in Germany, and the consequences for Europe and the world were most profound. After the disappointment of 1848, German nationalists looked for more effective means of bringing their dreams to fulfillment, and found an ally in the Prussian monarchy—thanks to a high Prussian official, Count Otto von Bismarck.

Born into an aristocratic landowning family, Bismarck was no liberal, nor even originally a nationalist. But he was devoted to the Prussian monarchy, and became convinced that the monarchy would benefit by alliance with German nationalism.

Map 21.3 **Languages and Nations**

Today's thirty-six major European languages are mostly descended from those of the ancient Romans and of early medieval Germanic and Slavic invaders. In 1815, languages most of whose speakers lived in united and independent countries amounted to only about one-quarter of the total, but language shortly became the main mark of nationhood. In today's Europe, speakers of three-quarters of languages form independent nations. © Cengage Learning

 Interactive Map

Language groups
- Slavic
- Latin
- Hellenic
- Germanic
- Celtic
- Baltic
- Other

Language-based nationhood achieved
FRENCH By 1815
GREEK 1815–1914
CZECH 1914–present
GAELIC No independent nation

He was sure that the German princelings would never join together through their own efforts, and he had only contempt for what "the people" might accomplish. "Not by speeches and majority votes," Bismarck declared, "are the great questions of the day decided—that was the mistake of 1848 and 1849—but by iron and blood"—and if the iron and blood of Prussia's army decided the great question of German unification, then the Prussian monarchy would dominate the new state. As chief minister to the Prussian king from 1862, Bismarck acted on this conviction and sought to remove, by diplomacy and war, whatever stood in the way of German unification.

 The Prussian King Receives a Much Needed Pep Talk Learn how Bismarck convinced the Prussian king to fight for German unification.

Austria was clearly the chief obstacle, for Metternich had managed to establish and maintain Austrian dominance in central Europe. Prussia cooperated with Austria in a military campaign to take the duchies of Schleswig and Holstein (whose population was mostly German) from Danish control, but the two powers quarreled over the division of their conquests. In 1866, the new model Prussian army (p. 400) invaded Austria and its allied German states, and defeated them in no more than seven weeks. The Austrians gave up all influence over northern Germany to Prussia. Metternich's German Confederation was abolished, and Bismarck raised in its place the North German Confederation, under the presidency of the king of Prussia.

The power of the Habsburg rulers of Austria was also shaken within their multinational realm, and to help hold it together, in 1867 they granted self-rule to its largest single territory, the kingdom of Hungary. That, too, was a victory for nationalism, though Hungary was itself a multinational land in which Hungarians were a dominant minority. In any case, from now on, the Habsburg realm was known as Austria-Hungary.

It was now France's turn to be uneasy, for the French, like the Austrians, had traditionally opposed a strong and united Germany. Aggressive factions in both Prussia and France viewed a military showdown as inevitable; diplomatic maneuvering and reciprocal insults led, in 1870, to a declaration of war by France. The Franco-Prussian War was another brilliant success for the Prussian armies. Napoleon III, humiliated by defeat and capture, lost his throne, and in 1871, William I of Prussia was proclaimed the emperor of a united Germany. Four south German states, which had remained aloof from the North German Confederation, took their places in the new country (Map 21.4). Bismarck, now the imperial chancellor, had achieved the central ambitions of

his career: Prussia was supreme in Germany, and Germany was supreme in Europe.

Italy

Meanwhile, the ambitious rulers of the Italian kingdom of Sardinia had been playing the same role in unifying Italy as Prussia in Germany, with the Sardinian prime minister, Camillo di Cavour, in the role of Bismarck. Since Sardinia was not a great power like Prussia, it needed outside help—above all against Austria, since 1815 the dominant power in Italy. Cavour won the support of Austria's rivals—first of all Napoleon III's France and then, when Napoleon cooled toward Italian unification, Bismarck's Prussia. With their help, Cavour was able to bring about Sardinian takeovers of territories in northern and central Italy, notably the States of the Church (p. 264). Meanwhile, in southern Italy, he was able to win the cooperation of the nationalist insurgent leader, Giuseppe Garibaldi (see photo). By

"I Greet the First King of Italy" In 1860 the insurgent leader Giuseppe Garibaldi's forces overran southern Italy, and the Sardinian King Victor Emmanuel II's army conquered most of northern Italy. The two men met and shook hands south of Rome, and Garibaldi (on the black horse) spoke the words by which he acknowledged the king as ruler of Italy north and south. This depiction by Pietro Aldi in Siena's ancient city hall shows the encounter that Italians still revere as the modern nation's founding moment.

Map 21.4 **A New Balance of Power**

By 1871, the traditional European balance of power had been overturned (Map 18.1 on page 336). The old balance between rival dynasties had depended on keeping Germany and Italy weak and divided but not dominated by any one of their stronger neighbors. Now united Germany was the single most powerful country on Europe's mainland, dynastic rivalries were turning into national ones, and the crumbling of Ottoman rule was creating a new area of weakness and division in the Balkans. © Cengage Learning

 Interactive Map

1870, a united kingdom of Italy already existed, but the pope still ruled in Rome, protected by troops of Napoleon III. Finally, when the French troops withdrew because of the war against Prussia, the kingdom of Italy sent in forces and annexed Rome, thereby completing national unification.

Italy and Germany, both of which had been divided for centuries, now became independent members of the European state system. This would be the central fact of international relations during the years to follow. The greater power, Germany, which had achieved unity and strength by the methods of authority, discipline, and militarism, was determined to win its "place in the sun" after its late arrival as a state. The successful revolutions of national unification were thus a prelude to European and global struggle, climaxed by the First and Second World Wars.

> **❝*The successful revolutions of national unification were a prelude to European and global struggle, climaxed by the First and Second World Wars.*❞**

 Listen to a synopsis of Chapter 21.

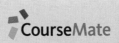

CHAPTER 22

INDUSTRIAL AND SCIENTIFIC SOCIETY, 1700–1900

LEARNING OBJECTIVES

AFTER READING THIS CHAPTER, YOU SHOULD BE ABLE TO DO THE FOLLOWING:

LO¹ Trace the Industrial Revolution from its beginnings to the present.

LO² Explain how business and economics changed as a result of the Industrial Revolution.

LO³ Discuss how labor and government challenged corporate power.

LO⁴ Identify some of the social changes that accompanied the Industrial Revolution.

LO⁵ Describe the progress of science and the emergence of the social sciences during the nineteenth century.

"FAST-MOVING TECHNICAL ADVANCE BECAME A SEEMINGLY PERMANENT FEATURE OF WESTERN CIVILIZATION."

The nineteenth century was the great turning point in the rise of the modern West. Not only the traditional power structure but also social and economic structures that were older than civilization itself were revolutionized in the course of a mere hundred years.

The single greatest nineteenth-century shift in civilization was what contemporaries themselves called the **Industrial Revolution**. The revolution began in eighteenth-century Britain with the invention of the steam engine and its use as a source of reliable power for machines to produce cotton textiles. In the nineteenth century, the partnership of machines to produce and use power spread to every branch of industry and agriculture, and from Britain to many other Western and non-Western countries. Fast-moving technical advance became a seemingly permanent feature of Western civilization.

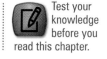

Test your knowledge before you read this chapter.

The result was the greatest change in human ways of life since the Agricultural Revolution (pp. 8–11). Giant capitalist corporations arose to finance and manage the new industries arising from technical advance. The elite came to be made up mainly of captains of industry, stock exchange tycoons, and government bureaucrats, rather than nobles. The sons and daughters of peasants crowded from the countryside into the cities to supply the vast forces of factory and office workers needed by the new industries. New social conflicts arose between management and labor over the distribution of the increased wealth produced by technology.

In the nineteenth century, too, the progress of scientific discovery became a broad advance on many fronts. Human understanding of the basic features of the physical universe and of the nature of living things expanded and changed out of all recognition, and this growth of theoretical knowledge became the main engine of industrial change. Impressed by these successes, social scientists (such as economists and sociologists) and human scientists (such as anthropologists and psychologists) began to apply measurement, observation, and experiment more or

What do you think?

The shift from manual labor to mechanized labor made life better for most people.

Strongly Disagree						Strongly Agree
1	2	3	4	5	6	7

≪ **Mass Production** A Bessemer converter blows air through 30 tons of molten iron to remove impurities and turn it into steel in 20 minutes. The converter was developed in Britain in the 1850s, and this picture by Fritz Gehrke shows it operating in Germany about 1900. By that date the Industrial Revolution, and with it the mass production of a previously scarce and expensive metal, had become international.

less systematically to society, culture, and human nature itself. In these ways, science took its place beside religion as one of the main influences on the outlook and way of life of Western civilization.

LO¹ The Industrial Revolution

Many of the developments that had remade Europe and the rest of the world from the late Middle Ages onward also paved the way for the Industrial Revolution. The rise of capitalism had created a class of merchants and manufacturers who were willing to take risks, as well as new forms of business organization that were adaptable to the needs of large industrial enterprises (p. 284). In the technical field, waterwheels and gunpowder had furnished stronger sources of power in peace and war than human or animal muscles, printing had set a precedent for complex mass-production operations, and clocks had provided an example of accurately functioning automatic machines (pp. 196, 256–258). The Scientific Revolution had aroused the expectation that scientific discovery would result in practical benefits (p. 362). The growth of colonial empires had brought much of the world's trade to the countries of western Europe, giving them the wealth to invest in new technology and worldwide markets for their resulting products (p. 284). And as it happened, by the eighteenth century, all these developments had gone farthest in one European country: Britain. It was there that the Industrial Revolution began; the pattern of change then spread to the European mainland, North America, and Japan.

The Agrarian Transformation

Preceding and accompanying the British Industrial Revolution were significant changes in agriculture. In the course of the eighteenth century, landlords had increased their holdings and revenues by speeding up the practice of land enclosure, which had been going on since the end of the Middle Ages. Under the old manorial regime, the lord's tenants had enjoyed access to the common pasture, meadows, and woodland (pp. 191–192). By successive parliamentary acts of enclosure, these lands were gradually removed from common use and were rented to individuals to farm. Over the same period, the "open fields" of cultivated strips were also switched into single plots and fenced in for individual use. In this process of redistribution, the landlords usually gained additional land, while tenants often found that they could no longer make a living.

Although the redistribution brought hardship to thousands of farm families, it put large tracts of land under more efficient management. Whereas the typical small farmer clung to old-fashioned ways, the more ambitious landlords were willing to experiment with improved methods. They tried new farming

CHRONOLOGY	
CA. 1700	Newcomen develops steam engine
1770s	Arkwright, inventor of water-powered spinning machine, launches first spinning factory
1775	Adam Smith's *The Wealth of Nations*
1798	Thomas Malthus's *An Essay on the Principle of Population*
1817	David Ricardo's *Principles of Political Economy and Taxation*
1825	Age of railways begins
1833	Parliament passes laws to protect British workers
1859	Charles Darwin's *On the Origin of Species*
1864	Labor unions legalized in France
1880s	Germany introduces sickness and accident insurance and old-age pensions
1890	Sherman Antitrust Act moves to break up U.S. monopolies
1899	Freud's *The Interpretation of Dreams*
1905	Einstein announces his theory of relativity

tools and fertilizers, planted soil-renewing crops, and developed scientific breeding of livestock. The result was a substantial rise in output. This revolution in agriculture also created a pool of displaced farm workers, both men and women, who desperately sought employment. Some hired themselves out to successful farmers; others were ready to go wherever they could find work, including tending newly invented machines in newly built factories.

The Mechanization of Industry and Transportation

By 1750, Britain had built up a globe-circling trading system, and rich profits awaited those who could increase their exports. Among the goods that British merchants traded across the world were cotton textiles, a product of India that was popular in many markets because it was comfortable, decorative, and cheaper than similar cloths such as fine linen or silk. But the profits would be all the greater if cotton cloth could be manufactured in Britain rather than bought in India. To begin with, cotton textiles were produced, like woolen ones, by hand workers in their homes (p. 253)—but it so happened that cotton fibers were strong enough to be spun into thread and woven into cloth even by relatively crude machines.

Mass Production

From about 1760, inventors developed machines that could produce far larger amounts of thread and cloth that could be done by hand. But unlike traditional spinning wheels and looms, the new machines were too expensive for workers to buy and operate at home, and too big to be operated by hand. Instead, business owners, sure of worldwide markets for cotton textiles, bought the machines and installed them on the banks of swift-running rivers, where they could be powered by waterwheels. Since waterwheels themselves were large and expensive devices, it made sense for them to operate several machines at a time, in what soon came to be called a "factory." Richard Arkwright, the inventor of the first successful water-powered spinning machine, launched the first spinning factory in the 1770s, and soon he was employing hundreds of workers.

The greatest boost to the building of factories came from the development of efficient steam engines, which could be built to be more powerful than waterwheels and were not confined to riverbanks. The steam engine was initially developed by Thomas Newcomen about 1700 in response to a mining problem: the tunnels, always liable to fill with underground water, were being dug too deep for the water to be drained from them by animal-powered pumps as in the past. Newcomen, though no scientist himself, knew about seventeenth-century discoveries concerning the behavior of water when heated and cooled, and used his knowledge to build a machine that would do the job (see photo). In this way,

> *"The steam engine was the first modern technical device to owe its existence to the progress of science."*

The Spinning Mill Animation (http://www.bbc.co.uk/history/british/victorians/launch_ani_spinning_mill.shtml) See how a spinning factory operated in this animation.

the steam engine was the first modern technical device to owe its existence to the progress of science.

Later in the eighteenth century, James Watt made improvements on Newcomen's machine, greatly increasing its power and harnessing it to turn a wheel. As a result, steam engines eventually became the chief source of power for factories, enabling them to be built away from running water. The new power-producing machines were fueled by a cheap and plentiful mineral, the fossilized remains of land plants of ancient geological eras, which had previously been burned mainly in the fireplaces of a few big cities—coal. Eventually, coal would be joined as a fuel by the fossilized remains of microscopic sea creatures—petroleum. Mass production and consumption of fossil fuels would become essential to modern industrial economies, and their effect on the atmosphere and climate would lead to the twenty-first century's dilemmas and disputes over global warming (pp. 579, 635–636).

Mass Transportation

Later inventors made the steam engine so small and powerful that it could be used for both water and land transportation. The "age of railways" began in 1825 when the steam locomotive pioneer George Stephenson opened a stretch of line between the coal-mining town of Darlington and the harbor of Stockton, 20 miles

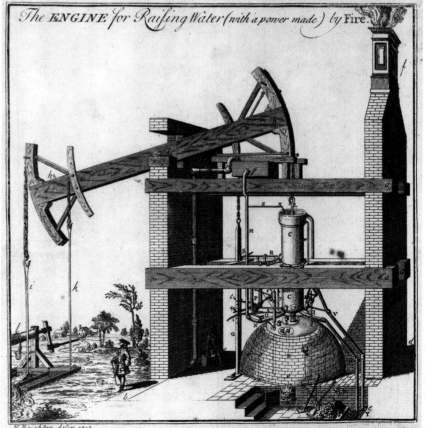

The ENGINE for Raising Water (with a power made) by Fire.

H. Beighton delin. 1717.

>> **The Newcomen Engine** This steam engine, installed at an English coal mine in 1717, is an enormous seesaw. The right end is pushed down by the atmosphere's weight when hot steam is cooled and condensed beneath a piston (sliding disk) in the cylinder; weights attached to the left end then pull that end down; and its up and down motion operates a pump in the mine to clear ground water. "Power made by fire" enabled mines to be deepened from 400 feet to 1,000 feet.

Science and Society Picture Library

Map 22.1 **Industrial England and Wales**

By 1850, the traditional dominant industry, woolen textiles, had been joined by coal-mining, production and manufacture of iron, pottery, and cotton textiles, and new and old industrial regions were linked by railroads. The industrial center of gravity had shifted from southern and eastern England to the country's center and north, to Wales—and to Scotland and northern Ireland, which had undergone the same changes. © Cengage Learning

 Interactive Map

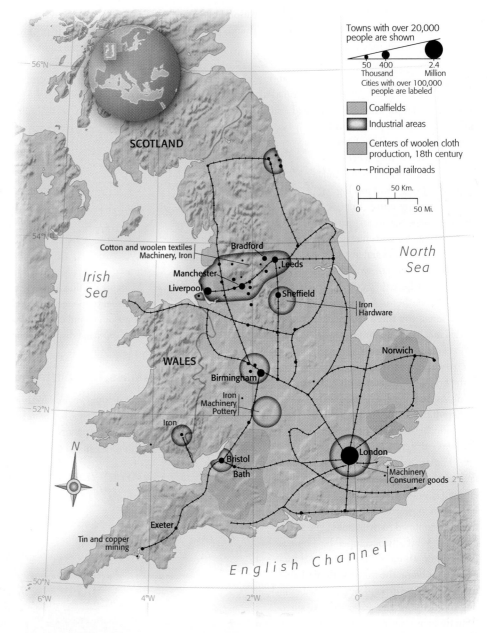

away, from which the coal moved to homes and factories by sea. Five years later, Stephenson linked two much more important centers—Manchester, the headquarters of the industrialized cotton industry, and Liverpool, the seaport through which Manchester imported raw cotton from the United States and exported finished textiles to customers in every continent. Within twenty years, steam trains were running between all the principal cities of Britain. With its cities linked by steam transportation, its coal mines deep beneath the earth, its mechanized cotton industry, and other industries following cotton's example, Britain provided the pattern for future industrialization around the world (see Map 22.1).

Permanent Industrial Revolution

At the middle of the nineteenth century, Britain's industrial productivity and technical progress were unique, but it did not keep this position for long. In the second half of the nineteenth century, with astonishing speed, the Industrial Revolution spread to other European countries, as well as to North America and Japan.

By the end of the century, the most productive and technologically advanced industrial power in Europe was Germany, while other countries such as France, Belgium, Italy, and Austria-Hungary were also important industrial producers. In the Far East, Japan was responding to the threat of U.S. and European imperialistic control by remaking itself into a modern industrial country (pp. 464–465). But the most productive of all, thanks to its vast natural resources, its population swelled by immigration, its scientific progress, and its technical know-how, was the United States.

Science, Industry, and Technical Progress

Industrialization not only spread from country to country, it also progressed. More and more traditional products came to be mass-produced, and more and more new products and manu-

INDUSTRIALIZATION SPREAD BEYOND BRITAIN TO COUNTRIES THAT POSSESSED CERTAIN KEY FEATURES:

Supplies of Natural Resources

· Other countries also had resources of coal and iron ore to power engines and forge steel.

Motivated Politicians, Business Owners, and Workers

· They too had middle-class business owners who were eager to build factories and landless country dwellers who were eager to earn wages in them.

· Landowning nobles wanted to farm their land more efficiently and profit from the coal and iron ore that might lie beneath it.

· Rulers seeking a role as leaders of national prosperity and power were well aware that industrial wealth and advanced weapons could only make them stronger.

facturing processes were invented. As scientific knowledge developed ever more broadly and swiftly, it divided into two fields: "pure" science, which made discoveries, and "applied" science, which turned them to industrial use. Practical engineers and backyard tinkerers could still make breakthroughs, but more and more inventors were professionally qualified scientists working in laboratories financed by industrial companies and national governments. Purposefully conducted and linked to the seemingly limitless progress of pure science, the surge of technological progress has continued down to the present day.

The new age of permanent Industrial Revolution linked to science began shortly after the middle of the nineteenth century. It was inaugurated by the development of new processes in the iron industry—mostly arising from better understanding of the chemistry of metallic ores—that enabled iron to be rapidly and cheaply transformed into a stronger form of the metal, steel (see photo on page 420). By the end of the century, steel had largely replaced iron for rails, bridges, shipbuilding, and other types of construction where great strength was required. Meanwhile, advances in the physics of heat, gas, electricity, and magnetism led to revolutionary inventions in the field of power production and distribution. A new and far more powerful form of steam engine, the turbine, was coupled with generators that turned steam power into electrical energy to make electric light and power.

At the end of the nineteenth century, steam and electrical power were joined by the internal combustion (gasoline or diesel) engine. Fueled by previously untapped petroleum resources—which could be located thanks to the rapidly developing science of geology—the new type of engine brought about yet more revolutions in transportation. Small, light, and yet powerful, it made possible the twentieth-century development of both automobiles and aircraft. With petroleum available in vast amounts to supply the needs of motorists and pilots, chemists also found ways to produce from it an endless variety of textiles and plastics. Other twentieth-century scientists, building on basic discoveries in physics from the late nineteenth century onward, created a whole range of electronic devices that have transformed the transmission and processing of information: radio, television, recording devices, and computers.

Each of these and many other inventions of the last century and a half has amounted to a revolution in itself. Whole industries—such as steel, oil, plastics, electronics, automobiles, and aircraft—have sprung from nothing to produce and sell these inventions. Usually in not more than twenty or thirty years after the initial invention, each new industry has developed its giant corporations, its massive production plants, and its labor force of hundreds of thousands.

This permanent worldwide Industrial Revolution has been far from painless. It has led to massive changes, usually accompanied by conflict and hardship, in the way businesses are organized and run and in the patterns of work and life of ordinary people. It has given rise to radical ideologies that have promised relief from the evils of capitalism and industrialization but in practice have often brought their own forms of mass suffering. It has altered the balance of power in the world, giving dominance to the industrialized and technologically advanced nations, subjecting nonindustrial ones to imperialistic control, and providing the weapons to fight wars more terrible than any in history. Much of this and the following chapters is concerned with exploring these aspects of the impact of the machine.

LO² The Business Corporation

As industrial operations grew in number and size, entrepreneurs had to raise capital from sources other than their own profits. Large undertakings, calling for heavy initial investment in buildings and equipment, required the pooling of money from hundreds of thousands of individuals. The device that business

corporation
A business or businesses funded by investors who have little involvement in daily operations and no liability beyond their individual shares in the business if it fails.

laissez-faire
The doctrine that if people are left free to follow their own nature and interests, this will promote the economic welfare of all.

leaders developed for raising and controlling such funds was called the *limited company* in Britain, the *corporation* in the United States.

The Structure and Control of the Corporation

The distinctive feature of the corporation or limited company is the financial protection it gives its stockholders. Its forerunner, the *joint-stock company* (p. 284), had first appeared in the seventeenth century as a means of financing trading ventures. Joint-stock companies had sold shares that could be bought and sold and had served as a means of risk sharing, but the stock owners collectively had been liable for the debts of the enterprise. The corporation, on the other hand, is a clever legal invention, a "fictitious person" created by law. It is authorized to hold property, borrow money, and sue and be sued—without direct involvement of the stockholders. Should the assets of the corporate "person" be lost, the stockholders would lose only the value of their shares of stock.

This idea of "limited liability" is of crucial importance, since it permits individuals far removed from the control of a business to invest money in its stock without the risk of losing other property that they hold. They delegate direction of the firm's operations to a small body, the board of directors, who are elected (usually routinely) by an annual vote of the stockholders. The board, in turn, chooses the executive officers of the firm. So long as the managerial group—the directors and the executives—produces profits for the stockholders, it normally remains in control. In fact, as corporations grew in size (especially after 1900), and as stockholders became increasingly numerous, more and more power went to the managers—a process that has been aptly called the "managerial revolution."

The Global Reach of Capitalism

Large corporations, from the very beginning, usually had important foreign interests. They sometimes sought to eliminate competition in world markets through private agreements (cartels), and by extending their investments abroad, they controlled the rate of economic growth in many lands. Industrial capitalism thus became a global force, with money and business seeking the best rates of return and with an international elite of owners, managers, bankers, and promoters. The push of industrialization was a major factor, along with liberalism and nationalism, in shaping Europe and the world in the nineteenth and twentieth centuries.

Investors were especially drawn to unindustrialized countries by the promise of extraordinary profits. Labor was cheap there, the demand for capital was high, and in some cases rich resources were awaiting exploitation. Overseas investments also aided the creation of an interdependent global economy geared to the interests of the industrial countries. Thus, European capital built railways in Africa that brought out raw materials to be manufactured in Europe and sold in markets around the world.

The industrialists of Great Britain had the jump on those of other nations. By 1914, British private investments overseas amounted to more than $18 billion. French capitalists were next, with some $7 billion. These figures are a fair index of the two nations' comparative penetration and influence in the "backward" continents. (United States capitalists had only $3 billion in foreign investments in 1914; by 1970, the figure was close to $150 billion.)

As early as 1900, some observers began to ask whether the concentration and expansion of economic power could go on without seriously disturbing political relations within and among nations. The corporate leaders knew well enough that their wealth was guiding politics both at home and abroad. They saw nothing wrong in this; in fact, they felt that their political influence was essential to the full development of the world's resources. Encouraged by the doctrines of economic liberalism, they believed that they could serve humanity best by the unrestricted pursuit of profit.

> **"** I have never known much good done by those who affected to trade for the public good. **"**
>
> —Adam Smith,
> *The Wealth of Nations*

Economic Liberalism: Theory and Practice

Such political and economic views were quite different from the doctrine of mercantilism, which was widely accepted up to the end of the eighteenth century. Mercantilism held that economic activities should be used to strengthen the state and that the state, in turn, should guide industry and commerce (pp. 334–335). The Scotsman Adam Smith had been the most effective critic of mercantilism during the eighteenth century. In *The Wealth of Nations* (1776), he attacked the notion that state intervention was the key to national prosperity. Basing his ideas on the widely held idea of natural law, he argued that there exists a "natural" economy geared to human selfishness. People, if left free to follow their own nature and interests (a doctrine known as **laissez-faire** [les-ey-FAIR]), will be led by an "invisible hand" to promote the economic welfare of all.

 **The Wealth of Nations: A Natural Law of Economy** Read Adam Smith's description of some of the "natural laws" of the economy.

Smith's writing reflected the optimism of the Enlightenment, but later theorists presented a darker outlook. An English clergyman, Thomas Malthus, noted the general misery of the poor and found the explanation in the pressure of population growth. Because of the sexual urge, said Malthus in *An Essay on the Principle of Population* (1798), people tend to increase faster than food supplies. Population growth is held down mainly by the "positive checks" of starvation, disease, and war. Seeing no way out of this condition (except the unlikely one of "moral restraint"), Malthus predicted continued suffering for the human race. Malthus thus called attention to one of the root problems facing the modern world.

 **Malthus Predicts Gloomy Prospects for the Human Condition** Read Malthus's gloomy predictions for the human race.

Another such theorist was David Ricardo, a financier who had made his fortune in Britain during the Napoleonic Wars. In his *Principles of Political Economy and Taxation* (1817), he set forth the main "laws" governing economic affairs, such as the law of supply and demand. He is best remembered, perhaps, for his "**iron law of wages.**" Ricardo declared that in a free-market economy with a plentiful supply of labor, wages must remain close to the level needed for bare subsistence of the workers. More than that would allow more of the workers' children to survive; this would increase the supply, which in turn would lower the "natural" price (wages). On the other hand, should wages fall so low that some workers died off, the supply of labor would then decrease, which would raise wages back to the subsistence level.

 The "Iron Law of Wages" Is Forged Read Ricardo on the iron law of wages.

Malthus and Ricardo agreed with Smith, however, that the production and consumption of wealth was a self-correcting process in which purposeful state intervention did more harm than good—a view that has come to be known as **economic liberalism**. On the whole, this view suited the captains of trade and industry. The pioneers of the science of economics provided respectable and compelling justifications for keeping wages down, for seeking profit when and where they could, and for working toward the elimination of unwanted government interference. Up to the middle of the nineteenth century, commercial and industrial interests often proved successful in striking down controls that were not to their liking. But later on, organized workers and governments eager for social peace insisted on changing the rules of the free market through collective bargaining and social reform.

LO³ Labor, Government, and Capitalism

There is no doubt that, in the long run, industrialization raised standards of living and lightened the burden of manual labor. But the rise of factories also took away one of the foremost functions of traditional families and households—industrial

production. Further, working conditions in the early factories were dangerous and oppressive, hours were long, and wages were low. The factory owners beat down the workers' protests and plowed profits back into more efficient machines. The capital accumulation and investment of the nineteenth century were thus drawn from the unhappy laborers, whose only choice was to work or starve. Often, in fact, even that choice was denied them, for nineteenth-century capitalism was a dynamic, unstable system in which good times (booms) alternated with bad times (depressions). Wage earners were hardest hit when the factories laid off workers. Under the doctrines of economic liberalism, they were bound to suffer for as long as the system endured.

iron law of wages
The theory that wages will always return to the level needed for bare subsistence of the workers.

economic liberalism
The view that the production and consumption of wealth are a self-correcting process in which purposeful state intervention does more harm than good.

trade union
A group of employees joined for the purpose of bargaining with employers or influencing legislation.

Trade Unions

The condition of workers in the early factories was not necessarily worse than those of farmhands or apprentices in small workshops. But the factory system also left the laborer at the mercy of a large-scale employer. With a surplus of hungry workers seeking jobs, wage-hands had no place to turn should they lose their jobs. In the early part of the nineteenth century, therefore, there was no bargaining over wages and hours; they were set by the employer, and the worker could either take them or leave them. Yet by bringing large numbers of workers together, factories made workers more aware of their common plight and gave them a sense of what their united power might be.

 An Austrian Girl Is Introduced to the Realities of the Workplace Read a young woman's account of sexual harassment in an Austrian factory.

Collective action for the purpose of bargaining with employers or influencing legislation offered some promise of relief to the laborers. They discovered, however, that whenever they tried to organize, the odds were against them. Local "trade clubs" had existed in Britain before the Industrial Revolution, but only in a few skills (printing, tailoring, weaving) and only in certain communities. When artisans tried to organize on a wider basis, their groups were broken up by the joint action of employers and the government. Generally viewed by the courts as "combinations" (conspiracies), **trade unions** had been prohibited in both France and Britain by 1800. Governments feared that they might lead to riots or uprisings; employers feared that they might lead to higher costs. Later legislation in Britain (1825) allowed unions to exist but closely limited their activities.

"SWEATED LABOR": A POOR WOMAN'S FATE

The British textile industry was the first to use machines for mass production, but in the mid-nineteenth century, finishing (the final steps in production) still had to be done by hand. The flood of half-finished products from the factories put enormous pressure on workers to keep up, and finishing work was typically done by "sweated labor." Nearly all the workers were women, often unmarried and with children to support, who were paid by the piece (based on how many items they completed). They worked for long hours, sometimes at home and sometimes in abysmal workshops; employers might at any time lower the piece rates or increase the quotas of items to be delivered. For many working-class women, this was their only option, since they were kept out of factory work by parliamentary reform legislation, as well as by the fear of male workers that cheaper female labor would drag down wages. In this selection dating from 1849, Henry Mayhew, an English journalist famous for his reports on the lives of poor people, presents the daily routine of one of these women, in her own words.

Money sums are given in shillings (abbreviated as "s.") and pence (pennies—"d." from the Latin for "penny," *denarius*). There were 12 pence to a shilling, and in 1849 one British penny was worth about two U.S. cents. "Second bread" is cheap bread left over from the previous day's baking.

I do the "looping." The looping consists in putting on the lace work down the front of the coats. I puts it on. That's my living; I wish it was not. I get 5d. for the looping of each coat; that's the regular price. It's three hours' work to do one coat, and work fast to do it as it's done now. I'm a particular quick hand. I have to find my own thread. It cost $1\frac{1}{2}$d. for a reel of cotton; that will do five coats. If I sit down between eight and nine in the morning, and work till twelve at night—I never enters my bed afore—and then rise between eight and nine again (that's the time I sit down to work on account of doing my own affairs first), and then work on till eleven, I get my four coats done by that time, and some wouldn't get done till two. It's an hour's work going and coming, and waiting to be served at the piece-master's, so that at them long hours it takes me a day and a half hard work to get four coats looped. When I first touched this work I could do eight in the same time, and be paid better; I had 7d. then instead of 5d.; now the work in each is nearly double in quantity, that it is.

I've got two boys both at work, one about fifteen, earning 3s. per week, and I have got him to keep and clothe. The week before last I bought him a top coat—it cost me 6s.—for fear he should be laid up, for he's in such bad health. The other boy is eighteen years, and earns 9s. a week. He's been in work about four months, and was out six weeks. At the same time I had no work. Oh, it was awful then! I have been paying 1s. 6d. a week off a debt for bread and things I was obliged to get on credit then.

My last boy is only nine years of age, and him I have entirely to keep. He goes to the charity school. It lets him have one coat and trousers and shoes and stockings every year. He wears a pinafore now to save his coat. My eldest boy is like a hearty man to every meal. If he hadn't got me to manage for him, may be he'd spend all his earnings in mere food. I get my second bread, and I go as far as Nassau-street to save two or three halfpence. Butter we *never* have. A roast of meat none of us ever sees. A cup of tea, a piece of bread, and an onion, is generally all I have for my dinner, and sometimes I haven't even an onion.

EXPLORING THE SOURCE

1. What does the woman do for a living? Describe her workday.

2. What is her family situation? How do they make ends meet?

Source: Adapted from Henry Mayhew, *The Morning Chronicle Survey of Labour and the Poor: The Metropolitan Districts* (Firle, UK: Caliban, 1980), 1:157–159.

Nevertheless, by the middle of the nineteenth century, steps had been taken in Britain to organize some skilled workers on a nationwide basis. The cotton spinners, for example, began to gain recognition for their associations and to develop modern collective bargaining procedures (supported by the power of strikes). Many legal battles still had to be fought and won by British labor unions, but by 1900, 2 million workers, skilled and unskilled, had been organized into effective bargaining associations. A similar pattern of struggle—legal, economic, and political—followed in the United States and in other industrial countries.

State Intervention

Many workers also looked to legislation as a means of remedying certain evils of industrialism. In Britain, the laboring classes themselves had virtually no political power until after midcentury; even before that, however, other social groups succeeded in bringing about some needed reforms through legislation.

Reform legislation was initiated by the Tory Party, which represented primarily the interests of the landed aristocracy. Since the landowners did not usually have large investments in industry, they could best afford to promote humane treatment of factory workers. Numerous intellectuals and humanitarians, without respect to party, also supported the Tory proposals. Even some of the industrialists themselves, after accumulating their fortunes, supported reforms. Factory owners as a group, however, bitterly fought all proposed limitations on their freedom to conduct their enterprises as they saw fit.

A series of parliamentary acts, beginning in 1833, removed the worst conditions in British industry. Employers were forbidden to hire children under nine years of age, and the labor of those under eighteen was restricted to nine hours a day. Women and children were excluded from mine labor (see photo), and better hours and safety devices were required in the mines. Government inspectors were hired to ensure that the regulations were observed. After wage earners themselves gained the right to vote (in 1867), additional measures were enacted for their protection and welfare.

On the continent of Europe, France and Germany began to catch up to the British in industrial growth. Napoleon III, who came to power in France partly on the promise of ending class conflict, sought to please both the bourgeoisie and the working class (p. 412). He took effective measures to promote agriculture, manufacturing, and commerce, but also legalized labor unions in 1864 and provided many social welfare institutions.

In the latter part of the century, as Germany became Europe's largest industrial producer, it also took the lead in social legislation. Labor unions, intellectuals, and religious groups helped bring about these reforms. After Bismarck became imperial German chancellor in 1871, he used social legislation in hopes of turning workers away from the growing Marxist labor movement, and more successfully, as a means of increasing the loyalty of citizens to the new German Empire. Laws passed in the 1880s provided for sickness and accident insurance and old-age pensions for workers. The crowning regulatory measure was the Industrial Code of 1891, which guaranteed uniform protection to workers (with respect to hours and conditions) throughout the nation. The Social Insurance Code of 1911 became a model for other industrialized countries.

In adopting measures of this kind, the United States was at least a generation behind western Europe—though in another field of government intervention, America was ahead. Giant industries developed rapidly after the Civil War; by 1890, mergers, trusts, and other forms of business combination were eliminating competitors and making huge profits. Many liberals, labor leaders, populists, and small entrepreneurs became alarmed by the growing concentration of economic power. They demanded legislation to check the expansion of monopolies and to keep enterprise "competitive and free."

Thus, in the name of liberalism, the power of the American government was called up as a counterforce to big business. The Sherman Antitrust Act of 1890 declared illegal "every contract, combination, or conspiracy in restraint of interstate commerce." The passage of this law was only the starting point of a long and tough contest in which government has sought to protect the public against the excesses of private economic powers; it was looked upon by those powers, however, as an encroachment on their freedom.

Child Labor Children had traditionally worked long hours at tasks like bringing in grain at the harvest, straightening threads for weavers, or even fetching powder for gunners aboard warships, but in the Industrial Revolution attitudes to child labor changed. This picture of a boy hauling coal along a mine tunnel comes from a report to the British Parliament in 1842. The working classes had little power in Britain at the time, but such depictions influenced middle- and upper-class politicians to pass labor legislation.

LO⁴ Urban and Consumer Society

Ever since the Middle Ages, European towns and cities had slowly grown in response to the gradual increase of local, regional, and worldwide trade. But in the nineteenth century, towns and cities grew so swiftly as to change the whole structure of society—from one that was traditionally rural to one that was becoming predominantly urban.

The Rural Exodus

Partly, this was because of a spectacular increase of the total population. In eight centuries up to 1800, the population of Europe had grown from about 40 million to about 150 million, but between 1800 and 1914, the population tripled to nearly 450 million. The extraordinary increase was the result of many factors that led to a lowering of the death rate. Chief among them were increased food production (aided by agricultural improvements), planting of more nutritious crops (the potato and Indian corn), advances in sanitation, and control of epidemics. In addition, the Industrial Revolution provided more purchasing power in the manufacturing countries, and that power was used to import more food from overseas.

By 1910, Germany, with 58 million inhabitants, had the largest population of any western European nation. Britain was next, with 42 million; then France, with 41 million; and Italy, with 36 million. The most striking growth was in the cities, fed by what came to be called the "rural exodus." Rising population and agricultural improvements made work harder to find in the countryside; in eastern Europe, the end of serfdom freed peasants to leave their villages; and factories, railroads, and offices offered far more city jobs than before.

Many of these jobs were across the Atlantic: between 1870 and 1914, over 26 million Europeans left their homes for the New World, more than half for the United States. But most of the migration was within countries—first of all in Britain. At the start of the Industrial Revolution, there were only four British cities with over 50,000 inhabitants; by 1850, there were thirty-one of that size, and half the population was living in cities—a proportion unprecedented in European history. Manchester, in the cotton-manufacturing region, was the largest and best known of the new industrial communities. Formerly a market town of 25,000 people, it had grown to half a million by 1850. Later in the nineteenth century, cities grew just as spectacularly in the main industrial regionss of central and western Europe (see Map 22.2).

 **Manchester Becomes a Thriving Industrial City** Read how the textile industry took root in Manchester.

The nineteenth-century growth of cities led to a momentous change in the way of life of the Western peoples. For thousands of years since the Agricultural Revolution, the average man or woman had lived on the land, either as a smallholding peasant or as an agricultural laborer. As late as 1800, in most European countries, 80 to 90 percent of the population was occupied in

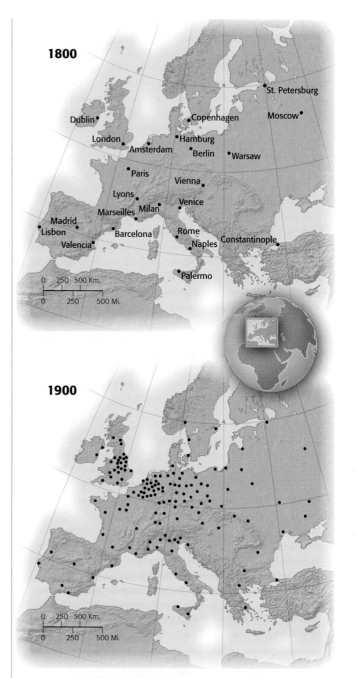

Map 22.2 Nineteenth-Century Urbanization

On both maps, a dot represents a city with a population of 100,000 or more. In 1820, Europe had 22 such cities, fairly evenly scattered from Ireland to Russia. In 1900, there were 152 cities of this size, and 99 of them (about two-thirds) were located in highly industrialized districts of the United Kingdom, the Netherlands, Belgium, northern France, northern Italy, and Germany. © Cengage Learning

Interactive Map

agriculture and only 10 to 20 percent earned a living from industry or commerce. By the late twentieth century, the proportion was exactly reversed. In western Europe and the United States, less than 10 percent of the population worked in agriculture, and much of the rest of the world was moving in the same direction.

Cities, Factories, and Offices

The "backwash" from industrialization and the swift overflow of people from towns and farms overturned deep-set patterns of family and community life that traced back to Neolithic times. As it brought an end to the traditional way of life, the factory carried the Western peoples from a world in which they were surrounded and dominated by nature to one that was more of their own making. And the new environment was ugly. The cities lacked sewers and paving. Housing for workers was cramped, rickety, and drab. Into the crowded, soot-blackened tenements poured the refugees from rural poverty—strangers in their own land. All this seemed to justify the words of Thomas Jefferson: "I view great cities as pestilential to the morals, the health, and the liberties of man."

Cities, in time, also brought much that was positive: better education, medical care, theaters, libraries, and merchandise from all over the earth. Even these advantages, however, were shared unequally, and poor people felt even more deprived in the presence of commodities they could not afford. Moreover, the factory system reduced workers to the tending of machines and subjected them to its rigid discipline. Narrowing specialization of tasks chained them to deadening, repetitive motions. Workers, like the machine and all its parts, became standardized, replaceable cogs in a production line that turned out standardized, replaceable things.

Alongside the factory, there grew up another institution that shaped the lives of millions of people from the late nineteenth century onward: the office. Business and government needed office workers and other "white-collar" employees even more than they needed factory workers. In pay and standards of living, white-collar employees (including increasing numbers of women) did not differ much from ordinary "blue-collar" workers, but since they did not do heavy or dirty manual labor, they considered themselves more respectable. Together with self-employed small business owners and storekeepers, they formed the lower middle class as opposed to the working class.

Mass Production and Mass Consumption

Mass production and maximum profits required not only standardized commodities but also mass demand. In order to keep capital and plant working at their full potential, advertising was

> "*Between 1870 and 1914, over 26 million Europeans left their homes for the New World.*"

The Nineteenth-Century American Trade Card Exhibit (http://www.library.hbs.edu/hc/exhibits/tcard/) Discover the "trade card," an early form of advertising.

developed to force-feed natural desires. Organized "buy" appeals supported and expanded the media of mass communication—overcoming local resistance and tending to make the demand for goods uniform and universal. As the twentieth century proceeded, the individual came to be viewed increasingly as a consumer of goods, a permanent target of the commercial persuaders. Daily choices (whether conscious or not) would be governed to a mounting degree by enticing propaganda.

Mass culture thus came into being, essentially as we know it today. Though it included numerous and varied subcultures, it held to one constant value: concern for material things. The machine now enabled people to produce wealth beyond their dreams, and the new salesmanship ensured that those dreams would never cease.

>> **Cathedral of Commerce** A Christmas and New Year's catalogue from the 1860s shows fancy toys, high-end kidswear, gloating kids, and the splendid exterior and thronged interior of a recently opened Paris department store. The novelist Émile Zola christened such places "cathedrals of commerce"—shrines of a new religion of middle-class mass consumption that sprang from the Industrial Revolution.

LO⁵ The Progress of Science

Accompanying the technological progress, social changes, and class conflicts of the nineteenth century were great leaps in pure science. The foundations of scientific organization and method had been laid in the seventeenth century (pp. 358–363), and science had continued to progress in the eighteenth century. But now the increase in knowledge became so fast as to make science what it has remained ever since—the intellectual enterprise that more than any other decides the destiny of the human race.

The influence and prestige of science rose to new heights, as industrialists, statesmen, generals, theologians, and philosophers sought to ally themselves with scientific doctrines. Social researchers of various sorts tried to model their methods of inquiry on those of mathematics, physics, or biology—and in the process to establish new branches of "social knowledge" that might draw the kind of respect paid to natural science.

Energy and Matter

Physical scientists continued to build on the foundations of Galileo, Newton, and Boyle. One of the most important subjects of their investigations was energy. Experimenters proved the equivalence of heat and energy and formulated two basic laws of thermodynamics. The First Law states that the total energy (or heat) in the universe remains constant, though it is continually changing its form. The Second Law states that energy systems tend toward degradation (heat, for example, flows from a hotter body to a colder one); hence the amount of useful energy is diminishing in the universe. These generalizations provided a basis for further advances in physics and chemistry.

Physics

In addition, new discoveries were made, with far-reaching practical applications, about electricity, magnetism, and light. Newton had observed that when sunlight passes through a prism, it spreads into a band of colors, or a *spectrum*—red at one end and indigo (dark blue) at the other. Scientists of the nineteenth century discovered that each chemical substance, when heated to incandescence (strongly enough to emit light), yields a spectrum distinct from every other. Spectrum analysis was developed as a tool for chemists—and for astronomers in studying sources of light in space. In addition, researchers made progress in identifying the actual nature of light as a series of vibrations or waves: in the spectrum, red is longer-wavelength light, and indigo is light of shorter wavelength.

These results were in turn linked with new findings about the nature of electricity and magnetism. Ever since the Renaissance, researchers had been investigating these two forces and had gradually come to suspect that they were in some way closely related. Finally, about the middle of the nineteenth century, Michael Faraday proved that this was so, and devised many ingenious experiments in which he used magnetism to produce electric currents and vice versa. In others, he used electricity in one coil of wire to cause a flow of current in another with which it was not connected. Out of these experiments, inventors soon developed electrical generators and motors, and Alexander Graham Bell devised the first telephone; thus the modern electrical and communications industries were born.

Meanwhile, in 1861, a Scottish physicist, James Clerk Maxwell, used Faraday's results to produce an exact mathematical description of the behavior of electricity and magnetism—which turned out to be exactly the same as that already discovered for the behavior of light. Evidently, all three were simply different forms of one and the same phenomenon—*electromagnetism*. True, only light was visible to the human eye, but invisible electromagnetism, too, must be able to travel in wavelike form with no obvious pathway to conduct it. As a result of Maxwell's findings, in 1887, Heinrich Hertz was able to build the first devices to transmit and receive these invisible electromagnetic waves.

Chemistry

The nineteenth century also witnessed many discoveries in chemistry and the theory of matter. The ancient Greek Democritus had theorized that matter was reducible to invisible, indivisible particles or atoms (p. 72). John Dalton, a British schoolteacher, accepted this general notion but found, early in the nineteenth century, that each chemical element was composed of atoms of different weights. Scientists later assumed the existence of *molecules*—combinations of atoms of the same or different elements. Most material substances, they concluded, are made up of molecules. In the nineteenth and early twentieth centuries, much chemical research was devoted to the analysis of molecules and the synthesis (artificial creation) of new ones, with astonishing results: basic understanding of the way in which atoms combine to form molecules; the invention of new dyestuffs, explosives, drugs, and the earliest plastics; and the identification of many substances found in living tissue.

The Atom, Space, and Time

All these advances took place within the understanding of the workings of nature that had developed on the basis of Newton's discoveries (pp. 362–363), but further developments starting shortly before 1900 began to correct or modify this "classical physics" in various ways.

Inside the Atom

Toward the end of the nineteenth century, it was discovered that certain chemical elements, such as uranium, emitted rays without being heated, electrified, or otherwise stimulated—a phenomenon that the Polish scientist Marie Curie, who was mainly responsible for identifying the elements concerned, called "radioactivity."

Subsequent research showed that radioactive and other types of rays in fact consisted of streams of tiny particles, which were evidently smaller than the atoms out of which the emitting substances must be composed. Clearly, for this to happen, something must be going on within the atoms, which must themselves be built up of still smaller particles. By studying various forms of radioactivity, Ernest Rutherford and Niels Bohr introduced their model of the atom (about 1910), which they saw as a miniature solar system, containing a nucleus of one or more *protons* with encircling *electrons* moving through space. Later research would show the atom to be even more complex than Rutherford or Bohr at first believed, but their concept was the starting point for modern atomic physics.

 The Life and Work of Marie Curie (http://www.aip.org/history/curie/contents.htm) Learn more about Marie Curie's life and work.

Relativity

In this way, one of the main assumptions of classical physics, the solidity of objects, began to dissolve. At the same time, the German physicist Albert Einstein attacked some other major classical assumptions—those that concerned mass, energy, space, and time. In his special theory of **relativity**, announced in 1905 and later extended to a general theory, Einstein

Michael Faraday in His Laboratory A painting from the 1850s by Harriet Moore shows the kind of kitchen-like space in which nineteenth century scientists made their discoveries. To Faraday's left on the counter stands an early version of a Bunsen burner, invented by himself. Perhaps he is at work on pollution in London's River Thames or the preservation of old-master paintings—matters of applied science with which he was busy at the time, having refused to help the British government develop chemical weapons. The Royal Institution, London/The Bridgeman Art Library

recognized that Newtonian physics "worked" well enough for ordinary purposes, but he believed that it did not truly describe the universe of nature. Newton had conceived of space and motion as *absolute*—exactly measurable regardless of the position in time and space of any observer who measured them. He assumed the existence of an "ether," a kind of immovable substance that fills space. All dimensions and motions, he thought, could be measured absolutely by reference to this ether. But experiments in the late nineteenth century proved that no such substance exists.

"E = mc² Explained" (http://www.pbs.org/wgbh/nova/einstein/experts.html) Listen to top physicists on Einstein's E = mc².

Einstein met this puzzlement with a radically different approach. Matter and motion are not absolutes, he declared, but are *relative*—their dimensions and motion vary according to the position in time and space of the observer who measures them. Einstein believed, further, that objects have a *space-time* dimension that affects their other dimensions. As bodies move toward or away from a given point, their size and mass change as observed from that point. The alterations are not noticeable in ordinary motions, but they become significant as bodies approach the speed of light. The speed of light is the one constant he found in the universe; it remains the same for all physical systems. In another way, too, mass is not an absolute but can be converted into energy. The tiny atomic "solar systems" that make up physical objects can be completely destroyed, releasing all the enormous energy contained within them—the basic concept behind the development of nuclear power and nuclear weapons (p. 516).

Medicine and the Structure of Life

Alongside these spectacular advances in physical science, the nineteenth century was just as much an era of biological and medical progress. Drawing on seventeenth-century descriptions of cellular structure in plants, Theodor Schwann developed the cell theory to explain organic (living) matter. It was realized by about 1835 that all living things consist of tiny cells whose health and growth determine the physical fate of the total organism.

Likewise the germ theory of disease developed out of the study of microorganisms. These tiny forms of life had been seen through the primitive microscopes of the seventeenth century, but little attention was given to them until after 1850. It was a French chemist, Louis Pasteur, who first theorized that bacteria (germs) were the cause of many deadly illnesses. Physicians knew of the existence of bacteria but thought them the result, rather than the cause, of disease. Pasteur also believed that these illnesses could be prevented by inoculation—injection with dead or weakened bacteria. The practice of vaccination—injecting people against smallpox with fluid from body tissue of people

who had had a weaker but related disease, cowpox—was already well established, but it only worked for that disease. After years of ridicule, Pasteur at last had the opportunity to demonstrate that his theory was correct, and hence that preventive inoculation against a wide range of diseases besides smallpox would be possible. His first successful test was against an epidemic of anthrax disease in sheep.

Once the germ theory was accepted, it led quickly to the identification, treatment, and prevention of countless diseases, as well as to antiseptic procedures in surgery and improvements in public hygiene and sanitation. The mass killers—bubonic plague, typhus, smallpox, and cholera—were at last subject to human control. No other development in science can match the importance of the germ theory in its effect on the world's death rate—and the consequent upward curve of human population.

The Development of Life: Evolution

The work of Charles Darwin, the main originator of the theory of **evolution**, may be compared with that of Isaac Newton two centuries earlier. As Newton completed the overturn of ancient ideas about the physical universe, so Darwin completed a revolution of thought with respect to living creatures—from the view that all species (kinds of animals and plants) had existed unchanged since the earth came into being to the view that they evolved (developed) over time.

Evolution Before Darwin

The change began with a Swedish botanist, Carl Linnaeus, who in the 1730s devised an unprecedentedly complete and systematic classification of species into groups and subgroups, based on the physical features that they had in common. Linnaeus believed firmly in unchanging species, but his classification made clearer than ever before that different species tended to cluster in groups that shared many features. Even humans, he thought, belonged in such a group: he classified them together with apes as "anthropomorphs" ("human-shaped species").

In the early nineteenth century, new theories and new evidence further undermined the view of unchanging species. In particular, the time since the earth came into being came to seem much longer than had previously been thought. Prior to the appearance of Charles Lyell's *Principles of Geology* in 1830, most educated people believed that the earth's history had been relatively short and that the earth's surface had undergone sudden and drastic changes. Lyell, however, argued that geological change had been slow and gradual and that the earth's age ran into hundreds of millions of years—a view that opened the door to the possibility of slow and gradual change in life forms. In addition, Thomas Malthus offered a key to how this process of change might take place. He pointed out that reproduction in animals advances at a rate that outstrips the supply of food. Hence the fate of all nature's creatures is one of struggle for survival—a struggle that eliminates some individuals, while others survive.

Darwin: The Process of Evolution

As a result, even before Darwin published *On the Origin of Species by Means of Natural Selection* in 1859, the theory of change in species had been accepted by some naturalists and thinkers. Darwin focused his life's work on that theory and established it securely on the basis of his observations and reasoned explanations.

According to Darwin, all forms of life are descended from a few original creatures, in the same kind of way that humans breed many varieties from a single type of plant or animal. Instead of intentional selection, however—as when humans breed larger dogs to produce German shepherds and smaller ones to produce Chihuahuas—this has taken place through what Darwin called "natural selection." Species come into existence as the result of a Malthusian struggle among individual creatures for survival in changing natural environments. Continuing slight variations in physical features give an advantage to some individuals over others; the losers in the struggle die out, while the winners survive to breed and pass on their distinctive features to their offspring; and as these features accumulate, new species arise. But unlike human selection, natural selection needs geological time. It takes a sweep of centuries beyond human imagination to produce, in tiny steps, the kinds of changes that turned the earliest microorganisms into mammals.

According to Darwin, therefore, species are not purposefully created, but develop out of a self-regulating process similar to that of Newton's universe—or to the production of wealth according to liberal economics. Like Newton's theory, that of Darwin inspired fierce religious debates, as well as new views of human nature and society, which are discussed in Chapter 23.

After Darwin: The Process of Inheritance

Darwin believed that new features were passed on simply by inheritance from individuals to their offspring, but already in his time, research by the Austrian botanist Gregor Mendel was laying the basis for a different explanation of heredity. By lengthy experiments with successive generations of plants and careful analysis of the results, Mendel was able to show, among other things, that a plant could carry what he called "hereditary factors" for particular characteristics even if it did not possess those characteristics itself: thus a short plant could carry the "factor" for tallness.

Later researchers in the new science of genetics used Mendel's results to correct Darwin's understanding of heredity in a way that actually strengthened the theory of evolution as a whole. Evolution, they said, depended not so much on the physical characteristics of individuals as on an entire species' supply of "hereditary factors," or, as they came to be called, *genes*. Only widespread *mutations* (changes) in gene supply could cause a change in the species.

Early in the twentieth century, the new theory of genes was linked up with the results of research into the cells of which all living things are composed. Nineteenth-century researchers had discovered that both the growth of living things and also their reproduction (the generation of new living things by existing ones) take place by means of cell division (the splitting of one cell into two). They had also discovered that when a cell divides, threadlike structures called *chromosomes* form within it, and these are transferred by various processes into the new cells. In 1911, the American geneticist Thomas H. Morgan suggested that Mendel's genes are tiny physical entities that are somehow strung out along the chromosomes—thereby moving from cell to cell in both growth and reproduction so as to determine and regulate the physical characteristics of new organisms. Not only did this insight further filled in the picture of evolution, but out of it the twentieth-century science of molecular biology would eventually be born (p. 517).

The Social and Human Sciences

Ever since modern scientific method first began to develop in the seventeenth century, thinkers and rulers had sought to apply it to the study of human society and human nature. Hobbes's image of humans as machine-like beings driven by desire and fear, the mercantilist notion of the "balance of trade," and the rise of the idea of the European "balance of power" were early applications of scientific concepts of motion, force, and balance to what would later be called psychology, economics, and international relations (pp. 328, 335, 338).

In the eighteenth century, rulers and their advisers began carefully observing and measuring the societies they governed. Systematic surveys and censuses provided information about matters that were highly relevant to the balances of trade and power, but which had earlier been a matter of guesswork—the value of imports compared with exports, for instance, or the number of young men of military age, or the fertility of taxpaying peasant farms. Statistical information of this kind then helped economics to become a well-developed field of knowledge and analysis by the early nineteenth century. Later in the century, economics acquired the scientific features of an exact vocabulary, advanced mathematical techniques, and methods of prediction. And as the spectacular progress of the natural sciences made them appear a uniquely successful way of gaining new knowledge, there arose a whole range of what came to be known as the social and human sciences.

Sociology and Anthropology

One of the pioneers of social science was the Frenchman Auguste Comte (**kawnt**). A disciple of Saint-Simon (p. 440), Comte was a lifelong reformer. He shared with Saint-Simon the view that society is best managed by "experts," but he believed that the experts needed a more reliable body of knowledge about people and their social relations than was at hand.

Comte believed that the most useful knowledge is the sort that rests upon empirical evidence (p. 365)—"positive" knowledge, he called it—which was to be found in his day only in the natural sciences. But empirical methods can and must, he insisted, be extended to form a "science of society," which Comte was the first to call *sociology*. Human conduct is neither random nor altogether unpredictable, and it can be quantified, analyzed, and classified. From the resulting social "laws," the proposed managers of society would be able to draw guidance for social regulation and planning.

Comte died in 1857, before he could complete his ambitious studies directed toward reconstructing knowledge and society. (Before breathing his last, he is said to have sighed, "What an irreparable loss!") But the foundations of sociology had been laid, and they were extended by many nineteenth- and twentieth-century thinkers. At about the same time, a companion discipline, *anthropology*, came into being. This word means, literally, the "study of human beings," but the study has focused on physical evolution, prehistoric cultures, and comparative social institutions.

Psychology and Psychoanalysis

While anthropology analyzed and classified the broad patterns of social conduct, observed over time and geographical space, a new discipline, *psychology*, concentrated on individual human actions. In 1872, Wilhelm Wundt established in Leipzig, Germany, the first laboratory for the observation and testing of human and animal subjects. Soon thereafter, a Russian, Ivan Pavlov, gained worldwide notice by his remarkable experiments with dogs. He discovered the "conditioned reflex," a principle that could (and would) be extended to humans.

By 1900, psychology was moving in several directions. Followers of Pavlov's experiments developed a view called **behaviorism**. Believing that human thoughts and actions can be understood on a purely physiological basis, they dismissed as meaningless such concepts as "mind" and "soul." They studied the various systems of the body—nervous, glandular, muscular—and the mechanisms of "stimulus" and "response," and measured them. From the accumulation of such data, the behaviorists hoped to develop "positive" knowledge of human nature. Most theologians, philosophers, and humanists found such ideas distasteful. They argued that a person's true being is

> "*Comte believed that human conduct could be quantified, analyzed, and classified.*"

spiritual rather than physical—or, if only physical, that it is far more complex than the behaviorists imagined.

Other investigators, meanwhile, were trying to penetrate the dark interior of the individual by means of **psychoanalysis**. The Austrian physician Sigmund Freud was a bold leader in this effort to investigate the subconscious and unconscious depths underlying thought and action. His methods were neither quantitative nor statistical but rather clinical. Each human subject was examined, by means of free discussion and dream recollection, for clues to the inner self. Freud's understanding of human nature has had a vast influence on Western thought, art, and everyday understanding of human relations (pp. 520, 554).

Freud's onetime associate, the Swiss psychologist Carl G. Jung, also stressed the importance of the unconscious as a major part of "psychic wholeness." Jung believed that each individual, as a result of biological evolution, possesses a "collective" unconscious in addition to a "personal" unconscious. The "collective" contains emotion-filled instincts and images connected with long-past experiences of the species. Jung called these "archetypes"—such as the "Great Mother" figure, the Hero, the Sage, the Betrayer, the Savior-God, and other images that appear widely in popular myths and religions. In keeping with this view, he held that "great" works of art and literature are seen as great because they portray such figures—projected from the collective unconscious of their creators.

History

One of the most ancient studies concerned with human affairs, history, was also affected by the rise of science—especially in Germany, where Leopold von Ranke (**RAHNG-kuh**) started the "objective" school of historical writing. He announced that he and his students would describe the past as it "actually happened." Sentiment and national bias were to be set aside, and historical documents were to be collected and interpreted in a rigorously critical fashion. Near the end of the century, the "scientific" approach was carried by historians from German to American universities.

Ranke wrote some excellent histories, and his insistence on correct method was wholesome. He did not convince all historians, however, that it is possible to reconstruct a single true picture of what "actually happened." Serious philosophical and practical objections have been raised against his assumptions, and most twentieth-century historians concluded that the account of individuals and societies can never be told with anything like the precision of natural science. There are indeed "lessons" of history, but they are interpreted in different ways by different writers. For example, a prominent group of twentieth-century French authors (the school founded by Fernand Braudel) holds that events in history can be presented properly only in their total context—including climate, geography, and cultural heritage—a method referred to as "structuralism." Still others ("deconstructionists") argue that words in any source document are but words and can never truly equate with reality (p. 559). At any rate, the fact is that history has never been altogether at home among the social sciences. It belongs more fully with the humanistic disciplines, especially philosophy, literature, and the arts.

 Listen to a synopsis of Chapter 22.

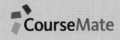

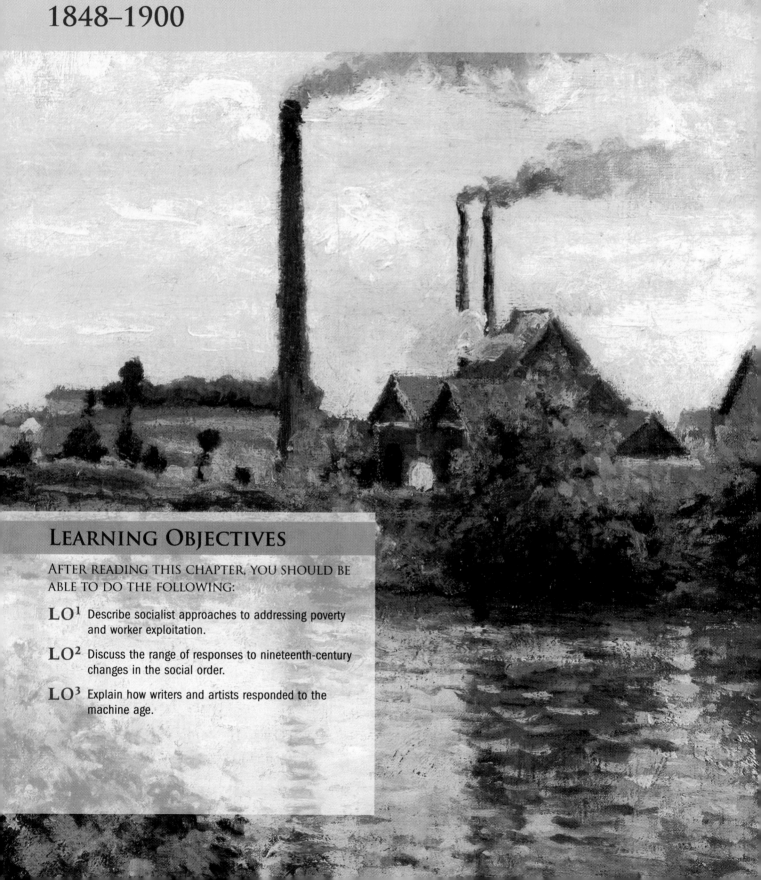

THINKERS AND ARTISTS IN A CHANGING WORLD, 1848–1900

LEARNING OBJECTIVES

AFTER READING THIS CHAPTER, YOU SHOULD BE ABLE TO DO THE FOLLOWING:

LO¹ Describe socialist approaches to addressing poverty and worker exploitation.

LO² Discuss the range of responses to nineteenth-century changes in the social order.

LO³ Explain how writers and artists responded to the machine age.

"WESTERN CIVILIZATION WAS TRANSFORMING ITSELF AMID DISPUTE AND CONFLICT."

Not only society and government, but also much of thought, literature, and art, were revolutionized in the course of the nineteenth century. An entire new ideology, that of socialism, proclaimed that out of the overwhelming social and economic changes and conflicts of the era a new world of equality and justice in human and social relations would be born. Christian thinkers sought to adapt their traditional social and economic values to provide guidelines for reforming unrestrained industrial capitalism. And both socialism and Christian social reform developed into powerful mass movements that influenced government and society in every country, while bitterly opposing each other. Ideological struggles were also waged over an advance in pure science, Charles Darwin's theory of evolution, which removed God's guiding hand from yet another vast area of the natural world—the origin and development of living beings. Furthermore, Darwin's idea of

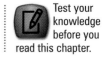

Test your knowledge before you read this chapter.

What do you think?

Economic equality is an impossible ideal.

Strongly Disagree					Strongly Agree	
1	2	3	4	5	6	7

the "survival of the fittest" was taken up by capitalists, nationalists, racists, and imperialists who saw human society as an arena of struggle, and wanted to feel that the victory of their side was both a scientific certainty and good for the human race.

Additional influence on people's ways of thinking was wielded by thinkers who responded to the nineteenth-century changes by giving up the quest for certainty, whether based on reason, faith, or tradition. Instead, they stressed the loneliness of the human person in the universe, and of the individual in mass society. The Christian thinker Søren Kierkegaard sought for contact with God through the "leap of faith"—the free choice to believe; the atheist Friedrich Nietzsche called for "supermen" who would live freely and nobly in disregard of meaningless modern values.

≪ *Factory near Pontoise* Early in the 1870s the factory age came to the small town of Pontoise (pawn-TWAHZ) near Paris, when a local company built a plant to process sugar beets into industrial alcohol. Soon after, the Impressionist painter Camille Pissarro captured this "impression" of a dark mass of buildings, starkly upright smokestacks, smoke drifting away beneath evening clouds, and broken reflections in brimming river waters. His painting expresses a changing perception of a changing world.

socialism
An ideology that aims to eliminate poverty and exploitation by transferring control of factories and farms from individual capitalists to society as a whole.

utopian socialism
A type of socialism based on an idealized society where owners give up their businesses and everyone works for the greater good.

The overwhelming nineteenth-century changes also had their effect on literature and the arts. The pull of the medieval, the classical, and even the Christian past began to weaken. Instead, to a greater extent than in previous eras, writers and artists found their themes in the life and objects of their own times—weary passengers in an overcrowded railroad car, for instance, or a middle-class woman awakening to the meaninglessness of her life of pleasing her husband. To depict such themes, new and contrasting styles evolved. The Realists treated their subjects in full and accurate detail, often accompanied by fierce denunciation of social evils. The Impressionists stripped detail to the bare minimum and carefully avoided social comment, so as to leave the most hauntingly evocative "impression" of the scenes they painted.

Because the Realists and Impressionists rejected so much that had traditionally seemed essential to the beauty and nobility of art, they were controversial. But they lived in a civilization that was in any case transforming itself amid dispute and conflict—a pattern that from now on became normal in the arts, too, as the West approached the great cultural divide that marked the beginning of the twentieth century.

LO¹ Socialist Thought and Action

The great problem of industrial capitalism was the persistence of poverty and exploitation in societies that were vastly wealthier than before. Governments and trade unions tried to remedy this by changing the behavior of capitalists and industrialists, but there were also those who said that the root of the problem ran deeper. The only way to eliminate poverty and exploitation was for society as a whole rather than self-interested individuals to own the factories and farms that produced wealth—an idea that in the 1830s first came to be called **socialism**. Social rebels of earlier centuries had sometimes approached this idea, but nineteenth-century thinkers sought to work out in detail how socialism would work and how to bring it about. Their ideas were compelling enough that socialism became the ideology of an international working-class movement with millions of supporters.

Utopian Socialism

Early socialist thinkers mostly drew up plans for a socialist society, with not much consideration of exactly how it would replace existing society. Later socialists criticized them for inventing "utopian" societies—ideal visions that had nothing to do with reality, like the Renaissance humanist Sir Thomas More in his book *Utopia* (p. 294). All the same, the vision of a future society that would be a basic improvement on existing ones has remained an inspiring hope for socialism—though often disappointed or betrayed.

One version of **utopian socialism**, that of the French aristocrat Count Henri de Saint-Simon (**san-see-MAWN**), involved a reorganization of society from the top, with state ownership of the means of production and control by a national board of scientists, engineers, and industrialists (technocrats). The purpose of industry would be production rather than profit, and workers and managers would be rewarded according to individual merit. In his chief work, *The New Christianity* (1825), Saint-Simon stressed philanthropic motives: "The whole of society ought to strive toward the amelioration of the moral and physical existence of the poorest class; society ought to organize itself in the way best adapted for attaining this end." Saint-Simon's disciples in France, some of whom became leaders in politics, were among the first modern advocates of a nationally planned society.

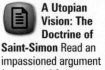 **A Utopian Vision: The Doctrine of Saint-Simon** Read an impassioned argument from one of Saint-Simon's disciples.

Charles Fourier, a younger contemporary of Saint-Simon, took a different approach. Resisting the idea of centralized economic control, he favored the creation of thousands of small

"PROPERTY IS THEFT": PROUDHON COMPARES PROPERTY AND SLAVERY

Pierre-Joseph Proudhon (**proo-DON**) was a printshop worker who became a leading radical writer and thinker in France in the 1840s. He shared with the utopian socialists the idea of a peaceful transition to a society where exploitation would disappear, but he took their ideas much further. He claimed that any kind of exercise of power over people was an evil that was doomed to disappear. His condemnation of power in general became a basic belief of the anarchist movement, and his attack on private property influenced Karl Marx—though Marx was contemptuous of Proudhon's utopian belief in peacefully revolutionizing society. In *What Is Property?* (1840), from which this excerpt is taken, Proudhon attacks the notion that property is a right that cannot be interfered with.

"'93" means 1793, the year of the Jacobin dictatorship, when the French revolutionary government confiscated whatever resources it needed to supply its armies and destroy its enemies.

If I were called upon to answer the following question: *What is slavery?* and I replied: *It is murder*, my meaning would be comprehended immediately. There would be no need for amplification to demonstrate that the power to deprive a man of his thought, will, and personality is the power of life and death and that to make a man a slave is to kill him. Why, therefore, may I not meet this other question: *What is property?* by replying: *It is theft*, without feeling certain I shall be misunderstood, although this second proposition is no more than a transformation of the first?

I am taking it upon myself to discuss property, the essential principle of our government and our institutions. I am within my rights. I may be deceived in the conclusion to which my researches lead me. I am within my rights. It pleases me to state my conclusion at the outset. I am still within my rights.

Such and such an author preaches that property is a civil right, generated by labor and sanctioned by law. Another maintains that it is a natural right which derives its origin from work. Both these doctrines, contradictory though they may appear, are endorsed and promoted. It is my contention that neither labor, nor business, nor law can create property: that it is an effect without a cause. Should I be reproved for this?

Yet I hear murmurs arising!
—*Property is theft!* This is the slogan of '93! This is the rallying cry of revolution.

Reader, reassure yourself. I am not an instrument of discord, a seditious incendiary. I am anticipating history a little; I am revealing a truth the march of which we are attempting in vain to halt. I proclaim the preamble of our future constitution. If our prepossessions would permit us to consider it, the definition *Property is theft*, which you deem heretical, might prove a lightning rod to deflect the thunderbolt. But how many interests, how many prejudices stand in the way! Philosophy, alas, will not alter the progress of events. Destiny will fulfill itself regardless of prophecy. . . .

EXPLORING THE SOURCE

1. Besides claiming that property is theft, Proudhon says it is "the essential principle of our government and institutions." What, then, does Proudhon think of existing government and institutions?

2. Proudhon also says that all he is doing with his claim that property is theft is "anticipating history a little." What does he mean by that?

Source: Geoffrey Bruun, ed., *Revolution and Reaction, 1848–1852* (Princeton, N.J.: D. Van Nostrand, 1958), pp. 109–110.

production units, which he called "phalanxes." Limited in size to four hundred families, each phalanx would contain a residential hotel, school, market, health service, and other public facilities—in addition to its own farms and manufacturing plants. All these were to be community property, and the rule governing labor and distribution would be "*From* each according to his *ability; to* each according to his *needs*." (The Marxists were later to adopt this slogan.) Surplus production would be exchanged for other goods by barter among the phalanxes; within each plant, workers would change jobs often in order to reduce the monotony of performing repetitive tasks.

Fourier's ideas attracted numerous followers, and a few

A Utopian's Response to Women's Poverty Read a French woman's plea in support of Fourier's proposal.

Marxist socialism
A type of socialism based on the ideas of Karl Marx, who believed that historical forces, not individual reformers, would bring about the end of capitalism.

"From *each according to his* ability; to *each according to his* needs."

—Karl Marx

believed that these developments were leading toward the collapse of capitalism independent of the will of individuals. According to **Marxist socialism**, therefore, the proper task of workers and intellectuals is to understand the trend of history and to participate in its forward movement.

isolated phalanxes were actually established in America—notably Brook Farm, near Boston. Each phalanx had its own internal problems, and each was doomed to failure. Success for Fourier's plan would have required whole societies to be reorganized in phalanxes, and there was no chance for this to happen.

The efforts of Robert Owen, an industrialist and utopian planner, failed for the same basic reason. A successful cotton mill owner in New Lanark, Scotland, Owen was distressed by the poverty, ignorance, and immorality of his employees. He determined to change matters and succeeded in setting up a model factory and community in New Lanark. He was not satisfied, however, with his own local reforms and sought to reform the whole industrial order. Owen observed that the factory system had not freed workers—it had enslaved them. Under laissez-faire, their condition remained at a miserable level. Morals had fallen along with material standards of living, and the traditional ties of compassion between master and servant had been broken. Owen had fair success in promoting remedial factory legislation, but he failed to persuade factory owners to follow his example at New Lanark.

 A Factory Owner with a Social Conscience Read Robert Owen on the evils of the factory system.

After his failure with factory owners, Owen decided to bring about change by turning to the working people themselves. He proposed that they be organized into cooperative, self-sufficient villages, and several producers' cooperatives grew out of his efforts, including one overseas—at New Harmony, Indiana. Founded in 1824, this venture, like the others, lasted only a few years. Owen nonetheless left his mark on public thought and on the struggle to lighten the harshness of industrialism. But it took another, more rigorous thinker to produce a tougher brand of socialism that would meet the capitalist system head on.

A History of New Harmony (http://www.usi.edu/hnh/history.asp) Learn about the American utopian community of New Harmony.

Marxist Socialism

The utopian socialists failed above all because they relied on human good will—on industrialists to give up their property without resistance, and on workers to share and share alike without quarrels and self-seeking. Karl Marx, however, had no such illusions. His study of history told him that events are shaped by underlying economic developments rather than by idealistic reformers, and he

For this reason, Marx and his followers regarded his doctrine as "scientific." Marx set forth certain theories and sought to prove them by the evidence of history. Materialist, rationalist, atheist, libertarian, and revolutionist, Marx was an heir of the Enlightenment—who drew upon the leading scientific, economic, and philosophical ideas of the nineteenth century. But reflecting also the Romantic spirit of his age, Marx's teachings contain strong elements of faith and feeling as well as of reason and science.

 Introduction to "Heaven on Earth: The Rise and Fall of Socialism" (http://www.pbs.org/heavenonearth/video_hour1_intro.html) Watch a brief introduction to early socialism.

Marx and Engels

Marx was the child of middle-class Jews in western Germany who had converted to Lutheranism. He began studying to become a lawyer like his father, but became attracted to history and philosophy. He would have liked to qualify himself for a professorship, but he feared that his Jewish background and his liberal political views would block his chances of winning a university appointment, for this was the period of the conservative reaction in Germany. Caught up by the revolutionary stirrings of the 1840s, he turned instead to journalism and pamphleteering.

With his lifelong friend and associate Friedrich Engels, Marx organized revolutionary groups and wrote *The Communist Manifesto* in 1848. After participating in the insurrections of that year in the Rhineland, he escaped to London, where he remained for the rest of his life. He was one of the first critics to stress the international character of working-class movements—thus placing himself in opposition to the mounting spirit of nationalism in Europe. From London, Marx continued his association with revolutionary movements in various countries and helped found the First (Socialist) International in 1864. He also spent long hours in the British Museum library studying history and economics.

Class Struggle and Revolution

The most famous product of Marx's labors, *Das Kapital* (Capital), consisted chiefly of theory and analysis and is closely related to the writings of the classical liberal economists (pp. 426–427). Working largely from their principles, Marx concluded that all economic value is produced by human labor and that the capitalist unjustly takes over a portion of this value. The system, he claimed, promises nothing but misery to the laborers and contains contradictions that ensure its own destruction.

But Marx's economic conclusions were perhaps the least important of his ideas. His enormous influence would come from the fact that he was able to join his criticism of capitalism with a revolutionary program based on a unified view of history, politics, and morals. The philosopher Hegel gave Marx the key to his general view. History is an unceasing process, said Hegel, governed at any moment by the "dialectic" struggle between a dominant idea and its opposing idea (pp. 403–404). Marx was excited by Hegel's dialectic principle, but he had no use for the notion that ideas are the prime forces in history. After much study and reflection, he concluded that the "mode of production" (the way in which society is organized to produce material goods) is the main determining force in a given society; its opposing force arises from technological changes that are no longer appropriate to the established economic structure. Thus did Marx "turn Hegel upside down." The flow of history and the growth of ideas and institutions, Marx thought, are all shaped by changes in the mode of production. And this evolution had passed through four principal stages: "the Asiatic, the ancient, the feudal, and the modern bourgeois methods of production."

Each mode of production, Marx said, involves "class struggle," for each serves a particular "ruling" class, which takes advantage of its opposing "exploited" class. The ancient world had its masters and slaves, and the feudal age, its nobles and peasants. As for the capitalist age, it had its increasingly wealthy and powerful class of business owners, managers, and stockholders and its increasingly numerous and poverty-stricken class of industrial wage-hands. Marx called the first of these groups by the French name for the class of better-off townspeople, the **bourgeoisie**, and the second by a name derived from that of the propertyless citizens of ancient Rome, the **proletariat** (pp. 97–98). Marx believed that the ruling class of each age provides laws and institutions to guarantee its continued exploitation of the opposing class. The state itself thus becomes a mechanism of suppression. The government of the nineteenth-century capitalist state, he declared, was "a committee for managing the common affairs of the whole bourgeoisie."

Social revolutions occur, according to Marx, when a new mode of production—taking shape within the framework of the old—bursts the bonds of established laws and relationships. The agents of the revolution are the "new" class, which in time becomes the ruling class. Thus, he argued, the seventeenth- and eighteenth-century revolutions in England, North America, and France, as well as those of 1830 and 1848, had been "bourgeois revolutions." The effect of these revolutions had been to overthrow feudalism and its noble ruling class, thereby paving the way for a new capitalist economic order in which the ruling class would be the bourgeoisie. Marx regarded the bourgeoisie's exploitation of the proletariat as the most brutal in history. Nevertheless, he felt that the bourgeoisie had played a constructive and progressive role, essentially by destroying the previous feudal order and creating the liberal state, within which the proletariat could prepare for its own proletarian revolution. This was in keeping with his (and Hegel's) view of history as moving irresistibly toward higher and higher goals of human fulfillment.

bourgeoisie
In Marxist thought, the ruling class of wealthy and powerful business owners, managers, and stockholders.

proletariat
In Marxist thought, the poverty-stricken class of industrial wage-hands.

Proletarian Revolution, Socialism, and Communism

But the hour had struck for the bourgeoisie, as it had earlier for the nobility. The potential of expanding technology could not be realized within the structure of private capitalism; and the capitalist system of production, hit by increasingly severe depressions, was stumbling toward its end. In accordance with the dialectic principle, the old system had already brought into existence the class that would overthrow it and build a new order upon the ruins. This class, the proletariat, was being drawn into the industrial centers in ever-larger numbers. All it needed in order to help history along was Marxist instruction and organization.

Marx predicted that the mounting clashes between the proletariat and the bourgeoisie would lead to the triumph of the working class—either by peaceful means, within the framework of the liberal state, or more likely through violent revolution. This victory would bring an end to the historic class struggle, for all individuals would then be included in one body of workers. Dismantling the old social order and taking over the means of production would be carried out under the "dictatorship of the proletariat." This would be followed, in turn, by an intermediate period of democratic "socialism," during which individuals would "work according to their ability and receive according to their output." Socialism would lead eventually to pure "communism."

Once communism had been reached, the state would "wither away," Marx believed, because without a class struggle, there would be no reason for the existence of a state. Thus would come into being, for the first time in civilized history, "true" liberty for all. In the vaguely outlined communist society, voluntary associations would plan and carry out production; individuals would work according to their abilities and receive according to their needs; private persuasion and restraint would replace police, prisons, and war.

"All the proletariat needed to help history along was Marxist instruction and organization."

 "Working Men of All Countries, Unite!" Read an excerpt from *The Communist Manifesto*.

Marx's vision of communism was not much different from the ideal societies of the utopian socialists, and like them, it had to be accepted on faith. Marx was its prophet, and his vision of

TWO DIFFERENT FORMS OF MARXISM DEVELOPED:

"Evolutionary" Marxism in Most of Western and Central Europe

- Marxism there grew into a mass movement.

- Marxists found a voice in trade unions and in legislatures (see photo).

- With this acceptance and influence, evolutionary Marxists argued that it was better to work within the existing system.

- They stressed democracy, parliamentary methods, and class cooperation as means of achieving further reforms.

- Eduard Bernstein, a German socialist, was the leading advocate for this view.

"Revolutionary" Marxism in Eastern Europe

- The absence of effective representative government prevented change by peaceful, legal methods.

- Contrary to Marx's expectation that worldwide revolution would begin in the most highly industrialized countries, it was in relatively unindustrialized Russia that the socialist revolution would take place.

---

the end of capitalism leading to communism resembled the vision of the end of the world making way for the coming kingdom. At a time when the foundations of "old-fashioned" religion and liberalism were being challenged, Marx created a new worldview of the facts, theories, and hopes of the industrial age. Its promise appealed to the working class, but it appealed also to many intellectuals who felt alienated from industrialism and were looking for some kind of total reorientation. Marxism offered a unified view and a psychological substitute for traditional religion.

Revolutionary and Evolutionary Marxism

Like traditional religion, too, Marxism has been open to differing interpretations. Had capitalism faltered and collapsed during the nineteenth century, as Marx himself expected, the division among his followers might have been less profound. But the established order proved much tougher, much more adaptable, than he had expected. Reform laws and unions strengthened capitalism (as did Marxist criticism), improved the distribution of purchasing power, and bettered the conditions of the workers. The rich were getting richer, as Marx had predicted, but the poor (at least in the West) were not getting poorer. And

in the United States, the young giant of capitalism, no strong revolutionary feeling or class consciousness appeared among the wage earners.

>> **"1,341,587 Social Democratic Voters"** A headline in a newspaper of Germany's Marxist party trumpets the party's triumph in the second round of voting in a general election in 1890. There has been a "567,405 Increase" over the first round, giving the Social Democrats the largest single share of voters. A banner proclaims: "The World Is Ours, No Matter What"; a poem celebrates "The First Act" of revolution. But did success within bourgeois politics mean that violent revolution was unnecessary? That question would eventually divide the Marxist movement.

How did the Marxists deal with this indefinite postponement of the day of revolution? The movement split into two broad camps: evolutionary and revolutionary.

A different sort of attack upon the established order of the nineteenth century took the form of **anarchism**. This view holds that any use of authority—economic, religious, or political—is an unjustified interference with the individual. Believing that human beings are basically good, the anarchists claimed that voluntary, harmonious relationships could be achieved among individuals if the power of the state were removed. Some, like the Russian writer Leo Tolstoy and the American essayist Henry David Thoreau, firmly opposed the use of violence as a means of realizing their ideas, but others sought to undermine the state by assassination of government officials, terrorism, and insurrection.

Though these anarchist ideas were first expressed in western Europe, it was Mikhail Bakunin (**buh-KOO-nyin**), a Russian nobleman, who exerted the largest influence. Bakunin died in 1876; his followers succeeded in killing (among others) Tsar Alexander II of Russia, President Sadi Carnot of France, King Humbert I of Italy, and President William McKinley of the United States. Such acts of terror horrified the powerful everywhere but failed to produce an effective movement for social change or for the abolition of state power. Nevertheless, these acts were forerunners of terrorist killings in the twentieth century.

> "*Capital cannot do without labor, nor labor without capital.*"
>
> —Leo XIII

LO² Reforming, Affirming, and Rejecting the Nineteenth Century

Marxism was not the only way of thinking about economic and social affairs, and human destiny in general, that developed in the nineteenth century. The authority of both traditional religion and modern science was drawn upon to criticize or extol the nineteenth-century changes; and influential thinkers denied both these authorities and rejected the changing world in which they lived.

Christian Social Reform

It was unthinkable that the established churches of the West could ignore the impact of industrial capitalism or the Marxist (and anarchist) attack upon it. While the one appeared destructive of certain Christian values and virtues, the other appealed openly to class hatred and violence. Both were roundly condemned, at last, by the most powerful spokesman of Western Christendom, the pope. In 1891, Leo XIII addressed his bishops through an *encyclical*

 **A Papal Encyclical Analyzes the Modern World** Read an excerpt from Pope Leo's encyclical.

(from the Greek for "going round"—to many recipients) entitled *Rerum Novarum* (Of New Things). In this carefully drawn, comprehensive statement, he set forth the position of his church on the relations between capital and labor.

The pope's immediate concern was for the "misery and wretchedness which press so heavily at this moment on the large majority of the very poor." The workers, he went on, "have been given over, isolated and defenseless, to the callousness of employers and the greed of unrestrained competition." Going still further, he declared that "a small number of very rich men have been able to lay upon the masses of the poor a yoke little better than slavery itself."

But the socialist remedy, the pontiff declared, called for the destruction of private property. Such action would be unjust to the present lawful owners of property and would deprive workers of the main object of their labors. He also rejected the socialist idea of equalizing wealth as being "against nature." The overriding mistake of the Marxists, however, was their feeling that social classes must be mutually hostile, "that rich and poor are intended by nature to live at war with one another." On the contrary, stated Pope Leo, "it is ordained by nature that these two classes should exist in harmony. . . . Capital cannot do without labor, nor labor without capital."

Quoting freely from the leading Catholic philosopher of the Middle Ages, Thomas Aquinas (p. 236), who was known for his efforts to harmonize conflicting positions, the pope urged a Christian "middle course." Moderation and cooperation should guide the common affairs of employers and employees. Working people must give honest work and never injure the owners or their property; the owners must never make excessive demands on their employees' labor or pay them less than the needs of their families require. For the purpose of mutual help and wage bargaining, workers should be allowed to form unions; and if workers find themselves too weak to defend their rightful interests, the government must intervene with protective legislation. At the same time, however, the government must preserve absolutely the sanctity of private property.

Rerum Novarum gave little comfort to aggressive entrepreneurs on the political right or to angry critics of capitalism on the left. But it offered a guide for moderates who wished to see the rewards of labor improved while avoiding industrial violence. It also prompted the founding of new Catholic trade unions and Catholic political parties in most of the countries of Europe. These organizations have exercised notable influence to the present day. Finally, *Rerum Novarum* pointed the way, morally and philosophically, to the democratic welfare states of the twentieth century.

Because of its organizational structure, it was possible and logical for the Roman Catholic Church to present a unified response to the disturbing economic changes of the nineteenth century. The response by Protestant churches, on the other hand, reflected their historical divisions into numerous national and denominational groups. In the wake of scientific findings and rising secularism in the Western world, Christian (and Jewish) believers were already torn between "modernists," who accepted the new science, and "fundamentalists," who rejected it and adhered to the "higher truth" of the literal Bible. Now another serious split was developing with respect to the impact of industrialization. Most Protestant preachers and congregations remained essentially conservative on economic issues, but an activist minority began to speak out for increased social consciousness, measures to assist the poor, and greater "economic justice."

The Impact of Darwinism

Darwin's theory of evolution was not just an advance in biology; it called into question the place of humans in the universe and their relationship with God. If every living thing had come about through brutal struggle, how could one trust the Bible story of a creator who had looked at his handiwork and seen that "indeed, it was very good"? And if humans were the descendants of ape-like creatures, how could one believe that the creator had made them "a little lower than God, and crowned them with glory and honor"? This was not just a question of whether the Bible was a reliable guide to science, as with Galileo (p. 359). Darwinism could be taken to mean that killing and dying were no aberration caused by sin, but were built into the workings of the universe—and that humans were animals just like any other (see photo). The reaction of many religious believers was to deny and disparage Darwinism; skeptics and atheists took it as confirming their unbelief, though they also sought to uphold the special value of the human race.

All the same, by the end of the nineteenth century, the theory of evolution was widely accepted in the West, and from the start, there were philosophers, statesmen, industrialists, and theologians who welcomed the doctrine and sought to extend it beyond the biological field. Herbert Spencer, a self-educated advocate of evolution, was one of those most excited by Darwin's writings. It was he who stressed Darwin's phrase "survival of the fittest" to describe the process of natural selection. In addition, he claimed that the survival of the fittest applies not only to living creatures but to human institutions, customs, and ideas as well. All of these, he reasoned, have their cycle of origin, growth, competition, decay, and extinction. Thus there can be no "absolutes" of religious or moral truth; there is only the passing truth of ideas that have evolved and have (so far) survived.

These convictions, however, did not drive Spencer to atheism. He insisted that behind evolution there must exist a supernatural power—one that humans cannot fully know. He believed, however, that moral standards can be established on the basis of what we do know. Spencer put forward a "science" of ethics based on the principles of natural evolution: moral acts are those that contribute to human adaptation and progress. Moral perfection will be reached, he concluded, by "the completely adapted man in the completely evolved society."

Spencer's philosophy of morals did not pass unchallenged. If morality is geared to the evolutionary processes of nature,

MR. BERGH TO THE RESCUE.

THE DEFRAUDED GORILLA. "That *Man* wants to claim my Pedigree. He says he is one of my Descendants."
Mr. BERGH. "Now, Mr. DARWIN, how could you insult him so?"

>> **Evolutionist and Humanitarian** Among the most disturbing of Darwin's ideas was the claim that humans had not been created by God in his own image but had evolved from lower animals. A cartoon of 1871 by the American Thomas Nast targets both Darwin and Henry Bergh, founder of the American Society for the Prevention of Cruelty to Animals. Nast mocks Darwin for ruthlessly lowering humans to the animal level, and Bergh for sentimentally raising animals to the human level.

The Granger Collection, New York

what becomes of one's own moral responsibility and freedom? What has science to do with ethics? And how could nature, so brutal in its workings, serve as a foundation for morals? Some, indeed, saw magnificence in the new view of nature; Darwin himself found it thrilling: "Thus, from the war of nature, from famine and death, the most exalted object which we are capable of conceiving, namely the production of the higher animals, directly follows. There is grandeur in this view of life . . . from so simple a beginning endless forms most beautiful and wonderful have been, and are being evolved."

Social Darwinism

In this way, Darwinism replaced the idea of a static world, of fixed relations and values, with the idea of continuous change and struggle. And if this was true of the workings of nature and the moral development of humanity, it must also be true of the workings and development of actual societies. Karl Marx declared that *On the Origin of Species* furnished a "basis in natural science for the class struggle in history" and sent Darwin a copy of *Das Kapital*, though the scientist probably did not read it. But most admirers of Darwin also admired the industrial capitalism of their time, and believed that the survival of the fittest applied in economic and social life as well as in nature. As Herbert Spencer explained, "The poverty of the incapable, the distresses that come upon the imprudent, the starvation of the idle, and those shoulderings aside of the weak by the strong, which leave so many 'in shallows and miseries,' are the decree of a large far-seeing benevolence."

The American billionaire John D. Rockefeller once used a vivid metaphor to explain how, in his opinion, the theory of natural selection worked to the advantage of all. The man who had built Standard Oil into a giant monopoly by beating out his competitors compared his work to the breeding of a lovely flower. The American Beauty rose, with its splendor and fragrance, could not have been produced, Rockefeller told a Sunday school audience, except by sacrificing the buds that grew up around it. In the same way, the development of a large business is "merely survival of the fittest . . . merely the working-out of a law of nature and a law of God."

Rockefeller and other titans of industry were eager promoters of what came to be known as **Social Darwinism**. Essentially, this ideology approved a struggle of "all against all," in the manner of the jungle. And the idea readily passed from one of battle among individuals to one of battle among races and nations. Darwin's theory strengthened the convictions of slave owners, racists, militarists, and extreme nationalists. Many individuals, including some respected philosophers, glorified war as a "pruning hook" for improving the health of humanity. "Making war is not only a biological law," declared a German general, "but a moral obligation, and, as such, an indispensable factor in civilization."

> "*God is dead. God remains dead. And we have killed him.*"
>
> —Nietzsche, *The Gay Science*

Rejection of Traditional Systems and Values: Kierkegaard and Nietzsche

Social Darwinism The idea that some individuals, races, and nations are "fitter" than others and will thereby dominate or destroy weaker rivals.

Socialists and Darwinists found meaningful patterns in human destiny, and Christian social reformers adapted long-standing traditions to the changing present. But there were also thinkers for whom the nineteenth-century changes seemed to call into question all traditions and values, and even meaning and certainty in general. Their views, too, powerfully influenced people at the time and down to the present.

Kierkegaard

Søren Kierkegaard (**KEER-ki-gahrd**), a Danish theologian-philosopher who lived in the first half of the nineteenth century, attacked Hegel's view that the world is rational and that it represents the unfolding of a divine plan (pp. 403–404). How can any person, a particular part of an uncompleted scheme, know what the completed form will be? If the world is a system, only God can know it! It follows, therefore, that people cannot presume that they occupy a specific place in a known scheme of things.

Instead, Kierkegaard saw human beings as alone in the universe—existing "outside" nature, possessing the power to think about the universe and to choose what they will believe and how they will act. This very freedom, thought Kierkegaard, gives individuals both responsibility and anxiety (*Angst*). They must suffer anxiety, for they can never be certain about the consequences of their own free choice—including the choice to make the "leap of faith" toward the God of Christianity.

Nietzsche

Friedrich Nietzsche (**NEE-chuh**), a German philosopher who died in 1900, challenged not just the traditional view of human nature but the entire institutional and ideological heritage of the West. When he said, "God is dead," he meant not only the God of traditional monotheism but the whole range of philosophical absolutes, from Plato down to his own day. Because all Western values had been linked to those ultimate "eternal" values, they crashed to earth with "God's death."

Nietzsche's most revealing work is his most poetic, *Thus Spake Zarathustra* (1884). In it, he allowed his unconscious self to speak freely, without regard to logical organization. The book is a flowing stream of images, symbols, and visions, some of which have not yet been fully understood. In *Zarathustra* and other works, notably *Beyond Good and Evil* (1886), Nietzsche considered the various conditions of human beings and their relation to the universe. He was one of the first thinkers to stress the absurdity of human existence: the inability of our reason to comprehend our surroundings—though we are born to try.

All existing systems, whether based on reason or revelation, appeared false to Nietzsche. He focused his attack on the bourgeois civilization of the late nineteenth century: on science, industrialism, democracy, and Christianity. As an untamed individualist, he rejected theism (belief in God as Creator and Ruler), mechanism, and any other idea that would deny human freedom. What he hated most was the reduction of people to narrowly specialized creatures and their subjection to a Christian ("slave") morality.

Nietzsche presented these ideas most fully in *The Genealogy of Morals*, published in 1887. He longed for a return to the heroic Greek idea of the "whole man"; this goal could be achieved only by the overthrow of current values and the permitting of determined individuals ("supermen") to recover their wholeness through disciplined struggle and sacrifice. Nietzsche left unanswered many questions as to how these aims could be accomplished. His importance lay primarily in his bold challenge to "sacred" beliefs and in his bitter protest against the smothering of the individual by the "herd."

LO³ Literature and Art in the Machine Age

Writers and painters responded sharply to the changes in civilization triggered by science and the machine. They developed, by the middle of the nineteenth century, new goals and forms that would eclipse Romanticism in European literature and art.

The Response of Writers: Realism

The new trend in literature was known as **Realism**. It started in France with Honoré de Balzac (**BAHL-zak**), who began writing successful novels late in the 1820s. (His collected works were later published as *The Human Comedy*.) Balzac placed under close examination men and women of all stations in society. A keen observer, he set the style of insightful reporting of human strengths and weaknesses that marked French literature for the rest of the century.

>> **"Please Sir, I Want Some More"** An illustration by George Cruikshank shows Dickens's boy-hero Oliver Twist, an inmate of a workhouse—an institution for destitute people where conditions were deliberately kept harsh to discourage applicants—making an unprecedented request. The scandalized workhouse master hauls him before the workhouse board and makes the stunning announcement: "Oliver Twist has asked for more!" A horrified board member declares: "That boy will be come to be hung." In spite of Dickens's satire, the British workhouse system was not abolished until 1930.

In England, Realism spotlighted the social effects of the Industrial Revolution. Charles Dickens, one of the most popular authors of the era, called the attention of his readers to the cruelties and hardships of the urban working class (see photo). In the generally lighthearted *Pickwick Papers* (1837), he nevertheless exposed the grim debtors' prisons; in *Oliver Twist* (1839), he revealed the horror of the English workhouses (places of forced labor for the poor; see photo). Though his many novels range widely over human themes and problems, they have a strong note of social protest, and Dickens's books helped bring about the reform legislation of the nineteenth century.

 The BBC Companion Site to Its Production of Charles Dickens's *Bleak House* (http://www.bbc.co.uk/drama/bleakhouse/animation.shtml) Watch an animated summary of Charles Dickens's *Bleak House*.

The continental writer who addressed himself most directly to the problems of his day was a Norwegian, Henrik Ibsen. The son of a once-prosperous businessman, Ibsen grew up with contempt toward his own society, especially the new bourgeois. In *Pillars of Society* (1877), he revealed the corruption and hypocrisy he had observed among "established" Norwegian families. His next plays dealt with such issues as female emancipation (*A Doll's House*) and the conflict between commercial interests and personal honesty (*An Enemy of the People*). Not surprisingly, these

Private Collection/Ken Welsh/The Bridgeman Art Library

works brought hostile reactions from middle-class audiences. In his later plays, Ibsen gave up his challenges to the social system and created memorable portraits of individuals (*Hedda Gabler*).

George Bernard Shaw, a brilliant Irish author, was among Ibsen's admirers, and he turned his own pen to the cause of social criticism. A most prolific writer, Shaw composed nearly fifty plays during the course of his long life. Virtually every one of them contains both satire and "message"; his characters, accordingly, tend to be two-dimensional, serving mainly as bearers of intellectual argument.

The relation of literature to social questions during the latter part of the nineteenth century is underlined by the fact that Shaw was a self-taught economist and one of the founders of English socialism. "In all my plays," he once said, "my economic studies have played as important a part as a knowledge of anatomy does in the works of Michelangelo." The drama that first attracted public attention was his *Widowers' Houses* (1892), a condemnation of slum landlordism. This was followed by *Mrs. Warren's Profession*, showing the economic roots of modern prostitution, and *Arms and the Man*, satirizing the military profession. Later dramas dealt with such matters as poverty, war, religious faith, and eugenics (human genetic improvement).

In the nineteenth century, Russian writers for the first time became leading figures in Western literature, beginning in the Romantic era with Alexander Pushkin and Nicolai Gogol. Pushkin was the first Russian writer whose poems, plays, and short stories were read and admired in the rest of Europe. In his homeland, he is still revered as a writer of genius whose own short life was filled with passion and adventure and as the forefather of modern Russian literature in general. Gogol's *Taras Bulba* (1835) tells of adventures and conflicts among the high-spirited Cossacks, warrior-horsemen who fought the Tartar enemies of Russia.

> "*In all my plays, my economic studies have played as important a part as a knowledge of anatomy does in the works of Michelangelo.*"
>
> —George Bernard Shaw

Later in the century, however, the finest Russian novelists, Feodor Dostoevsky (**dos-tuh-YEF-skee**) and Leo Tolstoy, worked under the influence of Realism. The best known of their works are Tolstoy's *War and Peace* (1868), describing the inner life and struggles of Russian aristocrats against the epic background of the struggle with Napoleon; and Dostoevsky's exploration of sin and redemption set among provincial landowners, *The Brothers Karamazov* (1880).

The Response of Artists: Realism, Impressionism, Expressionism

In the arts, social protest was expressed in the works of only a few individuals. Honoré Daumier (**doh-MYEY**), for instance, rebelled against the Romantic tradition, sympathized with the poor, and felt that art should correspond to social facts. His oil painting *A Third-Class Carriage* depicts modern life in an untraditional way (see photo). Earlier artists had painted groups of people united by some event like Christ's death or a wedding feast (see photos on pages 295, 350). In Daumier's painting, nothing is happening, and the only thing that holds these weary people together is that they are sitting in the same railroad car. Still, the nursing mother and the woman with the basket are movingly noble, patient, and strong. Daumier both reports on working-class life in the age of mass transportation and expresses his veneration for the people who have to live it.

>> *A Third-Class Carriage* Mid-nineteenth-century French railroad companies offered three types of passenger accommodation: first class, for "people of quality"; second class, for "respectable citizens"; and third class, for "laboring people." Daumier also depicted first- and second-class passengers, but as satirical caricatures; passengers in the lowest class were the only ones that he depicted with admiration and respect.

Impressionism
A style of painting that sought to record the fleeting appearance of objects as they appear to the eye.

Expressionism
A style of painting that sought to capture an emotional or spiritual reality.

Giraudon/Art Resource, NY

>> *Impression: Sunrise* "Something I'd made in Le Havre, from my window, sun in the mist and a few masts of boats sticking up in the foreground." That was Monet's description of the painting whose title inaugurated Impressionism, and the reason he gave for the title he chose was: "Landscape is nothing but an impression, and an instantaneous one."

Daumier's rejection of the traditional "grand" subjects for paintings was part of a larger movement toward the depiction of contemporary life that continued with **Impressionism**. Unlike the Realists, the Impressionists were not concerned to send a message of social satire or protest. Instead, they sought to record the appearance of objects immediately as they saw them at a particular instant, regardless of their prior knowledge of their shape and color—a break with traditional painting. The eye does not see clearly what it is not directly looking at, and it does not see under strong and even light; so the Impressionists made their pictures looked blurred and "unfinished."

 The National Gallery of London's Guide to Impressionism (http://www.nationalgallery.org.uk/paintings/learn-about-art/guide-to-impressionism/guide-to-impressionism) Take a gallery tour of Impressionist paintings.

The new style developed gradually in France from midcentury onward, but it received its name from an unfriendly critic in 1874 when Claude Monet **(moh-NEY)** and like-minded artists held an exhibition in Paris that included his *Impression: Sunrise* (see photo). Monet had carefully studied Turner, but unlike the sunset in *The Fighting Téméraire* (see photo on page 408), Monet's murky dawn over a busy seaport is not meant to inspire awe. Instead, the paint-dappled surface of the canvas guides the viewer's imagination to form an "impression" of a complex, changing scene. The waves are streaks of paint, the fishing boats are blobs, the cranes and masts and smokestacks are fuzzy scribbles. Even without seeking to send a message, Monet's painting reflects the new world of the nineteenth century.

 Impressionism Defined Read a nineteenth-century writer's explanation of Impressionism.

The same is true in different ways of other Impressionist painters. In France, Auguste Renoir **(REN-wahr)** painted female nudes without graceful poses or ideal beauty, and Edgar Degas **(dey-GAH)** depicted ballerinas tying on their shoes rather than pirouetting across the stage; in the United States, Mary Cassatt unsentimentally recorded informal scenes of mothers bathing and playing with their daughters. In all cases, the effect, as the French novelist Émile Zola said of Monet, is "living, profound, and above all truthful"—truthful to the new era in which they lived.

Impressionism was a beginning, not an end. The ultimate success and popularity of the Impressionists gave all artists a fresh sense of freedom and power. The traditional rules that had required "dignified" or "worthy" subjects, correct drawing, and balanced composition were coming into doubt. Paul Cézanne **(sey-ZAN)**, who came to Paris in 1861, further undermined the rules, for example, in his *The Peppermint Bottle* (see photo), one of hundreds of such pictures that he painted. "Still lifes"—finely detailed paintings of food and utensils—were pioneered by seventeenth-century Dutch painters. In the nineteenth century, Cézanne leaves details to photographers. Instead, he looks for the inner structure that gives objects solidity and permanence—"treating nature," as he put it, "by the cylinder, the sphere, the cone." In addition, Cézanne has broken with the rules of perspective (showing three-dimensional scenes on a flat surface) that artists had followed since the Renaissance (p. 298), so that together, these luminously solid objects form a flat pattern on the surface of the canvas. In his search for underlying truth, Cézanne has taken another step away from reproducing exact appearances.

A younger artist, Suzanne Valadon, undertook the same search for truth with similar methods. Valadon began as a model with Impressionist painters, taught herself to paint, and became

Paul Cezanne, The Peppermint Bottle, 1893/1895, Chester Dale Collection, Image courtesy National Gallery of Art, Washington, D.C. oil on canvas, .659 x .821 (26 x 32-3/8). 1963.10.104. (1768)/PA.

◄◄ Flat Patterns and Solid Objects
Flattening out a few household items on a table against a back wall, Cézanne creates a maze-like pattern of colors and lines. Yet the flask and bottle tower over the napkin and cloth like massive buildings over a landscape of swelling hills and valleys. His painting is one-dimensional and three-dimensional at the same time—a new and complex depiction of everyday reality

from recording the outward appearances of things; instead, he used the methods of Impressionism to express his own deep feelings about nature and life. Van Gogh was thus the pioneer of the modern school of **Expressionist** painters.

Extraordinary spiritual and mental stress marked van Gogh's brief life. The son of a Dutch Protestant minister, he sensed a divine creative force within nature and all forms of life and sought to show this force in his paintings. His works were the products of an emotional frenzy that passed into periods of mental illness. Finally, when he feared that he would no longer be able to paint, he took his own life (1890).

But in the years before his death, beginning with a stay at Arles in southern France, van Gogh produced a series of remarkable canvases. Stimulated by the sun-drenched countryside, he painted it with fevered excitement,

a leading artist in her turn. Late in her life, she painted a self-portrait, known from the surroundings in which she depicted herself as *The Blue Room* (see photo). Actually, she reclines in a cavernous array of blue fabric, plumped up beneath her and hanging above her. The fabric, as well as Valadon's pants and her upper body, are both massively solid yet form a splendid pattern of contrasting colors—a Cézanne-like way of depicting the appearance of objects. Her pose is a standard one of female nudes dating back to the *Venus of Urbino* (see photo on page 300), but the pose actually stresses the contrast between herself and those traditional figures—between Renaissance goddesses who symbolize desire and ideal beauty, and a twentieth-century woman who wears baggy pants and sticks a cigarette between her lips.

> *"Impressionism was a beginning, not an end."*

Expressionism

Meanwhile, Vincent van Gogh was moving even farther away

►► The Blue Room Suzanne Valadon, renowned as a painter of female nudes, here depicts herself informally clothed but in a pose made famous by nude paintings of the Renaissance. The result is a glowing pattern of color, massive solidity and depth, a wry comment on the tradition of nude painting, and an insightful self-portrait all in one.

CNAC/MNAM/ Reunion des Musees Nationaux/Art Resource, NY

Literature and Art in the Machine Age   **451**

Van Gogh Museum, Amsterdam/Art Resource, NY

>> *Wheatfield with Crows* Even more than Monet or Cézanne, Van Gogh conveys a truth that is different from "what things actually look like." In this landscape painted not long before his suicide, the wheat and crows, the sky and the rutted track, are all recognizable. But the intense colors and the jagged and twisting streaks of paint convey something else—the turbulence and menace that the artist finds in the scene, and which originate in himself. The truth here is not about the landscape but about the artist.

applying color with greater vigor and freedom than any painter had done before him. He did not try to imitate the hues of nature; the colors represented his feelings. Yellow, his favorite color, was his means of expressing the ever-present love of God. Blue, pale violet, and green expressed rest or sleep. A striking example of van Gogh's last works is *Wheatfield with Crows* (see photo), a view of a landscape near Paris finished just before his death. It presents "vast stretches of wheat under troubled skies," expressing, as he wrote, "sadness and the extreme of loneliness."

Such was the final response of a great and sensitive talent in the closing years of the nineteenth century.

 Listen to a synopsis of Chapter 23.

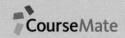 **Access to the eBook with additional review material and study tools may be found online at CourseMate for WCIV. Sign in at www.cengagebrain.com.**

{ Learning Your Way }

89% of students surveyed found the interactive online quizzes valuable.

We know that no two students are alike. **WCIV** was developed to help you learn Western Civilization in a way that works for you.

Not only is the format fresh and contemporary, it's also concise and focused. And, **WCIV** is loaded with a variety of supplements, like Chapter in Review cards, flash cards, a robust eBook, and more.

At **CengageBrain.com**, you'll find plenty of resources to help you study no matter what your learning style!

PART V

THE WEST AND THE WORLD IN THE ERA OF GLOBAL CIVILIZATION,

1900–PRESENT

A s spectacular as were the nineteenth-century shifts in Western civilization, by the end of that century they had only begun to make their full impact felt. Science and technology, capitalism and urbanization, liberalism and nationalism, and artistic and cultural experiment were forces that had almost limitless potential for change. Furthermore, these forces could not be confined to Western civilization's European and North American heartland, but were bound to take effect throughout the world.

The results, from the late nineteenth to the early twenty-first century, have been continued spectacular change within Western civilization, a rapid merging of Western and non-Western civilizations, and the growth of a new pattern of modern global civilization, replacing the traditional pattern of the past.

Over the last century and a half, the Western changes have moved in different and often shifting directions, and the terms of the merger between West and non-West have been continually redefined. This has taken place through an immensely complex process of interaction among individuals, nations, social classes, religions, and cultural groups that still continues today. At stake in this process are both the organization of modern global civilization—its distribution of wealth and power among all those groups—and its culture and values—its prevailing patterns of thought and art, feeling and behavior.

The shaping of modern global civilization has involved conflict both within and among Western and non-Western peoples. The era has been one of continual upheavals of social, political, and international orders, among them the rise and fall of colonial empires, of fascism, and of communism. The era has also been one of erosion of old beliefs, values, and patterns of behavior by new ones: the challenge of secular ideologies to traditional religions; drastic alterations in artistic techniques of representing human experience; a historic shift in the balance of status and power between men and women. The era has also seen the deliberate infliction of suffering on the largest scale in the history of the human race: the trench warfare and indiscriminate bombing of the world wars; the genocide of the Jews; the Soviet gulag and the Chinese "Cultural Revolution"; the killing fields of Kampuchea and Rwanda; terrorist attacks on an unprecedented scale of horror. And global civilization has even devised the means to destroy itself through nuclear war or environmental disaster.

Just as important in the coming into being of modern global civilization, however, have been processes of peaceful accommodation and interchange. In Western democratic countries, captains of industry and finance have more or less willingly consented to government intervention in the economy and the creation of welfare states, in the interests of economic stability and social peace. National governments have pooled some of their treasured sovereignty in regional and worldwide trading and financial organizations, in hopes of spreading the benefits and limiting the damage of economic globalization. Critics of global mass culture complain of the "McDonaldization" and "Coca-Colonization" of the world by the United States—but meanwhile, martial arts academies and Chinese take-outs spring up at countless U.S. street corners and shopping malls.

This worldwide accommodation and interchange are symbolized by global civilization's "patron saints"— revered figures who express its yearning for a harmonious future. Notable examples are Mohandas Gandhi, India's leader against both foreign colonialism and its own caste system, eager student of Western literature and thought, and Hindu holy man; and Martin Luther King, disciple of Gandhi, campaigner for African American civil rights in the name of racial harmony, and Bible-quoting Protestant minister. Such people combine in their persons and their deeds ancient religious traditions, modern secular goals, Western and non-Western origins and influences, canny use of mass organization and propaganda, and the waging of bitter conflicts without the use of force.

The realities of the coming into being of global civilization have often been very different from the ideals that such people embody. Time will tell whether the human race becomes a more or less harmonious worldwide community through accommodation and interchange, or undermines itself by worldwide conflict. The final verdict on the role of Western civilization in the destiny of humankind will depend on which of these possibilities comes to pass.

THE IMPERIALIST WORLD ORDER, 1871–1914

LEARNING OBJECTIVES

AFTER READING THIS CHAPTER, YOU SHOULD BE ABLE TO DO THE FOLLOWING:

LO¹ Explain the motives and methods at work in the new imperialism.

LO² Describe the partitioning of Africa.

LO³ Discuss European attempts to dominate Asia.

LO⁴ Identify the failures of the new imperialism.

> **"THE RISE OF GLOBAL CIVILIZATION BEGAN WITH THE SUDDEN APPEARANCE IN THE NINETEENTH CENTURY OF HUGE WORLDWIDE EMPIRES."**

The rise of global civilization began with the sudden appearance in the nineteenth century of huge worldwide empires. This development was closely linked with the other nineteenth-century Western economic, social, and political changes. A few countries in which these changes had gone farthest—most of them in Europe, but including also the United States and Japan—became more powerful than the rest of the world. These countries swiftly divided up the world among themselves, bringing about the first genuinely worldwide order in history. Peoples across the world were interconnected by Western-style imperialism, but Western-style democracy and national independence were privileges of a few nations, and those nations were fierce rivals for worldwide power and influence.

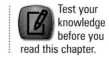 Test your knowledge before you read this chapter.

What do you think?

Imperialism was necessary to bring the benefits of industrial capitalism to the world.

Strongly Disagree						Strongly Agree
1	2	3	4	5	6	7

≪ *The Inauguration of the Suez Canal, 1869* In Edouard Riou's picture, Egyptians watch ships bearing French, Austrian, and Turkish royalty along the new link between the Mediterranean Sea and the Indian Ocean. Thousands of laborers drafted by the local Turkish viceroy died to build this engineering wonder, and British troops soon occupied the strategic waterway and the rest of Egypt. The canal's completion was a milestone in the growth of worldwide trade and travel during the Industrial Revolution, but in that era globalization went together with imperialism.

new imperialism
The era of imperialism that began in the mid-nineteenth century as highly industrialized capitalist countries sought control of global resources and markets.

LO¹ The New Imperialism

Imperialism—the drive for empire, in which one people rules over many subject peoples—is as old as civilization itself. Usually, empire builders are driven by a combination of motives. They are eager for wealth, power, and glory, they may be afraid of being conquered themselves, and they may have reason to be sure of their military superiority, so that the opportunities seem to be there for the taking. Often, too, empire builders believe that they are specially favored by divine power or in some other way uniquely entitled to rule; and they are liable to see themselves as bringers of peace and other benefits to the peoples they conquer. The results of imperial expansion range from vicious exploitation by conquerors and savage revolts by the conquered to welcome prosperity and cultural exchange for both sides. Empire builders always lose their power in the end, but the social and cultural changes that they bring can outlast them for hundreds or even thousands of years.

All these things had often happened over the centuries on a regional or continental scale, and they began to happen again on a worldwide scale after European overseas exploration began in the fifteenth century. About 1760, however, European overseas empires actually shrank: New World settlers won independence, and Europeans at home were busy with a traumatic restructuring of their political, social, and industrial order. But the countries that underwent these changes built up a much wider margin of political, military, and technological supremacy over the rest of the world than ever before. About the middle of the nineteenth century, there began the era of the **new imperialism**, when a small group of well-organized industrial and capitalist countries soon came to dominate the entire world. This group included not only European countries but also two non-European countries that underwent similar political and industrial changes—the United States and Japan.

New Motives

This was not the only way in which the new imperialism differed from the old. With the changes in imperialist countries, new variations on old motives for empire building appeared (pp. 270–272). Alongside the desire of the clergy to spread the Christian gospel, there appeared the nonreligious belief in racial superiority. More powerful than the traditional desire of monarchs for dynastic power and glory was that of whole peoples for nationalistic self-assertion; and the desire of the merchants for gold was replaced by that of industrialists for raw materials and markets, and of bankers for investment outlets.

> *"Empire builders always lose their power in the end, but the social and cultural changes that they bring can outlast them for hundreds or even thousands of years."*

CHRONOLOGY

1842	Opium War ends with British victory over China, weakening Chinese internal control
1850	Russians found city of Vladivostok on Pacific coast
1854	Japan opens ports to foreign vessels
1858	British crown assumes control of India
1885	Europeans agree on ground rules for the partitioning of Africa
1887	French Indochina established
1894	Japan wins Taiwan and claims to Korea from China
1898	United States gains control of the Philippines, also annexes Puerto Rico
1905	Japan defeats Russia, strengthening claim to special rights in Korea, Manchuria, and Port Arthur, China

The economic motive was stronger than ever, but with the growth of industrial capitalism, it took new forms. Factories that mass-produced goods needed mass deliveries of raw materials and mass sales to worldwide markets; steamships and railroads gave them the means of access to both. Capitalists, with more large-scale profits to invest, bought bonds of overseas governments and shares in railroad, mining, and plantation companies in distant continents. When countries with the same level of industrial and financial expertise did business with each other, all this happened on equal terms. But when countries with different levels of expertise did business, the terms soon became unequal—particularly because imperialist governments were prepared to use force to help their capitalists and industrialists get their way. Here, too, countries with advanced industry and technology had the advantage. In 1901, not long after Hiram Maxim's invention of the machine gun, the English writer Hilaire Belloc cynically pointed out that if his countrymen ran into trouble with the "natives" in some distant country,

 Imperial Conquest: The Nation's Savior Read a French writer's economic argument for France becoming a colonial power.

Whatever happens, we have got
The Maxim gun, and they have not.

But the economic motive was only one of the forces behind imperialism. Just as important was the drive for national power and prestige. European nationalism had come of age by 1870; the United States renewed its sense of unique national purpose and mission after the end of the Civil War; and Japan, as the one Asian country to successfully adapt the nineteenth-century Western model, developed its own militant nationalism. The pride and effort that went into achieving self-determination for nations led easily to the desire to control other nations (see photo).

 The "Poet Laureate of Empire" Issues a Word of Warning Read British poet Rudyard Kipling's warning about pride as a driving force behind imperialism.

Humanitarian intellectuals, in the spirit of the Enlightenment, began to speak and write of their nation's "civilizing mission," leading the rest of the human race forward on the march of progress. Social Darwinists, on the other hand, saw imperialism as a matter of survival of the fittest. They divided humankind into "higher races"—which usually meant the particular nation, or group of ethnically related nations, that one happened to belong to—and "lower races," which meant everyone else. The "higher races" must exploit and dominate the "lower races," or be overwhelmed by them. Ordinary citizens thrilled to phrases like "advance of the flag," the "white man's burden," and "manifest destiny," and many members of the upper and middle classes sought careers in the overseas services. Men, women, and children of all classes studied the new global maps showing their nation's overseas possessions in distinctive colors. The vocal minorities that protested against imperialism on practical or moral grounds were swept aside as "small-minded" or unpatriotic.

One old feature of imperialism did not change, however: its competitive nature. The imperialist countries were not collaborators but rivals. In 1875, for instance, the British bought a huge block of shares in the French-owned

(above, center) **Pride and Profits** A souvenir plate for Queen Victoria's diamond jubilee as ruler shows the queen and her heir, Edward Prince of Wales, with colonists and "natives" loyally clustering round Britannia. A map shows Britain's worldwide possessions, and the circle above it proclaims the slogan "The Empire on Which the Sun Never Sets." Figures below the map give nine-figure statistics of land area and population, as well as the bottom line of empire: a 100-million-pound surplus of British national exports over imports. Courtesy, Gallery Oldham, Oldham, UK. Photo: Sean Baggaley

Suez Canal Company from the heavily indebted ruler of Egypt, thereby gaining a stake in a recently completed transportation link of global economic and strategic importance (see photo on page 456). This was taken in France as a national humiliation by "perfidious" Britain. In the 1890s and 1900s, as Japan joined the ranks of imperialist countries, many in the West saw this as points scored against the "white" by the "yellow" race. With the opportunities there for the taking, if one country did not take them, another would, thereby winning an economic, national, or "racial" victory—so it was best to step in first. In this way, as in earlier centuries of European exploration and empire building, imperialist rivalry actually speeded the growth of empire.

New Methods

Likewise, the new imperialism involved new variations on old methods of imperial rule. Earlier empires had often used indirect methods of domination, taking tribute from subject peoples and enforcing obedience on them without actually ruling them. Likewise, the new imperialism did not always mean colonies. Control could be informal, exercised through the influence over local rulers of businesspeople and diplomats from imperialist countries, backed by the threat of force, as often happened in Latin America. Formal control (exercised through actual conquest and rule) did not always mean that local rulers were overthrown. Many rulers in Africa and Asia continued to wield power, but their countries became **protectorates**: they were answerable to a local representative of whichever imperialist power took them under its "protection," and ran their countries with the help of officials from that power.

Many economic and political experts preferred informal control, because it was cheaper and enabled a nation to avoid many risks and responsibilities. Prior to 1870, the British, with their shipping and financial strength, had proved especially skillful at securing economic privileges abroad. But informal and formal relations were woven together into a single fabric of empire: trade with informal control if practicable, trade with rule when necessary. The United States pursued a similar strategy in Latin America, where it was the dominant power. Though it annexed Puerto Rico and secured special constitutional privileges in Cuba (1898),

protectorate
A country under imperialist control whose ruler is still in office but is answerable to the local representative of an imperialist power.

> *"Imperialist rivalry actually speeded the growth of empire."*

EUROPEAN IMPERIALISM IN AFRICA: A VETERAN EXPLAINS THE RULES OF THE GAME

In the 1870s, the Welsh-American adventurer-explorer-journalist Henry M. Stanley made several well-publicized and heavily armed expeditions through southern Africa. In 1879, Stanley was hired by King Leopold II of Belgium to establish ties with the tribes along the Congo River with the aim of imposing Belgian control over Central Africa. Stanley set off on another well-armed expedition, made treaties with many African chiefs along the left bank of the river that put their tribes under the "protection" of Belgium, and forced African villagers to work as road builders. The extension of Belgian control in the Congo, which was soon matched by the French who set up protectorates on the right bank of the river, marked the beginning of the Scramble for Africa. In this excerpt from his autobiography, Stanley summarizes his formula for success in Africa.

Some explorers say: "One must not run through a country, but give the people time to become acquainted with you, and let their worst fears subside."

Now on the expedition across Africa I had no time to give, either to myself or to them. The river bore my heavy canoes downward; my goods would never have endured the dawdling requirement by the system of teaching every tribe I met who I was. To save myself and my men from certain starvation, I had to rush on and on, right through. But on this expedition, the very necessity of making roads to haul my enormous six-ton wagons gave time for my reputation to travel ahead of me. My name, purpose, and liberal rewards for native help, naturally exaggerated, prepared a welcome for me, and transformed my enemies of the old time into workmen, friendly allies, strong porters, and firm friends. I was greatly forbearing also; but, when a fight was inevitable, through open violence, it was sharp and decisive. Consequently, the natives rapidly learned that though everything was to be gained by friendship with me, wars brought nothing but ruin.

When a young white officer quits England for the first time, to lead blacks, he has got to learn to unlearn a great deal. We *must* have white men in Africa; but the raw white is a great nuisance there during the first year. In the second year, he begins to mend; during the third year, if his nature permits it, he has developed into a superior man, whose intelligence may be of transcendent utility for directing masses of inferior men.

My officers were possessed with the notion that my manner was "hard," because I had not many compliments for them. That is the kind of pap which we may offer women and boys. Besides, I thought they were superior natures, and required none of that encouragement, which the more childish blacks almost daily received.

EXPLORING THE SOURCE

1. If you were to witness Stanley's expedition traveling through the Congo region, what kind of activities would you see going on?

2. Who does Stanley say he was harder on, Africans or Europeans? What reason does he give for the different treatment?

Source: Henry Morton Stanley, *The Autobiography of Henry Morton Stanley*, ed. Dorothy Stanley (New York: Houghton Mifflin, 1909), pp. 342–343.

---

the United States controlled the rest of the Caribbean republics through economic influence ("dollar diplomacy"), aided when necessary by the Marines.

When rival states began to challenge British economic privileges in particular areas, Britain responded by seeking exclusive arrangements. Thus after 1870, it sought treaty rights, **"spheres of influence,"** and colonies. Other European nation-states, as well as the United States and eventually Japan, joined in the sweepstakes. The countries of Asia and Africa found themselves helpless before this combined onslaught of countries that held the advantages of aggressive purpose, superior organization, and advanced technology.

LO² The Scramble for Africa

For centuries, Europe had had close links of trade and travel with Muslim northern Africa, where powerful local rulers governed as more or less independent vassals of the Ottoman Empire. In the nineteenth century, two European countries on the other side of the Mediterranean Sea, France and Italy, were able to conquer their neighbors to the south in lengthy and brutal campaigns. They were joined by Britain, whose fleets and naval bases made it, too, a Mediterranean power. By 1914, these three countries dominated most of Muslim Africa, with the single largest share going to France.

Meanwhile, south of the Sahara Desert lay vast lands that were unknown to Europeans, apart from their coastal footholds that mainly served as bases for the slave trade (p. 280)—but now the time had come to "open up" the "Dark Continent." Pious humanitarians dreamed of saving heathen souls, curing disease, and ending the slave trade. Explorers were thrilled by romantic hopes of discovery and adventure. Capitalists and rulers dreamed of vast natural resources that must be there for the taking. And in fact, it was a ruler who was also a capitalist who began what came to be known as the **Scramble for Africa**—King Leopold II of Belgium.

A Brief Biography of Henry Morton Stanley (http://www.theatlantic.com/past/docs/issues/96sep/congo/hmsbio.htm) Learn about Sir Henry Morton Stanley, British explorer of the Congo.

Belgium was a small country that had gained independence only a generation before (p. 411), had no overseas possessions, and had no interest in acquiring any. Leopold's venture was therefore entirely private. He formed a company with himself as president, and sent agents into the Congo region. Taking the view that the African interior was open for sale to the white race, Leopold acquired "possession" of an enormous area by making "treaties," in exchange for trifling gifts, with hundreds of tribal chieftains. He thus created a "Congo Free State" under his personal rule—recognized as legal by the major powers in 1885. The boundaries enclosed an area equal to that of the United States east of the Mississippi River.

Though Leopold claimed scientific and humanitarian purposes for his venture, his prime purpose was personal gain. His eye was fixed on the booming industrial demand for rubber: the Congo had rubber trees and a large supply of African laborers. But the Africans could be forced to work only by the harshest methods. Leopold's agents used up the trees and people of the Congo without restraint, and the annual value of its rubber exports reached $10 million by 1908. But Leopold used much of the income for personal extravagance and borrowed huge sums from the Belgian government. In return, he mortgaged the Congo Free State to the government, which took it over at his death. As the Belgian Congo, the region received somewhat better treatment, but it remained a shocking example of human and resource exploitation.

sphere of influence
An area or region where an outside power has strong influence or control.

Scramble for Africa
The race among European countries to claim African territories, resulting in almost total partitioning of the continent by 1914.

The Kimberley Diamond Mine In 1867 a European colonist's son found a shiny 1½-ounce pebble on a hillside in southern Africa, which turned out to be a diamond. The photo shows what 13,000 European claim holders and 30,000 African laborers, wielding picks and shovels, did to the hill in the next five years. Besides leading thousands of hopeful wealth-seekers to rush to a single hill, the fabulous find also helped inspire ambitious European powers to scramble for control of the "Dark Continent" as a whole. Bettmann/Corbis

treaty system
A system of European control in China, in which European powers were allowed to establish their own settlements in Chinese port cities, free from Chinese authority.

Leopold's taking of the Congo attracted the attention of other European states to the prizes of Africa. A conference was held in Berlin in 1884–1885 to give some order to the carving up of the remainder of the continent. Certain ground rules were agreed upon: a nation with possessions on the coast had a prior right to the related hinterlands, but for a claim to any territory to be recognized, it must be supported by the presence of administrators and soldiers. The conference agreement was thus a signal to all competitors to move in with civilian and military forces.

 **European Imperialism in Africa** (http://www.youtube.com/watch?v=OJe1W_HlWmA&feature=related) Watch documentary footage of European imperialism in Africa (4:08).

The methods employed were similar to those used by Leopold's agents. White men trekked into the interior in search of tribal chiefs who would sign treaties. The chiefs seldom understood what the treaties meant or had the authority to transfer property rights, but the whites acted as if they did. These "rights" were then transferred to some European government, and a colony was thereby established. The only serious difficulties arose when rival nations secured overlapping grants in the same region. Such problems were usually referred to the European capitals for settlement.

By 1914, almost the entire continent had been partitioned. France held most of the bulge of West Africa, which was largely desert; the British held the richest lands, running from South Africa in the south to Egypt in the north. The main possessions on the southern and eastern coasts and in the central region were those of Portugal, Germany, Italy, and Belgium (Map 24.1). Of the continent's many nations, only the ancient East African kingdom of Ethiopia had managed to preserve its independence.

> **"By 1914, almost the entire continent had been partitioned."**

LO³ The Partition of Asia

In Asia, unlike in Africa, there were no areas that Europeans regarded as "dark" or "unoccupied." On the contrary, Europeans were so impressed by the efficient government of China and Japan by the reverence that their rulers received, and by the vast size of China that they called both of them "empires," though in neither of them did a single nation rule over different subject peoples. Both had done their best to insulate themselves from earlier Western influences (pp. 279–280), but now they faced intrusions that they could not resist. The Chinese empire, too unwieldy to cope easily with European imperialists, became their victim; Japan. smaller and more adaptable, joined the ranks of the imperialist powers.

China Outstripped by Europe

The wealth and power of China and its scientific and technical knowledge had traditionally been superior to that of Europe, and the excellence of its fine arts, scholarship, philosophy, and literature had impressed European travelers ever since Marco Polo (pp. 270–271). But China did not match the scientific and technological advances of the West after 1500, and in the eighteenth century it had deliberately kept European contacts to a minimum. Thus, when the Europeans eventually decided to penetrate the Chinese "wall" of isolation from foreigners, they were better organized and armed for warfare and made effective use of this advantage.

What the Europeans wanted initially were trading privileges. They coveted the luxury goods of China (silks, precious stones, porcelain) and wanted to secure them in exchange for their factory-made products. The Chinese, however, did not want such articles. The one item they would buy in substantial quantities was the narcotic drug opium, grown in India and smuggled into China. When the Chinese government tried to stop the illegal importation of opium, Britain started the so-called Opium War.

 **Frontline: Opium Through History** (http://www.pbs.org/wgbh/pages/frontline/shows/heroin/etc/history.html) Learn more about the history of the opium trade.

The treaty forced upon China at the end of the Opium War (1842) was the first of countless impositions on that country. According to the treaty's terms, the opium trade was to be resumed without further interference. In addition, Britain demanded and won possession of the harbor of Hong Kong on China's southern coast. Within the next few decades, other countries made their own demands. Under the "**treaty system**," a dozen Chinese port cities were opened to European traders (Map 24.2), and in each port city, the leading European powers were allowed to establish their own settlements, free from Chinese authority. European nationals, under further agreements, were allowed to travel inside China, subject only to the laws of their own homelands. The Chinese government was deprived of control over its external commerce; the European powers required that no tariff of more than 5 percent be placed on imports and that the tariffs be collected by Europeans. A good portion of this revenue was then siphoned off as "war indemnities" to the invaders.

The results for China were massive economic and social dislocation. The entry of low-priced manufactured goods in the nineteenth century upset the structure of the Chinese economy, above all in trade and industry. By building factories in the free ports and using the cheapest labor, the Europeans undermined Chinese handicrafts and demoralized the regular workforce. Quick fortunes were made from these enterprises by foreign traders and manufacturers, but the cost to the Chinese people was beyond measure.

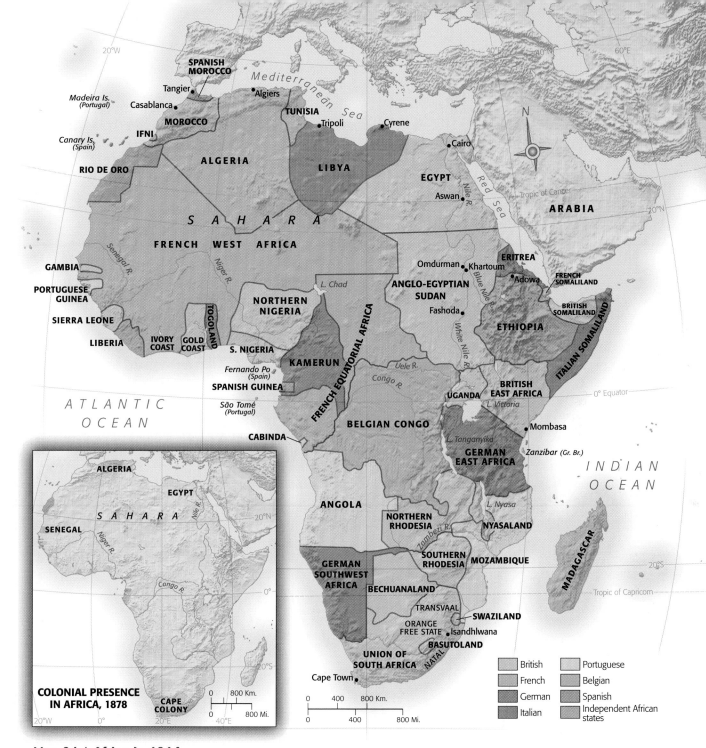

Map 24.1 **Africa in 1914**

Ilt took about 40 years for seven European powers to divide up all of Africa except for Ethiopia and Liberia. In North Africa, the Europeans took over existing Muslim states; elsewhere, the new borders reflected what each European power could lay its hands on, regardless of existing tribal and ethnic groupings. This division lasted mostly unchanged for another 40 years until the 1950s. Then, in only 20 years, European rule in Africa collapsed (see Map 29.1 on page 543). © Cengage Learning

Interactive Map

The Modernization of Japan

Like the Chinese rulers, the Japanese had closed their ports to foreign vessels in the seventeenth century. They did not reopen them until 1854, when the American commodore Matthew Perry threatened naval bombardment and thereby persuaded the rulers to negotiate a commercial treaty. The Japanese soon yielded to the idea that they must accept industrialization if they were to survive in the modern world. But they were determined to develop it themselves, without disruptive

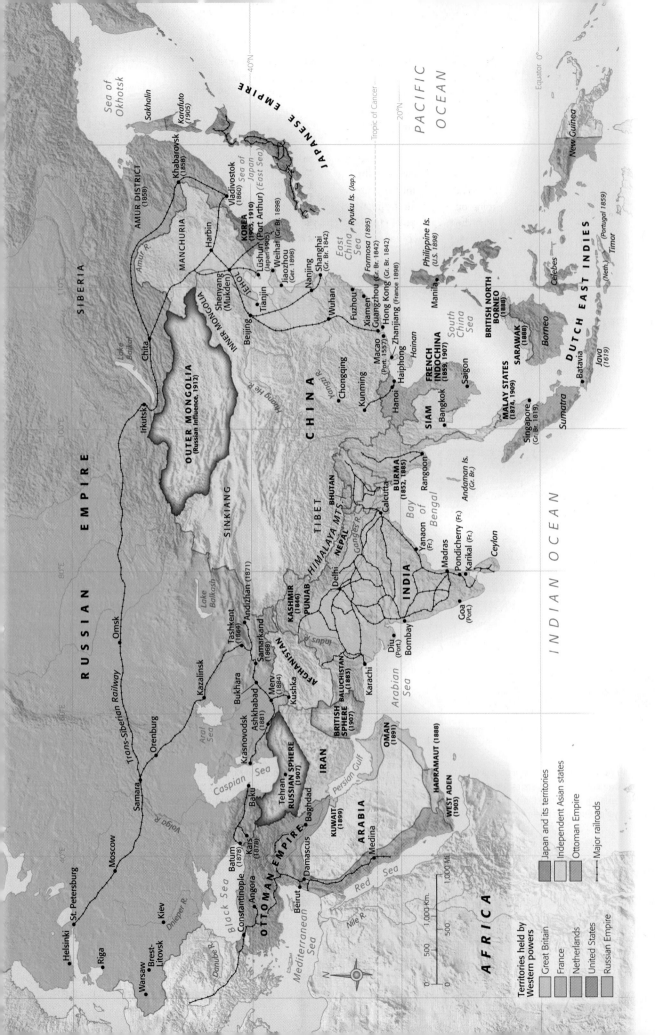

Interactive
Map

Map 24.2 Asia in 1914

In the mid-nineteenth century, Siberia, the Middle East, India, and the East Indies already belonged to outside rulers. By 1914, Japan had itself joined the imperialists; Afghanistan, China, Persia (Iran), and Siam (Thailand) were under powerful imperialist influence; and the rest of Asia was under outright imperialist control. Japan would soon try to expand its share of the spoils and would thereby begin the collapse of all imperial rule, including its own (see Map 29.2 on page 543). © Cengage Learning

interference by foreigners. They jealously guarded control over their finances and tariffs, and in an extraordinary national effort, they modernized their economy and armed forces.

By 1890, the Japanese were able to meet the Westerners on their own terms and even to become an imperialist power in their own right (see photo). In 1894, they drew China into war over clashing rights in Korea, and their Western-style army won easily. China was compelled to cede to Japan the large island of Taiwan, as well as its claims to Korea (Map 24.2).

Black Ships and Samurai: Commodore Perry and the Opening of Japan (1853–1854) (http://ocw.mit.edu/ans7870/21f/21f.027/black_ships_and_samurai/index.html) See Perry's encounter with the Japanese through images by artists on both sides.

The Struggle for East Asia

The Europeans were astonished by this demonstration of Japanese will and strength. Now that it appeared that China might be falling prey to greedy neighbors, they decided to protect their interests by seizing control of whatever territories they could. The Germans, French, Russians, and British pressured the Chinese government to give them vital coastal zones in addi-

Battle at the Machine Works, Tianjin A Japanese print shows a scene from the Boxer Rebellion, a massive antiforeign uprising in China in 1900. Chinese regular troops allied with the rebels are making a stand against a joint force of imperialist powers, on their way to Beijing to rescue besieged foreign diplomats and refugees. British attackers are in disarray, but Japanese soldiers are dauntlessly charging. Japan, says this picture, has not only joined the ranks of imperialist powers, it is in their forefront. The Granger Collection, New York

tion to their settlements in the "treaty ports." Only suspicions and disputes among the great powers saved the rest of China from complete partitioning at this time.

The intervention of the United States, which had become a Pacific power in 1898 when it took the Philippine Islands from Spain, had only a minor effect on the situation. The Americans feared that their commerce with China would be cut off if the foreign interests already there succeeded in spreading their territorial holdings. The secretary of state, John Hay, therefore pushed vigorously in 1899 for the acceptance of an **Open Door policy** in China, which would guarantee the "territorial integrity" of the country against further losses and extend to all nations equally the commercial privileges that had been won from the Chinese government.

Britain supported the Open Door policy, for it promised to block the threat of more annexations by China's neighbors. The other powers viewed it coolly, however, for they hoped to pounce on portions of the faltering empire. Ignoring the Open Door principle, Japan determined to tighten and extend its grasp. In both Korea and Manchuria (**man-CHOOR-ee-uh**), Japan faced a rival imperialist power, Russia. The Russians had begun, about 1850, to develop their long-neglected Siberian possessions, founding the city of Vladivostok (**vlad-ee-VOS-tok**) ("Ruler of the East") on the Pacific Ocean. Then they, too, had turned their attention to Manchuria and Korea. After failing to negotiate an agreement for two separate "spheres of influence" and fearing Russian advances, the Japanese decided to settle the issue by force.

Japan opened hostilities in 1904 with a surprise naval attack on the Russian fleet and base at Port Arthur in China, declaring war a few days afterward. This strike was a glaring violation of international law (repeated by the Japanese some forty years later in their sneak attack on American forces at Pearl Harbor). The tsarist government never recovered from this opening blow and was roundly beaten on sea and land (in Manchuria) during the Russo-Japanese War. As a result, Russian expansion in this area was checked, and Japan strengthened its special rights in Korea and Manchuria, as well as in Port Arthur. Japan also gained enormous international prestige for having humbled the supposedly mighty Russian Empire.

Meanwhile, the rest of Asia had been gobbled up. Over the years, the French had taken control of large areas of Southeast Asia; they combined them in 1887 to form French Indochina (Map 24.2). The British had begun to plant settlements in India

back in the seventeenth century; in the nineteenth century, the crown assumed direct control of the Indian government and extended its grip to Burma and Malaya. The Dutch widened their earlier holdings in the East Indies, while Persia and Afghanistan were split into British and Russian spheres of influence (1907). Russia also established a protectorate over Mongolia in 1913.

South Asian History: Colonial India (http://www.lib.berkeley.edu/SSEAL/SouthAsia/india_colonial.html) Learn more about colonial India in this extensive archive.

LO⁴ The New Imperialism, the West, and the World

At last, this era of seemingly limitless conquest came to an end. In not much more than half a century, the relationship between the West and the rest of the world had been transformed. The ancient civilizations and cultures of Africa and Asia, which had so far not felt the full force of Western influence, and even the Latin American countries with their regional version of Western civilization—nearly all were by 1914 directly ruled or indirectly controlled by a small group of Western or Westernized countries. The new imperialism had added 5 million square miles to the British Empire: in 1900, the empire included nearly 400 million people, of whom only one-tenth lived in Britain itself. French possessions had expanded by almost as much. Substantial areas had been acquired by Germany, Russia, Belgium, Portugal, Italy, Holland, the United States, and Japan.

In some ways, imperialism brought advantages to colonial peoples. It pushed them abruptly into the mainstream of world development. Roads, railways, sanitation, hospitals, and schools were introduced, while tribal wars and the slave trade were stopped. But these benefits must be measured against the physical and psychic blows inflicted by imperialism: forced labor, heavy colonial taxes, land confiscations, inferior status compared to European immigrants, destruction of traditional institutions and ways of life. The new imperialism left its subject peoples with a lasting sense of confusion, defeat, and degradation.

But the newly arisen empires were destined to short lives. This was partly because they were the work of countries most of which more or less wholeheartedly accepted individual freedom, national independence, and material well-being as universal principles. Like all empires, those of the nineteenth century were vehicles of cultural exchange, and in this case, at

> *"Japan gained enormous international prestige for having humbled the supposedly mighty Russian Empire."*

least to start with, the main influences were from the imperialist countries to the subject peoples. Ironically, to the extent that the colonial peoples learned and sought to imitate the ways of their rulers, this led them not to submission but to resistance and rebellion—to demand the freedom, independence, and prosperity that the imperial nations proclaimed as the birthright of the whole human race.

In addition, the outward thrust of the new imperialism had intensified the forces that were pushing the world's most powerful nations, above all those of Europe, toward war among themselves. Imperialists claimed to look after the problems of "backward" peoples, but they proved unable to solve their own. Europe was about to explode in a frightful conflagration, leading to the eventual collapse of the colonial empires.

 Listen to a synopsis of Chapter 24.

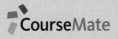

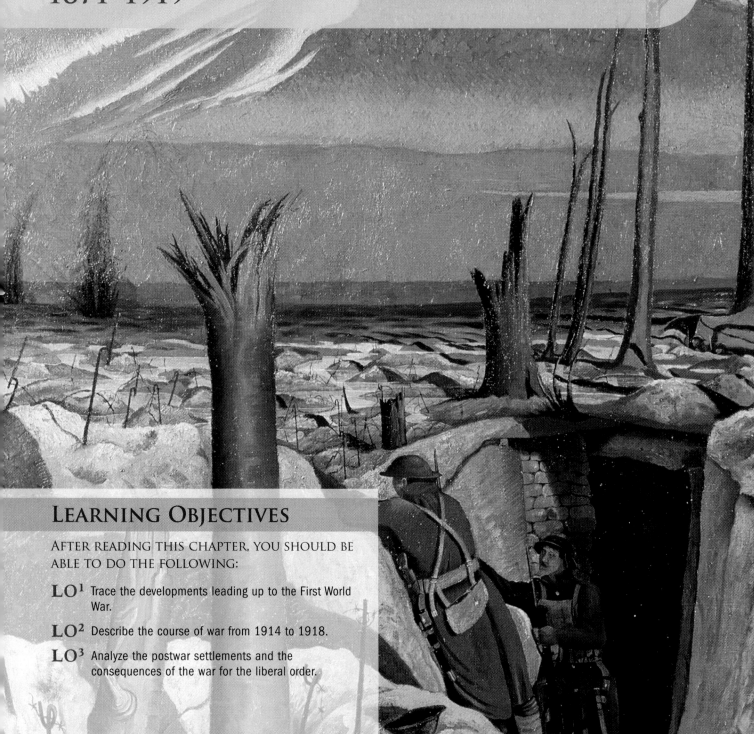

CHAPTER 25

"THE LAMPS ARE GOING OUT": THE FIRST WORLD WAR, 1871–1919

LEARNING OBJECTIVES

AFTER READING THIS CHAPTER, YOU SHOULD BE ABLE TO DO THE FOLLOWING:

LO¹ Trace the developments leading up to the First World War.

LO² Describe the course of war from 1914 to 1918.

LO³ Analyze the postwar settlements and the consequences of the war for the liberal order.

"OUT OF THE COMPETITIVE IMPERIALISMS AND RIVAL NATIONALISMS OF THE RULERS AND PEOPLES OF EUROPE THERE EMERGED TWO OPPOSING GROUPINGS OF GREAT POWERS, AND IN 1914 THEY WENT TO WAR."

The imperialist world order was an unstable one—mainly owing to conflicts among its privileged peoples, who continued their long-standing Western tradition of mutual strife. Out of the competitive imperialisms and rival nationalisms of the rulers and peoples of Europe there emerged two opposing groupings of great powers, and in 1914 they went to war. In the already close-knit world of the early twentieth century, the war eventually became a struggle between two intercontinental coalitions—Britain, France, Russia, the United States, and Japan against Germany, Austria-Hungary, and the Ottoman Empire. But most of the fighting was in Europe, where the progress of technology made the war the most devastating in history so far.

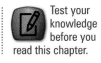 Test your knowledge before you read this chapter.

What do you think?

"If you want peace, prepare for war" is a foreign policy that invites conflict.

Strongly Disagree						Strongly Agree
1	2	3	4	5	6	7

In the end, victory went to the most powerful members of the larger coalition, which were also homelands of capitalism, nationalism, and liberalism: Britain, France, and the United States. The losers were undemocratic hereditary monarchies and multinational empires: Russia (defeated in 1917), and Germany, Austria-Hungary, and the Ottoman Empire (all defeated in 1918). The winners now hoped to reform the prewar world order by widening the privileged group of nations entitled to democracy and independence, making imperial rule more benevolent, and resolving conflicts through collective international action. But bitter frustrations and grievances were left over from the war; the nightmarish ordeal had inspired widespread disillusionment with hopes of peace and progress. Instead of hammering out a permanent settlement, all the peacemakers achieved was a twenty years' truce.

≪ *Oppy Wood, 1917, Evening.* Oppy is a village of northern France, situated amid wheat fields, cattle pastures, and patches of woodland. Allied and German armies confronted each other there from the fall of 1914 onward. This painting by an artist-soldier, John Nash, shows the effect on the landscape of three years of trench warfare.

LO¹ The Road to War

In 1914, Europe had been spared a general war for a hundred years since the downfall of Napoleon. The advance of science, liberal institutions, and material well-being was indisputable. The years before 1914 were a time of expansiveness and optimism, with the promise of the Enlightenment apparently nearing fulfillment. Given another half-century of peace, Europe might have made the liberal order secure.

But there was another, gloomier side to the European picture. Technology had created forces that were dissolving the foundations of traditional liberalism, and imperialism had opened wounds, both in Europe and overseas, that continued to fester. There was, too, a rising romantic mood, irrational and illiberal, associated with mystical ideas of racial purity and national "soul." Above all, the desire for national unity and independence had not brought international harmony as Mazzini had hoped (p. 416). Instead, it had become a source of conflict, especially when it became connected with militarism and military alliances among the great powers.

Nationalism and Militarism

By the close of the nineteenth century, the nationalist ideal had hardened into a self-centered and self-destroying passion. Its characteristics were the same in every Western land: the people of each nation believed in their own superiority, sovereignty, and special mission in the world. Nationalism had become the "religion of the fatherland," with its founders and heroes as its apostles and martyrs, and its political charters revered as holy texts.

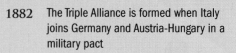

1882	The Triple Alliance is formed when Italy joins Germany and Austria-Hungary in a military pact
1897	Theodor Herzl founds the World Zionist Organization
1900	The Nobel Foundation is established to award annual prizes in literature, science, and the promotion of international peace
1907	The Triple Entente is formed when Britain joins France and Russia in a military alignment
1913	The last of the Turkish-ruled Balkan nations (Albania) gains independence, signaling the end of the Ottoman Empire in Europe
1914	Archduke Ferdinand of Austria and his wife are assassinated by Bosnian terrorists; war begins
1917	Russia's government and army fall apart in revolution; the United States enters the war on the Allies' side
1918	Germany agrees to end the fighting on Allied terms

National Conflict, Anti-Semitism, and Zionism

This patriotic enthusiasm fell hard on ethnic minorities within states, who were usually not allowed public schooling in their own languages and were in other ways disadvantaged and harassed. In most states, Jews in particular were resented as an alien element if they did not assimilate (conform to the culture of the nation among whom they lived); on the other hand, if they did assimilate, they were suspected of "Judaizing" the nation.

In reaction, some Jews began to think of securing a national state of their own, and in 1897, an Austrian journalist, Theodor Herzl, founded the World Zionist Organization. Zion is the name of the hill that had once been the site of King Solomon's temple and palace in Jerusalem (p. 38), and **Zionism** fit in with an age-old yearning for return to the ancient Jewish homeland. But instead of waiting for God to send his Messiah who would gather the Jews and convert the Gentiles, the Zionists sought

> **"By the close of the nineteenth century, the nationalist ideal had hardened into a self-centered and self-destroying passion. "**

by human action to organize the Jews into a modern nation-state like those among which they lived in Europe. Like other leaders who felt that their nation's past was more glorious than its present, they claimed the territory that their nation had occupied at the height of its power—in this case, Palestine. Herzl and his successors appealed to world leaders to support their cause, leading, a half-century later, to the creation of the state of Israel (p. 544).

The armed forces of each nation became the principal embodiment of its sovereign spirit and honor. They served, at the same time, as the ultimate means of pursuing national aims; both pride and interest, therefore, moved public officials and citizens to respect and strengthen the army and navy. Germany's midcentury victories led every major power except Britain to adopt universal male conscription. Most young men served for a couple of years and then were liable to be recalled if needed, so that peacetime armies numbered in the hundreds of thousands and could be swiftly expanded on the outbreak of war into million-strong forces of ready-trained soldiers (see photo on page 477).

In this way, nationalism was fatefully joined to **militarism**—the belief that preparation for war provides sound moral training and the best safeguard of peace and the national interest. But strength is relative, and each of the major nations wanted to be the strongest. Democracy, parliaments, and the influence of public opinion and a free press made no difference to the power rivalries that had been a feature of Western civilization since the fall of Rome. Instead of being mainly among dynasties and ruling elites, these rivalries came to involve whole peoples.

The Peace Movement

True, there was also a widespread movement of **pacifism**. Among the movement's most prominent leaders was an Austrian aristocrat, Bertha von Suttner. In 1889, Suttner published *Lay Down Your Arms*, the fictional autobiography of a Viennese woman who loses many loved ones to battle and disease in the wars of Italian and German unification (pp. 416–418) and becomes a pacifist as a result. The book became a bestseller in many languages, and gave Suttner the standing to become the leader of an international network of peace organizations. In 1896, her friend the Swedish industrialist Alfred Nobel left part of his fortune to establish prizes to be awarded yearly for high achievement in literature, various fields of science, and also to whoever "shall have done the most or the best work for fraternity between nations, for the abolition or reduction of standing armies and for the holding and promotion of peace congresses." The prize's fifth recipient, in 1905, was Suttner herself.

 The Official Website of the Nobel Prize (http://nobelprize .org/) Learn more about Nobel's endowment and the history of the Nobel Prize.

Governments took the peace movement seriously enough to send official representatives to such conferences, notably those at The Hague (in the Netherlands) in 1899 and 1907. Representatives of twenty-six nations who assembled there failed to agree on a proposal for arms control, but they did conclude several treaties on the "law of war" and the "rules of warfare." They pledged not to use poison gas or other weapons that were considered especially inhumane or indiscriminate. They also

created an international court of arbitration to which countries might submit their disputes. In this way, there began a search for binding alternatives to the use of force in international relations that has continued—alongside countless deeds of horrendous violence—down to the present day.

> " *Since the Jew is nowhere at home, nowhere regarded as a native, he remains an alien everywhere.* "
> —Leo Pinsker on the need for a Jewish state, 1882

militarism
The belief that preparation for war provides sound moral training and the best safeguard of peace and the national interest.

pacifism
Opposition in principle to war as a means of settling disputes.

The Alliance System

The responsible leaders of the era leading up to the First World War found the call to "lay down your arms" naïve. Instead, they relied on the traditional belief that "If you want peace, prepare for war"—war that could be expected to be ever more terrible as the progress of technology made weapons ever more devastating. Of course, no nation could expect to defeat any possible combination of rivals, so governments also relied

>> **Dropping the Pilot.** The British cartoonist John Tenniel shows Bismarck, who had piloted the German ship of state through the storms of national unification into calm waters protected by alliances and alignments with most of the other great powers, going off board after disagreements with the new captain, Emperor William II. William and his new navigators would steer once more into stormy seas, and ultimately to shipwreck. CartoonStock Limited

A VISION OF THE COMING WAR

Jean Jaurès (**zhoh-REZ**), the son of a small farmer in the south of France, became a leading figure in the French socialist movement in the years leading up to the First World War. He had a Marxist view of capitalist society as the scene of vicious exploitation and class struggle, and he was inspired by the French revolutionary ideal of "Liberty, Equality, and Fraternity" in which the whole human race must share. However, he also saw both international war and violent revolution as disasters that would hinder or defeat the worldwide struggle for a truly humane socialism. He labored to make the international working-class movement into a force for peace, but in July 1914, a few days before the European powers began to mobilize their armies and issue declarations of war, he was assassinated by a French nationalist. Jaurès and his ideals were casualties of a war that split the working-class movement, with most socialists rallying to their nation's cause.

In this excerpt from a speech that Jaurès gave in 1911, he foretells the horrors of a future war and the disasters that it will bring in its wake. The precedents he mentions are those of a short-lived revolutionary takeover in Paris following the Franco-Prussian War of 1870–1871 and of the Russian revolution of 1905 (pp. 418, 487).

But no matter what we do, gentlemen, we remain surrounded by an atmosphere of suspicion and mistrust from which, it seems to me, the clouds of war may descend upon us at any minute. As far as it is our responsibility, as far as it is the responsibility of a great people, we must constantly apply ourselves to dissipate this atmosphere of mistrust and to combat the causes of the renewed danger of conflicts. It is our primary duty to reject the pessimism and the fatalism of those who say that war is inevitable.

Gentlemen, I do not disregard the forces for war in this world; but one also has to see and to recognize the forces for peace and to salute them. In its own way, war fosters peace—since the horrors of a modern war are frightening. Gentlemen, when one sometimes speaks lightly of the possibility of this terrible catastrophe one forgets the hitherto unknown extent of the horror and greatness of the disaster that would occur. . . .

The present-day armies of each nation represent entire peoples, as in the times of primitive barbarism; but this time they would be let loose amidst all the complexity and wealth of human civilization. Each of these nations would employ instruments of terrifying destruction created by modern science. Do not imagine that it will be a short war, consisting of a few thunderbolts and flashes of lightning. On the contrary, there will be slow and formidable collisions like the ones which have taken place over there in Manchuria between the Russians and the Japanese. Untold numbers of human beings will suffer from the sickness, the distress, the pain, the ravages of this multiple explosion. The sick will die of fever; commerce will be paralyzed; factories will stop working; oceans, which

steamboats nowadays cross in every direction, will again be empty and silent as in former times.

This terrible spectacle will over-stimulate all human passions. Listen to the words of a man who is passionately attached to the ideals of his party and who is convinced that we must revolutionize our form of property holding, but who also believes that it will be the greatness of this movement to proceed in an evolutionary manner, without unleashing the destructive hatreds which have hitherto accompanied all great movements for social reform throughout history. But we must watch out, for it is in the fever of wars that passions for social reform are aroused to a paroxysm of violence. It was during the War of 1870 and the siege of Paris that convulsions seized that city; it was during the Russo-Japanese War that the fever broke out in Russia. Therefore, the conservatives should be the ones who desire peace more than any others, for once peace is broken the forces of chaos will be let loose. . . .

EXPLORING THE SOURCE

1. What reasons does Jaurès give to explain why the next war will be disastrous and will be accompanied by revolutionary violence?

2. How far and in what ways did Jaurès's predictions come true?

Source: Jean Jaurès, *Oeuvres de Jean Jaures*, ed. Max Bonnafous, vol. 7: *Pour la Paix: Europe Incertaine, 1908–1911* (Paris: Rieder, 1934), pp. 423–434.

Map 25.1 **Balance of Power**

The map shows the rival alliances of 1914. When war broke out, these alignments shifted: most importantly, Italy fought on the Entente side and the Ottoman Empire allied with Germany and Austria-Hungary. But the basic balance of forces never changed. A stronger but scattered group of countries confronted a weaker but more compact one. The stronger group would win in the end, but it would take four years of slaughter and ruin. © Cengage Learning

Interactive Map

on making alliances with nations with which they had interests in common. Instead of rival nations, Europe came to be divided between rival alliances, which served only to make the war fires hotter and more widespread when they flared up.

Rival Alliances

At the center of these rivalries stood Germany, whose unification in 1871 had made it the dominant power on mainland of Europe. Bismarck, Germany's unifier (p. 416), wished to maintain his country's new dominance. His motives were no doubt defensive; he feared that the French, stung by their defeat in the Franco-Prussian War (1870), would seek revenge. And so he arranged an alliance with another vanquished rival, Austria-Hungary, in 1879. Italy, seeing in Germany a stronger and more reliable ally than France, joined this pact a few years later, making it the Triple Alliance (Map 25.1).

At the same time, Bismarck took care to keep Germany on good terms with two other leading great powers, Russia and Britain. He was respectful of Russia's interests in eastern Europe and of Britain's position as the leading worldwide power. He hoped, in this way, to preserve German dominance by peaceful means: his friendships and alliances were designed not to fight a war but, by their overwhelming strength, to deter it. But if Germany's allies and friends ever lost their trust in Germany as a peaceful partner, they would turn against it, and Bismarck's war-deterring structure would crumble.

This began to happen when the isolation of France was broken soon after Bismarck fell from office in 1890 (see photo on page 471). His fall was due in part to the ambitions of the new German emperor, William II, who replaced Bismarck's cautious policy with one that would propel Germany into its "rightful" place as both a European and a world power. The emperor's policy was an open challenge to both Russia and Britain, and both responded by developing closer relations with France.

The French, of course, had not forgotten 1870 and had long been seeking military partners. They looked first to the power on Germany's eastern border. Russia—autocratic and conservative—was ideologically closer to Germany than to liberal and progressive France. But as so often before in the endless competition of European states, the needs of power politics outweighed ideology, and the two countries entered into a Dual Alliance in 1894. This action confronted Germany with the threat that Bismarck had most feared—the possibility of a two-front war.

All the same, William II was determined that Germany should find its "place in the sun"—overseas as well as in Europe. Convinced of the importance of sea power to overseas commerce, colonies, and national prestige, he was determined to have a great navy as well as the world's finest army. Beginning in 1898, Germany began to lay out huge expenditures for a fleet of warships. Britain, alarmed, reacted with still larger sums, insisting on the principle that its navy remain the equal of any other two. And though traditionally committed to "splendid isolation" from European "entanglements," the British now began to consider European alliances to counter the rising power of Germany (Map 25.1).

William II Offers Characteristic Bombast Read William II on the importance of the German navy.

As a result, Britain found itself swinging ever closer to France and Russia. The French accepted British advances in Africa that they had earlier opposed, and persuaded Russian diplomats to settle long-standing disputes with the British in the Middle East. For their part, the British made no formal military commitments, but in 1907, an "understanding" (*entente*) was reached by Britain, France, and Russia. British and French military officers began to coordinate their war plans. The Dual Alliance was thus extended into a Triple Entente.

Instead of a single overwhelming group of powers, there were now two rival groups. Statesmen on each side still hoped to keep the peace by what would from now on be mutual deterrence. They liked to think of the alliances as balancing each other and thereby giving stability to the Western-dominated world order. But the alliances also created a deadly danger: if

> *"Should, however, any one attempt to affront us, or to infringe our good rights, then strike out with mailed fist."*
>
> —William II to his naval officers

deterrence failed and any two powers went to war, the other alliance members would have little alternative but to join in. Any local conflict was almost certain to turn into a general European war.

The Balkans: The End of the Ottoman Empire

What brought this about was a combination of local and great power conflicts in the Balkans (southeastern Europe), a region that had long been an object of great power rivalries. In the nineteenth century, these rivalries worsened as the Ottoman Empire, the traditional ruler of the Balkans and the Middle East, gradually fell apart.

In the first half of the nineteenth century, however, the Balkans began to respond to the spirit of nationalism that was spreading through all of Europe. The Greeks, for example, had won their independence in 1829, and the Romanians, Bulgarians, and others were waiting for a chance to throw off the Turkish yoke. But the Balkan nations were divided among themselves. Most of them were of Slavic ethnic origin, but some belonged to other ethnic groups that had lived in the Balkans for longer than the Slavs. Most were Eastern Orthodox Christians, but some were Roman Catholic or had become Muslim under Turkish rule. And each was eager to claim the largest possible share of territory and population for itself, at the expense of fellow subject nations as well as the Turks. (For the background of religious and ethnic conflict in the Balkans, see Chapters 9 and 12.)

This was a situation that was bound to lead to interference by the great powers—each with different and competing aims. In the 1870s, the power with the greatest ambitions in the area was Russia, which had two objectives: to liberate fellow Slavs and Orthodox Christians who would then become grateful allies; and to win control of the Black Sea coasts, thereby gaining a "warm water" outlet (that would not be icebound in the winter like Russian ports on the Baltic Sea and Arctic Ocean) through the straits linking the Black Sea and the Mediterranean. But Austria-Hungary (pp. 417–418), which wanted to expand its trade and influence in the region and was afraid of the spread of Balkan nationalist unrest to its own territory, resented growing Russian prestige there. In addition, so long as Bismarck kept Germany's interest in the Balkans to a minimum, Britain considered Russia its main opponent there. Russia's southward push seemed a threat to Britain's own "line of empire," which ran through the Mediterranean via the Suez Canal (p. 459) to India, and it therefore sought to keep Russia bottled up in the Black Sea.

The tsar nearly achieved Russia's objectives in 1878 when he invaded the Turkish Empire and crushed its forces. But Austria-Hungary and Britain demanded, upon threat of war, that the Russians reduce their peace demands. At the ensuing Congress of Berlin, presided over by Bismarck acting as an

THE END OF OTTOMAN POWER IN THE BALKANS POSED A THREAT TO THE HABSBURG EMPIRE:

- Austria-Hungary, which stretched from central Europe to the Balkans, consisted of a dozen different nationalities.

- In the Balkans, the empire included Catholic Slovenes and Croats, Muslim Bosnians, and Orthodox Serbs, who differed in religion but all counted as

- South Slavs—members of the south-ernmost group of Slav peoples.

- The leaders of Serbia, besides gaining territory from the Ottoman Empire, also wanted to unite all the South Slavs—including those who lived in Austria-Hungary—into a single inde-pendent state.

- As a first step, they began agitation in the neighboring, Austrian-ruled ter-ritories of Bosnia and Herzegovina.

- If the South Slavs won independence, the Czechs, Slovaks, Romanians, and other nationalities would probably demand it too, and the empire would fall apart.

"honest broker," Russia gained only a few harbors and border territories. But Romania, Serbia, and Montenegro were recognized as independent states, and Bulgaria secured self-rule under the Turkish sultan (ruler).

For a time, the pressure on the Ottoman Empire eased as Russia turned to imperialist ventures in East Asia, and until the early twentieth century, the Turks lost only a few outlying territories. In 1912, however, Serbia, Montenegro, Bulgaria, and Greece invaded and liberated most of what remained of European Turkey—and immediately went to war among themselves over the division of territory and population. Another international conference gave independence to the last of the Turkish-ruled Balkan nations, Albania. By 1914, nothing was left of the Ottoman Empire's European territories except its capital, Constantinople, and a small surrounding area.

But liberation from Ottoman rule did not bring the local and international rivalries in the Balkans to an end. Competition among the great powers for influence there grew more intense than ever, particularly when the assertive Germany of William II joined in. To open up the Middle East to German economic and political penetration, the Germans had begun work on a Berlin-to-Baghdad railway—which in turn meant that Germany became closely aligned with the power that still ruled much of the Middle East, the Ottoman Empire. Britain, Russia, and France regarded the German enterprise as an intrusion into their own spheres of interest, and Britain now began to see Germany rather than Russia as the main threat to its interests in the Balkans and the Middle East.

The Balkans: Austria-Hungary Endangered

The Ottoman losses in turn raised another threat: that Austria-Hungary might now be broken apart by nationalist forces, encouraged by its Balkan neighbor, Serbia (see Reasons Why).

The explosive situation also affected the alliance system, on which the general peace of Europe seemed to hang. If Austria-Hungary were to break apart, the Triple Alliance would be decisively weakened. Germany, the senior partner of the alliance, therefore kept in anxious touch with Vienna. On the opposing side, the Russians did all they could to encourage Serbia. Here was a conflict between two great powers that was important enough to draw them into war—and with them, their friends and allies.

> "*Liberation from Ottoman rule did not bring the local and international rivalries in the Balkans to an end.*"

The Alliances Go to War

The South Slav movement was largely peaceful, but it included Bosnian terrorists with links to Serbian military intelligence. The efforts of this group reached a climax in the streets of the Bosnian capital, Sarajevo, in June 1914, when one of them succeeded in assassinating the Archduke Francis Ferdinand (the heir to the Austrian throne) and his wife. World leaders were shocked by the murders, and the Austrian government—having made sure of German support—decided to use the occasion for a showdown with Serbia. Believing that the Serbian government was involved in the assassination plot, the Austrians sent a harsh ultimatum (a demand backed by threat of war if not agreed to). The Serbs, having in turn made sure of Russian backing, accepted most but not all of the requirements. The Austrians rejected their response as unsatisfactory, broke off diplomatic relations, mobilized their army, and declared war on Serbia.

 An Unanswerable Demand: The Austro-Hungarian Ultimatum to Serbia Read the Austrian ultimatum to Serbia.

The decisive step in widening the war was the tsar's order to mobilize the Russian army. Because of the vast distances and

"General Mobilization Order" A government poster orders every Frenchman liable for military service to follow "the instructions on the colored pages" in his mobilization booklet for rejoining his unit. Like the booklets, the poster is ready in advance, except for a gap after "The first day of mobilization is . . . ," which a clerk has filled in with a date stamp: Sunday, August 2, 1914. As war loomed, this poster went up all over France, and similar posters were going up all over Europe.

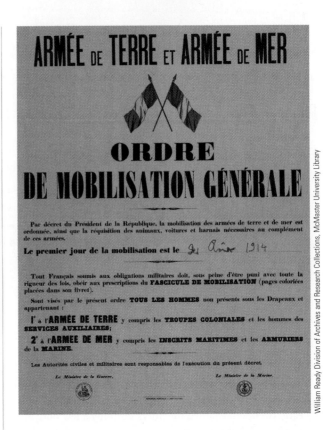

William Ready Division of Archives and Research Collections, McMaster University Library

sparse rail network of Russia, the process of calling up reservists and moving them to their attack positions was slower there than in countries farther west, and the Germans had counted on this to give them the chance of swiftly defeating France and then Russia in turn, rather than having to fight them both at the same time. The German leaders decided that they could not lose the time they needed to attack France while Russian mobilization went ahead, so they sent a telegram demanding that the Russians halt their call-up within twelve hours. Failing to receive a positive reply, the Germans declared war on Russia on August 1, 1914. The French, who had urged Russia to avoid any compromise that might be humiliating to the Triple Entente, could not now abandon their closest ally, nor could they let the German mobilization get ahead of theirs. They therefore refused a German demand to stay out of the fighting, and mobilized their own army in turn (see photo). As a result, Berlin declared war on France as well. The catastrophe that nobody wanted but many feared had at last come about.

Though Britain had made no public pledge to aid France, its ministers had privately promised to help if the French were attacked by Germany. Parliament put aside any reluctance it might have had to make good on this promise when the Germans, according to their war plan, invaded Belgium. Britain, as one of the guarantors of Belgian neutrality and security (p. 411), now had a legal basis for action. Parliament declared war on Germany on August 4. On the evening of the day before, watching from his office window as a lamplighter turned on the gas lights in the street below, the British foreign secretary, Sir Edward Grey, said to a friend: "The lamps are going out all over Europe, we shall not see them lit again in our lifetime."

 The British Rationale for Entering World War I Read Sir Edward Grey's argument for entering the war.

 "Take Up the Sword of Justice," British Recruitment Posters (http://www.library.georgetown.edu/dept/speccoll/britpost/posters.htm) View British recruitment posters.

LO² The Great War

The opposing alliances were still not quite complete. Japan, Britain's treaty partner in the Pacific, soon entered on the side of the "**Allies**," while the Turks, renewing their struggle with Russia, joined the "**Central Powers**" (Austria and Germany). Italy, a member of the Triple Alliance, remained neutral until 1915, when secret promises of extensive territorial rewards won it over to the Allied side. Many smaller nations were gradually drawn into the war (at least formally), but they did not influence its outcome.

The strategy of the First World War was basically simple. The Allies, with their worldwide power and resources, were sure of winning a long war of attrition. The Central Powers aimed for a quick, decisive victory based on superior military technique and forces already in place. They also enjoyed the advantage of interior lines of communication, which meant that they could concentrate their troops swiftly on chosen fronts. To make their first blow against France as swift and overwhelming as possible before turning against Russia, the German generals did not hesitate to sweep through tiny Belgium, violating the treaty guaranteeing Belgium's neutrality. The treaty, explained the Germans, was but a "scrap of paper"; the invasion was a matter of "military necessity."

 Aircraft of World War One (http://www.century-of-flight.net/new%20site/frames/WW1%20aircraft_frame.htm) See images of World War One fighter planes.

The Western Front: The Routine of Slaughter

The German attack, which aimed to roll up the French army in a grand, wheeling movement, stalled at the Marne River, near Paris (Map 25.2). After the first few weeks, the battle on the Western Front changed from one of movement to one of

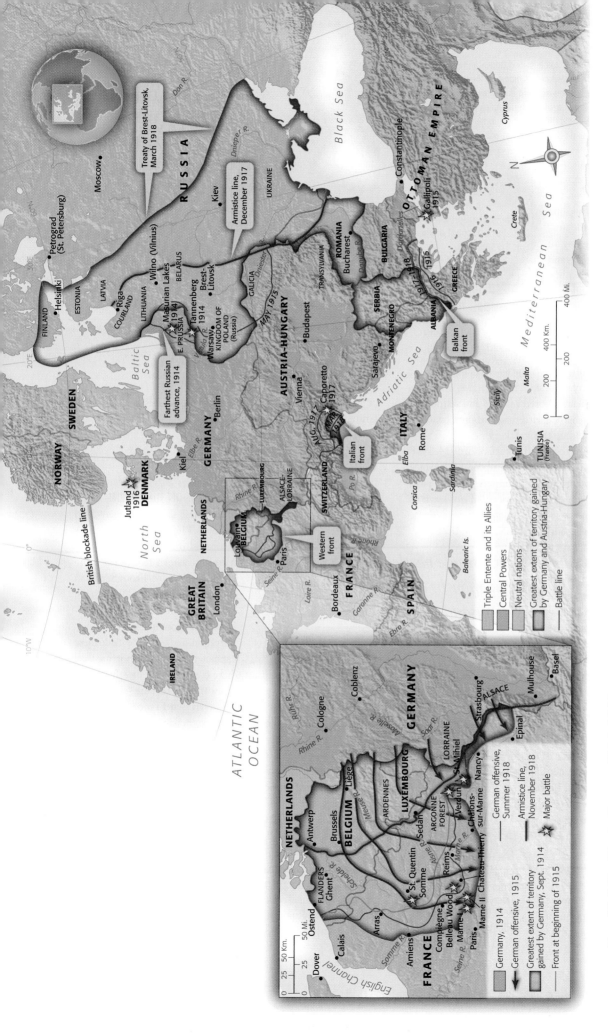

Interactive
Map

Map 25.2 The War in Europe, 1914–1918

The First World War was fought in Africa and Asia and on the world's oceans as well as in Europe, but the most decisive theaters were the Eastern Front, where the Central Powers and Russia struggled across vast spaces until Russia collapsed; the Western Front, where huge armies packed into a narrow space held each other in check; and the eastern Atlantic Ocean, where German U-boats failed to strangle Britain and France, but a British surface blockade eventually crippled Germany's fighting power. © Cengage Learning

Enemies and Companions Wounded soldiers—two British and one captured German—make their way rearward from fighting on the Western Front in 1916. They are a tiny few among the one and a half million casualties of the five-month Battle of the Somme, in which the Allies pushed the Germans back a maximum of six miles. The Britons huddle together for support with the German, who holds a cigarette that was probably given him by one of them. Hulton Archive/Getty Images

fixed positions. Now the advantage shifted to those who were on the defensive. Trench warfare became a routine of slaughter for the next four years (see photo). The dug-in positions of the Western powers and the Germans faced each other in a continuous, four-hundred-mile line across northern France. Again and again, the opposing armies tried to break through each other's lines, using the most terrible devices of modern science and industry: million-shell artillery bombardments, poison gas, the earliest armored vehicles and warplanes. But other modern devices—barbed wire, machine guns, counter-bombardments—always held up the attackers.

The World of the Trenches: A Deadly Life Read a German soldier's account of life in the trenches.

"The Trenches: Symbol of the Stalemate," from PBS's The Great War Series (http://www.pbs.org/greatwar/chapters/ch1_trench.html) Watch archival footage of life in the trenches.

Besides, in an important respect, the warfare of 1914–1918 was still backward. The armies were too large to control by voice command, by runner, or by drums and trumpets, as in the past, but they had no radios. Army commanders could not learn of suddenly arising attack opportunities until they were long past, and local commanders had no way of being quickly alerted to changes of plan. The troops must advance according to rigid plans and time-tables, and when the unexpected happened—as it usually did—the result was blood-soaked chaos. Attackers might manage to push the defenders back a few miles, or defenders might force attackers back to their original lines. Neither side would be willing to accept the result as final, so that a single battle might go on for months and cost hundreds of thousands of lives.

> **"** *A single battle might go on for months and cost hundreds of thousands of lives.* **"**

Both sides tried to cripple each other's ability to fight such battles by depriving each other of the food and raw materials their industrial economies needed. The Allies used their surface fleets to blockade the Central Powers' worldwide imports and exports, and Germany tried to do the same to the Allies, above all Britain, with submarines (U-boats—from the German *U-Boot*, short for *Unterseeboot*, "under-sea-boat"). The Allied fleets were effective but slow-working; the German submarines were defeated by the introduction of convoys—merchant ships sailing

His Imperial German Majesty's U-boats in World War I (http://www.uboat.net/history/wwi/) Learn more about Germany's use of U-boats during the war.

in groups with warship escorts—and worse still, provoked the United States into joining the Allies.

Winners and Losers, 1917–1918

In the south, Italian and Austrian armies also fought a trench war, except that in their Alpine borderlands, the trenches clung to mountain slopes and steep-sided valleys. There were also bitter struggles on the European and Middle Eastern frontiers of the Ottoman Empire. From Serbia in the Balkans to the Middle Eastern land of Armenia, millions of civilian deaths from massacre, disease, starvation, and genocide made these campaigns even more horrific than those on the Western Front where civilians were mostly spared. But from the strategic point of view they were mere "sideshows."

Only one theater of land war rivaled France in strategic importance: the Eastern Front. Here the land was vast and flat, and armies were thinly spread across a thousand miles of front line instead of a mere four hundred as in the West. On this front a war of movement was possible, and in three years of fighting, though both sides struck mighty blows, the tsar's armies gradually lost ground. The soldiers were less plentifully equipped and supplied for modern warfare than their German and Austrian opponents, the business of equipping and supplying the armies took an even greater toll on the people, and distrust of the rulers had been growing among all classes already before the war. Russia still stretched for thousands of miles eastward

The Home Front in Vienna Read an Austrian woman's account of food shortages and other wartime hardships.

from the front lines, but in 1917, its government and army fell apart in revolution (pp. 487–488).

In the same year, however, this loss to the Allies was more than balanced by the entrance of the United States on their side. Americans had been generally sympathetic with the British and French from the start of the war, and in the end, the country's traditional opposition to "entangling alliances" was overcome by a combination of forces: the American government, fearing the strategic consequences of a German victory, pushed for intervention on the side of the Allies; and the public, angered by reports of German atrocities and the sinking of commercial vessels by German submarines, rallied in support of joining the European war.

By bringing in fresh troops and equipment and by pledging the resources of their continent, the Americans ensured ultimate victory for the Allies. In 1918, a final German offensive on the Western Front, reinforced by armies from the east, almost broke through but was blocked by the British, the French, and a half-million-strong American army. Now it was the turn of the Germans to lose ground, and for their army and government to begin falling apart. The Germans at last responded favorably to President Woodrow Wilson's offer of a moderate settlement on Allied terms—a "peace without victory." In November 1918, they agreed to lay down their arms, and the Great War, as it was called at the time—there being, as yet, no second and even greater war to follow it—was over.

 A New Diplomacy: The Fourteen Points Read Wilson's "Fourteen Points," outlining his terms for a lasting peace settlement.

LO³ Repairing the World Order

At the peace conference, which met in Paris, separate treaties were arranged with each of the Central Powers—each signed in a different location in the palace and park of Versailles, the former palace of the Bourbon kings just outside the capital. None of the defeated nations was given any effective voice in the settlements; it turned out to be a victor's peace after all, in which France, Britain, and the United States laid down the conditions. Delegates from the Central Powers protested bitterly, but they were compelled to accept under threat that the war would be renewed.

 "War Without End," from PBS's **The Great War Series** (http://www.pbs.org/greatwar/chapters/ch4_war.html) Watch archival footage of the Paris Peace Conference and learn more about the postwar mood.

The Peace Treaties: War Guilt and National Self-Determination

In a vengeful stroke, the French required the Germans to sign their treaty in the Hall of Mirrors at Versailles (see photo on page 349), where, in 1871, Bismarck had proclaimed the German Empire. It was a suitable gesture for a treaty that was a good deal less ruthless than the Germans had made with defeated Russia and had planned to make if they had won in the West, but it was still intended to weaken Germany for years to come.

Peacemaking in Europe

Under the provisions of the treaty, Germany lost the provinces of Alsace and Lorraine (which it had taken from France in 1871), its overseas colonies, and valuable lands on its eastern frontiers. Germany also had to surrender most of its merchant shipping and to dismantle its armed forces. But the most objectionable part of the Versailles treaty, from the German point of view, was the "war guilt" clause—which stated that Germany and its partners accepted responsibility for all loss and damage caused by the war. The guilt clause reflected popular sentiment in the Allied countries and also justified huge claims by the victors for "**reparations**"—compensation for damage inflicted by the Central Powers in the course of the fighting. The Germans, on the other hand, did not feel that they alone were to blame, and that the payment of reparations would inflict on them endless undeserved hardship. Only small amounts of reparations were ever collected, but the "war guilt" clause aroused among Germans a violent and lasting hatred of the treaty.

 A Defeated Germany Contemplates the Peace Treaty Read Germany's acting chancellor on the harshness of the Versailles treaty.

The treaties with the other defeated powers (1919–1920) provided for the remaking of the map of central and eastern Europe, for now three empires (the Russian, Austrian, and Turkish) were in partial or total dissolution (Map 25.3). The guiding principle in drawing the new frontiers was Woodrow Wilson's principle of "self-determination" for nationalities. Seven new national states came into being. In northeastern Europe, there were Finland and the Baltic states of Estonia, Latvia, and Lithuania. In central Europe, there were Poland and Czechoslovakia (where there lived two closely related Slav nations, the Czechs and Slovaks). In the Balkans, there was Yugoslavia (at first called the Kingdom of the Serbs, Croats, and Slovenes), which fulfilled the dream of the Sarajevo assassins—the new country's name meant "Land of the South Slavs" in the Serbian and other local languages. Within Yugoslavia's borders, there lived not only Orthodox Serbs and Catholic Croats and Slovenes, but also Muslim Bosnians and Albanians, and other groups. Austria and Hungary were separated and reduced to small landlocked states.

Despite the general application of national self-determination, the problem of national conflict continued to plague Europe. The diverse nationalities were so intermixed that no state boundary could be drawn that did not leave a national minority on the "wrong" side. Since the boundaries were drawn by the victors, these minorities usually came from nations that had lost the war:

Map 25.3 **Twenty Years' Truce**

Following the First World War there were more nation-states in Europe than before, but some were "satisfied" ones that gained territory, such as France, Poland, Czechoslovakia, and Romania, while others, such as Germany and Hungary, as well as the multinational Soviet Union, were bitterly "dissatisfied." It was the same situation that had led to war in the first place. As a French delegate to the Paris Peace Conference said, "This is not a peace; it is a twenty years' truce." © Cengage Learning

Interactive Map

the new nation-states of central Europe and the Balkans were full of aggrieved minorities, mainly Germans and Hungarians. And in Yugoslavia and Czechoslovakia, nations that were ethnically related but divided by history and religion had endless opportunities for conflict within their "joint" nation-states.

Peacemaking Beyond Europe

The peace treaties also had to settle the future of lands beyond Europe that had belonged to the empires of Turkey and Germany. Turkey lost all of its Arab-inhabited Middle Eastern territories and was supposed to give up much more territory—in the west to Greece and in the east

to the rival Muslim nation of the Kurds. But nationalist revolutionaries led by a Turkish army officer, Mustapha Kemal, refused to accept the peace treaty, and in a brutal war with Greece, they were able to form an independent Republic of Turkey that included all of Asia Minor and a small area in Europe surrounding Constantinople—soon officially known by its Turkish name, Istanbul. One and a half million Greeks were compelled to leave their 2,700-year-old communities in western Anatolia (p. 50), making way for about a million Turks forced out of Greece. The Kurds, on the other hand, remain under Turkish rule to the present day, often rebellious and often harshly repressed (p. 626).

"A Merciless Sea of Crosses." That was how the author Rudyard Kipling, who lost a son in the First World War, described the sight of a war cemetery. Along the line of the Western Front there are hundreds of such seas of crosses. This one is the resting place of Frenchmen who died defending the city of Verdun against repeated German attacks in 1916. The building in the background contains the bones of 130,000 soldiers of both nations whose remains were too scattered or decayed to be identified. Jochen Schlenker/Masterfile

The Arab lands of the Ottoman Empire, as well as Germany's former colonies across the world, were deemed by the peacemakers to be "inhabited by peoples not yet able to stand by themselves under the strenuous conditions of the modern world," so that "the tutelage of such peoples should be entrusted to advanced nations who by reason of their resources, their experience or their geographical position can best undertake this responsibility." Above all, this meant Britain and France, which were entrusted with large territories in the Middle East and Africa as **mandates** from the newly formed **League of Nations**. The League, which was written into the Treaty of Versailles, was the international organization charged with underpinning the repaired world order by committing all countries to peaceful settlement of their disputes and collective action against disturbers of the peace (pp. 502–503).

In practice, the mandate system meant that the empires of the two leading imperialist powers became larger than ever before. By this time, however, their subject peoples were expecting to share in the individual freedom, national independence, and material well-being that their rulers preached. Furthermore, having been mobilized by the hundreds of thousands to help fight the war in Europe, the colonial peoples were expecting some reward for their services. The bloated empires of the European victors would soon become a source of trouble for their owners.

The deeper consequences of the war went far beyond the treaties and the breaking and making of states. The war had brought a catastrophic loss of lives and treasure (see photo). Of the more than 60 million men mobilized, nearly 10 million were killed. Total civilian deaths amounted to 7 million; economic costs ran into trillions of dollars. The spirit of Europe, especially of its surviving aristocracy, was broken. The youth who had lived through the war, and wondered why, regarded themselves as a "lost generation." The old beliefs and slogans had for them become

mandate
A region to be administered by an outside government, as authorized by an international organization such as the League of Nations.

League of Nations
The international organization created in the aftermath of the First World War to settle disputes and take collective action against aggressor nations.

mockeries; traditional morals, manners, and standards seemed, at best, irrelevant.

The Threat to the Liberal Order

Men and morals were not the only casualties of the war. The liberal order, which in 1914 had appeared firm, was badly damaged. Liberalism was rooted in the Enlightenment, with its optimistic faith in humanity, reason, nature, and progress. But this faith had been crushed in the agony and futility of the war. Could liberalism survive after its supporting faith had collapsed? Disenchanted Europeans were unsure. Some drifted into skepticism (doubting all), cynicism (scorning all), or nihilism (rejecting all). Other Europeans were drawn toward Marxist socialism or toward fascism, a new and more virulent strain of nationalism.

The war had undermined specific liberal institutions as well. This was most evident in the economic sphere, where "free enterprise" had been jealously guarded during the nineteenth century. Every nation at war was forced to clamp controls on business; just as the draft on manpower was compulsory, so was the call on economic resources. Raw materials, exports and imports, banking, wages, prices—all had been regulated in the pursuit of victory. Laissez-faire principles (pp. 426–427) had been ignored "for the duration," and this experience of government planning and direction continued into the future. The war had also disrupted the intricate mechanism of international trade, and a chain of financial dislocations after 1918 marked the end of historic laissez-faire. It would be demonstrated time and again that private enterprise, both domestic and international, was

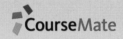

"Men and morals were not the only casualties of the war."

not always "self-regulating" in the public interest. To maintain employment and save business from mass failures, Western governments would be called on to take action.

The war had been fought, declared President Wilson, to make the world "safe for democracy." As he looked at Europe from Versailles in 1919, he might well have thought that the goal was now within reach. Prussian militarism had been defeated, long-standing empires had been reduced to ruins, and proud monarchies had been toppled. Democracy (as well as nationalism) appeared triumphant. Yet Wilson and others of liberal-democratic convictions were to suffer bitter disappointment. For most of the new democracies were only superficially democratic, and the older democracies were soon to lose their once-liberal character. Moreover, the shock and aftershock of the war were to open the doors of revolution in several countries. From the underground of the nineteenth century sprang the promoters of new social and international orders—who were radically opposed, in theory as well as in practice, to both liberalism and democracy. The world was about to enter an era of struggle between rival ideologies, social systems, and global orders that would continue for most of the century.

Listen to a synopsis of Chapter 25.

{ Listen Up! }

CHAPTER 26

THE WEST DIVIDED: COMPETING WORLD ORDERS,

1917–1939

LEARNING OBJECTIVES

AFTER READING THIS CHAPTER, YOU SHOULD BE
ABLE TO DO THE FOLLOWING:

LO¹ Trace the rise of communism in Russia.

LO² Compare and contrast fascism in Italy and Germany.

LO³ Explain how Britain and the United States responded
to economic depression.

"Out of the turmoil of the war there emerged two formidable movements against the existing order of Western and worldwide civilization: communism and fascism."

Out of the turmoil of the war, there emerged two formidable movements against the existing order of Western and worldwide civilization: communism and fascism. Each was inspired by a different secular ideology that had arisen within Western civilization, and their rise led to an era of struggle over the power structure of the West and the world that lasted for most of the twentieth century.

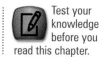

Test your knowledge before you read this chapter.

Communism, derived from nineteenth-century Marxism, took power in defeated Russia. It stood for the revolutionary overthrow of the existing world order on behalf of the victims of capitalism and imperialism, leading to a world of ideal social justice and international harmony. As Russian rulers, the communists concentrated on remaking the vast country into a formidable power base, the Soviet Union, through centralized economic control and massive bloodshed and coercion. Their worldwide following grew, however, as capitalism sank into depression and colonial peoples grew restive under imperialism.

What do you think?

In hard economic times, people tend to grant more power to their leaders.

Strongly Disagree						Strongly Agree
1	2	3	4	5	6	7

Fascism gained power in other defeated countries or ones where the spoils of victory had been unsatisfactory—notably Germany, Italy, and Japan. Its sources were injured national pride, resentment at the war's unavailing bloodshed and its aftermath of depression and unemployment, fear of rising communism, and in Europe, hatred of the Jews. Influenced by nineteenth-century Social Darwinism, fascism gloried in the "struggle for existence" among nations and races. European fascists also yearned for a Leader with a capital "L"—a man of brutal authority and power who would embody the collective might of the nation and its collective anger at its enemies within and without.

≪ **"Workers of the World, Unite!"** A poster from 1928 by the Soviet artist Dmitry Moor shows May Day demonstrators holding up banners with the international communist slogan in German, French, Italian, English, Chinese, and other world languages. Communism, the poster proclaims, is a worldwide movement that will destroy the existing world order and create a new one.

Interfoto/Alamy

communism
Term used in the West for a political and economic system derived from Marxist thinking under which the Communist party alone controls the state as well as social and cultural life, and the state controls the economy. Countries under communist rule generally called themselves "socialist," as they considered "communism" to be a final stage of political and economic development that they had not yet reached.

fascism
A political system led by a dictator who embodies the collective might of the nation and its collective anger at its enemies.

intelligentsia
In nineteenth-century Russia, a class of educated upper- and middle-class people, distinct from the elite of nobles and wealthy merchants.

In Britain, France, and the United States, victory confirmed liberal and national ideals, but their societies were damaged by wartime bloodshed and postwar unemployment. Political and labor movements arose that promised to change the workings of capitalism, and governments brought the welfare state "safety net" into being. The basic features of capitalism—private ownership and competition—remained largely untouched, however, for the welfare state was meant to uphold the existing order by reforming it.

LO¹ Communism in Russia

The first and longest-lasting of the movements to overturn the existing social and worldwide order was that of communism. In Russia, communism began as a revolutionary movement and developed into a whole new political, social, and economic alternative to that of democratic capitalism—an order that later spread to include a quarter of the human race, until in the late twentieth century, it suddenly collapsed.

Russia Before the Revolution

Russia in 1914 was a vast multinational empire, stretching eastward from Europe to the Pacific Ocean. Most of the population lived in European Russia (which then included Poland, Belorussia (present-day Belarus), Ukraine, and the Baltic lands), and in 1914, it totaled about 140 million. More than 80 percent of these people were peasants, who had been freed from serfdom only recently, in 1861. They held more than half the arable land of the country, either individually or as members of village communities, and they had gained limited political rights. Nevertheless, they remained largely illiterate and were regarded by the landed aristocracy (less than 10 percent of the population) as an inferior caste. Over all was the heavy hand

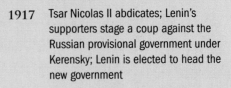

CHRONOLOGY

1917	Tsar Nicolas II abdicates; Lenin's supporters stage a coup against the Russian provisional government under Kerensky; Lenin is elected to head the new government
1918	The new Soviet government under Lenin signs a peace treaty with the Central Powers and distributes land to the peasants; the Whites launch an unsuccessful counterrevolution
1921	Britain falls into a chronic economic depression that lasts until World War II
1922	Mussolini takes over the government of Italy
1923	The Soviet constitution establishes the USSR as a federation of self-governing republics under the Supreme Soviet run by the Central Committee; Hitler leads an abortive coup against the Bavarian state government and is arrested, writes *Mein Kampf*
1928	Stalin announces the Communist party's first Five Year Plan
1929	Crash of the U.S. stock market, beginning of the Great Depression
1933	Hitler becomes chancellor of Germany, declares the beginning of the Third Reich; Roosevelt enacts the "New Deal" to combat the U.S. economic depression

of the imperial government, headed by the tsar, whose title proclaimed him "Autocrat of All Russia"—the last of Europe's absolute monarchs.

Russia and the West

Under its absolute rulers and often with their encouragement, nineteenth-century Russia was gradually changing on the Western pattern. The government set up universities and professional schools to supply the bureaucrats and experts that it needed, and Russian scholars and scientists were in the international forefront of their fields. Educated upper- and middle-class people became a whole new social element, distinct from the existing elite of nobles and wealthy merchants—the **intelligentsia** ("intellectual element"). Likewise, by 1914, the Industrial Revolution had begun to take hold. Substantial investments went into factories, mines, and railroads, and Russia became active in the world trading system.

But capitalist development was still limited in comparison to that of Britain or Germany. Industrial wage earners made up only a small fraction of the total labor force, and their working conditions resembled those in England fifty years earlier. The capitalist class was very small and had to share the economic field with numerous state-owned enterprises. Furthermore, the intelligentsia, the bureaucrats, and the tsars themselves all felt caught between the powerful traditions of autocratic, Orthodox, and peasant Russia and Western models of change that they found both attractive and dangerous. This unease was inspiring for thinkers and creative artists, whose achievements made Russian literature, music, and thought an admired model for other lands. But in the field of government policy, it resulted in half-hearted modernization and switches between liberalization and repression. Under Tsar Nicholas II, who came to the throne in 1894, this led to two ominous developments—growing internal opposition and humiliating defeat in war.

> "*Russia's future hinged upon the struggle for power between the provisional government and the Soviet.*"

The Autocracy Under Siege

Around 1900, the rising business and professional class, in combination with liberal land-owners, formed a political party known as the Constitutional Democrats. Eager to follow the example of western Europe, they wanted to convert Russia's autocracy into a liberal, constitutional government. At about the same time, two radical parties were founded—the Social Revolutionaries and the Social Democrats, both drawn mainly from the intelligentsia. The former was an agrarian party; its goals were to give more land to the peasants and to strengthen the functions of the village communities in accordance with Russian tradition. The Social Democrats were inspired by a Western ideology, that of Marxism. They viewed the peasantry as hopelessly backward and believed that for a revolution to be possible, Russia must first change on the Marxist pattern. Capitalism and industry must grow, the bourgeoisie must take over, and only then would the proletariat triumph (p. 443). For the moment, Marxists must organize and spread their message, but not try to bring about a proletarian revolution until the time was ripe.

Meanwhile, Russia's imperialist ambitions in East Asia led it into war with Japan (p. 466). By the end of 1904, the war was going very badly, bringing the tsar and his advisers into discredit. In 1905, a large body of protesting workers gathered in front of the tsar's Winter Palace in Saint Petersburg and was fired on by troops. This "Bloody Sunday" set off insurrections across the country that were supported and used in various ways by the opposition parties. As a means of restoring order, the tsar promised a constitution and civil liberties and further agreed to the creation of an elected legislative body, the Duma. But discontent still rumbled among most classes of the population. Only by means of a hated secret police was the tsar able to keep down the opposition. Even so, some revolutionaries resorted to terrorism, and no public official was safe from assassination. The grandfather of Tsar Nicholas, Alexander II, had been killed by a bomb, and Nicholas's prime minister was shot dead in 1911.

The Triumph of Lenin

What opened the way to successful revolution were Russia's renewed military disasters in the First World War. Soldiers and sailors, poorly supplied and hungry, at last refused to continue the hopeless fight against the Germans. In March 1917, food riots and strikes in Saint Petersburg (renamed Petrograd, because "Petersburg" sounded German) led to mutinies among the garrisons of the capital. The tsar abdicated on the advice of his generals; thus the Romanov dynasty ended, and Russia became a republic. A provisional government, composed chiefly of the reformist leaders in the Duma, now assumed power. This government was challenged, however, by the Petrograd Soviet (Council) of Workers' and Soldiers' Deputies, a body dominated by the radical parties. Local soviets had first appeared during the insurrection of 1905. They were formed again in 1917, supposedly speaking for the peasants, city workers, and soldiers; and the Petrograd Soviet began to act as a shadow government. The country's future now hinged upon the struggle for power between the provisional government and the Soviet.

The Struggle for Power

In April 1917, Vladimir Lenin arrived in Petrograd. Lenin was the son of a middle-class civil official, but in 1886, at the age of sixteen, after the execution of his elder brother for alleged participation in a terrorist plot, he made revolution his life career. Lenin spent most of his years in exile—first in Siberia, later in western Europe. An early convert to Marxism, he joined the Russian Social Democratic party and looked for ways to bring about a revolution sooner rather than later, in spite of Russia's lack of a strong proletariat. The more orthodox wing of the party appeared to outnumber Lenin's faction, but at a meeting in 1903, he temporarily secured majority backing for the radical position. His followers thenceforth called themselves Bolsheviks (**BOHL-shuh-viks**), from the Russian word meaning "majority"; their rivals came to be known as Mensheviks (from the word for "minority"). In 1912, the Bolsheviks broke away completely from the Social Democrats and formed an independent revolutionary party. They changed the name to Communist in 1918.

Lenin spent the First World War in neutral Switzerland, and returned to Petrograd in 1917 with help from the Germans, who hoped that his activities there would help take Russia out of the war. First, however, he had to take power from the provisional government, which was trying to restore internal order and uphold Russia's obligation to its allies to continue fighting the Germans. But conditions grew steadily more desperate in the country. Though Russia's economy had not developed to the point at which a proletarian revolution in the Marxist pattern could be expected, Lenin became convinced that the war had opened a shortcut to socialism. He saw that the bulk of the Russian people wanted three things above all: peace, land, and food. The provisional government, headed after July by Alexander Kerensky, a Social Revolutionary, had failed to satisfy these longings. If the "bourgeois" government was overthrown and Russia left the war, then proletarians in the other warring countries would surely rise up. In this way, "backward" Russia could start an international proletarian revolution.

The Bolshevik Takeover

Lenin's road to power was through the Petrograd Soviet. Though the Bolsheviks were a minority within the Soviet when Lenin arrived, he cleverly outmaneuvered the Mensheviks and the Social Revolutionaries, and his repeated promises of peace and land won growing popular support for the Bolsheviks. In October 1917, Lenin's faction won the upper hand in the Soviet and elected Lenin's close ally, Leon Trotsky, chairman. As Kerensky's power slipped and as soldiers once more began to desert their units, Lenin decided to move against the provisional government. On November 7, with the support of the Petrograd military garrison, a revolutionary force occupied the telephone exchanges, power plants, and railway stations of the capital. Kerensky found no troops to defend his government; he escaped, and the rest of his ministers fled or were captured.

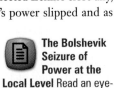 **The Bolshevik Seizure of Power at the Local Level** Read an eyewitness account of the Bolshevik takeover.

On the afternoon of the coup, according to plan, Lenin arranged a meeting in Petrograd of delegates from soviets in other parts of the country. This "all-Russian" congress, controlled by the Bolsheviks, declared the provisional government at an end and claimed full authority. It approved decrees for an immediate peace with Germany and for the distribution of land to the peasants. The congress also elected a Council of People's Commissars ("commissioners") to run the government, with Lenin at its head.

A small group, shrewdly and boldly led, had moved into the confused situation and taken command. Could such a government, facing enormous internal and external problems, keep itself in power? Its only organs of administration were the Bolshevik party, the soviets, and the Council of Commissars. The commissars established a secret police and authorized the recruiting of a new military force, the Red Army. The military commissar, Trotsky, was to be its builder and leader.

Holding onto Power

The first challenge to the Bolsheviks' hold on power came with the meeting of a national Constituent Assembly in January 1918. This body had been authorized months before by the provisional government and was to write a liberal con-

stitution for the country. The delegates had been chosen in a general election in which 36 million citizens voted, and a majority of them belonged to the Social Revolutionary party. When it appeared that the Bolsheviks could not dominate the assembly, Lenin sent a company of sailors to stop its meetings.

Not long afterward, in March 1918, the new Soviet government signed a peace treaty with the Central Powers, by which it agreed to surrender vast territories won by the tsars—Finland, Ukraine, much of Poland, and the Baltic territories of Lithuania, Latvia, and Estonia (see Map 25.2 on page 477). It was a bitter defeat, but it freed the Soviets' hands to face the next challenge to their rule. Former tsarist generals organized and led counterrevolutionary forces (the Whites) in several regions of the country. They were joined by property owners, reactionaries, liberals, and anti-Bolshevik revolutionaries. In addition, the Western Allies sent military units to aid the Whites against the Reds, to keep Russia in the war and help destroy communism. But after two years of frightful civil war, marked by the use of terror on both sides, the Bolsheviks emerged victorious.

 Video Footage of Lenin (http://www.encyclomedia.com/video- vladimir_ lenin_ .html) Watch documentary footage of Lenin and the early Soviet era (2:55).

The Red triumph owed much to the extraordinary will of Lenin and to the military and organizing genius of Trotsky. And it owed something to the confusion and splits among the counterrevolutionary groups and their association with foreign powers. But it owed most to the attitude of the common people. Many of the commoners, to be sure, opposed the new regime. But the majority feared that a White victory would probably lead to continued hopeless war with Germany and to the withdrawal of land from the peasants. Lenin's strategy for taking and keeping power had worked.

> "*The Red triumph owed most to the attitude of the common people.*"

In one respect, however, Lenin had been wrong: the revolution in Russia had not led to successful proletarian uprisings in any of the warring countries. For the moment, at least, communist Russia was on its own in a capitalist world.

Socialism in One Country

To survive as rulers of Russia, the Communists had first of all to make good the devastation of years of warfare. During the civil war, they had resorted to drastic measures to gain resources—later called "war communism." These included the drafting of workers into labor teams and forced deliveries of food from the peasants, in order to relieve hunger in the cities. Lenin was eager to start building socialism, but economic conditions were still so bad in 1921 that his plans had to be postponed.

Policy Changes and Power Struggles

Food was the primary problem; drought had made matters worse, and famine now stalked large areas of the country. In accord with the Soviet land

kulaks
The richer peasants in the Soviet Union who resisted collectivization.

collectivization
Under communism, the grouping of peasants into large farming units under orders from the state.

≪ **Digging Up Grain** Members of a collectivization brigade dig up grain that peasants have buried on a farm in western Siberia. Peasant holdings in this region were often quite large, so this grain probably belonged to a kulak family who wanted to hide it from the state's grasp. The peasants on the right have probably led the brigade to the hiding place, either under coercion or as willing denouncers.
Sovfoto

distribution decree of 1917, the peasants of each community had divided the properties of the landowning aristocracy among themselves, and something had to be done quickly to spur their efforts and encourage them to market their produce. The New Economic Policy (NEP), launched in 1921, aimed at doing just that. Now peasant farmers were permitted to hire laborers and to sell or lease land as they saw fit. Forced food deliveries were stopped, and the growers could market as they wished. The NEP was also extended to industry and commerce. While the state kept its grip on public utilities and other large industries (which had been nationalized in 1918), it encouraged private entrepreneurs to undertake new business ventures.

The NEP helped with reconstruction, but it fell short of the hopes and promises of the Communists. By 1928, output was at about the same level as it had been in 1913, and the momentum of the NEP seemed to slacken. Meanwhile, in 1924, the revered Lenin had died, and his former colleagues were maneuvering to take his place. Trotsky was the best known, probably the most talented, and certainly the most radical. In 1926, he openly criticized the NEP, complaining in particular about the new bourgeois and about the richer farmers or **kulaks** (from the Russian word for "fist," expressing their reputation for toughness). He called for the **collectivization** of agriculture—grouping peasants into large farming units that would use modern methods and respond to the needs of the state as a whole—as well as for vigorous expansion of heavy industry, a master plan for balanced and rapid economic growth, and renewed efforts to bring about international proletarian revolution.

But Trotsky could not gain the support of the majority of the party. Joseph Stalin, who held the post of party secretary, had quietly and skillfully built a following for himself as Lenin's heir. He appealed to those who wanted to concentrate on the revolution inside Russia, to those who looked inward rather than to the world. The party congress expelled Trotsky in 1927; he

was first sent to Siberia and then deported. Branded a communist heretic ("deviationist"), Trotsky was assassinated at Stalin's orders in Mexico in 1940.

Planning, Liquidations, and Purges

With Trotsky and other rivals out of the way, Stalin in 1928 commenced the building of "socialism in one country"—using the policies of rapid planned development that Trotsky had called for. He announced the party's first Five Year Plan, which concentrated on the collectivization of farming and the accelerated development of industry. State-controlled planning was the fulfillment of an idea that had been worked out by Marx's collaborator, Friedrich Engels, many decades before. Engels had noted that planning was indispensable to the efficient operation of individual factories and industries. The logical and ultimate goal, he thought, was the creation of a unified and complete national plan, embracing all parts of the economy.

Stalin's first plan ran into near-ruinous resistance. Collectivization brigades (party officials and workers from the towns charged with enforcement in the villages) scoured the countryside, joining private farms into large collectives of 1,000 or more acres each. Strictly speaking, the farmers of each collective, as a "cooperative" unit, retained possession of the land, but individual farmers no longer controlled any portion of the land as their own. The poorer peasants usually submitted to these forced measures, but the kulaks fought collectivization bitterly (see photo).

 Collectivization in the Soviet Union: A Peasant's Report Read a poor peasant's complaint about the injustices of collectivization.

The government at last decided to coerce the resisting kulaks by "liquidating them as a class." Most of the 2 million kulaks and their families were shipped off to labor camps in

THE TRIAL OF THE ANTI-SOVIET TROTSKYITE CENTER

Karl Radek was an Old Bolshevik (p. 492) who had worked closely in exile with Lenin before the First World War, and had returned with him to Russia after the February Revolution. He had been active in efforts to spread the revolution abroad, had sided with Trotsky in the disputes among party leaders after Lenin's death, and had been expelled from the party (his "first exile" in this excerpt). Eventually, he made his peace with Stalin and was readmitted to the party, but he was caught up all the same in the purges of the 1930s.

Although the purges involved millions of people, the centerpiece of each wave of arrests and executions was a "show trial" of prominent Communists, in which they were charged with ludicrous crimes backed up by only one real piece of evidence—their own written confessions, which they then repeated in court. Of course, these confessions were extracted by brutal physical and psychological torture. Generally, the defendants confessed to having belonged to "centers" or "blocs"—conspiratorial groups that had carried out such activities as espionage, "wrecking" and "diversion" (sabotage in industrial and agricultural enterprises), and terrorist assassinations.

Radek was tried in January 1937 as a member of the "Anti-Soviet Trotskyite Center"—supposedly an offshoot of the "Trotskyite-Zinovievite Center," another group of leading Communists who had already been tried and shot in 1936. (Grigory Zinoviev was another prominent leader who had been briefly allied with Trotsky in the 1920s.) This excerpt is taken from the closing statements of the procurator (chief prosecutor) Andrei Vyshinsky, and of Radek himself, before the Military Collegium (Board) of the Soviet Supreme Court, which had jurisdiction over both military and counterrevolutionary offenses. The court sentenced Radek to a mere ten years in a labor camp, but the secret police murdered him there in 1939.

The President: The session is resumed. Comrade Vyshinsky, Procurator of the U.S.S.R., will speak for the Prosecution.

Vyshinsky: Comrade Judges and members of the Supreme Court of the Union of Soviet Socialist Republics. In proceeding to perform my last duty in the present case I cannot but deal with several highly important specific features of the present trial.

In my opinion these specific features are, first of all, that the present trial, in a certain sense, sums up the criminal activities of the Trotskyite conspirators who for many years have systematically, and with the assistance of the most repulsive and despicable weapons, fought against the Soviet system, against the Soviet state, against the Soviet power and against our Party. This trial sums up the struggle waged against the Soviet state and the Party by these people, who started it long before the present time, started it during the life of our great teacher and organizer of the Soviet state, Lenin. While Lenin was alive these people fought against Lenin; and

after his death they fought against his great disciple, that loyal guardian of Lenin's behests and the continuator of his cause—Stalin.

Another specific feature of this trial is that it, like a searchlight, illuminates the most remote recesses, the secret byways, the disgusting hidden corners of the Trotskyite underground.

This trial has revealed and proved the stupid obstinacy, the reptile cold-bloodedness, the cool calculation of professional criminals with which the Trotskyite bandits have been waging their struggle against the U.S.S.R. They stuck at nothing—neither wrecking, nor diversions, nor espionage, nor terrorism, nor treason to their country.

When several months ago, in this very hall, in this very dock, the members of the so-called united Trotskyite-Zinovievite terrorist centre were sitting; when the Supreme Court, represented by the Military Collegium, was trying those criminals, all of us listened to the story of their crimes that unfolded itself like a nightmare scene before us, with horror and revulsion.

Every honest man in our country, every honest man in every country in the world could not then but say:

This is the abyss of degradation!

This is the limit, the last boundary of moral and political decay!

This is the diabolical infinitude of crime!

Every honest son of our country thought to himself: such hideous crimes cannot be repeated. There cannot be in our country any more people who have fallen so low and who have so despicably betrayed us.

But now we are again overcome with the sentiments that we felt not long ago! Once again across our anxious and wrathful vision pass frightful scenes of monstrous crime, of monstrous treachery, of monstrous treason. . . .

Many years ago our Party, the working class, our whole people, rejected the Trotskyite-Zinovievite platform as an anti-Soviet, anti-socialist platform. Our people banished Trotsky from our country; his accomplices were expelled from the ranks of the Party as traitors to the cause of the working class and socialism. Trotsky and Zinoviev were routed, but they did not subside; they did not lay down their arms.

The Trotskyites went underground, they donned the mask of repentance and pretended that they had disarmed. Obeying the instructions of Trotsky, Pyatakov and the other leaders of this gang of criminals, pursuing a policy of duplicity, camouflaging themselves, they again penetrated into the Party, again penetrated into Soviet offices, here and there they even managed to creep into responsible positions of state, concealing for a time, as has now been established beyond a shadow of doubt, their old Trotskyite, anti-Soviet wares in their secret apartments, together with arms, codes, passwords, connections and cadres.

Beginning with the formation of an anti-Party faction, passing to sharper and sharper methods of struggle against the Party, becoming, after their expulsion from the Party, the principal mouthpiece of all anti-Soviet groups and trends, they became transformed into the vanguard of the fascists operating on the direct instructions of foreign intelligence services. . . .

The President: Accused Radek.

Radek: Citizen Judges, after I have confessed to the crime of treason to the country there can be no question of a speech in defence. There are no arguments by which a grown man in full possession of his senses could defend treason to his country. Neither can I plead extenuating circumstances. A man who has spent 35 years in the labour movement cannot extenuate his crime by any circumstances when he confesses to a crime of treason to the country. I cannot even plead that I was led to

err from the true path by Trotsky. I was already a grown man with fully formed views when I met Trotsky. And while in general Trotsky's part in the development of these counter-revolutionary organizations is tremendous, at the time I entered this path of struggle against the Party, Trotsky's authority for me was minimal.

I joined the Trotskyite organization not for the sake of Trotsky's petty theories, the rottenness of which I realized at the time of my first exile, and not because I recognized his authority as a leader, but because there was no other group upon which I could rely in those political aims which I had set myself. I had been connected with this group in the past, and therefore I went with this group. I did not go because I was drawn into the struggle, but as a result of my own appraisal of the situation, as the result of a path I had voluntarily chosen. And for this I bear complete and sole responsibility—a responsibility which you will measure according to the letter of the law and according to your conscience as judges of the Soviet Socialist Republic.

. . . this trial has revealed two important facts. The intertwining of the counter-revolutionary organizations with all the counter-revolutionary forces in the country—that is one fact. But this fact is tremendous objective proof. Wrecking work can be established by technical experts; the terrorists' activities were connected with so many people that the testimony of these people, apart from material evidence, presents an absolute picture. But the trial is bicentric, and it has another important significance. It has revealed the smithy of war, and has shown that the Trotskyite organization became an agency of the forces which are fomenting a new world war. . . .

And finally, we must say to the whole world, to all who are struggling for peace: Trotskyism is the instrument of the warmongers. We must say that with a firm voice, because we have learned it by our own bitter experience. It has been extremely hard for us to admit this, but it is a historical fact, for the truth of which we shall pay with our heads. . . .

EXPLORING THE SOURCE

1. Judging from the tone and wording of Vyshynsky's statement, what seems to be the purpose behind the trial?

2. According to Radek's statement, what are the two main "facts" that the trial has shown? Why, in the late 1930s, should the Soviet authorities have been eager to have defendants admit to these "facts"?

Source: Thomas Riha, ed., *Readings in Russian Civilization* (Chicago: University of Chicago Press, 1964), 3:662–663, 667–668, 671.

totalitarianism
A political system in which the government aims to control every aspect of the citizens' lives and thoughts.

Siberia; others were forced into obedience, and many were killed. Some of them, in a final act of defiance and sabotage, destroyed their animals and implements before yielding. The heavy losses, and government manipulation of the surviving supplies, brought renewed famines in the early 1930s. Nevertheless, the collective-farm program was driven through; Stalin pursued it as a means of effecting complete state control over the rural population and of increasing agricultural efficiency and output.

Stalin's farm policy aroused sharp protests within the ruling bodies of the Communist party. His most notable critic was Nikolai Bukharin, a veteran activist and theoretician, who was a longtime associate of both Lenin and Stalin. Bukharin condemned the use of force against the peasants; he supported a flexible economic policy, based on persuasion, compromise, and gradual development.

But Stalin outmaneuvered his opponents. In 1930, Bukharin was shunted out of party influence and was later denounced as an "enemy of the revolution." Following a rigged show trial, he was sentenced to be shot in 1938. Many other communist leaders, together with almost all the "Old Bolsheviks" (who had belonged to the party before the Revolution), together with millions of lower-ranking party members, government officials, and ordinary citizens, were also arrested in a series of massive purges, which probably originated in Stalin's determination to suppress criticism and opposition but developed a momentum of their own. The victims were coerced into confessions, usually of crimes involving treason, espionage, and sabotage, and sent to labor camps or in many cases shot.

In these same years of famine and mass murder, Soviet industry boomed, thanks to the combination of socialist planning and state exploitation of labor that made rapid modernization possible. At a time when capitalism was in a seemingly incurable crisis of financial collapse and mass unemployment, the words of a foreign visitor in the 1920s, the American journalist Lincoln Steffens, seemed to make sense: "I have been over into the future, and it works." The industrial successes were trumpeted to Soviet workers and peasants, who developed a fierce pride in the country's accomplishments. "Backward Russia" seemed to be at last catching up with the West. To do so, it had destroyed its old ruling class, turned the life of its peasantry upside down, and was doing its best to smother its own religious traditions. But as the world's "first socialist country," the Soviet Union still had a unique character and mission, like the Russia of old.

Communist Totalitarianism

The price of all this, in addition to the years of bloodshed and hardship, was the domination of every aspect of life by the Communist party and government (**totalitarianism**). The Orthodox Church was stripped of its property and influence, other traditional faiths were barely tolerated, and Marxism became, in effect, the state religion. There was no free press, free speech, free unions, or freedom of assembly. Political power remained a monopoly of the party, which was supported—and at times dominated—by the secret police. Dissenters, under Stalin, were put down or destroyed by systematic terror: show trials, purges, labor camps, and mass executions. Using these modern tools of control, the Soviet government succeeded in deadening virtually every nerve of resistance.

The major political institutions of the new state had been formed before Lenin's death. According to the constitution of 1923, the Union of Soviet Socialist Republics (USSR) was a federal, democratic state. The former Russian Empire had embraced some fifty nationalities, and the Communists wanted to avoid openly suppressing national feeling. Each nationality became a self-governing republic, or a self-governing region within a republic, and by 1940, there were fifteen republics. The largest were the Russian Republic, which contained over half the USSR's total population of 190 million; the Ukrainian Republic (retaken by the Reds during the Civil War), with about 40 million; and the Belorussian Republic, with 9 million.

The highest body in the federal structure was the Supreme Soviet, which enacted national legislation. However, this body met for only a short time each year, when it elected a Presidium of some thirty members, to which its functions were delegated. The Soviet capital was moved in 1924 from Petrograd—renamed Leningrad—to Moscow.

The controlling power of the USSR lay in the Communist party rather than in the agencies of the state. It was not a party in the liberal-democratic sense but a disciplined organization whose self-appointed mission was to run the country. Accordingly, the constitution of 1923 authorized it to carry out this special role. One did not have to be a party member to vote or run for office in the Soviet Union, but party officials determined whose names would be placed on the election ballot. Within the party itself, organization and authority followed the principle of "democratic centralism": officers and delegates to higher bodies were elected at several levels from the smallest party "cell" to the All-Union Party Congress, which normally met every other year.

> **"***Dissenters, under Stalin, were put down or destroyed by systematic terror: show trials, purges, labor camps, and mass executions.***"**

One Woman's Struggle Against Stalinist Terror Read how the personal and political were entangled in one Russian woman's life.

Though the Congress was recognized as the highest party authority, actual control resided in its Central Committee, to which the Congress delegated its power. Once policy was decided upon there, it was the duty of every Communist to work for its fulfillment. Without this military-like organization, the party

COMMUNISM SPLIT THE INTERNATIONAL SOCIALIST MOVEMENT IN SEVERAL WAYS:

Left-wing socialists joined the Third International

- Left-wing socialists of other countries, impressed by Lenin's stand and by the Russian Revolution itself, readily accepted radical leadership.

- During the 1920s, the methods of the Soviet party were adopted by the new association.

- Tight organization, centralized control, and the name "Communist" were imposed on the international body and on each of its national parties.

Less radical socialists rejected communism

- Less radical socialists, who still preferred to call themselves Social Democrats, saw the totalitarian society that was growing up in the Soviet Union as a betrayal of socialist ideals.

- Communists and Social Democrats became bitter rivals, each accusing the other of splitting the international socialist movement.

could not have held power amid the vast and often chaotic changes that its own policies produced. In the long run, however, this monopoly of power by a single party—with its stultifying bureaucracy and lack of accountability—would prove incapable of satisfying the desires of the subject peoples.

International Communism

Marx himself had given socialism an international character, regarding national states as narrow creations of the bourgeoisie. In 1864, he had organized the First (Socialist) International. During the rest of the nineteenth century, however, the international socialist movement was weakened by internal differences and ultimately by rival patriotisms. A Second International, associating the socialist parties of many nations, fell to pieces with the start of the First World War. A radical minority refused to support their war governments, but most "reformist" socialists supported the "patriotic fronts" of their homelands.

As Marxists, the Soviet leaders did not give up hope of world revolution, but they scorned the reformist parties as bourgeois. In 1919, Lenin invited left-wing socialists throughout Europe to join the Soviet Communist party in forming a Third International (the Communist International or Comintern). This, Lenin declared, would be a "pure" successor to Marx's original organization. Free of the reformist socialists, it pledged itself to worldwide revolution and the dictatorship of the proletariat.

On the whole, Communist parties did not do as well as Social Democrats in Western countries. They were rightly suspected of "taking orders from Moscow," and they were liable to repression by national governments—as well as to damaging purges ordered by Stalin. Meanwhile, Social Democrats attracted more support by looking to reform the existing order more or less thoroughly by legal and democratic reforms. Communists did best in countries where the political and social order was most unstable. In China, driven into anarchy by rival imperialisms after the end of the war, the Communists began their rise to power. And Communists and other radical revolutionary groups became strong within two European great powers, Italy and Germany. But in these countries, the strength of the revolutionary Left contributed to a movement in a very different direction—that of fascism.

LO² Fascism in Italy and Germany

Strictly speaking, *fascism* is the name of the radical right-wing movement that took power in Italy in 1919, but the word is also used to refer to similar movements in other countries, including the Nazis in Germany. The Italian and German movements both sprang from two conditions: a social crisis that arose in the wake of the First World War, and the weaknesses of liberal-democratic government. Moreover, the movements were propelled by violent nationalisms growing out of the frustrations of the war. Whereas the communists focused on class and interclass struggle, the fascists stressed the nation and international struggle.

There was another significant difference between the two kinds of revolution. The communist uprisings in Europe had been anticipated in the decades of Marxist organization, propaganda, and threats of action. Fascism, on the other hand, came as a surprise. It had forerunners in nineteenth-century

> "*Whereas the communists focused on class and interclass struggle, the fascists stressed the nation and international struggle.*"

Social Darwinist and extreme nationalist movements, but it had no ideological founders, authoritative books, or international organization before 1918. Instead, its explosive appearance represented a breaking out of strong ideas and passions, some open to view and some hidden, that were opposed to liberalism, democracy, and rationalism. Though revolutionary, fascism had a broad appeal to privileged groups as well as to ordinary people. Its militant nationalism aroused all patriots, and its support of class interests satisfied individuals of property and power.

Fascism in Italy: Mussolini

Italy after 1918 provided a favorable setting for the rise of fascism. Its parliamentary institutions were less than fifty years old and had never won much loyalty or enthusiasm from the people—in fact, even male citizens were mostly not entitled to vote until 1912. Furthermore, the Italian legislature seemed incapable of dealing with postwar inflation and unemployment, and most Italians were bitterly disappointed over their country's role in the war. Though they finished on the side of the victors, their armies had experienced hardships, losses, and humiliating defeats. And at war's end, the Allies gave Italy only a portion of what they had promised as a reward for Italy's entering the conflict on the Allied side.

Mussolini and the Fascist Takeover

Many voters turned to the Socialists in the hope that they would do something about the worsening economic situation. The elections of 1919 gave the Socialist party one-third of the seats in the national Chamber of Deputies. The other large mass party was the Catholic Popular party, and mutual distrust between Catholics and Marxists made cooperation between them impossible. Instead, in 1920, the Socialist trade unions began to take direct action, occupying a number of factories and trying unsuccessfully to operate them. The workers soon withdrew, but their action had given the propertied classes a fright. In the following year, the Socialist party split over the question of whether or not to join the Comintern, thus losing what chance it might have had of becoming a dominant political force. It was on this scene of confusion, discontent, and fear of communism that Benito Mussolini presented himself as the national savior.

Born into a Socialist family, the son of a blacksmith, Mussolini was a man of the laboring class. He went to school to become a teacher but turned to journalism and radical agitation. In 1912, he became editor of the Socialist party newspaper in Milan and soon gained a reputation as a dynamic radical leader and opponent of militarism. In October 1914, however, he reversed himself by urging Italian entry into the war against the "militarist" Central Powers. He was expelled from the party, joined the army, and fought at the front until he was injured in an accident in 1917.

Returning to politics as editor of his own newspaper, he tried to stir popular support for the flagging war effort. He turned wholly against socialism after the Russian Revolution, growing more and more militant and nationalistic. He opposed the floundering parliamentary government of his own country

and, like many other veterans of the war, became attracted to violence as a way of life and as a means of securing change. He organized his followers into black-shirted "combat leagues"— *fasci di combattimento*—whose individual members were called *fascisti*—fascists. In Italian, *fascio* originally meant a thick staff made of many tightly bound sticks, such as had been carried by the bodyguards of ancient Roman magistrates, and it had stirring implications of individually insignificant people uniting into a single, overwhelmingly powerful force. Sure enough, the Blackshirts fought in the streets with socialists and others they disliked, smashed opposing party and newspaper offices, and assassinated some of the opposing leaders.

Mussolini next organized his forces into a fascist political party, even though he had only contempt for the parliamentary party system. In the national election of 1921, the Fascists won thirty-five seats in the Chamber of Deputies. As their leader, Mussolini made fiery nationalist appeals and attacks on socialism. He began to gain widespread support, especially from the shopkeepers and white-collar class, but from the rich as well. Young people were strongly attracted by the uniforms, parades, mass rallies, and calls for action. In 1922, his Blackshirts drove the legally elected socialist city governments out of Italy's northern industrial centers, and later that year, a huge Fascist assembly in Naples called for a march on Rome.

The constitutional king of Italy, Victor Emmanuel III, was now faced with the prospect of black-shirted bullies converging on his capital. His prime minister, unable to secure an effective legislative majority, urged him to declare martial law. But the king, probably fearing socialist revolution, invited Mussolini to come from Milan and form a new administration. The Fascists, camped near Rome, marched into the city, while Mussolini arrived by railway car to take over the government. To mark the world-wide significance of the event, on its fifth anniversary in 1927 the Fascists inaugurated a new calendar. Instead of "A.D." and "B.C.," Italians were to count years in the "Fascist Era," beginning with the takeover of power (see photo).

Video Footage of Musso-lini (http://www.encyclomedia.com/video-benito_mussolini.html) View documentary footage of the Fascists' march on Rome, along with clips of Mussolini (2:24).

Fascist Dictatorship

The new prime minister, who preferred his party title of *Duce* (DOO-chey) ("Leader"), was not long in consolidating his position. The Chamber of Deputies, which had surrendered to the Blackshirt threat without a fight, quickly voted Mussolini dictatorial power for one year. In the election of 1924, the party won about 70 percent of the total national vote. Despite its unclear aims and its fondness for violence, the party received the support of many moderates who hoped that they could exercise a restraining influence on the Duce. Subsequent elections, however, were rigged one-party votes (see photo).

The collapse of Italian democracy was clearly due to its own failures, but Mussolini's triumph resulted from a variety of factors. Critical among them was the backing of the army and the great industrialists of the country. Mussolini did not

The Leader and the Nation A poster by the Modernist artist Xanti Schawinski celebrates Mussolini's victory in elections in 1934 (Year XII in the new Fascist calendar). Figures in the "I" of "SI" ("Yes") give the results: more than 10 million people have voted Yes to Fascist candidates (the only ones on the ballot), and only 15,201 people (less than 0.15 percent) have voted No. The Duce's body is made up of countless tiny Italians: he is a colossus who personally embodies the nation.

have to create a new army (as did Lenin), for the regular army came readily to his side. Many of its high officers had had fascist sympathies from the beginning, and the Duce's glorification of militarism and his extravagant support of the army gained their active loyalty.

The industrial leaders, for their part, had been uncertain about Mussolini at first. They approved his smashing of the Socialist party and the unions, but they were worried about his intentions toward business. In 1925, the associated industrialists signed an agreement with the Duce. In return for their support of the Fascists, the industrialists were given a recognized position in the government, with the authority to regulate the nation's industrial affairs. The major employers in agriculture and commerce were later given similar authority. Together with handpicked labor and professional bodies, these regulatory groups made up what Mussolini called the "corporate state." In theory, this state represented a harmonizing of all the economic and social interests in the country, and the corporate associations gradually became the basis for political representation in the national legislative body. In fact, however, the corporate state

was an instrument of the dictator, through which he permitted the leading capitalists to administer the nation's economic affairs.

Mussolini completed his structure of power by negotiating an alliance with the pope. The papacy had never recognized the Italian state, which had come into existence partly by conquering the lands in central Italy that the popes had traditionally ruled (pp. 418–419). In 1929, however, Mussolini and Pius XI negotiated the Lateran Treaty and Concordat. The pope gained sovereignty over the area of Saint Peter's Basilica and its surroundings (the Vatican City), as well as state financial aid and a special position in the educational system for the Italian Church. In return, Pius gave his weighty support, and that of the Italian clergy and laity, to the fascist state. Mussolini was himself an atheist, but like Napoleon before him (p. 392), he sealed his position as dictator by a bargain with the Church. Afterward, not surprisingly, he violated the terms of the Concordat as he saw fit.

The Fascist party itself resembled, in many ways, the Communist party of the Soviet Union. It was the only legal party, it consisted of only a fraction of the total citizenry, and its members were drawn from the ranks of select youth organizations. Corresponding to the Communist Central Committee was the Grand Council of Fascism. Its members generally held high offices in the government in addition to their party positions; this connection, too, paralleled the interlocking of party and state officials that existed in the Soviet system.

The Fascist Ideology

In the beginning, as Mussolini himself admitted, fascism was largely a negative movement: against liberalism, democracy, rationalism, socialism, and pacifism. This negative feeling flowed from Mussolini's personal experience and that of countless other Europeans during and after the war. They had been cast adrift, let down by failed hopes of progress and happiness. The Fascists found an answer to this emptiness by arousing extreme nationalism. One could get an emotional lift by forgetting one's problems as a person and by giving oneself to something larger and grander—the nation. Mussolini and his associates developed this idea into the myth of the "organic state."

 The "Fundamental Ideas" of Fascism Read Mussolini's ideas about the fascist state.

The Fascists asserted that the state is a living entity, above the individuals who compose it. "The state," declared Mussolini, "is a spiritual and moral fact in itself." It encompasses every sphere of life; the state alone can "provide a solution to the dramatic contradictions of capitalism." And as a living organism, the state must expand in order to express its vitality. This meant a continuous and disciplined *will to power*, which requires unity within the nation, militarism, imperialism, and war.

The fascist myth rejected the liberal reliance on reason and replaced it with a mystical faith. Stridently anti-intellectual, it held that the "new order" would spring from the conviction of the "heart." Fascists therefore looked upon intellectuals as outmoded and suspicious characters, unduly concerned with their private mental fancies. Yet most Italian intellectuals willingly cooperated with the Fascists, thus confirming Mussolini's view that they were lacking in honesty and courage. The few who opposed the government were either silenced or forced into exile—the Fascist secret police struck down any active opposition.

Most ordinary Italians accepted fascism with enthusiasm. The individual, who formerly felt alone and unneeded, enjoyed a new sense of "belonging"; this feeling of personal identification and participation was deepened by the paternalistic measures of the government. Many types of workers wore distinctive uniforms, and mass rituals were staged in the great public squares of Rome and other cities. By 1930, fascism appeared to have gained the firm support of most of the Italian people, as well as the admiration of many conservatives abroad.

Fascist ideology frankly supported rule by an elite (the "chosen" best). While Marxists taught that the state and its officeholders would gradually disappear after the abolition of capitalism, the Fascists believed in permanent rule by their "natural" leaders. These would be individuals of rare intuitive power, capable of rising above self-interest and of sensing the character and desires of the nation. Their superiority, the Fascists declared, came chiefly from action rather than from thought: it was basic that the leaders would have fought for the fatherland, taken part in the Fascist revolution, and helped build the "new order."

The Nazi Compound of Fascism and Racism: Hitler

Fascism, like communism, was a worldwide movement. It won a substantial following in Austria, Portugal, Spain, and Argentina; but its world-shaking triumph was in Germany. Here, fascism as a doctrine fused with deeper and older forces in the German tradition; here, the fierce words of elitism and imperialism turned into deeds of conquest and **genocide**.

Germany's humiliation at Versailles (p. 479), coupled with severe economic problems after the war, prepared the ground for right-wing revolution. In 1919, Germany became a democratic republic, known from the name of the city where an assembly met to draft a new constitution as the Weimar (**VAHY-mahr**) Republic. But the new republic lacked the necessary minimum of consensus among its citizens. As in Italy, the largest voting blocs, the Marxists and the Catholics, bitterly distrusted each other, and the Marxists split into warring Social Democrat and Communist wings. The republic was also blamed for the military defeat. In the closing days of the war, the German generals had shrewdly left the country's surrender to a civilian government hastily appointed by the kaiser, and it was the republic's leaders who signed the Versailles Treaty. Much of the elite—industrialists, officials,

professors, and last but not least, generals—hankered after the Hohenzollerns under whom Germany had been prosperous and strong. And many who despised the Hohenzollerns for leading Germany to disaster were just as contemptuous of the new government that had accepted defeat. Those who had lost their belief in the Germany of the imperial past and despised the Germany of the republican present often put their hopes in a future "Germany Reborn through Blood and Iron"—the title of a book published in 1919, one of whose readers was Adolf Hitler.

The Nazi Rise to Power

Hitler had been born of middle-class parents in Linz, a city in the ethnically German part of Austria-Hungary. Early in life, he had become an ardent German nationalist, and though he spent some years in Vienna, he eventually moved to Munich in southern Germany—the country of his real loyalty. A moody drifter, he did not find a place for himself until the outbreak of the First World War. When he enlisted in the German army, Hitler experienced the comradeship and discipline of military life and exulted in his service to his adopted fatherland.

In 1919, embittered by the war's outcome, he returned to Munich—one of many unemployed veterans and political dissidents there. Hitler joined a budding group that called itself the National Socialist German Workers party, which became known to its opponents by a slang name derived from the word for "National"—the Nazis. He soon became the party's Leader (*Führer*) (**FYOOR-er**), a role that provided an outlet for his deep-seated hatreds and ambitions. He attracted to the Nazi banner others who shared his intense nationalistic feeling and hatred for Jews. Among his supporters were Hermann Goering, a swaggering pilot-hero; Dr. Josef Goebbels, a university-trained journalist; and General Erich Ludendorff, one of Germany's military commanders during the First World War.

 A Nazi Describes the Early Years Read a Nazi's account of his attraction to Hitler's ideas.

Hitler had only limited formal education, but he had an intuitive grasp of the concerns that were disturbing his fellow Germans, especially the middle class: deep anxieties about the decline of "culture," the threat of social revolution, and the mixing of the races. And like Mussolini, he had a gift for rousing speech-making. The early 1920s were a time of restlessness and disorder in Germany; street clashes and rioting were commonplace. In 1923, Hitler led an abortive coup against the Bavarian state government and was imprisoned for nearly a year. He used his enforced leisure to write *Mein Kampf* (**mahyn KAHMPF**) (*My Struggle*), the statement of his life and beliefs.

After Hitler's release, he revived his party. For a time, it made little headway, but the international economic crisis of 1930, a

> *"It was worse than hell sometimes . . . but nothing was able to turn me away from an intractable belief in the Führer and ultimate victory."*
>
> —A Nazi organizer, on the early days of the Party

product of the dislocations stemming from the war, gave the party its great opportunity. Rising numbers of unemployed men were looking desperately for work. Many of them found "jobs" as brown-shirted Nazi stormtroopers—brutal strong-arm forces like Mussolini's Blackshirts. The party gained electoral strength steadily during the years of economic hardship. And when, at one point, it ran out of funds, some powerful industrialists came to the rescue. In January 1933, Hitler received from them a promise to pay the wages of his stormtroopers and the party's debts. German business leaders generally preferred the familiar conservative politicians to Hitler. But in this time of crisis, they turned to the Nazis as a "bulwark against communism"—and to make sure that if the Nazis took power, they would be favorable to business.

A few weeks later, backed by conservative politicians and generals, Hitler succeeded in pressuring the aged president of the republic, Paul von Hindenburg, to appoint him head of the national government (chancellor). The Nazis had the largest number of elected delegates in the legislature (Reichstag), but they still did not have a majority. However, after the Reichstag building was mysteriously burned, Hitler enforced a suspension of constitutional guarantees, banned the Communist party, and had its leaders imprisoned. The Nazis, with the support of other conservative parties, then passed the Enabling Act of March 1933, giving the government power to rule by decree for a four-year period. Hitler next replaced the flag of the republic with the Nazi swastika (the "crooked cross") and declared the beginning of the "Third" Reich (Empire)—successor to the medieval Holy Roman Empire and the Hohenzollern empire.

Soon afterward, Hitler outlawed all parties save his own; by mid-1933, his political opponents were either in jail, in exile, or murdered. A year later, after Hindenburg's death, he became head of state—under the title of Führer—as well as chancellor. This act was ratified in a vote of overwhelming approval by the German electorate. Thus, the apostle of violence became the sole ruler of one of strongest country on the mainland of Europe. He proceeded, with the cooperation of the army and leading industrialists, to marshal the country's manpower and resources. Hitler's aim was to make Germany the most powerful nation in Europe and, ultimately, the world.

The Art of Propaganda: A Master Reveals His Secrets Read an excerpt from *Mein Kampf*.

of struggle and will, the glorification of militarism, insistence on authority and discipline, rule by an elite, and a mystical faith in the Leader. But in Germany, there were added elements of violent racism and nihilism. The first came largely from the nineteenth century; the last was mainly an outgrowth of the war and took the form of a mindless lust for power.

For the Jews of Europe, the Nazi racial theories led toward genocide. In the course of the nineteenth century, the liberal philosophy of equal civil rights for all had liberated Jews from the ghetto in most parts of Europe. However, the decline of discrimination on *religious* grounds was counterbalanced by the rise of new theories of *racial* difference. Writers in France, England, and Germany began to assert the supremacy of the "Nordic" or "Aryan race" of northwestern Europe over others—but also the danger that the "lower races" might swamp the highest one. The Slav, "Negroid," and "Mongoloid races" were all a threat, but the greatest danger came from the local representatives of the "Semitic race," scattered across Europe and newly free of traditional restrictions—the Jews.

Hitler and his associates, resentful of Jewish social and cultural influence in postwar Germany, embraced these racial ideas and made them a central part of their program. They became vicious anti-Semites, portraying the Jew as a seducing, bloodsucking fiend who longed to pollute Nordic "purity." Building on that passion, they enacted discriminatory legislation, outlawed marriage and sexual relations between Jews and citizens "of Aryan blood," forced Jews to wear a humiliating badge, burned their synagogues, and laid plans for the systematic annihilation of the Jewish people (see photo).

The Centerpiece of Nazi Racial Legislation: The Nuremberg Laws Read a selection of the Nuremberg Laws aimed at the Jews.

Like the Fascists, the Nazis had contempt for reason and intellectuals. Hitler saluted the German peasantry and declared that its way of life based on "blood and soil" would be the foundation of the new Germany. Yet under Hitler, the country became increasingly industrialized and urbanized. Cleverly, the Nazis covered up the disturbing reality of technological change by encouraging popular belief in the myths of rustic purity and racial superiority. Millions became converts to the Nazi faith during the 1930s. It suited the traditional romantic yearnings of most

Nazi Ideology

Nazism had much in common with Italian fascism. Both rested on the myth of the "organic state," the importance

>> **"Germans! Defend Yourselves! Don't Buy from Jews!"** A Nazi stormtrooper grins as he fixes a poster on the window of a Jewish-owned store in Berlin in April 1933, while a policeman "keeps order." A woman looks mildly regretful that from now on it will be unwise to buy dresses here, or even to window-shop. One month after the Nazi takeover, party thugs and officers of the law are already collaborating in intimidation and persecution. Deutsches Bundesarchiv Berlin, 102-14468-3, photo: o.Ang.

welfare state
A state that actively works to protect and advance the material well-being of the citizens.

Germans, offered a total view of life in place of fragmentation and alienation, appealed strongly to national and racial pride, and released the urge to violence.

Although Hitler roused powerful support for his measures in Germany, some individuals and groups struggled to resist him. The Roman Catholic hierarchy criticized many of the Nazi policies, but the Church generally looked to its own survival first and was able to secure its functioning while enduring an uneasy relationship with the state. More vulnerable were the German Protestant churches, which Hitler determined to organize into a supporting force for his party. Most of them yielded more or less willingly, but some individuals refused; they formed a separate "Confessing Church," which openly opposed Nazi power. They failed to stop Hitler and paid the high price of conscience: their chief leader, the Lutheran pastor Martin Niemöller, was arrested in 1937 and remained in a concentration camp until liberated by the Allies at the end of the war. Also arrested, imprisoned, and executed (in 1945) was the distinguished theologian Dietrich Bonhöffer, among many others.

LO³ Democracy in Britain and the United States

While totalitarian societies were taking shape in Germany, Italy, and the USSR, in the Scandinavian lands, France, Britain, and the United States, prewar social and government institutions appeared to hold firm. But none was secure from the disturbances that followed the war or from the ceaseless march of science and technology.

In response to these forces, democratic governments intervened more and more in matters formerly considered to be private. And as their functions expanded, governments left behind some of the principles and practices of historic liberalism and built up democratic-capitalist **welfare states**.

A European Example: Britain

Even before the war, the British had traveled a substantial distance away from liberalism (p. 429). Trade unions had become a distinct force between individual workers and their employers, and Parliament had passed numerous laws regulating industrial conditions. By 1914, the foundations had been laid also for compulsory national insurance, which protected workers against the costs of accident, sickness, unemployment, and old age. The revenues to support such programs were to be drawn in large measure from progressive income taxes. The First World War then brought new problems that demanded further action by the government. During the war itself, additional regulations were viewed as a matter of

necessity; that experience made it easier for the British to accept growing state intervention in the postwar period.

Britain had suffered severe losses of manpower and wealth during the struggle against Germany, and its most pressing problem at war's end was to recover its financial and trading position in the world. One obstacle to the effort was the country's aging industrial plants. Another was organized labor: the unions, accustomed to high wages during the war, would not agree to lower wages afterward. For these reasons, Britain failed to regain the lost markets, and after 1921, the country fell into a chronic depression that lasted until the Second World War. Unemployment and poverty became a way of life for several million Britons.

The Great Depression in Britain: The "Special Areas" Read a report on the causes and effects of unemployment during the British depression.

Organized labor grew into a powerful force in British politics during the 1920s. The unions, in combination with moderate socialists, had formed the Labour party in 1892. By 1924, it had the largest number of seats in Parliament and stood as a challenge to the dominant Conservative party. The working class discovered, however, that its exercise of political power did not guarantee a better standard of living for workers or a solution to the country's economic problems. The domestic policies of Labour governments did not, in fact, depart sharply from those of Conservative governments. Both parties agreed that the protection and advancement of the public well-being required continuing and widening intervention by the state.

As the British depression grew deeper during the early 1930s, laws were passed that ended the traditional policy of free trade. Tariffs were enacted to guard the home market against imports, especially from the United States. (This action was explained as a countermeasure against high tariffs in America.) The government also went off the gold standard in 1931 and devalued its money, the pound, in terms of other currencies. The latter step was taken as a means of aiding British exports, but its effect was shortly undone by corresponding devaluations of other currencies in capitals around the world. When key industries, like coal, proved unable to compete, they were voted subsidies by Parliament. Extensive plans were also laid by the government for the general development of British industry and agriculture.

The American Experience: Roosevelt

As a consequence of the First World War, the United States became the strongest capitalist country. During the 1920s, the nation pulled away from its military adventure overseas and from the domestic controls imposed during the mobilization for war. It was the decade of "normalcy," a word coined by the amiable and easygoing President Warren Harding.

Normalcy, however, soon proved anything but normal, and the government of the United States, during the 1930s, was

> *"Cleverly, the Nazis covered up the disturbing reality of technological change by encouraging popular belief in the myths of rustic purity and racial superiority."*

pushed into the kind of intervention that had become common in other Western democracies. The economic boom of the postwar years had brought temporary prosperity to the nation, but the boom was driven by artificial and unstable forces. In the spectacular stock market Crash of 1929, many of the inflated values were wiped out within a few hours. More serious, the Crash signaled the coming of the Great Depression—a long and bitter experience for millions of Americans.

> *"Both parties agreed that the protection and advancement of the public well-being required continuing and widening intervention by the state."*

The Great Depression

President Herbert Hoover, the Republican leader, was in office when the Crash occurred. A competent administrator and a well-meaning humanitarian, Hoover never understood that a system and an era had ended. Although he approved limited government measures to assist some financial institutions and railroads, he held stubbornly to the view that business in general would recover by itself. While Hoover was telling a worried public, repeatedly, that recovery was "around the corner," production and employment skidded downward. They struck bottom during the winter of 1932–1933. By then, production had fallen nearly 40 percent from the 1929 level; wages were down by the same proportion; farm income was reduced by half. Construction had nearly ceased, and about 15 million people were out of work.

 The Library of Congress Memory Project, Photographing the Great Depression (http://memory.loc .gov/learn///features/ timeline/depwwii/art/ people.html) View photographs of the Great Depression taken by New Deal photographers.

Depressions were by no means a new experience in capitalist countries. This depression, however, was the worst in history, and there was reason to believe that "normal" recovery forces were unlikely to prove effective. This was due to several factors: rigid price and wage structures, rapid technological advances in industry (which displaced workers), and the near-hopeless situation of farmers, who were producing for a depressed and uncontrollable world market. Given enough time, some kind of balance in the economy would no doubt have come about through "natural" forces. But the economy had grown so complex and interdependent that these forces would have been too slow. So many individuals and families would have been crushed in the process that the strain on the social system could have proved intolerable.

Roosevelt and the New Deal

In the presidential election of 1932, the American people turned to Franklin D. Roosevelt, who promised that he would act in this crisis—that he would lead the federal government in an attack on the depression as if it were an attack on a human enemy. The temper of the country was such that had he not promised to act, more radical leaders might well have gained a mass following. After an overwhelming electoral victory for his Democratic party, Roosevelt began the first hundred days of his "**New Deal**" program. This program marked a shift from the traditional policy of limited governmental interference to one of acceptance by the government of responsibility for the "general welfare."

The New Deal was new only to a degree, since it built on the ideas and policies of earlier American "progressives" as well as the wartime experience of industrial mobilization. But Roosevelt realized that the challenges were now far greater and that they demanded a new boldness. He proposed remedies in a frankly experimental fashion, with no developed ideology. The New Deal was not anticapitalist; on the contrary, it aimed at preserving and strengthening the capitalist system.

Roosevelt classified his measures under the headings of relief, recovery, and reform. Among the most important and enduring were legislative provisions for the Social Security system, bank deposit insurance, regulation of the securities exchanges, stabilization of agricultural production, direct relief for needy citizens ("welfare"), guarantees for labor collective bargaining, and natural resources conservation. The New Deal programs did not cure all of the nation's ills, but most of them worked, at least to a degree, and they placed the federal government in a new and generally accepted role in the social and economic life of the country. Though FDR, a well-to-do landowner, was attacked by some of his opponents as a "traitor to his class," he saw himself, simply, as a popularly elected president making necessary reforms in light of new economic realities.

> *"Roosevelt promised to lead the federal government in an attack on the depression as if it were an attack on a human enemy."*

In the United States, as in Britain, the expansion of the welfare state did not bring an end to high unemployment. What finally brought the workers back into the factories was the needs of rearmament and then, once more, of worldwide total war—a war brought about by the failure of the victors in the First World War to peacefully uphold the world order they had tried to repair in 1919.

 Listen to a synopsis of Chapter 26.

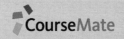

CHAPTER 27

THE WEST'S DARKEST HOUR: THE SECOND WORLD WAR, 1919–1945

LEARNING OBJECTIVES

AFTER READING THIS CHAPTER, YOU SHOULD BE ABLE TO DO THE FOLLOWING:

LO¹ Describe the collapse of the Versailles settlement and the fascist challenge to the world order in the 1930s.

LO² Trace the rise and fall of the fascist world order from 1939 to 1945.

> **"FASCISM PROVED ITSELF THE MOST SINISTER AND DESTRUCTIVE SYSTEM THAT EVER GOVERNED A SIZEABLE REGION OF THE WORLD."**

Following the First World War, it was up to victorious Britain, France, and the United States to uphold their repaired world order against its fascist and communist opponents. But the victor countries feared a renewal of bloodshed, and many of their citizens admired one or other rival system. The communists, too, wanted peace so as to build their power base in the Soviet Union. For the fascist nations, this was the chance to exploit the hesitations and mutual distrust of all their rivals. They swept aside the treaties that had ended the First World War, began the Second World War on favorable terms, and won its early stages in both Europe and Asia.

For a few short years, especially in Europe, fascism came into effect on an international scale, and proved itself the most sinister and destructive system that ever governed a sizeable region of the world. But the fascist countries' ideology of brutality and force made them reckless. They united the United States and Britain, the undefeated guardians of the existing world order, with the Soviet Union against them, and the superior combined resources of this new coalition enabled it eventually to crush the fascist challenge. The first round of the struggle over the future organization of Western and world civilization had ended. The next round was about to begin.

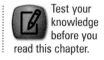

Test your knowledge before you read this chapter.

What do you think?

Negotiating with aggressor states is never effective as a foreign policy.

Strongly Disagree						Strongly Agree
1	2	3	4	5	6	7

Battle of Korsun, February 1944 (oil on canvas), Krivonogov, Petr Alexsandrovic (1911-1967)/Private Collection/The Bridgeman Art Library

◀◀ *After the Battle of Korsun, February 1944* As the Red Army drove Hitler's armies back across the Soviet Union late in the Second World War, it trapped a 60,000-strong German force in a "pocket" in central Ukraine. Most of the force fought its way out, but a third of its soldiers surrendered or fell victim to Soviet tank and artillery fire, along with all its heavy equipment. This painting by the Soviet artist Pyotr Krivonogov shows the results of what, by the standards of the Eastern Front, was a fairly small-scale battle.

sanction
An economic or military action intended to elicit cooperation from an aggressor state.

collective security
The idea that by banding together against potential aggressors, nations can protect the peace.

LO¹ The Collapse of the Versailles Settlement

When President Woodrow Wilson led the United States into the First World War in 1917, he declared that it was a "war to end all wars." When that conflict ended, Wilson began a determined effort to make his promise come true. He urged the Allies to put into effect the peace proposals that had persuaded the Germans to quit the war—his widely publicized "Fourteen Points." These included the goals of "open" diplomacy (no more secret treaties), freedom of the seas, arms reductions, removal of trade barriers, and political "self-determination" (independence) for peoples everywhere.

The fourteenth and crowning point was Wilson's proposal for a "general association of nations," to guarantee their independence and boundaries. And with a view to ensure that this association be established, Wilson traveled to Paris after the war and took part personally in the peace conferences. At his insistence, the plan for a League of Nations was written into the Treaty of Versailles in 1919.

The League of Nations

Most of the European diplomats at Paris, still nationalists to the core, had little enthusiasm for the League. They approved it largely to please Wilson, who, in return, made concessions to them on the other provisions of the treaty. Wilson believed that the League, once established, could correct such injustices and lay the foundation for a warless world—an emerging idea that now had substantial popular support. Ironically, the Treaty of Versailles, including the League plan, was later ratified by all the Allied governments except the United States. Its defeat in the Senate was due to a combination of factors: persisting nationalism, disillusionment with the late "crusade" in Europe, Wilson's refusal to accept amendments to the treaty, and the constitutional requirement of a two-thirds affirmative vote for ratification.

Whatever chance the League may have had to fulfill its high purpose was crippled by America's failure to join it. Both Germany and the Soviet Union were excluded from membership for a number of years, so the organization was far from being universal. Nevertheless, it had some strong supporters, and it carried on in the hope that the United States would one day become a member. Disillusionment with the war and the later miseries of the Great Depression, however, turned Americans inward.

The League performed many useful international functions, including overseeing the conduct of plebiscites (popular votes) in disputed territories, returning prisoners of war to their homelands, and providing aid to refugees. Through its commissions, it also arranged for the exchange of scientific and cultural information and the collection of social and economic statistics.

CHRONOLOGY

1919	The League of Nations is created under the Treaty of Versailles
1932	The Council of the League of Nations fails to sanction Japan for aggression against Manchuria
1935	Hitler defies Treaty of Versailles and announces plan to rearm Germany
1936	Mussolini annexes Ethiopia, withdraws from League of Nations, and forms "Rome-Berlin Axis" with Hitler
1937	Japan, Germany, and Italy ally in Anti-Comintern Pact
1938	France and Britain agree to Hitler's demand for a portion of Czech territory (Munich Pact)
1939	Fascists, led by Franco, are victorious in Spanish civil war; Stalin signs Nonaggression Pact with Hitler; Germany invades Poland; France and Britain declare war on Germany; Soviets annex eastern Poland, Estonia, Latvia, and Lithuania
1940	The Netherlands, Belgium, and France fall to Nazis; Italy formally enters conflict on the German side
1941	Germany attacks the Soviet Union; Japan attacks the U.S. naval fleet in Pearl Harbor; the United States declares war on Germany and Japan
1942	The Nazi operation to exterminate the Jews reaches full-scale implementation
1945	Germany surrenders in May, ending the war in Europe; Japan agrees to surrender in August, ending the war in the Pacific

But its sponsorship of disarmament conferences proved completely fruitless, for the participating nations viewed proposals for arms reduction as another arena for the continuing power struggle.

> "*Whatever chance the League may have had to fulfill its high purpose was crippled by America's failure to join it.*"

THE PRINCIPLE OF COLLECTIVE SECURITY FAILED TO MAINTAIN WORLD PEACE AFTER THE FIRST WORLD WAR:

The leading world powers did not act collectively against aggressors

- The leading powers did not put an overriding priority on stopping aggressors.

- In and out of the League of Nations, each nation continued to pursue its own particular aims.

- Each leading power (including the United States) refused to act except when its own immediate interest seemed to be threatened.

The aggressors were too powerful to be deterred by sanctions from other countries

- Although Japan and Italy were on the winning side of the First World War, they were disappointed with their shares of the spoils.

- Germany, which was the strongest remaining loser of the First World War, gained additional strength by aligning with Japan and Italy. Together, they came to be known as the "dissatisfied powers."

- The balance between countries wishing to preserve the repaired world order of Versailles and the "dissatisfied powers" proved to be too nearly equal for the collective security idea to succeed.

The primary purpose of the League, as planned by Wilson, was to prevent war. The treaty required that member states submit their disputes to arbitration (decision by an impartial umpire) and, if that failed, to the Council of the League. The Council, which consisted of representatives of the principal countries, could, by unanimous vote only, call for economic or military actions ("**sanctions**") by member states against any aggressor state. The principle underlying this provision was that of "**collective security**," that is, the idea that if all "peace-loving" countries acted collectively against *any* violator of the peace, the violator would be overwhelmingly defeated. Potential aggressors, once convinced that collective action against them was a certainty, would not start acts of conquest. While the principle made sense in theory, it did not work in practice.

> *"Little more than a decade after the First World War, the hope for collective security lay shattered."*

The Fascist Challenge to the World Order

Japan was the first country to test the will of the League's members. In 1931, Japanese soldiers occupied Manchuria, driving out the legal Chinese authorities. Responding to China's appeal, the League sent an investigating commission to Manchuria; in 1932, the commission concluded that Japan was guilty of aggression and recommended appropriate action. But the Council of the League could not agree on sanctions. Britain, with extensive interests in Asia, was reluctant to offend the Japanese, who had a powerful Pacific fleet. Unable to secure a guarantee of assistance from the United States should sanctions lead to war with Japan,

the British decided that nothing should be done. And Britain was the most influential member of the League and its Council.

The militarists in Tokyo, having successfully defied the League, strengthened their grip on Japanese politics and prepared for more ambitious conquests in China and beyond, and the League's failure encouraged aggressors in Europe as well. Little more than a decade after the First World War, the Wilsonian hope for collective security lay shattered. The great powers were already on the road to the Second World War.

The Dissatisfied Powers Against the World Order

Benito Mussolini viewed the League's failure with special satisfaction. In keeping with the fascist ideology of militarism and imperialism, he was seeking to expand Italian control in Africa. During the 1920s, he had attempted by negotiation to gain a foothold in the ancient empire of Ethiopia. But the Ethiopian emperor, Haile Selassie (**suh-LAS-ee**), had stubbornly refused. Mussolini, after observing the impotence of the League, decided to move by force of arms.

The emperor's tribesmen, armed with primitive weapons, could not hold out against the artillery and aerial bombardment of the Italians. Within a year, Ethiopia was beaten and annexed to Italy (1936). In this affair, Britain had been more deeply aroused than in the case of Manchuria; it had persuaded the Council of the League to call for economic sanctions against Italy, the declared aggressor. The measure was only partially effective,

>> **"Someone Is Taking Someone for a Walk"** This comment by the British cartoonist David Low appeared in 1939, when Germany was at war with Britain and France but on friendly terms with the Soviet Union, thanks to the Nonaggression Pact signed by the two countries earlier that year. The "someone" who was being taken for a walk was Stalin. On June 14, 1941, the Soviet government declared: "Rumors of the intention of Germany to break the pact are completely without foundation." Eight days later, the Germans attacked.

SOMEONE IS TAKING SOMEONE FOR A WALK

however, and Mussolini continued to receive needed supplies from Germany. Italy resigned from the League; Japan and Germany had already pulled out; and the "Rome-Berlin Axis," joining the two fascist states of Europe, was formalized in 1936. In the following year, the militaristic and profascist government of Japan joined Germany in an Anti-Comintern Pact, which Italy joined the following year. The pact was intended, supposedly, to check the spread of communism by the Comintern in Moscow (p. 493); actually, it was a general alignment of the dissatisfied powers that signaled their intention to cooperate in undermining the world order of 1919. And the strongest member of the alignment, Germany, was preparing to strike.

In 1935, Adolf Hitler had announced his decision, in defiance of the Treaty of Versailles, to rearm Germany. His army and air force were growing steadily in strength. Though he moved cautiously at first, Hitler continued to violate the 1919 peace settlement. His troops crossed into Austria in 1938, and the Führer announced the absorption of that state into the Third Reich (p. 497).

A year earlier, Hitler had extended his influence southward by supporting an army rebellion, led by General Francisco Franco, against the newly established Republic of Spain. The government—which had been elected by a "Popular Front" of democratic, socialist, and communist parties—appealed to the Soviet Union for help against the rebels, and the war soon became a bloody theater for the ideological struggle between Left and Right in Europe. It also proved to be a testing ground for new weapons and tactics of war. Hitler and Mussolini sent equipment, troops, and pilots in decisive numbers to Franco (now called *Caudillo*, "Leader"). The war ended in 1939 with total victory for the fascists. With the support of the Spanish Church, Franco established a tough, repressive government that was to endure until his death in 1975.

 Germany Rearms Learn more about the rearming of Germany in this video.

> *" All is over. Silent, mournful, abandoned, broken, Czechoslovakia recedes into the darkness. "*
>
> —Winston Churchill on the Munich Pact

 Hitler Plans the Next European War Read Hitler's 1937 plan for German expansion.

 Austria Falls Learn more about the fall of Austria in this video.

Britain and France were by now thoroughly alarmed, but popular antiwar sentiment and political incompetence kept them from responding effectively to the fascist threat. The Soviet Union seemed to be the only power that could check Hitler. France had concluded a defensive alliance with the Soviets in 1935, but the agreement proved short-lived. One reason for the collapse of the Franco-Soviet alliance was the failure of France and Britain to honor their treaty obligations to defend Czechoslovakia. (The Soviets also had an agreement to aid the Czechs—but only if the French acted with them.) At Munich, in September 1938, the two Western powers, ignoring Soviet concerns, agreed to Hitler's demand for a portion of Czech territory. Six months later, the Nazis took over the rest of Czechoslovakia.

Joseph Stalin's suspicions of the Western powers were strengthened by their act of "**appeasement**." The Soviet dictator feared (rightly) that some British diplomats were secretly hoping that Hitler would smash eastward into the Soviet Ukraine, thus reducing or eliminating one or both of the Nazi and Soviet threats; he himself hoped that if Germany and the Western powers went to war, that would weaken the capitalist world and thereby strengthen the Soviet Union. In fact, Hitler did intend eventually to invade and destroy the Soviet Union and use its population and resources for German benefit, but for the moment, he needed peace with the Soviet Union while he overawed or actually fought the Western powers. Accordingly, the two countries negotiated the Nazi-Soviet Nonaggression Pact of 1939, which provided, in return for mutual pledges of nonaggression (and territorial promises

 Munich Pact Learn more about the Munich Pact in this video.

 Allied Appeasement Denounced: The Shame of Munich Read Winston Churchill's critique of Britain's decision to appease Hitler.

to the Soviet Union), that Stalin would not interfere with Hitler's next territorial grab in Europe.

LO² The Rise and Fall of the Fascist World Order

The Nazi-Soviet Pact opened the way for Germany to pounce on Poland on September 1, 1939. In a desperate effort to deter or contain Hitler, the British and French had given pledges of assistance to the Poles. This time, they stood by their word and declared war on Germany. The Second World War was under way—for the moment, as a conflict between three of the leading European powers. It would expand to the point where the two sides, known as the **Allied** and **Axis Powers**, would include nations from around the world.

Germany's "New Order" and Japan's "Co-Prosperity Sphere"

Poland was crushed militarily within a month as the Germans displayed new tactics of mobile warfare. Swift tank formations, supported by motorized infantry and aircraft, and coordinated by radio communications, paralyzed and surrounded the Polish troops. Soviet troops, meanwhile, by prior agreement with the Nazis, moved into the eastern portion of Poland, where most of the population was not Polish, but belonged to two nations of the Soviet Union, the Belorussians and Ukrainians. To create a further "defensive buffer," on the Baltic Sea, the USSR also occupied and annexed the newly independent states of Estonia, Latvia, and Lithuania (see Map 25.3 on page 480).

 Nazis Invade Netherlands Learn more about the Nazi invasion of the Netherlands in this video.

In 1940, the Netherlands, Belgium, and France fell before the German **blitzkrieg**, and Italy formally joined the conflict on the side of the Germans.

The fascist forces, having seized the initiative, had scored astonishing gains in the early period of fighting, securing control of most of continental Europe and much of North Africa. The boundaries and power balances of 1919 had been overthrown and replaced by what the Nazis called a "New Order" in Europe. Only Britain held out defiantly against Nazi bombers and threats of invasion (see photo)—one of the main factors that eventually decided the outcome of the six-year war, since Britain could still mobilize the worldwide resources of its empire and serve as a platform for the struggle against Germany in the West. But Britain could not roll back Germany's conquests on its own, and for the moment, Hitler felt relatively secure as master of western and central Europe. The only possible rival was the Soviet Union, which controlled most of the lands in eastern Europe that Hitler wanted for Germany's "living space." Accordingly, ignoring his nonaggression pact with Stalin, he savagely attacked the Soviet Union in June 1941.

For the time being, furthermore, the fascist conquest of western Europe weakened the British, Dutch, and French hold on their Asian empires, and that in turn encouraged

Allied Powers
The coalition that opposed the Axis in the Second World War, led (after 1941) by Britain, the Soviet Union, and the United States.

Axis Powers
The coalition that opposed the Allies in the Second World War, led by Germany, Italy, and Japan.

blitzkrieg
"Lightening war," the Nazi tactic of paralyzing the enemy through a swiftly executed and coordinated strike by mechanized forces.

>> **"London Can Take It"** This photograph of Saint Paul's Cathedral was taken during the Blitz, the eight-month German bombing campaign against London in 1940 and 1941. The image of the British national shrine (p. 350) towering unscathed above the burning city became an international symbol of the country's survival despite the worst that Hitler could do—and of hope for ultimate victory over the Nazis.
Keystone/Getty Images

the Japanese to bring to pass long-held ambitions. Japanese forces had occupied large areas of China before 1941, and now they hoped for further gains. But they had run into determined opposition from the United States, and six months after the German attack on Russia, they struck the United States' Pacific fleet at Pearl Harbor, Hawaii. They then launched spectacular moves, winning mastery of the western Pacific Ocean and its islands and conquering the British colonies of Burma and Malaya, French Indochina, the Dutch East Indies, and the American-controlled Philippine Islands. They combined all of these lands into an allegedly anti-imperialist "Greater East Asia Co-Prosperity Sphere," which in fact functioned as a system for supplying foodstuffs and raw materials to Japan.

> **"***At both ends of the Eurasian landmass, the fascist powers sought to lay the foundations of a new global order.***"**

At both ends of the Eurasian landmass, the fascist powers sought to lay the foundations of a new global order in which they would at the very least be the equals of the traditionally dominant worldwide powers. And their efforts were now linked. As soon as the Japanese attacked Pearl Harbor, Germany declared war on the United States, partly in hopes that Japan would attack the Soviet Union in Asia, and partly to enable U-boats to act more freely to cut communications between America and Britain.

A Detailed Overview of the Pearl Harbor Attack (http://www.history.navy.mil/faqs/faq66-1.htm) Learn more about the Japanese attack on Pearl Harbor.

Defeating the Fascist Challenge

The Japanese never fulfilled the German hopes, and the U.S. administration of Franklin Roosevelt, which had already been helping Britain in many ways but was held back by the opposition of public opinion to joining in yet another distant conflict, was now free to fight a full-scale war against both Germany and Japan. United States industrial power, which enabled it to build up formidable forces in both Asia and Europe while also massively supplying Britain and the Soviet Union with food and equipment, was another main factor in the outcome of the war (see photo). "So we had won after all," British Prime Minister Winston Churchill, the leader of his country's difficult struggle

Arsenal of Democracy Women workers–half a dozen out of the millions recruited by U.S. war industries–check out a batch of warplane bomb-aiming windows. The windows may end up being used by American, British, or Soviet airmen, among many others, for this aircraft type, the Douglas A-20 fighter-bomber, was delivered to practically every Allied air force. The A-20, in turn, was only one item in the vast mass of equipment that U.S. industry supplied to its own and Allied forces.

for survival, remembered saying to himself on hearing the news of Pearl Harbor.

The War in Europe

The third main factor in the defeat of Germany was the armies of the Soviet Union, which for four years bore the brunt of the fighting in Europe. After their surprise attack on the Soviet Union, the Nazis had penetrated deep into the country and had nearly toppled the regime. However, they were stopped at last, just short of Moscow, having suffered heavy losses. A year later, the Soviets halted a German offensive into southern Russia at Stalingrad (since renamed Volgograd; Map 27.1), and surrounded and destroyed twenty-two Nazi divisions, numbering some 300,000 soldiers. In the next two years, they forced the Germans back across the Soviet Union's borders into neighboring lands to

A German Soldier's Last Letter
Home Read a German soldier's description of the Russian front.

Map 27.1 The Second World War in Europe and North Africa

The basic strategic pattern was the same as in the First World War. The Axis powers confronted a stronger but scattered group of opponents. This time, however, the opponents distrusted each other, and faced an additional threat from Japan in East Asia. For a time, the Axis powers made spectacular conquests until the rival coalition mobilized enough resources, determination, and mutual cooperation to squeeze and crush the bloated Axis domain. © Cengage Learning

Interactive Map

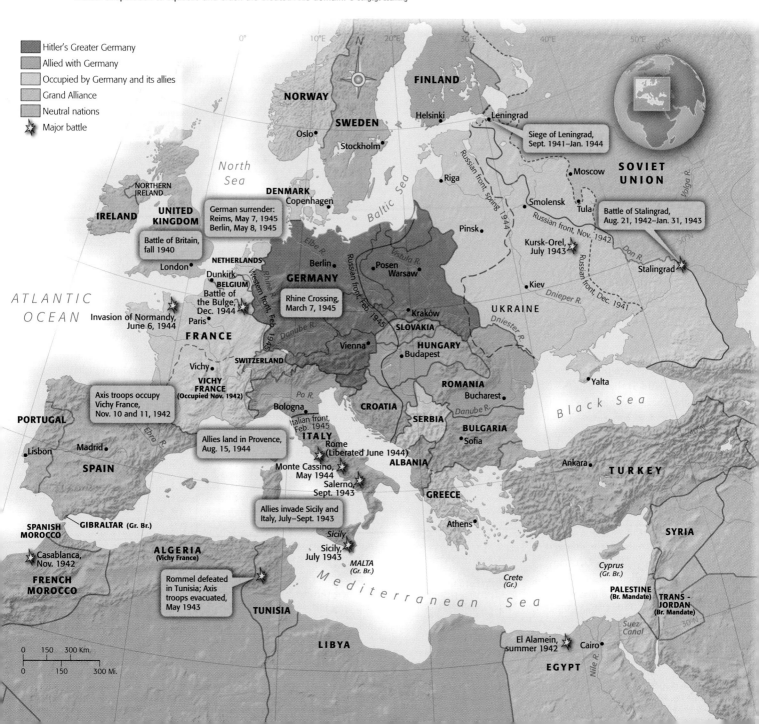

SKIRMISH IN THE STEPPES

By mid-August 1941, eight weeks after the German armies launched their attack on the Soviet Union, they were already hundreds of miles inside the frontier. In Ukraine, at the time a Soviet republic, they had reached the River Dnieper (**DNYEH-puhr**). Beyond the river lay steppes (flat grasslands) that stretched all the way to the Pacific, as well as the coal mines and steelworks of eastern Ukraine. As the Germans began to cross the river, once again the Soviets fell back. Caught up in the fighting was Fryderyk Wirski (**VEER-skee**), a draftee from a part of Poland that the Soviets had occupied in 1939, who was serving in an artillery regiment. After a pause in his unit's withdrawal, its retreat began again. Here is Wirski's account of what followed.

For several days nothing happened. The Germans did not advance. Nor did we retreat, we just stood at our posts. We didn't dare shoot, as we had very little ammunition. I myself sat about with the infantrymen, bored stiff, and to kill time killed lice.

Then one evening after about a week of louse-hunting, the Germans launched a regular attack. For us, of course, this meant a regular retreat. The twenty kilometers to Poltava we covered in one night. In Poltava they were erecting barricades and digging antitank ditches. We had barely arrived in the city when it was subjected to a violent and most unexpected bombardment. We consequently made a hurried exit and marched straight for the steppes. From regimental H.Q. I found that the defense staff of Poltava considered our forces so poor in numbers compared with the enemy's that they had decided not to risk such a one-sided fight. . . . So on we marched, over the Ukrainian steppe in the direction of Kharkov. On the way I

discovered that our contingent was composed of no more than three to four thousand infantry, a few light tanks, motorcycles, about thirty guns of various caliber, some horse supply columns, and one or two cavalry detachments. . . .

For two days we continued marching north up the Vorskla [a tributary of the Dnieper], then turned sharp east. We avoided all villages which, according to the patrols, had been completely evacuated. We now had a chance to observe the results of the National Defense Committee's order to destroy anything that could be useful to the invader. The houses, if not burnt, had their roofs pulled off; all agricultural machinery was smashed; the wheat had been set on fire and the wells filled with mud. The roadsides were lined with all types of tractors, their engines blown up, often by a grenade thrown under the hood.

By the third day it was no longer a secret that our H.Q. was utterly ignorant as to the whereabouts of the enemy's

---

the west, and finally into Germany itself.

The Americans and British, for their part, were pushing back German and Italian armies in North Africa, invading Italy itself, gradually mastering the German U-boat offensive that threatened the vital routes across the Atlantic between North America and Britain, and systematically bombing German cities by day and night. Then, on D-Day (June 6, 1944), Allied forces based in Britain executed a massive landing on the beaches of Normandy, in northwestern France. Once on the European mainland, they moved across France and into Germany, while their Soviet allies advanced from the east. The Germans surrendered in May 1945, thus ending the conflict in Europe.

 Soviet Propaganda Posters in Support of the War Effort (http://www.graphicwitness.org/undone/rp.htm) View a collection of Soviet war posters.

 D-Day Learn more about D-Day in this video.

 Europe at War Learn more about war in Europe in this video.

The War in Asia

Meanwhile, Japanese forces were finding it beyond their strength to fight an endless war in China that tied down most of their army, while also trying to batter their way into India against the resistance of British imperial forces, and to defend their gains in the Pacific against the United States. The Americans built up a whole new Pacific navy—both submarines that cut off the flow of supplies from the conquered lands of the "Co-Prosperity Sphere" to the Japanese homeland, and surface fleets that enabled ground forces to "island-hop" to bases within aerial range of the Japanese home islands (Map 27.2 on page 510). The Japanese population centers were now open to unlimited attacks from the sky. By mid-1945, virtually every Japanese city had been reduced to ashes by giant bombers (B-29s), which finally dropped the world's first atomic bombs on Hiroshima and Nagasaki, incinerating tens of thousands of

 "Pro and Con on Dropping the Bomb" (http://seattle times.nwsource.com/special/trinity/supplement/procon.html) Discover the arguments for and against the U.S. decision to drop the bomb.

forces and our own. Nobody knew who was on our left, on our right, who behind us, or if the country ahead was still in Soviet hands. We moved very slowly, sending out motorcycle patrols in every direction. That evening one of these patrols returned with the alarming news that a small village ahead was occupied by Germans. . . . Suddenly, in front of us and on both our flanks, three-colored flares—white, green, and red—shot up into the sky. Only the Germans used this kind of flare. We were confused, but when the flares shot up from our rear as well, the situation became clear to everyone: we were surrounded. . . .

Since the ring seemed equally strong on all sides, our colonel decided to try an attack ahead so that, in the event of success (in which, of course, nobody believed) we could continue our retreat to Kharkov. . . .

I was up front with the infantry, to check up on the firing of my battery. The village, invisible in the dark, was situated on a flat steppe, with no stream or river between us and it. I felt that my military career was about to come to an end.

At about three o'clock in the morning our poor thirty guns started making as much noise as they could. Their fire was well aimed. The infantry began moving up fast so that it found itself on the outskirts of the village by the time the firing ceased. We heard the usual "Urraa" and a moment later the thunder of shooting.

"They're in the village," whispered the observer of the neighboring battery. Both of us had climbed a tree from which we stood a better chance of directing the fire. Reaching its climax with a tremendous roar, the firing suddenly calmed down. There fell a sinister silence. What on earth had happened?

Suddenly I saw one of our motor bikes speeding toward us. I jumped from the tree and stopped the messenger.

"The victory is ours!" shouted a pink-faced brat, as though he had just destroyed an entire army singlehanded. . . .

We then discovered what had happened. A powerful force of five hundred German motorcyclists commanded by a twenty-three-year-old captain had advanced on its own. Reaching the village and meeting no resistance, it stopped. As we approached, the Germans, with unbelievable daring, tried to deceive us with a trick—which almost worked. They sent out a few patrols with orders to fire flares. The patrols drove around us in wide circles, with results described above. Seeing our confusion, the remaining Germans calmly went to sleep. They had calculated that we would retreat and sooner or later run into their regular forces advancing from the rear. Our barrage, and particularly our infantry attack, had caught them so unprepared that they made no attempt to resist. Most of them were killed, and the rest, including the young captain, were taken prisoner.

EXPLORING THE SOURCE

1. Judging from this account, what would have been the advantages and risks for the Soviets of retreating under German attack?

2. What does the story suggest about what the Germans hoped to achieve and what they risked by pursuing the Soviets so far and so fast?

Source: Fred Virski, *My Life in the Red Army* (New York: Macmillan, 1949), pp. 158–161.

---

men, women, and children. These superscientific devices for mass killing assured the quick and total victory of the Allies; Japan surrendered unconditionally in August 1945.

Destroying and Moving Populations

The new weapons confirmed a radical shift in the nature of all-out warfare: from attacking opposing armed forces to destroying whole populations. In six years of warfare, perhaps 25 million soldiers, sailors, and airmen had been killed in battle or died of ill treatment in prisoner-of-war camps—about three-quarters of them in Europe and the rest in Asia. In addition, however, between 30 and 40 million civilians—about half each in Europe and Asia—had died as a result of massacres, bombing, disease, starvation, exposure, and systematic genocide. This was a far higher proportion of civilian to military deaths than in what now came to be called the First World War (p. 481).

The Holocaust

In the Soviet Union and elsewhere in eastern Europe, the Nazis not only sought swift military victories but also launched a ruthless program of exterminating all Jews and a portion of the Slavic peoples, whom they regarded as racially inferior (*Untermenschen*). The operation grew gradually in scale and intensity between 1939 and 1942, as the German armies advanced eastward into territories that had held the majority of the world's Jews since the western European persecutions of the Middle Ages (pp. 218–219). The Germans began by separating the Jews from the rest of the local population and placing them in ghettos or in concentration camps, where many died from brutality, hunger, and disease. Mass shootings and gassings by special "task forces" followed. Then came extermination camps, most infamously at Auschwitz, Maidanek, and Treblinka in Poland, to which Jews from all over Europe were transported and selected either for immediate gassing or for hard labor under conditions that usually resulted in death. In all, about 6 million Jews perished in the

 The Ghettoization of the Jews: Prelude to the Final Solution Read an eyewitness account of the ghettoization of Jews in the town of Czernowitz.

Holocaust
The systematic genocide of Jews in Europe during the Second World War; also applied to the mass murder of all those, Jewish and non-Jewish, deemed to be racially inferior by the Nazi regime.

Holocaust, together with about 4 million mostly Slavic non-Jews.

The extermination campaign required an enormous German diversion of men, supplies, and transport from the war effort. It benefited from the cooperation of governments and often of non-Jews throughout occupied Europe, as well as from the passivity of the Allied governments and the Christian churches. There was widespread armed resistance in the ghettos, most famously in Warsaw in 1943, where Jewish fighters held out for a month against two thousand German troops; on the other hand Jews also staffed the administration of the ghettos, under "Jewish Elders" who sometimes functioned as cogs in the machinery of the Holocaust (see photo). More than any other of the horrific event of the twentieth century, the Holocaust stands as a warning of the possibilities of evil released by the combined technical advances and inner conflicts of modern civilization in general and Western civilization in particular.

 "A Very Grave Matter, the Extermination of the Jews" Read Heinrich Himmler, head of the concentration camps, on the mass execution of the Jews.

 The End of the Line: Auschwitz Read a survivor's account of Auschwitz.

Map 27.2 The War in East Asia and the Pacific

"I shall run wild for the first six months or a year, but I have utterly no confidence for the second or third year." With these words, the planner of the attack on Pearl Harbor, Admiral Yamamoto, spoke the truth. By mid-1942, Japan had reached almost to Alaska, Australia, and India; in 1943 it mostly held its ground; in 1944 it lost control of the Pacific; and in 1945 it collapsed on every front. © Cengage Learning

 Interactive Map

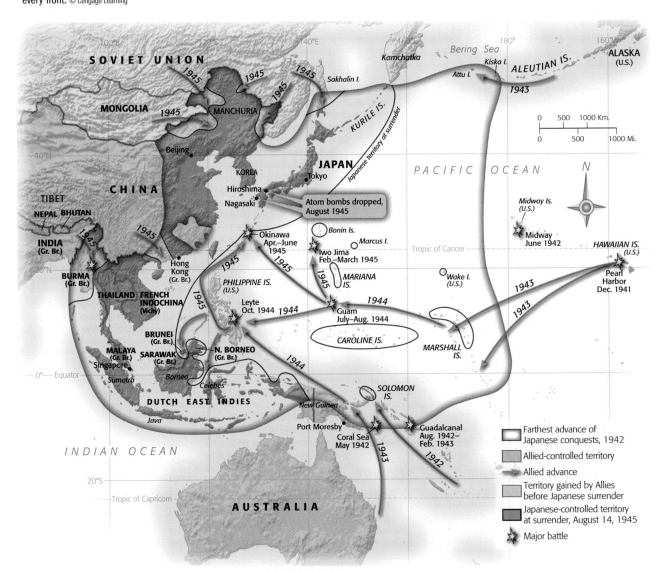

Bekanntmachung Nr. 372.

Betr.:

AUSSIEDLUNG

Wie mir bekannt wurde,
wurden Gerüchte verbreitet,
dass die Aussiedlung abgestellt ist.

**DIES ENTSPRICHT NICHT
DER WAHRHEIT,**

sondern geht

die **Aussiedlung weiter.**

Die auszusiedelnden Personen
müssen sich also wie bisher
unbedingt pünktlich
zu dem bestimmten Termin
an dem in Frage kommenden Treffpunkt einfinden,
**andernfalls sie ohne Gepäck
ausgesiedelt werden.**

Litzmannstadt-Getto,
den 25. März 1942.

(—) **CH. RUMKOWSKI**
Der Älteste der Juden in Litzmannstadt

באקאנטמאכונג נר. 372

וועג

אַרויסזיקן.

ווי מען ניט מיר איבער
ווערן פארשפרייט קלאנגען,
אז די ארויסזיקונג איז אָפגעשטעלט.

די דאזיקע קלאנגען
שטימען נישט מיט אמת,

די ארויסזיקונגען
קומען ווייטער פאָר.

די צום ארויסזיקן באשטימטע פערזאנען
מוזן דעריבער ווי ביז אהער
אומבאדינגט פינקטליך
צום באשטימטן טערמין
זיך איינשטעלן אין אנגעגעבענעם ערזאמ-פונקט,
אין קעגנפאל וועלן זיי ארויסגעשיקט
ווערן אן וועלכן עס איז באגאזש.

(—) מרדכי חיים רומקאווסקי

USHMM Collection, Gift of Malwina Gerson Allen

years in "DP camps" before dispersing across Europe and worldwide to any country that would take them, above all the United States and Israel.

Mass Deportations

In addition, whole populations had been rounded up and loaded into freight cars or sent on forced marches bound for distant destinations by conquerors who found their presence in their previous places of residence objectionable but did not necessarily intend to kill them. Whichever the conqueror, 50 kilograms (110 pounds) per family became the standard allowance of possessions that deportees were allowed to take with them from their homes; everything else they must leave behind.

Many of these mass deportations turned out to be temporary, particularly if carried out by countries that lost the war. Such were the expulsion of Poles from lands intended for German "living space," and the importation of forced laborers from many countries into Germany to replace workers drafted into the army. After the war, about half a million such deportees were unwilling to return to eastern European homelands that were under communist rule, and there were also half a million Holocaust survivors who were unwilling to return to those same countries for fear of anti-Semitic violence. These million people together formed a long-lasting class of "displaced persons" who spent

> " *We can say, that we have fulfilled this most difficult duty for the love of our people. And our spirit, our soul, our character has not suffered injury from it.* "
>
> —Heinrich Himmler, on the mass murder of German Jews

 "Displaced Persons," from the U.S. Holocaust Memorial Museum Website (http://www.ushmm.org/wlc/en/article.php?ModuleId=10005462) Learn more about the plight of displaced persons following the war.

Moving Populations to Suit Borders

Deportations by the victors, on the other hand, permanently changed the traditional ethnic makeup of central and eastern Europe. Among the deportees were a million and a half Poles living in lands that the Soviet Union had taken from Poland in 1939 and intended to keep. They were "exchanged" against half a million Ukrainians expelled from territory that still belonged to Poland. Furthermore, at least 12 million Germans were forced from their country's prewar eastern territories, as well as from Czechoslovakia, Hungary, Romania, and Yugoslavia. The Germans either fled the Red Army's advance, or were expelled by order of postwar governments, or were "transferred" with the blessing of the United States, Britain, and the Soviet Union, when their leaders met at the former residence of the Hohenzollern rulers of Prussia in Potsdam near Berlin in the summer of 1945. Most of the eastern German territories went to Poland in compensation for its losses to the Soviet Union (see Map 29.1 on page 535); other central and eastern European countries also rid themselves of Germans and other troublesome national minorities.

In this way, some of the national conflicts that had helped bring about the war were ruthlessly ended. The new Polish borders and the new ethnic pattern became basic facts of the postwar order in central and eastern Europe, which remained unchallenged throughout the era of the Cold War and after the eventual collapse of communism.

> " *Deportations by the victors permanently changed the traditional ethnic makeup of central and eastern Europe.* "

 Listen to a synopsis of Chapter 27.

SCIENCE AND MODERNISM IN THE TWENTIETH CENTURY,
1900–1960

LEARNING OBJECTIVES

AFTER READING THIS CHAPTER, YOU SHOULD BE ABLE TO DO THE FOLLOWING:

LO¹ Identify some of the major areas of achievement in twentieth-century science.

LO² Describe the variety of philosophical and religious responses to the modern world.

LO² Trace the development of Modernism in literature and the arts.

"THE ARTS OF THE TWENTIETH CENTURY REFLECTED THE CONFLICTED AND CHANGING MENTALITY OF MODERN GLOBAL CIVILIZATION."

The rise of global civilization has taken place amid an explosion of invention and discovery and of new ways of thinking, feeling, behaving, and creating. Most of these changes have originated in Western civilization, but non-Western peoples have increasingly participated in them.

These drastic changes have had opposing effects on the mentality of modern global civilization. On the one hand, there is a heady sense of liberation from traditional ignorance of the workings of nature and the mind, irrational codes of behavior and morality, and conventional limits on the themes and methods of art. But there also is a disturbing awareness of loss of tradition and stability, of individual helplessness against social forces or government and commercial manipulation, of the littleness of humanity compared with the vastness of nature.

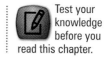 Test your knowledge before you read this chapter.

What do you think?

The impact of twentieth-century science and technology has been largely positive.

Strongly Disagree						Strongly Agree
1	2	3	4	5	6	7

The sharpening of this double feeling has resulted above all from the progress of science and technology. Today, humanity is reaching toward ultimate understanding of the universe as a whole and the medium of space and time in which it exists, as well as of the almost infinitely tiny yet unimaginably complex "worlds" that make up both living and nonliving matter. Technology, firmly hitched to the scientific juggernaut, has provided safety, comfort, and abundance on a scale that earlier generations would have considered miraculous. Yet science has also made the human race seem unimportant within the universe and made whatever ultimate reality lies behind the universe seem more distant than ever, while technology has given the human race the power to enslave and destroy itself.

In the twentieth century, the effect of the rise of science was strongly felt in philosophy and religion, which have traditionally guided the human race's thinking about itself and the universe. Twentieth-century philosophers often restricted themselves to studying and refining the basic methods of philosophy, or they protested against a universe that seems indifferent and unknowable and

«« **The Australia Telescope Compact Array** Nearby planets—the moon and Venus—look down on a telescope that collects radio signals from sources hundreds of light years away over the Southern Hemisphere. These seventy-foot dishes are part of a single observing instrument with a total of six dishes, which can roll as much as four miles apart. To see how the scale of science has grown in recent centuries, compare Tycho Brahe's observatory or Michael Faraday's laboratory (see photos on pages 357, 433).

Graeme L. White and Glen Cozens (James Cook University, Australia)

societies that seem materialistic and conformist. In the monotheistic religions, "fundamentalist" believers held to their sacred books as authoritative guides to knowledge about humanity and the universe, and opposed changes in traditional codes of behavior and morals. "Conservatives" accepted both the universe of science and the one God who exists beyond it and has given humanity a unique place in it, but found no way of combining these into a single whole. And "liberals" regarded traditional beliefs as no more than compelling myths, while affirming drastic changes in behavior and morality.

The arts of the twentieth century, too, reflected the conflicted and changing mentality of modern global civilization. The most admired artists generally depicted the complexities and problems of the modern world. Often, they found the traditional conventions of storytelling and depicting appearances inadequate to their purpose, preferring to view human experience through the lens of their own or others' subjective consciousness. Even when artists used more traditional methods, they did so mostly in order to cry out against the horrors of modern civilization. Celebrating the consensus values of society, an important function of art in traditional civilizations, was mostly left to mass entertainment.

LO¹ The Onrush of Science and Technology

The accelerating nineteenth-century progress of science (pp. 432–435) turned in the twentieth century into a headlong rush of discovery that left no aspect of nature unexplored. In the process, science has become a large-scale social undertaking, employing tens of thousands of highly trained people and supported by massive state subsidies (though these are only a small fraction of total government budgets). Scientists used to do their experiments in surroundings that looked much like kitchens or pharmacies, but it has taken the combined resources of twenty European nations to build the Large Hadron Collider in Switzerland—a machine that hurls subatomic particles at each other over a distance of 17 miles so that physicists can produce collisions violent enough to break the particles down into their still more basic constituents.

Furthermore, in some ways, the pursuit of scientific knowledge

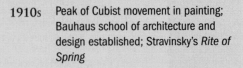

CHRONOLOGY

1910s	Peak of Cubist movement in painting; Bauhaus school of architecture and design established; Stravinsky's *Rite of Spring*
1920s	Hubble theorizes that the universe is expanding; Heisenberg announces the principle of uncertainty; Eliot's "The Love Song of J. Alfred Prufrock," Joyce's *Ulysses*, and Woolf's *To the Lighthouse*; the "Jazz Age" in America
1930s	Freud's *Civilization and Its Discontents* and Sartre's *Nausea*; Calder begins creating mobiles; Henry Moore begins creating abstract sculpture; Wright's Kaufmann House ("Fallingwater"); Fermi succeeds at nuclear fission
1940s	U.S. Department of Defense sponsors the first computer; Abstract Expressionism in painting begins; Paul Tillich's *Shaking of the Foundations*
1950s	Crick and Watson present double-helix model of the DNA molecule

has become the single most highly respected of human endeavors. Of all the ways in which the present-day world honors individuals as benefactors of humanity, perhaps the most prestigious are the Nobel Prizes, established by the Swedish industrialist Alfred Nobel in 1904. Of the six prizes annually awarded, one each is given for literature, economics, and peace, and the other three (physics, physiology and medicine, and chemistry) are all given for science.

The reason for this high valuation of science is not just that science has unlocked so many secrets of nature. It also has to do with the fact that the explosion of scientific knowledge has transformed every other aspect of human life on this planet: politics and warfare, industry and the economy, social life and culture. Most of the matters dealt with in the final chapters of this book, from the atom bomb to the "pill," and from the Green Revolution in agriculture to the revolution in politics produced by television, would never have happened without the onrush of science, towing technology in its wake at vastly accelerated speed.

> "*Our future as an industrial country depends both on the ability of our scientists to discover the secrets of nature and on our speed in applying the new techniques that science places within our grasp.*"
> —British Parliament, 1955

The Universe and the Atom

Among the countless twentieth-century achievements of science, perhaps the most significant—both as discoveries in themselves and in their consequences for human life and thought—are those that have taken humanity to the outermost edges of the universe, and to the innermost structure of both nonliving matter and living organisms.

The Expanding Universe

Twentieth-century changes in understanding of the universe's working were almost as revolutionary as those of the sixteenth and seventeenth centuries (pp. 356–363). These new changes were partly the result of other scientific and technical discoveries, which enabled astronomers to see ever farther into space. In the nineteenth century, spectrum analysis (p. 432) of the light emitted by stars showed that they are made of the same basic elements known on earth; comparison with geological estimates of the earth's age also indicated that the stars must somehow have the capacity to "burn" hot and bright for billions of years. From about 1900 on, huge new telescopes revealed that stars are clustered throughout space in galaxies similar to our Milky Way, the aggregation of 200 billion stars in which the sun was already known to be located. Further, spectrum analysis of the galaxies themselves indicated that they are moving away from one another at vast speed. In the 1920s, the American astronomer Edwin Hubble found that the farther apart galaxies are, the faster they seem to move away from each other, so that the totality of galaxies—that is, the universe itself—must be expanding.

This, in turn, led astronomers to a scientific theory about the probable origin of the universe—one as imaginative and ingenious as any earlier creation myth or philosophical speculation. If the universe has been growing larger over time, then there must have been a moment in the past—most likely about 15 billion years ago—when it was infinitely small; and if the galaxies are still today hurtling away from each other, then the reason must be that "in the beginning," the original tiny universe exploded outward with unimaginable violence. In the 1960s, a new type of observing device, radio telescopes that detect radio signals emitted by stars and other objects in space (see photo on page 512), confirmed this theory. It turned out that the entire universe is saturated with radio signals, all of the same very short wavelength, that have no source in any individual object(the remains of the mighty outburst of electromagnetic radiation (p. 432) given off by the original "**big bang**."

Relativity and Space-Time

To explain these discoveries, and for guidance in searching for such things in the first place, astronomers turned to Albert Einstein's theory of relativity (pp. 433–434). Only the large-scale conversion of matter into energy, as proposed by Einstein, could provide a "fuel" powerful enough to keep the stars "burning" for billions of years at a time. Only the concept of space and time, matter and energy, being related to one another allowed astronomers to conceive of how all four could originally have been packed into a tiny point, and then have expanded outward into a universe that grows without having an actual boundary but where space and time simply curve back on themselves. This new view of the universe did not prove Copernicus and Kepler, Galileo and Newton wrong, as they had proven Aristotle and Ptolemy wrong. But it became clear that what the sixteenth- and seventeenth-century giants had discovered was only part of the reality of the universe. Their twentieth-century successors were exploring the full outlines of the whole awesome structure of mass and energy extending through time and space.

> "*It became clear that what the sixteenth- and seventeenth-century giants had discovered was only part of the reality of the universe.*"

big bang
According to astronomers, the explosion that brought the universe into existence and caused it to expand ever since.

subatomic particles
The constituent parts of an atom.

quantum (plural, **quanta**)
Tiny particle-like "packets" of energy.

Inside the Atom

While astronomers searched for the origins of the universe, physicists explored the inner secrets of the atom. In the early twentieth century, Rutherford and Bohr had found that the atom is not a basic unit of matter, but itself a tiny structure or system, with its own constituent parts (p. 433). What exactly are these constituent parts, or **subatomic particles**? What forces keep them in balance with each other to form a stable system, and what kind of changes within the atom produce such things as radioactivity or light? What is the best way of describing the particles and forces at work in the atom, and how can such tiny entities be detected and measured? In the course of the twentieth century, atomic physicists came a long way toward answering these questions.

The theories that guided the physicists were devised mostly between 1900 and 1930. What they said was that, just as on the ultralarge scale of the universe as a whole, so in the ultrasmall world of the atom, the "classical" scientific concepts that seem to do well enough for the vast range of "middle-sized" items, such as falling apples or planets in their orbits, do not apply. To make sense of the world of the atom, it turned out to be necessary to think of many subatomic particles sometimes as tiny pieces of matter orbiting within the atom, and sometimes as tiny packets of energy lapping wavelike around it. Likewise, forms of energy that might be emitted by the atom, such as light, which it had become customary to think of as traveling in waves, now came to be regarded also as streams of tiny particle-like packets of energy, or **quanta**. Major contributors to these new

principle of uncertainty
In physics, the concept that it is impossible to observe at the same time both the position and the motion of a subatomic particle.

nuclear fission
The breaking apart of an atom's nucleus, a process that releases a vast amount of energy.

nuclear fusion
The joining of nuclei to form a heavier atom, a process that releases an even vaster amount of energy than nuclear fission.

concepts were Einstein—the most universal of scientific theorists since Newton—together with the German Max Planck and the Austrian Erwin Schrödinger (**SHROH-ding-er**).

It was also necessary to define very carefully how the world of the atom could be observed at all. In the 1920s in Germany, Werner Heisenberg announced a new basic concept of physics: the **principle of uncertainty**, which states that it is impossible to observe at the same time both the position and the motion of a subatomic particle. The reason is that the particle is so tiny that there is no way of observing it without significantly influencing either its position or its motion. The uncertainty principle led physicists to give up hope of ever "looking" at an individual atom, as Galileo had looked at Jupiter and its moons (p. 359).

Still, physicists could theorize on the basis of large numbers of atoms to predict what the "average atom" would most likely do—like market researchers who can never know for certain what brand of breakfast cereal an individual consumer will buy, but by studying many consumers, can accurately predict which brand the average consumer will purchase. And even if subatomic particles could not be directly observed inside the atom, they could be knocked out of atoms by powerful beams of rays or streams of other particles; their probable paths could be indirectly tracked and measured once they had been released in this way; and from these data it was possible, by complex calculations, to "read back" to conditions within the atom. Thus an array of increasingly powerful "atom-smashing" and later "particle-smashing" devices has made atomic physics one of the most spectacular and expensive branches of science.

With the help of concepts and devices such as these, physicists were able to perceive how the atom works to produce many features of the physical world as we know it. They knew that the differences among chemical elements are due to the different numbers of various subatomic particles among the atoms that make up the elements. They also knew that radioactivity consists of particles emitted by atoms; that electricity is produced by particles flowing among atoms; and that light is a result of the change of position of particles within atoms. In turn, this theoretical knowledge led to new technological revolutions. For example, understanding of the flow of electrons among atoms in certain types of solid materials—the "semiconductors"—made possible the miniaturization of electronic components, so that complex devices like televisions and computers could become cheap, compact, and hence widespread.

Fission and Fusion

Meanwhile, from the 1930s onward, the original model of the atom devised by Rutherford and Bohr, of a proton-filled nucleus with electrons orbiting around it, grew increasingly complex. New atom- and particle-smashing devices revealed ever more subatomic particles that theoretical physicists then had to incorporate into the model; or the theorists themselves, in order to account for discrepancies in the model, would think up new particles, or new forces acting on the particles, for which the atom- and particle-smashing devices would sooner or later provide actual evidence.

Some of the most significant discoveries made in this way concerned the structure and behavior of the atomic nucleus. This turned out to consist of two kinds of particles, protons and neutrons, clamped together by the action of a hitherto unsuspected force, the "strong interaction." Nevertheless, in 1938, Enrico Fermi succeeded in breaking apart some of the relatively large clumps of particles that formed the nuclei of uranium atoms. About ten years later, it became clear that the relatively small clumps of particles that formed the nuclei of hydrogen atoms could be forced together to create larger nuclei.

Either way, these processes of **nuclear fission** and **nuclear fusion** involved the conversion of tiny amounts of mass into vast amounts of energy according to Einstein's principles. Furthermore, they released neutrons that would hit the nuclei of neighboring atoms and start the same processes there, initiating *chain reactions* of enormous power. These discoveries led to the atom and hydrogen bombs, which make use of uncontrolled fission and fusion chain reactions, respectively; and to the use of controlled fission in nuclear power stations. Scientists still hope to learn how to control fusion reactions to fulfill the dream of cheap, plentiful, and nonpolluting energy.

 Witness to the Birth of the Atomic Age Read a top-secret report on the first full-scale test of an atom bomb.

 The Atomic Beast Harnessed: The Peaceful Use of Nuclear Power Read how the British Parliament of the 1950s viewed nuclear science.

Toward a Grand Unified Theory

Recently, the complex picture of particles and forces at work in the atom has been simplified in various ways. In the 1960s, physicists began to suspect that many of the newly discovered particles could be regarded as differing combinations of no more than three still tinier entities—*quarks*, as they were christened by one of the originators of this idea, the American Murray Gell-Mann. Another American, Steven Weinberg, together with a Pakistani, Abdus Salam, showed that two of the forces at work within the atom, electromagnetism and the "weak interaction" among particles outside the nucleus, were in fact one and the same force.

Atomic physicists hope that discoveries such as these are stepping-stones toward a "Grand Unified Theory," which in the not too distant future may show that all the various forms of matter and energy in the universe are all manifestations of a very few basic particles and perhaps only a single force. If this is in fact achieved, at least some physicists believe, it will mark the end of a stage in the Western quest for rational understanding of the "nature of things" that began in ancient Greece more than 2,500 years ago (pp. 71–72).

Inside the Living Cell

Similar progress toward what seems like an ultimate explanation of one of the main features of the natural world has been made by scientists investigating the basic structure of living organisms and the ways in which they reproduce and grow.

Already in the nineteenth and early twentieth centuries, there had been many advances in this field. Biologists had found that organisms are built up of cells, and that growth and reproduction take place by means of cell division. They had come to believe that hereditary characteristics are transmitted from one organism to another by means of **genes** and that the genes are somehow present in the central structure of the cell, the **nucleus**. Chemists had found that cells are made up of some of the same elements, and formed in the same way into molecules (although far bigger and more complex), as nonliving matter. They had identified many of the resulting substances, which seemed to be basic building blocks of life, as well as two substances of unknown function within the cell: *ribonucleic* and *deoxyribonucleic acid* (RNA and DNA).

Later-twentieth-century researchers assembled these scattered pieces of evidence and followed where they pointed—and more and more, the researchers found that they were led to the mysterious substances RNA and DNA. By the 1940s, it was known that the molecules of both consist of extremely lengthy strands built up of four basic units, the order of which continually varies along the strands. Experiments with bacteria showed that a type with a rough-coated exterior could be altered to have a smooth exterior when "fed" with DNA from a closely related, smooth-coated type. It seemed that somehow, within its molecular structure, DNA carried the genes, and had the ability to transfer them from one cell to another. But how did it do this?

The Double Helix

In 1953, an Englishman, Francis Crick, and an American, James D. Watson, opened the way to answering this question with their famous "double-helix" model of the DNA molecule. The molecule consists, they said, not of one but of two identical strands, interconnected along their lengths and twisted around each other. In the course of cell division, the two strands break apart and untwist, so that each can carry its genes into a new cell. Then, as each strand settles down within the newly formed nucleus, by chemical combination with surrounding substances it produces for itself a new "partner" strand. Thus these two, in turn, can separate when the time comes, thereby transferring their genes to yet further cells.

On the basis of this insight, molecular biologists have been able to build up as full a picture of the inner workings of the living cell as physicists have done with the atom. All of the following

are now fairly well understood: the way in which DNA strands sometimes replicate themselves in the slightly different form of RNA; how RNA, in turn, combines with surrounding substances to produce the many complex chemicals that make up living organisms; the actual "genetic code," the different sequences of the four basic chemical units along the strands of DNA and RNA; and details of the ways in which these processes are speeded, blocked, or altered to foster or discourage cell growth, or to produce different kinds of cells and hence different organisms.

> **gene**
> The basic unit of heredity.
>
> **nucleus**
> In biology, the central structure of a cell.

High Technology

Ever since the link between science and technology was forged in the nineteenth century, the human race has lived in a state of "permanent" industrial revolution (pp. 424–425). But in the twentieth century, this revolution accelerated as science reached the point of unlocking truly cosmic powers, and technology found ways of harnessing these powers for use (and abuse) by society. The result, from about the middle of the century onward, was an explosion of new types of machines, processes, materials, medicines, and weapons that seemed so marvelous (or so threatening) that as a group they came to be called "high technology."

Of course, the rise of high technology was not the result of scientific advance alone. To translate "pure" scientific knowledge into usable technology takes "applied" scientists and engineers obsessed with technical problems, and corporation executives hungry to stake the biggest claim in new and profitable markets. In the second half of the twentieth century, more than in earlier times, it also often took generals and admirals bent on victory in wars or arms races. The fact that the United States

"Two Sides to Every Coin" A cartoon by the American Mike Thompson, inspired by the human genome project, expresses the mixture of hope and fear with which the human race greets the explosion of scientific knowledge. By permission of Mike Thompson and Creators Syndicate, Inc.

had plenty of all three types, as well as massive resources for investment and a massive home market for new products, helped make it, more than any other country, the homeland of high technology.

Computers and Electronics

That, for example, is why the United States led the world in the single most spectacular field of high technology, computers. It was advances in the "pure" mathematical field of information theory that made computers possible, and discoveries in the "pure" science of semiconductor physics that made them cheap and small enough to be everywhere. Generals and admirals, wanting to win the Second World War and then the Cold War, spent the money to jump-start many computer technologies at a time when they seemed too risky and unprofitable for private companies. In the 1940s, the U.S. Department of Defense sponsored the first-ever computer in hopes of speeding up the production of mathematical data needed for heavy artillery; in the 1950s, it invested in computer-controlled machine tools that would accurately make complex parts for state-of-the-art warplanes; in the 1960s and 1970s, its scientists developed ways of linking military and government research computers into "inter-active networks" that would be so decentralized that not even a hydrogen bomb hit could totally knock them out. And once all these basic technologies had been proved, the engineers and corporation executives moved in. The results were mainframes and laptops, smartphones and "fire-and-forget" missiles, the Internet and the World Wide Web.

Biotechnology

At the end of the twentieth century, another, very much older field of technology had been pulled forward by "pure" science to the point where it was producing just as spectacular results as computers—that of biotechnology.

For thousands of years, humans have manipulated living things, or products derived from living things, by such processes as selective breeding, cooking, brewing, and distilling. What turned biotechnology into high technology was the rise of new methods and processes derived from "pure" biochemical understanding of the living cell as a chemical "factory." In the 1970s, an American molecular biologist, Paul Berg, managed to "cut" DNA strands and recombine the pieces in a different order, thereby altering also the order of their basic chemical units to produce new types of genes. Many different types of recombinant DNA were developed, which could be implanted in the DNA of bacteria to alter their genetic makeup. In this way, new strains of bacteria could be created, with the "hereditary" capacity to produce biological substances useful to humans—for example, insulin, an essential medicine for people with diabetes.

The result, in the 1980s and 1990s, was the growth of a whole new industry of **genetic engineering**. In this new industry, "pure" and "applied" science were hard to tell apart. As a result, "pure" scientists were often directly involved in genetic engineering, and it was mainly sponsored by civilian bureaucrats eager to get a return on government funding for pure science, and by college presidents dreaming of patent royalties from discoveries made by their biochemistry departments.

In any case, genetic engineering became a massive industry as computers had before, and early in the twenty-first century, it passed an important milestone. In the 1990s, scientists came to realize that for this new industry to reach its full potential, it would be necessary to be able to identify the location of the genes in the DNA molecules of various species, ranging from bacteria to mice, that were commonly used in genetic engineering—and also, most ambitiously, of humans themselves. Without this information, genetic engineers were like readers in a library with many stacks, tens of thousands of books, and no catalogue or floor plan. The completion in 2000 of the human "genome-mapping" project meant that the catalogue and floor plan were now available to anyone who needed them, though most of the books themselves were still unopened.

 **Official U.S. Human Genome Project Site** (http://www.ornl.gov/sci/techresources/Human_Genome/project/about.shtml) Learn more about the Human Genome Project.

LO² Thought and Belief in a New Era

Science and technology, along with the traumatic happenings of the era, had a great deal to do with several differing trends in twentieth-century philosophy and religion. Many thinkers developed the idea of the individual in one way or another in conflict with vast natural and social forces—either struggling against them, or forced into a straitjacket of social expectations and obligations. Religious thinkers challenged the idea that science provides the only knowable kind of truth, and they proclaimed an absolute spiritual truth that lay either beyond the material universe or within themselves. And some of them, recoiling from the century's human-made horrors, turned back to traditional doctrines of evil and sin.

The Authentic Life: Sartre

One of the most powerful responses to the scientific progress and mass atrocities of the twentieth century was that of **existentialism**. This way of thinking had nineteenth-century forerunners, notably the Christian Søren Kierkegaard and the atheist Friedrich Nietzsche (pp. 447–448). Kierkegaard had stressed the nakedness and loneliness of human beings in the universe—"condemned to be free" and able to reach God only by a "leap of faith." Nietzsche had protested against Christianity, technology, bourgeois codes of behavior—every force in Western

THE RISE OF SCIENCE AFFECTED MANY OTHER FIELDS OF THOUGHT AND CULTURE—AND VERY OFTEN THE RESULT WAS UNSETTLING:

Scientific explanations seemed to undermine long-held beliefs about humans and God

- If human beings could be explained as complex assemblages of molecules, where did such things as consciousness and free will fit in?

- If the universe could be explained as the outcome of the interactions of a few grandly simple forces and particles, where did a creating and intervening God fit in?

Scientific theories suggested the impossibility of finding "ultimate" reality

- Scientific theories were constantly modified or discarded in the light of new knowledge; knowledge was always to be subject to revision rather than fixed.

- Scientific explanations of phenomena in terms of probabilities and the viewpoint of observers also pointed to knowledge and reality as relative and uncertain.

- The traditional philosophical, religious, and artistic ideals of truth were thus upturned.

New technologies threatened the individual's autonomy and world security

- The World Wide Web, for example, seemed a symbol of the freedom and power offered by technology.

- Even an ancient and prestigious institution like the British monarchy was just another "vendor," offering information, entertainment, and products to the passing surfer (see photo).

- But the surfer's path from website to website could be tracked keystroke by keystroke by anyone who had the expertise and equipment to do so.

- Thus technology also offered the possibility of an "anthill society" where individuals were controlled and manipulated.

- Technology also created the threat of environmental disaster or nuclear extinction.

---

civilization that seemed to him to stunt the full unfolding of human personality. Existentialists, likewise, saw the individual increasingly depersonalized and alienated by the forces of modern society, such as huge economic organizations, mechanization, and bureaucratization. They sought to awaken in each person a sense of individuality and the possibility of an *authentic* life—one that would be true to a person's inner nature rather than falsified by fear of the consequences, obedience to social expectations, or conformity to mass opinions and emotions.

The philosopher, novelist, and playwright Jean-Paul Sartre (**SAHR-truh**) brought the existentialist view to the educated public through *Nausea*, *No Exit*, and other works. Sartre, partly through his own experience in the French Resistance against the Nazis, came to believe that personal commitment and action are essential to genuine living. He felt this especially during the war, in his daily decision making and risk taking. He proved to himself that even in extreme situations, the individual possesses the irreducible liberty of saying "no" to overpowering force. Such a force, Sartre inferred, might be an occupying army—or it might be the conformist cultures in which most of us live.

The freedom to say "no," even to "disaffiliate" oneself from the system, is the individual's ultimate defense against being swallowed up as a person.

Existentialism Defined Read Sartre's defense of existentialism against its critics.

>> **Tweet from the Queen** For 1,000 years the British monarchy has presided over the nation, but it is also part of the global culture of mass information and mass entertainment. Either way, it needs the Internet to reach its subjects and the world. When this tweet appeared in July 2010, the monarchy had 52,000 followers—a respectable number, but less than 1 percent of the figure for the world's most followed tweeter, Britney Spears.

Ewitter

Have an account? Sign in »

Get short, timely messages from TheBritishMonarchy.

Twitter is a rich source of instantly updated information. It's easy to stay updated on an incredibly wide variety of topics. Join today and **follow @BritishMonarchy.**

Sign Up ›   Get updates via SMS by texting **follow BritishMonarchy** to **40404** in the United States. Codes for other countries

BritishMonarchy

Gallery: The Prince of Wales talks to medical staff during a visit to meet Service personnel being treated at...
http://www.royal.gov.uk/Tj
about 3 hours ago via Royal Household

Verified Account

Name TheBritishMonarchy
Location United Kingdom
Web http://www.royal....
Bio http://www.princeofwales.g ov.uk The latest news on Royal events

0   53,363   1,678
following   followers   listed

Tweets   3,714

Favorites

Following

By permission Website Team, Buckingham Palace, per Twitter guidelines

>> **The Psychoanalyst's Couch** A photograph by Freud's friend Edmund Engelmann shows the psychoanalyst's consulting room in Vienna. While patients lay on the couch, Freud, seated in the chair, conducted "the removal, layer by layer, of the pathogenic psychic material, which I like to compare with the excavation of a buried city." The pictures on the corner walls come from such a city—Pompeii (p. 112), whose burial and rediscovery had deep meaning for Freud as a symbol of his work. © Edmund Engelman

After the war, having carefully studied the works of Karl Marx, Sartre conceded the powerful grip of social conditioning on personality—yet insisted that each individual nevertheless has the ability (and the responsibility) to "make something out of what is made of him." Sartre's idea of limited freedom contrasted with the optimistic, rational liberalism of the Enlightenment (pp. 365–366). It was closer to the "tragic view" of the ancient Greek poets and dramatists, who likewise saw pain and absurdity in the human condition, yet held that one remains responsible for what one is and does within an established order (pp. 70–71).

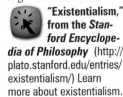 **"Existentialism,"** from the *Stanford Encyclopedia of Philosophy* (http://plato.stanford.edu/entries/existentialism/) Learn more about existentialism.

Instinct vs. Civilization: Freud

Another thinker who came to be looked up to as a guide to living in the world of the twentieth-century West was Sigmund Freud. As a pioneer of psychology (p. 436), Freud was a practicing physician whose initial interest was in curing the mental ailments of his patients (see photo). In the course of his clinical work, however, he discovered aspects of the human mind and personality that had long lain hidden. Freud published his first significant work, *The Interpretation of Dreams*, in 1900, but his broader impact on thought was not felt until after the First World War.

Though Freudian psychology has been disputed and amended (especially his views on female sexuality), much of it gained acceptance as an explanation of humans in society. Freud held that human beings are not rational machines, consciously directing their appetites and will. On the contrary, beneath the surface of conscious life are unconscious and subconscious drives, which are the chief engines of motivation; these include the desire for sexual gratification, love, power, and even death. In addition, behavior is influenced by physiological responses and acquired attitudes.

Society, Freud wrote in *Civilization and Its Discontents* (1930), compels individuals to *repress* many of their desires, and without some repression, civilization would be impossible. The "normal" person accepts the damage without breaking down, but the neurotic (or psychotic) person cannot do so. The Freudian view

> **"** *The freedom to say 'no,' even to 'disaffiliate' oneself from the system, is the individual's ultimate defense against being swallowed up as a person.* **"**

of the individual in relationship to society posed a sharp challenge to traditional morals, religion, and politics. All those had rested on a base of supposed rationality and conscious control. According to the new view, those traditions were not geared to psychological reality and might therefore be dangerously false. Freud believed that human personality would suffer even under "enlightened" social codes of behavior, because there exists an inescapable conflict between personal drives and the social order. Hence, "perfectionist" social dreams can never be fulfilled, and the goal of complete individual happiness is a tormenting mirage.

God Still Lives: Barth, Tillich

Leading theologians of the twentieth century also looked back to Kierkegaard, with his sense of the distance between humans and God. Karl Barth (**Bahrt**), an influential Swiss Protestant theologian, stressed human dependence on God but concluded that there is no straight line from the mind of humans to God: "What we say breaks apart constantly . . . producing paradoxes which are held together in seeming unity only by agile and arduous running to and fro on our part." Rather than preaching that there are compelling reasons for believing in God, religious thinkers like Barth would say, "This community of faith invites you to share in its venture of trust and commitment."

In addition to seeing religious faith as a matter of trust instead of something "objectively" proven, many theologians of the twentieth century sought to reconstruct the ancient symbols and myths. They believed that the traditional Christian image of God and the universe had crumbled under the bombardment of scientific findings and historical scholarship, so that the vision of reality expressed in the Bible was no longer believable. They were convinced that if Christianity was to endure as a meaningful teaching, it would have to create images that fitted with scientific knowledge.

To some religious thinkers, this was another way of saying, like Nietzsche, "God is dead." For the German-American theologian Paul Tillich (**TIL-ik**), this meant simply that the ancient image of God had passed into history. This did not mean that Christianity was obsolete but rather that it had to find, as it had found in the past, new forms to carry its message to the living. The idea of a Supreme Being "out there" or "up there" is not an essential part of Christian truth. Tillich dissented from Barth's view that God lives outside humankind; he insisted that God is not a special part of creation but rather Ultimate Reality itself. Modern people, Tillich suggested in *Shaking of the Foundations* (1948), must look for God as the depth and center of their culture and their lives.

> "*Many theologians of the twentieth century were convinced that if Christianity was to endure as a meaningful teaching, it would have to create images that fitted with scientific knowledge.*"

LO³
Modernism in Literature, Art, and Music

Nineteenth-century writers and artists had already begun to depart from traditional themes and methods of depicting reality so as to convey changing human experience in a changing civilization, and many of their twentieth-century successors often broke entirely with the past. Supporters of this tendency thought of it as a natural reflection of a changing civilization, while opponents saw it as a symptom of regrettable cultural decadence. Either way, the tendency seemed to be something typically "modern," and hence it came to be known as the *Modern movement*, or **Modernism**.

New Forms and New Insights in Literature

Modernist literature flourished throughout the first half of the twentieth century. It brought radical innovations in the forms of writing, as well as new insights into the human condition.

Breaking the Rules of Storytelling: Joyce, Woolf

James Joyce was a pioneer of the new literature. Born in Ireland, he abandoned his homeland and his Catholic faith to live on the European continent. From this distance, he wrote fiction inspired by his memories of Dublin—of his own life there and his fellow Dubliners, of the city's streets and shoreline, its churches and museums, its pubs and brothels.

Joyce's novel *Ulysses*—the Latin name for Odysseus—is patterned after Homer's *Odyssey*, but the many deliberate contrasts between Joyce's tale and its ancient model suggest some of what was "modern" about Modernist literature. Odysseus was a warrior-king, descended from a god; the hero of *Ulysses*, Leopold Bloom, is a small-time advertising salesman and the baptized offspring of an Irishwoman and an immigrant Hungarian Jew. Odysseus wandered for ten years by land and sea through many heroic adventures on his way back to his faithful wife Penelope; Leopold Bloom wanders around Dublin for a day, bumping into acquaintances, trying to rustle up business, and fitting in a couple of off-beat sexual encounters, until he comes home to Molly, who has spent the afternoon with the latest of her twenty-five lovers. Odysseus defeated a monstrous cave-dwelling, man-eating giant; Leopold Bloom has a run-in in a pub with an Irish superpatriot and anti-Semite who suspects him of keeping quiet about winning a racetrack bet so as not to have to pay for a round of drinks. Bloom the lower-middle-class wanderer between nations and religions becomes a symbol of the uncertainties of modern times, when the heroic life seems out of date.

To make his epic tale as evocative as possible, Joyce breaks many traditional rules of literary narration and language. He uses a different style for every one of Bloom's adventures: the encounter with the patriot is slangy and pompous by turns, evoking an echoing giant's cave; when a teenage girl notices that Bloom is eying her, the language is lush and kitschy like a romance magazine story. And often Joyce makes a kind of "unedited tape recording" of his characters' inmost thoughts, which appear, disappear, and reappear in a running jumble of sense and nonsense, mixing past, present, and future. The effect of these "interior monologues" is as carefully calculated as that of the most classic prose, however—most famously, when Molly Bloom lies awake with Leopold asleep beside her, his wanderings over. Her thoughts rush from one memory, feeling, and desire to the next, with no punctuation for pages on end. They are an epic in their own right, full of twists and turns like the *Odyssey*, until they arrive at the memory of her and Leopold's first passage of love: "his heart was going like mad and yes I said yes I will Yes." Perhaps Molly is in her way a faithful Penelope—and perhaps Leopold, in his way, is a heroic Odysseus.

Joyce's English contemporary, Virginia Woolf, took the method of interior monologue even further. Her novel *To the*

SEARCHING THE UNCONSCIOUS: SIGMUND FREUD ANALYZES A DREAM

Freud theorized that human behavior results from the conflict that arises when the primitive desires buried in the unconscious are forced to conform to the needs of living in society by the conscious mind. These two elements of the mind are in constant conflict, and when the conflict cannot be contained, the result is neurotic behavior. Freud believed that mental health can be restored by making patients aware of their unconscious desires and fantasies through a process that he called *psychoanalysis*.

Among his most trusted methods of revealing these desires and fantasies was analysis of his patients' dreams, which he believed were the outcome of processes taking place in the unconscious. He came to this conclusion in the 1890s, on the basis of his work as a physician in Vienna specializing in the new human science of psychology. His book, *The Interpretation of Dreams* (1900), describes and gives examples of his method of analyzing dreams and outlines the theory of the human psyche that he was to develop throughout the rest of his life.

In this excerpt, Freud uses an example to show that "dreams which are apparently guileless turn out to be the reverse of innocent." He uses the medical term *trauma* ("wound") to mean an experience that does lasting harm to the mental and emotional health of the person who undergoes it. "Transference" and "displacement" both refer to the process by which the memory of such experiences is disguised by directing the unwelcome feelings that they arouse onto some other object. "Blacky, save yourself!" translates a German slang phrase meaning "Get away from me!"—which happens to sound like the German words for "black raddish."

An intelligent and refined young woman, who in real life is distinctly reserved, one of those people of whom one says that "still waters run deep," relates the following dream: *"I dreamt that I arrived at the market too late, and could get nothing from either the butcher or the greengrocer woman."* Surely a guileless dream, but as it has not the appearance of a real dream I induce her to relate it in detail. Her report then runs as follows: *She goes to the market with her cook, who carries the basket. The butcher tells her, after she has asked him for something: "That is no longer to be obtained," and wants to give her something else, with the remark: "That is good, too." She refuses, and goes to the greengrocer woman. The latter tries to sell her a peculiar vegetable, which is bound up in bundles, and is black in colour. She says: "I don't know that, I won't take it."*

The connection of the dream with the preceding day is simple enough. She had really gone to the market too late, and

---

Lighthouse tells the story of two visits by an upper-middle-class family, the Ramsays, and some of their friends to a vacation home on the coast of Scotland. The visits take place ten years apart, before and after the First World War. On a tiny island a short distance across the sea is a lighthouse. It would be both an enjoyable trip and a good deed to sail over and bring gift parcels to the keepers who are cooped up there. For most of the story no one actually makes the trip, but the possibility—or impossibility, depending on the weather—of doing so evokes thoughts and memories in the members of the group that reveal their characters and relationships.

Events in the story are mostly seen through the eyes of the characters rather than independently narrated. The thoughts and memories of one character often end in his or her perceiving some object or incident; another character then reacts to the same object or incident with new thoughts and memories; and the effect is that of a single, constantly shifting "stream of consciousness." Near the end of the novel, Mr. Ramsay, made bereft by Mrs. Ramsay's death during the war and that of a soldier son, insists on making the trip to the lighthouse. The thoughts of his children with him in the boat turn to different possible meanings that the trip might hold for him. But at this final moment, his own thoughts are not revealed. "He rose and stood in the bow of the boat, very straight and very tall, for all the world, James thought, as if he were saying 'There is no God,' and Cam thought, as if he were leaping into space, and they both rose to follow him as he sprang lightly like a young man, holding his parcel, onto the rock."

Woolf also used her writing skills to advance the cause of equal opportunity for women—for education and careers. Her views are eloquently set forth in a book-length essay composed in the form of a lecture for college girls. She entitled it *A Room of One's Own* (1929), a unique and challenging blend of autobiography and advocacy.

had been unable to buy anything. *The meatshop was already closed,* comes into one's mind as a description of the experience. But wait, is not that a very vulgar phrase which—or rather, the opposite of which—denotes a certain neglect with regard to a man's clothing?[1] The dreamer has not used these words; she has perhaps avoided them; but let us look for the interpretation of the details contained in the dream.

When in a dream something has the character of a spoken utterance—that is, when it is said or heard, not merely thought—and the distinction can usually be made with certainty—then it originates in the utterances of waking life, which have, of course, been treated as raw material, dismembered, and slightly altered, and above all removed from their context. In the work of interpretation we may take such utterances as our starting-point. Where, then, does the butcher's statement, *That is no longer to be obtained,* come from? From myself; I had explained to her some days previously "that the oldest experiences of childhood are *no longer to be obtained* as such, but will be replaced in the analysis by 'transferences' and dreams." Thus, I am the butcher; and she refuses to accept these transferences to the present of old ways of thinking and feeling. Where does her dream utterance, *I don't know that, I won't take it,* come from? For the purposes of the analysis this has to be dissected. "I don't know that" she herself had said to her cook, with whom she had a dispute the previous day, but she had then added: *Behave yourself decently.* Here a displacement is palpable; of the two sentences which she spoke to her cook, she included the insignificant one in her dream; but the suppressed sentence, "Behave yourself decently!" alone fits in with the rest of the dream-content. One might use the words to a man who was making indecent overtures, and had neglected "to close his meat-shop." That we have really hit upon the trail of the interpretation is proved by its agreement with the allusions made by the incident with the greengrocer woman. A vegetable which is sold tied up in bundles (a longish vegetable, as she subsequently adds), and is also black: what can this be but a dream combination of asparagus and black radish? I need not interpret asparagus to the initiated; and the other vegetable, too (think of the exclamation: "Blacky, save yourself!"), seems to me to point to the sexual theme at which we guessed in the beginning, when we wanted to replace the story of the dream by "the meat-shop is closed." We are not here concerned with the full meaning of the dream; so much is certain, that it is full of meaning and by no means guileless.[2]

EXPLORING THE SOURCE

1. What are the main points of Freud's analysis of his patient's dream? Do they seem to be good evidence for the explanation that he gives in the footnote? Why or why not?

2. What seems to be Freud's attitude to his patient as a woman, and to women in general?

"Searching the Unconscious: Sigmund Freud Analyzes a Dream"—from Sigmund Freud, *The Interpretation of Dreams*, in *The Basic Writings of Sigmund Freud*, ed. and trans. E. J. Brill. Copyright © 1938. Reprinted with permission of the Estate of A.A. Brill.(New York: Modern Library, 1938), 251-252.

[1]Its meaning is "Your fly is undone." [Translator's footnote]

[2]For the curious, I may remark that behind the dream there is hidden a phantasy of indecent, sexually provoking conduct on my part, and of repulsion on the part of the lady. If this interpretation should seem preposterous, I would remind the reader of the numerous cases in which physicians have been made the object of such charges by hysterical women, with whom the same phantasy has not appeared in a distorted form as a dream, but has become undisguisedly conscious and delusional.—With this dream the patient began her psychoanalytical treatment. It was only later that I learned that with this dream she repeated the initial trauma in which her neurosis originated, and since then I have noticed the same behaviour in other persons who in their childhood were victims of sexual attacks, and now, as it were, wish in their dreams for them to be repeated. [Freud's footnote]

Prophesy and History

Some leading authors used traditional methods of writing, though the themes they depicted were often new. *Brave New World* (1932), for instance, by the Englishman Aldous Huxley, reveals a "probable" world to come, based on the rapid strides in the physical and social sciences. He sees a world state—achieved, at last, as the only means of avoiding suicidal nationalistic warfare. And to eliminate conflicts within the society, he sees the planned use of genetic engineering, social conditioning, easy sex, and safe drugs. Efficiency and "happiness" are the goals of this future society—at the cost of losing individuality, dissent, and struggle. Another "anti-utopia" of the period is *1984*, the work of another Englishman, George Orwell. Published in 1949, the novel is a prophecy of a future society built on totalitarian lines, one even more repressive than that of *Brave New World*. It uses psychological terror, rather than pleasure, as the primary means of social control (see photo on page 524).

In the Soviet Union, where totalitarianism was a fact, not a prophecy, some great literature appeared in the tradition of Dostoevsky and Tolstoy (p. 449). Notable is Boris Pasternak's *Dr. Zhivago* (1958), an epic historical novel about Russia before, during, and after the Communist revolution. Another giant is Aleksandr Solzhenitsyn (sohl-zhuh-NEET-sin), a voice of furious dissent against totalitarianism. He first became known for his *One Day in the Life of Ivan Denisovich* (1963), which draws on the author's experience as a prisoner in a Russian labor camp and highlights the struggle of one individual to uphold his spirit against determined efforts to crush it.

In the United States, some of the finest prose writing of the century was that of Edith Wharton. Among her numerous works, the best known are her romantic, ironic novel *Ethan Frome* (1911), which takes place in rural New England, and *The Age of Innocence* (1920), set in her native New York City. This novel focuses on the wealthy upper class of society and describes in rich detail its strict code of customs, dress, and manners. Underlying these, Wharton exposes the universal conflict between peer pressure to conform and the individual's own aspirations.

Experiment in Poetry and Drama

The major Modernist poet was T. S. Eliot, an American by birth who moved to London in 1914 and soon began to write poems that were rich in symbols and imagery; like Joyce's *Ulysses*, they broke with traditional forms yet were full of echoes from the literary past. His early works, such as "The Love Song of J. Alfred Prufrock" (1917), reflect a profound disenchantment with modern civilization, a sense of its emptiness and sterility. After Eliot became a devout Anglican Christian, he began to write more cheerfully about the human condition. If the waters of God's grace have dried up within us, he said, we must discover how to make them flow again. In a bid to reach a wider public, he turned to the theater; his most successful dramatic work, a modern morality play, is *Murder in the Cathedral* (1935).

Drama, like prose and poetry, came under subjectivist and experimentalist influences. Such notable playwrights as Eugene O'Neill, Tennessee Williams, and Arthur Miller dealt with ancient themes in new ways; they did not hesitate to alter methods of staging, as well as plot, form, and dialogue. The "theater of the absurd" reflected meaninglessness and the failure of human communication. The Irishman Samuel Beckett was perhaps the best known of the "absurdists." In *Waiting for Godot* (1948), his characters find themselves trapped in a nonsense world of neither logic nor decency.

Technology and Art: The Mass Media

The twentieth century brought four entirely new means of expression to world culture: the motion picture, radio, television, and the Internet. Producers of motion pictures drew on most of the established arts, including writing, drama, music, and photography; but what they created was a unique art form. As a product of technology, this form seemed perfectly suited to the new era. From experimental beginnings prior to the First World War, films grew into an immensely popular medium of entertainment. They are truly international in character, with writers, directors, and actors coming from many cultures. But the largest single source of filmmaking is the United States (chiefly, Hollywood).

Radio broadcasting was developed during the 1920s, offering a flexible and powerful new dimension in the field of communications. It has flourished worldwide, featuring information programs and music of all types. However, radio has been overshadowed since about 1940 by still another new medium: television. In some respects, TV is a projection of motion pictures, but it has special capabilities that give it enormous influence on its own. Millions of viewers in Western nations

"Big Brother Is Watching You" In a 1956 movie version, Winston Smith, a would-be rebel against totalitarian dictatorship in Orwell's *1984*, sprints past a poster of the all-watching, all-knowing, and all-ruling Big Brother. "Does Big Brother exist?" he later asks the interrogator-counselor-torturer charged with reshaping his mind. "Of course he exists. The Party exists. Big Brother is the embodiment of the Party." "Will Big Brother ever die?" "Of course not. How could he die? Next question." Photofest, Inc.

faithfully watch the daily "soaps," talk shows, and "sitcoms"; and most persons now rely mainly on television for news and for watching sports events. This medium has also become a prime carrier for commercial advertising and has revolutionized the conduct of political campaigns in democratic countries.

> *" The artistic shifts of the late nineteenth century became a general upheaval in the first half of the twentieth century. "*

The Inner World of Painters and Sculptors

Modernism in painting and sculpture expressed many of the same feelings and ideas that moved novelists and poets. The artistic shifts of the late nine-

A Violin Hanging on the Wall In this painting, Picasso not only takes a violin apart, but shows the parts at whatever angle and in whatever degree of distortion he desires. The result is an "abstraction" from the actual appearance of a violin.

Guernica In the 1930s the fear was widespread that in the "next war," bombers would spread havoc far beyond the fighting lines, and at Guernica this fear became a reality. Picasso's painting expressed the international horror and revulsion at the deed, and became a worldwide symbol of anti-fascism. The painting spent many years in "exile" while the fascists ruled Spain, and its homecoming to Madrid in 1981 signaled that the country's fascist era was well and truly over.

teenth century (pp. 449–452) became a general upheaval in the first half of the twentieth century.

Taking Nature to Pieces: Picasso

Pablo Picasso, a Spaniard who made his home in France, was the giant of Modernist art. A gifted draftsman trained at the Barcelona Academy of Fine Arts, Picasso began painting in a fairly conventional manner and quickly achieved mastery of the Expressionist style (pp. 451–452). But he moved restlessly on through successive experiments (he called them "discoveries"). From Cézanne, he took the idea of reducing natural subjects to their basic "cubes, cones, and cylinders" (p. 450), but he took it much further and became a leading exponent of a Modernist art movement that called itself Cubism.

Cubist art involved essentially a breaking down and reordering of nature. For example, the title of Picasso's painting *A Violin Hanging on the Wall* proclaims it a still life (see photo)—an exploration of the outward appearance of everyday objects, which Cézanne had turned into an analysis of their underlying forms. But Picasso turns analysis into abstraction. He takes the violin to pieces and rearranges it so that it is no longer a realistic object in three-dimensional space but a mysterious yet coherent pattern of flat colored surfaces. In mischievous contrast, he depicts the wood veneer patterns of the furniture with meticulous realism. The painting, in fact, is Picasso's personal but disciplined response to the *idea* of a violin.

Such inward creations have not been easily understood by the general public. In time, however, Modernist art became quite widely accepted—perhaps exactly because of its strangeness, which reflected the breaking down of traditional culture and values. Besides, the methods of Modernist art, for all their stress on the artist's personal vision, could also be used to comment memorably on public events. Picasso's *Guernica* (see photo) uses these methods to commemorate a fascist air raid against

 Works by Picasso from the Museum of Modern Art Collection (http://www.moma.org/collection/browse_results.php?criteria=0%3AAD%3AE%3A4609&page_number=&template_id=6&sort_order=1) View additional works by Picasso.

civilians in a small town during the Spanish Civil War (p. 504). Earlier artists had aroused pity and terror at the horrors of war by showing what those horrors actually looked like (see photos pages 247, 407). Picasso's *Guernica*, however, treats war like his violin on the wall. He shows nothing of the bombing of Guernica but assembles images that could be of any war—screaming women, a dead baby, a terrified horse, a warrior's corpse still grasping a broken sword. The resulting combined pattern uses techniques of Expressionism and Cubism to express the indiscriminate and hideous character of war in general.

Breaking with Outside Reality: Pollock

More often, however, artists in the forefront of Modernism moved farther and farther away from actually depicting any person, object, or scene. Their art became more and more **abstract**—separated from any outside reality—as in the works of Abstract Expressionist artists in the United States after the Second World War. Jackson Pollock, one of the most notable of these artists, preferred to begin painting with no pattern in mind, and instead responded spontaneously to his strong inner feelings. He allowed one brush stroke to lead to another; he would actually pour, spray, and drip his paints from a scaffold onto a large canvas below. He spoke of his designs as creating themselves; he did not know what the final appearance would be while he was "still in the painting."

Number 1, 1950 (Lavender Mist) (see photo) is a result of this creative process. Works of art usually show images that can be identified in words—prehistoric rhinoceroses, *The Birth of Venus* (see photos pages 29, 300), or even Picasso's violin. Pollock's painting is identified only as the first that he made in 1950, and its subtitle is simply the name of a standard commercial paint shade. The painting is about nothing that can be conveyed in words or recognizable images, but it hauntingly expresses an inner force that acts through the artist to leave its tracks on the canvas.

Stable and Mobile Sculpture: Moore, Hepworth, Calder

In sculpture, too, the trend was away from traditional forms of representation. The English sculptor Henry Moore began by going only some of the way. His *Recumbent Figure* (see photo) does recognizably suggest a female body, in accordance with his belief that "because a work does not aim at reproducing natural appearances, it is not, therefore, an escape from life—but may be a penetration into reality." To penetrate reality in this way, he combines the body's living masses and hollows with those of ancient weathered stone, transforming the appearance of both to suggest a female figure of superhuman power and permanence. Unlike Michelangelo's human forms, this one is not "liberated from the stone" (p. 302). Instead, the figure and the stone are one.

In time, Moore's work became more fully abstract, as did that of his friend and fellow student Barbara Hepworth. Both were impressed by three-dimensional models that mathematicians used in the study and teaching of advanced geometry—models that

Works by Pollock from the Museum of Modern Art Collection (http://www.moma.org/collection/browse_results.php?criteria=0%3AAD%3AE%3A4675&page_number=1&template_id=6&sort_order=1&section_id=T068492#skipToContent) View additional works by Jackson Pollock.

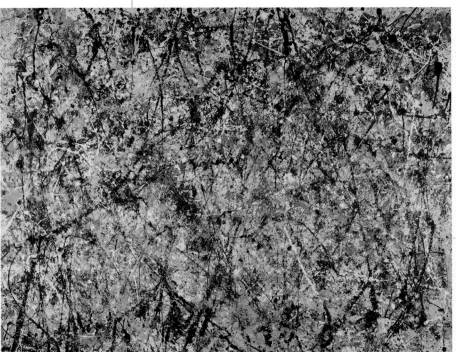

>> *Number 1, 1950 (Lavender Mist)*
"Numbers are neutral. They make people look at a picture for what it is—pure painting." That was how Jackson Pollock's wife Lee Krasner explained the fact that he numbered rather than named his paintings. Krasner was herself a leading Abstract Expressionist painter, and her statement expresses the creed of the movement as a whole.

Recumbent Figure Moore carved this statue for the terrace of an uncompromisingly Modernist house set amid the Downs, the rolling hills of southern England. He recalled: "My figure looked out across a great sweep of the Downs, and her gaze gathered in the horizon. The sculpture had no specific relationahip to the architecture . . . but it so to speak enjoyed being there, and I think it introduced a humanizing element. It became a mediator between the modern house and the ageless land."

Hepworth once described as "sculptural working out of mathematical equations." Like Pollock's *Lavender Mist*, Hepworth's sculpture *Stringed Figure (Curlew), Version II*, is partly an object for its own sake—in her case, a particular version of a "stringed figure." But unlike Pollock's work, Hepworth's stringed figure also represents something outside itself—a curlew is a kind of seabird (see photo). The carefully curved and shaped brass plates and the twisting patterns of strings recall the abstract concepts of three-dimensional geometry, yet the sculpture also evokes spread wings and soaring flight. Hepworth has devised a new way of fulfilling one of sculpture's traditional tasks—to give a motionless object the appearance of movement.

The American sculptor Alexander Calder was also absorbed by the problem of representing movement; in fact, he was the first sculptor to design works that actually moved, called *mobiles*. He would link components of wire and flat pieces of carved metal, hang them from a ceiling, and balance them carefully so that they would move in response to air currents or a slight touch. Instead of seeing motionless objects, viewers would see ever-changing structures. But Calder also constructed *stabiles*—static forms that transmit a feeling of motion, for example, *La Grande Vitesse* (see photo on page 528). As an abstract sculptor, Calder was not obliged to use materials like bronze or marble, which lend them-

 **Alexander Calder: In-Depth from the National Gallery of Art** (http://www.nga .gov/feature/artnation/ calder/index.shtm) View additional works by Alexander Calder.

selves to reproducing natural appearances. Here, industrial materials—steel beams and plates—are fabricated into a complex shape that suggests "high speed"—the meaning of *La Grande Vitesse* and a pun on the name of Grand Rapids, Michigan, where the sculpture stands. The city is proud of the sculpture, which appears on its street signs and municipal letterheads and lends it some of the international prestige and progressive image of modern art.

Architecture and Technology

Architecture was affected far less than painting and sculpture by the urge to express the inner world of the creator. Architects can never simply express themselves, since the buildings that they design have to meet the needs of the people who live and work in them. But overwhelming changes in life and work, as well as in the materials and technologies of building, led, in the first half of the twentieth century, to Modernist innovations in styles of architecture that paralleled those in the other visual arts.

Architecture in the nineteenth century had been a mixture of revival styles, none of which came from the technology of the times. During the 1890s, a number of designers in Europe and America began to rebel against the practice of putting up a

Stringed Figure (Curlew), Version II This is a 1959 "edition," as Barbara Hepworth called it, of a sculpture that she originally made in 1956 and repeatedly re-created for eager buyers, helped by assistants in her workshop. Successful artists of the past like Rubens (p. 345) had often worked with assistants, but the fact that a female Modernist artist needed help to meet the demand for her work was a sign of the changing taste and changing society of the twentieth century.

Form and Function: Wright, Gropius

Wright created impressive public and industrial buildings, but he is especially respected for his designs of private dwellings. Wright's Kaufmann House ("Fallingwater"), built as a mountain retreat above a waterfall for a Pittsburgh department store owner in 1936, is a spectacular example of organic architecture (see photo). Modern reinforced concrete (strengthened inside by steel rods or mesh) made it possible to extend the floors a long way into the open air by means of cantilevers—horizontal structures supported at only one end. As a result, the house's geometrical forms flow in and out of each other not like the elements that make up Picasso's violin, yet also seem to grow from the natural landscape. Wright called the house an "extension of the cliff beside a mountain stream, making living space over and above the stream upon which a man who loved the place sincerely, one who liked to listen to the waterfall, might well live."

European architects were deeply impressed by Wright's functional ideas—above all a German, Walter Gropius (**GROH-pee-uhs**). He designed a complex of buildings for the Bauhaus ("House of Architecture," the name of a school of art and architecture that he headed) in the eastern German town of Dessau according to the new principles. Gropius, like Wright, emphasized that attention

 Works by the Bauhaus from the Metropolitan Museum of Art Collection (http://www .metmuseum.org/toah/ hd/bauh/hd_bauh.htm) View works produced by the Bauhaus.

structure by modern engineering methods and then adding on Gothic windows or Roman columns. Among the leaders of this rebellion was an American, Frank Lloyd Wright. One should break entirely, he declared, with the forms and decorations of the past. One should try to utilize whatever kind of beauty modern technology and materials are capable of producing and allow "form to follow function." An authentic (true) style is one that provides the kind of space suited to a particular kind of human activity (work, rest, or play); its beauty will lie in the character of the building materials themselves. Because his structures were designed around the needs and desires of the people who occupied them, and because they preserved the natural appearance of the materials, Wright called his style "organic."

The Kaufmann House ("Fallingwater") With its cantilevered terraces, Wright's design made demands that went beyond what the reinforced-concrete technology of the 1930s could in the long run fulfill. A lifetime later, the terraces were sagging, internal beams were cracking, and the house was in danger of collapse. But in 2003 a newer technology, post-tensioning (inserting steel cables and pulling them tight) saved this classic of modern architecture for future generations.

to function is the first principle of architecture; a good design in an object, no matter what it is, ensures its beauty. His Bauhaus became a model of what today is called the International Style. When creatively applied to large buildings—factories and offices—this style aptly expresses the precision and efficiency of the machine age. On the other hand, the "glass boxes" that have made cityscapes across the world bleak and monotonous are the result of the International Style used without taste or imagination.

The International Style: Mies, Pei

The most brilliant architect in the International Style was Ludwig Mies van der Rohe, Gropius's successor as director of the Bauhaus, who emigrated to the United States after the Nazis came to power. Mies's masterpiece, the Seagram Building in New York (see photo), was designed for a Canadian distilling company. The building is a simple geometrical form with unadorned walls of tinted glass to retain heat and admit light. But Mies held that function alone is not enough to ensure beauty. The Seagram Building's walls are held in place by strips of expensive bronze; by day, they reflect the urban landscape, and at night, they glow with internal light. The building used the architectural language of simplicity

"Light is the Key" The East Building of the National Gallery of Art is an example of I. M. Pei's philosophy. Crowds of visitors make their way into, out of, and across a central space with many staircases and gangways under a vast skylit roof. The roof continues over the side galleries, so that natural light illuminates the masterpieces of modern art that they house.
Ezra Stoller © Esto © 2010 Artists Rights Society (ARS), New York

and utility to proclaim elegance, luxury, and power on behalf of a modern capitalist corporation just as effectively as a Baroque palace did for an absolute monarch (p. 348).

The influence of Modernism lasted well beyond the middle of the twentieth century, notably in the work of the Chinese-American I. M. Pei, a strong believer in what he calls the "tradition" of the pioneers of Modernist architecture. In the glass-roofed central hall of a new wing of the National Gallery of Art in Washington, D.C., he carried the tradition a step further. The hall's simple geometrical forms and self-revealing structures combine, contrast, and interlock to make a hall that is spacious and monumental yet also varied and intimate (see photo). Instead of intimidating visitors with Modernist austerity, the hall leads them on to explore the surrounding exhibits.

Modernism and Beyond: Le Corbusier

Another leading exponent of architectural Modernism was the Swiss architect Le Corbusier (luh kawr-byoo-ZYEY), who strongly believed that if architecture used modern technology uncompromisingly in the service of utility and convenience, the result would be aesthetically satisfying buildings: "A house," he declared, "is a machine

≪ The Seagram Building Mies owed the commission to design this building to Phyllis Lambert, the architect daughter of the chief of the Seagram Corporation, Samuel Bronfman. "Mies forces you in," Lambert told her father. "You might think this austere strength, this ugly beauty, is terribly severe. It is, and yet all the more beauty in it." Ezra Stoller © Esto © 2012 Artists Rights Society (ARS), New York/VG Bild-Kunst, Bonn

for living." Yet late in his life, he used the resources of technology to produce architecture that seems to reject the machine. In his chapel of Notre-Dame du Haut (Our Lady of the Hilltop), completed in 1955 near Ronchamp in a mountainous region of eastern France (see photo), reinforced concrete is bent into irregular curves. These shapes serve no engineering function, but instead express features of Christianity: hands folded in prayer; the wings of a dove, standing for both peace and the Holy Spirit; and the image of the Church as a ship navigating the stormy seas of this world. Here, modern architecture speaks speaks neither of well-being through technology nor of luxury and power, but of ancient religious faith. And modern technology enables this building, instead of expressing engineering logic, seemingly to defy it—a possibility that late twentieth-century architects would exploit to the maximum (p. 567).

> **" 'A house,' Le Corbusier declared, 'is a machine for living.' "**

New Patterns of Music

The changes that swept through the arts around the turn of the century affected music as well. Some composers turned to Impressionism, which was inspired in part by the movement in painting (p. 450). Musical Impressionism, as developed by the Frenchman Claude Debussy (**deb-yoo-SEE**), was anticlassical as well as anti-Romantic. It sought to record the composer's fleeting responses to nature (clouds, sea, moonlight). Departing from traditional patterns of melody, tone scales, and rhythms, Debussy's music has a dreamy, shimmering quality.

Modernism in Music: Schönberg, Stravinsky

As in painting, the musical Impressionists were followed by Expressionists, among them the Austrian Arnold Schönberg. Just before the First World War, he turned from the large orchestral productions of the nineteenth century and began writing string quartets and other forms of chamber music. Abandoning tonality, Schönberg stressed melodic distortion and the chance coincidence of notes—often producing a harsh dissonance. Later in life, he adopted a unique tone scale of his own invention. Musically, Schönberg was not unlike van Gogh or Picasso in seeking vigorous and disturbing means of expression.

Modernist composers, like painters or sculptors, freed themselves from the traditions of their craft and chose whatever musical elements they wished. The result was an unbounded diversity of individual styles. One of the best known and most successful of the musical Modernists was Russian-born Igor Stravinsky. Younger than Schönberg, he, too, worked with established forms before discarding them. He also decided to ignore public tastes (as the painters had done) and to write "abstract" music to suit his own ideas. The chief characteristics of his mature works were stress on polyphony, free use of dissonance, and quickly changing rhythms.

A Performance and Discussion of Stravinsky's *Rite of Spring* (http://video.pbs .org/video/1295282238/) Learn about and listen to Stravinsky's *Rite of Spring.*

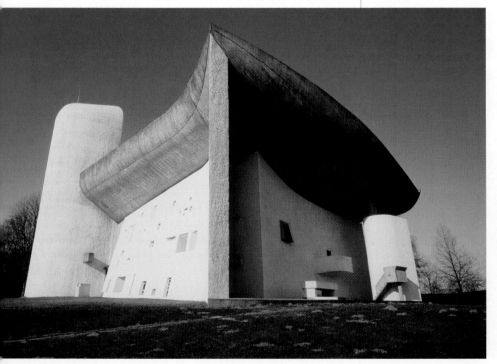

≪ **Notre-Dame du Haut** "In building this chapel I wished to create a place of silence, of prayer, of peace, of inner joy." Le Corbusier, an agnostic of Protestant background, spoke these words as he formally handed over the Chapel of Our Lady of the Hilltop to the local Catholic bishop. To create such a place, the architect stretched the bounds of Modernism with a building whose form does not follow its engineering function, but consists of startling and mysterious sculptured masses. Herve Hughes/Hemis/Corbis © 2012 Artists Rights Society (ARS), New York/ADAGP, Paris/F.L.C.

Musicals, Jazz, and Beyond

In popular culture, the Broadway-type "musical" proved highly successful in the United States and Europe. The leading geniuses of this entertainment medium were three Americans: Frederick Loewe, Alan Jay Lerner, and Cole Porter; their most acclaimed productions included *My Fair Lady*, *Camelot*, and *Kiss Me, Kate*.

The most original American contribution to world music, however, was *jazz*. Europeans, who had been creators and exporters of classical compositions for centuries, became eager importers of jazz. African rhythms are the foundation of this musical innovation, which flowered chiefly among the writers and musicians of black America. But the principal feature is its unending novelty and the improvisations of its interpreters; among the greatest of these were the prolific composer-conductor "Duke" Ellington and the trumpet-playing "Ambassador of Jazz," Louis Armstrong. A brilliant white composer, George Gershwin, created a unique blend of jazz rhythms and classical styles. He is best remembered for his piano *Rhapsody in Blue* and the folk opera *Porgy and Bess* (first performed in 1935). More than any other type of artistic expression, jazz seems to incorporate the spirit of rebellion against traditional forms and restraints.

 Excerpts from the Los Angeles Opera Production of *Porgy and Bess* (http://www.youtube.com/watch?v=M5o4e5ofRcw) Watch a compilation of scenes from *Porgy and Bess*.

Rock music, which first became popular in the 1960s, has a similar appeal. It grew out of black rhythm and blues and white country and western music into its own unique form. Rock is directed mainly at young adults; its sensual beat, electronic amplification, and frank lyrics excite audiences around the world. By means of the mass media, it quickly created idols (and legends) like Elvis Presley, John Lennon, and Michael Jackson. The power of rock was further extended in the 1980s through another new art form: music video.

These and other forms of mass entertainment, the world-changing outcome of the encounter between art and technology, originated in nineteenth-century universal education and high-speed printing, but it was twentieth-century electronic technology that made them central to the lives of individuals and societies. In the global village of the twenty-first century, mass entertainment plays the same role that gossip among neighbors, religious rituals, and community celebrations play in real villages. It is a glue that holds a changing world together, as civilization breaks with its past and moves toward whatever the future holds.

 Listen to a synopsis of Chapter 28.

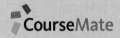

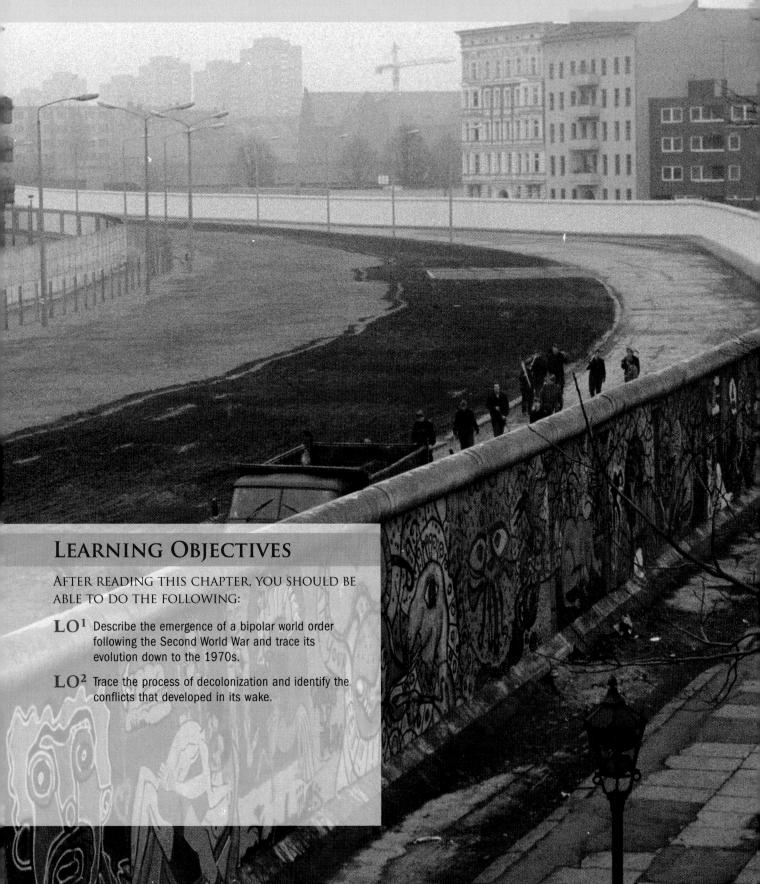

CHAPTER 29

THE SUPERPOWERS,
1945–1960s

LEARNING OBJECTIVES

AFTER READING THIS CHAPTER, YOU SHOULD BE
ABLE TO DO THE FOLLOWING:

LO¹ Describe the emergence of a bipolar world order
following the Second World War and trace its
evolution down to the 1970s.

LO² Trace the process of decolonization and identify the
conflicts that developed in its wake.

> **"WITH THE DEFEAT OF FASCISM IN THE SECOND WORLD WAR, THE SECOND ROUND OF THE STRUGGLE OVER THE FUTURE POWER STRUCTURE OF WESTERN AND WORLD CIVILIZATION BEGAN."**

With the defeat of fascism in the Second World War, the second round of the struggle over the future power structure of Western and world civilization began. This time, the contest was between the defenders of the democratic-capitalist world order and their communist challengers.

To safeguard the existing order, the West, now led by the United States, made more drastic reforms than ever before. Departing from the Western tradition of power struggles, they formed a single group of liberal democratic and capitalist nation-states upheld by overwhelming American power. Other war-winning countries like Britain and France, as well as the defeated fascist ones, gave up their claims to worldwide power and empire and were content to be junior partners in this wide democratic-capitalist grouping.

Political differences, economic competition, and the linking of many countries in the European Community did not change this basic pattern of cooperation under the leadership of a superpower. Together, the democratic-capitalist countries dominated the international economy; pursued the modern Western goals of health, education, leisure, and abundance for all more vigorously than ever before; and built up massive military power.

Meanwhile, the communist challenge to the world order grew more formidable than before, as communism spread from the victorious Soviet Union into eastern Europe and Asia. Up to the 1970s, communist planned economies grew faster than those of many capitalist countries, and European communist dictatorships dominated their societies in spite of occasional revolts. The vast size and state-controlled economy of the Soviet Union enabled it to build up armed forces that eventually matched those of the United States. Thus communism became a second group of countries under the leadership of a superpower.

Test your knowledge before you read this chapter.

What do you think?

The arms race was necessary to prevent a communist take-over of the world.

Strongly Disagree   Strongly Agree

| 1 | 2 | 3 | 4 | 5 | 6 | 7 |

‹‹ **The Berlin Wall** For nearly 30 years, the Antifascist Protective Rampart—its official communist name—encircled West Berlin to prevent East Germans escaping to the West, and thereby became a symbol of the Cold War division of Europe. As perfected after several rebuildings, the "rampart" had two walls enclosing a 100-yard death strip where guards could easily shoot down would-be escapers. Graffiti artists painted psychedelic images along the West Berlin side, to mock the repression that the wall represented.

Thierry Noir, Galerie Noir © 2012 Artists Rights Society (ARS), New York/VC Bild-Kunst, Bonn

533

Cold War
A period of military buildup and political hostility between the superpowers of the United States and the Soviet Union.

The communist and capitalist-democratic rivalry was primarily a conflict within Western civilization, pitting the countries of its North American and western European heartland against its outlying region of Russia and eastern Europe. Meanwhile, the non-Western peoples of Asia and Africa, together with the Western outlying region of Latin America, underwent the single greatest change in the world order that resulted from the war: decolonization. Following the war, defeated imperialist countries lost their empires and spheres of influence, victorious but weakened countries more or less willingly and completely gave them up, and intercontinental empires vanished even more swiftly than they had arisen a century earlier. Often they left a legacy of strife among the liberated peoples that interacted with the overriding rivalry of the democratic-capitalist and communist groupings.

In earlier times, the two sides would certainly have gone to war like the rival European alliances in 1914, but in the age of nuclear weapons, they settled for something less—the **Cold War**. They built up world-threatening armaments against each other that they intended never to use, and competed for influence and control over the ex-colonial world. But they generally respected each other's vital interests, built up enough mutual trust to avoid mutual annihilation, and sometimes practiced partnership as well as rivalry.

LO¹ The Bipolar World Order

The political consequences of the Second World War were decisive. Japan was stripped of imperial sovereignty and placed under American military occupation, and Italy lost its possessions in Africa. Germany was divided into occupation zones by the leading victor countries—the United States, Britain, liberated France, and the Soviet Union—and Berlin, within the Soviet zone, was also shared among the four occupying powers (see Map 29.1).

But Britain and France, as well as Germany, Italy, and Japan, all of them countries that a generation before had dominated global affairs, had now fallen to the rank of secondary powers. Instead, the United States, untouched at home by the ravages of battle, emerged as the strongest military and economic power in the world. The Soviet Union, however, though it had suffered enormous losses and damage from the Nazi invasion, extended its control in Europe (see Map 29.1). As it recovered from the

CHRONOLOGY

1945	United Nations is formed
1947	Truman announces the containment policy in response to Greek civil war; India and Pakistan become independent states
1948	UN authorizes an independent Palestine, with two states, Arab (Palestine) and Jewish (Israel)
1949	NATO alliance formed; Mao Zedong establishes the communist People's Republic of China
1952	United States develops hydrogen bomb
1954	*Brown v. Board of Education of Topeka*; Laos and Cambodia gain independence from France
1955	Warsaw Pact formed
1956	Soviet troops restore communist regime in Hungary; Britain, France, and Israel attempt to overthrow Gamal Abdel Nasser, the leader of Egypt
1957	Soviets' *Sputnik I* orbits Earth; European Economic Community (EEC) is formed

war, determined leaders built it into a military superpower, and communism continued to have worldwide appeal. The time was ripe for a lengthy conflict between the supporters of the democratic-capitalist world order and their communist challengers. The result, for the moment, was a *bipolar* world order in which the two superpowers were usually rivals and sometimes partners.

The End of Allied Unity

President Franklin Roosevelt, who had been the principal leader of the victorious alliance until his death in April 1945, anticipated the new distribution of power. During the war, he had joined in top-level ("summit") conferences with the British prime minister, Winston Churchill, and the Russian dictator, Joseph Stalin. The "Big Three," by working together despite grave differences, succeeded in defeating their common enemies.

Roosevelt hoped that when the war was over, the major powers could continue to cooperate for peace as they had for victory. The key to this accomplishment, he thought, was American-Soviet understanding. It was in part to develop such understanding and cooperation that Roosevelt proposed a new international organization, the United Nations. Its general

Map 29.1 Europe After the Second World War

The map shows the main border changes in Europe during and after the war—the Soviet Union's expansion at the expense of its western neighbors, the westward shift of Poland, the division of Germany and Austria among four occupying powers, the communist takeovers in eastern Europe, and the line along which NATO confronted the Warsaw Pact. © Cengage Learning

Interactive
Map

THE COLD WAR WAS DRIVEN BY A NUMBER OF FACTORS:

A Clash of Ideologies

- The Western side stood for triumphant worldwide democracy, with its belief in universal rights, and for world-wide capitalism, with its faith in free enterprise.

- The Soviet side stood for victori-ous communism, with its belief in a worldwide overthrow leading to a classless society and shared control of economic resources.

Fear of Aggression

- The Western powers had intervened in Russia against the Bolsheviks in 1918, and Soviet leaders still suspected that the West was out to destroy "the world's first socialist state."

- On the Western side, fear of com-munist expansion also traced back to 1917, but now it was heightened by

the presence of Soviet military power in central and eastern Europe.

Contested Actions

- The Americans and British protested vainly against Stalin's failure to provide free elections (as he had promised) and the imposition of com-munist-dominated regimes in Poland, Romania, Bulgaria, Hungary, Czecho-slovakia, Yugoslavia, and Albania.

---

outlines were approved by the Big Three at the Yalta Conference (1945), and the organization came into being some months later, after Roosevelt's death.

In planning the United Nations, Roosevelt had sought to avoid what he regarded as the visionary and rigid aims of his predecessor, Woodrow Wilson. The United Nations remained a forum of political discussion and debate, but it appeared unable to act as a "collective" power, and there was no evidence of a trend toward a unitary world or even a world "police force." Although the United Nations was similar in structure to the disbanded League of Nations, it was not based on the failed principle of collective security (pp. 502–503). Nor was it viewed as a world government or anything approaching it. The organization, thought Roosevelt, might be a step in that direction, but its immediate function was to serve as an instrument that would enable the two superpowers to maintain world order.

Within a few months of the president's death, a chill descended on East-West relations; as this chill deepened into the Cold War, hopes for cooperation evaporated. In 1946, Churchill declared that "an iron curtain has descended across the Continent" of Europe. The reasons for the deterioration in relations have been sharply debated by diplomats and scholars.

 A Soviet Assessment of American Post-war Intentions Read a Soviet view of western intentions.

Containment

The decisive turn in Western policy toward the Soviet Union came in 1947, when communist-led guerrilla fighters threatened the Western-supported government of Greece. President Truman responded vigorously by sending military and economic aid to Athens.

 President Truman's Plan to Contain the Soviet Union Read Truman's speech on the policy of containment.

More important, he declared a general American policy of **containment** of communism, which pledged military assistance to any regime threatened by "armed minorities or by outside pres-sure." In support of this policy, he undertook a multibillion-dollar program of aid for economic recovery and integration in western Europe (the Marshall Plan, named for his secretary of state). The Greek anticommunists prevailed in a brutal civil war, but in 1948, communists seized power in the only more or less democratically ruled country among those that the Soviets had occupied, Czechoslovakia (see Map 29.1).

 An American Plan to Rebuild a Shattered Europe Read George Marshall's plan for aiding Europe.

NATO and the Warsaw Pact

In 1949 came the final steps in the division of Europe into two rival blocs The Americans, British, and French merged their German occupation zones into an independent state (the Federal Republic of Germany). In addition, the North American and western European countries concluded a twelve-nation military alliance (the North Atlantic Treaty Organization, NATO) for unified defense against the Soviets. Huge arms expenditures by the United States, corre-sponding to these expanding overseas commitments, would lead to the creation of the most powerful military strike forces ever assembled.

The Soviets responded with a military buildup of their own, and in 1955, they formed a military alliance to counter NATO. Consisting of the communist states of eastern Europe (except Yugoslavia), it came to be known as the Warsaw Pact. In addi-tion, the Soviet zone in eastern Germany became the German Democratic Republic (GDR), one of eight **satellite states** that now existed in eastern Europe (see Map 29.1). The satellite states nearest to western Europe, the GDR, Czechoslovakia, and Hungary, gradually turned their western borders into a real

Iron Curtain of barbed wire, watchtowers, and minefields so as to prevent an exodus of discontented citizens. What became the most infamous portion of this barrier was the Berlin Wall, built around West Berlin (the part occupied by the Western powers) in 1961 by the GDR to stem the outflow of its citizens to the prosperity and freedom of the Federal Republic (see photo page 532). Its destruction in 1989 would signal the end of the Iron Curtain and the Cold War.

> *"The energy released in the hydrogen device was hundreds of times greater than that of the Hiroshima bomb."*

 Berlin Wall History Learn more about the history of the Berlin Wall.

The Balance of Terror

The American nuclear monopoly was the most decisive single fact in world politics immediately after the war. It caused deep worries in Moscow, where leaders feared that some American generals might gain backing for a "preventive" war against the USSR. Soviet scientists worked feverishly to build a bomb of their own as a counter to the American weapon, aided by secret information supplied by agents in the West. This they succeeded in doing in 1949, much to the surprise of scientists and military leaders in the United States.

It soon became evident that even without the help of spies, the Russians were a match for the Americans in advanced technical undertakings. When the United States exploded its first hydrogen (fusion—p. 516) device in 1952, the government revealed that the energy released was hundreds of times greater than that of the Hiroshima (fission) bomb (see photo). Within a year, the Soviets announced the explosion of their own hydrogen bomb, and in 1957, they became first in space by rocketing *Sputnik I*, the first artificial satellite, into orbit around the earth. In a real sense, these Soviet demonstrations lent a degree of stability to the international situation. With each side in the Cold War capable of destroying the other with aircraft or intercontinental missiles, a new kind of balance was struck—a **balance of terror**.

 American Civil Defense Posters and Ads (http://civildefense museum.org/artgal/ artgallery.html) See how Americans responded to the Soviet bomb in these civil defense posters.

containment
The American foreign policy goal of stopping the spread of communism by aiding countries threatened with Soviet rule.

satellite states
Eastern European states under the control of the Soviet Union.

balance of terror
The matching of nuclear arsenals and destructive power on each side of the Cold War.

Castle Bravo A 1954 test with this codename, of the first hydrogen bomb small enough actually to be dropped on a city, was the biggest U.S. explosion ever, equivalent to 1,000 atom bombs of the type that had destroyed Hiroshima. Local Pacific islanders and the crew of a Japanese fishing boat sickened from the unexpectedly large fallout cloud, and a Japanese crewman died. Seven years later the Soviets exploded a bomb more than three times as powerful as this one.

"AN IRON CURTAIN HAS DESCENDED ACROSS THE CONTINENT"

In 1946, as the alliance against Nazi Germany was beginning to break apart, Britain's wartime leader Winston Churchill traveled to Fulton, Missouri, to receive an honorary degree. He took this opportunity to deliver an address assessing Soviet future intentions, in which he coined the phrase "Iron Curtain" to describe the growing division of Europe. More broadly, the speech expressed growing Western distrust of the Soviet Union, and foreshadowed the policies that the Western powers would follow in dealing with the Soviets throughout the Cold War.

The United States stands at this time at the pinnacle of world power. It is a solemn moment for the American democracy. With primacy in power is also joined an awe-inspiring accountability to the future. As you look around you, you feel not only the sense of duty done but also feel anxiety lest you fall below the level of achievement. Opportunity is here now, clear and shining, for both our countries. To reject it or ignore it or fritter it away will bring upon us all the long reproaches of the aftertime. It is necessary that constancy of mind, persistency of purpose, and the grand simplicity of decision shall guide and rule the conduct of the English speaking peoples in peace as they did in war. . . .

A shadow has fallen upon the scenes so lately lighted by the Allied victory. Nobody knows what Soviet Russia and its Communist international organization intends to do in the immediate future, or what are the limits, if any, to their expansive and proselytizing tendencies. I have a strong admiration and regard for the valiant Russian people and for my wartime comrade, Marshal Stalin. There is sympathy and good will in Britain—and I doubt not here also—toward the peoples of all the Russias and a resolve to persevere through many differences and rebuffs in establishing lasting friendships.

We understand the Russian need to be secure on her western frontiers from all renewal of German aggression. We welcome her to her rightful place among the leading nations of the world. Above all, we welcome constant, frequent, and growing contacts between Russian people and our own people on both sides of the Atlantic. It is my duty, however, to place before you certain facts about the present position in Europe.

From Stettin in the Baltic to Trieste in the Adriatic, an iron curtain has descended across the continent. Behind that line lie all the capitals of the ancient states of Central and Eastern Europe. Warsaw, Berlin, Prague, Vienna, Budapest, Belgrade, Bucharest, and Sofia, all these famous cities and the populations around them lie in the Soviet sphere and all are subject, in one form or another, not only to Soviet influence but to a very high and increasing measure of control from Moscow. Athens alone, with its immortal glories, is free to decide its future at an election under British, American, and French observation. . . .

The "Free World" Confronts the "Socialist Camp"

During the years of the Cold War, from the 1950s through the 1980s, the two blocs were the most powerful forces in both upholding and destabilizing the bipolar world order. Besides its geographical north and south poles, the world now had military and political "West" and "East" poles, in Washington and Moscow. The term "the West," previously used to mean the North American and western European heartland of Western civilization, acquired a second meaning. It also came to be used—as it still is today—to refer to the political and military grouping of the NATO countries.

The West, together with other countries with both Western and non-Western traditions of civilization that were aligned with it, called itself the "Free World." "The East," in addition to being often used to describe non-Western civilizations in general, now also meant the communist countries, though their prevailing ideology had originated within Western civilization. They usually called themselves the "Socialist Camp," since according to their Marxist ideology, they were still "building socialism," preliminary to passing into the final stage of communism (pp. 443–444).

The Socialist Camp

The monolithic ("rocklike") unity of the Socialist Camp began to dissolve soon after it appeared. Even before Stalin died in 1953, Marshal Tito of Yugoslavia, though a communist, took actions that were increasingly independent of Moscow. After Stalin's death, the new Soviet leader, Nikita Khrushchev (KROOSH-chef), uncovered the massive crimes committed by Stalin and initiated a policy of internal relaxation, "peaceful

Free World
Term the democratic-capitalist countries used to define themselves as a group opposed to communism.

Socialist Camp
Term the communists used to define themselves as a group opposed to the Free World.

If now the Soviet government tries, by separate action, to build up a pro-Communist Germany in their areas, this will cause new serious difficulties in the British and American zones, and will give the defeated Germans the power of putting themselves up to auction between the Soviets and the Western democracies. Whatever conclusions may be drawn from these facts—and facts they are—this is certainly not the liberated Europe we fought to build up. Nor is it one which contains the essentials of permanent peace.

In front of the iron curtain which lies across Europe are other causes for anxiety. In Italy the Communist party is seriously hampered by having to support the Communist-trained Marshall Tito's claims to former Italian territory at the head of the Adriatic. Nevertheless, the future of Italy hangs in the balance. Again, one cannot imagine a regenerated Europe without a strong France. . . .

However, in a great number of countries, far from the Russian frontiers and throughout the world, Communist fifth columns are established and work in complete unity and absolute obedience to the directions they receive from the Communist center. Except in the British Commonwealth, and in the United States, where communism is in its infancy, the Communist parties or fifth columns constitute a growing challenge and peril to Christian civilization. These are somber facts for anyone to have to recite on the morrow of a victory gained by so much splendid comradeship in arms and in the cause of freedom and democracy, and we should be most unwise not to face them squarely while time remains. . . .

Our difficulties and dangers will not be removed by closing our eyes to them; they will not be removed by mere waiting to see what happens; nor will they be relieved by a policy of appeasement. What is needed is a settlement, and the longer this is delayed, the more difficult it will be and the greater our dangers will become. From what I have seen of our Russian friends and allies during the war, I am convinced that there is nothing they admire so much as strength, and there is nothing for which they have less respect than for military weakness. For that reason the old doctrine of a balance of power is unsound. We cannot afford, if we can help it, to work on narrow margins, offering temptations to a trial of strength. If the Western democracies stand together in strict adherence to the principles of the United Nations Charter, their influence for furthering these principles will be immense and no one is likely to molest them. If, however, they become divided or falter in their duty, and if these all-important years are allowed to slip away, then indeed catastrophe may overwhelm us all.

EXPLORING THE SOURCE

1. What does Churchill see as the main methods of Soviet expansionism, and how does he suggest they should be countered?

2. Read "A Soviet Assessment of American Postwar Intentions" (website link in this chapter). Does Churchill or Novikov make the better case for his view of the other side, and why?

Source: Winston Churchill—March 5, 1946.

---

coexistence" with the West, and somewhat greater freedom of action for the satellite countries.

Khrushchev's "thaw" was not supposed to undermine communist dictatorship or ultimate Soviet control of the satellite countries, however. He and his successors still expected the worldwide victory of communism. The limits of the freedom of the satellite countries were driven home to the Hungarians in 1956, when "de-Stalinization" ended in the overthrow of the communist regime until Soviet troops intervened to restore it. In 1968, there was another Soviet military intervention, this time to suppress a liberalization movement for "socialism with a human face" in Czechoslovakia. Following this intervention, Khrushchev's successor Leonid Brezhnev (**BREZH-nyef**) declared: "When forces that are hostile to socialism try to turn the development of some socialist country towards capitalism, it becomes not only a problem of the country concerned, but a common problem and concern of all socialist countries." His statement, which became known in the West as the "Brezhnev doctrine," reflected both communist ideology and Soviet fears that the defection of the satellite states, most of which were historically anti-Russian, would deprive the Soviet Union of its defensive buffer against the West.

China

Most weighty of the changes within other communist lands was the growing power of China. In 1949, Mao Zedong (**MOU zuh-DOONG**) had led his revolutionary forces to victory over Chiang Kai-shek's (**CHANG kahy-SHEK**) Nationalists, bringing the most populous country on earth under the Red banner. Chiang transported his retreating army from the mainland to the nearby island province of Taiwan, which had been returned by its Japanese conquerors in 1945. There he established a rival "Republic of China," with its capital at Taipei and a claim to authority over the whole nation.

After a period of dependence on Soviet aid, the Communist Chinese (the "People's Republic") began to regard Mao as the principal ideologist of Marxism, and Beijing as the true capital of proletarian revolution. By 1962, a bitter split had opened between the two communist giants. Mao accused the Soviets of ideological "revisionism" (backsliding toward capitalism) and collaboration with the United States; Brezhnev replied with charges of Chinese defection from the Socialist Camp. The harsh verbal exchanges during the 1960s were accompanied by military clashes along their common frontiers in Central Asia, and in 1965, China successfully tested a nuclear weapon—to deter the Soviet Union as much as the United States.

Soviet concern over the growing power of China grew stronger during the 1970s, when the United States reversed its policy toward the People's Republic. John Foster Dulles, the American secretary of state under President Dwight D. Eisenhower, had previously sought to contain the communist regime through diplomatic and economic strangulation. But as other nations recognized and opened commerce with China, it became apparent that the Dulles policy had failed. President Richard M. Nixon, a longtime opponent of communism, made the practical decision to abandon the American policy and come to terms with the People's Republic. Guided by his national security adviser (and later secretary of state), Henry A. Kissinger, Nixon made a dramatic visit to Beijing in 1972. Diplomatic missions were soon afterward established in the two capitals, and "friendship" replaced hostility.

The Chinese aim was clear: to neutralize the American threat as a means of improving their position with respect to the Soviets. By pursuing at the same time a policy of relaxation toward the Soviets, Nixon and Kissinger thus initiated a triangular power relationship among the three rival nations.

The Rise of Europe

While the Socialist Camp was becoming less monolithic, NATO was being similarly transformed, due in large measure to the swift postwar recovery of western Europe. The recovery, helped by massive American aid through the Marshall Plan, was linked to the creation in 1957 of the European Economic Community (EEC)—the "Common Market." It consisted initially of six countries: France, West Germany, Belgium, the Netherlands, Luxembourg, and Italy. In 1973, Britain, Ireland, and Denmark joined the EEC, which sought to draw the separate European economies into a single trading area. Tariffs and trade restrictions were steadily reduced within the Community, and a common set of tariffs was adopted for imports from outside the EEC.

The consequences were dramatic: during the 1960s and 1970s, Europe experienced the most rapid economic advance in its history, and the rising standards of living were shared in some degree by all classes of the population. Food and housing were better than before the war; travel became more widespread, and class lines were blurred by increasing social mobility. This prosperity also had its effects on internal politics and ideology. The Communist parties of western Europe turned away from the Soviet political model and worked out their own platforms of "democratic" Marxism (Eurocommunism).

While the western European nations now accepted lesser roles in global affairs, they did not give up the urge to reassert their traditional character and independence. Britain, whose scientists had shared atomic secrets with the United States during the Second World War, decided to develop its own nuclear force in the 1940s in hopes of maintaining some of its traditional world standing, Even a left-wing politician, Aneurin Bevan, declared that the country could not "go naked to the conference table." France followed suit in the 1950s, and under the guidance of President Charles de Gaulle, it sought to reduce or eliminate the strong influence that American politicians, generals, and business representatives had exerted in Europe after the Second World War. In 1966, de Gaulle ordered U.S. military forces and bases out of France. Within the EEC, he opposed any growth in power of the Community's central institutions at the expense of national governments while trying to build up France's influence in Europe in partnership with Germany. Though somewhat softened, de Gaulle's policies have been carried on ever since by his political successors in Paris.

Détente

A contributing factor in Europe's mounting spirit of independence was a lessening of the earlier fear of the Soviet Union. The American-Soviet balance of terror cast a protective cloak over Europe, and Kremlin policy after Stalin's death gave no indication of a desire for military adventure in Europe. Responding to this new situation, the chancellor of the German Federal Republic, Willy Brandt, sought to turn off the Cold War in the region (see photo). In 1970, he undertook successful talks in Moscow, accepting for his prospering country the postwar political boundaries of central and eastern Europe.

Brandt's initiative marked a dramatic step toward **détente** (day-TAHNT—easing of tension) in Europe. It was capped in 1975 by a summit meeting at Helsinki, Finland, where heads of thirty-five countries (including the United States) signed a pact for European "security and cooperation." The Helsinki agreement pledged all the signatories to recognize the international borders resulting from the Second World War—a key demand of the Warsaw Pact countries, especially the Soviet Union, Poland, and the German Democratic Republic—and to ensure "human rights" for their own citizens—a Western requirement that gave some protection to dissidents in communist countries.

Even so, neither bloc showed any sign of dissolving. Within the Socialist Camp, the economy and armed forces of the Soviet

> "*During the 1960s and 1970s, Europe experienced the most rapid economic advance in its history.*"

"I Suddenly Got This Feeling—Standing Isn't Enough" In December 1970, visiting Warsaw to sign a treaty recognizing Poland's postwar borders, West German chancellor Willy Brandt laid a wreath and then knelt before a monument to the Warsaw Ghetto uprising (p. 510). His kneeling came to be seen as repentance both for the Holocaust and for the havoc wreaked by Nazi armies throughout eastern Europe, and hence as a decisive contribution to détente. Today the deed is itself commemorated by a plaque in nearby Willy Brandt Square. Bildarchiv Preussischer Kulturbesitz/Art Resource, NY

Union dwarfed those of all its allies as well as those of its rival, China, and most of the eastern European countries remained faithful satellites of Moscow. In the West, the dominance of the United States was less oppressive. Most western European countries saw no need to challenge U.S. leadership as forcefully as France, since the transatlantic relationship rested on an unwritten but well-understood bargain between the two sides. The United States would use its military power to defend its allies and even bear more than its fair share of defense costs. In all diplomatic and military matters, it would act in their interests as well as its own and consult them whenever it expected their cooperation. The allies, for their part, would accept U.S. military command, consult the United States when making major diplomatic moves, and in times of crisis, act together under U.S. leadership. Even France held to this last condition—thereby acknowledging that its security, too, depended in part on U.S. power.

Furthermore, the rivalry of the blocs continued unabated. "Détente," Brezhnev told the 1976 congress of the Soviet Communist Party, "does not in the slightest abolish and cannot abolish or alter the laws of the class struggle." On the contrary, he believed that it helped turn the worldwide "correlation of forces" in the Soviet Union's favor. In the West, meanwhile, the fear of countries "going communist" was as lively as ever. Now, however, Cold War fears and ambitions were focused on the world beyond Europe, with each side trying to steer in its favor the forces released by the end of the nineteenth-century intercontinental empires.

LO² The Liquidation of Imperial Rule

The end of the nineteenth-century empires was the other great change, besides the superpower rivalry, that came out of the Second World War.

Most of the countries that had built those empires, such as Britain, France, and Japan, had been weakened or defeated in the war. In most cases, imperial rule had produced leaders in the colonial countries who opposed imperialism in the name of Western ideas of nationalism and progress. These leaders now saw the chance to steer their nations to independence.

Sometimes the imperial countries resisted the demand for independence, and the result was brutal wars of colonial liberation. For the most part, however, the empires now seemed no longer a source of strength and prosperity for their owners but an economic and military burden. As for the superpowers, though they both had their own imperialist traditions, they opposed the practice of imperialism by anyone else. For all these reasons, the colonial empires mostly disappeared over about twenty years between the late 1940s and the 1960s (see photo).

Decolonization was not just a struggle between the colonial peoples and the imperial countries, however. Often it involved bitter conflicts among the colonial peoples themselves as they disputed control of the territories that the imperial countries gave up—conflicts that in many cases are still unresolved today.

The End of the British Empire

The British took the most realistic and enlightened view of decolonization, in hopes of salvaging what they could from the colonial wreckage. Already in the eighteenth century, the loss of the American colonies had taught the British that overseas empires were hard to hold together by force. In the nineteenth century, at the height of their worldwide power, the British had begun granting what amounted to independence, though with the British monarch as head of state with very limited power, to countries like Canada and Australia where the people were mostly European immigrants.

Britain's leaders now sought to follow the same policy with countries where the people were mostly non-European, changing the "British Empire" into the "British Commonwealth of Nations." They hoped thereby to keep a measure of political influence around the globe and to benefit from established ties of commerce and culture. Perhaps the best sign of the organization's success, ironically, is the fact that the word "British" was eventually dropped from its name. The many formerly colonial nations that belonged to the Commonwealth valued it enough to want to feel that it was their common property, not that of any one member.

(above, center) **From the Gold Coast to Ghana** By 1900, after many fierce wars, Britain conquered a West African colony known by the European name of its shoreline, the Gold Coast. After 1945 more peaceful resistance revived, Britain made concessions, and independence came swiftly in 1957. The former colony had large stocks of colonial stamps still on hand, which it overprinted with its new name—that of a medieval African empire, Ghana. As Ghanaians sent out their mail, they could rejoice in their change of status. Brendan Howard/Shutterstock

India and Pakistan

The freeing of India from British rule was the largest single step in the ending of colonialism. With its 400 million inhabitants, India had by far the largest population of any territory of the British Empire, and a mass organization opposed to British rule, the Indian National Congress, had grown up there before the First World War. After the war, the organization's most prominent leader was Mohandas Gandhi, whose nonviolent methods of resistance, combining Hindu religious principles with Western methods of agitation and propaganda, made him revered in India, respected by the British, and admired around the world as the *Mahatma* (the Great Soul).

Shortly before the Second World War, India was granted limited self-rule, and at the war's end, the Congress insisted on full independence. But India lay on the boundary between the worlds of Hinduism and Islam, and as British rule weakened, the Muslim regions were unwilling to join a Hindu-ruled state. Finally, in hopes of avoiding civil war, the British agreed in 1947 to divide India into two independent states. The larger, mainly Hindu portion of the subcontinent kept the name of India. Two smaller, mainly Muslim portions formed the state of Pakistan (Map 29.2).

Even so, tens of thousands of Muslims and Hindus, dissatisfied with the terms of the division, launched reciprocal atrocities and expulsions. In the course of the troubles, Gandhi himself was murdered by a Hindu extremist who considered him too easy on the Muslims. There was bitter fighting over the northern territory of Kashmir, where a Hindu prince, who had ruled a majority Muslim population under ultimate British control, handed over his authority to India. In 1949, the territory was divided along a cease-fire line that has remained in place ever since, but this has not prevented many disputes and armed conflicts between India and its unwilling Kashmiri citizens, as well as between India and Pakistan.

The two territories of Pakistan, one in the west and the other in the east of the subcontinent, were separated by nearly 1,000 miles. In 1971, the eastern territory rebelled against the central government, which was located in the west. After months of fighting, the rebels established an independent state, Bangladesh. This poor, war-torn land thereafter depended on aid from India and other outside powers. The remaining state of Pakistan encountered stubborn difficulties in achieving stability, arising out of the conflict with India, ethnic divisions, political corruption, and the rise of Islamic fundamentalism (p. 617).

Independent India's leading statesman was Gandhi's close associate Jawaharlal Nehru, a graduate of Cambridge University who shared much of the way of thinking of anti-imperialist and

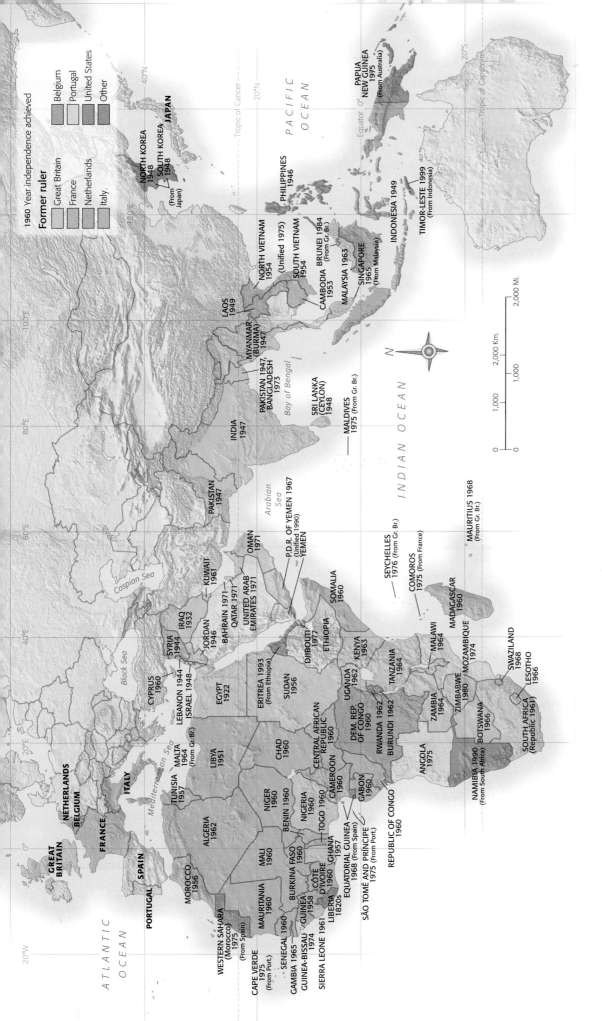

Map 29.2 Decolonization in Asia and Africa

In much of Asia and the Middle East, decolonization came swiftly after the war: 12 of 24 countries ruled by western European countries, Japan, and the United States gained independence between 1944 and 1948, though Russia held its Asian domain until 1991 (see Map 31.1 on page 587). In Africa, decolonization started later but was even swifter: 36 out of 51 countries, or nearly three-quarters, gained independence between 1956 and 1968. © Cengage Learning

 Interactive Map

Map legend

1960 Year independence achieved

Former ruler

Great Britain	Belgium
France	Portugal
Netherlands	United States
Italy	Other

Map labels

GREAT BRITAIN
FRANCE
SPAIN
PORTUGAL
NETHERLANDS
BELGIUM
ITALY

ATLANTIC OCEAN
PACIFIC OCEAN
INDIAN OCEAN

Caspian Sea
Black Sea
Mediterranean Sea
Arabian Sea
Bay of Bengal

Tropic of Cancer
Tropic of Capricorn
Equator

NORTH KOREA 1948
SOUTH KOREA 1948 (From Japan)
JAPAN
PHILIPPINES 1946
TIMOR-LESTE 1999 (From Indonesia)
PAPUA NEW GUINEA 1975 (From Australia)
INDONESIA 1949
BRUNEI 1984 (From Gr. Br.)
SINGAPORE 1965 (From Malaysia)
MALAYSIA 1963
CAMBODIA 1953
SOUTH VIETNAM 1954
NORTH VIETNAM 1954 (Unified 1975)
LAOS 1949
MYANMAR (BURMA) 1947
PAKISTAN 1947, BANGLADESH 1973
SRI LANKA (CEYLON) 1948
MALDIVES 1975 (From Gr. Br.)
INDIA 1947
PAKISTAN 1947

P.D.R. OF YEMEN 1967
YEMEN (Unified 1990)
OMAN 1971
UNITED ARAB EMIRATES 1971
QATAR 1971
BAHRAIN 1971
KUWAIT 1961
IRAQ 1932
JORDAN 1946
SYRIA 1944
LEBANON 1944
ISRAEL 1948
CYPRUS 1960
MALTA 1964 (From Gr. Br.)
EGYPT 1922
LIBYA 1951
TUNISIA 1957
ALGERIA 1962
MOROCCO 1956
WESTERN SAHARA 1975 (Morocco) (From Spain)

MAURITANIA 1960
MALI 1960
NIGER 1960
CHAD 1960
SUDAN 1956
ERITREA 1993 (From Ethiopia)
DJIBOUTI 1977
ETHIOPIA
SOMALIA 1960
KENYA 1963
UGANDA 1962
CENTRAL AFRICAN REPUBLIC 1960
CAMEROON 1960
NIGERIA 1960
BENIN 1960
BURKINA FASO 1960
TOGO 1960
GHANA 1957
COTE D'IVOIRE 1960
LIBERIA 1820s
GUINEA 1958
GUINEA-BISSAU 1974
SIERRA LEONE 1961
SENEGAL 1960
GAMBIA 1965
CAPE VERDE 1975 (From Port.)
EQUATORIAL GUINEA 1968 (From Spain)
SÃO TOMÉ AND PRÍNCIPE 1975 (From Port.)
GABON 1960
REPUBLIC OF CONGO 1960
DEM. REP. OF CONGO 1960
RWANDA 1962
BURUNDI 1962
TANZANIA 1964
MALAWI 1964
ZAMBIA 1964
ANGOLA 1975
MOZAMBIQUE 1974
ZIMBABWE 1980
BOTSWANA 1966
NAMIBIA 1990 (From South Africa)
SOUTH AFRICA (Republic 1961)
SWAZILAND 1968
LESOTHO 1966
MADAGASCAR 1960
COMOROS 1975 (From France)
SEYCHELLES 1976 (From Gr. Br.)
MAURITIUS 1968 (From Gr. Br.)

Scale

0   1,000   2,000 Km.
0   1,000   2,000 Mi.

N

20°W 0° 20°E 40°E 60°E 80°E 100°E 120°E
20°N 40°N

left-wing Westerners. He wanted India to become a British-style parliamentary democracy with a partly capitalist, partly government-run economy such as moderate European socialists called for, a secular state in which the distinction of Hindu and Muslim would no longer matter, and a great power that would command respect in both the Free World and the Socialist Camp without belonging to either. Ethnic and religious strife within the country's borders, conflict with Pakistan, rivalry and actual warfare with China, rural poverty, and unbridled capitalism have made the reality of India fall short of Nehru's ideal. Even so, independent India has made itself into a rising military and industrial power and a federal democracy with a population nearly four times that of the United States.

The Middle East and the Arab-Israeli Conflict

In the Middle East as in the Indian subcontinent, the end of the British Empire led to lengthy feuding among the peoples it formerly ruled—above all in Palestine (Map 29.3). In ancient times, the territory had been the homeland of the Jews, but under Roman rule, the Jews became a minority there, and after the rise of Islam, most of the population were Arabs.

When the British took control from the dissolving Turkish Empire at the close of the First World War, they opened the way for Jews to return, inspired by the Zionist ideal of reestablishing their "national home." Zionism as an organized movement had appeared in Europe at the turn of the century (p. 470). It was seen by many Jews as the only permanent solution to their age-old problem of repeated persecution and discrimination in Christian states. During the First World War, the British cabinet had responded to Zionist appeals by promising support for a national home in Palestine (the Balfour Declaration of 1917).

Following the Nazi extermination of two-thirds of Europe's Jews a generation later, the need for a place of refuge seemed even more desperate; thousands of Jews (chiefly from central and eastern Europe) made their twentieth-century exodus to the "Promised Land." The Arabs of Palestine (and elsewhere) saw this migration as a new form of Western imperialism. They believed the Jews, with their European ways, to be an expansionist colony on the Arab shore.

Violence broke out between Jewish and Arab armed factions in 1946; there were also terrorist acts, by both sides, against each other and the British. Two years later, Britain withdrew, and the United Nations voted for an independent Palestine, divided into two separate states, Arab (Palestine) and Jewish (Israel). Many Arab states of the Middle East and North Africa, newly liberated from British and French rule, refused to accept this division and joined with the Palestinians in unsuccessfully trying to overthrow the new state of Israel.

 **Israel Founded** Learn more about the founding of Israel.

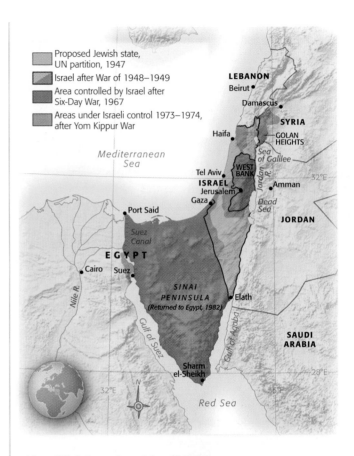

- Proposed Jewish state, UN partition, 1947
- Israel after War of 1948–1949
- Area controlled by Israel after Six-Day War, 1967
- Areas under Israeli control 1973–1974, after Yom Kippur War

Map 29.3 Israel and Its Neighbors

The map traces modern Israel's growth from a Jewish foothold centered on the Mediterranean coast to a state possessing or occupying much of the territory of ancient Israel at its largest (Map 2.2 on page 38). But the main centers of Jewish population remained in coastal regions, and Israel's rivals for "ownership" of the Holy Land, the Palestinians, held out in Gaza and in the inland region, the West Bank, where ancient Israel had first arisen. © Cengage Learning

Interactive Map

"Independent India has made itself into a rising military and industrial power and a federal democracy with a population nearly four times that of the United States."

During the war, Israeli forces expelled many Palestinians, and afterward the Israeli government refused reentry to many more who had left to avoid the fighting. Most ended in refugee camps in Palestine and surrounding territories, where their descendants still live today. Only one Arab country, Jordan, was willing to give Palestinian refugees full citizenship, though in any case, the Palestinians had an interest in maintaining a separate identity so as to keep their claim on Palestine. Meanwhile, many Jews fled government harassment and mob violence in Arab countries and settled mostly in Israel.

The Jewish state gained recognition from most non-Arab nations, and defended its existence against continuing Arab pressures and threats. It soon found allies—to begin with, Britain and France, which were eager to keep what they could of their influence in the Middle East. In 1956, the three countries tried to overthrow Gamal Abdel Nasser, the nationalist leader of Egypt, who had sponsored guerrilla attacks against Israel, nationalized the British-owned Suez Canal, and helped the Algerian revolt against French rule. But the attempt came to nothing because the United States and the Soviet Union, both of which opposed any continuation of European imperial power, pressured all three nations to call off the war.

The Suez affair was an important moment not only in the Middle East, but also in the changing balance of world power in general. From Suez, the French drew the lesson that Britain and the United States were not to be relied on, so that France could never again exercise worldwide influence except as a member of the European Community. The British decided that they would never again act independently of the United States, but that they also needed to be part of Europe. Israel decided that in future, it must rely for its survival, apart from itself, on the United States alone. All three countries have held to these decisions ever since.

> *"The wind of change is blowing through this continent. Whether we like it or not, this growth of national consciousness is a political fact."*
>
> —Prime Minister Harold Macmillan, 1960

Africa

The failure at Suez also hastened the departure of the British from the continent that held the largest proportion of their empire's land area. The British granted freedom to the Gold Coast (Ghana) in 1957 and to Nigeria in 1960. In the same year, the British prime minister told the South African parliament: "The wind of change is blowing through this continent. Whether we like it or not, this growth of national consciousness is a political fact." In acknowledgment of that fact, by the end of the 1960s, most of Britain's other African territories were independent members of the Commonwealth (see Map 29.2).

In some African territories of the British Empire, the end of imperialism was slowed by the fact that the European population did not consist only of officials and soldiers who could easily be withdrawn. There were also communities of European settlers who were unwilling either to leave countries that had become their homes or to give up their position as privileged elites. In Kenya, the result was what amounted to a vicious civil war between white settlers and "Mau Mau" rebels. The British crushed the rebellion partly by force but also by concessions to Africans that in 1963 led on to independence. In Southern Rhodesia a few years later, Britain was from the start determined to liquidate imperial rule even over the opposition of settlers. The settler leader Ian Smith declared independence from Britain in 1965, and held power for fifteen years against international economic sanctions and an African insurgency. In 1980, the Smith government collapsed, and an African government headed by the former guerrilla chief Robert Mugabe took over in what was now called Zimbabwe, after an ancient city of the region.

Of all the African territories of the British Empire, the one that had the largest white population was South Africa. Originally, the territory had been a Dutch colony, but in the course of the French revolutionary wars, it came under British rule. Thanks to its resources of gold, diamonds, and coal, it developed into the wealthiest and most advanced country in Africa south of the Sahara. The business elite and professional classes were mainly of British origin, but a larger population of working-class and farm-owning Afrikaners ("Africans" of Dutch origin) ran the government through their elected representatives.

This arrangement was at the expense of the native Africans, Indian immigrants, and "Coloureds" of mixed race, who outnumbered whites by ten to one. The better jobs and advanced education were reserved for whites, and very few nonwhites were able to vote. As was inevitable in an industrial society, nonwhites made gains all the same, and in the late 1940s, radical Afrikaner politicians came to power who were determined to hold the nonwhites down. The new leaders institutionalized the privileges of whites in the system of **apartheid (uh-PAHRT-heyt)** (separateness), which prohibited interracial marriage, mandated residential segregation, deprived black Africans of permanent residential rights outside their tribal "homelands," and obliged them to carry "passes"—identification documents that were used to track their employment and movements. The main African political organization, the African National Congress, was banned in 1960. Its leader, Nelson Mandela, was convicted of sabotage in 1964 and spent the next quarter of a century in prison. Apartheid violated the values of the by now multiracial Commonwealth, and in 1961, South Africa withdrew from the Commonwealth to avoid being excluded. For another quarter of a century, while empires collapsed around it, South Africa held out as a democracy for whites and a police state for most nonwhites.

apartheid
In South Africa, a policy of segregation and discrimination based on race.

 Apartheid Museum (http://www.apartheidmuseum.org/) Explore the history of apartheid in this online museum.

The End of Other European Empires

In contrast to the British, the French at first attempted to bring their colonies into closer political association. They offered them membership in a "French Union," which integrated overseas territories with continental France. This approach proved a failure; it appealed only to a limited number of colonial subjects who had been educated in French schools and who had come to respect and admire French culture. Moreover, Charles de Gaulle, who led the Free French movement during the Second World War, had promised the colonies that assisted him a free choice of status after peace was won. They chose independence, though most of them joined the French Community, a short-lived association that resembled the British Commonwealth. Regardless of their political choice, the former French territories in Africa have continued to rely heavily on French military aid, investment, and trade.

 **Third World Advocate Decries Colonized Peoples' Loss of Identity** Read an analysis of the effect of French colonial rule on the people of Antilles.

In two areas—Algeria, where there was a large minority of European settlers, and Indochina, where the independence leaders were communists—the French resorted to war in a vain attempt to hold power. After brutal fighting and heavy losses, they were at last compelled to withdraw from both. Algeria became independent in 1962. Portions of Indochina—Laos and Cambodia (now known as Kampuchea [**kam-poo-CHEE-ah**]) gained independence from France in 1954, but the remainder—Vietnam—was temporarily divided by an international conference into a communist-ruled north, with its capital in Hanoi, and a noncommunist south, ruled from Saigon. The two halves soon fell into a prolonged and bloody civil war, and now that the French had given up, the United States took up the struggle and intervened to forestall an expected communist victory in the southern half of the country (p. 573).

The smaller colonial nations—the Netherlands, Belgium, and Portugal—tried to regain or hold on to their colonies after the Second World War. The Dutch, who had lost their rich holdings in the East Indies to Japanese forces in 1942, sought to reestablish their control. But they were compelled in 1949 to recognize the newly formed state of Indonesia, with a population of nearly 100 million. Belgium made little preparation for the transition of the Belgian Congo to independence, but in 1960, the rising tide of nationalism forced the Belgians to agree to freedom—without adequate preparation. The result was temporary chaos, followed by the formation of the independent state of Zaire (later renamed the Democratic Republic of Congo) under military rule (see Map 29.2).

The Portuguese were determined to keep their grip on the vast southern African territories of Angola and Mozambique, which they continued to view as part of Portugal. The African resistance forces, however, through guerrilla tactics, at last broke the will of the colonial masters. Portuguese commanders in the field, observing the futility of their own military efforts, brought about a turnover in the imperial home government in Lisbon. The new Portuguese government, veering toward the political left, granted independence to both these territories in 1975. In both countries, independence was followed by many years of war. Rival ideological and tribal factions endlessly fought each other, the white Southern Rhodesian and South African governments intervened against African resistance movements based in Angola and Mozambique, and the United States, the Soviet Union, and Cuba helped opposing groups with troops and supplies.

Racial Equality in the United States

One of the justifications for nineteenth-century imperialism had been the idea of the superiority of the white race over the other races of the world. The nonwhite races, imperialists argued, were incapable of governing themselves on the Western level, or at least they would need many decades or even centuries of white rule before they were up to the task.

These ideas had always been contested even in the imperialist countries, and the Nazi atrocities had shown the horrors to which racism could lead. After the Second World War, the fact that so many white imperial countries were losing their empires made it hard to claim that peoples of European origin were in some way superior to other peoples of the world. As a result, the idea of white racial superiority ceased to be respectable even among whites themselves, and social and political orders based on this idea came to be recognized as oppressive.

Among the countries that were most affected by this result of decolonization was the United States. Its overseas empire—that is, the countries that it directly ruled, as opposed to those that it indirectly influenced—had never been large, and some of those countries, such as the Philippines, had already won independence before the Second World War. But unlike every other imperialist country, the United States had itself come into being as a result of European expansion. It had wrested its actual home territory from earlier inhabitants as well as from the rival European-dominated state of Mexico, and within that territory, it had practiced slavery on a massive scale.

Accordingly, racism and racial oppression had a long history within the borders of the United States, directed first of all against Native Americans, then against conquered Hispanic populations and Asian immigrants. But the most visible victims have been African Americans. The end of slavery as a result of the Civil War was followed by reconciliation between the northern and southern states at the expense of the former slaves, who became free but second-class citizens in the South, and massive early-twentieth-century migration brought racial resentment and segregation to the cities of the North. It was not until the middle of the twentieth century that African Americans began to move toward equality with whites in civil, political, social, and economic affairs.

The change began in 1954 with a landmark decision of the U.S. Supreme Court, *Brown v. Board of Education of Topeka*, putting an end to the earlier principle of "separate but equal" education for black children and calling for progressive integration of the races in public-supported schools and colleges. The decision was bitterly resisted by whites in many communities, but by 1970, it appeared to have been widely accepted in principle. Meanwhile, black leaders worked harder than ever to end separate seating in transportation and public service

 Civil Rights Movement Veterans (http://www.crmvet.org/) Learn more about the Civil Rights movement through the stories of its activists.

The Cleveland Avenue Bus This is the vehicle in which one of the founding events of the U.S. civil rights movement took place in Montgomery, Alabama in 1955: the refusal of Rosa Parks to give up her seat to a white man. The photo in front of the bus shows Parks at a commemorative ceremony in 2001, but her deed was recognized as historic much earlier. Already in 1970, the bus was auctioned off to the museum that currently holds it for no less than $400,000.

facilities and to place more blacks on voter registration rolls. These efforts, backed by sit-ins, boycotts, mass demonstrations, and civil disobedience, proved largely successful during the 1960s (see photo). In the forefront of the drive were aggressive legal actions guided by the National Association for the Advancement of Colored People (NAACP) and the leadership of the Baptist minister Dr. Martin Luther King Jr.

King stood squarely for full integration of the races, equal opportunity, and nonviolence. In the late 1960s, however, some of the younger members of the black community began to fall away from his leadership. Blacks still endured poor food and housing, especially in the urban ghettos, and unequal opportunity for jobs, health care, and schooling. Some concluded that more forceful methods were needed to persuade the white power structure that more must be done for blacks. Cries arose for "black power," militancy, and violence. The police became a particular target of hatred; in the eyes of most blacks, they patrolled black neighborhoods like soldiers of an occupying army. Clashes with the police sometimes erupted into riots, burnings, and lootings—such as

those in the Watts neighborhood of Los Angeles (1965) and in Detroit and Washington (1967). A "white backlash," meanwhile, heightened racist feelings and sharpened the "law and order" issue in the country. Police forces were enlarged and more heavily armed; they sought out militants like the Black Panthers, kept them under surveillance, raided their headquarters, and often brought court charges against their leaders. The assassination of Martin Luther King in 1968 brought renewed disturbances, but in death, the murdered leader, like Gandhi in India, became the symbol of a nation's highest aspirations.

Business recessions have borne most heavily on nonwhites, especially the young, in spite of "affirmative action" programs designed to employ more minorities in industry and public service. In any case, the white majority of the country resented these programs as "reverse discrimination" and supported moves to repeal them. Nevertheless, the result of civil rights and affirmative action was also the growth of a large and prosperous black middle class, as well as a growth in political and government power, especially at the local level, with African American mayors elected in many large cities—notably, Detroit, Los Angeles, Philadelphia, Atlanta, and Washington, D.C.

 Listen to a synopsis of Chapter 29.

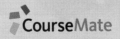

CHAPTER 30

SHIFTING VALUES, THOUGHT, AND ART:
THE SIXTIES AND AFTER

LEARNING OBJECTIVES

AFTER READING THIS CHAPTER, YOU SHOULD BE ABLE TO DO THE FOLLOWING:

LO¹ Describe the attitudes and goals of the sixties counterculture.

LO² Trace the shift in gender relations that accelerated in the sixties.

LO³ Identify the different ways that the Christian churches responded to social and moral shifts.

LO⁴ Discuss the Postmodern outlook.

LO⁵ Identify key trends in Postmodern art and architecture.

"WESTERN PEOPLES CAME TO LOOK BACK ON THE SIXTIES AS A WATERSHED IN MANY BASIC FEATURES OF BEHAVIOR AND CULTURE."

In the decade of the 1960s, some of the shifts in Western values and culture that had been going on since the nineteenth century reached a point of no return. Ideals and artistic styles that had been mainly those of social outsiders and cultural avant-gardes suddenly gained greater influence over Western societies than before. True, there was no complete break with the Western past. The new values and cultural forms were passionately contested, and as they became widespread in society, they were often diluted and combined with traditional ways. All the same, in the half-century that followed what came to be called "the sixties," Western peoples came to look back on the decade as a watershed in many basic features of behavior and culture.

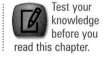

Test your knowledge before you read this chapter.

Perhaps the most far-reaching changes that spread through Western societies in the sixties concerned sexual behavior and family life. The unequal balance of status and power between men and women that seemingly arose with the Agricultural Revolution began to shift faster than before, and single parenthood and homosexuality claimed acceptance as part of the social order alongside heterosexuality and marriage. These changes originated long before the sixties. The emancipation of women, for instance, was partly driven by vast, impersonal, and long-continued social forces—by the tide of industrialization that swept millions of women out of homes and families and deposited them in factories and offices. Yet the women's liberation movement, the latest stage of emancipation, sprang from the protest of the sixties **counterculture** against mass society in the democratic-capitalist countries, with its manipulation of individuals into accepting predetermined social roles.

What do you think?

College students are the most effective agents of cultural change in modern society.

Strongly Disagree						Strongly Agree
1	2	3	4	5	6	7

≪ "People We Like" Among the crowd on the cover of the 1967 Beatles album *Sgt. Pepper's Lonely Hearts Club Band* are Einstein, Freud, and Marx, as well as Marlon Brando, Shirley Temple, and Snow White. Several revered Hindu gurus are also present; so is the writer Aldous Huxley, publicizer of the uplifting spiritual effect of the psychedelic substance mescaline. The names suggest some of the vast range of intellectual and cultural influences that helped make the sixties.

Redferns/Getty Images

549

counterculture
A protest movement against the values and conformity of mainstream society, originating in the United States and western Europe during the sixties.

Postmodernism
A cultural movement that criticized the goals and methods of Modernism in literature and art, and more generally attacked the search for inherent truth and universal values.

Closely linked with the sixties rebellion in values and behavior was the rise of a new cultural movement, **Postmodernism**. In thought, Postmodernists denied the possibility of finding ultimate truth through either reason or faith, and instead held out the hope of human fulfillment through the liberation of inner human energies. In social life, Postmodernists opposed rules of behavior that all must obey, and highly organized power structures that required and enforced such behavior. Instead, they spoke up for groups that broke the rules or were held down by power structures, especially in the areas of gender, race, and sexuality. In literature and art, Postmodernists produced works that embodied their view of the irrationality of the world, rejected the idealized abstraction of Modernism, or proclaimed the nobility and suffering of the groups they supported.

One of the main targets of Postmodernists was Western civilization itself, since most of the cultural traditions that they criticized were Western ones. Doubting the possibility of finding truth, as well as undermining social conformity, were themselves ancient Western traditions, however, and Postmodern thought and art were mainly influential within the lands of Western civilization. For the time being, it was not clear whether the rest of the world would follow the Western shifts of the sixties, or whether the shifts would create a new division between West and non-West within global civilization.

LO¹ The Sixties Rebellion and Its Legacy

In 1960, the heartland countries of the West seemed to be evolving into comfortable consumer societies, in which capitalism and the welfare state cooperated to fulfill the Western dream of prosperity and security for all. The power structures of worldwide imperialism and of segregation in the U.S. South were beginning to crumble. Science and technology were working unheard-of miracles—transistor radios, earth-orbiting satellites, "electronic brains." Yet alongside the dream, there were also nightmares. The Second World War, with its campaigns of starvation, bombing, expulsion, and genocide, overshadowed the recent past. New wars and atrocities accompanied the weakening of imperialism and segregation. The Cold War had turned into a terrifying absurdity—a stalemate

> *"It was in this world, torn between complacency and anxiety, that the sixties rebellion was born."*

CHRONOLOGY	
1949	De Beauvoir's *The Second Sex*
1961	Jacobs's *Death and Life of American Cities*
1965	Joint Working Group links Catholic and Protestant churches in dialogue
1966	National Organization for Women founded; Foucault's *The Order of Things*
1968	Students in Paris take to the barricades
1970	Kent State students are killed during an antiwar protest; Smithson's *Spiral Jetty*
1973	*Roe v. Wade*
1977	Said's *Orientalism*
1979	Chicago's *The Dinner Party*
1984	Eco's *The Name of the Rose*

between two mighty power structures, upheld by their ability to destroy each other and the rest of the world. And capitalism and the welfare state were themselves power structures that could only work if employees fulfilled expectations, citizens obeyed bureaucrats, and consumers responded to advertising. It was in this world, torn between complacency and anxiety, that the sixties rebellion was born.

By the 1960s, many among the postwar generation felt free to create a way of life alternative and opposed to that of the society to which they were supposed to adjust—a counterculture. Though uncertain and groping, they shared some central goals: humaneness in personal relations, self-discovery and independence, sexual freedom and equality, simple enjoyments, love of nature and peace. As a badge of these beliefs, the young revolted against adult styles of dress and began to develop styles of their own. Long hair, beards, fatigue jackets, and jeans—so repugnant to older believers in clean-shaven, starch-shirted efficiency and conformity—were symbolic challenges to the established order of values. Likewise, the young tended to be suspicious of governments, corporations, and military organizations. And they often scorned intellectualism in favor of spontaneous experience.

College students formed a leading part of the larger youth culture. After the Second World War, universities had mushroomed, into vast aggregations of researchers, teachers,

THE SIXTIES REBELLION HAD ITS ROOTS IN POSTWAR DEVELOPMENTS:

Intellectual Climate

- Philosophical and psychological barriers to doubt and idol-breaking had largely dissolved under the influence of thinkers like Freud, Sartre, and Tillich.

- These thinkers encouraged authenticity and warned about repression.

Alienation from "the System"

- Children of the middle class grew up in a time of rapid economic growth that made possible widespread affluence and leisure.

- The dominant materialistic morality placed high value on competitiveness, achievement, and success.

- A substantial minority of young people believed that the system generated a great deal of hypocrisy, violence, and injustice.

- They also felt that the system expected conformity and thwarted their personal identity and expression.

and students. They represented a huge capital investment and served as the principal workshops for the production and spread of specialized knowledge. Many students saw their universities as examples of corporate bureaucracy—huge machines that reduced the individual to a number. They conceived of the university also as a service center for the larger society, turning out what German students called "specialist idiots"—technicians for business and industry, researchers for the military, and obedient servants of the state (see photo). Individual courses and curricular requirements seemed arbitrary, sterile, and lacking in "relevance" to the urgent problems of campuses and societies.

In the 1960s, student discontent turned into protest at many educational centers around the world. In Europe, the headquarters of student protest were the Free University of Berlin and the University of Paris West at Nanterre (nahn-TAIR). Both universities were new, huge, and expanding. The Free University

>> **"We Participate, They Select"** In this poster, designed in May 1968 by a student-run "People's Studio" for a French high-school student group, the educational system is a giant processing plant. A hopper receives the raw material, most of which falls straight through into a garbage bin for the "workforce." Smaller amounts of higher-level products drop into a bucket and a can, and a wine glass receives the tiny fraction that is distilled into the elite.

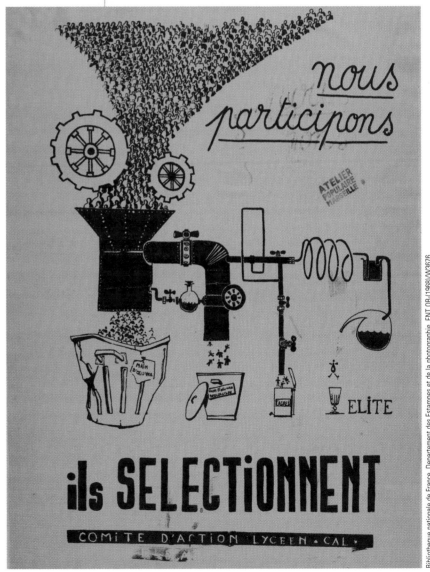

"ON STUDENT WRETCHEDNESS": PROTEST AT A FRENCH UNIVERSITY

In 1966, a scandal erupted at the University of Strasbourg, France, when left-wing students got together with radical writers and artists to produce a pamphlet "On Student Wretchedness in Its Economic, Political, Psychological, Sexual, and Particularly Its Intellectual Aspects, and Several Means for Remedying It." Students who were officers of the student union illegally used union funds to print 10,000 copies, some of which were distributed at the university's assembly marking the beginning of the academic year. The students were taken to court and the union was shut down. At the time, they were ahead of their fellow students in linking campus grievances with general social issues, but their ideas spread widely, and their pamphlet, translated into many languages, became a founding document of the international student movement.

The *École normale supérieure* (Higher School of Education) is not a teacher training college as its name suggests, but an elite school for future leaders of government, business, and the universities. The "Sorboniqueurs" are students at the Sorbonne—the University of Paris, named after its thirteenth-century benefactor Robert de Sorbon (p. 235). The UNEF is the National Union of French Students, and the FGEL is another student organization, the French Federation of Liberal Arts Groups. The "Encyclopaedists" were figures of the eighteenth-century Enlightenment who produced the *Encyclopedia*; Hegel was a thinker of the era following the Enlightenment (pp. 336, 403–404).

In their ideological existence French students come to everything too late. All the values and illusions that are the pride of their cloistered world are already doomed as untenable illusions which history has long ago made ridiculous.

Because they share a little of the University's crumbling prestige, students are still pleased to be students. Too late. The mechanical, specialized teaching they receive has fallen as abysmally low (in comparison with the former level of bourgeois general culture)[1] as their own intellectual level at the time they enter it, due to the single fact that the reality that dominates it all, the economic system, calls for mass production of untutored students incapable of thinking. Being unaware that the University has become an institutionalized organization of ignorance, that "higher education" itself is disintegrating at the same tempo that mass production of professors progresses, and that *all* of these professors are morons, most of whom would set any high school student body into an uproar, students continue, therefore, to listen respectfully to their teachers, with the conscious determination to rid themselves of all spirit of criticism, the better to commune in the mystic illusion of having become "students," i.e., persons who are seriously occupied with acquiring *serious* knowledge in

had been founded in 1948 to rival Berlin's original university, which had come under the control of the communist GDR; the vast educational complex at Nanterre, intended to cater to France's exploding student population, only opened in 1964. In addition, instead of having many buildings scattered across their cities, as was traditional for European universities, both were built on the campus pattern, newly imported from the United States. Rapid growth and isolation from the surrounding cities highlighted everything that was wrong with postwar higher education and the societies it served.

The U.S. counterpart of Berlin and Nanterre was the University of California, Berkeley—an old-established school, but one that had doubled in size since the end of the war. The Berkeley Free Speech Movement of 1964 sought a larger exercise of student political rights on campus; it also demanded (among other things) that the highly regarded and highly paid professors spend more of their time teaching students. Demonstrations,

sit-ins, and classroom "strikes" followed in support of these demands. The protests soon spread to hundreds of other U.S. campuses, and student demands were combined with demands on the nation as a whole: end the war in Vietnam (p. 573), check the power of the "military-industrial complex," stop discrimination against African Americans and other minorities. The student actions were generally led by small numbers of committed radicals, who hoped to bring on a general change of the social order. Their immediate demands, however, often won the support of moderate students as well. When college administrations overreacted, still larger numbers of students joined the action.

European student protests followed the same pattern of educational discontents leading to rebellion against the surrounding society and its governing authorities. The targets, too, were often the same: NATO, militarism, racism, the Vietnam War, and the Cold War policies of the United States. But there

the hope that they will be entrusted with ultimate truths. This is a menopause of the mind. Everything that is taking place today in school and faculty lecture halls will be condemned in the future revolutionary society as just so much socially harmful *noise*. From now on, students make people laugh.

Students don't even realize that history is also changing their absurd, "cloistered" world. The famous "crisis of the University," which is a detail of the more general crisis of modern capitalism, remains the subject of a deaf men's dialogue between different specialists. It expresses quite simply the difficulties of belated adjustment by this special production sector to overall transformation of the production apparatus. The leftovers of the old ideology of the liberal bourgeois University become commonplaces as its social basis disappears. The University could consider that it was an autonomous power at the time of free-trade capitalism and liberal government, which left it a certain marginal freedom.

It was in fact closely dependent on the needs of this type of society which were: to give a privileged minority who were pursuing studies an adequate general culture before they joined the ranks of the ruling class, which they had hardly left. Hence the ridiculous position of certain nostalgic[2] professors, embittered at having lost their former function of watchdogs of future leaders for the much less honorable one of sheep dogs leading flocks of "white collar" workers, according to the planified needs of the economic system, along the path to their respective factories and offices. They are the ones who oppose their archaic ideas to technocratization of the University and continue imperturbedly to impart scraps of the culture called "general" to future specialists who won't know what to do with it.

More serious, and therefore more dangerous, are the modernists on the left and those in the UNEF led by the "ultras" of the FGEL, who demand "structural reform of the University," "re-introduction of the University into social and economic life,"

that is to say, its adaptation to the needs of modern capitalism. From having been the dispensers of "general culture" for the use of the ruling classes, the various *facultés* [departments] and schools, still draped in anachronistic prestige, have been turned into quick-breeding factories for lower and medium cadres. So far from protesting against this historical process that directly subordinates one of the last relatively autonomous sectors of social life to the demands of the mercantile system, our progressives protest against the delays and lapses that beset its realization. They are the champions of the future cybernetically run University, which is already apparent here and there. The mercantile system and its modern hirelings are the real enemy.

EXPLORING THE SOURCE

1. What, according to the writers of the pamphlet, is the situation of mid-twentieth-century students and professors, and how has it changed over time?

2. What do the writers of the pamphlet think is wrong with the ways in which most students and professors respond to their changed situation?

Source: Used with permission of Beacon Press from The French Student Uprising by Alain Schnapp and Pierre Vidal-Naquest, eds., 1971; permission conveyed through Copyright Clearance Center, Inc.

---

[1]We do not mean the culture of the *École normale supérieure* or of the "Sorboniqueurs," but that of the Encyclopaedists, or of Hegel.

[2]Not daring to claim kinship with philistine liberalism, they invent references for themselves to the academic freedoms of the Middle Ages, which was the time of "non-freedom democracy."

---

were also local targets: British nuclear weapons; French economic policies that stressed growth and held down wages; West German public figures who were linked with the Nazi past. In West Germany, where many students had grown up in the GDR, Soviet-style dictatorship was also a target.

> **Jean-Paul Sartre Interviews Daniel Cohn-Bendit** Read the goals of the May 1968 Paris protest according to a student leader.

In the late 1960s the student movement reached its peak. There was street violence in many German cities in 1967 between police and students protesting what they claimed were unfair press attacks. In May 1968, students in Paris took to the barricades, industrial workers showed signs of joining them, and the government of General de Gaulle was nearly toppled. In the United States, the climax came in May 1970, when National Guardsmen shot and killed four students at Kent State University in Ohio who were protesting the U.S. invasion of Cambodia (p. 573).

In the 1970s, college campuses grew more peaceful. Societies beyond the campuses tended to blame protesters for violence and rejected most of their political demands. In French parliamentary elections in June 1968, President de Gaulle's party won by a landslide on the slogan of "defense of the Republic," and in November, Richard Nixon won the U.S. presidency on a "law and order" platform. Besides, for many sixties students, campus activism—like college in general—was an interlude between adolescence and the "real life" of necessary striving for jobs, families, and success. Later generations of students were intent on spending the college interlude preparing for adulthood in what they knew would be a harsher economic

Video Footage and a Report on the Paris Student Protests of May 1968 (http://news.bbc.co.uk/onthisday/hi/dates/stories/may/13/newsid_2512000/2512413.stm) Watch footage from the Paris student protests of May 1968.

sexual revolution
A change in sexual attitudes and practices toward freedom from traditional constraints, associated with the sixties.

feminism
A social movement that criticizes and seeks to change the traditional economic, political, and social status of women and advocates for gender equality.

climate. The tradition of countercultural protest persisted in the environmental and antiglobalization movements of the 1980s and 1990s, but it was no longer at center stage of politics and national affairs as in the sixties.

LO² The Shifting Balance of Gender

In spite of rejecting the student movement's political demands, society beyond the campuses was beginning to value the freedoms of lifestyle that the students had asserted. Students themselves often took these freedoms with them as they left the campuses. In many fields of business and industry, sixties-style clothing became accepted attire, and turning up for work in a suit and tie became as eccentric as appearing in blue jeans would once have been. That was a telling sign that the counterculture was beginning to merge with the society against which it protested.

In addition, the counterculture acted as a catalyst for general social changes that were in any case under way. Among the most visible of these were new sexual attitudes and practices—the "sexual revolution."

The Sexual Revolution

Many long-term shifts contributed to this change. The transition from an economy based on households to one based on factories and offices made it less necessary for people to restrain their feelings and desires in the interests of family survival. Cultural movements like Romanticism and Realism celebrated the untamed passions of the heart, and condemned the hypocrisy involved in upholding the traditional rules. The world wars and other horrors of the twentieth century eroded people's confidence in traditional restraints, while the rise of consumer society made the pursuit of pleasure more respectable than before. Freudian psychology identified sexual repression as a source of neurosis, and the belief grew up that freeing the sexual impulse was necessary for mental and psychological health. After the Second World War, the walls of literary censorship were leveled in nearly every Western nation; in 1960, science produced a convenient new method of birth control, the "pill"; and in the next few years, student movements in many countries included among their demands an end to separate dormitories for men and women. The era of sexual liberation was at hand.

In some ways, however, the breakdown of sexual restraints disappointed its idealistic supporters. People who hoped that it would be part of a general lightening of social pressures were disappointed. On the contrary, it provided a new means for advertisers to manipulate consumers, and helped turn "soft-core" and "hard-core" pornography into growth industries. In the United States, one of the first symptoms of this development was the rise of the magazine *Playboy*, first issued in 1953. Its self-made publisher, Hugh Hefner, also built a thriving entertainment business around his magazine, geared to the theme of guilt-free sensual enjoyment—of women by men.

This development was linked with another disturbing result of the sexual revolution that surfaced in the student counterculture—that the men often treated the women in traditional fashion as underlings in the movement, but with the loosening of sexual restraints, now also regarded them as easily "available." Among the many kinds of liberation that the movement proclaimed, calls began to be heard for "women's liberation"; and this in turn helped catalyze another change that had been a long time in the making: a new shift in the general balance of status and power between women and men.

The Women's Movement

Between the end of the First World War and the middle of the twentieth century, the long-term changes making for this shift had continued. Women worked outside the home and attended universities in greater numbers; improved contraceptive devices, especially ones whose use was under women's control like the pill, began to bring an end to the frequent pregnancies that had kept women at home ever since the Agricultural Revolution (p. 10).

In addition, feminist critics began to chip away at the image of woman as basically different from and inferior to man. In *The Second Sex*, published in 1949, the French author Simone de Beauvoir **(duh bo-VWAH)** distinguished between "sex" and "gender"—between the unchanging biological differences between women and men, and the shifting images and roles that societies create for them. Two thousand years before, Plato had claimed that women and men have the same general capacities, but that the belief in women's inferiority was necessary for real-world families and societies (pp. 75–76). Now, as the real world was in any case changing, feminists proclaimed that families and societies must define the genders as equal and act on that definition.

The Second Sex: Existential Feminism Read an excerpt from *The Second Sex*.

In the United States, the key work that undermined the traditional image of woman was Betty Friedan's *The Feminine Mystique*, published in 1963. She pointed to the social and psychological pressures that kept women in the home, the false notions about female sexuality, and the persisting stereotypes of female intellect and behavior. Friedan became a political activist in order to further her cause: she was one of the founders of the National Organization for Women (NOW) in 1966. Though much of the organization's inspiration came from advocates of "women's liberation" within the counterculture, it soon developed into a powerful interest group operating like any other within the politics of the wider society.

History of NOW (http://www.now.org/history/) Learn more about the founding and history of NOW.

Like all new and powerful social forces, the women's movement has provoked opposition—from women as well as from men. In the United States, its single most ambitious undertaking, the passage of an Equal Rights Amendment to the U.S. Constitution, has still not become law—partly because many women feared that it might take away from them such existing advantages as exemption from military conscription and protective laws in hazardous occupations. In the field of abortion rights—for feminists, a matter of a woman's right to control her own body—the U.S. women's movement has been more successful. It was lawyers linked with the movement who brought the *Roe* v. *Wade* case that led the U.S. Supreme Court to declare the criminalization of abortion unconstitutional in 1973—a decision that still stands, though it has been a mobilizing issue in conservative politics ever since.

In any case, in the last quarter of the twentieth century, gender equality, in the sense of the right and duty of both women and men to fill any and every role in the family and society, has become a generally accepted Western value. Like all generally accepted values, this one is often violated in practice. But the automatic identification of women with domesticity is now frowned on, harassment and discrimination in the workplace bring legal consequences, and Westerners often pride themselves on their shift to gender equality as a sign that they are still ahead of the rest of the world. Furthermore, two women have in recent times risen to supreme power in Western democracies, Margaret Thatcher in Britain and Angela Merkel in Germany—and these successors of Winston Churchill and Otto von Bismarck (pp. 416–417, 506–507) both belong to conservative parties. The values of the women's movement, which began on the countercultural left, have moved rightward to pervade Western societies.

> *"It made no sense for Christians to stress their disagreements when their influence in many societies seemed to be melting away."*

Homosexuality

The Western shifts on sexuality and gender encouraged the rise of another social movement, "gay liberation." Homosexuals, historically subject to contempt and abuse, called for the right to live freely according to their own sexual natures. In the 1970s, gay men and lesbians sought changes in laws and institutional practices that would prohibit acts of discrimination against them. Because their aims ran counter to traditional moral teachings and ingrained social attitudes, the movement to win public acceptance for sexual diversity encountered fierce hostility.

This feeling was intensified in the 1980s by the sudden appearance of a mysterious sexually transmitted disease that at the time seemed mainly to affect homosexual men. Eventually named the acquired immunodeficiency syndrome (AIDS), the disease was usually fatal. In the 1990s, however, the AIDS threat receded in advanced Western societies as drugs to manage the disease were developed, and the general level of tolerance for male and female homosexuality seems to have increased. Fierce conflicts have continued, especially in the United States, over such issues as "gays in the military," and more recently over gay marriage. But these conflicts are also signs that the gay and lesbian movement is following the same path as the women's movement. Originally countercultural, it now seeks recognition for its members as full participants in some very traditional activities of mainstream society: family, marriage, and warfare.

LO³ Christianity in a Changing World

The late-twentieth-century shifts in values and behavior created a crisis of decision for the traditional guardians of Western belief and morality, the Christian churches. In some ways, the crisis was a familiar one. For 2,000 years, the churches had proclaimed the belief in an unalterable truth and unchanging standards of behavior within societies that had constantly changed, and many times, they had had to decide whether and how much to adjust their beliefs and practices accordingly. Yet the changes that societies were now undergoing, for example in the balance of status and power between men and women, were without precedent in the era since Christianity had arisen—and the churches, as ever, were very much part of these societies. How far could the churches follow the new social and moral shifts?

United Responses

One thing on which most Christian churches were agreed was that the time had come to end their mutual hostility. Their theological disagreements persisted, but all of them were challenged, as never before, by the antireligious ideology of Marxism; by the pleasure-seeking values of consumer society; and by the sixties rebellion against traditional rules of sexuality and gender. It made no sense for Christians to stress their disagreements when their influence in many societies seemed to be melting away.

 **World Council of Churches Website** (http://www.oikoumene.org/en/home.html) Learn more about the activities of the World Council of Churches.

On the Protestant side, an important step was taken in 1948 when the World Council of Churches was formally established at Geneva, Switzerland. It included most Protestant churches, as well as Anglicans and Orthodox groups. The Catholic Church, holding to its claim to ultimate authority over all Christians, did not join the council, which would have made it merely one among a group of equals. In 1965, however, Rome and Geneva formed a permanent Joint Working Group that linked them closely together.

In addition, most churches have successfully decolonized themselves: non-Westerners now routinely become ministers, priests, bishops, and cardinals—and are mostly active on the conservative side of disputes within the churches arising from the sixties changes in the West. And most churches have undergone an important change of language: in the Catholic Church, from Latin to present-day tongues; and in the Protestant churches, from the language forms of the Reformation era (such as "thou" and "thee' in English) to those of today (such as "you"). In this way, Christianity has renounced some of its reverence-inspiring antiquity for the sake of identifying with the fast-moving present.

Divided Responses: Protestants

In other ways, however, the churches have been divided in their responses to the present-day changes. "Conservative" Protestants generally upheld their traditional belief in the literal truth and unchanging applicability of the Bible in every field—"In the beginning, God created the heaven and the earth"; "Wives, submit yourselves unto your own husbands, as unto the Lord"; "Let your women keep silence in the churches." "Liberal" Protestants, who were in any case more willing than conservatives to shrink the area of unchanging Christian belief, generally accepted many of the late-twentieth-century shifts in society. Women, for instance, moved from the important role they had occupied since the Reformation as ministers' wives (p. 315) to become ministers in their own right.

The divide between "liberal" and "conservative" ran right through some churches, and in the Anglican Church in the early twenty-first century, it threatened to turn into outright schism. In the predominantly liberal U.S. church, an openly gay man and an openly lesbian woman were elected bishops, and bishops in Africa and Asia issued strongly worded condemnations, refused to recognize the unwelcome bishops, or declared North America a "mission area."

Divided Responses: Catholics

About half the world's Christians belonged to the Catholic Church, which in the nineteenth and early twentieth centuries had seen itself mainly as a bulwark of divinely upheld stability in an era of chaos. In the middle of the twentieth century, however, the Church began its encounter with a changing world—especially after the election of Pope John XXIII in 1958. The new pontiff undertook a sweeping program of what he called *aggiornamento* (ad-jorn-a-MEN-toe)—"updating." This included a fresh attitude of humility and affection toward the "separated brethren" (no longer "heretics")—and toward "men of good will" beyond the fold (no longer "atheists"). In his encyclical *Pacem in Terris* (Peace on Earth), issued in 1963, the pope called for the harmonious coexistence of all faiths and social systems.

Like earlier popes who had wanted to make wide-ranging

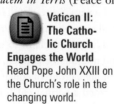 **Vatican II: The Catholic Church Engages the World**
Read Pope John XXIII on the Church's role in the changing world.

changes in the Church, Pope John also determined to summon all the bishops to a council whose decisions they would then put into effect. The Second Vatican Council (1963–1965) eventually met under John's successor Pope Paul VI. Among other measures of *aggiornamento*, it decreed the use of present-day languages in church services; ordained that priests should face believers while celebrating Mass, as a sign of unity between clergy and laity; and renounced the traditional Christian condemnation of the Jews. Pope Paul himself dramatized the new openness of the papacy by breaking its historic confinement to Rome and making visits to such places as the Holy Land, India, Latin America, and the United Nations headquarters in New York.

But the era of the Vatican Council was also the era of the sixties, and the changes of that decade raised difficult new problems. For most of its 2,000 years, the Church had been a highly organized power structure to which its members were expected to conform—and conformity within power structures was exactly what sixties rebels most detested. For 2,000 years, too, the Church had valued virginity and celibacy—and sixties rebels identified virginity and celibacy with unhealthy sexual repression. The Catholic Church was deeply interwoven with the societies in which it operated, and in the Western heartland countries, millions of believers—including priests, monks, and nuns—were influenced by or actually took part in the sixties rebellion. Laypeople began to openly protest against the Church's prohibition of contraception, recruitment to the priesthood began to dry up, and priests, monks, and nuns began to give up their calling. For all his openness to the world, in these respects Pope Paul held to the Church's traditions, and Catholics in turn began to divide between "liberals" and "conservatives," with the pope tending more and more to the conservative side.

In 1978, Pope Paul was followed by two popes in the same year, both of whom took the name of John Paul—combining the names of the pope of *aggiornamento* and the pope who had held the line. That was a statement of future policy, and after the sudden death of John Paul I, it was up to John Paul II to carry it out. The new pope had been the archbishop of Cracow, in Poland—the first non-Italian elected to the office in over four hundred years. His appealing and forceful personality had enabled him to rally Catholic believers under a communist dictatorship, and would now give him the standing to define the Church's response to a changing world.

In many ways, John Paul was a pope of *aggiornamento*. He gave up the portable throne, carried by gorgeously attired bearers, that popes had used on ceremonial Vatican occasions for a thousand years. Instead, he was driven round city streets in his "popemobile," on visits to distant countries that became media superevents, both rallying Catholics and impressing millions of non-Catholics. He consistently urged national leaders to avoid war, and he approved a pastoral letter (statement to the faithful) of the U.S. Catholic bishops opposing any "first use" of nuclear arms (p. 580), and appealing for immediate international agreements to end their testing and production. He maintained friendly relations with the Protestant and Orthodox Churches, and visited the synagogue of Rome, where he spoke of the "fraternal love" that ought to unite Catholics and Jews—a precedent that his successor Pope Benedict XVI followed (see photo). And in March 2000, at Mass in Saint Peter's Basilica, he asked God's forgiveness for past sins "by children of the Church" during the entire 2,000 years of the Church's existence. He declared that this "purification of memory" was essential as the Church moved forward into the new millennium with its evangelical mission. Though not specifying individual events, he placed them in seven categories: general sins; sins in the service of truth; sins against Christian unity; against the Jews; against respect for love, peace, and cultures; against the dignity of women and minorities; and against human rights.

On the other hand, John Paul held strictly to clerical celibacy, the prohibition on the use of contraceptives, and the exclusion of women from the priesthood. He appointed bishops whom he could trust to uphold these traditions, and strongly supported groups within the Church that favored self-sacrificing com-

mitment of laypeople to a traditional Catholic life. He rallied traditional-minded Catholics against what he called the modern "culture of death," including "mercy killing," capital punishment, and abortion. The aspect of the "culture of death" that bishops, priests, and conservative believers stressed more than any other was opposition to abortion.

Late in John Paul's reign and under Benedict XVI, the Church's power structure was nevertheless undermined by an ugly scandal that surfaced first in the United States and then in many other countries: revelations of sexual abuse of children and teenagers, mainly boys, by Catholic clergy whom bishops had neither reported to the police, nor dismissed from office, nor even removed from contact with the young. Liberal Catholics, and many outside the church, blamed the scandal on the existence of a hierarchical, unmarried, all-male clergy. Conservative Catholics blamed the influence of the sexual revolution in general and the new tolerance of homosexuality in particular. Where both sides agreed was in condemning the behavior of the bishops, who had sought to maintain confidence in the clergy by covering up evildoing. Benedict himself, a renowned theological conservative who was himself alleged to have been too indulgent with evildoers as a cardinal, began accepting the resignations of bishops.

Pope and Rabbi Pope Benedict XVI is a theological conservative who as a cardinal declared that non-Christians "are in a gravely deficient situation" regarding their salvation. But he is also a pope in the post-*aggiornamento* Church and a German who has spent his life in the shadow of the Second World War. In 2009, in a synagogue in a German city, Cologne, a cantor (chanter) intones the Kaddish (mourning prayer) for victims of the Holocaust, flanked by Pope Benedict and Rabbi Natanael Teitelbaum. Oliver Berg/Getty Images

Nearly five centuries earlier, in his "Rules for Thinking with the Church" (p. 321), Ignatius Loyola had declared that in dealing with evildoing, "we must . . . never attack superiors before inferiors. The best course is to make private approach to those who have power to remedy the evil." Catholic liberals, conservatives, and the pope himself now seemed to be coming round to the view that in the changing world of the early twenty-first century, the Church could no longer follow Loyola's advice.

LO⁴ Between Protest and Affirmation: The Postmodern Outlook

In the era of the Cold War and after, Western thought and art continued to respond to and influence changes in the civilization of which they were part. Following Realism and Impressionism and then the rise of Modernism, in the late twentieth century a movement arose that came to be known as Postmodernism. Like the earlier movements, Postmodernism gave rise to bitter disputes, but its influence has been widely felt in the Western, and to a lesser extent in the non-Western, world.

Postmodernism was closely linked with the shifts in social values of the sixties—above all, with the rebellion against social structures, expectations, and elites. Ideologies that pressed the individual into the service of some universal ideal, reverence for works of art as objects separate from and above the life of their times, and the assumption that the experience of Western civilization in thought, art, and every other field should establish the norm for the human race as a whole—all these were cultural values that Postmodernism sought to undermine.

The name Postmodernism suggested that the movement it described came after Modernism, and that Modernism had therefore come to an end. In fact, however, Postmodernism took many of its features from the Modernist artistic styles and the ideologies that it criticized, as well as from earlier Western thinkers and artists back to the ancient Greeks. Postmodernism is best seen as a new phase of Modernism, and of Western thought and art in general, which has developed as the West encounters the rest of the world in the era of the birth of global civilization.

The Background of Postmodernism

One of the main themes of Western thought and art has been that of the search for a single truth about the universe and the human race—a search that has taken many different forms over the centuries. There has been the philosophical search of thinkers from Plato onward, the religious search of Jewish prophets and Christian saints, the scientific search of Newton and Darwin. These and other searchers after truth have often

and bitterly debated whether they have actually found it or not. Whatever their differences, however, Western searchers after truth have proclaimed that a single truth exists; that it is valid for the world and the human race as a whole; that all societies throughout the world ought to reflect and uphold it; and that all individuals ought to recognize and obey it.

In ancient and medieval times, Western societies had only limited power to enforce truth within their own territories, let alone in the rest of the world. But in modern times, when exploration and empire building gave Western civilization worldwide reach, and individuals became part of highly structured mass societies, Western hopes grew high of spreading knowledge of truth and making individual human behavior conform to it throughout the world.

However, there is also an opposing Western tradition of denying the existence or the possibility of finding such a truth and questioning the motives of those who search for it. Doubting philosophers since the ancient Greek Sophists have argued that truth and moral standards vary for different individuals and communities, and writers and artists from ancient Greek and Roman comic playwrights onward have endlessly celebrated the theme of desire bursting through social constraints and group boundaries (pp. 72, 107). And in the nineteenth and twentieth centuries, with their highly structured mass societies and their secular ideologies proclaiming many competing versions of universal truth, thinkers such as Nietzsche, Kierkegaard, and Sartre turned doubt and denial into outright protest against the ideas of the search for truth and the enforcement of behavior (pp. 447–448, 519–520).

In addition, proclaimers of rival ideologies themselves undermined each other's searches for truth by declaring them to be motivated by one form or another of the urge to power. Marxists claimed that the Enlightenment values of universal freedom and equality were disguises for bourgeois exploitation of the proletariat, while bourgeois opponents of Marxism insisted that the idea of the dictatorship of the proletariat actually meant the tyranny of self-appointed intellectuals. Meanwhile, science set limits to its own search for truth with the principles of relativity and uncertainty, and Freudian psychoanalysts portrayed the human personality as a battleground between the conscious mind, formed by external social pressures, and formless urges welling up from within. Postmodernism has drawn on all these sources in its own protest against the search for truth and its own celebration of liberated desire.

> **"***Postmodernism gave rise to bitter disputes, but its influence has been widely felt in the Western, and to a lesser extent in the non-Western, world.***"**

Postmodernism in Thought

Postmodernism thought originated in France in the 1960s. Like most leading Western countries at the time, France had a capitalist-democratic social order bolstered by a burgeoning consumer society. In addition, it had a powerful Communist Party, but the party was losing its revolutionary zeal to consumerism, and in any case, the Soviet dictatorship was discrediting communism as an ideal. Then came the student demonstrations of 1968. When the protests threatened to spread to workers who had been left behind by consumer society, however, the Communist Party joined forces with the government to suppress the movement.

The events of 1968 confirmed the belief of some Marxist thinkers that democracy and consumerism were means by which capitalism manipulated the masses, and that the Soviet-led international communist movement, so far from overthrowing capitalist conformism, was actually in league with it. It was among these disillusioned French Marxists that Postmodernism was born.

Foucault: Discourse, the Other, and Desire

One of the most influential pioneers of Postmodern thought was a historian, Michel Foucault (**foo-KOE**). Impressed by the power and resilience of the capitalist and democratic world order of the West but convinced that it was fundamentally oppressive, Foucault looked into the past to discover the origins of this oppression and found it in the tradition of the search for truth and the enforcement of behavior.

Foucault's criticism of this tradition, and especially of the way it has developed in modern times, was the most radical in Western history. Essentially, he turned upside down one of the basic assumptions behind the Western scientific outlook: that if we perceive the truth about something, we can control it or at least predict how it will behave. Foucault, on the contrary, made the basic assumption that how we perceive things depends on our need to control them. We develop means of *representing* (describing) them, such as written or spoken language, numbers, or pictures (all of which Foucault called *texts*), in accordance with this need for control. We then form texts into *discourses*—general systems of interpreting the world in such a way that it becomes subject to our power.

According to Foucault, one such discourse is that of truth as something outside and apart from human beings and their needs. Another is that of human beings themselves as standing outside and apart from each other and the rest of the world, and able to acquire knowledge by observing each other and the world. These discourses are what make it possible to claim that power is exercised in the name of known truth, and that claim in turn justifies power in the eyes of both those who wield it and those who are subjected to it.

In one of his most influential books, *The Order of Things* (1966), Foucault examined how these discourses operated in the medical, social, and human sciences. These sciences, he said, did not objectively describe and predict true facts as they claimed. Rather, they controlled the human body, mind, and behavior by framing general laws that enabled distinctions to be made between the "normal" *One* and the "deviant" or *Other*. In other books, Foucault applied this concept to the history of insane asylums, hospitals, and prisons, where individuals defined as mad, sick, or criminal

The Fundamental Codes of a Culture "Deconstruct the Order of Things" Read an excerpt from *The Order of Things*.

are *marginalized*—confined to the outskirts of society—and subjected to the *gaze* (controlling observation) of doctors and guards.

Foucault's last work, *The History of Sexuality* (1976–1984), was a sustained attack on modern scientific attitudes to sexual behavior. Far from liberating people from sexual ignorance and repression, he claimed, the "sciences of sex" were discourses that controlled the most intimate aspects of human feeling and behavior, defining only one behavior (heterosexual marriage) as normal and all others as deviant. This was an example of how, in the name of reason and mind, modern Western discourses operated to hold down the underlying urges of the human personality, which Foucault called *desire*. These urges, he believed, are capable of taking many different shapes in human feeling, thought, and action. Consequently, true freedom would consist in allowing desire to fulfill all its possibilities of expression.

Foucault for Students (http://www .theory.org.uk/foucault/) Learn more about this influential thinker.

Derrida: Texts, Authors, and Deconstruction

Another leading Postmodern thinker, Jacques Derrida (**deh-ree-DAH**), shared many of Foucault's basic ideas but concentrated on one particular means of representation in thought and art, written language. Like Foucault, he believed that language is not an instrument with which people can exactly express themselves and accurately perceive the world; on the contrary, the structure of language determines what people express and perceive. Furthermore, language is an instrument with a life of its own. Individual words have a long history and are used in many different ways, so that they have many different meanings and evoke many different associations. "Art" can mean anything from creative endeavor to common slyness (as in "artful"); the associations of "thought" range from the deepest wisdom to Tweety Bird (as in "I tawt I taw a puddy tat").

As a result, Derrida believed, authors (all who compose written texts in any field of thought, art, or everyday life) cannot be sure that their words will have the same meanings and associations for their readers as for themselves. Hence, they cannot be sure that readers will grasp exactly what they intend to say. In fact, since authors formulate their own intentions in slippery words, and since their intentions are ultimately determined by shapeless desire, they themselves cannot know what they intend to say. Written texts, therefore, are *ambiguous* (carrying multiple meanings) and *indeterminate* (not the product of a single definable intention on the part of an author), and have an existence of their own, independent of authors. Derrida's name for the process of analyzing a text so as to reveal this indeterminacy, ambiguity, and independent existence is **deconstruction**. The concept of deconstruction has had wide influence on philosophical argument and literary criticism, on writers themselves, and in other fields of art.

Lyotard: Knowledge Production and Narratives

Of the leading Postmodern thinkers, Jean-François Lyotard (lee-o-TAR) was the one who dealt most directly with political and social matters. It was Lyotard who first used the term "postmodern" to describe late-twentieth-century culture and society in general in his book *The Postmodern Condition* (1979).

Lyotard shared the Postmodern belief that freedom consists in the release of desire to take what forms it will. People and groups *produce* knowledge to satisfy desire, he believed, rather than *acquiring* knowledge by the use of reason. The production of knowledge takes place by means of *narratives*—systems of interpretation that are much the same as Foucault's discourses. Such narratives must necessarily be *incommensurable* (mutually incompatible), but that is what freedom is all about. A free society is one in which many different individuals and small groups use *little narratives* to produce "knowledges" that they recognize as true only for themselves and do not wish to impose on others.

Often, however, the process of knowledge production takes place through *grand narratives* that claim that the knowledge they produce is true everywhere and always and for everyone. Examples of such grand narratives are Christianity, Marxism, and the *Enlightenment project*—the hope, first proclaimed by thinkers of the eighteenth-century Enlightenment, of mastering nature and reconstructing the human race on the basis of truths discovered by reason. In postmodern society, Lyotard believed, all grand narratives have been discredited, but large social structures such as governments, corporations, and the mass media can still control the production of knowledge and thereby manipulate individuals. The result is repression without violence and without grand narratives to justify it.

Individuals and small groups must therefore insist all the more on their own little narratives. They should seek to influence politics, for example, not by forming permanent mass parties but through coalitions of groups uniting for specific short-term purposes and then going their separate ways, or through larger and longer-lasting movements, each of which unites around a single issue. Many recent political movements, such as the antiglobalization campaign and the efforts of various underdog contenders in recent U.S. struggles for nomination as presidential candidates, have indeed taken this form, though without so far bringing about basic changes in the economic or political order. In any case, Lyotard saw postmodern society as one in which the mass power of governments, corporations, and the media can be caught off guard by what amounts to political guerrilla warfare.

Postcolonialism

Such themes as knowledge as power and control, and the normal One versus the deviant Other, are obviously relevant to the relationship between the Western heartland countries and the rest of the world, both Western and non-Western. The most influential thinker to explore this relationship from a Postmodern viewpoint was Edward W. Said (sah-EED), a Palestinian-American cultural historian and literary critic. His most influential book, *Orientalism* (1977), dealt with the Western study of other civilizations of the Eastern Hemisphere. Said did for orientalism, especially the Western study of Islam, what Foucault did for the study of criminality or madness. He attacked orientalism as yet another controlling discourse, which defined "West" and "East" as opposites, subjected the East to the West's controlling gaze, and described the features of both in such a way as to establish Western domination and Eastern subjection as the natural order of things.

Postcolonial thinkers criticize not only social and cultural attitudes of the Western heartland but also those of the ex-colonial countries themselves. The Postcolonialists reject such Western discourses as those of nationalism, progress, and traditional Christianity, all of which have considerable appeal in the non-Western world, as well as locally produced grand narratives such as Islamic fundamentalism. For this reason, **Postcolonialism** has actually had less influence on the non-Western world than on the Western heartland and Latin America. Edward Said, for example, was a very prominent figure, revered by some and detested by others, in literary and cultural circles in the United States and other Western countries. However, the revolutionary nationalists and Islamic fundamentalists who dominated Palestinian affairs paid little attention to him. So far, at least, the main effect of Postcolonialism has been to modify attitudes within Western civilization to the rest of the world.

Critics of Postmodernism: Conservatives, Liberals, Marxists

Postmodern thought has quickly come to pervade Western societies, and few can escape its influence. Today, people who feel neglected or ignored complain of being "marginalized"; debaters tearing apart opponents' arguments see themselves engaged in "deconstruction"; and political consultants devise strategies to "define the narrative" of campaigns. None of these items of everyday speech existed before the 1970s. Postmodern thought has altered the way people speak—a sure sign that it has also altered the way they think.

But this does not mean that the Western doubters and deniers have won their age-old battle with the Western searchers after truth. On the contrary, the battle rages more fiercely than ever before, and on many fronts. Conservatives accuse Postmodernists of actually suppressing individual freedom by defining knowledge and consciousness in terms of ethnic, gender, and sexual group identities—gay and straight discourses, white male and African American female narratives, and so on. Among liberals, the German philosopher Jürgen Habermas, a strong believer in the ideals of universal freedom and progress and the breaking down of barriers to communication among human beings, sees Postmodernism as itself conservative because it denies these ideals and erects barriers to communication. And Marxists see Postmodernism, with its rejection of grand narratives of "overthrow" and "revolution" in favor of little narratives of

Sidewalk Bubblegum ©1997 Clay Butler

Rival Narratives Postmodernism is widely distrusted on account of its denial of universal truths and values and its alleged popularity among college professors. The creator of this comic strip, Clay Butler, is an "alternative" cartoonist (in the tradition of the sixties counterculture), but he, too, shares this distrust. Sidewalk Bubblegum © 1997 Clay Butler

"subversion" (undermining society) and "transgression" (breaking rules), as actually working to uphold capitalist oppression. In Marxist eyes, Postmodernism functions as a safety valve in conformist modern society, relieving pressure so as to prevent an explosion.

All these criticisms of Postmodernism are variations on the traditional replies of searchers after truth to doubters and deniers (see photo). If there is no such thing as truth or if it cannot be discovered, how can the doubters know that what they themselves say is true, and why should others take them seriously? If societies cannot establish rules for all to follow that are generally accepted as good according to some truthful standard, how can societies exist at all? And if we think that a society's rules are in fact bad, how can we make that judgment and change that society unless we know the good rules and the truthful standard that we wish to adopt?

Feminism Between Grand and Little Narratives

The present-day social movement that has felt the force of the arguments for and against Postmodernism more than any other is feminism. On the one hand, Postmodern ideas have great attraction for many feminists because these ideas correspond in various ways to their hopes and experiences. On the other hand, it is only by operating as a grand narrative that feminism has brought about actual changes in the status and power of women in society.

Already before Postmodernism, Simone de Beauvoir described Western thought in general as a system in which man is central

and woman marginal, serving as the Other against which man can define himself. More recently, a leading French thinker, Luce Irigaray (**ear-re-GAR-ay**), has advocated that women should construct their own "feminine symbolic order" (system of thought and culture) parallel to and separate from that of men. Many feminist thinkers have carried the Postmodern logic even farther, claiming that since women are in fact divided by such factors as class, race, and sexual orientation, there can be no grand narrative for all women but rather there must be many feminine little narratives.

But ever since Olympe de Gouges proclaimed the universal "Rights of Women" in exact parallel to the French National Assembly's universal "Rights of Man" (p. 387), feminism has sought to replace one set of social rules, enforcing the superiority of men to women in status and power, by another set of rules, enforcing the equal status and power of men and women. It has done so in the name of equality, freedom, and justice—standards recognized as true for both men and women, by which male superiority is judged to be *wrong* and gender equality is judged to be *right*. These are the assumptions that inspire the work of women's organizations like the National Organization for Women in the United States when it campaigns for laws against sex discrimination in the workplace or for the election of women to public office. Many feminists therefore reject Postmodernism, in the belief that without a standard recognized as true for men and women alike, and social rules to enforce that standard, neither women nor men can ever be truly free.

This dilemma between grand narratives and little narratives is felt even by Postmodern feminists. They often claim that because female discourses express the desires of marginalized women, they are *truer* than male discourse. Underlying the thought of all thinkers claiming to represent nonwhite, non-male, and nonheterosexual groups is the belief in a standard of equality and freedom that allows them to declare it *wrong* for their groups to be marginal Others. Derrida himself recognized that this dilemma is one of Postmodernism in general when he wrote: "I cannot conceive of a radical critique [of society and culture] that would not be motivated by some sort of affirmation, acknowledged or not."

Thus in spite of being a movement of doubt and denial, so far as Postmodernists wish to influence society, they cannot do without the ideas of truth and order that they oppose. And perhaps Western searchers after truth and enforcers of behavior, for their part, cannot do without the humility that ought to come from thinking it possible they may be mistaken.

LO⁵ Postmodern Literature and Art

Postmodern forms of literature and art first appeared in the 1960s, when many writers and artists came to feel that the continuing Western social and cultural changes had outstripped the potential of the prevailing modern styles to express human experience. Abstract painting and "stream of consciousness" writing (pp. 521–522, 524–527), as practiced in the middle of the twentieth century, seemed to convey little or nothing of the changes in individuals' perceptions of the world brought by mass media or consumer culture, of the horrors of totalitarianism and genocide, or of the irrationality and chaos that haunt highly structured modern societies.

Writers and artists had consciously striven to depict changing human experience within a changing society and culture ever since the middle of the nineteenth century, and the pioneers of Modernist literature and art had continued this striving. All the same, many writers and artists of the 1960s felt that more recently, Modernist literature and art had deliberately turned away from life. Modernism had become "high art"—the status symbol of a privileged few, who looked down on the low pleasures of mass entertainment. It had become self-absorbed, concentrating on empty word play and experiments with visual form and color, instead of expressing or commenting on human experience. It was time, it seemed, for art to go back to depicting life—the endlessly fluid and changing life of the middle and late twentieth century, where there seemed to be more information and less certainty than ever before, where universal freedom was preached yet everyone lived as part of huge organizations, and where dreams, realities, and nightmares seemed to merge.

To begin with, the writers and artists who shared these beliefs worked independently of Postmodern thought, but in the 1970s and 1980s, many of them took Postmodernism as their inspiration and guide. All the same, Postmodern literature and art are a continuation of the modern Western striving to depict changing experience in a changing society and culture, not a break with it.

Postmodern Literature

This continuity was strongest in prose literature, where traditional methods of storytelling in fact often proved equal to the task of conveying the trauma and confusion of the twentieth century. In the 1950s, writers like Pasternak and Solzhenitsyn successfully used realistic narrative to depict the bitter experiences of the Russian Revolution and the Soviet gulag (p. 523). The British author Evelyn Waugh, in his series of novels *Sword of Honour* (1952–1961), used a style of disciplined elegance to mock (among other things) the irrationality lurking within a huge and highly structured organization, the British Army in the Second World War. And the Italian writer Primo Levi, in his novel *The Truce* (1963), used a narrative form dating from the Renaissance, the tale of comic adventure, to convey the chaos of eastern Europe just after the war as experienced by a Jewish prisoner newly released from Auschwitz.

Other writers, however, stretched the rules of storytelling farther than ever before. Joseph Heller's *Catch-22* (1961) did for the U.S. Air Force in the Second World War what Waugh did for the British Army, but it did so by deliberately breaking the rule that fictional events should follow the pattern of real life. The U.S. Air Force never had the "Catch-22" of the title—the rule that anyone who applies to be discharged on grounds of insanity must be sane, because any sane person would want to leave the wartime air force, so the application must be denied. But the improbable invention vividly conveys the lunatic logic of large organizations at war.

Likewise, in *One Hundred Years of Solitude* (1967), a story of a fictional Latin American community by the Colombian writer Gabriel García Márquez, supernatural events occur alongside natural ones, and flashbacks from the long past take place as if in the present. By breaking the flow of time and the rules of probability, this technique of "magic realism" ties together the past and the present, realities and illusions, to encapsulate the total experience of Latin America since the Spanish conquest.

More recently, the Indian Postcolonial writer Salman Rushdie, resident in Britain, "rewrote" the life of the Prophet Muhammad in *The Satanic Verses* (1989) in a way that mixed fact with fantasy. Rushdie's work was in line with the Postmodern belief that one way to deconstruct grand narratives—in this case, fundamentalist Islam—and thereby weaken their power is to "transgress" them in spectacular ways. Ayatollah Khomeini, the supreme leader of Iran at the time, convened a council of Muslim jurists that issued a *fatwa* (decree) condemning Rushdie to death for blasphemy, the sentence to be executed by any Muslim who had the opportunity. Rushdie went into hiding, and cultural leaders around the world protested against the *fatwa* in the name of the Western grand narratives of religious tolerance and freedom of speech. The *fatwa* was lifted in 1998, but Rushdie's transgression had deconstructed Islamic fundamentalism only in the eyes of people who already opposed it.

The Postmodern outlook is memorably expressed in *The Name of the Rose* (1984), by the Italian Umberto Eco. It is a tale of the medieval past, set in a Benedictine monastery (p. 144) with its routine of work and prayer, its mountaintop serenity disturbed by loves and hatreds among the monks and by the conflicts of the outside world, and its library, a vast and mysterious warren of texts, brooding over all. But the novel is also a detective story, in which a peerless reasoner and his naive companion investigate a seeming murderous plot within the community. In the end, the great detective's search for truth leads him to a conclusion that makes no sense: "There was no plot, and I discovered it by mistake!" Unquestionably, however, the events in the monastery are linked with a clash between rival versions of ultimate truth, those of the Catholic Church and its heretic opponents. About this, too, the investigator comes to a conclusion: "The only truth lies in learning to free oneself from the insane passion for truth."

The works of such writers as García Márquez and Eco have not only been acclaimed by critics familiar with their ideas and literary techniques, but have also been widely read and admired

> **"*The only truth lies in learning to free oneself from the insane passion for truth.*"**
> —from *The Name of the Rose*

by readers who do not necessarily know or share the outlook and convictions that inspire these authors. The reason is that Postmodern writing at its best is simply a new way of doing justice to the richness and strangeness of human experience, which is fiction's traditional task.

Postmodern Art

The keynote of a great deal of work in the visual arts that is identified as Postmodern has been to turn back some or all of the way from abstraction to the depiction of things as they appear to the eye. The general intent has been to bridge the gap between art and life that appeared to have been opened by abstraction. However, the purposes of bridging that gap, the methods of bridging it, and the views of life that artists have expressed have all varied widely—often under the influence of Postmodern thought.

Pop Art and Superrealism

Artists, like writers, began to turn away from the dominant trend in Modernism even before they discovered Postmodern thought—first and most spectacularly with the **Pop Art** movement. Pop Art began in Europe in the 1950s as a way of criticizing the consumer culture of the time, and spread to the United States, where artists used it for the opposite purpose—to celebrate that country's culture of mass entertainment.

A "classic" example is Roy Lichtenstein's *Hopeless* (1963; see photo). The painting realistically shows a young woman weeping, but it is not in fact a depiction of hopelessness. Instead,

Hopeless Roy Lichtenstein once told an interviewer: "I think art since Cézanne . . . has had less and less to do with the world; it is utopian. Outside is the world, it's there. Pop Art looks out into the world"—in this case the world of comic books, a prominent feature of the mid-twentieth century cultural scene.

it is an outsize (4-foot-by-4-foot) picture of a comic-book picture of a young woman weeping, accurate down to the dots of the color printing process, which are faithfully reproduced by the painter's brush. The "original" was an actual frame (single picture) that appeared in a romance comic book, *Run For Love!* in 1962. The frame was of course part of a strip telling a story, but by showing the frame without the story, Lichtenstein focuses the viewer's attention on the general character of comic books: their bold drawing and coloring, their strong and simple emotions—in this case, teenage female emotion—and their Americanness. The painting, a single handmade permanent object just like the *Mona Lisa* (see photo page 301), affectionately and even admiringly imitates a mass-produced throwaway comic-book picture. It is as if Lichtenstein is announcing the merger of popular art (which appeals to people on a level of basic entertainment) and high art (which is supposed to appeal to people on a more idealistic and intellectually demanding level).

 Pop Art and Its Legacy (http://www.tate.org.uk/collection/artist rooms/theme.do?id= 1000008) Learn more about Pop Art and its legacy.

The merger of traditional painting and other media, as well as of mass entertainment and artistic tradition, was carried farther still by a later school of painting, **Superrealism**. A leading artist of this school is the American Audrey Flack. Her painting *Marilyn* (1977; see photo page 564) is a still life—a highly traditional form dating back to the seventeenth century, in which everyday objects—some symbolizing the passage of time and the brevity of life—are depicted in lifelike detail. In this case, lifelike detail is carried to the point of photograph-like accuracy—a blown-up photograph, since the picture is 8 feet by 8 feet in size. The story the painting tells is also a traditional one: an ordinary girl finds a magic spell that brings her beauty, fame, and untimely death. The objects that tell the story, however, are mostly modern ones—photographs, makeup items that are the tools of enchantment, an hourglass in a plastic frame. And the story is in fact a contemporary one, involving an iconic figure of mass entertainment: the transformation of an ordinary girl, Norma Jean Baker, into the ill-starred sex goddess Marilyn Monroe, who took her own life in 1962.

Neo-Expressionism

Another motive for Postmodern artists to step back from abstraction has been the desire to express the experiences and identities of human groups. Anselm Kiefer's *Nigredo* (1984; see photo page 564) depicts another traditional subject, in this case a landscape. The depiction is not painstakingly detailed like those of Lichtenstein and Flack, but the huge 18-by-11-foot painting is realistic enough to suggest a vast, dark, and brooding scene—the

Collection of The University of Arizona Museum of Art & Archive of Visual Arts, Tucson. Museum Purchase with funds provided by the Edward J. Gallagher, Jr. Memorial Fund. Acc. No 1982.035.001

≪ *Marilyn* Present-day artists often disregard the saying that a picture is worth a thousand words, and paint words into a picture that spell out its meaning. Here, Flack painstakingly reproduces pages from a biography telling how the young Norma Jean Baker, instead of being punished for running away from home, was consoled by having her face powdered—a foretaste of the process of beautification that would one day turn her into Marilyn Monroe.

fire, in line with ancient scientific and mystical ideas. Through suggestion and symbolism, the painting is intended to evoke the deeds and experiences of the German nation in the recent past which still haunt the present, as well as the hope of the nation's transformation into something more noble.

Reinventing Artistic Creation

Mass entertainment and consumer culture, symbolism and different levels of meaning, and the collective experience of groups are also themes of Postmodern thought. Many recent artists have specifically sought to express or embody Postmodern ideas in their works—especially the Postmodern criticism of the idea of human beings as standing apart from and objectively observing the rest of the world. This has led them to try to revise the process of artistic creation so as to create new kinds of art objects.

painting's title is a Latin word meaning "blackness." The atmosphere is not unlike that of Van Gogh's landscapes (see photo page 452), and Kiefer's style of painting is often called **Neo-Expressionism**. Are the rows of white lines graves of fallen soldiers or the stubble of fields where battle has raged? Are the dark objects in the foreground tents or huts of some kind of camp? Perhaps Kiefer himself was not sure, though for him, the color black, so prominent in the foreground of the painting, symbolized both death and the transformation of substances by

Nigredo The title of Kiefer's painting is a technical term in the mystical art of alchemy, the transformation of base metals (those thought to be of lower quality) into the noblest of metals, gold. The term describes a stage of "darkness darker than dark," before metals in process of transformation gain the brightness of the sun. The belief is a myth, but for Kiefer it symbolizes the horrific deeds and experiences of twentieth-century humanity and the hope of a more noble future.

Nigredo, Anselm Kiefer, German, born 1945. Oil, acrylic, emulsion, shellac, and straw on photograph and woodcut, mounted on canvas, 1984, 10 feet 10 inches x 18 feet 10-1/2 inches. Gift of the Friends of the Philadelphia Museum of Art in celebration of their twentieth anniversary, 1985 © 2012 Artists Rights Society (ARS), New York/ ADAGP, Paris

Spiral Jetty "He would raise each rock up and roll it around, then he would move this one, change that one until it looked exactly right. He wanted it to look like it was a growing, living thing, coming out of the center of the earth." That was Robert Smithson's creative procedure, according to the building contractor from whom Smithson rented two dump trucks, a tractor, and a front-loader to create his earthwork.

Neo-Expressionism
A style of painting that aims to depict scenes and objects in a strongly emotional way, often in order to express the experiences and identities of human groups.

earthwork
An artwork that is part of a landscape rather than separate from it, and thereby expresses an aspect or aspects of nature.

installation
An artwork that sets up an environment for the viewer to experience and explore.

The traditional process of artistic creation, such artists claim, is a controlling discourse just like the idea of humans objectively observing the world. The process begins with an artist standing apart from human experience, subjecting it to his gaze, and imposing a pattern on it. The artist then creates an object that itself stands apart from the experience and duplicates the pattern that he has imposed. Finally, the object is exposed to the gaze of viewers so as to uphold the controlling discourse that it incorporates. If by any chance a work of art incorporates the discourse of a marginalized Other, it is itself marginalized—for example, by being placed in a museum. According to the Postmodern artist Robert Smithson, "Museums, like asylums and jails, have wards and cells—in other words, neutral rooms called 'galleries.' . . . The function of the warden-curator is to separate art from the rest of society. Next comes integration. Once the work is totally neutralized, ineffective, abstracted, safe, and politically lobotomized, it is ready to be consumed by society."

One way in which Smithson hoped to solve this problem was by means of a new art form, the **earthwork**. His best-known creation of this kind is *Spiral Jetty* (1970; see photo). The work is not exactly realistic; that is, it does not accurately depict something different from itself. Instead, it actually is what its title says it is—a jetty (a structure extending into a body of water) that is

> "*Once the work is totally neutralized, ineffective, abstracted, safe, and politically lobotomized, it is ready to be consumed by society.*"
> —Robert Smithson

spiral in form. All the same, it is intended to express something other than itself, namely the play of earth forces that Smithson perceived in the scenery on the shoreline of the Great Salt Lake, Utah, where the jetty is located. But the jetty is not separate from the scenery, let alone confined in a museum. Instead, it is part of the scenery and changes with it, disappearing beneath the water when the lake is full and appearing above water only in times of exceptional drought. For Smithson, the idea of a human depiction of nature as part of the nature that it depicts was part of an environmentalist discourse of humans as one with nature, as against the discourse of humans separate from and controlling nature.

Postmodern feminism, too, sees the traditional artistic process as part of a controlling (in this case male) discourse and looks for ways to replace it. A notable example is Judy Chicago's *The Dinner Party* (1979; see photo page 566). The work is an **installation**—an object that escapes the bonds of museum confinement and the viewer's gaze in the opposite way to an earthwork: instead of being part of the scene that it depicts, it creates and encloses the scene, setting up an environment that also includes the viewer.

In this case, both the artwork and the scene itself are a table set for dinner. The work is made not by the traditional process of an artist observing experience, but by a process of "women's work" (pp. 10, 13)—exercise of crafts traditionally assigned to women such as

360° View of Judy Chicago's *The Dinner Party* (http://www.brooklynmuseum.org/eascfa/dinner_party/place_settings/webtour/) Get a 360° view of Judy Chicago's *The Dinner Party*.

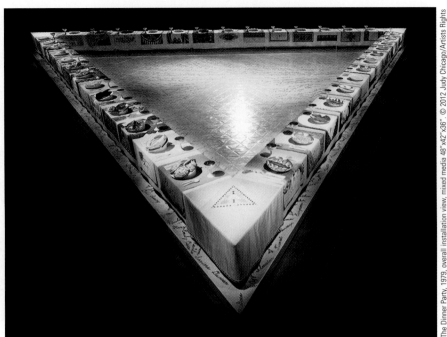

The Dinner Party, 1979, overall installation view, mixed media 48"x42"x36" . © 2012 Judy Chicago/Artists Rights Society (ARS), New York

needlework and china painting. There is plenty of symbolism. The triangular shape of the table is an ancient female symbol, the thirteen place settings on each side are the number of witches in a coven, and the plates are painted with patterns of butterflies and female sexual organs, standing for liberation and female sexuality. The names of thirty-nine principal guests, including the Egyptian pharaoh Hatshepsut, the U.S. women's rights activist Susan B. Anthony, and the British writer Virginia Woolf (pp. 23, 521–522), appear at the place settings, and the names of 999 other distinguished women are inscribed in the floor.

Opinions among feminists about *The Dinner Party* were divided. Some praised it for subverting the sexist cultural hierarchy that places traditionally female pursuits like needlework lower than traditionally male pursuits like painting and sculpture. Others criticized it exactly for glorifying traditional "women's work," and for proclaiming women's sexual and reproductive functions. Chicago certainly sought to deconstruct old discourses and construct a new one, but the new discourse was ambiguous. Like Postmodern feminism in general, *The Dinner Party* speaks both of women's separate identity from that of men and of their underrated role in a civilization that they share with men.

Postmodern Architecture

At first sight, it would seem impossible for a building, especially a large one, to be Postmodern. Postmodernism stresses fluidity, indeterminacy, and little narratives. A large building, however, has to have a massive and unchanging structure and has to be the work of a highly organized society. To build it, clients (usually wealthy and powerful organizations), real estate developers, local governments, architectural design bureaus, construction companies, trucking firms, and industrial manufacturers all have to work toward a single common end. Any large building, in fact, is a grand narrative in steel and concrete.

All the same, Postmodernism has been a leading trend in present-day architecture; in fact, it was in the architectural field that the word "Postmodernism" was first used in the sense of a turning away from Modernist styles of art. The reaction began in the United States in the 1960s with the publication of two influential books, Jane Jacobs's *Death and Life of American Cities* (1961) and Robert Venturi's *Complexity and Contradiction in Architecture* (1966). Both attacked the "glass box" style of Modernist architecture (p. 529), Jacobs for destroying the human scale and unplanned diversity of city life and Venturi for frustrating the human need for variety and complexity. Against Mies van der Rohe's Modernist slogan "less is more," Venturi proclaimed that "less is a bore." That did not mean, however, that either was opposed to bigness as such. Venturi, a practicing architect, designed individual residences, but he also praised bigness so long as it was also playful and showy—the hotel architecture of Las Vegas, for example. And many of the most striking Postmodern buildings have in fact been large ones.

The way that Postmodern architects strive to make large buildings interesting is by rejecting the idea that form should follow function—that the appearance of a building should reveal its structure, as in Modernist buildings or Gothic cathedrals (pp. 227–230, 528–529). Instead, they follow a rival architectural tradition of using the structure of a building to support an exterior that proclaims its own message. The columns on the west façade of Saint Peter's Basilica in Rome, for instance, do not support the structure, which consists of the walls and internal arches (see photo page 348). They are an external decoration, intended to impress worshipers with the majesty and permanence of the Roman Catholic Church. The messages that Postmodern buildings send are different, but their method of sending them is the same as in Baroque structures.

Sometimes the message that Postmodern buildings are intended to send is simply one of transgressing the grand narrative of Modernism, and of freedom to choose among the decorative styles of the past. A well-known example is the AT&T Building in New York City, which recalls the massive entrance arches and vertical stone ribs of skyscrapers at the turn of the twentieth century, as well as the elaborately carved tops of colonial-style chests of drawers (see photo). One of the designers,

Philip Johnson, had a change of heart after collaborating with Mies van der Rohe on the severely modern Seagram Building (see photo page 529). With its playful mixture of old-fashioned styles, the AT&T Building (recently sold and renamed the Sony Building) forms an ironic contrast with the glass boxes in its neighborhood—so far as any 660-foot corporate skyscraper can be playful and ironical.

Other recent buildings celebrate the Postmodern delight in chaos and confusion. Perhaps because it is hard for organizations to do business or people to live in structures that are designed to be disorienting, most buildings of this kind are intended to be visited rather than lived and worked in. Most of all, in spite of the Postmodern distrust of places where art objects are subjected to the public gaze, they tend to be galleries and museums.

Architecture and Sculpture "I don't know where you cross the line between architecture and sculpture. For me, it is the same. Buildings and sculpture are three-dimensional objects." The Guggenheim Museum in Bilbao expresses this belief of its designer, Frank Gehry. Its mostly window-less titanium-clad exterior is like the surface of a piece of modern sculpture, allowing the eye to follow the complex curves and irregular masses into which it is "carved."

The best-known such building is the Guggenheim Museum in Bilbao, chief city of the Basque Country of northern Spain (see photo), designed by the Canadian architect Frank Gehry. Architectural theorists call the museum's style Deconstructivist, from Derrida's term for the process of revealing ambiguity and indeterminacy in texts. Gehry himself has a simpler description of his preferred style: "Every architect who's any good, no matter what they say, is trying to make some kind of personal mud pie." But to make this particular "mud pie" and fit it onto an internal load-bearing structure took ingenious design that stretched computer technology to the limit. The building's sleek and fluid lines, so complex and indescribable that they seem almost to stretch the limits of three dimensions, make an unforgettable statement of the ancient idea that change governs all (p. 72).

 Guggenheim Bilbao Virtual Tour (http://www.guggenheim-bilbao.es/visita_virtual/visita_virtual.php?idioma=en) Take a virtual tour of the Guggenheim Bilbao.

 Listen to a synopsis of Chapter 30.

The AT&T Building Designed in 1984, the building looks old-fashioned in contrast with the surrounding modern office blocks. A quarter of a century before and a few streets away in New York City, the Seagram Building also contrasted with its neighbors—only the contrast was between a modern office block and old-fashioned apartment buildings. Philip Johnson, who worked on both buildings, had a simple explanation for the change: "We were getting bored with the box."

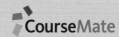 **Access to the eBook with additional review material and study tools may be found online at CourseMate for WCIV. Sign in at www.cengagebrain.com.**

CHAPTER 31

AFTER THE END OF EMPIRE: NEW POWER STRUGGLES AND NEW PROBLEMS,
1970s AND 1980s

LEARNING OBJECTIVES

AFTER READING THIS CHAPTER, YOU SHOULD BE ABLE TO DO THE FOLLOWING:

LO¹ Compare and contrast Third World responses to Western power in the postcolonial era.

LO² Describe the new challenges facing the world in the later part of the twentieth century.

LO³ Trace the end of the Cold War.

> **❝FOR THE MOMENT, THE SCHISM WITHIN WESTERN CIVILIZATION HAD ENDED, AND ITS HEARTLAND COUNTRIES ONCE AGAIN CONTROLLED THE WORLD ORDER.❞**

Following the end of the nineteenth-century empires, their former subject peoples were not sure what they wanted next or how to get it. Did they, like ex-colonial India, want to share the Western privileges of national independence, individual freedom, and widespread prosperity? If so, should they work with or against the democratic-capitalist nations, which already had these privileges? Would they seek the communist goal of overthrowing the existing world order in the name of social justice and national power? If so, would they be vassals of the Soviet Union, or would they compete with it like ex-colonial China? Would they turn their backs on these rival goals and values of divided Western civilization in the name of some updated version of non-Western traditions like Islamic fundamentalism? The ex-colonial peoples endlessly argued, wavered, and fought over these and other ends and means, or pursued varying combinations of them.

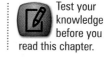

Test your knowledge before you read this chapter.

What do you think?

Industrialization has created unsustainable levels of consumption.

Strongly Disagree						Strongly Agree
1	2	3	4	5	6	7

Meanwhile, leaders and peoples across the entire world came to realize that they all faced grave threats arising out of the spectacular growth of modern civilization's technical and industrial capacities and its vulnerability to disruption: the interrelated problems of population growth, resource use, and pollution; the inequality between wealthier and poorer nations; the development and large-scale

≪ Third World Warriors, Cold War Backers Afghan mujahideen (holy warriors), fighting a Marxist government upheld by the Soviet Union, line up triumphantly on a downed Soviet helicopter gunship. Such aircraft, able to douse ground targets with automatic cannon fire, were invulnerable to the warriors' rifles and bazookas, but the mujahideen also had high-tech shoulder-fired antiaircraft missiles, supplied by the United States.

manufacture of nuclear weapons; and the increasing use of terrorism as a weapon in national, ethnic, religious, and social conflicts.

There was a great deal of argument about whose fault these problems were and how they should be solved, as well as about which problems were truly serious enough to count as grave dangers to the human race as a whole. Was the earth getting warmer, and if so, was it because power stations and automobiles were pouring carbon dioxide into the atmosphere or because of long-term natural trends? Was deterrence or disarmament the most reliable means of avoiding nuclear war? Was terrorism more the fault of terrorists who committed atrocious deeds or of oppressors whom they blamed for their grievances? Disputes over these and similar questions have continued down to the present, but few disagreed that the human race faced worldwide threats that needed worldwide measures to counter them.

The ex-colonial ferment and the newly recognized worldwide problems also interacted with the rivalry of the democratic-capitalist and the communist groupings, which seemed to be a permanent feature of the world order. In the 1980s, however, the dictatorships and state-run economies of the socialist camp turned out to be too rigid to adapt to the latest round of technical advance, the information revolution. Production stagnated, living standards dropped, and the burden of the arms race became ever harder to bear. Communism lost appeal in the ex-colonial world, where the fastest-growing economies were those that limited state planning like South Korea or Taiwan—or even China, which also loosened economic controls.

Finally, leaders took over in communism's superpower, the Soviet Union, who tried to restructure the system drastically. Not content with relaxing economic controls, they permitted freedom of information and discussion, and even the formation of noncommunist political organizations. The result, however, was not reform but the shriveling of communist power. First the eastern European countries broke away, and then the Soviet Union itself peacefully disintegrated. The democratic-capitalist countries had outlasted the communist challenge. For the moment, the schism within Western civilization had ended, and its heartland countries once again controlled the world order.

CHRONOLOGY

1955	Third World countries meet in Bandung, Indonesia, to form a nonaligned movement
1959	Castro takes control of Cuba, nationalizes agriculture and industry
1963	Cuban missile crisis
1965	President Johnson begins full-scale deployment of American troops in Vietnam
1967	Israel wins the Six-Day War
1968	Worldwide Nuclear Nonproliferation Treaty goes into effect
1973	President Allende of Chile is assassinated in a U.S.-backed coup; Arab oil embargo
1975	North Vietnam wins control of South Vietnam
1978	Camp David peace agreements between Israel and Egypt
1979	Iranian revolution ousts the shah; hostage crisis in Iran begins; a pro-Soviet government is installed in Afghanistan
1980	Saddam Hussein of Iraq attacks Iran, with military support from the United States, the Soviet Union, and wealthy Arab states
1982	Israeli invasion of Lebanon
1986	Chernobyl nuclear reactor disaster
1989	Beginning of successful popular movements against communist regimes in eastern Europe
1991	Failed coup brings about end of USSR
2000	World population reaches 6 billion

LO¹ The Third World and the West: Resistance, Cooperation, and Islamic Fundamentalism

The leaders of the liberated peoples of Asia and Africa—as well as of Latin American nations that hoped for freedom from foreign dominance in the newly decolonized world—knew that there was no going back to the old times before the colonial empires. Instead, what they wanted for their peoples was the chance to reproduce some of the achievements of their former imperial rulers—in particular, national freedom, unity, and power, and the possibility of health, wealth, and leisure for all. Independence was to be the first step in political and economic **development**—the building of powerful nation-states and wealthy industrial economies—so that the nations of Asia, Africa, and Latin America could take their rightful place in the world.

The ex-colonial leaders also knew very well that in the world in which they had won independence, the former imperial nations still had the lion's share of wealth and power—even if those nations were now divided between the West (the NATO countries) and the socialist camp. In the rush of optimism that followed independence, many Asian, African, and Latin American nations hoped to change the bipolar world order into a "tripolar" one that would better reflect their interests and values. A conference at Bandung, Indonesia, in 1955 led to the formation of the so-called nonaligned movement of mostly ex-colonial nations—a united movement of the **Third World**, as it came to be called, that would stand apart from both the rival blocs of the First (capitalist) and Second (socialist) Worlds.

The ideal of a united Third World as a pillar of a reformed world order has great appeal in Asia, Africa, and Latin America, but from the start, many realities worked against it. The Third World countries had widely different traditions of civilization—Islamic, Hindu, Chinese, and (in Latin America) Western. In many cases, their borders had originally been drawn by colonial powers regardless of these differences, as well as of well-established ethnic and tribal territories. Many Third World countries were peasant societies in which a few powerful groups—such as landowners, religious and tribal leaders, and generals—held most of the wealth and competed fiercely for power. All this often led to corruption, government instability, rule by dictatorial strongmen, and horrific civil and international wars.

In addition, it was hard for Third World countries to escape their traditional economic role as suppliers of raw materials and foodstuffs to the countries to whose empires they had earlier belonged. They continued to depend on these countries for access to markets, financial credit, and technical aid, and as often as not, for help in upholding their governments.

As a result of these internal conflicts and economic weaknesses, many Third World countries found that even after independence, they were still caught in a web of political and economic dependency on their former rulers or on the United States—that is, on the leading countries of the West.

Given these realities, there seemed to be two possible paths along which Third World countries might find their way to national power and industrial wealth. One was the path of resistance—to treat development as a continuation of the struggle for liberation, and hence to oppose the political and economic dominance of the West on the pattern of earlier opposition to imperial rule. The other was the path of cooperation, of working in partnership with the West—a partnership that was bound to be unequal, but could speed development and lead in the end to equality.

Few Third World countries chose either of these paths exclusively, and many altered course from time to time when the chosen path led to failure or conflict. In Muslim countries, in the course of such failures and conflicts, an international movement of Islamic fundamentalism grew up that rejected both partnership with the West, as well as resistance just for the sake of escaping political and economic dependency. Instead, the new movement proclaimed *jihad* (holy war, p. 162) against the West in the name of the one truth about the one God. It still sought unity and power, but on a religious rather than a national basis. It was not necessarily opposed to the pursuit of wealth, health, and leisure for all—so long as these things were pursued by societies that upheld the one Islamic truth.

The Path of Resistance

Many Third World countries found one or other leading nation of the West still standing in the way of their hopes and ambitions even after independence. Others were on fairly good terms with the West, but their governments nevertheless wanted to declare economic and social as well as political independence. All such countries were likely to follow the path of resistance more or less wholeheartedly. Internally, they were likely to take such measures as nationalizing foreign-owned companies and introducing government planning. Externally, they sought to take advantage of the bipolar world order by playing one bloc against the other so as to get the maximum help from both without depending on either.

But there were also Third World countries where the West—most often, the United States—wielded indirect control through wealthy and corrupt elites, which were then undermined by national and social liberation movements. These movements would bring down on themselves the anger of the Western patron country and turn for support to the socialist camp. And resistance would turn into confrontation—not just between local radicals and the patron country, but also between the rival blocs. The most noteworthy of these confrontations took place in Cuba and Vietnam.

Cuba

The Caribbean island of Cuba won independence from Spain with the help of the United States in 1898, but this did not lead

> **"***Cuba became an authoritarian model of 'national liberation' from a foreign-controlled political and economic establishment.***"**

to real independence either before or after the Second World War. The United States kept a heavy hand in Cuban affairs. From 1933 through 1959, it exerted its influence chiefly through one man, a former army sergeant—Fulgencio Batista. With or without elections, he remained the real force in most of the Cuban governments of that period. But in 1959, Fidel Castro led a revolutionary movement that ousted the dictator. One of Castro's first acts in power was to nationalize the country's agriculture and industry, both of which had been owned in substantial part by Americans. Cuba thus became an authoritarian model of "national liberation" from a foreign-controlled political and economic establishment.

In carrying his program forward, Castro faced not only grave internal handicaps but an external enemy as well: the United States. Despite public professions of the right of all peoples to self-determination, the American government (both Democratic and Republican) took a hostile attitude toward social revolutions—on the ground that they violated human rights and that they were or might become communist. In keeping with this policy, the United States began a trade embargo against Cuba, and President John F. Kennedy in 1961 approved the "Bay of Pigs" invasion by anti-Castro Cubans, guided unsuccessfully by the Central Intelligence Agency. Following the invasion's failure, the CIA subsequently plotted (though it did not carry out) the assassination of Castro.

Meanwhile the Soviet Union welcomed Cuba into the expanding socialist camp, subsidized its economy against the U.S. embargo, and in 1963 sought to protect Cuba against U.S. invasion and change the strategic balance in its own favor by stationing ballistic missiles there (see photo). U.S. warships

Reconnaissance over Cuba On a U.S. photo of a Soviet missile site in western Cuba, labels identify the most threatening features: missile-carrying trailers and "erector launchers" for raising the missiles upright for liftoff, to strike with 2-megaton warheads anywhere in the United States. The U.S. government released such photos at the time to rally public opinion and prevent Soviet denials; the photos also contributed to a worldwide sense of being on the brink of nuclear war. United States Department of Defense Photo: John F. Kennedy Library, Boston

MRBM FIELD LAUNCH SITE
SAN CRISTOBAL NO 1
14 OCTOBER 1962

ERECTOR/LAUNCHER EQUIPMENT

TENT AREAS

EQUIPMENT

ERECTOR/LAUNCHER EQUIPMENT

8 MISSILE TRAILERS

CONSTRU

blockaded Cuba, and for a week, the world watched in suspense while maps showed Soviet supply ships drawing ever nearer to the blockading fleet. Finally the superpowers compromised: the Soviets dismantled their missiles, while the United States declared that it would not seek the military overthrow of the Cuban regime, and later withdrew missiles that it had stationed near the Soviet borders. Having come to the brink of nuclear war, the superpowers from now on took measures to avoid direct confrontation. Indirect confrontation involving Third World conflicts continued on a massive scale, however—above all in Vietnam.

 An Account of the Cuban Missile Crisis (http://www.hpol .org/jfk/cuban/) Learn more about the Cuban missile crisis and listen to Kennedy's reports to the nation.

Vietnam

What had begun in that country in 1946 as a postwar revolt against French colonial rule led by a communist and nationalist revolutionary, Ho Chi-Minh (**chee-MIN**), turned into a desperate civil war between the communist-ruled northern and the noncommunist southern halves of the country. After the French pulled out in 1954, Americans replaced them in South Vietnam— first as "advisers," then as special forces (combat soldiers). In 1965, as the South Vietnamese proved unable to suppress a guerrilla uprising inspired from the North, President Johnson decided on full-scale American involvement.

Johnson sent hundreds of thousands of troops to South Vietnam to aid the Saigon army; they were supported by hundreds of warships and thousands of aircraft, which also ranged northward to pour bombs on "enemy" installations. By the end of the war, the total tonnage dropped by the United States in Indochina amounted to more than three times the tonnage dropped by the United States in all areas during the Second World War.

But the communist forces showed exceptional skill and courage, and were massively aided by China and the Soviet Union—whose supply ships the Americans did not attack, for fear of starting the nuclear war that they and the Soviets had avoided over Cuba. Meanwhile, American voters were becoming increasingly opposed to the continuing slaughter, and protests over the war nourished the student counterculture of the 1960s (p. 552). American war deaths already exceeded 40,000; Vietnamese deaths were estimated at more than a million; dollar costs had risen to hundreds of billions. President Johnson at last stopped the military escalation and announced that he would not run for reelection.

The next president, the Republican Richard Nixon, tried to placate growing doubts and opposition at home, while nevertheless holding South Vietnam. He carried the war into neighboring Laos and Cambodia to disrupt communist supply lines running through those countries. He sought to "Vietnamize" the struggle—to build up the South Vietnamese army and gradually withdraw American combat forces. And he sent his security adviser, Henry Kissinger, to Paris to negotiate with the North Vietnamese what he hoped would be "peace with honor."

Under the resulting agreement, U.S. ground combat forces began to withdraw from Vietnam, but the war itself continued, and in spite of Nixon's policies, so did opposition at home. A Democratic Congress cut financial aid to South Vietnam; as U.S. support wavered, the South Vietnamese government and army began to lose the determination to fight on; and in 1975, all of South Vietnam was swiftly taken over by "liberation" troops. The communist victory had a horrendous aftermath of mass arrests, mass deaths in prison camps, and the mass flight of "boat people"—refugees, often ethnic Chinese, who fled by sea in small boats, risking death by starvation, thirst, and piracy to escape the victors' vengeance. Eventually the fury died down and reconstruction got under way. The United States recognized united Vietnam in 1995, and in the globalization era of the 1990s, Vietnam, like China, loosened socialist economic controls, achieved swift economic growth, demanded less conformity from its citizens, but held to the system of rule from above by a powerful organization that still called itself the Communist Party.

Cambodia

The Vietnam War's most disastrous sequel unfolded in Cambodia. Caught in the drawn-out Indochina battle, Cambodia fell to the Khmer Rouge, an extreme Marxist group that had fought for years as guerrillas against various governments in Phnom Penh (**NOM PEN**), the capital. Its leader, Pol Pot, sealed off the country in 1976 (save for contacts with China) and proceeded to transform the nation by force into a collectivized agrarian society. People were uprooted from the cities and compelled to clear new lands or work on irrigation projects and farms. As a result of these shocking dislocations and accompanying repression, malnutrition, and disease, several million Cambodians perished.

In 1978, this genocidal government was overturned by Cambodian rebels and Vietnamese troops, though the Khmer Rouge (and other groups) fought on as guerrillas. The Vietnamese, unpopular in Cambodia, subsequently withdrew, and the United Nations intervened to attempt to settle the political and military situation but could not prevent further prolonged fighting. Finally the UN succeeded, in 1993, in establishing a democratic government in Phnom Penh headed by an astute and respected constitutional monarch, the former ruler Norodom Sihanouk (**SEE-uh-nook**). At first, the Khmer Rouge refused to participate, but in 1996, a large group came over to the government. Since then, the country has been largely free of civil war, and the Cambodian monarchy has survived a coup, rigged elections, the abdication of Norodom Sihanouk, and the succession of his son Norodom Sihamoni—though the "King-Father" still holds considerable power.

Latin America

In the 1970s, Chile was the scene of an effort to pursue the path of resistance through peaceful and democratic methods. Salvador Allende (**ah-YEN-dey**), an avowed Marxist, was elected president in 1970 by regular constitutional procedures. He had the direct support, however, of only a plurality of the voters, not a majority. While in office, Allende sought authority for sweeping landholding reforms and for state ownership of banks and basic industries; with equal vigor, he defended democratic methods, legality, and civil liberties. The president's conservative

fundamentalists
In religion, those who wish to uphold traditional beliefs and practices at all costs, often in an updated form that is stricter and more combative than in the past.

> *"Cooperation was not a certain and speedy path to development any more than resistance, but some East Asian countries had spectacular success with it."*

opponents made full use of the press, their control of the Chilean Congress, and their economic power to block Allende's legislative program and his efforts to increase national production. Faced with staggering inflation, internal unrest, and secret intervention by the American CIA, Allende had reached an impasse by 1973. Then, as some observers had predicted, his generals and admirals struck against his democratic government in a bloody military coup. Allende, holding to his principles to the end, stayed at his desk in the presidential palace, where he was gunned down by the rebel soldiers.

The new military government, headed by General Augusto Pinochet (pin-o-SHAY), proceeded to destroy its opponents by relentless harassment, torture, and executions. It was promptly recognized by the United States government, and with the aid of American loans and financial advisers, Pinochet set out to establish a laissez-faire economy within the bounds of his anticommunist dictatorship. The Chilean economy was thus stabilized, though it later stagnated. Meanwhile, the experience of dictatorship led moderate left-wing and right-wing forces to cooperate against the regime, and in 1989, Pinochet left office. Ten years later, he managed to avoid prosecution for the crimes of his regime on grounds of age and ill health.

Elsewhere in Latin America, most countries remained under the control of the wealthy, the Catholic Church, and the military—even when democratic forms of government were adopted. Though liberalism had been the declared ideal of the first independent states of Latin America, the twentieth century brought chiefly dictatorships and repression. However, while the higher clergy continued generally to defend the established social order, many parish priests began to preach, toward the end of the century, a new "liberation theology" that aimed to improve the conditions of the poor. Catholic power as a whole was diminished by the rapid spread of evangelical Protestant faiths in the area. In any case, it was economic modernization that became the principal goal of the Latin nations, and with it came the impact of foreign capital. American business was the major outside influence, buttressed by the CIA.

The Path of Cooperation: The East Asian Model

For a variety of reasons, many Third World countries sought national power and industrial wealth through cooperation with the West rather than resistance to it. Following independence, some felt more threatened by the Soviet Union or China than by the United States or their former colonial rulers, or they

hoped for the West's help in disputes with other Third World countries. Others had unpopular governments that needed the help of the West in order to hold on to power, or were so poor that they could not keep going without aid from their former rulers. Such countries were likely to welcome Western investment, to keep their economies on a capitalist path, and to align themselves more or less closely with the West against the socialist camp.

Cooperation was not a certain and speedy path to development any more than resistance, but some East Asian countries had spectacular success with it. Their particular form of cooperation—the "Far Eastern" or "East Asian" model of development—in time became an attractive one for Third World countries to follow.

Japan

The East Asian model originated in Japan—not a Third World country, but one that had already learned from the West so successfully that, by 1900, it had joined the ranks of the imperialist powers (pp. 463–466). Following their crushing defeat in the Second World War, the Japanese had powerful reasons to cooperate with and learn new lessons from the West—a benevolent U.S. occupation, fear of its communist neighbors the Soviet Union and China, and most of all, perhaps, the obvious failure of militaristic confrontation to bring Japan a dominant place in the world. Thus, postwar Japan was bound by its peace treaty and its constitution to a nonmilitary foreign policy, it renounced the veneration of the emperor as divine and adopted a fully democratic system of government, and it relied for security on a close alliance with the United States. As it rebuilt after the war, Japan transformed itself from a devastated country into a low-wage supplier of basic industrial products and then became a high-wage exporter of every kind of high-quality manufactured goods.

South Korea

As the Japanese economy grew, it pulled along with it the economies of various Third World countries in its neighborhood. Among them was the southern half of Japan's former imperial possession of Korea—a nation adjacent to China that was given divided independence by the victors of the Second World War (see Map 29.2 on page 543). The northern half was turned into a communist state under Soviet guidance; the southern half, under American guidance, was organized as a democratic-capitalist state. Each area was ruled by a dictatorial strongman dependent on one of the superpowers.

In 1950, North Korean troops, with Soviet arms, attacked the south, which was saved only by swift Western military intervention, authorized by the United Nations Security Council but carried out mainly by the United States. China, in turn, intervened to prevent the Americans from overrunning the

BY 1970, JAPAN GREW TO THIRD PLACE GLOBALLY IN GROSS NATIONAL PRODUCT FOR SEVERAL REASONS:

Business Practices

- Japan followed a capitalist pattern of economic reconstruction—but it was capitalism in the service of national prosperity and power.

- Companies worked closely with each other and with the government to identify new markets and promote new technologies.

- Business leaders limited the power of labor unions, partly by ruthless strikebreaking but also by rarely laying off workers.

Protectionist Policies

- Many formal and informal barriers prevented foreign investors from gaining control of Japanese companies.

- Barriers also made it difficult for competing foreign goods to enter the Japanese market.

---

north. After hard fighting, a cease-fire was arranged in 1951, but two more years of drawn-out negotiations passed before a final truce was signed. Korea, bloodied and devastated, remained divided.

 MacArthur Outlines His Objectives in Korea Read American General MacArthur's reaction to the Chinese intervention in Korea.

South Korea, traditionally the agricultural half of the country, came out of the war as a devastated peasant society, kept going by United States aid and held together by military rule. Then, in the 1960s, the increasingly prosperous Japanese began to look to South Korea as an outlet for investment and a source of low-cost components for their advancing industries. The South Koreans needed Japanese money and machinery, but they were afraid of yielding control of their economy to their former imperial occupiers. The answer was to use Japanese methods as a precaution against the Japanese—close cooperation between government and business, barriers to foreign control of South Korean companies, and guaranteed employment to keep workers loyal. Since this still left plenty of room for the Japanese to invest profitably in South Korea, the country's economy took off, and by 1980, it was well on the way to becoming an advanced industrial society—though still, for the time being, under the authoritarian government of generals or ex-generals.

Meanwhile, the communist dictatorship in North Korea had followed exactly the opposite trajectory, from speedy recovery in the 1950s to stagnation and poverty. The country's problems were made worse by the grotesque cult of its "Great Leader" Kim Il-sung and by the pursuit of military superiority over the south, to include, in time, nuclear weapons (pp. 581, 630). By 1980, the contrast between the two halves of Korea was already deeply embarrassing to the socialist camp in its competition with the West.

In addition, by 1980, Japanese investment and Japanese-style economic and industrial practices were also bringing prosperity to other East Asian countries, above all Taiwan, Malaysia, Singapore, and Thailand. Famous companies in leading American and European industries now vied for markets with East Asian competitors—Volkswagen with Hyundai, Harley-Davidson with Yamaha, IBM and Philips with Hitachi and Sony. The United States, Japan's conqueror and protector, owed that country billions of dollars and could not persuade it to change its restrictive policies on imports. The path of cooperation had turned the East Asian countries into both partners and rivals of the West.

Islamic Fundamentalism

Islam, like other monotheistic religions, claims for its believers a special knowledge of and a special closeness to the one almighty God. It has traditionally been a formative and directing force in countless societies that stretch right across the Eastern Hemisphere from West Africa to Indonesia. In recent centuries, however, it has been challenged by new secular ideologies and by deep social changes, and as a result, a new division has appeared in the Islamic world. On the one hand, there are "modernizing" Muslims who are influenced by secular ideologies and are optimistic about the effect of social change. On the other hand, there are **fundamentalists** who wish to uphold traditional beliefs and practices at all costs—often in an updated form that is stricter and more combative than in the past.

The split between modernizers and fundamentalists is found in Christianity and Judaism too, but with Islam, there are two differences. First, the changes and challenges that Islam faces today originated outside the Muslim world, in the West. Hence Muslim modernizers are not just seeking to adapt to new ways and beliefs in general, but also to introduce into their societies the ways of a region dominated partly by the rival monotheism of Christianity, and partly by nonreligious and antireligious secular ideologies. Second, Muslim modernizers have in general failed to give Islamic societies a place in the world equal or superior to that of the West. Nineteenth-century Muslim rulers introduced many reforms, but even so, their countries mostly ended as part of one or other European-ruled empire. Then came decolonization, and a new generation of modernizing leaders of Islamic countries who were committed to the Third World goal of reproducing the achievements of the West. But there were also Third World problems, such as corrupt elites, ethnic and tribal rivalries, struggles over the inheritance of the colonial empires, and dependency on one or other of the power blocs.

Mainly for these reasons, fundamentalism has been more radical in Islam than in Christianity or Judaism. Its appeal is felt exactly among those groups in Islamic societies whose lives have changed the most under Western influence, such as college students or peasants who move to the towns. In spite of its traditionalism, its belief and practice are far more rigorous than was usual in the Islamic past, and are promoted by up-to-date Western-style methods of organization and propaganda. Thus, fundamentalism amounts to a kind of religious dictatorship that is actually an innovation in Islam. And Islamic fundamentalism sees the ultimate source of evil as an outside enemy, namely, the West—above all, Israel as the Western bridgehead in the Muslim world, and the United States as Israel's closest ally, the West's leading country, and the main exporter of Western values.

> "*Islamic fundamentalism sees the ultimate source of evil as an outside enemy, namely, the West.*"

To begin with, the problems that gave rise to Islamic fundamentalism were worst in the Middle East. Both the superpowers had vital interests there: the Western industrial societies needed Middle Eastern oil in order to survive, and the Soviet Union did not want the West to become too powerful in a region that lay directly on its southern border. In addition, the Middle East was the scene of the Islamic modernizers' single greatest failure—the inability of secular-minded Arab nationalist leaders to stop Israel from coming into being, developing into the region's most successful modern country, continuing to expand its area of settlement, and conquering Jerusalem.

Israel and the Arabs: The Continuing Conflict

For nearly twenty years after its independence in 1948, Israel was a beleaguered country, outnumbered by well-armed Arab enemies while building up a modern economy and armed forces. But then came the Six-Day War of June 1967. In a lightning attack against a threatening Arab mobilization, the Israelis smashed the Egyptian, Syrian, and Jordanian armies. They wrested the West Bank of the Jordan River from Jordan, the Golan Heights from Syria, and Gaza and the Sinai from Egypt (see Map 29.3 on page 544). All of a sudden, Israel was revealed as the strongest military power in the Middle East.

Even so, the Israeli triumph did not end the conflict. The Arabs continued to refuse to recognize the Jewish state, and acquired new arms from the Soviet Union, which desired to expand its own influence in the Middle East. The UN Security Council passed a resolution calling in general terms for Israeli withdrawal in return for a settled peace. Not all Arab states accepted the resolution even in principle, however. Furthermore, many Zionists felt that Israel both needed the West Bank and Gaza for its security and had a historic right to those areas—above all the West Bank, which had been the core of the ancient Israelite kingdom (Map 2.2 on page 38). Israel therefore held on to the occupied territories and began to settle its citizens in them.

Eventually, the Egyptians and Syrians tried to regain their lost lands by a surprise attack on the Jewish holy day Yom Kippur in October 1973, and the Arab oil-exporting states imposed an embargo on shipments to all nations aiding Israel. Israeli forces, hastily reinforced by weapons from the United States, recovered from heavy initial losses and turned to the offensive. With the United States and the Soviet Union poised to enter the war, each to protect its client states, the United Nations stepped in and secured acceptance of a cease-fire. Since the United States was a major importer of Middle Eastern oil, it pressed Israel to come to an agreement with the Arabs, and eventually, Israeli forces withdrew to the lines they had occupied before the Yom Kippur War.

Partly as a result of the way the war had ended through U.S. mediation, Egypt shifted from its reliance on the Soviet Union to a close relationship with the United States. It now realized that only the United States (exactly because it had become the only ally that Israel relied on, p. 545) was in a position to influence the Israeli course of action. That in turn led to the first break in the feud between Israel and the Arabs. In 1977, Anwar Sadat (suh-DAHT), the Egyptian president, made a "surprise" flight (in fact the result of lengthy secret negotiations among Egypt, Israel, and the United States) from Cairo to Jerusalem. In a speech before the Israeli parliament, he called for the Jewish state to withdraw from all lands occupied in 1967 and proclaimed the right of return of Palestinian refugees from 1948 (p. 544). The following year, he settled for much less. At a series of meetings chaired by President Jimmy Carter at Camp David outside Washington, he and the Israeli prime minister, Menachem Begin (BEY-gin), agreed that Israel would return the Egyptian territory that it occupied in Sinai, in return for recognition by Egypt and the establishment of normal diplomatic relations.

The Camp David agreements were hailed in the West as a step toward peace, but in some ways, they intensified the conflict. Other Arab states, in particular Libya, Syria, Jordan, Iraq, and Saudi Arabia, furiously denounced both the agreements. Arab and Muslim public opinion felt humiliation and resentment at the sight of Sadat referring to Begin, the leader of the "Zionist entity," who had been involved in terrorism during the early struggles in Palestine, as "my friend." In 1981, Sadat was assassinated by Islamist militants, and though his successor Hosni Mubarak honored the agreements, the relationship between Egypt and Israel was one of "cold peace."

Furthermore, Begin fully intended for Israel to hold and settle all the other occupied territories, and had taken the risk of giving up Sinai partly because he hoped this would make Israel's expansion easier. But to digest the occupied territories, Israel also needed to crush the main political force there, the

Palestine Liberation Organization (PLO), led by Yassir Arafat, which called for the destruction of the Jewish state and used terrorism to further its cause. For this purpose, in 1982, the Israeli army invaded the neighboring country of Lebanon to clear out the PLO, which operated freely in Palestinian refugee camps. Besides, in Lebanon there lived many different Muslim and Christian groups who were in the midst of a vicious and many-sided civil war. The Israelis planned to end the war and install a friendly government, dominated by Christians who would follow the Egyptian example and sign a peace treaty.

In the course of the invasion, Israeli bombing killed thousands of civilians, causing fury in Arab and Muslim lands and revulsion in Israel itself. Meanwhile, U.S. president Ronald Reagan ordered American peacekeeping forces to the capital, Beirut, which were seen by most Lebanese and other Arabs as support for an Israeli effort to set up a puppet government. In 1983, a suicide bomber drove a truck full of explosives into a barracks building that was being used by U.S. marines, killing 240 of them. The president uttered defiant words, but within a few months, the Americans pulled out. Israeli troops also suffered from guerrilla attacks and withdrew gradually; after 1985, they occupied only a small "security" strip north of Israel's border. Instead, the neighboring Arab state of Syria, which had encouraged the campaigns against the American and Israeli forces, became the dominant influence in Lebanon. Its troops occupied most of the country and brought an end to the civil war. In the 1990s, Lebanon developed into an uneasily functioning democracy, where different religious groups each had their share of power and Syria had the last word.

The Lebanon war made it clear to the Israelis that in spite of their military superiority, they were not strong enough to impose peace on any Arab country by force. Arab militants drew the lesson that both the Israelis and the Americans would back down in the face of truck bombs. Fundamentalist denunciations of the Israelis as ruthless invaders and occupiers, the Americans as their henchmen, and moderate-minded Arabs as lackeys of both, came to seem more convincing than before. And many of those denunciations now came from a powerful country where fundamentalists had actually taken over: Iran.

Iran: Westernizing Monarch and Islamic Reaction

Iran had a history dating back well before Islam to the ancient Persian Empire. After the rise of Islam, it remained a separate state with rulers who kept the ancient title of *shah* (king), and it became the main center of the Shia branch of Islam (pp. 162–163), with its highly organized clergy led by revered *ayatollahs* ("Signs of God"). Iran managed to keep its independence during the era of imperialism, though Britain and Russia competed vigorously for influence there—especially after the discovery of huge oil reserves in the early twentieth century. After the Second World War, Iran turned to the United States as a counterweight against Soviet pressure from the north. Then, in 1951, a nationalist leader, Mohammad Mossadegh (**MOH-sah-dek**), came to power and took control of the oil fields away from American and British companies. With American help, Iran's ruler, Mohammad-Reza Shah Pahlavi, overthrew Mossadegh and for the next quarter of a century ruled Iran as an absolute monarchy.

The shah made full use of American aid and his government's oil revenues. He lavished funds on his armed forces and started a program of rapid modernization and industrialization. The oil prosperity helped swell the Iranian middle class, but most of the benefits were channeled to a privileged few. The shah's modernization efforts were also directed against Islamic tradition. He used repression and harassment to undermine the power of the clergy, made clear his sympathy with Western secular ways, and promoted a cult of himself as successor of the Persian kings of the times before Islam.

Public resentment grew in the 1970s, involving numerous groups and parties, but the clergy were the principal promoters of the swelling protest. In 1979, the pent-up pressures exploded against the shah. Riots and street demonstrations mounted in anger and violence. Thousands of people were imprisoned, tortured, or killed by the military during this period, but at last, the shah's soldiers refused to shoot at their rebelling fellow Iranians. The monarch was compelled to flee for his life; and the Ayatollah Khomeini (**khoh-MEY-nee**), who had been guiding the revolt from his exile near Paris, returned in triumph to the capital, Tehran.

Once the revolutionaries were in power, they moved to establish the theocratic (clergy-ruled) Islamic Republic of Iran. The new Revolutionary Council tracked down hundreds of the shah's military and civilian officials, put them on trial, and executed them. It also enforced strict Muslim rules and punishments respecting dress and behavior, especially for women. At the same time, the regime mobilized women in political and social organizations, recognized their right to vote and stand in elections, and continued the shah's policies of expanding women's education at every level from grade school to college. What the Iranian fundamentalists wanted to do was not to oppose every aspect of modern society but to build a modern society on a foundation of Islamic religious values instead of Western secular ones.

Direct confrontation with America began in November 1979 when the shah was received in New York City for medical treatment. Iranian militants protested by seizing the American embassy in Tehran and taking the staff hostage. In return for their release, the militants demanded return of the shah for trial (see photo page 578), recovery of the enormous wealth he had transferred abroad, and an end to American

 An Account of the Iran Hostage Crisis (http://www .jimmycarterlibrary.org/ documents/hostages .phtml) Learn more about the Iran hostage crisis and read from a hostage's journal.

interference in Iran's affairs—demands that the Islamic government supported.

The public reaction in the United States was one of surprise and anger. President Carter reacted by freezing Iranian assets in the United States (amounting to many billions of dollars) and cut off all trade with Iran, including imports of oil. He also appealed to the United Nations and his European allies to

take diplomatic and economic actions against these flagrant violators of international law. (Embassies have always been considered part of a nation's territory abroad.) But it was not until 1981, after a failed rescue mission by the Americans, that the Iranians finally released the hostages in exchange for the unfreezing of Iranian assets and a pledge of noninterference in Iranian affairs.

"The American Shah" A poster on the wall of the occupied U.S. embassy compound in Tehran shows the exiled and ailing ruler cravenly terrified at the thought of the fate that awaits him if the Americans meet the occupiers' demand to return him to Iran. "The American Shah Must Be Hanged" was a popular slogan in Iran at the time.

Afghanistan

The "loss" of Iran was a heavy blow to American prestige and interests, and the Soviets were at first delighted by the humiliation of the United States. However, they feared that the revolutionary Islamic tide might flow from Iran to a neighboring Muslim country, Afghanistan—or even to the millions of Muslims who lived in the southern republics of the USSR. It was this concern, in part, that moved the Soviets to send troops into Afghanistan late in 1979 to install a pro-Soviet regime. This move, in turn, caused a negative reaction in the United States and Europe, jeopardized the frail détente with Russia (pp. 540–541)—and also made the Soviets as much a target of Muslim resentment as Israel and the United States (see photo page 568).

Two things prevented Iran from becoming the center of international Islamic fundamentalism, however. It belonged to the smaller, Shia branch of Islam, which was viewed by the Sunni majority as a heresy; and it was not an Arab country. In a neighboring country, mostly Arab Iraq, a Sunni minority dominated a Shia majority, and the Arab nationalist Baath ("Rebirth") party, led by Saddam Hussein, held a monopoly of power. Saddam feared the spread of Iran's Shia revolution but also hoped that Iran had been weakened by its internal upheaval. In 1980, he attacked Iran, beginning a war that lasted for eight years, ended in stalemate, and probably cost 1 million dead. The Iraqi side received massive financial support and arms deliveries from the United States, the Soviet Union, and wealthy Arab states—a sign of the fear that Shia fundamentalism inspired in the West, the socialist camp, and traditional Sunni rulers.

LO² Worldwide Problems

A quarter of a century after the end of the Second World War, the rivalry and partnership of the First and Second Worlds,

with the Third World uncomfortably straddling the other two, seemed a permanent fact of the world order—even, perhaps, a guarantee of worldwide stability. But other dangers now loomed over the peoples of the world that seemed to arise out of the very nature of modern civilization—its explosive growth of technology, population, and production, and its intricate structure that could be unbalanced by small-scale violent acts.

Population, Resources, and Pollution

Advances in science and technology were primarily responsible for sweeping changes in social conditions. After 1800, the decrease in death rates, flowing chiefly from improvements in food production and medical practices, led to a sharp rise in the number of people in the world (p. 430). The rate of increase grew even steeper in the twentieth century; the numbers being added to the world's population each year were greater than ever before. In the decade of the 1980s, the cumulative increase amounted to more than 1 billion people—bringing the total to more than 5 billion in 1990. By the year 2000, the total reached 6 billion.

 The Dangers of Unregulated Growth and Technological Innovations Read an analysis from the 1970s on the dangers of unregulated growth.

For the time being, the food supply kept up with population growth but allowed little improvement in nutrition. The so-called **Green Revolution**, which introduced better grain seeds during the 1970s, lifted yields, but the increases were limited by inadequate supplies of water and fertilizer. The poor two-thirds of the globe (Asia, Latin America, Africa), where numbers rose the fastest, suffered from endemic malnutrition, and in Africa in particular, there were periodic famines. Meanwhile, the average American or European consumed many times more calories and proteins than the average Asian or African.

Other resources also came up short. Residents of the industrialized countries were shocked into an awareness of this reality by the unexpected Arab oil embargo of 1973, followed by dramatic price hikes by the Organization of Petroleum Exporting Countries (OPEC). Suddenly, the wheels of factories and automobiles slowed. In a few years, oil became plentiful and cheap again, but that in turn raised further threats: environmental pollution caused by rising energy consumption, industrial wastes, and the use of chemicals, and global warming caused by the consumption of both oil and coal on an ever vaster scale.

The dangers of pollution were highlighted in 1985 by the accidental release of a deadly gas from an American plant in Bhopal, India. Thousands of people were killed in a matter of hours or days. But pollution was easier to control than the emission of carbon dioxide gas caused by the burning of coal and oil—a "greenhouse gas" that traps the heat of the sun within the atmosphere. In the 1980s, scientists detected an increase in the temperature of the atmosphere and the oceans, and began to predict apocalyptic consequences, such as flooding of low-lying areas by rising oceans as ice caps melted, and devastating storms as the amount of energy trapped within the atmosphere increased.

But industrial society could not survive without mass production of energy, and ever since the Industrial Revolution, the main source of energy had been the burning of fossil fuels (p. 423). How could fossil fuels be replaced? Atomic energy, produced by nuclear reactors, was one answer. But this created new problems, such as operational safety, misuse by terrorists of the plutonium produced, and above all disposal of radioactive wastes that would remain deadly for thousands of years. The world was sharply alerted to such dangers by a reactor explosion in 1986 at the Ukrainian town of Chernobyl, then in the USSR, which spread a cloud of radioactive debris across much of the Northern Hemisphere (see photo). "Green technologies," using the force

of wind and tides and the heat of the sun to generate electricity, were another answer, but it would be a long time, if ever, before these technologies could mass-produce energy on the necessary scale. As the evidence for global warming mounted, it began to seem the most daunting worldwide problem of the human race.

The Third World and the First World

The problems of population and resources also had a decisive influence on relationships between the poorer and wealthier countries—which mainly meant those of the Third World and the First World, respectively. In order to reach at least survivable standards of living, the poorer countries asked for the creation of a "new international economic order" based on fairness and sharing rather than on power and inequality. They wanted control, for their own benefit, of whatever resources and natural advantages they possessed. And they demanded changes in the terms of trade, the relation between prices received for their exports and prices paid for their imports.

For their part, the wealthier countries accepted the fact of global interdependence, but they insisted on being the ones to decide what "adjustments" were to be made. The "North-South dialogue" of the 1970s and 1980s (between the rich and the poor nations) produced little help for development of the Third World. The poor countries, partly because of their own mistakes in economic planning and execution, were worse off in the 1980s than they were in the 1970s.

A side effect of the contrasting living standards among nations was a steep rise in the number of immigrants to the better-off states. In the nineteenth century, millions of Europeans migrated to the New World (p. 430). In the twentieth century, as Europe became more prosperous, the main flows of emigration came to be from Third World countries, either to the United States or to former imperial ruling countries in Europe. These migrants were joined by refugees from political repression,

> "*As the evidence for global warming mounted, it began to seem the most daunting worldwide problem of the human race.*"

deterrence

In global politics, the capacity of one nation to deter another from attacking it by the threat of retaliating in kind.

first-strike capability

The ability to destroy enough of the opponent's nuclear weapons (in a surprise attack) so that the opponent's retaliatory strike would cause only limited losses to the attacker.

Images from Sebastiao Salgado's Migrations: *Humanity in Transition* **Series** (http://www.pdngallery.com/legends/legends10/) View a collection of photographs documenting the world's migrations.

"ethnic cleansing," or social chaos (as in Rwanda, Somalia, and the former Yugoslavia). A United Nations study documented the alarming increase in the numbers of refugees: their count in 1973 was 2.5 million; within twenty years, in 1993, it was 19 million. And the number was swelled by millions more who migrated for the simple reason of crushing poverty in their homelands. Private humanitarian aid agencies were unable to meet their needs, and governments were strained to deal with them.

Most of the industrialized countries faced the inflow—Germany, France, Britain, the United States, and others. Immigration, legal and illegal, became a daunting problem, especially for housing, education, and medical care. The resulting financial cost, job competition, and social frictions with the newcomers disturbed the established residents and produced worrisome consequences. Antiforeign and racist sentiments mounted, and in some of the affected nations, such as France and Germany, extremist right-wing political parties began exploiting the situation to their advantage.

Nuclear Weapons and Terrorism

In the bipolar and ex-colonial world of the 1970s and 1980s, the relative distribution of strength was military as well as economic. Recognition of this fact speeded the race for weaponry, both nuclear and "conventional." The superpowers, notwithstanding their existing "overkill" capabilities and their lip service to arms control, spent hundreds of billions of dollars annually in a technological struggle for superiority. As each side matched the new weaponry of the other, neither gained in security or influence. On the other hand, if either side fell behind, it might lose in security and influence by no longer having the capacity of **deterrence**—to deter the other side from attacking it by the threat of retaliating in kind.

The Superpower Balance of Terror

The most dangerous and costly contest was in nuclear arms. The race had started in 1945 with the dropping of the first atomic bomb on Japan. This action by the Americans let the world know of their ability and will to use these "ultimate" weapons when they saw fit. The Soviets responded by building nuclear bombs of their own; during the 1950s, the race went onward for more efficient warheads and for faster and more accurate means of delivery. In this race, the Americans generally kept ahead, both in technological advances and in numbers of deliverable warheads.

Though many types of weapons were designed—for such purposes as short-range ("tactical") use against armies and for use at sea against submarines—the most critical area of competition was in long-range ("strategic") weapons that could reach the homeland of the other superpower. The Soviets put most warheads of this type into land-based missiles, placed in underground silos. The United States put most of theirs in nuclear-powered submarines, as well as in land-based missiles and bombers.

No matter what the differences in numbers and locations, it was clear by 1970 that each side had more than enough warheads to wipe out the population of the other side. Nevertheless, each side sought a breakthrough, by technological advance or sheer numbers, that would give it superiority over the other side. Essentially, this meant gaining a **first-strike capability**: that is, the ability to destroy enough of the opponent's nuclear weapons (in a surprise attack) so that the opponent's retaliatory strike would cause only limited losses to the attacker. The superpower that gained first-strike capability would supposedly have the final say in disputes with its rival. That is why each side wanted the advantage—and, even more important, why it could not permit the other side to gain it.

As it became obvious that neither side would be permitted to win superiority by adding more offensive weapons (because the other side would add more also), nuclear war planners turned to defensive weapons as a way to gain the advantage. If one side had a "near-perfect" defense against enemy warheads while the other did not, the first side would then have gained the desired first-strike capacity. So a race began about 1970 to build antiballistic missile (ABM) defenses.

However, this simply added another threatening and expensive side to the arms race—one that, again, neither side could win nor yet afford to lose. In 1972, President Richard Nixon and the Soviet leader, Leonid Brezhnev, signed a treaty limiting the building of ABM systems. This agreement was followed by further efforts to achieve limitations on or reductions of offensive weapons. A promising advance was achieved in 1979, when a Strategic Arms Limitation Treaty (SALT) was signed by Brezhnev and a new president, Jimmy Carter. However, after the Soviet intervention in Afghanistan, the U.S. Senate would not ratify the treaty, and the race in offensive weapons remained open.

Nuclear Proliferation

By the late 1960s, Britain, France, and China also possessed nuclear arsenals, though much smaller than those of the superpowers. For them, this was partly a matter of national prestige: a nation, to be considered a first-class power, now had to belong to the "nuclear club." In addition, they viewed their weapons as a deterrent threat against any nation that might plan to attack them. The five nuclear powers, however, did not want other countries to follow their example. The more nuclear weapons "proliferated" (spread), the greater the risk of a "small" nuclear catastrophe somewhere, which might also ignite a total catastrophe should the major nuclear powers become involved. Many nonnuclear countries, sharing this fear, supported and promoted the idea of a worldwide **Nuclear Nonproliferation Treaty (NPT)**. Signatories that possessed nuclear weapons would agree not to help other countries develop them; signatories that did not have such weapons would undertake never to acquire them. The treaty came into effect in 1968, and over the next twenty years nearly all countries of the world joined it.

Four countries, however, did not join. Israel, resented by its neighbors, developed nuclear arms to be used if invading armies seemed about to conquer it. At the insistence of its U.S. ally, which wanted the Arab states to join the NPT, Israel did not publicly announce its nuclear arsenal, but the fact that it had one was well known. South Africa, also unpopular in its region, built half a dozen atom bombs—also unannounced—but later dismantled them when apartheid collapsed. India, wanting to match China and intimidate Pakistan, tested a bomb in 1974; and Pakistan began developing nuclear arms with a view to deterring India. Some other countries, such as Iraq, Iran, and North Korea, joined the NPT but worked on nuclear weapons in violation of their obligations. Many signatories, though glad not to possess such weapons, have come to resent the legal division of the world into a privileged "nuclear club" and a mass of nonnuclear "outsiders." Still, most countries have abided by their NPT undertakings in spite of the conflicts that divide them.

Terrorism

The success of the NPT did not prevent nonnuclear countries from building up other types of arms, whose power and accuracy were also growing remarkably. In addition, the vulnerabilities of modern civilization made **terrorism** attractive as a type of armed force.

Deliberate and indiscriminate killing and destruction in order to inspire widespread fear, cause societies to cease to function, and thereby achieve political and military goals are nothing new. Conquerors throughout history have suppressed uprisings by massacring villagers and burning their crops; all sides in the Second World War indiscriminately bombed cities. But to achieve their purposes, these deeds were always on a vast scale, whereas terrorism generally involves not large-scale but relatively small-scale (though still indiscriminate) killing and destruction. Modern civilization itself then spreads the fear through the mass media, and widens the damage through its complex web of transport and communications.

 The Troubles in Ireland: An IRA Leader Reveals Its Ultimate Aims Read a 1979 statement of goals by the leader of the nationalist Irish Republican Army.

This is what makes terrorism a suitable weapon for small unofficial groups claiming to represent repressed populations. It expresses rage against real or imagined injuries arising out of religious, ethnic, social, and national conflicts, and it satisfies the need for revenge. To crush terrorist groups costs efforts out of all proportion to their size, and often leads repressors to atrocities that keep hatred against them alive. Even if a terrorist group does not achieve its stated political and military goals, therefore, it can produce a bloody stalemate that hurts the repressors as much as the terrorists (see photo page 582).

To begin with, in fact, terrorism sometimes did achieve its goals. Following the Second World War, it was successfully used by some nationalist movements against weakening imperialist countries—for example, by Arab nationalists against the French in Algeria and by Zionist extremists against the British in Palestine. The success of these early campaigns, together with new opportunities for spectacular operations presented by the growth of airline travel, led to new campaigns in the 1960s and 1970s—by Cuban opponents of the government of Fidel Castro, by Palestinian exiles against Israeli and Jewish targets following the 1967 Six-Day War, and by Irish nationalist opponents and British loyalist supporters of British rule in Northern Ireland.

These new campaigns had much less chance of success. Car bombs might encourage the British to evacuate Palestine, which was not a vital national interest for them. Against airplane hijackings intended actually to overthrow communist rule or the Jewish state, however, the governments of Cuba and Israel had no choice but to stand and fight. But from the point of view of the terrorists, bloody stalemate was better than no conflict at all. This view was shared by the rulers of countries under Arab nationalist or Islamic fundamentalist rule like Syria or Libya, which sponsored terrorism as a weapon against adversaries like Israel or the United States. By the 1980s, terrorism had become common enough to constitute a recognized worldwide problem, though it was not generally regarded as so serious as nuclear proliferation or the balance of terror. In the 1990s, however, the priorities would change and the problems would merge.

LO³ The End of the Cold War

During the 1980s, changes got under way in the political and economic order that had existed throughout the West since the Second World War. There was a widespread sense of frustration with the functioning of the welfare state, which came to seem a

Nuclear Nonproliferation Treaty (NPT)
An international agreement that nations in possession of nuclear weapons will not help other nations develop them, and that those that do not have such weapons will never acquire them.

terrorism
Deliberate and indiscriminate killing and destruction conducted on a relatively small scale in order to inspire fear and achieve political and military goals.

brake on economic growth and rising standards of living. A new militancy appeared in relations with the socialist camp, whose worldwide power seemed to be increasing even while oppressive dictatorships continued to rule its home countries.

Neither of these changes represented a total break with the past. No Western political leader seriously tried to dismantle the welfare state, and few politicians of any stripe doubted that the socialist camp would be the West's rival and partner for the indefinite future. But meanwhile, frustrations and disappointments were growing among the political leaders of the socialist camp as well. At the end of the decade, it was the socialist countries that made a total break with the past, and of their own accord gave up the effort to build a world order alternative to that of the West.

Political and Economic Changes in the West: Thatcher and Reagan

During the 1980s, many Western countries swung toward conservative domestic policies. This was primarily a reaction against the "liberal" policies that had generally prevailed in the West from the 1930s to the 1970s. In the eighteenth and nineteenth centuries, the terms "liberal" and "liberalism" had been equated with individualism and with the revolt against hereditary privilege and absolute monarchy (pp. 397, 413–416). In the twentieth century, liberalism still stood for individual rights (civil liberties) and openness to social reform but came to be most strongly identified with social democracy and the welfare state (pp. 496–497). The social and moral changes that accompanied the welfare state also came to be linked with liberalism.

"Thatcherite" Britain

Although the conservative reaction to these changes proceeded unevenly in most countries of the West, it took decisive form in Britain and the United States. Margaret Thatcher was chosen as leader by Britain's Conservative Party in 1979, and she led her party to victory in Parliament during the ensuing decade. With large majorities in the elected House of Commons, she was able to enact sweeping reforms. Many government-owned enterprises were **privatized** (sold off to private corporations); the educational system was overhauled at all levels—and at reduced cost; the power of trade unions was curbed; and taxation policies shifted ever more to favor the rich. Although these changes were not altogether pleasing to many British voters, Thatcher gained and held power largely because of splits within the opposition Labour Party. By 1990, her public support had fallen sharply, and she resigned as party leader and prime minister. But many of the "Thatcherite" changes survived their originator's downfall to become permanent features of the British way of life.

The "Reagan Revolution"

In the United States, the conservatives did not achieve a full grip on the federal government. This was due to the constitutional provision for "checks and balances," which distributes authority among the legislative, executive, and judicial branches. The election and reelection of Richard Nixon as president in 1968 and 1972 had signaled widespread disillusionment with liberal social reforms, but Nixon had disappointed conservatives by upholding both the welfare state and détente. He had then left office in 1974 under threat of impeachment, following the discovery of his role in covering up a political burglary at the Watergate office and apartment complex in Washington, D.C., as well as in numerous other abuses—illegal financial contributions, misuse of government agencies, campaign "dirty tricks," and obstruction of justice. It took several years for the conservatives to regroup and rally under another leader—Ronald Reagan, the governor of California.

The conservatives, like the liberals, had a considerable range of interpreters, but the central thrust of the movement was becoming quite clear. They objected to many of the features of the welfare state introduced in 1933 by Franklin Roosevelt's New Deal (p. 497) and to some of the social and ethical changes that had come about during the sixties (pp. 554–555). Many liberals themselves, who found that these changes had gone

≪ **Martyrs and Fighters** In twentieth-century Northern Ireland, Catholic-Irish nationalist and Protestant-British loyalist groups both committed terror and revenge killings of civilians. A wall painting in a Catholic suburb of the capital, Belfast, commemorates militants who died on hunger strike in prison in 1981, portrayed at top; below, a detachment of "Belfast B Company" of the Irish Republican Army "secures" a local street. Anger at British repression and fear of Protestant attack make "B Company" popular here, regardless of its murderous methods. Peter Montson/AP Photo

farther than they had expected or wanted, changed their political allegiance and became **neoconservatives**. Opposition was thus a principal part of the conservative program—opposition to the expanding functions of government (business regulation, welfare services, deficit spending, high taxes), and opposition to social "permissiveness"—feminism, abortion, pornography, and busing to improve racial balance in the public schools. The affirmative aims of American conservatives included a more assertive foreign policy, military superiority over the Soviet Union, restoring laissez-faire economic policies, strengthening "law and order," rejuvenating the traditional family and morals, and returning to religious "fundamentals."

The issues between conservatives and liberals found clear focus in the elections of both 1980 and 1984. The Republican Party, which had stood in opposition to most of the reforms of the New Deal, remained the political stronghold of conservatism. The Democratic Party, beginning with the New Deal, had become identified with liberalism. The Republicans won the presidency for Ronald Reagan in 1980, as well as control over the Senate. The election results signaled that conservatives had gained the balance of power in the nation—politically, psychologically, and philosophically—and the new president began to pursue a genuinely conservative agenda, the "Reagan Revolution."

As president, Reagan sought to reverse the tendency, which dated back to Franklin Roosevelt, of looking to government as a positive agency for solving the nation's problems and aiding its citizens. Reagan, rejecting that view, declared that "government is not the solution; it is the problem." In keeping with that declaration, he cut income tax rates, which in turn put heavy pressure on Congress to make up for the loss in government revenues by cutting spending on social programs. But Reagan insisted, at the same time, on large increases in military spending. As a result, the federal budget could not be balanced, and the huge annual deficits (money shortages) had to be made up through government borrowing, much of it from foreign investors. The tax cuts left more money for businesses to invest and consumers to spend and thereby stimulated substantial economic growth, but it left the country with a mountain of government debt (in addition to an unprecedented level of private debt)—a situation that would recur in the United States and other wealthy countries in future years.

In addition to reducing tax rates, Reagan pushed for deregulation of the economy. This was favored by the business community, but contributed to some serious negative results. Lax supervision of the savings and loan industry, for example, was a factor in permitting gross mismanagement and risky lending there. And since Congress had guaranteed depositors' savings accounts, it had to come up with hundreds of billions of dollars to make up the losses—the first great taxpayer bailout of financial institutions that had run themselves into unrepayable debt.

Relations with the "Evil Empire"

Reagan became president at a time when the Soviet Union had engaged in a lengthy buildup of nuclear and conventional arms. This was partly in order to force the United States to treat it as an equal in their bipolar partnership, but also to gain the advantage in their bipolar rivalry.

Soviet intervention in Afghanistan, as well as their support for the spread of left-wing governments and guerrilla insurgencies in Central America and southern Africa, seemed to be changing the bipolar balance of power and thereby undermining détente. Reagan, whose intense anticommunism went back to his earliest years in politics, was eager to take up the challenge. As president, he aimed, through a military buildup, to deal with the Soviets from a "position of strength"—which meant superior strength. He believed that this policy would stop communist expansionism and, by overstraining the Soviet economy, would lead to the undermining of the "evil empire."

In confrontations with communism throughout the world, Reagan took a hard line. When the Caribbean island of Grenada fell into a political crisis under its Marxist leaders in 1982, he sent United States military forces to occupy the island and install a prodemocratic government there. He supported the government of the Central American republic of El Salvador in a brutal war against Marxist guerrillas, while also backing guerrilla uprisings against Marxist governments in neighboring Nicaragua and in the southern African republic of Angola. None of these wars was as easy to win as that against Grenada, and in all three countries, they dragged on, at huge cost in human suffering, until the end of the Cold War. Once the Marxists could no longer count on Soviet support and the United States no longer saw the opponents of the Marxists as allies against communism, the conflicts ended in compromise.

Besides redressing the general balance of power with the Soviet Union, Reagan was eager to change the nuclear balance of terror in favor of the United States. By 1980, the nuclear arms race with the Soviet Union had come to a standoff. The superpowers had reached rough equality ("parity") in offensive power. But Reagan and his advisers were not satisfied with parity, and they began steps to regain nuclear superiority—which the United States had enjoyed right after the Second World War. They believed this could be done through a massive buildup of arms: annual military spending doubled from $150 billion for the year 1981 to about $300 billion in 1985—and continued to increase thereafter. The Soviets, however, matched the buildup, and the strategic standoff persisted.

With the effort to gain superiority through offensive weapons at a dead end, in 1983, Reagan proposed to build a defensive system against intercontinental nuclear missiles. This was a return to an earlier idea in the arms race, which had been rejected by both sides in 1972 when they signed the ABM treaty. But advances in technology—lasers, computers, space mirrors—had led some weapon scientists to advise the president that another try should be made. Reagan therefore determined to give up the "stability" of the existing nuclear balance and seek to construct a space-based system—one that could give the United States a first-strike capacity. Reagan called his plan the Strategic Defense Initiative, but it was quickly dubbed "Star Wars" by the news media. It soon became clear that even if the technical problems could be solved, a workable Star Wars sys-

neoconservatives
Liberals who changed their political allegiance in reaction against the welfare state and societal changes.

PROLETARIANS STRIKE AGAINST SOCIALISM: THE TWENTY-ONE DEMANDS OF THE LENIN SHIPYARD WORKERS

In August 1980, workers at the Lenin Shipyard in the Polish port city of Gdańsk went on strike after the government decreed the latest of many increases in meat prices and the shipyard management dismissed a crane operator, Anna Walentynowicz **(vah-len-tee-NOV-ich)**, for distributing an unofficial labor newspaper. The government had broken shipyard strikes before by shooting down workers, but this time, the movement spread to factories throughout the city. The workers formed an Interfactory Strike Committee, chaired by an electrician who had earlier been discharged as a troublemaker, Lech Wałęsa **(vah-WEN-sa)**.

The strikes spread far and wide through Poland, and the strike committee became the center of a nationwide free trade union movement (as opposed to the official unions linked with the Communist Party), Solidarity. Eventually the government declared martial law and banned Solidarity, which continued as an underground movement, reemerged in the Gorbachev era, and took over the government.

As soon as it was formed, the strike committee posted in the shipyard a handwritten list of twenty-one demands concerning economic and political reform—demands that foreshadowed the eventual dismantling of Polish communism under Lech Wałęsa as the country's president.

1. Acceptance of Free Trade Unions independent of both the Party and employers, in accordance with the International Labor Organization's Convention number 87 on the freedom to form unions, which was ratified by the Polish government.
2. A guarantee of the right to strike and guarantees of security for strikers and their supporters.
3. Compliance with the freedoms of press and publishing guaranteed in the Polish constitution. A halt to repression of independent publications and access to the mass media for representatives of all faiths.
4. (a) Reinstatement to their former positions for: people fired for defending workers' rights, in particular those participating in the strikes of 1970 and 1976; students dismissed from school for their convictions.
   (b) The release of all political prisoners . . .
   (c) A halt to repression for one's convictions.

tem would cost hundreds of billions of dollars, and the Soviets indicated that if the system went into operation, they would build up their offensive missile force so that it would overcome any defense system by sheer weight of numbers. Neither side was eager for a new round of the arms race that would be more costly than any before it, and the time seemed ripe to reduce tension between the superpowers.

The Star Wars issue was one of the main subjects discussed at the Geneva summit meeting in November 1985 between Reagan and a new Soviet leader, Mikhail Gorbachev **(GOR-buh-choff)**. Responding to concessions and fresh initiatives from Gorbachev, Reagan displayed a definite shift in his tone and words to the Soviets. This shift proved to be a critical turning point, built upon later by both leaders, toward slowing down the arms race between the superpowers, and the Star Wars

 CNN In-Depth Special Report on the Reagan Years (http://www.cnn.com/SPECIALS/2001/reagan.years/index.html) Learn more about the Reagan years.

project was eventually shelved. In addition, the revelation that what the Soviet leaders called the "correlation of forces" was not moving in their favor contributed both to the end of the Cold War and to the fall of communism.

The Revolutions in Eastern Europe: Gorbachev, Yeltsin

While conservative reforms were gradually taking shape in western Europe and America during the 1980s, the Socialist Camp showed little change on its surface. On the contrary, when the Polish "Solidarity" labor movement challenged communist authorities in the early 1980s, the Polish government, both fearing for its own survival and urged on by the Soviet leaders, repressed Solidarity temporarily by placing the country under martial law. Everything seemed to be normal in the Socialist Camp, until the end of the decade, when it suddenly fell apart.

5. The broadcasting on the mass media of information about the establishment of the Interfactory Strike Committee (MKS) and publication of the list of demands.

6. The undertaking of real measures to get the country out of its present crisis by:
   (a) providing comprehensive, public information about the socio-economic situation;
   (b) making it possible for people from every social class and stratum of society to participate in open discussions concerning the reform program.

7. Compensation of all workers taking part in the strike for its duration with holiday pay from the Central Council of Trade Unions.

8. Raise the base pay of every worker 2,000 zlotys per month [about 44 dollars at the time] to compensate for price rises to date.

9. Guaranteed automatic pay raises indexed to price inflation and to decline in real income.

10. Meeting the requirements of the domestic market for food products: only surplus goods to be exported.

11. The rationing of meat and meat products through food coupons (until the market is stabilized).

12. Abolition of "commercial prices" and hard currency sales in so-called "internal export" shops.

13. A system of merit selection for management positions on the basis of qualifications rather than Party membership. Abolition of the privileged status of MO [police], SB [Internal Security Police], and the party apparatus through: equalizing all family subsidies; eliminating special stores, etc.

14. Reduction of retirement age for women to 50 and for men to 55. Anyone who has worked in the PRL [Polish People's Republic] for 30 years, for women, or 35 years for men, without regard to age, should be entitled to retirement benefits.

15. Bringing pensions and retirement benefits of the "old portfolio" [pensions dating from earlier years that carried no cost-of-living increase] to the level of those paid currently.

16. Improvement in the working conditions of the Health Service, which would assure full medical care to working people.

17. Provision for sufficient openings in daycare nurseries and preschools for the children of working people.

18. Establishment of three-year paid maternity leaves for the raising of children.

19. Reduce the waiting time for apartments.

20. Raise per diem [for work-related travel] from 40 zlotys to 100 zlotys and provide cost-of-living increases.

21. Saturdays to be days off from work. Those who work on round-the-clock jobs or three-shift systems should have the lack of free Saturdays compensated by increased holiday leaves or through other paid holidays off from work.

EXPLORING THE SOURCE

1. Judging from these demands, what were the main features of the Polish socialist economy that disadvantaged workers?

2. Judging by the demands, what were the workers' main grievances against Polish socialism other than strictly economic ones?

Source: Lawrence Weschler, *The Passion of Poland, from Solidarity Through the State of War* (New York: Pantheon, 1984), pp. 206–208.

For some seventy years since the Russian Revolution of 1917, the Communist Party's grip on the Soviet Union had appeared to be unbreakable. So too seemed its forty-year grip on the satellite countries of East Germany, Poland, Czechoslovakia, Romania, Hungary, and Bulgaria. There had been some outspoken dissidents, like Aleksandr Solzhenitsyn (p. 523), but the socialist camp's instruments of control and repression were seemingly so systematic and so powerful that no major change could erupt from below. The sudden collapse of communism, when it came, was the "historical surprise" of the century.

Although largely unknown to foreign observers, serious doubts about the communist system had begun to grow within the Soviet Union during the 1980s. More and more party members (as well as ordinary citizens) were concluding that the longtime

> *"The sudden collapse of communism, when it came, was the 'historical surprise' of the century."*

promises of communism were not being fulfilled. They viewed with envy the rising prosperity of the capitalist West that socialism seemingly could not match, and they were discouraged by the failure of many years of weapons buildup to change the "correlation of forces" between the Soviet Union and the United States. As a result, they became convinced that changes had to be made to rescue their faltering economy—and that if only to lighten the burden of military spending, these changes must include an end to the worldwide power struggle with the West. But could the system be reformed without destroying it?

Perestroika and Glasnost

In 1985, the central committee of the party chose Mikhail Gorbachev as their agent of

glasnost
The "opening up" of Soviet society, including new freedoms of expression, assembly, and political activity.

perestroika
The "restructuring" of the Soviet economy in the direction of a market economy.

change. He moved quickly in two directions: what he called **glasnost (GLAS-nost)**, the "opening up" of Soviet society and **perestroika (per-uh-STROI-kuh)**, the "restructuring" of the economy. Gorbachev had powerful domestic critics on both "left" and "right" (those who wanted to move faster and those who tried to hold back reforms). Nevertheless, swift action was taken to implement glasnost. Thousands of political prisoners were released, and free expression and free assembly were permitted. Perhaps the most significant constitutional reform was the abolition of the Communist Party's monopoly on political power. New elections took place throughout the USSR, with rival nonparty groups vying for office.

Gorbachev's principal frustrations lay in the area of perestroika—the restructuring of the economy. Some individuals wanted to move as quickly as possible from the existing system of centralized control to a full-fledged market economy. Others believed that such a rapid move would be too disruptive and painful to workers and consumers; they favored a "go-slow" approach. Gorbachev, walking the tightrope, proposed a plan combining features from both sides. In October 1990, his compromise was approved by the newly elected Soviet Parliament—and he was authorized, as president, to set it in motion by executive decree. But Gorbachev's economic plan proved to be too little and too late: it caused widespread hardship by disrupting the workings of the socialist economy, without liberating the economic forces that socialism had confined.

 The Last Heir of Lenin Explains His Reform Plans: Perestroika and Glasnost Read Gorbachev's plans for economic and political reform in the USSR.

The Liberation of Eastern Europe

In foreign affairs, Gorbachev urged "new thinking"—for his own and other countries, and supported his words with action by pulling Soviet troops out of Afghanistan in 1988. The Cold War and its confrontational policies had proved enormously wasteful dead ends. A new era of cooperation in addressing the real problems of the planet was called for. But the "retreat from empire" signaled by the withdrawal from Afghanistan, together with the political and economic reforms at home, also precipitated revolutions in the eastern European satellite states.

The economies of the satellites had suffered from the same growing paralysis that the Soviets were enduring, and their governments held power through repression backed by the threat of Soviet intervention. Once the Soviet Union began to dismantle its economic and government system, it no longer made sense for it to uphold the same system in the satellite countries, and Gorbachev signaled that force would no longer be used to hold them in tow. No doubt, he expected that they

From Prisoner to President A month before demonstrators displayed this poster in November 1989 in the Czechoslovak capital, Prague, Václav Havel had been locked in the city's central jail. It was not the first time the prominent man of letters had done time as a "dissident"—a public opponent of his country's hardline communist rulers. Now, as communism crumbled, the demonstrators had no need to name the man they wanted "For President." The month after, the ex-convict would move into the Prague Castle, the presidential palace. Peter Turnley/Corbis

> "The Cold War and its confrontational policies had proved enormously wasteful dead ends."

would reform themselves on the same pattern that he was attempting in the Soviet Union. Instead, in 1989 and 1990, popular movements—mostly nonviolent—exploded against the communist regimes in Poland, East Germany, Hungary, Romania, Bulgaria, and Czechoslovakia (see photo).

In complex negotiations, the West Germans persuaded both their NATO allies and their former Warsaw Pact opponents that they would not use reunification as a springboard for reversing the results of the Second World War, and Germany was reunited as a single country. Czechoslovakia, on the other hand, was divided in 1993, by joint consent of its two predominant nations, into the Czech Republic and Slovakia. Though Yugoslavia had not been part of the Warsaw Pact, that country took a similar course of democratization and separation into its component republics—followed in this case by civil war.

 A Presidential Address to the People of Czechoslovakia on New Year's Day Read a speech by Václav Havel, the new leader of Czechoslovakia, a year after communism fell.

The Breakup of the Soviet Union

The liberation of the satellite states, as well as Gorbachev's general policy of repudiating the use of military force to uphold regimes, opened the door to long-pent-up desires for independence in the multinational Soviet Union itself. The three Baltic republics (p. 505) were the first to break away. The Russian Republic, the largest by far of the fifteen, quickly followed, along with Ukraine, Georgia, Azerbaijan (ah-zer-bahy-JAHN), and most of the other republics. How could a multinational economic plan work if each of the now sovereign states took off on its own plans? This dilemma was highlighted in the case of the Russian Republic. Boris Yeltsin, a former communist turned radical reformer, was elected president of that new republic in 1991. He declared, with the support of the republic's parliament, that Russia would change over to a full market economy "in five hundred days."

The momentous happenings of August 1991 gave added force to Yeltsin's plan. The political "right," backed by the secret police, ranking army officers, and Communist Party conservatives, launched a coup against Gorbachev (still officially the president of the USSR) and the reformers in the Russian parliament. But the coup lasted only seventy-two hours as thousands of Muscovites filled the streets to defend their parliament—and the deployed army units were pulled back.

The failed coup thus damaged the reactionaries—and gave decisive impetus to the supporters of democracy, market economy, and independence for the constituent republics. Within days, the reformers in the parliament initiated far-reaching measures: to deprive the Communist Party of any effective role in government, alter drastically the functions of the secret police, loosen controls over the media, and ensure that the armed forces were kept under the command of loyal officers. The way was also cleared for achievement of complete independence by the individual republics—whose elected leaders would now be free to negotiate their relations with one another and with foreign countries (see Map 31.1).

Collapse of the Soviet Union (http://video.google.com/videoplay?docid=-8953962851459266994#) Watch footage of the three days that changed Soviet history.

Map 31.1 "The Greatest Geopolitical Catastrophe of the Century"

That was the later verdict of Russian president Vladimir Putin on the events of 1991, whereby Russia lost all the territory that the tsars had gained in four centuries of westward and southward expansion, and millions of Russians were left on the "wrong" side of new borders. Most of the non-Russian peoples of the Soviet Union rejoiced more or less wholeheartedly in independence, but like all breakups of empires, this one left plenty of room for future conflicts. © Cengage Learning

Interactive Map

Shortly afterward, the governing organs of the USSR ceased to exist. In early December 1991, the presidents of three of the new republics—Russia and its western neighbors, Ukraine and Belarus (formerly Belorussia)—met and announced the creation of a substitute version of the union, which they called the Commonwealth of Independent States (CIS). In addition, the three presidents agreed on a declaration that the Russian Republic was to be accepted as the principal inheritor of the assets and obligations of the Soviet Union—including, especially, control over its nuclear missiles and its commitments to reduce their numbers. This declaration was welcomed by the United States and the European Community.

The CIS was quickly joined by most of the other new republics. Modeled after the idea of the British Commonwealth of Nations (p. 542), the CIS functioned as an international organization with limited powers. Many of its members have since taken steps for economic cooperation, and in 1997, Russia and Belarus agreed on a "union" with a common currency and citizenship, though still remaining separate and independent states.

On Christmas Day 1991, Mikhail Gorbachev, responding to these events, officially resigned his empty office as president of the now-dissolved Soviet Union. Gorbachev had aimed to reform socialism and to maintain the unity of its political domain. But in the country's critical time of troubles, he was swept aside by the swelling popular demand for radical economic change and national self-determination. The long struggle between the West and the socialist camp had ended in the socialist camp's voluntarily admitting defeat. Communism had collapsed suddenly, easily, and relatively peacefully. The process of replacing it, however, would be long, hard, and full of conflict.

 Listen to a synopsis of Chapter 31.

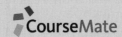 Access to the eBook with additional review material and study tools may be found online at CourseMate for WCIV. Sign in at www.cengagebrain.com.

{ Speak Up! }

"...love the book and the online resources help a lot. The design makes reading much easier and everything is more inviting than a regular textbook. Thanks a lot!"

—Justin Jensen, Student at Western Illinois University

WCIV was built on a simple principle: to create a new teaching and learning solution that reflects the way today's faculty teach and the way you learn.

Through conversations, focus groups, surveys, and interviews, we collected data that drove the creation of the version of **WCIV** that you are using today. But it doesn't stop there—in order to make **WCIV** an even better learning experience, we'd like you to SPEAK UP and tell us how **WCIV** worked for you. What did you like about it? What would you change? Are there additional ideas you have that would help us build a better product for next semester's Western Civilization students?

At **CengageBrain.com,** you'll find all of the resources you need to succeed in Western Civilization—flash cards, interactive online quizzes, a robust eBook, and more!

Speak Up! Go to **CengageBrain.com.**

CHAPTER 32

THE WEST REUNITED?
1990s

LEARNING OBJECTIVES

AFTER READING THIS CHAPTER, YOU SHOULD BE
ABLE TO DO THE FOLLOWING:

LO¹ Analyze the present-day notion of the world as
forming a single international community.

LO² Compare and contrast the economies of the United
States and Europe after the Cold War.

LO³ Trace developments in eastern Europe in the
aftermath of communist rule.

"THE END OF THE COLD WAR WAS FAR FROM ENDING THE RIFTS WITHIN WESTERN CIVILIZATION CREATED BY THE RISE OF COMMUNISM AND THE FORCES OF NATIONALISM."

The fall of communism opened a new stage in the worldwide process of conflict, accommodation, and interchange that is shaping the future organization of Western and world civilization. Having triumphed in the Cold War, the Western partnership of North American and western European capitalist and democratic countries now hoped to steer the world in a direction that would correspond to both their ideals and their long-term interests. Their goal was a harmonious worldwide community of independent nation-states, sharing the Western privileges of democratic freedom and capitalist prosperity, of which they would be the leaders and guardians.

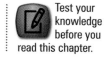

Test your knowledge before you read this chapter.

What do you think?

The threat of outside military action is the best way to prevent "ethnic cleansing."

Strongly Disagree						Strongly Agree
1	2	3	4	5	6	7

True, changes were under way within the Western partnership. The U.S. capitalist economy grew both harsher and more productive than those of its partners as it shrank its welfare state safety net. As the western European countries pooled their resources in the European Union, however, they came to wield almost as much economic power as the United States. Even so, the Western partnership continued close enough to remain the single strongest influence in world affairs, and the United States was still its senior partner.

In addition, the Western partnership expanded far into the lands of the former East. By the early twenty-first century, many eastern European countries that had once belonged to the socialist camp had joined NATO and the European Union, and others were on the way. But still farther eastward lay Russia, for which

≪ **Winners of the Cold War** At a fiftieth anniversary session of the North Atlantic Treaty organization in 1999, the celebrators included representatives of three former members of the Warsaw Pact, the Czech Republic, Hungary, and Poland. Without a Warsaw Pact to confront, the alliance was not sure of its role in world affairs, but other countries of the former East were eager to join it, and it was about to undertake its first-ever actual military operation, a bombing campaign to stop ethnic cleansing in Kosovo by Serbia.

the end of the Soviet Union turned out to mean not so much liberation from communism as national defeat and humiliation. And in the Balkan land of Yugoslavia, what the end of communism mainly liberated was vicious national conflict, leading to atrocities on a scale not seen in Europe since the end of the Second World War. In these respects, the end of the Cold War was far from ending the rifts within Western civilization created by the rise of communism and the forces of nationalism.

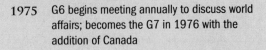

CHRONOLOGY

1975   G6 begins meeting annually to discuss world affairs; becomes the G7 in 1976 with the addition of Canada

1986   Single European Act provides for the free movement of capital and labor across the frontiers of Common Market states

1991   Yugoslav republics declare independence; ethnic cleansing begins

1993   Treaty of Maastricht establishes European Union

1994   NATO countries agree to extend membership to former Soviet satellites

1995   Bosnia, Croatia, and Serbia enter into a peace agreement; NATO peacekeepers move into Bosnia

1997   The G7 becomes the G8 with the addition of Russia

1999   Conflict reignites in the Balkans; the United States forces the Serb army to retreat from Kosovo

2002   A NATO-Russia Joint Council is established

LO¹ The West and the Postcommunist World: The Ideal of an International Community

With the collapse of communism, the bipolar world order had come to a relatively peaceful end. It no longer seemed appropriate, in this world with neither blocs nor colonial empires, to speak of the free world and the socialist camp, the imperial and colonial nations, or even of the First, Second, and Third Worlds. Another term was needed—one that would express the world's renewed hopes for harmonious diversity. More than before, government leaders, diplomats, and journalists began to speak of the world as a single community of nation-states—an **international community**. Now that the blocs had disappeared, it seemed, the time had come for this community truly to emerge.

> **"***Now that the blocs had disappeared, it seemed, the time had come for an international community truly to emerge.***"**

Institutions, Outlaws, and Leaders

Like all communities, this one had its common institutions, principally the United Nations (UN) and its affiliated organizations. It had its volunteer groups, which summoned dedicated activists to help solve its problems—**nongovernmental organizations (NGOs)** like Amnesty International (which devoted

itself to the plight of political prisoners), Oxfam (the Oxford Committee for Famine Relief), or Médecins sans frontières (Doctors Without Borders). But the community also had its bitter internal conflicts, which often tore apart individual nation-states—**failed states**, as such victims of conflict came to be called—and which the common institutions could hardly contain. And there were also **rogue states**—outlaws who would not obey the community's rules, and whom the common institutions were not strong enough to master.

In addition, the international community had its leading citizens, members of the world's most exclusive club: the Group of Seven (G7) leading democratic and capitalist countries, whose leaders had met yearly since 1975 to discuss world affairs in a relaxed and informal atmosphere. Six of these countries—Britain, Canada, France,

Strengthening the Role of Nongovernmental Organizations: Partners for Sustainable Development, from the United Nation's Agenda 21 (http://habitat.igc.org/agenda21/a21-27.htm) Read how the United Nations views the role of NGOs in creating a sustainable future.

Germany, Italy, and the United States—were located in North America and western Europe, the heartland of modern Western civilization. The seventh, Japan, was the non-Western country that had most successfully striven to gain equality with the West by adopting and adapting Western ways of doing business and running countries.

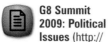 **G8 Summit 2009: Political Issues** (http://www.g8italia2009.it/static/G8_Allegato/G8_Declaration_08_07_09_final,0.pdf) Read the latest assessment of world affairs from a recent summit of the former G7, now the G8.

All of the G7 countries had already been prominent and privileged in the world at the end of the nineteenth century, and had managed to keep this position through all the ups and downs of imperialism, two world wars, decolonization, and the Cold War. Together with the smaller western European countries, they now formed the political and economic West—with Japan counting as fully Western in this political and economic sense.

The International Community and the West

To maintain their leadership, the democratic-capitalist countries would have to continue to share the ideals and interests that had held them together during the Cold War. In addition, the peoples of the rest of the world, in spite of their enormous diversity and endless conflicts, would have to feel that they too had a stake in a capitalist-democratic world order. If the West maintained its unity, followed its ideals as well as its interests, and was able to operate by consensus with the rest of the world, then perhaps it could steer the world to the benefit of all. Ethnic, religious, and international rivalries would be contained, economies would be able to grow, and nations outside the Western heartland besides Japan would gain influence and power equal to that of the West. In that case, the international community might become a reality, and democratic freedom and capitalist prosperity might be genuinely shared among the nations of the world.

Alternatively, the democratic and capitalist countries might become divided, follow their interests and neglect their ideals, and seek to impose their will on the rest of the world. In that case, the international community would not be a reality but an illusion, disguising a far less benign world order. There would be a fierce "struggle for existence" among nations, ethnic groups, religions, and economic competitors, and the "fittest" countries, Western and non-Western, would hold down the rest by economic power, technical supremacy, and military force. And there were even worse possibilities—of gradual environmental disaster produced by an overindustrialized world, or of sudden catastrophe resulting from the use of nuclear or other weapons of mass destruction by states or terrorist groups.

If the best alternatives came about, the democratic and capitalist countries would certainly have to share the credit with the rest of the world. If the worst possibilities were realized, it would just as certainly not be the fault of these countries alone. For the moment, however, the single strongest influence on the future distribution of wealth and power within global civilization was theirs, for it was they that had won the Cold War.

LO² The West in the 1990s: Continuing Partnership, Evolving Partners

The end of the Cold War was a victory not just for democracy and capitalism, but also for the new international power structure that had grown up within the Western heartland. In the past, Western civilization had sometimes been ruled by universal empires like Rome's and sometimes been divided among many rival states. Since the Second World War, however, the West had become a partnership in which the United States was the senior partner but usually operated in consensus with its junior partners, mostly in western Europe. This new power structure remained very much in effect in the 1990s, in spite of the disappearance of the communist adversary that had brought it into being. Shared democratic values, economic links of trade and investment, and the dangers and uncertainties of the postcommunist world were strong forces binding the partners together, even though their economic and social policies were growing apart, and the European partners were forming stronger links among themselves.

The United States: Economic Success and Its Costs

Bill Clinton was elected president in 1992 as a centrist Democrat who would concentrate on improving the U.S. economy. The conservative Republicans remained a powerful force, however, and from 1994 onward, Clinton faced opposing majorities in both the House and the Senate, committed to a program of shrinking the U.S. welfare state. Clinton found that when he proposed extensions of the welfare state, such as a plan for universal health care, the Republicans could defeat him. On the other hand, if he himself proposed less drastic versions of Republican policies, he could siphon off their support among voters and make them look dangerously radical.

With this strategy, Clinton won reelection in 1996 and kept control of government policy out of the hands of the Republican majorities. The fury and frustration of the Republicans led them to look for scandals that could bring him down. Their efforts came to a head when the House of Representatives impeached him on charges arising out of his efforts to conceal improper relations with a White House intern. The Senate acquitted Clinton, and the affair added a great deal of poison to the political atmosphere.

Meanwhile, economic expansion that had begun in the mid-1980s continued into the Clinton years. The president and his advisers benefited from the "Cold War dividend" (a reduction in defense spending following the disappearance of the Soviet threat) and made politically astute concessions to

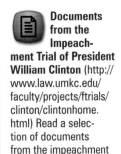

Documents from the Impeachment Trial of President William Clinton (http://www.law.umkc.edu/faculty/projects/ftrials/clinton/clintonhome.html) Read a selection of documents from the impeachment proceedings.

the Republicans' desire to cut welfare spending. As a result they were able to reduce the federal deficit in gradual steps, thereby avoiding the negative impact upon the economy of sudden cuts in government spending. With shrinking deficits and a lower tax burden, consumers had money to spend to keep the economy growing, and unemployment was low. Much of the consumers' spending went on goods imported from abroad, so that the United States regularly imported more than it exported. But foreign investors, confident in the size and strength of the U.S. economy, were willing to lend money to make up the difference between what the United States sold and what it bought in foreign countries. Furthermore, deregulation of financial markets—another area where the Clinton administration cooperated with its Republican opponents—helped borrowing and lending to become easier than ever before, a development that at the time seemed to be in the interests of an expanding economy.

The economic system that came out of the uneasy cooperation between the president and the Republicans was harsher than in the era before the rise of conservatism under Reagan. It offered less security, particularly for unemployed people, and the jobs it created were mainly in low-paying service industries, since technology and global competition were reducing the need for high-paid workers in manufacturing. But at a time when many other advanced industrial economies were stagnant or beset by crises, the United States seemed a model of capitalist economic success.

Western Europe: Welfare States and Closer Union

The U.S. economy produced goods and services and created jobs on a massive and growing scale, but it did so in part by making workers work long hours for low pay and by shrinking the welfare state safety net. Most western European countries, reacting to the same trends of industrial advance and worldwide competition, preferred to uphold the welfare state safety net and

regulation of pay and hours, so that their economies did not grow like that of the United States. All the same, the western European countries worked more intensively than ever on a project that, together with their partnership with the United States, represented a historic change in the power structure of Western civilization: the pooling of some of their national sovereignty in common institutions.

"Eurosclerosis"

In the 1990s, the western European economies hardly grew at all and sometimes even shrank, since government spending on welfare states left less money to invest in factories and businesses. Western Europe also lost millions of jobs, since employers were not eager to hire workers to whom they would be compelled by law to pay high wages. Economists and business leaders considered this lack of growth an alarming economic ailment, which they called "Eurosclerosis." But western European voters—even those who were unemployed, since there was no time limit to their benefits—mostly accepted the trade-off between jobs and production on the one hand, and welfare state security on the other.

Western European governments often announced policies of privatization (selling state-owned businesses to private corporations), budget trimming, and confrontation with labor unions, but in most countries, these measures were less radical than in the United States. The basic features of the system were maintained, regardless of whether center-left or center-right parties ran governments. Even Margaret Thatcher, the pioneer of conservative revival in Britain (p. 582), did not try to tear down the welfare state safety net, and in 1990, after she had insisted on pushing through Parliament a local government tax system that favored the wealthy, her support among voters rapidly dropped and her own party forced her to resign. By the early twenty-first century, however, as government spending on welfare states continued to grow, worldwide competition increased, and ten low-wage eastern European and Mediterranean countries prepared to join the European Union, the western European countries faced difficult problems upholding their model of capitalism.

> *"Economists and business leaders considered this lack of growth an alarming economic ailment, which they called 'Eurosclerosis.'"*

The Treaty of Maastricht

The process of building common institutions had been under way among the western European nations since shortly after the end of the Second World War (p. 540). In 1957, it had passed an important milestone with the founding of the **European Economic Community (EEC)** or **Common Market**. The building of common institutions had never gone smoothly, for too many national interests and identities were at stake. But year by year, the community's *acquis* (a-KEE) ("accumulation"—the body of commonly applicable treaties, laws, and regulations) grew larger and

THE PREAMBLE TO THE TREATY OF MAASTRICHT

In December 1991, leaders of the member countries of the European Economic Community, meeting in the Dutch city of Maastricht, negotiated what was officially called the Treaty on European Union. The treaty was signed in February the following year, and came into effect in November 1993.

Like all international agreements, this one begins with a preamble (opening statement) listing the signatories and their objectives in making the treaty. The signatories are formally listed as the monarchs and presidents of the countries concerned, but except in France, policymaking authority in these countries actually belongs to prime ministers and their cabinets rather than to heads of state. The list of objectives, therefore, shows what these democratically elected government chiefs hoped to achieve by transforming the European Economic Community into the European Union.

HIS MAJESTY THE KING OF THE BELGIANS,
HER MAJESTY THE QUEEN OF DENMARK,
THE PRESIDENT OF THE FEDERAL REPUBLIC OF GERMANY,
THE PRESIDENT OF THE HELLENIC REPUBLIC,
HIS MAJESTY THE KING OF SPAIN,
THE PRESIDENT OF THE FRENCH REPUBLIC,
THE PRESIDENT OF IRELAND,
THE PRESIDENT OF THE ITALIAN REPUBLIC,
HIS ROYAL HIGHNESS THE GRAND DUKE OF LUXEMBOURG,
HER MAJESTY THE QUEEN OF THE NETHERLANDS,
THE PRESIDENT OF THE PORTUGUESE REPUBLIC,
HER MAJESTY THE QUEEN OF THE UNITED KINGDOM OF GREAT BRITAIN AND NORTHERN IRELAND,

RESOLVED to mark a new stage in the process of European integration undertaken with the establishment of the European Communities,

RECALLING the historic importance of the ending of the division of the European continent and the need to create firm bases for the construction of the future Europe,

CONFIRMING their attachment to the principles of liberty, democracy and respect for human rights and fundamental freedoms and the rule of law,

DESIRING to deepen the solidarity between their peoples while respecting their history, their culture and their traditions,

DESIRING to enhance further the democratic and efficient functioning of the institutions so as to enable them better to carry out, within a single institutional framework, the tasks entrusted to them,

RESOLVED to achieve the strengthening and the convergence of their economies and to establish an economic and monetary union including, in accordance with the provisions of this Treaty, a single and stable currency,

DETERMINED to promote economic and social progress for their peoples, within the context of the accomplishment of the internal market and of reinforced cohesion and environmental protection, and to implement policies ensuring that advances in economic integration are accompanied by parallel progress in other fields,

RESOLVED to establish a citizenship common to nationals of their countries,

RESOLVED to implement a common foreign and security policy including the eventual framing of a common defence policy, which might in time lead to a common defence, thereby reinforcing the European identity and its independence in order to promote peace, security and progress in Europe and in the world,

REAFFIRMING their objective to facilitate the free movement of persons, while ensuring the safety and security of their peoples, by including provisions on justice and home affairs in this Treaty,

RESOLVED to continue the process of creating an ever closer union among the peoples of Europe, in which decisions are taken as closely as possible to the citizen in accordance with the principle of subsidiarity [decentralization of decision making],

IN VIEW of further steps to be taken in order to advance European integration,

HAVE DECIDED to establish a European Union . . .

EXPLORING THE SOURCE

1. What did the makers of the Treaty of Maastricht hope would be the main features of relations among countries, the government system, and the social order in the future Europe?

2. Of the specific measures mentioned, which do the treaty makers seem most definite about, which do they seem more tentative about, and why?

Source: *Official Journal of the European Communities* C 191, July 29, 1992.

European Union (EU)
The name of the common economic and political institutions of the European countries following the Treaty of Maastricht in 1992.

eurozone
The region of Europe where the euro is the common currency and the European Central Bank sets interest rates.

more complex: most notably, the Single European Act of 1986 provided for free movement of capital and labor across the frontiers of the member countries. From time to time, furthermore, the community gained new members. By the time of the fall of communism, the original six nations (Belgium, France, West Germany, Italy, Luxembourg, and the Netherlands) had been joined by Britain, Denmark, Greece, Ireland, Portugal, and Spain, so that the community included most of western Europe.

After communism's fall, the *acquis* grew faster than ever before, above all because of the reunification of Germany. The Germans, once again the most powerful single nation in Europe, did not want their western neighbors to turn against them as had happened before the two world wars, and those neighbors were eager not to allow Germany too much freedom of action. For both sides, the answer seemed to be to pool still more of their sovereignty. The result was the Treaty of Maastricht, signed in 1992, which changed the community's name to the **European Union (EU)** and announced measures to establish a common citizenship (see photo), a common currency, common economic and social policies, and common foreign and security policies.

Building the European Union

The Treaty of Maastricht made membership of the EU much more demanding on the individual nations than before, and progress in putting it into effect was uneven. The member nations were unable to agree on specific common foreign and security policies, which would have limited their ability to pursue their individual national interests. In economic matters, by 2002, most of the EU countries were able to agree on limiting their budget deficits, establishing a European Central

Bank to set common interest rates, and adopting a common currency, the *euro*. By doing so, these **eurozone** countries gave up much of their power to regulate their economies as they saw fit. But three EU countries—Britain, Denmark, and Sweden—were unwilling to make this sacrifice, and stayed out of the eurozone. France and Germany, on the other hand, joined the zone but regularly disregarded its rules on budget deficits, which were eventually loosened to meet their needs.

 At a Glance: Euro Basics (http://news.bbc.co.uk/nol/shared/spl/hi/europe/02/euro_primer/html/default.stm) Learn more about the debate in Britain over adopting the euro.

The pooling of sovereignty also led to bitter conflicts over the distribution of government power. In the Council of Ministers, the body through which national governments control EU policies, small countries feared being outvoted by large ones, and large ones complained of being underrepresented as against small ones. In every EU country, the public complains of being at the mercy of remote and imperious "Eurocrats"—officials of the European Commission, the EU's executive arm, headquartered in Brussels. This "democratic deficit" could be reduced if the European Parliament, which is directly elected in each country, gained greater power over the actions of the Commission and the Council of Ministers. But any increase in the power of the European Parliament would have to come at the expense of the power of the national legislatures—something that public opinion in every EU country would certainly also resent.

All these disputes arose because the EU countries remained independent nation-states, each pursuing its own national interests. Even so, the member nations found it in their interests to pool enough of their sovereignty to turn the EU into an economic superpower. Indeed, the EU's production of goods and services was not much smaller than that of the United States.

Furthermore, following the fall of communism, many more European nations found it in their national interests to pool some of their sovereignty in the EU. Austria, Finland, and Sweden, neutral countries that had stayed out of the EEC so long as the blocs existed, joined in 1995. (Among western European countries, only Norway, where the voters twice disallowed efforts by their government to join the EEC and then the EU, stayed outside the union.) In 2003, ten more, mostly ex-communist countries were admitted: Cyprus, the Czech Republic, Estonia, Hungary, Latvia, Lithuania, Malta, Poland, Slovakia, and Slovenia (see Map 32.1).

> "*The member nations found it in their interests to pool enough of their sovereignty to turn the EU into an economic superpower.*"

(above, center) **Separate Countries, Common Citizenship** These passports identify the bearers as natives of a particular European country, whose name—the Polish Commonwealth—and its coat of arms are prominently displayed. But above the country's name is that of the international grouping to which it belongs, the European Union, and the bearers are entitled freely to enter and leave, live and work in any other member country. Shutterstock

Interactive Map

Map 32.1 Europe After Communism's Collapse

In postcommunist Europe, Germany is again united, and the multinational Soviet Union, Czechoslovakia, and much of Yugoslavia have been divided into states in which one nation predominates. Many minorities live on "wrong" sides of borders; some new states in former Yugoslavia proclaim themselves multiethnic; nearly all states wish to pool some of their power in the European Union. But the main building block of the new Europe is the united and self-governing nation-state. © Cengage Learning

The European nations, however, did not find it in their interest to pool enough of their sovereignty to turn Europe from an economic into a military and political superpower. The Cold War bargain with the United States, whereby they accepted U.S. leadership and military command in return for being able to influence U.S. policy and save money on defense (p. 541), was still very much in their interests. Without it, they would have had difficulty upholding their welfare states and would hardly have been able to pursue their project of building their community. Even so, their influence for good or ill on the power structure of global civilization was second only to that of the United States, and that seemed a good reason for the United States to hold to its end of the Cold War bargain.

LO³ The Former East: Joining the West on Equal Terms?

From Germany's eastern borders all the way to the Pacific Ocean, two dozen countries that had once belonged to the Soviet Union or had been its satellite states coped with the aftereffects of the collapse of communism (see Map 31.1 on page 587, and Map 32.1). Except for the predominantly Muslim states of central Asia, most of the ex-communist countries had been outlying territories of Western civilization, with religious and cultural identities not too different from those of the Western heartland. What their peoples now mostly wanted was quickly and easily to join the democratic-capitalist world order on equal terms with its leading countries. In practice, the process turned out to be long and hard, and success was uneven.

The Former Satellites: Moving Westward

For most ex-satellite countries, becoming members of the EU was a second economic and political step toward joining the West. The first step was a military one: becoming members of the North Atlantic Treaty Organization (NATO, p. 536). In 1994, in response to urging from the westernmost ex-satellites, the Czech Republic, Hungary, and Poland, the NATO countries decided that the organization should expand eastward. In 1999, those three countries joined the alliance. Five years later, NATO further expanded to include all the other former satellite countries—Albania, Bulgaria, Romania, and Slovakia; two countries that had been part of Yugoslavia—Macedonia and Slovenia; and three Baltic countries that had belonged to the Soviet Union—Estonia, Latvia, and Lithuania.

Meanwhile, the westernmost ex-communist countries, the Czech Republic, Hungary, Poland, Slovakia, and Slovenia, seemed to be making harsh but successful political and economic transitions to Western-style democracy and capitalism. In many cases, the transitions involved cooperation and conflict among leaders of anticommunist resistance who now became national heroes,

eager privatizers who wished to introduce free-market capitalism overnight, and communist parties that changed their names, accepted democracy, and called for slower economic changes.

This call had wide appeal, for the adjustment to capitalism proved to be much harder than expected. Many noncompetitive industries had to be closed down almost overnight, causing massive unemployment. Hasty privatization led to corruption, stock market crashes, and sell-offs of assets to Western companies and local speculators. People began to miss the economic security of communism, even while they valued democratic freedoms. Late in the 1990s, government regulation and intervention made free markets less chaotic, and the large numbers of well-educated and unemployed workers began to attract global corporations to build plants and offices. In 2003, all five countries joined the European Union—a sign of their continued confidence, as well as that of the EU itself, in their democratic and capitalist future.

With this expansion, the EU reached the early medieval border between Catholic and Orthodox Europe (Map 10.3 on page 179). Beyond that line, the problems of economic and political adjustment were much worse. Romania and Bulgaria, traditionally much poorer countries than those farther west, were nevertheless beginning the process of joining the EU. In the countries fringing Russia in Europe, the Caucasus, and Central Asia, however, poverty and corruption were endemic, and former Communist Party bosses had in many cases made successful transitions to become nationalist dictators.

Russia: A Time of Troubles

In Russia itself, Boris Yeltsin, the victor over both the communist conservatives and the communist reformers in 1991 (p. 587), promised as president to turn Russia almost overnight into a modern capitalist democracy. Yeltsin was the third Russian ruler—the first two being Peter the Great and Stalin (pp. 337, 489–492)—to seek equality of wealth and power with the West through a program of breakneck Westernization. He was far less successful than the other two.

 **Russia: Economic Reform in the 1990s** (http://country studies.us/russia/57 .htm) Learn more about the transformation of the Russian economy in the 1990s.

Yeltsin presided over almost a decade of Russian national misfortune and humiliation. True, there seemed to be general acceptance (even within the still powerful Communist Party) that traditional communism was dead and would never be resurrected, and a rough-and-tumble version of democratic politics seemed to have won legitimacy. But in the ten years after the end of the Soviet Union, most Russians sank into poverty and squalor far worse than those of communism. Privatization led not to the modernization of industry and the economy but to the plundering of the country's assets by wealthy tycoons and gangsters, the spreading of an East Asian financial crisis to Russia in 1998, and a loan from the International Monetary Fund (p. 608) to prevent bankruptcy. Instead of growing, the economy's production of goods and services declined to two-thirds that of flourishing

BOTH THE FORMER SATELLITES AND THE NATO COUNTRIES SAW THE BENEFITS OF JOINING FORCES:

Advantages to Former Eastern European Satellites

· For the nations of eastern Europe, democratic freedom and capitalist prosperity were unthinkable unless they first won genuine independence.

· They believed that both Russia and the newly reunited Germany might threaten their independence.

· They also needed a structure that would suppress their own mutual rivalries and conflicts.

· NATO was now far stronger than Russia; it included Germany; and within it, Germany was balanced off by other powerful countries, especially the United States.

Advantages to NATO Countries

· The NATO countries shared the desire to avoid rivalries and conflicts in eastern Europe.

· The non-German NATO countries, too, wanted to eliminate the possibility of either Russia or Germany dominating eastern Europe.

· To achieve successful reunification, Germany needed the trust of its fellow NATO members and a peaceful eastern Europe in which it would not be drawn into rivalry with Russia.

Makdonalds The first McDonald's in Russia opened in 1990, just as the country's time of troubles was beginning. The fast-food chain has gradually expanded through all the ups and downs of Russia's relations with the West, and by the end of 2010 there were expected to be 45 outlets. The roof sign on this one advertises a *Makzavtrak* ("McBreakfast"), the Russian name for a Big Breakfast. Sovfoto

China. In international affairs, Russia fell far from its former status as a superpower, and lost much of its influence even in countries just outside its borders: the newly independent Baltic republics made their way into NATO, and U.S. oil companies took over oil fields in Central Asia. The Russian government could not collect taxes, the armed forces were in decay, and the space program, once the pride of the Soviet Union, was kept going only by U.S. subsidies.

Yeltsin's handpicked successor, Vladimir Putin—elected president in 2000—promised to strengthen the state, rein in the tycoons and gangsters, and restore Russia's standard of living and pride in itself. By 2004, he had gone some way toward accomplishing the first two of these objectives, and Russia's economy had begun to grow again. Few Russians had become more prosperous as a result, and Putin's methods included manipulation of the mass media and intimidation of opponents. Nevertheless, he gained genuine and widespread trust and respect among the voters and was reelected president in a landslide.

> *"Yeltsin presided over almost a decade of Russian national misfortune and humiliation."*

The Chechen War

Both Yeltsin and Putin had to deal with an ethnic and religious conflict within Russia's borders that was unleashed by the collapse of the communist dictatorship. Chechnya (**CHECH-nee-uh**), a territory within Russia whose Muslim population had a long history of resistance to rule from Moscow, moved in 1995 to achieve complete independence. Yeltsin treated the matter as a test of the strength of the Russian state and his own effectiveness as president, and decided to use force to put down the secession. A bitter war ensued between the Russian army and Chechen militants in which the Russians suffered many setbacks and eventually withdrew, leaving Chechnya apparently set for eventual independence. But Islamic fundamentalist forces in Chechnya provoked Moscow with raids on neighboring territories and terrorist bombings, and the conflict resumed in 1999. This time, the Russians reoccupied the territory with savage bombardments and systematic destruction, and installed a regime led by a former rebel clan that damped down further resistance by means of brutality and corruption combined with assertions of Chechen identity and Muslim piety.

The Chechen war weakened Russia at a time when turning it into a prosperous and powerful modern country was a vast and still unaccomplished task. If only because Russia still had a world-destroying arsenal of nuclear weapons left over from Soviet times, the Western countries could not afford to treat it too disrespectfully. In 1997, Yeltsin was invited to the annual meeting of the G7 leaders, who from then on became the **Group**

of Eight (G8). NATO treated Russia as a partner to be consulted rather than an adversary to be contained. The partnership was severely strained by NATO's eastward expansion, but in 2002, a NATO-Russia Joint Council was established that provided for the partners to take joint decisions and actions to deal with common threats. For the moment, however, Russia remained in a state of resentful dependence on its former capitalist rivals, and was still a long way from truly joining the West on equal terms.

Challenge to the West: The Yugoslav Wars

The fall of communism in eastern Europe unleashed many long-suppressed national conflicts, but usually these conflicts did not lead to war. The most destructive national passions in the region had already been released, and mostly satisfied, in an orgy of genocide and expulsions of national minorities during and after the Second World War (pp. 509–511). Most eastern European nations were therefore content with their existing borders, and even dissatisfied ones knew that nationalist wars would lay them open to German or Russian interference and prevent them from fulfilling their overriding ambition to join the West on equal terms. Furthermore, the United States and the EU countries, which were now the outside powers with the strongest influence in the region, were determined to damp down national conflicts.

The Yugoslav Background

In the Balkan country of Yugoslavia, however, national ambitions were still unsatisfied. Early medieval barbarian invasions, the schism of the Greek and Latin churches, and centuries of Turkish rule had made this territory one of half a dozen small, mostly Slavic nations, and of three religions—Catholic, Orthodox, and Muslim. Rival nationalisms, great power intervention, and two world wars had often turned these nations against each other. After the First World War, they had united for the first time in their histories to form Yugoslavia, but their rivalries and disputes had continued. (For details see Chapters 5, 7, and 14.)

Following the Second World War, the Communist Party, headed by Marshal Tito, took over power and organized Yugoslavia as a federal state of six republics. In each republic, one or other nation predominated, but in all of them except the northernmost republic of Slovenia, which had already expelled its German- and Italian-speaking minorities at the end of the war, there were strong minorities of other nations.

Communism and federal ties both weakened after Tito's death in 1980, and nationalist ambitions resurfaced, first of all in the Serb republic. The Serbs are an Orthodox nation with a glorious medieval past and a more recent history of resistance to foreign rule, terrible sufferings in both world wars, and conflict with neighboring nations. They dominated Yugoslavia's federal government, but many of their nation lived as minorities in the neighboring republic of Bosnia-Herzegovina (alongside Roman Catholic Croats and Muslim Bosniaks), as well as in the main Croat territory, the republic of Croatia. A Serb Communist leader, Slobodan Milošević (**mee-LOSH-eh-vich**), reinvented himself as an extreme nationalist and called for a "Greater Serbia," to include the entire nation.

Breakup and War

Partly out of fear of Serbia and partly to fulfill their own national ambitions, most of the republics declared their independence in 1991, and at that point, their hostilities exploded. Serbia was the principal inheritor of the former federal state and its army. Together with the neighboring republic of Montenegro, it formed a new and smaller Yugoslavia, but it also tried to use its power to gain control of the territories of Serb minorities in Croatia and Bosnia. Serbs most of all, but also Croats and Bosniaks, attacked the other groups, forcing them out of the areas they lived in, occupying those areas with their own people, and giving this common twentieth-century practice a new name—"**ethnic cleansing**." Only ethnically homogeneous Slovenia avoided massacres and ethnic cleansing, and was able to join less troubled eastern European countries on the path to EU membership.

The United Nations decreed sanctions against Serbia and established a war crimes tribunal in the Dutch city of The Hague. The European Union negotiated cease-fires, and NATO sent in western European peacekeeping troops. In spite of all these measures, the ethnic cleansing and accompanying massacres went on for four years. The main reason was that the armed forces of the EU countries were not strong enough to intimidate the warring parties, and the United States was unwilling to risk its own forces in this European dispute.

Finally, however, an alliance of Bosnian Croats and Bosniaks, and an army from the Croatian republic organized and armed with unofficial U.S. help, tipped the balance against the Serbs. A U.S. initiative then succeeded in bringing the parties to a general peace agreement. Bosnia, Croatia, and Serbia recognized each other as independent states with the same borders that they had had as republics within the old Yugoslavia. Bosnia became a loose union of a Bosniak-Croat "entity" and a Serb "entity," with NATO forces and an EU "High Representative" to keep the peace. United States, British, French, and other NATO forces moved into Bosnia in December 1995 (Map 32.2).

Serbia struck again in 1999, this time against the main national minority in the Serb republic, Albanians of Muslim faith in the province of Kosovo (p. 251). The Albanians were seeking to regain the autonomy they had enjoyed under Tito as a first step toward independence and possible union with the neighboring independent country of Albania (Map 32.2). The Yugoslav army, helped by local Serbs, drove the Albanians out of

their province—the largest-scale ethnic cleansing since the expulsions at the end of the Second World War. The United Nations failed to act for fear of a veto in its Security Council by Russia, which sympathized with the Serbs as a Slav and Orthodox nation. All the same, the members agreed that the Serbian crimes must be stopped and the refugees allowed to return.

After long hesitation, the United States used its military power to enforce this decision. Its air forces attacked the Serb army and targets inside Serbia until Milošević gave in. Most Albanians returned to their smashed homes, and some fled to other countries. Once again, NATO troops and administrators moved in, and normal life was gradually restored for most of the Albanian population; except in the northern part of the province where they were a majority, the Serbs were subject to occasional outbreaks of church-burning and ethniuc cleansing from Albanians thirsting for revenge.

> **ethnic cleansing**
> The practice of members of one group, usually ethnic or religious, attacking members of another such group, forcing them out of their home areas, and occupying those areas with their own people.

 Frontline: War in Europe: NATO's 1999 War Against Serbia over Kosovo (http://www.pbs.org/wgbh/pages/frontline/shows/kosovo/) Watch documentary footage of the 1999 war against Serbia over Kosovo.

The Fall of Milošević

This renewed disaster finally led to the ouster of Milošević as leader of Serbia. In 2000, he was defeated in a bid to win reelection as president, and when he tried to hold on to power in spite of the elections, he was forced out by massive street demonstrations in the capital city of Belgrade. His fall was welcomed by the NATO countries, and it meant the end of Serb efforts to unite their entire nation within a single state. Subsequent elections brought to power a Serbian government resolved on cooperation with the West and eventual membership of the EU.

> "*Milošević's fall was welcomed by the NATO countries, and it meant the end of Serb efforts to unite their entire nation within a single state.*"

With the fighting stopped and Milošević out of the way, the United States and the EU encouraged the leaders of the various republics of the former Yugoslavia, now nearly all independent states, to cooperate with each other. To the extent that they did so, they received financial help and were offered the hope of eventual membership in the EU. The same inducements were offered to the leaders of the different nations within the republics to work together.

The governments of the republics were also expected to arrest suspected war criminals and send them for trial before the tribunal at The Hague (see photo). The Serbs handed over Milošević himself in 2002, and he behaved in the courtroom as a defiant victim of a Western conspiracy against the Serb nation—as did Radovan Karadžić (**KAH-rad-zhich**), the main civilian leader of the Bosnian Serbs, after his arrest in 2008. Victims of ethnic cleansing were given shelter, food, and help with returning to their homes. Often this help came from NGOs based in western Europe and the United States that mobilized dedicated and idealistic volunteers more efficiently than governments, and for this reason gained official cooperation and financing.

 Milošević Trial Public Archive (http://hague.bard.edu/) Watch footage from the trial of Milošević.

Repairing Failed States: Nation Building and Civil Society

In Yugoslavia, the West faced an open challenge to its hopes for a harmonious postcommunist world order. It tried to deal with the challenge partly by applying lessons derived from the experience of western Europe during and after the Second World War. Military force and what amounted to military occupations would restore order and force warring nations apart. Financial help would ease the task of reconstruction. Reconciliation and cooperation among states would bring prosperity and harmony so that national grievances would no longer matter. The punishment of war criminals by legal trials would discourage vengeance and make nations repent of the crimes committed in their names. And the approval of the United Nations would provide legitimacy and a guarantee of impartiality for these and other measures.

It seemed, however, that Yugoslavia, with its complex ethnic and religious mosaic and its peoples unfamiliar with modern democratic government, needed more than the experience of postwar western Europe to help solve its problems. Accordingly, Western leaders turned from the lessons of their own recent past to two seemingly promising theoretical concepts.

One of these was the concept of **nation building**. This idea had originally been developed by political scientists, notably the U.S. scholar Reinhard Bendix, reflecting in the 1960s on the processes whereby Western nation-states had come into existence and on how to apply the lessons of these processes to the decolonized nations of Africa and Asia. According to Bendix, a human group acquires the status of a

nation in three ways. It acquires a feeling of common identity that supersedes earlier tribal, ethnic, and religious allegiances; it develops economic links of trade, travel, and communication that overcome the isolation of the smaller communities that make it up; and it creates a powerful and effective yet democratic government. These three processes, furthermore, interact so as to push each other forward: an effective democratic government, in which all citizens participate, for example, helps to give them a sense of common national identity.

The concept of nation building had obvious relevance to the newly independent Yugoslav republics, especially Bosnia and Kosovo. United Nations, EU, and NATO administrators in those lands must wield sticks and carrots, NATO peacekeeping troops must stand guard, and Western NGOs must provide disinterested help and advice, to promote reconciliation and economic development, and to foster effective government institutions in which all groups would have a stake. In this way, it would be possible to turn the Bosniaks, Croats, and Serbs of Bosnia, and the Albanians and Serbs of Kosovo, into "multiethnic"

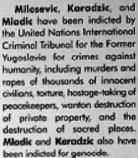

>> **Wanted Poster** The men on this poster, issued by the U.S. State Department in 2000 as part of an antiterrorist program, bore high-level responsibility for ethnic cleansing by Serbs in Bosnia. The Serbian government handed over Milošević to the Hague War Crimes Tribunal in 2001, so no reward was paid. U.S. officials denied a report that the full amount was paid for information leading to the arrest of Karadžić in 2008. Mladić, the Serb military commander, was still at large in 2010. Department of State, Diplomatic Security Service

nations—ones in which ethnic and religious groups would live as a single nation without losing their individualities, and without being compelled to do so by repression and force.

An idea allied to that of nation building was the concept of **civil society**. This idea dated back to Enlightenment beliefs about the social contract and about rulers as agents of society (pp. 344–345, 366–367), and it was revived in the 1970s by eastern European dissidents (opponents of communist rule), notably the Polish thinker Leszek Kołakowski **(ko-wak-OFF-skee)**. Under communism, the state had tried to control all organizations and activities, no matter how remote from politics, whereas Kołakowski believed that the direction of control should be exactly the other way round. For Kołakowski and like-minded thinkers, "civil society" denoted grassroots networks of orga-

nizations and activities separate from the state but influencing and controlling it, which in their view formed the foundation of democracy. Inspired by this school of thought, Western government leaders and diplomats believed that UN and NATO officials and NGOs must now help the peoples of Bosnia and Kosovo develop such civil societies, and thereby lay the foundations for true democracies and effective multiethnic nation-states.

nation building
The theory that disparate groups, usually ethnic or religious, can be deliberately formed into unified nations by fostering social, economic, and political processes believed to have a unifying effect.

civil society
The theory that grassroots networks of organizations and activities can provide the foundation of an effective nation-state.

Map 32.2 **Ethnicity, Nations, and Borders**

The map shows where peoples live as majorities and minorities in former Yugoslavia and nearby countries. For these peoples, ethnicity (a common language and traditions) is the main mark of nationhood (being a main constituent group of the human race, with rights such as united self-rule). Conflicts arising out of the intermingling of ethnic nations led to the wars in Yugoslavia; rival ethnic-national claims led to the peaceful breakup of Czechoslovakia; and the Hungarians consider themselves a single nation divided by frontiers. © Cengage Learning

 Interactive Map

The Results of Western Intervention

The combination of force, aid, processes of punishment and reconciliation, and grassroots reforms, all in the name of the international community, was successful in important ways. It stopped the massacres and ethnic cleansing, and enabled many victims of cleansing to return to their homes. In addition, it persuaded the former Yugoslav states to cooperate with each other on matters of common concern.

The more ambitious efforts for democratic nation building were less successful. The trials at The Hague were essential in the interests of justice, but they caused more resentment than repentance among the nations to which the defendants belonged. National minorities within each state lived in their own enclaves, resenting and resented by the majority population. Serbs in particular, as the main losers of the Yugoslav wars, found themselves in this position. Their population in Croatia had been reduced by ethnic cleansing once the tide of war turned there, and they were narrowly outvoted in a referendum on independence in Montenegro in 2006. And in two regions, post-Yugoslav conflicts involving Serbs were still unresolved in 2010: Bosnia and Kosovo.

All of Bosnia's neighbors, including Croatia and Serbia, recognized it, but it was weakened internally by the anger left over from the wars, by Croat resentment of Bosniak domination, and above all by the fact that the Serbs, one-third of the population, had no wish to belong to it. The new state endlessly teetered on the edge of breakup, and the resulting political uncertainty discouraged foreign investment and helped perpetuate widespread poverty. The way to overcome this weakness seemed to be to strengthen the state's central institutions as against its Bosniak-Croat and Serb "entities," but that was exactly what the Serb minority would never willingly accept. In 2010 the EU and the United States were looking for ways to make the Serbs accept it unwillingly.

Meanwhile in Kosovo, the Albanian majority was developing the institutions of an independent state under UN and EU supervision. Kosovo had been the heartland of the medieval Serbian empire (p. 219), the region where that empire had lost a decisive battle to the Turks, and the scene of many centuries of Orthodox Christian survival, and neither the Serbs of the province nor Serbia itself were willing to accept Kosovan independence. This was the one issue on which the reformed Serbia, otherwise eager for cooperation with its neighbors, the EU, and the United States, was unwilling to do the West's bidding. When efforts for a negotiated settlement between Kosovo and Serbia reached a dead end in 2008, the province unilaterally declared independence with the backing of the United States and most of the EU. The result was a lengthy dispute that not only pitted Serbia and the Kosovo Serbs against the new state, but also divided the international community.

One-third of the 192 UN member nations swiftly recognized the new state, in the belief that Kosovo deserved independence because of its sufferings at the hands of Serbia, and in the hope that independence would resolve a major issue remaining from the Yugoslav wars. But nearly half the UN members delayed a decision, and another one-fifth declared outright that they would not recognize Kosovo. The declared nonrecognizers included a minority of EU countries, Russia, and a quartet of powerful countries—Brazil, China, India, and South Africa—that were by this time emerging as the main challengers to the West's guidance of global economic affairs (pp. 635–636). Most of the declared nonrecognizers feared that Kosovan independence would encourage secessionist hopes among national minorities within their own borders, and they also resented the West's acting on its own to settle the destinies of nations just as they resented its leadership of the world economy.

In 2010 an effort by Serbia to improve its position against Kosovo backfired. Banking on the fact that the territorial integrity of states is an important principle of international law, Serbia tried to persuade the International Court of Justice in the Hague to find the Kosovan declaration of independence illegal, but a majority of the court ruled that the declaration as such did not violate international law. The majority explicitly declined to rule on whether or not Kosovo's actual secession and its existence as an independent state were in accordance with international law, however. The decision did not appear to change the minds of any of the outright nonrecognizers, nor did it lead to an immediate rush of recognitions by the UN members that were delaying a decision.

Meanwhile, Kosovo had developed into a corrupt ministate sustained by NATO forces and Western subsidies. Serbs living in isolated enclaves, reassured by the NATO presence and in need of government services, had begun to interact with the Kosovo Albanian authorities, but Serbs in northern Kosovo, which adjoined Serbia and where they were a solid majority, boycotted the Kosovo institutions and formed their own corrupt microstate sustained by subsidies from Serbia. Occasionally, politicians on both sides, as well as anonymous Western diplomats, talked of partition: Serbia would keep northern Kosovo, give up to Kosovo additional districts within its territory with an Albanian majority, and recognize Kosovan independence. For the moment, at least, both sides officially treated such suggestions as blasphemy, for each side hoped that if it stuck to its maximum demands the other side would eventually give in. Since Serbia needed Western economic help and wanted to join the EU, the Kosovo government and its Western backers seemed to have more leverage against Serbia and the Kosovo Serbs than the other way round. Still, Serbia had powerful supporters in the international community, and the dispute could last for a long time.

Whatever happened in Kosovo, it seemed unlikely that a single multiethnic Kosovan nation, distinct from the Serb and Albanian nations, would ever emerge there. This reflected the single most serious difficulty with the nation-building enterprise: that Albanians and Serbs—as well as Bosniaks and Croats—belonged to nations that had already undergone lengthy processes of building. Now, they were in effect being told to abort these nation-building processes and rebuild themselves as mere "ethnic" Albanians, Bosniaks, Croats, and Serbs—as "ethnicities" rather than as nations in their own right—belonging to new, multiethnic nations. Many among all four groups, however, felt that they had the same right to assert their existing national interests and identities as, for instance, Americans and Germans. Perhaps in acknowledgment of this, by 2010 Western diplomats and opinion makers were beginning to talk less of Balkan *nation* building and more of *state* building—of creating strong government institutions that reluctant minorities would willy-nilly have to accept, whichever nation they felt they belonged to. It remained to be seen how successfully this could be accomplished by outsiders who were unwilling to use force.

Listen to a synopsis of Chapter 32.

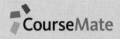

CHAPTER 33

THE WEST IN THE POSTCOMMUNIST WORLD, 1990s

LEARNING OBJECTIVES

AFTER READING THIS CHAPTER, YOU SHOULD BE ABLE TO DO THE FOLLOWING:

LO¹ Describe the tensions produced by the West's push for economic globalization.

LO² Analyze the limits of the West's ability to act as the leading force in the postcolonial world.

"THE MOST FORMIDABLE CHALLENGES FACING THE WEST WERE MILITANT ISLAMIC FUNDAMENTALISM, NUCLEAR PROLIFERATION, AND TERRORISM."

While the leading countries of the West saw themselves as leaders and guides of the international community, the rest of the postcommunist world had a mind—in fact, many minds—of its own about accepting Western leadership and guidance. There was widespread distrust of Western sincerity, particularly in the economic field. The West proclaimed the spread of capitalist prosperity through **globalization**—the unhindered worldwide movement of people, goods, and money—but Western countries made sure to shelter powerful domestic groups like bankers and farmers from globalization's hardships. The West, it seemed, was protecting its own interests at the expense of the rest of the world. How, then, could the world trust the West to steer it to prosperity?

Test your knowledge before you read this chapter.

What do you think?

Western countries should step in whenever an ethnic or religious dispute explodes or threatens to explode into war.

Strongly Disagree   Strongly Agree

| 1 | 2 | 3 | 4 | 5 | 6 | 7 |

In addition, many of the world's peoples were locked in national, ethnic, and religious conflicts that for them took priority over the pursuit of harmony, prosperity, and freedom. Many of these conflicts were already of long standing, unleashed by the earlier disappearance of colonial empires—Israel and the Arabs, India and Pakistan, and a whole series of ethnic and religious wars in Africa. Others were newly released by the fall of communism, like the wars in Yugoslavia (pp. 600–605). Either way, these conflicts came to be regarded both inside and outside the West as a test of its ability to steer the world.

Western mediation and more or less wholehearted military intervention, United Nations sanctions and war crimes tribunals, and help from Western-backed volunteer organizations often damped these conflicts down or relieved the suffering they caused. But the conflicts were mostly neither stopped before they inflicted tragic devastation nor truly resolved. Furthermore, the postcolonial conflicts,

◄◄ **Kwai Tsing Container Terminal, Hong Kong** At one of China's busiest ports in 1995, containers are stacked at dockside and on board ship. The steel cargo boxes come in a range of international standard sizes and can be quickly and easily moved between ships, truck trailers, railroad cars, and airplanes. Each box is bar coded, and can be tracked by computer across the world. This cargo-handling technology, developed in the United States in the 1960s, is one of the main factors behind economic globalization.

G. Bowater/Corbis

607

globalization
The unhindered world-wide movement of people, goods, and money.

Washington Consensus
A U.S.-based economic consensus on how unfettered globalization would bring worldwide prosperity.

resentment and distrust of Western power and influence, and growing evidence that Western power was not unlimited all strengthened three formidable challenges to the order of global civilization that the West wished to establish: militant Islamic fundamentalism, nuclear proliferation, and terrorism.

LO¹ The Global Economy: "The West and the Rest"

The postcommunist era of rising hopes for a single international community was also an era of economic globalization. People, goods, money, and information moved across the world on an unprecedented scale, and expectations grew for the reshaping of worldwide trade, industry, and finance into a single worldwide economy.

The globalization of the 1990s was the latest stage in an increase of worldwide travel and trade that had been going on for more than a thousand years. The main milestones of this process had been the rise of Islam, which strengthened links among the civilizations of the Eastern Hemisphere; European exploration and empire building, which linked the Old World and the New; and the first revolution in transport and communications, the nineteenth-century invention of steamships, railroads, and telegraphs. In the second half of the twentieth century, the increase of travel and trade passed another milestone, as transport and communications were once again revolutionized, this time by commercial jet aircraft, new methods of handling cargoes at seaports (see photo page 606), and advanced technologies such as the Internet.

In addition, for most countries of the world, the end of communism meant the end of any hope of finding prosperity by following a path of resistance to the West (pp. 571–574). Only one path remained open: that of seeking prosperity and power equal to that of the West but within the Western-dominated worldwide capitalist system. The great question of globalization was whether it would in fact provide such a path.

The Washington Consensus and Free Trade

Officials of Western governments, banks, and multinational corporations (those doing business in many countries) insisted that globalization would indeed bring worldwide prosperity, so long as all countries accepted it as quickly and completely as possible. They must abolish restrictions on movements of goods and money across their borders, privatize their economies, cut both taxes and government spending so as to release money for

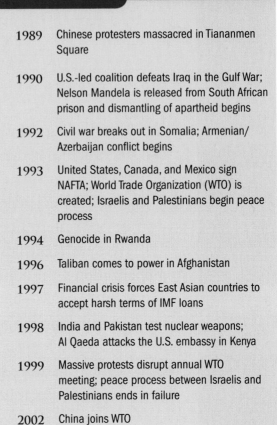

CHRONOLOGY

1989	Chinese protesters massacred in Tiananmen Square
1990	U.S.-led coalition defeats Iraq in the Gulf War; Nelson Mandela is released from South African prison and dismantling of apartheid begins
1992	Civil war breaks out in Somalia; Armenian/Azerbaijan conflict begins
1993	United States, Canada, and Mexico sign NAFTA; World Trade Organization (WTO) is created; Israelis and Palestinians begin peace process
1994	Genocide in Rwanda
1996	Taliban comes to power in Afghanistan
1997	Financial crisis forces East Asian countries to accept harsh terms of IMF loans
1998	India and Pakistan test nuclear weapons; Al Qaeda attacks the U.S. embassy in Kenya
1999	Massive protests disrupt annual WTO meeting; peace process between Israelis and Palestinians ends in failure
2002	China joins WTO

businesses to invest and consumers to spend, and loosen government regulation of business. Their economies, wide open to the increasing movement of people, goods, money, and information, would grow in step with the increase in travel and trade, and this would bring prosperity to their peoples.

This updated version of laissez-faire economics (pp. 426–427) became known as the **Washington Consensus**, because it was shared by four economic policymaking institutions based in the U.S. capital that together had considerable power to steer the global economy: the U.S. Treasury and the Federal Reserve Bank, which set policy for the largest national economy in the world; the World Bank, which lent money to countries in need of economic development; and the International Monetary Fund (IMF), established after the Second World War to help prevent worldwide economic crises like that of the 1930s by lending money to countries in financial trouble while supervising economic reforms.

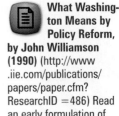

What Washington Means by Policy Reform, by John Williamson (1990) (http://www.iie.com/publications/papers/paper.cfm?ResearchID =486) Read an early formulation of the Washington Consensus.

The confidence of these institutions in laissez-faire economics grew from the fact that in the 1990s, the new and harsher U.S. economy grew faster not only than the EU economies, but also faster than Japan's. Since the end of the Second World

War, Japan had grown into a mighty economic power partly as a result of deliberate government intervention—fostering exports, discouraging imports, helping companies identify markets and develop new products, and raising barriers to foreign ownership of companies (pp. 574–575). These policies were successfully imitated by other East Asian countries, so that many economists and business leaders came to speak of a "Far Eastern" or "East Asian" model of capitalism, distinct from and more productive than the U.S. and European models. At the beginning of the 1990s, however, Japan's growth ended in a spectacular financial crash followed by seemingly endless economic stagnation. Japan still had the world's second largest economy and its people continued on the whole prosperous and secure, but the East Asian model of capitalism no longer seemed nearly so impressive as before.

Now, the Washington economic policymakers as well as U.S. business leaders and bankers believed, it was the turn of the United States to be the economic model for the world. True, in the World Bank and the IMF, the United States shared power with the EU countries and Japan. But however reluctant these other countries might be to adopt the laissez-faire model for themselves, their leaders tended to share the U.S. belief that unfettered globalization was good for the world as a whole.

President Clinton applied this belief to the United States itself, against considerable resistance from labor unions that supported his own Democratic Party, with the signing in 1993 of the **North American Free Trade Agreement (NAFTA)**. The agreement provided for gradual elimination of barriers to the movement of goods and money among the United States, Canada, and Mexico and anticipated the later addition of the other countries of the Western Hemisphere.

Even more sweeping than the NAFTA agreement was the 1993 revision of the **General Agreement on Tariffs and Trade (GATT)**, an arrangement for mutually agreed reductions of tariffs that was first signed in 1947 and had been periodically updated since then. The latest round of cuts, arrived at after years of hard bargaining by the major trading powers, was expected to have the effect of ending most tariffs on manufactured goods. The revised GATT also established, for the first time, an authorized agency for settling trade disputes among the signatory countries: the **World Trade Organization (WTO)**.

The Hardships of Globalization: The Global South and East Asia

In practice, globalization according to the strict requirements of the Washington Consensus often turned out to restrict the spread of capitalist prosperity. Rapid privatization enabled speculators

to bribe government officials and buy up valuable industries at knockdown prices, while workers in uncompetitive industries that no one wanted to buy lost their jobs overnight. That was one of the main reasons for the economic troubles of Russia and other postcommunist countries (pp. 598–600).

Furthermore, the Western countries and Japan refused to apply the Washington Consensus to their own farmers. They used tariffs and subsidies to foster domestic and export sales of products like sugar, soybeans, and rice, thereby locking many farmers in the rest of the world out of the benefits of globalization. Partly for this reason, in the 1990s, much of what now came to be called the *global South*—Africa and Latin America—made little or no progress along the path to economic growth and capitalist prosperity. Early in the twenty-first century, resistance in the rest of the world against Western agricultural protectionism was growing. A WTO conference in Cancún, Mexico, broke down over this divisive issue, and a further round of worldwide tariff reductions, scheduled for 2005, was still held up in 2010 (p. 635).

The Crisis of East Asian Capitalism

In addition, the loosening of currency controls combined with high technology made it possible to send tidal waves of money rolling across the world with a few computer keystrokes, thereby damaging many economies. Among the countries that suffered most from this were ones in East Asia that had successfully followed the Japanese model of economic growth, but unlike Japan, were vulnerable to international speculators because they depended heavily on foreign investment and credit. In 1997, several East Asian countries faced massive unemployment and business bankruptcies when speculators who had been scrambling to take advantage of the rise in value of those countries' currencies against the U.S. dollar suddenly grew nervous and pulled their money out.

The IMF then took advantage of the crisis to try to enforce the Washington Consensus and dismantle the East Asian model of capitalism. In order to get IMF loans to pay off debts to foreign banks and currency speculators, Thailand, South Korea, and

---

President Clinton's Remarks on the Signing of NAFTA (http://millercenter.org/scripps/archive/speeches/detail/3927) Hear President Clinton's remarks on the signing of NAFTA.

North American Free Trade Agreement (NAFTA)
An agreement providing for the gradual elimination of barriers to the movement of goods and money among the United States, Canada, and Mexico.

General Agreement on Tariffs and Trade (GATT)
An arrangement for the reduction and eventual elimination of tariffs among signatories.

World Trade Organization (WTO)
An international agency charged with settling trade disputes among the signatory countries to the GATT.

> *"Early in the twenty-first century, resentment in the rest of the world against Western agricultural protectionism seemed to be growing.*"

other countries had to cut many links between governments and private corporations and eliminate barriers to foreign ownership of those corporations. Their governments also had to balance their budgets by reducing spending on such activities as keeping down food prices for unemployed consumers or helping companies in financial difficulties. In Indonesia, where in 1998 the director of the IMF personally enforced exceptionally harsh terms on the country's corrupt and dictatorial President Suharto (see photo), the result was violent street protests and the overthrow of the regime. Elsewhere, there were no revolutions, but for many East Asian countries with basically sound economies, the 1990s ended not in prosperity but in hardship.

Globalization and the Spread of Prosperity: India and China

In spite of these hardships, many countries benefited from globalization—particularly ones that were large and powerful enough to ignore outside pressures to enforce the Washington Consensus rigorously, and instead were able to adopt it selectively. Among these countries were two that between them had one-third of the world's population—India and China.

India

Ever since independence, India had done its best to follow the Western model of the capitalist welfare state, with many state-owned industries alongside private corporations, a great deal of government planning, and strict controls on the movement of money in and out of the country. These policies had not brought prosperity to India's growing population, which reached 1 billion early in the twenty-first century. In the late 1980s, as socialism was plainly failing throughout the world, India's government followed a different Western example and began to privatize state-owned industries and loosen currency controls. All the same, the government did not give up fostering manufacturing industries, especially those using high technology, and it made great efforts to promote education in advanced technical fields.

When Hindu nationalists came to power in 1998, they continued these policies. As Hindu believers, they were suspicious of Western religious and cultural influences, but as nationalists, they believed that India must build its prosperity and power within the Western capitalist world. As a result, the Indian economy boomed, a rising middle class enjoyed some of the fruits of capitalist prosperity, and the country became a more influential member of the international community than ever before.

China

China, which had once competed with the Soviet Union to lead the communist challenge to the Western-dominated world order, began its long march back to capitalism in 1976 with the death of Mao Zedong and the rise to power of Deng Xiaoping (shou-ping), a veteran communist whom Mao had earlier persecuted for his relative moderation.

Deng's first move was to dissolve the large collective farms of the Mao era, returning land ownership to individual farm families. In the following years, Deng decentralized the management of the vast state-owned industrial enterprises, permitting greater flexibility and individual initiative. However, the government made sure to control the pace of change. It allowed domestic and foreign capitalists to invest in new industries, but moved very slowly to privatize existing ones. It also held down the value of China's currency against foreign currencies so that Chinese products would be cheap for foreigners to buy and exports would grow.

However, unlike the Soviet reformers of the Gorbachev era, Deng ruthlessly upheld the dictatorial authority of the Communist Party. In 1989, inspired by the Soviet and east European example, a swelling "democracy movement," centered in the universities and supported by many workers dissatisfied with their pay and conditions, challenged the party's authority. Finally, however, the army attacked thousands of demonstrators camped out in Beijing's central public space, Tiananmen Square. Perhaps as many as 2,600 people were killed, and the democracy movement collapsed.

≪ Controlling Gaze Michel Camdessus, director of the International Monetary Fund, looms over President Suharto in 1998 as the Indonesian leader signs on to harsh economic reforms for his bankrupt country in return for a multibillion-dollar loan. Camdessus later said that he adopted this schoolmaster-like pose only because there was nowhere to sit, and his mother had told him always to fold his arms when standing in public. But East Asians were enraged by this TV image of an Asian leader being humiliated by a Western power wielder.
Muchter Zakaria/AP Photo

The effect of this combination of political dictatorship and carefully managed economic liberalization, at least for the time being, was to channel the energies of the Chinese population into striving for prosperity within the global economy. Throughout the 1990s and on into the twenty-first century, China's economy grew without a pause, and in 2002, under Deng's successor, Jiang Zemin (**zuh-MIN**), the government showed its confidence in the country's global future by joining the WTO. In China as in India, millions began to enjoy modest fruits of capitalist prosperity.

But there were many millions in both China and India to whom capitalist prosperity did not spread. Bitter contrasts appeared between the newly rich and the still poor, which were unlikely to disappear at all soon. In both countries, more than 70 percent of the population were farmers, who were generally less well-off than the urban population and created an enormous reserve of cheap labor that kept factory and office wages low. In both countries, the dream of wealth, leisure, and well-being for all had been only partly realized, and disappointed hopes could still lead to social conflict.

 BBC On this Day: June 4, 1989, Massacre in Tiananmen Square (http://news.bbc.co.uk/onthisday/hi/dates/stories/june/4/newsid_2496000/2496277.stm) Learn more about how events unfolded on June 4, 1989, in Tiananmen Square.

> "*In India and China, the dream of wealth, leisure, and well-being for all had been only partly realized.*"

Globalization and the West

Economic globalization led to disputes and conflicts within Western countries just as in the rest of the world. The main wielders of economic power in governments, corporations, banks, and stock exchanges wholeheartedly supported it. Many labor unions, churches, and charitable organizations, as well as a widespread, mostly youthful, international protest movement, criticized and opposed it.

For and Against Globalization

The opponents of globalization blamed it for many evils and hardships within the West and throughout the rest of the world. The loss of high-paying industrial jobs and the decline of union membership in the West, the desperate poverty of the global South, the ruthless exploitation in Asian sweatshops, the overuse of natural resources, and the destruction of the natural environment—all were laid at the door of economic globalization. In 1999, the annual meeting of the WTO in Seattle was accompanied by massive protest demonstrations that turned violent. Such demonstrations, with or without disorders, became a regular accompaniment to the meetings of the World Bank and the IMF as well as the WTO.

Defenders of globalization insisted that the loss of industrial jobs was due to automation rather than free trade, and that cheap imports from overseas raised the standard of living of consumers. They claimed that Asian workers who found jobs in sweatshops, however badly they were exploited, were still taking a first step away from alternatives that were even worse, such as starvation and prostitution. They argued that in tropical lands, peasants in need of farms to feed their families destroyed just as much rain forest as multinational corporations eager to sell timber or soybeans on the global market.

The arguments on both sides were much the same as those that had raged in the nineteenth-century Industrial Revolution over such issues as the growth of cities, conditions in the factories, and tariffs and trade. As with nineteenth-century industrialization, many on both sides of the argument recognized that globalization was unstoppable. The real questions were how much and in what ways it could be managed and controlled, and who should manage and control it.

> "*The single biggest source of public indignation was the feeling that the leading countries of the West were using globalization to exploit the rest of the world.*"

Globalization and Western Legitimacy

Outside the countries of the Western heartland, this last issue aroused more concern than any other. As disturbing as the destruction of the environment or conditions in sweatshops might be, the single biggest source of public indignation was the feeling that the leading countries of the West were using globalization to exploit the rest of the world.

In actual fact, the West did not escape some of the hardships of globalization, and many countries in the rest of the world gained from it. In 1996, furthermore, the G7 countries put into effect a policy of forgiving part of the many billions of dollars owed them by the most heavily indebted poor countries, and they extended this measure in 1999. But although the international community's richest citizens could afford to be generous once in a while, they also did not hesitate to use their power to solve their economic problems at the expense of the rest of the world when they saw a chance to do so.

In the 1993 GATT negotiations, for example, the West held out for free trade in financial services (such as banking and stockbroking), where it had an overwhelming competitive edge—but successfully resisted free trade in farm products, which would expose Western farmers to the competition of cheap foodstuffs from the global South. Likewise, the IMF's solution to the East Asian financial crisis of 1997 threw millions of workers out of jobs and enabled Western investors to buy up businesses at bargain prices—but it also ensured that no Western bank went out of business, even though imprudent Western loans and currency transfers to East Asia had helped cause the crisis in the first place.

In 1998, furthermore, when the East Asian financial crisis led to crises in North America and Europe as well, the Federal Reserve Bank helped organize a multibillion-dollar loan to Long Term Capital Management, a huge private financial company that faced bankruptcy as a result of failed international speculations in government bonds. If the Federal Reserve had not intervened, the company's failure might well have led to a severe and lengthy stock market crash that would have thrown many U.S. workers out of their jobs. But this was just the kind of action that the IMF, with Washington's backing, was forbidding to one East Asian government after another, regardless of the loss of jobs in that region.

Nothing was more damaging to the legitimacy of the Western countries as would-be leaders of the international community—that is, to the community's willingness to accept their leadership as rightful and beneficial—than their unwillingness to abide by the rules that they tried to decree for the global economy as a whole. The image of the director of the IMF seemingly treating an Indonesian leader, however brutal and corrupt, like a misbehaving schoolboy (see photo page 610) symbolized a new division that threatened to appear within the world—a division between what observers of the global scene began to call "The West and the Rest." In addition, the mistakes and failures of globalization under Western leadership contributed to other problems and conflicts in the postcolonial world of Asia and Africa.

 A Student's Guide to Globalization (http://www.globalization101.org/) Learn more about the issues and debates over globalization.

LO² The Postcolonial World: The Limits of Western Leadership

Along with the conflicts and rivalries let loose by the fall of communism, those that had earlier been unleashed by the end of colonialism in Africa and Asia continued just as before. When postcolonial ethnic and religious disputes exploded or threatened to explode into war, the Western countries, as leaders of the international community, could not easily avoid responsibility for settling these disturbances of the community's peace and order. Thus every postcolonial dispute was to a greater or lesser extent a challenge to the West.

In meeting these challenges, the Western countries were at a disadvantage in many ways. With so many challenges to deal with, Western governments had limited time to spend on any one of them, and they spent much of that time arguing among themselves over what was to be done and which government was to bear the burden of doing it. In any case, Western voters were reluctant to spend money and risk lives in peacekeeping interventions, let alone in ones where their troops might actually have to fight. Often, too, Western countries were interested parties in the disputes they claimed to judge. Trade, travel, and the Internet might be shrinking the world, but it was still too vast and chaotic for anyone easily to steer it.

The Hope of Harmony: The Gulf War and the End of Apartheid

Closely following the end of communism came two events that held out the promise of what the U.S. president, George H. W. Bush, called a "New World Order"—one of harmonious diversity in which the international community would combine to punish the breakers of its rules.

The Gulf War

The first great challenge to the postcommunist international community came in the Persian Gulf in August 1990, when Iraq occupied the neighboring country of Kuwait (see Map 29.2 on page 543). Western countries had favored earlier expansionist efforts by the Iraqi leader Saddam Hussein against Islamic fundamentalist–dominated Iran. Kuwait, however, was a pro-Western Arab state with rich oil fields, and the occupation looked like Saddam's first step to conquering Saudi Arabia, the West's single largest oil supplier.

Five months later, with the backing of the UN Security Council including the Soviet Union, the United States led a coalition force against the invaders numbering nearly a million troops from thirty-four countries—about 70 percent Americans, 20 percent Arabs, and the rest mainly Europeans. The coalition quickly and decisively routed the Iraqis, and Kuwait's independence was restored. A U.S.-backed rebellion by the Kurds, a nation living in the north of Iraq whom Saddam had earlier repressed with poison gas attacks, achieved self-government. UN inspections forced Saddam to dismantle all or most of his programs to develop atom bombs, poison gas, and killer germs.

 Frontline: The Gulf War (http://www.pbs.org/wgbh/pages/frontline/gulf/) Learn more about the Gulf War in this multimedia presentation.

This successful demonstration of collective action in turning back aggression raised hopes for developing effective means for providing global security. In some ways, however, it showed the limits of what collective action could do. The Gulf coalition's Arab members did not want a Western-led coalition to overthrow their fellow Arab, Saddam. As Sunni Muslims, they distrusted the Shia of Iraq who had also rebelled—a feeling that the Western governments shared, since the Shia were presumed to be pro-Iranian fundamentalists. For these reasons, Saddam was able to stay in power, cruelly repress the Shia, and in various ways violate his obligations under the cease-fire agreements. Trade sanctions stayed in place, and from time to time, U.S. and British air raids retaliated for Saddam's misdeeds. The international community had won, but the outlaw was still able to show his defiance.

THE APARTHEID SYSTEM IN SOUTH AFRICA COLLAPSED UNDER PRESSURE FROM SEVERAL SOURCES:

Black South African leaders gained the world's respect and attention

- Growing unrest in the black communities led to countless protest marches, clashes with police, and hundreds of deaths and imprisonments.

- Nelson Mandela, the chief of the banned African National Congress (ANC), the main black political organization, received a life sentence in prison for treason against the apartheid government.

- Mandela's message of racial harmony and resistance against oppression gained him a worldwide moral status like that of Gandhi or Martin Luther King.

- Desmond Tutu, an Anglican priest who was also seen as a moral leader in the quest for racial equality, was promoted to become archbishop of Cape Town.

- Tutu urged South Africa's main economic partners, the leading Western countries, to cut their commercial and financial links with the country.

White South Africans suffered from global isolation

- English-speaking white South Africans, though they benefited from apartheid, saw themselves as part of a larger world that had mostly turned against them.

- When South Africa's main economic partners in the West began to cut their commercial and financial links with the country, South African business leaders joined the calls for an end to apartheid.

The End of Apartheid

Not long after the Gulf War came the dismantling of the last African outpost of colonial rule in the Republic of South Africa. Since the 1940s, the leaders of the Afrikaners (white South Africans of Dutch origin) had tried to build a state and society based on apartheid—separation of races—which in fact had the effect of making whites a privileged ruling group (p. 545). Even during the Cold War, this had isolated South Africa in the world, since both the rival blocs, as well as the decolonized countries, proclaimed their official belief in racial harmony. Nonetheless, a well-trained army, an efficient secret police, and South Africa's continued trading and financial links with other advanced capitalist economies successfully upheld apartheid into the 1980s. Late in that decade, however, the system began to unravel (see Reasons Why).

The sense that the end of apartheid was near encouraged blacks and discouraged whites, and the regime was faced with possible collapse. Among the discouraged whites was F. W. de Klerk, an Afrikaner and a strong supporter of apartheid who became prime minister in 1989. De Klerk now came to believe that only one policy and only one leader could save South Africa from civil war. The policy was to end apartheid, and the leader was Nelson Mandela.

Over the next five years of contentious partnership between de Klerk and Mandela, apartheid was peacefully ended and South Africa became a multiracial state with majority rule under Mandela as president. To banish the ghosts of the past, Tutu headed a Truth and Reconciliation Commission that—uniquely, after such a drastic regime change—investigated and exposed the crimes of apartheid without putting anyone on trial, and criticized misdeeds of antiapartheid groups including the ANC, as well as those of the former authorities. Meanwhile, in token of its willingness to become a good citizen of the international community, South Africa joined the Nuclear Nonproliferation Treaty and destroyed its atom bombs—the only country possessing such weapons ever to renounce the status of nuclear power.

The restructured state had plenty of problems. There was massive unemployment among blacks as well as continued hostility between the races and among black ethnic groups. AIDS (p. 555) was spreading disastrously, though the government for a long time ignored this problem under Mandela's successor, Thabo Mbeki, elected president in 1999. All the same, South Africa remained an advanced economy, a regional power, and an example of peaceful resolution of a historic conflict (see photo on page 614).

 Nelson Mandela's Address to Rally in Cape Town on His Release from Prison (1990) (http://www.anc.org.za/ancdocs/history/mandela/1990/release.html) Read Nelson Mandela's address to a rally in Cape Town on his release from prison.

The Threat of Anarchy: Failures of the International Community

Besides these spectacular victories of the international community, however, there were also spectacular defeats. In the postcolonial world of Africa and Asia, many other conflicts arose that the international community was unable to prevent from exploding into war, massacres, and ethnic cleansing. There were other postcolonial conflicts that smoldered on amid repression and terrorism without actually bursting into full-scale war, but which the international community could not resolve.

Asian and African Wars

In Asia, the international community took no action to stop a vicious ethnic war accompanied by ethnic cleansing between two former Soviet republics, Armenia and Azerbaijan, which lasted from 1992 to 1994. In that same time span, a U.S.-led peacekeeping force failed to stop a chaotic civil war in the East African country of Somalia (see Map 29.2 on page 543), and finally withdrew after both U.S. and Pakistani troops were killed in skirmishes with local armed gangs. And in the summer of 1994, ethnic fighting in Rwanda, in Central Africa, killed at least half a million people, besides another hundred thousand who died of disease in refugee camps. It was the worst single act of genocide since the atrocities in Kampuchea in the 1970s, and the international community, under the leadership of the triumphant West, did nothing to stop it.

Other African civil wars were more successfully ended by interventions authorized by the United Nations and carried out sometimes by French or British troops and sometimes by local peacekeepers led by regional powers such as Nigeria. Very often, the United Nations and Western-based NGOs supplied food relief, medical aid, and help with reconstruction. But the chaos in Africa in particular showed the limits of the international community's capacity to maintain peace and order, and of the West's ability and willingness to lead the community when its own vital interests were not involved.

Israel and the Arabs

The end of the Cold War, the end of apartheid, and the united action of Arab states under U.S. leadership in the Gulf War all seemed to point to an end to another lengthy conflict, that of Israel and the Arabs. Already, it was clear that the Arabs could not destroy Israel by force, and a leading Arab country, Egypt, had recognized the Jewish state a dozen years before. Likewise, the Israelis had learned in Lebanon (p. 577) that they were not strong enough to force Arab states to make peace simply by invading and occupying them.

Since 1987, furthermore, Israel had faced an uprising of Palestinians (the *intifada*, or "shaking off") in the lands west of the river Jordan (the West Bank) and the huge refugee camps

Back in Jail In 1994 Nelson Mandela revisited a cell he had occupied in South Africa's maximum security prison on Robben Island, where he had spent 18 years of his life. Some photos of his visit show him thoughtful and solemn, but here he cannot resist smiling and waving through the bars—a symbol of his triumph over his own imprisonment and that of a nation. Louise Gubb/Corbis

of Gaza, which it had conquered in 1967 (see Map 29.3 on page 544). It was clear that the Jewish state could hold on to these territories only by endless repression and force. In addition, the United States, Israel's main supporter and the backer of many Arab governments as well, was eager for a settlement that would help consolidate a harmonious international community under Western leadership.

The key to resolving the conflict, it seemed, was a settlement between Israel and the Palestinians in the West Bank and Gaza. In 1993, after lengthy negotiations in the Norwegian capital, Oslo, a crucial agreement was at last concluded. The Israeli government of Yitzhak Rabin (**rah-BEEN**) officially recognized the Palestine Liberation Organization (PLO), headed by Yassir Arafat, as the sole representative of the Palestinian people in return for the PLO's recognition of Israel. It also granted limited Palestinian self-rule in Gaza and the city of Jericho on the West Bank, under an interim government known as the Palestinian Authority, of which Arafat was elected president. This agreement was followed by an Israeli peace pact with the neighboring kingdom of Jordan.

The Israeli-Palestinian agreement was not in fact a final peace, but the beginning of a "peace process" that would require both sides to give up cherished national ambitions. The Israelis would have to evacuate most or all of the lands they had occupied

GIVING PEACE A CHANCE: YITZHAK RABIN AND YASSIR ARAFAT SPEAK OF THEIR PEOPLES' HOPES FOR PEACE

On September 13, 1993, the agreement that Israeli and Palestinian representatives had hammered out at Oslo was formally signed on the White House lawn. At the invitation of President Bill Clinton, the Israeli prime minister, Yitzhak Rabin, and the chairman of the executive committee of the Palestine Liberation Organization, Yassir Arafat, attended and spoke. In their statements excerpted here, they expressed the aspirations of their peoples, which must be fulfilled if peace was to come about.

The first speaker was Prime Minister Rabin.

President Clinton, Your Excellencies, ladies and gentlemen,___

This signing of the Israeli-Palestinian Declaration of Principles, here today, is not so easy—neither for myself, as a soldier in Israel's wars, nor for the people of Israel, and not for the Jewish people in the Diaspora, who are watching us now with great hope, mixed with apprehension.. . .

We have come from Jerusalem, the ancient and eternal capital of the Jewish people. We have come from an anguished and grieving land. We have come from a people, a home, a family, that has not known a single year—not a single month— in which mothers have not wept for their sons.

We have come to try and put an end to the hostilities, so that our children and our children's children will no longer have to experience the painful cost of war, violence, and terror. We have come to secure their lives, and to ease the sorrow and the painful memories of the past—to hope and pray for peace.

Let me say to you, the Palestinians: We are destined to live together, on the same soil in the same land. . . . we who have fought against you, the Palestinians—we say to you today in a loud and clear voice: Enough of blood and tears. Enough.

We have no desire for revenge. We harbor no hatred towards you. We, like you, are people who want to build a home, to plant a tree, to love, live side by side with you—in dignity, in empathy, as human beings, as free men. We are today giving peace a chance and again saying to you: Let us pray that a day will come when we will say, enough, farewell to arms.

We wish to turn over a new chapter in the sad book of our lives together—a chapter of mutual recognition, of good neighborliness, of mutual respect, of understanding. We hope to embark on a new era in the history of the Middle East. . . .

Chairman Arafat then spoke as follows. (Resolutions 242 and 338 are peacemaking resolutions of the UN Security Council, passed at the time of the Six-Day and Yom Kippur Wars [p. 576].)

In the name of God the most merciful, the compassionate. Mr. President, ladies and gentlemen: . . . Mr. President, I am taking this opportunity to assure you and to assure the great American people that we share your values for freedom, justice, and human rights—values for which my people have been striving.

My people are hoping that this agreement, which we are signing today, marks the beginning of the end of a chapter of pain and suffering which has lasted throughout this century. My people are hoping that this agreement which we are signing today will usher in an age of peace, coexistence and equal rights. We are relying on your role, Mr. President, and on the role of all the countries which believe that without peace in the Middle East, peace in the world will not be complete.

Enforcing the agreements and moving toward the final settlement, after two years to implement all aspects of U.N. resolutions 242 and 338 in all of their aspects, and resolve all the issues of Jerusalem, the settlements, the refugees and the boundaries, will be a Palestinian and an Israeli responsibility. It is also the responsibility of the international community in its entirety to help the parties overcome the tremendous difficulties which are still standing in the way of reaching a final and comprehensive settlement.

Now, as we stand on the threshold of this new historic era, let me address the people of Israel and their leaders, with whom we are meeting today for the first time. . . .

Our people do not consider that exercising the right to self-determination could violate the rights of their neighbors or infringe on their security. Rather, putting an end to their feelings of being wronged and of having suffered an historic injustice is the strongest guarantee to achieve coexistence and openness between our two peoples and future generations.

Our two peoples are awaiting today this historic hope. And they want to give peace a real chance. . . .

EXPLORING THE SOURCE

1. Which themes does each of the speakers choose to feature prominently, which are the same in both statements, and which are different?

2. What would be the reasons for these similarities and differences?

Source: http://www.dadalos.org/int/vorbilder/vorbilder/Rabin/zitate.htm (d@dalos, International UNESCO Education Server for Civic, Peace and Human Rights Education); http://electronicintifada.net/bytopic/historicalspeeches/99.shtml (The Electronic Intifada)

and settled in the West Bank. The Palestinians would have to give up hope of returning to the homes they had lost in what was now Israel. And both sides would have to reach agreement about Jerusalem, which each claimed as its national capital and which was holy to Jews, Muslims, and Christians throughout the world.

Strong forces on both sides opposed compromise on any of these issues, and the official leaders were unwilling to challenge these opponents. No Israeli government could bring itself to stop the confiscation of land and expansion of settlements in the West Bank and end oppressive restrictions aimed at keeping Palestinians a minority in Jerusalem. Arafat made only token efforts to stop terrorism by Islamic and nationalist groups, who now began the practice of sending suicide bombers on missions to kill civilians inside Israel.

In 1995, the Palestinian Authority's area of control was extended to include most large Arab towns in the West Bank, which had always been expensive and dangerous for the Israelis to occupy. The countryside, however, with its land available for settlement, stayed under Israeli control. Finally, the Israeli prime minister, Ehud Barak, elected in 1999, made a renewed effort for peace with all Israel's neighbors. He withdrew Israeli forces from southern Lebanon and began negotiations for peace with Israel's other northern neighbor, Syria, as well as for a final settlement with the Palestinians.

But intensive negotiations between the Israelis and the Palestinians, leading to face-to-face meetings of Barak, Arafat, and Clinton in the United States, only revealed the depth of the remaining disagreement. Barak was willing to evacuate most of the occupied territories over twenty-five years, but wanted to keep 10 percent of the West Bank together with continued rights of military control and intervention in the new Palestinian state. Arafat could not bring himself to compromise over the right of return of Palestinian refugees to homes in Israel. Neither side was willing to offer more than token concessions over Jerusalem. The result was the breakdown of the negotiations, an outbreak of fierce fighting between Palestinians and the Israeli army, and the election as Israeli prime minister of Ariel Sharon, the main backer of the settlements in the occupied territories. Meanwhile, negotiations with Syria were stalled by disagreement over Israeli evacuation of Syrian territory captured in 1967, and then by the death of Syrian president Hafiz Assad after many years of power.

In all these dealings between Israel and the Arabs, the United States had been active in coaxing and pressuring both sides to compromise, and the western Europeans had supported the peace process as best they could by subsidizing the Palestinian Authority. The halting of the peace process showed the limits of the power of the Western countries to end conflicts when one party or both parties were unwilling to make the sacrifices necessary for compromise.

India and Pakistan

The same was also true of Western power to influence another long-standing conflict, that of India and Pakistan. The two countries had compromised as well as fought each other in the past, but in the postcommunist era, rival fundamentalisms drove them onto a collision course.

In Pakistan, there was an uneasy balance of power between the army and increasingly fundamentalist Muslim political parties, which had growing success in elections. Army generals were usually able to overthrow politicians whom they considered corrupt, or who tried to bring the military under civilian control. But overthrowing politicians was one thing, and challenging the growing power of fundamentalist Islam was quite another. The generals themselves had to compromise with fundamentalism or risk revolution in the country—and mutiny among their own troops. In 1991, in a period of civilian rule, the Pakistani parliament passed legislation making *Sharia* (Islamic religious law) valid in many legal matters, and the army did not challenge this measure. Besides, the army and Islamic fundamentalists had an important common project: that of undermining Indian rule over a Muslim majority in the part of the disputed territory of Kashmir that India controlled (p. 542).

There were parallel developments in India—a secular democracy under firm civilian control, but one where Hindu nationalism became an increasingly powerful force. Hindu nationalism, like Islamic fundamentalism, is a movement that reasserts traditional religious belief in a stricter form than was usual in the past, despises other religions, and is deeply suspicious of cultural influences emanating from the West. Unlike Islamic fundamentalism, however, it is not an international movement but a nationalist one. Indian Hindu revivalists have made little effort to spread their influence to other Hindu peoples in southern Asia, but they have been intent on building up the power and prosperity of India.

During the 1990s, Hindu nationalist parties became an increasingly formidable threat to the secular Congress Party, which had steered India to independence and had nearly always been the main governing party since then. The rise of Hindu nationalism was accompanied by repeated bloody clashes with India's religious minorities—Sikhs, Christians, and above all the country's 140 million Muslims, who make up nearly one-sixth of the population. In Kashmir and elsewhere, Hindu militants burned Muslim shrines and tried to turn them into Hindu temples. Finally, in 1998, the main Hindu nationalist party, the Bharatiya Janata (Indian People's) Party, took over from Congress as the largest party in the Indian parliament.

One of the new governing party's first decisions was to authorize underground tests of three atomic weapons and of two more after the United States imposed mild economic sanctions. India had already tested a nuclear device in 1974, but since then, as the Indians knew, Pakistan had been working hard on its own nuclear program. The main point of holding tests now was to show that India was a great Hindu nation that could not be trifled with—not by Pakistan, nor by the United States. The Pakistanis quickly assembled and detonated their own atom bombs two weeks later and celebrated their own Islamic triumph. Once again, the United States imposed mild sanctions.

A year later, in 1999, the two South Asian nuclear powers almost went to war after Muslim militants based in Pakistan made incursions into Kashmir, and U.S. diplomats hastened to mediate a military stand-down by both sides. But that made no difference to the fact that two important non-Western members of the international community had shown that they could ignore the community's wishes, in particular those of its leading Western member.

Rebels and Outlaws: Islamic Fundamentalism, Terrorism, and Weapons of Mass Destruction

In Chechnya and Yugoslavia, in Palestine and Kashmir, and in other postcommunist or postcolonial conflicts, Muslims were involved as both victims and oppressors. The hatreds resulting from these struggles helped nourish the one international ideology that still rejected and sought to overthrow the Western-dominated world order, Islamic fundamentalism—and fundamentalist Islam, in turn, added fuel to the flames of many conflicts. In addition, the continuing conflicts also made two of the threatening problems of the 1980s even more menacing than before: terrorism and the proliferation of nuclear and other weapons of mass destruction.

Islamic Fundamentalism

In the 1980s, Islamic fundamentalism had developed into an international movement opposed to the existing world order like communism before it. As with communism, there were countries where Islamic fundamentalism was in power, countries where it was a strong movement without actually being in power, and countries where it was repressed. Of course, unlike communism, it had no worldwide appeal but affected only Muslim communities—and exactly for that reason, even countries that repressed it had to find a way of living with it. In addition, unlike communism, Islamic fundamentalism was an unstructured movement with no single claimant to worldwide authority—but that, if anything, helped it to spread.

The leading Islamic fundamentalist country remained Iran (pp. 577–578). If Iran was any guide, the future of Islamic fundamentalism as a Muslim alternative world order did not look promising. After the disastrous war against Iraq in the 1980s, Iran no longer sought to subvert governments in other Muslim countries, and restored normal relations with most Western countries other than the United States. Internally, there were signs of a reaction within Iranian society against extreme fundamentalism. The relatively moderate Mohammad Khatami was elected president in 1997, and a struggle began between "reforming" and "conservative" groups. The result was a stalemate in which the conservatives usually had the upper hand. But even the conservatives had lost their militancy, and so far as they were in control, the country seemed condemned to political and economic stagnation. If the reformers ever won, the result might well be a liberalized though still strongly Islamic society but no longer a militant challenge to the world order.

As Iranian militancy died down, the lead in Islamic extremism passed to Afghanistan. Soviet troops had been withdrawn from that country in 1988, and after years of civil war, the fundamentalist Taliban ("students of religion") movement came to power in 1996. The new regime imposed the strictest version of Islamic law yet seen, including prohibitions on any kind of activity by women outside the home—in contrast to the Iranian fundamentalists, who mobilized women for their own religious and political purposes. The Taliban regime was ostracized by most of the world and had unfriendly relations even with Iran—partly because the Taliban, who were Sunni Muslims, regarded the Shia Iranians as infidels.

 **The Bamiyan Buddha Project** (http://dsal .uchicago.edu/images/ aiis/bamiyan/) View images and learn more about the destruction of the Bamiyan Buddhas by the Taliban.

The failure of Islamic fundamentalism in the main country where it was in power did not prevent the movement from spreading widely across the Muslim world. Besides its appeal to religious tradition and resentment of the West, it used many modern methods, such as political parties, TV stations, and websites. In chaotic and poverty-stricken Muslim regions, such as Gaza or Shia districts in Lebanon, fundamentalists often brought food relief and medical help—performing the same tasks, in fact, as Christian missionary organizations and Western NGOs, and gaining supporters in the process.

Often, Islamic fundamentalism was an opposition movement, seeking to overthrow both secular Arab nationalist governments like those of Iraq, Syria, or Algeria, and those that were backed by the United States, like that of Egypt. In all these countries, it was cruelly repressed, but in others, like Pakistan, the territories under the Palestinian Authority, Saudi Arabia, and Nigeria, fundamentalist movements had more or less freedom to operate and a larger or smaller share of government power. Even countries that repressed fundamentalist opposition, however, had to give the movement some room. Often they allowed stricter religious preaching and practice and permitted radical propaganda against the United States, Israel, and the West in general.

Nuclear Proliferation and Terrorism

In the postcommunist era, India and Pakistan were not the only countries that wanted nuclear weapons as a symbol of national power and a deterrent against attack. Atom bombs remained expensive and difficult to produce, however, and some countries also looked to new and deadly poison gases as well as to new and lethal strains of bacteria as cheaper substitutes. Research, development, and actual use of all these types of weapons was nothing new, but as more countries made efforts to produce them they acquired a new and sinister name: weapons of mass destruction (WMDs).

Iraq's efforts to make such weapons were ended by UN inspection after the Gulf War, and seemingly were not successfully revived even after it expelled the inspectors in 1998. But late in the 1980s, North Korea, losing the protection of the dissolving Soviet Union and alienated from an increasingly capitalist

China, began to develop nuclear weapons. So did Iran, where both conservatives and reformers were eager for nuclear prestige and power against Israel and the United States; Libya's radical Muslim dictator Muammar al-Gaddafi also sought the prestige and reassurance of nuclear weapons. To help solve the problems of making atom bombs, all these countries made use of the services of the head of Pakistan's nuclear program, A. Q. Khan, who ran a well-organized and profitable international network to supply them with plans and parts (see photo). All these countries also established laboratories and production plants for the more easily developed poison gas and killer germs.

Most of these WMD efforts made slow progress in the 1990s, but terrorism became increasingly formidable. It kept all its old attractions as a way for unofficial groups to carry on conflicts against organized states and for weaker states to harass stronger ones. State-of-the-art communications technologies, the Internet, and e-mail made it easier for terrorist groups to organize and spread their messages. And terrorist deeds became harder to stop as perpetrators appeared who were not hampered by the wish to save their own lives—suicide bombers.

Suicide bombing had first been used by Syrian-backed Muslim groups against U.S., French, and Israeli troops in Lebanon in the 1980s (p. 577). In the 1990s, the use of suicide bombers against civilians became widespread. The Tamil Tigers, an organization fighting a brutal war for independence for their Hindu ethnic group in the South Asian country of Sri Lanka (formerly Ceylon; see Map 29.2 on page 543), sent suicide bombers against politi-cians and ordinary people belonging to the Buddhist majority. Suicide bombing was then taken up by Hamas (the Islamic Resistance Movement), a Palestinian fundamentalist organiza-tion, as a way of disrupting the peace process by infuriating the Israelis and weakening the Palestinian Authority.

Both the Tamil Tigers and Hamas had widespread support among the peoples they claimed to represent, and mass media throughout the Arab world acclaimed the anti-Israeli suicide bombers as martyrs. Saddam Hussein saw to it that the families of such "martyrs" received large gifts of money, and both Arab nationalist Syria and the Iranian hard-line fundamentalists sheltered and helped terrorist groups in various ways.

Al Qaeda

Alongside these long-established terrorist organizations, a new and formidable terrorist group or network of groups was arising, which seemingly received little or no support from the traditional state backers of terrorism. This was partly because its creator, Osama bin Laden, was the son of a wealthy Saudi Arabian build-ing contractor with a vast fortune of his own. A Sunni Muslim fundamentalist who despised the secular dictatorships of Syria and Iraq as well as the Shia fundamentalism of Iran, bin Laden first "invested" his wealth in recruiting fighters against the Soviet occupation of Afghanistan (p. 578). On arrival in that country, the recruits had to register in camps or "bases" financed by bin Laden, and soon he began calling his recruitment organization "The Base"—in Arabic, **Al Qaeda**.

In addition, after the Soviets evacuated Afghanistan, bin Laden turned his organization into a global network of ter-rorist groups, headquartered first in the East African country of Sudan, and later in Afghanistan under the rule of the Sunni fundamentalist Taliban movement. He also chose a new target that was more dangerous to attack than Israel or rival Arab countries—the United States.

For bin Laden, as for most militant fundamentalists, the United States was the single most deadly threat to Islam. He saw it as the source of cultural contamination, the backer of the Jewish state, and the puppetmaster of many Arab governments, including that of Saudi Arabia. Above all, by stationing its unbelieving troops in Saudi Arabia during and after the Gulf

≪ Nuclear Contraband The crates contain centrifuges—devices for separat-ing higher-radioactivity uranium suitable for atom bombs from unsuitable lower-radioactivity uranium. The centrifuges were designed in Pakistan, manufactured in Malaysia with blueprints supplied by A. Q. Khan, the head of the Pakistani nuclear program, and sold to Libya (among other countries) in the 1990s. Libya eventually gave up its nuclear weapons program in 2003 and handed over these centrifuges to the United States. Courtesy, Knoxville News Sentinel Photo: Paul Efird

War, the land of the holiest of mosques in the cities of Mecca and Medina, it insulted God himself. In retaliation for these alleged offenses against Islam, in 1995 and 1996 groups affiliated with Al Qaeda carried out truck bombings of U.S. installations in Saudi Arabia, and in 1998 there followed the car bombing of the U.S. embassy in Kenya.

Terrorism was of its nature a threat to the international community, both because of its inhumanity and because it was a kind of private violence on an international scale. In addition, the international community was in principle opposed to the development of WMDs. Treaties against the development of nuclear and biological weapons had been negotiated in the 1970s (pp. 580–581), and most nations had signed on to them; and in 1993, a similar treaty went into effect against chemical weapons. Terrorism and the proliferation of WMDs were certainly against the interests of the international community's leading Western members, against whom they were mostly directed.

Compared with the wars in Yugoslavia or Africa, however, the casualties of terrorist attacks were few and the dangers of proliferation seemed remote. In 1995, the bombing of a government building in Oklahoma City by a U.S. antigovernment group made domestic terrorism an issue for a time. But there were no more such atrocities, and in 1998, the bombing of the embassy in Kenya and retaliatory U.S. air raids on Al Qaeda training camps in Afghanistan preoccupied the public for a far shorter time than the year-long drama of the president's sex life.

Meanwhile, however, bin Laden and his collaborators were making plans. None of their attacks so far had involved suicidal "martyrs," and nearly all had been far from the United States. They wanted to strike a devastating blow against the United States itself that would unite all Islam behind Al Qaeda. Already, in 1993, a Muslim extremist group that was perhaps affiliated with Al Qaeda had unsuccessfully tried to destroy the World Trade Center in New York, for them a unique symbol of the American wealth and power they detested, with a truck bomb. Perhaps another effort, combining the old terrorist technique of airplane hijacking (p. 581) and the newer method of suicide bombing, would be more effective. By the end of the 1990s, a horrific deed was already in the making that would lead to a more drastic upheaval in the international community than any single event since the fall of communism.

 Listen to a synopsis of Chapter 33.

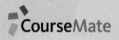

CHAPTER 34

WESTERN CIVILIZATION IN THE WORLD OF TODAY,

2000s

LEARNING OBJECTIVES

AFTER READING THIS CHAPTER, YOU SHOULD BE ABLE TO DO THE FOLLOWING:

LO¹ Describe how the U.S. approach to the international community, the Western partnership, and the Muslim world changed after 9/11.

LO² Analyze the erosion of Western economic and political dominance in the early twenty-first century.

> "In response to terrorist attacks, the United States launched an ambitious effort to change the way in which the West steered the world."

Early in the twenty-first century, Muslim tensions and resentments that had grown since the fall of communism exploded in terrorist attacks on the United States. In response, the United States launched an ambitious effort to change the way in which the West steered the world, by using force or the threat of it more readily than before and by purposefully encouraging the spread of secular democratic government and values to Muslim countries. In the service of these aims, it invaded Iraq and overthrew its tyrannical regime. Rather than remolding Iraq according to its own design, the United States presided over a period of horrendous turmoil, which it was able gradually to dampen down partly by force, but also by means of a complex process of negotiation and compromise with the religious and ethnic groups that it had liberated. The United States did not give up hope of persuading the Muslim world to adopt more Western structures and values than in the past, but it seemed to accept that this would have to happen on Muslim rather than on Western terms.

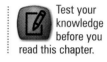

Test your knowledge before you read this chapter.

What do you think?

Using force against outlaw states and movements before they attack can be justified in certain cases.

Strongly Disagree						Strongly Agree
1	2	3	4	5	6	7

Meanwhile, the postcommunist predominance of the political and economic West was being gradually eroded. Within the West, the European Union encountered difficulties in adapting to an influx of new members, and U.S. economic successes of the 1990s turned into a crisis that spread to the rest of the world in the 2000s. Outside the West, Russia began to reassert its power, and countries that had prospered in the era of globalization began to deal with the West on more equal terms. Worldwide decision-making power was coming to be more widely shared, but that also made it hard to take effective decisions—notably in regard to what was perhaps the world's most menacing long-term problem, that of climate change.

≪ **Antiquity Greets Modernity** Fireworks explode and laser beams shoot upward at Giza, Egypt, on January 1, 2000, to mark the new millennium; behind them looms the pyramid of King Khafre, builder of the Great Sphinx (p. 26). Symbolic of the endurance of civilization, a 4,500-year-old monument looks down upon a 21st-century celebration; symptomatic of the global reach of Western civilization, a date in the Western time reckoning is marked by a predominantly Muslim country.

LO¹ September 11, the West, and Islam

Ten years after the fall of communism, the project of an international community steered toward harmony, prosperity, and freedom by the West was very much a work in progress. Globalization had spread prosperity in many poor countries but also inspired resentment between the West and "the Rest." Postcommunist and postcolonial conflicts were usually damped down or died down in the end, but remained a continually renewed source of destructive anarchy. The Islamic fundamentalist challenge to the Western-dominated world order was mostly held down by repressive governments in the Muslim world, but had increasing popular support in Muslim countries where it was not in power. Many states that the West suspected of seeking nuclear weapons had been blocked from making progress in developing them, but India and Pakistan had found ways around the obstacles, and North Korea was near to doing so. Terrorist movements within the countries of the Western heartland were mostly losing momentum, but Islamic terrorism was more active and better organized than ever before.

Such was the state of the world when Al Qaeda attacked and destroyed the World Trade Center in New York City and badly damaged the Pentagon in Washington on September 11, 2001.

 **9/11** Watch a report on the events of September 11, 2001.

The U.S. Response: Restructuring the International Community

The attacks were not just against people and buildings, or even against the United States, but against the whole idea of a harmonious international community with the West at the helm. At first, the result seemed to be to reinforce the community's solidarity, as Iraq's attack on Kuwait had done ten years earlier. By the end of the year, the administration of President George W. Bush, the conservative Republican successor to Clinton, had won the support of NATO for the use of force, and then seen to the overthrow of the fanatically Islamist Taliban government that harbored Al Qaeda in Afghanistan. In 2002, peacekeeping troops from Britain, France, Germany, and other NATO countries, UN advisers, and nongovernmental volunteers moved in alongside the Americans to help the Afghans with the task of building a nation and a civil society, according to the recipe for rebuilding failed states that had been devised in Bosnia and Kosovo (see photo).

Rebuilding Afghanistan

In the next few years, millions of Afghan refugees, displaced by twenty years of civil war and brutal repression, returned to their homes and resumed something like their normal lives. Rival ethnic and religious groups hammered out a national constitution that was democratic but far from secular: it declared itself to be adopted by "We the

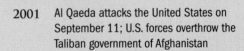

2001	Al Qaeda attacks the United States on September 11; U.S. forces overthrow the Taliban government of Afghanistan
2003	The United States invades Iraq and overthrows the government of Saddam Hussein, beginning the Iraq War
2004	The "Orange Revolution" in the Ukraine overturns a fixed election won by a pro-Russian candidate, initiating a strained relationship with Russia
2006	Responding to U.S. pressures, the Palestinian president agrees to elections; the Islamist movement Hamas wins the majority; with U.S. approval, Israel bombs and invades Lebanon to crush Hezbollah; a financial crisis gets under way in the United States and involves much of the rest of the world
2007	The U.S.-backed leader of Pakistan is ousted
2008	The United States and Iraqi governments agree to a complete U.S. troop withdrawal by the end of 2011; Russia invades Georgia in support of pro-Russian separatists; the global financial crisis reaches its peak
2009	Barack Obama becomes U.S. president and announces a change of approach to U.S.-Muslim relations; the European Union is reorganized in the Treaty of Lisbon; the international community takes a step to address climate change with the Copenhagen Accord
2010	The Obama administration announces a temporary troop increase in Afghanistan, to be followed by a withdrawal in 2012; the United States bows to the wish of other wealthy countries to set goals for reducing government deficits

people of Afghanistan," acting "In the name of God, the merciful, the compassionate."

However, the nation-building project soon ran into problems. By the time that the Democratic administration of Barack Obama took over in 2009, alongside the soldiers and development officials of the United States and its partners there existed in Afghanistan a corrupt and incompetent national government run by President Mohammed Karzai (**KAHR-zeye**) and his clan relatives that soon falsified national elections to stay in power, as well as a widespread and brutal Taliban guerrilla movement. Ruthless local warlords held power by maneuvering among all

three groups, and all three groups were more or less feared and resented by much of the population. Osama bin Laden lived free and unpunished, though seemingly with little influence on events, in the wild lands on the border of Afghanistan and Pakistan. And voters in the NATO countries were disillusioned with the constant trickle of casualties that seemingly was leading to no more than stalemate.

In 2010 the new Democratic U.S. administration of Barack Obama decided to break the stalemate by temporarily increasing its forces in Afghanistan. It would use the extra troops partly to hold and protect regions where the Taliban had been driven out, but also to train an effective Afghan army so that NATO troops could leave the country in 2012. Essentially Obama was betting on the chance of making quick gains against the Taliban and instilling a sense of urgency into the Afghan government, against the possibility that the Taliban would simply lie low for two years and then fill the gap left by NATO's departure.

The Superpower and the International Community

Even if the Afghan nation-building project was in trouble, at least the United States and its Western partners had from the start worked together to accomplish it, and they had the more or (in the case of most Muslim states) less enthusiastic blessing of the rest of the world. In the United States, however, September 11 aroused not only national sorrow, pride, and anger, but also a widespread feeling of frustration at the way the world had operated since the fall of communism. For ten years, the United States, the world's only superpower, had tried to operate by consensus, and the result had been the first successful attack on its mainland territory since the British burned Washington in 1812. President Bush expressed this mood in his speeches declaring a general "war on terror," implicitly threatening countries that did not wholeheartedly join it, and naming three specific countries that sought or were thought to be seeking nuclear weapons—Iraq, Iran, and North Korea—as an international "Axis of Evil."

Quite soon after the September 11 attacks, the Bush administration decided that, in the future, the United States would use force—including preemptively (without having been attacked first)—or the threat of force against all the outlaw and rebel states and movements that had troubled the world since the fall of communism. Terrorist movements and states that aided them, states that tried to acquire nuclear and other weapons of mass destruction, Islamic fundamentalist states and movements—all would be liable to U.S. attack. The plan derived partly from the traditional U.S. conservative belief that the United States should accept no limits on its freedom of action and no resistance to its will, and partly from the neoconservative (pp. 582–583) belief that the Islamic world had no legitimate grievances against the West, and that its resentments came from a backward mind set that needed to be changed. The Bush administration chose to first apply these principles to the defiant Iraqi dictatorship of Saddam Hussein.

President Bush's January 2002 State of the Union Speech (http://archives.cnn.com/2002/ALLPOLITICS/01/29/bush.speech.txt/) Read and watch President Bush's 2002 State of the Union address, in which he speaks of the "Axis of Evil."

> "*September 11 aroused not only national sorrow, pride, and anger, but also a widespread feeling of frustration at the way the world had operated since the fall of communism.*"

In support of their argument that the United States had the right to take military action against another country without a

THE BUSH ADMINISTRATION HOPED TO ACHIEVE THREE AIMS BY OVERTHROWING SADDAM HUSSEIN:

To prevent Iraq from using weapons of mass destruction

- After the Gulf War, Iraq's efforts to make such weapons were ended by UN inspection.

- However, Saddam expelled the UN inspectors in 1998.

- In 2001, the intelligence services of many countries suspected that Iraq's efforts to develop weapons of mass destruction (WMDs) might still be under way.

To intimidate other dangerous leaders

- By making a spectacular example of Saddam, U.S. planners hoped to intimidate other rebels and outlaws.

- Acting against Saddam would send a message to such potentially dangerous leaders as North Korea's Kim Jong-il.

To transform the Islamic world through the introduction of secular democracy

- U.S. conservatives imagined replacing Saddam's sadistic tyranny with a beneficent U.S. occupation that would remake Iraq into a secular democracy.

- This would in turn give the rest of the Islamic world an attractive alternative to militant fundamentalism, thereby leading to the integration of Islam into a secular and democratic world order.

"permission slip" from other nations, conservatives questioned the legitimacy of the institutions of the international community. They pointed, for example, to the fact that the UN Human Rights Commission had been taken over by countries that were tyrannies and dictatorships: in 2002, these countries had elected Libya, where torture and imprisonment without trial were routine, to be the commission's president. Did not the United States, the world's pioneer and model of democracy and human rights, have far greater moral authority than the feeble and hypocritical United Nations to be the lawgiver and law enforcer of the international community?

> **"One way or another, the United States would save the world from rebels and outlaws and nightmarish threats."**

In the course of heated arguments within the U.S. administration, international-minded Republicans, notably Secretary of State Colin Powell, were able to make NATO collaboration and UN authorization part of the plan. At U.S. urging, the UN Security Council would issue an ultimatum to Iraq to readmit UN inspectors, whom it had earlier expelled, to search for WMDs; Iraq would refuse, or not cooperate properly with the inspectors; and the Security Council would then authorize the United States to go to war as its enforcer.

If the U.S. administration could not get cooperation from the institutions of the Western partnership and the international community, however, it was determined to act without these institutions, and to replace them with a "coalition of the willing"—that is, of those countries that would be willing to join with it against Iraq. One way or another, the United States would save the world from rebels and outlaws and nightmarish threats. Either the institutions of the international community would follow its lead, or it would set those institutions aside and dominate the community through a league of states directly headed by itself.

The International Community and the Superpower

It soon appeared that only a minority of governments and almost no peoples were prepared to accept the United States in the role of trustee for the interests of the world. The reason was that just as the United States was dissatisfied with what it regarded as the feebleness and hypocrisy of the international community, so much of the community was discontented with what it perceived as the high-handedness of the United States as its single leading citizen.

Partly, this was because the United States was the main target of resentment among the "Rest" against the West for its self-interested globalization policies (pp. 608–612). But issues were also arising that pitted the United States even against its Western partners. For example, many nations including the United States, meeting in Kyoto, Japan, in 1997, had agreed upon a protocol (an amendment to an earlier international treaty) establishing a procedure for reducing emissions of burned fuel suspected of causing global warming (p. 579). The Bush administration, however, refused to submit the Kyoto Protocol to the Senate for ratification. Most nations that accepted the Kyoto Protocol did not do so because they were sure beyond a doubt that global warming was a clear and present danger caused by humans. Rather, they acted on what climatologists called the "precautionary" principle—namely, that with global warning, it was better to be safe than sorry. The United States in effect refused to subject itself to painful economic constraints on the basis of an uncertain judgment about global warming, even though this judgment was taken seriously by most of the nations of the world.

Now, however, the United States wanted the nations of the world to risk the lives of their troops in war and peacekeeping on the basis of its own uncertain judgment about Iraqi WMDs. Most of the community, however, was wary of a leading citizen that intended to command but refused to obey. This wariness only increased when Iraq, contrary to U.S. expectations, admitted UN inspectors and cooperated with them more or less to their satisfaction, and the inspectors found no WMDs—because, as the invaders later found, the Iraqis no longer had any.

> "*French president Jacques Chirac declared: 'no one can act alone in the name of all.'*"

Europe, Islam, and the War

As a result, the United States did not lead a united international effort as it had done in the 1991 Gulf War and against Afghanistan. Instead, the United States dragged the international community along behind it, with some governments going farther and more eagerly, and others pulling back with all their might. Britain, true to its twentieth-century "special relationship" of mutual loyalty with the United States, sent a third of its army to take part in the invasion of Iraq. Unlike in 1991, however, Britain was the only country apart from the United States to send a large force, though other European governments approved the war and sent small peacekeeping forces. Kuwait and other small Arab states in the Persian Gulf allowed their territories to be used as jumping-off points for the invasion, but not a single Arab soldier took part in war or peacekeeping.

Furthermore, two leading members of the Western partnership, France and Germany, openly refused to do the United States' bidding. France, true to its tradition of accepting U.S. leadership only in times of clear and present danger as in Afghanistan, pushed its opposition to the point of threatening to veto the Security Council resolution that would have authorized the invasion of Iraq. When the war began, the German chancellor Gerhard Schröder declared in a televised speech to his nation: "A wrong decision has been taken"; and in a speech to the United Nations six months later, French president Jacques Chirac declared: "no one can act alone in the name of all."

In France, Germany, and other European countries, both governments and public opinion to a greater or lesser extent shared the U.S. administration's belief that where traditional Islamic values and modern Western ones were in conflict, it was Islam that must change its ways. The only Muslims whose ways the Europeans felt it was urgent to change, however, were the growing immigrant populations within their own borders. In France, for example, by 2003 about 8 percent of the population was made up of Muslim immigrants from former colonies in North Africa and their French-born children. Partly because the Muslims faced widespread distrust and discrimination, they asserted their religious identity more strongly than before, and many families took to sending their daughters to school wearing the *hijab*, the Muslim headscarf.

One of the most prized French national values, however, was *laïcité* (lah-ee-see-TEH)—the understanding of the nation as a community that was separate from and took precedence over any religious affiliation. In addition, the country had undergone many of the sixties changes in gender values (pp. 554–555). In 2004, only a year after France had prevented the Security Council from authorizing the U.S. invasion of Iraq, the French parliament passed a "Law on the Wearing of Conspicuous Religious Symbols in Public Educational Institutions" up to high school. The law applied to symbols of every religion, but there was no doubt about the real target. The headscarf was seen as a symbol of religious identity and female subjection that did not belong in public schools where young citizens were being prepared for equal membership in the all-embracing community of the French nation.

As alarming as the French government (and a majority of non-Muslim French citizens) found headscarfs in the schools, however, Iraq's possible WMDs seemed to them less threatening than the prospect, as they deemed it, of an international community that was dominated and its institutions commandeered by the United States. This feeling was shared in countries outside the Western partnership like Russia and India, even though they had fought their own wars against Muslim extremists (pp. 600, 616–617). Meanwhile, Muslim governments were dismayed, and Muslim peoples reacted with fury, to what they considered a brazen U.S. effort to impose its values and its will on them, gain control of Middle Eastern oil fields, and bully the Arabs into submission to Israel. As a result, in April 2003, the United States went to war without UN backing and with limited international support.

"**What Are the Issues Related to the Headscarf Ban in France?**" (http://www.awid.org/eng/Issues-and-Analysis/Library/What-are-the-issues-related-to-the-headscarf-ban-in-France) Read three different perspectives on the headscarf issue by women's rights advocates.

Rebuilding Iraq

The "coalition of the willing" conquered Iraq in six weeks, and following the war, the resisters of the U.S. action all voted in favor of legitimizing and authorizing UN cooperation with the U.S.-led occupation administration in Iraq. In this way, by confronting the institutions of the international community with an accomplished fact and daring them to oppose it, the United States was able to extract a measure of agreement from them. But the agreement was not enthusiastic, and to judge from opinion polls, even in countries where governments stood by the United States, the peoples were mostly against the war. The hitherto popular and respected British prime minister Tony Blair, who had led his country into the war, soon came to be reviled as "Bush's poodle."

 **"Bush's War"** (http://www.pbs.org/wgbh/pages/frontline/bushswar/) Get an in-depth look at "Bush's War."

The main U.S. hope of gaining real international support for its actions, winning acceptance of its claim to a dominant worldwide role, and changing the mood of the Muslim world rested on rebuilding Iraq as a prosperous, secular, and democratic state. The U.S. administration seemingly made no detailed plans in advance for how to achieve this, partly because it expected that it would be a relatively easy task. The Iraqi people, grateful for liberation from Saddam Hussein's tyranny, would eagerly set to work to rebuild their country under U.S. guidance; U.S. oil companies would set the Iraqi oil industry, devastated by years of sanctions, back on its feet; and the country's reconstruction would be paid for out of its oil revenues. Thus, there would be no need for a lengthy occupation with a large army, and no burden on U.S. taxpayers.

Turmoil in Iraq

In actuality, these expectations turned out to be incorrect—above all, because not many people inside Iraq wanted it to become the kind of country that the United States planned for it to be, nor did they have their own united vision of what kind of country they wanted to live in. Iraq had come into existence in 1920, by decree of the British following the collapse of the Ottoman Empire (pp. 479–480). The three main Iraqi ethnic and religious groups had no sense of common nationhood, but each had its own historic identity and its own vision of a future Iraq, which turned out to be different from that of the United States.

The Shia Muslims, Arabs living mainly in the south of Iraq who formed about two-thirds of the population, hoped for an Iraq where they would be the dominant force. They were eager to live in a democracy and did not want direct clerical rule as in Iran, but they also did not want Iraq to be a secular state. The Sunni Arabs, who had been privileged under Saddam Hussein, were unwilling to live as a minority in a state with a Shia majority. And the deepest wish of the non-Arab and Sunni Muslim Kurds, a fragment of a large and ancient nation the rest of which lived in Turkey, Iran, and Syria, was not to be part of Iraq at all. Instead, they wanted a self-governing territory in the north of Iraq that would be the core round which a united and independent Kurdistan would one day form.

To begin with, the U.S.-dominated Coalition Provisional Authority planned a lengthy period in which it would govern Iraq from above, supervising its reconstruction and gradually introducing it to democratic and secular government. However, it soon became clear that the expected gratitude and devotion to the liberators were not forthcoming, except from the Kurds—who did not, however, let gratitude and devotion prevent them from determinedly pursuing their national ambitions.

Among the Iraqi Arabs, the Sunni regions became the scene of a vicious guerrilla insurgency that persisted even after the U.S. forces captured the former dictator, while the Shia majority began to lose patience with their status as wards of a non-Muslim and non-Arab occupation regime. Above all to placate the Shia Arabs, the United States soon changed course. First, it announced a handover of sovereign power to an Iraqi government by the middle of 2004. Then, in response to massive demonstrations called by the most influential Shia cleric, Ayatollah Ali al-Sistani (see photo), it agreed that nationwide elections would take place early in 2005, far sooner than it had originally intended. In Iraq, it seemed, the irresistible force of the world's only superpower had met an immovable object in the form of a leader who wielded the formidable power of Islam over the life and society of its believers.

Meanwhile, the Sunni insurgency turned into a full-scale religious rebellion, in which volunteers from many Sunni countries, organized and recruited by Al Qaeda, played a leading role. The insurgents attacked not only U.S. troops but also Shia targets, which in turn led to Shia retaliation. For three years, the Arabs of Iraq lived and died amid an inferno of kidnappings, torture, murder, suicide bombings, car bombings, and mortar and rocket bombardments by rival militias and death squads. The result was one of the most massive of postcommunist ethnic cleansings. Tens or perhaps hundreds of thousands of people were killed; 2 million ended as refugees abroad, mostly in neighboring Syria and Jordan; and perhaps as many as 3 million became "internally displaced persons," living as refugees inside Iraq.

On the Way to Recovery?

Late in 2007, the Bush administration carried out a successful temporary "troop surge" directed mainly against a Shia militia in Baghdad, the Mahdi Army, that was among the largest-scale ethnic cleansers. Meanwhile, Sunni militias grew resentful at domination by brutal religious extremists from foreign countries, and began allying with the Americans in the "Sunni Awakening." By that time, too, there were hardly any areas left where Shias and Sunnis lived closely enough side by side that they could attack each other. Quite soon the country seemed on the way to recovery from actual civil war. But terrorism was more common in Iraq than anywhere else in the Middle East, its government ministries were full of U.S. advisers, its army was backed by a U.S. garrison, its oil industry was run down, 5 million of its people were refugees at home or abroad, and following elections in March 2010, the

"Yes, Yes to Elections! No, No to Occupation!" In January 2004, 100,000 Shia Iraqis demonstrated in Baghdad against a U.S. plan for a gradual transition to democracy that it would be able to guide, and in favor of immediate elections. In a rare direct political intervention, Ayatollah Ali al-Sistani had personally rejected the U.S. plan and called for elections, and the demonstrators held portraits of him high. The United States swiftly complied with the ayatollah's demand. Marco Di Lauro/Getty Images

rival parties could not agree on a new government. Muslim public opinion had little reason to see Iraq as a model of reform.

Furthermore, if Iraq ever did fully recover, it would not necessarily be the kind of secular democracy that the United States had originally intended. For example, its constitution, like those of every other Arab state, proclaimed that "Islam is the official religion of the State and is a foundation source of legislation." Furthermore, there were limits to how close the Iraqis wanted any future partnership with the United States to be. In 2008, the Bush administration and the Shia-dominated government negotiated agreements that provided for all U.S. forces to leave by the end of 2011, while the two countries would maintain "a long-term relationship in economic, diplomatic, cultural, and security fields." It was the Iraqis who insisted on

> *"Muslim public opinion had little reason to see Iraq as a model of reform."*

a definite and relatively short deadline for the U.S. troops to leave, and they also inserted a clause into the long-term relationship agreement that "the United States shall not use Iraqi land, sea, and air as a launching or transit point for attacks against other countries"—meaning Iran. As a Shia country, an enemy of Saddam Hussein, and the land where many Iraqi Shia leaders had taken refuge from Saddam, Iran wielded influence in Iraq second only to that of the United States, and the Iraqi government generally sought to balance between its rival foreign backers rather than to choose between them. A fully recovered Iraq, it seemed, would be friendly to Iran, not a U.S. ally against it; and it would be an Islamic democracy, not a secular one.

 Iraq in Pictures (http://www.guardian.co.uk/Iraq/pictures/0,,942091,00.html) View photo essays chronicling the Iraq War.

Reform and Change in the "Greater Middle East"

As the Iraq project got under way, the United States also made efforts to foster secular democracy in what the Bush administration called the "Greater Middle East"—a region that stretched from

A U.S. PRESIDENT SPEAKS TO THE MUSLIM WORLD

On June 4, 2009, at Giza, the site of the Great Pyramid near Cairo, President Barack Obama spoke to an audience, including students, that had been jointly invited by Egypt's two most prestigious universities: al-Azhar (al-AZ-har) ("the Most Glorious"), a thousand-year-old center of Muslim learning, and the century-old, mainly secular Cairo University. The speech was intended to help repair the strained relationship between the United States and the Muslim world by stressing what both sides had in common, but also by honestly listing six "sources of tension" between them, and explaining what he thought each side should do to eliminate these.

The sources of tension that Obama named were violent extremism; Israel and the Arabs; Iran and nuclear weapons; democracy; religious freedom; women's rights; and economic development. Excerpted below are his general explanation of the reasons for the strained relationship, and his remarks on two issues of political structures and social values: democracy and women's rights.

. . . We meet at a time of great tension between the United States and Muslims around the world—tension rooted in historical forces that go beyond any current policy debate. The relationship between Islam and the West includes centuries of coexistence and cooperation, but also conflict and religious wars. More recently, tension has been fed by colonialism that denied rights and opportunities to many Muslims, and a Cold War in which Muslim-majority countries were too often treated as proxies without regard to their own aspirations. Moreover, the sweeping change brought by modernity and globalization led many Muslims to view the West as hostile to the traditions of Islam.

Violent extremists have exploited these tensions in a small but potent minority of Muslims. The attacks of September 11, 2001 and the continued efforts of these extremists to engage in violence against civilians have led some in my country to view Islam as inevitably hostile not only to America and Western countries, but also to human rights. All this has bred more fear and more mistrust.

So long as our relationship is defined by our differences, we will empower those who sow hatred rather than peace, those who promote conflict rather than the cooperation that can help all of our people achieve justice and prosperity. And this cycle of suspicion and discord must end.

I've come here to Cairo to seek a new beginning between the United States and Muslims around the world, one based on mutual interest and mutual respect, and one based upon the truth that America and Islam are not exclusive and need not be in competition. Instead, they overlap, and share common principles—principles of justice and progress; tolerance and the dignity of all human beings.

. . . The fourth issue that I will address is democracy. (Applause.)

I know—I know there has been controversy about the promotion of democracy in recent years, and much of this controversy is connected to the war in Iraq. So let me be clear: No system of government can or should be imposed by one nation by any other.

northwestern Africa to southern Asia. With U.S approval and sometimes at its urging, monarchies such as Jordan and Kuwait took measures to increase popular participation in government. Generally, however, these measures were designed to make sure that Islamic religious parties, which usually had wide popular support, would be unable to win majorities in legislatures, or to control governments if they did win majorities. Other undemocratic governments in Muslim countries, such as Egypt's authoritarian presidency, Saudi Arabia's absolute monarchy, and post-Soviet dictatorships in central Asia, continued exactly as before, confident that so long as they were pro-Western and repressed Islamic terrorist movements, the United States would not bother them.

Democracy and the Arab-Israeli Conflict

Apart from Iraq itself, the most spectacular unintended result of the U.S. democratization project came in the Palestinian territories in 2006. Two years earlier, following the death of Yassir Arafat, one of his aides, Mahmoud Abbas, had been elected president of the Palestinian authority. Abbas supported a settlement with Israel and unlike Arafat, was willing to turn forcefully against terrorist sections of the Palestinian movement. Both the United States and the Europeans approved of him, and the violent struggles with Israel died down in the West Bank (p. 616). In the spirit of its democratization policy, the United States then pressed Abbas to hold long-delayed elections to the Palestinian legislature so that he and his secular

That does not lessen my commitment, however, to governments that reflect the will of the people. Each nation gives life to this principle in its own way, grounded in the traditions of its own people. America does not presume to know what is best for everyone, just as we would not presume to pick the outcome of a peaceful election. But I do have an unyielding belief that all people yearn for certain things: the ability to speak your mind and have a say in how you are governed; confidence in the rule of law and the equal administration of justice; government that is transparent and doesn't steal from the people; the freedom to live as you choose. These are not just American ideas; they are human rights. And that is why we will support them everywhere. (Applause.) . . . And we will welcome all elected, peaceful governments—provided they govern with respect for all their people.

This last point is important because there are some who advocate for democracy only when they're out of power; once in power, they are ruthless in suppressing the rights of others. (Applause.) So no matter where it takes hold, government of the people and by the people sets a single standard for all who would hold power: You must maintain your power through consent, not coercion; you must respect the rights of minorities, and participate with a spirit of tolerance and compromise; you must place the interests of your people and the legitimate workings of the political process above your party. Without these ingredients, elections alone do not make true democracy.

. . . The sixth issue—the sixth issue that I want to address is women's rights. (Applause.) I know—I know—and you can tell from this audience, that there is a healthy debate about this issue. I reject the view of some in the West that a woman who chooses to cover her hair is somehow less equal, but I do believe that a woman who is denied an education is denied equality. (Applause.) And it is no coincidence that countries where women are well educated are far more likely to be prosperous.

Now, let me be clear: Issues of women's equality are by no means simply an issue for Islam. In Turkey, Pakistan, Bangladesh, Indonesia, we've seen Muslim-majority countries elect a woman to lead. Meanwhile, the struggle for women's equality continues in many aspects of American life, and in countries around the world.

I am convinced that our daughters can contribute just as much to society as our sons. (Applause.) Our common prosperity will be advanced by allowing all humanity—men and women—to reach their full potential. I do not believe that women must make the same choices as men in order to be equal, and I respect those women who choose to live their lives in traditional roles. But it should be their choice. And that is why the United States will partner with any Muslim-majority country to support expanded literacy for girls, and to help young women pursue employment through micro-financing that helps people live their dreams. (Applause.)

EXPLORING THE SOURCE

1. What basic beliefs about the relationship between America and the Muslim world does Obama express, and how does he think they ought to influence U.S. policy toward the Muslim world in the areas of democracy and women's rights?

2. Judging from Obama's remarks, how does he think that Muslims themselves ought to handle the issues of democracy and women's rights?

Source: The White House, Office of the Press Secretary

nationalist **Fatah** movement, which sought a settlement with Israel by negotiation, would acquire democratic legitimacy. Instead, the winner was the Islamist movement Hamas (p. 618), which called for Israel's destruction and an Islamic Palestinian state.

After a year of uneasy coexistence, Fatah and Hamas came to blows: Hamas took over power in its stronghold of Gaza, and in the West Bank, Fatah crushed the Hamas organization. The Americans and Israelis—in this case, with strong support from Europe—refused to deal with Hamas but aided Fatah in the West Bank. Their hope was that the people of Gaza, cut off from the world by a trade and travel embargo, oppressed by Hamas's religious strictness, and seeing relative prosperity and freedom in the West Bank, would turn against their Islamist rulers.

While the West was waiting for this to happen, the Israelis, provoked in 2006 by an incursion on their northern border, turned on **Hezbollah**, a movement armed and financed by Syria and Iran that ruled the Shia community in Lebanon as an all but independent territory. This seemed a good moment to crush Hezbollah. Lebanese Christians and Sunnis had grown increasingly resentful at Syrian domination of their country (p. 577). When an anti-Syrian prime minister, Rafik Hariri, was murdered in 2005, massive demonstrations and U.S. threats—again, with European support including from France, Lebanon's former ruler—had forced Syrian troops that had been stationed there since the early 1990s to leave. If only Hezbollah could be uprooted, or at any rate disarmed and discredited, Israel would be more secure, the United States and France would replace Syria as the dominant foreign influences in Lebanon, and Middle Eastern democracy would have moved another step forward.

With U.S. approval, the Israelis bombed and invaded. But the massive destruction and loss of life turned all Lebanon against Israel, and Hezbollah was applauded throughout the Arab world, Sunni as well as Shia, for its unexpectedly strong resistance and its massive rocket attacks on the Jewish state. An eventual cease-fire left the movement as powerful in Lebanon as before, though it now avoided armed actions against Israel. Not long after the war started, U.S. secretary of state Condoleezza Rice spoke of it as "the birth pangs of a new Middle East." But in Lebanon and throughout the Middle East, the war ended in business as usual.

Much the same happened again in 2009 after the Israelis fought another brief war against Hamas in Gaza. Rocket attacks from Gaza against nearby Israeli towns and Israeli raids into Gaza finally escalated into a massive Israeli attack in which many civilians were killed. Once again, by lashing out, Israel deterred a foe from further violence, but Hamas still ruled Gaza.

Pakistan and Iran

From time to time, undemocratic governments in Muslim countries were threatened or actually overthrown by popular protests, but these did not shake the position of Islam as a force that acted directly on politics and government. In Pakistan in 2007, the latest of many U.S.-backed military rulers, Pervez Musharraf, fell from power when he took measures of repression that the educated classes found intolerable and that rival generals were unwilling to support. The main forces in the restored democracy were the secular-minded Pakistan People's Party and the religiously inclined Pakistan Muslim League, with the army and a ruthless militant Islamic movement linked with the Afghan Taliban looming in the background. The most prominent victim of the terrorists was the People's Party leader Benazir Bhutto, whose hereditary standing as the daughter of a prominent leader executed by an earlier military dictator helped her rise to power even though she was a woman. But throughout her political career, she was careful to wear the *hijab* in public.

Meanwhile in Iran, the fundamentalist Mahmoud Ahmadinajad **(ahh-mah-dee-nah-ZHAHD)** had been elected in 2005 on a swing of the pendulum against reformists who had succeeded neither in liberalizing the country nor in bringing prosperity (p. 617). After four years, in which he had strengthened religious repression while himself being none too successful in managing the economy, he was challenged for reelection by a reformist, Hossein Mousavi. The government falsified the vote to make Ahmedinajad the winner, and used its military, paramilitary, police, and Islamic vigilante forces to crush massive protest demonstrations. But Mousavi was a strong supporter of Iran's nuclear development program that the West wanted to dismantle, and the slogan that his supporters shouted from the rooftops of Tehran was "God is Great!"

"A New Beginning"

By 2008, Iraq had not become the kind of model of secular democracy that the Bush administration had originally had in mind, nor had the other two countries of Bush's original "Axis of Evil," been intimidated by Iraq's fate. In 2006 North Korea claimed—perhaps falsely—to have exploded an atom bomb, and it certainly did so in 2009. Neither the Iraq invasion, nor UN sanctions, nor vague threats of U.S. or Israeli attack deterred Iran from pursuing a nuclear development program that it claimed was peaceful and that the United States and its allies—united on this issue—believed was aimed at building a bomb.

Furthermore, instead of being easy and cheap, the Iraq project had cost the United States very dear. The country had lost more than 4,000 dead and 30,000 wounded; it had spent $900 billion; one-third of its armed forces had been tied down in Iraq or retraining and reequipping at home. The cost in trust and reputation had also been heavy. There had been scandals involving incompetence and corruption among U.S. officials and private contractors in Iraq; there was strong suspicion that the Bush administration had squeezed from U.S. intelligence agencies dire assessments of Iraqi WMDs that it needed to start the war; the use of degrading and brutal methods of interrogation at the detention camp at Guantánamo in Cuba, and at secret jails elsewhere, had caused dissension at home and fury in the Muslim world. It seemed that as wealthy and powerful as the United States might be, it had neither the resources nor the popular consensus necessary for overthrowing outlaw regimes, rebuilding countries, changing the values and structures of the Muslim world, and in general acting as the lawgiver and law enforcer of the international community.

In June 2009, the recently elected U.S. President Barack Obama announced to an audience in a university auditorium near the Egyptian capital: "I've come here to Cairo to seek a new beginning between the United States and Muslims around the world." He condemned both Palestinian terrorism and Israeli settlements in the West Bank. He justified the war in Afghanistan and vowed to continue the U.S. relationship with Iraq, but admitted that "events in Iraq have reminded America of the need to use diplomacy and build international consensus to resolve our problems whenever possible." On women's rights, a defining issue between Islam and the post-sixties West, he declared: "I reject the view of some in the West that a woman who chooses to cover her hair is somehow less equal, but I do believe that a woman who is denied an education is denied equality."

The speech was far from rejecting the ultimate goals of the Bush administration. Part of Obama's message was that, for their own good, Muslims must learn from the example of the present-day West, and that the United States would actively encourage this process. But his message was also that it was up to Muslims to learn in accordance with their traditions and needs, not to the United States to teach and decide the curriculum. The Bush administration had already sometimes acted on this maxim, with its concessions to Islamic traditions and feelings in Iraq and Afghanistan, but it had not changed its rhetoric of shaking up Islam. Encountering a Muslim world where democratic constitutions enshrined Islam as the state religion, female politicians covered their hair, and protesters against Iranian vote-fixing called out the declaration of faith, Obama seemingly wanted to make what Bush had sometimes done into an avowed and consistent policy.

LO² Shifting Power Balances of the Twenty-first Century

"September 11 changed everything" was a common saying in the months and years after that dreadful event, which certainly brought a sudden and drastic change in the U.S. approach to the international community, the Western partnership, and the Muslim world. In other ways, however, the postcommunist world continued to move on paths that it had taken since the 1990s. More countries joined the European Union; some countries prospered under globalization, while others were left behind; Russia struggled with its postcommunist troubles, regardless of the upheavals in the Middle East. But about the turn of the century these changes seemed to reach a tipping point—not a sudden and drastic one, but one that took the world in a direction different from the one that the United States had in mind. Gradually, the hold of the political and economic West on worldwide leadership and guidance, which had always been subject to protest and challenge, began to weaken.

A Less Successful West

Partly, this was because the West was itself divided by the Iraq War and the U.S. claim to a new kind of world leadership. In 2005 and 2007, leaders came to power in Germany and France, Angela Merkel and Nicolas Sarkozy, who were less distrustful of the Bush administration than Chirac and Schröder, and from then on, the rifts in the Western partnership narrowed. Still, by that time, European countries that had sent peacekeeping troops to Iraq were withdrawing them exactly when the turmoil there was at its worst and the United States most needed help. And Sarkozy, though he praised the United States as the leader of the world, also declared the Iraq War a "historic mistake." In addition, both the European Union and the United States had problems of their own that made it hard for them to act as leaders and guides for the rest of the world.

The European Union: Struggling with Success

After the European Union's triumph in 2003 when it admitted ten countries, eight of them postcommunist, it faced many problems arising from its enlargement. Now that the EU had expanded so far eastward, to "eurofederalists" the time seemed ripe for reforms that would weld it into a still closer union. The union should become a single legal entity instead of a collection of agencies, each operating under the provisions of different clauses of different treaties. It should be easier for the decision-making Council of Ministers to pass measures for the whole union by majority vote rather than unanimously. There should be an EU minister of foreign affairs who would give the union greater international weight by coordinating the foreign policies of the member states. And to reduce the "democratic deficit" (p. 596), the European Parliament should have greater powers of "advice and consent" over a wider range of issues.

> **eurofederalists**
> Strong believers in European integration.

But these and other measures raised many difficult questions. Should voting in the Council of Ministers be weighted by population, which would allow larger countries to steamroller smaller ones, or should voting be by country, which would allow smaller countries to defy the wishes of European majorities? If the powers of the European Parliament were increased, how much power would national parliaments lose? Should the EU minister of foreign affairs be a political leader of high international standing whose views must be heeded by the member countries, or a lesser figure who could be safely ignored? Questions like these led to fierce disputes among larger and smaller countries, high-wage western European veteran EU nations and low-wage postcommunist newcomer ones, and eurofederalist and "euro-skeptical" politicians and electorates.

Because of these disputes, it took until 2009 to reorganize the European Union. To begin with, in 2004, the governments of the member states agreed on a "Treaty Establishing a Constitution for Europe." To come into effect, the treaty then had to be ratified (approved) in every member country—mostly by national parliaments, but the governments of some countries had promised to hold referendums. In 2005, French and Dutch voters rejected the constitution, and it seemed likely that euro-skeptical electorates in other countries would do the same. The treaty was therefore withdrawn, and two years later, in the Portuguese capital, Lisbon, the member states agreed on a new treaty that was no longer a constitution, but merely amended existing European treaties. In fact, the Treaty of Lisbon included most of the reforms in the earlier constitution, but since it was not the same document, governments that had promised to hold referendums on the constitution did not have to do so—except in Ireland, where the voters again rejected it but accepted it on a new vote in 2009. In this backdoor manner, the European Union grew closer than before, but the disputes and conflicts that had held up the process of integration were far from banished.

 "Treaty of Lisbon: Taking Europe into the 21st Century" (http://europa.eu/lisbon_treaty/index_en.htm) Read the European Union's own guide to the Treaty of Lisbon.

Whatever the EU's problems, most European countries believed that their region's future peace and prosperity depended on it, and nonmembers wanted to join it. Bulgaria and Romania joined in 2007, and the hope of joining was a powerful motive for the former Yugoslav countries to lay their conflicts to rest. In addition, a large and low-wage eastern European country, Ukraine, was eager to join, and so was Turkey, which since the Middle Ages had been a more or less unwelcome European state as well as a Muslim one. Would the EU governing system become impossibly unwieldy as more countries joined, and would the system be able to contain the quarrels and changes in power balances that would inevitably arise? Could the EU's high-wage and low-wage members coexist without the high-wage countries exploiting the low-wage ones, or the low-wage countries dragging down the high-wage ones? What, ultimately, was Europe's cultural, ideological, and religious identity, and where were its boundaries? These questions had arisen exactly out of the EU's success, and they might well find satisfactory answers. But while the EU wrestled with them, it was in no position to lead and guide the rest of the world.

> *"What, ultimately, was Europe's cultural, ideological, and religious identity, and where were its boundaries?"*

The United States: Economic Mistakes and Misfortunes

Meanwhile, a crisis was building up in the U.S. economy that exploded in the mid-2000s, spread to the global economy as a whole, and undermined faith at home and abroad in the laissez-faire model that the United States had followed and prescribed for the rest of the world since the 1980s.

Already in 2000, the economic expansion of the Clinton presidency had ended in the collapse of a speculative stock market boom, an economic downturn, and a rise in unemployment. The recovery that followed under the Bush administration was slow in producing jobs and was accompanied by unprecedented government deficits—excesses of spending over revenues, which had to be made up for by borrowing. The new administration was committed to one conservative principle, that of low tax rates, but not to its accompanying principle of cutting government spending. Instead, the administration was betting that as the economy recovered from recession, the government would take in more money in taxes, even if tax rates were low.

What made it possible for the Bush administration to make this bet was the fact that in many countries with expanding economies, especially in East Asia, governments, companies, and individuals preferred to save and invest their increasing wealth rather than spend it, and lending to the United States seemed a safe and profitable investment. As a result, the United States could buy far more abroad than it sold there, the U.S. federal and state governments could spend far more on foreign wars and the welfare state than they took in from taxes, and individual Americans could get auto, college, and home loans on an unprecedented scale, all by tapping into this worldwide "savings glut."

The combination of profit-seeking worldwide investors and U.S. governments and consumers hungry for loans led during the Bush years to a new speculative boom, this time not on the stock exchange but in borrowing and lending. An international chain of financial institutions, each lending to the next, acted as middlemen between the ultimate lenders around the world and the ultimate borrowers in the United States. Everyone along the chain made fabulous profits, especially on higher-interest loans—that is, on riskier ones. Commercial banks, which deal mainly with the public, operated toward the borrowing end; investment banks, which deal among themselves and with other financial institutions such as pension funds and insurance companies, were active toward the lending end.

Financial experts devised new forms of lending and borrowing that supposedly limited the risk. For example, loans to consumers, especially mortgages and home equity loans, were "bundled" together, and interest-bearing shares in these bundles ("mortgage-backed securities") were sold along the borrowing and lending chain: individual loans might go bad, but a bundle as a whole would supposedly still be safe. As in every speculative boom, a great deal of sharp practice crept in. Huge loans were made to disappear from the books of the financial institutions that had taken them out, thereby making these institutions look more trustworthy than they actually were; ratings companies, which assess the reliability of stocks and bonds, gave overoptimistic assessments to mortgage-backed securities issued by banks that paid their fees. Furthermore, late in the Clinton administration, the president and Congress had agreed on legislation that limited government regulation of practices such as the issue of mortgage-backed securities, in the belief that "financial innovation" was good for economic growth. The result was the rise of a "shadow banking system," in which huge financial services companies could borrow the money from profit-seeking investors to make risky loans, and could do so on a vast scale with few or no legal limits.

Like all speculative booms, this one eventually collapsed when the weakest link in the chain of borrowing and lending failed—in this case, the notorious "subprime mortgages." Easy borrowing and lending had helped lead to many years of increases in real estate values. Demand from families and businesses wanting to own homes, offices, and factories, as well as from speculators expecting to profit by buying and reselling these properties, had driven up prices. Mortgage lenders had profited to the utmost by providing loans even to "subprime" buyers whose ability to repay was doubtful, and then selling the loans on up the borrowing and lending chain. But in 2006, real estate prices rose beyond what the demand would sustain, and finally began to fall. Subprime buyers who found they could not afford their mortgage payments could no longer refinance (take out new mortgages) at a lower rate, and instead they defaulted (stopped repaying).

As soon as one link in the chain broke, all the other links were strained beyond their strength. Mortgage lenders could not repay the money they had borrowed to make the subprime loans in the first place. Commercial banks, which had bundled the loans together with less risky ones to sell mortgage-backed securities, could not pay the interest due on the securities. Investment banks that had bought the securities had used them as collateral (pledged them) to borrow from other financial institutions around the world—so-called "collateralized debt obligations." When the ultimate lenders "foreclosed" on the investment banks in their turn, demanding that they hand over the pledged securities, they found that no one knew how many bad mortgages were in the bundles on which the securities were based. Until the bad mortgages were unscrambled from the good ones, the bundles were unsaleable and therefore value-less—and in a crisis when lenders are clamoring to be repaid, no one has time to do any unscrambling. Meanwhile, insurance companies that had issued policies to lenders to protect them against bad loans ("credit default swaps"), and had enjoyed an incoming flood of premium payments, suddenly faced an incoming flood of claims that were far beyond their ability to pay.

> **"The international community's leading citizen, chastened by its economic mistakes and misfortunes, now bowed to the wishes of the community's majority."**

In the resulting chaos, flagship companies of U.S. capitalism went bankrupt, like the 160-year-old Lehman Brothers investment bank, or were sold off at knockdown prices to less endangered companies, like the 96-year-old Merrill, Lynch, which became the investment banking division of Bank of America. To protect themselves, surviving banks stopped not just speculative lending, but the everyday lending to consumers and businesses without which economies cannot function. Without access to credit, consumers stopped buying and businesses laid off workers. The "credit crunch" caused the entire U.S. economy to slow down, as well as those of countries across the world that sold goods and lent money to the United States; countries that had borrowed money from abroad like the United States to fuel their own speculative booms made their own smaller contributions to the global crisis.

At the height of the crisis, in the fall of 2008, the only institutions that still seemed trustworthy enough to be able to borrow and lend were governments themselves and the central banks, such as the U.S. Federal Reserve Bank, that were linked with them. Accordingly, governments and central banks began lending money to financial institutions in danger of collapse, buying up their untrustworthy bundles of mortgages, and taking actual ownership shares in them. The alternative seemed to be the drying up of the entire flow of lending and borrowing on which wealthy economies depend: as Ben Bernanke, the head of the Federal Reserve, put it one Thursday in September 2008, "If we don't do this, we may not have an economy on Monday."

The Aftermath of the Credit Crunch

In all, the governments and central banks spent about $4 trillion on these "bailout" measures, in addition to money they spent on efforts to create jobs and help nonfinancial businesses in trouble. By 2010 the worldwide financial system was for the time being more or less back in order, but the crisis left many unsolved problems behind. One of its causes had been the excesses of the unregulated shadow banking system: How much and what kind of government regulation would prevent such excesses in future, without choking off the necessary flow of lending and borrowing? In the United States and most European countries, the flow of lending and borrowing was still weak, and unemployment was still high. Should governments, having used their borrowing and lending ability to prop up the financial system, now do the same to jump-start their general economies, for example by cutting taxes or by spending money to create jobs? These issues set unemployed workers against overpaid banking tycoons, taxpayers against people in need of welfare state benefits, and thriftier countries against those that had been more extravagant.

Behind these problems there loomed another that was just as menacing: How far could governments and central banks themselves borrow and lend without loading their taxpayers and their economies with crippling burdens of debt repayment, and without facing their own day of reckoning when lenders would lose confidence in their ability to repay? Should governments reduce their borrowing, and if so, should they cut spending, raise taxes, or both? But if governments did not spend money to jump-start their economies, were they not condemning their unemployed workers to years of despair and anger?

In 2010, the pendulum seemed to be swinging toward spending cuts, as several European governments came face to face with the day of reckoning. The Greek government in particular, which had overspent for decades on its welfare state, was forced to make harsh cuts in return for international help to pay its debts, regardless of the resulting strikes and street clashes. The EU established a bailout fund for future sovereign (government) debt crises, but it was clear that any government it bailed out would also have to cut its spending drastically. And an international meeting in Toronto of leaders of the Group of 20—the world's twenty wealthiest countries (p. 635)—agreed that they would all reduce their government deficits by one-third in the next three years. The agreement was against the wishes of the Obama administration, which believed that in the short term, spending to reduce unemployment was more urgent than cutting deficits, but the other countries overrode the United States and the United States went along. Unlike in the prelude to the Iraq war, the international community's leading citizen, chastened by its economic mistakes and misfortunes, now bowed to the wishes of the community's majority.

The Weakening of Western Global Predominance

Besides their own problems, another factor that weakened the Western partners as worldwide leaders and guides was the fact that countries outside the political and economic West were becoming stronger and more assertive than before.

Russia: Stemming Decline

That was the case, for example, with Russia. At the very time that the Bush administration was prescribing democracy as a solution to conflicts across the world, as well as to the problems of relations between Islam and the West, President Vladimir Putin was turning Russia into an authoritarian state ruled by an interlocking elite of secret police chiefs, armed forces commanders, government ministers, and "oligarchs"—billionaire tycoons subservient to himself. When he came to the end of his second term as president in 2008, which was all the Russian constitution allowed, he simply switched jobs with his prime minister, Dmitry Medvedev (**mehd-VYEH-dehf**). What enabled Putin to turn away from democracy was partly the rising price of Russia's oil and natural gas, which strengthened the country economically, and partly the strong support of the Russian people after the chaos and humiliations of the 1990s. That, in turn, helped Russia successfully to oppose the West in disputes on its borders.

The first of these disputes arose in Ukraine in 2004, when street protests—the so-called Orange Revolution, from the color of the protesters' banners—overturned a fixed presidential election that had been "won" by a pro-Russian candidate, and a new election brought a pro-Western candidate, Viktor Yushchenko (**YOOSH-chehn-kaw**), to power. The victory for democracy fitted in with the U.S. agenda at the time, and the winner was eager for Ukraine to join not only the EU but also NATO—an ambition that the Bush administration supported, and which Russia regarded as a deadly threat. In the next few years, disputes over Ukraine's payments for Russian gas supplies—a matter on which Russia had been easygoing before Yushchenko came to power—escalated into crises in which Russia cut off supplies not only to Ukraine but also to much of Europe. The EU responded not by backing Ukraine but by calling on both countries to settle their disputes without harming third parties. Yushchenko, for his part, announced that Ukraine would not renew Russia's lease on naval bases left in Ukrainian territory by the collapse of the Soviet Union, which would have crippled Russian power in the Black Sea.

Ukraine, however, was an ethnically and religiously divided country. Its people included strong nationalists and more moderate ones; Catholics loyal to Rome; followers of the Ukrainian Orthodox patriarch in the capital, Kyiv (Kiev); followers of the Russian Orthodox patriarch in Moscow; and a large minority of actual Russians. Many people in Ukraine felt the pull of the West, but many also felt strong ties to Russia—and besides, unseemly rivalries within the government cost it public support. In 2010, Viktor Yanukovych (**yah-noo-KOH-vihch**), Yushchenko's opponent in 2004, won the presidency in a free and fair election, dropped his country's application to join NATO, agreed to renew Russia's lease on its naval bases, but also proclaimed his country's continued eagerness to join the EU. "We should not be forced to make the false choice between the benefits of the East and those of the West," he declared.

Meanwhile, in 2008 Russia fought a brief war against a post-Soviet republic on its southern border, Georgia. Separatist national minorities in Georgia had received Russian help ever since the breakup of the Soviet Union, but in 2003, a Harvard-educated politician, Mikheil Saakashvili (**SAH-ah-kahsh-VEE-lee**), came to power through street protests against fixed elections, took a hard line against the separatists and their Russian backers, and sought NATO membership for his country. The Bush administration was eager to admit Georgia to NATO, but the France and Germany of Merkel and Sarkozy made sure that the process was delayed—precisely because good relations with resurgent Russia seemed more important to them than backing up Georgia. In 2008, when Saakashvili tried to crush the separatists by force, the Russians invaded, but withdrew once the separatist regions were secure.

"Russia-Georgia Conflict Has Deep Roots" (http://www.npr.org/templates/story/story.php?storyId=93525210) Learn more about the roots of the Russia-Georgia conflict.

Russia seemed determined not to let countries on its borders take actions that it deemed to threaten its security and its standing as a great power, but it also showed no desire to reestablish the old Soviet Union—an undertaking for which its leaders knew that it lacked the strength. They had no desire to start a

≪ **Reset Button** At a meeting in Geneva in 2009, U.S. Secretary of State Hilary Clinton presented Russian Foreign Minister Sergei Lavrov with a mock reset button, in token of the U.S. desire to reset the two countries' relationship. Clinton asked Lavrov whether the Russian word on the button was right. "You got it wrong," Lavrov, a fluent English speaker, smilingly answered. "It should be *perezagruzka*."This says *peregruzka*, which means 'overcharged.'" Smilingly, Clinton replied: "We won't let you do that to us." Fabrice Coffrini,Pool/AP Photo

new Cold War; on the contrary, they were glad to belong to a worldwide international community, but as members of high standing and on their own terms. For years, Russia responded with protests and threats against the stationing by the Bush administration of antimissile rockets in Poland and the Czech Republic to defend against possible Iranian missile attacks. When the new Obama administration withdrew the missiles and indicated its desire to "reset" its relationship with Russia, however (see photo), Russia and the United States fairly swiftly agreed on a drastic reduction in their nuclear arsenals, as a joint contribution to "the achievement of the historic goal of freeing humanity from the nuclear threat."

The Changing Balance of Global Economic Power

While Russia strove to bring its decline to an end, the economic tug of war between the West and the "Rest" continued, with the "Rest" gradually becoming more assertive, notably over the issue of worldwide tariff cuts. In the 1990s, the countries of the economic and political West, in spite of having many trade disputes among themselves, had been able to enforce tariff reductions that were on the whole favorable to them as a group (p. 611). But in a new round of negotiations that got under way shortly after September 11, four countries—Brazil, China, India, and South Africa—took the lead in opposing the West. As a result, a stalemate developed that continued through many meetings and discussions in the 2000s, mainly because of the traditional disputes over protection of farmers by the West and barriers to industrial imports by many countries among the "Rest."

Both sides were eager for a deal, but too much was at stake, and the balance of power between the West and the four leading countries of the "Rest" was too even, for either side to give way. The four countries were certainly not opposed to globalization as such. On the contrary, what made them effective opponents of the West was exactly the fact their economies had grown spectacularly in the era of globalization. Economists might deplore the continuing stalemate, but it was also a sign that globalization was shifting the worldwide balance of power.

A telling sign of the strength of this shift was the growing importance of the **Group of 20**—the countries with the world's twenty largest economies, which by 2000 included not only the traditional Western economic leaders but Brazil, China, India, South Africa, and other newly wealthy countries. In 1997 the G20 finance ministers and central bank chiefs had begun holding regular meetings; from 2008, in response to the global financial crisis, the group's heads of state and government started holding regular yearly meetings; and in 2009 the G20 took over from the Group of 8 (pp. 592–593, 600) as the world's main economic forum. The Western countries fully supported this change: given the West's large share of responsibility for the financial crisis and the growing strength of the newcomers, it was much more in the West's interest to admit them to the global forum than to keep them out.

The same shift was seen in dealings on another global issue that seemed to need a global response, but where different countries had different interests that made global agreement exceedingly difficult: the problem of climate change. The wealth of countries depended on a cheap and plentiful supply of energy, which could only come from coal, oil, and natural gas—the very fuels that produced carbon dioxide when burned, thereby slowing the loss of heat from the earth's atmosphere. If carbon dioxide emissions were to be reduced, this could only come at substantial economic cost, which would have to be shared among three groups: the West, above all the United States, which until 2009 was the largest single emitter; rapidly growing countries like China, which overtook the United States in total emissions in 2009 (though it was still far behind in emissions per head of population); and the world's poorest countries, which were the smallest emitters but would have to avoid increasing their consumption of fossil fuels in the future.

Naturally, the question of who should bear how much of the burden led to endless arguments within and among the three groups, which came to a head at a contentious world-wide conference in the Danish capital, Copenhagen, in 2009. Climate change protesters clashed with police in the streets, nongovernmental organizationss and advocacy groups held side events intended to put pressure on the conference to reach an agreement, and the representatives of 138 governments spent a good deal of discussion time blaming each other in advance for the meeting's expected failure. Finally, the heads of state of many countries appeared in person, and a small group of them came up with an agreement that most other countries signed on to—mainly because they were not asked to "comply with" it, but only to "take note of" it.

The **Copenhagen Accord** set a target of maintaining world temperatures at an average of only two degrees centigrade above what they were estimated to have been during the past few thousand years. It asked each country to officially announce its own target of progressively cutting carbon dioxide emissions to help meet the target. It also committed wealthier countries to aid poorer countries with large amounts of money and technology to help them bear their share of the burden yet also develop their economies. Climate change experts were disappointed that the conference had not done more, yet hopeful that it would shortly lead to more ambitious and binding agreements.

The countries whose leaders were mainly responsible for drawing up the Copenhagen Accord were the United States, more sympathetic to reduction of emissions under Obama than under Bush, and Brazil, China, India, and South Africa—the same four countries that were leading the "Rest" against the

Group of 20 (G20)
A group of the countries with the world's twenty largest economies, which in 2009 took over from the G8 as the world's main economic forum.

Copenhagen Accord
A 2009 international agreement to address global warming.

West in trade negotiations. All five countries depended heavily on fossil fuels and were unwilling to be the first to make painful economic sacrifices, but all five accepted the reality of global warming. The European Union was also a major emitter, but it was more willing to impose government targets on private companies than the United States, and less in need of rapid development than the leaders of the "Rest"; it therefore called for a much stronger agreement. The poorest countries were deeply suspicious of anything decided on by the other groups that might foreclose their possibilities of future development, and wanted an agreement that would impose no sacrifices on them. The solution proposed by the United States and its four negotiating partners seemed the best way to finesse these disputes. This time, the shifting worldwide power balance had weakened but not paralyzed worldwide decision making—and the West's leading country had joined with the leading countries of the "Rest" as the main deciders.

Issues and Destinies of Global Civilization

At the present day, it seems as if the U.S. effort, in the wake of September 11, to determine on its own initiative the power structure and the prevailing values of global civilization has run its course. Instead, a world is growing up in which the United States, and the political and economic West as a whole, are sharing power with new leading citizens of the international community. In this world, some values that originated in the West, notably the pursuit of material well-being for everyone as a realistic possibility, have become universally accepted. Other Western values, notably gender equality, are more and more widely officially proclaimed and to some extent—though only to some extent—accepted in practice. And still other Western values, notably the separation of religion and the state in the Islamic world, and full democracy in countries such as Russia and China, seem to be low on the agenda of many governments and peoples.

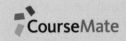

> "*A world is growing up in which the United States, and the political and economic West as a whole, are sharing power with new leading citizens of the international community.*"

In any case, present-day issues concerning the structure and values of the international community are simply the latest version of issues that are as old as civilization itself. Who is to be the community's lawgiver and law enforcer, and how far should these functions be combined? How are the community's wealthier and more powerful members and its poorer and weaker ones to share the benefits of community life and the power to make community decisions? What beliefs and values are to prevail within the community, and how much freedom is to be given to those who dissent from or transgress these values—including those who hold to older values when the community's values change?

Within Western civilization alone, such questions as these have received countless different answers—from democratic and oligarchic Greek city-states; from pagans and Christians in the Roman Empire; from the medieval papacy and Holy Roman emperors; from nobles and peasants; from factory owners and labor unions. In the twenty-first century, these questions again demand answers, and this time, the answers that they receive will determine the destiny of global civilization as a whole. Will it fulfill its yearning for harmonious diversity, or collapse under the pressure of its internal conflicts? Will it become a single worldwide entity, or will new civilizations arise, or updated versions of old ones, for which global civilization will provide no more than a common basic pattern? Will Western civilization preserve its individuality and its dominance, or will it be submerged by other civilizations that learn from it and then surpass it? All these questions are suggested by humanity's experience of the past. Only the future can answer them.

 Listen to a synopsis of Chapter 34.

INDEX

guilds, 200; Mesopotamian, 12, 17; technology and, 195

Cranach, Lucas, the Elder (1472–1553), *308–309*

Cranmer, Thomas, archbishop of Canterbury (1489–1556), 325

Crassus, Marcus (d. 53 B.C.), 100

Creation of Adam, The (Michelangelo), *302,* 303

Crete, Minoan civilization on, 49, *49*

Crick, Francis (1916–2004), 517

Critique of Pure Reason (Kant), 403

Croatia (Croats), 157, 179, 601, 603*(map),* 604

Cromwell, Oliver (1599–1658), 341–342

Cross-vault, 112, *112*

Cruciform plan, in churches, 227

Cruikshank, George (1792–1878), *448*

Crusades, 204, 212–219; Bernard of Clairvaux and, 215–217; Byzantium and, 213–214, 217–218, 219; castles of, *202–203;* First (1096–1090), 214–215, 217*(map);* papacy and, 212–214, 218, 249; Second (1147–1149), 215–217 *and map;* Third (1189–1192), 217 *and map;* Fourth (1202–1204), 217–218 *and map,* 219, *407*

Cuba, 546, 581; United States and, 459, 571–573

Cubism, in art, *525,* 525–526

Culture. *See* Art and artists; Counterculture; Mass culture

Cuneiform writing, 13, 14, 18

Curie, Marie (1867–1934), 433

Currency: Chinese, 610; coins, *51,* 55, 135, 138, 284; devaluation, 498; euro, 596

Cuzco, Peru, 278

Cynic philosophy, 85

Cyprus, 272, 596

Cyrillic alphabet, 177–178, 219

Cyrus the Great (Persia, 558–528 B.C.), 35

Czechoslovakia (1917–1993), 479, 480*(map),* 504, 511, 585. *See also* Czechs; Slovakia; division of, 586, 597*(map);* Soviet occupation of, 536, 539

Czech Republic, 586; in EU, 596; in NATO, 598

Czechs, 157, 220, 250, 327, 377, 603*(map);* nationalism and, 414–415

Dacia, 113. *See also* Romania

Dalton, John (1766–1844), 432

Damascus, 162

Danelaw (England), 177, 178

Danes, 174. *See also* Denmark

Dante Alighieri (1265–1321), 239–240, 248, 288, 290

Darius I (Persia, 521–486 B.C.), *30–31,* 56

Darwin, Charles (1809–1882), 434, 435, 439, *446*

Darwinism: ethics and, 446–447; religion and, 446; scientific theory, 446–447; social, 459, 485

Daumier, Honoré (1808–1879), *449,* 449–450

David, Jacques-Louis (1748–1825), 371, *372,* 406

David (Israel, c. 1010–970 B.C.), 38, 372

David (Michelangelo), 301–302, *302*

D-Day invasion (1944), 508

Death and Life of American Cities (Jacobs), 566

Debussy, Claude (1862–1918), 530

Decameron, The (Boccaccio), 290

Declaration of Independence (1776), 381–382, 388

Declaration of Pillnitz (1791), 388

Declaration of the Rights of Man and the Citizen (1789), 387–388

Declaration of the Rights of Woman and the Female Citizen (de Gouges), 387

Decolonization, 534, 541–546, 543*(map). See also* Third World

Deconstruction, 559; in architecture, 567, *567*

Deductive argument, 236

Degas, Edgar (1895–1900), 450

De Gaulle, Charles (1890–1970), 540, 546; student protests and, 553

De Gouges, Olympe (1748–1793), 387, 561

Deism, 364, 368, 375, 388, 390; Romanticism and, 405

De Klerk, F. W. (b. 1936), 613

Delacroix, Eugène (1799–1863), 406–407, *407*

Delphi, oracle of Apollo at, 50, 63, 70

Demeter, 51, 63, 84

Democracy: Arab–Israeli conflict and, 628–630; in Athens, 52, 56–59, 81; in Britain and United States, 498–499; First World War and, 482; Islam and, 624, 626–631; movement for, in China, 610

Democratic-capitalist nations, 534, 569

Democratic Party (United States), 499, 573, 583, 609; Obama and, 622, 623

Democritus of Abdera (460–362 B.C.), 71–72, 87, 432

Demosthenes (c. 382–322 B.C.), 82

Deng Xiaoping (1904–1997), 610

Denmark, 359; in EEC, 540, 596; Lutheranism in, 316; Norsemen

from, 174; in Thirty Years' War, 327, 328*(map)*

Department of Defense, United States, 518

Depression (1930s), 498, 499, 502

Derrida, Jacques (b. 1930), 559, 561, 567

Descartes, René (1596–1650), 361, 365

Despotism, 404; Enlightened, 374–377; in Italy, 263–265; oriental (Hegel), 404

Détente, Cold War and, 540–541, *541,* 578, 583

Deterrence, nuclear, 580

Dialectic, of Hegel, 403–404, 443

Diamond mines, in South Africa, *4 61,* 545

Dias, Bartolomeu (d. 1500), 273, 275

Diaspora, Jewish, 39, 124

Dickens, Charles (1812–1870), 448, *448*

Dictatorship, 624; in Central Asia, 628; in China, 610–611; in fascist Italy, 494–495; Islamic fundamentalist, 576; Jacobin, in France, 389–391; in Latin America, 574; in Nazi Germany, 496–497; in North Korea, 575; in Soviet Union, 487–490

"Dictatorship of the proletariat," 443

Diderot, Denis (1713–1784), 366

Diet of Augsburg (1555), 315, 316

Diet of Worms (1521), 314, 315

Dinner Party, The (Chicago), 565–566, *566*

Dioceses (Roman Empire), 137

Diocletian (Rome, 284–305): Baths of, *112,* 114; restructuring of empire under, 136–138

Dionysus, 63, *66,* 69, 70

Directory (France), 391

Discourse on Method (Descartes), 361

Discourses, The (Machiavelli), 265

Discus Thrower, The (Myron), 65, *66*

Disease: AIDS, 555, 613; Black Death, 245, 247, 249*(map),* 271; epidemics, in ancient world, 81, 134; germ theory and, 434; Native Americans and, 277, 278, 279; smallpox, 277, 278, 434

Displaced persons (DPs), in Second World War, 511

Dissenters (Calvinists) in England, 342, 344. *See also* Puritans

Divine Comedy (Dante), 239–240, 290

Divine kingship: in China and Japan, 279; of Egyptian pharaohs, *22–23;* of Hellenistic kings, 85–86; of Roman emperors, 104–105, 137

Divine right of kings, 338, 340

DNA. *See* Genetics

"Doctrine of Ideas" (Plato), 73, 404

Domes, Roman use of, 112, *112,* 113

Fundamentalism: *See also* Islamic fundamentalism; monotheistic religions and, 514

Gaddafi, Muammar al- (b. 1924), 618
Galen of Pergamum (c. 130–200), 110, 132, 362
Galerius (Rome, 305–310), 136
Galileo Galilei (1564–1642), 359–361, 362; Jupiter observations of, 359, *360*
Gallican Church, 260, 334
Gama, Vasco da (1469–1524), 274*(map)*, 276
Gandhara, art of, *78–79*
Gandhi, Mohandas (1917–1948), 455, 542
García Márquez, Gabriel (b. 1928), 562
Gargantua and Pantagruel (Rabelais), 304
Gargoyles, 227
Garibaldi, Giuseppi (1807–1882), *418,* 418–419
Gattamelata (Donatello), 299, *299*
Gaul. *See also* France; Celts of, 100, 119; Franks in, 141; Rome and, 97, 100
Gaza Strip, 576, 614, 616, 617, 629
Gda_sk, shipyard strike in (1980), 584–585
Gehry, Frank (b. 1929), 567, *567*
Gelasius (pope, 492–496), 147, 319
Gell-Mann, Murray (b. 1929), 516
Gender relations: *See also* Marriage; Women; Agricultural Revolution and, 10–11; among hunter-gatherers, 7; in ancient Egypt, 23; in Athens, 59; barbarian, 47; in Hebrew Bible, 41–42; in Plato's *Republic*, 74–75, 110; in Renaissance Italy, 290–292; in Roman Republic, 94; in Sumer, 13; women's movement (1960s) and, 554–555; women's work and, 7, 10, 13, 58, 192, *194*
Genealogy of Morals, The (Nietzsche), 448
General Agreement on Tariffs and Trade (GATT), 609, 611
General will, 367
Genetic engineering, 518
Genetics, 435, 517, 518
Geneva (Switzerland), 555; Calvinism in, 317–318, 319–320; U.S.-Soviet summit in (1985), 584
Genghis Khan (Mongols, 1206–1227), 223, 271
Genoa, 250*(map)*; Black Death and, 247; trade of, 247, 256, 272
Genocide: *See also* Holocaust; in Armenia, 478; in Cambodia, 573; "ethnic cleansing," in Yugoslavia, 600, 601, 602; in Rwanda, 614
Genre painting, Dutch, *350,* 350–351

Gentiles, 133; Jews and, 124, 127–128, 142
Gentileschi, Artemisia (c. 1597–c. 1651), 345–346, *346*
Geocentric theory, 357–358
Geometry, art and, 298, 526–527, *527*
George III (Britain, 1769–1810), 381
Georgia (Caucasus), 587 *and map,* 634
German Confederation, 400, 401*(map),* 414, 417, 418
German Democratic Republic (East Germany), 536–537, 540, 553, 585; reunification and, 586
Germanic kingdoms, 151, 152–155. *See also* Frankish kingdom; inheritance in, 154–155; warrior-landowners of, 152
Germanic peoples: Rome and, 123, 124, 135, 136; Rome invaded by, 139–141
Germany, 424. *See also* German Democratic Republic; West Germany; African colonies of, 462, 463*(map)*; alliances of, 473, 474, 475; alliance with Italy, 504; Bauhaus in, 528–529; division of, after Second World War, 535*(map),* 536; fascism in, 493, 496–498, 504; in First World War, 469, 476–478 *and map*; in G7 countries, 593; Holocaust and, 509–510, *541*; Holy Roman Empire and, 267; immigration to, 580; League of Nations and, 502; literature, 406; nationalism in, 400, 413, 414; Nazism in, 496–498; reparations and, 479; reunification of, 586, 596, 597 *(map)*; in Second World War, 505, 506–509; social legislation in, 429; in Thirty Years' War, 327; unification of, 398, 416–417, 419; urban growth in, 430 *and map*; U.S. invasion of Iraq and, 625
Germ theory, 434
Gershwin, George (1898–1937), 531
Ghana (Gold Coast), *542,* 545
Ghirlandaio, Domenico (1449–1494), *286–287*
Gibbon, Edward (1737–1794), 365
Gilgamesh, epic of, 15
Giotto di Bondone (1266–1337), 295, *295*
Giza, Great Pyramid of, *23, 26, 620–621*
Glasdale, William (d. 1429), 261
Glasnost (Soviet reform), 586
Global civilization, 454–455, 457, 636
Global economy, 608–612, 632. *See also* Globalization; changing balance of power in, 635–636; East Asian crisis and, 609–610
Globalization, 455, 610–612; India and China, 610–611; Vietnam and, 573;

Western domination and, 607, 608, 611–612, 622, 624
Global South, 609, 611
Global warming, 579, 635–636; Copenhagen Accord (2009), 635; Kyoto Protocol (1997) and, 624–625
Globe Theater (London), 305–306
Glorious Revolution (Britain, 1688), 342–343, 367, 382
Gnostics, 130–132, 212
God, the one: *See also* Monotheism; Christian (Trinity), 127, 145–146, 319; in Islam, 159, 160, 161; in Judaism, 37, 38–43
Godfrey, duke of Lorraine (c. 1060–1100), 214
"God is dead" (Nietzsche), 447, 521
Godric of Finchale (c. 1065–1170), 196–197
Gods and goddesses: *See also* Divine kingship; God, the one; Egyptian, 22, 23–25, *27*; Germanic, 152–153; Greek, *60–61, 62–63,* 65; Hellenistic, 84; Indo-European, 47; Neolithic, 10; Roman, 93, *94*; Sumerian, 14–15, 16–17, 18, *18*
Goebbels, Josef (1897–1945), 496
Goering, Hermann (1893–1946), 496
Goethe, Johann Wolfgang von (1749–1832), 406
Gogol, Nicolai (1809–1852), 449
Gold: in Africa, 271, *271,* 280, 545; in Americas, 284; jewelry, *49, 90;* gold standard, 498
Golden Ass, The (Apuleius), 119
Golden Mean, 76
Goliardic poets, 237
Gorbachev, Mikhail (b. 1931), 584, 585–586, 587, 588
Gospels, 126, 127, 129, 132. *See also* New Testament
Gothic architecture: churches, 227–232; revival of, 408–409, *409*
Government and politics: absolute monarchy, 332–339; African Americans and, 547; bank regulation, in United States, 632, 633; Bossuet's theory of, 338; Carolingian dynasty, 171; corporate influence in, 426; East Asian crisis and, 610; Egyptian, 22; English law and, 189–190; European privatization and, 594; European Union, 596, 631–632; federalism, in United States, 382–383; feudal, 184–190; Frankish kingdom, 155; French economy and, 334–335; in French Revolution, 388–391; Great Depression and, 498, 499; Greek city-states, 52–53, 73–76; Hobbes's theory of, 338–339; in India, 610; Italian city-states,

education, 173, *224–225*, 232–237; trade and towns in, 194–201

Medina, 159

Meditations (Marcus Aurelius), 110

Mediterranean Sea: agriculture in lands surrounding, 37; bubonic plague in, 156 *and map*; Egyptian trade in, 26; Greek trade and settlement in, 50; Islamic conquests in, 163; Italian trade in, 253, 272; Phoenician trade and settlement in, 32–33, 50; Roman rule of, 97

Medvedev, Dmitry (b. 1965), 634

Meeting, The (Fragonard), 370, *371*

Megaliths, 46, *47*

Mein Kampf (Hitler), 496

Men. *See* Gender relations; Marriage

Mendel, Gregor (1822–1884), 435

Menkaure (Egypt, c. 2500 B.C.), *26*

Mensheviks (Russia), 487, 488

Mercantilism, 335, 426

Mercenaries (soldiers), 246, 272; Carthage and, 95; Greek, 51, 83; Italian, 253, 265, 291

Merchants and traders, 422. *See also* Markets; Trade (commerce); Arab, 160, 162, 272, 276; Aramaean, 33; early capitalism and, 245, 252, 253; European, in China, 462; Italian, 253, 263–264, 272; in medieval Europe, 197, 200; Mesopotamian, 12; Phoenician, 32–33; wool industry, 253

Merkel, Angela (b. 1954), 555, 631, 634

Merovingian dynasty (Franks), 153, 155

Merrill, Lynch (investment bank), 633

Mesopotamia, 5, 17–20; Aramaeans in, 32, 33; Babylonia, 18–19; Chaldeans in, 32, 33, 34, 39; early empires in, 17–18; expansion of civilization, 19–20; Hammurabi code, 18–19; Jews deported to, 39; Kassites of, 19, 32; nomads, 17; papyrus in, 25; Sumer, 11–17, 63

Messiah: Jesus as, 127, 128, 132, 133; in Judaism, 124, 125; in monotheism, 37; Persian, 35

Metalworking, 255. *See also specific* metals; in Anatolia, 20; bronze casting, 196, 256, *298*, *299*; Sumerian, 14

Metropolis cities, 86

Metternich, Prince Klemens von (1773–1859), 399–400, 411, 413, 417

Mexico, NAFTA and, 609

Mexico City, 277

Michael and Eutychius of Thessalonica (13th century), *221*

Michelangelo Buonarroti (1475–1564), 301–304; architecture of, *303*,

303–304; painting and sculpture of, 301–303, *302*; Roman art and architecture and, *112*, *115*

Middle Ages: *See also* Late Middle Ages (1300–1500); Medieval civilization; defined, 148–149

Middle class: *See also* Bourgeoisie; Aristotle on, 76; consumption of transoceanic products, 284; English, 374; Enlightenment and, 363; humanism and, 289; imperialism and, 459; Iranian, 577; Nazi Germany, 496; 1960s rebellion and, 551; Roman citizenship and, 121; Russian, 486; white-collar workers, 431

Middle East, 474, 475. *See also specific countries*; after First World War, 480–481; Arab-Israeli conflict in, 544–545 *and map*, 576–577, 581, 614–616, 618, 628–630; Bush's "Greater Middle East," 627–630

Mies van der Rohe, Ludwig (1886–1969), 529, *529*, 566, 567

Migration. *See also* Mass explusion; Nomads; of displaced persons, in Second World War, 511; early Greek, 49–50; Etruscan, 90; of Europeans to Americas, 430, 579; Germanic, 140–141; Germans, into Eastern Europe, 220–221; in Hellenistic era, 86; Indo-European, 20, 47; of Jews to Israel, 544; of Muslims, to Europe, 625; rural-to-urban, in Europe, 430 *and map*; Slavic, 156–157; from Third World, 579–580

Milan, 284; despotism in, 263, 265

Militarism: *See also* Armies; War (warfare); fascism and, 495, 497; Japanese, 503, 504; nationalism and, 470–471

Mill, John Stuart (1806–1873), 413–416

Miller, Arthur (1915–2005), 524

Milošević, Slobodan (1941–2006), 601, *602*

Minerva, 93

Ming Dynasty (China), 270

Mining, 255. *See also* Coal mining; *specific metals*; diamond, in South Africa, *461*, 545

Minoan civilization, 49, *49*

Miracle plays, 239

Missionaries, 155, 272; in England, 154; Jesuit, in China, 279, 321; to Slavs, 177–178

Moctezuma (Aztecs, 1480–1520), 277

Modernism, 521–531. *See also* Postmodernism; in architecture, 527–530, *530*; in literature, 521–524,

562; in music, 530–531; in painting and sculpture, 524–527, *527*

Molecular theory, 432

Mona Lisa (Leonardo da Vinci), 300, *301*

Monarchy (emperors; kingship): *See also* Absolute monarchy; Assyrian, 33–34, 34; British, *519*; Carolingian, 167; constitutional, in France, 410–411; Egyptian (pharaohs), 22–23, 25, 27–28; English, 188, 189–190, 262, 339–345; feudalism and, 187–190; Frankish, 153–154, 155; French, 178, 187–188, 259–262; Greek, 52, 55, 56; Hellenistic era, 84–86, *86*; Hittite, 20; Holy Roman Empire, 178, 187–188, 211, 327–328; Israelite, 38, 40–41; Macedonian, 82; Mesopotamian, 12; papacy and, 188, 211, 248; Persian, 36; power of, in Late Middle Ages, 259; Roman, prior to Republic, 91; Roman Empire, 123, 136, 137, 147; Spanish, 262–263; Sumerian, 13; wars of religion and, 323

Monasteries (monks and nuns): closing of, in Austria, 375; closing of, in England, 325; closing of, in France, 388; in early Christianity, 144, 145, 155; education of, 232; Rabelais's view of, 304; reform of, 208; reopened, in France, 392

Monck, George (1608–1670), 342

Monet, Claude (1840–1926), 450, *450*

Moneylending, by Jews, 218, 254. *See also* Banking

Mongol Empire, 222 *(map)*, 223, 270–271

Mongolia, 466

Monophonic music, 373

Monotheism, 31; Christian (Trinity), 127, 145–146, 319; Egyptian, 25, 37; Islamic, 159, 160, 161, 162; Jewish, 37–43; Persian, 35

Monroe, Marilyn (1926–1962), 563, *564*

Montaigne, Michel de (1533–1592), 304–305

Montefeltro, Federico da (Duke of Urbino; 1422–1482), 291, *291*

Montenegro, 475, 601, 603 *(map)*, 604

Montesquieu, Charles-Louis de Secondat, Baron de (1689–1755), 366–367, 382

Monteverdi, Claudio (1567–1643), 374

Moor, Dmitry (1883–1946), *484–485*

Moore, Harriet (1801–1884), *433*

Moore, Henry (1898–1986), 526–527, *527*

Morality plays, 239